MEMOIRS ILLUSTRATING

THE HISTORY OF

JACOBINISM

Real View Books

Reprints of Catholic Classics Series★

J.-B. Bossuet, *History of the Variations of the Protestant Churches*, xxxiv+678pp

J. H. Newman, *Anglican Difficulties*, xli+268pp

A. Carrel, *Voyage to Lourdes*, 95pp

J. H. de Groot, *The Shakespeares and the Old Faith*, 276pp

K. A. Kneller, *Christianity and the Leaders of Modern Science*, xxviii+430pp

A. Barruel, *Memoirs concerning the History of Jacobinism*, xxxvii+846pp

H. E. Manning, *The True Story of the Vatican Council*, xxxii+206pp

Saint John Fisher, *The Defence of the Priesthood* (with his Sermon against Luther), xxix+182pp

C. Hollis, *Erasmus*, xxxii+323pp

H. Wilberforce, *Why I became a Catholic*, 76pp

J. H. Newman, *Conscience and Papacy* [Letter to the Duke of Norfolk], lxxxix+188pp

(★each title with an Introduction and Notes by Stanley L. Jaki)

A. BARRUEL

MEMOIRS ILLUSTRATING
THE HISTORY OF
JACOBINISM

with an Introduction by

Stanley L. Jaki

RealView Books

2002

Hardcover edition

(First RealView Book edition, 1995)

RealView Books
4237 Kinfolk Court
Pinckney, MI 48169
www.realviewbooks.com

All rights reserved. No part of this publication may be reproduced, stored in a retrieval system, or transmitted, in any form, or by any means, electronic, mechanical, photocopying, recording or otherwise, without prior permission from the publisher.

© (Introduction) Stanley L. Jaki

A. Barruel (1741-1818)
1. French Revolution—Jacobinism—Freemasonry—Illuminism
2. Antichristian, antimonarchical and antisocial conspiracy.

ISBN 1-892548-28-3

Printed in the United States of America

CONTENTS

INTRODUCTION by Stanley L. Jaki — xi

PART ONE

THE ANTICHRISTIAN CONSPIRACY

	PRELIMINARY DISCOURSE	1
Chap. I	Of the Principal Actors in the Conspiracy	9
Chap. II.	Of the Existence, Object, and Extent of the antichristian Conspiracy	19
Chap. III.	The Secrecy, the Union and the Epoch of the Conspiracy	25

MEANS OF THE CONSPIRATORS

Chap. IV.	First Means of the Conspirators—The Encyclopedia	32
Chap. V.	Second Means of the Conspirators—The Extinction of the Jesuits	41
Chap. VI.	Third Means of the Conspirators—Extinction of all the Religious Orders	53
Chap. VII.	Fourth Means of the Conspirators—Voltaire's Colony	61
Chap. VIII.	Fifth Means of the Conspirators—The Academic Honors	64
Chap. IX.	Sixth Means of the Conspirators—Inundation of Antichristian Writings	68
Chap. X.	Of the Spoliations and Violences projected by the Conspirators, and concealed under the Name of Toleration	76
Chap. XI.	Part, Mission, and private Means of each of the Chiefs of the Antichristian Conspiracy	80

CONTENTS

ADEPTS AND PROTECTORS

CHAP. XII.	Progress of the Conspiracy—First Class of Protectors—Crowned Adepts.	94
CHAP. XIII.	Second Class of Protectors—Princes and Princesses	104
CHAP. XIV.	Third Class of Protectors—Ministers, Noblemen, and Magistrates	112
CHAP. XV.	The Class of Men of Letters	130
CHAP. XVI.	Conduct of the Clergy toward the Antichristian Conspirators	141
CHAP. XVII.	New and more subtle Means of the Conspirators to seduce even the lowest Classes of the People	147
CHAP. XVIII.	Of the General Progress of the Conspiracy throughout Europe.—Triumph and Death of the Chiefs	158
CHAP. XIX.	Of the great Delusion which rendered the Conspiracy against the Altar so successful	169

PART TWO

THE ANTIMONARCHICAL CONSPIRACY

	PRELIMINARY DISCOURSE	185
CHAP. I.	First Step in the Conspiracy against Kings—Voltaire and D'Alembert passing from the Hatred of Christianity to the Hatred of Kings	189
CHAP. II.	Second Step of the Conspiracy against Kings—Political Systems of the Sect—D'Argenson and Montesquieu	204
CHAP. III.	Jean Jaques Rousseau's System	228
CHAP. IV.	Third Step of the Conspiracy—The general Effect of the Systems of Montesquieu and Jean Jaques—Convention of the Sophisters—The Coalition of their Plots against the Throne, with their Plots against the Altar	239
CHAP. V.	Fourth Step of the Conspiracy against Kings—Inundation of Antimonarchical Books—Fresh Proofs of the Conspiracy	254

CONTENTS

Chap. VI.	Fifth Step of the Conspiracy against Kings—The Democratic Essay at Geneva	273
Chap. VII.	Aristocratical Essay in France	281
Chap. VIII.	Essay of the Sophisters against Aristocracy	288

OF MASONRY

Chap. IX.	Of the General Secret, or Lesser Mysteries, of Freemasonry	299
Chap. X.	Of the Grand Mysteries or Secrets of the Occult Lodges	308
Chap. XI.	New Proofs of the System and Mysteries of the Occult Masons	325
Chap. XII.	Proofs of the Origin of Free-masons drawn from their own Systems	337
Chap. XIII.	Farther Declarations of the Free-masons as to their Origin—The real Founder of Masonry—True and first Origin of their Mysteries and of all their Systems	355
Chap. XIV.	Sixth Degree of the Conspiracy against Kings—Coalition of the Sophisters and of the Free-masons	366

PART THREE

THE ANTISOCIAL CONSPIRACY

	PRELIMINARY OBSERVATIONS	393
Chap. I.	Spartacus-Weishaupt; Founder of the Illuminees	400
Chap. II.	Code of the Illuminees—General System and Division of the Code	408
Chap. III.	First Part of the Code of the Illuminees—Of the Brother Insinuator, or the Recruiter	415
Chap. IV.	Second Part of the Code of the Illuminees—First preparatory Degree; of the Novice and of his Teacher	427
Chap. V.	Third Part of the Code of the Illuminees—Second Preparatory Degree—The academy of Illuminism, or the Brethren of Minerva	440

Chap. VI.	Fourth Part of the Code of the Illuminees—Third Preparatory Degree—The Minor Illuminee	446
Chap. VII.	Fifth Part of the Code of the Illuminees—Fourth Preparatory Degree—The Major Illuminee or Scotch Novice	453
Chap. VIII.	Sixth Part of the Code of the Illuminees—Intermediary Class—The Scotch Knight of Illuminism; or Directing Illuminee	460
Chap. IX.	Seventh Part of the Code of the Illuminees—Class of the Mysteries—Of the Lesser Mysteries; the Epopt or Priest of Illuminism	469
Chap. X.	Continuation of the Discourse on the Lesser Mysteries	486
Chap. XI.	Eighth Parth of the Code of Illuminees—The Regent, or the Prince Illuminee	495
Chap. XII.	Ninth Part of the Code of the Illuminees—Of the Grand Mysteries; the Mage or the Philosopher, and the Man-King	502
Chap. XIII.	Tenth and last Part of the Code of the Illuminees—Government of the Order—General Idea of that Government, and of the Share which the inferior Classes of Illuminism bear in it	525
Chap. XIV.	Of the Government and Political Instructions for the Epopts	530
Chap. XV.	Instructions for the Regent or Prince Illuminee, on the Government of the Order	541
Chap. XVI.	Continuation of the Instructions on the Government of the Illuminees—Laws for Local Superiors	549
Chap. XVII.	Instructions for the Provincial	558
Chap. XVIII.	Of the National Directors, of the Areopagites, and of the General of Illuminism	563

PART FOUR

ANTISOCIAL CONSPIRACY. HISTORICAL PART

	PRELIMINARY DISCOURSE	581
Chap. I.	First Epoch of Illuminism	584

CONTENTS

CHAP. II.	Of the principal Adepts during the first Epoch of Illuminism	596
CHAP. III.	Second Epoch of Illuminism—The Illuminization of Freemasonry—Weishaupt's attempts on the Masonic Lodges—Acquisition of Knigge, and his first Services	617
CHAP. IV.	Congress of the Freemasons at Wilhemsbaden—Of their divers Sects, and particularly of that of the Theosophical Illuminees.	628
CHAP. V.	Knigge's Intrigues and Successes at the Congress.—Official Reports of the Superiors of the Order—Multitude of Masons illuminized at this Period	645
CHAP. VI.	New means practised, and new conquests made by Knigge and Weishaupt on Masonry—Disputes between these two Chiefs of Illuminism—Their designs on the German Masons consummated before Knigge's retreat	660
CHAP. VII.	Third Epoch of Illuminism—Discovery of the Sect	674
CHAP. VIII.	Continuation of the Discoveries made in Bavaria as to the Illuminees—Proceedings of the Court with respect to the Chiefs of the Sect—A few Remarks on and a List of the principal Adepts	690
CHAP. IX.	New Chiefs and new Means of the Illuminees.—Device of the Jesuits Masonry and Success of that Imposture	703
CHAP. X.	The Germanic Union—Its principal Actors, and the Conquests it prepared for the Illuminees	712
CHAP. XI.	Fourth Epoch of Illuminism—The Deputation from Weishaupt's Illuminees to the Freemasons of Paris—State of French Masonry at that period—Labours and Successes of the Deputies—Coalition of the Conspiring Sophisters, Masons, and Illuminees, generating the Jacobins	726
CHAP. XII.	Application of the three Conspiracies to the French Revolution	749
CHAP. XIII.	Universality of the Success of the Sect explained by the universality of its Plots	779
CONCLUSION		817
[APPENDIX]	[Barruel's] OBSERVATIONS *on some Articles published in the* MONTHLY REVIEW, *relative to the* "MEMOIRS ON JACOBINISM"	839

INTRODUCTION

TODAY the word Jacobinism is largely a linguistic relic of which most learn only from textbooks on modern history. But in its heyday Jacobinism meant a violent stream of history that carried the French Revolution within four short years to its reign of Terror. During those years down went the monarchy, the aristocracy and, in all appearance, the Church as well. With an uncompromising brute force Jacobinism demolished all that had set the tone of public life in France for the previous thousand or so years.

What happened obeyed the logic that radicalism can only feed on more radicalism. But both logic and radicalism are abstractions, whereas history, or the interaction of many concrete individuals, is not. One is therefore prompted to assume that a process, so logical in its course and so terrifying in its dénouement, had to be directed by a relatively small group of powerful personalities. Historians are unanimous in seeing Jacobins playing a prominent part in that group. Jacobins stood for radicalism from the moment the process, subsequently known as the French Revolution, formally started with a splendid religious procession in Versailles on May 4, 1789. In two more months the Bastille was stormed under the protective eyes of a National Assembly, the designation which the Third Estate, as emphatically distinct from both aristocracy and clergy, had just bestowed upon itself. Soon that Assembly, under the pressure of Jacobins, set itself up as the Constituent Assembly.

The reconstitution of everything was now under way, including some of the most personal decisions a human being can make. Freely taken religious vows were declared to be illegal, while accolades were being heaped upon the freedom of the individual. Almost on the very first anniversary of the assault on the Bastille, the Constituent Assembly revealed the stunning extent to which it was already prisoner of a maddening logic animating the Jacobins. By asserting its right over every aspect of the Church, it committed, as recalled by a chief Jacobin, Prince Talleyrand, its "greatest political mistake . . . quite apart from the dreadful crimes which flowed therefrom."

Now a civil Constitution, whatever its legitimacy, pitted itself against a perennial constitution which is known as the freedom of conscience, including the freedom to obey the voice of a conscience that thinks in terms of eternity. It was at that juncture that the spine of the vacillating Louis XVI began to stiffen to the point of facing up bravely to what, in a sense, was a martyrdom. After all, it was not he who committed the sins of Louis XV, who also added long decades of absolutist rule to the no less lengthy absolutism of Louis XIV.

The King saw his fate sealed after he had to take refuge with the Constituent Assembly following the bloody confrontation, in August 1792, at the Tuileries between the crowd and his own Swiss Guards. The next month is remembered as the September massacre. Mme Roland, a great devotee of the Revolution, whose husband was at that time the Minister of the Interior, had to admit: "Women were brutally violated before being torn to pieces by those tigers; intestines cut out and worn as turbans; bleeding human flesh devoured." To save her father, the daughter of an aristocrat drank, with utter revulsion, the blood freshly squeezed from the body of one of the victims. Under the windows of the Queen the decapitated head of Madame Lamballe, a confidante of hers, was paraded. Another female victim was finished off with fire lit between her distended legs. Among the victims were two hundred and fifty priests. Violette, who presided at the execution of many of them in the Vaugirard section, reported the next day: "I do not understand, they seemed happy. They went to death as to a wedding."

Their judges and executioners could still pretend that those priests, refusing to take the oath to the civil constitution legislated for the Church, paid the penalty of high treason. But that pretense was wearing very thin when even the Sundays were abolished, and finally simple nuns could unmask it with ease. Fanaticism was the crime with which Fouquier-Tinville, president of the revolutionary court in Compiègne, accused sixteen Carmelite nuns there. But when asked by one of them as to what he meant by fanaticism, the true nature of the crime, "foolish attachment to your stupid religious practices," was made so clear as to let her draw the only logical inference: "There you are, sisters: we have been condemned for our religion. . . . What a happiness to die for our God!" They went to the scaffold singing the *Veni Creator* which continued until the voice of the last of them was stilled by the guillotine.

By then, July 17, 1794, the *sansculottes* (the kind of rabble ready for any hatchet job) had been the arm of Fate for more than two years. They added ruthless muscle power to that equally ruthless power-politics which was the chief trademark of the Jacobins. These were at first known as those delegates from Brittany to the National Assembly who formed the Breton Club. They rightly believed that even a small parliamentary group can wield considerable power if it carefully plans its strategy. Thus when the Assembly moved to Paris and forced the King to follow suit, members of the Breton Club quickly looked for a place where they could plan their further moves. They chose, not without reason, the refectory of the Dominican Convent, named after St. Jacques (James) in the rue St. Honoré, a locale close to the place where the Assembly was meeting. They were soon being called Jacobins, first a label of scorn and ridicule, and subsequently an appellation formally assumed by those radicals themselves, possibly because they felt powerful enough to pour scorn on ridicule. Indeed, they saw their power increase with hardly a setback.

Finally they disposed of the Girondists, their chief rivals in the corridors of power, who were only a shade less radical. The Jacobins increasingly relied on the *sansculottes* who in turn provided the naked ruthlessness which an ideological radicalism cannot dispense with if it is to keep its momentum.

Paris and France were now in the grip of the Terror, brought about by the Jacobins who themselves were to be devoured by it. Once the guillotine finished off their chief Girondist rivals, it was the turn of leading Jacobins. These may have found comfort in the conviction that their chief target and antagonist, the Church, had already gone down. For by the time it was the turn of Robespierre, thousands of priests, religious and nuns had been executed, at times in circumstances that were called the "dry guillotine," or the horrid holds of former slave ships. By then some twenty thousand French clergy were living in exile, ten thousand of them in England, a country which Pius VI thanked for its generous hospitality in a letter written to King George III on September 7, 1792. William Pitt, the King's Prime Minister, remembered those exiles in the following words: "Few will ever forget the piety, the irreproachable conduct, the long and dolorous patience of those men, cast suddenly into the midst of a foreign people different in its religion, its language, its manners and its customs. They won the respect and goodwill of all by a life of unvarying godliness and decency." Among the ones praised by Pitt, very prominent was the Abbé Augustin Barruel, the author of this book.

His fame had preceded him by the time he arrived in England, after having made his escape from France at practically the last minute, in the late summer of 1792, just before the September massacre. Born in 1741, in Villeneuve-de-Berg (near Viviers, in the mountainous Vivarais region of the Ardèche), in a recently ennobled family, he entered, at the age of fifteen, the Society of Jesus. Following his novitiate, he taught the humanities in the Jesuit college in Toulouse. But by the time he was ready to take his perpetual vows, Louis XV had signed the edict that banished the Jesuits from France. Barruel decided to continue his Jesuit training in Poland, but on his way he was retained in Prague by the Jesuit Provincial of Bohemia. He resumed his theological studies, was ordained priest, and after some teaching assignments in Bohemia and Moravia, he became attached to the faculty of the Teresianum in Vienna. It was there that he learned about the supression of the Jesuits by Pope Clement XIV on August 7, 1773. He therefore had to become a secular priest and a year later returned to France as tutor to the children of Prince François-Xavier of Saxe, a distant cousin of Louis XVI. In 1777 Barruel became the almoner of the Princesse Conti in Paris, a position that left him with leisure and means to devote himself entirely to studies and writing.

He greeted the ascent to the throne of Louis XVI with an ode that sold 12,000 copies. It made his name cherished in Royalist circles and odious in the circles of *philosophes* whose thinking and strategies were increasingly becoming Barruel's chief concern. He did his best to expose the fallacies of the *philosophes* in his *Les Helviennes*, a fictive exchange of letters between a young Parisian and a "Helvien" or youngster from Vivarais, the area occupied in

Roman times by the Helviens. The book, first published in 1781, was reprinted three more times between 1784 and 1788. But, it must be admitted, Barruel could not match the *philosophes* in pouring subtle ridicule on one's opponents. Barruel's strength was in marshalling evidence, which he used effectively in the pages of the *Année littéraire*, a periodical founded by Fréron, a resolute opponent of the *philosophes*.

Barruel opposed with no less resolve those among the clergy who thought that an accommodation was possible with the *philosophes*. One of those priests was the abbé Soulavie, author of a book on Genesis. Barruel's critique of it was so effective that the Sorbonne dissociated itself with its author, who in turn sued Barruel for libel. The result was that Barruel's book, *La Genèse selon M. Soulavie*, had to be destroyed. No copy is known to exist. Soon Barruel took over the editorship of the *Journal ecclésiastique*, which he kept publishing, often at his own expense, until August 10, 1792. Then he had to go into hiding in Paris, until he could escape to Normandy and from there, in mid-September 1792, to England.

Three years earlier Barruel had sat with the clergy in the National Assembly and opposed the schemings of the Jacobins from the start. By then he had already probed into their motivation in a book, *Discours sur les vraies causes de la révolution* (1789). No sooner had the Jacobins pressed for civil marriage and the legalization of divorce, than Barruel stepped in the breach by his *Lettres sur le divorce: les vraies principes sur le mariage*, published a year later. In the former book Barruel specifies two causes that made the Revolution a reality. One cause is supernatural, or divine Providence that punishes France for having acted as the breeding place of an ideology destructive of Christian society. The other cause is natural: the conspiracy of the *philosophes* to destroy Church and State. His analysis of that conspiracy was to appear eventually on a grand scale in the book here reprinted.

In 1791, the year that saw the new Constitution enacted and subsequently signed by Louis XVI, though with great reluctance and much delay, Barruel took up his antirevolutionary cudgels again with a book, *Question nationale sur l'autorité et sur les droit du peuple dans le gouvernment*. His chief annoyance was the civil reconstitution of the Church in France. He saw clearly that the new status accorded to French bishops and priests could not be reconciled with the idea that the Church in France was but a part of a Church that had its authority from above and therefore was not subject to civil authorities in matters relating to its divine mission. Less satisfactory was Barruel's rallying squarely behind the divine right of the monarchy. The teaching of Thomas Aquinas and of Bellarmine, that the people were the ultimate source on earth of political authority and power, was not something that Barruel would fully appreciate. However, he would have found an excuse in the difference between an abstract proposition and the concrete reality. With the Jacobins in ever wider control of political power, a free and dispassionate consultation of the people had to appear nothing short of a pipedream.

The extent to which the Jacobins were in control by mid-1793 is best attested by the fact that the combined membership of Jacobin clubs was by then close to half a million. Those clubs were the chief driving force behind the bizarre religious rites, of which the one performed in honor of the Goddess of Reason at Notre Dame in Paris became the most remembered, partly because of the debaucheries connected with it. Along with this the Jacobin clubs did not tire of imposing the study of the chief works of the *philosophes,* full of invectives against the Christian religion. When Robespierre's deist theology became the law of the land, notices of this were duly affixed on the doors of each and every Church.

All this well reflected the fact that the radicalism of the Jacobins was fuelled by a religion of their own, a religion radically different from Christian religion. The latter was anchored in the conviction that supernatural reality, as manifested in biblical revelation and especially in Jesus Christ, was the supreme reality. The religion professed by the Jacobins stood for exactly the opposite, that is, the very denial of the supernatural taken in that specific sense. Any other form of "supernaturalism," or cavorting in pseudoreligious rites, was not only tolerated, but eagerly cultivated in Jacobin circles. Clearly, a cult, in this case the Christian Cult, could not be replaced except by another cult. And the Jacobins' cult, insofar as it had rituals, was distinctly Freemasonic. There will be nothing surprising in this for anyone aware of the large influx of Freemasons into Jacobin clubs from the moment the Jacobins appeared to be riding the crest of the political wave. Following the creation of the Grand Orient in 1772, French Freemasony kept flexing its muscles under the Grand Mastership of the Duc d'Orléans, a cousin of Louis XVI. Within seventeen years, the number of Masonic lodges associated with the Grand Orient grew from 23 to 65 in Paris, and from 71 to about 600 in the country. Freemasonic religion and its ceremonies posed no problem for Voltaire when he was inducted, with great fanfare, into the Lodge in 1776. Two years later the rank anti-Christian character of Voltaire's funeral shocked even some leading Masons, such as the Marquis de Condorcet.

Some Catholics, who should have known better, were particularly slow in coming to their senses. In 1782 Joseph de Maistre, the future stalwart of ultramontanism, still hoped that the international collaboration of the Lodges would achieve the unity of all Christian denominations. The Cistercians of St. Bernard's Clairvaux formed a Lodge of their own. Had not some of the Dominicans of their convent in rue St. Honoré been dutiful members of the Lodge, the Jacobins would not have turned to them for accommodations.

It was then that Freemasonry began to dominate Jacobin clubs. In fact, Freemasons were responsible for the founding of many Jacobin clubs throughout France. Whatever was conspiratorial in this, it certainly evidenced that birds of the same feather flock together, especially when mutual interests demand it. The Jacobins could only be pleased to see their ranks swollen by aristocrats and men of letters, who were the mainstay of the Grand Orient and its affiliates, as well as by the still independent Lodges, of which the Loge des

Neufs Sœurs was the most prominent. The Lodges in turn could but see a golden opportunity in corralling the political power of the Jacobins for the promotion of their grand objective. It is still expressed (cagily enough) in the motto *novus ordo saeclorum* that graces each and every one dollar bill. The motto stood for the replacement of the order set by the *Novum testamentum* by a new order, in which the New Testament was acceptable only inasmuch as its miracles, prophecies, and above all its central figure, Jesus Christ, were taken for a mere stepping stone toward the supreme form of religion, the religion of Reason as interpreted and celebrated in the Lodges.

For celebrations and rituals were of the essence of the Freemasonic dispensation. Nothing can indeed silence so effectively latter-day glorifiers of the "rationality" of the Enlightenment than a brief reference to the "rites" to which its leaders readily submitted either in the salons or in the Lodges. And what about their taking Masonic vows of obedience and secrecy, while those who had taken the traditional religious vows had to run for dear life?

Of course, by 1793, when the Grand Orient was disavowed by its Grand Master, the Duc d'Orléans, many lesser Freemasons knew that the Lodges, inasmuch as they looked for and worked hand in hand with the Jacobins toward a quick instauration of the New Order, had their prospects darkened. As the Revolution devoured itself in its terrorist frenzy, so were decimated Jacobin clubs and Lodges as well as their combinations. They served further evidence to the truth of the biblical words: "When they sow the wind, they shall reap the whirlwind" (Hos 8:7). Jacobinism as such perished in the storm of its own making. As to the Lodges, they had to settle with an indefinite future in which to bring about the New Order. But that New Order has remained what it was meant to be from the start: an uncompromising replacement of Christian religion standing for supernatural truths, with the only supreme Truth, Reason as interpreted by the Lodges.

The thorough unity of this new start with its erstwhile beginnings was nowhere better summed up than in *The Revolution and Freemasonry, 1680-1800* by Bernard Fay, a Freemason himself. It ends with the statement: "The Catholic Church worshiped openly a mysterious God. Freemasonry honored mysteriously a logical principle. The Great Architect was simply an idea, a tool of the human mind, which needed it for its scientific work and social peace. The Masonic god had no mystery, while the Masonic society was all mystery. With a great scorn for dogmas, a complete independence of kings and religion,—wrapped in its mystery, which shone around it like a black and luminous cloud,—Freemasony had the supreme dexterity to replace a mysterious Divinity by a divine mystery." It still works with that supreme dexterity and secrecy, lulling countless Christians, weak in their faith, into the belief that one can be a genuine follower of Christ, while still being a good Mason.

The Abbé Barruel correctly diagnosed all this and took it for his guide in setting out, no sooner had he landed in England, to write his *magnum opus*, the work here reprinted in its English translation. To complete and see through the press a four-volume book in so many years would have been a great scholarly feat even if it had been done with one's own library close at hand. To do this in exile, even if that exile was London, added to the measure of Barruel's efforts. Already by the time he made his last-minute escape from France, most likely he had completed much of the manuscript of his *Histoire du Clergé pendant la Révolution française*. It came out in London in 1793 as a book of over 400 pages and saw six re-editions during the next six years.

But Barruel's great project was the present book, published in four volumes in 1797-98 under the title: *Mémoires pour servir à l'histoire du Jacobinisme*, reissued in Hamburg (1798-99), in Augsburg (1799), Brunswick (1800), and Hamburg again (1803). Publication in France had to wait until 1818, with another edition appearing in 1837. Meanwhile a one-volume abridged edition appeared in London (1798) which during the next twenty years was republished eight times in various places, the last of them being Paris. This edition (1817) was supervised by Barruel himself.

Almost simultaneously with the French original there appeared, in four volumes, an English translation by the Honorable Robert Edward Clifford (1767-1817) who one year later, in 1798, brought out a second edition that contained (especially in volume I) many stylistic corrections as well as revised and far more detailed references to sources quoted. About the same time Clifford's translation was printed in New York as well. It is the second London edition which is reset here in full, with all its orthographic idiosyncrasies, including some quaint spellings, such as Jean-Jaques and Lewis XVI, and the use of a comma before subordinate clauses introduced with 'that'. Last but not least, French words were printed with an almost complete omission of French accents. To the modern reader, "Nismes," "Besancon," "etre" or "pretre" or "abbe" will give a touch of the times. He will have the same experience on coming across English words such as "murthered," "recal," "skreen," "secresy," and the like. Inconsistency in spelling is exemplified in the gradual shifting from Free-masonry to Freemasonry. Those familiar with the German idiom will certainly be transported to late eighteenth-century Bavarian dialect and spelling as they read the German quotations, most of them in the notes. Only here and there were changes made in the text, such as when either an "is," or an "are," or a "the" was obviously missing.

The T. or Trans. at the end of some notes refer, of course, to the translator, Robert Clifford. He was the scion of the vast baronial family of the Cliffords of Chudleigh (in Devonshire) that originated when Charles II knighted Thomas Clifford for bringing about the treaty of Dover in 1670. Shortly afterwards Lord Clifford gave valuable advice to the King on how to replenish his treasury. But in 1673 he had to resign the post of Secretary of the Exchequer, because the Test Act, which he bravely contested in Parliament, barred Catholics from public office. It mattered not that he had showed signal bravery in the naval war against the Dutch.

During the next hundred or so years the descendants of Thomas Clifford grew into a huge clan, with much credit to the Catholic cause in England and elsewhere. In the mid-19th century a Clifford was the bishop of the new Catholic bishopric of Clinton in Wales and a trusted friend of John Henry Newman. About the translator of Barruel's book Joseph Gillow states in his *A Literary and Biographical History, or Bibliographical Dictionary of the English Catholics,* that he was the third son of Hugh, fifth Lord of Clifford, and lived mostly in France. In addition to his translation of Barruel's book, four other publications of his are listed by Gillow. Of the four, three make it abundantly clear that Robert Clifford was indeed a close observer of the French Revolution. Between 1789 and 1794 he dashed off a large number of brief accounts of current events in Paris. Another entry is his application of the lessons of Barruel's work to the spread of secret societies in Ireland. According to Gillow, Clinton translated into English Louis Marie Prudhomme's *Histoire générale et impartiale des erreurs, des fautes et des crimes commis pendant la Révolution française.* The fifth entry indicates, mistakenly, a book, the translation of a work by a A. Q. Budé, actually the Abbé Adrien-Quentin Buée. A strong critic of priests favorable to the civil constitution of the clergy, Buée left France for England about the same time as Barruel did. Buée's "Parallel of Romé de l'Isles's and the Abbé Haüy's Theories of Crystallography," was a mere essay, published, in Clifford's translation, in the *Philosophical Magazine* in 1804, or thirteen years after Clifford was elected Fellow of the Royal Society. Clifford was also a Fellow of the Royal Antiquarian Society.

Clearly, the translator of Barruel's work was a scholar in his own right, who most likely was in contact with Barruel prior to the latter's escape to England. Barruel may indeed have been a protégé of the Cliffords in London, although he found accommodations with a fellow Jesuit, Father Strickland. Robert Clifford must have had easy access to the manuscripts of Barruel's work, otherwise his translation would not have appeared almost simultaneously with the original. This closeness between the two would explain Barruel's easy access to many major documents and the fact that in all appearance important channels of communication remained open to him during the particularly difficult years that lasted until the Terror's fury consumed itself. Close ties with an English Catholic baronial family, such as the Cliffords, had to be of great advantage to Barruel, even as an author, let alone as a priest and a religious. The two chief printed sources from which Barruel gathered much of his material for the *Memoirs* must have, of course, been readily available in London. One of them was the *Oeuvres complètes de Voltaire,* published in 70 volumes in Paris between 1784 and 1789, the last thirty volumes being Voltaire's correspondence. It was edited by Kehl, whose *Vie de Voltaire* Barruel often made use of. In addition, Barruel could have hardly written volumes III and IV of the *Memoirs,* had not the Weimar police brought the scheming of Weishaupt, the head of the Illuminati (called *illuminees* throughout the *Memoirs*), into full daylight by quickly publishing his manuscripts after their confiscation on October 12, 1786.

One did not have to be an English Catholic aristocrat in order to sympathize with the thesis Barruel set forth with massive documentation. No

INTRODUCTION xix

sooner had Burke read in January 1790 a sermon which Richard Price, an eminent dissenting clergyman, preached two months earlier on the noble visions of the Constituent Assembly in Paris, than he set out to voice in his *Reflections on the French Revolution* the very different sentiments which many other commoners in England shared. They certainly resonated to the *Reflections*' most celebrated passage that followed Burke's bemoaning of the fact that no multitude of swords leapt from their scabbards to avenge even a threatening look at the Queen: "But the age of chivalry is gone. That of sophisters, oeconomists, and calculators has succeeded and the glory of Europe is extinguished forever." And Burke had not yet seen the *sansculottes* on the rampage and the Queen of France being ignominiously guillotined.

Burke's *Reflections* did much to enlighten the English Establishment about the true nature of the French Revolution, which at first was looked upon with favor in leading English circles, imbued as these were with Freemasonic ideas. It is easy to guess the kind of essay-review Burke would have written had he not died on July 9, 1797, just two months or so after the first volume of Barruel's magnum opus had come off the printing press. For as soon as Burke received that volume, he wrote, on May 1, to Barruel:

> I cannot easily express to you how much I am instructed and delighted by the first Volume of your History of Jacobinism. The whole of the wonderful narrative is supported by documents and proofs with the most juridical regularity and exactness. Your reflexions and reasonings are interspersed with infinite judgment, and in their most proper places, for leading the sentiments of the reader, and preventing the force of plausible objections. The tendency of the whole is admirable in every point of view, political, religious, and, let me make use of the abused word, philosophical.

He praised the French style as being "of the first water" and expressed his wish that the book, through a suitable abridgment, might find "a great circulation in France." To that end, he stated, he was glad "upon the scale of a poor individual, to become a liberal subscriber." Then he touched on a point which was to become the focus of debates about Barruel's book:

> I have known myself, personally, five of your principal conspirators; and I can undertake to say from my own certain knowledge, that so far back as the year 1773, they were busy in the plot you have so well described, and in the manner, and on the principle you have so truly represented. To this I can speak as a witness.

Such was a priceless testimony on the part of a lawyer, who always looked far beyond legal technicalities for the often unspoken assumptions that led his antagonists and who could size them up as if by instinct. So it was no boasting on Burke's part to refer to that visit of his to Paris in 1773. Then he certainly met Mirabeau, one of those five conspirators. The other four whom Burke most likely met were Diderot, Necker, Turgot, and the Duc d'Orléans. Compared with the testimony of Burke on behalf of Barruel's thesis, the raving reviews of the *Memoirs* in the conservative *Anti-Jacobin Review* and *The British Critic* may seem of secondary importance.

Barruel's book had much to offer to a great variety of readers. Undoubtedly the French Royalists saw in it a godsend. It had to please all Catholics, and even Christians whose faith was more than an embellished Deism. It had to please all those who were eager to know the truth about what were the driving forces behind the French Revolution. But the book was received with mixed feelings on the part of those—and there were many of them in the high echelons of the English political and ecclesiastical establishment—who complacently took Freemasonry for a natural ally of a properly tamed and civilized Christianity. Barruel knew, of course, the difference between English and French Freemasonry. But he warned that England would not escape the French Revolution, once its Lodges resembled those he was at pains to unmask. And in the same context (see pp. 257-59) he made a most important qualification about Freemasons. He held most of them, especially in England, to be unaware of the real intentions of their leaders. The more sinister, he added a few pages later, were the deliberations taken in the innermost recesses of the Lodges, the more the historian has to insist that the great multitude of Freemasons was unaware of them.

It would have been to deny the obvious if one disagreed with the themes which Barruel developed in the first volume of his work. The French Revolution was heavily fuelled by an anti-Christian conspiracy. Nor could there be any dispute about the fact, developed in the second volume, that the Revolution had fanatically anti-monarchical forces behind it. But beyond those themes there was a thesis, namely, that the fairly fast ascendency of the anti-Christian and anti-monarchical forces in the Constituent Assembly was the conspiracy of a relatively small group of Jacobins, Freemasons, and *illuminees* of whom more will be said shortly. Yet, the vast evidence Barruel marshalled on behalf of that thesis did not amount to a smoking gun, nor even to what Courts usually look for in the way of legal evidence.

But it was as a historian that Barruel wanted to convict those three groups. Now, if a historian has to wait in each case until he finds legal evidence, let alone a smoking gun, he will have few cases on which to take a firm stand. For the process of history is not a chain of logical steps that can be specified at every turn because they had been put on paper and carefully preserved for posterity. History, as Newman memorably put it, can be written only if one accepts the fact that "broad outlines and broad masses of colour rise out of the records of the past," even though the records are far from complete enough to satisfy the canons of minutious documentation which at times prevent their devotees from seeing the forest for the trees.

At any rate, what logic could be assigned to the somewhat meek yielding of Louis XVI to the pressure of the mob that he should transfer his residence from Versailles to Paris? But Barruel, the historian, rightly made much of the fact that long before Louis XVI ascended the throne, the *philosophes* had been busy with their propaganda. They were systematically piling up a kindling ready to be ignited by sparks, however unforeseen or unpredictable. No *philosophe* could foresee the disastrous harvest of 1788 that could but fuel an already seething discontent.

It is not for the historian to ponder imponderable questions: Would there have been a Revolution if Louis XVI had removed himself from Versailles, as he was urged, a month or two before some thirty thousand women of Paris, clamoring for bread, had descended on him on October 4, 1789? And could they have confronted the King *en masse*, had they not found a gate of the palace unlocked? Would the King have had better presence of mind on that fateful afternoon, had he not spent the morning in carefree hunting? Would the women have clamoured for bread in the first place, had not an unusually long drought stopped many watermills working over much of France? And, most importantly, could it really be in the plans of the Jacobins that strong detachments of the National Guard should follow those women? Was not Louis XVI's yielding to the demand that he and his entire family move to Paris something which no plan of the Jacobins could have included? But once the King assented, his cause was lost. Such was at least the reaction of a young American, Jefferson, who happened to be in Versailles on that ominous day.

When, finally, the King tried to escape from France with his family, only to be stopped at Varennes, he lost out on a desperate gamble. Yet had fortune favored the King, this too might have acted as a spark igniting a conflagration against him and the Monarchy. After all, months before the King's removal from Versailles to Paris, and three full years before the battle of Valmy, the Duc de Broglie, commander of the Royal Guards, saw matters all too clearly: The Royal Guards, he told the King, could not secure the transfer of the Royal Family to Metz, because the route there led through a country ready to revolt. His moving to Metz would have right there and then turned the Revolution into a holy cause to save France. Eventually Louis XVI invited Prussian and Austrian troops against his own country. This became the chief charge for which he had to suffer capital punishment and also the factor that raised French patriotic fever to a high pitch. But that fever was to have a fateful grip on France for almost twenty years. And just as a body comes out gravely weakened from a high and long fever, France too lost its earstwhile strength as Europe's leading power. Nothing of this was foreseen or planned by the Jacobins.

Still the history of the French Revolution, though full of decisive turning points that are less than half-logical, is also permeated by trends. As to the former the word chance alone applies where all reasoning and analysis fail. But the historian is not a calculator of probabilities that point in a direction at stark variance with trends. There were enough in France to make a revolution, which is hardly ever the work of a majority. Even in the United States, only one third of the population wanted independence, another third was resolutely against it, while still another third could not have cared less. It is in vain to speculate whether by relying on Fénelon as against Bossuet, the Court could have set in motion a gradual transition from an absolutist to a constitutional Monarchy. Even in England, one king had to be beheaded and another chased into exile, so that William, Prince of Orange, could be dictated the terms under which he could ascend the throne of a Monarchy "constituted" by Parliament.

The trend toward an explosive demolition of the *ancien régime* shows several components—political, religious, cultural, and economic. Barruel was particularly myopic about the economic as well as the cultural parameters. There was more to that latter parameter than the Enyclopedists' heavy plagiarizing of the *Dictionnaire* connected with the Jesuits' *Journal de Trévoux*. There are no traces in the *Memoirs* of the kind of observations which legitimately could be made about not infrequent cases of most abject poverty throughout France. The religious problems Barruel saw all too well, without speculating on effective means and procedures for their solutions. As to the political problems, he blamed the King's opponents for the stalling of much needed reforms. Yet much stalling was done by the King and the aristocracy around him, and this could only precipitate matters in the long run. But as in ordinary conflagrations, here too it was indispensable that the atmosphere be made highly inflammable. The *philosophes* saw to this and they did so in a concerted and conspiratorial manner. They would not have embraced the Lodges, had these in turn not found most germane to their purposes the ideological agitation against Altar and Throne. By the time the Jacobins, and their union with Freemasons, came along, the all important climate of thought had been in place. Here only by ignoring the role which the climate of thought plays in history can one argue with Barruel.

Barruel weakened his main contention by attributing a decisive role to the *illuminees,* as organized by Adam Weishaupt (1748-1830), professor of Law at the University of Ingolstadt. In volumes III and IV, a still unsurpassed portrayal of the ideas and activities of Weishaupt and his *illuminees,* Barruel claims to have found, so to speak, the smoking gun whereby he can indict French Freemasonry as penetrated by the *illuminees,* the braintrust, according to him, behind the events that constituted the French Revolution.

Barruel was not the first to hold that conspiracy theory. In the same year, 1797, when Barruel's *Memoirs* began to be published, it was proposed, independently of him and on a fairly large scale, by John Robison, an Edinburgh philosopher, who contributed a number of articles on scientific and technological topics to the *Encylopedia Britannica*. Robison's *Proofs of a Conspiracy against all the Religions and Governments of Europe, carried on in the Secret Meetings of Free Masons, Illuminati, and Reading Societies* relied heavily on the published texts of Weishaupt's manuscripts. Robison took up the Jacobins only in his book's fourth and last chapter where he dealt with the French Revolution itself. In the three first chapters, each about a hundred pages long, he discussed Freemasonry, the Illuminati and their German union. But once Barruel's *Memoirs* had been made available, any advocate of the conspiracy theory, or simply anyone who held the *philosophes* (together with or without the Freemasons and the Illuminati) responsible for the Revolution, had to make much of the material there. Such was certainly the case with Johann August Starck, professor of theology in Königsberg and author of the two-volume *Der Triumph der Philosophie im 18th Jahrhundert* (1803).

Awareness among French Catholics about a conspiracy against the Church was fairly strong. The Abbé Lefranc, superior of the major seminary at Coutances, and later a victim of the September massacre (and still later beatified by the Church), was one of those who early called attention to a "Masonic conspiracy." Of that conspiracy some Masons gave now and then a revealing hint. Upon returning from a major masonic congress in Wilhelmsbad in 1782, Henry de Virieu told a friend who asked him about secret information he might have brought back: "The whole business is more serious than you think. The plot has so carefully been hatched that it is practically impossible for the Church and the Monarchy to escape." By then that art of hatching had been going on for some time. A telling proof of this is a letter of Voltaire from April 1761, which Barruel quoted at the very beginning of chapter seven of Part One. There Voltaire wrote to D'Alembert that not only should the *philosophes* form a union as closely knit as Freemasons, but they too should do so in utter secrecy.

Freemasons did not have to protest publicly Barruel's thesis that they were strongly involved in that conspiracy. The work was done for them by Jean-Joseph Mounier, a moderate royalist deputy during the early days of the Constituent Assembly and in exile by the time of the Terror, who gladly took public office under the Consulate. Mounier's book, *De l'influence attribuée aux philosophes, aux franc-maçons et aux illuminés sur la révolution de France*, published in Tubingen in 1801, was immediately brought out in English in London, translated from the manuscript itself. Clearly, it was judged advisable by some to do the job with all possible speed! (The original French was republished, along with a lengthy Notice on Mounier, in Paris in 1822, twenty years after his death). The English translation was quickly reviewed in *The British Critic*, a review noteworthy because it focused, and rightly so, on Mounier's chief tactic. It was to insist that the word *conspiracy* denotes a meticulously planned co-operation to carry out a very specific plan.

Barruel, of course, could not document all details of that "meticulous" planning. He could not find in the published writings of the *philosophes* and of Masons traces of "specific" data as to how to proceed in the political arena at each and every step. But he could amply document their continually expressed intention of spreading ideas indispensable for fueling efforts that inevitably led to the overthrow of Altar and Throne. Last but not least, he could document many of their moves to place their own people into positions of influence and power.

Concerning the fact of conspiracy, Mounier's refutation of it would nowadays support the arguments of those who claim that, for instance, the Rosenbergs proved to be Soviet spies only after evidence against them has become available from former KGB archives. But there is an even more telling point against Mounier's grand conclusion that "the Freemasons had no influence whatsoever in the promotion of the French Revolution." The point, made very clear by the reviewer of Mounier's book in *The British Critic*, is Mounier's taking the word "conspiracy" in an extremely restricted sense. But as the reviewer recalled, Samuel Johnson, the great originator of modern English dictionaries, attributed a very broad meaning to the word *conspiracy*. (The same word had and still has, it is well to note, in French too a very broad meaning, as can be seen by a mere look at the words *conspirer* and its derivatives in *Dictionnaire alphabétique et analogique de le langue française*, the French counterpart of the *Oxford English Dictionary*.) Equally defective, in the eyes of the reviewer, was Mounier's use of the words *philosophy* and *superstition*. Moreover, Mounier almost paraded as a Freemason in that he heavily relied on Freemasonic connections for advice and material. Indeed, he praised Freemasons as "the friends of humanity and the defenders of the principles of tolerance and justice," while denouncing their adversaries, including Barruel, as "the apostles of superstition and slavery." Yet those apostles of toleration did their best to prohibit the publication of Barruel's book wherever they could, and to treat him as a rule with silence.

There was also the charge, made by a reviewer in *The Critical Review* (1797), that Barruel was not accurate in his documentation, a charge sharply renewed recently by Amos Hofman in his "Opinion, Illusion, and the Illusion of Opinion: Barruel's Theory of Conspiracy" (in *Eighteenth-Century Studies*, vol. 27, Fall 1993). According to Hofman "Barruel's book is indeed full of misquotations, unfounded conclusions and assertions based upon evidence that he seems reluctant to disclose. He often insisted on the anonymity of his sources, contending that his informants' lives might be in danger if their identities were revealed." Such a sweeping indictment of Barruel's veracity remains a slur as long as it is documented with a reference to merely two or three pages in the *Memoirs*. The one serious study of Barruel's use of his sources is by René Le Forestier, who in his *Les Illuminés de Bavière et la Fanc-Maçonnerie allemande* (1914) wrote in reference to the third volume of Barruel's *Memoirs* that it constitutes not only its most considerable but also its "most solidly and, in spite of its author's partiality, most conscientiously established part." According to Le Forestier Barruel "read everything" on the subject, and he praised Barruel's translations of the many passages he had quoted from the German as "somewhat free but reliable."

Most importantly, Barruel speaks even from his grave to those who appreciate a voice echoing principles much higher than the ones provided by sociology and political science, to say nothing of most "cultural" studies, whose authors either simply abstract from cults or treat all of them as equally relevant or irrelevant. Barruel did not for a moment try to conceal that he was a professed devotee of the cult called Roman Catholicism, and as such committed to a distinction between truth and error, right and wrong. It is to make a mockery of the *Memoirs* (and of the historical method) to find, as

Hofman does, its sole redeeming value in Barruel's turning the word "conspiracy" into a major tool of political interpretation.

According to Hofman, Barruel's chief problem was to explain how the absurd doctrines of the *philosophes* could quickly become a majority opinion in Catholic monarchical France and dominate political discourse and action. But this was not a problem for Barruel, who being the kind of priest and a theologian he was, had no illusions about the markedly unstable character of human nature. The problem exists for those who try to explain ontological and moral problems with references to sociological and political categories. Thus we see Barruel becoming in Hofman's hands a "prophetic" articulator of the Right versus Left dichotomy of modern political history inasmuch as through his use the word conspiracy has become a chief vehicle of power politics. The supreme accolade given by Hofman to the *Memoirs* is its being "an exceptionally powerful insight into the workings of revolution," that is, of all major political upheavals. "The idea of conspiracy, as Barruel explained," Hofman continues, "was the means by which revolutionary regimes (as well as those who opposed them) divided the world into those who were for and those who were against the newly created power."

This may do well for a political theorist, indifferent as to who are in power, but hardly for historians fond of logic. For even if Barruel's claim that the conspiracy of "specific men" brought about the French Revolution cannot "survive historical criticism," as Hofman would have it, there could still have been a conspiracy, and certainly in the broader sense of that word. Furthermore, if the mere appearance of conspiracy, or the artful indocrination of the public with the idea of a conspiracy, was alone needed to spark the Revolution, is not one in the presence of a conspiracy? Can the specter of conspiracy be exorcized by falling back on pleasing categories, smacking of Hegelian dialectic, about society in "constant conflict," where the rulers are replaced no sooner than the charge of conspiracy is skilfully made against them? But only if such is the case can conspiracy become the decisive political mechanism and Barruel be given major credit for formulating it, no matter how emphatically would he decline such an honor.

Thus is Barruel cast in a "prophetic" role, which, however, has nothing in common with the stance of the Prophets of old for whom the worship of Yahweh and of the Baals were not alternative forms of equally good or bad cults. Barruel would smile, because not only he, but his very opponents would protest the charge that they had merely propagated an illusion about views most dear to them, taken for so many illusory opinions. Their illusion would consist in mistaking political skills for the presumed truth of their views and the righteousness of their deeds. But if such an illusion is justified by political skills, what remains of moral arguments against Hitler, Stalin, and other most unusually skillful henchmen of modern history? Can one then take them to task on moral grounds for having continually renewed their claims about conspiracies being hatched against them?

Barruel—and let this be recalled once more in this age when prominent University Presses are eager to promote a catholicism void of dogmas, that is, Truths, writ large—was a Catholic. Therefore only superficialities of the real Barruel remain accessible to those who hold that all is relative and that this is the only absolute truth. This is not to suggest that today Barruel would be palatable to all Catholics. Gone are the days when a Gilson could congratulate Harvard philosophers for being so liberal as to invite him, an unabashedly dogmatic thinker, to deliver the William James Lectures. Nowadays Gilson might find himself be barred from many Catholic universities, dominated as they are by the dogma that there are no clearly identifiable dogmas.

In Barruel's own time his bent on principles earned him deep resentment even in his own camp, a camp ripped by factions. By the closing years of the eighteenth century French Catholics had been divided into four main groups. One was known as the "Petite Église," or clergy and faithful who rejected not only the Civil Constitution of the clergy but also refused to promise fidelity to Napoleon. Another group was formed by those, mainly under the unofficial leadership of Abbé Emery, head of St. Sulpice prior to its dissolution by the Revolution, who held out for an accommodation with the new secularist state, without siding with the church sanctioned by it. That Church was lead first by Talleyrand, the disgraceful bishop-diplomat, and later by the Abbé (and Senator) Grégoire. The Abbé, who had already made a name for himself by calling the Monarchy a "monster" to be done away with, refused to acknowledge any right of the Pope over French Catholics. In fact, it is most doubtful that he had any faith in the papacy. The fourth group was, of course, that of *émigré* Catholics, clergy and laity. For those in the first and the fourth group the Church and Monarchy were synonymous.

Strangely, but very significantly, these four groups would have been at one in one respect. They all would have been shocked, in different ways, had they heard in early 1798, when Barruel's *Memoirs* had already been widely circulating, that the bishop of Imola, Barnaba Chiaramonti (the future Pius VII) had just instructed his flock: "The form of democratic government adopted by you is in no way repugnant to the Gospel. . . . Be good Christians and be good democrats." Those around the Abbé Grégoire would have taken that instruction for a consummate ruse; those in the *Petite Église* would have sensed in it blasphemy, while most of the *émigrés* would have seen it as scandalous. Those around the Abbé Emery would have spoken of its utter impracticality. It is well to remember that a full hundred years later, many French Catholics found it very difficult to listen to Leo XIII as he urged them to participate fully in the political life of the Third Republic, even though it made a fetish of the Revolution and its ideology.

No wonder that the *émigrés* (to say nothing of the *Petite Église*) felt outraged when, sometime after Napoleon made his surprising offer of December 28, 1799, Barruel urged the French clergy to listen to Pius VII (elected on March 14, 1800), who took a positive view of it. For instead of asking an oath of loyalty from Catholics in support of the Constitution of 1797, Napoleon merely demanded a "promise of fidelity." Unlike the oath of loyalty to the Civil Constitution of the Clergy of 1791, the promise of fidelity to the Constitution of 1797 did not imply a break with the authority of Rome relating to the very structure of the Church and its discipline. Barruel, with many others, interpreted Napoleon's offer not so much as a clever ploy to exploit the Church eventually, but as an opportunity to restore the normal administration of sacraments that had already been greatly disrupted for seven or so years. Barruel published in London in 1800 two pamphlets on the subject. The result was that many fellow Catholics, in France and abroad, denounced him as a Jacobin, a heretic, and one whose celebration of the Mass was not to be attended by the faithful.

Barruel was vindicated, when, after a year and a half, following long negotiations with Napoleon, Rome approved of the offer. Part of the deal was that Rome should ask for the resignation of all French bishops, a demand previously unheard of in the history of the Church. Rome did so on August 15, 1801, after having signed the famed Concordat with Napoleon, which remained law until 1905. While 45 bishops submitted their resignation, 36 refused (among them 14 bishops living in London). The recusants were further incensed when later that year Pius VII replaced the 156 French bishoprics with 60 new dioceses. This too was a step unprecedented in the history of the Church. From the human viewpoint, Rome's action could but appear a huge gamble, an almost reckless trust in its power. After all, only a decade or so earlier, Rome merely confirmed the candidates which the "most Christian king of France" presented to this or that vacant see.

In fact two full years later 38 French bishops still sent "most respectful" remonstrations to Rome. It was at that point that Barruel's greatness as a Jesuit appeared in its best light. Barruel in his *Memoirs* had implied more than once that Altar and Throne were inseparable. He was not a "democrat" by a long shot. Humanly speaking it made little sense that Barruel should rally behind the Pope's policy, which could seem to be equivalent to fusing Altar and Revolution (minus Terror). Nowhere in the *Memoirs* did Barruel take the Revolution for an evolutionary step for something better. It is a howler to say, as Barruel's modern French biographer does, that he would today welcome Teilhard de Chardin's perspectives on evolution. Never a dreamer, Barruel was a hard-nosed arguer, always keen on facts and data and ever ready to turn inside out weak reasonings. He showed himself a consummate debater as he dashed off a refutation (reprinted at the end of this edition) of a British critic of the first edition of the English translation of his *Memoirs*, who tried to exculpate the Freemasons and other targets of Barruel.

However, Barruel would have come around to the repeated observations made by Angelo Roncalli as Nuncio to France and later as Pope John XXIII, that there was much good represented by various spokesmen of the Enlightenment. He would have come to agree that there were solid grounds for portraying in a truly sympathetic manner, as E. Kennedy did in his *Cultural History of the French Revolution,* the positive side of those turbulent years.

Barruel's conversion of mind would have had its principal motivation in his exemplary docility (as befitting a Jesuit) to the voice of the Pope. Barruel would have relied on that docility to cope with the special reaffirmation by Vatican II on the freedom of conscience. He would have also quickly noticed that with that emphasis the Church had greatly secured her own freedom of action in an increasingly pluralistic world. For Barruel's vision of the unity of Altar and Throne did not include a most dubious support of it, Gallicanism, which penetrated French Catholicism everywhere. He argued as an unabashed "ultramontane" in his long treatise, *Du Pape et de ses droits religieux à l'occasion du Concordat*. There he set forth theological reasons that revealed in him the genuine Jesuit who strengthens with a special vow the loyalty which every Catholic—priest and layperson—owes to the Pope as Peter's successor.

This distinctly "ultramontane" thinking made Barruel unacceptable to Napoleon's regime following his return to France in 1802. His being appointed by Cardinal Belloy, archbishop of Paris, as honorary canon of Notre Dame, brought him no monetary rewards. The prospects of material benefits that would have come to Barruel had he accepted from Pius VII the cardinalate did not make Barruel hesitate to decline that extraordinary offer. He wanted to remain a Jesuit in the hope that one day he would become a solemnly professed one. He kept supporting himself from what his parents left him. Prior to the fall of Napoleon, he published but a few articles, mostly to defend his defense of the papacy. Of course, Barruel's conservative critics among the clergy could cite, as the years went by, more and more evidence that Napoleon was far from willing to honor the Concordat. Indeed, what more proof of Napoleon's bad faith was needed than his making Pius VII a prisoner! Barruel in turn made abundantly clear his dislike of the ideology ruling in Napoleon's court when he republished in Paris, in 1812, his *Helviennes*.

By then Barruel had been living in France for ten years, but under constant police surveillance. His loyalty to the papacy earned him further difficulties when, on October 14, 1810, Cardinal Maury was nominated by Napoleon archbishop of Paris, in rank disregard of the wishes of the Pope, who later that year deprived the archbishop of all jurisdiction. Napoleon's police immediately arrested several leading ecclesiastics, among them Barruel, who was imprisoned for three weeks. In 1814 he once more rallied on behalf of the papacy when the abbé Grégoire pleaded for the people's sovereignty even in matters ecclesiastic. The word Jacobin, in the very title of Barruel's reply, *Du principe et l'obstination des Jacobins, en réponse au sénateur Grégoire*, befitted the most considered views of the author of the *Mémoires* as well as of the treatise *Du Pape et de ses droits religieux à l'occasion du Concordat*.

One can easily imagine the feelings of Barruel as he heard reports about how the people lined up along the roads to acclaim Pius VII on his way back to Rome, after several years of having been held captive by Napoleon. And he must have been familiar with Napoleon's reply, with a truly Jacobin ring, to the report that the Pope was ready to excommunicate him: "Does he think that the world has gone back a thousand years? Does he suppose the arms will fall from the hands of my soldiers?" What happened two years later to the Grande Armée on the snowy fields of Russia made even contemporary Protestant historians see matters in a superior light. Newman memorably quoted one of them, A. Alison, who avowed that "there is something in these marvellous coincidences beyond the operation of chance." Moreover, this happened not in connection with the medieval papacy, so well established in its secular powers as well, but to a papacy which the *philosophes* were ready to write off as moribund.

Barruel lived through those decades about which no one gave a more gripping portrayal than Newman, as he tried to convince Anglo-Catholics that very futile was their dream of a Catholic Church in England as independent of Rome as the Gallican Church tried to be. For those decades, Newman wrote, closed a century "upon the wondering world; and for years it wondered on; wondered what should be the issue of the awful portent which it witnessed, and what new state of things was to rise out of the old. The Church disappeared before its eyes as by a yawning earthquake, and men said it was a fulfilment of the prophecies, and they sang a hymn, and went to their long sleep, content and with a *Nunc Dimittis* in their mouths; for now at length had an old superstition been wiped off from the earth, and the Pope had gone his way. And other powers, kings, and the like, disappeared too, and nothing was to be seen." In speaking of prophecies Newman must have had in mind the ones uttered by the *philosophes* and the Illuminati, whether Freemasons or not. It is unimportant to know whether Newman was familiar with Barruel's *Memoirs*. He could not have summed up better its gist even if he had meant those lines to be the most concise abstract of that vast work.

What Barruel did not spell out in those *Memoirs,* but must certainly have had in mind, Newman spelled out in the next breath. For ultimately, the changes turned out to be at a total variance with those prophecies and expectations. It must have been bewildering to the "enlightened" that an apparently corrupt and unworthy French hierarchy was not the closing chapter of the Church in France: "Out of the ashes of the ancient Church of France has sprung a new hierarchy, worthy of the name and the history of that great nation." And even more painful to them must have been the great generalization that could be made: "The Church lives, the Apostolic See rules. That See has greater acknowledged power in Christendom than ever before, and that Church has a wider liberty than she had since the days of the Apostles. . . . The idea and the genius of Catholicism has triumphed within its own pale with a power and completeness which the world has never seen before." And those whose chief strategy against the Church was to find and exploit divisions within it had no answer to the fact, that "never was the whole body of the faithful so united to each other and to their head. Never was there a time when there was less of error, heresy, and schismatical perverseness among them."

And Barruel, whose soul was honed on the opening theme of the Exercises of St. Ignatius about two flags forever opposed to one another, would have but nodded approval to Newman's warning against the illusion about a final victory anytime before the final times: "Of course the time will never be in this world, when trials and persecutions shall be at an end: and doubtless such are to come, even though they be below the horizon. But we may be thankful and joyful for what is already granted to us; and nothing which is to be can destroy the mercies which have been."

If there was a mercy for which Barruel was most grateful, it was the restoration of the Society of Jesus and his official readmission into it on October 18, 1815. The five years left for him he devoted to the continuation of his campaign to shed light on the thinking of the antagonists of the Church. He started writing a long book along the lines of his *Helviennes*. In it he was to expose, on a grand scale, the deadly threat which the philosophy of Kant posed to genuine Catholicism. This is not a mere conjecture. In the closing part of the *Memoirs* (see pp. 802-03), Barruel held Kant's rationalism to be of no less a threat to Christianity than the one posed by Weishaupt's illuminism. For as Barruel rightly saw, the chief motivation of Kant the philosopher was the same as that of Weishaupt: to make the idea of Revelation appear utterly irrational and establish the total autonomy of human reason, thereby setting up man as his own sovereign and god.

That book of Barruel on Kant would have become a prophetic work, though unbeknownst to him. He could hardly suspect that a century or so later, many among his fellow Jesuits would take the view that Aquinas cannot be made meaningful to modern man unless Kant is grafted on him. Were Barruel alive today, he would perhaps write a huge "Memoirs Illustrating the History of Aquikantism." He certainly would not be taken in by a Boutroux or a Blondel, nor even by such confrères of his as Maréchal, Coreth, or Rahner. He would rather lament the fate of those among his confrères for whom an "appreciative" reading of Kant proved indeed very fatal, spiritually that is.

It is not known why Barruel, just a few days before his death, called for a big batch of manuscripts, the text of his critique of Kant, and asked it to be burned. But, judging by the unabashed sorrow and indignation he felt over priests, including some Jesuits, who had fallen in France to the deceptive words of the *philosophes* and in Germany to Kant's sophisms, it is reasonable to assume that his manuscript would have contained a chapter of great importance. It would have related to the fallacies with which Kant attacked the proofs of the existence of God, and to the readiness with which those victims justified their apostasies by claiming that those fallacies were sound reasonings.

In doing so, Barruel would have given the lie also to one of Péguy's memorable aphorisms: "Kantianism has clean hands, but it has no hands." In fact, the hands of Kantianism are metaphorically covered with blood. Many among the illustrious figures of nineteenth-century philosophical and literary culture justified their apostasies from Christianity and Church with a reference to the author of the *Critique of Pure Reason*. In recent decades cavorting with Kant took no less numerous victims among Catholic theologians and philosophers, who should have known better.

Anyone familiar with the contents of Barruel's *Memoirs* will know what to think of such dismissals of him as, for instance, the one offered in *L'histoire des idées dans l'émigration française* by Fernand Baldensperger, first published in 1924. Actually, Baldensperger undermines his own credibility by quoting, with obvious approval, the reply—"the mysterious rites bred by Freemasonry in France had no other effect than to mislead a few dupes,"—of Montmorin to the warning issued by Cardinal de Bernis, still the Ambassador of Louis XVI at the Holy Sea, in early 1790. In fact, Baldensperger seems to think that there were no secret societies at all. He also overlooks the fact that de Maistre thoroughly retracted his earstwhile benevolent appraisals of Freemasonry.

Baldensperger's anti-Barruel tactic is best summed up in his own words, because they give in a nutshell the pattern followed by almost all critics of Barruel. It is more devious than the tactic of damning with faint praise. It is venomous rhetoric taking cover under a pretence of utter superiority with respect to the knowledge of facts: Barruel's *Memoirs* are "the erection into a doctrinal system of the hypothesis about a secularist and concerted effort to subvert all authority in the world. A few clear ideas, cleverly connected, a documentation that inspires confidence, an extreme skill to throw the light of a blinding explanation on known but disjointed facts: such are the merits that established the author as an authority throughout Europe." Those who could be swayed by such a dismissal of the documentation which Barruel provided over almost 2000 pages in the original did not, of course, deplore the fact that Baldensperger failed to consider even one of the many facts marshalled by Barruel.

Where Baldensperger failed in respect to Barruel related not so much to ideology as to a method within which ideas are practically reified. In fact, the failure of Augustin Cochin, who certainly shared Barruel's ideology of monarchist Catholicism, is to be sought in the same direction. An unjustly overlooked historian of the French Revolution, Cochin, who in 1916 died, at the age of thirty-nine, a hero's death on the battlefields of the Marne, may, however, have found in Barruel's thesis the very key to his perspective within which the discontinuity between the *ancien régime* and post-revolutionary France loomed large. The discontinuity lay deeper than could be seen in the socio-political categories of monarchy versus democracy. The deepest layer touches on the difference whether one believes in the supernatural as given in Christ or rejects it. This contrast is factual insofar as it was powerfully acted out during the decades investigated by Barruel and therefore is a legitimate, and indeed obligatory topic for the historian.

There was therefore much more at issue than the rise of democracy on which François Furet has set so great a store. Thus even though Barruel largely ignored that point, a point emphasized by Furet in his slighting of Barruel, the latter's thesis remains as closely connected with facts as ever. In fact, when today, two centuries after the rise of democracy through the French Revolution, democracy all too often degenerates into monetary pragmatist politics, very visible are the naturalist shortcomings of Locke's theory of the State as having for its principal function the safeguarding of privaty property. Churchill's facetious statement that democracy is the best of all bad forms of government can have a meaning within Barruel's very supernatural perspectives, but hardly within the idealization (and idolization) of the natural, so dear to theorists like Furet, to say nothing of those of far lesser stature.

Had Barruel offered but rhetorical conjectures, the four volumes of his *Mémoires* would not have deserved the effort and expense of being translated into German, Italian, Russian, and Spanish. Nor, in that case, would the *Mémoires* have been re-edited in 1973 in the series *Les Maîtres de la Contre-révolution,* with all the corrections that Barruel himself provided in 1818, just two years before his death, on October 20, 1820. Yet the very strength of the massive documentation provided by Barruel is weakened by the charge made in the Introduction to that re-edition that Barruel failed in one basic respect, namely, for not having spelled out that ultimately Satan himself was behind the French Revolution. Being the kind of exemplary religious and priest he was, Barruel must have felt strongly about Satan's role. But, and this is acknowledged in that introduction, whenever the facts and his interpretation of them would have almost forced him to make more than a brief reference to Satan, he invariably pulled back. Clearly, such was the duty of the historian Barruel wanted to be. Time and again he reminded his readers that it was as a historian, not as a theologian, that he was addressing himself to them.

Of course, he would not be the kind of historian who denies to himself strong opinions and convictions, either because he has none, or because—and this is more typically the case—he is afraid of revealing them to be at variance with those approved within the ever more secularized climate of opinion. Thus, to recall only one instance from the closing chapter of the Part dealing with the antichristian conspiracy, he counted it to be "the historian's duty to tear off that mask of hypocrisy, which has misled such numbers of adepts, who, miserably seeking to soar above the vulgar, have only sunk into impiety, gazing after this pretended Philosophy." Today, he would assign the same task to the contemporary observer of the sophisticated skullduggery in which deconstructionism passes for a constructive enterprise, in fact, for the only such enterprise that can be justified.

In all this Barruel would see a strictly legitimate exercise of the craft of the historian. If he failed as a historian he did so inasmuch as he paid scant attention to the vastness of social and economic ills in eighteenth-century France. Nor did he see much of a changing world within which the absolute and divine right of kings, together with the Church's deep involvement in the political and economic structure, was gradually turning into an anachronism. Actually, it was far worse: often it amounted to a crime crying to high heaven. When Marie-Antoinette said—If the people have no bread, let them eat cake—she could claim only as a weak excuse her upbringing, sheltered from the cruel realities of poor peoples' lives. And the aristocratic background gave no more than the flimsiest excuse to that bishop who claimed not to have known that it was the Feast of Corpus Christi as he rode, with his hunting party, into a procession, leaving some dead in his wake.

It was, of course, another matter whether a reshaping of France along the model set by England, as a constitutional monarchy, would have remedied those ills. For let it not be forgotten that Burke, for instance, did not raise his voice about that child labor which already cast its horrid pallor over the lush English landscape. Nor is it known that Freemasonry has ever been in the forefront of the struggle for social justice. Ever since the regular, hard working masons had been sidelined in Freemasonic clubs in England, Freemasonry dutifully served the interests of its members, intent more on protecting their own wealth than anything else. To the supporters of such a policy the words of Christ about treasures that moth and rust cannot corrupt, had to be a supreme anathema.

The historian, which Barruel wanted to be, has the right to focus on a particular issue, though never too narrowly when the issue is broad indeed. The issue he wanted to shed light on was the ideology and dialectic of the "enlightenment" as held by those whom he refers to time and again as having formed a "triple conspiracy." In the end he seems to give most importance to the "Sophisters of Impiety," or the *philosophes*, and for very good reasons: The French Revolution quickly displayed itself as a profoundly anti-Christian movement. Yet Barruel would still consider it to be part of the historian's craft or method to keep the historical and the strictly supernatural in separate compartments. By respecting that separation, Barruel secured enduring respect to the facts he had marshalled at great pains and left intact the materials for the primary argument that must be used against all those who take cover in secrecy. The argument is that secrecy has no place in an "open society." The late Karl Popper, who gave so much currency to that Bergsonian phrase, was at least clear, though hardly in a profuse way, as to what he meant by it. In advocating a so-called "Democritean ethic," he certainly rejected openness to the supernatural.

Others of similar persuasion are far more taciturn, and this is especially true of Freemasons. In an open society, Freemasons, like anyone else, are entitled to their opinions. But, like anyone else, they also have the duty to be open about their views and aims. It is only on occasion that prominent Freemasons publicize their true intentions. It takes no small effort to find the original Freemasonic document wherein one can read, for instance, the declaration which Senator Delpech made in Paris in 1902 in the context of a Masonic banquet:

> The triumph of the Galilean has lasted twenty centuries; he is dying in his turn. The mysterious voice which once on the mountains of Epirus announced the death of Pan, today announces the death of the deceiver God who had promised an era of justice and peace to those who should believe in him. The illusion has lasted very long; the lying God

in his turn disappears; he goes to rejoin in the dust of ages the other divinities of India, Egypt, Greece, and Rome, who saw so many deluded creatures throw themselves at the foot of their altars. Freemasons, we are pleased to state that we are not unconcerned with this ruin of false prophets. The Roman Church, founded on the Galilean myth, began to decline rapidly on the day when the Masonic association was constituted. From the political point of view Freemasons have often varied. But in all times Freemasonry has stood firm on this principle: war on all superstitions, war on all fanaticism.

More recently it was Jacques Mitterand, twice Grand Master of the Grand Orient (1962-64 and 1969-71), who rebuked in his *La politique des Francmaçons* (1973) the Lodges of England for their insistence on belief in God, be it the pale God of deists. He said there that all "conservative, sectarian, narrow-minded Freemasonry, worshiping God instead of serving Man, is destined to extinction." He predicted all the more so the eventual demise of those individuals and groups who worship a God who revealed Himself, and of all those who substitute "the quest of eternal happiness through resignation to the quest of happiness on earth through action." And since he spoke of the Encyclical *Pacem in terris* of John XXIII as a document that would not dupe Freemasons, it should not be surprising that his strongest remark touched upon the claim of the Church to be "the teacher of Truth," a claim voiced even in the documents of Vatican II. He preferred to look back to the *philosophes*, the Encyclopedists, who, "although not all Freemasons, knew all the ardor of the thinking of [their Mason] Brethren and Friends." It was no accident that the administration of President Mitterand witnessed not only the first formal visit by the leaders of Grand Orient to the Élysée Palace in this century, but also a major renewed effort to impose secularist ideology on French Catholic schools. The resulting protest parade of three million French Catholics on the Champs Élysées undoubtedly gave food for thought to the Grand Orient about the number of the Pope's "divisions."

Those "divisions" are ready to take a stand, and for a very plain reason. They remember that Christ, the Galilean, emphatically distinguished between *his* peace and the peace the world promises. In speaking in such manner of the world, He had a special world in mind, the world as having fallen captive to His only real Antagonist, the Evil One who occasioned the first Fall. But since the Redemption prompted by that Fall was not an automatic cure-all, the world remained the theater of a mixture of good and evil, where the good did not represent all goodness and the evil did not lack good qualities.

Such is the only clue for drawing up a reasoned balance sheet about the French Revolution, whether engineered or not by the Jacobins. It ushered in a modern world which, for all its tragedies, has contributed much to keeping mankind on the threshold of hope, to quote a memorable phrase of John Paul II. This is so, because, as John Paul II told three hundred thousand youths gathered in Loreto on September 9, 1995, the idea of man presented by the French Enlightenment can be made complete only within a Christian perspective. It would be utopian to think that the threshold in question would ever be crossed in the sense of bringing about a Paradise on earth. If Christ likened even the Kingdom of God to a field, in which good seed and bad seed would forever grow side by side until the end of times, the prospects for the world at large can hardly be any better. Christ was therefore fully consistent when he warned his followers that they cannot be greater than their Master, and therefore would be forever under pressure and even persecuted. Fully aware that his chief antagonist was Satan, the great deceiver, He knew that there would be no end to deceptions, such as brandishing the words superstition and fanaticism and leaving them carefully undefined, that is, unexplained as to what was their real target. To leave things under cover is part and parcel of the art of conspiracy.

Compared with Freemasonic secretiveness, whatever there is of secretiveness in the Vatican should appear openness incarnate. The Vatican never hid the Christian creed, the Christian dogmas, the uncompromising duties of Christian morality. In that respect too, the chasm is infinite between the Church and the Lodge. It is indeed a clever abuse of words to complain, as does the noted French Freemasonic author, Alec Mellor, in his book, *Nos frères séparés les franc-maçons* (1961), about the refusal of the Vatican to consider Freemasons, like non-Catholic Christians, as so many separated brethren. Such an abuse of the expression "separated brethren" is a conspiracy with words, the very conspiracy which Voltaire, Diderot and D'Alembert—all Freemasons—turned into a high art.

For ultimately Barruel's chief (and non-theological) objection to the anti-Christian and anti-monarchical and anti-social conspiracy was the *fact* that it was a *conspiracy*, that it took cover most systematically as long as it had do to so. It was another matter whether the conspirators had control over every event in the process they planned, launched, and fuelled as much as they could, though as secretly as this was possible or advisable. In these days, when a chief argument against antisemitism is that relentless fomenting of hatred against Jews led to the Holocaust, it should not seem illogical at all to draw a parallel with some antecedents of a Revolution issuing in the Terror. Among those antecedents nothing was so sustained, so vicious, and so cunning as the concerted effort to stir and spread anti-Christian and antimonarchical sentiments. In that effort Freemasons, as heavily represented in the Jacobin clubs, played a significant role.

Indeed, Gaston Martin charged in his book, *La Franc-Maçonnerie française et la préparation de la Révolution* (1926), his late eighteenth-century French brethren not so much with the formulation of the idea of that Revolution, but with its very practice! What more is demanded to justify Barruel's thesis insofar as it bears on the Lodges? Is it then meaningful to try, as did Furet, in his *Interpreting the French Revolution,* to exculpate Freemasonry with a reference to the fact that not only the two brothers of Louis XVI, but the King too, were Freemasons. Such is a refutation that refutes itself, and only slightly less reprehensible than J. M. Roberts' dismissal, in his *The Mythology of Secret*

Societies (1972), of Barruel's *Memoirs* as being hardly more than "a farrago of nonsense."

But even those who grant, as Margaret Jacob does in her *Living the Enlightenment: Freemasonry and Politics in Eighteenth Century Europe* (1991), that Freemasonry was involved in making the French Revolution, though innocent of its Terror, have to face up to Freemasonry's continued "authoritarian paternalism in meritocratic ideologies," as a reviewer of Jacob's book observed. The charge implies that Freemasony has even today a decisive control over grants and promotions so that those ideologically opposed must feel as ones who "need not apply."

Today Barruel would remind those to his right and to his left along the ideological spectrum that there is little use in disagreeing with Freemasonry unless it is first taken to task on its proverbial secretiveness. Freemasonry's determination to take cover in secrecy should be enough to justify the now almost three-century-long position of the Church that one cannot be a Catholic and a Freemason at the same time. After all, Christian religion, steeped in the supernatural, can for genuine Freemasons be but a stepping stone to *their* religion, which consists in a resolute step away from the supernatural to the level of mere nature. This was the very point of Leo XIII's famed encyclical, *Humanum genus* (1884), on Freemasonry. And it was a Freemason who admitted in a letter to the Père Berteloot, a Jesuit, that "one outsider alone has really understood Freemasonry, namely, Leo XIII. His condemnation of Freemasonry is, of course, logical, necessary, and justified from the Catholic viewpoint. The Sovereign Pontiff went to the very root of Freemasonry. He found it harmful, wants it extirpated, and he has good reasons for it."

If there are low-echelon Freemasons unaware of the radically anti-Christian aims of Freemasonry, they can only be pitied as so many victims of a secretive tactic that lures before it captures. It is difficult to suppose that some Archbishops of Canterbury and York (and other dignitaries of the Church of England) have remained low-echelon Masons unaware that now even Anglo-Saxon Freemasonry is dedicated to the elimination of the supernatural. It was not without reason that the late Eric Mascall, a High-Church Anglican, wondered aloud why the Anglican hierarchy fails to speak out on Freemasonry. He did so in a Foreword to W. Hannah's book, *Christian by Degrees: Masonic Religion Revealed in the Light of Faith* (1954), a sequel to his *Darkness Visible: A Revelation and Interpretation of Freemasonry*.

It may indeed be the case that powerful Christian groups are conspiring with Freemasonry's staunch resistance to calls that its membership lists be made public. In an age when politicians, businessmen, and Churchmen are granted no protection from the glare of publicity, Freemasons can, in all appearance, easily ignore efforts, such as Stephen King's book, *The Brotherhood,* that pressure them to come into the open. Why is it, for instance, that after a prominent headline stated that most of the Edinburgh constabulary are Freemasons, the topic was duly dropped within a day or two? Would the press let this (and many other cases) be readily forgotten if some other group was so unequally represented in this or that social and economic context, let alone in a context that bears on public justice in a pluralistic society? Should one assume that Freemasons can pull many strings, even if from behind the scenes? But is not this what is meant by secretiveness? And does this not smack of conspiracy?

To be sure, in the civilized parts of the world it no longer passes for civility to hanker after the heads of priests, bishops, and popes. Far more sinister a threat to Christianity is to persuade Christians by cunning tactics that they can remain followers of Christ without holding with utter seriousness that He alone is the Way, the Light, and the Truth. Such Christians should at least consider the inevitable result when that Light is systematically discredited, whether by Freemasons or by others. Once more the light of Reason (even when not contaminated by strange rituals, Masonic or other) proves itself inadequate by itself to produce general conviction about absolute moral standards, without which society is fragmented into an increasingly anarchical state. Statistics about the number of children growing up without fathers are already being paralleled by statistics about the rapid growth of crime. Here too a critical magnitude may be within sight, no different in its devastating explosiveness than the critical mass responsible for an atomic chain reaction.

To speak out against the "privatisation of morality," as did the Archbishop of Canterbury recently, makes little sense if at the same time premarital sexuality is declared to be Christian on the ground that otherwise the Church will become so exclusive as to be unable to function as the inclusive organ befitting a Church "established" for a given nation. This may delight some Masons, but can only make the hearts of serious Christians sink. They should rather look toward that Church that even in the decades of an ecumenical euphoria did not lift its ban on Freemasonry and other secretive efforts to dilute the uniqueness of Christ's message of salvation. To imply otherwise, and with copious references to a "deepened" understanding of Freemasonry by Catholics, as done in a recent book, *Église et Franc-Maçonnerie* by L. Nefontaine, is to blind oneself to the shallowness of some new-fangled profundities.

A good safeguard against this is to ponder the Bulgarian proverb: Those who want to drown, should not torture themselves in shallow waters. One merely disarms oneself by pretending that there is no longer on hand a secrecy operating through cunning tactics. An opponent who hides is more dangerous than the one who openly throws down the gauntlet. If the facts and statements filling the hundreds of pages of Barruel's *Memoirs* proved only this much, his magnum opus deserves to be studiously remembered.

Stanley L. Jaki

MEMOIRS,

Illustrating the

HISTORY of JACOBINISM,

Written in FRENCH by

THE ABBÉ BARRUEL,

And translated into ENGLISH by

THE HON. ROBERT CLIFFORD, F.R.S. & A.S.

Princes and Nations shall disappear from the face of the Earth... and this REVOLUTION shall be the WORK OF SECRET SOCIETIES.
Weishaupt's Discourse for the Mysteries.

PART I.

THE ANTICHRISTIAN CONSPIRACY.

Second Edition, revised and corrected.

LONDON:
Printed for the TRANSLATOR,
By T. BURTON, No. 11, Gate-street, Lincoln's-Inn Fields.
Sold by E. BOOKER, No. 56, New Bond-street.

1798.

PRELIMINARY DISCOURSE.

At an early period of the French Revolution, there appeared a Sect calling itself JACOBIN, and teaching *that all men were equal and free!* In the name of their Equality and disorganizing Liberty, they trampled under foot the altar and the throne; they stimulated all nations to rebellion, and aimed at plunging them ultimately into the horrors of anarchy.

At its first appearance, this Sect counted 300,000 adepts; and it was supported by two millions of men, scattered through France, armed with torches and pikes, and all the fire-brands of revolution.

It was under the auspices of this Sect, and by their intrigues, influence, and impulse, that France beheld itself a prey to every crime; that its soil was stained with the blood of its pontiffs and priests, of its rich men and nobles; with the blood of every class of its citizens, without regard to rank, age, or sex! These were the men who, after having made the unfortunate Louis XVI, his Queen and Sister, drink to the very dregs the cup of outrage and ignominy during a long confinement, solemnly murdered them on a scaffold, proudly menacing the sovereigns of the earth with a similar fate! These are the men who have made the French revolution a scourge to all Europe, a terror to its Rulers, who in vain combine to stop the progress of their revolutionary armies, more numerous and more destructive than the inundations of the Vandals.

Whence originated these men, who seem to arise from the bowels of the earth, who start into existence with their plans and their projects, their tenets and their thunders, their insidious means and ferocious resolves? Whence, I say, this devouring Sect? Whence this swarm of adepts, these systems, this frantic rage against the altar and the throne, against every institution, civil and religious, so much respected by our ancestors? Can their primogeniture in the order of the revolution give them this tremendous power, or were they not anterior? Is it not their own work? Where then was their hiding place, their schools, their masters, where shall we find these, and who will dive into their future projects? This French revolution ended, will they cease to desolate the earth, to murder its kings, or to fanaticise its people?

These certainly are questions that cannot be indifferent to nations or their rulers, or to those who watch for the happiness and preservation of society; and these are the questions which I will attempt to answer. I will draw their solution from the very annals of the Sect, whence I will show their plans and systems, their plots and their means. Such, reader, will be the object of the following Memoirs.

Had I seen the conspiracies of the Jacobins end with the disasters they produced; had I even seen the cloud of our misfortunes dissipated with the French Revolution, still should I have remained convinced of the importance and necessity of disclosing to the world the dark recesses from which it burst into being.

When with aweful astonishment we read of plagues and other scourges that have desolated the earth, though the danger be passed, they are not to be considered as objects of mere curiosity. In the history of poisons we find the antidotes; in the history of monsters we learn by what weapons they were destroyed. When former calamities reappear, or are to be apprehended, is it not our duty to explore the causes which first promoted their destructive influence, the means by which they might have been opposed, and the errors whereby they may again be produced? The present generation is instructed by the misfortunes of the past; be then the future instructed by the history of ours.

But we have evils yet more pressing to encounter: the present generation has been deluded; and such delusions must be done away as may double our misfortunes in the instant when we think ourselves most secure. We have seen men obstinately blind to the causes of the French Revolution: we have seen men who wished to persuade themselves that this conspiring and revolutionary Sect had no existence anterior to the Revolution. In their minds the long series of miseries which have befallen France, to the terror of all Europe, were merely the offspring of that concourse of unforeseen events inseparable from the times. In their conceptions, it is in vain to seek conspirators or conspiracies, and as vain to search for the hand that directs the horrid course. The man who rules today, knows not the plans of his predecessor; and he that shall follow will, in their opinions, be equally ignorant of those of the present ruler.

Prepossessed with such erroneous notions, and acting under so dangerous a prejudice, these superficial observers would willingly make all nations believe, that the French Revolution ought to be to them no cause of alarm; that it was a volcano rapidly venting itself on the unfortunate country that gave it existence, while its focus and its origin remain unfathomable. "Causes unknown (they will say) but peculiar to your climate; elements less subject to ferment; laws more analogous to your character; the public fortune better balanced; these and such as these are reasons sufficient to make you regardless of the fate of France. But, alas! should such be your impending fate, vain will be your efforts to avert the threatening blow. The concourse and fatality of circumstances will drag you toward it; the very ramparts which you shall build against it will fall back upon you, and perhaps level the space that now divides you from the horrid scene of anarchy and desolation."

Who would conceive, that I have heard this very language fall from the mouth of those whom the unfortunate Louis XVI had called near his person to ward off the blows perpetually aimed at him by the Revolution! a language better calculated to lull all nations into that fatal security which portends destruction?—I have now before me the memorial of an ex-minister, consulted on the causes of this infernal Revolution, and particularly as to the chief conspirators (whom he should have better known) and on the plan of the conspiracy. I hear this man answer, that it would be useless to seek either a man or any set of men conspiring against the altar and the throne, or to suppose that any plan had been framed for that purpose. Unfortunate monarch! Are those who ought to watch for the safety of your person, for the security of your people, ignorant of the names, nay even of the very existence of your enemies! If then we behold both you and your people falling victims to their plots, can we or ought we to be astonished?

Strong in the facts, and armed with the proofs produced in the following Memoirs, we shall hold a very different language. We shall show what it is incumbent on all nations and their chiefs to be informed of: we shall demonstrate that, even to the most horrid deeds perpetrated during the French Revolution, every thing was foreseen and resolved on, was premeditated and combined: — that they were the offspring of deep-thought villany, since they had been prepared and were produced by men, who alone held the clue of those plots and conspiracies, lurking in the secret meetings where they had been conceived, and only watching the favourable moment of bursting forth. Though the events of each day may not appear to have been combined, there nevertheless existed a secret agent and a secret cause, giving rise to each event, and turning each circumstance to the long-desired end. Though circumstances may often have afforded the pretence or the occasion, yet the grand cause of the revolution, its leading features, its atrocious crimes, will still be found one continued chain of deep-laid and premeditated villany.

In revealing the object, and showing the extent of these plots, I meet a second error, more dangerous than the first. There are men who, though they hesitate not to believe that the French Revolution was premeditated, yet think that the intentions of the first authors were pure, and that they only sought the happiness and regeneration of empires; that if great misfortunes have since happened, they arose from the obstacles thrown in their way; that a great people cannot be regenerated without commotion, but that the tempest will subside, and a calm succeed the swelling billow; that then nations, astonished at the apprehensions they had entertained of the French Revolution, and true only to its principles, will be happy in imitation.

This error is the favourite theme of the *Jacobin missionaries*; it was this that gained them their first instruments of rebellion; that cohort of constitutionalists, who still look on their decrees of the RIGHTS OF MAN as the summit of legislative perfection, and still impatiently wait the fatal day when the world shall impetuously move in the sphere of their political rhapsody. It was this that gained them that prodigious number of votaries more blind than wicked, and who might have been mistaken for honest, if virtue could have associated with ferocity in search of happier days. It was this that gained them those men whose well-meant, though stupid credulity, misled them to believe in the necessity of the carnage of the 10th of August and of the horrid butcheries of the 2d of September; in a word, all those men who, in the murder of 3 or 400,000 fellow-creatures, in the extermination of millions of victims by famine, the sword, or the guillotine, seek consolation, in spite of this depopulating scourge, in the empty hope that this dreadful chain of horrors may be productive of happier days.

To confound these hopes, and to show the fallacy of these pretended good intentions, I will oppose the real views of this revolutionary Sect, their true projects, their conspiracies, and their means of execution. I will show them undisguised, for they must be divulged, the proofs being acquired. The French Revolution has been a true child to its parent Sect; its crimes have been its filial duty; and those black deeds and atrocious acts the natural consequences of the principles and systems that gave it birth. Moreover I will show that, so far from seeking future prosperity, the French Revolution is but a sportive essay of its strength, while the whole universe is its aim. If elsewhere the same crimes are necessary, they will be committed; if equal ferocity be requisite they will be equally ferocious; *and it will unavoidably extend wheresoever its errors shall be received.*

The reflecting reader will conclude, then, that either this Jacobin Sect must be crushed, or society overthrown; that all governments must give place to those massacres, those convulsive disorders, and to that infernal anarchy which rages in France. Indeed there is no other alternative, but universal destruction or extinction of the Sect. Let it however be remembered, that to crush a Sect is not to imitate the fury of its apostles, intoxicated with its sanguinary rage and propense to enthusiastic murder; it is not to massacre and immolate its adepts, or retort on them the thunders they had hurled. To crush a Sect, is to attack it in its schools, to reveal its imposture, and show to the world the absurdity of its principles, the atrocity of its means, and above all the profound wickedness of its teachers. Yes; strike the Jacobin, but spare the man; the Sect is a Sect of opinion, and its destruction will be doubly complete on the day when it shall be deserted by its disciples, to return to the true principles of reason and social order.

The Sect, I grant, is monstrous, but all its disciples are not monsters. Its care in hiding its latter projects, the extreme precaution with which it initiated the chosen of the elect, shews how much it feared the desertion of the multitude of its disciples, and its consequent destruction, had the horror of its mysteries been surmised. For my part, I never doubted, how depraved soever the Jacobins may have been, that the greatest part would have deserted the Sect could they have foreseen whither and by what means they were led. Could the French people have followed such chiefs, had it been possible to make them conceive to what lengths the plans and plots of the conspirators would carry them?

Though France were, like hell, a bottomless pit, impenetrable to every voice but that of the fiends of the Revolution, still it is not too late to acquaint other nations of their danger. They have heard of the crimes and horrors of that Revolution, let them contemplate the lot that awaits them should Jacobinism prevail; let them learn that they are not less within the grand revolutionary circle than France itself; that all those crimes, the anarchical and bloody scenes which have followed the dissolution of the French empire, equally await all other nations; let them learn that their altars and their thrones, their pontiffs and their kings, are doomed to the same fate with those of France: all are comprehended within the grand conspiracy.

When a phantom of peace shall seem to terminate the present war between the Jacobins and the combined powers, it certainly will be the interest of all governments to ascertain how far such a peace can be relied on. At that period, more than at any other, will it be necessary to study the secret history of that Sect, which sends forth its legions rather to shiver the sceptre than to fight the power; which has not promised to its adepts the crowns of princes, kings and emperors, but has required and bound those adepts by an oath to destroy them all. At that period we must recollect, that it is not in the field of Mars that the war against Sects is the most dangerous; when rebellion and anarchy are in the very tenets of the sectary, the hand may be disarmed, but war glows warmly in the heart.—The Sect, being weakened, may slumber for a time, but such a sleep is the calm preceding the irruption of the volcano. It no longer sends forth its curling flames; but the subterraneous fire winds its course, penetrates, and preparing many vents, suddenly bursts forth and carries misery and devastation wherever its fiery torrent rolls.

It is not the object of these Memoirs to treat of that state of war or of peace commenced between one power and another. In such cases it often happens that, all resources being exhausted, the sword must be sheathed, though the original grievances still subsist. Let the rulers of the people discuss the means of force; but we know there exists another sort of war, which a confidence in treaties only serves to render more fatal; we mean a war of plots and conspiracies, against which public treaties can never avail. Woe to that Power which shall have made peace without knowing why its enemy had declared war against it. What the Sect had done before it first burst forth, it will do again to prepare a second eruption. In darkness it will conspire anew, and calamities still more disastrous will teach all nations that the French Revolution was only the first step towards the universal dissolution which has so long been meditating and contriving by the Sect.

Such were the reasons by which I was impelled to investigate the plots and wishes, the tortuous means and nefarious nature of this Sect. We have witnessed the frantic rage and the ferocity of its legions; we have known them as the agents of the French Revolution, as the perpetrators of all its atrocious crimes and devastations; but few are acquainted with the schools that have formed them. Posterity, alas! will feel for many generations their dire effects. To trace their ravages, it will only have to cast its eyes around. The ruins of the palaces and the temples, the fallen cities, the mansions destroyed throughout the provinces, will paint in glowing colours the devastations of the modern Vandals. The lists of proscription, fatal to the prince and to so many of his subjects, the deserted villages, all, in a word, will long be the vouchers of those fatal lamp-posts, of that insatiable guillotine, of those legislative executioners supported by bands of assassins.

Circumstances so painful and so humiliating to human nature will not require to be recorded in these memoirs. It is not to shew what a Marat or a Robespierre has done, but to expose the schools, the systems, the conspiracies, and the masters that have formed a Philippe D'Orleans, a Syeyes, a Condorcet, or a Petion, and who at this very time are forming in all nations men that would rival Marat and Robespierre in their cruelties. Our object is, that, the Sect of the Jacobins and their conspiracies once known, their crimes shall be no longer matter of surprise; that their propensity to the effusion of blood, their blasphemies against Christ and his altars, their frantic rage against the throne, and their cruelties against their fellow-citizens, shall be as clearly understood as the ravages of the plague. And may nations in future as sedulously guard against the one, as they shun the other!

It was to attain this important object that all our researches into the Sect have been directed at its chiefs, its origin, its plots, its plans, and its progress; more desirous of investigating the means it employed to bring about the revolution, than to describe its conduct during that revolution.

The result of our inquiries, corroborated by proofs drawn from the records of the Jacobins, and of their first masters, has been, that this Sect with all its conspiracies is in itself no other than the coalition of a triple Sect, of a triple conspiracy, in which, long before the Revolution, the overthrow of the altar, the ruin of the throne, and the dissolution of all civil society had been debated and resolved on.

1st. Many years before the French Revolution men who styled themselves Philosophers conspired against the God of the Gospel, against Christianity, without distinction of worship, whether Protestant or Catholic, Anglican or Presbyterian. The grand object of this conspiracy was to overturn every altar where Christ was adored. It was the conspiracy of the *Sophisters of Impiety*, or the ANTICHRISTIAN CONSPIRACY.

2dly. This school of impiety soon formed the *Sophisters of Rebellion*: these latter, combining their conspiracy against kings with that of the Sophisters of Impiety, coalesce with that ancient Sect whose tenets constituted the whole secret of the *Occult Lodges* of Free-masonry, which long since, imposing on the credulity of its most distinguished adepts, only initiated the chosen of the elect into the secret of their unrelenting hatred for Christ and kings.

3dly. From the Sophisters of Impiety and Rebellion, arose the *Sophisters of Impiety and Anarchy*. These latter conspire not only against Christ and his altars, but against every religion natural or revealed: not only against kings, but against every government, against all civil society, even against all property whatsoever.

This third Sect, known by the name of *Illuminees*, coalesced with the Sophisters conspiring against Christ, and with the Sophisters who, with the Occult Masons, conspired against both Christ and kings. It was the coalition of the adepts of *impiety*, or the adepts of *rebellion*, and the adepts of *anarchy*, which *formed the* CLUB *of the* JACOBINS. Under this name, common to the triple Sect (originating from the name of the Order whose convent they had seized upon to hold their sittings), we shall see the adepts following up their triple conspiracy against God, the King, and Society. Such was the origin, such the progress of that Sect, since become so dreadfully famous under the name of JACOBIN.

In the present Memoirs each of these three conspiracies shall be treated separately; their authors unmasked, the object, means, coalition, and progress of the adepts shall be laid open.

Proofs of the most pointed nature are necessary, when such horrid plots are denounced to all nations; and it is to give these proofs the greater authenticity, that the title of MEMOIRS has been prefixed to this work. To have written the simple history of the Jacobins might have sufficed for many; but these Memoirs are intended for the historian, who will find a collection of proofs, both numerous and convincing, all extracted from the records and avowals of the conspirators themselves. Strong in these proofs, we shall not fear to proclaim to all nations, "that whatever their religion or their government may be, to whatever rank they may belong in civil society, if Jacobinism triumphs, all will be overthrown; that should the plans and wishes of the Jacobins be accomplished, their religion with its pontiffs, their government with its laws, their magistrates and their property, all would be swept away in one common mass of ruin! Their riches and their fields, their houses and their cottages, their very wives and children would be torn from them. You have looked upon the Jacobinical faction as exhausting itself in France, when it was only making a sportive essay of its strength. Their wishes and their oaths extend throughout Europe; nor are England or Germany, Italy or Spain, strangers to their intrigues."

Let not the Reader take this for the language of enthusiasm or fanaticism; far be such passions either from myself or my readers. Let them decide on the proofs adduced, with the same coolness and impartiality which has been necessary to collect and digest them. The order observed in the investigation of these conspiracies shall be exactly that in which they were generated. We shall therefore begin with the conspiracy against the whole religion of the Gospel, and which we have styled the ANTICHRISTIAN CONSPIRACY.

THE ANTICHRISTIAN CONSPIRACY

CHAP. I.

Of the Principal Actors in the Conspiracy.

ABOUT the middle of this century appeared three men who were leagued in the most inveterate hatred against Christianity. These were Voltaire, D'Alembert, and Frederic II, King of Prussia. Voltaire hated Religion because he was jealous of its Author, and of all those whom it had rendered illustrious; D'Alembert because his frigid heart was incapable of affection; and Frederic because he had never seen it but through the medium of its enemies.

To these a fourth must be added, and this was Diderot. Hating religion because he doated on nature, and enthusiastically wedded to the chaos of his own ideas, he chose rather to build a system on chimeras and form mysteries of his own, than submit to the light of the Gospel. Numerous adepts were afterwards drawn into this Conspiracy, and these were generally stupid admirers or secondary agents. Voltaire was the chief, D'Alembert the most subtle agent, Frederick the protector and often the adviser, and Diderot the forlorn hope.

Mary Francis Arouet was born at Paris, February 20, 1694, the son of an ancient notary of the Chatelet. Through vanity he changed his name to that of Voltaire, which he deemed more noble, more sonorous, and better suited to the celebrity at which he aimed: and never had there appeared a man with such versatile talents, and such a thirst of dominion over the literary world. Gravity of manners, a contemplative mind, or a genius for discussion or deep research, unfortunately were not among the gifts which Nature had lavished on him; and, more unfortunately still, in his heart were engendered all those baleful passions which render abilities dangerous. From his youth he seemed to direct them all at the overthrow of religion.

While only a student of rhetoric, in the college of Louis le Grand, he drew on himself the following rebuke from his professor, the Jesuit Le Jay. *Unfortunate young man, at some future day you will come to be the standard-bearer of Infidelity.*[1] Never was oracle more literally fulfilled.

On leaving college, he neither sought nor loved any other society than that of men whose profligate morals could strengthen his infidelity. He was particularly intimate with Chaulieu, the poet of voluptuousness, the Anacreon of his day; and with a few Epicureans who held their meetings at the Hotel de Vendôme. His first essays were in satire which gave offence to government, and in tragedy, in which we should have seen the rival of Corneille, Racine, and Crebillon, had he not at the same time emulated Celsus and Porphyrius, with all the other enemies of religion. At a time when licentiousness in opinion still met with obstacles in France, he sought an asylum in England. He there found men whom the writings of Shaftesbury, commented on by Bolingbroke, had trained up to Deism. He mistook them for philosophers, and was persuaded that they alone were esteemed by the English. If he was not then mistaken, opinions are since greatly changed. All those Sophisters whom Voltaire extols as the glory of Great Britain, if not forgotten, are more despised than read. Collins and Hobbes, when remembered, are classed with Tom Paine; an Englishman's good sense does not allow him to hate religion, nor make an ostentatious display of impiety. With him nothing is less philosophical, notwithstanding his toleration and variety of creeds, than that affected hatred to Christianity which marks our Sophisters, and which more particularly characterizes their plans to overthrow it.

Philosophism is said to have originated in England. I deny the fact. Philosophism is the error of every man who, judging of all things by the standard of his own reason, rejects in religious matters every authority that is not derived from the light of nature. It is the error of every man who denies the possibility of any mystery beyond the limits of his reason, of every one who, discarding revelation in defence of the pretended Rights of reason, Equality, and Liberty, seeks to subvert the whole fabric of the Christian religion.

Such an error may constitute a Sect. The history of ancient Jacobinism demonstrates that the Sect existed long since; but it was shrunk back to its dark abodes at the time when Voltaire appeared.

Such an error may be that of a few individuals. Many of the same sort had been broached during the two last centuries. Numerous were the Sects which had sprung from Luther and Calvin, each making its partial assault on the ancient tenets of Christianity; when at length there arose a set of men who attacked them all and would believe nothing. These were at first styled Libertines, the only denomination they deserved.

Voltaire might every where have met with some of these men, but more particularly at Paris under the Regency of the Duke of Orleans, who, though himself a monster of libertinism, yet, feeling the necessity of religion to the state, would not suffer it to be impugned in their publications.

It was in England, it is true, where, under their Collins and their Hobbes, the libertines first styled themselves Philosophers, and assumed the character of deep-thinkers, supported probably by some impious productions, which in any other part of Christendom would neither have enjoyed equal publicity nor even impunity. But it may be certainly concluded, that Voltaire would every where have been what he became in England; he would have been so, at least, wherever, from the lenity of the laws, he could cherish his insatiable appetite for the dominion over the empire of science or of literature.

It was in vain for him to aspire at the reputation of a Bossuet or a Pascal, or to affect the blaze of genius which had shone forth in defence of religion; but, hating their cause, and envying their glory, he dared to be jealous of their God: at his empire, therefore, he levelled his blows, and would be foremost in the ranks of the Philosophists.—He succeeded; but, to keep his pre-eminence, blushed not to blend Philosophy with impiety, and deliberately to contrive means for the overthrow of religion. England was the place where he first conceived a possibility of success. Condorcet, his adept, his confidant, his hisstorian, and his panegyrist, asserts this in positive terms: *There it was* (in England) *that Voltaire swore to dedicate his life to the accomplishment of that project; and he has kept his word.*[2]

On his return to Paris about the year 1730, he made so little a secret of his design, he had published so many writings against Christianity, and was so sanguine in his hopes, that Mr. Herault, the Lieutenant of Police, upbraided him one day with his impiety, and added, *You may do or write what you please, but will never be able to destroy the Christian religion.* Voltaire without hesitation answered, *We shall see that.*[3]

Stimulated by the obstacles he met with, and perceiving much glory in his enterprize, he would not willingly have shared it with any body. "I am weary," he would say, "of hearing people repeat that twelve men were sufficient to establish Christianity, and I will prove that one may suffice to overthrow it."[4] When he uttered these words, his malignity seemed to blind him to such a degree, as to hide from him the immense distance between the genius that creates, and the petty cunning of the mischievous monkey that destroys. The Sophister may conjure the clouds, or veil the world in darkness, but does not by that approach the God of truth. The virtues, the miracles, and all the divine knowledge of the apostles, were necessary to teach man the true path of life.

Although in his outset Voltaire flattered himself that he should enjoy alone the glory of destroying the Christian religion, which was his sole object, he nevertheless soon found that associates would be necessary. He even began to fear the noise of his undertaking, and hence resolved to move in the surer though humbler sphere of a Conspirator.—Already his numerous writings, either impious or obscene, had gained him many admirers and disciples, who, under the name of Philosophers, prided themselves in the hatred they bore to Christianity. From these he chose D'Alembert as the most proper person to second him in his new plan of attack; and he could not have chosen better.

Among the Sophisters we should compare Voltaire to Agamemnon, and D'Alembert to Ulysses. If the comparison be too noble, see the latter cunning, cringing, and even yelping like the fox.—Born of Fontenelle according to some, of Astruc the physician according to others, his birth was always a mystery to him. His mother Claudina Alexandrina Guerin de Tencin, an apostate nun from the convent of Montfleury in Dauphiny, was at the head of one of those societies of men of letters which were common in Paris, and she used to style them her *beasts*. Whether designed to conceal his birth or not, is unknown; but certain it is, that in the night between the 16th and 17th of November 1717, he was found, wrapped in swaddling cloaths, in the portico of the small church of St. John; and hence obtained the name of *Jean le Rond* at the Foundling Hospital whither he was carried and in which he was bred.

While yet a youth he enlisted under the banners of infidelity, thereby repaying with ingratitude the church that had charitably reared him. With the small sums given him for his education, he bought, like many other young men, all the profligate works written against a religion from whose proofs they impatiently flee, as wicked boys calumniate the kind master who thwarts their evil dispositions.

Both his heart and mind led him to be a disciple of Voltaire; and even their diversity of character and the immense difference of talents were soon confounded in their mutual bias to infidelity, and confirmed hatred to Christianity.

Voltaire was fiery, passionate and impetuous; D'Alembert cold, reserved, prudent and crafty.—Voltaire was fond of show, D'Alembert almost feared to be seen. The one, like the chief who is obliged to mask his battery, reluctantly used dissimulation while he wished to wage open war with Christianity, *and die on a heap of Christians*, whom he terms Bigots, *immolated at his feet*.[5]—The other, by instinct a dissembler, waged war like the partizan who, from behind a bush, smiles to see his enemy fall into the snares he has laid.[6] Voltaire, transcendent in polite literature, was but superficial in mathematicks. In the latter D'Alembert was profound, indeed he owed all his reputation to them; for in everything else he was a dry, finical, and confused writer; sometimes as mean and vulgar as Voltaire is noble, easy, and elegant, he would plod to turn a bad epigram, while the latter would have wittily filled whole volumes.

Voltaire, impudently daring, whether for or against, would quote the Scriptures, history, or the holy fathers, affirming, inventing, or traducing the passage as he wanted; for to wound was his only aim. D'Alembert carefully guards against the reply that may expose him; his steps mysterious and indirect conceal his design; shrinking from refutation, if attacked he flies, suppressing the fight lest he should proclaim his defeat. Voltaire on the contrary, seeks his enemies, and loudly calls to them; though a hundred times defeated, he returns to the charge; though his error be refuted, he will incessantly repeat it. It is not in defeat but in flight alone that he sees disgrace; and thus after a war of sixty years we still see him ranging on the field of battle. D'Alembert seeks the smile of every little assembly; and the applause of forty men in an academical circle constitutes his greatest triumph; while all the world, from London to St. Petersburg, from Sweden to America, to please Voltaire, must sound his fame.

D'Alembert enlists from around him the secondary adepts; he trains and initiates them, directs their missions, and holds petty correspondences. Voltaire will conjure kings, emperors, ministers and princes against his God; all must do homage to the sultan of infidelity. Among these latter personages history must distinguish that Frederic, which as yet it has only known by titles glorious to monarchs, whether conquerors or rulers.

In this Frederic II, the *Solomon of the North* according to the Sophisters, we see two distinct men. First that King of Prussia, that hero less worthy of our admiration displaying his vast military talents in the field of victory, than as the father of his people, giving life to agriculture and energy to commerce, protecting the arts, and counterpoising in some sort, by the justice and wisdom of his administration, exploits perhaps more brilliant than just. In the second (so beneath a monarch) we see the Sophister, the philosophic pedant, the conspirator of infidelity; less cruel and enthusiastic indeed than Julian the apostate, but much more artful and perfidious.

It is painful to disclose the dark mysteries of this impious prince; but history must be true, and herein especially. To trace the conspiracy against their thrones, kings must know what share their colleagues have had in the conspiracy against the altar.

Frederic, born with a mind worthy of a Celsus or his school, had not the help of a Justin or a Tertullian to guide his steps in religion, and unfortunately was surrounded by its calumniators. While only Prince-royal he was in correspondence with Voltaire, chiefly on religion or metaphysics; and even at that early age it appears he deemed himself a Philosopher; for he says—"To speak with my usual freedom, I must confess to you, that whatever regards the *God made man* displeases me in the mouth of a Philosopher, who should be above popular error. Leave to *the great Corneille*, when *doating and falling back to childhood*, the insipid talk of versifying the *Imitation of Christ*; and whatever you may give us, let it be your own. We may speak of fables, but merely as fables; and a profound silence in my opinion should be kept concerning those fables of the Christians which have been sanctified by time and the credulity of the absurd and stupid."[7]

Even in his first letters we find, with the ridiculous pride of a pedantic king, all the versatility and hypocrisy of a Sophister. Frederic denies, when Voltaire supports liberty.[8] With Voltaire, man is a pure machine; Frederic then maintains that man is free. In one place we are free, precisely because we can form a clear idea of freedom.[9] In another, man is all matter; yet one can hardly form, though it were with Frederic's own versatility,[10] a more absurd idea, than that of matter thinking, free, or arguing. He upbraids Voltaire with the praises that he had bestowed on Christ, and three years after is not ashamed to write—"For my part, I own that, whatever people may enlist under the banners of Fanaticism, I never shall. I may indeed compose a few Psalms to raise a good opinion of my orthodoxy. Socrates incensed the household Gods, so did Cicero, and he was not credulous. We must give way to the fancies of a frivolous people, in order to avoid blame and persecution; for, after all, what is most desirable in the world is to live in peace; let us then live foolishly with fools, that we may live quietly."[11]

The same Frederic had written, that the Christian religion *yielded none but poisonous weeds;*[12] and Voltaire had congratulated him, *as having above all Princes fortitude of soul, with sufficient perspicacity to see that for the seventeen hundred years past the* CHRISTIAN SECT *had never done any thing but harm*,[13] though we afterward find him the opponent of that work of Philosophic insight, or rather of infamous profligacy, *the System of Nature*. "One might be tempted," he says, "to suspect its author of want of sense and skill when, calumniating the Christian religion, he imputes to it failings that it has not. How can he with truth assert that religion can be the cause of the misfortunes of mankind! He would have been more correct, had he simply said, that men from ambition and self-interest, *concealed under the veil of religion*, had sought to disturb the world and gratify their passions. What is there reprehensible in the morals of the commandments? Were there in the whole Gospel but this single precept, *Do as thou wouldst be done by*, we should be obliged to confess, that those few words contained the whole quintessence of morality:—The forgiveness of injuries, charity, and humanity—were not these preached by Jesus in his excellent sermon on the mount?"[14]

When he wrote thus, how much had Frederic lost of that perspicacity which had so lately distinguished him from other princes! But, strange to say, after having viewed religion in so clear a light, he compliments Voltaire on being its scourge,[15] he still communicates plans for its destruction,[16] and foresees, that should it be preserved and protected in France, *the fine arts and higher sciences must fall*, and that *the rust of superstition will completely destroy a people, otherwise amiable and born for society*.[17]

Had this sophistical monarch *really* foreseen events, he would have seen *that* people, *otherwise amiable* and *born for society*, when it had lost its religion, terrifying all Europe with its horrid deeds. But, like Voltaire, he was to be the sport of his pretended wisdom, as he was of his philosophy; and, though we shall often see him judging shrewdly of the adepts, we shall always find him conspiring with them against the religion of Christ.

The correspondence that so clearly develops the two characters of the royal adept and of his idol Voltaire begins in 1736; and it was uninterrupted during their lives, some few years of the latter's disgrace excepted. It is in this correspondence that we must contemplate him. Incredulous and impious, divesting himself of his royal insignia, he is more emulous of the Philosophist than he was jealous of the Caesars, and to rival Voltaire becomes his servile copyist. A poet beneath mediocrity, a metaphysician on the lower form, he excels in but two things, his admiration for Voltaire and his impiety; in the latter he often outgoes his master.

In consideration of this zeal and homage, Voltaire overlooked his caprice, and the rough usage he sometimes met with, even to the correction of the cane inflicted on him by a major at Frankfort by order of the despotic Sophister. It was too essential that the Sect should secure at any expence the support of a royal adept, and we shall see how very much he served them. But first, in order to asecertain the extent of their mutual hatred to Christianity, let us attend to the vast obstacles they overcame; let us hear Voltaire pathetically describing his sufferings at Berlin a few years after his arrival, in a letter to Mad. Denis, his niece and confidant. He says, "La Metherie may in his Prefaces extol his extreme felicity in being with a great king who sometimes reads his poetry to him; yet in private he weeps with me; he would willingly return, though it were on foot. But why am *I* here? I will astonish you. This La Metherie, a man of no consequence, chats familiarly with the king when their readings are over. He speaks to me with confidence. He declared to me that talking to the king a few days ago of my supposed favour with his majesty, and of the jealousy it excited, the king had answered, *I shall certainly not want him above a twelvemonth longer; we squeeze the orange and then throw away the rind*. . . . I made him repeat these consolatory words; I questioned him again and again, but he only reiterated his declaration.—I have done my utmost not to believe La Metherie; and yet, in reading over the king's verses I found an epistle to one of his painters called Père, which begins thus:

> *Quel spectacle étonnant vient de frapper mes yeux?*
> *Cher Père, ton pinceau, t'égale au rang des dieux.*
>
> Tell me, what sight has struck my wond'ring eyes?
> Thy skill, dear Père, with gods immortal vies.

Now this Père is a fellow of whom he takes no notice, and yet he is the *dear Père, he is a God*; he may perhaps see me in the same light, and that is not saying much.—You may easily guess what reflexions, what a recoil upon myself, and what perplexity, nay what anxiety this declaration of La Meterie's has created within me."[18]

This first letter was sometime after succeeded by a second, as follows: "My sole views at present are, to desert in a genteel manner, to take care of my health, to see you again, and forget this three years dream. I plainly perceive the orange has been squeezed, and must think of saving the rind. For my own instruction I will compile a dictionary for the use of kings: *My friend*, signifies *my slave; my dear friend*, is as much as to say, *you are to me more than indifferent*: you are to understand by *I will make you happy, I will bear with you as long as I shall have need for you; sup with me to-night*, means *I will make game of you to-night*. This dictionary might be carried on to great length, and be not unworthy a place in the Encyclopaedia."

"Seriously this distresses me. Can there be truth in what I have seen? What! delight in making mischief among those that live with him! To say every thing that is kind to a person, and write pamphlets against him! To lure a man from his country by the most endearing expressions and solemn promises, and treat him with the blackest malice! What contrasts! And this is the man who wrote in such a philosophic strain, that I mistook him for a Philosopher, and styled him *the Solomon of the North*! Do you remember that fine letter, which never pleased you? You are a Philosopher (said he) and so am I. Upon my word, Sire, as to Philosophers we are neither of us so."[19]

Voltaire never spoke more truly; neither Frederic nor he could pretend to Philosophy in its true acceptation; but they were eminently so in the sense of the conspirators, with whom impiety and hatred to Christianity constituted its sole essence.

It was soon after writing this last letter, that Voltaire stole away from the court of his disciple, and received at Frankfort that corporal correction which made him the laughing-stock of all Europe. Established however at Ferney, he soon forgot the bastinado; Frederic was once more the *Solomon of the North*, and returned the compliment by saluting Voltaire as the Father of Philosophy. Though not in friendship, they were soon united in mutual hatred to Christianity; and though they never met again, their plans were more easily formed, and intelligently conducted, in their future correspondence.

As to Diderot, he flew spontaneously toward the conspirators. A heated brain; an enthusiastic rage for that Philosophism of which Voltaire had set the fashion; a confusion of ideas, the more evident as both his speech and pen followed all the explosions of his brain, pointed him out to D'Alembert as a man essential to the conspiracy, and who would say, or could be made to say, such things as he dared not speak himself. They were both, until death, as truly attached to Voltaire as the latter was to Frederic.

Had any thing but chaos been to have succeeded to Christianity, had any doctrine whatsoever been to have been taught, never were four men less fitted for such an undertaking.

Voltaire leaned to Deism, and seemed for some time to have adopted it; but, insensibly falling into Spinosa's systems, he knew not what to believe. Consulting at one time D'Alembert, at another Frederic, he was, during the remainder of his life, a prey to remorse, if doubts and anguish of mind void of repentance can be so called. At nearly fourscore he expresses himself in the following manner: "Doubts encompass us round, *and doubting is a disagreeable state*. Is there a God such as he is said to be? A soul such as is imagined? Analogies such as are laid down? Is there any thing to be hoped for after this life? Was Gilimer in the right to laugh, though stripped of his dominions, when brought before Justinian; or Cato in preferring suicide to the sight of Caesar? Is glory then but an illusion? Shall Mustapha, in the effeminacy of his harem, beaten, ignorant, proud, and committing every folly, be happier, provided he digests well, than the Philosopher who digests ill? Are all men equal before the Great Being that animates nature? In that case, could the soul of Ravaillac be equal to that of Henry IV, or had neither of them a soul? Let the heroic philosophers unravel all this; for my part I can make nothing of it."[20]

D'Alembert and Frederic, being alternately pressed by these questions, answered each after his own way. Unable to fix his own opinion, the former frankly confesses he has not the gift of solving them: "I own to you," says he, "that concerning the existence of God, the Author of the *System of Nature* seems too warm and dogmatic; and on this subject Scepticism seems the most rational. *What do we know about it?* is with me an answer to most metaphysical questions; and the natural reflection must be, that since we know nothing of the matter, it is, doubtless, unnecessary that we should know more."[21]

THE ANTICHRISTIAN CONSPIRACY

This remark on the unimportance of these questions was added, lest Voltaire, wearied out by the anxiety of his mind, should forsake a Philosophy unable to solve his doubts on questions by no means, in his opinion, indifferent to the happiness of man. Voltaire still insists; but D'Alembert, continuing in the same style, says, "*No*, in metaphysics, appears to me not much wiser than *yes*; and *non liquet* (it is not clear) is generally the only rational answer."[22]

Frederic was as impatient of doubts as Voltaire; and, perpetually wishing to stifle them, he was at length persuaded that he had succeeded.—"A philosopher of my acquaintance," says he, "a man pretty bold in his opinions, thinks that we have a sufficient degree of probability to constitute a certainty that *post mortem nihil est* (or, that death is an eternal sleep). He maintains that man is not twofold, but is only matter animated by motion; and this strange man says, that there exists no relation between *animals* and the supreme *intelligence*."[23]

This bold Philosopher, this strange man, was Frederic himself; and a few years after he makes no secret of it, for he more decidedly writes, "I am well convinced that I am not twofold; hence, I consider myself as a single being. I know that I am an animal organised, and that thinks; hence, I conclude that matter can think, as well as that it has the property of being electric."[24]

Verging toward his grave, but wishing to inspire Voltaire with confidence, he writes again: "The gout has successively run over all my body.—Our frail machine must needs be destroyed by time, which consumes every thing; my foundations are undermined; but all this gives me very little concern."[25]

As to the fourth hero of the Conspiracy, the famous Diderot, he is the very person whose decisions against God D'Alembert has found too warm and dogmatic; though oftentimes, in the same work, we find him, after deciding against the Deist, arguing in the same peremptory manner for or against the Sceptic and the Atheist. But whether writing for or against a God he always appears free from doubts or anxieties. He fairly wrote what he thought at the moment, whether *he crushed the Atheists with the weight of the universe*, and asserted that *the eye of a mite, the wing of a butterfly*, was sufficient to defeat them,[26] or declared *that glorious display did not give him even the most distant idea of any thing divine*,[27] and that this universe was but the *fortuitous result of motion and matter*;[28] whether, when the existence of God was to be left in doubt, *Scepticism at all times and in all places could alone preserve us from the two opposite excesses*,[29] or *he prays God for the Sceptics*, because he sees *they all want light*;[30] whether, in short, to form a sceptic, *it was necesssary to have a head as well organised as that of Montaigne the philosopher*.[31]

Never was a man more peremptory when affirming or denying any point, more perfectly void of constraint or care, or more impervious to remorse; for he was a perfect stranger to them even when asserting positively, that *between him and his dog he knows of no other difference but their dress*.[32]

With these extravagancies in their religious opinions, we find Voltaire impious and tormented by his doubts and ignorance; D'Alembert impious, but calm in his; while Frederic, impious and triumphant (or thinking he had triumphed) over his ignorance, left God in heaven, provided there were no souls on earth; and Diderot, by turns Atheist, Materialist, Deist, and Sceptic, but ever impious, ever frantic, was the better fitted for the various parts he was doomed to act.

Such were the men whose characters and whose errors were necessary to be known, in order to ascertain the Conspiracy of which they were the chiefs, of the existence of which we shall give undeniable proof, define its precise object, and unfold its means and progress.

1. Life of Voltaire, edit. of Kell, and Feller's Hist. Dict.
2. Life of Voltaire, edit. of Kell.
3. Ibid.
4. Ibid.
5. To D'Alembert, 20 April 1761, Vol. 68, Let. 85, P. 164.
6. From D'Alembert, 4 May 1762, Vol. 68, Let. 100, P. 199.
7. From Frederic, May, 1738, Vol. 64, Let. 53, P. 275.
8. Their Letters in 1737, Vol. 64.
9. From Frederic, 16 Sept. 1771, Vol. 66, Let. 12, P. 30.
10. From Frederic, 4 Dec. 1775, Vol. 66, Let. 100, P. 237.
11. From Frederic, 6 Jan. 1740, Vol. 64, Let. 107, P. 471.
12. From Frederic, 8 Jan. 1766, Vol. 65, Let. 143, P. 334.
13. To Frederic, 5 April, 1767, Vol. 65, Let. 159, P. 374.
14. Examination of the System of Nature, by Frederic, King of Prussia.
15. From Frederic, 12 Aug. 1773, Vol. 66, Let. 40, P. 94.
16. From Frederic, 29 July, 1775, Vol. 66, Let. 93, P. 216.
17. From Frederic, 30 July, 1774, Vol. 66, Let. 59, P. 137.
18. To Mad. Denis, 2 Sept. 1751, Vol. 54, Let. 208, P. 352.
19. To Mad. Denis, 18 Dec. 1752, Vol. 54, Let. 227, P. 518.
20. To Frederic, 12 Oct. 1770, Vol. 65, Let. 179, P. 426.
21. From D'Alembert, 25 July, 1770, Vol. 69, Let. 36, P. 68.
22. From D'Alembert, 4 Aug. 1770, Vol. 69, Let. 38, P. 72.
23. From Frederic, 30 Oct. 1770, Vol. 65, Let. 180, P. 429.
24. From Frederic, 4 Dec. 1775, Vol. 66, Let. 100, P. 237.
25. From Frederic, 8 April, 1776, Vol. 66, Let. 108, P. 257.
26. Philosophical Thoughts, No. 20.
27. The Code of Nature.
28. Philosophical Thoughts, No. 21.
29. Idem. No. 33.
30. Idem. No. 22.
31. Idem. No. 28.
32. Life of Seneca, Page 377.

CHAP. II.

Of the Existence, Object, and Extent of the Antichristian Conspiracy.

To say that there existed against the Christian religion a Conspiracy, of which Voltaire, D'Alembert, Frederic II, King of Prussia, and Diderot, were the prime authors and instigators, is not merely saying, that each of them individually was an enemy, and that their writings tended to the destruction of the religion of Christ; for, both before and after them, we have seen enemies of this same religion seeking to diffuse, by their writings, the venom of infidelity. France has had her Bayle and her Montesquieu; the first a true Sophister, undecided in his principles, and supporting the *pro* and *con* with equal facility; but destitute of that hatred which constitutes the Conspirator, and leads him to seek accomplices: the latter was but a youth when he wrote his *Persian Letters*, and had no fixed principle against that faith, to which he was one day to do homage, by declaring that *he always respected religion,* and that he looked on the Gospel *as the fairest gift that God had bestowed on man.*[1]

England has seen her Hobbes, her Woolastons, and her Collins, with many other disciples of infidelity; but each of these Sophisters was impious in his own way; they sought not to league together, though Voltaire and Condorcet strongly assert the contrary. Each made his partial attack on Christianity from his own heated brain, and that is not sufficient to constitute a Conspiracy.

In order to prove a real Conspiracy against Christianity, we must not only point out the wish to destroy, but also the secret union and correspondence in the means employed to attack, debase, or annihilate it. When, therefore, I name Voltaire and Frederic, Diderot and D'Alembert, as the chiefs of this Antichristian Conspiracy, I not only mean to shew that each individual had impiously written against Christianity, but that they had formed the wish, and had secretly concurred in that wish, to destroy the religion of Christ; that they had acted in concert, sparing no political nor impious art to effectuate that destruction; that they were the instigators and conductors of those secondary agents whom they had misled; and followed up their plans and projects with all that ardor and constancy which denotes the most accomplished Conspirators. My proofs shall be drawn from what we may very properly term the records of the conspiracy, I mean from their most intimate correspondence, a long time secret, or from their own assertions contained in their various writings.

When Beaumarchais gave us a complete edition of Voltaire's works, with all the magnificence of the Baskerville type, either the adepts, dazzled by their success, were persuaded that the publicity of this monstrous conspiracy could only give new lustre to its chief; or the Editors themselves were ignorant of the fact; or concluded that, being scattered and dispersed through forty large volumes of letters to all sorts of persons, and on all sorts of subjects, no man could at once seize the thread of a conspiracy, the work of many long years.—But whatever may have been their intentions, how great soever their art in suppressing parts of the correspondence, they have not effectually done away all means of discovery. Never should I have undertaken a work of such labour, so painful and so disgusting, had I not seen the possibility and the necessity of proving from the very records of the conspirators the reality of their plots; of denouncing to all nations, with proof in hand, the men who wished to mislead them, and sought to overturn every altar provided it was Christian. With them the altars of London or Geneva, of Stockholm or Petersburg, were to share the same fate with those of Paris or Madrid, of Vienna or Rome; thus adding, by their fall, a new though tardy proof of the universality of this conspiracy. Such then are their black and obscure crimes. Behold them conspiring against your God, in order to undermine your sovereign and your laws! Behold them seeking to overthrow all civil society, and to extend universally the evils of the French revolution.

I know that the importance of the charge requires strong evidence and clear proofs to justify it; if then my proofs should appear too numerous let the reader reflect on the magnitude of the charge.

In all conspiracies we find a secret language, or a watchword, which, though unintelligible to the vulgar, perpetually recalls the object to the mind of the conspirator. The words chosen by Voltaire must have been dictated by some fiend of hatred or of frantic rage: And what words! *Crush the wretch!* (*écrasez l'infame!*) What a signification is attached to these three words in the mouths of Voltaire, of D'Alembert, of Frederic, and of their disciples! They mean *Crush Christ, crush the religion of Christ, crush every religion that adores Christ.* Oh readers! restrain your indignation till you have seen the proof!

When Voltaire complains that the adepts are not sufficiently united in the war which they wage against *the wretch*, and wishes to revive their zeal, he recalls to their minds the hopes and projects he had conceived so early as 1730, when the lieutenant of the police of Paris warned him that he would not succeed in overturning the Christian religion, and when he daringly answered, *We shall see that.*[2]

When exulting in the success of the war and progress of the conspiracy against *the wretch*, he triumphs in the idea "that in Geneva, Calvin's own town, there are but a few beggarly fellows who believe in the consubstantial."[3]

When he wishes, during this war against *the wretch*, to give his reasons for tolerating the Socinians, it is, he says, *because Julian would have favoured them, and he hates what Julian hated, and despises what he* (Julian) *despised*.[4]

What (let us ask) is this hatred, common to the Socinians and to Julian the apostate, if not their hatred to the divinity of Christ? What is meant by the consubstantial fallen into disrepute, if not Christ? Or, how can the word *wretch* be otherwise interpreted in the mouth of him that has said, "I am weary of hearing people repeat that twelve men have been sufficient to establish Christianity, and I will prove that one may suffice to overthrow it;"[5] in the mouth of a man who, in his intrigues against *the wretch*, exclaims, "Could not five or six men of talents, and who rightly understood each other, succeed after the example of twelve scoundrels who have already succeeded?"[6]

In the mouth of this frantic infidel can we misconceive the sense of these words? The twelve apostles are called *twelve scoundrels*! and their divine master a *wretch*! I may dwell too long on the proofs, but the charges are too heinous to pass them over lightly.

All the men so much extolled by Voltaire for their ardor in *crushing the wretch*, are precisely those who attacked Christianity without the least decorum or decency; such as Diderot, Condorcet, Helvetius, Freret, Boulanger, Dumarsais, and other such infidels; and those whom he particularly wishes D'Alembert to rally, the more effectually *to crush the wretch*, are the Atheists, the Deists and Spinosists.[7]

Against whom then will the Atheist, the Deist, and the Spinosist coalesce, but against the God of the Gospel?

Voltaire proceeds to direct the zeal of the conspirators against the holy fathers, and against those modern authors who have written in defense of Christianity and of the divinity of Christ; both of these he wishes to see treated with the utmost contempt; and he thus writes to his adepts: "Victory is declaring for us on all sides; and I can assure you, that in a short time none but the rabble will follow the standard of our enemies; and that rabble we equally contemn whether for or against us. We are a corps of brave knights, defenders of the truth, and admit none among us but men of education. Courage brave Diderot, intrepid D'Alembert! Form with my dear Damilaville, and rush forward on those fanatics and knaves. Pity poor Pascal, but despise Houtville and Abbadie as much *as if* they were *fathers of the church*."[8]

Here then is clearly shewn, what Voltaire means *by crushing the wretch*. It is to undo what the apostles have done; to hate what Julian the apostate hated; to attack those whom the Deists, Atheists, and Spinosists always attacked. It is, in short, to rush on the holy fathers, or on any man who dares to defend the religion of Christ.

The sense of this atrocious watchword is equally clear in the mouth of Frederic. With this royal Sophister, as with Voltaire, *Christianity, the Christian Sect, the Christicole superstion* (La superstition Christicole), and *the wretch*, are all synonymous terms. With him, as with Voltaire, *the wretch yielded none but poisonous weeds*; the best writings against *the wretch* are precisely the most impious, and if any in particular deserve his highest esteem, it is, *that since Celsus, nothing so striking had been published* against Christianity. The fact is, that Boulanger, unfortunately more known by his impiety than by his conversion, *is still superior to Celsus himself.*[9]

As to D'Alembert, we may see, that though he seldom uses this shocking word, he was well acquainted with its meaning. This is evident by his answers to Voltaire, by the means he suggests, and by the writings he approves and seeks to circulate as fittest *to crush the wretch*; which writings are precisely those that most directly tend to eradicate religion from the minds of the people. We may see, when, wishing to shew his zeal for the progress of the conspiracy against *the wretch*, he professes his eagerness to support Voltaire, and his sorrow that from local circumstances he cannot speak with the same freedom against Christianity. His expressions and the numberless letters hereafter quoted, will leave no more doubt of him than of Voltaire or Frederic.[10]

Such was the general acceptation of the watchword among all the conspirators. Condorcet, indeed, laying aside the word *wretch*, positively asserts that Voltaire had sworn *to crush Christianity*;[11] and Mercier says, *to crush Christ.*[12]

That the views of the conspirators were *to crush Christ*, is not too strong an expression. In the extent of their projects no shadow of his worship was to remain: it is true, that among the Christians they honoured the church of Rome with their chief hatred. But Luther and Calvin, the Churches of England and of Geneva, though separated from Rome, had retained their belief of Christ, and were therefore to share the fate of the former.

The whole Gospel of Calvin is ridiculed by Voltaire *as the fooleries of Jean Chauvin*;[13] and it is of these fooleries that he speaks when, writing to D'Alembert, he says, *in Calvin's own town* (Geneva) *there were but a few beggarly fellows who believed in the consubstantial*, that is to say, *who believed in Christ*. He particularly exults in the approaching fall of the Church of England when he extols *the English truths*,[14] that is, the impieties of Hume; and when he thought himself authorized to write, that *in London Christ was spurned.*[15]

Those disciples who paid him the homage of their philosophic science, adopting his style, write thus: "I don't like Calvin, he was intolerant and poor. Servetus fell a victim to him; and it is a fact, that he is no more spoken of at Geneva than if he had never existed. As to Luther, though he had not much wit, as is easily perceived in his writings, he did not persecute; he only loved wine and women."[16]

It is observable, that for a considerable time the conspiring sophisters found particular satisfaction in their successes against the Protestant churches. With what excessive joy would Voltaire write, that England and Switzerland were over-run with men *who hated and despised* Christianity *as Julian* the apostate *hated and despised it*;[17] and that *from Geneva to Berne not a Christian was to be found.*[18] Frederic, on his side, writes with equal joy, *In our protestant countries we go on much brisker.*[19]

Such was the extent of this conspiracy; it was to overturn every altar where Christ was adored. A superficial historian might have been misled by seeing the adepts solicit, more than once, the recal of the Protestants into France; but at the very time that Voltaire is expressing how much he laments to see the petition made by the minister Choiseul rejected, he hastens to add (fearing that his disciples might imagine he wished to spare the Huguenot more than the Catholic) that the Huguenots and the Calvinists *are not less mad than the Sorbonists or the Catholics*; that they were even *raving mad*;[20] nay, sometimes he saw *nothing more atrabilarious and ferocious than the Huguenots*.[21]

All this pretended zeal of the conspirators to calvinize France, was but a preparatory step to unchristianize it with the greater ease and expedition. We may trace the ground of their intended progress in the following words of D'Alembert to Voltaire: "For my part I see every thing in the brightest colours; already I behold toleration established; *the Protestants recalled*, the Priests married, confession abolished, and fanaticism crushed, *without its being perceived*."[22] *Fanaticism* and *wretch* in D'Alembert's mouth are synonymous, the latter is even made use of in the same letter, both meaning *Christ* or *his whole religion crushed*.

There is however an exception often made by Voltaire, which might have left to Christ some few worshippers among the rabble. He seems little jealous of that conquest when he writes to D'Alembert, "Both you and Damilaville must be well pleased to see the contempt into which *the wretch* is fallen among the better sort of people throughout Europe; *they are all we wished for* or that were necessary; we never pretended to enlighten *house-maids and shoemakers*; we leave them to the apostles."[23] Again, he writes to Diderot, "Whatever you do, have your eye *on the wretch. It* must be destroyed among the better sort; but we may *leave it to the rabble* for whom *it* was made;"[24] or when, in fine, he writes to Damilaville, "I can assure you, that in a short time none but the rabble will follow the standard of our enemies; and that rabble we equally despise whether for or against us."[25]

Voltaire, despairing of more enlarged success, would sometimes except *the clergy and the great chamber of Parliament*. But in the sequel of these memoirs we shall see the conspirators actively extending their principles, and instilling their hatred against Christianity into every class of men from the cottage to the throne, and not even excepting their so-much-despised rabble.

1. Vid. Montesquieu, Feller's Hist. Dict.
2. To D'Alembert, 20 June, 1760, Vol. 68, Let. 66, P. 118.
3. To D'Alembert, 28 Sept. 1763, Vol. 68, Let. 119, P. 253.
4. To Frederic, 8 Nov. 1773, Vol. 66, Let. 46, P. 112.
5. Life of Voltaire by Condorct.
6. To D'Alembert, 24 July, 1760, Vol. 68, Let. 70, P. 127.
7. To D'Alembert, 27 July, 1770, Vol. 69, Let. 37, P. 70.
8. To Damilaville, 19 Nov. 1765, Vol. 59, Let. 123, P. 216.
9. See Let. of the King of Prussia, No. 143, 145, 153, anno 1767, et passim Vol. 65.

10. See D'Alembert's Letters, 100, 102, 151, Vol. 68.
11. Life of Voltaire.
12. Mercier's Let. No. 60, of M. Pelletier.
13. To Damilaville 18 Aug. 1766, Vol. 59, Let. 239, P. 424.
14. To the M. D'Argence de Dirac, 28 Apr. 1760. Vol. 56. Let. 133, p. 276.
15. To D'Alembert, 28 Sept. 1763, Vol. 68, Let. 119, P. 254.
16. From the Landgrave of Hesse, 9 Sept. 1766, Vol. 66, Let. 64, P. 410.
17. To D'Alembert, 8 Feb. 1776, Vol. 69, Let. 151, P. 257.
18. From Frederic, 8 Nov. 1773, Vol. 66, Let. 46, P. 112.
19. From Frederic 8 Jan. 1766, Vol. 65, Let. 143, P. 334.
20. To Marmontel, 2 Dec 1767, Vol. 60, Let. 200, P. 336.
21. To the M. D'Argence de Dirac, 2 March 1763, Vol. 58, Let. 36, P. 74.
22. From D'Alembert, 4 May 1762, Vol. 68, Let. 100, P. 201.
23. To D'Alembert, 2 Sept. 1768, Vol. 68, Let. 234, P. 486.
24. To Diderot, 25 Sept. 1762, Vol. 57, Let. 242, P. 475.
25. To Damilaville, 19 Nov. 1765, Vol. 59, Let. 123, P. 216.

CHAP. III.

The Secrecy, the Union and the Epoch of the Conspiracy.

IN conspiracies it is not enough for the agents to have a particular watchword, or formula, in order to conceal their common object; but they must also have peculiar names, by which they distinguish each other, but which are wholly unintelligible to the public. They always carefully conceal their correspondence; but if they apprehend discovery, they then use these precautions lest their names, or the object of the plot, be exposed.

Such means were not neglected by Voltaire or D'Alembert. In their correspondence Frederic is often called *Luc*,[1] D'Alembert *Protagoras*,[2] though he often styles himself *Bertrand*. Both were well applied to him, the former to denote the infidel, the latter to typify the means of his impiety by the shifts of *Bertrand* in Fontaine's fable of the Monkey and the Cat: when D'Alembert is *Bertrand* (the monkey), Voltaire is *Raton*[3] (the cat). Diderot personates *Plato* or *Tonpla*;[4] and the general term for the conspirators is *Cacouac*.[5] They say he is a good Cacouac when he can be perfectly depended upon. They are often too, and particularly Voltaire, called brothers, as in Masonry. They also give peculiar imports to entire phrases of their enigmatical language; for example, *the vine of Truth is well cultivated*; is tantamount to saying, we make rapid progress against religion.[6]

Of this secret language they particularly made use when they suspected that their letters were opened or stopped, a suspicion which often gave Voltaire and D'Alembert great uneasiness. It was for this reason that many of their letters were directed to fictitious persons, to merchants, or to some clerk in office who was in the secret. It does not appear that they ever made use of cyphers, which would have been much too tedious, considering Voltaire's immense correspondence. Those were reserved for conspirators not less ardent, perhaps, but of a deeper policy. False directions, and not signing their names, seem to have given them sufficient confidence in their style; and if perchance any of their letters are more enigmatical than common, they are easily explained by those preceding or following them. It was by these shifts, that they wished to leave an opening for excusing or explaining away what they had already written; but they are not sufficiently obscure to prevent discovery, and that with very little trouble, when once surprised.

Some few, however, are certainly more difficult to be understood than others; for example, the letter written by Voltaire to D'Alembert, the 30th of January 1764, of which the following is an extract: "My illustrious Philosopher has sent me the letter of Hippias, B. This letter of B proves that there are T...'s and that poor literature is falling back into the shackles which *Malesherbes* had broken. That demi-scholar as well as demi-citizen, D'Aguesseau, was a T.... He would have hindered the nation from thinking! I wish you had but seen that brute of a *Maboul*, he was a very silly T... to be at the head of the customs upon ideas under the T... D'Aguesseau. Then followed the under T...'s, about half a dozen miserable rascals, who, for the pitiful salary of 17l. per annum, would erase from a book everything that was worth leaving in it."[7]

Here it is evident that T stands for *Tyrant*, one of which tyrants is the chancellor D'Aguesseau, the other Maboul, the comptroller of the press. The under T's, or tyrants, are the public censors, whose salaries were about 17l. per annum. As to *Hippias B,* his person is not so clear; he was most probably some tyrant who wished to stop the circulation of those works which directly tended to the overthrow of the altar and the throne. But who can see, without indignation, the chancellor D'Aguesseau, the ornament of the magistracy, called a tyrant, a demi-scholar, a demi-citizen. It is, however, forbearance in Voltaire, not to abuse him more grossly; we must expect to see him and D'Alembert, throughout this correspondence, lavishing the lowest terms of blackguardism on every man who differs from them in opinion, whatever be his merits in other respects; but especially on those who laboured for or wrote in defense of religion.

But, openly as the Conspirators expressed themselves to each other, secrecy was strictly recommended to them with respect to the public; and Voltaire perpetually apprizes the adepts of its importance. "The mysteries of Mytra (he would make D'Alembert write to the adepts) are not to be divulged;....the *monster* (religion) must fall, pierced by a hundred invisible hands; yes, let it fall beneath a thousand repeated blows."[8]

This secrecy, however, was not to be so much with respect to the object of the conspiracy, as the names of the Conspirators, and the means they employed; for it was impossible for the rancorous hatred of Voltaire to disguise the wish of annihilating Christianity; but he had to fear on one side the severity of the laws, and on the other the contempt and infamy which would certainly attach to himself and his disciples, for the impudence of their falsehoods and the effrontery of their calumnies, had it ever been possible to trace their authors and abettors.

It is not the fault of history if it be obliged to represent the Chief of the conspiracy as at once the most daring and most unrelenting in his hatred to Christ, yet the most desirous of concealing his attacks. Voltaire secretly conspiring and masking his means, is the same man as when bold and blaspheming. He is the same Sophister, whether openly attacking the altars of his God, veiling the hand that strikes, and seeking in the dark to undermine the temple. It is hatred that fires his rage, and the same hatred that leads him through the tortuous ways of the Conspirator. To unmask this dissimulating man shall be a leading object in the following Memoirs.

In his character of Chief, the mysteries of Mytra, as well as the intrigues of the Conspirators, could be of no small concern to him; and the following were his secret instructions: "Confound *the wretch* to the utmost of your power; speak your mind boldly; but when you strike *conceal your hand*. You may be known; I am willing to believe there are people sufficiently keen-scented, but they will not be able to convict you."[9]

"The Nile is said to spread around its fertilizing waters, though it conceals its head; *do you the same*, and you will secretly enjoy your triumph. I recommend *the wretch to you*.[10] We embrace the worthy knight, and exhort him *to conceal his march* from the enemy."[11]

No precept is oftener repeated by Voltaire than this, *strike, but conceal the hand*; and if by indiscretion any adept occasioned discovery, he would complain most bitterly, he would even deny works that were the most notoriously his. "I know not (says he) why people are so obstinately bent on believing me the author of the *Philosophical Dictionary*. The greatest service you can do me is to assert (though you even pledge your share in Paradise) that I had no hand in that hellish work. There are three or four people who perpetually repeat that I have supported the good cause, and that I fight mortally against the wild beasts. *It is betraying one's Brethren to praise them on such an occasion; those good souls bless me, but they also ruin me.....*It is certainly his, they say; it is his style and manner. Ah, my Brethren, what fatal words! you should on the contrary cry out in the public streets, It is not he; *for the monster must fall pierced by a hundred invisible hands; yes, let it fall beneath a thousand repeated blows.*"[12]

It was in this art of secrecy, and the skill of concealing his steps, that D'Alembert so much excelled. Him it was that Voltaire recommended to the Brethren for imitation, *as the hope of the flock*. "He is daring (would he say to them), but not rash; he will make hypocrites (that is, religious men) tremble, without giving any hold against himself."[13]

Frederic not only approved of this secrecy,[14] but we shall see him playing off all the artifices of a dark policy to ensure the success of the conspiracy.

In every plot union is as essential to the conspirator as secrecy to the cause, and therefore it is often and particularly recommended. Among others, we find the following instructions: "Oh, my Philosophers, we should march closed, as did the Macedonian phalanx, which was only vanquished when it opened. Let the real Philosophers unite in a brotherhood like the Freemasons; let them assemble and support each other, and let them be faithful to the association. Such an academy will be far superior to that of Athens, and to all those of Paris."[15]

If any dissension, by chance, happened among the Conspirators, the Chief immediately wrote to appease them: "Ah, my poor Brethren (he would say), the primitive Christians behaved themselves much better than we do. Have patience; do not let us lose courage; God will help us, provided we remain united;" and when he wished to insist more particularly on the object of that union, he would repeat his answer to Herault, *We'll see whether it be true, that the Christian religion cannot be destroyed.*[16]

Most of these dissensions arose from the difference of opinion in the Conspirators, and the discordancy of their Sophisms against Christianity, which often made them thwart each other. Voltaire, aware of the advantage it gave to religious writers, immediately enjoined D'Alembert to seek, if possible, a reconciliation with the Atheists, Deists, and Spinosists. "The two parties (says he) must necessarily coalesce. I wish you would undertake that reconciliation; say to them, *if you will omit the emetic, I will overlook the bleeding.*"[17]

This Premier Chief, always fearful lest their ardor should subside, and wishing to animate their zeal, would write to the other chiefs, "I fear you are not sufficiently zealous; you bury your talents; you seem only to contemn while you should abhor and destroy the monster. Could not you *crush* him in a few pages, while you modestly hide from him that he falls by your pen? It was given to Meleager to kill the boar. *Hurl the javelin, but hide your hand.* Comfort me in my old age."[18] He would write to a young adept, who might be dejected through ill success, *Courage! do not suffer yourself to be dejected.*[19] Again, to bind them by the strongest ties of interest, he would tell them, through the medium of D'Alembert, "Such is our state, that we shall be the execration of mankind if we have not the better sort of people on our side. We must therefore gain them, cost what it will; labour then in the vineyard, *and crush the wretch; oh, crush the wretch.*"[20]

Thus clearly is every distinctive mark of the conspirator, as enigmatical language, a common and secret wish, union, ardor and perseverance, to be seen in these first authors of the war against Christianity. Hence the historian is authorised to represent this coalition of Sophisters as a real conspiracy against the altar. At length Voltaire not only avows it, but wishes every adept to understand, that the war of which he was the chief was a true plot, and that each individual was to act the part of a conspirator. When he feared an excess in their zeal, he would write himself, or through D'Alembert, that in the war which they waged, *they were to act as conspirators, and not as zealots.*"[21]

When the chief of these infidels makes so formal a declaration, when we find him so clearly ordering them to *act as conspirators*, it would be absurd to seek farther proofs as to the existence of the conspiracy. I fear they have already been too numerous for the reader; but in a matter of such importance, I was to presume him equally rigid as myself with respect to its demonstration. Now as nobody, unless blind to conviction, will deny this to have been a real conspiracy of the Sophisters against Christ and his Church, I will, before I close this Chapter, try to ascertain its origin and epoch.

If this conspiracy were to be dated from the day on which Voltaire consecrated his life to the annihilation of Christianity, we should look back to the year 1728, that being the time of his return from London to France; and his most faithful disciples inform us, that he made his determination when in England.[22] But Voltaire lived many years ruminating alone his hatred against Christ.—It is true, he was already the officious defender of every impious work that had the same tendency; but these were only the isolated productions of Sophisters, writing singly, without any of the appurtenances of the conspirator. To form adepts, and to instil his hatred into them, must be the work of time; and his efforts, unfortunately crowned with success, have greatly augmented their number, when, in 1750, he, by the express desire of the King of Prussia, took his departure for Berlin. Of all the disciples whom he left in Paris, the most zealous were D'Alembert and Diderot; and it is to these two men that the coalition against Christ can be traced. Though it might not then have acquired all its strength, it certainly existed when the plan of the Encyclopedia was decided on; that is to say, the very year that Voltaire left Paris for Berlin. Voltaire had formed his disciples; but D'Alembert and Diderot united them in one body to make that famous compilation, which may truly be styled the grand arsenal of impiety, whence all their sophisticated arms were to be directed against Christianity.

Voltaire, who alone was worth a host of infidels, labouring apart in the war against Christianity, left the Encyclopedists for some time to their own schemes; but though his disciples had been able to form the coalition, they were incapable of carrying it on. Their difficulties augmenting, they sought a man able to remove them, and without hesitation fixed on Voltaire, or rather, to use the words of his historian, *Voltaire, by his age, his reputation, and his genius, naturally became their chief.*

At his return from Prussia, about the year 1752, he found the conspiracy complete. Its precise object was the destruction of Christianity; the chief had first sworn it; the secondary chiefs, such as D'Alembert, Diderot, and even Frederic, notwithstanding his quarrels with the premier, were ever after leagued with him in the same bonds. At this period, the adepts were all that Voltaire could number as his disciples: but from the day of the coalition between the premier, the secondary chiefs, and the adepts' agents or protectors, from the day that the object of this coalition to crush Christ, under the appellation of *wretch*, and his religion, had been decreed, until the grand object of the coalition was to be consummated by the proscriptions and horrid massacres of the Jacobins, near half a century was to elapse; for so much time was necessary for the harbinger of blood and corruption to prepare the way for the Philosophist of destruction and murder. During this long period of time, we shall see this sophistical Sect, that had sworn to *crush,* naturally coalescing with the Sect, which, under the name of *Jacobin,* really does *crush* and masssacre.

Where then is the difference between the sophistical Sect under Voltaire and D'Alembert, anticipating the murders of the French revolution by their wishes and their conspiracies, and those Sophisters who, under the name of *Jacobins,* overthrow the Altar and imbue its steps with the blood of its priests and pontifs? Do not they proscribe the religion of the same Christ, of the same

God, whom Voltaire, D'Alembert, Frederic, and all that impious clan of adepts, have sworn to crush and abhor? Will any one tell us that there is any difference between the sophisms of the former and the pretexts of the latter, between the school of Voltaire and the maxims of the Jacobinical den?

The Jacobins will one day declare that all men are free, that all men are equal; and as a consequence of this Equality and Liberty they will conclude that every man must be left to the light of reason. That every religion subjecting man's reason to mysteries, or to the authorities of any revelation speaking in God's name, is a religion of slavery and constraint; that as such it should be annihilated, in order to re-establish the indefeasible rights of Equality and Liberty, as to the belief or disbelief of all that the reason of man approves or disapproves: and they will call this Equality and Liberty the reign of reason and the empire of Philosophy. Can the intelligent reader believe, that this Equality and Liberty is not apposite to the war carried on by Voltaire against Christianity? Had ever the chiefs or adepts any other view, than that of establishing their pretended empire of Philosophy, or their reign of reason, on that self-same Equality and Liberty applied to revelation and the mysteries in perpetual opposition to Christ and his Church?

Did not Voltaire hate the church and its pastors because they opposed that Equality and Liberty applied to our belief, because nothing was *so contemptible* and *so miserable* in his eyes, as to see one man have recourse to another in matters of faith, *or to ask what he ought to believe?*[23] Reason, Liberty, and *Philosophy*, were as constantly in the mouths of Voltaire and D'Alembert, as a means of overthrowing Revelation and the Gospel, as they are at this day in the mouths of the Jacobins.[24] When the adepts wish to extol the glory of their chiefs, they will represent them as *perpetually reclaiming the independence of Reason,* and devoutly expecting those days *when the sun shall no longer shine but upon free men acknowledging no other master but their own reason.*[25]

When therefore, on the ruins of the temple, the Jacobins shall have erected the idol of their Reason, their Liberty, or their Philosophy, will they have fulfilled any other wish, confirmed any other oath, than that sworn by Voltaire and his adepts?

When the Jacobins shall apply the axe to the foundations of the temples, whether Protestant or Catholic, or indeed of any Sect acknowledging the God of the Christians, will they have more widely extended their systems of destruction, than Voltaire did conspiring against the Altars of London or Geneva equally as against those of Rome?

When their grand club shall be filled with every infidel that the French revolution can produce, whether Atheist, Deist, or Sceptic, will their revolutionary cohorts be differently formed from those which D'Alembert was to quicken and stir up against the God of Christianity?

In short, when one day these legions sallying from this den of impiety, from the grand club of the Jacobins, shall triumphantly carry to the Pantheon the ashes of Voltaire, will not that be the consummation of the Antichristian Conspiracy, will not that be the revolution so long planned by Voltaire? The means may differ; but the object, the spirit, and the extent of the conspiracy will remain. We shall see that the very means employed, the revolution that destroys the altar, that plunders and massacres its priests by the hand of the Jacobin, were not foreign to the wishes or intentions of the first adepts. The most dreadful and disgusting parts of this irreligious revolution only differs from their plans by a difference in terms; *one* WISHED *to crush, the other* DID *crush.* The means were such as the times suggested, both were not equally powerful.—We will now proceed to tear the veil from those dark intrigues successively employed by the Sophisters during the half century which preceded and prepared such scenes of blood and confusion.

1. From D'Alembert, 17 Nov. 1760, Vol. 68, Let. 77, P. 145.
2. To Thiriot, 26 Jan. 1762, Vol. 57, Let. 157, P. 320.
3. From D'Alembert, 22 March 1774, Vol. 69, Let. 128, P. 216.
4. To Damilaville, 11 Aug. 1766, Vol. 59, Let. 237, P. 420. In French Plato is spelled *Platon*, the anagram of which is *Tonpla*; hence Plato and *Tonpla* are to be looked upon as synonymous.
5. From D'Alembert, 18 Oct. 1760, Vol. 68, Let. 76, P. 141.
6. To D'Alembert, 17 Nov. 1760, ut supra.
7. Vol. 68, Let. 128, p. 278.
8. To D'Alembert, 1 May 1768, Vol. 68, Let. 229, P. 478.
9. To D'Alembert, 20 April *and* 8 May, 1761, Vol. 68, Lett. 85-6, P. 164-6.
10. To Helvetius, 11 May, 1761, Vol. 57, Let. 53, P. 110.
11. To Mr. de Villevielle, 26 April, 1767, Vol. 60, Let. 102, P. 180.
12. To D'Alembert, 1 May 1768, Vol. 68, Let. 229, P. 178.
13. To Thiriot, 19 Nov. 1760, Vol. 56, Let. 228, P. 453.
14. From Frederic, 29 Juin, 1771, Vol. 66, Let. 10, P. 26.
15. To D'Alembert, 20 April, 1761, Vol. 68, Let. 85, P. 162.
16. To D'Alembert, 20 Juin, 1760, Vol. 68, Let. 66, P., 118.
17. To D'Alembert, 27 July, 1770, Vol. 69, Let. 37, P. 70.
18. To D'Alembert, 28 Sept. 1763, Vol. 68, Let. 119, p. 253.
19. To Damilaville, 15 Juin, 1761, Vol. 57, Let. 70, P. 143.
20. To D'Alembert, 13 Feb. 1764, Vol. 68, Let. 129, P. 282.
21. To D'Alembert, 19 Sept. 1764, Vol. 68, Let. 142, P. 316.
22. Life of Voltaire, edit. of Kell.
23. To Duke D'Ufez, 19 Nov. 1760, Vol. 56, Let. 226, P. 450.
24. See the whole of their correspondence.
25. Condorcet's Progress of Reason, 9th Epoch.

CHAP. IV.

First Means of the Conspirators.—The Encyclopedia.

*T*O *crush the wretch* in the sense of Voltaire, or to attain the destruction of the altars of that God whose worship had been taught by the Apostles, nothing less could suffice than the total subjection of the public opinion, and the annihilation of the faith of all Christian nations. To extirpate it by force was above the strength of the rising coalition. Force was only to be resorted to when, by a revolution in all religious ideas, things had been brought to that state in which our Jacobin legislators found them; or when, by infidelity, the courts, the senates, the armies, in short, men of all descriptions, had been gained over to a blind confidence in and submission to their Sophistry. Indeed the necessary growth of impiety and corruption supposed too long a period for Frederic or Voltaire ever to flatter themselves with the hope of seeing it.[1] It was then too early for them to grasp the falchion of the butchering Jacobin; nor must we expect, in the following pages, to read of guillotines, or forced requisitions in battle array against the altars of Christianity.

In the beginning their intrigues are hidden and silent, slow and tortuous; but more insidious from their secrecy, more certain from their slowness; the public opinion was to perish, as it were, by inanition, before they dared lay the axe to the altar. This mode of proceeding, we find, is perfectly understood by Frederic when he writes to Voltaire, that *to undermine the edifice in silence is to oblige it to fall of itself;*[2] and still better understood by D'Alembert, when, upbraiding Voltaire with being too hasty, he says, *If mankind grow enlightened, it is because we have used the caution to enlighten them by degrees.*[3] Convinced of the necessity of this gradation, D'Alembert bethought himself of the Encyclopedia, as the grand means of philosophising mankind, and of *crushing the wretch.* His project is no sooner conceived, than it is enthusiastically adopted by Diderot; and Voltaire more than once animated their drooping courage, by his constant attention to the undertaking.

To judge of what prodigious importance the success of this famous dictionary was to conspiring chiefs, we must be acquainted with its plan, the method of its execution, and how it was to become the infallible agent of infidelity, and its most powerful weapon in perverting the public opinion, and overturning all the principles of Christianity.

The Encyclopedia is at first ushered into the world as the aggregate, the complete treasure of all human arts and sciences, of Religion, Divinity, Physics, History, Geography, Astronomy, and Commerce; in a word, of whatever can constitute a Science: of Poetry, Oratory, Grammar, Painting, Architecture, Manufactures, and whatever can be the object of useful or pleasing arts. This great work was to comprehend the very minutiae of different trades, from the manufacturer to the labourer; it was to be of itself an immense library, and to supply the place of one. It was to be the work of scientific men, the most profound in every branch that France could produce. The discourse in which it was announced by D'Alembert to all Europe was written with so much art, and had been so profoundly meditated and so nicely weighed; the concatenation of the sciences and the progress of the human mind appeared so properly delineated; whatever he had borrowed from Bacon or Chambers on the filiation of ideas so completely disguised; in short, the plagiary Sophister had so perfectly decked himself in the plumage of others, that the prospectus of the Encyclopedia was looked upon as a masterpiece, and its author, of course, considered as the most proper person to preside over so stupendous a work.

Such were their mighty promises, but these were never intended to be fulfilled; while, on the other side, they had their secret object, which they were determined to accomplish. This was, to convert the Encyclopedia into a vast emporium of all the sophisms, errors, or calumnies, which had ever been invented against religion, from the first schools of impiety, to the day of their enterprize; and these were to be so artfully concealed, that the reader should insensibly imbibe the poison without the least suspicion. To prevent discovery, the error was never to be found where it might be supposed. Religion was not only to be respected, but even advocated in all direct discussions; though sometimes the discussion is so handled, that the objection they seem to refute is more forcibly impressed on the mind of the reader. The more to impose on the unthinking, D'Alembert and Diderot artfully engaged several men of unblemished character to partake in this vast and laborious undertaking. Such was Mr. de Jeaucourt, a man of great learning and probity, who has furnished a number of articles to the Encyclopedia: his name alone might have been thought a sufficient guarantee against all the art and perfidy of its principles; and it was further declared, that all points of religion were to be discussed by divines well known for their learning and orthodoxy.

All this might have been true, and yet the work only prove the more perfidious; for D'Alembert and Diderot had reserved to themselves a three-fold resource for forwarding their Antichristian Conspiracy.

Their first resource was that of insinuating error and infidelity into those articles that might be deemed the least susceptible of them; such, for example, as History or Natural Philosophy, and even into Chemistry and Geography, where such danger could not have been surmised. The second was that of references, a precious art, by which, after having placed some religious truth under the reader's eye, he is tempted to seek further information in articles of a quite different cast. Sometimes the mere reference was an epigram or a sarcasm; they would, for instance, after having treated a religious subject with all possible respect, simply add, *See the art.* PREJUDICE, or SUPERSTITION, or FANATICISM. Lastly, when our referring Sophisters feared this shift could not avail them, they would not hesitate at altering and falsifying the discussion of a virtuous co-operator or at adding an article of their own, whose apparent object was to defend, while its real intention was to refute what had already been written on the subject. In fine, impiety was to be sufficiently veiled to make it attractive; but at the same time to leave place for excuse and subterfuge. This was the peculiar art of our barking Sophister D'Alembert. Diderot, more daring, was at first countenanced in the mad flights of his impiety; but in cooler moments his articles were to be revised; he was then to add some apparent restriction in favour of religion, some of those high-sounding and reverential words, but which left the whole of the impiety to subsist. If he was above that care, D'Alembert as supervisor-general took it upon himself.

Peculiar care was to be taken in the compiling of the first volumes, lest the clergy, those men of prejudice, as they were called, should take the alarm. As they proceeded in the work they were to grow more bold; and if circumstances did not favour them, nor allow them to say all they wished to say, they were to resort to supplements, and to foreign editions, which would at the same time render this dangerous work more common and less costly to the generality of readers.

The Encyclopedia, perpetually recommended and cried up by the adepts, was to be a standing book in all libraries; and insensibly the learned was to be converted into the Antichristian world. If this project was well conceived, it was impossible to see one more faithfully executed.

It is now our duty to lay before the reader the proofs, first as to the fact, secondly as to the intention. For the first it will be sufficient to cast the eye on divers articles of this immense collection, especially where the principal tenets of Christianity, or even of natural religion, are treated, and to follow them through the divers references which the Sophisters have prepared for the reader. We shall find the existence of God, free agency, and the spirituality of the soul, treated in the style of a Christian Philosopher; but a *vide* DEMONSTRATION, or a *vide* CORRUPTION, will be added to pervert all that had been said; and the article to which D'Alembert and Diderot more particularly refer the reader, are exactly those where the doctrine of the Sceptic or the Spinosist, of the Fatalist or the Materialist, is chiefly inculcated. [*See note at the end of the Chapter.*]

This cunning could not escape those authors who wrote in the defence of religion.[4] But Voltaire, resorting to calumny in order to defend their Encyclopedia, would represent these authors as enemies of the state, and bad citizens.[5] Such, indeed, were his usual weapons; and had he perfectly succeeded in deceiving people, it would have been sufficient to have examined his confidential correspondence with the very authors of the work, to be convinced of the wickedness of their intentions.

At a hundred leagues from Paris, and not thwarted by the obstacles which D'Alembert had to combat, he often complains, that the attacks are not sufficiently direct. He is often ruffled by certain restrictions usual to D'Alembert, and at length he breaks out on those which are visible in the article BAYLE. D'Alembert answers, "This is an idle quarrel indeed on Bayle's Dictionary. In the first place, I did not say, *happy would it have been had he shown more reverence to religion and morality*. My phrase is much more modest: and beside, in a cursed country like this where we are writing, who does not know that such sentences are but a mere matter of form, and only a cloak to the truths additionally conveyed? Every one is aware of that."[6]

During the time that Voltaire was busied with the articles he so frequently sent to D'Alembert for the Encyclopedia, he often complained of his shackles, and was unable to dissemble how much he desired to attack religion openly. He writes, "All that I am told about the articles of Divinity and Metaphysics grieves me to the heart; *O how cruel it is to print the very reverse of what one thinks.*"[7] But D'Alembert, more adroit, sensible of the necessity of these palliatives, *lest he should be looked upon as a madman by those whom he wished to convert,*" foresaw the day when he could triumphantly answer, "If mankind is so much enlightened to-day, it is only because *we* have used the precaution, or had the good fortune, *to enlighten them by degrees.*"[8]

When Voltaire had sent certain violent articles, under the name of the priest of Lausanne, D'Alembert would immediately write, "We shall always receive with gratitude whatever comes from the same hand. We only pray our heretic to draw in his claws a little, as in certain places he has shown his fangs a little too much. *This is the time for stepping back to make the better leap.*"[9] And to show that he never lost sight of this maxim, he answers Voltaire's animadversions on the article HELL: "Without doubt we have several wretched articles in our divinity and metaphysics, *but with divines for censors, and a privilege, I defy you to make them better.* There are articles *less exposed* where *all is set to rights again.*"[10]

Can there be a doubt left of the precise and determined intention of the Encyclopedists, when Voltaire exhorts D'Alembert to snatch the moment, whilst the attention of government is drawn off by other concerns: "During this war *with the parliament* and the *bishops*, the Philosophers will have fine play; *You have a fair opportunity of filling the Encyclopedia with those truths that we should not have dared utter twenty years ago,*"[11] or when he writes to Damilaville, "I can be interested by a good dramatic performance, but could be far more pleased with a good philosophical work that should for ever crush the wretch. *I place all my hopes in the Encyclopedia.*"[12] After such an avowal it would be useless to seek farther proof of this immense compilation being no other than the grand arsenal for all their sophisticated arms against religion.

Diderot, more open, even in his ambush reluctantly employed cunning. He does not hide how much he wished boldly to insert his principles; and those principles are explained when he writes, "The age of Louis XIV only produced two men worthy of co-operating to the Encyclopedia," and these two men were Perrault and Boindin. The merits of the latter are more conspicuous than those of the former. Boindin, born in 1676, had lately died a reputed Atheist, and had been refused Christian burial. The notoriety of his principles had shut the French academy against him, and with such titles he could not have failed being a worthy co-operator.

Such then the object, such the intention of the conspiring authors. We see by their own confession, that they did not wish to compile for science, but to compile for science, but for infidelity; that it was not the advancement of arts they sought, but to seize the moment, when the attention of the ruling authorities was drawn off, to propagate their impious calumnies against religion. They hypocritically utter some few religious truths, and *print the contrary of what they believed* on Christianity, but only the better to cover the Sophisms which they printed against it.

In spite of all their arts, however, men zealous for religion forcibly opposed the work. The Dauphin, in particular, obtained a temporary suspension of it; and various were the obstacles encountered by its authors. D'Alembert, wearied, had nearly forsaken it, when Voltaire, sensible of the importance of this first tool of the conspiracy, roused his drooping courage. He, far from abating, rather redoubled his efforts, asking for and incessantly sending fresh articles. He would extol perseverance, he would show D'Alembert and Diderot the ignominy and shame redounding to their opponents.[13] He would urge them, conjure them by their friendship, or in the name of Philosophy, to overcome their disgust, and not to be foiled in so glorious an undertaking.[14]

At length the Encyclopedia was brought to a conclusion, and it made its appearance under the sanction of a public privilege. Triumphant in their first step, the conspirators saw in it but the forerunner of their future successes against religion.

That no doubt may exist as to the particular drift of this compilation, the reader must be made acquainted with the co-operators chosen by D'Alembert and Diderot, especially for the religious part. Their first divine was Raynal, a man just expelled from the Order of the Jesuits on account of his impiety, that very thing which constituted his chief and strongest recommendation to D'Alembert. Every one, unfortunately, knows how well he verified the judgement of his former brethren by his atrocious declamations against Christianity; but few are acquainted with the anecdote of his expulsion from among the co-operators; and that connects his story with that of another divine, who, without being impious himself, had been unfortunately drawn into the company of the Sophisters.

This was the Abbé Yvon, an odd metaphysician, but an inoffensive and upright man; often in extreme indigence, and living by his pen when he thought he could do it with decency. In the simplicity of his heart he had written *The Defence of the Abbé de Prades*. I have heard him assert that not a single error could be found in that work, and on the first argument give up the point. With the same simplicity I have heard him relate, by what means he had co-operated in the Encyclopedia. "I was in want of money (said he); Raynal met me and persuaded me to write a few articles, promising me a good reward. I acceded, and when my work was delivered at Raynal's study I received twenty-five Louis-d'ors. Thinking myself very well paid, I imparted my good fortune to one of the booksellers employed for the Encyclopedia, who seemed much surprised that the articles furnished by Raynal should not be his own. He was furious at the trick he suspected. A few days after this I was sent for to the office; and Raynal, who had received a thousand crowns for his pretended work, was obliged to refund me the hundred Louis-d'ors he had kept for himself."

This anecdote will not surprise those who are acquainted with Raynal's plagiary talents. His impiety was not indeed sufficient to prevent his dismission, but it preserved him within the pale of the fraternal embrace.

I must add, that the articles on GOD and on the SOUL, furnished by the Abbé Yvon, are exactly those which grieved Voltaire to the heart, and for which D'Alembert and Diderot were obliged to have recourse to their art of references.

The third divine, or as D'Alembert styles him the second, for he never dared mention Yvon to Voltaire, was the Abbé de Prades, obliged to fly to Prussia for an attempt to impose on the Sorbonne by advancing his own impious propositions as those of religion. It was the cunning of this thesis which had misled the Abbé Yvon. but being soon discovered the parliament took it up. The author, nevertheless, was put under the protection of the King of Prussia by Voltaire and D'Alembert.[15]

We also owe it to the memory of the Abbé De Prades to relate (what his protectors would willingly conceal) that three years afterward he publicly retracted all his errors in a declaration signed the 6th of April 1754, bewailing his intimacy with the Sophisters, adding, *that one life could not suffice to bewail his past conduct.*"[16] He died in 1782.

Another of their divines was the Abbé Morrelet, a man dear to Voltaire and to D'Alembert, who, playing on his name, called him the Abbé *Mord-lès* (Bite 'em), because, under pretence of attacking the Inquisition, he had fallen on (bitten) the church with all his might.[17]

Were we to enumerate the lay writers who co-operated in this work, we should find far worse than these divines. But we will only mention the celebrated Dumarsais, a man so infamous, that the public authorities were obliged to interfere and destroy a school he had formed solely to imbue his pupils with the venom of his impiety. This unfortunate man also retracted his errors, but not till he lay on his death-bed. The choice of this man's pen shows the kind of co-operators which D'Alembert sought.

Far be it from me to confound in this class, such men as MM. de Formey or Jaucourt, particularly the latter, to whom, as we have already said, they were indebted for many articles. The only reproach that can attach to him is, that he should have continued his labours after he either saw or should have seen the drift of that vast compilation, wherein, intermixed with his toils, lay all the sophisms and calumnies impiety could invent.

Excepting these two men, we may comprehend nearly all the rest of the Encyclopedian writers in the following picture, drawn by Diderot himself. "All that detestable crew, who, though perfectly ignorant, valued themselves on knowing every thing; who, seeking to distinguish themselves by that vexatious universality to which they pretended, fell upon every thing, jumbled and spoiled all, and converted this pretended digest of science *into a gulph, or rather a sort of rag-basket, where they promiscuously threw every thing half-examined, ill-digested, good, bad, and indifferent, but always incoherent.*" What a precious avowal as to the intrinsic merit of their work! especially after what he says as to their views, in describing the pains they had taken, the vexations it had caused them, and the art it had required to insinuate what they dared not openly write against prejudices (religion), in order to overthrow them without being perceived.[18]

But all these follies of the *rag-dealers* contributed to the bulk and accelerated the appearance of the volumes, the chiefs carefully inserting in each volume what could promote the grand object. Being at length terminated, all the trumpets sounded, and the journals of the party teemed with the praises of this literary achievement. The learned themselves were duped. Every one would have an Encyclopedia. Numerous were the editions, of all sizes and prices; but in every successive one, under the pretence of correction, greater boldness was assumed. About the time when the antichristian revolution was nearly accomplished, appeared *L'Encyclopédie par ordre des Matières*. When it was first undertaken, some deference was still paid to religion. A man of eminent merit, Mr. Bergier, a canon of Paris, thought it incumbent on him to yield to the pressing solicitations of his friends, lest the part treating of religion should fall into the hands of its greatest enemies. What was easy to foresee came to pass. The name of a man who had combated the impious work of a Voltaire or a Rousseau naturally served as a cloak to this new digest, styled *The Encyclopedia methodised*. This was on the eve of the French revolution, so that the petty infidels charged with the work, observed no farther bounds with regard to religion. This new work is more completely impious than the former, notwithstanding some excellent tracts of Mr. Bergier and of some others; and thus the Sophisters of the day perfected the first tool of the antichristian conspirators.

Note to CHAP. IV.
vide Page 34. Of the devices of the Encylopedia.

Look for the article GOD (Geneva edition), and you will find very sound notions, together with the direct, physical, and metaphysical demonstration of his existence; and indeed under such an article it would have been too bold to have broached any thing even bordering on Atheism, Spinosism, or Epicurism; but the reader is *referred* to the article DEMONSTRATION, and there all the physical and metaphysical cogent arguments for the existence of a God disappear. We are there taught, that all direct demonstrations *suppose the idea of infinitude, and that such an idea cannot be very clear either to the Naturalist or the Metaphysician.* This, in a word, destroys all confidence the reader had placed in the proofs adduced of the existence of God. There again they are pleased to tell you, that a single insect, in the eyes of the Philosopher, more forcibly proves *the existence of a God, than all the metaphysical arguments whatever* (ibid.); but you are then *referred* to CORRUPTION, where you learn how cautious you must be of asserting in a positive manner that corruption can never beget animated bodies; that such a production of animated bodies by corruption seems to be countenanced by *daily experiments*; and it is precisely from these experiments that the Atheists conclude the existence of God to be unnecessary, either for the creation of man or animals. Prepossessed by these *references*, against the existence of God, let the reader turn to the articles of ENCYCLOPEDIA and EPICURISM. In the former he will be told, *that there is no being in nature that can be called the first or last, and that a machine infinite in every way must necessarily be the Deity.* In the latter the *atom* is to be the Deity. It will be the primary cause of all things, by whom and of whom every thing is active, essentially of itself, *alone unalterable, alone eternal, alone immutable*; and thus the reader will be insensibly led from the God of the Gospel to the heathenish fictions of an Epicurus or a Spinosa.

The same cunning is to be found in the article of the SOUL. When the Sophisters treat directly of its essence they give the ordinary proofs of its *spirituality and of its immortality.* They will even add in the article BRUTE, that the soul cannot be supposed *material*, nor can *the brute be reduced to the quality of a mere machine, without running the hazard of making man an Automaton.* And under NATURAL LAW we read, that if the determinations of man, or even his oscillations, arise from any thing *material, and extraneous to his soul, there will be neither good nor evil, neither just nor unjust, neither obligation nor right.* Then *referred* to the article LOCKE, in order to do away all this consequence, we are told that it is of no importance *whether matter thinks or not; for what is that to justice or injustice, to the immortality of the soul and to all the truths of the system, whether political or religious*; the reader, enjoying the Equality and Liberty of his reason, is left in doubt with regard to the spirituality, and no longer knows whether he should not think himself all matter. But he will decide when, under the article ANIMAL, he finds *that life and animation are only physical properties of matter*, and lest he should think himself debased by his resembling a plant or an animal, to console him in his fall, they will tell him, article ENCYCLOPEDIA and ANIMAL, *that the only difference between certrain vegetables, and animals such as us, is, that they sleep and that we wake, that we are animals that feel, and that they are animals that feel not*; and still further in the article ANIMAL, that the sole difference *between a stock and a man is, that the one ever falls, while the latter never falls, after the same manner.* After perusing these articles *bona fide*, the reader must be insensibly drawn into the vortex of Materialism.

In treating of Liberty or free agency we find the same artifice. When they treat of it directly, they will say, "Take away Liberty, all human nature is overthrown, and there will be no trace of order in society—Recompense will be ridiculous, and chastisement unjust.—The ruin of Liberty carries with it that of all order and of police, and legitimates the most monstrous crimes.—So monstrous a doctrine is not to be debated in the schools, but punished by the magistrates, &c. *Oh Liberty!* they exclaim, *Oh Liberty, gift of heaven! Oh, Liberty of action! Oh, Liberty of thought!* thou alone art capable of great things." [*See articles* AUTHORITY and the PRELIMINARY DISCOURSE.] But at the article CHANCE (*fortuit*) all this liberty of action and of thought is only *a power that cannot be exercised, that cannot be known by actual exercise*: and Diderot in the article EVIDENCE, pretending to support Liberty, will very properly say, "This concatenation of causes and effects supposed by the Philosophers, in order to form ideas representing the mechanism of the Universe, is as fabulous as the Tritons and the Naïads;" but both he and D'Alembert will descant again on that concatenation, and, returning to CHANCE (*fortuit*), will tell us "That though it is *imperceptible*, it is not the less *real*; that it *connects* all things in nature, and that *all events depend on it*; just as the wheels of the watch, as to their motion, depend on each other; that from the first moment of our existence, we are by *no means masters of our motions*; that were there a thousand worlds similar to this, simultaneously existing, and governed by the same laws, every thing in them would be done in the same way; and that *man, in virtue of these same laws, would perform at the same instants of time the same actions* in each one of these worlds." This will naturally convince the uninformed reader of the chimera of such a Liberty or free agency, which cannot be exercised. Not content with this, Diderot in the article FATALITY, after a long dissertation on this *concatenation of causes*, ends by saying, that it *cannot be contested* either *in the physical world,* or *in the moral* and *intellectual world.* Then what becomes of that Liberty without which there no longer exists *just* or *unjust, obligation* or *right.*

These examples will suffice to convince the reader of the truth of what we have asserted, as to the artful policy with which the Encyclopedia had been digested; they will show with what cunning its authors sought to spread the principles of Atheism, Materialism, and Fatalism, in short, to plant every error incompatible with that religion for which at their outset they professed so great a reverence.

1. From Frederic, 5 May, 1767, Vol. 65, Let. 160, P. 377.
2. From Frederic, 13 Aug. 1775, Vol. 66, Let. 95, P. 222.
3. From D'Alembert, 31 July, 1762, Vol. 68, Let. 102, P. 207.
4. See *Religion Vindicated*, the writings of Gauchat, of Bergier, our Helvian Letters, &c.
5. To D'Alembert, 16 Jan. 1757, Vol. 68, Let. 18, P. 31.
6. To D'Alembert, 10 Oct. 1764, Vol. 68, Let. 145, P. 323.
7. To D'Alembert, 9 Oct. 1755, Vol. 68, Let. 4, P. 9.
8. From D'Alembert, 16 July, 1762, Vol. 68, Let. 102, p. 207.
9. From D'Alembert, 21 July, 1757, Vol. 68, Let. 30, P. 51.
10. Ibid. Page 52.
11. To D'Alembert, 13 Nov. 1756, Vol. 68, Let. 11, P. 20.
12. To Damilaville, 23 May, 1764, Vol. 58, Let. 196, P. 360.
13. See his letters of the years 1755-6.
14. Letters of 5th Sept. 1752, 13th Nov. 1756, and particularly of 8th Jan. 1757, Vol. 68.
15. To D'Alembert, 5 Sept. 1752, Vol. 68, Let. 3, P. 7.
16. Feller's Hist. Dict.
17. From D'Alembert, 16 Juin, 1760, Vol. 68, Let. 65, P. 115—and to Thiriot, 26 Jan. 1762, Vol. 57, Let. 157, P. 320.
18. The text in the original is far more extensive, where Diderot treats of the deficiencies of the Encyclopedia; but, not having it at hand, we quote from Feller's Hist. Dic. art. DIDEROT.

CHAP. V.

*Second means of the Conspirators.—
The Extinction of the Jesuits.*

THE hypocrisy of Voltaire and D'Alembert had triumphed over every obstacle. They had so perfectly succeeded in their abuse of all who dared oppose the Encyclopedia, whom they represented as barbarians and enemies to literature; they had found such powerful support during the successive ministries of D'Argenson, Choiseul, and Malesherbes, that all the opposition of the grand Dauphin, of the clergy, and of the religious writers, could not avail, and this impious digest was in future to be looked upon as a necessary work. It was to be found in every library; whether at home or abroad, it was always to be referred to. Thence the simple mind in quest of science was to imbibe the poison of infidelity, and the Sophister was to be furnished with arms against Christianity. The conspirators, though proud of their first invention, could not dissemble that there existed a set of men whose zeal, whose learning, whose weight and authority, might one day counteract their undertaking. The church was defended by her bishops and all the lower clergy. There were, moreover, numerous orders of relogous always ready to join the seculars for her defence in the cause of Christianity. But before we treat of the means employed for the destruction of these defenders of the faith, we must show the plan formed by Frederic, whence they resolved on the destruction of the Jesuits, as the first step toward dismantling the church, and effecting the destruction of her bishops and of her different orders of priesthood.

In the year 1743 Voltaire had been sent on secret service to the Court of Prussia; and among his dispatches from Berlin we find the following written to the minister Amelot. "In the last interview I had with his Prussian majesty, I spoke to him of a pamphlet that appeared in Holland about six weeks back, in which the secularization of ecclesiastical principalities in favour of the Emperor and Queen of Hungary was proposed as the means of pacification for the Empire. I told him that I could wish, with all my heart, to see it take place; that what was Cæsar's was to be given to Cæsar; that the whole business of the church was to supplicate God and the princes; that by his institution, the Benedictine could have no claim to sovereignty, and that this decided opinion of mine had gained me many enemies among the clergy. He owned that the *pamphlet had been printed by his orders*. He hinted, that he should not dislike to be one of those kings to whom the clergy would conscientiously make restituion, and that he should not be sorry to embellish Berlin with the goods of the church. This is most certainly his grand object, and he means to make peace only when he sees the possibility of accomplishing it. It rests with your prudence to profit of this his secret plan, which he confided to me alone."[1]

At this time the court of Lewis XV began to be overrun with ministers who on religious matters thought like a Voltaire or a Frederic.—They had no ecclesiastical states, no ecclesiastical electors to pillage; but the possessions of the numerous religious orders dispersed through France could satiate their rapacity, and they conceived that the plan of Frederic might be equally lucrative to France. The Marquis D'Argenson, counsellor of state and minister of foreign affairs, was the great patron of Voltaire. It was he who, adopting all his ideas, formed the plan for the destruction of all religious orders in France. The progress of the plan was to be slow and successive, lest it should spread alarm. They were to begin with those orders that were least numerous; they were to render the entrance into the religious state more difficult; and the time of professions was to be delayed until that age when people are already engaged in some other state of life. The possessions of the suppressed were artfully to be adapted to some pious use, or united to the episcopal revenues. Time was to do away with all difficulties, and the day was not far off when, as lord paramount, the Sovereign was to put in his claim to all that belonged to the suppressed orders, even to what had been united, for the moment, to the sees of the bishops; the whole was to be added to his domains.

That the French ministry often changed, but that the plans of the cabinet never did, and that it always watched the favourable opportunity, was the remark of a shrewd and observing legate.—The plan for the destruction of religious orders had been made by D'Argenson, in the year 1745, though forty years after it still lay on the chimney-piece of Maurepas, then prime minister. I owe this anecdote to a person of the name of Bevis,[2] a learned Benedictine, and in such high repute with Maurepas, that he often pressed him to leave his hood, promising him preferment as a secular.—The Benedictine refused such offers; and it was not without surprise that he heard Maurepas tell him, when pressing him to accept his offer, *that secularization would one day be his lot*; he then gave him D'*Argenson's* plan, which had long been followed and would soon be accomplished.

Avarice alone could not have suggested this plan; as the mendicant orders, as well as the more wealthy, were to be destroyed.

It would have been folly to attempt its execution before the Encyclopedian Sophisters had prepared the way; it therefore lay dormant many years in the state offices at Versailles. In the mean time the Voltairean ministry, fostering infidelity, pretended to strike, while they secretly supported, the sophistical tribe. They forbade Voltaire to enter Paris, while *in amazement he receives a scroll of the king*, confirming his pension, *which had been suppressed twelve years before!*[3] He carries on his correspondence with the adepts, under the covers and under the very seals of the first secretaries and of the ministers themselves, who were perfectly conversant with all his impious plans.[4] It was this very part of the Antichristian Conspiracy that Condorcet meant to describe when he says: "Often a government would reward the Philosopher with one hand, whilst with the other it would pay his slanderer; would proscribe him, while it was proud of the soil that had given him birth; punished him for his opinions, but would have blushed not to have partaken of them."[5]

This perfidious understanding between the ministers of his most Christian Majesty and the Antichristian Conspirators hastened their progress, when the most impious and most despotic of ministers judged that the time was come for the decisive blow to be struck. This minister was the Duke of Choiseul; during the whole time of his power he was the faithful adept and admirer of Voltaire, who says, "Don't fear opposition from the Duke of Choiseul; I repeat it, I don't mislead you, he will be proud of serving you:"[6] or to Marmontel, "We have been a little alarmed by certain panics, but never was fright so unfounded. The Duke of Choiseul and Mad. de Pompadour know the opinions of the *uncle* and of the *niece*. You may send any thing without danger." In fine, he was so secure in the Duke's protection against the Sorbonne and the church, that he would exclaim, "*The ministry of France for ever; long live the Duke de Choiseul.*"[7]

This confidence of the premier chief was well placed in Choiseul, who had adopted and acted upon all the plans of D'Argenson. The ministry prognosticated a great source of riches to the state in the destruction of the religious, though many of them did not seek in that the destruction of religion; they even thought some of them neessary, and the Jesuits were excepted. Unfortunately, these were the very men with whom Choiseul wished to begin, and his intention was lready known by the following anecdote:—Choiseul, one day, conversing with three ambassadors, one of them said, "If I ever chance to be in power, I will certainly destroy all religious orders excepting the Jesuits, for they are at least useful to education."—"As for my part (answered Choiseul), I will destroy none but the Jesuits; for, their education once destroyed, all the other religious orders will fall of themselves;" and his policy was deep! There can be no doubt but that destroying the Order in whose hands the majority of the colleges were at that time, would be striking at the very root of that Christian eduction which prepared so many for the religious state; in spite, therefore, of the exception, Choiseul still sought to sway the council by his opinion.

The Jesuits were tampered with, but in vain; so far from acceding to the destruction of the other Orders, they were foremost in their defence; they pleaded the rights of the church; they supported them with all their weight, in their writings and their discourses. This gave occasion to Choiseul to remonstrate with the council, and to persuade them, that if they wished to procure to the state the immense resources of the religious possessions, it was necessary to begin with the *destruction of the Jesuits*.

This anecdote I only cite as having heard it among the Jesuits, but their subsequent expulsion strongly corroborates its veracity. Whether these religious deserved their fate or not is alien to my subject; I only wish to point out the hand that strikes, and the men who, as D'Alembert says, *gave the orders* for their destruction. Treating of the Antichristian Conspiracy, I have only to ascertain whether the destruction of the Jesuits was not conceived, urged, and premeditated, by the Sophistical Conspirators, as a means powerfully tending to the destruction of Christianity. Let us then examine what that body of men really was, and how necessarily odious they must have been to the conspirators from their general reputation. Let us, above all, hear the Sophisters themselves; let us see how much they interested themselves in their destruction.

The Jesuits were a body of twenty thousand men spread through all Catholic countries, and particurly charged with the eduction of youth. They did not, however, on that account, neglect the other duties of the ecclesiastic, but were bound by a particular vow to go as missionaries to any part of the globe, if sent, to preach the gospel. From their youth brought up to the study of literature, they had produced numberless authors, but more particularly divines, who immediately combated any error that might spring up in the church. Latterly they were chiefly engaged in France against the Jansenists and Sophisters, and it was their zeal in the defence of the church that made the King of Prussia style them *The Life-guards of the Pope*.[8]

When fifty French prelates, cardinals, archbishops or bishops, assembled, were consulted by Louis XV on the propriety of destroying the Order, they expressly answered, "The Jesuits are of infinite service to us in our dioceses, whether for preaching or the direction of the faithful, to revive, preserve, and propagate faith and piety, by their missions, congregations, and spiritual retreats, which they make with our approbation, and under our authority. For these reasons we think, Sire, that to prohibit them from instructing would essentially injure our dioceses, and that it would be difficult to replace them with equal advantage in the instruction of youth, and more particularly so in those provincial towns where there are no universities."[9]

Such in general was the idea entertained of them in all Catholic countries; it is necessary for the reader to be acquainted with it, tht he may understand of how much importance their destruction was to the Sophisters. At the time, the Jansenists had the honor of it, and indeed they were very ardent in its promotion. But the Duke of Choiseul and the famous courtezan La Marquise de Pompadour, who then held the destiny of France, under the shadow and in the name of Louis XV, were not more partial to the Jansenists than to the Jesuits. Both confidants of Voltaire, they were consequently initiated in all the mysteries of the Sophisters,[10] and Voltaire, as he says himself, *would willingly have seen all the Jesuits at the bottom of the sea, each with a Jansenist hung to his neck*.[11]

The Jansenists were nothing more than the hounds employed in the general hunt by Choiseul, the Marquise de Pompadour, and the Sophisters; the minister spurred on by his impiety, the Marquise wishing to revenge an insult (as she called it) received from Père Sacy, a Jesuit. This Father had refused her the Sacraments, unless by quitting the Court she would in some sort atone for the public scandal she had given by her cohabitation with Louis XV. But, if we judge by Voltaire's letters, they neither of them needed much stimulation, as they both had always been great protectors of the Sophisters, and the minister had always favoured their intrigues as far as he could consistently with circumstances and politics.[12] The following pages will show these intrigues; and we shall begin with D'Alembert, who writes in the most sanguine manner on their future victory over the Jesuits, and on the immense advantages to be derived to the Conspiracy by their downfall. "You are perpetuallky repeating *Crush the wretch*; for God's sake let it fall headlong of itself! Do you know what Astruc says? It is not the Jansenists that are killing the Jesuits, but the Encyclopedia; yes, the Encyclopedia: and that is not unlikely. This scoundrel Astruc is a second Pasquin, and sometimes says very good things. I for my part see every thing in the brightest colours; I foresee the Jansenists naturally dying off the next year, after having strangled the Jesuits this; I foresee toleration established, the Protestants recalled, the priests married, confession abolished, and *fanaticism* (religion) *crushed*; and all this without its being perceived."[13]

The express words of the Conspirators show what part they had in the destruction of the Jesuits. They were indeed the true cause. We see what advantage they hoped to reap from it. They had kindled the hatred, and procured the death warrant. The Jansenists were to serve the Conspirators, but were themselves to fall when no more wanted. The Calvinists were to be recalled, but only to perish in their turn. To strike at the whole Christian Religion was their aim; and Impiety, with its Sophisters, was to range uncontrolled throughout an infidel world.

D'Alembert smiles at the poreblind parliaments seconding with all their might the plans of the Conspirators. It is in this idea that he writes thus to Voltaire: "The laugh is no longer on the side of the Jesuits, since they have fallen out with the Philosophers. They are now at open war with the Parliament, who find that the society of Jesus is contrary to *human* society. This same society of Jesus on its own part finds that the *order* of the Parliament is not within the *order* of those who have common sense, and *Philosophy would decide that both the society of Jesus and the Parliament are in the right*:"[14] and again, when he writes to Voltaire, "This evacuation of the College of Louis le Grand (the Jesuits College at Paris) is of more importance to us than that of Martinico. Upon my word this affair is becoming serious, and the people of the Parliament don't mince the matter. They think they are serving religion, while *they are in reality forwarding reason without the least suspicion*. They are the public executioners, and *take their orders from Philosphy without knowing it*."[15] Rapt in this idea, when he sees the Encyclopedian commands nearly executed, he openly avows the cause of his revenge, and even implores Heaven that his prey may not escape him. "Philosophy (says he) is on the eve of being revenged of the Jesuits, but who will avenge it of the other fanatics?—Pray God, dear Brother, that reason may triumph even in our days."[16]

And this day of triumph comes. He proclaims the long-concerted exploit: "At length," he cries, "on the sixth of next month, we shall be delivered from all that Jesuitical rabble; but will reason by that have gained, or *the wretch* have lost ground?"[17]

Thus we see, that under this shocking formula the destruction of Christianity is linked with that of the Jesuits. D'Alembert was so thoroughly convinced of the importance of their triumph over that Order, that, hearing one day of Voltaire's pretended gratitude to his former masters, he immediately wrote to him, "Do you know what I was told yesterday? – nothing less than that you began to pity the Jesuits, and that you were almost tempted to write in their favour; as if it were possible to interest any one in favour of people on whom you have cast so much ridicule. *Be advised by me; let us have no human weakness.* Let the Jansenitical rabble rid of us the Jesuitical, and do not prevent one spider from devouring another."[18]

Nothing could be more ill-grounded than this alarm. Voltaire was not the writer of the conclusions drawn by the Attorney-Generals of the Parliament (as D'Alembert had been informed, who himself had been the author of Mr. de la Chalotais, the most artful and virulent piece that appeared againstthe Jesuits). Voltaire, however, was not less active in composing and circulating memorials against them.[19]

If he suspected any great personage of protecting the Jesuits, he would write and use his utmost endeavours to dissuade them. It was for that purpose he wrote to the Mareschal de Richlieu, "I have been told, my Lord, that you have favoured the Jesuits at Bourdeaux:—try to destroy whatever influence they may have[20]." Again, he did not blush to upbraid Frederic himself with having offered an asylum to these unfortunate victims of their plots.[21] Full as rancorous as D'Alembert, he would express his joy at their misfortunes in the same gross abuse; and his letters show with what adepts he shared it. "I rejoice with my brave *chevalier* (writing to the Marq. de Villevielle) on the expulsion of the Jesuits; Japan led the way in driving out those knaves of Loyola; China followed the example of Japan; and France and Spain have imitated the Chinese. Would to God that all the Monks were swept from the face of the earth; they are no better than those knaves of Loyola. If the Sorbonne were suffered to act, it would be worse than the Jesuits. One is surrounded with monsters: I embrace my worthy chevalier, and exhort him to conceal his march from the enemy."[22]

What examples does the Philosophist of Ferney adduce! the cruelties of a Taikosama, who, while expelling and crucifying the missionary Jesuits, also murders thousands and tens of thousands of his subjects, in order to eradicate Christianity; and the Chinese, less violent indeed, but with whom every persecution against the missionaries has always been preceded or followed by a prohibition to preach the Gospel. Can a man build upon such authorities without forming the same wish?

It is to be remarked, that Voltaire dares not cite the example of Portugal, or of its tyrant Carvalho.[23] The truth is, that, with the rest of Europe, he is obliged to confess that the conduct of this minister in Portugal, with regard to the Father Malagrida and the pretended conspiracy of the Jesuits, *was the height of folly and the excess of horror.*[24]

It is always worthy of remark, that the conspiring Sophisters spared no pains to throw the odium of the assassination of Louis XV on the Jesuits; and more particularly Damilaville, whom Voltaire answers in the following manner: "My Brethren may easily perceive that I have not spared the Jesuits. But posterity would revolt against me in their favour, were I to accuse them of a crime of which all Europe and Damien himself has cleared them. I should debase myself into the vile *echo of the Jansenists*, were I to speak otherwise."[25]

Notwithstanding the incoherency in their accusations against the Jesuits, D'Alembert, convinced of Voltaire's zeal in this warfare, sends him his *pretended history* of these Religious; a work, of the fallacy of which his own pen is the best guarantee, when he speaks of it as a means for the grand object: "I recommend this work to your protection (he writes to Voltaire); I really believe it will be of service to the common cause, and that *superstition*, notwithstanding the many bows I pretend to make before it, will not fare the better for it. If I were, like you, far from Paris, I would certainly *give it a sound threshing* with all my heart, with all my soul, and with all my strength; in short, as they tell us we are to love God. But, *situated as I am, I must content myself with giving it a few fillips*, apologizing for the great liberty I take; and I do think that I have hit it off pretty well."[26]

Could the reader for a moment suppress his indignation at the profligacy of the style, would not the hypocrisy, the profound dissimulation, of which these Sophisters speak so lightly, rouse it anew? If the annals of history should ever be searched, it would be in vain to seek a Conspiracy the insidiousness of whose intrigues was of a deeper cast; and that from their own confession.

As to Frederic, his conduct during the whole of this warfare is so singular, that his own words alone can give a proper idea of it. He would call the Jesuits, *The life-guards of the court of Rome, the grenadiers of Religion*; and, as such, he hated them, and triumphed with the rest of the Conspirators in their defeat. But he also beheld in them a body of men highly useful and even necessary to his state; as such, he supported them several years after their destruction, and was deaf to the repeated solicitations of Voltaire and his motley crew. One might be almost led to think that he liked them; for he openly writes to Voltaire, "I have no reason to complain of Ganganelli; he has left me my dear Jesuits, who are the objects of universal persecution. I will preserve a seed of so precious and so rare a plant, to furnish those who may wish to cultivate it hereafter."[27] He would even enter into a sort of justification with Voltaire on his conduct, so opposite to the views of the party.

"Although a heretic, and what is still more an infidel," says he, "I have preserved that Order after a fashion, and for the following reasons:

"Not one Catholic man of letters is to be found in these regions, except among the Jesuits. We had nobody capable of keeping schools; we had no Oratorian Fathers, no Purists (Piarists, or Fathers of Charity-schools)....There was no other alternative, but the destruction of our schools, or the preservation of the Jesuits. It was necessary that the Order should subsist to furnish professors where they dropped off, and the foundation could suffice for such an expence; but it would have been inadequate to pay the salaries of laymen professors. It was moreover at the university of the Jesuits that the divines were taught, who were afterwards to fill the rectories. Had the Order been suppressed, there had been an end of the university; and our Silesian divines would have been obliged to go and finish their studies in Bohemia, which would have been contrary to the fundamental principles of our government."[28]

Such was the language of Frederic, speaking in his regal character, and such were the political reasons he so ably adduced in support of his opposition to the Sophisters. Alas! as I have already said, in Frederic there were two distinct men; one the great king, in which character he thinks the preservation of the Jesuits necessary; the other the impious Sophister, conspiring with Voltaire, and triumphant in the loss which religion had sustained in that of the Jesuits. In the latter character we find him freely exulting with the Conspirators, and felicitating D'Alembert, on this happy omen of the total destruction of Christianity. In his sarcastic style he writes, "What an unfortunate age for the Court of Rome! she is openly attacked in Poland; her life-guards are driven out of France and Portugal, and it appears that they will share the same fate in Spain. The Philosophers openly sap the foundations of the apostolic throne; the hieroglyphics of the conjuror are laughed at, and the author of the Sect is pelted; toleration is preached, and so all is lost. A miracle alone could save the church. She is stricken with a dreadful apoplexy, and you (Voltaire) will have the pleasure of burying her, and of writing her epitaph, as you formerly did that of the Sorbonne."[29]

When that which Frederic had foreseen really came to pass in Spain, he wrote again to Voltaire: "Here is a new victory that you have gained in Spain. The Jesuits are driven out of the kingdom. Moreover, the courts of Versailles, of Vienna, and of Madrid, have applied to the Pope for the suppression of divers convents. It is said that the holy Father, though in a rage, will be obliged to consent. O cruel revolution! what are we not to expect in the next century? The axe is at the root of the tree. On one side, the Philosophers openly attack the abuses of a sainted superstition; on the other, *princes, by the abuses of dissipation*, are forced to lay violent hands on the goods of those recluse who are the props and trumpeters of fanaticism. This edifice, sapped in its foundations, is on the eve of falling: *and nations shall inscribe on their annals, that Voltaire was the promoter of the revolution effected during the nineteenth century in the human mind.*[30]

Long fluctuating between the feelings of the king and the Sophister, Frederic had not yet yielded to the solicitation of the conspirators. D'Alembert was particularly pressing in his. We see how earnestly he was bent on its success by the following letter which he wrote to Voltaire: "My venerable Patriarch, do not accuse me of the want or zeal in the good cause; no one perhaps serves it more than myself. You would not guess with what I am occupied at present? With nothing less, I assure you, than the expulsion of the Jesuitical rabble from Silesia; and your former disciple is but too willing on account of the numerous and perfidious treacheries which, as he says himself, he experienced through their means, during the last war. I do not send a single letter to Berlin without repeating, *That the Philosophers of France are amazed at the king of Philosophers, the declared protector of Philosophy*, being so *dilatory* in following the example of the kings of France and Portugal. These letters are read to the king, who is very sensible, as you know, to what the true believers may think of him; and this sense will, without doubt, produce a good effect by the help of God's grace, which, as the Scripture very properly remarks, turns the hearts of kings like a water-cock."[31]

It is loathsome to transcribe the base buffoonery with which D'Alembert was accustomed to season his dark plots; and to observe his clandestine persecution against a society of men whose only crime was their respect and reverence for Christianity. I pass over many more expressions of this stamp, or not less indecent. It will suffice for my purpose to show how little, how empty, how despicable, these proud and mighty men were, when seen in their true colors.

In spite of all these solicitations Frederic was invincible; and, fifteen years after, he still protected and preserved *his dear Jesuits*. This expression in his mouth, who at length sacrificed them to the conspiracy, may be looked upon as an answer to what D'Alembert had written of their treachery to the king. It might prove with what unconcern calumny, or supposed evidence of others, were adduced as proofs by him; for in another place he says, "Frederic is not a man *to confine within his royal breast* the subjects of complaint he may have had against them," as had been the case with the king of Spain, whose conduct in that respect had been so much blamed by the Sophisters."[32]

These sophistical conspirators were not to be satisfied by the general expulsion of the Jesuits from the different states of the kings of the earth. By their reiterated war-hoop, Rome was at length to be forced *to declare the total extinction of the Order*. We may observe this by the manner in which Voltaire particularly interested himself for a work, whose sole object was to obtain that extinction. At length it was obtained. France too late perceiving the blow it had given to public education, without appearing to recoil, many of her leading men, sought to remedy the mistake, and formed the plan of a new society solely destined to the education of youth. Into this the former Jesuits, as the most habituated to education, were to be admitted. On the first news of this plan, D'Alembert spread the alarm. He sees the Jesuits returning to life. He writes again and again to Voltaire. He sends the counter-plan. He lays great stress on the danger that *would result thence to the state, to the king, and to the Duke D'Aiguillon,* during whose administration the destruction had taken place. *He also insists on the impropriety of placing youth under the tuition of any community of priests whatever:* they were to be represented *as ultramontanes by principle, and as anti-citizens.* Our barking Philosophist then concluding in his cant to Voltaire, says, "*Raton* (cat), *this chestnut requires to be covered in the embers, and to be handled by a paw as dextrous as that of Raton; and so saying I tenderly kiss those dear paws.*" Seized with the same panic, Voltaire sets to work, and asks for fresh instructions. He considers what turn can be given to this affair, much too serious to be treated with ridicule alone. D'Alembert insists,[33] Voltaire at Ferney writes against the recall, and the conspirators fill Paris and Versailles with their intrigues. The ministers are prevailed upon; the plan is laid aside; youth left without instruction; and it is on this occasion that Voltaire writes, "My dear friend, I know not what is to become of me; in the mean time let us enjoy the pleasure of having seen the Jesuits expelled."[34]

This pleasure was but short; for D'Alembert, seized with a new panic, writes again to Voltaire: "I am told, for certain, that the Jesuitical rabble is about to be reinstated in Portugal in all but the dress. This new Queen appears to be a very *superstitious Majesty.* Should the King of Spain chance to die, I would not answer for that kingdom's not imitating Portugal. *Reason is undone should the enemy's army gain this battle.*"[35]

When I first undertook to show that the destruction of the Jesuits was a favourite object of the conspirators, and that it was essentially comprised in their plan of overthrowing the Christian religion, I promised to confine myself to the records and confessions of the Sophisters themselves. I have omitted, for brevity's sake, several of great weight, even that written by Voltaire fifteen years after their expulsion, wherein he flatters himself *that by means of the court of Petersburg* he could succeed in getting them expelled from China, because "*those Jesuits, whom the Emperor of China had chosen to preserve at Pekin, were rather* CONVERTERS *than Mathematicians.*"[36]

Had the Sophisters been less sanguine or less active in the extinction of this order, I should not have insisted so much on that object. But the very warfare they waged was a libel on Christianity. What! they had persuaded themselves tht the religion of the Christians was the work of man, and that the destruction of a few poor mortals was to shake it to its very foundations? Had they forgotten that Christianity had flourished during fourteen centuries before a Jesuit was heard of? Hell might, indeed, open its gates wider after their destruction, but it was written that they should not prevail. The power and intrigues of the ministers of France, of a Choiseul or a Pompadour, plotting with a Voltaire; of a D'Aranda in Spain, the public friend of D'Alembert, and the protector of infidelity; of a Carvalho in Portugal, the ferocious persecutor of the good; and the arts of many other ministers, dupes or agents of the sophistical conspiracy, rather than politicians, may have extorted the bull of extinction from Ganganelli, by threats of schism: but did that pontiff, or any other Christian, believe that the power of the Gospel rested on the Jesuits?

No: the God of the Gospel reigns above, and he will one day judge the pontiff and the minister, the Jesuit and the Sophister.—It is not to be doubted that a body of twenty thousand religious dispersed throughout Christendom, and forming a succession of men attending to the education of youth, and applying to the study of science both religious and prophane, must have been of the greatest utility both to church and state. The conspirators were not long before they perceived their error; and though they had done the Jesuits the honour to look upon them as the base on which the church rested, they found that Christianity had other succours left, that new plots were yet necessary; and we shall see them with equal ardor attacking all other religious orders, as the third means of the Antichristian Conspiracy.

1. To Mr. Amelot, 8 Oct. 1743, Vol. 53, Let. 229, P. 474.
2. He was in London at the time the first edition of this Volume was printing.
3. To Damilaville, 9 Jan. 1762, Vol. 57, Let. 152, P. 310.
4. To Marmontel, 13 Aug. 1760, Vol. 56, Let. 173, P. 353.
5. Condorcet's Sketch on History, 9th Epoch.
6. To D'Alembert, 9 July, 1760, Vol. 68, Let. 68, P. 121.
7. To Marmontel, 13 Aug. 1760, Vol. 56, Let. 173, P. 352, and 2 Dec. 1767, Vol. 60, Let. 200, P. 336.
8. From Frederic, 10 Feb. 1767, Vol. 65, Let. 154, P. 361.
9. Opinion of the Bishops, 1761.
10. To Marmontel, 13 Aug. 1760, Vol. 56, Let. 173, P. 352.
11. To Chabanon, 21 Dec. 1767, Vol. 60, Let. 215, P. 362.
12. To Marmontel, 13 Aug.1760.
13. From D'Alembert, 4 May 1762, Vol. 68. Let. 100. P. 201.
14. From D'Alembert, 9 July, 1761, Vol. 68. Let. 88, P. 168.
15. From D'Alemert, 4 May, 1762, Vol. 68, Let. 100, P., 201.
16. From D'Alembert, 8 Sept. 1761, Vol. 68, Let. 90, P. 173.
17. From D'Alembert, 31 July, 1762, Vol. 68, Let. 102, P. 208.
18. From D'Alembert, 25 Sept. 1762, Vol. 68, Let. 105, P. 218.
19. To the M. D'Argence de Dirac, 26 Feb., 1762, Vol. 57, Let. 174, P. 352.
20. To the Duc de Richelieu, 27 Nov. 1761, V. 57, Let. 139, P. 281.
21. To Frederic, 8 Nov. 1773, Vol. 66. Let. 46. P. 112.
22. To the M. de Villevielle, 27 April, 1767, V. 60, Let. 102, P. 180.
23. I have seen well-informed persons, who thought that the persecution in Portugal was not entirely unconnected with the conspiracy of the Sophisters; that it was only a first essay of what might be afterwards attempted against the whole body. This might be. The politics and power of Choiseul, and the character of Carvalho, may add weight to this opinion. I candidly confess that I have no proof of their secret co-operations; and beside, the ferocious wickedness of Carvalho has been set in so strong a light, (he was the jailor and murderer of so many victims declared innocent by the decree of the 8th of April 1771) that it would be useless to seek any other stimulator than his own heart in that shocking series of cruelties which distinguished his ministry. *See the*

Memoirs and Anecdotes of the Marq. of Pombal; and The Discourse on History by the Comte D'Albon.
24. Voltaire's Age of Louis XV. chap. 33.
25. To Damilaville, 2 March, 1763, Vol. 58, Let. 35, P. 72.
26. From D'Alembert, 3 Jan. 1765, Vol. 68, Let. 151, P. 333.
27. From Frederic, 7 July, 1770, Vol. 65, Let. 173, P. 408.
28. From Fred. 18 Nov. 1777, Vol. 66, Let. 127, P. 300.
29. From D'Alembert, 10 April, 1767, Vol. 65, Let. 154 p. 361.
30. From Frederic, 5 May, 1767, Vol. 65, Let. 60, P. 378.
31. From D'Alembert, 29 Dec. 1763, Vol. 68, Let. 124, P. 269.
32. From D'Alembert, 4 May, 1767, Vol. 68, Let. 206, P. 434.
33. From D'Alembert, 22 March, 1774, Vol. 69, Let. 128, P. 216.
34. To D'Alembert, 27 Apr. 1771, Vol. 69, Let. 64, P. 105.
35. From D'Alembert, 23 June, 1777, Vol. 69, Let. 182, P. 301.
36. To D'Alembert, 8 Dec. 1776, Vol. 69, Let. 173, P. 289.

CHAP. VI.

Third Means of the Conspirators— Extinction of all Religious Orders.

THE favorite measure of those who were inimical to religious orders, has been to endeavour to show their inutility both to church and state. But by what right shall Europe complain of a set of men, by whose labours she has been enabled to emerge from that savage state of the ancient Gauls or Germanni, by whom two-thirds of her lands have been cultivated, her villages built, her towns beautified and enlarged? Shall the State complain of those men who, sedulously attending to the cultivation of lands which their predecessors had first tilled, furnish sustenance to the inhabitants? Shall the inhabitant complain, when the village, the town, the country, from whence he comes would not have existed, or would have remained uncultivated, but for their care? Shall men of letters complain, when, should they even have been happy enough to have escaped the general ignorance and barbarity of Europe, they would perhaps, but for them, have been now vainly searching ruins in hopes of finding some fragment of ancient literature? Yes, complain; all Europe complain! It is from them that you learned your letters, and they have been abused without mercy. Alas! our forefathers learned to read, but we read perversely; they opened the temple of science, we half shut it again; and the dangerous man is not he who is ignorant, but the half wise who pretends to wisdom.

Had any one been at the trouble of comparing the knowledge of the least learned part of the religious orders, with that of the generality of the laity, I have no doubt but the former would greatly have excelled the latter, though they had received their ordinary education. It is true, the religious were not versed in the sophisticated science of the age; but often have I seen those very men who, upbraided with their ignorance, were happy in the sciences which their occupations required. Not only among the Benedictines, who have been more generally excepted from this badge of ignorance, but among all other orders, I have met with men, as distinguished by their knowledge, as by the purity of their morals. Alas! that I could extend this remark to the laity! This, indeed, is a language very different from that which the reader may have seen in the satiric declamations of the age; but will satire satisfy his judgement? In the annals of the conspiring Sophisters shall he find testimony borne of their services; and every scurrilous expression shall be a new laurel in their crown.

The Jesuits were destroyed; but the conspirators saw Christianity still subsisted, and they then said to each other, We must destroy the rest of the religious orders, or we shall not triumph. Their whole plan is to be seen in a letter from Frederic, to which Voltaire gave occasion by the following: "Hercules went to fight the robbers and Bellerophon chimeras; I should not be sorry to behold Herculeses and Belerophons delivering the earth both from Catholic robbers and Catholic chimeras."[1] Frederic answers on the 24th of the same month: "It is not the lot of arms *to destroy the wretch*; it shall perish by the arm of truth, and interested selfishness. If you wish me to explain this idea, my meaning is as follows:—I have remarked, as well as many others, that the places where convents are the most numerous, are those where the people are most blindly attached to superstition. No doubt, if these asylums of fanaticism were destroyed, the people would grow lukewarm, and see with indifference, the present objects of their veneration. The point would be *to destroy the cloisters*, at least to begin by lessening their number. The time is come: the French and Austrian governments are involved in debts; they have exhausted the resources of industry to discharge them, and they have not succeeded; the lure of rich abbeys and well-endowed convents is tempting. By representing to them the prejudice cloistered persons occasion to the population of their states, as well as the great abuse of the numbers of *Cucullati*, who are spread throughout the provinces; and also the facility of paying off part of their debts with the treasures of those communities, who are without heirs; they might, I think, be made to adopt this plan of reform; and it may be presumed, that after having enjoyed the secularization of some good livings, their rapacity would crave the rest.

"Every government that shall adopt this plan *will be friendly to the Philosophers*, and promote the circulation of all those books which attack popular superstition, or the false zeal that would support it.

"Here is a pretty little plan, which I submit to the examination of the patriarch of Ferney; it is his province, as father of the faithful, to rectify and put it in execution.

"The patriarch may perhaps ask *what is to become of the bishops?* I answer, it is not yet time to touch them. To destroy those who stir up the fire of fanaticism in the hearts of the people, is the first step; and when the people are cooled, *the bishops will be but insignificant personages, whom sovereigns will, in process of time, dispose of as they please.*"[2]

Voltaire relished such plans too much not to set a great value on them, and of course thus answered the King of Prussia: "Your plan of attack against the *Christicole Superstition*, in that of the friar-hood, is worthy a great captain. The religious orders once abolished, *error* is exposed to universal contempt. Much is written in France on this subject; every one talks of it, but as yet it is not ripe enough. People are not sufficiently daring in France; bigots are yet in power."[3]

Having read these letters, it would be ridiculous to ask of what service religious orders could be to the church. Certain it is, that many had fallen off from the austerity of their first institutes; but even in this degenerate state we see Frederic making use of all his policy to over-turn them, because his antichristian plots are thwarted by the zeal and example of these religious, because he thinks the church cannot be stormed until the convents are carried as the outworks; and Voltaire traces the hand of the great captain, who had distinguished himself so eminently by his military science in Germany, in the plan of attack against the *Christicole Superstition.* These religious corps were useful then, though branded with sloth and ignorance; they were a true barrier to impiety. Frederic was so much convinced of it, that when the Sophisters had already occupied all the avenues of the throne, he dared not direct his attacks against the Bishops, nor the body of the place, until the outworks were carried.

Voltaire writes to him thus on the 29th of July 1775: "We hope that Philosophy, which in France *is near the throne,* will soon *be on it.* Yet that is but hope, which too often proves fallacious. There are so many people interested in the support of error and nonsense, so many dignities and such riches are annexed to the trade, that the hypocritres, it is to be feared, will get the better of the sages. Has not your Germany transformed your principal ecclesiastics into sovereigns? Where is there an elector or a bishop who will side with Reason, against a Sect that allows him two or three hundred thousand pounds a-year?"[4]

Frederic continued to vote for the war being carried on against the religious. It was too early to attack the bishops. He writes to Voltaire, "All that you say of our German bishops it but too true; they are the hogs fattened on the tythes of Sion." (Such is their scurrilous language in their private correspondence). "But you know likewise, that in the Holy Roman Empire, ancient custom, the golden bull, *and such antiquated fooleries as these,* have given weight to established abuses. One sees them, shrugs one's shoulders, and things jog on in the old way. If we wish to diminish fanaticism, *we must not begin with the bishops.* But if we succeed in lessening the friarhood, especially the mendicant orders, the people will cool, and, being less superstitious, will allow the powers *to bring down the bishops* as best suits their states. *This is the only possible mode of proceeding.* Silently to undermine the edifice hostile to reason, is to force it to fall of itself."[5]

I began by saying, that the means of the conspirators would give new proofs of the reality of the conspiracy, and of its object. Can any other interpretation, than that of an Antichristian Conspiracy, be put on the language made use of in their correspondence? How can we otherwise understand, *such is the only possible mode of proceeding, to undermine* the edifice of that religion which they are pleased to denominate the *Christicole Superstition,* as fanatic or unreasonable; or in order to overthrow its pontiffs, to seduce the people from its worship? What then is conspiracy, if those secret machinations carried on between Ferney, Berlin, Paris, in spite of distance, be not so? What reader can be so infatuated as not to see, that by the establishment of Reason is only meant the overthrow of Christianity? It is indeed a matter of surprise, that the Sophisters should so openly have exposed their plans at so early a period.

In the mean time Voltaire was correct when he answered Frederic, that the plan of destruction had been ardently pursued in France ever since the expulsion of the Jesuits, and that by people who were in office. The first step taken was, to put off the period of religious professions until the age of twenty-one, though the adepts in ministry would fain have deferred it till the age of twenty-five. Of course, of a hundred young people who might have embraced that state, not two would have been able to follow their vocations; for what parent would let his child attain that age without being certain of the state of life he would embrace? The remonstrances made by many friends to religion caused the age fixed on by the edict to be that of eighteen for women, and twenty-one for men. This nevertheless this was looked upon as an act of authority exercised on those who chose to consecrate themselves more particularly to the service of their God, and rescue themselves from the danger of the passions at that age when they are the most powerful. This subject had been very fully treated in the last Œcumenical Council, where the age for the profession of religious persons had been fixed at sixteen, with a term of five years to reclaim against their last vows in case they did not choose to continue the religious life they had undertaken. And it had always been looked upon as a right inherent to the church to decide on these matters, as may be seen in Chappelain's discourse on that subject. It would be ridiculous, after what has been said in this chapter, to repeat the favourite argument of their inutility to France. What! pious works, edification, and the instruction of the people, useless to a nation! Beside, France was a lively example that the number of convents had not hurt its population, as few states were peopled in so great a proportion. If celibacy was to be attacked, she might have turned her eyes to her armies, and to that numerous class of worldlings who lived in celibacy, and who perhaps ought to have been noticed by the laws. All further reclamations were useless. What had been foreseen came to pass according to the wishes of the ministerial Sophisters. In many colleges the Jesuits being very ill replaced, the youth, neglected in their education, left a prey to their passions, or looking on the number of years they had to wait for their reception into the religious state as so much time lost, laid aside all thoughts of that state, and took to other employments. Some few, from want, engaged; but rather seeking bread than the service of their God, or else prone to vice and to their passions, which they had never been taught to subdue, reluctantly submitted to the rules of the cloister. Already there existed many abuses, but these daily increased; and while the number of religious was diminishing, their fervour languished, and public scandals became more frequent. This was precisely what the ministers wanted, in order to have a plea for the suppression of the whole; while their masters, still more sanguine if possible, made the press teem with writings in which neither satire nor calumny were spared.

The person who seemed to second them with the greatest warmth was he who, after having persuaded even his companions that he had some talent for governing, at length added his name to those ministers whom ambition may be said to have blinded even to stupidity. This man was Briennes, Archbishop of Toulouse, since Archbishop of Sens, afterwards prime minister, then a public apostate, and at last died as universally hated and despised as Necker himself appears to be at this day. Briennes will be more despised when it shall be known that he was the friend and confidant of D'Alembert, and that in a commission for the reform of the religious orders he wore the mitre and exercised its powers as a D'Alembert would have done.

The clergy had thought it necessary to examine the means of reforming the religious, and of re-establishing their primitive fervor. The court seemed to enter into their views, named counsellors of state to join the bishops in their deliberations on this subject, and called it the *Commission of Regulars*. A mixture of prelates who are only to be influenced by the spirit of the church, and of statesmen solely acting from worldly views, could never agree; some few articles were supposed to have been settled; but all was in vain, and many, through disgust, abandoned the commission. Among the bishops were Mr. Dillon, Archbishop of Narbonne; Mr. de Boisgelin, Archbishop of Aix; Mr. de Cicè, Archbishop of Bourdeaux, and the famous Briennes, Archbishop of Toulouse.

The first, majestic in his person and lofty in his eloquence, seems to have had but little to do in this affair, and soon withdrew. The talents and zeal shewn by the second in the national assembly in defense of the religious state will convince the reader that he might have given an opinion which the court did not wish to adopt; he also abandoned the commission. In the third we see, that though by accepting of the seals of the revolution, and by affixing them to the constitutional decrees, he could err; by his repentance and retraction sufficiently prove he never would have engaged in, had he known the plans of the conspirators.

Briennes was the only man of this commission who enjoyed the confidence of the court, or had the secret of D'Alembert, and the latter knew well how to prize the future services Briennes was about to render to the conspiracy. On his reception into the French academy, D'Alembert says to the patriarch, "We have in him a good brother, who will certainly prove useful to letters *and to philosophy*, provided *Philosophy does not tie up his hands by licentiousness*, or that the general outcry does not force him to act against his will."[6] In fewer words he might have said, he will attack his God and his religion with all the hypocrisy worthy a conspiring Sophister.

Voltaire, thinking he had reason to complain of the monstrous prelate, is answered by D'Alembert, who was a connoisseur in brethren, "For God's sake don't judge rashly;- - - — I would lay a hundred to one that things have been misrepresented, and that his misconduct has been greatly exaggerated. I know too well his way of thinking, not to be assured, that he only did on that occasion what he was indispensibly obliged to do."[7]

Voltaire complained at that time of an order published by Briennes against the adept Audra, who at Toulouse openly read lectures on impiety, under pretence of reading on history. On the enquiries made in favor of the adept by D'Alembert, he writes that Brienne "had withstood, during a whole year, the joint clamours of the parliament, the bishops, and the assembly of the clergy;" and that it was absolutely necessary *to compel him to act*, to prevent the youth of his diocese from receiving such lectures. His apologist continues, "Don't suffer yourself to be prejudiced against Briennes; and be assured, once for all, that Reason (that is, our Reason) will never have to complain of him."[8]

Such was the hypocrite, the mitred Sophister whom intrigue had placed in the commission to deliberate on the reform of the religious orders. Seeking disorder and destruction, supported by the ministry, without attending to the other bishops of the commission, he solely dictated in this reform.

To the edict on the age for professions he added another, suppressing all convents in towns that consisted of less than twenty religious, and elsewhere when their number was under ten, on the specious pretence, that the conventual rules were better observed where the number was greater. The bishops, and the cardinal de Luynes in particular, represented the great services rendered in country places by these small convents, and how much they helped the curates; but all to no purpose; and Briennes had contrived to suppress fifteen hundred convents before the revolution. He would soon have advanced more rapidly; for by promoting and encouraging the complaints of the young religious against the elder, of the inferiors against the superiors, by cramping and thwarting their elections, he spread dissensions throughout the cloisters. On the other side, the ridicule and calumnies contrived by the Sophisters were so powerful that few young men dared take the habit, while some of the ancients were *ashamed of wearing a gown covered with infamy.*[9] Others at length, wearied out by these shuffling tricks, themselves petitioned to be suppressed.

Philosophism, with its principles of Equality and Liberty, was even gaining ground in their houses with all its concomitant evils. The good religious shed tears of blood over those persecutions of Briennes, who would alone have carried into effect those dreaded schemes planned by Voltaire and Frederic. Their decline was daily more evident; and it was a wonder that any fervor yet remained, though a greater prodigy still, to see the fervor of many of those who had petitioned for their secularization revive in the first days of the revolution. I know for certain, that not one-third of those who had petitioned dared take the oath, for apostacy stared them in the face. The tortuous intrigues of a Briennes had shaken them; but the direct attacks of the National Assembly opened their eyes, and in their suppression, they beheld with astonishment, the grand attack which had been levelled against Christianity.

Voltaire and Frederic did not live to see their plans accomplished; Briennes did; but while claiming the honour, he only reaped the ignominy of them. Shame and remorse devoured him.— With what pleasure we can speak of the piety of those chaste virgins consecrated to the service of their God!

With them his intrigues had been useless. They, more immediately under the direction of their bishops, had not been exposed to the anarchy and dissentions of a Briennes; their seclusion from the world, their professions at an earlier age (eighteen), their education within the walls of the convent, these were barriers against his intrigues. But with what admiration do we behold those who, from the pure motives of religion, spent their lives in the service of the sick; whose charity, whose chaste modesty, though in the midst of the world, could make man believe them to be angels in human forms! These were far above the reach of calumny, or of a Briennes: a pretence could not even be devised.

With a view to diminish the number of real nuns, he thought that if he augmented those asylums for canonesses who have a much greater communication with the world, and are therefore more easily perverted, novices would not be so numerous. But by an inconceivable oversight (unless he had some very deep and hidden scheme) these canonesses were in future to prove a certain number of degrees of nobility to enter these asylums, which before had been open to all ranks in the state. One might have thought, that he meant to render the real nuns odious to the nobility, and the latter to all other classes, by applying foundations to particular ranks which had ever been common to all.

These were reflections to which Briennes little attended. He was laying his snares, while D'Alembert smiled at the idea that ere long both nuns and canonesses would add to the common mass of ruin; but these sacred virgins baffled all their cunning. Nothing less than the whole despotic power of the Constituent Assembly could prevail against them. They were to be classed with the martyrs of that bloody September; their fervor was impassible. — Edicts worthy of Nero exulting in the flames of burning Rome are necessary to drive them from the altar; cannons, and the satellites of that Constituent Assembly, march against them to enforce those edicts; and *thirty thousand women* are driven from their convents, in contradiction to a decree of that same assembly promising to let them die peaceably in their asylums. Thus was the destruction of religious orders completed in France. It was forty years since this plan had been dictated by the Sophisters to the ministers of his most Christian Majesty. But when accomplished, ministers are no more! . . . The sacred person of the king a prisoner in the towers of the Temple! . . . The object of the abolition of religious orders was fulfilled; and religion was savagely persecuted in the person of its ministers! But during the long period that preceded the triumph of the Sophisters they had resorted to many other means with which I have yet to acquaint my reader.

1. To Frederic, 3 March, 1767, Vol. 65, Let. 157, P. 369.
2. From Frederic, 24 March, 1767, Vol. 65, Let. 158, P. 370.
3. To Frederic, 5 April, 1767, Vol. 65, Let. 159, P. 375.
4. Vol. 66, Let. 93, P. 217.
5. From Frederic, 13 Aug. 1775, Vol. 66, Let. 95, P. 222.

6. From D'Alembert, 30 June, 1770, Vol. 69, Let. 32, P. 62—and 21 Dec. 1770, vol. 69, Let. 53, P. 93.
7. From D'Alembert, 4 Dec. 1770, Vol. 69, Let. 48, P. 85.
8. From D'Alembert, 21 Dec. 1770, Vol. 69, Let. 53, P. 92.
9. To Frederick, 5 April, 1767, Vol. 65, Let. 159, P. 375.

CHAP. VII.

*Fourth Means of the Conspirators—
Voltaire's Colony.*

WHILST the conspirators were so much occupied with the destruction of the Jesuits, and of all other religious orders, Voltaire was forming a plan which was to give to impiety itself both apostles and propagandists. This idea seems first to have struck him about the year 1760-61. — Always ruminating the destruction of Christianity, he writes to D'Alembert, "Could not five or six men of parts, who rightly understood each other, succeed, after the example of twelve scoundrels who have already succeeded."[1] The object of this understanding has already been explained in a letter before quoted. "Let the real Philosophers unite in a brotherhood, like the Freemasons; let them assemble and support each other; let them be faithful to the association. This secret academy will be far superior to that of Athens and to all those of Paris. But every one thinks only of himself, and forgets that his most sacred duty *is to annihilate the wretch.*"[2]

The Conspirators never lost sight of this most sacred duty; but they met with various obstacles; religion was still zealously defended in France, and Paris was not yet a proper asylum for such an association. It appears also that Voltaire was obliged for some time to lay this plan aside; but taking it up again a few years afterwards, he applied to Frederic, as we are told by the editor of their correspondence, for leave "to establish at Cleves a little colony of French Philosophers, who might there freely and boldly speak the truth, *without fearing ministers, priests, or parliaments.*" Frederic answered with all the desired zeal, "I see you wish to establish the little colony you had mentioned to me.—I think the shortest way would be, for those men, or your associates, to send to Cleves, to see what would be most convenient for them, and what I can dispose of in their favor."[3]

It is to be lamented that many letters respecting this colony have been suppressed in their correspondence; but Frederic's answers are sufficient to convince us of the obstinacy of Voltaire in the undertaking, who, returning again to the charge, is answered, "You speak of a colony of Philosophers who wish to establish themselves at Cleves. I have no objection to it. I can give them every thing, only excepting wood, the forests having been almost destroyed by your countrymen. But on this condition alone, that *they will respect those who ought to be respected*, and that they will keep within the *proper bounds of decency in their writings.*"[4]

The meaning of this letter will be better understood when we come to treat of the Antimonarchial Conspiracy. Decency in their writings, one should think, would be of the first necessity even for their own views; as otherwise this new colony must have spread a general alarm, and governments would have been obliged to repress their barefaced impudence.

While on one side Voltaire was imploring the succour and protection of the King of Prussia for these apostles of impiety, on the other he was seeking Sophisters worthy of the apostleship. He writes to Damilaville, that he is ready to make a sacrifice of all the sweets of Ferney, and go and place himself at their head. "Your friend," says he, "persists in his idea. It is true, as you have observed, that he must tear himself from many objects that are at present his delight, and will then be of his regret. But is it not better to quit them through Philosophy than by death? What surprises him most is, that many people have not taken this resolution together. Why should not a certain philosophic baron labor at the establishment of this colony? Why should not so many others improve so fair an opportunity?" In the continuation of this letter we find that Frederic was not the only prince who countenanced the plan: "Two sovereign princes, *who think entirely as you do*, have lately visited your friend. One of them offered a town, provided that which relates to the grand work, should not suit."[5]

It was precisely at the time when this letter was written, that the Landgrave of Hesse Cassel went to pay homage to the idol of Ferney. The date of his journey, and the similarity of his sentiments, can leave little doubt that he was the prince who offered a town to the colony should Cleves prove inconvenient.[6]

Meanwhile the apostles of this mock Messiah, however zealous as they were for the grand work, were not equally ready to sacrifice their ease. D'Alembert, idolized by the Sophisters at Paris, saw that he could be but a secondary divinity in the presence of Voltaire. That Damilaville, who was celebrated by the impious patriarch as personally hating God, was necessary for carrying on the secret correspondence in Paris. Diderot, the certain philosophic baron, and the remaining multitude of adepts, reluctantly cast their eyes on a German town where they could not with equal ease sacrifice in luxury and debauchery to their Pagan divinities. Such remissness disconcerted Voltaire. He endeavoured to stimulate their ardor by asking: "If six or seven hundred thousand Huguenots left their country for the *fooleries of Jean Chauvin*, shall not twelve sages be found who will make some little sacrifice to Reason, which is trampled on?"[7]

When he wishes to persuade them that their consent is all that is necessary to accomplish the grand object, he writes again, "All that I can tell you now by a sure hand is, that every thing is ready for the establishment of the manufacture. More than one Prince envies the honor of it; and from the borders of the Rhine unto the Oby, Tomplat (that is Plato Diderot) will be

THE ANTICHRISTIAN CONSPIRACY 63

honored, encouraged, and live in security." He would then repeat the grand object of the conspiracy, in hopes of persuading the conspirators. He would try to inflame their hearts with that hatred for Christ which was consuming his own.—He would repeatedly cry out, *Cruch, crush the wretch! oh, crush the wretch—then crush the wretch.*[8]

His prayers, his repeated solicitations, could not avail against the attractions of Paris. That same reason which made Voltaire willing to sacrifice all the pleasing scenes of Ferney, to bury himself in the heart of Germany, there to consecrate his days and writings to the extinction of Christianity; that reason, I say, taught the younger adepts that the sweets of Paris were not to be neglected. They were not the Apostles of the Gospel preaching temperance and mortification both by word and example; and in the end Voltaire, obliged to give up all hopes of expatriating his sophistical apostles. He indignantly expresses his vexation to Frederic a few years afterwards: "I own to you, that I was so much vexed and so much ashamed of the little success I had in the transmigration to Cleves, that I have never since dared to disclose any of my ideas to your Majesty. When I reflect that a fool and an ideot like St. Ignatius should have found twelve followers, and that I could not find three Philosophers who would follow me, I am almost tempted to think that Reason is useless."[9] "I shall never be reconciled to the non-execution of this plan; it was there that I should have ended my old age."[10]

Violent however as Voltaire was in his reproaches against the other Conspirators, the sequel of these Memoirs will show that he was unjustly so. D'Alembert in particular had far different plans to prosecute. He grasped at the empire of the academic honors; and, without exposing his dictatorship, or expatriating the adepts, by distributing these honors solely to the Sophisters he abundantly replaced Voltaire's so-much-regretted plan. This object, and the method by which it was promoted, shall be the subject of the ensuing Chapter.

1. To D'Alembert, 24 July, 1760, Vol. 68, Let. 70, P. 127.
2. To D'Alembert, 20 April 1761, Vol. 68, Let. 85, P. 163.
3. From Frederic, 24 Oct. 1765, Vol. 65, Let. 142, P. 330.
4. From Frederic, 7 Aug. 1766, Vol. 65, Let. 146, P. 340.
5. To Damilaville, 6 Aug. 1766, Vol. 59, Let. 234, P. 415.
6. To the Landgrave, 9 Sept. 1766, Vol. 66. Let. 64, P. 409.
7. To Damilaville, 18 Aug. 1766, Vol. 59, Let. 239, P. 423.
8. To Damilaville, 25 Aug. 1766, Vol. 59. Let. 243, P. 433.
9. To Frederic, Nov. 1769, Vol. 65, Let. 162, P. 383.
10. To Frederic, 12 Oct. 1770, Vol. 65, Let. 179, P. 426.

CHAP. VIII.

Fifth Means of the Conspirators.—The Academic Honors.

THE protection which the sovereigns had given to men of letters had brought them into that repute which they so well deserved, until, abusing their talents, they turned them against religion and governments. In the French Academy glory seemed to be enthroned; and a seat within its walls was the grand pursuit of the orator and the poet; in short, of all writers, whether eminent in the historic or any other branch of literature. Corneille, Bossuet, Racine, Massillon, La Bruyère, La Fontaine, and all those authors who had adorned the reign of Louis XIV were proud of their admission within this sanctuary of learning. Morals and the laws seemed to guard its entrance, lest it should be prophaned by the impious. Any public sign of infidelity was a bar against admission even during the reign of Louis XV. Nor was the famous Montesquieu himself admitted, until he had given proper satisfaction as to certain articles contained in his Persian Letters. Voltaire pretends that he deceived the Cardinal de Fleury by sending him a new edition of his work, in which all the objectionable parts had been omitted. Such a mean trick was beneath Montesquieu; repentance was his only plea, and in his latter days little doubt can be left of his having repented sincerely. On his admission, however, impiety was openly renounced, and religion publicly avowed.

Boindin, whose infidelity was notorious, had been rejected, though a member of several other academies. Voltaire, for a long time unable to gain admission, at length succeeded merely through the influence of high protectors, and by the practice of that hypocrisy which we shall see him recommending to his disciples. D'Alembert, with great prudence, concealed his propensity to infidelity until he had gained his seat; and though the road to these literary honours had been much widened by the adepts who surrounded the court, he nevertheless thought that it would not be impossible, by dint of intrigue, to turn the scale; that if impiety had formerly been a ground of exclusion, it might in future be a title to admission, and that none should be seated near him but those whose writings had rendered them worthy abettors of the Conspiracy and supporters of its sophisticated arts. His *forte* was petty intrigue, and so successfully did he practice it, that in latter times the titles of Academician and Sophister were nearly synonimous. It is true that he sometimes met with obstacles; but the plot formed between him and Voltaire for the admission of Diderot will be sufficient to evince what great advantages they expected would accrue to their conspiracy by this new means of promoting irreligion. D'Alembert first proposes it. Voltaire receives the proposal with all the attention due to its importance, and answers, "You wish Diderot to be of the academy, it must then be brought about." The king was to approve of the nomination, and D'Alembert feared ministerial opposition. It is to this fear that we owe the account Voltaire has given of Choiseul. He therein mentions his partiality to the Sophisters, and declares that so far from obstructing their plots, he would forward them with all his power. "In a word," he continues, "Diderot must be of the academy; it will be the most noble revenge that can be taken for the play against the Philosophers. The Academy is incensed at le Franc-de-Pompignan; and it would willingly give him a most swinging slap.—I will make a bonfire on Diderot's admission. Ah! what a happiness it would be, if Helvetius and Diderot could be received together."[1]

D'Alembert would have been equally happy in such a triumph; but he was on the spot and saw the opposition made by the Dauphin, the Queen, and the Clergy. He answers, "I should be more desirous than yourself to see Diderot of the academy. *I am perfectly sensible how much the common cause would be benefited by it*; but the impossibility of doing it is beyond what you can conceive."[2]

Voltaire, knowing that Choiseul and La Pompadour had often prevailed against the Dauphin, ordered D'Alembert not to despond. He takes the direction of the intrigue on himself, and places his chief hopes on the Courtesan. "Still further, (says he), she may look upon it as an honor, and make a merit of supporting Diderot. Let her undeceive the king, and delight in quashing a cabal which she despises."[3] What D'Alembert could not personally undertake, Voltaire recommends to the courtiers, and particularly to the Count D'Argental: "My divine Angel! (would he write) do but get Diderot to be of the Academy; it will be the boldest stroke imaginable in the game that reason is playing against fanaticism and folly (*that is, religion and piety*).... Impose for penance on the Duke de Choiseul, to introduce Diderot into the Academy."[4]

The secretary of the academy, Duclos, is also called in as an auxiliary by Voltaire, who gives him instructions to insure the success of the recipiendary adept. "Could not you represent, or cause to be represented, how very essential such a man is to you for the completion of some necessary work? Could not you, *after having slyly played off that battery*, assemble *seven or eight of the Elect*, and form a deputation to the King, to ask for Diderot as the most capable of forwarding your enterprize? Would not the Duke of Nivernois help you in that project, would not he be the speaker on the occasion? The bigots will say, that Diderot has written a metaphysical work which they do not understand: *Let him say that he did not write it, and that he is a good Catholic—it is so easy to be a Catholic.*"[5]

It may be an object of surprise to the reader and to the historian, to see Voltaire straining every nerve, calling on dukes and courtiers, not blushing at the vilest hypocrisy, advising base dissimulation, and that merely to gain the admission of one of his fellow Conspirators into the Academy; but this surprise will cease when they see D'Alembert's own words: *I am perfectly sensible how much the common cause would be benefited by it*; or in other words, the war we are waging against Christianity. These words will explain all his anxiety. And to get admitted within the sanctuary of letters the man the most notorious for infidelity, would it not be confirming the error which the government had committed, in letting itself be led away by the hypocritical demonstrations of a Voltaire or a D'Alembert? Would it not have been crowning the most scandalous impiety with the laurels of literature, and declaring that Atheism, so far from being a stain, would be a new title to its honors? The most prejudiced must own it would have been an open contempt for religion; and Choiseul and La Pompadour were conscious that it was not yet time to allow the Conspirators such a triumph. D'Alembert even shrunk back when he beheld the clamours it would excite, and for the present desisted. But the critical moment was now come, when the ministers secretly abetted what they publicly professed a desire to crush. D'Alembert persisted in his hopes, that with some contrivance he might soon be able to exclude from literary honours all writers who had not offered some sacrifice at least to the Antichristian Sophistry; and he at length succeeded.

Having shown how highly D'Alembert had conceived of the importance that the French Academy, converted into a club of irreligious Sophisters, would be to the Conspiracy, let us examine the merits of some of those who were admitted among its members. And, first, we find Marmontel, perfectly coinciding in opinion with Voltaire, D'Alembert, and Diderot. Then, in succession, La Harpe the favorite adept of Voltaire; Champfort, the adept and hebdomadary co-adjutor of Marmontel and La Harpe; one Le Mierre, distinguished by Voltaire as *a staunch enemy to the wretch*, or Christ;[6] an Abbé Millot, whose sole merit with D'Alembert was his total oblivion of his priesthood,[7] and with the public his having transformed the history of France into an antipapal one; a Briennes, long since known to D'Alembert as an enemy to the church, though living in its bosom; a Suar, a Gaillar, and lastly a Condorcet, whose reception enthroned the fiend of Atheism within the walls of the academy.

It does not appear why Mr. de Turgot did not succeed in his election, though aided by all the intrigues of D'Alembert and Voltaire.[8] The reader who casts an eye on their correspondence will be surprised to see of what concern it was to them to fill this philosophical Sanhedrim with their favorite adepts. There are above thirty letters on the admission of them, and on the exclusion of those persons who were friendly to religion. Their intrigues, whether through protection or any other means, were at length so successful, that in a few years, the name of Academician and Atheist or Deist were synonimous. If there were yet to be found among them some few men, especially bishops, of a different stamp from Briennes, it was a remains of deference shown them, which some might have mistaken for an honour; but they should have looked upon it as an insult, to be seated next to a D'Alembert, a Marmontel or a Condorcet.

There was however among the forty a layman much to be respected for his piety. This was Mr. Beauzée. I one day asked him, how it had been possible, that a man of his morality could ever have been associated with men so notoriously unbelievers? "The very same question (he answered), have I put to D'Alembert. At one of the sittings, seeing that I was nearly the only person who believed in God, I asked him, how he could ever have thought of me for a member, when he knew that my sentiments and opinions differed so widely from those of his brethren? D'Alembert, (added Mr. Beauzée) without hesitation answered, I do not wonder at your question; but we were in want of a skilful grammarian, and among our party not one had made himself a reputation in that line. We knew that you believed in God; but we cast our eyes on you, being a good sort of man, for want of a Philosopher to supply your place."

Thus was the sceptre wrested from the hands of science and virtue, by the hand of impiety. Voltaire had wished to place his conspirators under the protection of the Royal Sophister; D'Alembert stopped their flight, and made them triumph in the very states of that monarch who gloried in the title of Most Christian. His plot, better laid, conferred the laurels of literature solely on the impious writer, whilst he who dared defend religion was to be covered with reproach and infamy. The French academy, thus converted into a club of infidels, was a far better support to the Sophisters conspiring against Christianity, than any colony which Voltaire could have conceived. The academy infected the men of letters, and these perverted the public opinion by that torrent of impious productions which deluged all Europe. These were to be instrumental in bringing over the people to universal apostacy, and will be considered by us, as the sixth means for the Antichristian revolution.

1. To D'Alembert, 9 July 1760, Vol. 68, Let. 68, P. 121.
2. From D'Alembert, 18 July 1760, Vol. 68. Let. 69, P. 123.
3. To D'Alembert, 24 July, 1760, Vol. 68, Let. 70, P. 126.
4. To the Count D'Argental, 11 July 1760, Vol. 56, Let. 153, P. 315.
5. To Duclos, 11 Aug. 1760, Vol. 56, Let. 171, P. 349.
6. To Damilaville, 15 June, 1761, Vol. 57, Let. 70, P. 143.
7. From D'Alembert, 27 Dec. 1777, Vol. 69, Let. 190, P. 312.
8. To D'Alembert, 8 Feb. 1776, Vol. 69, Let. 151, P. 256.

CHAP. IX.

Sixth Means of the Conspirators.—Inundation of Antichristian Writings.

THAT for these forty years past, and particularly for the last twenty of Voltaire's life, all Europe has been overrun with most impious writings, under the forms either of pamphlets, systems, romances, or feigned histories, is one of those self-evident truths which needs no proof. Though I shall in this place confine myself only to a part of what I have to say on the subject, I will show how the chiefs of the conspiracy acted in concert, in the production, the multiplication and distribution of them, in order to disseminate their poisons throughout Europe.

The method to be observed in their own works was particularly concerted between Voltaire, D'Alembert, and Frederic. We see them, in their letters, imparting to each other the different works they are writing against Christianity, their hopes of success, and their methods of insuring it. We see them smile at the snares which they have laid against religion; and that particularly in those works and systems which they affected most to consider as indifferent to, or as rather promoting than attacking religion. In that style D'Alembert was inimitable. The following example will convince the historian, or the reader, of the consummate art of this crafty Sophister.

It is well known with what immense pains the Philosophers of our day have been forming their pretended physical systems on the formation of the globe, their numerous theories and genealogies of the earth. We have seen them diving into mines, splitting mountains, or digging up their surface in search of shells, to trace old ocean's travels, and found their epochs. These numerous researches (according to them) had no other end but the advancement of science and of natural Philosophy. Their new epochs were not to affect religion; and we have reason to believe, that many of our naturalists had no other object in view, as many of them, real men of learning, of candour in research, and capable of observation, have rather furnished arms against, than forwarded those vain systems by their studies, labours, and peregrinations: not such was the case with D'Alembert and his adepts. They soon perceived that these new epochs and systems drew the attention of divines, who had to maintain the authenticity of, and the truth of the facts contained in the books of Moses, the rudiments of Revelation. To baffle the Sorbonne and all the defenders of holy writ, D'Alembert writes a work under the title of *The Abuse of Criticism*, a palpable defense of all those systems. The main drift of the work was, while showing a great respect for religion, to prove that neither revelation, nor the credibility of Moses, could be in the least affected by these theories or epochs, and that the alarms of the divines were ungrounded. Many pages were occupied in proving that these systems could only serve to raise our ideas to the grand and sublime. That, so far from *counteracting the power of God, or his divine wisdom,* they only *displayed it more clearly;* that considering the object of their researches, *it less became the divine, than the natural Philosopher to judge them.* Divines are represented as *narrow-minded, pusillanimous, and enemies to reason,* and terrified at an object which did not in the least concern them. He is very pointed in his writings against those feigned panics; and among other things, says, "They have sought to connect Christianity with systems purely philosophical. In vain did religion, so simple and precise in its tenets, constantly throw off the alloy that disfigured it; it is from that alloy that the notion has arisen of its being attacked in works where in fact nothing was farther from the minds of the writers."[1] These are precisely the works in which *a much longer space of time is required* for the formation of the universe, than the history of the creation, as delineated by Moses, leaves us at liberty to suppose.

Who would not have thought D'Alembert convinced, that all those physical systems, those theories, *and that longer space of time,* so far from overturning Christianity, would only serve to raise the grandeur and sublimity of our ideas of the God of Moses and of the Christians? But that same D'Alembert, while seeking this *longer space of time,* anticipated his applause to the lie which his travelling adepts were about to give to Moses and to revelation. Those adepts, rambling in the mountains of the Alps or the Appenines, are the men whom he points out to Voltaire *as precious to Philosophy.* It is he who, after having been so tender for the honor of Moses and revelation, writes to Voltaire, "This letter, my dear companion, will be delivered to you by Desmarets, a man of merit and of sound Philosophy, who wishes to pay his respects to you on his journey to Italy, where he purposes *making such observations on natural history, as may very well give the lie to Moses.* He will not say a word of this to the master of the sacred palace; but if, perchance, *he should discover that the world is more ancient than even the septuagint pretends, he will not keep it a secret from you.*"[2]

It would have been difficult to use more art, though it were to point the hand of an assassin; D'Alembert would sometimes direct Voltaire, when shafts were to be sent from Ferney which could not yet be shot from Paris. On these occasions the theme was already made, and only needed the last gloss of Voltaire's pen.

When, in 1763, the Sorbonne published that famous thesis which foretold what the French revolution has since taught the sovereigns of Europe on the evil tendency of this modern Philosophism to their very thrones, D'Alembert, in haste, informs Voltaire of the necessity for counteracting an impression so detrimental to the conspiracy. He shews Voltaire how to impose on the kings themselves, and how to involve the church in all their doubts and suspicions. In tracing this master-piece of art and cunning, he reminds him of the contests long since extinct between the priesthood and the empire, and instructs him in the art of throwing odium and suspicion on the clergy.[3] Many other plans are proposed to the patriarch according to circumstances.[4] Those were (in his style) *the chestnuts* that *Bertrand* (D'Alembert) *pointed out under the ashes*, and which *Raton* (Voltaire) was to help him draw out of the fire with *his delicate paw*.

Voltaire did not fail, on his part, to inform D'Alembert and the other adepts of what he himself wrote, or of the steps he took with ministry. Thus, as a prelude to the plundering decrees of the revolution, he gave Count D'Argental notice of the memorial he had sent to the Duke de Praslin, to prevail on that minister to deprive the clergy of part of its maintenance by abolishing tythes.[5]

These secret memorials, the anecdotes, whether true or slanderous, against the religious writers, were all concerted among the conspirators and their chiefs.[6] Even to the smiles, the witticisms, insipid epigrams of the adepts, were under the direction of Voltaire, and used by him as forwarding the conspiracy. He, better than any man, knew the powers of ridicule, and would often recommend its use to the adepts in their writings and their conversation. "Do your best (he writes to D'Alembert) to preserve your cheerfulness; always endeavour to *crush the wretch*. I only ask five or six witticisms a day; they would suffice. *It* would not get the better of them. Laugh, Democritus; make me laugh, and the sages shall carry the day."[7]

Voltaire was not always of the same opinion with regard to this attack on Christianity. This method was not sufficiently elevated for a Philosopher! and he soon after adds, in his quality of chief, "*To the flood of jests and sarcasms*, there should succeed, *some serious work, which however should be worth reading*, for the justification of the Philosophers, and the confusion *of the wretch*."[8] This work, notwithstanding the exhortations of the chief, and his union with the adepts, never was executed. But, on the other side, the press teemed with deistical and atheistical works fraught with calumny and impiety. Monthly or weekly some new production of the most daring impiety was printed in Holland. Such were the *Philosophic Soldier, The Doubts, Priestcraft, Blackguardism unveiled*,[9] which are among the most profligate that the Sect has produced. One might have thought (such was his zeal in promoting the sale of them) that Voltaire alone had monopolized this traffic of impiety. He received notice of the publications, which he communicated to his brethren at Paris. He recommended their procuring and circulating them; upbraided them with their little ardor in spreading them abroad, while he himself dispersed them all around him.[10] To stimulate them, he would write that it was out of these works *that all the German youth learned to read; that they were the universal catechisms from Baden to Moscow*.[11]

When he thought that Holland could not sufficiently infect France with these profligate writings, he would select those which D'Alembert was to get privately printed at Paris, and then distribute them by thousands. Such, for example, was the pretended *Survey of Religion* by Dumarsais. "They have sent me, (these are Voltaire's own words) *a work of Dumarsais,* ASCRIBED *to St. Evremond*. It is an excellent work (that is to say, precisely one of the most impious). I exhort you, my dear brother, to prevail on some one of our faithful and beloved to reprint this little work, which may do a great deal of good."[12] We find the like exhortations, or rather more pressing, with regard to the *Last Will of Jean Meslier*, of that famous Curate of Etrepigni, whose apostacy and blasphemies could make a still stronger impression on the minds of the populace. Voltaire would complain that there were not so many copies of that impious work in all of Paris, as he himself had dispersed throughout the mountains of Switzerland.[13]

D'Alembert was himself obliged to apologize as if he had been indifferent and deficient in point of zeal; but particularly for not having dared, at the entreaties of Voltaire, to *print* in Paris *and distribute four or five thousand copies of John Meslier's Last Will*. His excuse manifests the consummate conspirator, who knows how to wait the proper moment, and take precautions to ensure that success which too great precipitancy might have ruined.[14] By what he writes to Voltaire on a master-piece of impiety entitled *Good Sense*, we see that he was perfectly aware of the effect which these impious works had on the minds of the people; that he knew when they were to be multiplied, or cast into the hands of the vulgar; he says, "This production (*Good Sense*) is a work much more to be dreaded than the *System of Nature*." It really was so, because, with greater art and unconcern, it leads to the most unqualified Atheism; and for that reason we see D'Alembert setting forth the advantages to be derived from it to the conspiracy, if it were abridged, though already so small *as to cost no more than five-pence, and thus to be fitted for the pocket and the reading of every cook-maid*.[15]

These low intrigues, however, were not the only means to which the Sophisters resorted to evade the law, and overrun all Europe with these Antichristian productions. They were supported at court by powerful men, or ministerial adepts, who knew how to silence the law itself; or, if it ever was to speak, it was only to favour the better this impious traffic, at another time, in spite of the magistracy. The duke de Choiseul and Malesherbes were again the promoters of this grand plan for robbing the people of their religion, and insinuating the errors of Philosophism. The former, with the assurance of ministerial despotism, threatened the Sorbonne with all the weight of his indignation, when by their public censures they sought to guard the people against those ephemerous productions. It was this strange exertion of authority which made Voltaire exclaim, *Long live the ministry of France; above all, long live the Duke of Choiseul!*[16]

Malesherbes, who, having the superintendency over the whole trade of printing and bookselling, was hence enabled to evade the law both in the introduction and circulation of these impious writings, was on that point in perfect unison with D'Alembert. Both would willingly have hindered the champions of religion from printing their replies to that legion of infidels then rising in France; but the time was not yet come. With his pretended toleration, Voltaire was indignant, that under a philosophic minister the apologists of the Gospel should still have access to the press; and D'Alembert is obliged to plead in his defence, that Malesherbes, so far from favoring the antiphilosophic works, had reluctantly been obliged *to submit to superior orders which he could not resist.*[17] Not content with a simple connivance, such excuses were unsatisfactory to Voltaire; nothing less than the authority of kings could satisfy his zeal, and he has again recourse to Frederic. This inundation of impious books was to have been the prime object of his colony. As yet unconsoled for the failure of that plan, he writes to the king of the Sophisters, "Were I younger and had I health, I would willingly quit the house I have built and the trees I have planted, to go and dedicate with two or three Philosophers the remainder of my life, under your protection, to the printing of a few useful books. *But, Sire, cannot you, without exposing yourself, have some of the Berlin booksellers encouraged to reprint them, and to distribute them throughout Europe at a price low enough to ensure their sale.*"[18]

This proposal, which transformed the King of Prussia into the hawker-general of Antichristian pamphlets, did not displease his protecting majesty. "You may (answers Frederic) *make use of our printers as you please*; they enjoy perfect liberty, and as they are connected with those of Holland, France, and Germany, I have no doubt but that they have means of conveying books whithersoever they may think proper."[19]

Even at Petersburg Voltaire had found hawkers of these impious productions. Under the protection and by the influence of Count Schouvallow, Russia was to petition Diderot *for leave to be honoured with* the impression of the Encyclopedia, and Voltaire is commissioned to announce that triumph to Diderot.[20] The most impious and most seditious work that Helvetius had written was then reprinting at the Hague, and the Prince Gallitzin dared to *dedicate it to* THE EMPRESS OF ALL THE RUSSIAS. Here Voltaire's zeal was out-run by his success. He could not help remarking, with what amazement the world would see such a work inscribed to the most despotic sovereign on earth; but while he smiled at the imprudence and folly of the Prince adept, he exultingly beheld *the flock of sages silently increasing*, for princes themselves were no less eager than himself in the circulation of these antichristian writings. We find this account repeated three different times in his letters to D'Alembert; so great was his joy, and so confident was he of annihilating all idea of Christianity in the minds of the people by these means.

In this chapter we have treated only of the solicitude with which the chiefs sought to infuse the poison of their writings into the minds of the people; hereafter we shall see the means employed by the Sect to extend it to the hovel or the cottage, and to imbue the rabble with its impious principles, though we have seen Voltaire despising such a conquest.

Note to CHAP. IX.

On the Works more particularly recommended by the Conspirators.

Were I not pretty well acquainted with a certain numerous class of readers, I might consider as superfluous the observations I am about to make on the doctrine of those works which the chiefs of the conspiracy, independently of their own, sought to circulate through all classes of society. I have not only to satisfy men hard to convince, but to persuade men who will resist evidence itself, unless it overwhelms them. In spite of all the proofs we have already adduced of the Conspiracy formed and carried on by Voltaire, D'Alembert, Frederic, Diderot, and their adepts, against the vitals of Christianity, will nobody again assert, that the Sophisters only levelled their writings at the abuses, or at least that Catholicism was their only aim; and that they never meant to attack the divers other religions that are within the pale of Christianity, whether at Geneva or London, in Germany or Sweden. The extreme falsity of such an argument renders it absurd. If we do but reflect for a moment on the nature of those works which the Sophisters circulated with so much zeal, can we suppose that they wished to disseminate other principles than those preached up in these works? Let us appeal to them, and see if the destruction of abuses, or even of Catholicism alone, could have been their sole object.

We have seen that the works so highly recommended by Voltaire and D'Alembert are particularly those of Freret, Boulanger, Helvetius, John Meslier, Dumarsais, and Maillet; or at least they bear the names of those Sophisters. They are, as we have before said, THE PHILOSOPHIC SOLDIER; THE DOUBTS OF THE SAGE'S SCEPTICISM; *and* GOOD SENSE; whose authors remain unknown. I will lay before the reader the divers opinions broached by the writers so much commended by the Sophisters, concerning those points which cannot be invalidated without overthrowing the very foundation of Christianity; and then let any one conclude that the Conspiracy only impugned abuses, or some particular branch of Christianity.

The belief of the existence of a God belongs to every religion that is Christian; let us then examine their doctrine as to a GOD.

FRERET tells us expressly, "*The universal cause, that* GOD *of the Philosophers, of the Jews, and of the Christians, is but a chimera and a phantom.*" The same author continues: "Imagination daily creates fresh chimeras, which raise in them that impulse of fear; and such is the phantom of the Deity."[21]

The author of GOOD SENSE, that work which D'Alembert wishes to see abridged, in order to sell it for five-pence to the poor and ignorant, is not so emphatical; but what is his doctrine? "*That the phenomena of nature only prove the existence of* GOD *to a few prepossessed men,*" that is to say, full of false prejudices; that the "*wonders of nature, so far from bespeaking a* GOD, *are but the necesssary effects of matter prodigiously diversified.*"[22]

THE PHILOSOPHIC SOLDIER does not deny the existence of GOD; but he starts, in his first chapter, with a monstrous comparison *between Jupiter* and *the* GOD *of the Christians*; and the pagan god carries all the advantage of the discussion.

According to CHRISTIANITY UNVEILED, which appeared under the name of Boulanger, it *is more reasonable* to admit with Manes of a *twofold God*, than of the GOD of Christianity.[23]

The author of THE DOUBTS, or of Scepticism, informs the world, "That they cannot know whether a GOD really exists, or whether there is the smallest difference *between good and evil, or vice and virtue.*" Such is the drift of the whole of that work.[24]

We find the same opposition to Christianity in their doctrines on the spirituality of the SOUL. With FRERET, "every thing that is called *Spirit*, or SOUL, *has no more reality* than *the phantoms, the chimeras,* or *the sphinxes.*"[25]

The Sophister of the pretended GOOD SENSE heaps up arguments anew to prove, that it is the body that feels, thinks, and judges; and that the SOUL *is but a chimera*.[26]

HELVETIUS pronounces, "That we are in an error when *we make of the* SOUL *a spiritual being*; that *nothing* can be *more absurd*; and that the SOUL *is not a distinct being from the body*."[27]

BOULANGER tells us decidedly, "That *the immortality of the* SOUL, so far from stimulating man to the practice of virtue, is nothing but a *barbarous, desperate, fatal tenet*, and contrary to all legislation."[28]

If from these fundamental tenets, essential to every religion as well as to Catholicism, we pass on to MORALITY, we shall find FRERET teaching the people that "all ideas *of justice and injustice, of virtue and vice, of glory and infamy*, are purely arbitrary and dependent on custom."[29]

HELVETIUS will at one time tell us, that the only rule by which *virtuous actions* are distinguished from *vicious ones*, is the law of princes, and public utility. Elsewhere he will say, "that *virtue*, or *honesty*, with regard to individuals, is no more than the *habit of actions personally advantageous*, and that *self-interest* is the sole scale by which the actions of man can be measured;" In fine, "that if the virtuous man is not happy in this world, we are justified in exclaiming, O *Virtue! thou art but an idle dream*."[30]

The same sophister also says, that "*sublime virtue and enlightened wisdom* are only the fruits of those passions *called folly*; or, that stupidity is the necessary consequence of the cessation of passion. That to moderate the passions is to ruin the state.[31] That *conscience* and *remorse* are nothing but the *foresight* of those physical penalties to which crimes expose us. That the man who is above the law can commit, without remorse, the dishonest act that may serve his purpose."[32] That it *little imports* whether *men are vicious*, if they be but enlightened.[33]

The fair sex too will be taught by this author, that "MODESTY is only an *invention of refined voluptuousness*:—that MORALITY has nothing to apprehend from *love*, for it is the passion that *creates genius*, and *renders man virtuous*."[34] He will inform children, that "the commandment of loving their father and mother is more the work of education than of nature."[35] He will tell the married couple, that "the law which condemns them to live together becomes *barbarous and cruel* on the day they cease to love each other."[36]

In vain should we seek among the other works that the chiefs of the conspirators wished to circulate a more Christian MORALITY. DUMARSAIS, as well as Helvetius, knows no other virtue but what *is useful*, nor vice but that which *is hurtful* to man upon earth.[37] The PHILOSOPHIC SOLDIER thinks that so far from being able to offend God, *men are obliged to execute his laws*.[38] The author of GOOD SENSE so much praised by the leaders, tells them that to think we can offend God, is *to think ourselves stronger than God*.[39] He would even teach them to answer us, "If your God leaves to men the *liberty of damning* themselves, *why should you meddle with it*? Are you *wiser* than that God whose rights you wish to avenge?"[40]

Boulanger, in the work so much admired by Frederic and Voltaire, asserts that the *fear of God*, so far from being the beginning of wisdom, *would rather be the beginning of folly*.[41]

It would be useless to the reader, and irksome to ourselves, were we to carry these quotations any farther. Those who wish to see these texts, and numberless others of the same kind, may peruse the HELVIAN LETTERS. But certainly here is enough to demonstrate, that conspirators who wished to circulate such works, were not levelling solely at the Catholic religion, much less at a few abuses. No; it is evident, that every altar where Christ was adored was to be overthrown, whether Anglican, Calvinist, or Protestant.

The base project of throwing into circulation four or five thousand copies of John Meslier's Last Will would fully prove the design of annihilating every vestige of Christianity, since this Last Will or Testament is nothing but a gross declamation against the doctrines of the Gospel.

1. The Abuse of Criticism, Nos. 4, 15, 16, 17.
2. From D'Alembert, 30 June, 1764, Vol. 68, Let. 137, P. 302.
3. From D'Alembert, 18 Jan. 1773, Vol. 69, Let. 90, P. 150, and 9 Feb. Let. 96, P. 160.
4. From D'Alembert, 26 Feb. 1774, Vol. 69, Let. 125, P. 210, and 22 March, Let. 128, P. 216.
5. To the Count D'Argental, 20 June, 1764, Vol. 58, Let. 130, P. 243.
6. To D'Alembert, 16 Jan. 1757, Vol. 68, Let. 18, P. 31, and 23 Jan. Let. 20, P. 35.
7. To D'Alembert, 30 Jan. 1764, Vol. 68, Let. 128, P. 279.
8. To D'Alembert, 23 June, 1760, Vol. 68, Let. 67, P. 119.
9. Le Militaire Philosophe, Les Doutes, l'Imposture Sacerdotale, Le Polissonisme devoilé.
10. See his letters to Count D'Argental, to Mad. du Dessant, and particularly to D'Alembert, 13 Jan. 1769, Vol. 69, Let. 2, P. 5.
11. To Ct. D'Argental, 26 Sept. 1766, Vol. 59, Let. 270, P. 480.
12. To D'Alembert, 13 Dec. 1763, Vol. 68, Let. 122, P. 263.
13. From D'Alembert, 31 July, 1762, Vol. 68, Let. 102, P. 207, and to D'Alembert, 15 Sept. Let. 104, P. 214.
14. From D'Alembert, 31 July, 1762, ibid.
15. From D'Alembert, 15 Aug. 1775, Vol. 69, Let. 146, P. 249.
16. To Marmontel, 2 Dec. 1767, Vol. 60, Let. 200, P. 336.
17. From D'Alembert, 28 Jan 1757, Vol. 68, Let. 21, P. 37.
18. To Frederic, 5 April, 1767, Vol. 65, Let. 159, P. 374.
19. To Frederic, 5 May, 1767, Vol. 65, Let. 160, P. 378.
20. To Diderot, 25 Sept. 1762, Vol. 57, Let. 242, P. 475.
21. Letter from Thrasybulus to Lucippus, P. 164 and 254.
22. No. 36 et passim.
23. Page 101.
24. Particularly No. 100 & 101.
25. Letter from Thrasybulus.
26. No. 20 and 100.
27. Of the Spirit, and of Man and his Education, No. 4 and 5.
28. Antiquity Unveiled, p. 15.
29. Letter of Thrasybulus.
30. On the Mind. Discourse 2d and 4th.
31. Idem. Discourse 2d and 3d, chap. 6, 7, 8, and 10.
32. Idem. Of Man, vol. 1st, sect. 2d, chap. 7.
33. Idem. No. 9, chap. 6.
34. Idem. Disc. 2d, chap. 4 and 15, &c.
35. Of Man, ch. 8.
36. Of Man, sect. 8, &c.
37. Essay on Prejudices, chap. 8.
38. Chap. 20.
39. Sect. 67.
40. Sect. 135.
41. Christianity Unveiled, in a note to P. 163.

CHAP. X.

Of the Spoliations and Violences projected by the Conspirators, and concealed under the Name of Toleration.

OF all the arts put in practice by the conspirators, none, perhaps, has succeeded better with them, than the perpetual appeal in all their writings to *toleration, reason, and humanity,* which Condorcet tells us they had made their *war-hoop.*[1] In fact, it was natural enough, that men who appeared so deeply impressed with these sentiments should gain the attention of the public: But were they real? Did the conspiring Sophisters mean to content themselves with a true toleration? As they acquired strength, did they mean to grant to others what they asked for themselves? These questions are easily solved; and it would be useless for the reader to seek the definition of each of these high-sounding words imposed upon the public, when their private and real sentiments are to be seen in their continued cry of *Crush Religion.* To cast an eye on their correspondence, is sufficient to identify the plans of these conspiring Sophisters with those of the Jacobins their successors. Do not the Petions, the Condorcets, and the Robespierres, adopt their wishes and execute their plans under the same mask of toleration?

Plunder, violence, and death have marked the toleration of the revolutionists. Nor were any of these means foreign to the first conspirators, whose language the latter had adopted. As to spoliations, I have already said that Voltaire, as early as the year 1743, was plotting with the King of Prussia to plunder the Ecclesiastical Princes and the Religious Orders of their possessions. In 1764, we have seen him sending a memorial to the Duke of Praslin on the abolition of tythes, in hopes of depriving the clergy of their sustenance.[2] In 1770, he had not abandoned his plan when he writes to Frederic, "I wish to God that Ganganelli had some good domain in your neighbourhood, and that you were not so far from Loretto.... It is noble to scoff at these Harlequin *Bull-givers;* I like to cover them with ridicule, but *I had rather* PLUNDER *them.*"[3]

These various letters prove to the reader, that the chief of the Conspirators only anticipated the plundering decrees of the Jacobins, and the revolutionary incursion their armies have made to Loretto.

Frederic, assuming the kingly tone, seems for an instant so shocked at these spoliations, as to have forgotten that he had been the first to propose them. He answers, "Were Loretto adjoining to my villa, I would not touch it. Its treasures might tempt a Mandrin, a Conflans, a Turpin, a Rich . . . . or their fellows. It is not that *I* reverence donations consecrated by sottish stupidity; but what the *public* venerates should be spared. When one looks upon one's self as gifted with superior lights, compassion for others, and commiseration for their weakness, should make us unwilling to shock their prejudices. It is to be lamented, that the pretended Philosophers of our days are not of the same way of thinking."[4] But the Sophister soon prevails over the monarch; and Frederic is no longer of opinion that spoils of the church are to be left to a Mandrin: the very next year, coinciding with Voltaire, he writes to him, "If the new minister of France is a man of sense, he will neither be weak nor foolish enough to restore Avignon to the Pope."[5]—He recurs to his means of *silently undermining the edifice*, by first plundering the Religious Orders, that they might then strip the bishops.[6]

D'Alembert, on his side advised, that the clergy should be first deprived of that consequence they enjoyed in the state, before they were plundered of their possessions. Sending to Voltaire his task, almost ready made, that *he* might speak out what D'Alembert dared not utter himself, he tells him, "that he must not forget (if it could be done delicately) to add to the first part a little appendix, or an attractive postscript, on the danger both to states and kings, in suffering the clergy to form a separate and distinct body, with the privilege of holding regular assemblies."[7]

As yet this doctrine was new both to kings and states; they had never perceived this pretended danger of letting the clergy form a distinct body in the nation, as did the nobility and the third order; but these conspiring chiefs were anticipating the horrors of the revolution, the plunders and murders of their Jacobin successors and disciples.

Violent and sanguinary edicts, decrees of deportation and of death, were not foreign to the wishes of the conspiring chiefs. How frequent soever the words of toleration, humanity, and reason, may be in Voltaire's mouth, it would be a great error in judgment to think that those were the only arms he wished to employ against the Christian Religion. When he writes to Count Argental, "Had I but a hundred thousand men, I well know what I would do with them,"[8] and to Frederic, "Hercules went to fight the robbers and Bellerophon chimeras; I should not be sorry to behold Herculeses and Bellerophons delivering the earth both from Catholic robbers and Catholic chimeras;"[9] it was not toleration that dictated those wishes; and one is tempted to conclude, that he would not have been sorry to behold the massacre of the Clergy by the Herculeses and Bellerophons of the sanguinary September. Have we not observed him wishing to behold *every Jesuit at the bottom of the ocean, each with a Jansenist hung to his neck?* When, with the view of avenging Helvetius and Philosophism, he does not blush to ask, *Could not the moderate and discreet proposal of strangling the last Jesuit with the guts of the last Jansenist*, bring matters to some compromise? In reading this, can we reasonably infer, that the humanity and toleration of Voltaire would have been greatly shocked at the sight of ships stowed with the Catholic Clergy by a Le Bon, as a preparatory step to submerging them in the ocean!!!

Frederic seemed to be nearer to simple toleration when he thus answered Voltaire: "It is not the lot of arms to destroy *the wretch.—*It will perish by those of truth."[10] At length he begins to think that force must strike the last blow at Religion. He is not averse to this force, and we see him willing to employ it had the occasion offered when he writes to Voltaire, "To Bayle, your forerunner, and to yourself, no doubt, is due the honor of that Revolution working in the minds of men. But, truly to speak, it is not yet complete; bigots have their party, and *it will never be perfected but by a superior force: from government must the sentence issue that shall crush the wretch.* Enlightened Ministers may forward it, *but the will of the sovereign must accede.* Without doubt this will be effectuated in time; but neither of us can be spectators of that long-wished for moment."[11]

There can be no doubt but that the long-sought for moment was that, when impiety, enthroned, should cast aside the mask of toleration, with which it had necessarily disguised itself: Julian-like, would not Frederic also have resorted to superior force at that desired period? Would he not have seconded the Sophisms of the Conspirators with that sentence which was to issue from the Sovereign? He would have spoken as a master; and under Frederic might not the reigns of a Domitian or a Julian have been renewed, when apostacy, exile, or death, were the only alternatives left to a Christian's choice.— But to reconcile this superior force, this sentence of the government that is *to crush*, with what D'Alembert says of that Prince in a letter to Voltaire, is difficult: "I believe him at his last shift, and it is a great pity. Philosophy will not easily find a Prince like him, tolerant through indifference, (which is the true style) and an enemy to superstition and fanaticism."[12]

But with D'Alembert even that mode of tolerating, through indifference did not exclude underhand persecutions; nor would it have been incompatible with this man's rage and phrenzy, so openly expressed in his letters to Voltaire, to see a whole nation destroyed solely for having shewn its attachment to Christianity. Could toleration through indifference dictate the following lines? "*A-propos* of the King of Prussia, he has at length got a-head again. And I, as a Frenchman and a thinking being, am quite of your opinion, that it is a great happiness both for France and for Philosophy. Those Austrians are a set of insolent capuchins who hate and despise us, *and whom I could wish to see annihilated with the superstition they protect.*"[13]

It would be useless to remark in this place, that these very Austrians whom D'Alembert wishes to see annihilated, were then the allies of France, at war with that very King of Prussia whose victories he celebrates. These circumstances might serve to show, how much more philosophism swayed the heart of the Sophister, than the love of his country; and that toleration would not have hindered the Conspirators from betraying their king or country, could they by that event have made a new attack on Christianity.

THE ANTICHRISTIAN CONSPIRACY.

We plainly see, that all these inhuman wishes were rather expressed by inadvertency, than the avowed object of their correspondence. They were preparing the road for those seditious and ferocious minds, that were to perpetrate what the Sophisters could at that time only devise.—The day of rebellion and murder was not yet come; with the same wishes circumstances had not distributed to them the same parts to act. Let us then examine what characters the first chiefs performed, and by what services each one in particular, signalizing his zeal in the Antichristian Conspiracy, prepared the reign of his Revolutionary adepts.

1. Sketch on History. Epoch 9.
2. To the Count D'Argental, 20 June, 1764, ut supra.
3. To Frederic, 8 June, 1770, Vol. 65, Let. 172, P. 405.
4. From Frederic, 7 July, 1770, Vol. 65, Let. 173, P. 409.
5. From Frederic, 29 June, 1771, Vol. 66, Let. 10, P. 25.
6. From Frederic, 13 Aug. 1775, Vol. 66, Let. 95, P. 222.
7. From D'Alembert, 9 Feb. 1773, Vol. 69, Let. 96, P. 161.
8. To the Count D'Argental, 16 Feb. Vol. 57, Let. 28, P. 60.
9. To Frederic, 3 March, 1767, Vol. 65, Let. 157, P. 369.
10. From Frederic, 25 March, 1767, Vol. 65, Let. 158, Page 370.
11. From Frederic, 8 Sept. 1775, Vol. 66, Let. 97, P. 230.
12. From D'Alembert, 27 Jan. 1762, Vol. 68, Let. 95, P. 187.
13. From D'Alembert, 12 Jan. 1763, Vol. 68, Let. 113, P. 237.

CHAP. XI.

Part, Mission and private Means of each of the Chiefs of the Antichristian Conspiracy.

IN order to attain the grand object of the conspiracy, in short to crush the Christ whom they pursued with unrelenting hatred, all the general plans and means they had concerted were judged insufficient. Each individual was to concur with his own means, with those which his faculties, his situation, or peculiar mission, enabled him to exert.

Voltaire was endowed with all those talents which adorn the eminent writer; and no sooner was the confederacy formed than he turned them all against his God. During the last five and twenty years of his life, he declares himself, that *he had no other object in view than to vilify the wretch.*[1] Before that period he had shared his time between poetry and impiety; but henceforward he is solely impious. One might have thought that he wished to vomit forth himself more blasphemies and calumnies against the God of Christianity, than had the whole class of Celsi, or Porphyrii during all ages. In the large collection of his works (more than forty volumes in 8vo.) Romances, Dictionaries, Histories, Memoirs, Letters and Commentaries, flowed from his pen, embittered with rage and breathing the wish of crushing Christ. "I finish all my letters," would he write, "by saying, *crush the wretch*, as Cato was used to finish his harangues. Such is my opinion and *let Carthage be destroyed.*"[2]

In this immense collection it would be in vain to seek any particular system of Deism, of Materialism, or Scepticism. They all form one common mass. We have seen him conjuring D'Alembert to unite all these diverging Sects in the common attack against Christ; and his own heart may be said to have been their focus. He cared not whence the storm arose, or whose the hand that struck; the subversion of the altar was his only aim. The religious authors, and we ourselves, have shown him fickle in his systems, and daily adopting new opinions, and that from his own works;[3] we behold twenty different men in him alone, but each of them equally hateful. Rage accounts for his contradictions; even his hypocrisy flows from the same source. This latter phenomenon is not sufficiently known; it must have its page in history; but let Voltaire himself speak as to the extent and original cause of so base a conduct.

THE ANTICHRISTIAN CONSPIRACY

During that inundation of Antichristian books in France, government would sometimes, though remissly, take cognizance of their authors. Voltaire himself had been prosecuted on account of his first impious writings. When declared premier chief, he thought that more caution became his pre-eminence, lest any legal proof should be acquired of his impiety. The better to attack, and the more securely to *crush Christ*, he conceals himself under his very banners; he frequents his temples, is present at his mysteries, receives into his mouth the God he blasphemed; and if annually at Easter he received, it was but more audaciously to blaspheme his God. To so monstrous an accusation incontestable proofs shall be brought.

On the 14th of Jan. 1761, Voltaire sends a performance, (I know not what, but which the editor of his works supposes to be an epistle to Mademoiselle Clairon, a famous actress in those days,) to one of his female adepts, the Countess of Argental, whom he styles his angel. Beyond a doubt, it was a most scandalous production; since only the chosen of the elect are favored with it, or rather since to them alone Voltaire *dared* send it. In short, whatever was the subject, it was accompanied with the following letter.

"Will you amuse yourself with the perusal of this scrap: will you read it to Mademoiselle Clairon? None but yourself and the Duke de Choiseul are in possession of it; you will tell me presently that I grow very daring, and rather wicked in my old age. Wicked! No; I turn Minos, and judge the wicked. But take care of yourself. There are people, I know, who do not forgive; and I am like them. I am now sixty-seven years old. I go to the parochial mass. I edify my people. I am building a church. *I receive communion there*; and, zounds, I will be buried there, in spite of all the hypocrites. I believe in Jesus Christ consubstantial with God, and in the Virgin Mary mother of God.—Ye base persecutors, what have you to say to me? Why, you have written *La Pucelle*. No, I never did. You are the author of it; it was you that gave ears to Joan's palfrey. I am a good Christian, a faithful servant of the king, a good lord of the parish, and a proper tutor for a daughter. I make curates and Jesuits tremble. I do what I please with my little province about as big as the palm of my hand (his estate extended about six miles); I am the man to dispose of the Pope whenever I please. Now, ye raggamuffins, what have you to say to me?—These, my dear angels, are the answers I would make to the Fantins, Grisels, Guyons; or to the little black monkey, &c.&c."[4]

The female adepts might indeed laugh at the tone and style of such a letter; but will the judicious reader see it in any other light, than as the production of an insolent old man, who, proud of his protections, is nevertheless determined impudently to lie, and to set forth the most orthodox profession of faith, should religious writers accuse him of impiety, and to combat the laws with denials or make a merit of his sacrilegious *communions*; and the infidel talks of hypocrites and base cowards!

Such odious artifice seems to have shocked the Count D'Argental himself; for on the 16th of February following, Voltaire writes to him, "Had I a hundred thousand men, I would know what use I would make of them;

but as I have them not, *I will receive at Easter,* and you may call *me hypocrite as much as you please*; Yes, by God! I will receive the sacrament, and that in company with Mad. Denis and Mademoiselle Corneille; and if you say much, I will put the *Tantum ergo* into verse, and that in cross rhimes."[5]

It appears that many more of the adepts were ashamed of this meanness in their chief. He himself at length thinks it necessary to write to D'Alembert on the subject; to whom he says, "I know there are people who speak ill of my Easter devotions. It is a penance I must resign myself to, in expiation of my sins.----*Yes, I have received my Easter communion, and what is more, I presented in person the hallowed bread;*----after this, I could boldly defy both Molinists and Jansenists."[6]

If these last words do not sufficiently declare the motives of his hypocrisy, the following letter, also to D'Alembert, will do away all doubt; it is only three days posterior to the last: "What, in your opinion, should the sages do when surrounded by senseless barbarians? There are times when *one must imitate their distortions, and speak their language. Mutemus clypeos* (let us change our bucklers). In fact, what I have done this year, *I have already done several times before*; and please God I will do it again."[7] This is the same letter too in which he particularly recomends that *the mysteries of Myrtra should not be divulged*, and which he concludes with this terrible sentence against Christianity. *The monster must fall pierced by a hundred invincible hands; yes, let it fall beneath a thousand repeated blows.*

With this profound dissimulation,[8] Voltaire combined all that dark-dealing activity, which the oath of crushing the God of Christianity could suggest to the premier chief of the Antichristian Sophisters. Not content with his partial attacks, he had recourse to whole legions of adepts from the east to the west; he encouraged, pressed, and stimulated them in this warfare. Present every where by his correspondents, he would write to one, "Prevail on all the brethren, to pursue *the wretch in their discourses and in their writings, without allowing him one moment's respite."*—To another he would say, *"make the most earnest, though the most prudent efforts to crush the wretch."* Should he observe any of the adepts less ardent than himself, he would extend his Philippics to all: *"They forget* (says he) *that their principal occupation ought to be to crush the monster."*[9] [The reader has not forgotten that *monster, wretch,* and *Christ* or *Religion,* are synonymous in his mouth.] Satan could not have been more ardent, when, in the war of hell against heaven, he fought to stir up his legions against the Word. He could not more urgently exclaim, We must triumph over the Word, or meanly serve: shame in defeat could not be expressed more forcibly by Satan than by Voltaire, when he cries out to his adepts, *"Such is our state, that we shall be the execration of mankind, if* (in this war against Christ) *we have not the better sort of people on our side*; we must therefore gain them cost what it will; labour then in the vineyard; *oh, crush the wretch,*[10]----*I tell you, crush the wretch."*

So much zeal had made him the idol of the party. The adepts flocked from all parts to see him, and went away fired with his rage. Those who could not approach, consulted him by letter, and laid their doubts before him; they would crave to know whether there really was a God, if they really had a soul, &c. Voltaire, who knew nothing of the matter, smiled at his own power; but always answered, that the God of the Christians was to be crushed. Such were the letters he received every week.[11] He himself wrote a prodigious number in the same blasphemous style. The reader must have seen the collection in order to believe that the heart or hatred of one single man could dictate, or that one hand could pen them, and that without considering his many other blasphemous works. In his den at Ferney, he would be informed of, and see all; he would personally direct every thing that related to the conspiracy. Kings, princes, dukes, marquisses, petty authors or citizens, might write to him, provided they were but impious. He would answer them, strengthen them, and encourage them all in their impiety. In short, to extreme old age, his life was that of a legion of devils, whose sole and continued object was to crush Christ and overthrow his altar.

Frederic the Sophister, though on a throne, was not less active, nor less astonishing in his activity. This man, who alone did for his kingdom all that a king could do, and even more than both king and ministers in most other countries do, out-stripped the Sophisters also in their Antichristian deeds. As a chief of the conspiracy, his part, or rather his folly, was to protect the inferior adepts, if any of them chanced to fall under prosecution by what was called fanaticism. When the Abbé Desprades was obliged to fly the censures of the Sorbonne and the decrees of Parliament, the sophistical monarch presented him with a canonicate at Breslaw.[12] Etallonde de Morival, a hair-brained youth, flies the vengeance of the laws, after having broken the public monuments of religion; he is received, and the colours of a regiment are entrusted to his hands.[13] If his armies require money, his treasures are exhausted; but not so to the adepts. In the very height of war, their pensions, and particularly D'Alembert's, are regularly paid.

He was sometimes, it is true, seen to lay aside the Sophister, and think it beneath a monarch to be connected with a set of *blackguards, coxcombs, and visionary fools*.[14] But those were little sallies which the Sophisters easily overlooked; his philosophism would return; he was one of their's again; and his hatred to Christianity would once more engage his whole attention. He would then spur on Voltaire himself; he would urge and solicit him impatiently for new writings, and the more impious the work, the more he approved of it.—Then with Voltaire and D'Alembert he would demean himself even to their artifices; he would, above all, admire the hand that struck unseen, or, as he expresses himself, that method of filliping the *wretch,* while loading him with civilities.[15]

Then, assuming the tone of disgusting flattery, he would stile Voltaire the God of Philosphy. "He would fancy him ascending Olympus, loaded and satiated with glory, *the conqueror of the wretch,* supported by the genii of Lucretius and Sophocles, of Virgil and Locke, seated on a car beaming with light, and placed between Newton and Epicurus."[16] He paid homage to him for the Antichristian Revolution which he saw preparing.[17] Unable to triumph by so many titles himself, he would acquire that of being laborious; and even those impious works, whether in rhyme or in prose, published under his name, are not the only productions of the royal Sophister. Many he privately ushered into circulation, and which never could have been thought to be those of a man who had the duties of a throne to fulfil. Such, for example, was his extract of Bayle. More impious than Bayle himself, he only rejects the useless articles, in order to condense the poison of the rest. His *Akakia* too, and that *Discourse on the History of the Church* so much extolled, as well as its preface, by the abettors of impiety. In short, his productions were numberless, in which Voltaire finds no other fault but the eternal repetitions (like his own) of the same arguments against religion.[18]

Hence we see, that it was not enough for Frederic to forward the conspiracy by his counsels, and to give refuge to its agents; but he would also, by his constancy and application to infect Europe with his impieties, aspire to the rank of chief. If he was inferior to Voltaire, it was in his talents, and not in his hatred; but had Voltaire been destitute of the support of a Frederic, he could not have risen to the height he aimed at. Possessed of the secret, he would willingly have initiated all kings to the mysteries of the conspiracy; and of all, he was the king who gave it the chief support. His example was still more powerful than his writings; and it may be justly said, that his reign was that of a sceptered infidel.

Placed in an humbler sphere, Diderot and D'Alembert began their several missions with a game that well characterized their apostleship. Both were actuated by its spirit; but neither had yet acquired that reputation which they afterwards gained more by their impiety, than by their abilities. The coffee-houses at Paris were their first stage. There unknown, first in one then in another, they would begin an argument on religious matters, Diderot the assailant and D'Alembert the defendant. The objection was forcible and pointed, the energy and tone of Diderot was invincinble. The reply was weak, but made with all the apparent candour of a Christian, who wished to maintain the honor and truth of his religion. The idle Parisians, who generally resorted to these places, would hearken and admire, and sometimes take a part in the dispute. Diderot then insisted, resumed, and pressed the argument. D'Alembert, in return, owned that the difficulty appeared unanswerable, and then withdrew as if ashamed, and regretting, that neither his divinity, nor his love for religion, could furnish him with arguments for its defense. Our two disputant friends would soon meet to felicitate each other on the good success of their sham conflict, and on the impression they had made upon the crowd of ignorant hearers, who had been completely duped. They then make a fresh appointment; the dispute was taken up again; the hypocritical advocate for religion makes a new display of his zeal, but submits to the superior arguments of Atheism. At length the police, informed of their game, attempted to put a stop to it: but it was too late; these sophisms had spread through the different societes, never to be eradicated. Hence arose, in great part, that fury which soon became fashionable with all the youth of Paris, of disputing on matters of faith; and that still greater folly, of looking on objections as insuperable which immediately disappear when, in search of truth, we seek to know it, and follow it, in spite of those passions which militate against it. It was on occasion of the coffee-house disputations, that the lieutenant of the police upbraiding Diderot with propagating Atheism, that madman proudly answered, *It is true, I am an Atheist, and I glory in it.* "Why Sir," replied the minister, "you would know, were you in my place, that even had no God existed, it would be necessary to have invented one."

However much the brain of this Atheist might have been heated, the fear of the Bastille put a period to his apostleship. The minister would have been more correct in his office, had he threatened him with Bedlam. We refer the reader to the Helvian Letters, where are recorded his numberless titles to a place there.[19] He was in fact the boasting madman of the conspiracy. They wanted a man of this cast, who would utter all the absurd and contradictory impieties which his brain could invent. Such are the ideas with which he filled his different writings his pretended *Philosophic Thoughts*; his *Letter on the Blind;* his *Code,* and his *System of Nature.*

This last work gave great offense to Frederic, who even refuted it, for reasons we shall explain in the Antimonarchial Conspiracy. And indeed D'Alembert always kept the author's name a profound secret. He would not even own it to Voltaire, though he was as well acquainted with it as myself. But Diderot was not the sole author of this famous system. To build this chaos of nature, which, destitute of *intelligence,* had made man intelligent, he had associated with two other Sophisters, whose names I will not mention for fear of error, not having paid sufficient attention to them to be certain; but as to Diderot I am certain, being previously acquainted with him. It was he who sold the manuscript, to be printed out of France, for the sum of one thousand livres. I had the fact from the man who paid them, and who owned it when he came to know better those impious Sophisters.

Notwithstanding all these follies, Diderot, was nevertheless, in Voltaire's eyes, the *illustrious philosopher, the brave Diderot,* and one of the most useful *knights* of the conspiracy. The conspirators proclaimed him the *Great Man;* they sent him to foreign courts as the *Admirable Man;* yet whenever he had been guilty of some notable piece of folly, they were silent, or even disowned him. This was the case in particular when at the court of Empress of Russia.

Formerly, at all courts a fool was kept for amusement; fashion had substituted a French Philosopher, and little had been gained in point of common sense. But the Empress Catherine soon perceived, that much might be lost with respect to public tranquillity. She had sent for Diderot, judging his *imagination to be inexhaustible.* She classed him *among the most extraordinary men that ever existed;*[20] and she was correct in her judgement, for Diderot behaved himself in such an extraordinary manner, that her majesty thought it necessary to send him back to the place he came from. He consoled himself, in his disgrace, with the idea that the Russians were not yet ripe for the sublimity of his philosophy. He set off for Paris in a bannian, with a velvet cap on his head. His footman, like a king at arms, preceded; and when they were to pass through any town or village, he would cry out to the gazing multitude, "it is Diderot the *Great Man* that is passing."[21] Such was his equipage from Petersburg to Paris. There he was to support the character of the extraordinary man, whether writing in his study, or dealing out in divers companies his philosophic absurdities; always the bosom friend of D'Alembert, and the admiration of the other Sophisters. He finished his apostleship by his *Life of Seneca*, in which he sees no other difference between him and his dog, but that of their dress; and by his *New Philosophical Thoughts*, where God is supposed to be the *Animal Prototype*, and mortals so many little particles flowing from this great animal, and successively metamorphosed into all sorts of animals until the end of time, when they are all to return to the divine substance whence they had originally emanated.[22]

Diderot would madly utter in public all those absurdities which Voltaire would impiously assert. It is true, that none of them gained credit; but religious truths were enfeebled by these assertions wrapped in frothy discourse and philosophic pomp. Men cease to believe the religion of Christ, thus perpetually reviled in these writings; and that was all the Sophisters aimed at. The part which Diderot acted was thereby rendered so essential to the conspiracy.

Who can reconcile this antichristian zeal, ever emphatic, and in a state of ebullition when his imagination is heated, with that real admiration which he often expressed for the Gospel? The following is an anecdote I had from Mr. Beauzée, a member of the academy. Going one day to see Diderot, he found him explaining a chapter of the Gospel to his daughter, as seriously and with as much concern as the most Christian parent could have done. Mr. Beauzée expressed his surprize. "I understand you," said Diderot, "but in truth where could I find better lessons to give her?"

D'Alembert would never have made such an avowal as this. Though the constant friend of Diderot, we find throughout their lives, and their philosophic course, that same difference which marked their first essays in the apostleship. Diderot spoke out whatever he thought at the moment, D'Alembert never said a word but what he wished to say. I will defy any one to find his real opinion on *God*, or on the *soul*, except in his private correspondence with the conspirators. His works have all the obscurity and cunning of iniquity, but he is the fox that infects and then burrows himself. Easier would it be to follow the meanderings of the eel, or trace the windings of the serpent gliding through the grass, than to discover the tortuous course he follows in those writings which he owns.[23]

No body was ever more true to Voltaire's maxim of *strike, but hide your hand*. The avowal he makes of his *bows* to religion, while he is striving to pull it to pieces,[24] might save the historian the trouble of seeking those numerous proofs with which the works of this Sophister abound. To make himself amends for this perpetual restraint under which, from his dissimulation, he was himself forced to write, by means of his pupils, or in their productions, he would speak more boldly. When he returned them their works, he would artfully insinuate an article, or plan a preface; but so much the worse for the pupil, if he underwent the punishment incurred by the master. Morellet, still a youth, though already a graduate among the divines of the Encyclopedia, had just published his first essay in philosophism. This was a manual with which Voltaire was enchanted; above all he valued the Preface; *it was one of the finest lashes ever given by Protagoras.* The youth was taken up and sent to the Bastille. The real Protagoras, or D'Alembert, who had so well taught him the art of *lashing*, never owned the whip, as may be supposed.[25]

On the whole, D'Alembert would have been but of little use to the Conspirators, had he confined himself to his pen. In spite of his quibbling style, and of his epigrams, his talent of wearying his readers left them an antidote. Voltaire, by giving him another mission, better suited his genius. He had reserved to himself the ministers, dukes, princes, and kings, and all those sufficiently initiated to forward the Conspiracy; but charged D'Alembert with the care of training the young adepts: "*Endeavour,*" he writes expressly, "*endeavour on your part to enlighten youth as much as you are able.*"[26]

Never was mission more actively, more zealously, nor more ably fulfilled. It is to be remarked, that however secret D'Alembert may have been in all the other parts he acted in the conspiracy, he was not unwilling that his zeal in this particular should be observed. He was the general protector of all young men who came to Paris possessed of any talents. Had they any fortune of their own, he dazzled them with crowns, premiums, and even with the academic seats, of which he absolutely disposed, either as perpetual secretary, or as being irresistible in all those petty intrigues wherein he so much excelled. The reader has already seen what a master-stroke it was for the Conspirators to have filled with their adepts this tribunal of European Mandarines presiding over the empire of letters. But his power in this point extended far beyond Paris. He writes to Voltaire, "I have just got Helvetius and the Chevalier de Jeaucourt admitted into the academy at Berlin."

D'Alembert was particularly attentive to such of the adepts as were intended to train others, or to fulfil the functions of private or public professors, or of tutors in private families; but particularly in the latter, when the pupil, by his rank or wealth, might hereafter be a protector of the Conspirators, or more amply remunerate his teacher. This was the true method of imbuing youth with the real principles of the conspiracy. D'Alembert was perfectly aware of its importance, and took his measures so well that he succeeded in spreading such tutors and preceptors throughout all the countries of Europe, and deserved the title of the most fortunate propagator of philosophism.

The proofs he cites of their progress will suffice to show the choice he had made. "Here is, my dear Philosopher," he exultingly writes to Voltaire, "here is what was pronounced at Cassel on the 8th of April, in presence of his highness the Landgrave of Hesse Cassel, of six princes of the empire, and of a most numerous assembly, by *a professor of History which I gave to his Highness the Landgrave.*" This was a discourse full of the grossest invectives against the Church and the Clergy, as *obscure fanatics, praters crosiered or unmitred, with or without a cowl.* Such was the style of the professor and such the proofs adduced by D'Alembert of the victories daily gained by his adepts over religious ideas, and of the sentiments they instilled into their pupils.[27]

It was, above all, of importance to the conspirators to place such tutors about young princes and children hereafter destined to govern nations. The correspondence of Voltaire and D'Alembert lays open their intrigues on this point, and the powerful support which they expected from it.

The court of Parma was seeking men worthy of presiding over the education of the young infant; and when they placed the Abbé de Condilhac and De Leire at the head of his Instructors, they flattered themselves with having succeeded; as they little thought that these two men were to inspire the young prince with the irreligious ideas of the Sophisters. The Abbé de Condilhac, in particular, had by no means the reputation of an Encyclopedian Philosopher; and it was long ere they became sensible of their error, which could only be remedied by the total subversion of all that these two tutors had done. The whole would have been foreseen, had they known that Condilhac was the particular friend of D'Alembert, who always looked up to him as a man precious to the self-created Philosophers; or had they known that the choice of these two men was only the effect of an intrigue in which Voltaire glories, when he writes to D'Alembert, "It appears to me that the Parmesan child will be well surrounded; he will have a Condilhac and a De Leire. If, with all that, he is a bigot, *grace must be powerful indeed.*"[28]

These wishes and artifices of the Sect were so well propagated,, that in spite of Louis the XVI's attachment to religion, they sought to place new Condilhacs about the heir to the crown; and as they succeeded in discarding the bishops from the education of the young Dauphin, they would willingly have excluded all ecclesiastics; but, despairing of so complete a success, they sought to make the choice fall on some clergyman, who, like Condilhac, would inspire the illustrious pupil with the principles of the Sophisters. I am acquainted with one of those men with whom they dared to tamper. They offered him the place of tutor to the Dauphin, being, as they said, sure of getting it for him, and of thereby making his fortune; *but on condition* that when he taught the young prince his Catechism, he would take care to insinuate, that all religious doctrine, as well as all the mysteries of Christianity, were only prejudices and popular errors, of which a prince should indeed be informed, but which he should never believe; and that in his private lessons he would instil, as true doctrine, all the errors of Philosophism.— Fortunately, this priest answered, that he knew not how to sacrifice his duty to his fortune; more fortunately still, Louis XVI was not a man to encourage such intrigues. The Duke D'Harcourt, named to preside at the education of the Dauphin, took the advice of some bishops, and chose (to read lectures on religion to his pupil) a clergyman perfectly competent to the task, as he was then superior of the College of La Fleche. Alas! why must we felicitate this tender youth on his premature death? While yet the Sophisters of infidelity could not flatter themselves with the subversion of the throne of his ancestors, were they not infusing their poisons to transform him at least into an impious king? And when the throne was overturned, would he, more than his young brother, have escaped the hands of the Sophisters of rebellion?

Many other adepts, with the same zeal to enthrone Philosophism and to prepare the way for the Antichristian Revolution in divers other courts, showed the same activity. At Petersburg they had beset the Empress; they had persuaded her, that some Sophister, and that of the first class, ought to be entrusted with the education of her son. D'Alembert was named, and the Count Schouvallow was ordered by his sovereign to make the proposal in her name.—D'Alembert simply received the offer as proof *that Voltaire had no reason to be displeased with his mission, and that philosophy was sensibly reaching the throne.*[29] Whatever advantages he might have expected to reap from such a commission, he prudently declined; he preferred the petty empire he swayed in Paris as chief of the adepts, to the precarious favor of courts, and of that in particular whose distance from the center of the conspiracy could not have permitted him to act the same part in it.

King of the young adepts, he did not confine his protection to those of Paris alone, but to the remotest parts of Russia would he extend his paternal care; he would follow their progress, share their destiny, or protect them in adversity.—When he found his power insufficient, he would have recourse to Voltaire's credit; he would write, for instance: "The poor Bertrand is not lucky. He has petitioned fair Kate (the Empress of Russia) to restore to liberty five or six giddy-headed Velches. He had conjured her, in the name of Philosophy; he had drawn up, under that sacred name, the most eloquent pleading that from memory of monkey was ever made, and Kate pretends not to understand it."[30] This was as much as to say to Voltaire, try in your turn whether you can succeed better, and do for them what you have so often done for other adepts whose misfortunes I have made known to you.

This understanding equally subsisted in all that regarded the conspiracy; little satisfied with pointing out works that were to be refuted, or with giving the sketch of some new impious brochure, he would also be the spy over every religious author. It has often been an object of surprise, to see Voltaire, so familiar with the anecdotes of the private lives of those whose works he pretended to refute, though generally they are slanderous, sometimes ridiculous, but always foreign to the question. He was indebted to D'Alembert for them. Whether true or false, the latter always chose such as could attach ridicule to the person of the authors, knowing how well Voltaire could substitute ridicule for proof, or wit for sound argument. Those who doubt this fact may consult D'Alembert's letters on the Père Bertier, or the Abbé Guenèe, whom Voltaire himself could not but admire; or those concerning Messrs. Le Franc, Caveirac or Sabbatier, and on many others whom Voltaire hardly ever combats, but with the weapons that D'Alembert had furnished.

Voltaire on his part spared nothing that could raise the importance of D'Alembert. He would recommend him to all his friends; he would introduce him into every little society, or petty philosophic club; for these were already forming in Paris, to be one day absorbed by the great club of the Jacobins. Some indeed would have been styled aristocratical, as they were the weekly meetings of *Counts, Marquisses* or *Chevaliers*, personages already too consequential to bend their knee before the altar of their God. Here would they debate on prejudices, superstition, or fanaticism. They would scoff at J. C. and his priests, or smile at the simplicity of the adoring populace. They also thought of shaking off the yoke of religion, leaving indeed just what was necessary to keep the rabble in awe. The female adept, the Countess du Deffant, held the chair, and continued her philosophic education under the particular direction of Voltaire, by whose orders she studied Rabelais, Polymbrock, Hume, the Tale of the Tub, and other such romances.[31]

D'Alembert was far from being at his ease in these aristocratical clubs; he even disliked this female adept. Voltaire on the contrary, knowing what advantages were to be drawn from them, wished him to belong to them all, and would introduce him by his letters. His introduction was less difficult into some other clubs, and particularly into that where Mad. Necker presided, when she had snatched the sceptre of Philosophy from the hands of all the other adepts of her sex.[32]

Our two chiefs mutually assisted each other by imparting their plans for drawing off the people from their religion. One, in particular, cannot certainly be omitted in these memoirs; it denotes too clearly the intentions of the conspirators, and it shows how far their views extended. It was not indeed the invention of D'Alembert; but he was aware of the advantages Philosophism would derive from it, and, strange as was the plan, he flattered himself with the execution of it.

It is well known what strength the Christian religion draws from the fulfilling of the prophecies, and particularly from those of Daniel, and of Christ himself, on the fate of the Jews and of their temple. Julian the apostate, in order to give the lie to Christ and to the prophet Daniel, had sought to rebuild the temple. It is also known, that flames bursting forth from the earth at divers times, and devouring the workmen, had obliged him to desist from the undertaking. D'Alembert was not ignorant of this act of the divine vengeance having been ascertained by a multitude of eye-witnesses. He had undoubtedly seen it recorded in Ammianus Marcellinus, an author of unquestionable authority, for he was a friend of Julian, and like him a Pagan. But this did not hinder him from writing to Voltaire, "You probably know, that at this present time, there is in Berlin one of the circumcised, who, expecting Mahomet's paradise, is in the mean time gone to wait on your former disciple in the name of the Sultan Mustapha. Writing to that country the other day, I mentioned, that if the king would but say a word, it would be a fine opportunity to have the temple of Jerusalem re-built."[33]

That word was not said by the former disciple, and D'Alembert gives the following reason to Voltaire: "I have no doubt but that we should have succeeded in our negotiation for the re-building of the temple of the Jews, if your former disciple had not been afraid of losing some circumcised worthies, who would have carried away thirty or forty millions with them."[34] Thus, in spite of all their inclination to give the lie to the God of the Christians, even the sordid interest of the Conspirators was to add a new proof to his doctrines.

Voltaire had not, eighteen years after, given up the plan, nor lost all hopes of accomplishing it. Seeing that D'Alembert had not succeeded with Frederic, he endeavoured to prevail with the Empress of Russia. He writes to her, "If your Majesty is in a regular correspondence with Ali Bey, I implore your protection with him; I have a little favor to ask of him; it is to re-build the temple of Jerusalem, and to recal the Jews, who will pay him a large tribute, and thereby make a mighty lord of him."[35]

Voltaire when nearly eighty still persisted in this plan, by which he was to prove to the people, that Christ and his prophets were impostors. Frederic and D'Alembert were also far advanced in their career; and the time was not far distant, when they were to appear before that very God whom they had daringly styled a *wretch*, and against whom they had never ceased to direct their malice.

I have now laid before my readers the means and the industry with which they sought to overturn the altars, to annihilate the dominion of the faith, to destroy the priests of God, and to substitute the hatred and ignominy of him whom the Christians adore, to his religion. I had promised not so much the history, as the real demonstration of the Conspiracy; and in exposing its object, its extent, or its means, I have not resorted to hearsay or vague report, for proof.—My proofs are their own words; the comparison of their letters and of their mutual communications carries conviction. My readers may henceforth reconcile this conspiracy, and its means, with that revolution operated by the Jacobins. They may already perceive, that the latter, in destroying the altars of Christ, only execute the plots of the Sophisters their fore-runners and masters.

Was there a temple to be overthrown, a depredatory decree against the church to be passed by the Jacobins, of which we have not already seen the plan? Are not the Marats and the Robespierres figured by Voltaire in his Hercules and Bellerophon? And if whole nations are to be crushed in hatred to Christianity, have we not seen that wish formally expressed by D'Alembert? Every thing teaches us (the hatred of the father gaining strength in the breast of the son, and the plots propagating), that when force shall coalesce with impiety, they can only generate a race brutal and ferocious.

But this force to be acquired by the Conspirators supposes a successive progress. Before it could throw off the mask, it was requisite that the number of adepts should be augmented, and that the arms of the multitude should be secured to them. I am about to show their successes under the reign of corruption in the divers orders of society during the lives of the chiefs.—Hence history will hereafter more easily conceive and explain what they were during the reign of terror and devastation.

1. Letter to Damilaville, May, 1761, Vol. 57, Let. 58, P. 117.
2. To Damilaville, 26 July, 1762, Vol. 57, Let. 225, P. 446.
3. See Helvian Letters, and particularly letter 34 and 42.
4. Vol. 57, Let. 8, P. 15.
5. Vol. 57, Let. 28, P. 60.
6. To D'Alembert, 27 April 1768, Vol. 68, Let. 228, P. 476.
7. To D'Alembert, 1 May 1768, Vol. 68, Let. 229, P. 477.
8. If I may credit men who knew Voltaire in the earlier part of his literary triumphs, he was then no stranger to this profound hypocrisy. The following anecdote I learned from men who knew him well. It was singular enough, that Voltaire had a brother, an arrant Jansenist, who professed all the austerity of manners which that Sect affected. The Abbé Arouet, heir to a considerable fortune, would not see his impious brother, and openly declared that he would not leave him a halfpenny. But as his health was weak, and his life could be of no long duration, Voltaire did not give up all hopes of the inheritance; he turned Jansenist and acted the devotee. On a sudden he appears in the Jansenistical garb; with a large slouched hat, he runs from church to church, taking care to choose the same hours as the Abbé Arouet; and there, with a deportment as contrite and humble as Deacon Paris himself, kneeling in the middle of the church, or standing with his arms crossed on his breast, his eyes cast on the ground, on the altar, or on the Christian orator, he would hearken or pray with all the compunction of the penitent sinner reclaimed from his errors. The Abbé believed in his brother's conversion, exhorted him to persevere, and died leaving him all his fortune. The Jansenist's cash was, however, all that Voltaire retained of his conversion.
9. See Letters to Thiriot, Saurin, and Damilaville.
10. To D'Alembert, 13 Feb. 1764, Vol. 68, Let. 129, P. 282.
11. To Mad. du Dessant, 22 July, 1761, Vol. 57, Let. 87, P. 181.
12. To D'Alembert, 5 Sept. 1752, Vol. 68, Let. 3, P. 7.
13. To D'Alembert, 8 Dec. 1772, Vol. 69, Let. 82, P. 134.
14. His Dialogues of the Dead.
15. From Frederic, 16 March, 1771, Vol. 66, Let. 6, P. 16.
16. From Frederic, 25 Nov. 1766, Vol. 65, Let. 151, P. 353.
17. To Frederic, 10 Feb. 1767, Vol. 65, Let. 154, P. 361.
18. Correspondence of Voltaire and the King of Prussia, Let. 133, 151, 159, &c. &c. Vol. 65.
19. Letters LVII. and LVIII.
20. From Catherine, 7 Jan. 1774, Vol. 67, Let. 134, P. 286.
21. Feller's Historical Dictionary.
22. New Philosophical Thoughts, Page 17 and 18. The whole is exposed in the Helvian Letters, XLIX.

23. From the criticism made of his works in our Helvian Letters the result is this: D'Alembert will never declare himself a sceptic, or whether he knows of the existence of a God or not. He will even let you think that he believes in God; and then begin by attacking certain proofs of a Deity; he will tell you that, from zeal for the Deity, man must know how to choose among those proofs. He will end by attacking them all, with a *yes* on one object, and a *no* a little while on the same; he will entangle the minds of his readers, he will raise doubts in them, and smile to see them fallen without perceiving it, into the very snare he had prepared for them. He never tells you to attack religion, but he will tempt you with a stand of arms, or place them in your hands ready for combat. (*See his Elements of Philosophy and our Helvian Letters, Let.* xxxvii). He will never declaim against the morality of the church or the commandments of God; but he will tell you that *there does not exist a single catechism on morality fitted to the capacities of youth*; and that it is to be hoped there will at length appear a Philosopher who will supply that *desideratum* (See *Elem. of Phil.* No. 12). He will not pretend to deny the sweets of virtue; but he will tell you, "that philosophers would have better known our nature, had they been satisfied with simply confining the happiness of this life to the exemption from pain." (*Preface of the Encyclopedia*). He will not offend his reader by obscene descriptions, but he will tell him, Art. HAPPINESS, "Men all agree as to the nature of happiness; they declare it to be the same as pleasure, or at least they are indebted to pleasure for all that is most delicious in it." And thus his young pupil is transformed into an Epicurean without knowing it.
24. From D'Alembert, 3 Jan. 1765, Vol. 68, Let. 151. P. 333.
25. To Thiriot, 26 Jan. 1762, vol. 57, Let. 157, P. 320.
26. To D'Alembert, 15 Sept. 1762, Vol. 68, Let. 104, P. 214.
27. From D'Alembert, 1 July, 1772, vol. 69, Let. 77, P. 124.
28. To D'Alembert, 17 Nov. 1760, Vol. 68, Let. 77, P. 174 and from D'Alembert, 3 Jan. 1765, Let. 151, P. 335.
29. To D'Alembert, 25 Sept. 1762, Vol. 68, Let. 106, P. 219, and the 2 Oct. following.
30. From D'Alembert, 18 Jan. 1773, Vol. 69, Let. 90, Page 151.
31. Letters of Voltaire to Mad. Dessant, particularly 13 Oct. 1759, Vol. 56, Let. 90, P. 182.
32. To D'Alembert, 21 June, 1770, Vol. 69, Let. 31, P. 59, and to Mad. Fontaine, 8 Feb. 1762, Vol. 57, Let. 167, P. 336.
33. From D'Alembert, 8 Dec. 1763, Vol. 68, Let. 121, P. 261.
34. From D'Alembert, 29 Dec. 1763, Vol. 68, Let. 124, P. 269.
35. To Catherine, 6 July, 1771, Vol. 67, Let. 82, P. 172.

CHAP. XII.

Progress of the Conspiracy.—First Class of Protectors.—Crowned Adepts.

VOLTAIRE's grand object, as we have seen, was to hurry away that whole class of men, styled by the conspirators the better sort, and infuse into them his hatred for Christ and his religion; to have left his gospel to none but the rabble, and to them only in case they could not efface it from their minds. Under this denomination of *the better sort*, they comprehended all who were distinguished either by power, rank, or riches; and, after them, all people of education or instruction, and honest citizens ranking above what Voltaire calls rabble, footmen, cooks, &c. It is an observation worthy the historian, that the Antichristian Conspiracy first makes its progress in the most illustrious part of this class; among princes, kings, emperors, ministers and courts; among those, in short, who may be styled the great.

If a writer dares not utter these truths, let him throw aside his pen; he is too base and unworthy of treating such important subjects of history. He who has not the courage to tell kings, that they were the first to league in the conspiracy against Christ and his religion, and that it is the same God who has permitted the conspirators first to threaten, shake, and silently undermine their thrones, then openly to scoff at their authority; the man, I say, who dares not hold such language is only abandoning the powers of the earth to their fatal blindness. They would continue to hearken to the impious, to protect impiety, and support its dominion, to let it circulate and spread from the palace to the city, from the towns to the country, from the master to the servant, from the lords to the people. And would not such crimes call down vengeance from heaven? Will not heaven have crimes too numerous to avenge upon nations not to curse them with luxury and discord, with ambition and conspiracies, or with all those scourges which portend the downfall of nations? Had the monarch alone throughout his empire raised his head against his God, who has told us that the crimes of the chief shall not be avenged upon his people? Once more, I say, let the historian be silent, if he dares not utter the truth. Should he seek the causes of a revolution in its agents, he would meet a Necker, a Brienne, a Philippe D'Orleans, Mirabeaux, and Robespierres; a confusion in the finances, factions among the great, insubordination in the armies, the people agitated and disquieted, and at last seduced. Will he, by that, know whence these Neckers, Mirabeaux, or Robespierres, have arisen; whence this confusion in finance, this spirit of faction, this insubordination of the armies, or the seduction of the divers classes of the state? He will have seized but the last thread of the conspiracy. He will have seen empires in their agony, but he will have overlooked that slow fever which consumed them, while the violence of the fit is reserved to that last crisis which precedes dissolution. He will describe the calamities which every one has seen, but will he be the nearer to the remedy? Let the historian reveal the secrets of the masters of the earth, to ward from them the conspiracy which shall fall back upon them; and what secrets do we reveal? secrets publicly printed for these ten years past in their own correspondence with the chief of the conspiracy. It is too late to attack us on that point. Those letters were printed, to the great scandal of the public, to discover the favor of the impious man with the sovereigns of the earth; and when we show this protection avenged upon the sovereigns, it is not their shame we are seeking to divulge, it is their misfortunes and those of their people that we make known; the remedy then spontaneously manifesting itself, may avert or prevent much greater evils. Such a motive is more than an equivalent to all that could induce us to be silent.

In the correspondence of the conspirators there is more than one letter which deposes against the Emperor Joseph II with all the possible evidence of such testimony, that he was initiated and had been admitted into all the mysteries of the Antichristian Conspiracy by Frederic.

In the first of these letters Voltaire announces his victory in these terms: "You have afforded me great pleasure by reducing the infinite to its real value. But here is a thing far more interesting: *Grimm assures us, that the Emperor is one of ours. That is lucky*, for the Duchess of Parma, his sister, is against us."[1]

In another letter, Voltaire, exulting in so important a conquest, writes to Frederic: "A Bohemian of great wit and Philosophy, called Grimm, has informed me that you have initiated the Emperor into our holy mysteries."[2] In a third, Voltaire, after enumerating the princes and princesses whom he reckoned among the adepts, adds these words: "You have also flattered me with the Emperor's being in the way of perdition; *that would be a good recruit for Philosophy*."[3] This alludes to a letter written by Frederic to Voltaire a few months before, in which he says, "I am setting off for Silesia, and shall meet the Emperor, who has invited me to his camp in Moravia; not to fight, as formerly, but to live as good neighbors. He is an amiable prince, and full of merit. *He likes your works and reads them as often as he can*. He is the *very reverse of superstitious*. In fine, he is an Emperor such as Germany has not for a long time seen. We neither of us like the ignorant and barbarous, but that is not a reason for exterminating them."[4]

Now that we are acquainted with Frederic's idea of a prince, *The very reverse of superstitious,* and *who reads Voltaire's works as often as he can,* his encomiums are easily understood. They truly point out an Emperor such as Germany *had not for a long time seen,* that is, an Emperor as irreligious as Frederic himself. Both the date and the last words, *but that is not a reason for exterminating them*, recalls to our mind a time when Frederic, thinking the Sophisters too daring and hasty, sought himself to repress their imprudence, lest it might overthrow the whole political system of governments. It was not yet time to employ *superior force,* or to pass the *last sentence.* The war aginst Christ then resolved on between Frederic and Joseph was not to be a war of Neros and Dioclesians; it was silently to undermine. Such was that which Joseph waged, as soon as the death of Maria Teresa left him at liberty to act. He carried it on with hypocrisy; for Joseph, as unbelieving as Frederic, wished to be looked upon as a very religious prince, and would often protest that the slightest attack on Christianity was the most distant from his ideas. During his travels through Europe he continued to take the sacraments, and perform his Easter devotions at Vienna and Naples, with that exterior piety, which could not seem to coincide with the hypocrisy of those of Voltaire at Ferney. He carried his dissimulation so far, that in passing through France he refused to call at Ferney, though very near and fully expected there by Voltaire. It is even said, that in turning away he affectedly observed, *That he could not bear to see a man, who, by calumniating religion, had given the severest blow to humanity.* What credit is to be given to this affirmation I will not pretend to decide; but certain it is, that the philosophers did nevertheless look upon Joseph as one of theirs. The flight of Voltaire was soon pardoned. It was everywhere asserted, that the Emperor's admiration had not diminished for the premier in impiety; that he would have willingly visited him, but that he had refrained through regard to his mother, *who at the solicitations of the priests had made him promise that he would not see him during his journey.*[5]

Notwithstanding his reserve and his dissimulation, the war which Joseph waged soon became one of authority and oppression, of rapine and violence; and was very nigh ending in the extermination of his own subjects. He began by the suppression of a large number of monasteries; this, we have seen, was a leading feature in Frederic's plan: he seized on a great part of the ecclesiastical property; so would Voltaire have done, for he exclaims, *But I had rather plunder them*: Joseph II tore from their cells and cloisters even to those Carmelite nuns whose extreme poverty could afford no bate to avarice, and whose angelic fervor left no room for reform. He was the first who gave to the world the public spectacle of holy virgins driven to wander into distant countries, even as far as Portugal, to seek an asylum for their piety. Innovating at pleasure in the church, he only anticipated that famous constitution of the clergy called *civil* by the Jacobin legislators, and which prepared the way to the butchery at the Carmes. The sovereign pontiff thought it incumbent on him to leave Rome and pass into Austria, and, in the capacity of common father of the faithful, personally to represent to the emperor the laws and rights of the church. Joseph II received him with respect, and permitted all that homage and public veneration to be shown to Pius VI, which his virtues and his dignity equally demanded. He did not, however, discontinue his war of oppression. He did not expel the bishops, it is true, but he gave them much trouble; for, constituting himself as it were the superior of a seminary, he would permit no lectures to be read, but by those professors whom he had chosen, and whose doctrine, like that of *Camus*, tended only to forward the grand apostacy. At length these secret persecutions and depredations gave rise to murmurs. The wearied Brabanters revolted. Since that, we have seen them call in those very Jacobins who, promising them the free exercise of their religion, and more artful than Joseph, are now consummating his work. Had they been less tormented in matters of faith by Frederic's adept, the Brabanters would have been less impatient under the yoke of Austria; had they been fraught with greater zeal and affection for the Emperor Joseph, they would have better seconded, and had more confidence in the virtues of Francis II. They would with greater force have opposed that invasion which we have seen extend to the very banks of the Danube. Should history lay the blame on Joseph, let it look back to that day when he was, by Frederic, initiated into the mysteries of Voltaire. It is the emperor *adept* that shall be found guilty of this war of extermination, which has threatened even the throne of his successors.

In the sequel of this work we shall see Joseph repenting of the war he had waged against Christ, when he beheld philosophism attacking both himself and his throne. He will then attempt, but too late, to repair his fault. He will fall a melancholy victim.

Many other sovereigns are mentioned in the correspondence of the conspirators, as having imprudently engaged in these plots. D'Alembert complaining to Voltaire of the obstacles he sometimes encountered from the public authorities, and which he terms *persecutions*, at length consoles himself by adding, "But we have on our side the Empress Catherine, the King of Prussia, the King of Denmark, the Queen of Sweden and her son, many Princes of the Empire, and all England."[6] Much about the same time Voltaire writes to the King of Prussia, "I know not what Mustapha thinks (on the immortality of the soul); my opinion is, that he does not think at all.... As for the *Empress of Russia, the Queen of Sweden your sister, the King of Poland, and Prince Gustavus* son of the Queen of Sweden, I believe that I know what they think."[7]

Voltaire effectually knew it. The letters of these sovereigns could not leave him in the dark; but had we not those letters to adduce in proof, we now see an Emperor, an Empress, a Queen, and four Kings, already enlisted under the banners of the conspirators.

In bringing to light this horrid Conspiracy, let not the historian abandon himself to false declamation, nor draw inferences still more deceptive. Let him not pretend to say to the people, Your kings have shaken off the yoke of Christ; it is but just that you should throw off that of their dominion. Such reasoning would be to blaspheme Christ, his doctrines, and his examples. The arm of vengeance is reserved to God alone. For the happiness of subjects, to preserve them from revolutions and all the horrors of rebellion, he alone can smite the apostate on the throne. Let not the Christian apostatize, but let him be subject to his lawful prince. To join revolt to impiety is not averting the scourge of heaven; it is only adding anarchy, the most terrible of all political scourges; it would not be a bar against the Sophister of impiety, but the consummation of the Conspiracy of the Sophisters of sedition against the throne and all the laws of civil society. Such was the fate of the unfortunate Brabanters when in rebellion against the Emperor Joseph. They pretended to the right of rejecting their lawful sovereign, and they are become the prey of Jacobins; they called insurrection to the aid of religon, and that religion proscribes insurrection against all lawful authority. At the time that I am now writing, the fulminating reports made to the Convention forbode those dreadful decrees which, levelling the religious worship, the privileges, and the churches of the Brabanters to the standard of the French revolution, shall punish them for their error. When therefore the historian shall report the names of those sovereigns who unfortunately were initiated, and conspired against their God, let his intention be to recal them to their religion; let him not be led away by false inferences so adverse to the peace of nations. No; let him insist on the duties which religion imposes on the people; let him teach them what they owe to Caesar and to every public authority.

Of the royal protectors all are not to be classed with Voltaire, Frederic, or Joseph. All had tasted of the impious cup of infidelity, but all did not equally wish to imbue their people with its poison.

Immense was the distance between Frederic and this Empress, in whom the conspirators placed so much confidence. Seduced by the talents and homage of their premier chief, Catherine may have owed to him her first taste for literature; she almost devoured those works which she had mistaken for masterpieces, whether in history or philosophy, totally ignorant of their being disguised solely to forward the ends of impiety. On the fallacious encomiums of the Sophisters she boldly pronounced, *That all the miracles in the world could never wipe out the alleged disgrace of having hindered the printing of the Encyclopedia.*[8] But we never see her, like Frederic (to obtain the fulsome flattery of the Sophisters) pay to impiety a degrading court. Catherine would read their works;—Frederic would circulate them, compose himself, and wish to see them devoured by the people. Frederic would propose plans for the destruction of the Christian religion, Catherine rejected all those proposed to her by Voltaire. She was tolerant by nature, Frederic only from necessity. He would have been no longer so, had his policy permitted him, in following the dictates of his hatred, to call in *a superior force* to effect the overthrow of Christianity.[9]

Nevertheless, Catherine was a royal adept; she had the secret of Voltaire, and applauded the most famous of our infidels.[10] She was even willing to entrust the heir of her crown in the hands of D'Alembert; her name constantly appears among the protecting adepts in the writings of the Sophisters, nor can the historian suppress the fact.

The claims of Christiern VII, King of Denmark, to the title of adept are also founded on his correspondence with Voltaire. Among the numerous services rendered by D'Alembert, I should not have omitted the pains he had taken to prevail on different powers and great personages to subscribe to the erection of a statue in honor of Voltaire. I could have shown the Sophister of Ferney modestly pressing D'Alembert to collect these subscriptions, and in particular that from the King of Prussia, who hardly waited their solicitations. This triumph of their chief was too desirable for the Conspirators, and Christiern VII eagerly contributed.

A first letter, with a few compliments, might not be thought sufficient to constitute an adept, but we have Voltaire's own authority for naming the King of Denmark; and beside, among those compliments we find one exactly in the style of Frederic, "You are now occupied in delivering a considerable number of men from *the yoke of the clergy, the hardest of all others;* for the duties of society are only imprinted in their heads, *and never felt in their hearts. It is well worth while to be revenged of the barbarians.*"[11] Unfortunat Monarchs! Such was the language held to Marie Antoinette, in the days of her prosperity, by those corruptors. But in her misfortunes, when she witnessed the loyalty and the sensibility of those *barbarians* at the Thuileries, she exclaimed, "Alas! how we have been deceived! We now plainly see how much the clergy distinguish themselves among the faithful subjects of the king."[12] May the king that is led away by Philosophism never be reduced to the same experiment; may he learn at least from one revolution, that there is a yoke more *hard* and terrible than that of the clergy, which Voltaire his master had taught him to calumniate.

It is our duty to add, that with regard to this prince, as well as to many others who were seduced by the Sophisters, the conspirators had taken advantage of their youth. At that period of life, the writings of Voltaire could easily make impression on men who were not, because they were kings, better versed than other people in what they had not learned; nor were they able to discriminate truth from error, in objects where the want of knowledge is more to be dreaded than inclination or the passions.

At the time of his journey into France Christiern was but seventeen years of age; but even then, young as he was, he had, to use D'Alembert's expression, *the courage to say at Fontainebleau* that Voltaire *had taught him to think.*[13] Men about the court of Lewis XV, of a different way of thinking, wished to hinder his young majesty from learning to think still more like Voltaire, and from seeing in Paris the adepts or most celebrated of his disciples. These however obtained admission; and to judge how well they understood improving their opportunity, we need only observe D'Alembert writing to Voltaire, "I had seen that prince at his own apartments, together with several of your friends. He spoke much about you, *of the services that your works had rendered, of the prejudices you had rooted out,* and of the enemies that *your liberty in thinking* had made you. You easily guess what my answers were."[14] D'Alembert has a second interview, and again writes, "The King of Denmark scarce spoke to me but of you.-----I can assure you, he had rather have seen you at Paris, than all the entertainments with which they have surfeited him."[15] This conversation had been but of short duration; but D'Alembert made amends in a discourse on Philosophy which he pronounced at the academy, in presence of the young monarch. Numerous were the adepts who were present, and they loudly applauded; the youthful monarch joined in the applause. Such, in short, is the opinion he carries away with him of that pretended Philosophy, (thanks to D'Alembert's new lectures!) that no sooner is he informed of a statue to be erected to the premier chief of the conspirators, than he sends a very *handsome subscription*, for which Voltaire acknowledges himself to be indebted to the lessons of the academical adept.[16] How much these lessons have since been forgotten by Christiern VII, I cannot pretend to say. Events have taken place since his Danish Majesty had learned *to think* from Voltaire, sufficient to have given him a very different opinion of the *services* that the WORKS of his master have rendered to empires.

Similar artifices were made use of with regard to Gustavus, King of Sweden. That prince also came to Paris, to receive the homage and lessons of the self-created philosophy. He was as yet but Prince Royal, when, already extolling him as one whose protection was insured to the Sect, D'Alembert writes to Voltaire, "You love REASON AND LIBERTY, my dear brother; and one can hardly love one without the other. Well then, I here present to you a *worthy republican philosopher,* who who will talk PHILOSOPHY and LIBERTY with you. It is Mr. Jennings, chamberlain to the King of Sweden.—He has compliments to pay you from the *Queen of Sweden and the Prince Royal, who in the North* PROTECT *that philosophy* so ill received by the princes in the South. Mr. Jennings will inform you of the *progress that* REASON *is making in Sweden* under those happy auspices."[17]

At the time that D'Alembert was writing this letter, Gustavus, who was soon to restore royalty to the rights it had lost long since in Sweden, was no doubt ignorant that those great men, which he so much protected, were *Philosophers* superlatively *republican*. He was equally blind to the ultimate (and to him fatal) fruit of this conspiring Philosophy, when on his accession to the throne he wrote to their premier chief, "I daily pray the Being of beings, that he may prolong your days, so precious to humanity, and so necessary to the progress of REASON and TRUE PHILOSOPHY."[18]

The prayer of Gustavus was heard; the days of Voltaire were prolonged; but he who was suddenly to shorten the days of Gustavus was born; he, grasping the dagger, was soon to sally forth from the occult school of Voltaire. For the instruction of kings, let the historian compare the gradual steps of this unfortunate prince, and those of the adept and assassin.

Ulrica of Brandenbourg had been initiated into the mysteries of the Sophisters by Voltaire himself. So far from rejecting his principles, she did not even feel herself offended at the declaration of a passion which he was daring enough to express.[19] When Queen of Sweden, she more than once pressed the Sophister to come and end his days near her person.[20] She knew no means of giving a stronger proof of her staunchness in the principles she had received, than, during Voltaire's first residence at Berlin, to make the infant king imbibe them with his milk. She initiated Gustavus, and wished to be the mother of the Sophister as well as of the king; and indeed we constantly see

THE ANTICHRISTIAN CONSPIRACY. 101

both the mother and the son ranking together among the adepts of whom the Sophisters thought themselves the most secure. Such then was the gradation of the unfortunate Gustavus. Voltaire initiated Ulrica, and Ulrica initiated her son.

On the other hand, Voltaire initiated Condorcet, and Condorcet, seated in the club of the Jacobins, initiated Ankestron. A pupil of Voltaire, Ulrica, teaches her son to ridicule the mysteries and scoff at the altars of Christ. Condorcet also, a disciple of Voltaire, teaches Ankestron to scoff at the throne and sport with the lives of kings.

When public report announced that Gustavus III was to command in chief the confederate armies against the French revolution, Condorcet and Ankestron were members of the great club; and the great club resounded with the cry of, Deliver the earth from kings! Gustavus was doomed for the first victim, and Ankestron offers himself for the first executioner. He leaves Paris and Gustavus falls under his hand.[21]

The Jacobins had just celebrated the apotheosis of Voltaire, they also celebrate that of Ankestron.

Voltaire had taught the Jacobins that *the first of kings was a successful soldier:* they teach Ankestron, that the first hero was the assassin of kings; and they placed his bust beside that of Brutus.

Kings had subscribed to the erection of a statue to Voltaire; the Jacobins erect one to Ankestron.

Lastly, Voltaire's correspondence shows Poniatowski, King of Poland, to have been of the number of the protecting adepts. That king had known our Philosophers in Paris, and was one day to fall a victim to Philosophism! He had done homage to their chief, and written to him, "M. de Voltaire, every contemporary of a man like you, who knows how to read, who has travelled, and has not been acquainted with you, must feel himself unhappy; you might be allowed to say, *Nations shall pray, that kings may read me.*"[22] Now, when the king has seen men, who, like himself, had read and cried up the works of Voltaire, attempting in Poland the revolution they had wrought in France; when, a victim of that revolution, he has seen his sceptre vanish from his hand, how different must be his prayer? Does he not regret that nations have known Voltaire, or that kings have ever read his works? Those days which D'Alembert had foretold, and which he longed to see, are at length come, and that without being foreseen by the royal adepts. When the misfortunes of religion shall fall back upon them, let them read what D'Alembert says to Voltaire, "Your former illustrious protector (the King of Prussia) began the dance; the King of Sweden led it on; Catherine imitates them, and bids fair to outdo them both. How I should enjoy seeing the string run off in my time."[23] And indeed the string has begun to run with a vengeance. Gustavus, King of Sweden, dies by the dagger; Lewis XVI, King of France, on the scaffold; Lewis the XVII by poison: Poniatowski is dethroned:[24] the Stadtholder is driven from his country; and the adepts, disciples of D'Alembert and his school, laugh as he would have done himself at those sovereigns who, protecting the impious in their conspiracy against the altar, had not been able to foresee that the disciples of those same conspirators would conspire against their thrones.

These reflections anticipate, contrary to my intention, what I have to unfold in the second conspiracy; but such is the union of the Sophister of Impiety with the Sophister of Rebellion, that it is hard to separate the progress of the one from the ravages of the other. It is the intimacy of this union, which has forced us to lay before the eyes of the protecting monarchs one of the most important lessons that history could produce.

I cannot conclude this chapter without remarking, that among the kings of the North, in whose protection the Sophisters so often exult, the name of his Britannic Majesty is not so much as mentioned. This silence of the conspirators is above all the encomiums they could have bestowed. Had they sought a king beloved by his subjects, and deservedly so; had they sought, I say, a king good, just, compassionate, beneficent, zealous to maintain the liberty of the laws and the happiness of his empire, then George III might have been extolled as the Solomon of the North, he might have been their Marcus Aurelius, or Antoninus. They found him too wise to coalesce with vile conspirators who knew no merit but impiety, and hence the true cause of their silence. It is an honour for a prince to be omitted in their records, who in this terrible revolution has been so conspicuous by his activity in stopping its progress, and by his noble generosity in relieving its victims.

It is also a justice which the historian owes to the kings of the South, to say, that the conspirators, so far from ranking them among their adepts, complained that they had not yet attained to the height of their sophisticated Philosophy.

1. To D'Alembert, 28 Oct. 1769, Vol. 69, Let. 13, P. 27.
2. To Frederic, Nov. 1769, Vol. 65, Let. 162. P. 383.
3. To Frederic, 21 Nov. 1770, Vol. 65, Let. 181. P. 432.
4. From Frederic, 18 Aug. 1770, Vol. 65, Let. 175, P. 416.
5. See note to the letter of the Count de Touraille, 6 Aug. 1777, Vol. 63, P. 387.
6. To D'Alembert, 23 Nov. 1770, Vol. 69, Let. 47, P. 83.
7. To Frederic, 21 Nov. 1770, Vol. 65. Let. 181, P. 432.
8. From Catherine, 22 Aug. 1765, Vol. 67, Let. 3, P. 8.
9. Those who, as men of literature, shall criticize the correspondence of this Empress, will find an amazing difference between her manner and that of the King of Prussia. The former is that of a woman of wit, who often plays upon Voltaire in the most agreeable manner. With her light style and full of taste, she never forgets her dignity; she at least will not be seen to degrade herself to the gross dialect of scurrility and blasphemy; while Frederick in his, truly the pedantic Sophister, will be as void of shame in his impiety, as he is of dignity in his encomiums. When Voltaire wrote to Catherine, "We are three, Diderot, D'Alembert, and myself, who raise altars to you;" (22 *Dec.* 1766, *Vol.* 67, *Let.* 8, *P.* 17) she answers, "Pray leave me, if you please, on earth; there I shall be more near at hand to receive your letters and those of your

friends." (9 Jan. 1767, Let. 9. P. 18.)— Nothing so perfectly French can be found in Frederic's; we only have to regret, that it was addressed to a set of infidels. Catherine wrote Voltaire's own language in perfect purity, while Frederic could have had little pretensions to the hero, had he not handled his sword better than his pen.

10. From Catherine, 26 Sept. 1773, Vol. 67, Let. 129, P. 280, and 7 Jan. 1774, Let. 134, P. 285.
11. From Christiern, 15 Dec. 1770, Vol. 67, Let. 44, P. 371.
12. I heard this anecdote in the midst of the revolution; and such expressions were necesssary to shew that she was recovered from those prejudices she had imbibed against the clergy, and which appeared to have redoubled after the second journey which her brother made to Versailles.
13. From D'Alembert, 12 Nov. 1768, Vol. 68, Let. 239, P. 494.
14. From D'Alembert, 6 Dec. 1768, Vol. 68, Let. 240, P. 496.
15. From D'Alembert, 17 Dec. 1768, Let. 242, P. 496.
16. To D'Alembert, 5 Nov. 1770, Vol. 69, Let. 46. P. 81.
17. From D'Alembert, 19 Jan. 1769, Vol. 69, Let. 3, P. 7.
18. From Gustavus, 10 Jan. 1772, Vol. 67, Let. 51, P. 379.
19. It was for this princess that Voltaire composed the Madrigal *Souvent un peu de Vérité*.
20. Her letters to Voltaire, anno 1743 and 1751, Vol. 67.
21. Journal of Fontenai.
22. From Stanislaus, 21 Feb. 1767, Vol. 67, Let. 41, P. 367.
23. From D'Alembert, 2 Oct. 1762, Vol. 68, Let. 107, P. 221.
24. And since the publication of the first edition of this volume is dead. He died at Petersburg, Feb. 11, 1798.

CHAP. XIII.

Second Class of Protectors—Princes and Princesses

IN the second class of protecting adepts, I shall comprehend those persons who, without being on the throne, enjoy a power over the people nearly equal to that of kings, and whose authority and example, adding to the means of the conspirators, gave them reason to hope that they had not sworn in vain the destruction of the Christian religion.

In this class of protectors Voltaire particularly mentions the *Landgrave of Hesse Cassel*. The care with which D'Alembert had chosen the professor of history whom we have already mentioned, shows how much the Sophister abused his confidence. He was much imposed upon when he confided in the philosophy of Voltaire; he permitted him in some sort to direct his studies, and he could hardly have fallen into the hands of a more perfidious tutor. A letter, dated the 25th Aug. 1766, will suffice to show in what sources the august pupil was directed to seek lessons of wisdom. "Your Serene Highnesss has shown," the corruptor writes, "a desire of seeing some new productions worthy your attention. There is one that has just made its appearance, entitled *The Necessary Collection*. You will find there, in particular, a work of Lord Bolingbroke's, which appears to me one of the most forcible things ever written against superstition. I believe it is to be found at Frankfort; but I have a copy of it sewed, which I will send to your Highness, if agreeable."[1]

For a prince who really was desirous of instruction, what lessons were to be found in this collection! The name of Bolingbroke does not sufficiently denote how far they tended to pervert his religion; but we know that Voltaire often published, under that name, works far more impious than those of the English philosopher; and that he was the author of several of those which he particularly recommended in that collection.

Left to himself for the solution of doubts occasioned by such readings, and unfortunately prejudiced against those who might have solved them, he threw himself headlong into studies which he had mistaken for those of truth, and of the most transcendent philosophy. When he could receive these lessons from Voltaire himself, the illusion was so great, that his Highness would flatter himself, and really believe that he had found a means of soaring far above the vulgar. He would lament the absence which deprived him of the lessons of his master, and, thinking himself under real obligations, would say to him, "I left

Ferney with the greatest regret.... I am delighted to find that you approve of my way of thinking. I try as much as possible to divest myself of all prejudices; and if in that I differ in opinion from the vulgar, it is to my conversation with you, and to the perusal of your works, that I am solely indebted for it."[2]

That he might give some proof of his proficiency in the school of Philosophism, the illustrious adept was wont to impart to his master the new discoveries he had made, and which he looked upon as unanswerable objections against the sacred writ. "I have been making," he would write to his hero, "for some time past reflections on Moses, and on some of the historians of the New Testament, to me apparently just. Might not Moses be a natural child of Pharoah's daughter, whom that princess caused to be brought up? It is not credible that the daughter of a king should have taken such care of a Hebrew child, whose nation was so much abhorred by the Egyptians."[3] Voltaire could easily have solved such a doubt, by making his pupil observe that he was gratuitously slandering the fair sex, whose benevolence and tenderness would readily lead them to take compassion on a child exposed to such danger. Many would naturally do what Pharoah's daughter did, and would show it still greater care and attention, as the child was exposed to national enmities. Had Voltaire wished to give his illustrious pupil the rules of sound criticism, he would have hinted, that to destroy a fact both simple and natural, his Highness supposed one truly incredible: a princess who wishes to give her child a brilliant education, and begins by exposing it to be drowned, for the pleasure of going to seek it on the banks of the Nile at a given time; an Egyptian princess, who, loving her child, and knowing how much the Egyptians hated the Israelites, causes this child to be suckled by an Israelite, leaves it to believe that it was born of that nation, which its mother detests; and afterwards, to render this child odious to the Egyptians, persuades them of the same; a mystery still more singular is, that the birth of an infant who became the man the most tremendous to the Egyptians has always remained a secret; that the whole court of Pharoah obstinately believe him to be an Israelite, and that at a time when, to have declared Moses an Egyptian, would have sufficed to destroy his power with the Israelites and to have saved Egypt. Such arguments might have been used by Voltaire to make his Highness sensible of the impropriety, in sound criticism, of combating a fact both simple and natural by suppositions the most distant from probability. But such suppositions were consonant with that hatred which Voltaire bore to Moses and the sacred writ; he was better pleased to see his disciples ignorantly launching into infidelity, than to teach them the rules of sound criticism.

Voltaire again applauds his adept when his Highness pretends that the *brazen serpent*, isolated on the mountain, *did not a little resemble the god Esculapius* in the temple of Epidaurus, holding a stick in one hand and a serpent in the other, with a dog at his feet; that the cherubim, displaying their wings over the ark, *were not unlike the sphinx* with the woman's head, the four claws, body, and tail of a lion; that *the twelve oxen standing under the brazen sea,* and bearing that enormous vessel, twelve cubits in breadth and five in height, filled with water for the ablutions of the Israelites, bore a strong resemblance to the god Apis, or to the ox elevated on the altar and beholding all Egypt at its feet.[4]

His Highness concludes, that Moses appeared to have introduced among the Jews many ceremonies which he had taken from the Egyptians.[5] The historian will at least remark, that it would have been easy for the conspirators to have undeceived an adept who sought only to be instructed. While we lament his Highness having been the dupe to such masters, we are in justice obliged to show how frankly he sought the truth, when he continues writing to Voltaire: "As to what regards the New Testament, there are stories in it, of which *I should wish to be better informed*. I cannot understand the massacre of the innocents. How could King Herod have ordered all those infants to be slain, not having the power of life and death, as we see in the history of the Passion, where we find it was Pontius Pilate, governor of the Romans, who condemned Jesus Christ to death."[6]

Had he referred to the proper sources of history, had he consulted any other but that professor of history which D'Alembert had given him, or any other masters than those vain Sophisters, this prince, who wished for and deserved better information, would have seen this slight difficulty vanish from before his eyes. He would have learned, that Herod of *Ascalon*, surnamed the *Great*, and who might have been more properly called the ferocious, he who ordered the massacre of the innocents, was king of all Judea and of Jerusalem, and is not the person mentioned in the Passion. He would have further learned, that the latter was Herod *Antipas*, who had only been able to obtain of the Romans one-third part of his father's dominions, and being simply Tetrarch of Galilee, had not the same power over the other provinces. Hence there can be little room for surprise at his not exercising the power of life and death in Jerusalem, though we see Pilate inviting him to exercise that right by sending Jesus Christ before him, as he had before tried and sentenced St. John the Baptist.

As to the ferocious Herod of *Ascalon*, his Highness would have learned, that this prototype of Nero had caused the infants at Bethlehem to be slain by the same power with which he had murdered Aristobulus and Hircanus, the one the brother, the other an octagenarian, and grand-father to the queen; by the same power also did he put to death Marianne his queen and her two children; Sohemus his confidant, and numbers of his friends and nobles of his court, who had the misfortune to displease him. Reading of these numerous murders, of such unheard-of tyranny, and particularly that this Herod of *Ascalon*, on the point of death, and fearing lest the day of his decease should prove a day of public rejoicing, had caused all the chiefs of the Jews to be shut up in the Circus, commanding they should be massacred at the moment he himself expired; such lectures, I say, could have left little doubt in the mind of the illustrious adept, whether this Herod exercised the right of life and death. He would not then have suspected the Evangelists of forging a fact like that of the massacre of the innocents; a fact so recent, that many Jews then living had been witnesses to it. He would have reflected, that impostors would not expose themselves to be so easily discovered, or in so public a manner shamed; and all his objections against this massacre of the innocents would not have availed against his faith in the Gospel.

But he was nurtured in the same objections with his master; he studied the sacred writ through the same medium; and Voltaire, who had fallen into thousands of the grossest errors on those sacred writings, carefully avoided referring his disciples to those answers which he had received from the religious writers.[7]

Though we blend these slight discussions with our memoirs, we will not add to the bitterness with which so many princes, who have been seduced by these impious chiefs of the Sophisters, now reproach themselves. We will not say to them, "With what strange blindness were you smitten? It was your duty to study the sacred writings, to learn how to become better, and to render your subjects more happy; and you have debased yourselves by entering the lists with the conspirators, that like them you may dispute against Christ and his prophets. If doubts arise on religion, why appeal to those who have sworn its ruin. The day will come when the God of the Christians shall raise doubts on your rights, and will refer your subjects to the Jacobins for their solution. They are in your dominions, seated in your palaces ready to applaud, as Voltaire did, your objections against Christ and his prophets. Answer to their sword the objections they make to your laws." Let us forbear these reflections; let us simply remark, as history must, how very unfortunate these princes must have been, who, seeking instruction, had applied to men whose sole object was to make them efficient to the destruction of the altar, as the first step towards the overthrow of their thrones.

In the number of the protecting adepts history will find itself necessitated to insert the names of many princes whose states at this present moment feel the sweets of this new Philosophy. In the account given by D'Alembert to Voltaire of those foreign princes who would not travel through France without doing homage to the conspiring Sophisters, we see him extol the *Prince of Brunswick* as deserving *the kindest welcome*, and particularly so, when put in competition with the *Prince of Deux Ponts*, who only protects *Freron and such like rabble*, that is to say religious authors.[8] The Jacobin army at this day proves which of those two princes was most mistaken in his protection. It will be still better seen when in these memoirs we come to treat of the last and deepest conspiracy of the Jacobins.

To this prince we must add *Louis Eugene Duke of Wirtemberg*, and *Louis Prince of Wirtemberg*, who both equally gloried in the lessons they received from Voltaire. The former writes to him, "When at Ferney I think myself a greater philosopher than Socrates himself."[9] The latter, not content with encomiums on the premier chief, petitions for the most licentious and the most impious work Voltaire had ever penned, I mean the poem of Joan D'Arc, or the Maid of Orleans.

Charles Theodore, Elector Palatine, would at one time solicit the impious Sophister for the same master-piece of obscenity, or for philosophic lectures;

at another, he would press and conjure him to repair to Manheim, that he might there receive his lectures anew.[10]

Even those adepts who, through modesty, should have shrunk back at the very name of such a production, even the *Princess Anhalt-Zerbst*, sends thanks to the author, who had been impudent enough to send her a present more worthy of Aretine.[11]

The historian cannot but remark the eagerness of these mighty adepts for so profligate a work, as an awful testimony what charms depravity of morals gave to the productions of the Sophisters. The empire of the conspirators will cause less surprise when we reflect how prevalent their Sophisms became over the mind when they had once tainted and perverted the heart. This is a reflection we reluctantly make; but it is too apposite to the history of Philosophism, and to the cause and progress of the Antichristian Conspiracy, to be suppressed. We know the reverence due to great names, but we cannot on that consideration conceal the truth. Let those look to it whose shame is brought to the light; while longer to conceal it would be to betray at once their own interests, that of their people, the safety of their thrones, and that of the altar.

Her Highness Wilhelmina, *Margravine of Bareith*, ranking among the protecting adepts, affords to the historian the opportunity of laying open a new cause of the progress of the Antichristian Sophisters, of the weight they acquired from the vanity of their school, and from their pretensions to a superiority of light above the vulgar.

It is far from being the lot of all men to argue with equal success on religious or philosophical topics. Without being wanting in the respect due to that precious half of mankind, we may observe in general, I think, that women are not born with minds congenial with philosophy, metaphysics, or divinity. Nature has compensated this want of research and meditation by the art of embellishing virtue by that sweetness and vivacity of sentiment which often proves a surer guide than all our reasonings. They do the good peculiarly allotted to them better than we do.—Their homes, their children, are their real empires, that of their lessons lie in the charm of example, more efficacious than all our syllogisms. But the female Sophister, philosophizing like a man, is either a prodigy or a monster; and prodigies are not common. The daughter of Necker, the wife of Roland, as well as Mesdames du Deffant, D'Espinasse, Geofrin, and such like Parisian adepts, in spite of all their pretensions to wit, can lay no claim to the exception. If the reader is indignant when he finds the name of the Margravine of Bareith on the same line, let his indignation fall upon the man who inspired her with such pretensions. Let an opinion be formed of the masters, by the tone she assumed with them to insure their approbation. The following is a specimen of the style of this illlustrious adept, aping the principles and the jests of Voltaire, in order to captivate his approbation at the expence of St. Paul.

"Sister Guillemetta to Brother Voltaire, greetings.—I received your consoling epistle. I swear by my favorite oath, that it has edified me infinitely more than that of St. Paul to Dame Elect. The latter threw me into a certain drowsiness that had the effect of opium, and hindered me from perceiving the beauties of it. Yours had a contrary effect; it drew me from my lethargy, and put all my vital spirits in motion again."[12]

We have no knowledge of any Epistle of St. Paul to Dame Elect; but Sister Guillemetta, like Voltaire, burlesquing what she had, as well as what she had not read, means no doubt to speak of St. John's Epistle to Electa. This contains no other compliment but that of an apostle applauding the piety of a mother, who rears her children in the way of life, exhorting her charity, and guarding her against the discourse and schools of seducers. It is rather unfortunate, that such lessons should have been opium for the illustrious adept. It is probable that Voltaire would have found a dose in the following letter, had it come from any other hand but that of Sister Guillemetta. We will however copy it, as making an epoch in the annals of Philosophism. We shall see in it the female adept attempting to give lessons to Voltaire himself, anticipating Helvetius by mere dint of genius, and without perceiving it copying Epicurus. Before she commences, Sister Guillemetta assures Voltaire of the friendship of the Margrave, and had carefully invoked the *Genius of Bayle*.[13] One day she thought herself inspired with the whole of it, and immediately writes to *Brother Voltaire*, "God, you say (in the Poem of the Law of Nature), has bestowed on all men justice and conscience to warn them, as he has given them all what is needful. As God has bestowed on man justice and conscience, these two virtues must be innate in man, and become an attribute of his existence. Hence it necessarily follows, that man must act in consequence, and that he cannot be just or unjust, or without remorse, being unable to combat an instinct annexed to his essence. Experience proves the contrary. If justice was an attribute of our being, chicane would be banished. Your counsellors in Parliament would not lose their time as they do, in disturbing all France about a morsel of bread given or not. The Jesuits and the Jansenists would equally confess their ignorance in point of doctrine... Virtue is barely accidental... Aversion to pain and love of pleasure have induced men to become just---Disorder can beget nothing but pain. Quiet is the parent of pleasure, I have made the human heart my particular study, and I draw my conclusions on what has been, from what I see."[14]

There is extant a play intitled, *Divinity dwindled into a Distaff*. This letter of her Highness the Margravine of Bareith, dwindled into Sister Guillemetta, may perhaps furnish the same idea for Philosophy. But, consigning over the female Socrates to the Molieres of the day, the historian will draw from the errors of this female adept a more serious lesson on the progress of the Antichristian Conspiracy. He will behold a new cause in the mortifying limits of the human intellect, and the vanity of its pretensions, which in certain adepts seem precisely to expand itself, in as much as nature had, from the weakness of their understanding, seemed naturally to insinuate modesty and humility.

Sister Guillemetta fears for liberty, if it be true that God has given to man a conscience, the necessary sense of right and wrong. She was ignorant then, that man, with the eyes that God has given him to see and know his road, is nevertheless free to go where he pleases. She has made a particular study of the human heart, and she has not learned, that man often sees what is best, but will do the worst! She thinks herself in the school of Socrates; and, with Epicurus, she only sees the *aversion of pain and the love of pleasure*, as the principle of justice and virtue. She tells us, in short, probably without even perceiving it, that if chicane is not banished, it is because our attornies have not a sufficient aversion to indigence; that if our vestals are not all chaste, it is because they do not sufficiently love pleasure; and after that, in presence of *her Highness*, Parliaments, Jesuits, Jansenists, and undoubtedly the whole Sorbonne, with the whole faculty of divinity, must confess their ignorance *in point of doctrine*.

With more genius, but less confidence in his own lights, Frederic William, Prince Royal of Prussia, presents us with quite another species of adept. Indefatigable in the field of victory, he dares not answer for himself: he knows what he could wish to believe, but not what he ought to believe; he fears to lose himself in reasoning. His soul repeats that he must be immortal; he fears her voice misleads him, and Voltaire is to decide for him. When in the field of Mars, he has the confidence and activity of a hero; but when he is to reflect on futurity, he has all the modesty and the humility of a disciple, almost the unconcern of a sceptic. The authority of his master is to save him the trouble of research, and that master is Voltaire. "Since I have taken the liberty of conversing with you, he respectuously writes, suffer me to ask, for my own instruction only, whether as you advance in years you find no alteration necessary in your ideas on the nature of the soul—I don't like to bewilder myself in metaphysical reasonings; but I could wish not to die entirely, and that such a genius as yours were not to be annihilated."[15]

Like a man who can assume every tone, Voltaire answered, "The King of Prussia's family is much in the right, not to consent to the annihilation of his soul.---It is true, that it is not well known what a soul is, as nobody has ever seen one. All that we know is, that the eternal Master of nature has endowed us with the faculty of feeling and knowing virtue. That this faculty survives us after our death, is not demonstrated; but then the contrary is not better proved.---There are none but quacks who pretend to be certain; we know nothing of the first principles. Doubt is not an agreeable state, but certainty is a ridiculous one."[16]

I know not what effect this letter had on the serene and respectful disciple; but we see the premier chief varying his means of power over his princely adepts, as much as he did over the citizens of Haarlem. When the King, Frederic, wrote to him in so resolute a tone, *man once dead, there is nothing left*; he takes care not to reply, that certainty is *a ridiculous state*, that *quacks only are certain*. No; Frederic, King of Prussia, is always the first of philosophic kings.[17] And a week after, Frederic, Prince Royal, only wishes to be confirmed on the immortality of his soul; then it is, that, notwithstanding all the troubles and disquietudes of Scepticism, the dubitation of the sceptic is the only rational state for the true Philosopher. Such a state will suffice, as he then beholds his adepts no longer belonging to the religion of Christ, and that is sufficient for his plans. He will leave the king materialist, and resolute in his opinions, notwithstanding his own irresolution and uncertainty, by encomiums and admiration. He leaves Eugene of Wirtemberg in astonishment at the master he coincides with in opinion. Wilhelmina of Bareith, more daring than her master, is permitted to argue. He cuts short, and threatens with ridicule and quackery, the humble adept who seeks to reclaim and allay the ire of his master. To one he dictates his principles; to another he peremptorily declares that man is condemned to the total ignorace of the *first principles*; and he is not the less the idol of the astonished Princes. He does not the less transform them into the protectors of his school and of the conspirators; and such is the success with which he flatters himself, that, writing to his dear Count D'Argental, he says, "At present there is not a German prince who is not a Philosopher;"[18] that is to say, the Philosophist of impiety! There certainly are exceptions to be made from such an assertion; but it will prove at least how much these abettors of impiety flattered themselves with the progress they were making among sovereigns and princes,—and to whom impiety was one day to prove so fatal!

1. Vol. 66, Let. 63, P. 408.
2. To the Landgrave of Hesse Cassel, 9 Sept. 1766, Vol. 66, Let. 64, P. 109.
3. Ibid. 1 Nov. 1766, Let. 65, Page 411.
4. Ibid. 1 Nov. 1766.
5. Ibid.
6. Ibid.
7. See the errors of Voltaire in the Letters of some Portuguese Jews.
8. From D'Alembert, 25 June, 1766, Vol. 68, Let. 185, P. 396.
9. From Duke of Wirtemberg, 1 Feb. 1763, Vol. 66, Let. 43, P. 380.
10. The 20 Oct. and 29 Dec. 1754, Vol. 67, Let. 15 and 16, P. 336-7.
11. From the Princess Anhalt-Zerbst, 25 May 1751, Vol. 67, Let. 9, P. 329, and April 1762, Let. 35, P. 360.
12. 25 Dec. 1751, Vol. 66, Let. 7, P. 322.
13. 12 Juin, 1752, Vol. 66, Let. 12, P. 330.
14. 1 Nov. 1752, vol. 66, Let. 13, P. 331.
15. 12 Nov. 1770, Vol. 66, Let. 69, P. 416.
16. 28 Nov. 1770, Vol. 66, Let. 70, P. 417.
17. From Frederic, 30 Oct. 1770, Vol. 65, Let. 180, P. 429, and to Fred. 21 Nov. 1770, P. 433.
18. To the Count D'Argental, 26 Sept. 1766, Vol. 59, Let. 270, P. 480; and this is written as a proof of the great success the distribution of bad books had had in that unfortunate country.—*See above, Page* 69.

CHAP. XIV.

Third Class of Protectors.—Ministers, Noblemen and Magistrates.

It was in France that Philosophism had taken all the forms of a true Conspiracy; and it was in France also, that it had made its greatest ravages among the rich and powerful. It had not gained the throne of Bourbon as it had many of the northern thrones; but it would be in vain for history to dissimulate, that Lewis XV, without being of the Conspiracy, powerfully helped the Antichristian Conspirators. He never had the misfortune of losing his faith; he even loved religion; but during the last thirty-five years of his life, he so little practised it, the dissoluteness of his morals and the public triumph of his courtezans answered so little to the title of His Most Christian Majesty, that he might almost as well have been a disciple of Mahomet.

Sovereigns are not sufficiently aware of the evils they draw on themselves by swerving from morality. Some have supported religion only as a curb on their subjects; but woe be to them who only view it in that light. In vain shall they preserve its tenets in their hearts; it is their example that must uphold it. Next to the example of the clergy, that of kings is the most necessary to restrain the people. When religion is used only as a policy, the vilest of the populace will soon perceive it; they will look upon it as a weapon used against them, and sooner or later they will break it, and your power vanishes. If without morals you pretend to religion, the people will also think themselves religious in their profligacy; and how often has it been repeated, that laws without morals are a mere phantom? But the day will come when the people, thinking themselves more consequent, will throw aside both morals and tenets, and then where shall be your curb?

Such were the discourses often held by the Christian orators in presence of Lewis XV. He without morals was soon surrounded by ministers destitute of faith, who could have seldomer deceived him, had his love for religion been stimulated by practice. After the death of the Cardinal de Fleury some are to be found, the Marechal de Belleisle and Mr. de Bertin for example, who are not to be confounded in that class of adepts; but then we successively find near his person Mr. Amelot in the foreign department, Mr. D'Argenson in the same; the Duke de Choiseul, de Praslin and Mr. de Malesherbes, also the Marquise de Pompadour as long as she lived, and all these were intimately

THE ANTICHRISTIAN CONSPIRACY.

connected with Voltaire, and initiated in his Conspiracy. We have seen him make application to *Mr. Amelot* on the destruction of the clergy. This minister had sufficient confidence in Voltaire to intrust him with a secret and important mission to the King of Prussia; and Voltaire, in return, does not conceal from him the use he had made of his mission against the church. He confided no less in that *Duke de Praslin*, to whom he had sent his memorial on the tithes, in hopes of depriving the clergy of the greatest part of their sustenance.[1] This confidence from the premier chief sufficiently denotes the sentiments of those men to whom he sent his plans for execution.

A minister whose assiduity in corresponding with Voltaire indicates more clearly their perfect coincidence with each other, was the *Marquis D'Argenson*, whom we have already noticed tracing the plan for the destruction of the religious orders. It was he who first protected Voltaire at Court and with the Marquise de Pompadour; he was also one of the most impious of his disciples; and to him it is that Voltaire writes constantly, as to one of the adepts with whom he was most intimate. In fact, he appears more resolute in his antireligious opinions than his master; his Philosophism coincided more with that of the King of Prussia's; for he was also convinced that he was not two-fold, and that he had nothing to fear or hope for, when once his body should rest in eternal sleep.[2]

More zealous for the reign of impiety, and more active than the Marquis D'Argenson, the *Duke de Choiseul* better knew and more powerfully seconded the secrets of Voltaire. We have already seen him extolling this great protector in his quarrels with the Sorbonne; we have already seen why this Duke, adopting and pressing the execution of D'Argenson's plans against the religious orders, began by that of the Jesuits. It would be useless to dwell long on this minister; his impiety is too well authenticated.

Thus did this series of Antichristian ministers partially anticipate the Jacobins in the overthrow of the altar. It was to the man who was one day to see that very revolution in all its horrors, and at length fall a victim to it, that these impious chiefs pay their greatest homage; it was to him they were chiefly indebted: and this protector of the Conspiracy against his God, was *Malesherbes*. This name, I am aware, will recal to mind many moral virtues, it will recal his benevolence when alleviating the rigor of the prisons, when remedying the abuse of the *Lettres de Cachet*; but France shall, nevertheless, demand of him her temples that have been destroyed; for it was he who above all other ministers abused his authority to establish the reign of impiety in France. D'Alembert, who knew him well, always vouches for his reluctantly executing the *superior orders* issued in favor of religion, and for his favoring Philosophism whenever circumstances would permit; and unfortunately he knew but too well how to avail himself of circumstances. By his office he particularly presided over the laws relative to the press; but with a single word he effaced all distinctions in books, whether impious, religious, or seditious; he declared them all the be a *mere object of commerce*.

Let politicians of other nations argue on the liberty of the press in consequence of what experience has taught them in their own countries; but it is an incontrovertible fact, that France owes the misfortunes of the revolution to the great abuse of the press, and to an actual inundation of bad books at first only impious, but latterly both impious and seditious. There were also many causes peculiar to France which rendered the abuse of the press more fatal than elsewhere.

Without pretending to raise the merit of the French writers, it may be observed (and I have often heard foreigners repeat it) that there is a certain clearness, process, and method, peculiar to them, which by putting our French books more within the reach of the generality of readers, makes them in some sort more popular and thence more dangerous when bad.

Our frivolousness may be a failing; but that failing made a book more sought for in France than would the profoundest meditations of an Englishman. Neither truth nor error could please a Frenchman when latent; he likes to see clearly; epigram, sarcasm, and all what may be called wit, is what he delights in. Even blasphemy, elegantly spoken, will not displease a nation unhappily gifted with the talent of laughing on the most serious subjects, and who will pardon every failing in him who can divert them. It was to this unfortunate taste that the impious writings of Voltaire owed their chief success.

Whatever may be the reason, the English also have their books against the Christian religion; they have their Collins, their Hobbes, their Woolstons, and many others, among whom is to be found, in substance, all that our French Sophisters have only repeated after their way, that is to say, with that art which adapts every thing to the most vulgar minds. In England Hobbes and Collins are almost forgotten or unknown. Bolingbroke and other authors of the same class are little read, though of greater merit as literary men, by a people who knows how to occupy itself with other things. In France, from the idle Marquis or Countess to the attorney's clerk, or even to the petty citizen, who had far other occupations, these impious productions, and particularly Voltaire's, were not only read, but each would have his opinion, and criticise every new publication of the sort. The French, in general, were great readers, and every citizen would have his library. Thus in Paris a bookseller was sure of selling as many copies of the most pitiful performance, as are generally sold in London of a work of no small merit.

In France an author was as passionately cried up as a fashion; the Englishman, who deigns to read his work, passes judgment on it and remains unconcerned. Can this arise from good sense or indifference, or may it not be a mixture of both. Notwithstanding all the benefactions received from the English, I will not pronounce; neither flattery nor criticism is within my sphere; but an undoubted fact, and which ought to have taught Malesherbes, is, that in France, still less than elsewhere, a book either impious or seditious never could be looked upon as a mere article of commerce. The greater readers and arguers, and the more volatile the French people were, the more the minister superintending the press should have enforced the laws enacted to repress the licentiousness of it, which, on the contrary, he favored with all his power. His condemnation is recorded in the encomiums of the conspirators; it was he, they said, who *broke the shackles of literature*.[3]

In vain would it be objected, that the minister left the same liberty to the religious writers. In the first place, that was not always true, it was much against his will that he suffered works refuting the Sophisters to appear;[4] and what a minister allows with reluctance, he finds abundant means of preventing. Could a minister be innocent, when letting a poison infuse itself throughout the public, under pretext that he did not forbid the sale of the antidote? Moreover, however well written a religious work may be, it has not the passions to second it; much more talent is required to make such a performance palatable. Any fool may attract the people to the theatre, but the eloquence of a Chrysostom is necessary to tear them from it. With equal talent, he who pleads for licence and impiety will carry more weight than the most eloquent orator who vindicates the rights of virtue and morality. The religious apologist requires a serious and an attentive reading, with a stedfast desire of finding the truth, and such a study fatigues; whereas, depravity requires none; in a word, it is far more easy to irritate and throw the people into revolt, than to appease them when once put in motion.

At length *Malesherbes*, seeing the revolution consummated in the death of Lewis XVI, gave signs of a tardy repentance. His zeal in that moment did not hinder men who had deeply felt his fault from exclaiming, "Officious defender, cease to plead for that king you yourself betrayed; it is too late. Cease to accuse that legion of regicides who demand his head; Robespierre is not his first executioner; it was you that long since prepared his scaffold, when you suffered those impious works that called the people to the destruction of the altar and of the throne to be openly displayed and sold in the porticos of his palace. That unfortunate prince confided in you; he had imparted his authority to you to repress the impious and seditious writers, and you permitted the people to inhale blasphemy and hatred of kings from a Raynal, an Helvetius, or a Diderot, and you pretended only a wish to encourage commerce. If then, at the present day, this people, in the frantic crisis of those poisons which you have circulated in their veins, call aloud for the head of Lewis XVI, it is too late to make a parade of his defence, or to criminate the Jacobins."

Men of meditation and reflection had long since foreseen the reproach that history would one day make to Malesherbes. They never passed the galleries of the Louvre, without exclaiming in the bitterness of their souls, *Unfortunate Lewis XVI! It is thus that you are sold at the gates of your own palace!*

Malesherbes at length leaving the ministry, overpowered by the reclamations of the friends of religion, his successors undertook or pretended to undertake, to enforce the former laws. But soon, under the title of *Fables*, the Sophisters sought to spread their poison anew; and, charmed with their success, D'Alembert writes to Voltaire, "The luck of it is, that these fables, far superior to Esop's, are sold here (at Paris) pretty freely. I begin to think the trade (of bookselling) will have lost nothing by the retreat of Mr. de Malesherbes."[5] It in truth lost so little, that the writers in defence of the altar and the throne were the only ones thwarted in their publication.[6]

Meanwhile the conspirators carefully calculated their successes with ministry. At the period when Lewis XVI ascended the throne, they were so great, that Voltaire, writing to Frederic, expresses his hopes in the following terms: "I know not whether our young king will walk in your footsteps; but I know that he has taken *philosophers for his ministers*, all except one, who is unfortunately a bigot.... There is Mr. Turgot, who is worthy of your Majesty's conversation. The priests are in despair. THIS IS THE COMMENCEMENT OF A GREAT REVOLUTION."[7]

Voltaire, in this, is correct to the full extent of the term. I remember, in those days, to have seen venerable ecclesiastics bewailing the death of Lewis XV while all France, and myself among others, were in expectation of better days. They would say, the king we have lost had indeed many failings, but he that succeeds is very young, and has many dangers to encounter. They foresaw that same revolution which Voltaire foretels to Frederic, and in the anguish of their hearts they shed tears over it. But let not the historian blame the young prince for the unhappy choice in which Voltaire so much exults. Lewis XVI, to succeed the better in this choice, had done all that diffidence in his own abilities, or that the love of his subjects or of religion, could suggest. This we see by the deference he paid to the last advice he received from his father, from that Dauphin whose virtues had long been the admiration of France, and whose death plunged it into universal mourning. This is again to be seen in the eagerness with which Lewis XVI called to the ministry that man, who, in Voltaire's language, was unfortunately a bigot. This was the *Mareschal de Muy*. When the historian shall discover the throne surrounded by so many perfidious agents of its authority, let him remember to avenge piety and Christian fervor, courage, and fidelity, in short, all the virtues of a true citizen, when he shall treat of the memory of this Mareschal. Mr. de Muy had been the companion and bosom friend of the Dauphin, father of Lewis XVI, and such a friendship is more than an equivalent for the scurrilous abuse of Voltaire. The Mareschal de Saxe was soliciting, for one whom he protected, the place of companion (*menin*) to the young prince. On being told that it was intended for Mr. de Muy, he replied, *I will not do Mr. Le Dauphin the injury of depriving him of the company of so virtuous a man as the Chevalier de Muy, who may, hereafter, be of great service to France.* Let posterity appreciate such a commendation; and O that the Sophister could but hear and blush!

Mr. de Muy was the man who bore the greatest resemblance to the Dauphin who loved him. In him were to be found the same regularity and amenity of manners, the same beneficence, the same disinterested zeal for religion and the public welfare. It was through his means that the prince, unable to visit the provinces in person, was acquainted with the misfortunes and grievances of the people; he sent him to examine their situations, and they were occupied together in seeking those remedies which the prince's premature death, alas! hindered from being carried into execution. When, during the war, Mr. de Muy was called upon to give proofs of his fidelity in the victorious fields of Crevelt and Warbourg, the Dauphin would daily offer the following prayer for his safety: "My God, may thy sword defend, may thy shield protect the Count Felix de Muy, to the end, that if ever thou makest me bear the heavy burthen of a crown, he may support me by his virtue, his counsels, and his example."

When the God of vengeance inflicted on France with its first scourge, when the hand of death had struck the Dauphin, Mr. de Muy by his bedside, bathed in the tears of friendship, hears the prince, in a voice that might rend the heart asunder, pronounce these last words: "Do not abandon yourself to sorrow. Preserve yourself, to serve my children. Your knowledge, your virtues will be necessary to them. Be for them, what you would have been to me. Bestow on my memory that mark of kindness; but above all, let not their youth, during which God grant them his protection, keep you at a distance from them."

Lewis XVI, ascending the throne, recalled these words to Mr. de Muy, conjuring him to accept of the ministry. Though he had refused it in the preceding reign, he could not withstand the entreaties of the son of his departed friend. To a court universally assaulted by impiety, he taught that the Christian hero would, in no situation, be ashamed of his God.

When he commanded in Flanders he had the honor of receiving the Duke of Gloucester, brother to the King of England, at a time when the Catholic church commands abstinence from meat. True to his duty, he conducted the Duke to his table, saying, "My religion is strictly observed in my house; had I ever the misfortune to infringe that law, I should more carefully observe it on a day when I have so illustrious a prince, for a witness and censor of my conduct. The English punctually follow their religion; out of respect for your Royal Highness, I will not exhibit the scandal of a loose Catholic, who in your presence could dare to violate his."

If so much religion, in the eyes of Philosophism, is only unfortunately being a bigot, let it look to the thousands of unhappy creatures that religion relieved by the hands of Mr. de Muy. Let it behold the soldiery, rather led by his example than by the laws of courage and discipline. Let it learn, that the province in which he commanded still gratefully remembers and blesses their former governor, in spite of the revolution, which seems to have tinged the human mind with the black hue of ingratitude.[8]

One of the great misfortunes of Lewis XVI was to lose this virtuous minister at an early period. *Maurepas* was by no means the proper person to replace him in the confidence of the young king. His father even, who mentioned him in his will, had been misled by the aversion this former minister had shown to the Marquise de Pompadour, and his long exile had not wrought the change in him which the Dauphin had supposed. The attention, however, which the young prince paid to the counsels of his father shows how ardently he wished to surround himself with ministers who would promote his views for the good of the people. He might have made a better choice, had he known what had misled the Dauphin. Maurepas was now old and decrepid, but had all the vices of youth. Voltaire transforms him into a philosopher, and he coalesced with the Sect through levity and indolence. He believed in nothing; he was without hatred against the altar, as without affection for the Sophisters. He would with equal indifference wittily lash a bishop or D'Alembert. He found D'Argenson's plan for the destruction of the religious orders, and he followed it. He would have soon set aside the impious minister, had he known him that would conspire against the religion of the state. An enemy to all convulsions, and without any fixed principles of Christianity, he thought it at least impolitic to attempt its destruction. He certainly was not a man capable of stopping a revolution, but he did not forward it. He rather let others do the harm, than did it himself; but unfortunately that harm which he let others do was great. Under his administration philosophism made a terrible progress. Nothing proves it more clearly than the choice of that Turgot, whose nomination is celebrated by Voltaire as the *beginning of a great revolution*.

The philanthropy of this man has been much extolled; but it was that of a hypocrite, as the reader will be convinced by the following letter from D'Alembert to Voltaire: "You will soon receive another visit, which I announce to you. It is that of *Mr. de Turgot*, a master of Requests, full of Philosophy, a man of great parts and learning, a great friend of mine, and who wishes to pay you a sly visit. I say sly for *propter metum Judæorum* (for fear of the Jews); we must not brag of it too much, nor you neither."[9]

If at first sight the signification of the fear of the Jews is not understood, D'Alembert will explain it in a second portrait of his friend: "This Turgot," he writes, "is a man of wit, of great learning, and very virtuous; in a word, he is a worthy *Cacouac*, but has good reasons for not showing it too much, for I have learned to my cost, that the *Cacouaquery* (Philosophism) is not the road to fortune, and he deserves to make his."[10]

Voltaire had an interview with Turgot, and formed so true a judgment of him, that he answers, "If you have many sages of that stamp in your Sect, I fear for the *wretch, she* is lost to good company."[11]

To every man who understands the encomiums of Voltaire to D'Alembert, this is as much as to say, Turgot is a secret adept, he is an ambitious hypocrite, and will at once be a traitor to his God, his king, and his country: but by us, he is called virtuous; he is a conspirator of the true stamp, necessary to compass the overthrow of Christianity. Had Voltaire or D'Alembert spoken of an ecclesiastic, or a religious writer, who had only the virtues of a Turgot, what a monster we should have seen arise from his pen. Let the impartial historian examine and lay aside these usurped reputations of virtue; let him say with truth, that Turgot, rich, above the common rank of citizens, and still aiming at dignities and further fortune, cannot be called a real Philosopher. Turgot being the adept of the conspiring Sophisters, and a master of requests, is already perjured. He will be far more so when he arrives at the ministry. For by the standing laws of the state, he could only enjoy these dignities by affirming, both by himself and others, his fidelity to the king, to religion, and to the state. He had already betrayed religion and the state, and he will soon betray his king. He belonged to that Sect of Œconomists who detested the French monarchy, and only endured a king, in order to treat him as did the first rebels of the revolution.

At length advanced to the ministry by the cabals of the Sect, he uses all his power to inspire the young king with his disgust for the monarchy, and with his principles on the authority of a throne he had sworn to maintain as minister. He would willingly have transformed him into a Jacobin king. He first insinuates those errors which are one day to throw the sceptre into the hands of the people, and overturn the altar and the throne; if such are the virtues of a minister, they are those of a treacherous one; if errors of the mind, they are those of a madman. Nature had endowed him with the desire of relieving his fellow-creatures. He heard the declamations of the Sophisters against the remains of the feudal system, under which the people still labored; and what with the Sophisters a mere sign of their hatred for kings, he mistook for the cry of compassion. He was blind to what all the world saw, and that particularly on the Corvees. He would not hearken to the voice of history, which told him that the shackles of the feudal system had as yet been only broken by the wisdom and mature deliberation of the monarch, foreseeing the inconveniences and the means of covering the losses of the suppression. But he would be hasty, and he ruined every thing. The Sophisters thought his dismission was too early; but, alas! it was not early enough; for he had already tainted the throne with those revolutionary ideas on the sovereignty of the people; he had then forgotten that this was making all power dependant on their caprice; he pretended to make the people happy by placing arms in their hands, with which they destroyed themselves. He thought to re-establish the laws in all their purity, and he only taught rebellion; he misleads the youthful monarch, too inexperienced to unravel the sophisms of the Sect; and the very goodness of his heart leads him still more astray. In the pretended rights of the people, he only sees his own to be sacrificed; and it is from Turgot that we may trace that fatal error of his insurmountable patience and fatal condescension with that people whose sovereignty led to the scaffold himself, his queen, and his sister.

Turgot is the first minister who shows that revolutionary spirit at once antichristian and antimonarchial. Choiseul and Malesherbes were more impious than Turgot, Choiseul perhaps was even more wicked; but never before had a minister been known seeking to destroy the principles of that authority in the mind of the king which he imparted to him. It was reported, that Turgot had repented on seeing the sovereign mob threatening his person, on seeing them bursting open the magazines of corn, and throwing both corn and bread into the river, and that under pretence of famine. It was then, as reported, that, seeing his errors, he had laid open to Lewis XVI all the plans of the Sophisters, and that these latter ever after sought to destroy the idol they had set up. This anecdote, unfortunately for the honor of Turgot, is unfounded. Before his elevation to the ministry, he was an idol of the conspirators, and such he remained until his death. Condorcet has also been his panegyrist and historian, and he would not have been tolerant on the repentance of an adept.

Scourges have successively fallen on France since the revolution; but prior to it they had succeeded each other in the persons of Lewis XVIth's ministers. Necker appeared after Turgot, and Necker re-appears after Briennes; and his virtues were extolled by the Sophisters nearly as much as he extols them himself. This is another of those reputations which the historian must judge by facts, not for the mere pleasure of detecting the conspiring hypocrite, but because *these unmerited reputations were a means employed* for the consummation of the conspiracy.

Necker, when only banker's clerk, was employed by some speculators both as the confidant and agent in a business which was suddenly and greatly to augment their fortunes. They had the secret of an approaching peace, which was considerably to enhance the value of the Canada Bills; one of the conditions of the future peace being, the payment of those bills which had remained in England; they let Necker into the secret, on condition that, for their common emolument, he would write to London to have a number of these bills bought up at the low price to which the war had reduced them. Necker engaged in the association, and, through the credit of his master, the bills were monopolized. His associates returning to know the state of the bargain, he told them that the speculation had appeared so hazardous and bad, that he had desisted from and countermanded the purchase. Peace comes, and Necker is in possession of these bills on his own account alone, and these make near three million Tournois.—Such was the virtue of Necker when a clerk!

Now become rich, he calls the Sophisters to his table; his house becomes a weekly club, and the new Mecænas is well repaid for his good cheer by the encomiums and flattery of his guests. D'Alembert, and the chiefs of the conspirators, punctually attended these assemblies every Friday.[12] Necker hearing of nothing but philosphy, would be a philosopher, as suddenly as he became a lord, and the intrigue and encomiums of the Sect would transform him into a Sully. At length Lewis XVI, hearing so much of the talents of this man in finance, called him to the ministry as Comptroller General. Among the many means of the conspirators, the most infallible was to introduce disorder in the finances. Necker succeeded completely in this plan by those exhorbitant loans which nothing could have hidden from the public, but that blind confidence and those encomiums perpetually thrown out by the Sect.—But supposing Necker to have acted from the impulse of the conspirators, like an ignorant minister who knew not whither he was driven, or deliberately hollowed out the abyss, it is not his pretended virtue that is to plead his defence. Is it not probable that the man who, when recalled for the second time to the ministry, could dare to starve the people in the midst of plenty in order to convulse them into a revolution, might also attempt to ruin the finances to produce the same convulsive state? Such a virtue as his may be classed with nearly the blackest guilt.

At the time when Necker was recalled to replace Briennes in the ministry, at the time when his great generosity to the people was cried up, and that all France was stunned with his great feats; at that very time was he, in concert with Philippe D'Orleans, starving the people into revolt against their king, the nobles, and the clergy. This virtuous man had bought up all the corn, had ordered it to be shut up in store-houses, or sent it in barges from one place to another, forbidding the intendants to allow of the sale of any corn, until they had received his orders. The magazines remained shut. The boats wandered from port to port. The people clamorously called for bread, but in vain! The parliament of Rouen, concerned for the state to which the province of Normandy was reduced, desired its president to write to the minister (Necker) to demand the sale of a great quantity of corn which they knew to be then in the province. His letter was not answered. The first president received a second summons from his body, to remonstrate in the most pressing manner on the wants of the people; at length Necker answers, that he has sent his orders to the Intendant. His orders are executed, but the Intendant is obliged, for his own justification, to lay them before the Parliament; and so far were they from what was expected, that they were barely an instruction to put off the sale, and to invent divers pretexts and excuses to elude the demands of the magistrates, and to rid him of their applications. Meanwhile the vessels laden with corn proceeded from the ports to the ocean, from the ocean to the rivers, or simply to the interior of the provinces. At the period when Necker was driven from the ministry for the second time, the people were destitute of bread. The parliament had then obtained proof that the same boats, laden with the same corn, had been from Rouen to Paris, and from Paris back again; then embarked at Rouen for the Havre, and thence returned again half rotten.—The *Attorney General* profited of this second dismission to send circular orders to stop these proceedings, and to give the people the liberty of buying this corn. At the expulsion of this minister, the populace of Paris, stupidly sovereign, ran to arms, and demanded their Necker, carrying his bust through the streets with that of Philippe D'Orleans; and never were two assassins better coupled in their triumph. The populace would have its executioner, which it stupidly stiled its father; and Necker, on his return, starves it anew. Scarce had he heard of the orders which the *Attorney General* of the Parliament of Normandy had given, when the revolutionary agents are sent from Paris, the people are stirred up against the magistrate, his mansion is forced and pillaged, and a price is put upon his head!—Such were the virtues of the adept Necker, when minister and protector of the conspirators.

For the authenticity of these facts the historian will appeal to the chief magistrates of the parliament of Rouen. If, to shew the chief agent of such horrid deeds, I have been obliged to anticipate on the second part of this work; it is because Necker had conspired against the throne, equally as against the altar. It was through him that the Sophisters were to draw the Calvinists into their party, but though pretending to the faith of Geneva, he was really a Deist. Had not the Calvinists been blind to conviction, they could have seen it in his writings or in his universal connections with the impious; for this empty and vain man aimed at every thing. From a Clerk he became Comptroller-General; next a protecting Sophister, and thence imagined himself a divine. He published is ideas on Religious Opinions; and this work was nothing less than Deism; nor in saying this do I judge severely a work which does not look upon the existence of God as proved; for what can the religion of that man be who doubts of the existence of a God? This work obtained for its author an academic crown, as being the best production of the day; that is to say, that which could insinuate the most impiety in the most perfect disguise.

After what has been said of the minister *Briennes*, the intimate friend of D'Alembert, after the wickedness of this man has been made so public, I should not mention him, had I not to discover a plot, a parallel to which history would blush to show, and none but the annals of the modern Sophisters could produce. Under the name of Œconomists, the conspirators held secret meetings (which we shall hereafer lay open to the public), and impatiently waited the death of Mr. de Beaumont, Archbishop of Paris, to give him a successor, who, entering into their views, and under the pretext of humanity, kindness, and toleration, was as patiently to endure with Philosophism, Jansenism, and all other Sects, as Mr. de Beaumont had strenously opposed them. He was to be particularly indulgent as to the discipline of the parish clergy, even so much so as to let it decay in a few years. On tenets he was to be equally relaxed. He was to repress the zeal of those who appeared too active, to interdict and even to displace them as men too ardent or even turbulent. He was carefully to receive all accusations of this sort, and replace the over-zealous by men whom the Sophisters had prepared and would recommend, particularly for dignitaries.—By this plan the parish churches, hitherto administered by a most edifying clergy, were soon to be overrun by the most scandalous. Sermons and catechistical lectures becoming daily less frequent, all instructions running in the philosophic strain, and bad books daily multiplying, the people seeing in their parishes none but a clergy scandalous in their morals, and little zealous in their doctrine, were naturally inclined to abandon the churches and their religion. The apostacy of the capital was to carry with it that of the most essential diocese; and hence the evil was to spread far around. Thus without violence, *without being perceived*, but solely by the connivance of its chief pastor, religion was to be crushed in the capital; not but that Briennes might have given some exterior signs of zeal, had the circumstances required.[13]

Nothing but the ambition of a Briennes, and the wickedness of his heart, could have made him accept the archbishopric on such conditions.—The agreement made, the Sophisters put all their agents in motion. The court is beset; an artful man, of the name of Vermon, who had been made reader to the queen by Choiseul on the recommendation of Briennes, seized on this opportunity to make some return to his protector. The queen recommended the protector of Vermon, and she thought she was doing well; the king thought he did still better in nominating the man whose moderation, whose prudence, and whose genius, were so perpetual a topic, to the Archbishopric of Paris: and one day Briennes was actually named. But no sooner was it known at court and in Paris, than every Christian shuddered at the news. The king's aunts, and the Princess de Marsan in particular, immediately foresaw the scandal with which France was threatened; and the king, prevailed upon by their prayers, annulled what he had already done. The archbishopric was given to a man whose modesty, zeal, and impartiality would form the strongest contrast with the vices of Briennes. Unfortunately for France, neither the king nor the queen were sufficiently convinced to lose all confidence in the pretended virtues of this man; nor did the conspirators lay all hopes aside of hereafter raising him to a more exalted station.

As the thunder-bolt hidden in the clouds blackened by the tempest, and waiting the convulsion of the heavens to break forth, so did Briennes, from the dark cloud which threatened France, convulsed during the sitting of the Notables called by Calonne, burst forth prime minister. To show his subserviency to the Sophisters, he began by that famous edict which Voltaire had solicited twenty years before in behalf of the Huguenots, though he had looked upon them as *mad* and *raving mad*;[14] that edict so long wished for by D'Alembert, as a means of *duping* the Protestants and of *crushing* Christianity, without its *even being perceived*.[15] Offspring of the tempest, he is at length overpowered by those billows which carried Necker to the helm, and which Necker holds solely to immerse his king, the nobility, and the clergy into that sea of impious sophistry and frantic rage, which the conspirators had created. Briennes died covered with infamy, but without remorse, or sign of repentance.

By the same intrigue that had carried Briennes to the prime ministry, *Lamoignon*, whose ancestors had been an ornament to the magistracy, obtained the seals. He was notoriously, like many other courtiers, an unbeliever; but he was also one of the conspirators. His name is to be found in their most secret committees. On his disgrace, which soon followed that of Briennes, he *philosophically* shot himself.—Two such men at the head of the ministry! what means had they not of countenancing and forwarding the Antichristian Conspiracy!

Posterity will find it difficult to conceive that a monarch so religious as Lewis XVI should have been surrounded by such a set of impious ministers. Their surprise will be much lessened, when they consider that the Conspirators aimed mostly at the higher orders of society, and that they wished to destroy religion in those who approached the person of the monarch.[16] To the passions of this privileged class, let the facility of satisfying them be added; and we shall easily conceived with what facility Voltaire could attack a religion that so much militated against those passions. Without doubt, eminent virtues and the most distinguished piety were to be found among the nobility and grandees of the court: for instance, Madame Elizabeth, sister to the king; Mesdames de France the king's aunts, the Princesses de Conti, Louise de Condé, de Marsan, the Duc de Penthievre, the Mareschal de Mouchi, de Broglie, and many other distinguished personages who would have done honor to the brightest ages of Christianity. Among the ministers themselves history will except Mr. de Vergennes and Mr. de St. Germain, and perhaps some others who could not be challenged by impiety. Throughout the whole class of the nobility these exceptions may be more frequent than might be supposed; but, nevertheless, it is unfortunately true to say, that Voltaire had made surprising progress among the great, and that will easily account for the unhappy choices Lewis XVI had made. Virtue seeks obscurity and is little jealous of elevation. None but the ambitious were foremost on the ranks, and the Sophisters would stun the ill-fated monarch with the praises of those whom they thought would best second their views, and who had been initiated in their mysteries. Not only the throne, but the public itself was to be overpowered by the praises which they lavished on the adept whom they wished to elevate to the ministry. Their intrigues were more secret, and surpassed the art of courtiers themselves; besides, acting under the influence of public opinion, in what way could they not direct the choice of a young prince whose greatest failing was diffidence in his own judgment. By such arts were the Turgots, the Neckers, the Lamoignons, the Briennes successively forced into the councils of Lewis XVI; passing over in silence those subaltern ministers and first clerks, importantly great, whose services the conspiring Sophisters carefully secured.

Thus protected, impiety soared above the laws now almost silenced. It was in vain for the clergy to reclaim the hand of power, for it connived at the Conspirators; their writings were circulated, and their persons secure. Voltaire even writes to D'Alembert, "Thanks to a priest about the court, I should have been undone had it not been for *the Chancellor*, who at all times has shown me the greatest kindness."[17] This shows how little any reclamations of the clergy could avail against the chief of the Conspirators. This letters discovers a new protector of the Sophisters in the person of *Mr. de Meaupou*; his ambition, and his connection with the chief of the Conspirators, had always been hidden under the mask of religion.

In a letter written also to D'Alembert, we see of what immense use such protections were, not only to Voltaire but also to the other adepts. He speaks thus of Choiseul: "I am under the greatest obligations to him. It is to him alone that I owe all the privileges I have on my estate.— Every favor that I have asked *for my friends* he has granted."[18]

Some of these protectors also aimed at being authors, and without Voltaire's talents sought to inspire the people with the same principles. Of this number was the *Duke D'Ufez*, who, to verify the expression of Voltaire, that he was stronger in mind than in body, had undertaken a work in favor of Equality and Liberty applied to our belief in matters of faith, without consulting either church or pastor. Voltaire only wished to see it finished to declare the work as useful to society as it was to the Duke himself.[19] This work never appeared; we know not, therefore, how to class the genius of the noble divine.

In Voltaire's letters we find many other great personages, that swell the list of adepts and protectors, and many names already famous in history; such was the descendant of a *Crillon* or a *Prince of Salm*, both worthy of better days, according to Voltaire; but let not the reader mistake them for the age of the Bayards and of those bold knights of former times; no, it is of an age worthy of *their modesty and their philosophic science*.— We see Voltaire placing all his hopes in the *Prince of Ligne* for the propagation of his sophisticated science throughout Brabant; and the *Duke of Braganza* is as much extolled for the similarity of his sentiments.

Among the Marquisses, Counts, and Chevaliers, we find the *Marquis D'Argence de Dirac*, a brigadier-general, zealous in the destruction of Christianity in the province of Angoumois, and modernizing his fellow-countrymen with his philosophic ideas; the *Marquis de Rochefort*, colonel of a regiment, who through his Philosophism had gained the friendship of Voltaire and D'Alembert; the *Chevalier Chatellux*, bold but more adroit in the war against Christianity. In fine, were we to credit Voltaire, nearly all those whom he was acquainted with in this class were what (in a letter to Helvetius in 1763) he styles honest men.— "Believe me," he writes, "Europe is full of men of reason, who are opening their eyes to the light. Truly the number is prodigious.—I have not seen for these ten years past a *single honest man,* of whatever country or religion he may have been, *but who absolutely thought as you do.*"[20] It is probable, and it is to be hoped, that Voltaire greatly exaggerated his success. It would be impossible to conceive, that of the numbers of the nobility who went to contemplate the Grand Lama of the Sophisters at Ferney, the greatest part were not attracted by curiosity, rather than impiety. The surest rule by which we may distinguish the true adepts is by the confidence he placed in them, or whether he sent them the productions of his own pen or those of other conspirators; and at that rate the list would greatly extend. Many Duchesses and Marchionesses would be found, as philosophic as Sister Guillemetta. But let them be forgotten, those adepts more dupes than wicked; more unfortunate are they still, if they are above being pitied.

Of these protectors, the *Count D'Argental*, Honorary Counsellor of the Parliament, is to be particularly distinguished. Nearly of the same age as Voltaire, he always had been his bosom friend. All that Mr. de la Harpe says of the amiability of this Count may be true; but however amiable he might be, it will also be true to say, that both the Count and Countess D'Argental were the dupes of their admiration and friendship for Voltaire. He corresponds as regularly with these two adepts as he did with D'Alembert, and as confidently exhorts them to crush *the wretch*. He styles them his two angels. He employed the Count as general agent for all higher protections that he might stand in need of; and few agents were more devoted or more faithful; that is to say, more impious.[21]

A name of greater importance, that is not to be overlooked among the protecting adepts, is the *Duc de la Rochefoucault*. To him who knows how much the Duke must have been mistaken in his own wit, it will be matter of little surprise to see him so seldom mentioned in Voltaire's correspondence; but facts supply the place of written proofs. The Duke had been weak enough to be persuaded, that impiety and Philosophism could alone give him a reputation. He protected the Sophisters, and even pensioned Condorcet. It would have been happy for him had he not waited for the murderers sent by Condorcet himself, to learn what were the real principles of this Philosophism.

In foreign courts, many great personages thought to soar above the vulgar by this same Sophistry. Voltaire could not sufficiently admire the zeal of *Prince Gallitzin*, in dedicating the most impious of Helvetius's works to the Empress of all the Russias.[22] He was still more delighted with *Count Schouwallow*, the powerful protector of the Sophisters at that Court; and with all those, by whose intrigues D'Alembert had been nominated for the education of the heir to the Imperial diadem.

In Sweden, whence the *Chamberlain Jennings*, under the auspices of the King and Queen, had gone to announce to the patriarch of Ferney the great progress of Philosophism in that country,[23] an adept was to be found far more extolled by the Conspirators. This was the *Count de Creutz*, ambassador in France, and afterwards in Spain. He had so well blended his embassy with the apostleship of impiety, that Voltaire, enraptured, was inconsolable at his departure from Paris.— He writes to Madame Geofrin, "Had there been an Emperor Julian on earth, the *Count de Creutz* should have been sent on embassy to him, and not to a country where Auto-da-fés are made. The senate of Sweden must be gone mad, not to have left such a man in France; he would have been of use there, and it is impossible that he should do any good in Spain."[24]

But this Spain, so much despised by Voltaire, could produce a *D'Aranda*, whom he styles the *Favorite of Philosophy*, and who daily went to stimulate his zeal, in the company of D'Alembert, Marmontel, and Mademoiselle D'Espinase, whose club nearly equalled the French Academy.

Other Dukes and Grandees were to be found in Spain equally admiring the French Sophistry. In particular the *Marquis de Mora* and the *Duke of Villa Hermosa*.[25] In this same country, so much despised by the Sophisters, we find D'Alembert distinguishing the *Duke of Alba*. It is of him that he writes to Voltaire, "One of the first Grandees of Spain, a man of great wit, and the same person who was ambassador in France, under the name of Duke of Huescar, has just sent me twenty guineas towards your statue....Condemned, he says, secretly to cultivate my reason, I joyfully seize this opportunity of publicly testifying my gratitude to the great man who first pointed out the road to me."[26]

It was at the sight of so numerous a list of disciples, that Voltaire exclaimed, "Victory declares for us on all sides; I do assure you, that in a little time nothing but the rabble will follow the standard of our enemies."[27] He did not sufficiently dive into futurity, or he would have seen that rabble misled one day by the same principles, and sacrificing its masters on the very altar they had raised to impiety.

As to D'Alembert, he could not contain himself when informed of the numerous admirers that flocked to Ferney. "What the devil!" would he write, "forty guests at table, of whom two Masters of Requests and a Counsellor of the Grand Chamber, without counting the *Duke of Villars* and company!"[28] Dining at Voltaire's, to be sure, is not an absolute proof of the Philosophism of the guests, but it generally shows men who admired the Chief of that impiety which was one day to be their ruin.

It was not by chance that D'Alembert mentioned the Counsellor of the Grand Chamber. He was fully aware of what importance it was for the Conspirators to have protectors, or even admirers, in the higher orders of the magistracy. Voltaire was of the same opinion when he writes, "Luckily, during these ten years past that parliament (of Thoulouse) has been recruited by young men of great wit, who have read, and who think like you."[29] This letter alone denotes how much the tribunals were relaxed for many years preceding the revolution. They were vested with all the authority necessary for stopping the circulation of these impious and seditious works, and of taking cognizance of their authors; but they had so much neglected it, that in the latter times a decree of the parliament was a means of enhancing the price and extending the circulation of a work.

Voltaire, notwithstanding the numerous conquests made in these temples of justice, often complains of some of those respectable corps, as still containing magistrates who loved religion. But in return he extols the philosophic zeal of those of the South. "There (he writes to D'Alembert) you go from a *Mr. Duché* to a *Mr. de Castillon*, and Grenoble can boast of a *Mr. Servan*. It is impossible that reason and toleration should not make the greatest progress under such masters."[30] This hope was the better founded, as these three magistrates here named by Voltaire are precisely those who, by their functions of attorney or solicitor generals, were obliged to oppose the progress of that reason, synonimous with impiety in the mouth of Voltaire; and to uphold the power of the law against those daily productions and their authors.

Mr. de la Chalotais is of all others the solicitor general who seems to have been in the closest intimacy with Voltaire. It is in their correspondence that we see how much the conspirators were indebted and how grateful they were to him, on account of his zeal against the Jesuits, and how much the destruction of that order was blended with that of all other religious, in their plans for the total overthrow of all ecclesiastical authority.[31]

But in spite of all this Philosophism, which had crept into the body of the magistracy, we meet with venerable men, whose virtues were the ornament of the highest tribunals. The grand chamber of the parliament of Paris, in particular, appeared so opposite to his impiety, that he despaired of ever philosophizing it. He even does it the honor of ranking it with that *populace* and *those assemblies of the clergy* that he despaired of ever rendering *reasonable*, or rather impious.[32]

There even was a time when he expresses his indignation to Helvetius in the following terms: "I believe that the French are descended from the centaurs, who were half men and *half pack-horses*. These two halves have been separated, and there remained *men like you and some others;* and also horses, *who have bought the offices of counsellor* (in parliament), or who have made themselves doctors of the Sorbonne."[33]

It is an agreeable duty that I fulfil, when I show proof of this spite of the Sophisters against the first corps of the French magistracy. It is certain, that at the time of the revolution many magistrates were yet to be found, who, better informed of the intrigues of the Sophisters, would willingly have given greater vigour to the laws for the support of religion. But impiety had intruded even into the grand chamber. Terray, well known as a wicked minister, is not sufficiently so as a Sophister.

Whatever may be the turpitude of many facts mentioned in these memoirs, few are of a deeper hue than the following one:

The bookseller Le Jay was publicly selling one of those works, the impiety of which sometimes commanded the attention of the parliament. That sold by Le Jay was ordered to be publicly burnt, and the author and sellers to be prosecuted. Terray offered himself to make the necessary investigations, and was to report to parliament. He ordered Le Jay before him, and I will lay before the reader the very words I heard the bookseller use when he gave an account of what had passed on the occasion. As to the title of the work, I am not quite certain whether he mentioned it or not; but I perfectly remember what follows:—"Ordered before Mr. Terray, counsellor in parliament; I waited on him. He received me with an air of gravity, sat down on a sofa, and questioned me as follows:—Is it you that sell this work condemned by a decree of the parliament? I answered, Yes, my Lord. How can you sell such dangerous works? As many others are sold.—Have you sold many of them? Yes, my Lord.—Have you many left? About six hundred copies.—Do you know the author of this infamous work? Yes, my Lord.—Who is it? Yourself, my Lord!—How dare you say so; how do you know that? I know it, my Lord, from the person of whom I bought your manuscript.—Since you know it, all is over; go, but be prudent."

It may be easily conceived that this interrogatory was not reported to the parliament, and the reader will readily comprehend what progress the Antichristian Conspiracy made in a country where its adepts were seated in the very sanctuary of the laws.

1. To Count D'Argental, 20 June, 1764, Vol. 58, Let. 130, P. 243.
2. See, in the General Correspondence, the letters of Mr. D'Argenson.
3. To D'Alembert, 30 Jan. 1764, Vol. 68, Let. 128, P. 278.
4. To D'Alembert, 8 Feb. 1757, Vol. 68, Let. 24, P. 43.
5. From D'Alembert, 8 Dec. 1763, Vol. 68, Let. 121, Page 259.

6. We know of several excellent works which never could gain admission into France. Such was the case with Feller's PHILOSOPHICAL CATECHISM, because it contains an excellent refutation of the systems of the day. We are acquainted with several authors, and we might cite ourselves, to whom greater severity was shown than the law could countenance, whilst it was openly transgressed in favor of the conspirators. Mr. Lourdet, of the Royal College, the censor of our Helvian letters, needed all his resolution and firmness to maintain his prerogative and ours, by publishing that work which the Sophisters would fain have suppressed, and that before the first volume was half printed. The same censor invoked in vain the power of the laws to stop the publication of Raynal's works. That seditious writer had daringly presented his pretended PHILOSOPHIC HISTORY to the censor, and, instead of the probate, he received the reproaches of just indignation. In spite of censure or laws, however his work appeared the next day, and was exposed for public sale.
7. To Frederick, 3 Aug. 1775, vol. 66, Let. 94, P. 219.
8. See Mr. Le Tourneur de Tressol, on this Mareschal, also Feller's Hist. Dict.
9. From D'Alembert, 22 Sept. 1760, Vol. 68, Let. 74, P. 136.
10. From D'Alembert, 18 Oct. 1760, Let. 76, P. 141.
11. To D'Alembert, 17 Nov. 1760, Vol. 68, Let. 77, P. 144.
12. Vous qui chez la belle Hippatie *(Mad. Necker)*
    Tous les vendredis raisonnez
    De virtu, de Philosophie, &c.
    To D'Alembert, 21 *June* 1770, *Vol.* 69, *Let.* 31, *P.* 59.
13. See hereafter the declaration of Mr. Le Roi.
14. To Marmontel, 2 Dec. 1767, Vol. 60, Let. 200, P. 336.
15. From D'Alembert, 4 May, 1762, Vol. 68, Let. 100, P. 202.
16. To Diderot, 25 Sept. 1762, Vol. 57, Let. 242, P. 475, et passim, to D'Alembert and Damilaville.
17. To D'Alembert, 28 Sept. 1774, Vol. 69, Let. 133, P. 223.
18. To D'Alembert, 1 Nov. 1762, Vol. 68, Let. 110, P. 228.
19. To the Duke d'Usez, 19 Nov. 1760, Vol. 56, Let. 226, P. 450.
20. March, 1763, Vol. 58, Let. 50, P. 100.
21. See General Correspondence.
22. To D'Alembert, 2 Aug. 1778, Vol. 69, Let. 118, P. 199.
23. To D'Alembert, 19 Jan. 1769, Vol. 69, Let. 3, P. 7.
24. To Mad. Geofrin, 21 May, 1764, Vol. 58, Let. 193, P. 355.
25. To Marq. de Villevielle, 1 May 1768, Vol. 60, Let. 268, P. 469.
26. From D'Alembert, 13 May, 1773, Vol. 69, Let. 108, P. 182.
27. To Damilaville, 25 Sept. 1762, Vol. 57, Let. 242, P. 475.
28. From D'Alembert, 18 Oct. 1760, Vol. 68, Let. 76. P. 141.
29. To D'Alembert, 4 Sept. 1769, Vol. 69, Let. 11, P. 22.
30. To D'Alembert, 5 Nov. 1770, Vol. 69, Let. 46, P. 81.
31. See their Correspondence, particularly Voltaire's letter to Mr. Chalotaix, 17 May, 1762, Vol. 57, Let. 192, P. 393.
32. To D'Alembert, 13 Dec. 1763, Vol. 68, Let. 122, P. 264.
33. To Helvetius, 22 July, 1761, Vol. 57, Let. 86, P. 178.

CHAP. XV.

The Class of Men of Letters.

THEIR passions, and the facility of gratifying them, the yoke of religion once thrown off, had given the conspirators great power among the higher classes of society; and the empty hopes of a reputation brought over to their standards all those who pretended to literary fame. The great talents of Voltaire, and a success perhaps superior to his talents, proclaimed his sway absolute over the class of men of letters. Humbly those men followed his triumphant car who, above all others, will proudly flatter themselves with the perfection of their own ideas. It was only necessary for him to give the fashion. Like those frivolous nations where the high-flown courtezans, by their sole example, can introduce the most wanton fashions in attire, just so does the premier chief. Scarce had he shown his bias towards impiety, when the men of letters would all be impious.

From that cloud of writers and adepts a man shone forth who might have disputed with him the palm of genius; and who, for celebrity, needed not to resort to impiety. This was *Jean Jaques Rousseau*. That famous citizen of Geneva, sublime when he pleases in his prose, rivalling Milton and Corneille in his poetry, could have rivalled Bossuet under the banners of Christianity. Unfortunately for his glory, he was known to D'Alembert, Diderot, and Voltaire; and for a time he leagued with them, and sought like them the means of crushing Christ and his religion. In this synagogue of impiety, as in that of the Jews, testimonies did not agree; divisions ensued, but, though separated, their attacks were all bent against Christianity. This is to be seen in a letter from Voltaire to D'Alembert, where he says, "What a pity it is that Jean Jaques, Diderot, Helvetius and you, *cum aliis ejusdem farinæ hominibus*, (with other men of your stamp,) should not have been unanimous in your attacks on *the wretch*. My greatest grief is, to see the impostors united, and the friends of truth divided."[1]

When Rousseau seceded from the Sophisters, he did not at the same time forsake either his own or their errors; but separately carried on the war. The admiration of the adepts was divided. In either school impiety had only varied its weapons, nor were opinions more constant or less impious.

Voltaire was the most active, but vigor was given to Jean Jaques. With the strength of Hercules he also partook of his delirium. Voltaire laughed at contradiction, and his pen flew with every wind. Jean Jaques would insist on the paradoxes fostered in his brain, and, brandishing his club on high, would equally strike at truth or falsehood. The former was the vane of opinion, the latter the Proteus of Sophistry. Both equally distant from the schools of wisdom, both wished to lay the foundations and first principles of philosophy.

The *pro* and *con* was equally adopted by them, and both found themselves condemned to the most humiliating inconstancy. Voltaire, uncertain as to the existence of a God or of a future state, applies to Sophisters bewildered like himself, and remains perplexed. Jean Jaques, while yet a mere youth, says to himself, "I am going to throw this stone against that tree opposite to me: If I hit, let it be a sign of salvation; if I miss, a sign of damnation." Jean Jaques hits, and heaven is his lot. This proof sufficed for the philosopher long after his youthful days; and he was far advanced in years when he said, "After that, I never doubted of my salvation."[2]

Voltaire one day believed he could demonstrate the existence of the *Author of the Universe*; he then believed in an all-powerful God, who remunerated virtue.[3] The day after, the whole of this demonstration is dwindled into probabilities and doubts, which it would be ridiculus to pretend to solve.[4]

The same truth is one day evident to Jean Jaques, nor does he doubt of it after having demonstrated it himself. He beheld the Deity all around him, with him, and throughout nature, on that day when he exclaimed, "I am certain that God exists of himself."[5] But the day following the demonstration is forgotten, and he writes to Voltaire, "Frankly I confess that neither the *pro* nor *con* (on the existence of God) appears to me demonstrated." With Jean Jaques, as with Voltaire, *Theism and Atheism* could only found their doctrine on *probabilities*.[6] And they both believed in one only principle or *sole Mover*.[7] But at another time they could not deny but that there were two principles or two causes.[8]

Voltaire, after having written that Atheism would people the earth with robbers, villains, and monsters,[9] would pardon Atheism in Spinosa, and even allow of it in a Philosopher;[10] and he professes it himself when he writes to D'Alembert, "I know of none but Spinosa who has argued well."[11] That is to say, I know of no true Philosopher but he to whom all matter and this world is the sole God; and after having tried every Sect, he ends by pressing D'Alembert to unite all parties in the war against Christ. Jean Jaques had written that the Atheists deserved punishment; that they were *disturbers of the public peace*, and as such guilty of death.[12] Then, thinking he had fulfilled Voltaire's wish, writes to the minister Vernier, "I declare that my sole object in the New Eloisa was to unite the two opposite parties (the Deists and Atheists) by a reciprocal esteem for each other, and to teach the philosophers that one may believe in God without being a hypocrite, or deny him without being a rascal."[13] And this same man writes to Voltaire, that an Atheist cannot be guilty before God. That should the law find the Atheist guilty of death, it was the denounciator who should be burned as such.[14]

Voltaire would blaspheme the law of Christ, retract, receive the sacrament, and press the conspirators to crush the wretch! Jean Jaques would lay aside Christianity, or resume it again, and with Calvin partake of the Last Supper.[15] He will write the most sublime encomiums on Christ that human eloquence could devise, and then finish by blaspheming that same Christ as a fanatic.[16] If the Antichristian Revolution was one day to carry Voltaire triumphantly to the Pantheon, Rousseau had the same rights to the inauguration of the Sophisters of Impiety. We shall see him gain far other claims on the Sophisters of Rebellion. If the former secretly solicits kings to subscribe to his statue, the latter openly writes that at Sparta one would have been erected to him.

With so singular a conduct each of these chiefs had his distinctive characteristics. Voltaire hated the God of the Christians; Jean Jaques admired, but blasphemed him; pride wrought in the latter all that jealousy and hatred produced in the former; and it will long be a doubt which has been most injurious to Christianity, the one by his atrocious sarcasms and impious satire, or the other by his sophistry under the cloak of reason.

After their separation, Voltaire hated Jean Jaques, scoffed at him, and would have him chained as a madman.[17] But he could not hide his joy, when the Profession of Faith of the Savoyard Vicar, written by this madman, was the book out of which youth were taught to read.[18] Jean Jaques would at the same time detest the chiefs of the conspirators, expose them and be hated by them: he would preserve their principles, court their friendship and esteem anew, and that of the premier chief in particular.[19]

If to define the Sophister of Ferney be a difficult task, is it not equally so, to paint the citizen of Geneva? Jean Jaques loved the sciences, and was crowned by those who reviled them; he wrote against the theatre, and composed operas; he sought friends, and is famous for his breaches of friendship. He extols the charms of virtue, and he bends the knee before the prostitute de Varens. He declares himself the most virtuous of men, and, under the modest title of his Confessions, he retraces in his old age the dissolute scenes of his youth. To tender mothers he gives the most pathetic advice in nature; and, smothering in himself the cries of that same nature, he banishes his children to that hospital where, from the shame of its birth, the unfortunate babe is condemned to the perpetual ignorance of its parents. The fear of seeing them makes him inexorable to the entreaties of those who would have provided for their education.[20] A prodigy of inconsistency even to his last moments; he wrote against suicide, and perhaps it is treating him too favorably not to assert that he himself had prepared the poison which caused his death.[21]

However inconsistent, error is inculcated by the Sophister of Geneva with all the powers of genius; and many have lost their faith by his works, who would have resisted all other attacks. To be cradled in one's passions gave empire to Voltaire; but to resist Jean Jaques the acutest sophisms were to be penetrated: youth was led away by the former, while those who were advanced in age fell a victim to the latter, and a prodigious number of adepts owed their fall to these two writers.

Indignantly would the manes of *Buffon* see his name classed after that of Jean Jaques among the conspiring adepts; and impossible is it for the historian, when speaking of those who have adopted the fashion set by Voltaire, not to sigh at pronouncing the name of the French Pliny. He certainly was rather the victim than the associate of the conspirators. But who can erase Philosophism from his writings? Nature had lent her genius, and why would he not content himself with what she had placed before him? No; he would ascend higher, he would explain those mysteries reserved to revelation alone; and, soaring above his sphere, he often shows himself the disciple of Maillet and Boulanger. In giving the history of nature, he destroys that of religion. He was the hero of those men whom D'Alembert had sent to split mountains, and seek from the depths of the earth arguments to belie Moses and the first pages of holy writ. In the praises of the Sophisters he consoles himself for the censures of the Sorbonne; but the punishment attached to the fault itself, as he only belied his own reputation for a knowledge of the laws of nature. They appeared to be null when he treated of the earth formed by the waters, or by fire, and of his endless epochs. And to falsify the scriptures, he makes nature as inconsistent as his own systems. His style, elegant and sublime, has always been admired, but found insufficient to save his works from the smile of the real philosopher; and his glory, like his comet, vanished in his dreams of incredulity. Happy, if in retracting his errors he had been able to destroy that spirit of research in the adepts who only studied nature through the medium of Voltaire.[22]

After these two men, so justly distinguished by the grandeur of their style, the remaining adepts chiefly owe their celebrity to their impiety; nevertheless, two might have done honor to science by their learning. The first, *Freret*, had by his immense memory nearly learned Bayle's Dictionary by heart. But his letters to Thrasybulus, the offspring of his Atheism, shows that his vast memory was more than outweighed by his want of judgment.

The second was *Boulanger*, whose brain, overburdened with Latin, Greek, Hebrew, Syriac and Arabic, had also adopted all the extravagancies of Atheism; but who retracted in the latter part of his life, execrating the Sect that had misled him. We shall soon see that all the posthumous works attributed to these writers were not written by them.

Fain would the *Marquis D'Argence de Dirac* have figured among the *learned* Sophisters; but his *Chinese and Cabalistic Letters*, and his *Philosophy of Good Sense*, only prove, that to Bayle's Dictionary he was indebted for his pretended reputation. He was a long while a friend of Frederic's, and his impiety entitled him to that friendship. From his brother, the President D'Eguille, we have learned, that after several discussions on religion, with persons better versed in that science than Frederic, he submitted to the light of the Gospel, and ardently wished to atone for his past infidelity.

As to *La Metherie* the doctor, if he appeared to rave, it was only from the sincerity of his heart. His *man-machine*, or his *man-plant*, only caused the Sect to blush from the open manner in which he had said what many of them wished to insinuate.

Even in the first days of the revolution, the Sophisters conspiring against their God thought they could glory in the talents and co-operation of *Marmontel*. But let us not add to the sorrows of the man who needed only the first days of the revolution to shrink with horror from those conspiracies which had given it birth. Of all the Sophisters who have outlived Voltaire, Mr. de Marmontel is the one who most wished to hide his former intimacy with the Antichristian chiefs. But alas, it is to those connections that he owes his celebrity, far more than to his *Incas*, his *Belifarius*, or his *Tales*, intermingled with Philosophism. We could wish to hide it, but Voltaire's own letters convict the repenting adept of having acted, and that during a long time, a very different part among the conspirators. Voltaire was so well convinced of Mr. de Marmontel's zeal, that, thinking himself on the point of death, he bequeathed La Harpe to him. His last will is worded thus, "I recommend La Harpe to you, when I am no more; *he will be one of the pillars of our church.* You must have him received of the academy. After having gained so many prizes, it is but just that he should bestow them in his turn."[23]

With a taste for literature, and some talents, which in spite of his critics distinguish him above the common rank of the writers of the day, *Mr. de la Harpe* might have rendered his works useful, had he not, from his youth, been the spoilt child of Voltaire. At that age it is easy to believe one's self a Philosopher, when one disbelieves one's catechism; and the young La Harpe blindly followed the instructions of his master. If he never was the pillar, he might be correctly styled the trumpeter of the new church, by means of the *Mercure*, a famous French journal, by which its encomiums or its weekly criticisms nearly decided the fate of all literary productions.[24]

The encomiums which Voltaire lavished on that journal after La Harpe had undertaken the direction of it show how little governments are aware of the influence of such journals over the public opinion. Above ten thousand people subscribed, and many more perused the *Mercure*; and, influenced by its suggestions, they by degrees became as philosophic, or rather impious, as the hebdomadary Sophister himself. The Conspirators saw what advantage could be reaped from this literary dominion. La Harpe ruled the sceptre during many years; then Marmontel jointly with Champfort as Remi, who was little better, had held it before them. I one day asked the latter, how it was possible that he had inserted in his journal one of the most false and wicked accounts possible of a work purely literary, and of which I had heard him speak in the highest terms. He answered me, that the article alluded to had been written by a friend of D'Alembert's, and that he owed his journal and even his fortune to D'Alembert's protection. The injured author wished to publish his defence in the same journal, but it was all in vain.—Let the reader judge from this how powerfully the periodical papers contributed to the designs of the conspirators; in fact, it was by them that the public mind was chiefly directed to their desired object.

This Sect disposed of reputations by their praises or their censures, as best suited them.—By these journals they reaped the two-fold advantage of pointing out to those writers who hungered after glory or bread[25] what subjects they were to investigate, and of calling, by means of their literary trump, the attention of the public only to those works, which the Sect wished to circulate, or from which they had nothing to fear.

By such artifices the La Harpes of the day forwarded the conspiracy as much, if not more than the most active of the Sophisters, or their most impious writers. The sophistical author would mingle or condense his poison in his productions, whilst the journalist adept would proclaim it, and infuse it throughout the capital, or into all parts of the empire. The man who would have remained ignorant of the very existence of an impious or a seditious work, the man who would neither have spent his time nor his money on such productions, imbibed the whole of their poison from the insidious extracts made by the sophistical journalist.

Above all the adepts, far more than even Voltaire himself, did a fiend called *Condorcet* hate the son of his God. At the very name of the Deity the monster raged; and it appeared as if he wished to revenge on heaven the heart it had given him. Cruel and ungrateful, the cool assassin of friendship and of his benefactors, he would willingly have directed the dagger against his God, as he did against La Rochefoucault. Atheism was but folly in La Metherie and madness in Diderot; but in Condorcet it was the phrenzy of hatred and the offspring of pride. It was impossible to convince Condorcet, that any thing but a fool could believe in God. Voltaire, who had seen him when a youth, little foresaw what services he was to render to the conspiracy, even when he wrote, "My great consolation in dying is, that you support the honor of our poor Velches, in which you will be well assisted by the Marquis de Condorcet!"[26]

It could not have been on the talents of this man that the premier rested his hopes. Condorcet had learned as much geometry as D'Alembert could teach him; but as to the Belles Lettres, he was not even of the second class.—His style was that of a man who did not know his own language; and his writings, like his sophisms, required much study to be understood.—But hatred did for him what nature has done for others. Perpetually plodding at his blasphemies, he at last succeeded in expressing them more clearly; for the amazing difference which is observable between his former and his latter works can only thus be accounted for. It is more remarkable in his posthumous work on the human mind, where his pen can hardly be traced, excepting in a few passages, though his genius haunts every page. There he is to be seen, as during his life time, in his studies, in his writings or conversation, directing every thing towards Atheism, seeking no other object in this work than to inspire his readers with his own frantic hatred against his God. Long had he looked for the downfal of the altar, as the only sight his heart could enjoy. He beheld it, but was soon to fall himself. His end was that of the impious man, a vagabond and wanderer, sinking under pain, misery, and the dread of

Robespierre, without acknowledging the hand of God, that struck him by that of the ferocious dictator. Alas, if he died as he lived, will not the first moments of his conviction and repentance be those, when he shall hear that God, whom he blasphemed and denied, confessed by the mouths of those awful victims of eternal vengeance!!

During his lifetime, so great was his hatred, that adopting error, in order to rid men of that fear of an immortal God in heaven, he did not stop short of imagining that his Philosophism would one day render men immortal upon earth. To belie Moses and the prophets, he became himself the prophet of madness. Moses had shown the days of man decreasing unto the age at which God had fixed them, and the royal prophet had declared the days of man to extend from sixty fo seventy, and at the most to eighty years, after which all was trouble and pain. And to the oracles of the Holy Ghost, Condorcet would oppose his! When he calculates his philosophic revolution, which begins by dragging so many to their graves, he adds to the creed of his impiety that of his extravagancies; and without hesitation he pronounces that, "*we are to believe that the life of man must perpetually increase*, if physical revolutions do not obstruct it. That we are ignorant of the extreme term which it is never to exceed. We do not even know, *whether nature in its general laws* has fixed that extreme term!" Thus in his pretended *Philosophic Sketch of the Progress of the human Mind*,[27] after having built his entire history on the hatred of Christ, and left no hopes to man but in Atheism, we see this Sophister of falsehood, setting up for a prophet, and foreseeing all the fruits of his triumphant philosophy. It is in the very moment of the overthrow of the altar that he tells us, that henceforth the days of man shall be lengthened, and that in lieu of an eternal God in heaven, man may become immortal on earth, as if at the very moment of its triumph Philosophism and the pride of the whole Sect were to be humbled through the extravagancies of the most impious and dearest of its adepts. A life wholly spent in blasphemy could not fail to have frenzy for its end.

The name of Condorcet will appear again in these memoirs, and we shall see him hating kings nearly as much as he did his God. Helvetius, and many others before him, had fallen a victim to this double hatred, though their hearts seemed capable of neither.

The unfortunate *Helvetius*, the child of a virtuous father, followed his steps till beyond his early youth. An exemplary piety had been the fruit of a good education, till he became acquainted with Voltaire. He at first sought him as a master, and his love for poetry had inspired him with admiration for Voltaire. Such was the origin of their intimacy, and never was connection more perfidious. In lieu of poetry, impiety constituted his lectures; and in the space of one year Voltaire transforms his pupil into a more impious and determined Atheist than he was himself.—Helvetius was rich, and was at once agent and protector; laying aside the Gospel, like the generality of the Sophisters, who while they pretend to superior understanding in crediting the mysteries of Revelation, not only believe in all the absurdities of Atheism, but are the sport of their own puerile credulity in all that can be turned against religion. Helvetius's works on the *Spirit*, and which Voltaire calls *Matter*, is filled with ridiculous stories and fables, which he gives for truths, and which are all beneath criticism. This is nevertheless the work of a man who pretends to reform the universe, but who equally disgusts his readers by the licentiousness and obscenity of his morals, and by the absurdity of his materialism.

Helvetius also wrote on *Happiness*, but appears himself to have been a perfect stranger to it. In spite of all his Philosophy, he was so tender to the best-founded censure, that he lost his rest, quitted his country, and only returned to brood over the hatred he had vowed to kings and to the church.—Naturally of a good and gentle disposition, his work *on Man and his Education* proves how much Philosophism had altered that disposition. There he gives full scope to the grossest calumny and abuse, and denies facts daily occurring, and most publicly attested.[28]

I have already spoken of *Raynald*; it is not worth our while to call *Deslisle* from the oblivion in which both he and his work on the *Philosophy of Nature*, have so long been buried. Still less to speak of *Robinet* and his book *of Nature*, which is only remembered on account of his strange explanations of the intellect by *oval fibres*; of memory by *undulated or spiral fibres*; of will by *fretted fibres*; pleasure and pain by *bundles of sensibility*, and learning by *humps in the understanding*, and a thousand such like vagaries, if possible, still more ridiculous.[29]

I shall, however, mention *Toussaint*, as that man shows to what a height Atheism raged among the Conspirators. He had undertaken the part of the corruption of morals.[30] Under the mask of moderation, he succeeds by telling youth, that *nothing was to be feared from love*, this passion *only perfecting them*. That between man and woman *that* was a sufficient claim on each other without matrimony.[31] *That children are not more beholden to their fathers for their birth, than for the champagne they had drunk, or the minuet they had been pleased to dance*.[32] That, vengeance being incompatible with God, the wicked had nothing to fear from the punishments of another world.[33] Notwithstanding all this doctrine, the conspirators looked upon him as a timid adept, because he owned a God in heaven, and a soul in man; and to punish him they styled him the *Capuchin Philosopher*. Happily for him, he took a better way of punishing them, by abandoning their cause and recanting from his errors.[34]

In vain should I name a crowd of other writers of the Sect. Voltaire had so perfectly brought Antichristian productions into fashion, that this species of literature was the resource and livelihood of those miserable scribblers who fed upon their traffic in blasphemy. Holland in particular, that miry bog, where the demon of avarice, enthroned under the auspices of a few booksellers, would for a doit have made over every soul, every religion to impiety, was the grand asylum of these starving infidels. *Marc Michel Rey* appears to have been the bookseller who bought their blasphemies at the highest price. He kept in his pay one Laurent, a monk, who had taken refuge at Amsterdam, and is the author of the *Portable Divinity*, and so many other impious works recommended by Voltaire, particularly of the *Compere Mathieu*. This monk had other co-operators, whom Marc Michel Rey paid by the sheet. It is Voltaire himself who gives us this account, and these are the works of which he perpetually recommends the circulation, as those of a Philosophy which diffused a new light to the universe.[35]

We shall soon see the presses of the secret confraternity vying with those of Holland in deluging Europe with these vile productions. Their immense number brought them into such repute, that many years before the revolution there was not a petty poet, not a novel writer, but must needs pay his tribute to the Philosophism of impiety. One might have thought that the whole art of writing, and of obtaining readers, consisted in epigrams and sarcasms against religion; that all sciences, even the most foreign to religion, had equally conspired against the God of Christianity.

The history of mankind was transformed into the art of distorting facts, and of directing them against Christianity and Revelation; Physics, or the history of Nature, into Anti-Mosaic systems. Medicine had its atheism, and *Petit* taught it at the schools of surgery. *La Lande* and *Dupui* imbued with it their lectures on astronomy, while others introduced it even into grammar; and Condorcet, proclaiming this progress of Philosophism, exults in seeing it *descend from the northern thrones into the universities*.[36] The young men, walking in the footsteps of their masters, carried to the bar all those principles which our romancing lawyers were to display in the Constituent Assembly. On leaving the college, the attorneys clerks, or those of a counting-house, only seemed to have learned their letters in order to articulate the blasphemies of Voltaire or Jean Jaques. Such was the rising generation, who, since the expulsion of their former masters, were to be found prepared for the grand revolution. Hence arose the Mirabeaux and Brissots, the Caras and Garats, the Merciers and Cheniers. Hence, in a word, all that class of French literati, who appear to have been universally carried away by the torrent of the French Revolution.

An apostacy so universal does not necessarily prove that literature and science are prejudicial in themselves; but it shews that men of letters, destitute of religion, are the most dangerous subjects in the state. It is not absolutely in that class that a Robespierre and a Jourdan is found; but it can afford a Petion or a Marat. It can afford principles, sophisms, and a morality, which terminate in Robespierres or in Jourdans; and if these latter murder a Bailly, terrify a Marmontel, and imprison a La Harpe, they only terrify, murder, or imprison their progenitors.

1. To D'Alembert, 5 Feb. 1765, Vol. 68, Let. 156. P. 143.
2. His Confessions, book 6th.
3. Voltaire on Atheism.
4. Voltaire on Atheism; and on the Soul by Suranus.
5. The Emile and Let. to the Archbishop of Paris.
6. Letter to Voltaire, vol. 12. Quarto edit. of Geneva.

7. Voltaire on the Principle of Action.—Jean Jaques in the Emile, vol. 3, page 115, and Letter to the Archbishop of Paris.
8. Voltaire, Quest. Encyclop. vol. 9.—Jean Jaques, Emile, vol. 3, page. 61, and Let. to the Archbishop of Paris.
9. On Atheism.
10. Axiom 3.
11. To D'Alembert, 16 June, 1773, Vol. 69, Let. 113, P. 193.
12. Emile, vol. 4, page 68. Social Contract, Chap. 8.
13. Letter to Mr. Vernier.
14. Letters to Voltaire, Vol. 12, and New Eloisa.
15. D'Alembert writes to Voltaire, in speaking of Rousseau, "I pity him; and if his happiness depends on his approaching the Holy Table, and in calling holy a religion which he has so much vilified, I own that my esteem is greatly diminished." (25 *Sept.* 1762, *Vol.* 68, *Let.* 105, *P.* 217.) He might have said as much of Voltaire's communions, but he never dared. He even seeks to give him a plea for his hypocrisy, when he says, "Perhaps I am in the wrong; for certainly you are better acquainted than I am with the reasons that determined you." He does not mention his esteem being diminished; on the contrary, Voltaire is always his *dear and illustrious master*! 31 *May* 1768, *Vol.* 68, *Let.* 232. *P.* 482.
16. His Confessions and Professions of the Savoyard Vicar.
17. To Damilaville, 8 May 1761, Vol. 57, Let. 52, P. 108, and War of Geneva.
18. To the Count D'Argental, 26 Sept. 1766, Vol. 57, Let. 270, P. 478.
19. See his letters, and the Life of Seneca by Diderot.
20. See his Confessions.
21. See his life by the Count Barruel de Beauvert.
22. D'Alembert and Voltaire ridiculed all those vain systems of Bailly and Buffon on the antiquity of the world and of its inhabitants. They would call these systems, *Nonsense, Follies, an Excuse for the want of Genius, Shallow Ideas, Vain and ridiculous Quackery* (From D'Alembert, 6 March 1777, Vol. 69, Let 178, P. 296); but D'Alembert took care to keep his opinions secret on this subject. By discrediting these systems he feared lest he should discourage those adepts whom he and sent to forge new ones in the Appenines, in order to give the lie to Moses and the sacred writ.
23. To Marmontel, 21 Aug. 1767, Vol. 60, Let. 159, P. 272.
24. We learn, by the public newspapers, that Mr. de la Harpe was converted, when in prison, by the Bishop of St. Brieux. I should be little surprised at it. The examples of this prelate, with the fruits of Philosophism in this revolution, must strongly impress the man who, with a sound judgment, can compare them with the lessons and promises of his former masters. If the news of this conversion be true, I shall have shown him consecrating his talents to error; and nobody will applaud him more than myself, for consecrating them in future to truth alone.
25. The Sophisters were so well acquainted with the powers of a journal, that they mustered up their highest protections against the religious authors who would dispute one with them. When Voltaire was informed that Mr. Clement was to succeed to Mr. Freron, whose pen had long been consecrated to the vindication of truth, he did not blush at sending D'Alembert to the chancellor in hopes of hindering Mr. Clement from continuing Freron's journal. (To D'Alembert, 12 Feb. 1773, Vol. 69, Let. 97, P. 163.).

26. To D'Alembert, 2 March, 1773, Vol. 69, Let. 101, P. 170.
27. Epoch 10th, Page 382.
28. I would willingly have acquitted Helvetius of this posthumous work, by saying, that it might have been an offspring of that same committee which had fathered so many other impious works on the dead. But then Voltaire could not have mentioned that work to his brethren at Paris, as one that they must be acquainted with. In three successive letters, he attributes it to Helvetius. He censures him on history, as we have done; and D'Alembert, who could not be ignorant of its author, does not undeceive him. The shame then of this work must attach to Helvetius. This man writes (in a city where its archbishop and its pastors were remarkable for their care and charity to the poor) that the clergy were so hard-hearted, that the poor were never seen to beg an alms of them; though in that very city the rectors were perpetually seen surrounded by and alleviating the distresses of those same poor. (See his work on Man, &c.) Such were the calumnies his hatred invented, though contradicted by daily facts. He might have said with more truth, that many applied for alms to ecclesiastics and religious houses when they dared not ask them elsewhere.
29. Of Nature, Vol. 1, Book 4, Chap. 2, &c. &c.
30. On Morals, Part 2 and 3.
31. Ibid.
32. Ibid, Part 3, Art. 4.
33. Ibid. Part 2, Sect. 2.
34. See his Expostulations on the Book of MORALS.
35. To Count D'Argental, 28 Sept. 1761, Vol. 57, Let. 117, P. 241—To D'Alembert, 15 Jan. 1768, Vol. 68, Let. 223, P. 438, and 13 Jan. 1769, Let. 2, P. 6—To Mr. De Bordes, 4 Apr. 1768, vol. 60, Let. 260, P. 448.
36. See his artful Edition of Pascal, Advertisement, P. 5.

CHAP. XVI.

Conduct of the Clergy towards the Antichristian Conspirators.

WHILE apostacy bore sway in the palaces of the great, and in the schools of science; and while all the higher classes of citizens were led away from the worship of their religion, some by example, others by the artful Sophisms of the Conspirators; the duties of the clergy could not be doubtful. It was their part to oppose a bank to the fetid torrent of impiety, and save the multitude from being swept away by its waters. Far more than its honour or its interest, its very name called on the clergy, by the most sacred ties of duty and of conscience, to guard the altar against the attacks of the Conspirators. The least backwardness in the combat would have added treason to apostacy. Let the historian who dared speak the truth on kings be true on the merits of his own body; whether it redounds to the honour or disgrace of his brethren, let him speak the truth. Hence the future clergy will learn from what has been done the line of conduct they ought to follow. The Conspiracy against Christ is not extinct, though it may be hidden; but should it burst forth anew, must not the pastor know how far his conduct may influence or retard its progress?

If under the name of Clergy were comprehended all those who in France wore the half-livery of the church, all that class of men who in Paris, and some of the great towns, styled themselves Abbés, history might reproach the clergy with traitors and apostates from the first dawn of the Conspiracy. We find the Abbé de Prades the first apostate, and happily first to repent; the Abbé Morellet, whose disgrace is recorded in the repeated praises of Voltaire and D'Alembert;[1] the Abbé Condilhac, who was to sophisticate the morals of his royal pupil; and above all, that Abbé Raynal, whose name alone is tantamount to twenty demoniacs of the Sect.

Paris swarmed with those Abbés; we still say, the Abbé Barthelemi, the Abbé Beaudeau, again the Abbé Noel, and the Abbé Syeyes. But the people, on the whole, did not confound them with the clergy. They knew them to be the offspring of avarice, seeking the livings but laying aside the duties of the church ; or through economy adopting the dress, while by their profligacy and irreligious writings they dishonored it. The numbers of these amphibious animals, and particularly in the metropolis, may be one of the severest reproaches against the clergy. However great the distinctions made between these and the latter may have been, the repeated scandals of the former powerfully helped the Conspiracy, by laying themselves open to satire, which retorted upon the whole body, and affected the real ministers of the altar. Many of these Abbés, who did not believe in God, had obtained livings through the means of the Sophisters, who by soliciting dignities for their adepts sought to introduce their principles, and dishonour the clergy by their immorality. It was the plague that they spread in the enemy's camp; and not daring to face them in the field, they sought to poison their springs.

If under the title of Clergy we only comprehend those who really served at the altar, the Conspirators never prevailed against them. I have searched their records; I have examined whether among the bishops and functionary clergy any of these adepts were to be found, who could be classed with the conspiring Sophisters. Antecedent to the Périgords and d'Autuns, or the apostacy of the Gobets, Gregoires, and other constitutionalists, I only meet with the name of Briennes, and one Judas seated in the College of the Apostles during the space of thirty years is quite sufficient; or rather, is one too many.[2] Meslier, rector of Etrépigny in Champagne, might be added, were it certain that his impious *Last Will and Testament*, was not a forgery of the Sophisters attributed to him after his death.

In the times when the revolution drew near, Philosophism attached itself to the covenants of men, and soon produced Dom Gerles and his confederates, but these belonged to a different class of conspirators, which will be a future object of our Memoirs. At all times the body of the clergy preserved the purity of its faith; a distinction might have been made between the zealous edifying ecclesiastics, and the lax (not to say scandalous) ones; but that of believing and unbelieving could never stand. Never could the Conspirators exult in this latter distinction. Would they not have availed themselves of their decreasing faith, as they did of the incredulity of the ministers of Geneva?[3] On the contrary, the most scurrilous abuse is uttered against the clergy for their zeal in support of Christianity, and the satire of the Sophisters redounds to their immortal honor.

The purity of faith alone was not sufficient in the clergy; examples far more powerful than lessons were necessary to oppose the torrent of impiety. It is true that in the greater part of their pastors the people beheld it in an eminent degree; but the majority will not suffice. Those who are acquainted with the powers of impression know but too well, that one bad ecclesiastic does more harm than a hundred of the most virtuous can do good. All should have been zealous, but many were lax. There were among those who served the altars men unworthy of the sanctuary. These were ambitious men, who, while they ought to have been giving good example to their dioceses, preferred the intrigues and pomp of the capital. It is true, such a conduct could not have constituted vice in the worldling, but what may be venial in the world, is often monstrous in the church. The Sophisters in particular, with their morals, were not authorised to reprobate those of the delinquent clergy. Where is the wonder that some few unworthy members should have intruded on the sanctuary, when the enemies of the church had possessed themselves of its avenues, in order to prevent the preferment of those whose virtues or learning they dreaded? How could it be otherwise, when the bishops wishing to repel an unworthy member, Choiseul answered, "Such are the men we want and will have:" or when the irreligious nobleman only beheld in the riches of the church, the inheritance of a son not less vicious than his father?

The clergy might certainly have thus replied to their enemies. And true it is, that if any thing could astonish us, it is not that with all these intrigues and ambition some few bad pastors had been obtruded on the church, but rather that so many good ones, worthy of their titles, yet remained. But the crimes of the first instigators do not excuse those pastors who gave room for the scandal. Let the future clergy find this avowal recorded; let those men be acquainted with whatever influenced the progress of the Antichristian Revolution, whose duty essentially militates against that progress, and renders the least pretext given criminal in them.

History, however, must also declare, that if the remissness of some few may have furnished a pretext to the conspirators, the majority made a noble stand against them; and though some few spots could be found, the body was nevertheless splendent with the light of its virtues, which shone forth with redoubled lustre, when impiety at length, strengthened in its progress, threw off the mask. Then rising above its powers, the clergy were not to be intimidated by death, or the rigors of a long exile; and the Sophister unwillingly blushed at the calumnies he had spread, when he represented those men as more attached to the riches than to the faith of the church. Those riches remained in the hands of the banditti, while that faith crowns the archbishops, bishops and ecclesiastics butchered at the Carmes, or consoles those who have found in foreign countries a refuge from the armies and bloody decrees of the Jacobins: every where poor, and living on the beneficence of those countries, but powerfully rich in the purity of their faith and testimony of their conscience.

But the Clergy had not waited these awful days to oppose the principles of the Conspirators.—From the first dawn of the Conspiracy we can trace their opposition. Scarcely had impiety raised its voice, when the clergy sought to confound it: the Encyclopedia was not half printed when it was proscribed in their assemblies; nor has a single convocation been held for these fifty years past, which has not warned the throne and the magistracy of the progress of Philosophism.[4]

At the head of the prelates who opposed it, we find *Mr. de Beaumont*, archbishop of Paris, whose name history could not silently pass over without injustice. Generous as an Ambrose, he was fired with the same zeal, and equally stedfast against the enemies of the faith. The Jansenists obtained his exile, and the Antichristians would willingly have sent him to the scaffold; but there he would have braved their poignards, as he did the Jansenists; when he returned from his exile, he might be said to have acquired new vigor to oppose them both.

Many other bishops following his example, to the most unblemished manners added their pastoral instructions. *Mr. de Pompignan*, then Bishop of Puy refuted the errors of Voltaire and Jean Jaques; the *Cardinal de Luynes* warned his flock against the *System of Nature*; the Bishops of Boulogne, Amiens, Auch and many others, more powerfully edified their dioceses by their example than even by their writings; nor did there pass a single year, without some bishop combating the increasing progress of the impious Conspirators.

If the Sophistry of the Sect continued its ravages, it was not the fault of the Bishops or the religious writers. The Sorbonne exposed it in their censures. The *Abbé Bergier* victoriously pursues Deism in its very last intrenchments, and makes it blush at its own contradictions. To the sophisticated learning of the Conspirators, he opposed a more loyal application and a truer knowledge of antiquity and of the weapons it furnished to religion.[5] The *Abbé Guénée*, with all that urbanity and attic salt of which he was master, obliges Voltaire to humble himself at the sight of his own ignorance and false criticism of sacred writ.[6] The *Abbé Gérard* had found a method of sanctifying novels themselves. Under the most engaging forms, he reclaims youth from vice and its tortuous ways, and restores history to its primitive truth. The *Abbé Pey* had searched all the records of the church to reinstate it in its real rights, and under the simple form of a catechism, we see the *Abbé Feller*, or *Flexier Dureval*, uniting every thing that reason, truth, or science can oppose against the Sophisters.

Prior to all these champions of the faith, the *Abbé Duguet* had victoriously vindicated the principles of Christianity, and the *Abbé Houteville* had demonstrated the truth of it from history. From the first dawn of the Conspiracy, the *Père Berthier* and his associates had, in the Journal de Trevoux, particularly exposed the errors of the Encyclopedists. We see, therefore, that if the Celsi and Porphirii were numerous, religion had not lost its Justins or its Origens. In these latter times, as in the primitive days of Christianity, he who sincerely sought after truth must have found it in the victorious arguments of the religious authors, opposed to the Sophisms of the Conspirators. And it may be truly said, that many points of religion had been placed by these modern apologists in clearer light than they had been seen in before.

The Christian orators ably assisted the efforts of their bishops, and incessantly invoked the attention of the people to their danger. The refutation of Philosophism was become the object of their public discourses. The *Pere Neuville*, and after him *Mr. de Senez*, and the *Pere Beauregard* in particular, seem to have been fired by that holy zeal. That sudden inspiration with which he appeared to be seized in the Cathedral Church of Paris is not yet forgotten; when thirteen years before the revolution, expounding the different maxims and exposing the plans of modern Philosophism, he made the vaults of the temple resound with words too shamefully verified by the revolution, and exclaims in a prophetic strain: "Yes it is at the King—at the King and at religion that the Philosophers aim their blows. They have grasped the hatchet and the hammer, they only wait the favorable moment to overturn the altar and the throne.—Yes, my God! thy temples will be plundered and destroyed; thy festivals abolished; they sacred name blasphemed; thy worship proscribed. - But what sounds, Great God, do I hear! what do I behold!—to the sacred canticles which caused the vaults of this temple to resound to thy praises, succeed wanton and prophane songs! And thou infamous Deity of Paganism, impure Venus, thou durst advance hither, and audaciously, in the place of the living God, seat thyself on the throne of the Holy of Holies, and there receive the guilty incense of thy new adorers."

This discourse was heard by a numerous audience, collected by their own piety or attracted by the eloquence of the orator; by adepts themselves, who attended in hopes of carping at his expressions; by doctors of the laws with whom we were acquainted, and who often repeated them to us, long before we had seen them printed in various publications. The adepts cried out, Sedition and Fanaticism. The doctors of the law only retracted the severity of their censures after they had seen the prediction completely accomplished.

Such strong cautions from the clergy, and the means they opposed, retarded indeed the progress of the Sophisters; but could not triumph over the conspiracy. It was too deep, the black arts of seduction had been too well planned in the hidden dens of the conspirators. I have still to unfold some of their dark mysteries; and when light shall have shone upon them, with surprise shall the reader ask, not how was it possible, (with so much zeal on the part of the clergy) that the altar should be overthrown, but how the fall of the temple could have been so long delayed?

1. To D'Alembert, 16 June, 1760, Vol. 68, Let. 65, P. 115. To Thiriot, 26 Jan. 1762, Vol. 57, Let. 157, P. 320.
2. It is true that Voltaire in his correspondence, sometimes flatters himself with the protection of the Cardinal de Bernis, who was then but the youthful favourite of the Marquise de Pompadour, or the slender poet of the Graces. The mistakes of a young man are not sufficient to prove his concert with conspirators, whom he never supported unless in the expulsion of the Jesuits. But could not what D'Alembert said of the parliaments apply to him, "Forgive them, Lord, for they know not what they do, nor whose commands they obey." D'Alembert writes in a quite another style, when he speaks of Briennes; he shows him acting the most resolute part of a traitor, in support of the Conspiracy, and simply hiding his game from the clergy. (*From D'Alembert, 4 and 21 Dec. 1770, Vol. 69, Let. 48 and 53, P. 85 and 91.*)

I found some few letters also, mentioning the Prince Lewis de Rohan, seconding their intrigues on the reception of Marmontel at the Academy, condescending, as D'Alembert says, *from Coadjutor of a Catholic Church*, to become *the Coadjutor of Philosophy*. (*From D'Alembert, 8 Dec. 1763, Vol. 68, Let. 121, Page 260.*) If such an error in a prince, naturally noble and generous, proves that he was mistaken in thinking that he barely protected literature in the person of an adept, it does not necessarily follow that he musdt have been initiated into the secrets of those who abused his protection, and ended by sporting with his person.

3. See the Encyclopedia, article GENEVA; and letter of Voltaire to Mr. Vernes.
4. See the acts of the clergy since the year 1750.
5. His Deism refuted, and his Answer to Freret.
6. Letters to some Portuguese Jews.

CHAP. XVII.

New and more subtle Means of the Conspirators to Seduce even the lowest Classes of the People.

WHEN Voltaire swore to annihilate Christianity, he did not flatter himself with the hope of drawing the generality of nations into his apostacy. His pride seems often satisfied with the progress that Philosophism had made among those *who governed, or were made to govern*, and among *men of letters*;[1] for a long time he does not appear to envy Christianity the inferior classes of society, which he does not comprehend under the appellation of the *better sort*. The facts we are about to lay before the reader will show to what new extent the conspirators sought to carry their impious zeal, and by what artifices Christ was to be deprived of all worship even from the lowest populace.

A doctor known in France by the name of *Duquesnai* had so well insinuated himself into the favor of Lewis XV that the king used to call him his *thinker*. He really appeared to have deeply meditated on the happiness of the subject, and he may have sincerely wished it; nevertheless he was but a system-maker, and the founder of that Sect of Sophisters called Œconomists, because the œconomy and order to be introduced into the finances, and other means of alleviating the distresses of the people, were perpetually in their mouths. If some few of these œconomists sought nothing further in their speculations, it is certain, that their writers took no pains to conceal their hatred for the Christian religion. Their works abound in passages which at least show their wish of substituting natural religion to the Christian religion and revelation.[2] Their affectation of solely speaking of agriculture, administration, and œconomy, render them less liable to suspicion, than those conspirators who are perpetually intruding their impiety.

Duquesnai and his adepts had more especially undertaken to persuade their readers, that the country people, and mechanics in towns, were entirely destitute of that kind of instruction necessary for their professions; that men of this class, unable to acquire knowledge by reading, pined away in an ignorance equally fatal to themselves and to the state; that it was necessary to establish free schools, and particularly throughout the country, where children might be brought up to different trades, and instructed in the principles of agriculture. D'Alembert, and the Voltairian adepts, soon perceived what advantages they could reap from these establishments. In union with the Œeconomists, they presented various memorials to Lewis XV in which not only the temporal but even the spiritual advantages of such establishments for the people are strongly urged. The king, who really loved the people, embraced the project with warmth. He opened his mind on the subject to Mr. Bertin, whom he honored with his confidence, and had entrusted with his privy purse. It was from frequent conversations with this minister, that the memorial from which we extract the following account was drawn up. It is Mr. Bertin himself who speaks:

"Lewis XV," says that minister, "having entrusted me with the care of his privy purse, it was natural that he should mention to me an establishment of which his Majesty was to defray the expence. I had long since closely observed the different Sects of our philosophers; and though I had much to reproach myself with as to the practice, I had at least preserved the principles of my religion. I had little doubt of the efforts of the Philosophers to destroy it. I was sensible that they wished to have the direction of these schools themselves, and by that means seize on the education of the people, under pretence that the bishops and ecclesiastics, who had hitherto superintended them and their teachers, could not be competent judges in subjects so little suited to clergymen. I apprehended that their object was not so much to give lessons on agriculture to the children of husbandmen and trades-people, as to withdraw them from their habitual instructions on their catechism or on their religion.

"I did not hesitate to declare to the king, that the intentions of the Philosophers were very different from his. I know those conspirators, I said; and beware, Sire, of giving them your aid. Your kingdom is not deficient in free schools, or schools nearly free; they are to be found in every little town, and almost in every village, and perhaps they are already but too numerous. It is not books that form mechanics and plowmen. The books and masters sent by these Philosophers, will rather infuse system than industry into the country people. I tremble lest they render them idle, vain, and jealous; in a short time discontended and seditious, and at length rebellious. I fear, lest the whole fruit of the expence they seek to put your Majesty to, should be gradually to obliterate from the hearts of the people the love of their religion and their sovereign.

"To these arguments I added whatever my mind could suggest to dissuade his Majesty. I advised him, in place of sending and paying those masters whom the Phiosophers had chosen, to employ the same sums for multiplying the catechists, and in sesarching for good and patient men, whom his Majesty, in concert with the bishops, should support, in order to teach the poor peasantry the principles of religion, and to teach it them by rote, as the rectors and curates do to those children who do not know how to read.

"Lewis XV seemed to relish my arguments; but the Philosophers renewed their attacks. They had people about his person who never ceased to urge him, and the king could not persuade himself that his *thinker*, Duquesnai, and the other Philosophers, were capable of such detestable views. He was so constantly beset by those men, that during the last twenty years of his reign, in the daily conversations with which he honored me, I was perpetually employed in combating the false ideas he had imbibed respecting the Œconomists and their associates.

"At length, determined to give the king positive proof that they imposed upon him, I sought to gain the confidence of those pedlars who travel throughout the country, and expose their goods to sale in the villages, and at the gates of country seats. I suspected those in particular who dealt in books to be nothing less than the agents of Philosophism with the good country folks. In my excursions into the country I above all fixed my attention on the latter. When they offered me a book to buy, I questioned them what might be the books they had? Probably Catechisms or Prayer-books? Few others are read in the villages? At these words I have seen many smile. No, they answered, those are not our works; we make much more money of Voltaire, Diderot, or other philosophic writings. What! said I, the country people buy Voltaire and Diderot? Where do they find the money for such dear works? Their constant answer was, We have them at a much cheaper rate than Prayer-books; we can sell them at ten sols (5d.) a volume, and have a pretty profit into the bargain. Questioning some of them still farther, many of them owned that those books cost them nothing; that they received whole bales of them without knowing whence they came, but being simply desired to sell them in their journeys at the lowest price."

Such was the account given by Mr. Bertin, and particularly during his retreat at Aix la Chapelle. All that he said of those pedlars perfectly coincides with what I have heard many rectors of small towns and villages complain of. They looked upon these hawking booksellers as the pests of their parishes, and as the agents of the pretended philosophers in the circulation of their impiety.

Lewis XV, warned by the discovery made by his minister, at length was satisfied that the establishment of these schools so much urged by the conspirators, would only be a new instrument of seduction in their hands. He abandoned the plan; but, perpetually harrassed by the protecting Sophisters, he did not strike at the root of the evil, and but feebly impeded its progress. The pedlars continued to promote the measures of the conspirators; but this was but one of the inferior means employed to supply the want of their free schools, as a new discovery brought to light one far more fatal.

Many years prior to the French Revolution, a rector of the diocese of Embrun had had frequent contests with the school-master of the village, charging him with corrupting the morals of his pupils, and with distributing most irreligious books among them. The lord of the village, one of the protecting adepts, supported the school-master; the good rector applied to his archbishop. Mr. Salabert D'Anguin, Vicar-general, desired to see the library of the master. It was filled with these sort of works; but the delinquent, so far from denying the use he made of them, with a pretended simplicity, said he had always heard those works spoken of in the highest terms; and, like the hawkers, declared that he was not at the trouble of buying them, as they were sent to him free of all costs.

At about a league from Liege, and in the adjacent villages, masters still more perfidious carried their means of corruption to a far greater extent. These would assemble on certain days, at particulr hours, a number of trades-people and poor country fellows, who had not learned to read. In these meetings one of the pupils of the professor would read in an audible voice a chapter in some work with which he himself had already been perverted; for example, one of Voltaire's romances, then the *Sermon of the Fifty*, the pretended *Good Sense*, or other works of the Sect furnished by the master. Those that abounded in calumny and abuse against the clergy were read with particular emphasis. These meetings, the fore-runners of the Liege revolution, were only discovered by an honest and religious carpenter, who, working for a canon of that cathedral, declared the sorrow he had felt at finding his two sons in one of these meetings reading such lectures to about a dozen of country fellows. On this discovery, a proper search was made in the adjacent country; many school-masters were found guilty of the same perfidy; and, shocking to say, by the exterior practice of their religion, these men had done away all suspicion of such infernal dealings. The inquiry was carried still further, and the plots were traced up to D'Alembert. The following was the result of this new discovery; and it was the very person to whom the honest carpenter opened his mind, and who made the necessary inquiries on this important object, who gave me the information.

In seeking what men had been the prompters of these corrupters of youth, they were found to be men whose connexions with the Sophisters of the day were no secret. At length they were traced to D'Alembert himself, and his office for tutors. It was to this office that all those heretofore mentioned addressed themselves, who wanted the recommendation of the Sophisters to obtain a place of preceptor or tutor in the houses of the great or wealthy. But at this period private education was not the sole object of D'Alembert. He now had established a correspondence throughout the provinces and beyond the kingdom. Not a place of professor in a college, nor of a simple schoolmaster in a village, became vacant, but he or his coadjutors were immediately informed of it by his agents; as also of the persons who petitioned for these places, of those who should be accepted or rejected, and of the means necessary to be employed, or persons to be applied to, to obtain the nomination of an adept competitor, or of those who were to be sent from Paris; in short, of the proper instructions to be given to the elected with regard to local circumstances, or the greater or less progress that Philosophism had made around them. Hence the impudence of the school-master in the diocese of Embrun, and that hypocrisy in those of the principality of Liege, where a government totally ecclesiastical was to be feared, and where infidelity had not yet made the same ravages it had in France.

It is thus that D'Alembert, faithful to the mission Voltaire had given him, *to enlighten youth as much as lay in his power*,[3] had extended his means of seducing them. Voltaire no longer regretted the colony of Cleves. That *manufacture* of impiety, which was to have been its chief object, the philosophic *confraternity*, like *that of the Freemasons,* the SECRET ACADEMY, more zealous in crushing Christ and his religion, than any other ever had been in the propagation of science or learning, was now established in Paris. And it was in the capital of the Most Christian empire that these associations were held, the parents of the revolution that was to bring devastation on France, and destruction on Christianity throughout the world. This was the last *mystery of Mytra*; this was the deepest intrigue of the conspirators; nor do I know that it has been hitherto laid open by any writer. In the correspondence of the Sophisters no trace can be discovered of this intrigue, at least in what the adepts have published. They had their reasons for suppressing such letters; for even in the first days of the revolution the people would have been indignant at hearing of such means to wrest their religion from them; and never would such a mystery of iniquity have emerged from the darkness in which it had been conceived, if Providence had not ordained that the unfortunate adept of whom we are about to speak, stung with remorse, should make an avowal of it.

Before we publish his declaration, it is incumbent on us to say by what means we became acquainted with it, and what precautions we have taken to ascertain its authenticity. The honor and probity of the person who gave us the account placed its veracity beyond all doubt; nevertheless we requested to have it under his signature. Still further, seeing that a great nobleman was mentioned as a witness, and even as the second actor in the scene, we did not hesitate in applying directly to him. This nobleman, of distinguished honor, virtue, and courage, bears the first distinction of French knighthood, and is in London at this time. We attended to the recital he was pleased to make, and found it perfectly consonant with the signed memorial we had carried with us. If his name is omitted, it is only because he was loath to see it appear in a fact that criminates the memory of a friend, whose error was rather owing to the seduction of the Sophisters than to his own heart, and whose repentance in some sort atoned for the crime of which he had been guilty. The following is the fact, which will complete the proofs, as yet only drawn from the letters of the conspirators themselves.

About the middle of the month of September 1789, little more than a fortnight antecedent to the atrocious 5th and 6th of October, at a time when the conduct of the National Assembly, having thrown the people into all the horrors of a revolution, indicated that they would set no bounds to their pretensions, Mr. *Le Roy,* Lieutenant of the King's Hunt, and an Academician, being at the house of Mr. D'Angevilliers, Intendant of the Buildings of his Majesty, the conversation turned on the disasters of the revolution, and on those that were too clearly to be foreseen. Dinner over, the nobleman above-mentioned, a friend of Le Roy, hurt at having seen him so great an admirer of the Sophisters, reproached him with it in the following expressive words: *Well, this, then, is the work of* PHILOSOPHY! Thunderstruck at these words,

—Alas! cried the Academician, *to whom do you say so? I know it but too well, and I shall die of grief and remorse!* At the word *remorse*, the same nobleman questioned him whether he had so greatly contributed towards the revolution as to upbraid himself with it in that violent manner? "Yes," answered he, "I have contributed to it, and far more than I was aware of. I was secretary to the committee to which you are indebted for it; but I call heaven to witness, that I never thought it would go to such lengths. You have seen me in the king's service, and you know that I love his person. I little thought of bringing his subjects to this pitch, *and I shall die of grief and remorse!*"

Pressed to explain what he meant by this committee, this secret society, entirely new to the whole company, the Academician resumed: "This society was a sort of club that we Philosophers had formed among us, and only admitted into it persons on whom we could perfectly rely. Our sittings were regularly held at the Baron D'Holbach's. Lest our object should be surmised, we called ourselves Œconomists. We created Voltaire, though absent, our honorary and perpetual president. Our principal members were D'Alembert, Turgot, Condorcet, Diderot, La Harpe and that Lamoignon, Keeper of the Seals, who, on his dismision, shot himself in his park."

The whole of this declaration was accompanied with tears and sighs, when the adept, deeply penitent, continued: "The following were our occupations; the most of those works which have appeared for this long time past against religion, morals, and government, were ours, or those of authors devoted to us. They were all composed by the members or by the orders of the society. Before they were sent to the press, they were delivered in at our office. There we revised and corrected them; added to or curtailed them according as circumstances required. When our philosphy was too glaring for the times, or for the object of the work, we brought it to a lower tint; and when we thought that we might be more daring than the author, we spoke more openly. In a word, we made our writers say exactly what we pleased. Then the work was published under the title or name we had chosen, the better to hide the hand whence it came. Many supposed to have been posthumous works, such as *Christianity Unmasked*, and divers others, *attributed to Freret and Boulanger* after their deaths, were issued from our society.

"When we had approved of those works, we began by printing them on fine or ordinary paper, in sufficient number to pay our expences, and then an immense number on the commonest paper. These latter we sent to hawkers and booksellers free of cost, or nearly so, who were to circulate them among the people at the lowest rate. These were the means used to pervert the people and bring them to the state you now see them in. I shall not see them long, *for I shall die of grief and remorse!*"

This recital had made the company shudder; nevertheless, they could not but be struck at the remorse and horrid situation in which they beheld the speaker. Their indignation for Philosophism was carried still further when Le Roy explained the meaning of ECR: L'INF: (écrasez l'infame, *crush the wretch*), with which Voltaire concludes so many of his letters. The reader will perceive, that in the whole of these Memoirs we had uniformly given the same explanation; and indeed the context of the letters makes the sense evident; but he revealed what we should not have dared assert on our own authority, that all those to whom Voltaire wrote under that horrid formula were members or initiated into the mysteries of this secret committee. He also declared what we have already said on the plan of elevating Briennes to the archbishopric of Paris; and many other particulars which he related would have been precious to history, but have escaped the memory of those present. None of them could give me any information as to the exact time when this secret academy was formed; but it appears from the discovery made by Mr. Bertins, that it must have existed long before the death of Lewis XV.

I think it necessary, on this occasion, to lay before my reader a letter of March 1763, which Voltaire writes to Helvetius. "Why," says he to his zealous brother, "do the worshippers of reason live in silence and fear? They are not sufficiently acquainted with their own strength. *What should hinder them from having a little press of their own*, and from publishing small works, short *and useful, and which should only be confided to their friends*. This was the method followed by those who printed the Last Will of the good and honest curate (Meslier); his testimony is certainly of great weight. It is further *certain, that you and your friends could, with the greatest facility, pen the best works possible, and throw them into circulation without exposing yourselves in the least.*"[4]

There also exists another letter, in which Voltaire, under the name of *Jean Patourel*, heretofore a Jesuit, and in his ironical style seeming to felicitate Helvetius on his pretended conversion, describes the method employed for the circulation of those works among the lower classes. "In opposition to the *Christian Pedagogue*, and the *Think well on it*, books formerly so much famed for the conversions they had wrought, pretty little philosophic works are *cleverly* circulated; these little books rapidly succeed each other. *They are not sold, they are given to people who can be relied on, who in their turn distribute them to women and young people*. At one time it is the *Sermon of the Fifty*, attributed to the King of Prussia; at another *an Extract from the Will* of the unfortunate curate Jean Meslier, who, on his death-bed, implored forgiveness of his God for having taught Christianity; or, lastly, *the Catechism of the Honest Man*, written by a certain Abbé Durand, (that is, Voltaire himself)."[5]

These two letters may throw great light on the subject. First, we see Voltaire giving the plan of a secret society, which perfectly coincides with the one described by Le Roi; secondly, we find that one of a similar nature existed at Ferney; thirdly, that it had not taken place at the period when these letters were written, as he presses the establishment of it. But on the other side, the pretended posthumous works of Freret and Boulanger, which the adept Le Roi declares to have been issued from this secret academy holding its sittings at the Baron D'Holbach's, were published in 1766 and 1767.[6] It therefore appears that this secret committee was established at Paris between the years 1763 and 1766. That is to say, that for three and twenty years preceding the Revolution they had been incessantly endeavouring to seduce the people by those artifices and intrigues, the shame of which, drew the above avowal from its repenting secretary. Such would have been the manufacture of Voltaire's colony!

It was with truth that this unhappy adept repeated, *I shall die of grief and remorse*; for he did not survive his avowal three months. When he mentioned the principal members, he added that all those to whom Voltaire wrote under the abominable formula of *Crush the Wretch*, were either members, or initiated into the mysteries of this secret academy.

According to this clue the first of these adepts will certainly be Damilaville, who exulted so much on hearing that none but the rabble were left to worship Christ; for it is to him in particular that Voltaire always ends his letters by, *crush the wretch*. This man was himself very little above that rabble whom he so much despised. He had made a small fortune by being one of the clerks in the office for the tax called the Vingtiemes, and had a salary of about 18ol. per ann. His philosophy had not taught him to endure poverty, as we see Voltaire excusing himself on his not having been able to procure him a more lucrative employment.[7]

The distinctive character which Voltaire gives him in one of these letters is that of *hating God*. Could that have given rise to their great intimacy? It was through his means that he transmitted his most impious productions or particular secrets to the conspirators. We should have remained in the dark as to his literary talents, had it not been for a letter from Voltaire to the Marquis de Villevielle, which so perfectly describes the meanness of the Sophisters, and how distant they were from the true Philospher, ready to sacrifice every thing in the cause of truth. "No, my dear friend (says Voltaire to the Marquis), the modern Socrates will not drink hemlock. The Athenian Socrates, with respect to us, was a very imprudent man, an eternal quibbler, and who foolishly set his judges at defiance.

"The philosophers of our days are wiser than that. They are not possessed with that foolish vanity of putting their names to their works. They are invisible hands, who, from one end of Europe to the other, pierce fanaticism with the shafts of truth. Damilaville is just dead; he *was the author of Christianity Unmasked* (which he had published as a posthumous work of Boulanger's) and of many other writings. *It was never known, and his friends kept his secret with a fidelity worthy of Philosophy.*"[8]

Such then is the author of that famous work which the Sophisters had given us as flowing from the pen of one of their most learned adepts. Damilaville, under the name of Boulanger, from his public-office, sallies forth the phœnix of modern Philosophism, and with the courage of a Sophister shrinks from his own works, lest they cost him dearly if ever called upon to support his principles before the tribunals. He also would have shrunk from the hemlock potion, under the infamy and eternal shame with which such abominable calumnies as he had vomited forth against Christianity must have overpowered him.

This adept, so worthy of Voltaire's and D'Alembert's friendship, died a bankrupt clerk in office, and had been parted from his wife for the last twelve years. Voltaire is his panegyrist when he says, "I shall always regret Damilaville; I loved the intrepidity of his soul; he was enthusiastic like *Saul* Paul; he was a necessary man."[9] Decency forbids us to quote the remainder of the panegyric.

Next to this Sophister, whose chief merits appear to have been his enthusiastic Atheism, we find the Count D'Argental. I have already spoken of his intimacy with Voltaire, and now only mention him as one of those initiated in the secret mysteries of the secret academy; being one of those correspondents to whom Voltaire expresses himself in the most unreserved manner on his plan of crushing Christ.[10]

On the same claim a sort of scribbler called Thiriot is to be enumerated among the members of the academy. No more elevated than Damilaville in rank or fortune, he for a longer time subsisted on the benefactions of Voltaire, who first made him his disciple and then his agent. Brother Thiriot added ingratitude to his impiety, and Voltaire complained bitterly of him. But Thiriot, notwithstanding his ingratitude, always remained impious, which reconciled Voltaire to him, and preserved him within the fraternal embrace of the conspirators.[11]

It is with concern that Mr. Saurin is found to have been a member of this academy. Certainly it is not his literary works that raise this sentiment; for were it not for his Tragedy of Spartacus, both his prose and verse would equally be forgotten; but we are told that it was rather his want of fortune, than to his disposition, that he owed his connexions with the Sophisters. He is even said to have been a man of great probity; but that he was drawn into that society for the consideration of a pension of a thousand crowns which Helvetius paid him. What an excuse! And where is the probity of the man who will sacrifice his religion to his interest, and for a pension coalesce with those who conspire against his God? We see Voltaire writing to Saurin himself, and placing him on the same line with Helvetius and the initiated Brethren, entrusting him with the same secrets, and exhorting him to the same warfare against Christ. As we have never seen him disclaim the connexion, the shame of it must attach to him.[12]

A Swiss Baron of the name of Grimm must also necessarily find his place here. He was the worthy friend and co-operator of Diderot; like him travelling to Petersbourg to form adepts, then returning to Paris, he also joins in his absurdities, repeats after him, that *between a man and his dog there is no other difference than their dress*, and exults in being able to apprize Voltaire that the Emperor Joseph II was initiated into his mysteries.

We will terminate our list by the German Baron D'Holbach, who, destitute of abilities, lends his house. He had acquired at Paris the reputation of a lover and protector of the arts, nor did the Sophisters contribute a little to it. This was a cloak to their meetings at his house. Unable to vie with the poet, he wishes to be the Mecenas. Nor is he the only person who has owed his reputation to his purse, and to his having disposed of it in favor of the Sophisters. In spite of these pretences, used for coloring the frequent meetings of the adepts, the public repute of those who resorted to his house had thrown such an odium on him, as to cause it to be openly said, that to gain admittance at his house it was necessary, as in Japan, to trample on the cross.

Such then were the members of this famous academy, whose sole object was to corrupt the minds of the people and prepare the way to universal apostasy, under the pretext of public happiness, public œconomy, or the love and advancement of the arts. We have mentioned fifteen of its members, Voltaire, D'Alembert, Diderot, Helvetius, Turgot, Condorcet, La Harpe, the keeper of the seals Lamoignon, Damilaville, Thiriot, Saurin, the Count D'Argental, Grimm, the Baron D'Holbach, and the unfortunate Le Roi, who died consumed with grief and remorse for having been the secretary to so monstrous an academy.

If we now revert to the real founder of this academy, and to Voltaire's letter to Helvetius, already quoted, the following one to D'Alembert should be added: "Let the Philosophers unite in *a brotherhood like the Freemasons*, let them assemble and support each other; let them be faithful to the association. Then I would suffer myself to be burnt for them. This SECRET ACADEMY will be far superior to that of Athens, and to all those of Paris. But every one thinks only for himself, and forgets that his most sacred duty is to *crush the wretch*." This letter is dated 20th April 1761.[13] Confronting it with the declaration of Le Roi, we see how faithfully the Parisian adepts had followed the plans of the premier chief. Often did he lament his inability of presiding over their labours but at a distance; and it was difficult to persuade him, that the capital of the most Christian empire was a proper seat for so licentious an establishment. It is for that reason that we see him pursuing his favorite plan of the philosphic colony, even after the establishment of the secret academy. But the time came when the direful success of the latter more than compensated the loss of the former. Triumphant in Paris, and surrounded by the adepts, he was one day to reap the fruits of such unrelenting constancy in the warfare which during the last half century he waged against his God.

1. To D'Alembert, 13 Dec. 1763, Vol. 68, Let. 122, P. 264.
2. See the analysis of those works, by Mr. Le Gros, Prevost of St. Louis du Louvre.
3. To D'Alembert, 15 Sept. 1762, Vol. 68, Let. 104, P. 214.
4. Vol. 58, Let. 50. P. 99.
5. To Helvetius, 25 Aug. 1763, Vol. 58, Let. 91, P. 179.
6. See L'Antiquité dévoilée, Amsterdam, anno 1766, and l'Examen des Apologistes du Christianisme, anno 1767.
7. To Damilaville, 14 Dec. 1767, Vol. 60, Let. 211, P. 356.
8. 20 Dec. 1768, Vol. 60, Let. 331, P. 592.
9. To D'Alembert, 23 Dec. 1768, Vol. 68, Let. 243, P. 500, and 13 Jan. 1769, Vol. 69, Let. 2, P. 6.
10. See numbers of letters in the General Correspondence.

11. See Correspondence and Letters to D'Alembert, and letters from the Marchioness of Chatellet to the King of Prussia.
12. To Saurin, 2 Feb. 1761, Vol. 57, Let. 23, P. 52, and to Damilaville, 28 Nov. 1762, Let. 259, P. 506.
13. Vol. 68, Let. 85, P. 163.

CHAP. XVIII.

Of the Progress of the Conspiracy throughout Europe.—Triumph and Death of the Chiefs.

As the conspirators advanced in their arts of seduction, their hopes were daily heightened by some new success. Already was that success so great, that a few years after the Encyclopecia had first appeared we find D'Alembert confidently writing to Voltaire, "Let Philosophy alone, and in twenty years the Sorbonne, however much Sorbonne it may be, will outstrip Lausanne itself;" that is to say, that in twenty years time (and this was written 21st July, 1757[1]), the Sorbonne would be as incredulous and Antichristian as a certain minister of Lausanne (Voltaire himself), who furnished the most impious articles that are to be found in the Encyclopedia.

Soon after Voltaire, improving on D'Alembert, says, "Twenty years more, *and God will be in a pretty plight!*[2] That is to say, twenty years more, and not an altar of the God of the Christians shall remain.

Every thing indeed seemed to forbode the universal reign of impiety throughout Europe. The district in particular which had fallen to Voltaire was making such an awful progress, that eight years after he writes, *not a single Christian is to be found from Geneva to Berne.*[3] Every where else, to use his expressions, the *world was acquiring wit apace;* and even so fast, *that a general revolution in ideas threatened all around.* Germany in particular gave him great hopes.[4] Frederic, who as carefully watched it as Voltaire did Switzerland, writes, that "philospfy was beginning to penetrate even into superstitious Bohemia, and into Austria, the former abode of superstition."[5]

In Russia the adepts gave still greater hopes. This protection of the *Scythians* is what consoles Voltaire for the persecutions which befel the Sect elsewhere.[6] He could not contain himself for joy when he wrote to D'Alembert how much the brethren were protected at Petersburg, and informed him, that during a journey made by that court the Scythian protectors had each one, for his amusement, undertaken to translate a chapter of Belisarius into their language: that the Empress had undertaken one herself, and had even been at the trouble of revising the translation of this work, which in France had been censured by the Sorbonne.[7]

D'Alembert wrote, that in Spain Philosophism was *undermining* the Inquisition;[8] and according to Voltaire, a great *revolution was operating in ideas*

THE ANTICHRISTIAN CONSPIRACY. 159

there, as well as *in Italy*.⁹ A few years later we find that this Italy swarmed with men thinking like Voltaire and D'Alembert, and that their interest only prevented them from openly declaring for impiety.¹⁰

As to England, they made but little doubt of its falling an easy prey. According to them, it was overrun with Socinians who scoffed at and hated Christ, as Julian the apostate hated and despised him, and who only differed in name from the philosophers.¹¹

Finally, according to their calculations, Bavaria and Austria alone (this was during the lifetime of the Empress Queen) continued to support the divines and defenders of religion. The Empress of Russia *was driving them on gloriously*; and they were at *their last gasp in Poland*, thanks to the King Poniatowski. They were *already overthrown in Prussia*, through the care of Frederic; and *in the north of Germany* the Sect daily gained ground, thanks to the Landgraves, Margraves, Dukes and Princes, adepts and protectors.¹²

Far otherwise did matters stand in France. We often see the two chiefs complaining of the obstacles they had to encounter in that country, the favorite object of their conspiracy.

The perpetual appeals of the clergy, the decrees of the parliaments, the very acts of authority which the ministers, though friendly to the conspirators, were obliged to exert in order to hide their predilection, were not entirely ineffectual. The bulk of the nation still remained attached to its faith. That numerous class called the people, in spite of all the intrigues of the secret academy, still flocked to the altar on days of solemnity. In the higher classes, numerous were the exceptions to be made of those who still loved religion. Indignant at so many obstacles, Voltaire would perpetually stimulate his countrymen, whom he contemptuously calls his *poor Velches*. Sometimes however he was better pleased with them, and would write to his dear Marquis Villevieille, "*The people are mighty foolish; Philosophism nevertheless makes its way down to them*. Be well assured, for instance, that there are not twenty people in Geneva who would not abjure Calvin as soon as they would the Pope; and that many philosphers are to be found in Paris behind the counter."¹³ But, generally speaking, his complaints about France predominate in his correspondence with the conspirators; sometimes he would despair of ever seeing Philosophy triumph there. D'Alembert, on the spot, judged of matters very differently; and though every thing did not answer his wishes, he nevertheless thought himself authorised to flatter Voltaire, that though *philosophy might receive a temporary check, it never could be subdued.*¹⁴

About the period when D'Alembert wrote this, it was but too true that Philosophism could flatter itself with the hopes of triumphing over the attachment of the French nation to their religion. During the last ten or twelve years impiety had made a dreadful progress; the colleges had sent forth a new generation educated by new masters; they were nearly void of all knowledge, and particularly destitute of religion or piety. It perfectly coincided with Condorcet's expression, that Philosophism *had descended from the thrones of the North into the very universities*.¹⁵ The religious generation was nearly extinct, and the revealed truths were obliged to give place to the empty sounds of reason, philosophy, prejudices, and such terms. In the higher classes impiety made large strides, whether at court or in the tribunals. From the capital it gained the provinces, and the master set the example to the servant. Every one would be a Philosopher, whether minister or magistrate, soldier or author. He that wished to adhere to his religion was exposed to all the sarcastic irony of the Sophisters, and that particularly among the great, where it required as much courage to profess one's religion after the conspiracy, as it did audacity and rashness to declare one's self an Atheist before.

Voltaire was at that time in his eighty-fourth year. After so long an absence, and always under the power and lash of the law, he could only have appeared publicly in Paris to controvert those impieties which had brought the animadversion of the parliament on him. D'Alembert and his academy resolved to overcome that obstacle. In spite of religion they easily succeed, and ministers, chiefly adepts, abusing the clemency of Lewis XVI, obtain the recal of this premier chief, under pretence that this aged man had been sufficiently punished by his long exile; and that in consideration of his literary trophies, his failings might be over-looked. It was agreed that the laws should be silent with regard to him on his approach to Paris; the magistrates seemed to have forgotten the decree they had passed against him. This was all that the conspirators wished. Voltaire arrives in Paris, he receives the homage of the Sect, and his arrival constitutes their triumphal day. This man, bending under the weight of years spent in an unrelenting warfare, whether public or private, against Christianity, is received in the capital of his Most Christian Majesty, amidst those exclamations which were wont to announce the arrival of the favorite child of victory returning from the arduous toils of war.

Whithersoever Voltaire bent his steps, a croud of adepts and the gazing multitude flocked to meet him. All the academies celebrate his arrival, and they celebrate it in the Louvre, in the palace of the kings, where Lewis XVI is one day to be a prisoner and victim to the occult and deep conspiracies of the Sophisters. The theatres decree their crowns to the impious chief; entertainments in his honor rapidly succeed each other. Intoxicated through pride with the incense of the adepts, he fears to sink under it. In the midst of these coronations and acclamations he exclaimed, *You wish then to make me expire with glory!*— Religion alone mourned at this sight, and vengeance hung over his head. The impious man had feared to die of glory; but rage and despair was to forward his last hour still more than his great age. In the midst of his triumphs a violent hemorrhage raised apprehensions for his life. D'Alembert, Diderot, and Marmontel, hastened to support his resolution in his last moments; but were only witnesses to their own ignominy as well as to his.

Here let not the historian fear exaggeration. Rage, remorse, reproach, and blasphemy, all accompany and characterize the long agony of the dying Atheist. This death, the most terrible that is ever recorded to have stricken the impious man, will not be denied by his companions in impiety; their silence, however much they may wish to deny it, is the least of those corroborative proofs which could be adduced. Not one of the Sophisters has ever dared to mention any sign given of resolution or tranquillity by the premier chief during the space of three months, which elapsed from the time he was crowned at the theatre until his decease. Such a silence expresses how great their humiliation was in his death.

On his return from the theatre, and in the midst of the toils he was resuming in order to acquire fresh applause, Voltaire was warned, that the long career of his impiety was drawing to an end.

In spite of all the Sophisters flocking around him, in the first days of his illness he gave signs of wishing to return to the God he had so often blasphemed. He calls for the priests who ministered to *Him* who he had sworn *to crush*, under the appellation of *the wretch*. His danger increasing, he wrote the following note to the Abbé Gaultier. "You had promised me, Sir, to come and hear me. I intreat you would take the trouble of calling as soon as possible. *signed*, VOLTAIRE. Paris, the 26th Feb. 1778."

A few days after he wrote the following declaration, in presence of the same Abbé Gaultier, the Abbé Mignot, and the Marquis de Villevieille, copied from the minutes deposited with Mr. Momet, Notary at Paris.

"I, the underwritten, declare, that for these four days, having been afflected with a vomiting of blood at the age of eighty-four, and not having been able to drag myself to the church, the Rev. the Rector of St. Sulpice having been pleased to add to his good works that of sending to me the Abbé Gaultier, a priest, I confessed to him; and if it pleases God to dispose of me, I die in the *Holy Catholic Church* in which I was born; hoping that the divine mercy will deign to pardon all my faults: if ever I have scandalized the Church, I ask pardon of God and of the Church. 2d March 1778. *Signed*, VOLTAIRE: in presence of the Abbé Mignot, my nephew, and the Marquis de Villeveille, my friend."

After the two witnesses had signed this declaration, Voltaire added these words, copied from the same minutes: "The Abbé Gaultier, my confessor, having apprized me, that it was said among a certain set of people, that I should protest against every thing I did at my death; I declare I never made such a speech, and that it is an old jest attributed long since to many of the learned more enlightened than I am."

Was this declaration a fresh instance of his former hypocrisy? Unfortunately, after the explanations we have seen him give of his exterior acts of religion, might there not be room for doubt? Be that as it may, this is a public homage paid to that religion in which he declared he meant to die, notwithstanding his having perpetually conspired against it during his life. This declaration is also signed by that same friend and adept the Marquis de Villevielle, to whom eleven years before Voltaire was wont to write, "*Conceal your march from the enemy* in your endeavours to crush the wretch."[16]

Voltaire had permitted this declaration to be carried to the rector of St. Sulpice, and to the Archbishop of Paris, to know whether it would be sufficient. When the Abbé Gaultier returned with the answer, it was impossible for him to gain admittance to the patient. The conspirators had strained every nerve to hinder the chief from consummating his recantation, and every avenue was shut to the priest which Voltaire himself had sent for. The demons haunted every access; rage succeeds to fury, and fury again to rage during the remainder of his life. Then it was that D'Alembert, Diderot, and about twenty others of the conspirators who had beset his apartment, never approached him, but to witness their own ignominy; and often he would curse them and exclaim,—"Retire; it is you that have brought me to my present state; begone, I could have done without you all; but you could not exist without me; and what a wretched glory have you procured me!"

Then would succeed the horrid remembrance of his conspiracy. They could hear him, the prey of anguish and dread, alternately supplicating and blaspheming that God against whom he had conspired; and in plaintive accents he would cry out, Oh Christ! Oh Jesus Christ! And then complain that he was abandoned by God and man. The hand which had traced in ancient writ the sentence of an impious revelling king, seemed to trace before his eyes CRUSH THEN, DO CRUSH THE WRETCH. In vain he turned away his head; the time was coming apace when he was to appear before the tribunal of him he had blasphemed; and his physicians (particularly Mr. Tronchin), calling in to administer relief, retire thunderstruck, declaring the death of the impious man to be terrible indeed. The pride of the conspirators would willingly have suppressed these declarations; but it was in vain: the Mareschal de Richlieu flies from the bedside declaring it to be a sight too terrible to be sustained; and Mr. Tronchin says, that the ravings of Orestes could give but a faint idea of those of Voltaire.

Thus died on the 30th of May, 1778, rather worn out by his own fury than by the weight of years, the most unrelenting Conspirator against Christianity that had been seen since the time of the Apostles. His persecution, longer and more perfidious than those of Nero or Dioclesian, had YET only produced apostates; but they were more numerous than the martyrs made in the former persecutions. (*See the note at the end of the chapter.*)

The conspirators, in losing Voltaire, had lost every thing with respect to talents; but his arms of impiety they had remaining in his numerous writings. The art and cunning of D'Alembert proved more than a succedaneum to the genius of their deceased founder, and he was proclaimed chief. The secret committee of education in Paris, the country conventicles, and the correspondence with the village school-masters, owed their origin to him. He continued to direct the works of the secret academy in the propagation of impiety, until called upon to appear before that same God who had already judged Voltaire. He died five years after his patron, that is in November 1783.—Lest remorse should compel him to similar recantations to those which had so much humbled the Sect, Condorcet undertook to render him inaccessible, if not to repentance and remorse, at least to all who might have availed themselves of any homage that he might do to religion.

When the Rector of St. Germain's, in quality of pastor, presented himself, Condorcet, like a devil watching over his prey, ran to the door and barred his entrance! Scarcely had the breath left his body when the pride of Condorcet betrays his secret. D'Alembert really had felt that remorse which must have been common to him with Voltaire; he was on the eve of sending, as the only method of reconciliation, for a minister of that same Christ against whom he had also conspired; but Condorcet ferociously combated these last signs of repentance in the dying Sophister, and he gloried in having forced him to expire in final impenitence. The whole of this odious conflict is comprized in one horrid sentence. When Condorcet announced the decease of D'Alembert, and was relating the circumstances, he did not blush to add—*Had I not been there, he would have flinched also.*[17]

Frederic alone had succeeded, or pretended to have succeeded, in persuading himself that death was but an eternal sleep.[18] And he alone appears to have been an exception from among the chiefs of the conspiracy, with whom the approach of death had substituted, in lieu of their pretended hatred for the *wretch,* the fear of his judgments.

Diderot, that hero of Atheism, that conspirator who long since had carried to insanity his audacity against his Christ and his God, Diderot, I say, was he who was nearest to a true reconciliation. This is another of those mysteries of iniquity carefully hidden by the Antichristian conspirators.

When the Empress of Russia purchased Diderot's library she left him the use of it during his life. Her munificence had enabled him to have near his person, in quality of librarian, a young man who was far from partaking in his impiety. Diderot liked him much, and he had particularly endeared himself by the attentions he had shown Diderot during his last illness. It was he who generally dressed the wounds in his legs. Terrified at the symptoms he perceived, the young man runs to acquaint a worthy ecclesiastic, the Abbé Lemoine, then resident at the house called the Foreign Missions, Rue du Bac, Fauxbourg St. Germain. By his advice the young man prays for half an hour in a church, begging of Almighty God that he would direct him in what he should say or do to ensure the salvation of one who, though he detested his impieties, he could never forget was his benefactor. Rising from his prayers he returns to Diderot, and the same day, while dressing his wounds, he spoke as follows:

"Mr. Diderot, you see me this day more anxious than ever as to your fate. Do not be surprised; I am aware how much I am indebted to you; it is by your kindness that I subsist; you have deigned to put greater confidence in me than I had reason to expect. I cannot prove ungrateful; I should for ever accuse myself of ingratitude were I to hide from you the danger which your wounds declare you to be in. Mr. Diderot, you may have dispositions to make; and above all you have preparations to make for the world you are about to enter. I am but a young man, I know; but are you certain that your Philosphy has not left you a soul to save? I have no doubt of it; and it is impossible for me to reflect on it, and not warn my benefactor to avoid the eternal misery which may await him. Sir, you have still sufficient time left; and excuse an advice which gratitude and your friendship forces from me."

Diderot heard the young man with attention, and even melted into tears. He thanked him for his frankness, and for the concern he had shown for him. He promised to consider and to reflect what line of conduct he should adopt in a situation which he owned to be of the greatest importance.

The young man waited his decision with the greatest impatience, and the first signs were conformable to his wishes. He ran to inform the Abbé Lemoine that Diderot asked to see a clergyman, and the Abbé directed him to Mr. de Tersac, Rector of St. Sulpice. Mr. de Tersac waited on Diderot, and had several conferences with him.—He was preparing a public recantation of his past errors; but, unfortunately, he was watched by the conspirators. The visit of a priest to Diderot had given the alarm to the Sophisters, who thought themselves dishonored by the dereliction of so important a chief. They surround him;—they persuade him that he is imposed upon; that his health is not in so bad a state, but that a little country air would immediately recover him.—Diderot was for a long time deaf to all the arguments Philosophism could invent, but at length consented at least to try the country air. His departure was kept secret, and the wretches who carried him away knew that his last hour was fast approaching. The Sophisters who were in the plot pretended to think him still in Paris, and the whole town was misled by daily reports; while those jailors who had seized on his person watched him till they had seen him expire; then, continuing their horrid duplicity, they bring back the lifeless corpse to Paris, and spread the report that he had died suddenly at table. He expired the 2d of July 1784, and was represented as having died calm in all his Atheism, without giving any signs of remorse. The public are again misled, and thus many are confirmed in their impiety, who might have followed the example of this chief, had he not by the most unheard-of cruelty been deprived of all spiritual relief in his last moments.

Thus in the whole of this conspiracy, from its origin to the death of its first promoters, we have seen but one continued chain of cunning, art, and seduction; of the blackest, falsest, and most disgusting means employed in the tremendous art of seducing the people. It was on these horrid arts that Voltaire, D'Alembert, and Diderot had built all their hopes of working universal apostasy; and in their last moments they are a prey to those very arts. In that awful moment when glory vanishes, and the empty name he has acquired by their deceit is no more, the disciple of seduction lords it over his master. When reason calls on them to make use of that liberty, (so much cried up when opposed to their God) to reconcile themselves with him they had blasphemed, even their very remorse is sacrificed to the vanity of their school: when it calls on them to use that courage they had shown when blaspheming, it fails them in their repentance, and they show none but the slavish symptoms of weakness and fear. Under the subjection of their adepts they expire fettered in those chains which they themselves had forged, and consumed by that impiety which their hearts now abhor.

At the time of their death, hatred to Christianity and the Conspiracy against the Altar was not the only object of their school. Voltaire had been the father of the Sophisters of Impiety, and he lived to be the premier chief of the Sophisters of Rebellion. He had said to his first adepts, "Let us crush the altar, let the temples be destroyed, and let not a single worshipper be left to the God of the Christians;" and his school soon re-echoed with the cry of, "Let us break the sceptres, let the thrones be destroyed, and let not a single subject be left to the kings of the earth." It is from their mutual success, that the combined revolution is to be generated, which, grasping the hatchet, shall in France overthrow the altar and the throne, murder the pontiffs, strike off the head of the monarch, and proudly menace the kings of the earth and all Christian altars with a similar fate.—We have now given the history of the plots and of the means of the ANTICHRISTIAN CONSPIRACY, or of the *Sophisters of Impiety*. Before we begin that of the ANTIMONARCHIAL CONSPIRACY, or of the *Sophisters of Rebellion*, let us reflect on the extraordinary illusion which Philosophism has thrown over all nations, and which may be considered as having been one of the most powerful agents of the Sect.

Note to CHAP. XVIII

SOME person, on perusing the first edition of this work, thought proper to send a flat denial of the above account of Voltaire's death to the authors of the British Critic, under the initials D. J. They gave him no degree of credit; but it is to his anonynmous assertion thast we are indebted for the following letter from Mr. De Luc, a name that needs no observation to enhance the value of his testimony.

Letter from M. DE LUC *on the Death of Voltaire.*

"SIR, Your *Memoirs illustrating the History of Jacobinism* having been the other day the subject of conversation, it was objected, that the description of Voltaire (so prominent a feature in your Work) was so very dissimilar to that given by the other historians of his life, that persons at a distance from the source of information were at a loss what judgment to form. The difference between your account of his death, and that which appeared in *a Life of Voltaire* translated from the French by Mr. Monke, and published in London 1787, was particularly noticed, and incited me to consult that work. The Translator describes himself *as a young naval officer, who, while at Paris, wished to employ his recess from professional duty, both to his improvement and advantage.* Nothing but the youth of Mr. Monke, and his want of experience, can excuse his undertaking; for, to let his countrymen benefit by the proficiency he was making at Paris, he diffused among them, through the medium of this translation, all that poison which was then so industriously emitted, to produce an effect now but too well known, and which I hope he does not this day contemplate without horror.

"I will make no observations *on this Life of Voltaire*; you know from what source it came,[19] and how little capable it was of seducing any but heedless youths who, without any knowledge of the age they lived in, were still susceptible of a sort of admiration for every thing that was *great*, though in vice and villany. As one of the artifices of impiety is to represent its champions *calmly* breathing their last in the bed of honour, I feel it incumbent on me to confirm what you have said on one of those circumstances of the death of Voltaire which is closely connected with all the rest.

"Being at Paris in 1781, I was often in company with one of those persons whose testimony you invoke on public reports, I mean Mr. Tronchin. He was an old acquaintance of Voltaire's at Geneva, when he came to Paris in quality of first physician to the father of the late Duke of Orleans.—He was called in during Voltaire's last sickness; and I have heard him repeat all those circumstances on which Paris and the whole world were at that time full of conversation, respecting the horrid state of this impious man's soul at the approach of death. Mr. Tronchin (even as physician) did every thing in his power to calm him; for the agitation he was in was so violent, that no remedies could take effect. But he could not succeed; and, unable to endure the horror he felt at the peculiar nature of his frantic rage, he abandoned him.

"So violent a state in an exhausted frame could not be of long duration. Stupor, the forerunner of dissolution, must naturally succeed, as it generally does after any violent agitations generated by pain; and it is this latter state which in Voltaire has been decorated by the appellation of *calm*. Mr. Tronchin wished to discredit this error; and with that laudable view, as an eye witness, he immediately published in all companies the real facts, and precisely as you have stated them. This he did to furnish a dreadful lesson to those who calculate on being able in a death-bed to investigate the dispositions most proper to appear in before the judgment-seat of the Almighty. At that period, not only the state of the body, but the condition of the soul, may frustrate their hopes of making so awful an investigation. For justice and sanctity as well as goodness are attributes of God; and he sometimes, as a wholesome admonition to mankind, permits the punishments denounced against the impious man to begin even in this life by the tortures of remorse.

"But this inaccuracy respecting the death of Voltaire is not the only one with which the aforenamed author might be upbraided. He has suppressed many well known circumstances relating to his first disposition to return to the church, and his consequent declarations, which you have given on well-authenticated records, all anterior to that anguish of mind which his co-operators have wished to suppress, and of which they themselves were too probably the cause. They surrounded him, and thus cut him off from that which alone could restore tranquility to his soul, by employing the few moments he still had to live in making what reparation he could for the evil he had done. But this artifice could not deceive those who were better acquainted with Voltaire's character; for, not to notice the acts of hypocrisy which earthly considerations frequently made him commit, those of which the sudden fear of a future state have made him guilty are also known. I will give you an example of one, which was related to me at Gottinguen in December 1776, by Mr. Dieze, second librarian of that university; and you may, Sir, make what use of it you please.

"During Voltaire's residence in Saxony, where Mr. Dieze served him as a secretary, he fell dangerously ill. As soon as he was apprized of his situation he sent for a priest, confessed to him, and begged to receive the sacrament, which he actually did receive, showing all the exterior signs of repentance, which lasted as long as his danger; but as soon as that was over, he affected to laugh at what he called his *littleness*, and, turning to Mr. Dieze, "My friend (said he) you have seen *the weakness of the man*."

"It is also to *human weakness* that sectaries of his impiety have attributed the paroxisms of fear in him and some of his accomplices. Sickness, say they, weakens the mind as well as the body, and often produces pusillanimity. These symptoms of conversion in the wicked at the approach of death are, undoubtedly, signs of a great *weakness*; but to what is it to be attributed? Is it to their understanding? Certainly not; for it is in that awful moment that every thing vanishes which had clouded it during their life. That *weakness*, therefore, is to be wholly attributed to their *internal conviction* that they have sinned.

"Led away by vanity, or some other vicious passion, those men aspire at creating a Sect: Ignorance and the passions of other men second their undertaking. Inebriated with their triumph, they persuade themselves that they are capable of giving laws to the whole world: They boldly make the attempt, and the hoodwinked crowd become their followers.—Having attained the zenith of happiness for the proud and vain glorious soul, they abandon themselves to all the wantonness of imagination and desire. The world then, in their eyes, becomes a vast field of new enjoyments, the legitimacy of which has no other standard but their own inclinations; and the fumes of an incense lavished on them by those whom they have taught to scoff like themselves at every law, perpetuates their delirium. But when the sickness has dispersed the flattering cohort, has blasted their pleasures, and all hopes of new triumphs; when they feel themselves advancing, abandoned and naked, toward that awful *Eternity* on which they have taken upon themselves to decide, not only for themselves but for all those who have been led away in the whirlwind of their fictions—If in this terrible moment, when pride has lost its support, they come to reflect on the arguments on which they grounded their attack against the universal belief of a *Revelation* which was to serve man as a positive and universal rule in matters of faith.—The *weakness* then of their arguments (which they dare no longer attire in the garb of sophistry, stares them in the face; and nothing but the total extinction of their feelings can quell the terrors of a conscience which tells them that they are about to appear before the tribunal of the author of that same *Revelation.*

"It is to point out this real *weakness* of the Antichristian chiefs that we must labor throughout their whole history, for the benefit of those who, without any further examination (and persuaded that these opinions are grounded on deep research) become their dupes and disciples: It is, I say, incumbent on us to show that those men had not, any more than their sectaries, any real *conviction*, and that their obstinacy in their opinions solely proceeded from the narcotic fumes of the incense of their admirers. For this purpose it is my intention shortly to give to the public, in confirmation of what you have said of Voltaire, all that my former acquaintance with him has brought to my knowledge. The times in which we live makes it the duty of every man who has had a nearer view of the plots laid by the Sect against Revelation to unfold the circumstances of them, which are as shameful from their voluntary ignorance, as from their atrocity; and it is this sentiment, Sir, which makes me partake in common with all true friends to humanity, of that admiration and gratitude which are due to you for your generous exertions in this charitable career.

"I remain, Sir, your's, &c. &c.

De Luc"

Windsor, the 23d of October, 1797.

After such a testimony, let people talk of Voltaire dying with the calmness of a hero.

1. Vol. 68, Let. 30, P. 51.
2. To D'Alembert, 25 Feb. 1758, Vol. 68, Let. 44, P. 79.
3. To D'Alembert, 8 Feb. 1766, Vol. 69, Let. 151, P. 257.
4. To D'Alembert, 5 Apr. 1765, Vol. 68, Let. 162, P. 352.
5. From Frederic, 8 Jan. 1766, Vol. 65, Let. 143, P. 344.
6. To Diderot, 25 Dec. 1762, Vol. 57, Let. 242, P. 475.
7. To D'Alembert, July, 1767, Vol. 68, Let. 212, P. 445.
8. From D'Alembert, 13 May, 1773, Vol. 69, Let. 108, P. 182, and 5 April 1768, Vol. 68, Let. 226, P. 473.
9. To Riche, 1 March, 1768, Vol. 60, Let. 254, P. 434.
14. To D'Alembert, 16 June 1773, Vol. 69, Let. 113, P. 194.
11. To Frederic, 8 Nov. 1773, Vol. 66, Let. 46, P. 112.
12. To D'Alembert, 4 Sept. 1767, Vol. 68, Let. 219, P. 459.

13. 20 Dec. 1768, Vol. 60, Let. 331, Page 593.
14. From D'Alembert, 5 Nov. 1776, Vol. 69, Let. 49, P. 282.
15. See his Preface to his edition of Pascal's Thoughts.
16. 27 April 1767, Vol. 60, Let. 102, P. 180.
17. Historical Dictionary, Article D'Alembert. It is true that Condorcet, sorry for having inadvertently revealed the secret of his associate's remorse, sought to destroy the effect of it. It is true, that questioned another time on the circumstances of D'Alembert's death, he answered in his philosophic jargon, *that he did not like a coward.* In his first letter to the King of Prussia, dated the 22d Nov. 1783, he represents D'Alembert as dying with a tranquil courage, and with his usual strength and presence of mind. But it was too late to lead Frederic into error on that subject, as the adept Grimm had already written, *That sickness had greatly weakened D'Alembert's mind in his last moments* (11th of November 1783).
18. Vide supra.
19. I have seen this life of Voltaire. Mr. de Villette was the author of it; and Mr. Monke might just as well have exercised his talents in translating Condorcet.

CHAP. XIX.

Of the great Delusion which rendered the Conspiracy against the Altar so successful.

IN the first part of these Memoirs on Jacobinism, our object was to demonstrate the existence, to unmask the chiefs, and deduce the means and progress of a conspiracy, planned and executed by men, known by the name of Philosophers, against the Christian religion, without distinction of Protestant or Catholic, without even excepting those numerous Sects which had sprung up in England or Germany, or in any other part of the universal world, provided they did but adore the God of Christians. To unfold this mystery of impiety, we had promised to adduce our proofs solely from their own records, that is from their letters, writings or avowals, and we flatter ourselves with having given real historical demonstration of it, sufficient to convince a reader, the most difficult of conviction. Let us for a moment examine what pretensions its authors could have had to be styled PHILOSOPHERS, a name which gave them so much weight in their conspiracy.

The generality of men attending rather to words than things, this affectation of dominion over wisdom and reason proved a very successful weapon in their hands. Had they called themselves unbelievers, or the declared enemies of Christianity, Voltaire and D'Alembert would have been the execration of all Europe; while only calling themselves PHILOSOPHERS, they are mistaken for such. Is not their school to this day venerated by many as that of Philosophy, notwithstanding the numerous massacres and all the horrid disasters which we have seen naturally flowing from their conspiracy? And every man who will adopt their way of thinking on religion styles himself a Philosopher!—This is a delusion of more consequence than can be imagined, and has carried the number of adepts perhaps farther than any other of their artifices. As long as their school shall be mistaken for that of reason, numberless will be the thoughtless persons who, pretending to depth of thought, will adopt the sentiments of a Voltaire or a Diderot, of a D'Alembert or a Condorcet, and conspire like them, against the altar; and that disastrous blast will once more spread around the throne, and over all the orders of society. Their oaths, their wishes and their plots have been laid open; where then are their pretensions to wisdom? Is it not the historian's duty to tear off that mask of hypocrisy, which has misled such numbers of adepts, who, miserably seeking to soar above the vulgar, have only sunk into impiety, gazing after this pretended Philosophy. The empty sounds of *Reason, Philosophy*, and *Wisdom*, have made them believe themselves inspired, when, like Voltaire, they hated or despised the religion of Christ. But it is time they should know that they have only been the dupes of designing men. Let them hearken; the numerous proofs we have adduced give us a right to be heard when we tell them, "that at the school of the conspirators they have mistaken the lessons of hatred and phrenzy, for those of reason; they have been the dupes of folly and madness, under the cloak of wisdom; of ignorance, under the pretence of science; of vice and depravity, under the mask of virtue; and their zeal for Philosophy still makes them err through all the tortuous windings of wickedness and impiety." We do not pretend, in holding such language, to dispute the talents of the premier chief. That his poetic genius should enjoy itself in fictions, on the banks of Parnassus, or on the heights of Pindus, is much to be admired; but is he to be allowed to substitute those fictions for truths? The greater his genius, the less we are astonished to see him entangled when he has once adopted error. If stupidity can never attain to genius, the genius that dares to soar above reason is not the less within the regions of delirium. In a raging fever, your strength will be redoubled; but is there a more humiliating sight for man! Where then is the excuse of genius or of talents in the Sophister conspiring against his God? Can the adepts, who believe their master to be a Philosopher even to his last moments admire that frantic rage in which he expired? But first let them tell us what other titles he may have to the empire of reason.

What Philosophy can there be in that extraordinary *hatred* which Voltaire had sworn against the God of Christianity? That a Nero should have sworn to crush the Christians and their God may be explained, because the idea could only have been that of a cruel monster. That a Dioclesian should have sworn it may be understood, because the idolatrous tyrant thought to appease the anger of his gods and avenge their glory. That a Julian, mad enough to restore the worship of idols, should have sworn it, appears only to have been a consequence of his former delirium. But that a pretended sage, who neither believes in the God of the Christians nor in the Gods of the Pagans, and who knows not in what God to believe, should vent all his rage and fury precisely against Christ, is one of those phænomena of modern Philosophism which can be considered but as the delirium of the impious man.

I do not pretend by this to exclude from the school of reason every one who is not fortunate enough to be within the pale of Christianity; let that man rank with an Epictetus or a Seneca, or before the Christian era with a Socrates or a Plato, who has been unfortunate enough not to have known the proofs of Christianity. But this real Philosophy of reason sought what Voltaire has conspired to destroy. The greatest of Socrates's disciples pants for the coming of that just man who shall dissipate the darkness and the doubts of the sage. I hear him exclaim, "Let him come; let that man come who will teach us our duties toward the Gods, and our duty towards man. Let him come instantly;

I am ready to obey whatever he may ordain, and I hope he will make me a better man."[1] Such is the language of the Philosophy of reason. I think I behold him again, when in the bitterness of his heart he foresees that should this just man appear upon earth, he would be scoffed at by the wicked, buffeted, and scourged, in a word treated as the outcast of men.[2] That man has appeared, so much sought for by the Pagan Philosopher; and the conspiring Sophisters, a D'Alembert or a Voltaire, seek to crush him. and yet pretend to the Philosophy of reason. Let their disciples answer for them. If in the son of Mary they will not acknowledge the Son of the Eternal Father, let them confess him to be at least that just man sought for by Plato. What then are their pretensions to the Philosophy of reason in conspiring against him? If the awful testimony of the sun being darkened, the dead rising from their graves, the veil of the temple being rent, cannot convince them; let them at least admire the most holy, the justest of men, the prodigy of goodness and meekness, the apostle of every virtue, the wonder of oppressed innocence praying for his executioners. Where is their Philosophy when they conspire against the Son of Man? Yes, Philosophy they had; but it was that of the Jews, that of the synagogue, whence issued those blasphemous cries of, "Crucify him, crucify him!" or *crush the wretch!* Judas himself confesses him to be the just man; and shall he approach to perfection when compared to their school of modern Philosophy? Oh, what a Philosophy! that after seventeen centuries repeats the blasphemous cries which resounded in the courts of Pilate or Herod against the Holy of Holies!—In vain shall the disciple deny the hatred of Voltaire against the *person* of CHRIST; does he not particularly distinguish Damilaville for that hatred, does he not sign himself *Christ-moque* (Christ-scoffer), just as he terminates his letters by *crush the wretch*, or talks of the *Christicole* superstition. Yet while the Sophister denies the power of Christ, he cannot refuse acknowledging his wisdom, his goodness, and his virtue.

But they may object, that it is not so much at the person as at the *religion* of Christ they aim their blows. Where then is the Philosophy in attacking a religion whose essence is to enforce every virtue, and condemn every vice. Has there ever appeared, either before or since Christ, a Philosopher, who has even formed the idea of a virtue of which this religion does not give the precept or set the example? Is there a crime or a vice which it does not condemn and reprobate? Has the world ever seen a sage impressing such divine doctrines with more powerful motives? Did there ever exist, either before or since Christ, laws more conducive to the interior happiness of families, or to that of empires; laws that better teach men the reciprocal ties of affection; laws, in short, that more peremptorily command us to afford each other mutual assistance? Let the Philosopher appear who pretends to perfect this religion; let him be heard and judged. But should he, like Voltaire and his adepts, only seek to destroy it, let him be comprised in the common epithet of madman and of enemy to humanity.

But it is said to be only at the altars, at the *mysteries* of that religion, and not at the *morality* of it, that they aim their blows.—In the first place that is not true, as we have already seen and shall see again. Their attack was common on the morality of the Gospel, as well as on the mysteries or the altars of Christianity.—But had it been true, what is there to be found in these mysteries sufficient to render the Christian religion so hateful in the eyes of the Philosopher? Do any of them favor the crimes and faults of men? Do any of them counteract his affection for his neighbour, or render him less attentive to his own duties, less faithful to friendship or gratitude, or less attached to his country? Is there a single mystery which does not elevate the Christian, stimulate his admiration for his God, or spur him on to his own happiness and to the love of his neighbours? The son of God expiring on a cross to open the gates of heaven to man, to teach him what he has to dread, should he, by his crimes, be unfortunate enough to close them again; the bread of angels, given only to those who have purified themselves from the dross of sin; those words pronounced on the man repenting of his crimes, and firmly purposing rather to die than to fall into them anew; the awful sight of a God who comes to judge the living and the dead, to call to him those who have loved, cloathed, and fed their brethren, while he casts into eternal flames the ambitious man, the traitor and the tyrant, the hard-hearted rich, the bad servant, the violator of the nuptial tie; and lastly, all persons who have not loved and helped their neighbour: are all these, I say, mysteries against which the Philosopher should direct his hatred; or can reason, on such a plea, authorise his conspiracy against the religion of the Christians?

Should Voltaire and his disciples refuse to believe these *mysteries*, does it import to them that other people should not equally disbelieve them. Is the Christian more dangerous to them, because he that forbids me to injure my brother is the same God before whom we are both one day to appear in judgment. Is that God less tremendous to the wicked, or less favorable to the just, because on his word we believe him to be one in essence, though three in persons? This hatred of Voltaire must be a phrenzy which the very infidels themselves could not ground on such pretexts. What frantic rage must it be that blinds the Sophisters, when, in contradiction with themselves, they applaud the toleration of the ancient Philosophers, who, though disbelieving the mysteries of Paganism, never attempted to rob the people of their religion; while, on the other hand, they incessantly conspire against Christianity under pretence that it contains mysteries.

Another objection no less extravagant, is that against *Revelation* itself. It is God, they say, whom the Christians declare to have spoken; hence there can be no further liberty of opinion in man on matters of faith; the Sophister of Equaliy and Liberty is then authorised to rise in arms against Christianity and its mysteries. Such are their arguments. But to what lengths does their phrenzy carry them? Voltaire, D'Alembert, and Diderot, conspire to overthrow every altar, Roman or Lutheran, Calvinist or Anglican, and that in order to avenge the rights of liberty and toleration in matters of faith. What a bedlamite idea is this? Can reason be traced through plots and conspiracies, of which the sole tendency is the overthrow of the universal religion of Europe, under pretènce of liberty of worship? We have heard Voltaire invoking Bellerophon and Hercules to his aid, to crush the God of the Christians, and D'Alembert, expressing the frantic wish of seeing a whole nation annihilated for its attachment to that God and his worship. Have we not seen them for half a century past meanly conspiring and using all the artifice of cunning intrigue to rob the world of its religion? And because they utter the empty sounds of EQUALITY, LIBERTY, and TOLERATION, we must mistake their voice for that of Philosophy!—Far be from us the idea of such Philosophy. Terms themselves must have been changed, for this must be extravagance and absurdity; and is not such REASON madness and phrenzy? Such must be the explanation of these words to expound the REASON and PHILOSOPHY of a Voltaire or a D'Alembert conspiring to crush the religion of Christ.

I wished not to have had to mention Frederic again. I reflect that he was a king; but, alas! he is also the royal Sophister. Let us then examine how far philosophy misled him, and whether his wisdom extended beyond the genius of the meanest adept.

Frederic wrote; but why? It is a problem. Was it to impose on the public, or to delude himself? Decide it who can. Probably for both, and he seems to have succeeded. Frederic would sometimes write in favor of toleration, and he was believed to be tolerant. In the *Monthly Review*, October 1794, page 154, we see him cried up as a model of toleration, and the following passage of his works is quoted: "I never will constrain opinions on matters of religion. I dread religious wars above all others. I have been so fortunate, that none of the Sects who reside in my states have ever disturbed civil order. We must leave to the people the objects of their belief, the form of their devotion, their opinions, and *even their prejudices*. It is for this reason that I have tolerated priests and monks, IN SPITE *of Voltaire and D'Alembert, who have* QUARRELLED WITH ME ON THIS HEAD. I have the greatest veneration for all our modern Philosophers; but I am indeed compelled to acknowledge that a GENERAL TOLERATION is not the *predominant virtue in these gentlemen.*" From this the editors draw many excellent conclusions, by objecting the wisdom of Frederic's doctrine to the atrocious persecutions and ferocious intolerance of the French Sophisters; but the reader who has seen him stimulate these same Philosophers to overthrow the altar, *to crush the wretch;* who has seen him trace the plan so much admired by Voltaire as that of *a Great Captain* for the destruction of the priests and monks, in order to attack the bishops, and to compass the overthrow of religion; who has heard him decide that the Antichristian Revolution, which he so *much longed to see,* could only be accomplished *by a superior force,* and that *the sentence* which was definitively *to crush* religion was *to issue from government*; will that reader, I ask, recognize the toleration of the sophistical monarch! No, he will pass the same judgment on the Sophister which the editors have passed on the disciples of that school. "When SUCH MEN tell us their *object is to carry into practice all the perfection of theory,* we know not which it ought principally to excite, *our* DISGUST *or* INDIGNATION." But let us revere the Monarch; let us vent our indignation against that frantic Philosophism which involves in darkness the royal adept on his throne, as it did his masters in their sanhedrims and secret academies, eradicating from man every symptom of reason.

If any thing could paint the folly of the masters in stronger colors, it would be that empty pride of the adepts at the period when they look upon the grand object of their conspiracy as accomplished. Religion was mourning over her altars overthrown, her temples profaned when Concorcet exalting the triumph of Voltaire, exclaims: "Here at length it is permitted openly to proclaim the right, so long disused, of reducing all opinions to the standard of *our own reason*; that is to say, to employ, in order to arrive at the truth, the *only implement* that has been given us to recognize it. Man learns with a certain pride, that he is not designed by nature to believe on the affirmation of others; and the superstitions of antiquity, the degradation of reason in the phrenzy of a supernatural faith, are vanished from society as they were from Philosophy."[3]

Condorcet, when writing these words, no doubt meant to describe the triumph of reason over revelation and over the whole Christian religion. The adepts applaud, and, like him, believe in the pretended triumph of reason. But it had not less cause than religion to mourn over such triumphs. Was it then to reinstate man in his right of bringing his *opinions* to the test of *reason*, that the Sophisters had with unrelenting fury conspired against the religion of Christ? What could they have intended by this test? Was it to exercise the right of only believing what their reason, when convinced, invited them to believe? If so, where the necessity of conspiring? Does the religion of Christ command man to believe what his enlightened reason does not induce him to believe? Is it not to convince our reason that Christianity surrounded itself with incontestable proofs; that Christ and his Apostles wrought numberless miracles; that religion has preserved its records, and that her pastors invite the Christian to the spirit of research, that he may know what has been proved and what he ought to believe; that her apostles formally declare, that *his faith, his submission should be reasonable* (rationabile obsequium vestrum)? And can the Sophister hence infer, that conspiracies and the darkest plots are necessary to vindicate the rights of reason believing in religion? a religion whose God is the God of reason; whose tenets are the tenets of reason; whose rights are the rights of reason rejecting Sophistry and false prejudices; but whose duty is to believe, from the numerous proofs of the power, of the sanctity, of the wisdom and sublimity of the God who speaks, and on the authenticity of his word.

If by the rights of reason the Sophister means the right of only believing what his reason can conceive, and that ceases to be myterious, then these rights of reason must truly border on phrensy. The Sophister is no longer to believe in the light of the day nor the darkness of the night, till light and its action on man shall cease to be a mystery; no longer shall he believe in the oak towering over the forest, raised from an acorn; nor in the humble flower glowing in the brightest colors; no longer shall he believe in man, succeeding from generation to generation; nature shall be denied, and his own existence remain a doubt, until all is clearly conceived by his reason, and the veil of mystery spread over these various objects shall be rent asunder.—Thus to attain the honors of infidelity, he submits to the garb of folly.

How different is the language of the real sage! His reason declares that objects once proved are to be believed, however mysterious they may be, under the penalty of absurdity; for then they are believed to exist because their existence is demonstrated, and not, as the Sophister would pretend, because their nature is inconceivable.

But another right, equally inconceivable and triumphantly inculcated by Condorcet, is that of being reduced *in order to arrive at truth, to the only implement that has been given us to distinguish it!* If then nature has left me in the dark on objects of the greatest importance, on my future state, on the means of avoiding a destiny I dread, or of obtaining the lot I desire, the man who shall dissipate the mist with which I am surrounded, will have robbed me of my rights? Why did he not say that the right of the blind man is also to keep to the only instrument nature had given him, and that it would be encroaching on his rights if he that has eyes should attempt to lead him? Why did he not conclude that the blind man had also learned with a *sort of pride* that nature had never designed that he should believe in light on the assertion of another.—What philosophic pride is that of the Sophister! His reason is degraded by a *supernatural faith!*—Christianity, he thinks, has debased his reason by raising it above the sphere of this world; he thinks that the God of the Christians has vilified man by explaining to him his eternal destiny, and leaving him the memory of his miracles as a proof of his word.—Such a pretense was the grand plea for the Antichristian Conspiracy, and dared they invoke the name of reason? Were they believed to be Philosophers? And do many yet labor under this error?—But let us return to their masters, to Voltaire, D'Alembert and Diderot; let us show to the adepts the unfortunate dupes of ignorance also decorated with the title of Philosophers.—To accomplish this, it will only be necessary to point out the most formal avowals and mutual confidences of these pretended Philosophers.

Does God exist, or does he not?—Have I a soul to save, or have I not?—Is this life to be entirely spent for my present interest?—Am I to believe in a future state?—Is this God, this soul, and this future state what I am told; or am I to believe quite another thing?—Such certainly are the elementary questions of true science, of Philosophy the most apposite to the happiness of man both in itself and in its consequences. On questions of such importance, what do these assuming sages reply, what are their mutual answers to each other, at the very time they are conspiring against Christ? Has not the reader seen their letters, and their own expressions? Did not these men, who pretended to the empire of knowledge, formally and repeatedly declare that they were unable even to form an opinion on any of these questions? Voltaire, consulted by the citizen or by the prince, consults D'Alembert in his turn, whether there is a God, whether he has a soul; and a *non liquet* (I do not know), is the answer he receives—These must be strange Philosophers indeed, uncertain on the very principles of Philosophy. How can they assume the title of rulers of reason, who are ignorant of that science on which the morals, principles and basis of society rest; on which the duties of man, of the father of a family and of the citizen, of the prince and of the subject, on which, in short, their conduct and happiness entirely depend? What can be their science on man if they are perfectly ignorant of his nature? What can be their doctrine on his duties, on his grand concerns, if they are ignorant of his future destiny? What is that Philosophy which barely tells me that I am ever to be in the dark with regard to those objects which most concern me and those with whom I am to live?

We have seen D'Alembert, in order to conceal his ignorance, absurdly excusing it by answering, that it could be of little concern to man, not to be able to solve these questions on the soul, on God, or on a future state. We have seen Voltaire declaring that nothing was known of these first principles, yet owning that uncertainty was a disagreeable state, but pleading this uncertainty itself, he adds, that certainty is a ridiculous state and that of a quack. Thus because the former is ignorant on these questions, it can little import man to know whether his concerns extend no further than this mortal life, or whether a happy or an unhappy eternity is to be his fate. Because the latter is equally ignorant, though more unhappy in his ignorance, man is to despise whoever shall pretend to dispel his doubts; Christ and his Apostles are to be treated with ridicule, and certainty shall be the doctrine of a Quack!—This cannot be ignorance alone; it must be pride and folly. What! Man is to be buried in darkness, because the jealous eye of the Sophister is dazzled with the light.

Hatred, jealousy, and destruction, contain the whole science of these pretended sages. Hate the Gospel, calumniate its author, overthrow his altars, and your science will be that of the modern Philosopher. Profess yourself a Deist, an Atheist, a Sceptic, a Spinosist, in short, whatever you please; deny or affirm, set up a doctrine or a worship in opposition to the religion of Christ, or set up none, that is not what either the Sect or Voltaire himself requires to constitute a modern Philospher. When asked what doctrine he wished to substitute to that of Christ, did he not think himself authorised to answer, I have delivered them from the physicians (he called the clergy physicians), what farther service do they require? Require! have you not infected them with the plague? Have you not unbridled every passion? And what remedies have you left them? In vain were it for us to challenge Voltaire and his panegyrist Condorcet, they will not answer.—No; follow their example; declare all religious truths to be erroneous, false, or popular prejudices, to be superstition and fanaticism; glory in destruction, little troubling yourself with substituting science for ignorance, or truth for error. To have destroyed will suffice; and for that you shall be entitled to the high-sounding name of a modern Philosopher.

At this rate, the reader's surprise at the numerous tribe of Philosophers to be found in every rank, of all ages and sexes, must cease. But at such a rate can an honest man pride himself in the title of Philosopher: such a science is, alas! but too easily acquired. It is as yet a problem why Voltaire, on his outset, seemed to confine his views to the higher classes, to kings, nobles and the rich, why he should have excluded *beggars and the rabble*. On seeing the guests smile at the blasphemies uttered at table, will not the footman soon equal his master in the Philosophic science, will he not also learn to scoff at the pontiff and the pastor, at the altar and the gospel? Will not the butchering Marseillais, like Condorcet, glory in having cast off those vulgar prejudices, when in the bloody murders of September he overthrows the altar and stains its steps with the blood of its priests and pontiffs. Like Voltaire, will he not style this the Age of Reason, and of enlightened Philosophy: harangue the vilest of the populace; tell them that the priests are imposing on them, that hell is of their invention; that the time is come to throw off the yoke of fanaticism and superstition, and to assert the liberty of their reason; and in a few minutes, the ignorant plough-boy will rival, in Philosophic science, the most learned of the adepts. The language may vary, but the science will be the same. They will hate with the adept, and will destroy what he wished to crush. The more ignorant and ferocious they are, the more easily shall they adopt your hatred, which constitutes the whole of this sophisticated science.

If adepts are sought for in another line, it is easy to increase their numbers, but without adding to the science of the Sect. Thus let the daughter of Necker but find some impertinent sarcasm of hers against the Gospel taken for wit by D'Alembert, and she immediately becomes as Philosophic as he and as void of religious prejudices as sister Guillemetta. It had astonished many to see the numbers of young fops who were already styled Philosophers, at so early an age they scarcely had had time to read any thing except a few impious pamphlets. But this age of enlightened Philosophy can no longer be a subject of surprise.

What! shall every wanton coquette partake of this Philosophy; shall every husband or wife who scoffs at conjugal fidelity;, shall every son who throws aside all sentiments of duty, and denies the authority of a parent; shall they all be styled Philosophers? The courtier destitute of morals, or the man who is a slave to, and imprudently quits all control over his passions, these also will glory in the name of Philosophers! Voltaire, in spite of all their vices, rejects none of these from his school, provided they have the necessary requisites of scoffing at the mysteries, of insulting the priesthood, and hating the God of the gospel. Certainly these cannot be simply the dupes of ignorance mistaken for science. No; these must be the children of corruption substituted for the school of virtue. That folly, that frantic rage which consumes Voltaire, conspiring against his God, or setting heaven at defiance, when he writes to D'Alembert, *Twenty years more, and God will be in a pretty plight;* or when he repeatedly writes to Damilaville, *Crush, crush the wretch*; that, I say, may be more worthy of pity than of blame. Yes, Voltaire in the phrensy of his rage is to be pitied. That multitude of adepts, of noblemen, ministers, and citizens, are to be excused, who, without having the least idea of Philosophy, have believed themselves Philosophers, misled by those impious Sophisters. I will not even ask them since when could the bare title of Philosopher, assumed by Frederic and Voltaire, suffice to constitute them masters in a science of which they openly professed their ignorance and contempt: I will not tell them, that if Frederic, consummate in the art of war, could form warriors; that if Voltaire, rivalling Corneille, could give lessons to the poet, they were nevertheless both equally ignorant in point of religion. I will not say to them, that this latter is a science, like all others, requiring great application and study in order to excel; that it was absurd to look for masters and teachers in men who blasphemed what they neither understood nor sought to understand; in men who, often stammering out a petty sophism which they deemed unanswerable, resembled the child, who dashes the watch on the ground because the spring is hidden from him. Such would be the reflexions of common sense, which should have rendered the school of the Sophisters at least suspected, if not absurd and ridiculous to its adepts; when Frederic combats the Sorbonne, or Voltaire St. Thomas; when D'Alembert attacks St. Augustin, or Sister Guillemetta St. Paul.

It is possible, that all these great Sophisters, debating on divinity, religion, and tenets, may have been mistaken by the ignorant adepts for learned doctors. But when the whole school, treating of morality and virtue, pretend to direct them solely by the rules of natural religion, the very shadow of a pretext for their delusion disappears. Casting an eye on the Sect, could they perceive a single adept who, under the direction of Voltaire or D'Alembert, had quitted his religion to become a better father or a better son, a better husband or a better man; in short more virtuous! Would not the simple reflexion have sufficed, that this pretended Philosphy of virtue had regularly been the refuge of all those men who were publicly known to scoff at every duty, at all morality: that when the friends to religion reproached them with the dissoluteness of their morals, as constantly answered with a sort of sneer, "Such reproaches may do for men who have not as yet shaken off the prejudices of the Gospel; but we are Philosphers, and we know what to believe!!"

It would be impossible to dissemble that every vice was cloaked under such a Philosophy; the faithless wife; the profligate youth; the man practising every art, whether just or unjust, to attain his ends; even to the loose women, whose characters were openly disparaged;, all decorated themselves with the high-sounding name of Modern Philosophers. None would have dared to justify their criminal conduct by answering,—I am a Christian,—I believe in the Gospel.—Let not the chiefs charge the error and ignorance on the disciples. The adept knew but too well that nothing but the name of virtue remained in the school of the Sophisters; that the greater progress he made in their science, the more he adopted their principles, by setting at defiance the reproach of the virtuous man, and by smothering the cries of his own conscience. It is true, they had not barefacedly blasphemed the morality of the

Gospel; but they had erased from their code all those virtues *which religion maintains to be descended from heaven.* He had seen the long list of those which they called *sterile and imaginary virtues,* or *virtues of prejudice;* he had seen erased from their code all the list of real virtues, such as modesty and continence, conjugal fidelity and filial piety, gratitude, and forgiveness of injuries, disinterestedness, even probity itself.[4] To these virtues they had substituted ambition, pride, vain glory, the pleasures, and the passions. Their morality acknowledged no other virtue than that *which is advantageous;* nor vice but that *which is hurtful* in this world; and virtue is declared to be but *an empty dream* if the virtuous man is unhappy. Personal interest is laid down as the sole principle of all Philosophic virtues; they sometimes indeed name *beneficence* as one; but that is merely as an excuse to dispense them from the practice of every other virtue. *Friend, do good to us, and we will overlook every thing else,* is the express doctrine of Voltaire:[5] but that was not all. It was necesssary to bring the adepts to doubt even of the existence of virtue, to doubt whether in morality there existed a right and wrong, and it was to such a question that Voltaire did not blush to answer, *non liquet* (it is not known).[6] As a further step, they were to decide that all that is called "perfection, imperfection, righteousness, wickedness, goodness, falsehood, wisdom, and folly, only differed from each other by their sensations of pleasure or pain;"[7] that "the more the Philosopher examined the nature of things, the less he dared to assert that it depended any more on man to be pusillanimous, choleric, vicious, or voluptuous, than it did to be squint-eyed, hump-backed or lame."[8] Such were the lessons of the conspiring Sophisters; and can it be believed that such lessons could be mistaken for those of virtue and Philosophy?

Had the adept been certain as to the existence of vice and virtue, of what consequence would this distinction have been to him, when his masters teach him, that man is born for happiness, and that the latter consists *in pleasure, or the absence of pain;*[9] when laying aside all solicitude for his soul, he is taught that *the motto of the wise man ought to be to watch over his body;*[10] or that it is by *pleasure* that God *stimulates to virtue.*[11] Such are the lessons taught by Voltaire, Diderot and D'Alembert, the chiefs of the conspirators.

What motives to virtue did these chiefs suggest to their adepts when they declared that a God neither *regards their virtue nor their vices,* that *the fear of this* GOD *is an absolute folly*! or when, wishing to stifle all remorse of conscience, they tell them, that "the man void of fear is above the laws—That a bad action, when useful, can be committed without remorse—That remorse is no other than the fear of men and of their laws;" or again, when (carrying their doctrine beyond all absurdity) they on one side assert the liberty of opinions in order to leave man free to choose the false, while, on the other hand they destroy in him all liberty of action to smother all symptoms of remorse.[12]

Such was the doctrine of the Sophisters. In vain would they attempt to deny it; all their writings are full of it, and particularly those which they most extolled as their principal master-pieces. What could have been the conduct of these great Philosophers had they undertaken to draw up a code of villainy and depravity? What more could be required to demonstrate to the world that this pretended age of Philosophy was no other than that of vice, than that of wickness organized into principles and precepts for the use of the abandoned, to whom they might be advantageous.

The only plea that can be left to the numbers of adepts who styled themselves Philosophers, in alleviation of their criminality, is the amazing constancy and artfulness which it required from the chiefs to propagate their principles, and ensure the success of their conspiracy.

But with these artifices, these intrigues, what was their Philosophy? Let us suppose that during the life-time of Voltaire, of Frederic, or of D'Alembert, and before depravity had attained to such a height, the frequent and repeated orders given to the conspirators of *strike, but hide your hand* had been known; let us suppose that the people had been acquainted with all the tortuous means secretly used to seduce them; would any one then have traced the actions of the Philosopher in such dark hypocrisy, in such perpetual dissimulation, or in the ambushes which were their only means of success?

At the time when D'Alembert and Condorcet, Diderot, Helvetius and Turgot, held their sittings at the Hotel D'Holbach under the name of Œconomists, and under the pretence of meditating on the happiness of the people, had it been known by that same people, that they were only plotting against the altars of the God whom it adored; had it been known that those teachers, who had been appointed to instruct the rising generation, were only the impious emissaries of D'Alembert, sent to corrupt its morals; that all those hawkers of books sold at so low a rate were the agents of the secret academy, employed to circulate its poisons from towns to villages, and thence to the poorest cottages; would such means, I ask, have entitled the Sect to that respect and veneration which it has usurped? Their wicked plots once detected, could such sages have sufficed to have given to the century they lived in the appellation of the Philosophic Age? No:—without doubt, horror would have succeeded to this admiration; and if the laws had remained silent, public indignation would have avenged Philosophy of the infamous plots carried on under the cloak of its name.

Let then this age of pretended Philosophy cast off the delusion under which it has been led away, a delusion arising perhaps more from its own vices and corruption than from the arts of the conspirators; let it blush and repent. That unpolished multitude, confessing its inexperience in the ways of the Sophisters, whom instinctive virtue so long preserved from the arts of seduction, may be excusable; but let those thousand of adepts, who are to be found in the courts and palaces of the great, in the seats of literature, let them reflect on and scrutinize their past conduct. In adopting impiety they believed themselves Philosphers.—In throwing off the yoke of the Gospel, and laying aside its virtues rather than its mysteries, they mistook the empty sounds of *prejudice* and *superstition*, perpetually repeated by the Sophisters, for profound reasoning. They were ignorant that the word *prejudice* only signifies an opinion void of proofs; and that they themselves had become slaves to prejudice, by casting off a religion of which they gloried in not having studied the proofs, while they continued to read all the calumnies that its enemies could compile against it. Let them seek still further claims to this Philosophy in their own hearts. Was it not to a lukewarm weariness for the virtues of the Gospel that they were indebted for their admiration of the Conspirators? Was it not for the love of their passions which made them a prey to infidelity, far more than all the intrigues and ambushes of the Sophisters? It is much to be feared, that that man is already wicked who makes himself so happy and glories so much in following the apostles of wickedness; or small indeed must have been his portion of Philosophy, if such duplicity, such meanness, and such conspiracies, could have been mistaken for wisdom or virtue.

Whatever may have been the causes, it was ordained, that an age duped by the intrigues and conspiracies of impiety should glory in styling itself the *Age of Philosophy*. It was ordained that an age, a dupe to the frantic rage of impiety substituted to reason; a dupe to the oaths of hatred and the wish of crushing all religion, mistaken for toleration, for religious Equality and Liberty; to ignorance for science; to depravity for virtue; a dupe, in short, to all the intrigues and plots of the most profound wickedness mistaken for the proceedings and means of wisdom; it was ordained, I say, that this *Age of Philosophy* should also be a dupe to the plots of the rebellious Sophisters, mistaken for the love of society and the basis of public happiness.

The Conspiracy against the altar, the hatred sworn by the chiefs against their God, were not the only legacies bequeathed by the chiefs to this school of modern Philosophy. Voltaire was the father of the Sophisters of Impiety, and before his death he becomes the chief of the Sophisters of Rebellion. He had said to his first adepts, Let us crush the altar, and let not a single altar nor a single worshipper be left to the God of Christians; and his school soon resounded with the cry of, *Let us crush the sceptre*, and let not a single throne., nor a single subject, be left to the kings of the earth! It was from the mutual co-operation and success of these two schools, that the revolution was to be generated in France, which, grasping the hatchet, was at the same time to destroy the altar of the living God, and imbue its steps with the blood of its pontiffs; to overturn the throne, and strike off the head of the unfortunate Louis XVI; menacing all the altars of Christendom, all the kings of the earth, with a similar fate. To the plots contrived under the veil of Equality and Liberty *applied to religion*, and of religious toleration, are to succeed those begotten under the veil of *political* Equality and Liberty. The mysteries of the second conspiracy of the *Sophisters of Rebellion*, combining with those of *Impiety*, in order to generate the modern JACOBINS, will be the object of the Second Part of these Memoirs.

1. Plato in his second Alcibiades.
2. Ibid.
3. Sketch on the Progress of Mind, epoch 9.
4. See the original texts quoted in the Helvian Letters, vol. 5.

5. Fragments on divers subjects, Art. VIRTUE.
6. Philosophical Dictionary, Art. TOUT EST BIEN.
7. Let. of Thrasybulus.
8. Encyclopedia, Geneva edition, Art, VICE.
9. Encyclopedia, Art. HAPPINESS, and Preface.
10. D'Alembert on the Elements of Philosophy, No. 5.
11. Voltaire's Discourse on Happiness.
12. See their texts quoted in the Helvian Letters, vol. 3.

END OF THE FIRST PART

MEMOIRS,

Illuſtrating the

HISTORY of JACOBINISM,

Written in FRENCH by

THE ABBÉ BARRUEL,

And tranſlated into ENGLISH by

THE HON. ROBERT CLIFFORD, F.R.S. & A.S.

Princes and Nations ſhall diſappear from the face of the Earth ... and this REVOLUTION ſhall be the WORK OF SECRET SOCIETIES.
Weiſhaupt's Diſcourſe for the Myſteries.

PART II.

THE ANTIMONARCHICAL CONSPIRACY.

Second Edition, reviſed and corrected.

LONDON:
Printed for the TRANSLATOR,
By T. BURTON, No. 11, Gate-ſtreet, Lincoln's-Inn Fields;
Sold by E. BOOKER, No. 56, New Bond-ſtreet.

1798.

THE ANTIMONARCHICAL CONSPIRACY

PRELIMINARY DISCOURSE

IN this Second Part of the "Memoirs illustrating the History of Jacobinism," our object will be to show, how the *Sophisters of Impiety*, becoming the *Sophisters of Rebellion*, after having conspired against every altar, conspire against every throne. We shall demonstrate, that these men under the name of Philosophers, after having sworn to crush Christ and his altars, bound themselves in a second oath to annihilate all regal power.

We have said, in the former part of this work,[1] that the Sophisters of Impiety, when they were become the Sophisters also of Rebellion, had leagued with a Sect, long since concealed in the occult lodges of Freemasonry, whose adepts, like the modern Philosophers, had sworn hatred to the altar and the throne, had sworn to crush the God of the Christians, and utterly to extirpate the Kings of the earth.

This two-fold object naturally divides our Second Volume into two Parts. The first will develop the rise and progress of the Conspiracy of the Sophisters, called Philosophers: The second, of that sect, which we have denominated Occult Masons (*Arrières Maçons*), to distinguish their adepts from the multitude of brethren who were too virtuous to be initiated in the occult mysteries, too religious, and too faithful citizens to associate in their plots.

After having treated separately of these two conspiracies, though both tending to the same object, we shall show them leaguing together; and by their united efforts accomplishing that part of the French Revolution which effected the overthrow of Religion and Monarchy, of the altar and the throne; in a word, which murdered, basely murdered, the unfortunate Lewis XVI on a scaffold.

Confining ourselves to facts, and suppressing the powers of imagination, it seems incumbent on us to submit some few reflections to the reader, which, though naturally flowing from the subject, are yet requisite to enable him to follow the progress of the Sophisters in their second conspiracy, to show by what gradations they passed, or rather with what celerity they were hurried headlong, from the school of impiety to that of rebellion, by the inherent tendency of their principles.

While, under the direction of Voltaire, these pretended Philosophers had merely applied their principles of Equality and Liberty to matters of faith, and had thence conspired against the God of the Gospel, that each might be at liberty to form his own religion, or throw off every religious tie;—during that time, few were the obstacles they had to fear from those various classes of men, which it was chiefly their object to captivate.—During their war against Christianity, the passions proved their most powerful allies. There would be no great difficulty in deluding those unfortunate men, who combat the mysteries which they do not understand, merely to exempt themselves from the restraint of those precepts and the practice of those virtues which are unfavourable to their passions.

Sovereigns, seldom much versed in the science or history of religion; men who often, under the sanction of opulence and the splendour of rank, only seek to throw off all control on their moral conduct; others aspiring at fortune, and caring not by what unwarrantable means they acquire it; vain men panting after an empty name, and ready to sacrifice every truth to a sarcastic meteor, or some blasphemy mistaken for wit, and others who would have had little hope of celebrity had they not directed their genius against their God;—in short, all those men who, easily receiving sophisms for demonstrative proofs, never troubled themselves with the investigation of that *equality of rights*, and that *liberty of reason*, which the conspiring Sect represented to them as being incompatible with a religion revealed, and replete with mysteries.

Few even of the adepts had ever reflected on the absurdity of opposing the rights of reason to revelation; as if those pretended rights of our limited reason were to suspend the power of an infinite God who reveals himself, or were to depreciate the truth of his oracles, and of the mission of his Prophets and Apostles. They never had reflected, that the whole question of these rights of reason turned simply on this: to know whether God had spoken or not; and to believe and silently adore whatever might be the nature of the truths he had revealed.

Men so little able to comprehend and to defend the rights of their God, could not have been very dangerous adversaries for the Sophisters, who are perpetually setting this liberty of reason in opposition to the Gospel.

But how different the case, when the Sect applying this same Equality and Liberty to the empire of human laws and to civil society, concludes, that after having crushed the altar, it was also necessary to overturn every throne, in order that men might be reinstated in their original Equality and Liberty! A conspiracy on such principles, and drawing after it such consequences, must naturally have been combated by the interests and the passions of the Royal Sophisters, of the protecting Princes, and of all those adepts of the higher classes, who were so docile to the accents of liberty, when those accents only menaced the destruction of the religion of their God.

Voltaire and D'Alembert could not expect to find Frederic, Joseph II, Catherine III, or Gustavus of Sweden, much disposed to subvert their respective thrones. It was very probable too, that many other protecting adepts, such as ministers or courtiers, nobles, or wealthy persons distinguished by their rank, would soon perceive the danger of depending on a multitude, who, having thrown off all obedience, would soon grasp at sovereignty itself, and, as the first essay of its power, would level every species of property, and strike off every head which rose above that multitude.

On the side of the Sophisters themselves, though gratitude could have had but little weight with them, yet their interest, their very existence might have abated their eagerness against the throne. D'Alembert lived on pensions from the Kings of France and Prussia; his very apartment in the Louvre was a gift from Lewis XVI. The Empress of Russia alone supported Diderot's ruined fortune; and the Grand Duke pensioned the adept La Harpe. Damilaville would have been a beggar, if discarded from his office. The Philosophic Sanhedrim of that French Academy composed of so many adepts owed its existence, its means, its counters (*jetons*) to the generosity of the monarch. There were few other scribbling Sophisters who did not either look up to a pension, or had not already obtained one by the intrigues of the protecting ministers.

Voltaire had acquired an independent fortune; but he was not, on that account, the less elated when M. de Choiseul gave him back the pension which, twelve years before, he had lost, on account of his impious writings.[2] Beside, nobody knew better than did Voltaire, that he was chiefly indebted for the success of his Antichristian Conspiracy to the royal adepts. He was too proud of numbering among his disciples Imperial and Regal Sovereigns, to conspire against their very existence on earth.

All these motives, therefore, gave quite a different turn to the conspiracy against the Throne, from that which we have already seen erected against the Altar. In the warfare against the Gospel, Equality and Liberty could have been but a shallow pretence; it was their hatred against Christ by which they were hurried away. It is hardly possible that they could have concealed from themselves that it was rather a war waged by their passions against the virtues of the gospel, than a warfare of reason against the mysteries of Christianity. In the Antimonarchical Conspiracy, the pretext had grown into conviction. The Sophisters believed their principles of Equality and Liberty to be demonstrated, they did not even suspect an error in their principles. They believed the war which they waged against Kings to be a war of justice and of wisdom. In the former conspiracy, it was the passions inventing principles to combat the God of the Christians; in the latter, it was reason, misled by those same principles, seeking and glorying in the downfal of every crowned head.

Rapid had been the progress of the passions. From his very birth, Voltaire's hatred against Christ had been at its height. Scarcely had he known, ere he hated, scarcely hated when he swore to crush, the God of the Christians. Not such was the progress of the hatred against Kings. This sentiment had, like opinion and conviction, its gradations. The very interest of the Sophisters of Impiety thwarted for a long time the measures of those of Rebellion; many years were necessary to enable the sect to form its systems, to determine its plots, and resolve on its object. Were we to precipitate its steps, we should be guilty of misrepresentation. As faithful historians, it will be incumbent on us, to show this hatred against Kings in its infancy, that is, springing from the hatred against Christ, and successively applying those principles invented against the altar, to the destruction of the throne. This hatred against kings had even in the chiefs of the conspirators its gradations: but their systems will complete the delusion, and root it in the hearts of the adepts. It will bear absolute sway over their secret academy, and there will the same plots be contrived against the throne as Philosophism had framed against the altar. The same means and the same success will combine the conspiracies. The same crimes and the same disasters will combine the revolutions.

1. Preliminary Discourse, Vol. I, p. xxii [p. 6, Ed.].
2. To Damilaville, 9 Jan. 1762, Vol. 57, Let. 152, P. 310.

CHAP. I.

First Step in the Conspiracy of Kings.

Voltaire and D'Alembert passing from the Hatred of Christianity to the Hatred of Kings.

OUR attention to truth and justice with regard to a man, who was so far from both with respect to religion, obliges us to begin this chapter by a declaration, which might make Voltaire appear to be the farthest from an enemy, much less from being the author of a conspiracy against the throne. If this man, the most unrelenting chief when conspiring against Christianity, had followed the bias of his own inclinations; or had he been able to sway his adepts in politics as he had in impiety, never would that oath of destroying the throne have issued from his school.

Voltaire loved kings; their favor and their caresses were his delight; he was even dazzled with their greatness. His sentiments cannot be mistaken, after having seen him glory in singing the praises of Lewis XIV or Henry IV, kings of France; of Charles XII, king of Sweden; of the czar Peter, Emperor of all the Russias; of Frederic II, king of Prussia; and of so many other kings both of ancient and modern times.

Voltaire had all the habits and manners of the great, and at his court of Ferney acted the Grandee perfectly well. He had too high an opinion of his own abilities to assimilate himself, by Equality, to that multitude which he contemptuously stiles, the beggarly *canaille*.

He was not only partial to kings, but even to the monarchical form of government. When he gives a loose to his own sentiments, and in his historical writings, we see him invariably preferring the dominion of ONE to that of the MANY. He could not endure the idea of having so many masters as there were counsellors in the parliament;[1] how then could he adopt that liberty and sovereignty of the people which would have given him as joint sovereigns, the towns and suburbs, the peasantry and his own vassals. He who so much delighted in reigning in his own castle, who was so jealous of his prerogatives in the midst of his estates which he called his little Province, how could he wish to sanction an Equality and Liberty which was to level the castle with the cottage?

Beside, Voltaire's principal object was to annihilate Christianity; and he feared nothing so much as to be thwarted by the kings in his undertaking, on pretence that he equally aimed his blows at the throne as he did against the altar. It was for this reason that he perpetually warns the adepts of what consequence it was, that the Philosophers should be considered as faithful subjects. When assuring Marmontel how much he (Voltaire) was protected by Choiseul and the courtezan Pompadour, he writes, that they may send him any thing without danger. "They know that we love the king and the state. It was not among us that such people as Damien heard the voice of rebellion. I am draining a bog, I am building a church, and I *pray for the king.* We defy either Jansenist or Molinist to have a greater attachment for the king than we have. My dear friend, the king must be acquainted that the Philosophers *are more attached to him* than all the fanatics and hypocrites in his kingdom."[2]

It was the self-same motive which induced him to write to Helvetius (that Sophister whom we shall see so unrelenting in his hatred to kings), "*It is the king's interest* that the number of Philosophers should augment, and that of the Fanatics diminish. We are quiet, and they are all disturbers of the peace; *we are citizens,* they are the children of sedition.... *The faithful servants of the king,* and of reason, shall triumph at Paris, at Voré, and even at the Délices."[3]

Apprehensive, however, that the Philosophers might be suspected, notwithstanding all his protestations, he had already written thus to D'Alembert: "Do you know who the bad citizen is that wishes to persuade the Dauphin that France is overrun with the enemies of religion? They will not pretend to say, I hope, that Peter Damiens, Francis Ravaillac, and their predecessors were Deists and Philosophers." Nevertheless, he ends his letter by saying, "I fear that Peter Damiens will be a great detriment to Philosophy."[4]

Finally, if any thing can paint in strong colours Voltaire's attachment to kings, it will be the method in which he treats those of the adepts who dared attack the authority of the sovereign. The adept Thiriot had sent him a work on the *Theory of Taxation,* and Voltaire answers, "*Received the Theory of Taxation,* an obscure theory, and apparently to me an absurd one. All such theories are very ill timed, as they only serve to make foreign nations believe that our resources are exhausted, and that they may insult and attack us with impunity. *Such men are very extraordinary citizens indeed, and curious friends to man.* Let them come where I am on the frontiers, and *they will presently change their opinions. They will soon see how necessary it is that the king and the state should be respected. Upon my word, at Paris people see every thing topsy-turvy.*"[5]

The staunchest Royalist could not have insisted in a clearer manner on the necessity of supporting the Royal authority; nevertheless, he had already let fall many expressions which little denoted any zeal for the cause of kings. He had not adopted, as yet, that Philosophism of rebellion, of Equality and Liberty, which was to fanaticise the French people, and raise Robespierres and Marats in succession to the fanatics Ravaillac and Damiens.—There were times even when he would have treated the Mirabeaux, La Fayettes, and Baillys, as he used sometimes to treat those mad Œconomists, who, attacking the authority of kings, saw, through their pretended theory, every thing in a wrong light. But this love for his king was but a remnant of his first education, which Philosophism had often belied, and of which the very trace would soon be erased from the heart of the Sophister.

Had Voltaire, either from his own sentiments, or for the interest of the Sect, been still more desirous of being looked upon as a good citizen, or a faithful subject of the king, yet the adepts could have retorted the arguments he had perpetually repeated to stir them up against Christianity, in too powerful a manner against his arguments in favor of kings, for him to have been able to withstand them. It was but natural that men who had been taught to oppose their Equality and Liberty to the God of revelation, to his ministers and prophets, should also oppose them to the kings of the earth. Voltaire had taught them that the Equality of rights and Liberty of reason were incompatible with that power of the church and of the gospel commanding a submission to and a belief in mysteries which were inconceivable by reason. The adepts, as the next step, declare that the Equality of men, the Liberty of nature, were equally incompatible with any submission to the empire and laws of *one* man, or even of *many*, whether called parliaments or senates, lords or princes, pretending to the dominion over a whole nation, and dictating laws to the multitude, who had neither made them, discussed them, nor wished for them.

These principles, so forcibly insisted on by Voltaire when combating Christianity, might naturally be objected to his propositions respecting submission to the sovereign; and they were so. The adepts urged the consequences, and the premier chief was unwilling to lose the pre-eminence over his own school in what he called Philosophy. The process by which he was led from the Sophistry of Impiety to that of Rebellion, is too much blended with the progress of his anti-religious Philosophism, not to be worthy of investigation.

Voltaire had been actuated by no other passion than that of hatred against Christ, when in the year 1718 he caused to be publicly recited in his tragedy of Œdipus those two famous verses, which alone comprehend the whole of that anti-religious revolution which was to be accomplished seventy years afterward:

> Priests are now what they seem to vulgar eyes,
> In our credulity their science lies.[6]

These two lines only proclaim that Equality of rights and Liberty of reason which, disavowing the authority or mission of the clergy, leave the people at full liberty to form their religious tenets on whatever they may please to call their reason. But many years elapsed before Voltaire could form a correct idea of that Equality and Liberty which was to divest the monarch of his rights, as he had divested the church of hers. It even appears that he had not at that time any idea of deducing from this Equality and Liberty principles so fatal to monarchy; that he was perfectly ignorant of what Equality and Liberty, applied to civil society, meant, when he published his epistles or discourses on Equality and Liberty in 1738. The first lessons he received on the subject were from his *élève* Thiriot, whom he had left in England, and from whom he wished to learn what opinion the adepts had formed on those epistles. Or, as is more probable, Thiriot, knowing his master's bias for aristocracy, only wrote that he had not sufficiently *gone to the point*, and that he was not in complete possession of the true principles. Piqued at such a reproach, Voltaire, like a man who did not care to see himself outdone by his disciples, writes, "A word on the Epistles. Where the devil do you find that they do not go to the point. There is not a single verse in the first epistle, which does not show the *Equality of conditions*, nor one in the second which does not prove *Liberty*."[7]

Notwithstanding this reply, the disciple was in the right. He might have rejoined, that throughout the whole of the Epistles there was not a single verse which, philosophically speaking, was not a misconstruction; since, in the first, all that Voltaire aimed at proving was, that in all stations of life the sum total of happiness was nearly the same; and in the second, Liberty is considered much more as a physical faculty, than as a natural, civil, and political right. The inference drawn from the first is, that it is useless for man to trouble himself about the difference of stations as the same portion of happiness is nearly allotted to each; the second does not even mention that liberty which the adepts so much insist on against kings, and only asserts that liberty which so well demonstrates the distinction of right and wrong, and which the sect always looked upon as too favorable to religion.

Without seeming to submit to his disciples, Voltaire, nevertheless, gradually adopted their sentiments; vexed at having asserted the rights of free agency, he counteracted all the influence that doctrine might have had, and gave his definition of liberty[8] such a turn, that Predestinarians themselves could not have cavilled at it. In a word, he no longer asserted any other liberty than that which has proved such a powerful weapon against sovereignty in the hands of the Sect.

The corrections he made in his Epistle on Equality, had a more direct affinity to the system of the political revolution. In the first edition of that Epistle we read,

> Equal the state, in men the difference lies.[9]

The Sect wished him to have said,

> Equal are men, in states the difference lies.[10]

At length Voltaire understood their meaning, and blushed at finding that his own disciples had made a greater progress in the knowledge of Equality than he had himself; and to avoid their future criticisms he changed both his doctrine and his verses. He corrected, and almost reconstructed his Epistle on Equality; nor did he let his poetic genius rest, till he had shown the adepts that he understood the equality of man as well as they did, and that they could no longer reproach him with not *going to the point*. It was then that he wrote the following verses, which contain all that the revolutionary populace have alledged against the wealthy, the nobility, and kings, in proof of its equality.

> With calm indifference let my friend survey
> The pomp of riches and despotic sway;
> This world's a ball, where his undazzled eyes
> Pierce thro' each silly actor's vain disguise.
> My Lord, your Highness, are the masks that hide
> Their little beings and exalt their pride;
> *But, men are equal*; pride do what you can,
> *The mask may differ but the same the man.*
> The five weak senses by us all possest,
> Of good, of evil, are our only test.
> A slave has five, *six can the Monarch claim*?
> The same his body and his soul the same.[11]

This is precisely what the democratic rabble of Paris was wont to say, less elegantly indeed, when it asked whether kings and nobles were not made of the same clay as the simple clown? Whether those who enjoyed large fortunes had two stomachs? And of what use were all those distinctions of Sovereigns, Princes, or Chevaliers, since *all men were equal*?

It was with reluctance, it must be confessed, that Voltaire became the Apostle of Equality. For without having a body or soul of a different species from that of Pompignan, Freron, or Desfontaines, or of so many other men whom he was perpetually overwhelming with his sarcasms, he nevertheless was aware that in the same species, and with the same nature, there existed no small inequality among men; that without being endowed with a sixth sense, he felt the great distance there was between himself and the rabble he so much despised. At length he submitted to the criticisms of the adepts, and after having declared

> Equal the state, in men the difference lies.[12]

he writes in absolute opposition,

> The mask may differ but the same the man.[13]

As to that liberty which commences in the love of Republicanism, and ends in the hatred of Kings, it is probable that Voltaire would never have adopted it, had it not been necessary to establish that liberty which was essential to the hatred of Christ; but he had found himself too much thwarted by the authority of Kings in his first publications against Christianity. In Holland he enjoyed a greater liberty for printing his blasphemies; and it was to that circumstance, that he owed his bias for Republicanism. Those who have read his correspondence while in Holland, and particularly the following letter to the Marquis D'Argenson, dated from the Hague, will not have a doubt that this was the case. "I am," says he, "better pleased even with the abuses of the liberty of the press here, than with that sort of slavery under which the human mind is kept in France. If you continue on that plan, the simple remembrance of the glorious age of Lewis XIV will be all that will remain. This degeneracy almost inclines me to settle in the country I am now in.... The Hague is a charming residence; *liberty alleviates the rigors of the winter. I like to see the Rulers of the State no more than plain Citizens.* There are factions, it is true, yet they must exist in Republics: But faction does not damp patriotism, and I see great men contending with great men....On the other side, I see, with equal admiration, the chief members of the state walking on foot without servants, living in houses worthy of those Roman Consuls who dressed their own roots; you would like this government extremely, notwithstanding all those imperfections which are unavoidable in it. *It is entirely municipal, and that is what you admire.*"[14]

All these expressions naturally denote a man declining towards a Republican Equality and Liberty, and who impatiently bore the yoke of Kings. A few years after, we may observe this passion much more predominant in Voltaire, especially in a letter which he is supposed to have written to an Academician of Marseilles, and mentioned in Mr. de Bevis's Memoirs. "I should accept your invitation, were Marseilles still a Grecian Republic; for I greatly admire Academies, *but am much more partial to Republics.* How happy are those countries where our masters visit us, and are not affronted when we do not return to wait on them!"

In all this, however, we see nothing more than a partiality for Republics; it was not positively a hatred of Kings, nor an imputation of tyranny and despotism in the regal government. But a few years after this, that same rancour is directed by Voltaire against the throne, which he had already conceived against the altar. Such at least is clearly the purport of a confidential letter which he writes to D'Alembert, wherein he says, "As to Luc (the King of Prussia), sometimes biting sometimes bitten, he must be a most unhappy mortal; *and those men who put themselves in the way of a musket or a sabre for such gentry, are most abominable fools.* Don't betray my secret either to Kings or Priests."[15]

This, however, could be no secret to those who had observed the modern Sophisters trying to cast all the odium of war and its miseries on Kings and the nature of their governments, and wishing to persuade the people that their only way of acquiring happiness, and everlasting peace, was to take the government into their own hands by wresting it from their Royal Masters. This proposition, so evidently contradicted by that perpetual state of warfare, interior or exterior, so common to Republics, evinces that Voltaire had no care about proof, when he decided in so peremptory a stile, that those who were persuaded they were fighting for their country when rallied under the standard of their king, were most abominable fools.

We should particularly remark in this letter, how much his secret with regard *to Kings* is connected with that respecting *the Priesthood*; and he had more than once publicly divulged them both. The latter he had expressed in the verses already quoted from his Tragedy of Œdipus,

> Priests are not what they seem to vulgar eyes,
> In our credulity their science lies[16]

and as to the former, we see Voltaire by the same means teaching the people what they are to think with regard to Sovereigns, their rights, and their origin; or with regard to the Nobility, who are perpetually led and spurred on to the defence of their country in emulation of those services by which their ancestors distinguished themselves. It would be in vain to excuse the poet: it is a hatred of Kings, and not the genius of poetry, which inspires such artful turns, and makes the dramatic actor speak the sentiments of the Sophister. It certainly was not the love of Monarchy which dictated the following verses, and caused them to be spoken on the stage of a nation under the dominion of a King, and proud of the achievements of its Nobility. In his Tragedy of Mérope, he says,

> Some lucky soldier was the first of Kings;
> Who serves the state, no matter whence he springs.[17]

When Voltaire taught this doctrine to the French people, the Antimonarchical Revolution had made as great a progress in his mind, as the Antichristian formerly had, when the verses already quoted had been spoken against the Clergy. But nothing short of the most abandoned Jacobinism could testify applause when Voltaire continues, *Do you wish to be happy? Never own a master.*[18]

It was thus that Voltaire, carried away by his System of Liberty opposed to the Altar, daily cherished the sentiments of that liberty which was to combat the throne. Nor was it inadvertently that these maxims escaped from his poetic genius. In his correspondence with D'Alembert, his intention appears clearly when he points out to his confidant all those verses which may teach the subject to rise in judgment against his King, or even to become his assassin or executioner, should he ever chuse to view his Prince in the light of a tyrant or a despot. Exactly such are the passages which he wishes D'Alembert to notice, when he writes, "Last year I hurried over a Play called *The Laws of Minos*, which presently you will see hissed. In those *Laws of Minos*, Teucer says to Merion the Senator,

> Our laws a change, our state a King requires.[19]

The Senator answers:

> Of me, my treasures, and my life dispose;
> But should the pow'r this sovereign rank bestows
> Be turn'd against our laws and native land,
> Then shall my arm that guilty pow'r withstand.[20]

Had Voltaire ever met with such verses in the writings of a Clergyman, he would immediately have attacked him as an assassin and a traitor; he would have exclaimed, Behold the subject who raises himself in judgment against his Sovereign, who takes upon him the right of deciding between his King and the Laws, the right of attacking and combating his King, and of turning his sword against him, every time it may please him to believe, or to persuade the people, that the death of the Prince would restore energy to the laws.—Voltaire would have immediately added, there we see the people decidedly created both judge and sovereign over their Kings; such are the maxims which form Rebels, and produce Revolutions with all their concomitant horrors of democratic anarchy.

What Voltaire would very properly have said on this affectation of their making a distinction between the King and the Country, history may as properly apply to Voltaire himself; more particularly as nobody knew the consequences and danger of such maxims better than he did; nor did he even make any secret of their dangerous tendency when writing to his friends. He begins his letter to the Count D'Argental on sending him some of those seditious publications, by saying, "In the first place, promise me upon oath, that you never will let my *petit pâtés* out of your hands, that you will send them back to me, and inform me whether they are too highly seasoned, or whether the general taste of the day is more depraved than my own. *The forcemeat of my petits pâtés is not quite palatable to a monarchy*; but you told me *that a dish of Brutus* had been lately served up at the Count de Falkenstein's (the name under which Joseph II travelled), and that none of the guests had left the table."[21] Such language is not very enigmatical; but it paints Voltaire in very different colours from those we have seen him in, when reproaching his Parisian brethren with seeing every thing *topsy-turvy* in their attack on the King's power. It denotes an author who dares not yet show his sentiments so opposite to that power, but who wishes to go as far as possible without exposing himself to danger. We see him flattering himself that he has not been too daring, as Joseph II had been imprudent enough *to let a dish of Brutus be served up at his table*; that is to say, that monarch had heard broached at his table, without shewing his displeasure, doctrines the most dangerous and threatening to the lives of Sovereigns.

There are many other letters extant, which indicate how deeply this Antimonarchical liberty had rooted itself in the heart of Voltaire, and even how much he despised that love for their Sovereign at that time so universally prevalent among the French people. There is one in particular, in which he complains most bitterly, that strangers perfectly conversant in the catechism of liberty, and equal to the task of teaching it to the Parisians, are obliged to carry their systems elsewhere, before they have succeeded in teaching them to the French people; that if man was created to serve God, *he was also created to be free*. In short, what displeased Voltaire more particularly was, that while he was making such progress in this catechism of liberty, the French people, whom he calls his *Velches*, did not keep pace with him.[22] When the Historian shall treat of the progress which Voltaire was making in the arts of liberty, he shall not extenuate his error, by saying that Voltaire was not aware of the fatal consequences of a revolution, or that he would have started back from his purpose could he by possibility have foreseen them. Certainly his soul could not be so ferocious as to have aspired after the bloody reign of a Robespierre; but he complacently foretells, and offers up his prayers for a revolution, which he knows to be big with bloodshed and surrounded with firebrands; and, however disastrous such revolutionary scourges may appear to him, he nevertheless deems those persons happy, who, from their juvenility, may live to see them. He writes to the Marquis de Chauvelin, "Every thing is preparing the way to *a great revolution*, which will most *undoubtedly take place*; and I shall not *be fortunate enough to see it*. The French arrive at every thing slowly, but still they do arrive. Light has so gradually diffused itself, that on the first opportunity the nation will break out, *and the uproar will be glorious. Happy those who are now young, for they will behold most extraordinary things.*"[23]

Let the reader notice the date of this letter, which is twenty-five years anterior to the French revolution. During the whole of that long period we shall never observe Voltaire reproaching the adepts with seeing every thing *topsy-turvy*, when they attack the Royal prerogative.

Whether it was that the victories he had obtained over the altar gave him more confidence in his attacks against the throne; or that the success of his sarcastic attacks gradually made against kings with impunity, had persuaded him that they were not so formidable as he had believed them, either to himself or to his adepts; which of these was the true reason we cannot now determine. This however is certain, that so far from being startled at the principles of insurrection inculcated throughout the writings of his disciples, he hugs himself in the idea that their productions were becoming the catechisms of all nations.

When Diderot published his *System of Nature*, it was neither his attacks nor his frantic declamations against kings, that the Philosopher of Ferney sought to combat; but a kind of metaphysics the absurdity of which he feared would reflect on Philosophy. Yet, notwithstanding this absurdity, and the violent declamations against sovereignty, we find him exulting with D'Alembert in the success of that abominable work, and bragging of its being *so greedily read throughout all Europe*, that people *snatched it* from each other. When he saw the courtiers and princes encouraging new editions of Helvetius's work ON MAN AND HIS EDUCATION, notwithstanding the seditious and antimonarchical principles it contained, and which will be noticed in the course of this work, Voltaire, so far from fearing the indignation of kings, which such writings would naturally draw down on his school of Philosophers, smiles exultingly with D'Alembert at the great success of the work, and receives it as a proof that *the flock of sages silently increased.*[24]

Thus it is that all his fears of irritating sovereigns, by this apostleship of Equality and Liberty gradually subside, and are succeeded by that thirst of revolution, of *riot*, and of those tempestuous scenes which were to accompany the downfal of emperors and kings, in a word, of all sovereigns, or, in their philosophical cant, of tyrants and despots.

Our readers, and future ages, will naturally inquire, whether D'Alembert walked in the footsteps of his dear master; whether, as zealous as Voltaire for the Antichristian Liberty, he also adopted that liberty so inimical to royalty. Let D'Alembert speak for himself: his answer is contained in a letter already quoted, but which may throw new light on this question.

"You love REASON AND LIBERTY, my dear and illustrious brother; and a man can hardly love the *one* without loving *the other*. Well then, here is a worthy *Republican Philosopher* whom I present to you, who will talk with you on PHILOSOPHY AND LIBERTY: it is Mr. Jennings, chamberlain to the king of Sweden, a man of great merit and enjoying a high degree of reputation in his own country. He is worthy of your acquaintance, both for his own merit, and for the uncommon esteem he has for your writings, *which have so much contributed toward disseminating those two principles among persons worthy of feeling them.*"[25]

What an avowal is this for a man like D'Alembert, who was extremely cautious in his expressions, and always on his guard, lest he should utter any thing that might expose him to danger. *You love Reason and Liberty; and a man can hardly love the one, without loving the other.* A few lines lower, we find this *Reason* to be Philosophy; and the subsequent *Liberty* to be that of a Republican Philosopher; who nevertheless lives under a monarchy, loaded with the favors, and enjoying the confidence of his sovereigns. It is D'Alembert then who avows, that one can hardly love his pretended Philosphy, without loving Republicanism, or *that liberty* which he believes not to exist under Monarchy.

It is D'Alembert again who selects from among the numerous claims which may entitle the sophistical courtier to Voltaire's or his own esteem, that of his love for Republican Philosophy; though he certainly could not cultivate such a disposition, without secretly wishing to betray the cause of his King.

In short, it is D'Alembert who extolls the writings of his dear and illustrious brother, as peculiarly adapted to disseminate *those two principles of Republican Liberty and Republican Philosphy among persons worthy of feeling them*; or, in other words, as peculiarly adapted to fulfil the wishes of those pretended sages, who can find no liberty under the government of Kings, and who detest Monarchy in proportion to their love for Republics. He who believes himself worthy of feeling this *two-fold sentiment*, he who acknowledges no Philosphy as true if void of these two sentiments, could he, I ask, demonstrate in a more forcible manner, how ardently they glowed in his heart, or how much he panted after those revolutions which were to crush the throne, and establish Republicanism on its ruin?

In drawing these inferences, let not the reader suppose that we mean to confound in all cases a bias for Republics, or the love of Liberty, with the hatred of Kings, and the desire of subverting every Throne. We are perfectly aware, that there exist many worthy Republicans, who, while they love their own Government, are not unmindful of the respect due to those of other nations. Nor are we ignorant that true Civil Liberty is no less compatible with Monarchies than with Republics: indeed, it might not be difficult to prove, that the subject frequently enjoys a more real and extensive Liberty under a Kingly, than under a Republican Government, especially if a Democracy. But when we behold the Sophisters perpetually complaining of the Government of Kings under whom they live, styling their Sovereigns Despots, and sighing after the Liberty of the Republican Philosopher, we are certainly entitled to view their love for Liberty and Republicanism as blended with the hatred of Kings. If their blasphemies against Christ, if what they call their Philosophy be by any means thwarted, impatient of the rein, they burst forth into complaint, and they exclaim that *Reason is shackled*; that Despotism, *Decius like, perpetually persecutes them*; or, that *man is unfortunate indeed* when he lives under the eye of a Monarch, or of his Ministers.[26]

But to confine ourselves to D'Alembert, let us recal to mind, that in the warfare against the altar, he acted the part of the fox. We shall see him employing the same cunning in his attack against the Throne. He will excite and stimulate others, he will even guide their pens; but he carefully avoids every thing by which he might himself be eventually endangered. It is thus that he lauds Voltaire, that he extols the zeal with which his dear brother propagates the Republican Liberty and Philosophy; and fearing lest this zeal should sometime abate, he adds, "Continue to fight as you do, *pro aris et focis;* as for me, *my hands are tied by ministerial and sacerdotal tyranny*; I can only follow the example of Moses, and raise up my hands to heaven while you contend in fight."[27]

Again, we find him informing Voltaire of the eagerness with which he reads and devours all those writings in which that Premier Chief had combined his attacks against the Altar and the Throne. We see him applauding his sarcastic wit, and thus addressing him: "I am almost angry when I learn from public report, that without informing me of it you have given a slap to Fanaticism and Tyranny, and that without detriment to the swingeing blows which you apply in so masterly a manner on other occasions. You enjoy alone the privilege of covering with odium and ridicule those two pests of society."[28]

During this warfare, it was not the good fortune of all the adepts to gain the applause of D'Alembert. They had not, like Voltaire, the art of pleasing or amusing Kings, who did not perceive that the sarcastic wit and satire of his romances and historical productions fell on their own heads, though seemingly aimed only at the persons of other Kings.

It was not every one of the adepts that had the art of throwing the living into contempt, by striking at the dead; of flattering the person of the Sovereign, and rendering sovereignty odious; nor shall we find D'Alembert equally pleased with all those who appear in array against the Royal cause. Some of them, too eager, said too much; others were awkward in their attacks, and these he styles *bunglers who are to be found every where*.[29] Others again were not sufficiently bold. He will allow them wit, but he wishes *them to be less favorable to Despotism;* and the reader will easily conceive what he would have written himself if *his hands had not been tied,* when he confidentially writes to Voltaire, *I hate Despots almost as much as you do yourself.*"[30]

It would be futile to object, that the hatred of Despotism does not infer the hatred of Kings. We know that; but who are the Despots implied by our Sophisters, if not the Kings under whom they lived. Were the Emperor of the Turks, or the Grand Mogul, who had nothing to do with our Philosophers, the objects of their repeated complaints and hatred? Such objections are unworthy of being noticed. Their language is known; and sufficient proofs will occur to show, that with the Sect *Despots or Tyrants* and *Sovereigns or Kings* are synonymous terms. The very affectation of confounding them together shows that the hatred of the one and of the other were blended in the hearts of the Chiefs and of their Adepts.

In short, the compliments of D'Alembert are not the sole proofs with which the Adepts have furnished us of the great part Voltaire had taken in that Revolution so fatal to Monarchy, and which he so exultingly foresaw. Had he never aimed his sarcastic wit, so much admired by the sophisters, at the persons of Kings, still he would have been the man, at least in the eyes of his school, who had smoothed the way, who had sealed the rampart, to assail the Throne and shiver the Scepter of the pretended Tyrants; in a word, to contrive what the French Revolution has since accomplished, both with respect to the crown and person of the unfortunate Lewis XVI.

These important services are thus appreciated by Condorcet: "Shall (says he) men who would still have been slaves to prejudice if Voltaire had not written, accuse him of betraying the cause of Liberty!—They cannot understand that if Voltaire had inserted in his writings the principles of the elder Brutus, that is to say, those of the American Act of Independence, neither Montesquieu nor Rousseau could have published their works. Had he, as the Author of the System of Nature did, obliged all the Kings of Europe to support the ascendancy of the Clergy, Europe would still have remained *in the bonds of slavery and buried in superstition.* They will not reflect, that in our writings, as in our actions, we are to make no more than a necesssary display of courage."[31]

Condorcet, in writing this, seems to have considered himself as having displayed a sufficient courage, as he did not think it necessary to say, that the throne would have remained unshaken, if Voltaire had not begun by eradicating religion from the minds of the people. His brethren the hebdomadary adepts, criticized the panegyrist as not having sufficiently extolled the services which Voltaire had rendered. At that period the French Revolution was at its summit, Lewis XVI was reduced to a mere phantom of royalty in his palace, or rather prison, of the Thuilleries. The literary part of the Mercure was conducted by La Harpe, Marmontel, and Champfort; and these reviewers undertake to inform the unfortunate Monarch of the hand which had wrought the downfall of his throne. In giving an account of the life of Voltaire, written by the Marquis de Condorcet, the hebdomadary Philosophers speak in the following terms:

"It appears that it would have been possible to show in a clearer light, *the eternal obligation which human nature has to Voltaire*. Circumstances were favorable. *He did not foresee all that he has done, but he has done all that we now see*.—The enlightened observer and the able historian will prove to those who are capable of reflexion, *that the first Author of the great Revolution, which astonishes all Europe, which infuses hope into the hearts of nations, and disquiet into courts, was, without doubt, Voltaire*. He was the first who levelled that formidable rampart of Despotism, the religious and sacerdotal power. Had he not broken the yoke of Priests, that of Tyrants never could have been shaken off; both equally weighed upon our necks, and were so intimately interwoven, that the first once slackened, the latter must soon have lost its hold. The human mind is no more to be impeded in the career of independence than it is in that of slavery; and it was Voltaire who shook off the yoke, by teaching it to judge, in every respect, those who kept it in subjection. It was he who rendered reason popular; and if the people had not learned to think, never would it have known its own strength. The reflexions of the sage prepare *Political Revolutions*, but it is the arm of the people which executes them."[32]

Had I no other object in view than to demonstrate that these men, styling themselves Philosophers, and glorying in the school and name of Voltaire, chiefly aimed at the overthrow of Monarchy when they attacked religion; that it was to the successful warfare which Voltaire had carried on against the religion of Christ that they peculiarly attribute their success against the Throne; that by the appellation of Tyrant and Despot they point at the best of Kings and most rightful of Sovereigns: had this been my only object, I say, it would have been useless to continue these Memoirs on the Antimonarchical Conspiracy, or that of the Sophisters of Rebellion against every King.

And who are these Sophisters that declare so openly and so expressly the secret of the Sect? First view Condorcet, the most resolute Atheist, the dearest of the brethren, the steady support of Voltaire's hopes, the most intimate confidant of D'Alembert.[33] It is he who sets out by declaring, that, if Voltaire had not combated Religious prejudices, or that if he had attacked Regal authority in a more direct manner, France would have remained enslaved.

Next on the list we find the Journalists La Harpe, Marmontel, and Champfort, who, in the most celebrated journal of the Sect, complain that Condorcet has not shown sufficient courage, and that he is not sufficiently explicit on the pretended *eternal obligations* which mankind have to Voltaire, who by shaking Religion to its foundations has overturned the Throne, who by the ruin of the Pontiff has struck the Tyrant.

And who is the Tyrant, the Despot over whom they so loudly triumph? A King whose very name echoes to that of justice and goodness; a Monarch almost adored by his people, and who loved them to a degree of weakness; for he very often repeated, that he would not suffer one drop of his subjects blood to be spilt in his defence.

Will history believe, that the unfortunate Lewis XVI was the Despot over whom they triumph? And yet if any King upon earth should believe that he is not comprehended in the general subversion aimed at by the conspirators, let him hearken: It is not of France alone that they speak, but of *all mankind*: it is a mankind that they pretend to behold enslaved under Kings; and that *hope* which they had infused into the heart of man, is the same which they joyfully observe expanding itself through all nations! If now tranquil on his throne, let him remember, that he is destitute of the prudence which even the Conspirators suppose him to be endowed with. They believe *disquiet to be infused into every Court*; for they well know, that their principles and their lawless attempts openly menaced monarchy. Yes, that their conspiracy was universal, is already evident; history needs no farther proof: But before they dared proclaim it, that conspiracy had its gradations; its means are to be laid open. The first step is that hatred against the throne, flowing in the hearts of the chiefs, from the hatred they had conceived against their God. The second will be found in the investigation of those systems devised by the adepts to overthrow regal authority, and substitute another in its stead. The teachers of the Sect had applied the vague principles of Equality and Liberty to Religious tenets; and hence originated the hatred of Christ and his Church. From the same principles applied to politics arose those theories and systems of subversion, with which the Sect assails every Throne.

---

1. To the Duc of Richelieu, 20 May, 1771, Vol. 61, Let. 281, P. 490; and 20 July, Let. 293, P. 515.
2. To Marmontel, 13 Aug. 1760, Vol. 56, Let. 183, P. 352.
3. To Helvetius, 27 Oct. 1760, Vol. 56, Let. 220, P. 438.
4. To D'Alembert, 16 Jan. 1757, Vol. 68, Let. 18. P. 31.
5. To Thiriot, 11 Jan. 1765, Vol. 57, Let. 7, P. 14.
6. Les prêtres ne sont pas ce qu'un vain peuple pense;
   Notre credulité fait toute leur science.
7. To Thiriot, 24 Oct. 1738, Vol. 53, Let. 35, P. 88.
8. If we are to believe this definition, *Liberty* consists in *the power of doing what we will*. A true metaphysician would say, *The power itself, the faculty of willing or not willing*, that is to say *of determining one's will, of chusing and willing any thing, or the contrary*. These two definitions are very different. It is not the *power* but the *will* which is culpable. A righteous man has frequently the same power of committing the same crime as the wicked man; but one wills it, while the other does not. The wicked man is at liberty *not* to will it, as the upright man is at liberty to will it; otherwise, there can be no moral difference between the good and the bad man. For how could the latter be culpable, if he had not had it in his power to will the contrary? Suppose three men—the first *can* commit a bad action, but his will *freely rejects* it; the second *can* accomplish the same, and he *freely wills* it. The third not only *can* but he *irresistibly wills* it. The first of these men will be a virtuous man, the second a wicked man, the third a mere brutal machine, a madman who is neither master of his will nor of his reason. The wicked man and the mad one could and did will the same action. The

difference did not lie in the power of the action, but in the will itself more or less free to will or not to will. But Voltaire and his sophistical school had their reasons for not making such distinctions.

9. Les Etats sont égaux, mais les hommes diffèrent.
10. Les hommes sont égaux, et les états diffèrent!
11. Tu vois, cher Ariston, d'un œil d'indifférence
    La grandeur tyrannique, et la fière opulence.
    Tes yeux d'un faux éclat ne sont point abusés;
    Ce monde est un grand bal, où des fous déguisés,
    Sous les risibles noms d'Eminence et d'Altesse,
    Pensent enfler leur être et hausser leur bassesse.
    En vain des vanités l'appareil nous surprend;
    Les mortels sont égaux, le masque est différent.
    Nos cinq sens imparfaits, donnés par la nature,
    De nos biens, de nos maux sont la seule mesure.
    *Les Rois, en ont-ils six? et leur âme et leur corps
    Sont-ils d'une autre espèce? ont-ils d'autres ressorts?*
12. Les Etats sont égaux, mais les hommes diffèrent. *(1st and 2d Edit.)*
13. Les mortels sont égaux, le masque est différent. *(See the variations, edit. of Kell.)*
14. To D'Argenson, 8 Aug. 1743, Vol. 53, Let. 221, P. 455.
15. To D'Alembert, 12 Dec. 1757, Vol. 68, Let. 36, P. 60.
16. Les prêtres ne sont pas ce qu'un vain peuple pense;
    Notre crédulité fait toute leur science.
17. Le premier qui fut Roi, fut un soldat heureux,
    Que sert bien son Pays, n'a pas besoin d'ayeux.
18. Dialogues of the Philosophers on Happiness.
19. "Il faut changer de loix, il faut avoir un maître."
20. "Je vous offre mon bras, mes trésors & mon sang;
    Mais si vous abusez de ce suprême rang,
    Pour fouler à vos pieds les loix & la patrie,
    Je la defends, Seigneur, au péril de ma vie."
        To D'Alembert, 13 *Nov.* 1772, *Vol.* 69, *Let.* 81, *P.* 131.
21. To D'Argental, 27 Juin, 1777, Vol. 63, Let. 220, P. 377.
22. Letter to Damilaville, 23 May, 1764, Let. 196, P. 361, et passim.
23. To Chauvelin, 2 April, 1764, Vol. 58, Let. 171, P. 315.
24. Letter to D'Alembert, 3 July, 1773, Vol. 69, Let. 114, P. 195, et passim.
25. From D'Alembert, 19 Jan. 1769, Vol. 69, Let. 3, P. 7.
26. See Voltaire's and D'Alembert's Correspondence *passim.*
27. From D'Alembert, 19 Jan. 1769.
28. From D'Alembert, 14 July, 1767, Vol. 68, Let. 213, P. 446.
29. From D'Alembert, 24 Jan. 1778, Vol. 69, Let. 190, P. 313.
30. From D'Alembert, 25 Jan. 1770, Vol. 69, Let. 17, P. 34.
31. Life of Voltaire, edit. Kell.
32. Mercure de France, Saturday, 7th August, 1790, No. 18, p. xxvi.
33. See the first part of these Memoirs.

CHAP. II.

Second Step of the Conspiracy against Kings.

Political Systems of the Sect.

D'Argenson and Montesquieu.

AMONG the adepts who must have foreseen the consequences which naturally ensued from the application of a pretended equality of rights, and of an irreligious liberty, to politics, none could have done so more intuitively than the Marquis D'Argenson. This man, minister of the foreign department, had lived during the greater part of his life near the person of his Sovereign, and enjoyed that favour, to which he was thought to be entitled by having consecrated his life to the Royal service. Yet he was the man who, during the reign of Lewis XV, drew the outlines of those Sophisticated Systems, which were to oppose Regal authority, and gradually metamorphose the French Monarchy into a Republic.

We have seen Voltaire, as early as the year 1743, extolling the affection which this Marquis bore to Equality, to Liberty, and to the Municipal Government. These praises of the Premier Chief evidently show, that Mr. D'Argenson had already conceived his Municipalizing System, and all those wild plans, which the future rebels, under the title of a Constituent Assembly, were to adopt as one of the leading features of their Royal Democracy, at once the most senseless and most seditious as well as the most heterogeneous form of government that could be conceived, and more especially for Frenchmen: They also prove, that he made no secret of his plans to his confidents and co-operators.

His system consists in the division and subdivision of the Provinces into small States, first called *Provincial Administrations* by Necker, and afterwards termed *Departments* by Target and Mirabeau.

According to D'Argenson's plan, resumed and corrected by Turgot and Necker, each of those petty states was, under the inspection of the King, to be charged with the interior administration of its districts, and the levying of taxes; to superintend the different plans adopted for the relif of the people; to inspect the hospitals, the high roads, the establishments useful to commerce, and other such objects. The administrators could not determine on any subject of importance without the orders of his Majesty, and this was judged a sufficient fence to the Royal prerogative, especially as at the first formation of these provincial administrations, one half of the members were to be nominated by the King, which half when assembled chose the remaining moiety. The distinction of the three orders, of the Clergy, the Nobility, and the third Estate, was preserved, as it used to be in the States General.[1]

The towns and boroughs, and even the villages were to have their respective municipalities, all acting on the same plan, and under the direction of the Provincial Administrations, in their secondary districts.

Though at first sight this system appears extremely advantageous, yet, on examination, we shall find, that its sole tendency was to apply Republican forms, as much as circumstances would permit, to a Monarchical government; that its object was to cramp the authority of the Monarch, to clog and weaken it; and to annihiate the power of his officers, or direct agents, the intendants of provinces.

Soon was France by means of these assemblies and their committees, or permanent offices, to be filled with ambitious men starting forth in the new political career; men indeed who, in the first instance, would have recognized the authority of a King, but who would soon have considered themselves better informed of the wants of the people (being nearer to them) than his ministers, and therefore more fully acquainted with the means of alleviating their distresses. Remonstraces and philosophic reasonings would soon have followed, and sufficed to justify disobedience. The people, under a fond persuasion, that these provincial administrators supported their interests against the court, would easily have been brought to believe them the bulwark of their liberties and privileges, assigning every happy event to them, and attributing every misfortune to the King and his ministers. Each municipality coalescing with the administrators, a hundred petty Republics start into existence, ready to league against their Sovereign, who, under the title of King, would scarcely have retained the authority of a Doge.

In time we should have seen a swarm of polticasters, or petty tribunes, sallying forth from these administrative bodies, who would have left no means untried to persuade the populace that such a King was rather a burden than an advantage to the state; that it would be proper to lay him aside, since he was unnecessary; that the provincial and municipal administrations would then be able to follow up in a more effectual manner, the salutary measures they had conceived for the good of the people: and thus, step by step, the Monarchical government would have been overthrown, and a municipal administration established, with the freedom of which Voltaire and D'Argenson had been so fascinated in Holland. The man who could not readily foresee that such would be the consequence of this municipalizing system, must have been very ignorant of the character of Frenchmen, and especially of French Philosophers when drawn into the vortex of modern politics.

Even the admission of the clergy into these provisional administrations must have proved a fatal boon to the church, as it necessarily tended to change the spirit of its ministers. Priests and bishops were admitted, or rather called upon, to form a part of their administrations, so foreign to their sacred functions, for the conspiracy had not yet attained sufficient force to cast them off. The zeal for salvation was to be superseded by the wild ambition of moving in a sphere so contrary to their calling. Already were several prelates distinguished by this new title of Administrators. Soon should we have seen them become rather the disciples of D'Argenson, Turgot and Necker, than of Christ; soon seen the bishoprics conferred upon none but Morellets and Beaudeaux, with whom religion would have been a very subordinate object, when compared to the glorious enterprize of system-making, or of resisting the Ministers and the Sovereign. This was a sure method of ruining the church, by robbing her of the real bishops, and substituting petty politicians, who would easily be carried away by the torrent of impiety and ambition, and join with heart and hand a Brienne or an Expilli.

Whatever might have been the consequence to the church, it is very evident that all these new forms of administration tended directly to republicanize the state. Each of these petty administrators would soon have swelled himself into the representative of the province, and the aggregate would have styled themselves the Representatives of the Nation. The bare appellation of National Representative, combined with Modern Philosophism, sufficed to crush the Monarchy.

D'Argenson did not live to witness the experiment of his system; some may suppose that he had not foreseen its consequences. But it plainly appears, that if he even had foreseen them, so great an admirer of municipalized Republics would not have been much alarmed. At a time when the Sophisters had not sufficiently erased the love of religion from the hearts of the French to efface their affection for their Monarch, this system appeared to make but little impression; but we shall see the Sophisters afterward making it the particular object of their dissertations, to accustom the people to the idea of governing themselves.[2]

To the great misfortune of France, a man far more capable than D'Argenson of giving to any system the appearance of deep thought and erudition engaged in these political speculations.— The love of the commonweal may appear to have directed him toward this study; but the real cause is to be found in the restlessness of Philosophism, and in that liberty of thinking which is disgusted with every thing around it, and which would continue restless even after having attained the object of which it was in search. This man, who by so many claims commands the public veneration, was Charles Secondat, Baron de la Brede and De Montesquieu. He was born on the 18th of January, 1689, in the Château de la Brede, within three leagues of Bourdeaux; and in 1716, became president *à mortier* of that parliament. We have already mentioned, that his first productions were those of a young man who had no fixed principles of religion; and this is clearly perceptible in perusing the *Lettres Persannes*. At a riper age his duty called him to the study of the laws; but not content with the knowledge of those of his own country, and desirous of making himself conversant in those of foreign nations, he made the tour of Europe, stayed sometime in England, and then returned to France full of those ideas which he has developed in the two works that have chiefly contributed to his fame. The first is entitled, *Considerations on the Causes of the Grandeur and Decline of the Roman Empire*, and was published in 1733; the latter was *The Spirit of Laws*, which appeared in 1748.

It was obvious, on the first appearance of his work on the Romans, that Montesquieu had not acquired from his travels an additional esteem for the government of his own country. One of the prime causes to which he attributes the eclat of the Romans, is their love of a Liberty which begins by dethroning all Kings. The Sophisters, who were still less favorable to Monarchy, did not fail to adopt this idea, to make it the leading principle, and to inculcate it in all their discourses.[3]

Both Montesquieu and his panegyrists would have been more correct, had they traced back to this love of liberty all those scourges and intestine broils which harrassed Rome, from the expulsion of its Kings until the reign of the Emperors.—Liberty perpetually convulsed the people, and the senate could only free themselves from their clamours by habitual war and foreign pillage. This perpetual state of hostility rendered the Roman the most warlike of all nations, and gave them that immense advantage which they enjoyed over all other people. To the man who has read the Roman history, nothing can be more evident.—But if such be the merits of that liberty which expelled the Kings of Rome, that antisocial spirit, which, sowing discord in the interior economy of families, drives them from their homes, inures them to fatigue and the inclemency of the weather, and gives them all the advantage and strength of robbers, by forcing them to live on plunder, after having denied them the sweets of social life,—the antisocial spirit, I say, must needs possess the very same advantages.

Montesquieu was so strangely misled by his admiration for liberty, that he did not perceive the strangely paradoxical positions that he advanced. After having spoken of the public edifices, *which even to this day give us a great idea of the power and grandeur of Rome under its Kings*, after having said, "that one of the causes of its prosperity was, that its Kings were all great men; and that no country could ever shew *such a continued series of statesmen and great generals*;" he adds, nearly in the same page, "that on the expulsion of the Kings it must necessarily follow, either that Rome would change its government, or remain a poor and petty monarchy."[4] In a word, that if Rome arrived at that very high pitch of greatness, it was owing to his having *substituted annual Consuls* to the dethroned Kings.

This work teems with satyrical remarks on Rome, when again brought under the dominion of a Monarch; and his frequent expressions of regret for the loss of the Republican Liberty, could not but tend to diminish that love, that admiration, that enthusiasm so natural to Frenchmen for their king. One might really suspect that he wished to instil into the minds of the people a belief, that what sovereigns call establishing order, is another term for riveting fetters on their subjects.[5]

But the work that we have been considering was merely a prelude to the doctrines which he was about to teach (*in his Spirit of Laws*) to all nations governed by a monarch. Let us premise, and with great sincerity we say it, that had we to perform the task of a panegyrist, causes for admiration would abound; had we to answer those critics who reproach Montesquieu with having taken the motto, *prolem sine matre creatam*, and giving his work as if it were an original, though he may appear to have followed the footsteps of Bodin, celebrated for his work on Republics, we nevertheless think we may triumphantly answer, that the dross he may have borrowed from others cannot alloy the sterling value of his own production; and that in spite of the errors contained in the Spirit of Laws, it will for ever continue to be considered as the work of a wonderful genius.[6]

But it is not for us to assume the character, either of the critic or of the panegyrist. Our object is to investigate how far Montesquieu broached or influenced revolutionary ideas. It is the misfortune of a great genius, that his very errors are too often converted into oracles. Truth must often submit to error, when that error is supported by a celebrated name! That victory which he would have disclaimed, resulted merely from the celebrity of his name, and the weight of his authority. The distinction which he makes between the principles of monarchy and those of republicanism may convince the reader. In an ordinary writer, the whole of that part of the Spirit of Laws would have been looked upon as the sport of imagination playing upon words. But from Montesquieu they are received as the result of profound thought, sanctioned by the great name of history. Let us examine whether the notions branding monarchy with disgrace can originate from any thing but the abuse of terms.

Honour, in the general acceptance of his countrymen, was the fear of being despised, and a horror particularly of being looked upon as a coward. It was the sentiment of Glory and of Courage. When a more moral sentiment attached itself to *honour*, it was converted into the shame of having done, or of hearing oneself reproached as having done, some act unworthy of an honest man; for instance, as having broken one's word. Montesquieu, observing the despotic influence which this word exercised over his countrymen, adopted *honour* as the first principle, the main spring, the prime mover of monarchies, and flatters republics with having virtue for their first principle.[7] The chivalry of the French, pleased with the idea, applauds Montesquieu, but does not perceive that in adopting the word he falsifies the sentiment and metamorphoses it into a *false honour, a prejudice, a thirst of fame, an ambition for distinctions or for favor;* in a word, into all the vices of the courtier.[8] This was bewildering *honour;* it was telling those bold knights, so zealous for their king, that they were no more than effeminate courtiers, ambitious men, and slaves to a prejudice the source of all the vices of courts: an assertion the more evidently false, as many a Frenchman replete with true honour was entirely free from any of those vices. Such a distinction was not only odious and disgraceful, it was also delusive, and the delusion seems to have prevented Montesquieu from perceiving that hereafter Philosphism would adopt the principle, but would only repeat the word *honour* as the opposite to *virtue, the principle of Republics*, and brand the royalists with all the false prejudices, the ambition, and other vices, which he had artfully ascribed to *honour*.

This first error therefore was the offspring of delusion. Though, in one sense, as much may be said of the pretended principle of democracies. In another point of view, however, this principle may be introduced with more correctness; and this latter sense appears to be that to which Montesquieu at first alluded. It is undeniable, that virtue ought to be more particularly the principle of democracies than of any other form of government, they being the most turbulent and the most vicious of all; in which virtue is absolutely necessary to control the passions of men, to quell that spirit of cabal, anarchy, and faction inherent to the democratic form, and to chain down that ambition and rage of dominion over the people, which the weakness of the laws can scarcely withstand.

But it would have been satyric in the extreme to have adopted this latter sense; and Montesquieu's great admiration for the ancient democracies would never permit him to give such an explanation of the principle. He therefore generalizes or particularizes his definitions as suits his purpose. At one time *this virtue*, the prime mover of Republics, is *the love of one's country—that is to say, of Equality—is a political, and not a moral virtue*.[9] At another, this political virtue is *a moral one*, as it is directed to the public good.[10] In one place it is not *the virtue of individuals*,[11] though in another it is every thing that can be understood *by good morals*, or by the virtue of a people *who are preserved from corruption by the goodness of their maxims*.[12] Again, it is the most common virtue in that state where "theft is blended with the spirit of justice; the hardest servitude with excess of Liberty, the most atrocious sentiments with the greatest moderation;" in short, it is the virtue of that state where "natural sentiments are preserved without the tie of son, husband, or father, and where even chastity is denuded of modesty and shame."[13]

Whatever idea the reader may have formed of virtue through the mist which appears to have enveloped the genius of Montesquieu in enigmatic darkness, let us ask, which principle will he adopt, or which will he conceive to be the most clearly expressed? If asked, whether virtue was not also to be found in Monarchies, he will answer, "I know that virtuous Princes are no uncommon sight; but I venture to affirm, *that in a Monarchy* it is extremely difficult for the people to be virtuous;"[14] and this sentiment, so odious and so injurious to all Royalists, will in the end be the most clearly deduced of all the new opinions he has broached upon Monarchical Government. Whether such were his intentions or not, a day will come, when the Sophisters, repeating his assertions, will say to the people, "You only love your King because you have not a sufficient sense of Philosophy to raise yourselves above *the prejudices of ambition and of false honour*; because you are destitute of those *moral virtues which direct to the public good*; because you are not inflamed with *the love of your Country*; because you admire that form of Government, where it is *extremely difficult for the people to be virtuous*. You would admire *Democracy* were your *morals good*, and were you fired with the *amor patris*—but, destitute of virtue and unacquainted with Philosphy, you are only capable of loving your Kings."

Such, as every reflecting reader must perceive, is the real explanation of these principles. The Revolution has only brought them into practice. We have heard a Robespierre and a Sieyes, proclaiming to the people, that in crushing the Scepter, murdering their King, and constituting France a Republic, they had *only put virtue on the order of the day*. In the midst of massacres and bloodshed, they profaned the sacred name of virtue; and with virtue in their mouths they plunged the people into the most horrid scenes of vice and debauchery. But have we not seen Montesquieu teaching them how to blend virtue with the *most atrocious sentiments*, and how it may reign amidst the *hardest servitude, or the excess of Liberty*? To attribute such intentions to this celebrated writer would most certainly be doing an injustice to his memory; but still it is our duty to speak unreservedly on what he has written, and to shew what sentiments nations may have imbibed from his writings. It is awful (whatever may have been his intentions) to reflect on the terrible ravages which his opinions, suported by the authority of his name, have operated in the minds of men. Error is in its infancy with Montesquieu; but it is the same error that was afterwards, in the state of manhood, adopted by Robespierre. Montesquieu would have shrunk back with horror had he heard that Democratic villain place virtue *for the order of the day* with his sanguinary Republic; but what could the astonished master have replied, on being told, *that it was extremely difficult for the people to be virtuous under a Monarch*, or under Lewis XVI?

Let genius shrink back with horror at seeing its errors traverse the immense interval between Montesquieu and Robespierre; let it tremble at its despotic influence over the public opinion. Without designing any convulsion, by its very name it may raise the most dreadful storm. At first, its errors may be tender shoots; but, daily gaining bulk and strength, will they not in the form of massive limbs be wielded by a Condorcet, a Petion, or a Sieyes?

During a long period Montesquieu's opinions on the principles of Monarchies and Republics were entirely overlooked, and they might have remained in oblivion at any other time, when Philosophism was less active in its research after every means of rendering the Throne odious.—Almost as much may be said of that *Equality* which, he believed, "in Democracy limited ambition to the sole desire of doing greater services to our country, than the rest of our fellow-citizens:"[15] a virtue far too sublime for Monarchies, "where nobody aims at Equality; it does not so much as enter their thoughts; they all aspire to superiority. People of the very lowest condition desire to emerge from their obscurity only to lord it over their fellow-subjects."[16] Genius may have been so led away, as not to perceive how powerful a weapon it was forging for the Jacobin, who, extolling the merits of this Equality, and persuading the people that it was impracticable under the dominion of the Monarch, would also paint in glowing colours *that ambition of serving the country*, arising from the ashes of the Throne and the destruction of the Nobility. But there appeared another system in the *Spirit of Laws*, deeper laid, and replete with weapons more directly pointed at the Throne. They were the first on which Philosophism seized, while others adopted them through ignorance, from want of reflection, or from imprudence. They were too fatal in the hands of the first rebels not to claim a place in these Memoirs.

To form a correct idea of the Revolutionary tendency of Montesquieu's system, we must revert to the time at which it was published. Whatever may have been the Legislative forms in the primitive days of the French Monarchy, it is certain that at the time of his publication (and he avows it) not only the King of France, but most of the crowned heads united in their persons the rights of executing the Laws, of enacting those which they conceived necessary or conducive to the welfare of the State, and of judging those who had infringed the law.[17]

The reunion of this Triple Power constitutes an *absolute Monarch*, that is to say, a real Sovereign who in his person concentrates the whole power of the law. At that period the French were far from confounding this absolute power with the arbitratry power of the Tyrant or the Despot. This power was to be found in Republics and in mixt States. Here it existed in the Senate, or in the assembly of Deputies; there in the compound of the Senate and the King. The French nation beheld it in their Monarch, whose supreme will, legally proclaimed, was the utmost degree of political authority.

This supreme will, construed into law by the requisite forms, was equally binding on the King and on his subjects. It is not only Henry IV and his Minister Sully, who declare *that the first law of the Sovereign is to observe them all*; but it is Lewis XIV, that Prince whom the Sophisters affectedly style the Despot, who at the height of his glory openly proclaims this obligation in his edicts: "Do not let it be said," are his words, "that the Sovereign shall not be subject to the laws of the state. The rights of nations proclaim the contrary truth, which has sometimes been attacked by flattery, but which all good Princes have defended as the guardian of their states. How much more acurate it is to say, that to constitute the perfect happiness of a kingdom, it is necessary in order that the Prince should be obeyed by his subjects, *that the Prince should obey the Laws*, and that those laws should be just and directed to the public good!"[18]

This obligation alone in the Sovereign immediately destroys all despotic or arbitrary power.—For, in the idiom of modern languages, the Despot is the man who rules only by his passions and caprice; under whom no subject can be at ease, as he is ignorant whether his master will not punish him to-day for having executed the orders he had received from him yesterday.

In short, it may be justly said, that Political Liberty consists in two points: 1st, That every Citizen should be free to do all that is not forbidden by the law: 2dly, That the law should prescribe or forbid any particular action for the public good only. Experience will vouch for the correctness of this definition. And where could the honest and upright man, obedient to the laws of his country, enjoy greater security and freedom than he did in France?

It may indeed be objected, that there existed many abuses, but did not they originate from the genius of the French, or from an excess rather than a want of liberty? Were the conspirators to exclaim against the immoral and impious Minister for having abused the power with which he was entrusted, when these Sophisters had during many years conspired against the morals and piety of the whole nation? No; they had no right to complain that the law was often sacrificed to private passions; the exact observance of the law should have been their prayer, but they only sought after ruin and revolution.

One real abuse had crept into the French Government, which savoured much of Despotism.—This was the use of *Lettres de Cachet*. Undoubtedly they were illegal. On a bare order from the King the subject lost his liberty. I will not defend such an abuse by saying, that none but the higher classes or seditious writers were exposed to the effect of this arbitrary power. But, perhaps, few are acquainted with the origin of those Letters. It was to the moral character of the French, and to the notions particularly of the higher classes, that this abuse owed its origin; and it was necessary either to do away those notions, or to leave so formidable a power in the hands of the Monarch.

Such was the received opinion in France, that a family would have thought itself dishonored, if any child, brother, or near relation were brought to justice. Hence it was that families, fearing the arm of the law, applied to the King to obtain an order to imprison any profligate youth whose irregular conduct might disgrace the family. If any hopes of reformation could be conceived, the *Lettre de Cachet* was only temporary, and served as a correction; but where the offence was criminal and infamous, the culprit was imprisoned for life.

The reader must not be misled to suppose, that these Letters were granted on a mere request and without any inquiry into the case. After Mr. de Malesherbe's administration, the petitions sent to the King were transmitted to the Intendant of the Province, who immediately ordered his sub-delegate to call a meeting of the relations and witnesses, and to take minutes of their proceedings. On these informations, which were forwarded to the Ministers, his Majesty granted or refused the *Lettres de Cachet*.[19]

Under such restrictions it was evidently rather the authority of a common parent, which the King exercised over his subjects, than that of a despot enslaving them. With the notions which the French nation had adopted, it was the necessary means of preserving the honour of different families; and few were victims to this authority but those who were dangerous either to private or public society. From the use to the abuse of a thing, however, the distance is but small: a profligate minister might exercise this power against the citizen or the magistrate who had fulfilled his duty with the greatest integrity. Nor was it unexampled, that a minister, solicited by powerful men, rather consulted their private animosities, than public justice, or general utility. But a profligate minister abusing his authority does not make his King a despot. The morals of the higher classes being perverted, as we have seen, by Philosophism, the abuse of this prerogative might loudly call for reform; but are the Sophisters thence justifiable in seeking to overthrow the Monarchy?

In short, whatever may have been the cause of these abuses at the period when *The Spirit of Laws* appeared, it had never entered the minds of Frenchmen, that they lived under a despotic government. Let us hear Jean Jaques Rousseau lay down the law, he who created systems to overthrow it; and let the candid reader judge how far the Sophisters are authorized to represent the French government as arbitrary, oppressive, and tyrannical. "What (says Jean Jaques) is the true end of a political association? Is it not the preservation and prosperity of its members? And what is the most certain sign that they are preserved, and that they prosper? Is it not the increasing population? We need seek no further for the sign in dispute; but pronounce that government to be infallibly the best (provided there is no particular circumstance to make it stand an exception to a general rule) under which, without the application of any improper means, without the naturalization of strangers, without receiving any new colonists, the citizens increase and multiply: and that to be the worst under which they lessen and decay. Calculators, it is now your affair; count, measure, and compare them."[20]—The same author adds, "It is a long continuance in the same situation that makes prosperity or calamity real. When a whole nation lies crushed under the foot of despotism, it is then that the people perish; and it is then that their masters can hurl destruction among them with impunity, *ubi solitudinem faciunt, pacem appellant* (and call peace, the silence of the desert they have created). When the factions of the chief men of France had arisen to such a height as to agitate the kingdom, and the coadjutor of Paris judged it necessary to carry a dagger in his pocket every time he went into the parliament, the French people lived free and at ease, and they were happy and their numbers increased. The prosperity of a nation and its population depends much more *on liberty* than on peace."[21]

Thus, without taking on himself the task of calculator, Jean Jaques confesses that the French people, even in the midst of civil broils, *lived free and at ease*. But let us attend to one of his most faithful disciples, who undertook to calculate, and that at a time when the Revolution had done away every idea of exaggerating the happiness of the French people under the government of their Kings. The revolutionist Gudin, in his annotations on the above text, and in his Supplement to the Social Contract, has examined and calculated, year by year, the state of the population, the deaths, births, and marriages of all the principal towns in the kingdom during the course of this century, and then proceeds: "The author of the Social Contract spoke a grand truth when he exclaimed: Calculators, it is now your affair; *count, measure,* and *compare*. His advice has been followed; we have calculated, measured, and compared, and the result of all these calculations has demonstrated that the population of France is really twenty-four millions, though it had always been supposed to be under twenty; that the annual births amount to one million; and *that the population is daily increasing.*"

"Hence we may conclude, after Rousseau, that the government was very good. It really was better than it ever had been at any period since the destruction of that which the Romans had established in Gaul." Such are the words of the same author, and according to his calculations it was *in the reign of Lewis XIV,* whom the Sophisters represent as the haughtiest of despots, *that the population of France began to increase regularly and univerally throughout the whole kingdom,* notwithstanding all his wars.

"The long reign of Lewis XV (another alledged despot, under whose reign the Antimonarchical Conspiracy was begun and indefatigably conducted) was not exposed to such calamities; and it is certain," continues the revolutionist Gudin, "that during the whole monarchy there has existed no period when population increased in a more constant and uniform progression throughout the whole kingdom, than during that reign. It increased to that amazing height, that from twenty-four to twenty-five millions of souls were spread over a surface of twenty-five thousand square leagues, which makes about a million souls to a thousand square leagues, or a thousand inhabitants to every square league, *a population so unparalleled in Europe, that it might be almost looked upon as a prodigy.*"

Let us hear the same author on the state of France at the time when the Revolution broke out, which he is perpetually extolling; and let us remark, that the work whence we have extracted our documents was so acceptable to the Revolutionary Assembly, that by a particular decree of the 13th of November 1790, *it accepted the homage of it*: a stronger contrast cannot be sketched between that Revolution and its authors, whether distant or immediate, and the necessity of those plans by which they pretended to work the happiness of the Empire. The same author continues:

"The French territory is so well cultivated, that its annual produce is estimated at four thousand millions.

"Its currency amounted to two thousand two hundred millions, and the gold and silver employed in plate and jewels may be estimated at a similar amount.

"The Records of the Assinage Office in Paris attest, that the annual consumption or rather waste of refined gold, in gilding furniture, carriages, pasteboard, china, nails, fans, buttons, books, in spotting stuffs, or in plating silver, amounted to the enormous sum of eight hundred thousand livres.

"The profit on trade was annually computed at between forty and fifty millions.

"The taxes paid by the people did not exceed six hundred and ten or twelve millions, which does not amount to one third of the circulating medium nor to one sixth part of the gross territorial produce, and which probably cannot be computed at more than one third of the neat produce, a sum which in that proportion could not have been exorbitant if every one had paid according to his means.[22]

"In this kingdom were annually born upwards of 928,000 children; in short, nearly a million. The town of Paris contained 666,000 inhabitants. Its riches were so great, that it paid annually one hundred millions into the King's coffers, about one sixth of the whole taxation of France.

"But even this immense taxation did not overburthen Paris. Its inhabitants lived in affluence. If its daily consumption amounted to one million, at least from eighty to one hundred millions were necessary for its interior circulation.

"In short, calculators have estimated, that during the reign of Lewis XV *the population of the country was increased by one ninth*, that is to say, by two millions five or six hundred thousand souls.

"Such was the state of France and of Paris at the time the Revolution took place; and as no other state in Europe could exhibit such a population, nor boast of such revenues, it was not without reason that it *passed for the first kingdom on the Continent*."

The revolutionist Gudin, to whom we are indebted for all these particulars, concludes by saying, "I thought it necesssary to state in a precise and exact manner the population and riches of the kingdom at the period when *so grand a revolution took place*. I apprehended that this investigation would shew the future progress of the nation, and serve as a table by which we might calcuate the advantages that will accrue from the constitution when brought to perfection." Without doubt our author has by this time formed his opinion on the advantages of that constitution; but we can plainly see by his enthusiastic admiration of the revolution, and of the Philosophers to whom he attributes the honor of having effected it;[23] that he was very far from wishing to exaggerate the liberty and happiness of France under the Monarchy. By the foregoing long extract we have no other object in view, than that of furnishing the historian with the proper materials (all extracted from the greatest admirers or chief authors of the French Revolution) to enable him to judge of those systems in which the Revolution originated, and to appreciate properly the wisdom or the imprudence of its authors.—But to return to Montesquieu.

Precisely at that period when *L'Esprit des Loix* was published, the French were so happy and so pleased with their King, that the surname of *well-beloved (bien aimé)* had resounded from one extremity of the nation to the other. And, unfortunately for Montesquieu, it is from this publication that we are to trace all those Philosophical reveries on Equality and Liberty, which at first only produced disquiet and doubt, but which soon after created other systems, that misled the French people in their ideas on government, that weakened the tie of affection between the subject and the monarch, and generated at length the monster of Revolutions.

There is an essential difference to be perceived between Voltaire and Montesquieu. Voltaire, as we have shown, would willingly have endured a Monarch that should have connived at his impiety. He would have thought himself sufficiently free, had he been allowed publicly to blaspheme; and, generally speaking, he was more partial to the forms of Monarchy, or of Aristocracy, than to those of Democracy. It was his hatred to religion (and he hated religion more than he loved Kings) which plunged him into the municipalizing system.

With Montesquieu it was far otherwise. Though he was not indifferent on the subject of religious liberty, it was nevertheless Monarchy itself that he meant to investigate. He proposed to regulate all kingly power and authority according to his ideas of political liberty. Had religious liberty been carried to excess, still he would have looked upon himself as immersed in slavery in every state where the public authority was not subdivided, according to his system, into three distinct powers, *the Legislative, the Executive, and the Judiciary*. This distinction was new to the French nation, which had been accustomed to view its Monarch as the central point of all political authority. The peaceful ages they had passed under their Legislative Kings little inclined them to envy the boisterous liberty of a neighbouring country, perhaps more celebrated for its civil broils in quest of liberty, than for the wisdom of its constitution, which, at length fixing every mind and every heart, had scarcely terminated a long struggle between the Monarch and the People.

Without doubt we may admire, as much as Montesquieu, the wisdom of that nation which has known how to model its laws according to the experience it had acquired during those struggles. Laws indeed, congenial to the manners which characterize it, to its local situation, and even to its prejudices. But is that constitution, the most perfect perhaps existing for a nation surrounded by the ocean, to be equally perfect when transplanted into a continental state? Has not nature, by diversifying the soil, varied its culture? Are men so heterogeneous in their characters, men that may be viewed under so many different points, are they, in order to attain happiness and freedom, to be reduced to one only mode of government? No; it would have been madness to adopt the English constitution in France. The genius of the French nation must have been totally changed before a Frenchman would believe himself free where the Englishman does not even perceive the yoke of the law; before the former would refrain from abusing that liberty which the latter will scarcely taste of; and particularly before the Frenchman could be kept within those limits where the Englishman rests content.

We are willing to believe, that Montesquieu had never made these reflections, when, carried away by his admiration for foreign laws, he was inventing new principles, and presenting as constant and general such truths, as would make his countrymen view their Sovereign in the light of a real Despot, and the mild government they lived under, though so conformable to their interests and their genius, as that of a most horrid and shameful slavery.

It is painful to apply such a reproach to this celebrated writer; but can history refrain from observing the fatal impression which such doctrines must have made on a people so long accustomed to say, *si veut le Roi, si veut la loi* (as the King wills, so wills the law); the doctrines, I say, of him who dared assert as a demonstrated truth, that "when the legislative and executive powers are united in the same person or in the same body of magistrates, there can be no liberty; because apprehensions may arise lest the same Monarch or Senate should enact tyrannical laws, to execute them in a tyrannical manner."[24] But in laying down this principle, he had taken care to say immediately before, "the political liberty of the subject is a tranquillity of mind, arising from the opinion which each one has of his safety. In order to have this liberty, it is requisite that the Government be so constituted, as that one man need not be afraid of another."[25]

Either Montesquieu must have believed the French reader incapable of uniting those two ideas, or else he meant to say, "Frenchmen! You believe that under the government of your King you are in safety, and enjoy liberty. Your opinion is erroneous, it is shameful. Amidst that calm which you seem to enjoy *there is no liberty*; and none can exist so long as you repeat *si veut le Roi, si veut la loi*; in short so long as the Legislative and Executive Powers are united in the person of your King. He must be deprived either of the one or the other; or else you must submit to live in the perpetual terror of *tyrannical laws, tyrannically executed*."

This language is not held out to the French alone, but to every people governed by Kings, even to most Republics, where, as he himself remarks, these powers were often united. The whole universe was then in a state of slavery, and Montesquieu was the apostle sent to teach them to break their chains, chains so light that few were even sensible of their existence! A general Revolution was then necessary, that mankind might assert its liberty! I could wish to exculpate Montesquieu; but if on the one side I am afraid of attributing intentions to him which he never had, on the other I dare not revile genius by separating it from reason; by saying that he had laid down new principes without even perceiving their most immediate consequences. It is a hard task to represent Montesquieu brandishing the torch of discord between nations and their Kings, between the subjects even of Republics and their Senates, or their Magistrates; but would it not be something more or less than kindness, to behold the torch, and the man who wields it, without daring to intimate the intention of kindling a blaze? How chimerical must have been that terror of tyrannical laws tyrannically executed in a country where the legislator himself is bound by pre-existing laws, whose sole object is the preservation of property, liberty, and the safety of the subject!—What a phantom such a supposition must be in a country where the King was omnipotent in the love of his subjects, and null in tyranny; in a country where, if the representations of the Magistrates were insufficient, the Monarch could never resist those of the people, whose very silence was sufficient to disarm him, and he would abrogate any number of laws to make them return to their noisy acclamations. Montesquieu, who attributes so much influence to climates, might very well have taken into consideration the manners, the character, and the received opinions, acting so much more powerfully among his countrymen than in any other nation. But the fact was, that the French laws enacted by their Legislative Monarchs were not to be surpassed either in wisdom or mildness by the laws of any country; under those Legislative Kings they had seen their liberties, so far from being contracted, ascertained and extended, and facts are better authorities than systems.[26]

The same error, the same delusion shows itself when Montesquieu believes every thing to be ruined, if the Prince who has enacted a law has the power of judging the man who transgresses it. Such a fear might be reasonable in a country where the Legislative Monarch could be both judge and plaintiff, thus sitting in judgment on his own cause, and over those of his subjects of whom he might have reason to complain; or where the Legislative King beomes sole Magistrate and sole Judge, or violates the accustomed forms requiring a certain number of Magistrates and votes to condemn or absolve a subject. This was a chimerical terror in every true Monarchy, where, as in France, the first law is to observe those of nature, which will always preclude either Sovereign or Magistrate from sitting in judgment on their own causes, and on their private differences with the subject. A terror still more futile wherever, as in France, the King might be cast in his own tribunals, and where equally with any subject he was bound by the law. Hence nothing could ever have made the French unite the idea of Despotism to that of a Monarch the judge of his subjects. With what romantic ideas and tender affection they were wont to paint those happy days when Lewis IX, surrounded by his subjects as if they had been his children, would, under a shady oak, hear and determine their differences, with all the authority and justice of the first magistrate of his kingdom![27] How new must it then have been for the people to hear Montesquieu assert, that "there is no liberty, if the power of judging be not separated from the Legislative and Executive Powers! Were it joined with the Legislative, the life and liberty of the subject would be exposed to *arbitrary control*, for the Judge would then be the Legislator. Were it joined to the Executive Power, the Judge might behave with all the violence of an oppressor. There would be an end of every thing, were the same man, or the same body, whether of the Nobles or of the people, to exercise those three powers, that of enacting laws, that of executing the public resolutions, and that of judging the crimes, or determining the disputes of individuals."[28]

Montesquieu appears to have felt the danger of such lessons, when he really seeks to console nations by telling them, that "most kingdoms in Europe enjoy a moderate government, because the Prince who is invested with the first two powers leaves the third to his subjects." But such a distinction can little avail; of what consequence can it be, that the Prince should leave this third power to his subjects, when about twenty lines higher Montesquieu has laid down as a constant principle, that when the two first powers are united in the same person *there can be no Liberty*? And why does he immediately add, "In Turkey, where these three powers are united in the Sultan's person, the subjects groan under the weight of the most frightful oppression?[29]" Is it not very well known, that the Sultan generally leaves the judiciary power to the tribunals? Could the illustrious author have meant to address his countrymen in saying, "You who in every age of your history behold your Kings exercising this power, such as Hugues Capet judging Arnould de Rheims; as Lewis the Younger, the Bishop of Langres, and the Duke of Burgundy; as Lewis IX administering justice to all those of his subjects who had recourse to him; as Charles V judging the Marquis of Saluces, or Charles VII condemning the Duke of Alençon; as Francis I pronouncing on the Connetable de Bourbon, and Lewis XIII judging the Duke de la Valette; in fine, all you, I say, who behold your Monarchs exercising the judiciary power learn that there was *an end of every thing* under such Princes, who were real Sultans, by whom the subject was made to groan under the most *frightful despotism*, and that you are in danger of seeing it revived every time your Kings shall exercise the same powers."[30]

Would it not have been wiser and more correct if Montesquieu had said, that what constituted the despotic power in the Sultan was the power of capriciously and instantaneously pronouncing on all points, following no other guide but his passion and his momentary interest? He sends the bowstring and it is an order to die; but can such an order be deemed a judgment. He sends it because he wills it, little regarding the letter or decisions of the law; and it little imports whether such a will be assented to by a senate which may bear the title of judges, or whether he wills it alone, and in direct opposition to such a body of Magistrates. Such is the power which creates a Sultan, and which constitutes Despotism. But is it not chimerical to suppose, that in France the power of making a law and then pronouncing according to the decisions of that law antecedently made and promulgated, could constitute Despotism?

This erroneous assertion of so celebrated a writer is the more extraordinary, as we find it fully refuted in that part of his work where he treats of those ancient Dukes and Counts who, under the ancient government of the Franks, exercised the three powers. "It may be imagined perhaps, (he says) that the government of the Franks must have been very severe at that time, since the same officers were invested with a military and a civil power, nay, even with a fiscal power over the subjects, which in the preceding books I have observed to be distinguishing marks of Despotic Authority. But it is not to be believed, that the Counts pronounced judgment by themselves, and administered justice in the same manner as the Bashaws do in Turkey. In order to judge affairs, they assembled a kind of assizes where the principal men appeared. The Count's assistants were generally seven in nuber, and as he was obliged to have twelve persons to judge, he filled up the number with the principal men. But whoever had the jurisdiction, whether the King, the Count, the *Grafio*, the *Centenarian*, the Lords, or the Clergy, they never judged alone; and this usage, which derived its origin from the forests of Germany (as also did the *beautiful system* of the admirable constitution), was still continued even after the fiefs had assumed a new form."[31] He was not then to come and tell the French people, whose Kings did not judge alone in modern more than they had done in former times, that *all was over with them*, that Liberty was at an end, because the judiciary power was not separated from the legislative and executive powers.

It is easy to see what disquiet such principles must have created in the minds of his countrymen, and how they exposed the Royal Authority to odium and mistrust. But, alas! this work contains the origin of far greater evils.

Forewarned by experience of the trouble which accompanied the States-General, the French seldom recalled them to mind but to enjoy the peace and glory they had acquired under Monarchs, who by their wisdom had supplied the want of those ancient States. Montesquieu not only spread his false alarms on the legislative and executive powers of the Sovereign, but he was unfortunate enough to lay down as law to the people, that every state that wishes to believe itself free must only confide in itself, or its representatives, for the enacting of its laws. He was the first who said, *"As in a free State every man, who is supposed a free agent, ought to be his own governor,* so the legislative power ought to reside in the whole body of the people. But since this is impossible in large States, and in small ones is subject to great inconveniences, *it is fit that the people should execute by their Representatives what they cannot execute by themselves."*[32]

This is not the place to observe what a multitude of errors these assertions contain: the chief is that of having converted into a principle what he had observed in England, without considering that often what has conducted one nation to Liberty, may lead another into all the horrors of Anarchy, and thence to Despotism. On seeing this opinion laid down as a general principle, the French believed, that to become a free state it was necessary for them to return to their former States-General, and vest them with the legislative power. And in order to throw the fiscal power also into their hands Montesquieu adds, "If the legislative power were to settle the subsidies, not from year to year, but for ever, *it would run the risk of losing its Liberty,* because the executive power would no longer be dependent; and when once it was possessed of such a perpetual right, it would be a matter of indifference whether it held it of itself, or of another. The same may be said, if it should fix, not from year to year, but for ever, the sea and land forces with which it is to entrust the executive power."[33]

When we consider how little such a doctrine was ever thought of in France before Montesquieu had written; when we behold that swarm of scribbling copyists, who all repeat that Liberty is at an end wherever the people do not exercise the legislative and fiscal powers, either by themselves or by their representatives; when we compare this doctrine with that of the first revolutionary rebels, whether under the denomination of *Constitutionalists* or *Monarchists*; when we reflect that it was on such principles that Necker, Turgot, Barnave, Mirabeau, and La Fayette founded their systematic rebellion, do we not immediately infer (an awful truth indeed for Montesquieu, but which History can never hide), that it is to Montesquieu the French must trace that system which disjoints the sceptre and throws the Monarch into the hands of the people, who by means of their representatives proclaim their pretended laws; that system which recalls the States-general, who soon, styling themselves National Assembly, leave nothing to their King but the theatrical show of royal pageantry, until, carrying their consequences still further, the people assert their unbounded sovereignty by dragging the unfortunate Lewis XVI to the scaffold?

History will be astonished when it beholds Montesquieu, ignorant of his system having been precisely that which the most inveterate enemies of his country had formerly adopted, in hopes of diminishing the lustre and grandeur which it enjoyed under the dominion of its kings. For ever will the memory of those servile copyists, the Constitutionalists and Monarchists, be odious to their country, when it shall be remembered that their main object was to subject their Monarch to the authority of the States-General, and thus consummate the very plan concerted by the foreign enemy.

All these wonderful men, who were so well versed in the English constitution, might during their researches have learned what every English school-boy was acquainted with, who, in his most tender years, on receiving Salmon's Geography must have read the following passage: "January 16th, 1691, at the Congress of the Hague, consisting of the Princes of Germany, the Imperial, English, Italian, Spanish and Dutch ministers, a declaration was drawn up, wherein they solemnly protested before God, that their intentions were never to make peace with Lewis XIV, until the Estates of the kingdom of France should be established in their ancient liberties; so that the Clergy, the Nobility, and the Third-Estate, might enjoy their ancient and lawful privileges; nor till their kings for the future should be obliged to call together the said estates *when they desired any supply*, without whom they should not raise any money, on any pretence whatever, and till the parliaments of that kingdom and *all other his subjects were restored to their just rights*. And the confederates invited the subjects of France to join with them in this undertaking for restoring them to their *rights and liberties*, threatening ruin and devastation to those who refused."[34]

It is thus that, after thirty years of the most learned discussion and research on the part of Montesquieu, and forty years of new discussion on the part of his learned disciples, the Constitutionalists and Monarchists, that they adopt that plan for restoring their country to liberty which every English school-boy knew to have originated in the mind of the enemy, who wished to overturn the Throne, and tarnish the lustre which France had acquired under its Legislative Monarchs.

Had I already said it, I should nevertheless repeat, that the object here in debate is, not what the ancient constitution of France has been, nor whether their kings enjoyed the legislative power, (which has been very ill discussed by our modern politicians); still less are we disposed to agitate the question, which is the most perfect constitution in itself? Nobody will deny that government to be the best, under which the people are happiest at home, and most formidable abroad; and such a reflection will suffice to show how baneful the doctrines broached by Montesquieu and repeated by the Sophisters of

Rebellion must have proved to France: they who came to stun their countrymen with the pretended fears of despotism, alienating their minds from their own constitution to excite their admiration for foreign laws, and that at a time when the love of the subjects for their king was carried to enthusiasm after the tranquil ministry of the Cardinal Fleury, and the brilliant campaigns of the Marechal de Saxe in Flanders.

It may be difficult to decide how far this imprudent doctrine is to be looked upon as the error or as the perversion of genius; were we to appeal to the testimonies of his greatest admirers, we should not hesitate at the latter decision, and rank him among the Sophisters of Rebellion, as the sect appears to have done. D'Alembert rather accuses than defends him, when, answering those who complained of the obscurity of the *Spirit of Laws*, he says, "All that may appear obscure to common readers is not so to those whom the Author had particularly in view. Beside, *a voluntary obscurity* ceases to be obscure. Mr. de Montesquieu, often wishing to advance certain important truths, which, boldly and absolutely expressed, might have given offence to no purpose, *very prudently disguised them, and by this innocent artifice* hid them from those who might have been offended, without destroying their intended effect on the sage."[35] It is difficult to pass over this *voluntary obscurity* in a man who has advanced principles so subversive of the laws and government of his country. His pretended *innocent artifices* would almost convince the reader, that all those protestations of Montesquieu were hypocritical and sophistical, when we see him, after having strained every nerve to prove to most nations that they are perfect strangers to liberty, and that their kings are real despots, seeking every means to dispel any suspicion of his being of that disquiet, morose, and seditious temper which thirsts after revolutions.

Nor is the suspicion removed by D'Alembert when he compliments him as having "diffused that general light on the principles of government which has rendered the people more attached *to what they ought to love*." What can be the signification of "what they ought *to love*" in the mouth of this artful Sophister? Why should he not have said more attached to their King and the Government of their country? But we have already seen how little this Sophister was attached to either the one or the other.

It is equally unfortunate, that his panegyrist, now that the name of Encyclopedist is so justly covered with opprobrium, should extol his zeal for that monstrous digest, whose object remains no longer a secret, or when the most revolutionary among the Sophisters positively assert, that *Montesquieu would not have written* had not Voltaire written before him. Condorcet, by advancing such a proposition, clearly means, that if Voltaire had not succeeded so well in his Antichristian Conspiracy, Montesquieu would not have contributed so powerfully towards the political revolution;—that if the one had been less daring against the Altar, the other would have dared less against the Throne.

In solving this unfortunate problem, what "damning proof" would be acquired against Montesquieu if the authenticity of a letter which appeared in one of the London papers could ever be ascertained! Voltaire and D'Alembert conspired against the Jesuits, because they believed that society to be one of the firmest props to religion; Montesquieu, if the letter be genuine, presses for their destruction, because he thought them too much attached to the Royal authority. "We have a Prince," says he, "who is good, but weak. That society employs every art to transform the Monarch into a Despot. If it succeeds: I tremble for the consequences, civil war will rage, and streams of blood will inundate every part of Europe.—The English writers have thrown so great a light upon Liberty, and we have so great a desire of preserving what little of it we enjoy, that we should make the worst slaves in the world."

Were those violent and extreme measure which we have since witnessed already taken? This letter would indicate as much; beside, it is entirely written in the style of a conspirator. It is full of such expressions as these: "If we cannot write freely, *let us think and act freely*. We must wait patiently, but never cease working for the cause of Liberty. Since we cannot fly to the pinnacle, let us climb."

Could it be possible that Montesquieu had already formed the plan of driving out the Swiss guards, and of calling forth the national guards of the revolution? The following lines strongly denote such a plan: "What a point should we have gained, if we could once get rid of those mercenaries and foreign soldiers! *An army of natives* would declare for Liberty, at least the greater part of them would. But that is the very reason why foreign troops are maintained."[36] However difficult it may appear to vindicate Montesquieu from being a conspirator, if it be true that he was the author of the above letter, still I must say what may absolutely excuse him. This letter may have been written in a moment of anger, and be the effect of one of those fantastical contradictions from which the greatest genius is not always exempt. Montesquieu had bestowed the highest encomiums on the Jesuits in his *Spirit of Laws*;[37] but that did not hinder them from condemning several of his propositions. The resentment of the moment might have induced him to wish for their destruction. It is generally known, that he was much more tender to criticism than could be supposed for a man of his superior genius. All his love of Liberty could not hinder him from applying to the Marquise de Pompadour to obtain the despotic order for suppressing and even for burning Mr. Dupin's Refutation of his Spirit of Laws.[38]

We may observe various traits in this celebrated genius which are irreconcileable. He was very intimate with the Encyclopedian Deists and Atheists, but always desirous that his friends should die good Christians, and that they should receive all the rites of the church. At that awful period he was an Apostle or Divine, he would exhort and insist until the sick person assented; he would run, though it were at midnight, to call the clergyman whom he thought the most proper to complete the conversion; at least such was his conduct with respect to his friend and relation Mr. Meiran.[39]

His works are equally fantastical. He speaks of religion in terms of the highest panegyric; nevertheless we have to guard against many an attack which he makes against it. In defending Christianity against Bayle, he tells us, that perfect Christians "would be citizens infinitely more enlightened with respect to the various duties of life. That the more they believed themselves indebted to religion, the more they would think due to their country; that the Principles of Christianity deeply engrave on the heart should be infinitely more powerful than the false honour of Monarchies, than the human virtues of Republics, or the servile fear of Despotic States."[40] And yet he lays aside that religion, and continues to make this false honour and these human virtues the prime movers of Monarchies and Republics! He represents the Christian religion as the most consonant to Monarchy;[41] and he has said before, "There is no great share of probity or virtue necessary to support a Monarchical Government—That in well regulated Monarchies, they are almost all good subjects, and very few good men—That in a Monarchy it is extremely difficult for the people to be virtuous,"[42] that is to say, that the Christian religion is the most consonant with Monarchies,—but that it is the most difficult for the people to follow under that government. He writes in the midst of a people then the most distinguished for its love to its Sovereign, and his whole system appears to be calculated for a nation enslaved under the severest Despotism, and of which Terror is the prime agent. Certainly, either the beloved Monarch is not a Despot, or fear is not the prime agent of Despotism. Might not all this be comprised under what D'Alembert calls *innocent artifices*? but another cause may be surmised.

Montesquieu declared in his last moments, that if he had hazarded any expressions in his works which could cast a doubt on his belief, "it was owing to a taste for novelty and singularity; to a wish of passing for a transcendent genius soaring above prejudice and common maxims; to a desire of pleasing and of obtaining the plaudits of those men who directed the public opinion, and who were never more lavish of their praise than when one appeared to authorize them to throw off the yoke of all dependence and restraint."[43] This avowal would lead us to infer, that there was a greater taste for novelty and singularity in his political systems than in his religious ideas. He always preserved a sufficiency of his religious education to respect Christianity, though not enough to guard against those political systems which might and really did gain him that applause which he so much sought for, I mean that of the modern Sophisters, who, with their new-fangled ideas of Equality and Liberty, thought themselves authorized to shake off the yoke of all dependance. I cannot believe that he conspired with them; but that he forwarded their plans is too certain. And such will be our opinion, till the before-mentioned letter can be authenticated.[44] He did not conspire by setting up his systems, but his systems formed conspirators. He created a school, and in that school systems were formed, which, improving on his, rendered the latter more fatal.

1. See D'Argenson's plans, &c. on the nature of governments.
2. Suppl. to Social Contract, Part 3. Chap. 2, by Gudin.
3. Eloge de Montesquieu, by D'Alembert.

4. Considerations &c. &c. on the Romans.
5. Chap. 13.
6. We may safely assert, that if Montesquieu has borrowed such dross as the System of Climates from Bodin, he has thrown aside many articles which by no means coincided with his ideas. For example, the definition of a Sovereign given by Bodin could never agree with Montesquieu's notions of a free people, or of its representatives. The former is exaggerated. In Bodin's language, we might say, that the covenant by which the Sovereign is constituted, gives him the right of disposing at pleasure of the lives and fortunes of every citizen: That the sole distinction between the Tyrant and the lawful King is, that the former exercises his authority for the subjugation, while the latter exerts his for the happiness of the people. The generality of Montesquieu's principles appear not to recognize a sufficient Sovereignty in the real Monarch; but the opposite excess into which Bodin had fallen may, by disgusting Montesquieu, have driven him into the opposite extreme. In short, whether this criticism be correct or not is of little consequence, our object being to represent Montesquieu's ideas exactly as he has expressed them, in whatever part of the work they may be found.
7. Spirit of Laws, Book III. Chap. 3, and following.
8. Ib. Chap. 7, & *passim*, Book III and V.
9. Advertisement of the Author to the new Edition.
10. Note to Chap. 5, Book III.
11. Ibidem.
12. Chap. 2, Book I.
13. Chap. 6, Book IV.
14. Chap. 5, Book III.
15. Chap. 3, Book V.
16. Chap. 4, Book V.
17. Chap. 6, Book XI.
18. Edict of Lewis XIV, 1667; also the Treatise of the Queen's Rights on Spain.
19. Although these *Lettres de Cachet* did not generally regard the commonalty, yet the King, when petitioned, did not always refuse them to the lower classes. I was once ordered to attend one of those meetings as interpreter for an honest German, who, though low in life, had requested his Majesty to grant a *Lettre de Cachet* for his wife, who, violent and choleric, had attempted to stab him, but fortunately he had stopped her hand. The poor man, unable to live in peace or safety with this woman, and unwilling to bring her before a tribunal, had recourse to the King, who ordered the Intendant to take all the proper evidence. The relations and witnesses were secretly assembled. I saw the Subdelegate examine the facts with the greatest humanity. The whole being verified, the minutes were laid before his Majesty, and the *Lettre de Cachet* granted. The lady was confined; but in a few months she was permitted to return, and was ever after a model of gentleness and submission.
20. Social Contract, Chap. 9, Book. III.
21. Ib. in the note.
22. As this last sentence alludes to the privileges and exemptions of the Clergy and Nobility, I cannot but refer my reader to a work attributed to Mr. Senac de Meilhan, and which is very satisfactory on this point. It contains the following passage: "Mr. Necker at length, in a moment of pique against his ungrateful children, disclosed the

whole truth, and declared before the National Assembly, that the exemptions of the Clergy and Nobility, which had been represented in so odious a light, did not exceed seven millions of livres (381,181£) that the half of that sum belonged to the privileged persons of the *Tiers Etat*—and that the tax on enregistering (*droit de contrôle,*) which only bore on the two first orders, amply balanced the privileges they enjoyed with regard to the ordinary taxes. These memorable words were spoken in the face of all Europe, but were drowned in the cries of the victorious demagogues. The Clergy, the Nobility, and the Monarchy, all have perished,"—and perished under the pretence of an inequality of privileges (an empty assertion), which was more than amply compensated by a single tax on the privileged orders. This was the tax on all public acts. It was rated in proportion to the sum specified in the act, or to the *titles inserted*. Thus the Most High and Puissant Lord, Marquis, Count or Baron, was rated according to his birth, or rank, while a citizen only paid in the ratio of his obscurity." *Vid. that work, and note to chap. 6.*

23. Book III. Chap. on the Philosophers.
24. Chap. 6, Book XI.
25. Chap. 6, Book XI.
26. On the occasion we may cite Mr. Garat, a lawyer, whose opinion cannot be mistrusted, having with many others of his brethren distinguished himself by his philosophical zeal for the Revolution; and before that period he was one of the most obstinate sticklers for the sovereignty of the people.—Nevertheless he says, "at present all laws emanate from the supreme will of the Monarch, who no longer has the whole nation for his council. But his throne is so easy of access, that the wishes of the nation can always reach it." *Garat's Report: de Jurisprud. art.* Souverain.
27. See Joinville's Memoirs.
28. Chap. 6, Book XI.
29. Chap. 6, Book XI.
30. It might be objected, that some of the Kings, as in the case of Francis I, who sat in judgment on trials for High Treason were judges in their own cause. But in reality those are causes which interest the whole state. It might as well be objected, that a French Parliament could not judge a traitor to the state, because it is the cause of every Frenchman. This was an objection made against Francis I in the case of the Marquis de Saluces. It was quashed by the Attorney General. But its having been made is sufficient to prove that the King was no despot, since the laws of the country and a court of justice were to decide, whether he could exercise his power in that particular case.—(*Report: de Jurisprud. art.* Roy, *par M. Polverel*).
31. Chap. 18, Book XXX.
32. Chap. 6, Book XI.
33. Ibid.
34. Edit. 1750. Page 309.
35. Montesquieu's Elogy by D'Alembert, at the head of the 5th volume of the Encyclopedia.
36. It is earnestly requested of all persons who may have any further knowledge of that letter, or are in possession of the Newspaper in which it was published, that they will be kind enough to give such information to the Author, at Mr. Dulau's, Bookseller, No. 107, Wardour-street. He cannot question the veracity of the Abbé le Pointe, who gave him the translation of it, taken from an Evening Newspaper about the

latter end of 1795; but, not attaching the same importance to the letter which the Author would have done, the Abbé neither remarked the title nor the date of the paper which he translated it from, and *that* the Author hopes will plead his excuse for troubling his readers.

37. Chap. 6, Book IV.
38. See Feller's Historical Dictionary.
39. Ibid.
40. Chap. 6, Book XXIV.
41. Chap. 3, Book XXIV.
42. Chap. 3, Book XXIV.
43. See Historical Dictionary.
44. It is certainly a most extraordinary coincidence, that while our Author, though obliged to state the revolutionary principles laid down in Montesquieu's works, does all he can to exculpate him from any evil intention, Bertrand Barrere, the sanguinary Reporter of the successive Committees of General Safety which have butchered France, and who was himself at length involved in the downfal of Robespierre, after having been his agent during his whole reign of terror, should have been writing precisely at the same time a long declamatory pamphlet under the title of *Montesquieu peint par lui-même*, claiming the honours of the Pantheon for him, as one of the Doctors of Democracy and a Progenitor of the French Revolution. He even declares his object to be no other than to form an Edition of Montesquieu for the use of Republicans. Could it be possible that men of Barrere's stamp were the persons whom D'Alembert meant to design when he said, "All that may appear obscure to common readers, *is not so to those whom the author had particularly in view*; besides, a *voluntary obscurity* ceases to be obscure"? T.

CHAP. III.

Jean Jaques Rousseau's System.

HOWEVER cautiously Montesquieu may have expressed himself, the grand principle of all Democratic Revolutions was nevertheless laid down in his writings. He had taught in his school, "that in a free state, every man who is supposed a free agent ought *to be his own governor.*"[1] This axiom evidently implies, that no man nor any people can believe themselves free, unless they are their own legislators; and hence it was natural to conclude, that there hardly existed a nation on earth that had a right to believe itself free, or that had not some bonds to burst in order to extricate itself from slavery.

Scarcely could England even flatter itself with the real enjoyment of this liberty; and we see Montesquieu not venturing to assert it when he adds, "It is not my business to examine whether the English actually enjoy liberty or not. It is sufficient for my purpose to observe, that it is established by their laws, and I inquire no farther."[2] Though this may have satisfied the master, it might not be sufficient for all the disciples; and some one of them might answer, that according to his principle the English laws were far from granting that liberty inherent to a people governing itself.

It is evident, that to believe in their own freedom the English were obliged to deny this principle as too general, and certainly they were entitled to reply, "With us liberty consists in the right of freely doing all that the law does not forbid; and every Englishman, whether rich or poor, is equally free, whether he have the requisites for being an elector or not, whether he make the law by his direct vote, or by his deputies; or even if he does not in the least contribute toward it. For in all these cases he is certain of being judged by the same law. The Foreigner even is as free among us as ourselves, when he is willing to observe our laws, for he may do as freely as ourselves all that is not forbidden by the law."

If England could justly reproach Montesquieu with the generality of his principle, what must have been the case with other nations, such as France, Spain, Germany, or Russia, where the people do not partake either by themselves or by their representatives, of the power of enacting laws? What was to be said of all those republics, either in Switzerland or Italy, where the three powers are united in the senate, where, to use Montesquieu's expression, *the power being one,* he thinks *he discovers and dreads at every step a despotic Prince?*

228

It was a necessary consequence, either that this principle must have been done away; or that all Europe, persuading itself that it groaned under slavery, would attempt, by a general Revolution in all Governments, to cast off the yoke. Some great genius must have arisen who could have counteracted the fatal shock given by this illustrious author. But for the misfortune of Europe the very reverse came to pass.

Montesquieu was not only admired and extolled, as he deserved, in consideration of many parts of his Spirit of Laws; but he was more especially venerated for those passages in which, by means of his principles on Liberty, Equality, and Legislation, he aspersed the existing governments with the imputation of Slavery. The Sophisters easily overlooked his restrictions, his protestations, *his obscurities and his innocent artifices*, because they conceived it to be sufficient that he had opened the path, and shown how far it might lead.

The first who undertook to widen this path was Jean Jaques Rousseau, that famous citizen of Geneva, whom we have already seen so powerfully forwarding the conspiracy against the altar. He was in every shape the man of whom the Sophisters of rebellion stood in need to conduct them in their attack against the Throne. Born a citizen of a Republic, he imbibed with his milk, as he says himself, *the hatred of Kings*, as Voltaire had done that of Christ. He was better versed than Montesquieu in that dangerous talent of propagating error with the tone of importance, or of presenting paradox as the result of deep thought. He possessed, above all, that boldness which neither admits principles by halves, nor shrinks at their consequences. He surpassed his master, and in his political theories greatly outstripped him.

The *Spirit of Laws* appeared in the year 1748, and The *Social Contract* in 1752. Montesquieu had revived the ideas of Equality and Liberty; but Jean Jaques construes them into supreme happiness. "If we examine," says he, "in what the *supreme happiness of* ALL consists, which ought to be the grand object of every legislature, it will appear to center in these two points, LIBERTY AND EQUALITY. In *Liberty*, because all private dependence is so much strength subtracted from the body of the state; in *Equality*, because Liberty cannot subsist without it."[3]

Montesquieu had not dared to decide whether the English were free or not; and at the very time when he was passing the most severe criticism on other governments, he sheltered himself under the intention of not wishing to *vilify* or *debase* any one. Jean Jaques was above such cautions; he begins his work by saying, *Man is born free, and yet we see him every where in chains.*[4]

Montesquieu had surmised, that to believe himself free it was necesssary that *man should be his own governor*; that he should act according to his own laws, and according to his own will. But he judged the means of execution to be difficult in a small state, and impossible in a large one. Jean Jaques would have believed that principle false had he found it impossible in practice. But he believed the principle, as laid down by Montesquieu to be true in theory; and to surpass his master he had only to demonstrate its possiblity, and to facilitate its execution. This constitutes his favorite problem:

To find a form of association which "will defend and protect with the whole aggregate force the person and property of each individual; and by which every person, while united with ALL, *shall obey only* HIMSELF, *and remain as free as before the union*; such is the fundamental problem, says Jean Jaques, of which the Social Contract gives the solution."[5] This was in other terms precisely seeking to realize Montesquieu's principle; to give to each man who feels himself a free agent the means of being his own governor, and of living under no other laws than those which he has himself made.

How a man, after having entered into the Social Contract, is to find himself as free as if he had never engaged in it, is not easily conceived; or, how a man who has subjected himself to the will of the majority can be as free as when his actions were to be directed solely by his own will, is equally inconceivable. This was precisely saying, that the object of civil society is to preserve that Liberty which is anterior to government, or of the state of nature; though the Social Contract, according to all received ideas, expressly imports the sacrifice of part of that Liberty to preserve the rest, and to obtain at that price peace and security to one's person, property, and families; in short, all the other advantages of civil society.

The solution of this problem became more difficult when Jean Jaques asserted, that "it is evident, that the first wish and intention of the people must be, that the state should not perish."[6] According to their second maxim, it was not essentially necessary to be one's own governor, or to act always according to one's own will, and to live under laws enacted by oneself; but to have good laws, whoever might have been the legislator, and to be governed so as to save the State.

But contradictions could not thwart Jean Jaques in his career. He wished to realize Montesquieu's principle. He sets off on the supposition, that every man, a free agent, is to be his own governor; that is to say, that every free people are to obey those laws solely which they have themselves enacted: and in future he never views the law in any other light than *as the act of the general will*. Such a proposition immediatly annuls all laws which had ever been enacted by any King, Prince, or Emperor, without the participation of the multitude; nor does Jean Jaques hesitate in saying, "It is unnecessary to inquire to whom belongs the function of making laws, because the laws are but the acts of the general will. The legislative power belongs to the people, and can belong only to them. Whatever is ordered by *any* man of his own accord is not law. For the people, to be subjected to laws, must enjoy the right of making them."[7]

Such was the first principle which Jean Jaques deduced from his master's distinction of the three powers. The second was not less flattering for the multitude. All Sovereignty, according to Jean Jaques, resided in the power of Legislation. In giving this power to the people, he concluded *the people were Sovereign*; and so much so, that they had not the power *of submitting to another Sovereign*. All submission on the part of the people is represented in this new school as a violation of the very act by which every people exists; and to violate this act was to annihilate their own existence; and as a further consequence he concludes, that all submission on the part of any people is *null in itself*, for this great reason, that *by nothing nothing can be performed*.[8]

Lest he should not be understood, we see Jean Jaques frequently repeating both the principle and the consequences. "The Sovereignty, he says, being no more than the exercise of the general will, can never alienate itself. If therefore a people promise unconditionally to obey, the act of making such a promise dissolves their existence, and they lose their quality of a people; for at the moment that there is a *master* there is no longer a Sovereign; and the body politic is destroyed of course."[9]

It was impossible to say in a clearer manner to all nations, Hitherto you have been governed by Kings whom you looked upon as Sovereigns; if you wish to cease being slaves, begin by taking the Sovereignty to yourselves, that you may enact your own laws; and let your Kings, if you wish to keep them, be no more than servants, to obey your laws, and to see them observed by others.

Montesquieu feared that a legislative people would not be sufficiently enlightened for the discussion of laws and affairs in general; but this fear had not made him relinquish the principle. Jean Jaques, insisting on the principle, could see nobody more proper than the people to carry both principle and consequence into practice. In this new system, the general will of the people was not only to frame the laws, but in the making of those laws it became infallible. For he says, "the general will is always right, and tends always to the public advantage. The people can never be bribed, yet they may be deceived."[10] But in whatever manner they may be deceived, this *Sovereign people, by its nature, must, while it exists, be every thing that it ought to be.*"[11]

To compensate for the incapacity of the people in the framing of laws, Montesquieu proposed representatives, or men who should make the laws for them. Jean Jaques would not allow these men to be representatives in any thing but in name: He contended, that Montesquieu, in causing deputies to be chosen, placed the people under attornies and barristers, that is to say, under men who were to plead their cause as a guardian does that of his ward. But neither attornies nor guardians could be looked upon as real representatives. That these men, whose judgment the people would be obliged to receive as law, might differ both in will and opinion from the people; in fine, it was giving absolute legislators to the people, and thereby divesting it of the legislative power. He further observes, that the will of the people could be no more represented by these deputies than that of a ward by his guardian. And he adds, in spite of his master, "*The Sovereign*, (the people) *which is only a collective being, cannot be represented but by itself; the power may be transmitted, but not the will.* Besides, the Sovereign power may say, 'my will at present agrees with the will of such a man, or at least with what he declares to be his will;' but it cannot say, 'our wills shall likewise agree to-morrow,' as it would be absurd to think of binding the will for any time to come."[12]

From these reasonings certain qualities and rights are inferred, which Montesquieu would not perhaps have refused to the Sovereign people, but which he had not dared to express. This Sovereign made the law; and, whatever might be the law made by the people, *it could not be unjust*, as no person can be unjust towards himself.

The Sovereign people make the laws, but no law can bind them. "For, continues Jean Jaques, in every case the people are masters, to change even the best laws: for, if that body is disposed to injure itself, who has a right to prevent it?"[13]

In short, the great difficulty which Montesquieu found in free men being their own governors and legislators lay in the impossibility of holding, especially in great states, the assemblies of this legislative people. These inconveniences, or even impossibilities, vanish before Jean Jaques, because he felt that either the principle was to be abandoned, or the consequences to be followed up; and neither Parliaments nor States General could suffice for him; he wished for real assemblies of the whole people. "The Sovereign, having no other force but the legislative power, acts only by the laws; and the laws being only the authentic acts of the general will, the *Sovereign can never act but when the people are assembled*. Some will perhaps think, that the idea of the people assembling is a mere chimera: but, if it be so now, it was not so two thousand years ago; and I should be glad to know whether men have changed their nature? The limits of possibility, in moral things, are not so confined as many are apt to suppose them: it is our weakness, our vice, and our prejudice, that narrow the circle. The abject mind distrusts the very idea of a great soul; and vile slaves hearken with a sneer of contempt when we talk to them of Liberty."[14]

However confidently Jean Jaques may have laid down this doctrine, still the examples which he adduces to corroborate it were far from demonstrating that these assemblies of the Sovereign had ever existed. The citizens, for instance, of Rome or Athens were perpetually flocking to the forum; but those citizens, especially the people of Rome, were not the Sovereign people and every where Sovereign. The Empire was immense, and the people in this immense Empire, so far from being Sovereign, were a people enslaved by a Despotic Metropolis, by an army *of four hundred thousand soldiers* called Citizens, always ready to burst forth from an entrenched camp called *Rome*, to crush any town or province which should dare to assert its own liberties. Athens followed the same conduct with respect to its colonies and allied towns.

These examples adduced by Jean Jaques only showed what the French Revolution has, since, so well demonstrated: that when the inhabitants of an immense town, like Rome or Paris, take up their arms, they may style their Revolutions by the names of Equality and Liberty, but all the real distinction is, that in place of one King whom they may have banished or murdered, the inhabitants are transformed into four or five hundred thousand Despots and Tyrants over the Provinces, while they in their turn are tyrannized by their tribunes. Are not the ashes of Lyons, are not the unfortunate people of Rouen or Bourdeaux the unhappy examples that may be cited to show what fate awaited the miserable town that might attempt to shake off the yoke of the suburbs of St. Marceau, St. Antoine, or of the citizens of Paris? And has not that immense town paid its tribute to a Robespierre at one time, and at another to the five Kings?

At some times, however, Jean Jaques was sensible of these inconveniences. But he would not on that account abandon his grand principle of the Sovereignty of the people, nor even the general assemblies. He would, after Montesquieu's example, have recourse *to the virtue* of Republics or of the Sovereign people; but he would even reproach Montesquieu with a "frequent *want of precision* in not making the necesssary distinctions, and not perceiving, that, the Sovereign authority being every where the same, the same principle must prevail in every well constituted state." Then he would add, "that there is no government so subject to civil wars and internal agitations, as the democratic or popular one;" (that is to say, as the state of which virtue is the basis) "because there is not one which has so strong and so continual a tendency to change its form, which can only be preserved by the vigilance and courage employed to maintain it."[15]

He even then confesses, that "if there were a nation of Gods, *they* might be governed by a Democracy; but so perfect a government will not agree with men."[16] Yet then, lest, after Montesquieu's example, he should be wanting in precision, he proscribes all great empires from the sweets of liberty; he would allow of none but small states,[17] of one town in each state; and capitals are in his plan particularly excluded.[18]

His doctrine on this point is precise enough, when he says, "no city, any more than a nation, can be lawfully subjected to another, because the essence of the body politic consists in the perfect union of obedience and liberty, and because the words *Subject* and *Sovereign* are the identical co-relatives whose meaning is united in the word *Citizen*."[19] That is to say in a plain style, that all the Sovereigns and Subjects of a given state are only the burgesses of the same town. That a *Citizen*, subject and sovereign of London, has no authority at Portsmouth or Plymouth, and the citizens, subjects and sovereigns of these latter or any other towns cannot be subject to a sovereign which inhabits another town. And Jean Jaques continues, "It is always wrong to unite many cities in one (that is to say in one empire); it would be absurd to speak of the abuses prevalent in great states, to those who would wish to form only small ones. But is it proper to consider, how sufficient strength can be communicated to small states, to defend them from the attacks of great ones? The reply here is, that they must follow the footsteps of the Grecian cities, which formerly resisted the power of the great King; and of Holland and Switzerland who more recently withstood the house of Austria."[20] All which meant, that in this system of Liberty and Equality applied to the sovereign people it was necessary to subdivide the greater states into small federative democracies.

"In fine, if it be impossible to reduce a state within proper limits, (notwithstanding his admiration for Rome), there is still one measure to be adopted—that of not allowing a capital, or settled seat of government, but moving it in rotation to every city, and assembling the states of the country alternately in the same manner."[21]

Lest it should be objected to our Philosopher, that to form these little democracies, would only be subdividing the larger states into so many lesser provinces, which would be for ever a prey *to civil war and intestine divisions*, and always *tending to change their form*, which he declares to be the lot of all democracies, he is pleased to grant existence to aristocracies. These, and particularly "the Elective Aristocracy, which is the true one, are the best of all governments."[22] But whether Democracy, Aristocracy, or Monarchy be adopted, the people always remain sovereign; the general assemblies of the sovereign are always requisite, and they were to be frequent, "and so ordered as to assemble of course at the stated period, without being formally convened, not leaving it in the power of any Prince or Magistrate to prevent the meeting *without openly declaring himself a violator* of the laws, and an enemy to the state."[23]

Jean Jaques, more consequent than his master, follows up the principle he had borrowed from Montesquieu, and continues, "at the opening of these assemblies, whose object is the maintenance of the social treaty, two questions should always be proposed, and never on any account omitted; and the suffrages should be taken separately on each—The first should be, Does it please the Sovereign (the people) to preserve the present form of government? And the second, Does it please the people to leave the administration with those who are at present charged with it?"[24] That is to say, to continue the Magistrate, the Prince, or the King, whom they had chosen.

These two questions in the system of the sovereignty of the people are only consequences of the great principle laid down by Montesquieu, *that every man feeling himself a free agent ought to be his own governor*. For this man, or people, feeling themselves free agents, might not chuse to be governed to-day after the same manner they were governed yesterday. If they were unwilling, how could they be free agents, when obliged to maintain that government and those chiefs which they had formerly chosen.

Such a consequence would have made any Philosopher less intrepid than Jean Jaques abandon the principle. Without pretending to Philosophy, one might have told him, "that every people which foresaw the misfortunes that perpetual revolutions in their government exposed them to, might without vilifying or enslaving themselves, have chosen a Constitution and sworn to maintain it. They might have chosen Chiefs, Magistrates, or Kings, who were bound by oath to govern according to that Constitution: a compact which it would be no less criminal to violate, than the most sacred oath (and equally so to-morrow as to-day). If the people are supposed to sacrifice their Liberty by a compact of this nature, you will call every honest man by the degrading name of slave, who shall think himself bound by the promise he made yesterday, or the oath he took to live according to the laws of the state?" But such reasonings would have had little weight with Jean Jaques. In his opinion, it was a great error to pretend, that a Constitution equally binding for the people and their chiefs was a compact between the people and the chiefs they had chosen; because, (says he) "it would be absurd and contradictory to suppose, that the Sovereign should give itself a superior; and that, to oblige itself to obey a master, would be to reinstate itself in the fullness of Liberty."[25]

Such was the consequence naturally flowing from the idea of the sovereignty of the people, of the people essentially sovereign, who to be free must be their own governors, and who must retain, notwithstanding all their oaths, the right of annulling to-day those very laws, which yesterday they swore to maintain. This conclusion, however strange it may appear, is nevertheless that in the application of which the Revolutionary Sophister particularly exults when he says, "when it happens therefore that the people establish an hereditary government, whether it be Monarchical in family, or Aristocratical in one order of Citizens, *it is not an engagement which they make,* but a provisional form given to Administration, until it shall please the Sovereign to order otherwise."[26] That is to say, until it shall please the people to expel their Senate, Parliament, or King.

Let not the reader be astonished at seeing me insist so much in these memoirs on the exposition of such a system. The application of the causes to the effects will be more evident when the Historian treats of the acts of the French Revolution. But should he wish to know more particularly, how much our Philosopher of Geneva influenced the warfare which the Revolution had kindled against every throne, let him examine how this Sophister applies his principles to Monarchies, and the lessons that he teaches to all nations respecting their Kings.

Here again it was Montesquieu who had laid the ground-work, and Jean Jaques raised the superstructure. He, walking in the footsteps of his master, admits the absolute necessity of separating the Legislative from the Executive Power, but, always more daring than Montesquieu, he scarcely leaves to Monarchy its very name. "I therefore denominate every State a Republic which is regulated by laws, under whatever form of administration it may be; for then only the public interests governs, and the affairs of the public obtain a due regard.—*To be legitimate,* the government should not be confounded with the Sovereignty, but be considered as its administrator; and then the Monarchy itself would be a Republic."[27]

These last words seem to imply, that Jean Jaques recognized at least the legitimacy of a King who would receive the law from the people, and who, acquiescing in their sovereignty, would submit to be a simple administrator, in a word their slave. For, according to this system, the only free man is he who makes the laws, and the only slave he who receives them. The people were to make the law, the King to receive it; the King therefore is only the slave of the sovereign people.

On such conditions Jean Jaques consents to recognize a King in great empires; but he teaches the people at the same time, that it is owing to their own faults if a King be necesssary in such a state. They would have learned to govern themselves without one if they had reflected, that *the greater the enlargement of the state, the more Liberty is diminished;*[28] that their real interest would have been to occupy a space of ground a hundred times less extensive, in order to become a hundred times more free; that if it be difficult for a large state to be properly governed, it is still more so for it to be *well governed by one man.*

In fine, whatever states these may be, we are never to forget, according to this Philosopher, that the whole dignity of those men called KINGS "*is certainly no more than a commission,* under which, simply as officers of the sovereign power, they exercise in the name of the Sovereign the power delegated to them, and which may be limited, modified, or recalled at the will of the Sovereign."[29]

Even on these conditions, had Jean Jaques succeeded according to his wishes, Kings, though reduced to mere Officers or Commissioners for the Sovereign people, would not have had a long existence. This wish is clearly expressed throughout the whole of his Chapter on Monarchy.[30] There he has heaped up every argument against Royalty, whether hereditary or elective; there, extolling the supposed virtues of the multitude, he beholds the throne invaded by Tyrants, or vicious, covetous and ambitious Despots. Nor did he fear to add, that if we were to understand by KING him who governs *only for the welfare of his subjects,* it would be evident that *there had never existed one from the commencement of the world.*[31]

The direct consequences of this whole system evidently were, that every nation desirous of preserving its rights of Equality and Liberty, was in the first place to endeavour to govern itself without a King, and to adopt a Republican Constitution; that nations who judged a King necessary were cautiously to preserve all the rights of Sovereignty, and never to lose sight, in quality of Sovereigns, of their inherent right of deposing the King they had created, of shivering his scepter, and of overturning his throne, whenever, and as often as they pleased. Not one of these consequences startled the Philosopher of Geneva. He was obliged to admit them, lest it should be objected (as he had done against Montesquieu) that *he sometimes wanted precision!* and once more to leave the word a prey to slavery. Had it been objected, that it was precisely among those nations who carried their ideas of Equality, Liberty, and Sovereignty to the greatest lengths, that the greatest number of slaves were to be found, he would have contented himself with answering, "Such, it is true, was the situation of Sparta.—But as to you, people of the present day, you have no slaves, *but are yourselves enslaved.*—You purchase their Liberty at the expence of your own. Forbear then to exult in a presence which discovers, in my opinion, more of indolence than of humanity."[32]

It is evident that Rousseau, always more lively and more daring than his master, could not suppress any of the consequences which flowed from the principle laid down by Montesquieu. He brands every nation, even the English, with slavery, declaring them all to be slaves under their Kings.

To have surpassed his master in politics was not sufficient. Montesquieu is often lax, even insinuates error, and, notwithstanding all the eulogy he bestows on Christianity, appears sometimes to sacrifice the religious virtues to politics; yet he appeared too timid to his disciples. Jean Jaques, more dogmatic, declares openly that he knows of no Religion *more destructive of the social spirit* than that of the Gospel; and he paints a true Christian as a being always ready to bend his neck under the yoke of a Cromwell or a Catiline.

Montesquieu had mentioned the *Catholic Religion* as particularly adapted to moderate Governments and Monarcy; *the Protestant Religion* as appropriate to Republics.[33] Jean Jaques will neither allow of the Catholic nor of the Protestant Christian, and finishes his system with Bayle's famous paradox that Montesquieu had refuted. He conceived no Religion but Deism to be worthy a Sovereign, equal, and free people; and in order to undermine every throne, he banishes from the state every altar where the God of Christianity was adored.[34]

This conclusion alone raised Jean Jaques far above Montesquieu in the eyes of the Sophisters. Time was to decide which of these two systems should bear away the palm of victory. Let the historian compare the effects of each, observing their nature and the successive progress of opinion. He will then be less surprized at beholding that school triumph which is regardless of the sanctity of the Altar and of the authority of the Throne.

1. Chap. 6, Book XI.
2. Chap. 7, Book XI.
3. Social Contract, Chap. II, Book II.
4. Chap. 1, Book I.
5. Chap. 6, Book I.
6. Chap. 6, Book IV.
7. Chap. 6, Book II.
8. Chap. 7. Book I.
9. Chap 1. Book. II.
10. Chap. 3. Book II.
11. Chap. 7, Book I.
12. Chap 1. Book. II.
13. Chap. 12. Book II.
14. Chap. 12, Book. III.
15. Chap. 4, Book III.
16. Ibid.
17. Ibid.
18. Chap. 13, Book III.
19. Chap. 13, Book III.
20. Ibid.
21. Chap. 13, Book. III.
22. Chap. 5, Book III.
23. Chap. 18, Book III.

24. Chap. 18, Book III.
25. Chap. 16, Book III.
26. Chap. 18, Book III.
27. Chap. 6, and Note to Book II.
28. Chap. 1, Book III.
29. Ibid.
30. Chap. 6, Book III.
31. Note to Chap. 10, Book III.
32. Chap. 15, Book III.
33. Spirit of Laws, Chap. 5, Book XXIV.
34. See Social Contract, Chap. 8, Book IV.

CHAP. IV.

Third Step of the Conspiracy.

The general Effect of the Systems of Montesquieu and Jean Jaques.

Convention of the Sophisters—The Coalition of their Plots against the Throne, with their Plots against the Altar.

IN comparing the two Systems that we have just exposed, it is easy to remark, that the respective authors of those Systems have been biassed in their application of the ideas of Liberty and Equality to polity by the different stations which they held in life. The first, born of that class in society that is distinguished by riches and honours, participated less of those ideas of Equality which confound every class of citizens. Notwithstanding his great admiration for ancient Republics, he observes, that "In every state there are always persons distinguished by their birth, riches, or honours; but were they to be confounded with the common people, and to have only the weight of a single vote like the rest, the common liberty would be their slavery, and they would have no interest in supporting it, as most of the popular resolutions would be against them."[1]

It was this system which was at an after-period to induce the Jacobin Club to style Montesquieu the *Father of Aristocracy*; and it appears that he was led to the adoption of this idea by the supposition that the class of citizens (the parliament) to which he belonged, would become legislators and thus, enjoying his distinctive mark of liberty, would be their own governors, and would never obey any but their own laws. The care he had taken not to generalize his ideas, excepting when treating of the island where he had learned to admire them, screened him from all censure, and removed any imputation of his wishing to overturn the constitution of his countyry, in order to introduce that of another. But such a precaution did not repress that desire which he had kindled in the breasts of many of his readers, a desire of seeing that constitution, which he so much extolled, established in their own country, a desire also of the only laws congenial to liberty, those of a country where each person is his own governor.

The French at that period, little accustomed to political discussions, rather enjoyed the advantage of their government under the laws of their Monarch, than cavilled at his authority. They were free under their laws, nor did they lose their time in disquisitions on the possibility of being so, though they had not participated in the making of them. The novelty of the subject irritated the curiosity of a nation with whom the bare title of *Spirit of Laws* was sufficient to captivate their suffrages. Besides, it contained an immense fund of learning; and in spite of many witty reflections, even bordering on epigram, a strong feature of moderation and candour laid further claim to the public esteem. The English also admired it.—Notwithstanding Montesquieu's reserves, it was but natural for them to extol so great a genius, whose chief error lay in having believed that their laws and their constitution were sufficient to impart Liberty to all nations, whatever might be their moral or political position on the globe.

The esteem in which a nation, perhaps at that time its most worthy rival, had always held Great Britain, added much to the high repute of the Spirit of Laws. It was translated into several languages; and it would have been a disgrace for a Frenchman not to have been acquainted with it. I hope the expression I am going to make use of will be forgiven; that poison, that true source of the most democratic of all revolutions, infused itself without being perceived. The ground-work is entirely comprized in the principle, that *Every man who is supposed a free agent ought to be his own governor*, which is absolutely synonimous with another, viz., "*it is in the body of the people that the legislative power resides.*" Those members of the aristocracy who admired Montesquieu, had not sufficiently weighed the consequences of this grand axiom. They did not perceive that the Sophisters of rebellion would one day only change the terms, when they proclaimed that the *law* was but the *expression of the general will*, and hence conclude, that it is a right inherent in the people or multitude to enact or abrogate all laws; and that should the people change and overturn every thing at pleasure, they would do no more than exercise a right.

When Montesquieu passed over these consequences, or rather pretended not to see them; when, viewing the different Monarchies of Europe, he finds himself obliged to confess that he knew of no people, one excepted, who exercised the pretended right of governing themselves, and of making their own laws; when he adds, that the less they exercised that right, the more *the Monarchy degenerated towards Despotism*; when, declaring that Liberty was at an end wherever those powers which were generally concentrated in the person of the Sovereign, were not distinct, he seems to console nations, by flattering them with a greater or smaller portion of Liberty, for which they were indebted to what he calls prejudices, to their love *of the Subject's, the State's, and the Prince's glory*;[2] in what cloud could he have enveloped himself? After having laid down principles which stigmatize all nations as in a state of slavery, will he pretend to appease their minds by speaking of what little Liberty prejudice may have left them? Are not these some of the *voluntary obscurities* which D'Alembert styles *innocent artifices*? Or, are we to join with Jean Jaques in accusing Montesquieu *of not being precise, and being often obscure*?

Be this as it may, such were Montesquieu's principles, that it was impossible to adopt them either in France or elsewhere, without inviting those aweful revolutions which, snatching the most important branch of the Royal prerogative from the Monarch, invest the people with his spoils. After the *Spirit of Laws* only one thing was wanting to operate such a Revolution; and that was, a man who, sufficiently daring, would assert these consequences without fear, perhaps even complacently, because he beheld in them a means of annihilating all titles or distinctions, which decorate stations of life superior to his own. The son of a poor artizan, in a word Jean Jaques Rousseau, bred in a watchmaker's shop, proved to be this daring man. He grasped the weapons which Montesquieu had forged to assert the privileges of the multitude, and ascertain the rights of legislation and sovereignty in the poor workman as the former had in the rich man; in the commoner as in the nobleman. The whole aristocracy of Montesquieu was no more than a scaffolding for the Sophisters of rebellion; and if he ever uses the word *Aristocracy* as expressing the best government, it was only in its original signification; he does not understand by it the government of the wealthy and noble classes, but that of the *best* of each, whether rich or poor, who were to be chosen magistrates by the people; and then in the very aristocracy he constitutes the people Legislators and Sovereigns.

Montesquieu believed the Nobility to be necessary intermediates between the King and the People. Jean Jaques detested these intermediate bodies, and thought it absurd that a sovereign people should stand in need of them. Montesquieu parcels out the authority of Kings, to adorn the aristocracy of riches and nobility with one of its fairest branches. Jean Jaques, pennyless, shivers the scepter of his King, and proscribes the prerogative of nobility or wealth, and to assimilate himself to the Peer or Nobleman he invests the Sovereignty in the multitude. Both forboded Revolutions; both taught nations that they laboured under the yoke of slavery, whatever may have been their protestations to the contrary; both led nations to believe, that the liberty of the subject could never be ascertained until they had adopted new Constitutions and new Laws, and had chosen chiefs, who, more dependent on the people, would ensure the liberty of the subject at the expence of their own.

Both, in giving their ideas upon Liberty, instructed nations in what they ought to do to acquire this supposed Liberty. Public opinion, like the two systems, was to be restrained within certain limits with Montesquieu, or expand itself to any lengths with Jean Jaques, according to the strength, preponderance or multitude of disciples which interest might have enrolled under the banners of either of these modern politicians. Every reflecting person could already foresee, that all the rebels of aristocracy would follow Montesquieu as their chief, but that all the lower classes, and all the enemies of aristocracy, whether from hatred or jealousy, would fight under Jean Jaques.

Such must have been the natural effect of these two systems according to the progress they made in the public opinion. This effect, it is true, might have been counteracted by opinions still predominant among many nations, whom these false ideas of Liberty had not misled so far as to make them believe they lived in slavery because they were governed by the laws of their Princes.

All these revolutionary principles must have been fruitless in nations whose religious tenets teach and ordain submission to their lawful Sovereign, in nations where the Gospel was followed and respected, a Gospel which equally proscribes injustice, arbitrary and tyrannic power in the Prince, and rebellion in the Subject, which, teaching the true worship of the King of Kings, does not instil pride into nations by stunning them with the repeated proclamation of their sovereignty.

But the Sophisters of Impiety had undermined the foundations of the religion of the Gospel, and numerous were their impious adepts. Many had been led to impiety by their ambition, and by the jealousy they had conceived against those who enjoyed distinctions or exercised power, and they soon perceived that by means of these two systems, the same ideas of Equality and Liberty, which had proved such powerful agents against Christianity, might prevail also against all political Governments.

Till this period, the hatred which the school of Voltaire, or the brethren of D'Alembert, had conceived against Kings was vague and without any plan. In general, it was a mere thirst after Equality and Liberty, or a hatred of all coercive authority. But the necessity of a civil government stifled all their cries. Here they were convinced, that to destroy was not sufficient, and that in overturning the present laws, it was necessary to have another code to replace the former. Their writings teemed with epigrams against Kings, but they had not attacked their rights; Despotism and Tyranny were represented in the most fantastic light, though they had not yet decided that every Prince was a Despot or a Tyrant. But this was no longer the case when these two systems had appeared; Montesquieu taught them to govern themselves, and make their laws in conjunction with their Kings; and Jean Jaques persuades them to expell all Kings, and to govern and make their laws themselves. The Sophisters no longer hesitate, and the overthrow of every throne is resolved on, as they had before resolved on the destruction of every altar. From that period the two conspiracies are combined and form but one in the school of the Sophisters. It is no longer the isolated voice of a Voltaire, or of any particular adept who, following the explosions of his brain, raises a sarcastic cry against the authority of Kings; it is the combined efforts of the Sophisters leagued in plots of rebellion and impiety, aiming all their hatred, their means, their wishes and their artifices, at teaching all nations to destroy the throne of their Kings, as they had formerly excited them to overturn the altars of their God.

Such an accusation is important, it is direct; and the proofs are taken from the words of the conspirators themselves. It is not only the simple avowal of the Conspiracy, but the exulting pride of the Sophister who glories in his crime. He paints the hypocrisy, the wickedness, the hideousness of his crime in as glowing colours as if he had delineated the triumph of genius and wisdom, in a word of true Philosphy, in the cause of the happiness of mankind. Let us attend, and we shall hear them tracing the history of their plots, which they represent as the climax of human understanding in Philosophical learning.

The French Revolution had hurled the unfortunate Lewis XVI from his throne, when the most unrelenting conspirator, that monster Condorcet, thinks it incumbent on him to celebrate the glory of Philosophism, and trace the progress of this fiend which had kindled the torch of discord and had reared the Republic on crime, bloodshed, and the ruins of the throne. Lest the school whence these horrid deeds had issued, should not be known, he decribes it from its origin, and historifies all the monsters of iniquity and rebellion which each century had produced. He then descends to the new Republican æra. That history may carefully weigh his evidence and appreciate his avowal, his words shall suffer no alteration: without interruption from us he may extol his school and its pretended benefactions. He supposes us at the middle of this century, considers his reader as arrived at that period when the delirium of superstition is dispelled by the first rays of modern Philosophy. Then it is that he developes the following plot as the history and triumph of his false Philosophy.

"*There was a class of men which soon formed itself in Europe* with a view not so much to discover and make deep research after truth as to diffuse it: whose chief object was to attack prejudices in the very asylums where the Clergy, the Schools, the Governments, and the ancient Corporations had received and protected them; and made their glory to consist rather in destroying popular error than in extending the limits of science: this, though an indirect method of forwarding its progress, was not on that account either less dangerous or less useful.

"In England Collins and Bolingbroke, in France Bayle, Fontenelle, Voltaire, Montesquieu, and *the schools formed by these men*, combated in favour of truth. They alternately employed all the arms with which learning and Philosophy, with which wit and the talent of writing could furnish reason. *Assuming every tone, taking every shape*, from the ludicrous to the pathetic, from the most learned and extensive compilation to the novel or the petty pamphlet of the day, covering truth with a veil, which, *sparing the eye that was too weak*, incited the reader *by the pleasure of surmising it*, insidiously caressing prejudice in order to strike it with more certainty and effect; seldom menacing more than one at a time, and that only in part; sometimes flattering the enemies of reason *by seeming to ask but for a half toleration in Religon or a half Liberty in polity; respecting Despotism when they impugned religious absurdities, and Religion when they attacked tyranny; combating these two pests in their very principles, though apparently inveighing against ridiculous and disgusting abuses; striking at the root of those pestiferous trees, whilst they appeared only to wish to lop the straggling branches; at one time marking out superstition, which covers despotism with its impenetrable shield, to the friends of Liberty, as the first victim which they are to immolate, the first link to be cleft asunder; at another denouncing it to Despots as the real enemy of their power*, and frightening them with its hypocritical plots and sanguinary rage; but indefatigable when they claimed *the Independence of Reason and the Liberty of the Press* as the right and safeguard of mankind;—inveighing with enthusiastic energy against the crimes of Fanaticism and Tyranny; reprobating every thing which bore the character of oppression, harshness, or barbarity, whether in Religion, Administration, Morals or Laws; commanding Kings, Warriors, Priests and Magistrates in the name of nature to spare the blood of men; reproaching them in the most energetic strain with that which their policy or indifference prodigally lavished on the scaffold or in the field of battle; in fine, adopting *reason, toleration, and humanity* as their signal and watch-word.

"Such was the Modern Philosophy, so much detested by those numerous classes whose existence were drawn from prejudices—Its chiefs had the art of escaping vengeance, though exposed to hatred; *of hiding themselves from persecution, though sufficiently conspicuous to lose nothing of their glory.*"[3]

Had rebellion, impiety, and revolt wished to trace their means and ascertain their object, could they have made a better choice than the pen of Condorcet to delineate the actors, describe their detestable plots, and fix the epoch of their double conspiracy, which, first aiming at the altar, is afterward directed and pursued with fury against all Kings and Rulers of nations? How could their means and plots have been rendered more manifest? How could the hero of the plot, or the adept most intimately initiated in the mysteries of the conspiracy, have more evidently pointed out the object, the double tendency of the Sophisticated school; or shown in a clearer light the wish of destroying the throne springing from the league which they had formed against the altar?

Let the historian seize on this avowal or rather on this eulogy of plots. He will find concentrated and flowing from Condorcet's pen, every thing that the most daring and the deepest initiated conspirator could have let fall, to characterize the most authenticated and most universal conspiracy, planned by those men called Philosophers, not only attacking the persons of particular Kings but of every King, and not Kings only, but the very essence of Royalty and all Monarchy. The commencement of this conspiracy was when Collins, Bolingbroke, Bayle, and other masters of Voltaire, together with that Sophister himself, had propagated their impious doctrines against the God of Christianity.

We see it fast rising into eminence when Montesquieu and Jean Jaques, nearly his contemporary, applying their ideas of Equality and Liberty to Polity, had given birth to that disquiet spirit which sought to investigate the rights of Sovereigns, the extent of their authority, the pretended rights of the free man, and without which every subject is branded for a slave—and every King styled a Despot. In fine, it is that period when their systems, by means of empty theories, furnish the Sophisters with a means of supplying the want of Kings in the government of nations.

Until that period the sect seemed to have carried their views no further, than to the establishment of Philosophic Kings, or Kings at least who would let themselves be governed by Philosophers, but, despairing of success, they league in the oath of destroying all Royalty, the very isntant they shall have found in any system the means of governing without Kings.

The persons who compose this school of conspirators are strongly marked. They are the authors and adepts of this *Modern Philosophy*, who, before they resolved on the destruction of Monarchy, began by raising their heads against Religion; who, before they depicted every Government in the colours of Despotism and Tyranny, represent fanaticism and superstition as the sole growth of Christianity.

The extent, the means, the constancy of the conspiracy all are shown in the clearest light—Our conspiring Sophisters pretend to *ask but for a half-toleration in Religion or a half-Liberty in Polity; respecting* the authority of Kings *when they impugned Religion, and Religion when they attacked* Royalty. They pretend *to inveigh only against abuses*; but both Religion and the authority of Monarchs *are but two pestiferous trees*, at whose very *roots they strike*. They are the two giants whom they combat in their principles, that every vestige of their existence might be annihilated.

They assume every tone, they take every shape, and artfully flatter those whose power they wish to destroy. They spare no pains to deceive the Monarch whose throne they undermine. They *denounce* Religion *as the real enemy of their power*, and never cease reminding their adepts, that it is Religon which covers Kings with an *impenetrable shield: That it is the first victim to be immolated, the first link to be cleft asunder*, in order to succeed in shaking off the yoke of Kings, and in annihilating Monarchy, when once they should have succeeded in crushing the God of that Religion.

The whole of this wicked game is combined among the adepts; their action, their union cannot be better delineated. Their watch-word is *Independence and Liberty*. They all have their secret, and during the most vigorous prosecution of their plots *they sedulously conceal them. They nevertheless pursue them with an indefatigable constancy*. What can be called conspiracy, if this is not conspiring against all Kings; and how could the Philosophers more clearly demonstrate, that the war which they waged against Christ and his Altar, against Kings and their Thrones, was a war of extermination?

I still fear its being objected, that the Philosophers did not mean to point at Royalty by the words *Despotism and Tyranny*. I have already said, that the Despots and Tyrants whom the Sophisters were to destroy could be no other than those Monarchs under and against whom they did conspire; and if the unfortunate Lewis XVI was a Tyrant and a Despot in their eyes, the mildest and the most moderate of Monarchs must have been guilty of Tyranny and Despotism. But let it not be thought that these conspiring Sophisters were always restrained by a sense of shame from casting aside the veil of Despotism and Tyranny with which they had shrowded the hatred they had conceived against Royalty. The same Condorcet who may be supposed (at the head of the Sophisticated bands) to have attacked only Tyranny and Despotism, leaves us no room to doubt.

Scarcely had the original rebels called Constitutionalists left the name or phantom of a Monarch to France in the unfortunate Lewis XVI, so greatly had they abridged the regal authority; and most unjustly could that unfortunate Prince, in his degraded state at least, be accused of Despotism or Tyranny; nevertheless the designs of the Sophisters had not been fulfilled, and it is Condorcet who undertakes to shew the extent of their views. Royalty was still preserved as to the name, and Condorcet now no longer exclaimed, "Destroy the *Tyrant*, the *Despot*," but "*destroy the* KING." Speaking in the name of the Philosophic Sect, he proposes his problems on Royalty in the most direct language. He entitled them *Of the Republic*; and the first question he proposes is, *Whether a King is necessary for Liberty?* He answers it himself, and declares that Royalty is not only unnecessary and useless *but even contrary to Liberty*, that it is irreconcileable with Liberty; and after having solved this problem, he continues: "As to the reasonings which may be brought against us, we will not do them the honour of refuting them; much less shall we trouble ourselves to answer that swarm of mercenary writers, who have such good reasons for believing that a Government cannot exist without a civil list, and we will give them full liberty to treat those persons as madmen who have the misfortune to think as the sages of every age and nation have done before them."[4]

It is thus that, from the mouth of that Sophister, who was the most deeply initiated of the adepts, we learn, without the least subterfuge, the extent of their plots; such were the wishes of his pretended sages. It is not only Despotism but Royalty itself, it is even the empty name of an imprisoned King, that is incompatible with Liberty. What then is necessary to accomplish their last views with respect to Kings as well as to the Priesthood? These views are not confined to France alone, no, not even to Europe; but they extend to all nations, to the whole globe, to every region on which the sun shines. It is no longer a wish, it is a hope, it is the confidence of success, which makes the same Sophister, adopting the prophetic strain, announce to Kings and the Priesthood, that, thanks to the union, toils, and unrelenting warfare of the Philosophers, "the day will come when the sun shall shine on none but free men, a day when man, recognizing no other master than his reason, when Tyrants and their Slaves, when Priests, together with their stupid and hypocritical agents, will have no further existence but in history or on the stage."[5] At length the whole extent of their plots is revealed, and revealed by that adept who was at the head of the Sophisticated school; by him, whom the original masters had judged to be the most proper person to succeed them and as most strongly fired with their spirit; by him, in fine, who proves to be their *greatest consolation* in their last moments, as they leave a chief to their school worthy of themselves.[6] That their conspiracy might be complete, the *Royal Authority and the Priesthood* were not to exist but in history or on the stage. In the former, as the subject of calumny and all the imprecations of the Sect; on the latter, as an object of public derision.

Condorcet is not, however, the only one of the Sophisters, who, exulting in the success of their double conspiracy, lay open its source and shew it springing from that concert and understanding of the Sophisters, uniting their means, their labours, and directing them at one time against the throne, at another against the altar, with a common wish of crushing both the one and the other. Condorcet is, without doubt, the Sophister who betrays the greatest vanity on the subject, because he is the adept who, scoffing at all shame and disclaiming every moral sentiment, would blush the least in describing those artifices which he so complacently relates; for it was he that could with the least embarrassment reconcile that atrocious dissimulation, those tortuous plans, those snares laid at once for Priests, Kings, and Nations, to the rules of honour, probity, and truth; while the whole conduct of his school exhibits a concatenation of guilt and cunning, unworthy of the Philosopher, and becoming the odious conspirator only. Many other adepts speak their true sentiments, when they declare their belief that the publication of their proceedings can be no bar to the success of the conspiracy.

The Editors of the *Mercure*, La Harpe, Marmontel, and Champfort, had nearly been as explicit as Condorcet, when they published the following sentence, "It is the arm of the people that executes Revolutions, but it is the meditations of the sage that prepare them." These adepts, like Condorcet, represent our pretended sages as directing by silent and tortuous means, the minds of the people toward that Revolution which was to shiver the scepter of Lewis XVI and whose grand object was to *break* the pretended *yoke of the Priesthood* in order *to break that* of the pretended *Tyrants*, of Tyrants such as Lewis XVI, the most humane and just of Kings, and whose fondest pursuit was the happiness of his subjects. Before Condorcet and our Sophisters of the *Mercure* many other adepts had shewn this concert and union, and had claimed the honour of this Revolution menacing every throne, as the glorious achievements of their school. Let us hearken to a man illustrious in the annals of Philosophism, and whom as such we may suppose well informed as to their plots.

Mr. de la Metherie is not one of the common class of adepts; on the contrary, he was one of those who had the art of insinuating Atheism with all the seduction of natural science. So early as on the 1st of January 1790, this adept, who was deservedly looked upon as one of the most learned of the Sect, begins his observations and memoirs with these remarkable words: "At length the happy day is come when Philosophy triumphs over all its enemies. They are obliged to own, that it is the light which Philosophy has spread, more especially of late years, that has produced *the great events which will distinguish the end of this century*." What are these great events which the learned Atheist claims in the name of Philosophy? They are those of a Revolution which discovers man *breaking the shackles of slavery*, and shaking off the yoke with which *audacious Despots* had burthened them. It is the people recovering their *inalienable right*, of making alone the laws, of deposing Princes, of changing or continuing them according to their will and pleasure, and of viewing their Sovereigns in no other light than as men who cannot infringe these popular laws *without being guilty of treason to the people*. Lest the principles on which these pretended rights were founded should be forgotten, he repeats them with enthusiastic eloquence; lest the glory of such lessons and their consequences should be attributed to any but the masters of his school, lest, in short, the intention and concert of its authors should not be sufficiently evident, he tells us, and that at the very moment when the unfortunate Lews XVI is the sport of that legislative and Sovereign populace, "It is these truths repeated thousands and thousands of times by the Philosophers of humanity, that have operated those precious effects, so long expected;" he carefully adds, that if France is the first to burst the fetters of Despotism, it is beause the Philosophers had prepared them for such noble efforts *by a multitude of excellent writings*. And that we might be acquainted to what extent these successes prepared by Philosophy are to be carried by the concert of these lessons repeated *thousands and thousands of times*, the adept La Metherie continues, "The same lights are propagating throughout other nations, and soon they will cry out like the French, *we are determined to be free*—Let the brilliant success *which Philosophy has just gained* be a new spur to their courage—*Let us be persuaded that our labours will not be fruitless.*"

The foundation of this hope (and never let the historian lose sight of this obervation, since the Philosophers incessantly repeat it) rests on the prospect of an approaching Revolution in religious matters. It is because sects equally inimical to Royalty and Christianity are daily increasing in numbers and strength, particularly in *North America* and *Germany*. It is because the new tenets *are silently propagated,* and that all these sects unite their efforts with those of Philosophism.

He delineates the extent of their hopes, by declaring that Philosophy, after having conquered Liberty in America and France, will carry its conquests on the one side into Poland, on the other into Spain and Italy, and even into Turkey; nay, more, that it will penetrate into the most distant regions; and that Egypt, Syria, and India itself, shall be tributary to it.[7]

Were it necessary to seek further proof that this Revolution had been the work of the combined efforts, of the wishes and labors of our modern Sophisters, La Metherie will tell us, that he had clearly announced it to all Sovereigns when he said, "Princes, do not deceive yourselves—TELL *raises the standard of Liberty, and he is followed by his fellow citizens.* The whole power of Philip II could not prevail against Holland; and a chest of tea liberates America from the yoke of the English. In all energetic nations Liberty raises itself on the ruins of Despotism; but Joseph II and Lewis XVI were far from thinking this warning regarded them. May Kings, Aristocrats, and Theocrats profit by this example!" Should they continue deaf to his voice, the same sage will shrug his shoulders, and, pitying, say, "These privileged persons are bad calculators of the course of the human mind and of the influence of Philosophy; and let them remember that their fall in France was accelerated by the neglect of such calculations."[8]

Another Philosopher not less vain than La Metherie, extolling and revealing the plans, intentions, and plots of the sect, with nearly as much perspicuity as Condorcet, is also acknowledged by it for one of its profoundest adepts. This is Gudin, who, adding his reveries to those of Jean Jaques, makes the glory of his masters consist not only in the principles and the wish of the revolution, but in all they had done to bring it about, and which enabled them to *announce it as infallible*.

This adept Gudin goes much further; for he tells us, that it was not the intention of the Philosophers to operate this Revolution by the arm of the people, but by means of the King and his Ministers; that they had forewarned them that it was in vain for them to pretend to stop it. According to him, "these same Philosophers who, under the ancient order of things, had told the King, his Council, and his Ministers, *that these changes would take place in spite of them, if they would not adopt them*, say at this present day to those who oppose the constitution, that it would be impossible to return to the old form of government, whichever might be the party that carried the day, it being too imperfect and too much discredited even by the enemies of the new constitution."[9]

These men therefore, whom we see to-day, under the name of Philosophers, so numerous and such zealous partizans of that Revolution which dethrones Kings; which invests the Sovereignty in the hands of the people, and executes systems the most directly opposite to the authority of Monarchs; these men, before they attempted to accomplish their plans by the arm of the people, had already revolutionized the public opinion to that degree, and were so certain of their success, that they boldly threatened both Kings and their Ministers, if they would not adopt their Revolutionary ideas, with the completion of that long wished for Revolution, in spite of all opposition.

It would be endless to quote the multitude of proofs which attest, that Philosophism only waited for the success of its plots, to glory in having contrived them. The historian will find those proofs in the numerous discourses pronounced by the adepts, either at the legislative club called National Assembly, or at the regulating club called the Jacobins; scarcely will he hear the name of Philosophers pronounced in these revolutionary dens, without the grateful acknowledgment of their being the authors of the Revolution.

I could adduce proofs of a different nature.—The adepts, for example, who many years before the Revolution entrusted with their secret those whom they wished to gain over to their party. I could name that Counsellor, that Sophister Bergier, whom Voltaire mentions as the most zealous adept.[10] I am acquainted with the person to whom this secret was entrusted five years before the Revolution, in the Park of St. Cloud, to whom Bergier without the least hesitation said, that the time was not distant when Philosophy would triumph over Kings and the Priesthood. That as to Kings, their Empire was at an end, and that the downfall of the grandees and nobility was equally certain. That the plans had been too well laid, and things were too far advanced, to leave room for any doubt of success. But the man who has since entrusted me with these secrets, though he gave them to me in writing, will not consent to have his name mentioned. He, like many others, at that time believed the dogmatic assertions of the Sophister, whom he knew to be one of the most profligate of the Sect, to be those of folly. And at present, like many others, not conceiving how much it imports to history that facts of this kind should be authenticated by witnesses of known veracity, he sacrifices that grand object to the delicacy of not betraying what appears to have been but a confidential communication.

Bound by such scrupulosities, I am obliged to pass over many such anecdotes, that would show the Sophisters entrusting the secrets of their plots, and foretelling as clearly as Bergier did the downfall of Kings and the triumph of Philosophy. I will consent even to suppress the name of a French nobleman who, resident in Normandy, received the following letter: "Monsieur le Comte, do not deceive yourself. This is not a sudden storm. The Revolution is made and consummated. It has been preparing for these last fifty years, and that by some of the greatest geniuses in Europe. It has its abettors *in every cabinet*. There will be no other Aristocracy but that of the mind, and you certainly will have a greater claim to that than any body else."—This letter was written, a few days after the taking of the Bastille, by Alfonse le Roi, a physician. It needs no comment.

It is now time to call my reader's attention to that other Le Roi whom we have mentioned in the first part of our Memoirs. He is not the vain Sophister glorying in his plots, not a Condorcet, a La Metherie, a Gudin, or an Alfonse, who exultingly behold the triumph of Philospy in the crimes perpetrated and in the plots framed against the Altar and the Throne. No, this is the shamefaced and repenting adept, whom sorrow and remorse oblige to reveal a secret bursting from him in the agony of grief. But both the repentant and the proud adept perfectly agree in their evidence. For it would be a strange error to believe, that the declaration of Le Roi and the object of his remorse were confined to the Antichristian Conspiracy. At the period when he made his declaration neither the constitution nor the oath of apostacy had been decreed. It had not as yet been proposed to plunder and profane the temples, and to abolish the public worship. No blow had been given to the symbol of Christianity. All was prepared and daily starting into existence; but as yet the assembly had only trespassed against the political authority and the rights of their Sovereign. It was at the sight of these first crimes that Le Roi is reproached with the miserable effects of his school; and it was to this reproach he answered, *To whom do you say so? I know it but too well, and I shall die of grief and remorse.* When he disclosed all the heinousness of the plot framed by his secret academy at the Hotel d'Holbach, when he declares that it was there that the Conspiracy, whose dire effects they then beheld, had been formed and carried on; the plots which he detests are those that he sees attacking the Throne. If he declares those at the same time which had been formed against the Altar, it is because they had been the forerunners of the above, because it was necessary to show that the hatred which the people had conceived for their King, arose from that which had been instilled into them against their God. Thus while the declaration of this unhappy adept authenticates the conspiracy of the Sophisters against Religion, it equally demonstrates that contrived against the Throne.

It would be in vain to object that this unhappy man loved his King; he calls all present to witness that he is attached to the person of Lewis XVI; how could he then join in a conspiracy against him? But it is in vain, all is consistent, all is combined in this mind racked with remorse. This unhappy Secretary of the Conspiring Academy might have loved the person of the Monarch, but detested Monarchy, detested it at least as it existed, and in the light in which his masters had taught him to consider it, that is to say, as irreconcilable with their principles of Equality, Liberty, and Sovereignty of the people. We shall see hereafter, that opinions differed very much in this secret academy. Some wished to have a King, or at least to preserve the appearance of one in the new projected order of things; others, and they were to carry the day, objected to the very name or any appearance of Royalty, and both parties were unanimous in their attacks against Royalty as then existing. The one wished for a Revolution partly combined of Montesquieu's system, partly of Jean Jaques's. The other wished to establish it on the consequences which Jean Jaques had deduced from Montesquieu's principles. But both were leagued in Rebellion, and both conspired to bring about a Revolution. The repenting adept wanted a half Revolution, nor did he believe that the people, when put in motion, would proceed to those excesses which he detested. He flattered himself that the Conspiring Philosophers who stirred up the populace would be able to direct its motions; that they would inspire this populace with a proper respect for the person and even for the dignity of a Prince whom he loved and respected as a Frenchman and a Courtier, while as a Sophister he dethroned him. This is all that his remorse and his protestations of attachment for the person of Lewis XVI can indicate. He wished to make him a King subservient to the views and systems of the Sophisters, and he reduced the unfortunate Monarch to be the object of the licentious outrages of the populace; such are the real causes of his grief and remorse.

But the more this remnant of affection for his King appears in his declaration, the more it corroborates his avowal. It is not without cause that a man accuses himself of having pierced the bosom of the person he loves, or of having been concerned in a conspiracy against a Monarch whose Throne he with regret beholds menaced with ruin. People do not accuse themselves of crimes which they detest. Let us weigh the declaration of the repenting adept. What has Condorcet, proud and vainly exulting in the Conspiracy of Philosophism against the Throne, told us, which the unhappy Le Roi sinking under shame and remorse has not confirmed?

The haughty adept tells us, that of the disciples of Voltaire and Montesquieu, that is to say, of all the principal authors of that impiety and sophisticated polity of the age, a School or Sect was formed, uniting and combining their labors and their writings to effectuate the successive overthrow of the Religion of Christ and of the Thrones of Kings. The repentant adept shows us these same disciples of Voltaire, Montesquieu, and Jean Jaques, uniting and coalescing under the fictitious name of Œconomists at the Hotel d'Holbach; and he says it was there that the adepts dedicated their labors and their lucubrations to the perversion of the public opinion on the sacred subjects of Religion and the Rights of the Throne. "Most of those works (his declaration says) which have appeared for a long time past against *religion, morality, and government*, were ours, or those of Authors devoted to us. They were composed by the members or by the orders of the society."[11]—The unhappy Le Roi not only says against religion and morality, but also against *government*; and had he not said it, the one would be the natural consequence of the other; for the greatest part of the writings issued from this club of the Baron D'Holbach unite both objects. Soon we shall see them equally aiming at the overthrow of the Throne and of the Altar. They were the same Sophisters who had combined in one and the same plot the destruction of both.

The adept Condorcet complacently dwells on the art with which the coalesced Sophisters directed their attacks now at the Clergy then at Kings; covering truth with a veil which spared the eye that was too weak, artfully caressing religious opinions, to strike at them more surely, stirring up with still greater art Princes against the Priesthood, and the People against their Princes, fully resolved to overturn both the Altar of the Priest and the Throne of the Prince. Are not these the same stratagems which the repenting adept describes when he says, "before these impious and seditious books were sent to the press, they were delivered in at our office. There we revised and corrected them, added to or curtailed them according as *circumstances* required. When our Philosophy was too glaring for the times, or for the object of the work, we brought it to a lower tint; and when we thought that we might be more daring than the Author, we spoke more openly."[12] As to its object, its means, and its authors, we see the account of this double conspiracy perfectly coinciding, whether given by the haughty Condorcet or the repenting Le Roi. Both demonstrate this school conspiring against their God and against their King, flattering themselves with success against Monarchy, and generating that Revolution which was to overturn their Thrones, but not till that period when the faith of nations, long before disordered, weakened, and at length misled by the snares of the Sophisters, threatened but a slight resistance to their attacks either against the Altar or the Throne.

The enthusiastic pride of Condorcet, and the shame and remorse of the penitent Le Roi, certainly had never concerted this consistency in their depositions. The one, hardened in impiety and rebellion, preserves his secret till that period when he thinks he may violate it without endangering the success of his wicked pursuits. He enjoys at length, he glories in this success, and represents his accomplices as men to be revered as the benefactors of mankind. The other, as it were to extenuate his crime, the very instant his eyes are open to the heinousness of his past conduct, names those who have seduced him, discloses the place where they conspired, but to curse it; and throws all the weight of his crimes on his perfidious masters, on Voltaire, D'Alembert, Diderot, and their accomplices. He beholds these men who have seduced him in no other light than as monsters of rebellion. When such opposite passions, such different interests and sentiments agree in their depositions on the same conspiracy, on the same means, and on the same conspirators, truth can require no further proofs; it is evidence, it is demonstration itself.

Such then is the first problem of that Revolution so fatal to Monarchy. Voltaire forwards it with all his might in conspiring against his God, in spreading his doctrine of modern liberty, and in artfully attacking with his sarcastic wit and satire the pretended despots of his own country and of Europe. Montesquieu traced in his systems the first steps toward that disorganizing liberty. Jean Jaques adopts Montesquieu's principles and enlarges on their consequences. From the Equality of the *legislative* peope, he deduces the Equality and Liberty of the *sovereign* people; from the people essentially free and exercising the right of deposing their Kings at pleasure, he teaches the people to govern without them. The disciples of Voltaire, Montesquieu, and Jean Jaques, united and coalesced in their secret academy, league also in their oaths; and of those oaths that of crushing Christ and of annihilating Kings form but one. Had the proofs of these plots been supported neither by the boasting of the haughty Sophister exulting in success, nor by the declaration of the penitent adept ready to expire at the sight of such successes, still what we have to unfold of this mazy coalition, would equally demonstrate both its existence and its object from the publicity of the means employed by the Sect.

1. Spirit of Laws, Chap. 6, Book XI.
2. Chap. 7, Book XI.
3. Esquisse d'un tableau historique de l'esprit humain, 9 Epoque.
4. Of the Republic, by Condorcet, an. 1791.
5. Of the Republic, by Condorcet, epoch 10.
6. To D'Alembert, 27 March, 1773, Vol. 69, Let. 101, P. 170.
7. Observations on Experimental Philosophy and Natural History, January 1790. Preliminary Discourse.
8. *Idem*, January 1791, page 150.
9. Supplement to the Social Contract, Chap. 2, Part III.
10. Gen. Correspondence.
11. See Part the 1st of these Memoirs, P. 343 [p. 155, Ed.].
12. See Part the 1st of these Memoirs, page 325 [p. 149, Ed.].

CHAP. V.

Fourth Step of the Conspiracy against Kings.

Inundation of Antimonarchical Books.

Fresh Proofs of the Conspiracy.

THE very fact of the Conspiracy against Monarchy having been carried on by the same men and in the same secret academy where the Antichristian Conspiracy had been debated and conducted with such unrelenting fury, will induce the reader to suppose that many of the artifices employed against the Altar were equally directed against the Throne. The most fatal attack on Christianity, and on which the Sophisters had bestowed their chief attention, was that which they made with the greatest success to imbue the minds of the people with the spirit of insurrection and revolt. Nothing proves this with more certainty than the care with which they combined their attacks against the Throne with those against the Altar, in that inundation of Antichristian writings which we have seen flowing like a torrent through every class of society. This second inundation of Antimonarchical writings, by which the Sophisters were in hopes of perverting that sentiment of confidence and respect, which the people had for their Sovereign, into hatred and contempt, was only a continuation of those means which they had employed against their God. These writings are issued from the same manufactory, composed by the same adepts, recommended and reviewed by the same chiefs, spread with the same profusion, hawked about from the town to the village by the same agents of Holbach's Club, sent free of cost to the country school-masters, that all classes of people from the highest to the most indigent might imbibe the venom of their Sophistry. As it is certain that these writings were the grand means of the Sophisters in their conspiracy against Christ, so it is equally certain, that these same productions, monstrous digests of the principles of impiety and of those of rebellion, are irrefragable proofs that these same Sophisters had combined the most impious of plots against their God with the most odious machinations against all Kings.

One only difference is to be observed, that the first productions of the Secret Society were not so strongly tainted with the blast of rebellion. The grand attack against Monarchy was reserved until the sect should have reason to expect that their principles of impiety had prepared the multitude for their declamations against Royalty, as they had gradually swoln in those against the pretended superstitions of Christianity. Most of those violent declamations against Sovereigns are posterior not only to Montesquieu's and Rousseau's systems, but even to the year 1761, when we beheld Voltaire reproaching the Sophisters with seeing every thing topsy-turvy, because in some of their writings they trenched upon the Royal Prerogative.

The Philosophers of the Encyclopedia had only alluded very faintly, in their first edition of that incoherent compilation, to the principles of that Equality and Liberty which have been since so much extolled by the enemies of Royalty, though it was a cause of reproach to D'Alembert, that even in his preliminary discourse, *he sees but a barbarous right in the inequality of stations*; and though the Royalist or even the Subject of every state, of every Government, might have objected to the insertion in the Encyclopedia of that proposition which the Jacobins have since so often repeated, "that the subjection in which every man is born with respect to his father or to his Prince, has never been looked upon as a tie binding unless by his own consent."[1] In short, though the Encyclopedists were the first to enter the lists in defense of Montesquieu, yet the fear of alarming the public authorities make them act with great circumspection during many years on this subject. It was necessary to wait for new editions. That of Iverdun was still too early; and it was in the edition of Geneva that these revolutionary principles first make their appearance. Lest they should escape the notice of the reader, Diderot had repeated and condensed the poison, had decked them with all the array of Sophistry in at least three different articles.[2] There neither Montesquieu, Jean Jaques, nor all the admirers of the legislative and sovereign multitude, could have cavilled at a single link in this brilliant concatenation of Sophisms. This perhaps might have given rise to those fears which Voltaire expresses in his correspondence with D'Alembert, lest this edition should not obtain the free circulation which he wished for in France. These fears, however, were ill grounded, for it became the most common in use; but at that period, that is to say, in 1773, the Conspirators had begun the inundation of those Antimonarchical Writings from the secret academy, which the slightest examination will prove to have had no other tendency, as Le Roi has since declared, than to overthrow religion, morals, and *government*, and particularly those governments where the chief power is invested in the Monarch.

In order to show their concert on this last object as we have on the other two, let us suppress, if possible, the indignation which must naturally arise on reciting the lessons of the Sophisters. Let us say to all subjects of Monarchies, to all subjects of Aristocracies, and even of all Republicans not as yet jacobinized, 'If you tremble at the sight of revolutions which menace your government, learn at least to know the sect which prepares these revolutions by means of the principles which it artfully insinuates.'[3]

All religions and all governments are equally doomed to destruction by the Sophisters. They wish to establish every where a new order of things both in church and state. We see them all, or nearly all, teaching us, that there scarcely exists a single state on the whole globe where the rights of the equal and sovereign people are not most intolerably infringed. If we are to believe their writings and assertions, almost literally repeated by a swarm of these Sophisters, "ignorance, fear, chance, folly, superstition, and the imprudent gratitude of nations, have every where directed the establishment as well as the reformation of governments." These have been the sole origin of all societies, and of all empires which have existed until the present day. Such is the assertion of the *Social System* which the secret academy published as a Continuation of the Social Contract of Jean Jaques; such are the lessons taught in the *Essay on Prejudices*, which they gave to the public under the supposed name of Dumarsais; such again is the doctrine of the *Oriental Despotism* which they attributed to Boulanger; such in fine are the principles of the *System of Nature*, which Diderot, with the chosen of the elect, after having given it existence, so carefully seek to circulate.[3]

Jean Jaques, teaching *that man is born free, and yet that he is every where in chains*, asks *how this happens*; and answers, that *he is ignorant*.[4] His disciples of the secret academy were become either more learned or more daring.

The most moderate of these Sophisters, or at least those who, under the standard of the Œconomist Du Quesnay, wished to appear so, did not give the people a more flattering account of the origin or of the present state of their governments. "It must be owned," they tell us by the insipid pen of Dupont, "that the generality of nations still remain victims of an infinitude of crimes and calamities, which could not have happened if a well-conducted study on the law of nature, on moral justice, and on real and true politics, had enlightened the majority of intellects. Here prohibitions are extended even to thought; there nations, misled by the ferocious love of conquest, sacrifice the stock of which they stand most in need for the cultivation of their lands, to these plans of usurpation. Men are torn from their half-inhabited deserts, and the scattered riches which had been sparingly sown are seized for the purpose of shedding the blood of neighbouring states, and of multiplying elsewhere other deserts. On one side.... on the other....Elsewhere....Elsewhere...."

This fable picture is terminated by twenty or thirty lines of dots, leaving to the imagination of the reader to fill them up, or to tell us, as the gentle author will, "*Such is still the state of the world; such has always been the state of our Europe, and nearly of the whole globe.*"[5]

The reader will remark, that the men who broach such doctrines on Governments, and wish to instil them into the people, take care to insert them in those works which are peculiarly devoted to the instruction of country farmers. He will also remark how exactly they follow the steps of their master Jean Jaques. This latter, refusing to except England from the general sentence, that *man was every where in chains*, did not hesitate at saying, "The people of England deceive themselves when they fancy they are free: they are so, in fact, only during the interval between a dissolution of one Parliament and the election of another; for, as soon as a new one is elected, *they are again in chains and lose all their virtue as a people.* And thus, by the use they make of their few moments of liberty, they deserve to lose it."[6]

Reflecting adepts would have questioned Jean Jaques to know how his equal and sovereign people could enjoy a greater degree of Liberty than the English, and how it came to pass that they were not as much enslaved every where else as they were in their assemblies, since it was only in these assemblies that the people *could exercise their sovereignty*; and in these assemblies even their sovereignty was null, their acts were illegitimte and void unless they *had been convoked by the proper Magistrate*; since on all other occasions the sole duty of this sovereign people was to obey?[7] But our passive adepts preferred viewing the English Government in the light of one that was to be cried down with the rest. "Nations even that flatter themselves with being the best governed, such as England, for example, *have no further pleasure* but that of perpetually struggling against the Sovereign Power, and of rendering their natural imposts inadequate to the public expenditure.—Of seeing both their present and future revenues, the fortunes and mansions of their posterity, in short of half their island, sold and alienated by their representatives, &c.—England at this price, too dear by three fourths, forms a Republic, in which, luckily for her, *a couple of excellent laws* are to be found; but as to her constitution, notwithstanding all that Montesquieu has said to the contrary, it does not appear much to be envied."[8]

Our respect for that nation forbids us to continue our citations from this declamatory work.—What we have already quoted will suffice to show how much the Sophisters wished by means of these scurrilous harangues to persuade all nations, that, since the sovereignty of the people was so strangely violated even in England, and if it was necessary for her to overthrow her constitution to re-establish the people in their rights, how much greater must be the necessity of a Revolution for all other nations, being their sole hope of breaking their chains.

This was only an indirect attack of the Sophisters against Kings, under whose Government most nations live. Nor must the reader expect to see Philosophism circumscribing its effects to render every throne odious, within the narrow sphere of commenting on the seditious parts of Montesquieu, Jean Jaques, or Voltaire.

Montesquieu had represented prejudice as the prime mover of Monarchies. He had declared that it was very difficult for *the people to be virtuous* under that form of Government. Helvetius, sallying forth from his secret academy, and carrying these principles to greater lengths, exclaims, "The true *Monarchy* is no more than a constitution invented *to corrupt the morals of nations and to enslave them*; witness the Romans when they gave a King or a Despot to the Spartans and Britons."[9]

Jean Jaques had taught nations, that if *the authority of Kings* came from God, it was by the same channel through which *sickness* and other public scourges came.[10]—Reynal follows him to inform us, that "*these kings are wild beasts who devour nations.*"[11] A third Sophister presents himself who tells us, all "*your Kings are the first executioners of their subjects; and force and stupidity were the founders of their thrones.*"[12]—Another tells us, "Kings are like Saturn in the heathen Mythology, who devours his own children," others again say, "the Monarchical form of Government, placing such great force in the hands of one man, must by its very nature tempt him to abuse his power; and by that means, placing himself above the laws, he will exercise *Tyranny and Despotism*, which are the *two greatest calamities that can befall a state.*"[13] The most moderate of their declamations on Royalty supposes *too great a distance between the Sovereign and the Subject* for it ever to be looked upon as a wise Government;[14] and that if a King be absolutely necessary, we never should forget, that he only ought to be *the first Commissioner of the Nation.*[15]

But this necessity grieved the Sophisters to such a degree, that, to make their countrymen triumph over it, they incessantly repeat that France is under the yoke of *Despotism, whose peculiar property is to debase the mind and degrade the soul*; that their country even, governed by Kings, can find no remedy for its *misfortunes* but in falling *a prey to a foreign enemy*; that as long as they are swayed by the scepter of Kings, "they are *invincibly* and by the *very form of government brought down to brutal degradation*, and that it is in vain to diffuse light on *the French*, as it will only show them the misfortunes of Despotism without enabling them to withdraw from its oppression."

What they say to their countrymen they proclaim to all the nations of the earth. They have consecrated whole volumes to persuade them *that it is a pusillanimous fear alone that has created and still maintains Kings on their thrones.*[16] They proclaim to the English, the Spaniards, the Prussians, the Austrians, indiscriminately with the French, *that the people are as much slaves in Europe as they are in America*; that the only advantage *they enjoy over the Negroes is, that they may leave one chain to take another.* They proclaim that the *inequality of power* in any state whatever, and particularly the reunion of the supreme power in their chiefs, is *the height of folly*; that the spirit of *Liberty* and of *Independence* which cannot bear with a superior, much less with Kings and Sovereigns, *is the instinct of nature enlightened by reason.* They brandish that *parallel sword* which was to glide along the heads of Kings, and mow off those which *rose above the horizontal plane.*[17]

If nations, wise in experience, and despising the declamations of a seditious Philosophism, sought an asylum under the protection of a King, or if to crush anarchy they had extended the authority of the Monarch, it was then that one might behold the adepts exclaiming in their rage, "at this humiliating sight (of a nation of the North, of Sweden, re-establishing the rights of its Monarch), who is there that does not ask himself, *what then is man?* What is that profound and original sense of dignity with which he is supposed to be endowed? Is he then born for independence or for slavery? What, then, is that silly flock, called a nation. Mean populace! silly flock! What, content to groan when you ought to roar? Cowardly, stupid populace! since this perpetual oppression gives you no energy—since you are millions, and, nevertheless, suffer a dozen of children (called Kings) armed with little sticks (called scepters) to lead you as they please; obey, but submit without importuning us with your complaints, and learn to be unhappy, if you don't know how to be free."[18]

Had every nation murdered its Sovereign at the time when Philosophism broached such doctrine, what would they have done more than practise the lessons of the Sophisters? When we see that it was the very leaders of the Sect who held such language, an Helvetius or a Boulanger, a Diderot or a Raynal; when we know that it was those very productions in which such sentiments were advanced that endeared them to the Sect, what can we suppose was the meaning of this concert, of this union of the most celebrated adepts? What could be their plans? Where did they aim their blows, if not at the Throne as well as the Altar? Was it not against them that their rage was constantly let loose? What other Revolution did they meditate, if not that which buries the altar and the throne beneath the ruins of the state?

I know what is incumbent on History to add with respect to some of these Sophisters, to Raynal, for example. I know that when this adept beheld the Revolution, he shuddered at the sight of its excesses, that he even shed tears; and that when he appeared at the bar of the new Legislators, he dared reproach them with having o'erstepped the limits which Philosophy had prescribed. But this apparition of Raynal at the bar, or rather this comic scene which had been vainly prepared by the humbled and jealous Revolutionists, in opposition to the Revolutionists triumphant in their successes, only furnishes us with a new proof of the plots of the Sophisters.—For it was in their name that Raynal dares address the new Legislators, saying, "That is not what we wished for; you have broken through the Revolutionary line which we had traced."[19] What can such language mean, and are we not authorized to answer the man who holds it, 'These rebels do not follow the line which you and your sages had traced for the Revolution! There was then a Revolution which you and your sages had meditated and planned. Are the plans of Revolutions against Kings carried on without the plots of rebellion? Could those Revolutions which you planned differ from those which your lessons on Equality and Liberty prognosticated! or, when you brand every nation which suffers itself to be governed by its lawful King, or which *contents itself with groaning when it ought to roar* against its Sovereign, with the appellation of *a silly flock of cowards?*—And when these nations begin to roar why should you complain? So far from having transgressed the bounds you had prescribed, our Legislative Jacobins have not yet attained the goal you had pointed out. The *parallel sword* has not yet glided over the heads of Kings; wait then till there shall not exist a single King upon earth; and even then, so far from having overshot your doctrines, Jacobinism will only have followed them to the very letter.'

To such an answer, which Raynal so richly deserved, the National Assembly might have added, "Before you complain, begin by thanking us for the justice we have rendered you. One of our members,[20] friendly to Philosophers like you, has represented to us the injustice of Kings whom you had set at defiance, he has shown us in your person the sacred liberty of

Philosophy oppressed by Despotism. At the very name of Philosopher, we discovered our master, the worthy rival of Voltaire, D'Alembert, Jean Jaques, and of so many others, whose writings and concert hastened our successes. We have listened to the prayer of your friends, we have restored you to Liberty under the eye of that very King, whom you taught us to revile; go and peacefully enjoy the advantages of friendship, and of the decrees of the national assembly, while it will continue to run the course which you have marked out."

Thus even the vain protestations of humiliated Philosophism, reduced to blush at the excesses naturally attendant on its doctrines, every thing in short concurs to demonstrate the existence of their Conspiracies.

But partial attacks of the adepts are not sufficient; the reader must behold them encouraging each other, pressing the execution of their plots, and the insurrection of the people against their Sovereigns. Let him hear the same Raynal convoking the adepts, and calling out to them, "Sages of the earth, *Philosophers of* ALL NATIONS, make those mercenary slaves blush who are always ready to exterminate their fellow-citizens at the command of their masters. Make nature and humanity rise in their souls against such a perversion of the social laws. Learn that *liberty is the gift of God*, but *authority the invention of man*. Bare to the light *those mysteries which encompass the universe with chains and darkness*; and may the people, learning how much their credulity has been imposed upon, avenge the glory of the human species."[21]

The art and solicitude with which the Sophisters seek to preclude Kings from the succour they might one day have drawn from the fidelity of their troops, is worthy of attention. We see in these discourses by what means the French army first imbibed those principles which have been so often and so successfully employed by the revolutionists to restrain and damp their courage and their activity. We see how they succeeded in representing as rebels so many of their brethren, against whom humanity, nature, and the social laws, forbad them to turn their arms, though it were to defend the life and authority of their lawful Sovereign. We see these Sophisters, bearing down all opposition, and preparing a free course for all the fury of that horde of rebels or of pretended patriots, that they might brandish, without fear, the hatchet and the pike. The reader may observe them disposing the armies meanly to betray their Sovereigns under the pretence of fraternizing with rebels and assassins.

To these villanous precautions, which destroyed in the rebels the fear of the Royal forces, let us add the pains they took to rob Kings of what support religion and Heaven itself might have given them, that affectation of extinguishing all remorse in rebellion, and of pointing out the God who protects Kings as an object of detestation. How could it be possible for us to mistake the double tendency of doctrines at once dictated by the phrenzy of Rebellion and of Impiety!

"It is only in a numerous, fixed, and civilized state of society, that, wants daily multiplying, and interests differing, Governments have been obliged to have recourse to laws, public forms of worship, and uniform systems of religion. It is then that the governors of the people invoke that *fear of invisible powers, to restrain them, to render them docile, and to oblige them to live in peace*. It is thus that morality and policy form a part of the religious system. *Chiefs of nations*, often superstitious themselves, little acquainted with their own interests, or versed in sound morality, and blind to the real agents, believe they secure their own authority as well as the happiness and peace of society at large, by immerging their subjects in superstition, by threatening them with their invisible phantoms (of their divinity) and by treating them like children, who are quieted by means of fables and chimeras. Under the shadow of such surprizing inventions, and of which the chiefs themselves are often dupes, transmitting them from generation to generation, Sovereigns believe themselves excused from seeking any farther instruction. They neglect the laws, they enervate themselves in luxury, and are slaves to their caprices. They confide in the gods for the government of their people. They deliver over the instruction of their subjects to priests who are to render them very devout and submissive, and teach them from their earliest youth to tremble both before the visible and invisible gods."

"It is thus that nations are kept in a perpetual awe by their governors, and are only restrained by vain chimeras. When the happiness of man shall become the object of real investigation, it will be with *the gods of heaven* that the reform must begin. *No good system of government can be founded on a despotic god; he will always make tyrants of his representatives.*"

It is possible to combine their attacks in a more villanous manner against the God of Heaven and the powers of the earth? Tyrants or Kings have invented a god, and this god and his priests support alone the authority of these Kings and Tyrants. This perfidious assertion is perpetually repeated throughout the famous System of Nature, and this is the work which the secret academy disseminates with the greatest profusion. But neither Diderot nor his associates will hesitate at going to much greater lengths, notwithstanding the height to which they had carried their hatred in this famous system. If we are to believe them, all the vices and crimes of Tyrants, the oppression and misfortunes of the People, all originate in the attributes of the justice of the God of the Gospel. That God of *vengeance*, so terrible to the wicked; that God, the *remunerator*, the consolation, and the hope of the just man, is in the eyes of the Sophister *no more than a chimerical and capricious being, solely useful to Kings and Priests*. It is because Priests are perpetually stunning both Kings and People with this God of *vengeance* and *remuneration* that Priests are wicked, Kings despotic and tyrannic, in short the people oppressed. It is on that account, we see that *Princes even the most abjectly superstitious are no more than robbers; too proud to be humane, too great to be just*; and who are inventing for their own use a particular code of perfidy, violence, and treachery. It is on this account, that nations, degraded by superstition, will suffer *children*, or Kings *made giddy with flattery, to govern them with an iron rod*. With this God of vengeance and remuneration, *these children,* or foolish kings *transformed into gods, are masters of the law. It lies in their breast to decide what is just or unjust*. With this

God *their licentiousness has no bounds, because they are certain of impunity.—Accustomed to no other fear but that of God, they act as if they had nothing to fear.* This God of vengeance and remuneration is the cause *why history swarms with wicked and vicious potentates.*[22]

In transcribing these short extracts, we have abridged prolix chapters tending to infuse that hatred for God and kings into the minds of the people, which animated the leading adepts. Nobody could better express to what degree he was inflamed by it than Diderot himself. We have seen Voltaire, in a moment of phrenzy, wishing to see the last Jesuit strangled with the entrails of the last Jansenist. The same frantic rage had inspired Diderot with the same idea on Priests and Kings; and it was well known in Paris, that in his fits of rage he would exclaim, Ah! *when shall I see the last King strangled with the bowels of the last Priest!*[23]

The reader may be surprised at hearing that the System of Nature was not the most virulent production which the Club of Holbach had published to incite the people to rebellion and to persuade them to consider their Kings and Princes in no other light than as monsters to be crushed. The adept or adepts who had composed the *Social System* availed themselves of the impression Diderot's work had made. They are more reserved on Atheism, only to be more virulent against Kings. The object of this work is to persuade the people that they are the victims of a long state of warfare, which ended by throwing them under the yoke of Kings. But they were not to abandon all hope of breaking their chains, and even of loading their Kings with them, though they had been hitherto unsuccessful. There the imagination is worked upon, and the meanest subject is taught to say to his Sovereign, "We have proved the weakest, we have submitted to force; *but should we ever become the strongest, we would wrest that usurped power from you* whenever you exercised it for our unhappiness. It is only by your attention to our prosperity that you can make us forget *the infamous titles* by which you reign over us. *If we are not strong enough to shake off the yoke we will only bear it with horror.* You shall find an enemy in each of your slaves, and every instant you shall tremble on the thrones which you have unlawfully usurped."[24]

Such menaces will certainly be looked upon as the last stage of their conspiring fury. Nevertheless they found a higher tone; and, to teach nations to shudder at the very name of Monarchy, they roar like monsters.

Many years before the French Revolution their productions had teemed with every thing that a Petion, a Condorcet, or a Marat could have invented in their frantic rage against Sovereigns to excite the populace to bring the head of the unfortunate Lewis XVI to the scaffold; since many years after having told us, *that truth and not politeness should be the chief object of man*, to practise this doctrine they address Kings, saying, "*Ye tigers, deified by other tigers, you expect to pass to immortality?* Yes, answer they, *but as objects of execration.*"[25]

With the same excess of phrenzy, commenting on the axiom,

> Some lucky soldier was the first of Kings,

full of his Voltaire, like the Pythoness inspired by the devil, from the summit of his fiery tripod the same adept, addressing himself to all nations, tells them, "Thousands of executioners crowned with laurel and wreaths of flowers, returning from their expeditions, carry about in triumph an *idol* which they call *King*, Emperor, Sovereign. They crown this idol and prostrate themselves before it, and then, at the sound of instruments, and of repeated, senseless and barbarous acclamations, they declare it in future to be the *Sovereign Director* of all the bloody scenes which are to take place in the realm, and to be *the first executioner of the nation.*"

Then, swelling his chest, foaming at the mouth, and with haggard eyes he makes the air resound with the following frightful declamation:

"*To the pretended masters of the earth*, scourges of mankind, illustrious tyrants of your equals, *Kings, Princes, Monarchs, Chiefs, Sovereigns*, all you, in fine, who, raising yourselves on the throne, *and above your equals*, have lost all *ideas of equality*, equity, *sociability* and truth; in whom *sociability* and goodness, the beginnings of the most common virtues, have not even shown themselves, I cite you all at the tribunal of reason. If this miserable globe, silently moving through the etherial space, drags away with it millions of unhappy beings fixed to its surface, and fettered with the bonds of opinion; if this globe, I say, has been a prey to you, and if you still continue to devour this sad inheritance, it is not to the wisdom of your predecessors, nor to the virtues of the first inhabitants, that you are indebted for it; but *to stupidity, to fear, to barbarity, to perfidy, to superstition. Such are your titles.* I am not the person who pronounces against you; it is the oracle of ages, it is the annals of history which depose against you. Open them, they will assuredly furnish you with better information, and the numerous monuments of our miseries and of our errors will be proofs which neither political pride nor fanaticism can controvert.

"Descend from your thrones, and, laying aside both sceptre and crown, go and question the lowest of your subjects; ask him what *he really loves, and what he hates the most:* he will undoubtedly answer, that he really *loves but his equals, and that he hates his masters.*"[26]

It is thus that, assuming every tone from that of the epigram, pamphlet, romance, system, or tragic sentence, to the declamations of enthusiasm, or the roaring of rage, Voltaire's and Montesquieu's school, so well described by Condorcet, had succeeded in inundating all France and all Europe with works naturally tending to efface from the earth the very memory of a King.

To place in their true light the intention and the concert of the Sophisters, the Historian must never lose sight of the den from whence these productions were issued, and of the art with which and the men by whom they were spread from the palace to the cottage: By the Secret Society of the Hotel D'Holbach, in Paris; by the numerous editions in the provincial towns; by the hawkers in the country; by D'Alembert's office of instruction, and tutors, in wealthy families; and by the country school-masters in the villages, and among the workmen and day-labourers.[27] In their various attacks, let him remark the uniformity of their principles, of their sentiments, and of their hatred; and let him particularly remember, that the same authors who declaim most virulently against Kings, had already distinguished themselves by their hatred against religion. Should he hesitate at declaring the Sophisters of impiety to be also the Sophisters of rebellion; should the very evidence of the conspiracy lead him to doubt of its reality; in that case let us not refuse to solve even the doubts of the historian, and may the very objections be turned into fresh demonstrations!

I feel that it may be objected to me, that my proofs differ in their nature from those which I had chiefly drawn from the very correspondence of the Conspirators. In answer, it may be remarked, that if any cause of surprize existed, it would not be, that the letters of the Conspirators made public should contain nothing respecting the conspiracy against Kings; but it would be, on the contrary, that they had furnished us with so much evidence. We may be surprized at the assurance of the editors of those letters, who show us Voltaire conjuring D'Alembert not to betray his secret on Kings, who show us Voltaire panting after Republics; Voltaire bewailing the departure of those adepts who were expounding the new catechism of Republican Liberty in Paris itself; Voltaire praised by D'Alembert for the art he displays in combating Kings or pretended Despots, and in preparing Revolutions and their boisterous scenes; Voltaire, in fine, regretting that they were still too distant for him to flatter himself with living to see them. It is this same correspondence which points out D'Alembert furious at his *hands being tied*, and at not being able to deal the same blows on the pretended Despots as Voltaire did, but seconding him at least with his wishes in this rebellious warfare. When all these letters were made public by Condorcet and the other editors in 1785, Lewis XVI was still on the throne, and the Revolution at some distance. They had reason to fear the discovery of their plots; and it is easy to see, that many of the letters had been suppressed. Most certainly Condorcet, and the other adepts, must have had even then a strange confidence in their success, not to have suppressed many more. Besides, had these letters been entirely silent as to the Conspiracy against Kings, could even that silence invalidate the avowals of Condorcet, and of so many other adepts? The same artifices, the same calumnies, the same wishes against the Throne being combined with those against the Altar, in the productions of the Sect, could that silence weaken the evidence of the common plot for the destruction of both?

But if these plots were so visible, it will be said, are not the Magistrates to be blamed for their negligence and silence? How was it possible that these Conspirators could have escaped the severity of the laws? Here it would be sufficient to recall the favorite maxim of the Conspirators, *Strike, but hide your hand!* It would suffice, were we merely to repeat Condorcet's words when, after having exposed in the clearest terms the double conspiracy, the labors, and the concert of the Philosophers against the Altar and the Throne, he adds, that "the *Chiefs* of the Philosophers *always had the art of escaping vengeance, though they exposed themselves to hatred; and of escaping persecution, though sufficiently conspicuous to suffer no diminution of their glory.*"[28]

But this silence of the Magistracy is a false imputation. The Conspirators may have concealed themselves from the tribunals, but the Conspiracy was not on that account less evident to the sight of the Magistracy; and juridical denunciations will give new force to our demonstrations. If such proofs are necessary for the Historian, let us transcribe the words of a most celebrated magistrate; let us hearken to Mr. Seguier, Attorney-General of the Parliament of Paris, denouncing on the 18th of August 1770 this very Conspiracy of the Philosophers.

"Since the extirpation of heresies which have disturbed the peace of the church," said the eloquent Magistrate, "we have seen a system rising out of darkness, far more dangerous in its consequences than those ancient errors, always crushed as fast as they appeared. *An impious and daring sect has raised its head in the midst of us, and it has decorated its false wisdom with the name of Philosophy.* Under this authoritative title its disciples pretend to all knowledge. Its sectaries have taken upon themselves to be the instructors of mankind. *Liberty in thinking* is their cry, and this cry has resounded from the northern to the southern pole. *With one hand they have sought to shake the Throne, and with the other to overturn the Altar.* Their object is to abolish all belief, and to instill new ideas into the mind of man on *civil and religious institutions*; and this revolution may be said to have taken place; the proselytes of the sect have multiplied, and their maxims are spread far and wide. *Kingdoms have felt their ancient basis totter*, and nations, surprized to find their principles annihilated, have asked each other, by what strange fatality they became so different from themselves."

"Those who by their talents should have enlightened their contemporaries, have become the leaders of these unbelievers; they have hoisted the banner of revolt, and have thought to add to their celebrity by this spirit of independence; numberless obscure scribblers, unable to attain to celebrity by their abilities, have had the same presumption. In fine, religion can number nearly as many declared enemies, as literature can boast of pretended Philosophers. *And Government should tremble* at tolerating in its bosom such an inflammatory Sect of unbelievers, whose sole object appears to be to *stir up the people to rebellion, under pretence of enlightening them.*"[29]

The formal denunciation of the double Conspiracy of the Sophisters was grounded on the peculiar attention which they paid to the propagation of their impious and regicide principles in their daily productions, and more particularly in those which this great lawyer presented to the Court as most deserving of animadversion.

Foremost among those productions stood a work of Voltaire's, the honorary president of Holbach's club. It was one of the most impious of all, and bore the title of "*God and Men.*" The second, *Christianity Unveiled*, had been written by Damilaville, a zealous adept of that club. The third, the pretended *Critical Examination*, was published by this same club under the name of Freret, as the repenting Secretary Le Roi declared. The fourth was the famous *System of Nature* written by Diderot, and two others of this secret academy.—So true it is, that most of that pestilential blight both of Impiety and Rebellion which has overspread the greatest part of Europe, proceeded from that den of Conspirators.[30]

"From these different productions," continued the Magistrate, "a system of the most flagitious doctrine may be collected, which *invincibly proves*, that their proposed object is not to destroy the Christian Religion only—Impiety has not limited its plan of innovation solely to its dominion over the minds of men. *Its restless and enterprizing genius, averse to all dependence, aspires at the overthrow of every political institution, and its wishes will only then be fulfilled when it shall have thrown the Legislative and Executive Powers into the hands of the People, when it shall have destroyed the necesssary inequality of ranks and stations, when it shall have reviled the Majesty of Kings, and have rendered the authority precarious and dependent on the caprice of a blind multitude; when, in fine, by these astonishing changes, it shall have immersed the whole world in the horrors of Anarchy with all its concomitant evils.*"

To these denunciations of the public Magistrate may be added those of the general assemblies of the Clergy, those of a great many Bishops in their pastoral letters, those, in short, of the Sorbonne and of every religious orator or author, who never ceased refuting the Sophisters of the day, whether in their theses, their writings, or from the pulpit. It would be vain to say, that these denunciations were only made by people seeking to strengthen their own cause by confounding it with that of Kings. But are we not to hearken to an adversary even, when he speaks for us as well as for himself, and when he produces proofs? It would be imprudence in the extreme not to hearken, and even second him, when he comes and says, 'You are leagued with my greatest enemies, but they are equally yours; I forewarn you of their hostile intentions; and if they have conspired against me, it is only to ascertain the success of the plots they have formed against you.'[31] It would have been easy to discriminate, whether the Clergy denouncing these conspiracies were actuated by self-interest or the love of truth; a slight examination of the proofs adduced in testimony of their denunciations would have sufficed. These proofs were all drawn from the productions of the Sect, from productions replete with sarcastic declamations and calumny against Sovereigns, with invitations to the people to rebellion, sowing in the same page the seeds of Anarchy with those of Impiety. And these were evidently the two-fold productions of the same men, of the same academy of authors, of the same conspirators. Were not the Clergy then authorized to point out these same Sophisters as brandishing the torch, on one side to spread the blaze throughout the temple, on the other to kindle the flames which were to reduce the royal crown and sceptre to ashes?[32] Might they not be said to have conspired more desperately against the Throne than against the Altar; and might not the latter Conspiracy have been merely a preparatory step to the completion of the former? So far then from excluding the destruction of the Throne from their wishes, and confining them to the overthrow of religion, say that to overturn Government was their chief object: examine and compare their doctrines, behold their concert, their constancy, their assurance, and then candidly pronounce.

But the evidence of the Clergy shall, if it be required, be thrown aside as suspicious, though it is now too late to attaint it with falsehood. Will the testimony of a man who certainly had every reason to spare the Sect also be thrown aside? I have heard it asked, How it was possible, since the Sophisters were said to have conspired against the Throne, that Frederic II, the Royal Sophister, could have been deceived by and could have leagued during so long a time with the sworn enemies of his Throne, in short with the Sophisters of Rebellion? But she an objection will only serve to throw new light on the Conspiracy. Let the Royal Sophister be the accuser, let him cover his Sophistical Masters with ridicule. The inveteracy of his hatred against religion, his protection of the irreligious Encyclopedists, all his conduct in short, will corroborate his testimony when he paints these Sophisters as empty sages conspiring equally against the Altar and the Throne. And the time came when Frederic II perceived that his dear Philosophers, by initiating him into their mysteries of Impiety, had let him into but half their secret; that by employing his power to crush Christ, they had planned the destruction of his throne and the extirpation of Monarchy. Frederic was not the repenting adept, like the unhappy Le Roi, for his soul was too deeply immersed in impiety; but he was certainly ashamed of having been so strangely duped. Indignation and revenge succeed his admiration, and he blushes at having been so intimate with men who had made him their tool to undermine that power which he was most jealous of preserving.

He became the public accuser of those very Encyclopedists who owed the greatest part of their success to his protection. He warned Kings, that the grand object of those Sophisters was to deliver them over to the multitude, and to teach nations *that subjects may exercise the right of deposing their Sovereign when they are displeased with him.*[33] He gives notice to the Kings of France, that their Conspiracy is more particularly aimed at them.

The denunciation is clearly and formally expressed in the following terms: "*The Encyclopedists reform all Governments. France* (according to their plans) *is to form a great Republic, and a Mathematician is to be its Legislator.*—Mathematicians will govern it, and work all the operations *of the new Republic* by fluxions.—*This Republic* is to live in perpetual peace, and support itself without an army."

This ironic and sarcastic style was by no means in Frederic's natural disposition. The repute of the pretended wisdom of the Sophisters had given weight to the adepts, and contributed to the seduction of the people; and contempt was the most powerful weapon that could be employed against them. It is on this account that he represents these pretended sages as puffed up with their own merits and their ridiculous pride. But whatever may be his style, it is to guard Kings and Nations against their plots that he writes. "The Encyclopedists (says he) are a set of pretended Philosophers who have lately started into existence. They look upon themselves as superior to every school which antiquity has produced. *To the effrontery of the Cynic* they add the *impudence* of uttering every paradox their brain can invent. They are a set of *presumptuous* men, who never will own themselves to be in the wrong. According to their principles, the sage can never be mistaken, he is the only enlightened person: It is from him that the light emanates which is to dissipate the dreary darkness into which the silly and blind multitude have been deluded. And God knows how they enlighten them. At one time it is by unfolding the *origin of Prejudices;* at another, it is by a book *on the Mind*, or a *System of Nature*; in short, there is no end to them. A set *of puppies*, whether from fashion or an air they assume, call themselves their disciples. They affect to copy them, and take upon themselves to be the Deputy Governors of Mankind!"

While painting in such colours the pretensions and ridiculous pride of both Masters and Scholars, Frederic declares that *the madhouse* would be their most proper habitation, *where they might legislate over their crazy equals*; or else, to show the ignorance of their systems, and what innumerable disasters they would engender, he wishes "that some province which deserved *a severe punishment* should be delivered over to them. Then they would learn, says he, by experience, after having thrown every thing topsy-turvy, that they were a set of ignorant fellows; they would learn that to criticize is easy, but that the art of criticism is difficult; and above all, that no one is so apt to *talk nonsense as he that meddles with what he does not understand.*"[34]

Frederic, in support of regal authority, would sometimes lay aside his epigrammatic style, and think it incumbent on him to condescend to the refutation of the gross calumnies which his Sophistical Masters had invented against the Throne. It is thus that we see him refuting the System of Nature and the *Essay on Prejudice*, which latter the secret academy had published under the name of Dumarsais. There he principally devotes himself to exposing the cunning of the Sophisters; he shows with what wicked art the Conspirators, calumniating the Sovereigns and the Pontiffs, only seek to instigate the hatred of all nations against them. Among others we may distinguish the author of the System of Nature, who in an especial manner has undertaken to disparage all Sovereigns. "*I can venture to assert,*" he says, "*that the Clergy have never spoken to Princes all that nonsense* which the author pretends. If ever they may have represented Kings as the images of the Deity, it was doubtless only in an hyperbolical sense, to guard them by the comparison against any abuse of their authority, and to warn them to be just and beneficent, that they may imitate the general attributes given to the Deity by all nations. The author has dreamed, that treaties have been made between the Sovereign and the Ecclesiastic, in which Princes had agreed to honour and sanction the power of the Clergy provided the latter preached submission to the people. I will venture to affirm, that this is a shallow invention, and that nothing could be more ridiculous or void of foundation, than the supposition of such a fact."[35]

Though Frederic expresses himself thus on the Ecclesiastics, still the reader is not to suppose him more favourable to their cause. On the contrary, his Antichristian prejudices blind him to such a degree, that he does not so much blame the Sophisters for attacking Religion, as for having done it unskilfully; he even points out the weapons with which he wishes it had been assailed. But the more inveterate his hatred against Christianity, the more demonstrative are the proofs he alledges against those from whom he had imbibed it, and of their plots against the Throne. He pardons their attacks upon the Altar, he even supports their advances, but he defends the Throne. At length however he discovered and was convinced, that from the Conspiracy against the Altar the Sophisters passed to that against the Throne. It is this latter Conspiracy which he wishes to lay open; and it is with these latter plots that he charges the whole school in the person of Diderot, when he says, "The true sentiments of the Author, on Governments, are only to be discovered toward the end of his work. It is there that he lays down as a principle that subjects ought to enjoy *the right of deposing their Sovereigns* when displeased with them. And it is *to effectuate this* that he is perpetually crying out against great armies, which would prove too powerful an obstacle to his designs. A person would be tempted to think, it was Fontaine's fable of the Wolf and the Shepherd that he was reading. If ever the visionary ideas of our Philosophers could be realized, it would *be necessary to new-mould every Government in Europe*, and even that would be a mere trifle. It would be necessary again, though perhaps impossible, that *subjects setting up as the judges* of their masters should be wise and equitable; that those who aspired to the crown should be free from ambition; and that neither intrigue, cabal, nor the spirit of independence, should prevail."[36]

Nothing could have been more masterly applied in these observations than the comparison of the Wolf and the Shepherd. Frederic perfectly comprehended that the object of these declamatory repetitions of the Sect against the vain-glory of war, was not so much to instil the love of peace into the minds of the Sovereign, as to deprive him of the necessary forces to repress that rebellious spirit which Philosophism sought to infuse into the people. He overlooked all those common truths on the miseries of war, which the Sophisters described, as if solely capable of describing them; but when he clearly perceived their plots, the hatred he conceived for the Sect made him dedicate his talents to counteract the Philosophists in his own States, and to render them elsewhere as contemptible as he judged them dangerous.

It was then that he composed *those Dialogues of the Dead*, between Prince Eugene, the Duke of Marlborough and the Prince of Lichtenstein, in which he particularly developes the ignorance of the *Encyclopedists*; their absurd pretension of governing the universe after their own new-fangled doctrines; and, above all, their plan for abolishing the Monarchical form of Government, and of beginning by the subversion of the throne of Bourbon to transform France into a Republic.

At that period it was in vain for Voltaire or D'Alembert to solicit his protection for any of the adepts. Frederic would answer in *a dry and laconic style*, 'Let the scribblers of the sect go and seek a refuge in Holland, *where they may follow the same trade with so many of their equals.*' His indignation and contempt was expressed in such strong terms, that D'Alembert often thought it necessary to soften the expressions in his correspondence with Voltaire.[37]

Then it was that D'Alembert perceived the *great mistake* which Philosophism had committed in reuniting the Civil and Ecclesiastical power against them. It was then that Diderot and his co-operators in *the System of Nature* were nothing more than a set of *blunderheads.* Then it was that Frederic lost his title of *Solomon of the North,* and D'Alembert depicts him as a *peevish man,* or as a sick person whom the Philosophers might accost as Chatillon does Nerestan:

> My Lord, if thus it is, your favour's vain.

"Besides, he says, Mr. Delisle (the adept who was recommended and so ill received) might not have been happy in the place we wished to procure for him (to attend on the King of Prussia). *You know as well as I do what a master he would have had to do with.*"[38] As to Voltaire, who was equally in disgrace, he consoles himself by writing to D'Alembert, "What can we do, my dear friend, we must take Kings as they are, and GOD too."[39]

It is worthy of remark, that neither D'Alembert nor Voltaire seek to deceive Frederic as to the double Conspiracy which he attributed to their school. Silence, it is to be supposed, was judged the most prudent; and it really was so for men sensible that Frederic might bring further proofs, which would only expose their plots in a clearer light, and that before they could exult in their completion.

However numerous the proofs may be that we have already adduced of the Conspiracy against the Throne, whatever evidence may result from the wishes and the secret correspondence of Voltaire and D'Alembert, whatever may be the combination of the Systems adopted by the Sect, on one side throwing the authority of the laws into the hands of the people to constitute the Monarch the Slave of the multitude; on the other erasing the very name of King from the governments of the earth; however incontestable the object of those writings, all, or nearly all, issued from the secret academy of the Sophisters, may be,[40] all breathing hatred to Kings and annihilation to the Throne as well as to the Altar; whatever may be the force which the declarations of the penitent adepts, or of the accomplices exulting in their successes, may add to our demonstrations; however authentic the evidence of the public tribunals may be, denouncing to the whole universe the Conspiracy of the Sophisters against Monarchy: In short, however aggravating the indignation and denunciations of the royal adept against his former masters of impiety (reduced as he is to tear off their mask, to preserve his own throne) may be for the conspiring Sophisters, still these are only the beginning of the proofs which the Historian may hereafter collect from our Memoirs. We still have many gradations of the conspiracy to investigate, and each step will add new force to our demonstrations.

1. See the Philosophical Memoirs of the Baron XX. Chap. 2, on the Art. GOVERNMENT of the Encyclopedia.
2. See Edition of Geneva Articles, DROIT DE GENS, EPICURÉENS, ECLECTIQUES.
3. See these works, particularly the Social System, Chap. 2 and 3, Vol. II.
4. Chap. I, Book I. Social Contract.
5. Ephemerides du Citoyen, Vol. VII. Operations de L'Europe.
6. Social Contract, Chap. 15, Book III.
7. Chap. 12 and 13, Book III.
8. Dupont on the Republic of Geneva, Chap. IV.
9. Of Man, note to sect. 9, Vol. II.
10. Emile, Vol. IV. and Social Contract.
11. Philosophical and Political History &c. Book 19, Vol. IV.
12. System of Reason.
13. See Essay on Prejudice, the Oriental Despotism, and Social System, Chap. 2 and 3.
14. Ibid.
15. Helvetius on Man.
16. See the Oriental Despotism in particular.
17. See Philosophical and Political History, by Raynal, &c. Vol. III and IV *passim*.
18. Ibid.
19. Let the reader consult the discourse he pronounced at the bar of the National Assembly, and he will find that the whole drift of his speech turns on those two lines. I know that this Sophister at his retreat near Paris wept bitterly on the excesses of the Revolution, that he threw the fault principally on the French Calvinists, and cried out, "It is those wretches, I see it clearly, it is those men for whom I have done so much, that plunge us into all these horrid scenes." These words were related to me by an Attorney-General of the Parliament of Grenoble on the very day he had heard them, and a few days before the famous 10th of August, 1792. But what do such tears prove? Without doubt Raynal and his brotherhood did not wish for all those butcheries, the infamy of which he wishes to throw upon the Calvinists. But Rabaud de St. Etienne, Barnave, and the other Calvinists, whether deputies, actors, or leaders, were not the only men formed by his Philosophy. The masters wished for a Revolution after their fashion, but the disciples consummate it according to their own ideas. And by what right can those men who have formed the rebel, complain of the excesses, crimes, and atrocious deeds of his rebellion! Observe—We are told also, that in the end Raynal returned to his religion. He would be another great example to be added to La Harpe. If this be really the fact, if even those who have so greatly contributed to the Revolution by their impiety acknowledge that to return to that God they began by deserting, is the only means of expiating their crime, how culpable is it in those who, after having fallen a sacrifice to that Revolution, expose even in exile their impiety to public view! How unfortunate is it for them to be at once the victim of the Jacobin and the scandal of the Christian!
20. The honour of Raynal's recall was attributed to Mr. Malouet.
21. Ibid., Vol. I.
22. Ibid. Vol. II. Chap. 8.

23. It is with regret that I recollect having been credibly informed, that in the north of Ireland the disaffected part of the inhabitants frequently gave as a toast, *May the guts of the last Bishop serve as a rope to strangle the last King.* If this be true, the reader will not be at a loss to know whence they imbibed their principles. T.
24. Social System, Chap. I. Vol. II.
25. Ibid. note.
26. Social System, page 7 and 8.
27. See Vol. I. Chap. XVI.
28. Above, page 135 [p. 244, Ed.].
29. See *Requisitoire du 18 Aoust*, 1770.
30. There were also some few books translated from the English: But such only as are cast aside with abhorrence in England for their impiety; that, however, was the greatest of all recommendations with Voltaire and the club.
31. See the acts of the Assemblies of the Clergy, 1770. The pastoral letters of Mr. de Beaumont, archbishop of Paris. The sermons of Père Neuville, the works of the Abbé Bergier and of many others.
32. The burning of the crown and sceptre, with the other attributes of sovereignty, has been one of the favourite ceremonies of the Revolutionary agents. In France the crown and sceptre, at Venice and Genoa the chair and golden book were burnt. T.
33. See Refutation of the System of Nature, by the King of Prussia.
34. See Refutation of the System of Nature, by the King of Prussia.
35. See Refutation of the System of Nature, by the King of Prussia.
36. See Refutation of the System of Nature, by the King of Prussia.
37. From D'Alembert, 27 Dec. 1777, Vol. 69, Let. 188, P. 309.
38. Ibid.
39. To D'Alembert, 4 Jan. 1778, Vol. 69, Let. 189, P. 311.
40. After such a variety of proofs, and the declaration of the adept Le Roi respecting the hiding-place of the Sophisters at the Hotel d'Holbach, it would be useless for us to seek any further testimonies. Nevertheless, we think it incumbent on us to say, that since the publication of the first volume we have met with several people, who without being acquainted with all the particulars that we have given, knew the chief object of that meeting to have been the contriving and forwarding of the double conspiracy. I met with an English Gentleman in particular, who heard the academician Dusaux positively assert, that the major part of those books which have operated so great a change in the minds of the people with respect to Monarchy and Religion had been composed in that club of the Hotel d'Holbach. And certainly the testimony of Mr. Dusaux, a man so intimately connected with the Sophistical Authors of the Revolution, is as much to be depended upon at least as that of the repentant or exulting adepts of the Sect.

CHAP. VI.

Fifth Step of the Conspiracy against Kings.

The Democratic Essay at Geneva.

AT the very time when Frederic II was denouncing this impious Sect (which he had heretofore protected with so much tenderness) as inimical to all authorities, he was far from being acquainted with the real depth of their plans. It is chiefly to Voltaire that we see him complain of the temerity of those philosophers against whom he was obliged to defend his Throne;[1] and that at a time when Voltaire and the other Encyclopedian adepts, more particularly the Œconomists, were making the first essay that ever was made of the systems of the Sect.

Geneva, that town where none but a few *beggarly fellows* believed in Christianity,[2] had been chosen for this first essay. The democracy which Calvin had established in that Republic was not in unison with their new rights of man. They beheld the people subdivided into different classes. The first class was that of citizens or burgesses, and comprehended the descendants of the ancient Genevese, or those received into this class, and it was from among them alone, that the counsellors and other officers of the Republic were chosen. They particularly had their vote in the general council. Three other classes had been formed of those who were more recently annexed to the Republic, or who had never been incorporated into the class of citizens. These were the natives, the mere inhabitants of the town, and the subjects. All these could, under the protection of the Republic, with very few exceptions, follow their divers trades and professions, acquire and cultivate lands, &c. but were excluded from the councils and principal dignities of the Republic.

However odious such distinctions may have appeared to the Sophisters, nevertheless the man who appeals to sound judgment and real principles will easily agree, that a Republic, or any State enjoying Sovereignty, has a right to admit new inhabitants on certain conditions which may be just and oftentimes necessary, without establishing on that account a perfect equality between the real and the adoptive children of the State. He who asks to be admitted knows the conditions of his admission, and the exceptions he is exposed to. He was perfectly free to accept, to refuse, or to seek an asylum elsewhere; but certainly, having once accepted and admitted of these exceptions, he has no farther right to create disturbances in the Republic, on pretence that, all men being equal, the adoptive child is entitled to the same privileges as the ancient children of the State.

But such self-evident principles were not consonant with those of the Sect. Even Voltaire had laid them aside. From the perpetual repetition of his Equality and Liberty applied to religion, he had adopted the same doctrine with respect to politics. At the distance of six miles he had long since been observing the feuds which had arisen between the citizens and the magistrates, and thought that by working a political revolution there, he might add new laurels to those which he had gained by the religious revolution in which he so much gloried.

Hitherto these disputes between the magistrates and the citizens had been confined to the interpretation of certain laws, and of the constitution. The natives, and other classes who were excluded from the legislative power, were only spectators of the quarrel, when Voltaire and the other Sophisters judged this a favourable moment to change the very constitution of the Republic, and to make an essay of their new Systems of Equality and Liberty, of the Legislative and Sovereign people.

All Europe is acquainted with the troubles which agitated Geneva from the year 1770 till 1782. The public prints were filled with accounts of the disordered state into which the constitution of Geneva had been thrown; but the public prints have been entirely silent as to the part which the Sophisters took in it, and which it will be the particular object of our Memoirs to reveal. We shall lay open those intrigues and secret artifices, by which they hoped to establish an absolute Democracy according to the system of Jean Jaques Rousseau.

To form a sound judgment on these occult dealings, let men be questioned who, present on the spot, were capable of observing, and who acted the part of real citizens. Such has been the plan that we have adopted, and such inquiries will attest the authenticity of the accounts which we have followed.

Most certainly the systems of Jean Jaques, their countryman, first gave rise to the pretensions of the natives or inhabitants of Geneva to the legislative power. They were stimulated by the insinuations of Voltaire and of the other adepts who flocked to second him.

The part which Voltaire acted was, on one side to encourage the citizens in their disputes with the magistrates, whilst on the other he would insinuate to the natives and inhabitants that they had rights to assert against the citizens themselves. He would invited first one party, then the other to his table, and to each he broached the sentiments which he wished to instil into them. To the citizens he would urge, that their legislative power absolutely made the magistrates dependent on them; and he would persuade the natives or inhabitants, that living in the same Republic and subject to the same laws, the equality of nature assimilated their rights to those of citizens; that the time was come when they should cease to be slaves, or to obey laws which they had not made; that they were no longer to be victims of such odious distinctions, or subject to taxes disgraceful, inasmuch as they were levied without their having consented to them.

Such insinuations acquired new vigour from the numerous pamphlets flowing from the fertile pen of the Premier Chief. Under the name of a Genevese he published the *Republican Ideas*, which will always bear testimony of his hatred for Kings, and show how much ground Republican Liberty had gained in his heart as he advanced in years.

As to this hatred, he expresses it in the above pamphlet, by saying, "There never yet has existed a perfect government, because men are prone to their passions—*The most tolerable, without doubt, is the Republican, because, under that form, men approach the nearest to the equality of nature*. Every father of a family should be master in his own house, but is to have no power over the house of his neighbour. Society being an aggregate of many houses, and of many lands belonging to them, *it would be* a contradictory proposition to pretend that *one man* should have the sole dominion over all those houses and lands; *and it is natural, that each master should have his vote for the general welfare of society.*"[3]

This article alone was sufficient to incite the Genevese to revolt, particularly the natives and others who had acquired lands under the dominion of the Republic. He told them, that to deprive them of the right of voting was to rob them of a natural right inherent to them. But to express himself in still clearer terms, the true disciple of Montesquieu and Jean Jaques, he repeats their fundamental tenets; he tells the Genevese, "that civil government *is the will of* ALL, executed by *one* or *many,* by virtue of *laws which* ALL *have enacted.*"[4] With respect to finance, it is well known, that it is the right of the citizens to regulate and determine what is to be granted for the expences of the state.[5]

It was not possible to tell all those, who lived under the Genevese dominion without having voted at the enacting of the laws, or at the imposition of the taxes, that they were bound by no tie under their present government, and that no government could exist for them until the ancient constitution was overthrown. Let the reader judge what an impression such writings must have made, profusely spread about, and distributed with that art which we have seen Voltaire describing, when he wished to infuse his venomous doctrines into the lowest classes of the people.

But means still more perfidious were made use of. The Sophisters have been seen extolling the generosity of their Premier; and, as a proof, they cite the multitude of Genevese artizans who taking refuge at Ferney found a new country and protection in Voltaire's little province, and partook sufficiently of his riches to continue their trades and support their families. But when we interrogate those who on the spot could observe the secret motives of such a perfidious generosity, we hear them answer, "Voltaire, it is true, has been in some sort the founder of Ferney, of a new town;" but they will add, "how did he people it, if it was not with those factious citizens whom he had stirred up against their country, and which he reunites at Ferney and Versoi to form a focus of insurrection, which was to force the unhappy Republic, by the desertion of its natives and inhabitants, to receive the law from the Sophisters, and to substitute their systems to the ancient laws of the Republic?"

Unsatisfied with all these means and intrigues, the levelling Sect had other agents who forwarded the revolution at Geneva. It had already acquired that Clavière, who was hereafter to continue his revolutionary career at Paris; it had acquired a sort of petty Syeyes in the person of Berenger, and a true firebrand in Segère; but above all it gloried in seeing a French magistrate leaving his country, and laying aside the comely habit of the bench for the filthy round head of the Jacobin. This was Mr. de Servan, that Attorney-General of Grenoble, whom Voltaire in his correspondence with D'Alembert represents as one of the *greatest proficients* in modern philosophy, and as one of those who had chiefly *forwarded its progress*.[6] It is remarkable, that this letter bears date the 5th of November 1770, the very year of the Genevese Revolution. Like a true apostle of Equality and Liberty, Mr. Servan had hurried away to Geneva to unite his efforts to those of Voltaire. But Philosophism had not confined its succours to his talents and reputation alone. An attorney of the name of Bovier, of the same parliament, powerfully aided it with his pen. He appeared with all the arms of Sophistry. Whilst the other adepts were stirring up, in their clubs and private companies, the citizen against the magistrate, and the native and inhabitant against the citizen, Bovier, to raise his constitution of Equality from the midst of discord and civil broils, pretends to assert the real rights of the ancient constitution, not to form a new one; and from antiquity alone he appears to draw all his arguments in favor of the Equality and Sovereignty of the People.

The most revolutionary among the Genevese were surprized to see a foreign Sophister informing them, that till then they had been ignorant of their own laws; that all those distinctions of citizens, inhabitants, or natives, and all the privileges of the first, were novelties which had been usurped and introduced into the Republic so lately as the year 1707; that before that period a very short residence entitled every new comer "to the rights of citizen, and to be admitted into the general *sovereign and legislative* council. That afer one year's residence at Geneva, every man enjoyed his share of Sovereignty in the Republic; in short, that the most perfect equality had reigned among all the individuals of the State, whether of the town or country."[7]

This was nearly the same plan which the Sect followed at that time in France, always calling for the States-General in order to re-establish the pretended constitution of the Sovereign and Legislative people. Bovier was refuted in the most complete manner, but the Sophisters knew too well that a people in a state of revolution swallow every falsehood that favors their Sovereignty. They succeeded in putting them in motion, nor were they ignorant of the means of accelerating and perpetuating their vibrations.

At that time they published at Paris a periodical work under the title of *Ephémérides du Citoyen*. The Œconomists had the direction of it, and that class of adepts was perhaps the most dangerous. They, with all the appearance of moderation, with all the show of patriotic zeal, forwarded the revolution more efficaciously than the frantic rebels of Holbach's Club. The Sect had ordained that this journal should support the efforts of Voltaire, Servan, and Bovier, until they had succeeded in their democratic essay on Geneva. It was the hypocritical and smooth-tongued Dupont de Nemours, who was entrusted with the care of givig monthly a new impetus to the Revolutionists. His periodical publications, carefully directed towards that object, were regularly sent from Paris to Geneva to second the fury of the Democratizing Zealots.

To form a proper judgment of the artful manner in which Dupont fulfilled his trust, it would be necessary to run over all the articles which the *Ephemerous Citizen* has given us under the head *of Geneva*. There we should see the humane citizen lamenting the troubles which had already shortened the lives of some natives, and had banished many others from their country; then, fired by that love of peace and humanity which consumes the philosophic breast, he insinuates exactly such remedies as may throw the whole Republic into a flame. He represents their constitution as that of the most oppressive *Aristocracy*. He assimilates the natives and inhabitants of Geneva to the *Helots* or the slaves of Greece, who, under the dominion of free citizens, have nothing but the most abject slavery to look up to in the very heart of a Republic.[8] Then for the instruction of the Genevese *Helots* he lays down what he calls principles, or rather lessons of rebellion; such, for example, as these given to a people in the most violent ferment. "To say that men can tacitly or formally consent for themselves or their descendants to the privation of the *whole* or *part* of their liberty, would be to say, that men have the right to stipulate against the rights of other men, to sell and cede what belongs to others, to alienate their happiness, and perhaps destroy their very lives:—and of what others? of those whose happiness and whose lives should be the most sacred to them,—of their posterity. Such a doctrine would be a libel on the dignity of human nature, and an insult to its Great Creator."[9]

This certainly was insulting both reason and society in the grossest terms; for if every man who subjects himself to the empire of civil laws does not sacrifice a part of his liberty, he is then as free to violate those laws, though living in society, as he would be were he living among the savages in the woods of America. But it was through pity and humanity that they fed this people, in open revolution, with the most frantic licentiousness. It was to spare the effusion of blood in Geneva that Dupont taught the multitude of *natives, inhabitants*, and *burgesses*, to say to the senators, "Do you imagine the exercise of Sovereignty to be sufficient, as if the proper exercise of it were not an obligation? Do you know that when the people have once *recognized* your authority, you are imperatively and strictly obliged, under pain of the most deserved execration, to render them happy, to protect their liberty, to guarantee and defend their rights of property to the utmost extent? Republicans, if you wish your fellow-citizens to exercise Sovereignty, remember that even Kings only enjoy their power on these terms.

"Would you wish to be worse Sovereigns than the arbitrary Despots of Asia? And when even those who reign over nations buried in ignorance and fanaticism abuse their monstrous power to a certain excess........They are called tyrants. Do you know what happens to them? Go to the gates of the seraglios of the East, *behold the people calling for the* HEADS *of the Visirs and Athemadoulets*; and sometimes striking off those of the Sultans and Sophis. Now reign arbitrarily if you dare. Yes, dare it in your town, where the people are far from being ignorant, and, brought up with you from your childhood, have had many occasions, setting aside your dignity, to know that you are no better than they."[10]

Thus we see that our moderate and humane Sophisters would not lose an occasion, any more than Raynal, or Holbach's Club, of teaching the people to roar rather than to groan, and to wade through carnage preceded by terror to the conquest of their pretended rights.

Such lessons were intermixed with those which the Œconomists pretended to give to Sovereigns on the administration of finances. "One saw them, say the memoirs of the man who followed their operations with the greatest accuracy during the whole of this Revolution,—one saw them insinuating themselves into all affairs of the State, to seize every opportunity of infusing the doctrines of the Sect. Amidst their lessons on œconomy, that on the razing our fortifications is not to be forgotten; their pretence was the great expence and little utility of them. Geneva, they would say, cannot be considered as a state capable of defending a fortress should it be at war with any of the neighbouring States; and with respect to a surprize, it is the inhabitants of the country that are to prove its defence:[11] A most absurd proposition for a State about a league square. But that was not their object; they wished to establish the general principle, and to apply it hereafter to France, or any other State, when the opportunity should offer." In other words, it was the means of exposing the Sovereign to all the fury of a revolted people reclaiming by force of arms that Equality and Liberty which the Sophisters were perpetually representing to them as their inherent rights. This also was the object of those perfidious lessons which they pretended to give to the magistrates, representing them as oppressors, and presupposing the existence of that hatred against them which the adepts themselves had infused into the minds of the people. With the same art they thus again addressed us, says our observer, "The natural defenders of Geneva are the people of the country, the subjects of the Republic. It is possible, nay, it is easy, to attach them so much to the Republic, that they would form the most secure advanced posts possible. But it would be necessary that their country should be far otherwise than a *harsh, severe, and exacting master*; it would be necessary to restore them to the free exercise of the natural rights of man, and to guarantee their possession."[12]

The Sect reaped a twofold advantage from this journal. First, by spreading it through France, and preparing the multitude to hold at a future day a similar language to their Kings; secondly, to kindle anew the flame of discord at the beginning of every month among the unfortunate people of Geneva, for whom it appeared to be written. The brotherhood at Paris continued this work unilt Servan, and the other agents of the Sect, had seen their plots effectuate a Revolution in Geneva, and a total overthrow of the ancient laws of that Republic.

It is true, the Sophisters did not long enjoy their success, as Mr. de Vergennes, who at first had viewed this Revolution with indifference, soon learned its importance. Evidence at length convinced him that all that had come to pass at Geneva was nothing more than an essay which our modern Sophisters were making of their principles and systems; that neither their plans nor their plots were to be concluded by these first successes; that they were nothing more than a prelude to the revolutionary scenes with which they threatened all Europe, and which might ere long involve France itself in the common mass of ruin.

The Sophisters had the mortification to see these first fruits of their revolutionary principles blasted by a few battalions of French troops. It was reserved to Clavierre, and afterwards to Robespierre, to resume their plans, and to send the apostate Soulavie to consummate them by murder and exile, in short by all the revolutionary means which Philosophism had invented in the Castle of Ferney for the future benefit of the Jacobinical den.[13]

1. From Frederic, 7 July, 1770, Vol. 65, Let. 173, P. 409, and Correspondence of Voltaire and D'Alembert, 1770.
2. 1st Part, Page 32 [p. 22, Ed.].
3. Republican Ideas, No. 43. Edit. of Kell.
4. Ibid. No. 13.
5. Ibid. No. 42. Many people cannot conceive that Voltaire could have fallen into such Democracy. Let them read his latter works with attention, and particularly those from which we have made the above extracts, and they will find that he is even violent against the distinction of *Noble* (he who holds land by knights services) and *Roturier* (who holds lands in soccage). He even declares the origin and real signification of these two words to be no other than Lord and Slave.

    Let them read his *Commentary on the Spirit of Laws*, and they will see in what a light he viewed that nobility, among whom he nevertheless numbered so many admirers, and to whom he was so much indebted for the propagation of his Philosphism. It is not hatred which makes him say in this Commentary, "I could wish that the author (Montesquieu), or any other writer possessing such abilities, had explained more clearly why the *nobility* are essential to the Monarchical form of government. One should rather be tempted to believe, that it was the essence of the Feudal System, as in Germany, or of Aristocracy as at Venice." (No. 111.)

    To us it appears, that, whether young or old, Voltaire often confounds all his ideas. The idea of nobility, in general, represents to us the children of men distinguished by their services either civil or military, forming a body in the state whose sentiments and education, whose very interest, often fits them for those employments which are at the disposal of the Sovereign. Undoubtedly such a distinction may take place without the Feudal System of the Germans, or the Aristocracy of the Venetians. It is possible indeed to conceive a Monarchy without

a body of nobility; but most certainly such a distinction greatly tends to form a body of men more attached to the Monarch, and very useful to the State in those stations for which the general education of the multitude can seldom be a suitable preparative.
6. To D'Alembert, 5 Nov. 1770, Vol. 69, Let. 46, Page 81.
7. See the Memorial of Bovier from page 15 to 29; and the refutation of the natives of Geneva.
8. Ibid. Chap. I, and Note.
9. Ibid. Chap. 2.
10. Ibid. Chap. 2.
11. Ephem. du Citoyen, 1771, Vol. I.
12. Ephem. du Citoyen, page 176. I have sought in vain to learn what species of oppression the people of Geneva suffered under their magistrates; I have found that it was not possible for a people to be more fondly or more justly attached to their government; that the union between the magistrates and the subjects resembled that of a numerous family with its Chiefs. The Sophisters knew this too well; but they were not speaking for the Genevese alone. They pre-supposed discord, that they might create it where it did not exist, and add to it where it already began to spread.
13. The above Chapter, whether with respect to the general conduct of the Sophisters, or more particularly with respect to the conduct of Voltaire, Servan, or Dupont de Nemours, during the Revolution of Geneva, has been entirely formed by memoirs with which eye-witnesses have favored us, and on the writings of the Sophisters, which have been quoted with the greatest precision.

CHAP. VII.

Aristocratic Essay in France.

IN laying before the reader the proofs of the Conspiracy formed against Monarchy we have said, that there existed a set of Philosophers who held themselves so secure of bringing about a Revolution, that they had not scrupled to advise both the King and his Ministers to make the Revolution themselves, lest Philosophy might not be sufficiently powerful to direct the motion when once imparted. Among this class of Philosophers, who wished to be styled the *Moderates*, but whom Jean Jaques calls the *Inconsistents*, we are to distinguish Mr. de Mably, the brother of Condillac, and one of those Abbés who bore nothing of the Ecclesiastic but the dress, and who, bestowing great application on prophane sciences, was almost entirely ignorant of those necessary for an Ecclesiastic.

Without being impious like a Voltaire or a Condorcet, even though adverse to their impiety, his own tenets were extremely equivocal. At times his morality was so very disgusting, that it was necessary to suppose that his language was ambiguous, and that he had been misunderstood, lest one should be obliged to throw off all esteem for his character. At least such has been the defence I have heard him make to justify himself from the censures of the Sorbonne. He had the highest opinion of his own knowledge in politics, and during his whole life that was his favourite topic; he believed himself transcendant in that science, and he met with others who were led to the same belief. His *mediocre* talents would have been better appreciated, had he been viewed in the light of a man led away by the prejudices he had imbibed from a scanty knowledge of antiquity, and who wished to reduce every thing to the standard of his own ideas.

Mr. de Mably had also been led away by all those Systems of Liberty, of the Sovereignty and Legislative authority of the people, of the rights of self-taxation and of contributing to the public expences only in as much as they had voted the monies themselves or by their representatives.—He was persuaded that he had found these Systems of Government among the ancient Greeks and Romans, and more particularly among the ancient Gauls. He was perfectly persuaded, that without the States General the French Monarchy could not exist; and that to re-establish the ancient and real Constitution, it was necessary to resume those States General.[1]

Mably and his disciples, or more properly the adherents of Montesquieu, detested the feudal laws; but they did not reflect that it was to those very laws the States-General owed their former existence. When Philip le Bel and some other Princes had found themselves under the necessity of applying to those States for subsidies, the reason was, because under the feudal system the King, like the Counts of Provence, Champagne, and Thoulouse, or the Dukes of Brittany, had their fixed revenues and particular desmenes which were supposed to suffice for the exigencies of the state. And in fact wars of the longest duration could be carried on without its being necessary to augment the revenues of the Sovereign. Armies at that time were composed of the Lords and Knights serving at their own expence and defraying that of their vassals whom they led after them into the field. Neither Mably nor his disciples would reflect that at a period when France had acquired so many new Provinces, when the armies, general officers, and soldiers, waged war solely at the King's expence, it was impossible for the ancient crown lands to supply the wants of Government. They could not conceive, that in the new system of politics, it would have been the height of imprudence for the Monarch in France to be dependent (every time he found it necesssary to repel or anticipate an atttack of the foreign enemy) on the great and jealous Lord, on the seditious tribune, or on the surly deputy, perhaps even in the interest of the enemy, for the necessary subsidies on so pressing an occasion. Such reflections as these never occured to the minds of our Sophisters.

Filled with the idea, that Revolution and the States General were necesssary to break the chains of the French people, we are told by his strongest adherents, that Mably went still farther than merely inviting the Sovereign and his Minsters to commence the Revolution themselves:—"He upbraided the people in his Treatise *On the Rights of Citizens*, written *in the Year* 1771, with having missed the opportunity of making the Revolution; and he lays down the means of effecting it. He advised the Parliament in future to refuse to enregister any bursal edict, to declare to the King that he had no right to impose taxes on the people, who alone were vested with the fiscal power, *to ask pardon of the people* for having co-operated during so long a time in the levy of such unjust taxes, and to supplicate His Majesty to convoke the States-General. *A Revolution*, he adds, brought about by such means would be the more advantageous as it would be founded on the love of order and of the laws and not on licentious liberty."[2]

This system of a Revolution to be accomplished, according to Montesquieu's ideas, by vesting the legislative and fiscal powers in the hands of the people, or of their representatives in the States-General, found many supporters and abettors, and particularly among the aristocracy, as the distinction of the three states was still preserved. All that class of men which impiety had enrolled under the banners of Sophistry from among the Duke de la Rochfoucault's society, viewed this as a means for the Grandees to reassume their ancient influence in the state, and to conquer from the King and Court, that power which they had gradually lost under the preceding reigns. They were ignorant that other Sophisters were already prepared to enforce their systems of Equality in those States General, and to assert, that *the three estates being separate, of opposite interests, and jealous of each other, mutually destroyed each other's strength; and that to this distinction was to be attributed the inefficacy; and the very little good that had arisen from all the former States General.* The Grandees did not perceive this snare which the levelling Sophisters had laid for them; the levellers had conceived the greatest expectations from the dissentions which reigned at that period between Lewis XV and the Parliaments, and believed themselves on the eve of obtaining the convocation of those States General where they were to consummate their revolution.

These dissentions were principally owing to an opinion originating in Montesquieu's systems, which had crept into the first tribunals of the state. Such magistrates as, according to that system, believed Liberty to be entirely annulled in every state where the people or its representatives did not partake of the legislative and fiscal powers with the King, had construed their Parliaments into the representatives of the people, and pretended that the different Parliaments, though dispersed in different towns throughout the state, constituted but one and the same body, holding their powers directly from the people, whose perpetual representatives they pretended to be, whose rights they were to support against the encroachments of the crown, and exercising for them that inalienable and indefeasable right of making laws and voting subsidies; although they were resident magistrates and fixed in different towns by the King to administer justice in his name.

This was a system of Parliaments very widely different from the idea which the French Kings, who had created them without even taking the sense of the nation, had conceived of these Judiciary Courts. It was indeed extraordinary, that tribunals either ambulant or stationary, and which the King had created at their own will and pleasure, should belong to the very essence of the Constitution; that a body of Magistrates all named by the King should pretend to be the free chosen representatives of the people, and a magistracy so much at the disposition of the Sovereigns, that they had sold the offices; could then these men pretend to assimilate themselves to representatives deputed by the people to the States General.[3]

The states themselves never viewed the Parliaments in any other light, which is easy to be seen by what the President Hainault says on the states held in 1614: "On this occasion I must say, that as we recognize no other authority in France but that of the King, it is by his authority that laws are made. *As wills the King so wills the Law.* On that account the States General can only remonstrate and humbly supplicate. The King hearkens to their grievances and prayers in his prudence and his justice.—For, was he obliged to grant all that was asked of him, says one of our most celebrated authors, he would cease to be their King. *It is for that reason that during the sittings of the States General the authority of the Parliament suffers no diminution,* as exercising no other power but that of the King, which may be easily seen in the minutes of the last states."[4]

It was therefore a most extraordinary claim of these Parliaments, all created by, and exercising the authority of the King only, to pretend to be the representatives of the people in order to resist the power of that same King; styling themselves the habitual and permanent representatives of the States General, who had never formed the least idea of such representatives, and who had always looked upon them as the King's Magistrates. But when new systems had spread disquietude in every breast, and produced the thirst of Revolution, illusion easily banished truth. The most respectable Magistrates, overpowered by the weight of Montesquieu's authority, and spurred on by the Sophisters, were easily persuaded that every country was enslaved, and groaned under the most severe despotism, where the legislative and fiscal powers were not in the hands of the people or of their representatives. And, lest the whole code of laws which the King had made and the Parliaments proclaimed, should suddenly become null and void, these Magistrates, who had enregistered and proclaimed them, constituted themselves the representatives of the people.

These claims served as a pretence for the most invincible resistance to the orders of their Sovereign. The King's council, and particularly Mr. de Maupou, surmised a coalition aiming at nothing less than to disorder the Monarchy, to diminish the authority of the throne, to put the Sovereign under the habitual dependence of the Twelve Parliaments, and to create disturbances and disputes between the King and his Tribunals as often as any factious Magistrate, assuming the character of a tribune of the people, should oppose the pretended will of the nation to his Sovereign. Lewis XV resolved to annihilate such Parliaments, and to create new ones more limited in their powers, and which might be restrained within the bounds of their duty with greater ease.

This resolve was being put in execution, and the Sophisters rejoiced to see the disputes daily increase. Convinced that these dissentions would necessarily oblige the King to assemble the States General, where they should be able to find means of publishing their plans and of operating, at least in part, the Revolution they so ardently wished for, they brought forward that same Malesherbes, whom we have seen so active in seconding the Sophisters of Impiety. He was at that time President of the *Cour des Aides*, the first tribunal in Paris after the Parliament. He engaged his *company* to make the first signal step towards opposing the States General to the authority of the Monarch. He formed those remonstrances since so famous among the Philosophers, because, under the cloak of a few respectful expressions, he had broached all the new principles of the Sect and all their pretensions against the authority of their Sovereign.

In those remonstrances we see the demand for the States-General couched in the following terms: "Until this period at least the reclamations of the Courts supplied, though imperfectly, the want of the States-General; for, notwithstanding our zeal, we cannot pretend to say, that we have been able to make amends to the nation for the great advantages which must have accrued to it, by the intercourse between its representatives and the Sovereign.

But at present the sole resource which had been left to the people is torn from them. By whom shall their interests be asserted against the minister? The people dispersed have no common organ by which they may prefer their complaints. *Sire, interrogate then the nation itself*, since that alone remains to which your Majesty can hearken."[5]

The other parliaments who followed Malesherbes's example were ignorant of the intentions of the Sect which had prompted him to act. They abandoned themselves to the torrent, and were hurried away by the impulse given by the Sophisters and by the public opinion, which the system of Montesquieu on the Legislative and Fiscal Powers had new-modelled.

Misled by Malesherbes's example, the Parliament of Rouen also asked for the States-General in their remonstrances of the 19th March 1771. "Sire, Since the efforts of the Magistracy are fruitless, deign to consult the Nation assembled." But the former colleagues of Montesquieu, the Parliament of Bourdeaux, thought it incumbent on them to show more than ordinary zeal for his principles, as is to be seen by the pressing style in which their remonstrances of the 25th February 1771, are couched.

"If it be true (say these Magistrates), that the Parliament, become sedentary under Philip le Bel, and perpetual under Charles VI, is not the same as the Ambulant Parliament convoked during the first years of Philip le Bel's reign, under Lewis IX, under Lewis VIII, and under Philip Augustus; the same as the *Placita* convoked under *Charlemagne and his descendants*; the same as those ancient assemblies of the Francs of which history has preserved the memory both before and after the conquest; if the distribution of this Parliament to different districts has changed the *essence of its Constitution*, in short, Sire, though your Courts of Parliament should not have the right of examining and verifying the new laws which your Majesty may please to propose, *still the nation cannot be deprived of that right, it is a right that cannot be lost; it is inalienable. To attack that right is not only to betray the Nation but the King himself*. It would be to overthrow the constitution of the kingdom. It would be to attack the authority of the Monarch in its very principles. Will it be believed, that the verification of the new laws being made by your Courts in Parliament *does not compensate for this primitive right of the nation?* Can public order be benefited by this power being once more exercised by the nation? Should his Majesty deign to re-establish the people in their rights, he would see us no longer claiming that portion of *authority* which the Kings, your predecessors, have entrusted us with, as soon as the nation assembled shall exercise that power itself."

It is thus that the Parliaments, a prey to a faction with whose dark designs they were wholly unacquainted, were craving pardon as it were of the people for having forgotten their inherent and inalienable rights of Legislation and of Sovereignty, at least in part, in the Assembly of the States-General. They did not foresee that a day would come when they would have to ask pardon of the people for having called for those same States-General, so fatal to the King, to themselves and to the nation.

The Revolution would have been accomplished at that time had Lewis XV shown less resolution. It was precisely at that period when the Sect, painted in such true colors a few months before by the Attorney General of the Parliament of Paris, "*was seeking to excite the people to revolt under pretence of enlightening them*; when its disquiet and daring genius, inimical to all dependence, aspired at the overthrow of every political constitution, and whose views would only be accomplished when they had succeeded in throwing the legislative and executive powers into the hands of the multitude, *when the Majesty of Kings had been reviled, and their authority had been rendered precarious and subordinate to the capricious starts of an ignorant mob.*"

It was at that period "when the numbers of the proselytes were increasing and the maxims of the Sect were spreading far and wide, when kingdoms felt themselves shaken in their foundations; when nations, astonished, asked each other, whence arose the extraordinary changes which had been operated among them?" In a word, it was at that period when Mably and his disciples were conjuring a Revolution, when the Œconomists were circulating and infusing their principles into every class of the people, when the Philosophers *foresaw the Revolution, foretold it,* and proposed *the manner of accomjplishing it by means of a combination with the people.*[6]

From that period the convocation of the States-General must have infallibly brought about the Revolution. The Sophisters needed no longer to inspire the Magistracy with their systems. The principles were admitted, though the application of them might vary. The right of verifying and examining the laws had been recognized as *a primitive and inalienable* right inherent to the people. If the parliament in the days of its illusion only held this language to their Sovereign to assert their authority against his Ministers, still the Sophisters wished for no further declarations, *to revile the Majesty of Kings, and to render their authority precarious and subordinate to the capricious starts of an ignorant mob*. From the right of examining to the right of rejecting, or to the right of insurrection, in short, to all the rights of the Revolutionary Code, there was but one step further; and the Sophisters at the head of the multitude were ready prepared to bear down every opposition to that measure. Almost every existing law was null, because it had been made by the King without consulting the people; and all laws might be set aside, because the people had a right to examine them anew and hence proscribe them, if such was their will and pleasure.

Such a one, nevertheless, was to be a moderate Revolution in the language of the Sophisters. It was not only those Magistrates who, wresting from the Sovereign his rights and transferring them to the people, and hoping by that means to enjoy the whole power in their assemblies, were the abettors of this Revolution; but also that numerous class of the Aristocracy, whom we shall see hereafter carrying to the States-General all those systems of the legislative people; of a people preserving all the hierarchy of birth in their legislative assemblies; of a people adopting Montesquieu's principles only in as far as they applied to, and threw the power into the hands of the Aristocracy;

in fine, this revolution was forwarded and supported by all that class of Sophisters who, contented with having asserted the principles of the *Legislative and Sovereign people*, were pleased to continue the name of King to the first minister of that people.

Lewis XV was perfectly aware that he was on the eve of losing the most precious rights of his crown. Naturally humane, and an enemy to all acts of authority, he was nevertheless determined to transmit whole and unimpaired to his successor the power which he had received on ascending the throne. He wished to die as he had lived, a King: He dissolved the Parliaments, refused to convoke the States-General, and never permitted them even to be mentioned during the remainder of his reign. But he knew that in repressing the Magistrates he had not crushed the monster of Revolution. He more than once expressed his fears for the young Prince heir to his throne. He was even so much convinced that the Sophisters would make the most violent efforts against his successors, that he would say with a tone of disquietude, *I should like to know how Berri will get over all this*; meaning his grandson, afterwards Lewis XVI, who bore the name of Berri during the life-time of his father, who died Dauphin. Lewis XV however found means to stop the Revolution which menaced France during his life-time. The conspirators perceived it necessary to defer their plans. They were content with preparing the people for its execution. In the mean time the Sect made other essays of a different nature, which shall not be lost to History.

1. See his Rights of the Citizen.
2. Gudin's Supplement to the Social Contract, 3d Part, Chap. I.
3. The denomination of *Parlement* (Parliament) which had been given to the first Tribunals of the state, had greatly contributed to the illusion, which might have been easily avoided had the old term of *Plaid* (*court leet*) been preserved, which in the ancient history of France denotes sometimes those great assemblies which the King deliberated with on important questions respecting the state, at other times those ambulatory tribunals which administered justice. It was these latter only that our Kings had perpetuated under the name of Parliaments. The difference is the more evident, as those great Assemblies or States General never meddled with the Judiciary Power, the exercise of which constituted the sole functions of the ambulant Magistracy. In those great Assemblies or *National Plaids* the Clergy was always admitted as the first order of the state; whereas by the very nature of its duties, it was excluded from the *Judiciary Plaids* (see the President Hainault, ann. 1137, 1319, & *passim*); how then was it possible to confound the States General with the Judiciary Plaids or Parliaments?
4. History of France, anno 1614.
5. Remonstrance of the Cour des Aides, Feb. 28, 1771.
6. See Gudin, Suppl. to the Social Contract.

CHAP. VIII.

Essay of the Sophisters against Aristocracy.

THE distinctions of King and Subject, of the Sovereign making and the Multitude obeying the law, were not the only points which militated against the principles of a school that recognized no other law, whether religious or political, than *Equality and Liberty*. In all civil societies there exist men elevated above the horizontal plane of the multitude, men who are to be distinguished by their rank, by their titles, or by the privileges granted to their birth, to their own services, or to those of their ancestors; men who, by the industry of their forefathers, or by their own, have acquired riches and abundance, of which their fellow-citizens cannot partake; in fine, men who earn their bread by the sweat of their brow, while others enjoy the benefit of their labours in consideration of a salary which they pay them. If the distinctions of nobleman and commoner be not every where known, those of poor and rich are universally understood.

Whatever interest the numberless adepts in the higher classes might have had not to push too far the consequences of that Equality which they had applied to their God, there were many adepts in the lower classes who did not partake of any such restraint. Many of these latter were to be found in France, but a much greater number in Germany and Poland, and in many other parts of Europe, where the principles of our modern Sophisters had gained admittance.

As early as the year 1766, we have seen Frederic writing to Voltaire, "*That Philosophy was beginning to penetrate even into superstitious Bohemia, and into Austria, the ancient abode of superstition.*" And it is to that year that we are able to trace the first seeds of a plan which was to gratify the Sophisters with a new Republic in those countries, where the distinctions of Marquis or Clown, of Noble or Burgess, of rich or poor, were to vanish from before their sight.

The whole of what we are about to relate concerning this plan, and the various essays made by Philosophism to extend its branches to Austria and Bohemia, even to Hungary and Transilvania, will be extracted from two Memorials, with which we have been favoured by persons who, being on the spot, were enabled to oberve with the greatest precision, the one the causes, the other the effects, which enabled the German Sophisters to glory in having preceded our Carmagnols and Septembrizing butchers in their Revolutionary depredations.

Scarcely had the French Philosophism penetrated to the banks of the Moldaw, when those baneful principles of *Equality and Liberty* which formerly had led the Hussites and Thaborites to the enthusiastic murder of the Clergy and Nobility, to the laying in ashes the Castles and Monasteries, were seen to ferment anew. A conspiracy was formed at Prague, and it was to break out on the 16th of May. It was customary on that day for multitudes of the common people to throng into town, to celebrate the feast of St. Jean Nepomucene. At the time of this immense concourse of people from the country, some thousands of armed Conspirators were suddenly to appear; others were to make themselves masters of the bridge and gates; others again were to mix among the people; to harangue them, to announce the dawn of rising Liberty, and to exhort them to throw off the yoke of Slavery, and to take possession of those lands which they had so long watered with the sweat of their brows, and whose fruit only enriched a set of tyrannical, haughty, vain, and idle Lords.

Such language, it may easily be conceived, must have made a strong impression on men who, for the greatest part, cultivated lands which they only held at the pleasure of the Lord, in consideration of so many days work every week, employed in the culture of the Lord's lands.[1] Arms were to be distributed to this populace suddenly heated by the cry of Equality and Liberty. The Lords and the rich were to fall the first victims of their fury; the lands distributed to the murderers, and Liberty proclaimed, we should have behld Bohemia the first Republican offspring of Philosophism.

Secretly however as this plot was carried on, some of the adepts ere long betrayed the secret.—Maria Theresa, the Empress Queen, found means of stifling the whole, and her council behaved with so much prudence and dexterity, that the public journals of the time scarcely mention it. Perhaps the court judged wisely, and thought it prudent to gain over the chiefs, rather than by executions to call the attention of the public to principles which have but too often stained Bohemia with the blood of its best citizens.

Notwithstanding the very small success that had attended their attempt, the Sophisters of the Danube and Moldau did not lose all hopes of effectuating their schemes of Equality. They invented a plan which drew the Empress Queen into the delusion, and still more her successor Joseph II.—The apparent object of this plan was, that proprietors whose lands were so extensive that they were unable to cultivate them, should be obliged to cede a part of such lands to the peasantry. These, in return, were to pay an annual rent to the former proprietors equal in value to the estimated revenue. Each community was to engage to punish severely every peasant who should neglect either the cultivation of the land ceded, or the payment of the settled rent.

This plan was presented to the Empress Queen with so much art, that she was persuaded it had no other view than the enriching of the state by favouring the industry and encouraging the emulation of the real cultivators.

She therefore gave orders to various agents of government to send in Memorials on the subject: and herself tried the experiment by ceding some of the crown lands on the aforementioned conditions.

The Sophisters feared the delay attendant on such deliberations; and, to hasten the general execution of their projects, they spread their propositions and plans among the peasantry. Their most ardent missionary was an intriguing priest, who ran to and fro throughout the country, preaching up this reformation of property which he thought admirable. He found it no difficult task to infuse a portion of his enthusiasm into his rustic auditors. The Nobles, viewing this plan in no other light than as a means of despoiling them of their property under the pretence of a just compensation, objected that the peasantry, become masters and proprietors of the land, would soon find means of turning the whole profit to their own use; and that Philosophism would soon invent new reasons for paying no retribution whatever to the Lords (for would it not be doubly unjust to carry any part of the produce of lands to Lords who neither cultivated nor had any *property* in them); in fine, should it ever please the peasantry to league together and refuse all payments, the Lords would have lost both their lands and money, and the Nobility, thus reduced, would be able to find no other means of subsistence than by entering into the service of their *quondam* tenants.[2]

This opposition only contributed to stimulate the zeal of the levelling apostles. They had given the peasantry every hope of success, and it was easy to irritate them against their opponents. It was soon to be perceived that those vassals who had always been so mild and humble with respect to their Lords had now assumed a haughty and insolent mien. It was necessary to resort to punishments, which only added to their complaints and murmurs. The Empress Queen, still misled by the apparent justice of the plan, and the Emperor, whose Philosophism and ambition secretly enjoyed the hopes of humiliating the Nobility, were imprudent enough to receive the complaints of those whom the Lords had thought necessary to punish. This sort of connivance gave our rustic revolters reason to believe, that they had nothing to fear on the part of the government. The Sophistical Emissaries persuaded them, that they ought to obtain by force what in justice could not be refused them. Such insinuations naturally produced violence, and in 1773, the insurrection of the peasantry against the Nobility was almost universal throughout Bohemia.

The rustics already began to burn and pillage[3] the castles; the nobility and the rich proprietors were menaced with a general massacre. The Empress Queen came to a tardy sense of the fault she had committed; but then at least she lost no time to crush the growing evil. An army of 28,000 men received orders to march and to quell the rioters. The Sophisters had not the time necessary to organize their Revolutionary bands, and the revolters were soon defeated.

Those parts of Prussia and Silesia which border on Bohemia had felt the commotion, and it was then that Frederic first divined the intentions of the

Sophisters. He had not courted them so far as to disband his army. He was even more resolute than the Empress Queen in eradicating the spirit of revolt. He immediately hung up the mutineers; and our levelling Philosophists were still obliged quietly to behold those disgusting distinctions of Lords and peasants, of Nobles and rich. But they were only pacified for the moment, and never lost sight of their plans. The death of the Empress Queen gave them an occasion of making still more perfidious essays for the destruction of the Nobility.

Initiated in the Sophisticated mysteries, Joseph II had found means of combining the ideas of Equality and Liberty with those of the Despot, and, under pretence of reigning like a Philosopher, levelled every thing around him, that he and his systems might tower alone above the ruined plane. With his pretended Liberty of conscience, he would have been the greatest persecutor of his age, had not the French Revolution followed him so closely. With his pretended Equality, he only sought to vilify and plunder the Nobility, and to fling their fortunes into the hands of their vassals, in order to overthrow the laws of the Empire, and those of property as well as those of religion, that he might not meet with a greater opposition from the Nobility than he would from their vassals.—With all his pretensions to genius, the most awful lessons were necessary to persuade him that the real tendency of this Philosophism of Equality and of religious and political Liberty, was the destruction of the throne as well as of the altar.

Such was the Philosophy of that Prince: whatever may have been his intentions, his innovating genius was unfortunate enough to furnish the pretext for a most cruel insurrection against the Nobility of a large portion of his dominions. The celerity with which he was accustomed to make himself obeyed, may cast cruel doubts on the dilatory manner in which he went to the succour of the unhappy victims.

All that I am about to relate concerning this memorable event, the atrocious memory of which the court of Vienna vainly attempted to stifle, shall be extracted from a relation written by Mr. J. Petty, an English gentleman whom I knew to be one of those who had escaped from the massacre, and is now living at Betchworth near Darking, in the county of Surry. It was to his memorial I alluded when I spoke of one more particularly instructive as to effects. The other, from which I have extracted the greater part of what has been already seen in this Chapter, has a greater application to causes, and shows the connection between those facts and the progress of Philosophism and Jacobinism in the Austrian dominions. On considering these two memorials collectively, we see that it was at Vienna where the Sophisters, under the cloak of Humanity and Liberty, were inventing every means either for the destruction of the Nobility, or to oblige the Lords to renounce their ancient rights over their vassals and villains, and that the orders given by Joseph II for the mode of defence of the frontiers of Transilvania furnished the means or the occasion for executing their plans. These orders were such, that they were calculated either to rob the Hungarian Lords of their vassals, or to throw them into open rebellion against their masters.

Antecedent to this new plan adotped by the Emperor, the chain of troops destined for the guard of the Turkish frontiers was composed of peasants or villains, who were exempted from a part of their ordinary labours in consideration of this military duty; but were not on that account exempt from dependence on their masters. In the spring of the year 1781, Joseph II sent the Major General Geny to Hermanstadt, with orders to augment the number of these guards, and to put them on the same footing as the rest of the Imperial troops; that is to say, in a state of perfect independence on their former Lords. The proposed indemnifications did not, however, prevent numerous reclamations being made. What seemed to justify this opposition, and what was easy to be foreseen (which perhaps might have been the real object of the Sophisters), was, that the peasantry flocked in crouds to be enrolled, and by that means enfranchize themselves from all submission and from any services or duties to their Lords.—I must own with truth, and in unison with Mr. Petty, that the fate of the peasantry or villains was much aggravated by the harshness of some of their masters.

In the mean time, until an answer to the reclamations of the Nobility and proprietors could be obtained from Vienna, the commander in chief at Hermanstadt thought it incumbent on him to declare, that these new enrollments should be considered as operating no change in the political situation of the peasantry, until further orders and instructions should be received from the Emperor. But those orders did not arrive, and the commander in chief had made his declaration too late.—Those villains who had enrolled themselves not only looked upon their enfranchizement as complete, but committed such excesses against their former masters, that the Magistrates were obliged to apply to the commander in chief for the revocation of all the enrollments, as the only method of restoring order. But the revocation proved useless; it was well known that the Emperor had returned no answer. The peasantry, in lieu of peaceably submitting to their injured Lords, persisted in looking upon themselves as independent soldiers, when on a sudden there appeared a Valachian peasant of the name of Horja who gathered a multitude of them around him. He, decorated with a large star and bearing a patent written in golden letters, declared himself sent by the Emperor to enroll them all. He offered to put himself at their head and to restore them to their liberty. The peasantry flocked to their new general. The Lords and Proprietors sent daily information to the government and to the commander in chief at Hermanstadt of what was passing; of the secret committees which were held in different parts, and of the insurrection which was on the eve of bursting forth. Reproaches for their apprehensions and timidity were the only answers they received.

The day marked out by the Conspirators was approaching, and on the 3d November 1784 Horja appeared at the head of four thousand men. He formed different detachments and sent them to burn the castles and murder the Lords and proprietors. These forerunners of the Jacobin Galley Slaves of Marseilles executed his orders with that sanguinary fury which they had imbibed against the Nobility from the doctrines of Equality, and the rebels soon counted 12,000 men following their levelling standards. In a very short space of time fifty Noblemen were murdered. Carnage and desolation now spread from county to county; the houses of the Nobility were every where burnt and ransacked, and mere assassination could no longer satiate their sanguinary fury. The unhappy Noblemen who fell into their hands were put to the most excruciating tortures. Some were impaled alive, their hands and feet cut off, and roasted at a slow fire, for such is the humanity of levellers!!—But we will not attempt to comment on the relation we have before us; to extract is a task sufficiently distressing. "Among the castles which were reduced to ashes the most remarkable were those of the Counts D'Esterhazy and Tekeli; and of the Noblemen who were murdered the most distinguished were the two Counts and Brothers Rebiezi. The eldest was spitted and roasted; many others of the same family, men, women and children, were cruelly massacred. The unfortunate Lady Bradisador, with whom I had spent a few days (says Mr. Petty) also fell a melancholy victim.—These barbarians seized her, cut off her hands and feet, and then left her to linger in that state till she expired. But let us turn from such horrid subjects: They recall to my mind persons forever dear to me, who fell a most wanton sacrifice to cruelty, on which I have not the courage to dilate."

We also would gladly have withheld such bloody recitals from our readers; but, when compared to our Septembrizing Jacobins, they become marking features in history. And how much more striking would these lessons be, was it here the place to enumerate the many similar attacks against the nobility with which our Memoirs on Ancient Jacobinism are replete. We should there see that same Philosophism of Equality and Liberty forming the same plots and perpetrating the same atrocities against that part of society distinguished by its titles, rank, or riches; and the Aristocracy may learn from their own history the danger of encouraging sophisticated levellers, who never fawn on them but in hopes of tearing to pieces and devouring the whole of that class which is distinguished by riches and honors.

In making a comparison between the Jacobins of the present day and their forefathers, I should not conceal those horrid sights of noblemen roasting, of women mutilated, of whole families masssacred, or of the palpitating members of fathers, mothers and children in Transilvania.—Nor should I pass over those cannibals of the *Place Dauphine* burning at a slow fire (on the 3d of September 1792) the Countess of *Perignan* and her daughters, Madame *de Chevres*, and so many other victims, offering the flesh of those whom they had already butchered as food to those who were next to be sacrificed. Such horrid deeds are far from being novelties in the annals of the Sect.[4] Nor was it reserved to the Carmagnols of Paris or of Transilvania to show the example of such cruelties.

These statements I know will make my reader shudder with horror, but it is a salutary tremor. At length perhaps they will cease to hearken to those Sophistical Apostles of an Equality and Liberty less chimerical than atrocious, and whose systems assimilate man to the ferocious beasts of the forest. The error is too fatal; let us therefore guard against the delusions of pride by the remembrance of deeds humiliating to nature itself. We have witnessed the sanguinary consequences of these vain systems of Equality and Liberty in our own times; let us venture to examine for a moment what course they took in the days of our ancestors.

In 1358 France had its Jacobins, and their system was *Equality and Liberty*. Froissard, one of the most esteemed French Historians, paints their conduct as follows:

"In the month of May 1358 France was stricken with a strange desolation. Some country people, without a chief, and at first not one hundred in number, assembled in the Beauvoisis, declaring that the nobility were a dishonor to the nation, and that it would be a meritorious act to destroy them all. Their companions answered, 'It is true, and evil fall upon the man who shall not do his utmost to destroy the nobility.' They then gathered together, having no other arms than sticks tipped with iron, and knives, and immediately proceeded to the neighbouring mansion of a nobleman. After having murdered him, his wife and children, not sparing the infant babes, they set fire to his house. They then proceeded to another castle, where seizing on the Chevalier, they offered violence to his wife and daughter, and afterwards murdered them in his presence, with the rest of his children; they then butchered him, and levelled his castle with the ground.—They treated several other country houses and castles in the same manner. Their numbers increased to six thousand, and they were joined every where as they went by their equals; the others fled through terror, carrying their wives and children with them to the distance of ten or twenty leagues, leaving their houses and valuables at the mercy of the robbers. These wicked wretches, without chiefs, buffetted, burnt, and massacred every nobleman they met with, and offered the most unheard of violences to the wives and daughters of their victims. He who committed the greatest excesses and horrors (deeds that neither can nor ought to be described) was the most exalted among them, and looked upon as the most distinguished leader. I could not dare recite the treatment which women met with from them. Among other horrors which they committed, they seized a nobleman, murdered him, spitted him, and roasted him in the presence of his wife and children.[5] They forced this unhappy woman to eat of the flesh of her husband, and then made her undergo a most shocking death.

"These wicked wretches burnt and destroyed above sixty castles in the Beauvoisin and in the neighborhood of Corbie, Amiens, and Montdidier. They destroyed above a hundred in the county of Valois, and the bishopricks of Laon, Noyon, and Soissons."[6]

It is worthy of remark, that when these wretches were asked what induced them to commit such horrors, they answered, 'That they did not know.' Such was the precise answer which our first incendiaries gave when asked why they burned the castles; such also would have been the answer of our Transilvanian Carmagnoles. Whence did that clown who became their chief procure his star and his patents written in golden letters? Who had forged them, if not the same Sect that in 1789 forged the pretended orders of Lewis XVI sent to the peasantry in Dauphiné to burn the castles and chase the nobles? The pretext was every where the same, and the like evils flowed from the same, though *hidden, source.*

Besides, there is a most terrible cloud impending over this insurrection of the peasantry in Transilvania against the nobility. In the commencement the government of Hermanstadt refused to send succours on pretence that their alarms were groundless, when it was impossible to deny the horrors committed by the insurgents. Soldiers were sent, but without orders to act. At first appearance one would have thought they were in an understanding with the banditti, who continued their devastations without fearing to be repressed by the soldiery. The troops, having no orders, were reduced to be tranquil spectators of the castles in flames (the incendiaries even marching before them), and heard the unhappy victims calling for succour in the agonies of death, but in vain; they had not the power to act. At length such of the nobles as had escaped the general massacre, being joined by those of the neighbouring counties, formed themselves into a body, marched against the insurgents, and defeated them in various encounters; and Horja, with his followers who were still numerous, was obliged to retire into the mountains. He there gathered fresh forces, and renewed his devastating and sanguinary course. Then at least it was impossible not to give the troops orders to act. But the cloud becomes still more impenetrable. When the insurgents pillaged Abrud-Banga the *Caisse d'Escompte* belonging to the Royal Chyamber fell into their hands; but they would not touch it because it belonged to the Emperor: And soon after a detachment of a Lieutenant and only *twenty-four* men came to escort the chest to Zalatna. On their march a numerous party of Horja's followers might have seized it again, when one of the insurgents advancing proposed a parly between their Chief and the Lieutenant. The Chief advanced, saying, "We are not to be considered as rebels. We love and adore the Emperor in whose service we are. Our sole object is to throw off the tyrannical yoke of the Nobility, which we can bear no longer. Go and tell the Officers of the Chamber of Zalatna, that they have nothing to fear from us."

Notwithstanding the fidelity with which they adhered to their promise, it was necessary to order the troops to act; and in various encounters many prisoners were made from the insurgents. I could wish that it had fallen to my task to praise the generosity of the nobility on this occasion. But my Historian accuses them of having cruelly revenged themselves on a multitude of unhappy persons, who had only joined the revolters through compulsion. A cruel Magistrate condemned them all indiscriminately, and in such numbers, that an

Austrian Major threatened to make him responsible to the Emperor for all the innocent blood which he had spilt.

This harsh treatment of the prisoners stimulated Horja and his followers to new cruelties against the nobility. He intrenched himself again in the mountains, and they in vain offered him a general amnesty. He was beginning to renew his depredations the following year, when he was taken by a stratagem. The insurgents, disconcerted, craved peace, and laid down their arms.

Such was the conclusion of a conspiracy, which was no more than an essay made in those distant provinces by the Sophisters of Equality and Liberty of what they were contriving elsewhere, to level every head which towered above the vulgar. The apparent cause, and which might have greatly contributed in reality, was the excessive abuse of their rights and the oppression over their vassals exercised by the nobility of Transilvania. The tone of moderation and veracity with which the relation we have followed is written, leaves no room to doubt of these oppressions; and in that point of view this terrible insurrection would be foreign to the object of our memoirs. But the insurrection of the negroes may also be attributed to the harshness of the treatment they underwent; yet it is nevertheless universally known, that all the atrocious crimes and barbarities committed by the insurgent slaves against their masters at St. Domingo, Martinico, and Guadaloupe, are to be traced to the plots combined by the levelling Sophisters in Paris.

It is precisely in a similar light that the insurrection in Transilvania is represented in a narrative which we received from a person who was more in the way of observing the progress of Philosophism in Vienna and the other Austrian dominions. He was acquainted with their plots, he refuted the pretences, and foresaw the fatal consequences; he even more than once declared them to the Austrian government; but he was not more hearkened to than many others whose words have been but too fatally verified by the horrid Revolution.

In the memoirs of this accurate observer on the insurrection of Transilvania, I see him combine the efforts of our modern Sophisters with those of a Sect long since lurking in the Occult Lodges of Free-masonry.

At the epoch we are now describing such indeed was the union between the Sophisters and the Craft, and such was the mutual succour which they lent to each other, that it was impossible to develop the progress of the one without seeking the origin of the other, without exposing their common hatreds and common systems, and the combinations of their mutual plots into one and the same conspiracy against Christ and his altars, against Kings and their thrones. Our object therefore in the remaining chapters will be, to reveal the mysteries of Free-masonry, to explain the means and succours it afforded to the modern Sophisters in the French Revolution, and to show how fatal their union has already been, and how much it threatens the social orders of the whole world.

1. The peasantry called *Robota* were not all in an equal degree of slavery. Some held their lands for three, others for four days labour per week. However just the conditions of such a servitude were in themselves, it was nevertheless difficult for the traveller accustomed to other governments not to be persuaded, that these men were very unhappy. I was of that opinion, when an unexpected sight nearly reconciled me to that mode of administration. It was an immense granary belonging to the Lord. In the middle of a large hall were vast heaps of corn; around the place as many divisions as there were families in the village, and each division contained the corn belonging to one family. An overseer attended at the distributions, which were made once a week. If the stock of any particular division was exhausted, the necessary quantity was taken from the Lord's heap for the family in need, who were to replace the corn so taken at the ensuing harvest. By this means the poorest peasant was certain of his sustenance. Let the reader decide, whether such a government may not be as good as others, where the poor man may often starve in the possession of perfect Liberty. I know what might be wished for under every administration; but it is not the part of true Philosophy to overthrow existing governments in the chimerical idea of reducing, some day or other, every thing to its own plans.
2. This may serve to explain the theory of the French Emigration. A friend of mine, who had exercised an almost boundless charity in the manor of which he was Lord, was nearly murdered in the general insurrection of 1789, by that peasantry which he had preserved from the inclemency of the foregoing winter. He was however fortunate enough to escape the hands of the assassins, and, returning to his former mansion, was received with acclamations of joy. On expostulating with his tenants on the treatment he had lately received they begged his pardon in these words, saying, "Ah Sir, we were misled; we were made to believe that if we burnt your title deeds and got rid of you, we should have nothing to pay, and should remain proprietors of the lands we hold; but we ask pardon," &c. He thus escaped the agents, but was afterwards pursued by the revolutionary leaders called Deputies, and is at present involved in the general decree of death pronounced against the Emigrants. T.
3. The fate of France 1789.
4. In our *History of the Clergy during the French Revolution*, we mentioned these atrocious facts at the Place Dauphine, which some of our readers called in question, because they had not witnessed them, though in Paris at the time; but let it be recollected, it was a time when terror would scarcely permit them to raise their heads from their hiding places. Let them consult the writings of Mr. Girtanner, a Swiss physician, who was an eye witness to what he relates. They will learn that the work from which I had made the extract was only a translation from his work, nor did I know at that time that the *Baron de Pelessier Vien* was the translator, as I have since learned from himself. I have also seen Mr. Cambden, chaplain to one of the Irish regiments: He had printed the same account at Liege, and declared to me that he had only published it on the testimony of twenty different witnesses, who all assured him that Mr. Gertanner and myself had been so far from exaggerating the fact, that we had stopped far short of the horrors of that sanguinary scene.
5. When the unfortunate Chevallier Dillon was murdered by his own soldiers at Lisle, after having made him languish from nine in the morning till seven at night with a broken thigh from a pistol ball which one of the cuirassiers under his command had fired at him in the field. As he entered the gates of Lisle he received three more shots, which

put an end to his existence, and his body was dragged to the *Grande Place, where it was roasted, and pieces of his flesh sold for two-pence and three-pence to the standers-by*. On the 11th of August, I was eyewitness to the burning of the bodies of many of the Swiss in large bonfires, made of the wood-work of the guard-houses and out-houses of the Thuilleries, while men covered with blood and smoke were beating down with long poles the flesh which bloated up from the heat. Large piles of burnt bones lay by the fires, which had been kindled soon after the attack upon the palace the day before, which proved that such had been their amusement during the preceding night. T.

6. Froissard's Chronicle, Ed. of Lyons 1559, Chap. 182.

CHAP. IX.

Of the General Secret, or Lesser Mysteries, of Free-masonry.

IN treating of Free-masonry truth and justice rigorously compel us to begin with an exception that exculpates the greater part of those brethren who have been initiated, and who would have conceived a just horror for this association, had they been able to foresee that it could ever make them contract obligations which militated against the duties of the religious man and of the true citizen.

England in particular is full of those upright men, who, excellent Citizens, and of all stations, are proud of being Masons, and who may be distinguished from the others by ties which only appear to unite them more closely in the bonds of charity and fraternal affection. It is not the fear of offending a nation in which I have found an asylum that has suggested this exception. Gratitude on the contrary would silence every vain terror, and I should be seen exclaiming in the very streets of London that England was lost, that it could not escape the French Revolution, if its Free-mason Lodges were similar to those of which I am about to treat. I would say more, that Christianity and all government would have long been at an end in England, if it could be even supposed that her Masons were initiated into the last mysteries of the Sect. Long since have their Lodgees been sufficiently numerous to execute such a design, had the English Masons adopted either the means or the plans and plots of the Occult Lodges.

This argument alone might suffice to except the English Masons in general from what I have to say of the Sect. But there exist many passages in the history of Masonry which necessitate this exception. The following appears convincing.—At the time when the Illuminees of Germany, the most detestable of the Jacobin crew, were seeking to strengthen their party by that of Masonry, they affected a sovereign contempt for the English Lodges. In the letters of Philo to Spartacus we see the English adepts arriving in Germany from London dawbed all over with the ribbands and emblems of their degrees, but void of those plans and projects against the altar and the crown which tend directly to the point. When I shall have given the history of these Illuminees the reader will easily judge what immense weight such a testimony carries with it in favour of the English Lodges. It is glorious for them to see themselves despised by the most unrelenting enemies of the altar, of the throne, and of all society.[1]

For a considerable length of time a similar exception might have been made of the generality of Lodges both in France and Germany. Some of them not only published protestations, but seceded from Masonry as soon as they perceived it to be infected by those revolutionary principles which the Illuminees had infused among the brethren.[2] In short, the number of exceptions to be made for upright Masons is beyond the conception of those who are not thoroughly acquainted with the principles and proceedings of the Sect.—In fact, how is it possible to conceive, that in so numerous an association, where its members are united by bonds and oaths to which they are most religiously attached, so very few of its adepts should be acquainted with the grand object of the association itself? This enigma would have been easily understood had we published (as we hope to do) the history of ancient Jacobinism with that of the middle age, before we had digested these memoirs of modern Jacobinism. But to supply this deficiency, and to methodize our ideas on this famous association, we will begin by treating of the secret which is common to all degrees, that is to say, of what may be called the lesser mysteries; and thence proceeding to the secret and doctrine of the Occult Lodges, we will treat of the grand mysteries of Masonry. We will also treat of its origin and of its propagation; in fine, of its coalition with the conspiring Sophisters, and of the means it afforded them of executing their plans against the altar and the throne.

Until the 12th of August 1792, the French Jacobins had only dated the annals of their Revolution by the years of their pretended *Liberty*. On that day Lewis XVI, who forty-eight hours before had been declared to have forfeited his right to the crown, was carried prisoner to the Tower of the Temple (so called because it formerly belonged to the Knights Templars). On that day the rebel assembly decreed, that to the date of *Liberty*, the date of *Equality* should be added in future in all public acts, and the decree itself was dated the fourth year of *Liberty*, the first year and first day of *Equality*.

It was on that day, for the first time, that the secret of Free-masonry was made public; that secret so dear to them, and which they preserved with all the solemnity of the most inviolable oath. At the reading of this famous decree, they exclaimed, 'We have at length succeeded, and France is no other than an immense lodge. The whole French people are Free-masons, and the whole universe will soon follow their example.'

I witnessed this enthusiasm, I heard the conversations to which it gave rise. I saw Masons, till then the most reserved, who freely and openly declared, "Yes, at length the grand object of Free-masonry is accomplished, EQUALITY and LIBERTY; *all men are equal and brothers; all men are free*. That was the whole substance of our doctrine, the object of our wishes, THE WHOLE *of our* GRAND SECRET." Such was the language I heard fall from the most zealous Masons, from those whom I have seen decorated with all the insignia of the deepest Masonry, and who enjoyed the rights of *Venerable* to preside over Lodges. I have heard them express themselves in this manner before those whom Masons would call *the prophane,* without requiring the smallest secrecy either from the men or women present. They said it in a tone as if they wished all France should be acquainted with this glorious achievement of Masonry; as if it were to recognize in them its benefactors and the authors of that Revolution of *Equality and Liberty* of which it had given so grand an example to all Europe.

Such in reality was the general secret of the Freemasons. It was similar to what in the games of the ancients were called the lesser mysteries, common to all degrees; and though the word expressed the whole, it was not wholly understood by all.—Its progressive explanation, while it renders it innocent in some, renders it monstrous in others.—In the mean time, before we have accounted for this difference, let not the Mason, whatever may be his degree, inculpate us if as in Paris this famous secret ceases to continue one. Too many of the prophane were acquainted with it in that Revolutionary country, for it to remain a secret in others. Even those in England who may still wish to keep it, will vainly object that we have been misled; they will soon see whether it was possible for us to be so. Were we destitute of other evidence, we might safely assert, that those Masons did not mislead us, who were actuated by no other passion than that of the glory of the Sect when they revealed those mysteries which when secure of their execution ceased to be mysterious. Those again did not mislead us, who, formerly initiated into those mysteries, at length owned that they had been dupes: That all that Equality and Liberty which they had treated as mere play had already proved a most desperate game for their country, and might bring ruin on the whole universe. And I have met with many of these adepts since the Revolution, both in France and elsewhere, who had formerly been zealous Masons, but latterly confessing with bitterness this fatal secret, which reduces the whole science of Masonry, like the French Revolution, to these two words *Equality* and *Liberty.*

I once more conjure the upright Masons not to look upon themselves as accused of wishing to establish a similar Revolution. When I shall have verified this article of their doctrine, the essence and the basis of all their mysteries, I will show how it came to pass that so many noble and virtuous characters were initiated without even suspecting the ultimate design. But for the history of the Revolution, it is necessary that the most distant doubt should not subsist as to this *fundamental secret.* If this were not made clear, it would be impossible for the reader to comprehend the help which the Sophisters of Rebellion and Impiety acquired from Masonry. I shall therefore seek other proofs beside these avowals, which many others must have heard like me from the adepts, since their successes in France had made them regard secrecy in future as superfluous.

Antecedent to these avowals, there was an easy method of discovering that Equality and Liberty were the grand objects of Masonry. The very name of *Free*-mason carries with it the idea of Liberty; as to *Equality* it was disguised under the term *Fraternity,* which has nearly a similar signification. But who has not heard the Mason brag of the Equality which reigned in their Lodges, where Princes and Nobles, the rich and the poor, all were *equal*, all were brothers: that distinctions of rank no longer existed when once passed the Tyler;[3] and that the sole appellation used among them was that of Brother, the only name also which gives us an idea of perfect Equality.

It is true, that it was expressly forbidden to any Mason ever to write these two words *Equality* and *Liberty* consecutively, or give the least hint that their secret resided in the union of these two grand principles; and that law was so exactly observed by their writers, that I do not remember ever to have seen it transgressed among the numerous volumes which I have read, though of the most secret sort, on the different degrees. Mirabeau himself, when he pretended to reveal the secrets of Masonry, only dared reveal them in part. The order of Free-masonry, which is spread all over the world, he says, has for its objects, Charity, *Equality of stations*, and perfect harmony.[4]—Though this *Equality of stations* seems pretty well to denote the Liberty which must exist in this Equality, still Mirabeau, who was a Mason himself, knew that the time was not yet come, when his brethren would pardon him for avowing that in these two words consisted their general secret; but this very reservedness sufficiently denotes how much both the one and the other were held precious in their mysteries. If we refer to the hymns and songs sung in chorus at their festivals, we shall generally find some verses or stanza in honour of Equality or of Liberty.[5] In the same way we may often remark either the one or the other to be the subject of the discourses they have pronounced, and which are sometimes printed.

Were I even deprived of these proofs, still it would be incumbent on me to declare what personal knowledge I may have acquired.

Though I have seen so many Masons who since the famous decree of *Equality* have spoken in the most open manner of this famous secret (though the oath which they had taken should have made them more reserved on it than me, who never took any oath either in their Lodges, or to the Revolution of Equality and Liberty), I should nevertheless be perfectly silent on all that I have witnessed, were I not thoroughly convinced how much it imported all nations, to be acquainted with the ultimate tendency of Masonry. I should be sorry to see thousands of upright Masons, especially in England, take offence at the discovery of their secret; but such virtuous and upright men are not those who would prefer the vain-glory of their secret to the public welfare, or to the proper precautions to be taken against the abuses of Masonry; in a word against an abominable Sect who, under the pretence of virtue, wish to mislead the universe. I shall speak openly and without the fear of displeasing those Masons whom I esteem and revere; and shall but little trouble myself about the displeasure of others whose persons I contemn and whose plots I abhor.

During the last twenty years it was difficult, especially in Paris, to meet persons who did not belong to the society of Masonry. I was acquainted with many, and some were my intimate friends. These, with all that zeal common to young adepts, frequently pressed me to become one of their brotherhood.

As I constantly refused, they undertook to enroll me notwithstanding my refusal.—The plan settled, I was invited to dinner at a friend's house and was the only prophane in the midst of a large party of Masons. Dinner over and the servants ordered to withdraw, it was proposed to form themselves into a Lodge, and to initiate me. I persisted in my refusal, and particularly refused to take the oath of keeping a secret, the very object of which was unknown to me. They dispensed with the oath, but I still refused. They became more pressing, telling me that Masonry was perfectly innocent, and that its morality was unobjectionable: In reply, I asked whether it was better than that of the Gospel. They only answered by forming themselves into a Lodge, when began all those grimaces and childish ceremonies which are described in books of Masonry, such as Jachin and Boaz. I attempted to make my escape, but in vain; the apartment was very extensive, the house in a retired situation, the servants in the secret, and all the doors locked. I am questioned, and answer most of the questions laughing. I am received *Apprentice*, and immediately after *Fellow-craft*. Having received these two degrees, I was informed that a third was to be conferred on me. On this I am conducted into a large room. There the scene changes, and takes a more serious appearance. And though they dispensed with my undergoing all the more toilsome tests, they nevertheless were not sparing in a multitude of tiresome and insignificant questions.

On finding myself obliged to go through this farce, I had taken care to say, that since they had cut off every means of retreat, I was forced to submit; but that, if I perceived any thing either against honour or conscience, they should soon find with whom they had to deal.

As yet I had only perceived a mere childish play and burlesque ceremonies, in spite of all the gravity which the brethren affected; but I had given no offence by any of my answers. At length the Venerable with the utmost gravity put the following question: "Brother, are you disposed to execute all the orders of the Grand-Master, though you were to receive contrary orders from a King, an Emperor, or any other Sovereign whatever?" My answer was "*No*." "What *No*," replies the Venerable with surprize! Are you only entered among us to betray our secrets! Would you hesitate between the interests of Masonry and those of the prophane?—You are not aware then that there is not one of our swords but is ready to pierce the heart of a traitor." Notwithstanding the gravity with which this question was put, and the menaces which accompanied it, I could not persuade myself that he was in earnest; but I still continued to answer in the negative, and replied, as may easily be imagined, "That it was rather extraordinary to suppose that I who had only been brought in by force could ever have come there in order to betray the secrets of Masonry. You talk of secrets, and you have told me none. If in order to be initiated I must promise to obey a man that I know not, and if the interests of Masonry can be a bar to any part of my duty, good day to you Gentlemen. It is not too late as yet. I know nothing of your mysteries, nor do I wish to know more of them."

This answer did not disconcert the Venerable in the least, and he continued to act his part perfectly well; he pressed me more earnestly, and renewed his threats. I certainly believed the whole to be a farce; but even in joke I would not promise obedience to their Grand Master, especially on the supposition that his commands could ever be contrary to those of the Sovereign. I replied once more, "Gentlemen, or Brethren, I told you before, that if there was any thing in your games either against honor or conscience, you should learn whom you had to deal with. We are now come to the point. You may do what you please with me, but you shall never make me assent to such a proposition; and once more I say *No*."

Every one kept the most profound silence except the Venerable, though they were much amused with the scene. It at length grew more serious between the Venerable and me. He would not give up the point, and renewing his question over and over again, he was in hopes, by tiring my patience, to extort a YES. At length I found myself quite wearied out. I was blindfolded, I tore off the bandage, threw it upon the ground, and stamping with my foot, called out No, with every sign of impatience. Immediately the whole Lodge clap their hands in sign of applause, and the Venerable compliments me on my constancy. "Such are the men for us, men of resolution and courage."—"What," said I, "men of resolution! And how many do you find who resist your threats! You yourselves, gentlemen, have not you all said YES to this question: and if you have said it, how is it possible that you can persuade me that your mysteries contain nothing against honor or conscience."

The tone I assumed had thrown the Lodge into confusion. The brethren surrounded me, telling me I had taken things too much in earnest, and in too literal a sense: that they never had pretended to engage in any thing contrary to the duties of every true Frenchman, and that in spite of all my resistance I should nevertheless be admitted. The Venerable soon restored order with a few strokes of his mallet. He then informed me that I was passed to the degree of *Master*, adding, that if the secret was not given to me, it was only because a more regular lodge, and held with the ordinary ceremonies, was necessary on such an occasion. In the mean while he gave me the signs and the pass words for the third degree, as he had done for the other two. This was sufficient to enable me to be admitted into a regular Lodge, and now we were all brethren. As for me, I had been metamorphosed into *apprentice, fellow-craft,* and *master* in one evening, without having ever dreamt of it in the morning.

I was too well acquainted with those who had received me, not to believe their protestation sincere, when they declared that they had never pretended to engage in any thing contrary to their duty. And in justice I am bound to declare, that, excepting the Venerable, who turned out a violent Jacobin, they all showed themselves loyal subjects at the Revolution. I promised to be present at a regular meeting, provided the oath was never mentioned to me. They promised that it never should be insisted on, and they kept their words. They only requested that I would inscribe my name on the list, that it might be sent to the Grand Lodge of the East. I refused again, and asked time to consider of it; and when I had sufficiently attended to see what these Lodges were I retired, without even consenting to inscribe my name.

On my first appearance in a regular Lodge, I was quit for a fine speech on Masonry, of which I knew but little at that time, so chiefly dwelt upon fraternity, and on the pleasure of living with brethren.

They had agreed on that day to receive an apprentice, who was to have the secret given him with all the ordinary forms, in order that I might learn it, though only a spectator. It would be useless to swell this chapter by describing the ceremonial and the trials on such occasions. In the first degrees, they appear to be nothing more than a childish play. I may refer my readers to the Key of Masonry (La Clef de Maçons) or to the Free-masons Catechism, and some other books of the sort, which are perfectly exact as to the ceremonial of the three degrees which I received and saw conferred upon others, excepting in some very small points of no consequence.

The grand object for me was to learn the famous secret of Masonry. The moment at length comes when the postulant is ordered to approach nearer to the Venerable. Then the brethren who had been armed with swords for the occasion drawing up in two lines held their swords elevated, leaning the points toward each other, and formed what in Masonry is called the *arch of steel*. The candidate passes under this arch to a sort of altar elevated on two steps, at the farthest end of the Lodge. The Master, seated in an arm chair, or a sort of throne, behind this altar, pronounced a long discourse on the inviolability of the secret which was to be imparted, and on the danger of breaking the oath which the candidate was going to take. He pointed to the naked swords which were always ready to pierce the breast of the traitor, and declared to him that it was impossible to escape their vengeance. The candidate then swears, "that rather than betray the secret, he consents to have his head cut off, his heart and entrails torn out, and his ashes cast before the wind." Having taken the oath, the Master said the following words to him, which the reader may easily conceive have not escaped my memory, as I had expected them with so much impatience, "My dear brother, the secret of Masonry consists in these words, EQUALITY AND LIBERTY; *all men are equal and free; all men are brethren.*" The Master did not utter another syllable, and every body embraced the new *brother equal and free.*— The Lodge broke up, and we gayly adjourned to a Masonic repast.

I was so far from suspecting any further meaning in this famous secret, that I could scarcely refrain from bursting into a fit of laughter on hearing it, and with the greatest simplicity told those who had introduced me, If that was all their secret, I had known it a long time.

And certainly there was no occasion for being a mason to learn that man is not born for slavery, but to enjoy a *true Liberty* under the empire of the laws; or if they understand *by Equality* that as we are the children of one common parent, the creatures of the same God, we are to love and help each other as brethren; such truths certainly are better taught in the Gospel than by the childish rites of Masonry. I must say, that though the Lodge was numerously attended, I did not see a single craftsman who gave any other interpretation to this famous secret. The reader will see that it was necessary to go through many other degrees before they were initiated into a very different Equality and Liberty, and even that many who rose to higher degrees were never initiated into the ultimate sense of their famous secret.

Let not people be surprized that English Masonry should be chiefly composed of good and loyal subjects, whose main object is mutually to help each other on the principles of Equality, which with them is nothing more than Fraternity. Few English craftsmen are acquainted with more than the three first degrees already mentioned; and the reader may rest assured, that with the exception of the imprudent question on obedience to the Grand Master of the Order, there is nothing which can render the secret dangerous, were it not for the Jacobin interpretation. The English good sense has banished such an explanation. I have even heard of a resolution taken by some of the chief craftsmen, of rejecting all those who might seek to introduce the revolutionary liberty among them. I have read most excellent discourses and lectures on the avoiding of abuses, in the history of their Masonry. I have there seen the Grand Master telling the Brethren that the true Equality of the craft, does not authorize the Brother when out of the Lodge to derogate from that respect and deference due to the rank which any person bears in the world, or their different political degrees and titles. I have also remarked in the secret instructions of the Grand Master many excellent lectures to conciliate the Equality and Liberty of the craft, with fidelity and submission to the laws, in short, with all the duties of a loyal subject.[6] Hence it arises, that though the English have every thing in common with the craft of other nations, as far as the degree of Master inclusive; though they have the same secret, the same word, and the same signs to know each other by, yet as they generally stop at this degree, they never are initiated into the Grand Mysteries; or we should perhaps be more correct, if we said they had rejected them. They have found means of purifying Masonry. We shall soon see how little these grand mysteries could agree with the character of a nation which has given so many proofs of its wisdom.

1. See letter of Philo to Spartacus.
2. See the speech of a Master pronounced in a Bavarian Lodge.
3. The Officer standing at the door, with a drawn sword, to receive the sign, and admit only the real Members.
4. Essay on the Illuminees, Chap. 15.
5. It is for this reason, that amidst all their encomiums on benevolence, which is the chief object of their songs, we see the English always add some lines in the sense of the following:

> Masons have long been free,
> And may they ever be, &c.
> Princes and Kings our brothers are, &c.

These lines, however, notwithstanding their tendency to Equality and Liberty, are not to be understood in a Jacobinal light in the mouth of an English Mason.
6. See the 1st part of the History of English Masonry.

CHAP. X.

Of the Grand Mysteries or Secrets of the Occult Lodges.

WE comprehend under the designation of Occult Lodges, or the higher degrees of Masonry, all Freemasons in general who, after having past the first three degrees of *Apprentice, Fellowcraft,* and *Master,* show sufficient zeal to be admitted into the higher degrees, where the veil is rent asunder, where emblematical and allegorical figures are thrown aside, and where the twofold principle of Equality and Liberty is unequivocally explained by *war againt Christ and his Altars, war against Kings and their Thrones*!!! In demonstrating that such is the result of the grand mysteries of the Craft, it will not be the want, but the multiplicity of proofs that will embarrass us. These alone would fill a large volume, and we wish to comprize them in this chapter. The reader will at least dispense with the emblems, oaths, ceremonies, and trials which are peculiar to each of these higher degrees. To show their last object and to develop their doctrine is the essential point, and what we shall always have in view. We shall begin by general observations, which will enable the reader to follow these mysteries more accurately, according as they are explained.

Notwithstanding that in the first degrees of Masonry every thing appears to partake of puerile inventions, they nevertheless contain many things which the Sect have thrown out, merely to observe the impression which they made on the young adepts, and to judge from thence to what lengths they may be led.

1st. It declares the grand object it has in view to be at one time, *the raising of temples to virtue, and the excavating of dungeons for vice*; at another, to bring the adepts *to light*, and to deliver them from the darkness with which the *prophane* are encompassed; and by the *prophane* are understood the remainder of the universe. This promise is contained in the first Catechism of the Craft, and none will deny it. Nevertheless, this promise alone sufficiently indicates that the Craft acknowledge a morality and teach a doctrine which brands Christ and his Gospel with error and darkness.

2dly. The Masonic and Christian æra do not coincide. *The year of Light* dates with them from the first days of the creation: This again is what no Mason will deny. But that custom clearly demonstrates that their *lights,* their *morality,* and their *religious doctrines,* are anterior to the Evangelical Revelation, or even to Moses and the Prophets; they will, in short, be whatever incredulity may please to style the Religion of Nature.

3dly. In the Masonic language, all their Lodges are but one temple representing the whole universe; the temple which extends from the *East to the West, from the South to the North*. They admit into this temple with equal indifference the Christian or the Jew, the Turk or the Idolater, in fine, without distinction of Sect or religion. All equally behold the *light*, all learn the science of virtue, of real happiness, and all may remain members of the Craft, and rise in its degrees up to that where they are taught that all religious tenets are but errors and prejudices. Though many Masons may view this re-union in no other light than that of universal charity and benevolence, which ought to extend to all mankind, whether Jew, Gentile, Idolater, or Christian, it is nevertheless much to be feared, that this re-union of error and falsehood only tends to infuse an indifference for all religious tenets into the minds of the adepts, as a preparatory step to the denial of all in the higher degrees.

4thly. It is always under the most dreadful oaths of secrecy, that the Freemasons communicate their pretended lights or their art of building temples to virtue, and dungeons for vice. When both truth and virtue had every thing to fear from the reigning tyrants, it may be conceived that they taught their lessons in private; but, so far from exacting an oath of secrecy, they condemned silence as criminal when their lessons could be made public, and commanded that what had been learned under the shadow of the night should be preached openly at noon day. Either the doctrines of the Craft are conformable to the laws of Christianity, to the peace of states, and conducive to virtue and happiness (and then what has it had to fear from Kings and Pontiffs since Christianity was established?) or, their pretended science is in opposition to the religion and the laws of the Christian world (and then we have only to say, that the evil doer seeks to hide himself).

5thly. Most certainly the Freemasons do not make a secret of what is praise-worthy in their associations. It is not that fraternal affection for their neighbour which they hide, and which they only have in common with every religious observer of the gospel. Neither do they make a secret of the sweets of that convivial Equality which accompanies their meetings and their fraternal repasts. On the contrary, they are perpetually extolling their benevolence, and nobody is ignorant of the conviviality of their regales. Their secret must therefore contain something widely different from this fraternity, and something less innocent than the mirth of the Masonic table.

Such language in general might have been held to all Masons; such reasonings might have made them suspect that the higher degrees of their association contained mysteries which it was far more interested in hiding, than their fraternity, their signs, and pass-words. That affected secrecy on the first principlees of Masonry, *Equality* and *Liberty*, the oath never to reveal that such was the basis of their doctrines, premised that there existed such an explanation of these words as the Sect was interested in hiding both from the state and church. And in reality it was to attain to this explanation of the last mysteries that so many trials, oaths, and degrees were necesssary.

To convince the reader how much these surmizes are realized in the Occult Lodges, it is necessary for us to go back to the degree of Master, and relate the allegorical story of which the successive explanations and interpretations form the profound mysteries of the higher degrees.

In this degree of Master-mason the Lodge is hung round with black. In the middle is a coffin covered with a pall: the brethren standing round it in attitudes denoting sorrow and revenge. When the new adept is admitted, the Master relates to him the following history or fable:

"Adoniram presided over the payment of the workmen who were building the temple by Solomon's orders. They were three thousand workmen. That each one might receive his due, Adoniram divided them into three classes, Apprentices, Fellow-crafts, and Masters. He entrusted each class with a word, signs, and a grip by which they might be recognized. Each class was to preserve the greatest secrecy as to these signs and words. Three of the Fellow-crafts, wishing to know the word, and by that means obtain the salary, of Master, hid themselves in the temple, and each posted himself at a different gate. At the usual time when Adoniram came to shut the gates of the temple, the first of the three met him, and demanded the *word of the masters*; Adoniram refused to give it, and received a violent blow with a stick on his head. He flies to another gate, is met, challenged, and treated in a similar manner by the second: flying to the third door he is killed by the Fellow-craft posted there, on his refusing to betray the word. His assassins buried him under a heap of rubbish, and marked the spot with a branch of Acacia.

"Adoniram's absence gave great uneasiness to Solomon and the Masters. He is sought for every where: at length one of the Masters discovers the corpse, and, taking it by the finger, the finger parted from the hand; he took it by the wrist, and it parted from the arm; when the Master, in astonishment, cried out *Mac Benac*, which the Craft interprets by "*the flesh parts from the bones.*"

"Lest Adoniram should have revealed the *word*, the Masters convened and agreed to change it, and to substitute the words *Mac Benac*; sacred words, that Free-masons dare not pronounce out of the Lodges, and there each only pronounces one syllable, leaving his neighbour to pronounce the other."

The history finished, the adept is informed, that the object of the degree he has just received is to recover the word lost by the death of Adoniram, and to revenge this martyr of the Masonic secrecy.[1] The generality of Masons, looking upon this history as no more than a fable, and the ceremonies as puerile, give themselves very little trouble in searching farther into these mysteries.

These sports, however, assume a more serious aspect when we arrive at the degree of Elect (*Elu*). This degree is subdivided into two parts; the first has the revenging of Adoniram for its object, the other to recover the *word*, or rather the sacred doctrine which it expressed, and which has been lost.

In this degree of Elect, all the brethren appear dressed in black, wearing a breast-piece on the left side, on which is embroidered a death's head, a bone, and a poniard, encircled by the motto of *conquer or die*. The same motto is embroidered on a ribband which they wear in saltier. Every thing breathes death and revenge. The candidate is led into the Lodge blindfolded, with bloody gloves on his hands. An adept with a poniard in hius hand threatens to run him through the heart for the crime with which he is accused. After various frights, he obtains his life, on condition that he will revenge the father of Masonry in the death of his assassin. He is shown to a dark cavern. He is to penetrate into it, and they call to him, Strike all that shall oppose you; enter, defend yourself, and avenge our master; at that price you shall receive the degree of Elect. A poniard in his right hand, a lamp in his left, he proceeds; a phantom opposes his passage, he hears the same voice repeat, Strike, avenge Hiram, there is his assassin. He strikes and the blood flows.—Strike off his head, the voice repeats, and the head of the corpse is lying at his feet. He seizes it by the hair,[2] and triumphantly carries it back as a proof of his victory; shows it to each of the brethren, and is judged worthy of the new degree.

I have questioned divers Masons whether this apprenticeship to ferocity and murder had never given them the idea, that the head to be cut off was that of Kings, and they candidly owned that the idea had never struck them until the Revolution had convinced them of the fact.

It was the same with respect to the religious part of this degee, where the adept is at once Pontiff and Sacrificer with the rest of the brethren. Vested in the ornaments of the priesthood, they offer bread and wine, according to the order of Melchisedec. The secret object of this ceremony is to re-establish religious Equality, and to exhibit all men equally Priests and Pontiffs, to recall the brethren to natural religion, and to persuade them that the religion of Moses and of Christ had violated religious Equality and Liberty by the distinction of Priests and Laity. It was the Revolution again which opened the eyes of many of the adepts, who then owned that they had been dupes to this impiety, as they had been to the regicide essay in the former part.[3]

These mysteries are not sufficiently explained in the degree of Elect for all to comprehend them. The generality of Masons initiated in this degree give themselves little trouble to understand the real signification of them; and as long as they have any sentiments of religion or attachment to their Prince, they reject with indignation all interpretations which militate against either. Many of them are disgusted with the multiplicity of trials, and are content to remain in the inferior degrees, which suffice to give them the title of Masons, admit them to all the Masonic repasts, and even entitle them to the alms and benefactions which the Lodges bestow on their indigent brethren.—Those whose zeal is not cooled by this multiplicity of trials, are generally admitted from the degree of *Master*, or from that of *Elect*, to the three Scotch degrees. We shall not seek for the history and tendency of these three degrees in books which have been written to discredit the craft. The German adept who translated them into his language for the instruction of his brethren, is one of the most zealous knights for the doctrine therein contained. His whole genius is exerted in their defence, nor could we follow a more unexceptionable author. His object was to infuse light into his brethren; and we prophane beings may draw the following conclusions from his lectures.[4]

Every Mason who wishes to be admitted into the Scotch degrees, and even into all other degrees of Masonry, is first taught that until that period he has lived in slavery, and it is on that account only that he is admitted into the presence of the other brethren with a rope about his neck, praying that he may be delivered from his bonds. But when he aspires at the third Scotch degree, or at becoming a knight of St. Andrew, he must appear in a far more humiliating costume. The candidate is shut up in a dark cell, a rope with four flip knots is twisted round his neck, he is stretched upon the floor; there, by the dull light of a twinkling lamp, he is abandoned to himself to meditate on the wretched state of slavery in which he exists, and to learn properly to estimate the value of Liberty. At length one of the brethren comes and introduces him to the Lodge, leading him by the rope, holding a drawn sword in his right hand as if meant to run him through the heart, in case he made any resistance. After having undergone a long examination, and particularly after having sworn on the salvation of his soul, never to reveal the secrets with which he is entrusted, he is declared free. It would be useless to enumerate all the different oaths; it is sufficient to say, that each degree and subdivision of degree has its peculiar oath, and that they are all frightful; all call the vengeance of God and of the Brotherhood on the unhappy man who shall betray their secret. In future then we shall only treat of the doctrine of these secrets.

In the first degree of Scotch Knighthood the adept is informed, that he has been elevated to the dignity of *High Priest*. He receives a sort of benediction in the name of the *immortal and invisible Jehovah*, and in future it is under that title that he is to adore the Deity, *because* the signification of JEHOVAH *is far more expressive than that of* ADONAI.

In this first degree he receives the Masonic science only as descending from Solomon and Hiram, and revived by the Knights Templars.—But in the second degree he learns that it is to be traced to Adam himself, and has been handed down by Noah, Nimrod, Solomon, Hugo de Paganis, the founder of the Knights Templars, and Jaques de Molay, their last Grand Master, who each in their turns had been the favourites of *Jehovah,* and are styled the Masonic Sages. At length in the third degree it is revealed to him, that the celebrated *word* lost by the death of Hiram was this name of Jehovah. It was found, he is told, by the Knights Templars at the time when the Christians were building a Church at Jerusalem. In digging the foundations in that part on which the holy of holies of Solomon's temple formerly stood, they discovered three stones, which had formerly been parts of the foundation. The form and junction of these three stones drew the attention of the Templars; and their astonishment was extreme, when they beheld the name of Jehovah engraved on the last. This was the famous word lost by the death of Adoniram. The Knights Templars, on their return to Europe, took great care not to lose so precious a monument. They carried them into Scotland, taking particular care of that which bore the name of Jehovah. The Scotch sages on their part were not forgetful of the respect due to such precious monuments, they made them the foundation stones of their first Lodge; and as these first stones were laid on St. Andrew's day, they took the name of Knights of St. Andrew. Their successors are entrusted with the secret, and are at this day the perfect masters of Freemasonry, the High Priests of Jehovah.

If we lay aside the hermetical part of the science, or the transmutation of metals, such will be in substance the whole doctrine which is revealed to the adept initiated in the grand mysteries of the Scotch degrees.

In a sort of Cathechism, to which he answers to show that he has remembered every thing that he has seen, and all that has been explained to him in the Lodge, or, as it is then called, in Solomon's temple, the following question is asked, *Is that all you have seen?* To which he answers, *I have seen many other things, but, like the other Scotch Masters, I keep them secret in my heart.* This secret henceforth cannot be difficult to understand. It is only to view the *Scotch Master* in his new character of *High Priest of Jehovah*, or of that worship, that pretended Deism, which we have been told was successively the religion of Adam, Noah, Nimrod, Solomon, Hugo de Paganis, of the Grand Master Molay, and of the Knights Templars, and which at this day is to constitute the religion of the complete Master Mason.

These mysteries might have sufficed for the adepts. All who had obtained the Scotch degrees were declared free in future, and all were equally Priests of Jehovah. This priesthood ridded them of all the mysteries of the Gospel, and of all revealed religion. That liberty and happiness which the Sect declares to consist in the revival of Deism, sufficiently instils into the mind of the adept what he is to think of Christianity and of its divine Author. Nevertheless the grand mysteries are not exhausted. The adepts still have to discover who was the person that wrested the *word*, the famous name of *Jehovah*, from their predecessors; that is to say, who it was that destroyed their favourite worship of Deism. It was but too evident that the whole fable of Hiram or Adoniram and of his assassins was no more than an allegory, the explanation of which must naturally answer the questions, who is the real assassin of Adoniram? By whom was the Deistical form of worship destroyed? Who was it that wrested the famous word from the Sect? He is the person against whom the vengeance and the hatred of the Sect is directed, and it was necessary to instil the same spirit into the minds of its profound adepts. To effectuate this, we ascend to a new degree called the Knights *Rosæ Crucis*, or the Rosicrucians.

It is certainly a most atrocious blasphemy to accuse Christ of having destroyed by his religion on the doctrine of the unity of God; when on the contrary the most evident and the most attested of all facts is, that to his religion we owe the banishment of thousands and thousands of false gods, which the Idolators had made to themselves. The gospel, in declaring the unity of God, teaches us the Trinity of Persons; but this mystery like all others which we learn from revelation, humbles the Sophisters in their own minds. Fraught with ingratitude against him who has cast the idols on the dust, they have sworn an eternal hatred against the eternal Word, because he reveals a God whom in their madness they are not able to comprehend. *Christ himself* in their eyes is the destroyer of the unity of God, he is the great enemy of *Jehovah*; and to infuse the hatred of the Sect into the minds of the new adepts, constitutes the grand mystery of the new degree which they have called Rosicrucian.

As the adept was seldom initiated into this new degree before he had passed through the Scotch degrees, he is already aware, as the reader must observe, that *Jehovah* is no longer the word sought after, and here we shall see every thing related only to the author of Christianity. The ornaments of the Lodge appear to be solely intended to recal to the candidate the solemn mystery of Mount Calvary. The whole is hung in black, an altar is to be seen at the bottom, and over the altar is a transparent representation of the three crosses, the middle one bearing the ordinary inscription. The brethren in sacerdotal vestments are seated on the ground, in the most profound silence, sorrowful and afflicted, resting their heads on their arm to represent their grief. It is not the death of the son of God, who died victim of our sins, that is the cause of their affliction, the grand object of it is evident by the first answer which is made to the question with which all Lodges are generally opened.

The Master asks the Senior Warden what o'clock is it? The answer varies according to the different degrees. In this it is as follows: "It is the first hour of the day, the time when the veil of the temple was rent asunder, when darkness and consternation was spread over the earth, when the light was darkened, when *the implements of Masonry were broken*, when the flaming star disappeared, when the cubic stone was broken, *when the word was lost*."[5]

The adept who has attended to the progressive discoveries he has made in the different degrees, needs no further lessons to understand the meaning of this answer. He thereby learns that the day on which the *word* JEHOVAH was lost is precisely that on which the Son of God dying on a cross for the salvation of mankind consummated the grand mystery of our Religion, destroying the reign of every other, whether Judaic, natural, or sophistical. The more a Mason is attached to the *word*, that is, to his pretended natural Religion, the more inveterate will his hatred be against the author of Revealed Religion.

Neither is this *word*, which he has already found, any longer the object of his researches; his hatred has further views. He must seek for a new word, which shall perpetuate in his own mind and that of his brethren their blasphemous hatred for the God of Christianity; and for this they adopt the inscription of the cross.

Every Christian knows the significtion of INRI, I*esus* N*azarenus* R*ex* I*udæorum* (Jesus of Nazareth King of the Jews). The Rosicrucian is taught the following interpretation—the I*ew of* N*azareth* led by R*aphael* into I*udea*; an interpretation which, divesting Christ of his divinity, assimilates him to a common man, whom the Jew Raphael conducts to Jerusalem there to suffer condign punishment for his crimes. As soon as the candidate has proved that he understands the Masonic meaning of this inscription INRI, the Master exclaims, *My dear Brethren, the word is found again*, and all present applaud this luminous discovery, that — HE whose death was the consummation and the grand mystery of the Christian Religion was no more than a common Jew crucified for his crimes.

It is thus that the Sect have blasphemously adopted the very word, which recals to the Christian all that love which he bears for the Son of God expiring on the cross for the salvation of mankind, as their watchword of hatred. They repeat it to each other when they meet, and INRI is to perpetuate their spite against him who loved them even unto the death of the cross.

It is not on the authority of persons strangers to the craft that we have disclosed this atrocious mystery of Occult Masonry. What I have already said respecting my initiation to the first degrees put me in the way of conversing with those whom I knew to be more advanced, and in many of these interviews it happened that, notwithstanding all their secrecy, some unguarded expressions escaped the most zealous adepts, which threw light on the subject. Others lent me their books, presuming that their obscureness and the want of the essential words, or the method of discovering them, would baffle all my attempts to understand them. I nevertheless discovered some of these words, such as *Jehovah*, by uniting several pages and only taking the bottom letter of each. This famous word discovered, I soon got knowledge of that of *Inri*. I then combined all I had seen, all that I knew of the different degrees, with what I had collected from divers conversations I had had with certain Masons, whose Philosophism was otherwise known to me. I afterwards conversed with the most candid men whom I knew to be in the same degrees. I reprobated particularly those ceremonies so evidently in derision of Religion, and which they had never beheld but as games without any object. I never met with one who denied the facts as I have stated them. They owned the different reading of the word *Inri* in the degree Rosæ Crucis, but they denied the most distant idea of the consequences which I had drawn. Some, on reflection, acknowledged them to be well founded, while others considered them vastly exaggerated.

At the time when the Revolution took place, I combined my preceding discoveries, the decrees of the National Assembly, and the secret of the first degree, and no longer doubted that Masonry was but a society formed by men who, on the first initiation of their adepts, gave them the words Equality and Liberty as their secret, leaving to well-meaning and religious Masons to interpret them according to their own principles; yet reserving to themselves to interpret (in their Occult degrees) these same words according to the full extent of the French Revolution.

One of these Brethren, who had long since been admitted to the degree Rosæ Crucis, but who was at the same time a very virtuous and religious man, was much concerned at seeing me in this opinion. He tried every means to give me a better idea of a society in which he was proud of having filled the most honorable posts. This was a topic on which we had often conversed; and he wished much to make me a convert to Masonry. He was indeed almost affronted with me for saying that he was not initiated into all the mysteries of Masonry, though a Rosicrucian, or else that this degree had its subdivisions, and that he was only partially acquainted with them. At length I convinced him of the fact, by asking the explanation of some of the Masonic *Hieroglyphics*; he owned that he had asked their meaning, but the explanation of them had been refused him; yet he had no doubt of their being as innocent emblems as the Square, the Compass, the Trowel, and many others. I knew that he had but one degree more to take, and the veil would be rent asunder. I proposed or rather marked out the means by which he might acquire that degree; and then, I told him, all illusion as to the real object of the Occult Masons would vanish. He was too eager for being initiated not to make a trial of the means I proposed; but he was convinced that it would prove ineffectual, and only furnish him with new arms to combat my unjust prejudices against Masonry. A few days after I saw him enter my room; but in such a state of agitation, that his lips could scarcely utter, "O my dear friend, my dear friend—you were in the right—Oh, how much you were in the right!... Where have I been? My God! Where have I been?"—I easily understood these exclamations; but the poor man could scarcely recover himself so as to continue. He threw himself into a chair as if he were exhausted, perpetually repeating, "Where have I been?—Oh how much you are in the right!"—I earnestly desired him to give me some particulars with which I was unacquainted—"Oh how much you were in the right!" he repeated again, "but that is all I can tell you."—"Oh, unhappy man," I exclaimed, "you have then taken that execrable oath, and I am the person who has exposed you to that rash deed; I sincerely ask your pardon, but I protest upon my word, that I never reflected on that execrable oath when I suggested the means by which you might convince yourself, and learn to know those detested beings who have so horribly abused your credulity. I know that it had been better for you to have been for ever ignorant of that fatal secret, than that you should learn it at the expense of so horrid an oath. I really did not reflect on it, or I should never have exposed you to it; no, I could not in conscience." It was really true, that I never had reflected on this oath. Without examining whether such wicked oaths are binding, I feared being indiscreet. But it had been sufficient for me to have shown this gentleman that I was acquainted, at least in part, with these Occult mysteries. He saw clearly by my questions, that he had taught me nothing new by an avowal which alone proves the very essence of these Occult degrees.

His fortune had been ruined by the Revolution; and he declared to me, that it would from that moment be retrieved, provided he accepted of a proposal which had been made to him.—"If I chuse," said he, "to go to London, Bruxelles, Constantinople, or any other town I please, neither I, my wife, nor my children, will ever want for any thing."—"Yes," I replied, "but on condition only that you go there *to preach Equality and Liberty; in short, all the horrors of the Revolution.*"—"*You are right,*" replied he, *but that is all I can say*—Oh my God where have I been!—I beg you will not question me any farther."

This was sufficient for my present purpose; but I hoped in time to learn farther particulars. Nor were my hopes vain. The following is what I have gathered from various Masons who, finding me acquainted with the major part of their secrets, spoke the more openly to me, till at length, feeling how much they had been duped by this Occult Sect, they would willing have revealed all its mysteries, could they have done it without exposing themselves to danger.

The explanation which was given to an adept of all that he had seen before on his admission to the degree of Rosæ Crucis, depended entirely on the disposition they observed in him. If they had to do with a man who was proof against their impiety, they sought to divert him from the Church under pretence of regenerating his faith; they represented to him, that there existed an infinity of abuses in Christianity at present, with respect to Equality and Liberty of the children of God. With them the word to be recovered was, a wish for a Revolution which should revive those times when every thing was common among Christians, when the distinctions of rich, of poor, or of high and mighty Lords, were unknown. They were taught to look forward to the most happy regeneration of mankind, and almost to a new heaven and a new earth. Credulous and simple minds were caught by such magnificent promises. They looked upon the Revolution as that sacred fire which was to purify the earth; and these credulous adepts were seen to second the Revolution with the enthusiastic zeal of a holy cause. This may be called *Mystical Masonry*. Such was the craft of all those fools for whom the Occult Masons set up the Prophetess *La Brousse*, so famous in the beginning of the Revolution. Such again was the weak-minded *Varlet*, the Bishop *in partibus* of Babylon. I never could conceive where he had gathered his religious opinions, when with the greatest simplicity he complained that I had combated them. I was informed of it by a guest of his, whose reputation of great knowledge in Masonry had acquired him a seat at the Masonic repasts which the poor simple man used to give; and even at those dinners the difference was observable in the adepts, though of the same degree, each having received an explanation of the mysteries coinciding with his own disposition. Our simple Bishop viewed the whole science of the Craft in no other light than as the perfection of the Gospel; and even in his repasts he was ever mindful of the precepts of the Church, keeping abstinence on days appointed, &c. The Apostate Dom Gerles, on the contrary, was a Mason of a quite different system or explanation. He already sung those verses which in a letter since found among Robespierre's papers,[6] he delares to have addressed to truth alone:

> Ni Culte, ni Prêtres, ni Roi,
> Car la Nouvelle Eve, c'est toi.[7]

It was at these repasts that the Doctor La Mothe, a learned Rosicrucian, behaved with a modesty which seemed to prognosticate that one day he would equally hate both the craft of Varlet and of Dom Gerles. The latter paid his revolutionary debt to the guillotine; the other two are living, and I name them because I am not afraid of being contradicted, and because these sorts of anecdotes carry strong proof with them, and explain how persons of the most pious and charitable dispositions have been misled: how a Princess, the sister of the Duke of Orleans, was so blinded as even to pant after the Revolution, which in her eyes was to be nothing less than the regeneration of the Christian world.[8]

Such explanations of the Rosicrucian degree were only for those dupes in whom they remarked a certain bias towards mysticity. The generality were abandoned to their own interpretations; but when an adept testified a great desire of acquiring new lights, and was thought able to undergo the necessary trials, he was admitted to the degree of *Kadosch*, or of the *regenerated man*, where all ambiguity ceases.

It was to this degree that the adept of whom we have before spoken was admitted. Nor was the exhausted state in which he found himself after having undergone those trials to be wondered at. Adepts have told me, that no physical art is spared; that there is no machinery, spectres, terrors, &c. &c. which are not employed, to try the constancy of the candidate. We are told by Mr. Monjoye, that the Duke of Orleans was obliged to ascend, and then throw himself off a ladder. If that were all, he was most kindly treated. A deep cave, or rather a precipice, whence a narrow tower rises to the summit of the lodge, having no avenue to it but by subterraneous passages replete with horror, is the place where the candidate is abandoned to himself, tied hand and foot. In this situation he finds himself raised from the ground by machines making the most frightful noise. He slowly ascends this dark vault, sometimes for hours together, and then suddenly falls as if he were not supported by any thing. Thus mounting and falling alternately, he must carefully avoid showing any sign of fear. All this however is a very imperfect account of the terrors of which men, who had undergone these trials, speak. They declared that it was impossible for them to give an exact description of them; they lost their senses; they did not know where they were. Draughts were given to them, which, adding to their corporal strength, did not restore them to their mental faculties; but rather increased their strength only to leave them a prey to fury and terror.

Many circumstances relating to this degree made us believe at first sight that it was connected with *Illuminism*; but on examination we find it to be only a farther explanation of the Masonic allegory. Here again the candidate is transformed into an assassin. Here it is no longer the founder of Masonry, Hiram, who is to be avenged, but is is Molay the Grand Master of the Knights Templars, and the person who is to fall by the assassin's hand is *Philippe le Bel*, King of France, under whose reign the order of the Templars was destroyed.

When the adept sallies forth from the cavern with the reeking head, he cries *Nekom* (I have killed him). After this atrocious trial he is admitted to take the oath. I learned from one of the adepts, that at the time when he was about to take the oath, one of the *Knights Kadosch* held a pistol at his breast, making a sign that he would murder him if he did not pronounce it. On my asking if he believed that it was in earnest, he said that he certainly did believe so, though he could not be sure. At length the veil is rent asunder. The adept is informed, that till now he had only been partially admitted to the truth; that Equality and Liberty, which had constituted the first secret on his admission into Masonry, consisted in recognizing no superior on earth, and in viewing Kings and Pontiffs in no other light than as men on a level with their fellow men, having no other rights to sit on the throne, or to serve at the altar, but what the people had granted them, and of which they had the power of depriving them whenever they pleased. They are also informed, that Princes and Priests have too long abused the goodness and simplicity of the people; that the grand object of Masonry, in building temples to Equality and Liberty, is, to rid the earth of this double pest, by destroying every altar which credulity and superstition had erected, and every throne on which were only to be seen despots tyrannizing over slaves.

These documents concerning the degree of Kadosch are not merely taken from the works of Messrs. Monjoye and Le Franc, but from adepts themselves. Besides, it is easy to perceive how exactly this account corresponds with the avowal of the adept who was obliged to own that I was quite in the right when I told him that this was the final object of Freemasonry.

Oh how profound the combination of these mysteries! their progress is slow and tortuous; but how artfully each degree tends to the grand object.

In the first two degrees, that is to say, in those of *Apprentice* and *Fellowcraft*, the Sect begins by throwing out its *Equality* and *Liberty*. After that, it occupies the attention of its novices with puerile games of fraternity or Masonic repasts; but it already trains its adepts to the profoundest secrecy by the most frightful oaths.

In that of *Master*, it relates the allegorical history of Adoniram, who is to be avenged; and of the *word*, which is to be recovered.

In the degree of *Elect*, it trains the adepts to vengeance, without pointing out the person on whom it is to fall. It carries them back to the time of the Patriarchs, when, according to them, men knew no religion but that of nature, and when every body was equally Priest and Pontiff. But it had not as yet declared that all religion revealed since the time of the Patriarchs was to be thrown aside.

This last mystery is only developed in the Scotch degrees. There the brethren are declared free: The word so long sought for is, Deism; it is the worship of Jehovah, such as was known to the Philosophers of nature. The true Mason becomes the Pontiff of Jehovah; and such is the grand mystery by which he is extricated from that darkness in which the prophane are involved.

In the degree *Rosæ Crucis* he who wrested the *word*, who destroyed the worship of *Jehovah*, is Christ himself, the Author of Christianity; and it is on the Gospel and on the Son of Man that the adept is to avenge the brethren, the Pontiffs of Jehovah.

At length, on his reception as *Kadosch*, he learns that the assassin of Adoniram is the King, who is to be killed to avenge the Grand Master Molay, and the order of the Masons successors of the Knights Templars. The religion which is to be destroyed to recover the *word*, or the true doctrine, is the religion of Christ, founded on revelation. This word in its full extent is *Equality and Liberty*, to be established by the total overthrow of the Altar and the Throne.

Such are the incipient degrees, the process, and the whole System of Masonry; it is thus that the Sect by its gradual explanations of its twofold principle of *Equality and Liberty*, of its allegory of the founder of Masonry to be avenged, of the word to be recovered, leading the adepts from secret to secret, at length initiates them into the whole Jacobinical code of Revolution.

We are not to lose sight of the extreme care with which the adept is questioned on all that he has seen before, whenever he is initiated to a new degree, lest he should overlook the intimate connection subsisting between each; and thus in the first degrees *Equality and Liberty* are given to him as the secret, while the complete explanation and application of them form the mysteries of the last.[9]

The more frightful these hidden mysteries of the Lodges shall appear to the historian, the more strenuously it becomes his duty to insist on the numbers of honest Masons who never partook of these horrid mysteries. Nothing is more easy than to be duped in Masonry. Such may have been the lot of those who only seek to make acquaintances in the Lodges, or to pass their leisure hours with men apparently intimate at first sight. It is true, that this intimacy seldom extends beyond the walls of the Lodge; but the days of their meeting are often days of festivity. These repasts are certainly heightened by the temporary Equality, which adds much to the mirth of the meeting; and all cares subside for the day. What has been said of certain assemblies where decency was not respected, is most certainly the invention of calumny. The extreme order and morality of these meetings has often proved a snare to captivate those who are to be caught with outward appearances, and Cagliostro's infamous behaviour would have made many desert the Lodges. This monstrous Adonis disgusted all Strasbourg, and was betrayed by the cries of the Egyptian sisters. It was no longer the age when the mysteries of the Adamites could be approved of. He was driven from that town for having attempted to introduce them. He would in like manner have ruined the craft had he continued to confound his Lodges with those of the East. Such was not the behaviour of our modern Masonry; on the contrary it appeared, that it had neither Religion nor Government in view; and they were seldom mentioned in the generality of Lodges. It was only on the day of initiation, that the reflecting adept could surmise that it had any future object; but even on those very days the trials were rather a subject of diversion than of reflection; and, so far from meditating on the allegorical emblems, they were rather diverted from it by the Sect, until favourable dispositions had been discovered in them for their further initiation.—The Sect knew well, that a day would come when a small number of the Occult Masons would suffice to put all the inferior multitude of adepts in motion. It is thus that it may be easily explained how there have existed so many honest Masons, and how so many are still to be found who have never surmised any thing in their games but the mysteries of an innocent Equality and Liberty, no ways alluding either to Religion or the State.

In defence of English Masonry, we may add, that they allow only of the three first degrees.—Prudence and wisdom have made them reject the wish of avenging the death of Adoniram on his pretended assassin, a wish that we have seen converted in the Occult Lodges into a desire of revenging the Masons and their founder Molay, and then into a wish of avenging the Masonic Equality and Liberty by the extinction of all Kings. Nothing of this is to be found in the English Masonry; nor is that mysterious pursuit of the *word* which was lost by Adoniram to be traced. You are immediately informed that it is *Jehovah*. He who could wish to draw certain inferences from this, would have a long course of reasonings to run through, none of which appear to have ever been thought of by the English Masons. With them *Jehovah* is no more than the universal god of human nature; it is to be sure rather extraordinary that they should pretend to be the only people who have any knowledge of that God; but their conclusion is, that all mankind, and particularly the Freemasons, ought to live with and succour each other like brethren. Nothing appears in their mysteries tending towards the hatred of Christianity, or that of Kings.

Their laws and institutes with respect to Religion are comprehended in declaring, "That a Mason will never be a stupid Atheist nor an irreligious Libertine. That though in former times every Mason was obliged to profess the religion of the state or nation he lived in, at present, leaving every one to enjoy his own private opinions, they are only bound to follow the religion in which every body agrees, a religion which consists in being good, sincere, modest, and men of honour." Certainly such laws do not oblige the English Mason to be a Deist, but only to be an honest man, whatever may be his religion.

With regard to the civil powers, a part of their laws are expressed as follows: "A Mason shall be a peaceable subject, and cheerfully conform to the laws of the country in which he resides. He shall not be concerned in plots or conspiracies against Government; and he shall pay proper respect to the civil Magistrate. Should a brother be implicated in rebellion against the state, he shall not be supported in his rebellion." Such are the laws to be found in Thomas Wolson and William Preston, the one full of contempt, the other full of zeal, for English Masonry; both nevertheless agree as to the laws of the Lodges. We are not therefore to confound English Masonry with the occult Lodges, which they have prudently rejected.

We perfectly well know that many English are initiated in the occult mysteries of the Rosicrucians and Scotch degrees; but it is not their *Occult Science* which constitutes them English Masons; for the first three degrees are all that are acknowledged in England.

Having made these exceptions, we shall continue our proofs; for it is not on their degrees alone that we have founded our judgment of the occult Masons. Were we strangers to their rites and ceremonies, the reader will judge what opinions we should form on perusing the doctrines of their most celebrated writers.

1. See the degree of Master in the Works on Masonry.
2. The reader may easily conceive, that this corpse is no more than a mannikin containing bladders full of blood.
3. Were we less rigorous as to our proofs, we should treat in this place of the degree called the *Knight of the Sun*. But we are only acquainted with it through the medium of the *Voile Levé (the veil raised up)* a work of the Abbé Le Franc, certainly a man of the greatest virtue and undoubted veracity, and one of those excellent Ecclesiastics who preferred falling under the butchering poniards of the Septembrizers, to betraying their religion. But this author has neglected to inform us from what sources he had drawn his documents on the Masonic Degrees. Beside, we can remark, that he was not sufficiently acquainted with the origin of Masonry, which he only traces back to Socinus: His knowledge also of the Scotch degrees appears to have been acquired from inaccurate translations, which our French authors had vitiated according to their respective purposes.

    On the other side, we know for certain, that this degree of *Knights of the Sun* is a modern creation. Its author is to be known by his Teutonic style. If we are to believe what we have been told, it owes its origin to one of those Philosophists of very high life, who was too much attached to the high rank which he enjoyed, to adopt any other Equality than that which applied to the Masonic feasts and their impiety. And nothing is to be found in this degree which militates against the throne. It is much too perspicuous for many Masons, who would have been disgusted with any thing but emblematical figures susceptible of various explanations. Nevertheless, we were acquainted with several of these *Knights of the Sun* in France. This degree was only given to such of the adepts whose impiety was unequivocal. It was rather a degree of modern Philosophism than of ancient Masonry. Under that point of view it is worthy of notice; but we only give the following account as an extract from the Abbé Le Franc's work.

    When initiated into this higher degree, it was no longer possible for the adept to dissemble with himself how incompatible the Masonic code was with the slightest remnant of Christianity. Here the Master of the Lodge is styled *Adam*, while the introducer takes the name of *Veritas (Truth)*. The following are part of the lectures which brother *Veritas* repeats to the new adept while recapitulating all the allegories which he has seen in the former parts of Masonry.

    "Learn in the first place that the three implements with which you have been made acquainted—the Bible, the Compasses, and the Square, have a secret signification unknown to you. By the Bible you are to understand that you are to acknowledge no other law than that of Adam, the law which the Almighty had engraved on his heart, and *that is what is called the* LAW OF NATURE.— The Compass recalls to your mind, that God is the central point of every thing, from which every thing is equally distant, and to which every thing is equally near.—By the Square we learn, that God has made every *thing equal*—The Cubic Stone, that *all your actions are equal with respect to the sovereign good*.—The death of Hiram, and the change of the Master's word, teach you, that it is difficult to escape the snares of ignorance, but that it is your duty to show the same courage as our Master Hiram, who suffered himself to be massacred rather than hearken to the persuasions of his assassins."

The most essential part of this discourse is the explanation which Brother *Veritas* gives of the degree of Elect. Amongst others we read the following lines:

"If you ask me what are the necesssary qualities to enable a Mason to arrive at the centre of real perfection? I shall answer, that in order to attain it, he must have crushed the head of the serpent of worldly ignorance, and have *cut off* those prejudices of youth conerning the mysteries of the predominant religion of his native country. *All religious worship being only invented, in hopes of acquiring power, and to gain precedency among men; and by a flesh which covets, under the false pretence of piety, its neighbour's riches;* in fine, by Gluttony, the daughter of Hypocrisy, who, straining every nerve to restrain the carnal senses of those who possess riches, perpetually offer to them on the altar of their hearts, holocausts which voluptuousness, luxury, and perjury, have procured for them. This, my dear brother, is what you have to combat, such is the monster you have to crush under the emblem of the serpent. *It is a faithful representation of that which the ignorant vulgar adore under the name of religion.*

"It was the prophane and timid Abiram who, transformed by a *fanatical zeal into a tool of the Monkish and religious rites*, struck the first blows on the breast of our father Hiram; that is to say, who sapped the foundations of the celestial temple, which the ETERNAL had himself erected upon earth to sublime virtue.

"The first age of the world witnessed what I assert. *The most simple law of nature* rendered our first fathers the happiest of mortals. The monster Pride appears on earth, he bellows, he is heard by men and by the happy mortals of those days. He promises them happiness in another life, and persuades them by his mellifluous words, that he *taught men to adore the Eternal Creator of all things in a more extensive and more special manner* than any person had done before on earth. *This hydra* with an hundred heads misled and misleads those men who are subject to its laws, and will continue its deceptions until the moment when the *Elect* shall appear to combat and crush it entirely." (*See the degree of Knights of the Sun*). Such doctrines need no comment.

4. See the Scotch degrees printed at Stockholm, 1784.
5. See the degree Rosæ Crucis.
6. Proces Verbal, No. 57.
7. Nor Worship, nor Priests, nor King, for thou art the new Eve.
8. The art shown in this degree should prove a salutary lesson to those who, without any examination, adopt political and religious ideas, and sport them in every company that will submit to hear them. Had they only reflected on the persons who had instilled them into their minds, or on the authors of the works whence they had adopted their ideas, how mnay honorable but misguided persons would, on such an examination, find they were no more than the blind apostles of every religious and political

iniquity, and the agents of designing men! Abuses are certainly to be reformed, and our worship ought to be pure; but reflexion can never be detrimental to him who wishes to speak on either. T.

9. I am not ignorant of the existence of several other degrees in Occult Masonry, such as those of the *Star* and of the *Druids*. The Prussians have added theirs, and the French have done as much. We though it sufficient to attach ourselves to the most common ones, as most proper to delineate the conduct and spirit of the Sect.

CHAP. XI.

New Proofs of the System and Mysteries of the Occult Masons.

IN order to form a proper idea of the extent of the system of the Occult Lodges of Free-masonry, let us combine in this Chapter two essential points; first, the general doctrine of the most zealous and learned Masons; secondly, their divers opinions as to their origin.

Masonic writers in general divide Free-masonry into three classes, the Hermetic, the Cabalistic (which comprehends the Martinists), and the Eclectic Masonry. Let us first take a view of the religious tenets of these different classes, and we shall find that, like our modern Sophisters, they only agree in one point, and that is in their hatred to Christianity and Revelation; in all other points we shall find them in perfect opposition to one another with respect to their religious tenets or rather blasphemous impieties.

The Hermetic Masonry, or the Scotch degrees, who work in chymistry, have adopted *Pantheism or the true Spinosism*. With them *every thing is God, and God is every thing*. That is their grand mystery, engraved in one word *Jehovah* on the stone brought by the Knights Templars from the Holy Land.

Let the reader refer to the preface of the zealous Knight of St. Andrew, who has given us such a circumstantial account of these degrees. He will there see our Knight reducing the result of his whole doctrine to this famous text of Hermes Trismegistus, "All is part of God; if all is part, the whole must be God. Therefore every thing that is made made itself, and will never cease to act, for this agent cannot repose. And as God has no end, so can his works have neither beginning nor end." After having recited this passage, our Pantheistical adept tells us, "Such is the summary though expressive belief of the whole Hermetic System;" in a word the whole religious system of the Scotch degrees with the discovery of which he is so much pleased.

Let not the reader suppose that he attempts to explain away the expression *all is God*. In his opinion nothing but the grossest ignorance and prejudice can disapprove of the assertion. It is in vain to object, that, making the grain of sand, the Heavens, the Earth, the animal, or man, *a part of God*, is rendering the Deity divisible; for he will answer, that it is only the grossest ignorance which hides from us, that *those millions of millions of parts are so united together and so essentially constitute a God* WHOLE, *that to separate a single particle would be to annihilate the* WHOLE *itself, or the Great* JEHOVAH. But, lest the Knight of the Craft should be vain on finding himself a part of God, our Hierophant informs us, that *as the little finger is always less than the whole body; so is man, though a small particle of God, infinitely smaller than* JEHOVAH. Our adept may nevertheless rejoice, however small a particle he may be of the Deity, as the day will come when he is to be reunited to *the great* WHOLE, the day when, every thing being reunited to the great Jehovah, harmony will be complete, *and true Pantheism will be established for ever.*[1]

It is to be hoped that the reader does not expect us to trouble ourselves with the refutation of so monstrous a system. The preface however is not the only part of that work which lays down this system as the tenets of these degrees; for, after the description of them, we find what are called *Solomon's Thesis;* also the *Archetype world;* and these are productions all tending to strengthen them in their impiety.[2] We shall not therefore be accused of calumniating this branch of Masonry by attributing to it a system which makes the villain, like the just man, a constituent part of the Deity, and represents vice and virtue as the very action of the Deity; a system which promises the same destiny to the good and to the wicked, of being *reunited to the Deity;* and thus, after having ceased to be man, of being God to all eternity.

The Cabalistic system, without being less impious, is far more humiliating for the human understanding; and that especially in an age which pretends to the high-sounding appellation of the Philosophic age, of the age of light. It was in the Prussian Lodges of the Rosicrucians that this Cabalistic system was to be found; at least before their union with the Illuminees.[3] We have authentic information, that this was adopted by certain Lodges of Rosicrucians in France a few years before the Revolution, and particuarly at Bourdeaux. To prevent, however, all possibility of being mistaken, whatever we shall say on this subject shall be grounded on the Cabalistic lectures lately printed under the title of *Telescope de Zoroastre.* They are dedicated to one of those Princes whom the author does not name, but whose zealous pursuits in these mysteries are sufficiently known by public report. With such a guide we shall not be accused of imposing on our readers.

The JEHOVAH of this Sect is no longer the *God* WHOLE; but he is at once the *God* SISAMORO, and the *God* SENAMIRA. The first is joined by the *Genius* SALLAK, and the second by the *Genius* SOKAK. If these famous Cabalistic words are inverted, we have *Oromasis* or the *God* GOOD, and *Arimanes* the *God* EVIL, and the Genii will become *Kallas* and *Kakos, pretty correctly Greek for* GOOD *and* BAD.[4]

Thus in attributing to OROMASIS a multitude of *good* Genii or spirits like himself, and to ARIMANES *evil* Genii participating of his own wickedness, we have the JEHOVAH of *Cabalistic Masonry;* that is to say, the *word* to be recovered in their Lodges, or the tenets to be substituted to those of Christianity.

Of these good and evil Genii, some are more perfect spirits and preside over the planets, the rising and setting of the Sun, the increase and decrease of the Moon; others, inferior to the first, but superior to the human soul, exercise their empire over the Stars and Constellations; but in both these classes, the good are the angels of life, victory and happiness, while the bad are the angels of death and calamity. All know the secrets of the past, present, and to come, and can impart this great science to the adepts. To captivate their favour, the cabalistic Mason is to study what we should call the Conjuring-book. He must be well versed in the names and signs of the planets and constellations; he must also know whether it be a good or evil Genius which presides over it, and which are the numbers that represent them. By the word *Ghenelia*, for example, he must understand the rising Sun, a pure, mild and active spirit, presiding at births, and at all natural affections which are good. *Sethoporos*, on the contrary, is Saturn, the planet which may be looked upon as the head quarters of the evil Genii.

It is not our object to give a dictionary of all their Hieroglyphics, much less to describe the circles, the triangles, the table, the urns, and the magic mirrors, in a word all the science of the Cabalistic Rosicrucian. The reader has seen a sufficient specimen, to be convinced, that the whole is an incoherent system of the vilest and grossest superstition. It might be only humiliating to nature, did not the adept carry his impiety to such an extent, that he looks upon the communication with, and apparitions of the Devils, whom he invokes under the appellation of Genii, as a special favour, and on them he relies for the whole success of his enchantments. If we are to credit the masters of the art, the Cabalistic Mason will be favoured by these good and evil Genii, in proportion to the confidence he has in their power; they will appear to him, and they will explain more to him in the magic table, than the human understanding can conceive.

Nor is the adept to fear the company of the *evil Genii*. He must firmly believe, that *the worst among them, the most hideous of those beings which the vulgar call Devils, are never bad company for mortals*. In many cases he is to prefer the company of these evil Genii to that of the good; the latter frequently costing you your rest, fortune, and sometimes even your life; while we often have the greatest obligations to the former.[5]

From whencesoever these Genii or Devils may come, it is from them alone that the adept can learn the occult sciences, which will infuse into him the spirit of prophecy. He will be informed, that Moses, the Prophets, and the three Kings, had no other teachers, no other art, but that of Cabalistic Masonry, like him and Nostradamus.

When immersed in this delirium of folly and impiety the adept becomes dear to the Sect. He will have shown that he prefers the doctrine of *Sisamoro* and of *Senamira* to that of the Gospel; that he had rather be a madman than a Christian; and then he will have attained the grand object of the last mysteries of Cabalistic Masonry.

Those Masons who may have adopted a different course to arrive at the same end, are to take great care not to discredit the Cabal. Though they disbelieve the art themselves, let them say at least, "That there is nothing wonderful in judicial astrology but its means; that its tendency is extremely simple: That it is very possible, that at the hour of your birth a star should be in a certain position of the Heavens, and in a particular aspect, and that nature should follow a particular course, which, through a concatenation of causes, would be favourable or fatal to you." Then let them add a few Sophisms to corroborate this idea, and give themselves out for learned Philosophers, and the Sect will approve their conduct as tending to avenge the Cabalistic Mason, and bring his science into repute.[6]

Were I not writing for the Historian, I should fear to abuse my reader's patience with the enumeration of these absurdities of Occult Masonry. But in describing the grand causes of a Revolution *which threatens all Europe*, it is necessary at least to give a general idea of those systems of Impiety and rebellion whence it originated. We spare him the trouble of research, he will only have to verify our quotations; he will know from what sources he is to derive his proofs. Beside, one of the most dangerous arts of the Sect, is not only to hide its tenets and its variegated means of attaining its Revolutionary object, but it wishes even to conceal the very names of its different classes. That which may appear to be the farthest from Impiety or Rebellion may be the most strenuous in its attempts to revive the antique systems of the bitterest enemies to Governments and to Christianity.

It may be matter of surprize to many, to see me comprehend the Martinists among the latter; they are, nevertheless, the persons whom I had in view. As to the origin of Mr. de St. Martin, who has given them his name, we are ignorant; but we defy any body to show a greater appearance of probity, or to assume a more devout and mellifluous mystical strain, than the hypocrisy of this spurious offspring of Curbicus the slave.[7] We have been acquainted with men whom he had seduced, with others that he wished to seduce, and all spoke of his great zeal and respect for Christ and his gospel, and for Governments. We shall seek his doctrines and his views in his own writings, in the *Apocalypse* of his adepts, in his famous book OF ERRORS AND OF TRUTH. We have learned to our cost what labour and what pains are necessary to unravel this work of darkness; but surely the same perseverance should be shown by the disciples of truth as by the adepts of darkness.

Much patience is requisite to understand and to elucidate the code of the Martinist Mason, amidst its mysterious language of numbers and enigmas. We will spare as much as possible this trouble to our readers. Let the Hero of these doctrines appear, and he will be found to be no other than the servile copyist of the absurdities of the Heresiarch slave, and a rival of his hypocrisy. With all the tortuosities of MANES we shall behold him leading his adepts through the same paths, infusing into them the same hatred for the altars of Christianity, for the thrones of Sovereigns, and for all political establishments whatever. We will begin with his religious sytems; but though we shall compress whole volumes of impious absurdity into a few pages, still we must again appeal to the patience of the reader; for as their Martinist Masons contributed much to the Revolution, it is necessary that their sophistical reveries should be known.

We are, then, to form an idea of a *first being; one; universal; of himself; and the beginning of all principle*. At first sight, this *first being* appears to be the *God* WHOLE, or the *Jehovah* of Pantheism: and such really is the *first being* of the Martinists.[8] But this *God* WHOLE comprehends a twofold God; one the principle of *good*, the other of *evil*. The former, though produced by the *first being, holds of itself the whole of its power, and all its worth*. It is infinitely good, and can *only do good*. It produces another being of its own substance, a first good like itself, but which soon becomes infinitely bad, and can do nothing but evil.[9] The *God* GOOD, though it holds all its power of itself, could neither create this *world, nor any corporeal being, without the means of the God* EVIL:[10] the one *acts*, the other *reacts*, and from their conflicts the world is framed, and bodies are formed of the *sparks*, as it were, emanating from this struggle between the *God or principle of* GOOD, and the God or principle of EVIL.

"Man already existed at that time, *as no origin can be anterior to man*. He is antecedent to any being in nature; he existed before the birth of the Genii; nevertheless he only came after them.[11] Man at that time existed without a body, and a much preferable state to that in which he is at present; for, inasmuch as his actual state is limited, and replete with disgust, so was his former unlimited and abounding in delights."[12]

By the ill use he made of his Liberty, he erred from the centre at which the *God* GOOD had placed him; he then acquired a body, and that was the period of his first fall. But in his fall he preserved his dignity; he is still of the same *essence* as the *God* GOOD. To convince ourselves of it, "we have only to reflect on the nature of thought; and we shall soon perceive, that it being simple, one, and unalterable, there can be but one sort of being capable of it; as nothing can be common between beings of different natures. We shall observe, that if man has in himself an idea of a Supreme Being, of an active and intelligent cause which executes his will, he must be of the same essence as that superior Being."[13] Therefore according to the Martinist System, *the God* GOOD, *the God* EVIL, and every *thinking being* or, in other words, God, Man, and the Devil, are of the same nature, the same essence, and the same species.

If therefore the adept does not think himself God or Devil, it is not the fault of his teachers. There is, however, a remarkable difference between man and the *God* EVIL. For the Devil, or the principle of Evil, separated from the *God* GOOD, can never return to him; whereas man will return to the same state he was in antecedently to time and the *sparkling* conflict. "He erred by going from four to nine, but re-establishes himself by returning from nine to four."[14]

This enigmatical jargon becomes more intelligible as the adept advances in the mysteries. He learns that the number *four* signifies a *strait line*—number *nine* the *circumference* or the *curve line*:[15] then that the sun is a *quaternary* number; that number *nine* represents *the moon*, and consequently *the earth, of which it is but a satellite*:[16] and hence the adept concludes, that man anterior to time was in the sun or in the centre of light. That he flew from thence by the radius, and that, passing by the moon, he remains on the earth, until the time comes when he shall be reflected back to his centre, to be incorporated with the GOD GOOD.

In the mean time, till he can enjoy that happiness, "it is a most fallacious system to pretend to lead men to wisdom *by the frightful description of eternal flames in a life to come*. Such descriptions are of no avail when unfelt; therefore the blind teachers, who can only represent those torments to us in imagination, must necessarily produce but little effect upon us."[17]

The enlightened Martinist, soaring above such teachers, erases the pains of hell from his moral code; and it is worthy of remark, that this is the leading feature in the Systems of the Sophisters of the Occult Lodges, as well as of the Sophisters of the Secret Academy. We should be tempted to suppose, that they knew no means of working their salvation but by destroying the possibility of being damned; and that, by denying the existence of hell, they sought to harden themselves and all nations to crimes the most deserving of the divine vengeance.

The Martinist substitutes "*three temporal worlds*. There are but three degrees of Expiation, or three degrees of real F. M. (*Free-masonry*)." This is pretty clearly asserting, that the perfect Mason neither has sin to fear, nor penance to perform; but in every sense the reader can no longer doubt of the systematic impiety which reigns throughout these absurdities, in direct opposition to the Gospel. It was not sufficient for the Sect to renew in their hatred the ancient blasphemies of a senseless Philosophy; but the detestation of Laws, Sovereigns, and Governments, was to mingle with their mysteries; and in this our Martinist adept only primes over the Jacobin, by the art and cunning with which he infuses his spirit of Rebellion, and broods over the downfal of the Throne.

Let not the zealous adept appear, protesting his respect for the Throne or Government; I have heard their protestations, I have heard those of their masters; but I have also heard their doctrines, and seen their transactions. It is in vain for their chief to teach them privately, or to envelop them in enigmatic language; for, had I not hereafter to unfold the iniquitous mysteries of the Illuminees, the reader would be ready to pronounce, without hesitation, that of all the conspiring Sects the Martinist Lodges are the most dangerous.

Neckar, La Fayette, Mirabeau, notwithstanding their Sovereignty of the People, sought a Constitutional King;—Brissot, Syeyes, Petion, supported the Republican system;—conventions, compacts, and oaths, were admitted by both. But the Martinist denies the legitimacy of every Empire which may have originated in violence, force, or conquest; he denies all society whose foundation rests on conventions or compacts, though freely entered into. The former are acts of tyranny, which never can be legitimated; no antiquity, no *prescription*, can render them valid, *prescription* being a mere invention of tyranny, as a palliative to injustice, in direct opposition to the laws of nature, which knows of no such invention."The edifice formed on a voluntary association is equally imaginary as if it were on a forced association."[18] To prove these two assertions, and particularly the latter, is the main object of our hero's Sophistry. He easily decides, that it is *impossible that any social compact could have been freely entered into by all the individuals of a state.*—He asks, *whether it stands to reason that man should rely on those who had formed such a compact, or whether they ever had the power of forming it?* He examines the question, and concludes, "that a voluntary association is neither more just nor reasonable than it is practicable, since by such an act, man must invest other men with a right (his own liberty) which he cannot dispose of himself; and since he transfers a right which he has not, *he makes a convention which is absolutely void, and which neither himself, the chiefs, nor subjects can put into execution, since it can neither have been binding on the one nor the other.*"[19]

Then come the innocent artifices of protestations of fidelity and submission to the reigning powers, and invitations not to trouble the order of the existing laws and governments; but stupidity itself cannot be duped by such artifices. After the Martinist has told us, that social compacts, though freely formed, are null, and that associations formed by force are void, what can be the submission which the civil laws, the magistrates, or the Princes can exact from their subjects?

The hero of the Martinists also shudders at the very idea of revolt or of insurrection; but then it is because the individual is exposed to acts of violence resulting from *private authority.* When the mob shall have imbibed these principles, when *private* violences are no longer to be feared, what will all these restrictions and exhortations avail for the preservation of peace and submission to the constituted authorities? Does not the Martinist try every means to persuade that same mob that there never existed a legitimate Prince, nor a lawful Government? Is he not perpetually recalling them to their *first origin,* "when the rights of one man over another were not known, because it was impossible that such rights could exist among *equal beings?*"[20]

With them, it is sufficient to observe the variations of Governments, and their succession; that some have perished, others are perishing, or will perish before the end of the world, to be convinced that they are no more than the offspring of *the caprice of man, or of their disordered imaginations.*[21]

In fine, I know that the Martinist makes profession of a true government, a real authority of man over men, and that he pleases to call it a Monarchy. But notwithstanding all the subtleties of his mysterious language, this very profession will prove to be the most universal Conspiracy against every existing Government. He tells us, that there is a superiority to be acquired by one man over others, the superiority of learning, of means, of experience, which bring him nearer to his *original state;* and this is a superiority *of fact,* "and of necessity, because other men, having applied less and not having reaped the same advantages, will stand in need of him, from the poverty and dimness of their faculties."[22]—The reader will naturally conclude, that according to this system nobody could exercise a lawful authority over his equals, but in right of his virtues, his experience, and his means of being useful. And that is in reality the first artifice of the Sect, which immediately overthrows all idea of hereditary succession, which submits the rights of the Sovereign to the reveries of the factious and of the populace on the virtue, talents, and success of him who governs. But let us follow their windings, and unfold their mysterious writings.—"If every man," say they, "attained to the same degree of his own power, then every man would be a King."

These words evidently show, that in the sense of the Martinist, he only is not King who is not arrived at the last degree of *his power*, or of his strength in the *natural* state. A little further it appears, that this difference alone can constitute a real political authority, that such is the *principle of unity, the only one* by which nature allows the exercise of a legitimate authority over men, the *the only light which can reunite them in a body.*[23]

The reader may believe it to be a chimerical research to seek in the history of man for a society where he alone commands whose *powers* or faculties have been the best developed in the order of nature, where he alone obeys who has not acquired this *degree of power*; but the Martinist will carry him back "to those happy days said to have had no existence but in the imagination of the poets, because, distant from them, and strangers to their sweets, we have been weak enough to believe, that because we did not enjoy them, they could not exist."[24]

Should you not immediately perceive that the only legitimate authority is that exercised of old, or in the golden age, when each father of a family was the sole king; when the son, acquiring sufficient strength and age to develop his *powers*, became king himself; should you deny these consequences, and object, that no government had ever perpetuated itself since the commencement of the world, and that consequently the rule given to discover the only legitimate government pointed out none; you are then left to your own imagination, and the adept will continue, "Nevertheless, it is one of those truths which I can best affirm, nor do I pledge myself too far, when I certify to my equals, that there are governments which have *subsisted ever since man was first placed upon earth, and will subsist until the end*; and that for the same reasons which made me assert, that here below there has always been and always will be legitimate governments."[25] What then are or can be these legitimate governments which the Martinist recognizes? What can be these governments which have subsisted from the beginning, and will subsist until the end of time? None can be surmised, but that of the Patriarchs, or of the first families governed by the sole paternal authority. In later ages can any other be found than that of isolated families, or of the Nomades, the Tartars, or the savages roaming through forests without any other chief than the father of the family? And it is there alone, that those whose age has equally developed their strength and *their power*, will find themselves all *equal* and each *a king*, that is to say, each one recognizing no other law than his own, and each acquiring at the same age all the power of a father over his children. This government may perhaps be traced in civil society; each private family abstractedly taken may be said to perpetuate this government, and it has existed and will perpetuate itself until the end of time. Now let the reader reflect on what has been said on governments formed by force or free compact, on those governments which have perished, do perish, or will perish before the end of time, and which by this distinctive mark are known to be illegitimate. He will clearly perceive, that all the zeal of the Martinists for the *true monarchy*, for the *only legitimate* government, *the only one consistent with nature*, the only one lasting as the world, is nothing else but the wish of reducing all society, all legitimate authority, to that of a father governing his children; to overturn every throne and annihilate every law but that of the ancient patriarchs.

Such is the whole tendency of the political system of the Martinists. Many more blasphemies both religious and political might be extracted from this work; nor would it be impossible to prove, that in the sense of the Martinists, the *great adultery* of man, the true cause of all his misfortunes in this world, the real original sin of mankind, was his having divorced himself from the laws of nature, to subject himself to laws which nature condemns, to those of Emperors, of Kings, and even of Republics, in a word, to any other authority except the paternal.[26] But this matter would require us to follow all the windings of their mysterious language, a task that would be as tedious to my reader as to myself. I trust therefore that he will not be displeased with me for having spared him the labour of research, which I have endured in the task of gathering from admist these *voluntary obscurities* some of those luminous traits which now and then escape the Sect; and the re-union of which leave no doubt as to the grand object of this Apocalypse.

In reading over and studying this extraordinary code, one would be tempted to decide with Voltaire, *that there never was printed a more absurd, obscure, mad, or foolish work*; and we should be equally surprized that such a code had produced so many enthusiasts, or that we know not what *Dean* of Philosophy had been so much enchanted with it.[27] But it all probability this *Dean* had not sent the word of the enigma to Voltaire; he had not told him that this voluntary obscurity was one of the most powerful means employed by the Sect to crush the altar and the throne. The works of Voltaire himself had not the celebrity of Mr. de St. Martin's Apocalypse. The greater the obscurity the more it attracted the curiosity and piqued the vanity of his disciples; the adepts of the first class tutored and explained it to the young novices, and none were more eager than those of the fair sex. Their dressing-rooms were metamorphosed into secret schools, where the interpreting adept developed the mysteries of each page, and the novice in extasy applauded the mystery which was hidden from the vulgar. Little by little the novice herself became an interpreter, and founded a species of school.—This is not a mere assertion; such schools for the explanation of the code existed at Paris and in the Provinces, particularly at Avignon, the headquarters of the Martinists. I was and am acquainted with several persons who were introduced to these schools. They were the preparatory steps to initiation. There they learned the art of imposing on the simple by factitious apparitions, which ended by casting ridicule on the Sect; the art of conjuring up the dead; the art of making absent persons speak, or of seeing them at a thousand miles distance; in fine, all those arts which quacks and mountebanks of all ages have invented to delude the populace, and rob them of their money, the Martinist studied to enable them to make converts to Impiety and Rebellion.

This Sect made great progress in France and Germany; some even have reached England; and every where their grand object is to represent the French Revolution as the fire which is to purify the world.

Notwithstanding the multitude of the Martinist Masons, they are not nearly so numerous as the Eclectic Masons; and these indeed should naturally predominate in an age where the Philosophism of the Atheists and Deists only succeeds to the ancient heresies in order to absorb them all.

The appellation of Eclectic is applied to a Free-mason, as it was formerly to certain Philosophers. We are to understand by this word those of the adepts who, after having passed through the different degrees of Masonry, attach themselves to no particular system, either political or religious, into which they have been initiated, but adopt from them all whatever may best suit their political or religious views.[28] They are neither Hermetic, Cabalistic nor Martinist Masons; they are what they please, Deists, Atheists, Sceptics, an aggregate of all the errors of the Philosophism of the day. They, like the simple Sophisters of the age, have a twofold point of union. With respect to Religion, they all admit that Equality and Liberty which denies every authority but their own reason, and rejects all revealed religion; as to governments, they admit of no Kings, unless subservient to the will of the people in right of its sovereignty. I shall be very brief on this class; it is that of the Brissots, Condorcets or Lalandes; in a word of the Sophisters of the day, whom we shall soon see combining with Masonry to operate their Revolution. Were we to expose their systems it would only be a repetition of what has been said of the Sophsiters conspiring against the altar and the throne; and the multitude of these abettors of Impiety who were in our time aggregated to the Masonic Lodges would alone prove how peculiarly such plots coincided with their principles.

I know that there is another species of Eclectic Masons lately established in Germany. These not only make profession of appertaining to no particular system of Masonry, but assert also that they depend on none. According to them, all are independent, all have the right of making their own laws. It is for that reason that they have abolished the very names of Grand Lodge and of Scotch Lodge: and in this respect they may be said to have improved upon Masonic Equality and Liberty.[29]

In this light the Eclectic Masons could not have been very numerous in France, as the major part of them were under the inspection of the Grand Parisian lodge called the *Grand Orient*. But our modern Sophisters had introduced into all the Lodges the true Eclectic spirit of Impiety; and sentiment was a stronger tie than a professed opinion. This sentiment, to be uniform, must agree in hating Christ and his Religion, in detesting all Sovereignty and all Legislative Power, except that of the people. The Eclectic

Mason, like the Sophisters, are at liberty to substitute Deism or Atheism to Christianity, to replace Monarchy by Democracy or even by a Democratic Monarchy; but a step less towards Equality and Liberty would suffice to banish him from the Occult Lodges.

All classes therefore, every code of Masonry, Hermetic, Cabalistic or Martinists, and Eclectic, all and each forwarded the Revolution; and it little imported to the Sect which struck the blow, provided ruin ensued.[30]

I promised to add to these proofs those which more particularly result from the divers opinions of Masons on their origin. Let us here again be only guided by the most learned and zealous of the Sect. The reader will consider whether the parents they have adopted would not suffice alone to direct their judgement on the plots of their progeny.

1. Preface to the Scotch Degrees.
2. Second Part, Edition of Stockholm, 1782.
3. Letters from Philo to Spartacus.
4. Telescope de Zoroastre, page 13.
5. Ibid. Page 118 and 136.
6. See the *Continuation* OF ERRORS AND OF TRUTH *by an unknown Philosopher*. Masonic Era 5784, Chap. OF VICES AND ADVANTAGES. Notwithstanding the title of this book, it is far from being a *Continuation* of the work of which I am about to treat. It was only a snare laid by Holbach's club, who, seeing the immense run which Mr. de St. Martin's work had, adopted the title of *Continuation* OF ERRORS AND OF TRUTH to attract the curiosity of the Public. In this pretended continuation, whole pages are copied from the works of the club, coinciding in nothing with Mr. de St. Martin's system, excepting in its zeal for Masonry.
7. *Terebinthus,* or *Budda,* a disciple of *Scythian,* a conjurer, finding that the Persian Priests opposed his designs, retired to a *widow's house* in Palestine to whom he left all his money and books. She bought a slave named CURBICUS, whom she afterwards adopted and caused to be instructed in all the sciences of Persia. After her death he quitted the name of *Curbicus,* to blot out the memory of his first condition, and took that of MANES, which in the Persian language signifies *discourse*. For an account of his doctrines many learned writers, and particularly St. Augustin, may be consulted. They are represented as the common sewer of all the impieties of the times, and as the seat of empire which Satan had chosen to himself.

    Manes had the insolence to promise the King of Persia that he would cure his son by his prayers, and the credulous Prince, believing him, neglected the remedies of art, and sent away his physicians. The son died, and Manes was thrown into prison; but, escaping from thence, he fled into Mesopotamia; after various adventures however, falling into the hands of the King of Persia, he was flayed alive, and his carcase cast upon the dunghill to be devoured by wild beasts. His skin was stuffed, and hung up on one of the city gates.—His followers honoured him as a martyr, and, in memory of his being flayued with reeds, *they slept upon them*—(See the "Annals of the Church,"—Third Age). T.
8. Of Errors and Truth, 2d Part, page 149.

9. First Section.
10. Ibid. Of Temporal Causes and Concatenations.
11. Ibid. Of Primitive Man.
12. Ibid.—We think it necessary to inform our readers, that we have made use of the Edinburgh edition, which is the least enigmatical. As Philosophism and Impiety gained ground, the Martinists thought they might have fewer *voluntary* obscurities, and they have suppressed, or given in common print, what was originally only expressed in cyphers, in which the first edition abounds.
13. Ibid. Of the Affinities of Thinking Beings, page 205.
14. This was precisely the lesson Mr. de St. Martin was explaining to the Marquis de C——. He traced his circles on the table; then, pointing to the centre, he added, "You see how every thing emanating from the centre moves in the radius to reach the circumference."—"I perceive it," says the Marquis; "but I also observe, that having reached the circumference this body emanating from the centre may proceed in a tangent or a strait line; and then I do not understand how you can demonstrate that it must necessarily be returned back to the centre." This was sufficient to disconcert the learned Doctor of the Martinists. He nevertheless continued to teach, that souls emanating from God by the number four, would return to him by the number nine.
15. Ibid. 2d Part, Page 106, 126.
16. Ibid. Page 114 and 215.
17. Ibid. First Section.
18. Ibid. Sect. 5.
19. Ibid. Part II. Sect. 5, Page 9.
20. Ibid. Part II. page 16 and 17.
21. Ibid. Of the Instability of Governments, P. 34 and 35.
22. Ibid, P. 18.
23. Ibid. P. 29.
24. Ibid.
25. Ibid. Page 35 and 36.
26. Part II. Sect. 5. Art. ADULTERY
27. Let. of Voltaire to D'Alembert, Oct. 22, 1776.
28. See the Archives of the Free-masons and Rosicrucians, Chap. 3. Edition of Berlin, 1785.
29. See the Rules of their Association, Frankfort, 18th May, 1783, signed Rustner and Rottberg, secretaries.
30. La Metherie's Journal de Physique, 1790.

CHAP. XII.

Proofs of the Origin of Free-masons drawn from their own Systems.

LET us begin by rejecting the opinions of all those demi-adepts, who in their research on Masonry, led away by the similarity of name, really believe themselves descended from the Masons who built the Tower of Babel, or who raised the pyramids of Egypt, or more particularly from those who erected Solomon's Temple, or who worked at the Tower at Strasbourg; in fine, of those who laid the foundations of so many Churches in Scotland in the tenth century. These men of mortar had never been admitted to the mysteries. If it be true that they ever constituted a part of the Brotherhood, they were soon excluded; their minds were too blunt and not sufficiently Philosophic.[1]

They were no longer wanted, when once the trowel, the compasses, the cubic stone, the truncated or entire column, became nothing more than systematic emblems; and the learned adepts blush at an origin which they consider as too ignoble.

We will subdivide into two classes the divers opinions set forth in order to ennoble their origin. In the first class, we comprehend all those who ascend back to the mysteries of the Egyptian priests, to those of Eleusis or the Greeks, or those who pretend to filiate from the Druids, or even who call themselves descendants of the Jews. In the second class, we consider those who only trace themselves from the Knights Templars, or the age of the Crusades.[2]

If we examine ever so carefully the reasons on which the learned Masons ground their filiation from the ancient Philosophers, they will be found to contain merely this assertion: "that in those ancient times when men first began to desert the primitive truths, to follow a religion and morality founded on superstition, some sages were to be met with who segregated themselves from the general mass of ignorance and corruption. These sages, perceiving that the grossness or the stupidity of the people rendered them incapable of profiting by their lessons, formed separate schools and disciples, to whom they transmitted the whole science of the ancient truths and of the discoveries they had made by their profound meditations on the nature, the religion, the polity, and the rights of man. In these lessons some insisted on the unity of God or true Deism, others on the unity of the Great Being, or Pantheism. The morality deduced from these principles was pure; it was grounded on the duties of charity, on the rights of Liberty, and on the means of living peaceably and happily. Lest these doctrine should lessen in value, should be falsified or be entirely lost, these sages commanded their disciples to keep them secret.—They also gave them signs and a particular language by which they were to recognize each other. All those who were admitted to this school and to these mysteries were the children of Light and Liberty, while all the rest of mankind were with respect to them but *slaves and prophane beings*; and hence their contempt for the vulgar. This was also the reason why the disciples of Pythagoras observed such a profound silence, the origin of that particular and secret science of the divers schools. Hence the mysteries of the Egyptians and afterwards of the Greeks and of the Druids, even the very mysteries of the Jews themselves, or of Moses initiated in all the secrets of the Egyptians.

"These divers schools and the secrets of these mysteries have not been lost; the Philosophers of Greece transmitted them to those of Rome, and the Philosophers of all nations followed the same line of *conduct after the establishment of Christianity*. The secret was always preserved, because it was *necessary to avoid the persecutions of an intolerant Church and of its Priests*. The sages of divers nations by means of the signs which had been originally established, recognized each other, as the Free-masons do every where at this present day. The name only has been changed; and the secret has been handed down under the denomination of Free-masonry, as it was formerly under the sanction of the Magi, of the Priests of Memphis or of Eleusis, and of Platonic or Eclectic Philosophers. Such is the origin of Masonry, such are the causes which perpetuate it, and which render it the same in all parts of the world."[3]

This is the faithful result of what the most learned Masons have published on their origin.—It is not our object to examine how false are such ideas on the pretended doctrine of the Persian, Egyptian, Grecian, Roman or Druid sages, nor how contrary to all history. In the first place, can any thing be more absurd than to suppose, that there existed a unity of religious opinions, of morality, and of secrets among Philosophers, who have left behind them systems as variegated, and as opposite to each other, and as absurd as those of our modern sophisticated Philosophists?[4] Nor do I undertake to examine the erroneous assertion, that the mysteries of Eleusis had no other secret but the unity of God, and the purest morality.—How is it possible to suppose that those mysteries were not universally known to the people, when it is certain that all the citizens of Athens were initiated into both the lesser and the greater mysteries, according to their age?[5] Nor do I ask how it came to pass, that these same Athenians under ground were all taught their catechism on the unity of God, and how when above ground they adored such a multitude of Gods; or, again, how it happened that they condemned Socrates to death on the accusation that he did not adore all the Gods; or else, why all the Priests of the different idols only acquired by their initiation new zeal for the defence of that multitude of Gods and their altars. In fine, I will not ask how it is possible to persuade oneself that those Priests, so ardent and so zealous in their temples for the worship of Jupiter, of Mars, of Venus, and of so many other

Deities, should be the very persons who assembled the people during the solemnity of the grand mysteries, to tell them that all their worship of the Gods was nothing but imposture, and that they themselves were the authors, ministers, or priests of imposture!

I know that such reflections are more than sufficient to stamp with falsehood the origin in which the learned Masons glory. But let us for a moment suppose, that these mysteries were what they have represented them to be; the very pretension of a society springing from such ancestry and glorying in perpetuating their spirit and their dogmas,—this pretension alone, I say, must class this Brotherhood among the most ancient conspirators. It would entitle us to say to the Craft, 'Such then is the origin of your mysteries; such the object of your Occult Lodges! You then descend from those pretended sages, and those Philosophers, who, reduced to the lights of reason, had no farther knowledge of the true God than what their reason inspired. You are the children of Deism or Pantheism, and, replete with the spirit of your forefathers, you wish to perpetuate it! Like them you look upon every thing which the rest of mankind have learned from the lights of Revelation, as superstition and prejudice. Every Religion which adds to the worship of the Theist or detests the Pantheist, in a word Christianity and its mysteries, are with you objects of hatred and contempt! You abhor whatever the Sophists of Paganism, or the Sophists initiated in the mysteries of the idolatrous Priests, abhorred;—but those Sophists detested Christianity, and showed themselves its most inveterate enemies. From your own avowals, then, in what light can we view your mysteries, if not as a perpetuation of that hatred and of that wish of annihilating every other Religion but the pretended Deism of the Ancients!'[5]

'You also say that you are what those Jews were, and still are, who, for all their religious tennets, only acknowledge the unity of God (provided there have existed Jews who did not believe in the Prophets and in *Emmanuel* the Saviour).—You have then the same sentiments toward the Christian which the Jews have. Like them, you insist on *Jehovah*, but to curse Christ and his mysteries.'[6]

The more the Masonic works above-mentioned are read, the more conspicuous will be the justice of the reproaches we make. With some, matter is eternal; with others, the Trinity of the Christians is only an alteration of Plato's system.—Others again adopt the follies of the Martinists, or of the ancient Dualism.[7] Nothing then can be more evident. All these learned Masons who pretend to descend from the Egyptian Priests, from those of Greece, or from the Druids, only seek to establish what may appear to each to be the Religion of nature. Nor do they vary less as to its tenets than did both the ancient and modern Sophisters. They all agree in destroying faith in the minds of their adepts, by systems in direct opposition to Christianity. If they do not run into wild declamation like Voltaire, Diderot, or Raynal, it is because they wished themselves to deduce their consequences. To have expressed them too openly would have been divulging their mysteries; but one must be more than ignorant not to comprehend their meaning—How can we be blind to their intentions, when we peruse the writings of those who declare themselves to have originated in the Templars, or in those sectaries who infested all Europe under the name of Albigeois? These two sources have more analogy between them than may be supposed. Let us examine them separately, and then judge what we have to expect from men who glory in such an origin.

As to the Templars, let us even suppose that this famous order was really innocent of all the crimes which occasioned its dissolution; what object either religious or political can the Free-masons have in perpetuating their mysteries under the name or emblems of that order? Had the Templars brought into Europe a religion, or a code of morality, that was not known? Is that their inheritance?—In that case neither your religion nor your morality can be that of Christ. Is it their fraternity, their charity, which is the object of your secrets? Did the Templars really add any thing to those Evangelic virtues? Or is it the religion of *Jehovah*, or of the Unity of God, coinciding with the mysteries of Christianity?—If so, why do you reject all *Christians* who are *not Masons* as *prophane*?

It is too late to reply, that the alarms of religion are vain and ungrounded; that religion never was the object of the Lodges. What then is that name, that worship of *Jehovah*, which the learned Masons declare to have been handed down from the Knights Templars. Whether these Knights were the authors of it, or whether they received it by tradition, or borrowed it from the ancient mysteries of Paganism and of its sages, this name I say, this worship cannot be foreign to Christianity; and is not every Christian entitled to say, 'You would not be so secret nor so ardent to revenge it, if it were similar to the worship established throughout the Christian world?'

Should governments partake of the same alarms, to what subterfuge will the adepts have recourse who have sworn to avenge Equality, Liberty, and every right of their association, which has been so desperately outraged in the destruction of the Templars? It will be in vain to assert the innocence real or fictitious of those too famous Knights. That vow of vengeance which has been perpetuated for nearly five centuries can hardly fall on *Philip le Bel or Clement V,* or on the other Kings and Pontiffs who in the beginning of the fourteenth century contributed to the dissolution of that order? Nor will it be renewed in these days on account of the ties of blood, or through any pity for the particular individuals of the order? This vow, this oath of vengeance must be instigated by other causes—It has been perpetuated as the very object, the very doctrine of the school, as the principles and mysteries which the Masons have received from the Templars. What then can those men, those principles be, which can only be avenged by the death of Kings and Pontiffs? And what are those Lodges wherein for four hundred and fourscore years this vow, this oath of vengeance has been perpetuated?

It is evident: Nor is it necessary in this place to examine whether *Molay* and his Order were innocent or criminal, whether they were the real progenitors of the Free-masons or not; what is incontestable is sufficient; it is enough that the Masons recognize them for their ancestors; then the oath of avenging them and every allegory recalling that oath decidedly points out an association, continually threatening and conspiring against Religion and its Pontiffs, against Empires and their Governors.

But it may be asked, what lights can history throw on such an intimate connection between the mysteries of Masonry and the order of the Templars? Such a question requires much research, nor will I withhold from my reader the result of the inquiries which I have made on that subject.

The order of the Knights Templars established by Hugo de Paganis, and confirmed by Pope Eugenius III, was originally founded with all that charity which Christian zeal could inspire, for the service of those Christians who, according to the devotion of the times, went to visit the Holy Land. At first mere Hospitallers, these Knights, following the manners of the age, soon acquired great celebrity by their exploits against the Saracens. Their first repute originated in the services which were naturally to be expected from their great valor and eminent virtues: and such is the general testimony which history bears in their favour, making a wide distinction between the former and latter part of their existence. The Order soon spread through Europe, and acquired immense riches. They then began to forget their religious state, courted only the celebrity of the field, and were no longer led to it by the same spirit. It is worthy of remark, that many years before their dissolution, history already reproached them not only with being lax in their former virtue, but with those very crimes which caused their destruction. In the very zenith of their glory, and at a time when it required much courage to upbraid them with their vices, we see *Matthew Paris* accusing them of converting into darkness the lights of their predecessors, of having abandoned their first vocation for plans of ambition, pleasure, and debauchery, and of unjust and tyrannical usurpation. They were already accused of holding correspondence with the Infidels, which rendered abortive all the plans of the Christian Princes; they were accused particularly of having treasonably communicated the whole of Frederic II's plan to the Soudan of Babylon, who, detesting such perfidy, informed the Emperor of the treachery of the Templars.[8] This testimony, to which the Historian may add many others, will serve to render less surprizing the catastrophe which befel this famous order.[9]

In the reign of *Philip le Bel*, two men who had been imprisoned for their crimes declared that they had some important discoveries to make concerning the Knights Templars. Such a declaration under circumstances so peculiar could not be thought entitled to much credit; it sufficed nevertheless to make the King determine on the dissolution of the order, and he caused all the Templars in his kingdom to be arrested on the same day. This step may be thought too precipitate: But interrogatories and a thorough examination followed; and it is on those proofs alone, and the authentic minutes of that examination, that the Historian is to found his judgment. If their avowals are perfectly free, numerous, and coincident with each other, not only in different tribunals, but in different countries, enormous as their crimes may have been, still we are forced to believe them, or reject all history, and the juridical acts of the tribunals. These juridical minutes have survived the ravages of time, and their importance has caused them to be preserved in great numbers. Let the Historian refer to the collection made by Mr. Dupuy, the King's librarian; I know no other way of forming one's judgment, and of dissipating prejudices.

It has been said, that *Philip le Bel and Clement V* had concerted between them the dissolution of the Templars. The falsity of such an assertion is evident on the inspection of their letters. *Clement V* at first will give no credit to the accusations against the Templars; and even when he receives incontestable proofs from *Philip le Bel*, he had still so little concerted the plan with that Prince, that every step taken by the one or the other occasions disputes on the rights of the Church or of the Throne.

It was also said, that the King wished to seize on the great riches of these Knights; but at the very commencement of his proceedings against the order, he solemnly renounced all share in their riches; and perhaps no Prince in Christendom was truer to his engagement. Not a single estate was annexed to his domain, and all history bears testimony to the fact.[10]

We next hear of a spirit of revenge which actuated this Prince; and during the whole course of this long trial, we do not hear of a single personal offence that he had to revenge on the Templars. In their defence not the most distant hint either at the revengeful spirit, or at any personal offence against the King is given; so far from it, until the period of this great catastrophe the Grand Master of the order had been a particular friend of the King's, who had made him godfather to one of his children.

In fine, the rack and torture is supposed to have forced confessions from them which otherwise they never would have made; and in the minutes we find the avowal of at least two hundred Knights all made with the greatest freedom and without any coercion. Compulsion is mentioned but in the case of one person, and he makes exactly the same avowal as twelve other Knights, his companions, freely made.[11] Many of these avowals were made in *Councils* where the Bishops begin by declaring that all who had confessed through fear of the torture should be looked upon as innocent, and that no Knight Templar should be subjected to it.[12] The Pope, *Clement V*, was so far from favouring the King's prosecutions, that he began by declaring them all to be void and null. He suspended the Archbishops, Bishops, and Prelates, who had acted as inquisitors in France. The King accuses the Pope in vain of favouring the Templars; and *Clement* is only convinced after having been present at the interrogatories of seventy-two Knights at Poictiers in presence of many Bishops, Cardinals, and Legates. He interrogated them not like a Judge who sought for criminals, but like one who wished to find innocent men, and thus exculpate himself from the charge of having favored them. He hears them repeat the same avowals, and they are freely confirmed. He desired that these avowals should be read to them after an interval of some days, to see if they would still freely persevere in their depositions. He hears them all confirmed.

Qui perseverantes in illis, eas expresse et sponte prout recitatæ fuerant approbârunt. He wished still further to interrogate the Grand Master and the principal Superiors, *præceptores majores*, of the divers provinces of France, Normandy, Poitou, and of the Transmarine countries. He sent the most venerable persons to interrogate those of the superiors whose age or infirmities hindered them from appearing before him. He ordered the depositions of their brethren to be read to them, to know if they acknowledged the truth of them. He required no other oath from them than to answer freely and without compulsion; and both the Grand Master and the superiors of these divers provinces depose and confess the same things, confirm them some days after, and approve of the minutes of their depositions taken down by public notaries.[13] Nothing less than such precautions could convince him of his error: it was then only that he revoked his menaces and his suspension of the French Bishops, and that he allows the King to proceed in the trials of the Templars.

Let such pretexts be forgotten, and let us only dwell on the avowals which truth alone forced from these criminal knights.

Their depositions declare, that the Knights Templars on their reception denied Christ, trampled on the cross, and spit upon it; that Good Friday was a day which was particularly consecrated to such outrages; that they promised to prostitute themselves to each other for the most unnatural crimes; that every child begotten by a Templar was cast into the fire; that they bound themselves by oath to obey without exception every order coming from the Grand Master; to spare neither sacred nor prophane; to look upon every thing as lawful when the good of the order was in question; and above all, never to violate the horrible secrets of their nocturnal mysteries under pain of the most terrible chastisements.[14]

In making their depositions many of them declared they had only been forced into these horrors by imprisonment and the most cruel usage; that they wished, after the example of many of their brethren, to pass into other orders, but that they did not dare, fearing the power and vengeance of their order. That they had secretly confessed their crimes and had craved absolution. In this public declaration they testified by their tears the most ardent desire of being reconciled to the church.

Clement V, convinced at length, conceives whence the treachery proceeded, of which the Christian Princes so often complained they had been the victims in their wars against the Saracens. He permits the trials of the Templars to be continued, and a hundred and forty are heard in Paris.

All repeat the same deposition, except three, who declare they have no knowledge of the crimes imputed to their order. The Pope, not content with this information taken by religious Orders and by French Noblemen, requires that a new trial should take place in Poitou before Cardinals and others whom he himself nominates: Again, with the same freedom and for the third time, the Grand Master and other Chiefs in presence of Clement V repeat their depositions. Molay even requested that one of the Lay Brothers who was about his person should be heard, and this Brother confirms the declaration.

During many years these informations were continued and renewed at Paris, in Champagne, in Normandy, in Quercy, in Languedoc, in Provence. In France alone above two hundred avowals of the same nature are to be found; nor did they vary in England, where at the synod of London, held in 1311, seventy-eight English Knights are heard, and two whole months were spent in taking informations and in verifying their declarations. Fifty-four Irish were also heard, and many Scotch, in their respective countries. It was in consequence of these declarations, that the order of the Templars was abolished in those kingdoms, and that the Parliament disposed of their goods.[15] The same declarations were taken and proved in Italy, at Ravenna, at Bologna, at Pisa, and at Florence, though in all these councils the Prelates were very ready to absolve all those Knights who could succeed in their justifications.

When I hear the crimes of this order called in question, it appears to me that a sufficient attention has not been paid to the multiplicity of the avowals of these Knights, and of the diversity of nations which judged them. It would be one of the most extraordinary facts in history to see two hundred of these Knights accusing themselves of the greatest abominations. It would be a still greater atrocity to see so many Bishops, Noblemen, Magistrates, and Sovereigns, of different nations, sitting in judgment on the Templars, and publishing to the world, as free and uncontrolled, declarations which had only been extorted from them by the fear of torture. Such a conduct would be still more horrible than that of the Templars themselves; and would it not be equally extraordinary to see so many different nations agreeing to use the rack to extort such depositions from them? But for the honor of humanity such means were not employed in the trials of the Templars, by the Bishops and Grand Bailiffs, the King's Commissaries, the Cardinals, and Commissaries of Clement V nor by himself in France. Such methods were not resorted to by the councils nor by the tribunals of other nations. Never was a cause of greater importance pleaded; and, from the numerous and authentic documents which are still extant, it is evident, that Judges never were more fearful of confounding the innocent with the guilty.

Let not the dissolution of another celebrated Order, though in a very different way, be objected. The Jesuits were abolished, but they were not brought to trial; not a single member of the Order has been heard in its defence, nor have any members deposed against it. I should be the first to condemn them, could proofs similar to those against the Templars, be adduced against them.

Let us for a moment suppose the Templars entirely innocent of the crimes imputed to them, what could have been the virtue and courage of an order, which could demean itself so much, as to make such declarations against itself? How can the Free-masons glory in such an ancestry, who, if their crimes were not monstrous, must themselves have been monsters of the basest cowardice.

The vulgar may be led away by the tardy protestations of Guy and Molay; but do the vulgar ever distinguish between the obstinacy of despair and that serene firmness and constancy which are the attendants on virtue? They are not aware that false honor, like truth, may have its martyrs. During three years Molay persevered in his avowal, and he repeated it at least three times; when he pretends at length to deny it, his expressions are those of rage, and he throws down the gauntlet to whoever shall pretend to assert that he *had made any deposition* against his order; at the place of execution he declares *that all that he has said* against his order was false, and that if he deserved death it was *for having accused his order falsely* both before the Pope and the King. Amidst these contradictions, can the Historian receive such protestations of innocence? Much less is he to attend to the popular fable of Molay having cited Philip le Bel and Clement V to the tribunal of God within a year and a day, and that both the Pope and the King died within the year; for history not only varies as to the day, but even as to the year of Molay's execution.[16]

As a last resource in defense of the Order, the very nature and infamy of the crimes of which the Templars were accused have been alledged as a proof of their innocence. But most certainly the more infamous those crimes, the more debased must have been the members of the Order to accuse each other of them. But all these crimes, however infamous and incredible, only serve to discover the abominable Sect which introduced them among their adepts, and from whom the Templars evidently learned their frightful mysteries. That hatred of Christ, that execrable immorality, even to the atrocious infanticide, all are to be found in the tenets, they are even in the principles of that incoherent medley of *Begards, Cathares*, and of that shoal of sectaries which flocked from the East to the Western States about the beginning of the eleventh century.

I would willingly assert that it was the smaller part of the Templars who suffered themselves to be carried away by such abominations. Some even at Paris were declared innocent. In Italy a still greater number were absolved, of all those who were judged at the Councils of Mayence and Salamanca, none were condemned; and hence we may conclude, that of the nine thousand houses belonging to the Order many had not been tainted, and that whole provinces were to be excepted from the general stain of infamy. But the condemnations, the juridical depositions, the method of initiating the knights, almost become general; the secrecy of their receptions, where neither Prince nor King, nor any person whatever, could be present during the last half century, are so many testimonies which corroborate the divers accusations contained in the articles sent to the Judges; that is to say, that at least two— thirds of the Order knew of the abominations practiced, without taking any steps to extirpate them. *Quod omnes, vel quasi duæ partes ordinis scientes dictos errores corrigere neglexerint.*

This certainly cannot mean that two-thirds of the Knights had equally partaken of these abominations. It is evident on the contrary, that many detested them as soon as they were acquainted with them; and that others only submitted to them, though initiated, after the harshest treatment and most terrible threats. Nevertheless, this proves that the greatest part of these Knights were criminal, some through corruption, others through weakness, or connivance; and hence the dissolution of the Order became necessary.

Another reflection which strikes me as being of weight, though I do not know that any one has made it, is, that between thirty and forty thousand Knights not only survived the condemnation of the order, but also survived Philip le Bel and Clement V. The greater part of these had only been condemned to canonical penance, to so many days fasting or prayer, or to a short imprisonment.—They lived in different parts of the world, where they had nothing to fear from *their persecutors and tyrants*. Conscience, honour, and many other motives, should have induced these survivors to make their recantations after having made juridical depositions of such an abominable nature against their Order; most certainly if they had made them through fear or seduction, it was a duty incumbent on them. Nevertheless, of those thousands of Knights heard in so many different states there is not a single one that makes his retractation, not one who leaves such a declaration to be published after his death. What men are these Knights? If their depositions be true, how monstrous must that order have been by its crimes; if they be false, what monsters of calumny was it composed of? That fear may have made them swerve from truth during the reign of Philip le Bel, I will admit; but that King being dead, what becomes of such a plea?

Such nevertheless are the men whom the Masons glory in their descent from. Yes, and their descent is real. Their pretensions are no longer chimerical. Were they to deny it we should force them to recognize as their progenitors not the whole of the Order, but that part whose ancient corruption and obstinate hatred against the Altar and the Throne, when added to their thirst of revenge, must render them still more formidable to both Kings and Pontiffs.

Were we to trace the descent of the Freemasons by the Templars, we should not have the assurance of those who suppose the Grand Master Molay, when in the Bastile, creating the four *Lodges*, that of Naples for the East, of Edinburgh for the West, of Stockholm for the North, and of Paris for the South.[17] Yet, following nothing but the archives of the Free-masons themselves, and the apparent affinities which subsist between them and the Knights Templars, we are entitled to say to them—'Yes, the whole of your school and all your Lodges descend from the Templars. After the extinction of their Order, a certain number of criminal Knights, who had escaped the general proscription, formed a body to perpetuate their frightful mysteries. To their pre-existing code of Impiety they added the vow of vengeance against Kings and Pontiffs who had destroyed their Order, and against all Religion, which proscribed their tenets. They formed adepts who were to perpetuate and transmit from generation to generation the same mysteries of iniquity, the same oaths, and the same hatred against the God of the Christians, Kings, and Priests.—These mysteries have descended to you, and you perpetuate their impiety, their oaths, and hatred. Such is your origin. Length of time, the manners of each age may have varied some of your signs and of your shocking systems; but the essence is the same, the wishes, oaths, hatred and plots are similar. You would not think it, but every thing betrayed your forefathers, and every thing betrays their progeny.'

Let us then compare the tenets, language, and signs. What a similarity, and how many are common to both!

In the mysteries of the Templars, the Initiator begins by opposing the God who cannot die to the God who dies on the cross for the salvation of mankind. "Swear," he says to the candidate, "that you believe in *a God the Creator of all things, who neither did nor will die;*" and then follow blasphemies against the God of Christianity. The new adept is taught to say, that Christ was but a false prophet, justly condemned in expiation of his *own* crimes and not of those of mankind. *Receptores dicebant illis quos recipiebant, Christum non esse verum Deum et ipsum fuisse falsum Prophetam; non fuisse passum pro redemptione humani generis, sed pro sceleribus suis.*[18] Can any one here mistake the Jehovah of the Masons, or the I*ew of N*a*zareth led by R*a*phael into I*u*dea to suffer for his crimes?*[19]

The God of the Templars, who *never could die*, was represented by the *head* of a man, before which they prostrated themselves as before their real idol. This head is to be found in the Masonic Lodges in Hungary, where Freemasonry has preserved the greatest number of its original superstitions.[20]

This head is to be found again in the *Magic Mirror* of the Cabalistic Masons. They call it the Being of Beings, and reverence it under the title of SUM (*I am*). It represents their great *Jehovah*, source of all beings. And we may look upon it as one of the links which compose the general chain by which the Historian may connect the History of Masonry with that of the Templars.

These same Knights in hatred to Christ celebrated the mysteries of *Jehovah* more particularly on Good Friday, *præcipue in die Veneris Sancta*; and it is the same hatred which assembles the Rosicrucians on that day, according to their statutes, to dedicate it more particularly to their blasphemies against the God of Christianity.

Among the Templars, Equality and Liberty was masked under the name of Fraternity.

> Qu'il est bon, qu'il est doux, de vivre en freres,[21]

was the favorite canticle during their mysteries. It has since been adopted by the Masons, and is the mask that conceals all their political errors.

The Templars were bound to secrecy by the most terrible oaths, subjected themselves to the vengeance of the Brethren and to death itself, if ever they revealed the mysteries of the Order. *Injungebant eis per sacramentum, ne prædicta revelarent sub pœna mortis.* The same oath subsists among the Masons, and the same threats for any one who shall violate secrecy.

The precautions lest any *profane being* should be present at their mysteries are similar. The Templars always began by sending out of their houses whoever was not initiated. Armed brethren were placed at the doors to keep off all curious people, and sentries were placed on the roofs of their houses, which they always called Temples.[22] Hence originates the *Brother Terrible, or the Tyler*, who stands at the doors with a drawn sword, to defend the entrance of the Lodge against the prophane multitude. Hence that common expression among Masons the *Temple is covered*, to say the sentries are placed; no prophane Being can gain admittance, not even by the roof, we may now act with full liberty. Hence also the expression *it rains*, signifying the Temple is not covered, the lodge is not guarded, and we may be seen and over-heard.

Thus every thing to the very symbols,[23] their language, the very names of *Grand Master*, of *Knight*, of *Temple*, even to the columns *Jachin and Boaz*, which decorated the Temple of Jerusalem, and which are supposed to have been given to the care of the Templars, all in a word betray our Free-masons to be the descendants of those proscribed Knights. But what 'a damning proof' do we find in those trials, where the candidate is taught to strike with his poniard the pretended assassin of their Grand Master;[24] in common with the Templars it is on Philip le Bel that they wreak their vengeance; and in every other King the Sect behold this pretended assassin. Thus with all the blasphemous mysteries against Christ we see them perpetuating those mysteries of vengeance, hatred, and combination against Kings. The Masons then are correct when they claim the proscribed Knights for their forefathers. The same plans, the same means, the same horrors could not be more faithfully transmitted from father to son.

We shall conclude this chapter by a few observations which will not leave any subterfuge to those who may still entertain doubts concerning the crimes that brought dissolution on this proscribed Order. Let us suppose the whole of this Order to have been perfectly innocent of all the accusations of impiety, or of principles dangerous to governments. It is not in this state of innocence that they are recognized by the Masons as their forefathers. The profound adepts only acknowledge the Templars as their progenitors, because they are convinced that those Knights were guilty of the same impiety and of the same plots as themselves. It is in these crimes alone, and in these conspiracies, that they recognize their masters; and as infidels and conspirators it is that they invoke them.

Under what title do the Condorcets and the Syeyes, under what title does Fauchet or Mirabeau, Guillotin or Lalande, Bonneville or Volney, and so many others who are known to be at once the profoundest adepts of Masonry and the heroes of Impiety and Revolutionary Rebellion—under what title can such men challenge the Knights Templars as their progenitors, if not because they believe that they have inherited those principles of Equality and Liberty which are no other than hatred to Christ and hatred to Kings? When Condorcet, summing up the studious research of thirty years, falsifying all the facts of history, and combining all the cunning of Sophistry to extort our gatitude for those *secret associations destined to perpetuate privately and without danger among a few adepts,* what he calls *a small number of plain truths, as certain preservatives against the predominant prejudices*; when he extols the French Revolution as the triumph so long preparing and expected by these *secret societies*; when he promises to solve the question hereafter, whether the Knights

Templars, whose dissolution was the summit of *barbarity and meanness, are not to be numbered among these associations.*[25] When he holds such language, under what point of view can the Knights Templars have inspired him with such deep concern? With him, these secret associations, so deserving of our gratitude, are those of the pretended sages, "indignant at seeing nations oppressed, even in the sanctuary of their consciences, *by Kings, the superstitious or political slaves of the priesthood.*" They are the associations of those *generous* men "who dare examine the foundations of all power or authority, and who revealed to the people the great truths, *that their Liberty is inalienable; that no prescription can exist in behalf of tyranny; that no convention can irrevocably subject a nation to any particular family: that Magistrates, whatever may be their titles, functions, or powers, are only the officers, and not the masters of the people: that the people always preserve the right of revoking those powers emanating from them alone, whether they judge it has been abused, or consider it to be useless to continue them. In short, that the people have the right of punishing the abuse as well as of revoking the power.*"[26]

Thus we see Condorcet tracing back the germ at least of all the principles of the French Revolution to these *secret associations*, which he represents as the benefactors of nations, and as preparing the triumph of the multitude against the altar and the throne. All therefore he does or promises to do in future, when he proposes the question, whether the Knights Templars are not to be numbered among those secret associations, can only originate in the hope of tracing to them principles, oaths, and means which in time would operate similar revolutions. All this zeal of Condorcet for the secret association of the Templars, is no other than the hopes of finding them guilty of that same hatred against Royalty and the Priesthood with which his own heart is inflamed.

The secret which he has half disclosed, more daring adepts have betrayed; it has escaped them amidst their declamations. In the delirium of fury, and in the cavern as it were of their regicide trials, they publicly invoke the *reeking dagger*, they exclaim to their Brethren,—"Let the interval of ages disappear and carry nations back to the persecutions of Philip le Bel—*You who are or are not Templars*—help a free people to build in three days and for ever, a Temple in honor of Truth—*May tyrants perish*, and may the earth be delivered from them!"[27]

Such then is the explanation which the profound adepts give of the mysterious names of *Philip le Bel* and of the Templars. The first recalls to their mind, that in all revolutions Kings are to be immolated, and the second, that there existed a set of men leagued in the oath of delivering the earth from its Kings. That is what they call restoring Liberty to the People, and building the Temple of Truth!—I had long feared to exaggerate the depravity and the plots of the proscribed Knights; but what crimes can history impute to them which are not comprehended in this terrible invocation of the adepts at the dawn of the Revolution? It is when they grow more daring, and stimulate each other to those crimes which overthrow the altar and the throne; it is at that period that the most furious adepts, at once Masons and Jacobins, recall the name and the honor of the Templars to be avenged, and their oaths and plots to be accomplished. The Templars were then, what the Jacobin Masons are at this day; their mysteries were those of the Jacobins. It is not to us that objections are to be made on this accusation. Let the profound adepts of Masonry and Jacobinism defend their own assertions; let the offspring be persuaded that they have wronged their forefathers: and even could that be demonstrated, still it would be evident that the mysteries of the Occult Lodges consist in that hatred of the Altar and the Throne, and in those oaths of rebellion and impiety, which the adepts extol as their inheritance from the Templars.—Still it would be evident that the oath (the essence of Jacobinism) of overturning the Altar and the Throne is the last mystery of the Occult Masons, and that they only recognize the Templars as their progenitors, because they believed the mysteries of those famous though proscribed Knights contained all the principles, oaths, and wishes which operated the French Revolution.

1. I make this observation, as it is very possible that the name and implements of the Craft may be borrowed from the real Masons. Many mechanical arts, in France at least, had their signs, their ceremonies, their hidden language, which constituted the secret of the profession. This language and these signs served to distinguish the workmen, and denoted the degree they had acquired, whether of Apprentice or Master; and was a method of recognizing those who on the road asked for work, or for support to enable them to continue their journey. For all men of the same profession are naturally inclined to help each other in preference to strangers.

    It is very possible that in time some of the adepts initiated in the mysteries of the Sect gained admission among the mechanical Masons. These adepts may have formed others among those mechanics. Then, to form a separate society, it was only necesssary to adopt new signs, and choose different emblems from those workmen, and the Lodges were ready formed.

    What may corroborate this supposition is, that there exists in France another profession, which, had it not been for one obstacle, might have undergone a similar change. This is the profession of the FENDEURS *(Hewers of Wood)*. These men also form a confraternity. They have their signs, their watch-word, their secret and their convivial meetings. They call themselves *L'Ordre des* FENDEURS *(the Order of the Hewers of Wood)*. They admit Gentlemen and Burgesses into their order, who are initiated into the secret, and attend their meetings and repasts in the same manner as the Freemasons do theirs. I have known men who were both Masons and *Fendeurs*, and who from their birth and stations in life had far other occupations than splitting of wood. They were as reserved with respect to the secret of the *Fendeurs* as to that of Masonry.—I knew the sentiments of these Adepts, and should not be surprised that the sole reason why they took so great an interest in the secret of the Fendeurs was from its similarity to that of Masonry, or else, that in time, our Adepts of the town were in hopes of *Philosophizing* their Brethren of the woods. The grand obstacle to the propagation of these principles would be the difficulty and infrequency of their meetings, which are held in the midst of forests, far from the eyes of the prophane, and only in fine weather. Should the Philosophist take it into his head to convert theese repasts into those of Equality and Liberty, in a word, of the Golden Age, then Adepts would flock from all parts, Sophisticated dissertations and allegories would be introduced; but the uncouth inhabitants of the woods would no longer be able to comprehend the mysteries. Some of the signs would be changed, the emblems of the profession would be preserved, and the Sophisticated Lodges of the *Fendeurs,* established in the towns would cease to be open to the clownish mechanics from whom they had adopted their allegorical emblems. It is very possible that such may have been the case with the Mechanical Masons. This however is no more than a conjecture as to the mode of the Sect; our readers will soon see that we are not reduced to such uncertainty with regard to the origin of its secret and of its doctrine.

2. For these divers opinions let the reader consult from among the learned and zealous Masons of Germany, the GESCHICHTE DER UNBEKANNTEN, *or the History of the Unknown,* 1780, with this Epigraph—*Gens æterna est, in qua nemo nascitur*—ARCHIV FUR FREYMAURER, or *the Archives of the Freemasons, Berlin,* 1784—UBER DIE ALTEN UND NEUEN MYSTERIEN, or *of Ancient and Modern Mysteries, Berlin,* 1782—DIE HEBRAISCHE MYSTERIEN, ODER DIE ALTESTE RELIGIOSE FREYMAURERY, *the Mysteries of the Hebrews, or the most ancient religious Freemasonry, Leipsic,* 1788. Among the English Masons, he may consult THE SPIRIT OF MASONRY *by William Hutchinson*—and among the French *Guillemain de St. Victor* ON THE ORIGIN OF MASONRY, &c. &c.

Let the reader remember that several of these works might have been quoted for the greatest absurdities that Masonry is guilty of. For example in the ARCHIVES OF FREEMASONRY, several dissertations are to be found written by their Doctors on the Cabalistic art, and that even by an English Doctor, for the defence and instruction of the Rosicrucians.—I was really confounded, and almost ashamed, when among other absurdities I read, "ASTROLOGY is a science which by the situation of the stars reveals the causes of what has come to pass and foretells what is to come. This science has had its blots, but that destroys neither the foundation nor the *sanctity* of the art." And this is written by an English Doctor to justify the Rosicrucian Lodges, and to be preserved in their Archives. (*See these Archives in German, Part III. No. 18, page* 378). I have added this quotation, because I am always afraid of its being said, that I attribute incredible things to Free-masonry. I know that in one sense they are incredible, but they are so only to those who are strangers to the proofs. Were the books of Masonry in different languages to be consulted, especially those in German, they would be found to superabound in proofs.

3. An Extract from the divers works cited in the Note.

4. Let those who wish to be convinced of the discordancy of their systems consult CICERO *Questiones Academ.*—*De Natura Deorum*—*De Legib.*—*De Finibus Boni et Mali.*—*De Off: &c.*—or LACTANTIUS *Instit: Divin:* —or the last of the *Helvian* Letters; where the doctrines, the systems, and the absurdities of our modern Sophisters are compared with those of the ancient sages.

5. See Mr. de St. Croix's work on *the Mysteries of the Ancients.*

6. As for this Jewish part of the Craft, or the Free-masonry of the Jews, we recommend to our readers to peruse the treatise of a most learned and zealous Mason dedicated *Denen die es Verstehen, or to those who can understand.* He leaves no stone unturned throughout antiquity to prove the identity of the ancient mysteries of Eleusis, of the Jews, of the Druids, and of the Egyptians, with those of Free-masonry. And indeed when we reflect on the pretended history of the name of *Jehovah* lost by the

assassination of Adoniram, it may be very probable that the Jews had had a part in Masonry, "As it is drawn from the *Chaldaic Paraphrase*, and taken from a fable invented by the Rabbins to rob Christ of his divinity and power. They supposed, that Christ being one day in the Temple of Jerusalem had seen the Holy of Holies, where the High Priest alone had a right to enter. That he there saw the name of *Jehovah*—That he carried it away with him—and that in virtue of this ineffable name he had wrought his miracles." (See the Voile Levé).—The whole of this Fable is evidently directed against the tenets of the Christians on the Divinity of Christ. The importance which Masons annex to the recovering of the name of Jehovah, and particularly all their mysteries in the degree of *Rosæ Crucis*, has the same object in view.

7. See particularly the letter *Aux Illustres Inconnus*, or to the Real Free-masons, 1782.
8. See Matthew Paris, ann. 1229.
9. See Abbas Vispurgiensis in Chronica, an. 1227 & Sanut. Lib. III. Part 12, Cap. 17, &c. apud Dupuy Traité sur la condamnation des Templiers.
10. Layette, Tom. III. No. 13.—Rubeus Hist. Ravanensis—Bzovius ann. 1308.—Marianna Hist. Hispanniæ.
11. Layette, No. 20, Interrog. made at Caen.
12. See the Council of Ravenna. Rubeus Hist. Raven. Lib. VI.
13. Qui Magister & Præceptores Franciæ, Terræ ultra-marinæ, Normandiæ, Acquitaniæ ac Pictaviæ, coram ipsis tribus Cardinalibus præsentibus, quatuor tabellionibus publicis et multis aliis bonis viris, ad Sancta Dei Evangelia ab eis corporaliter tacta, præsteto juramento quod super præmissis omnibus, meram et plenam dicerent veritatem, coram ipsis, singulariter, liberè ac sponte, absque coactione qualibet et timore, deposuerent et confessi fuerunt. (*Epist. Clementis V. Regibus Angliæ, Galliæ, Siciliæ, &c.*)
14. See the Vouchers brought by Dupuy, and Extract of the Registers.
15. Vide Valsinger in Edvardum II et Ypodigma Neustriæ apud Dupuy.—Essai de Fred. Nicolai.
16. It has been said to have taken place in the different years 1311, 1312, and 1313. The first of these dates appears to me to be correct, because the execution of the Grand Master certainly took place while the Commissaries of the Pope were at Paris, and they only resided there from August 1309 till May 1311. It is in vain to alledge the protest of the Abbot of St. Germain as Lord of the Manor against the execution of two Knights Templars on his land; for, supposing this regarded the execution of Guy and Molay, we have the answer to the protest in date March 1313, whereas Clement V only died on the 20th April 1314; so that even in that case the citation must have been of no avail.

    Boccacio, who is so often quoted on the death of Molay, does not so much as mention it. When people make such a display of what this author has said concerning the constancy of the Grand Master and the other Templars executed at the same time, some attention should be also paid to his commencing with saying, that "these Knights were strangely fallen off, on account of their great riches, from their pristine virtue; that they were ambitious, voluptuous, and effeminate; that so far from making war in defence of the Christians, according to their institute, they left that duty to be discharged by people whom they had hired, or by valets; and that in the days of *Jaques Molay* their virtues had degenerated into vices." All that Boccacio says afterwards on the constancy and death of the Grand Master and his companions, which so greatly excites his enthusiasm, is solely grounded on the account his father gave him, who was a merchant and at Paris at that time; his ideas on the subject, as is easily perceived, are merely those of the vulgar. I shall always return to the same point. Let us examine the authentic documents and the minutes of the proceedings. When they are to be had, and they still exist in great numbers, they are real points by which we are to be guided. Such has been the line of conduct (the only satisfactory one) held by Mr. Dupuy, in his Treatise on the Condemnation of the Templars. This work is written with candor; and though he has not made the most of his proofs, he abounds in authentic documents and extracts from the minutes of the trials, and furnishes far more than are necessary to satisfy our judgment.

17. This account is to be found in an Almanac printed at Paris under the title of *Etrennes Interessantes* (1796-97). I don't know from whence the writer has drawn this anecdote, nor on what grounds he says that the Duke of Sudermania as Grand Master of the Mother Lodge of the North, was accessary to the assassination of the King his brother Anckarstroëm. Though this writer shows some knowledge of the Craft, he is so ignorant in other respects that it is impossible to take him for an authority:—For example, he says, that the Jesuits were Free-masons, that it was they who poisoned the Emperor Henry VII, and that the Emperor died *two hundred years* before a Jesuit existed. This fable of the Jesuits Free-masons is an artifice devised by the Illuminees, and we shall see them own to it, to divert the attention of States from their own Sect and conspiracies.

18. 2d Art. of their Avowals. See Dupuy, P. 48.

19. See above, P. 312 [p. 314, Ed.].

20. See Kleiner's Report to the Emperor Joseph II. I never saw this Report written by Kleiner, whom the Emperor Joseph II had ordered to get himself received, that he might know what he ought to depend upon with respect to the Masons and Illuminees. The Report was printed by order of the Emperor; but the Free-masons and Illuminees bought it up with such rapidity, that scarcely a copy escaped them. I am acquainted with a Nobleman who has read and even made extracts from it; and it was through his means that I learned this anecdote concerning the head being preserved in the Hungarian Lodges. It appears that some of the Templars revered it as the head of their first founder, while others worshipped it as the image of the God whom they adored.

21. How pleasing, how happy it is to live like brethren.

22. Ibid.

23. Without doubt there is a variety of other symbols which do not come from the Knights Templars, such are the flaming star, the sun, the moon, and the stars. The learned Masons in their secret journal of Vienna attribute these to the founder of the Rosicrucians, called Brother *Ros-Crux*. He was a Monk of the thirteenth century, who imported both his magic and mysteries from Egypt. He died, after having initiated some few disciples, who for a long time formed a separate association; they at length united with the Free-masons, and formed one of their occult degrees. Or it would be more correct to say that there exists now a-days in this degree nothing more than the name and the magic art of the ancient Rosicrucians, with the stars and other symbols borrowed from the firmament. Every other part is confounded with, and merged in, the mysteries and plots of Masonry.

24. See above, page 322.
25. Esquisse des Progres, &c. Epoque 7.
26. Ibid. Epoque 8.
27. Bonneville, Esprit des Religions, P. 156, 157, 175, &c.

CHAP. XIII.

Farther Declarations of the Free-masons as to their Origin.

The real Founder of Masonry.—True and first Origin of their Mysteries and of all their Systems.

THE learned adepts were not mistaken when they numbered the Knights Templars in the ancestry of Free-masons. We have seen by the comparative statement of their mysteries how much they coincided with each other; but it still remains to be shown whence the Templars had received their systems of impiety. This observation has not escaped those of the adepts who gloried so much in the impiety of their mysteries. They have extended their researches with that view, to ascertain whether there had not exited some of *those secret associations* in Europe whence they might trace their origin prior to the Templars. The Sophister, the famous adept shall speak. The result of his researches are only announced; death cut the thread of those ideas which he had promised to develop in the extensive work he was meditating on the *progress of the human mind,* and of which his admirers have only published the general plan under the title of *Esquisse d'un Tableau general sur les Progrès de l'Esprit humain (Sketch of a general Table of the Progress of the Human Mind).* But in this sketch we find more sufficient to dissipate the remaining cloud, and to rend the veil which as yet the adepts had not thought prudent entirely to withdraw. The text of this famous adept shall be laid before the reader: a very few reflections will then suffice to lead us to the fountain head whence sprung all the mysteries and systems of Free-masonry, and to develop to its full extent the true spirit with which it is actuated.

"In the South of France, says our Sophisticated and Masonic Adept, whole provinces united to adopt a Doctrine more simple, a Christianity more pure, where man, subject only to the Deity, judged according to his own lights what the Deity had pleased to reveal in the books emanating from him.

"Fanaticised armies, led by ambitious Chiefs, devastated these provinces. Executioners led by Legates and Priests immolated those who had escaped the fury of the soldiery; a tribunal of Monks was established, who were to condemn to the flames all that were suspected of hearkening to the dictates of reason.

"They nevertheless could not hinder this spirit of Liberty and research from gaining ground. Overpowered in the state where it had dared to appear, and where more than once intolerant hypocricy had combated it with savage war, it would reproduce and spread itself in a neighbouring country. It was to be found at all times until that period when, seconded by the invention of printing, it grew in power sufficiently to deliver a great part of Europe from the yoke of the Court of Rome.

"At that time there existed a class of man, who, despising all superstitions, were content secretly to despise them, or who at most took the liberty of making them, now and then, the objects of their sarcastic wit; the more stinging as they were worded in terms of the utmost respect."

As a proof of this spirit of Philosophism or Impiety at that period, Condorcet cites the Emperor Frederic II, his Chancellor Peter de Vigne, the works entitled LES TROIS IMPOSTEURS (*the three Impostors*), LES FABLIAUX and the DECAMERONE DI BOCACIO; it is then that he adds those words already cited in the preceding chapter, but necessary to be repeated, "We will examine whether at a time when Philosophic Proselytism would have been attended with danger, *secret associations were not formed, destined to spread and perpetuate privately and without danger, among a few adepts, a small number of simple truths as certain preservatives against the predominant prejudices.*

"We will examine whether that celebrated order (the Templars), against which the Popes and Kings so barbarously conspired, are to be numbered among these associations."[1]

I will avail myself of this indication of Condorcet. Those *men of the South*, among whom he promised to seek the origin of these secret associations, are known. They are that motley crew, followers of Manes, who during many ages, spreading from the East into the West, inundated France, Germany, Italy, and Spain at the time of Frederic the Second; they are that horde of sectaries known by the names of *Albigeois, Cathares, Patarins, Bulgares, Begards, Brabanters, Navarrese, Bearnese, Coteraux, Henriciens, Leonists, &c. &c.*; in fine, sectaries who, under a hundred different and uncouth names, recall to the mind of the reader every thing that had been broached by the most direful enemies of morality, government, and the altar, and that had *as yet* appeared in Europe. I have studied their tenets in their divers ramifications. I have viewed that *monstrous whole* of all the *Jehovahs* which Masonry could invent. In their twofold principle is to be found the twofold God of the Martinist and Cabalistic Mason. In the diversity of their opinions is to be found the concord of Eclectic Masonry against the God of Christianity. In their principles are to be seen the germ and the explanation of the most infamous mysteries of the Occult Lodges, and of their forerunners the Templars. They declare the flesh to have been created by the evil spirit, that they might have the right of prostituting it. All is in the direct line of succession, the Cathares, the Albigeois, the Knights Templars, and our Jacobins of the Occult Lodges, all proceed from the same parental stock. This is still more evident when we consider their disorganizing principles of Equality and Liberty, which declare that no submission is due *to the Spiritual or Temporal powers.*—This was the distinctive mark of the Albigeois; it was by this distinction they were pointed out to the Magistrates as the persons amenable to the laws enacted against the Sect. Let us follow them.

At that period when the multitude of the sectaries empowered them, with arms in their hands, to triumph over their opponents, we see them resorting to all the frantic rage of Jacobinized Masonry against the very name of Christian. Even before the spiritual and temporal authorities had united their efforts to subdue their savage rage, they had already exercised all the cruelties and ferocities of a Robespierre: Jacobin like, they went *beating down the churches and the religious houses, killing without mercy the widow and the fatherless, the aged parent and the infant child, making neither distinction of age nor sex; and, as the sworn enemies of Christianity, ravaged and destroyed every thing both in Church and State.*[2]

When at length the public authority had triumphed over these ferocious sectaries, they shrunk back into their dens or Occult Lodges, and reduced themselves again to secret associations. Then they had their oaths, their occult doctrines, their signs and their degrees, as the Occult Masons have their perfect masters; and their apprentices were only admitted partially to the secrets.[3]

In future we may dispense with Condorcet's researches on the secret associations of these famous sectaries. That is not the point to be sought for in their history. We know they had their oaths, their signs, their secret language, their fraternity, their propaganda, and, above all, *secrets which a father could not reveal to his children, nor a child to a parent; secrets which a brother could not mention to a sister, nor the sister to her brother.*[4]

What is the most remarkable is the coincidence pointed out by Condorcet between the mysteries of the sectaries, those of the Templars, and those again of the secret associations of our days. We know whence the sectaries of the South sprung; we know their common father; if he is to be the progenitor of Freemasonry, the stock is not honourable. To be sure it will trace the Masonic mysteries back to the immense space of sixteen centuries, but if this origin be true the adept need not glory in it. History has spoken clearly. The true parent of the *Albigeois*, of the *Cathares, Begards, Bulgares, Coteraux, and Patarins*, of all those sects in fine mentioned by Condorcet, is the slave sold to the Palestine widow; it is the slave *Curbicus*, more generally known under the name of *Manes*. It is not we who have traced the Masonic Lodges and their mysteries to this slave; it is Condorcet; he is the person to be blamed by the adepts. We were sorry to reveal so humiliating an origin; but we only raised the veil pointed at by Condorcet. He had seen that slave, indignant at the fetters which disgraced his youth, seeking to revenge himself on society for the baseness of his origin. He heard him preaching liberty, because he had been born in slavery; preaching equality, because born in the most degraded class of the human species. Condorcet did not dare say that the first Jacobin Mason was a slave; but he pointed out the offspring of Curbicus in the sectaries of the South, in the order of the Templars. He has shown the brethren, who have inherited from these sectaries and the Templars, to be the adepts in Masonry, and that was sufficiently saying that they all sprung from one common parent.

But let us beware of deciding on this single proof. If the mysteries of Masonry really are to be traced back to Manes, if he be the true father, the founder of the Lodges, we are first to prove it by his tenets, and then by the similarity and conformity of their secrets and symbols. We beg the reader's attention to the following comparative statement; the reesult will not be unimportant to history, and it particularly interests those who are to watch over the welfare of nations.

I. With respect to tenets, till the existence of Eclectic Masonry, that is to say, till the Impious Sophisters of the age introduced into the rites of the Lodges their impious mysteries of Deism and Atheism, no other God, no other *Jehovah* is to be found in the Masonic code but that of Manes or the universal Being, subdivided into the *God* GOOD and the *God* EVIL. It is that of the Cabalistic Masonry, and of the ancient Rosicrucians; it is that of the Martinists, who seem to have only copied Manes and his Albigeois adepts. A most extraordinary fact is, that in an age when the Gods of Superstition were to disappear before the Gods of our modern Sophisters, the God of Manes should have preserved his ascendancy in so many branches of Masonry.

II. At all times the follies of the Cabal, and of Magic founded on the distinction of this twofold God, had been received in the Masonic Lodges.—Manes also made magicians of his Elect.[5]

III. Manes in particular is the founder of that religious fraternity which the Occult Masons interpret into a total indifference for all religion.—That Heresiarch wished to gain over to his party men of every sect; he preached that they all tended to the same end, and he promised to receive them all with the same affection.[6]

IV. But above all, what we should particularly attend to, and compare both in the code of Manes and of the Occult Lodges, are the principles of disorganizing Equality and Liberty. That neither Princes nor Kings, Superiors nor Inferiors might exist, this Heresiarch taught his adepts, that all laws and all magistracy was the work of the evil principle.[7]

V. Lest there should be either poor or rich, he inculcated that the whole belonged to all, and that no person had the right of appropriating to himself a field, a house, &c.[8]

Such doctrines must naturally have suffered many modifications in the Occult Lodges as well as among the disciples of Manes. He aimed at the abolition of all laws and of Christianity, at the establishment of Equality and Liberty, by means of superstition and fanaticism; our modern Sophisters were to give his systems a new direction, that of their impiety. The Altar and the Throne were equally to be victims to them; and Equality and Liberty, in opposition to Kings and to God, were the last mysteries of Manes, as they are of our modern Sophisters.

VI. The same conformity is to be found between the degrees of the adepts before they are initiated in the profound secrets. The names are changed; but Manes had his *Believers*, his *Elect*, and his *Perfects*. These latter were impeccable, that is to say, absolutely free; because no violation of any law could inculpate them.[9] These three degrees correspond with those of *Apprentice, Fellow-craft,* and *Perfect Master*. The name of *Elect* has been preserved in Masonry, but it constitutes the fourth degree.

VII. The same terrible and inviolable oaths bound the disciples of Manes as bind the adepts of the Occult Lodges, to keep the secrets of their degree. St. Austin had been admitted to the degree of *Believer* nine years, without being initiated into that of *Elect*—"Swear or forswear yourself, but be true to your secret," was their motto.[10]

VIII. The same number and almost identity of signs. The Masons have three which they call the *sign*, the *gripe*, and the *word*. The Manichæans also had three, that of the *word*, of the *gripe*, and of the *breast*.[11] This latter was suppressed on account of its indecency; it can be traced to the Templars; the other two are still extant in the Lodges of Masonry.

Every Mason who wishes to know whether you *have seen the light*, begins by offering his hand to know whether you are acquainted with the gripe. It was precisely by the same method that the Manichæans recognized each other, and felicitated a Brother on having seen the light.[12]

IX. If we penetrate into the interior of the Masonic Lodges, we shall find representations of the sun, of the moon, and of the stars. These are nothing more than Manes's symbols of his *God* GOOD whom he brings from the sun, and of the different genii which he distributed in the stars. If the candidate is only admitted into the Lodge blindfold, it is because he is yet in the empire of darkness, whence Manes brings his *God* EVIL.

X. I do not know whether any of the Masonic adepts are sufficiently informed of their own genealogy to know the real origin of their decorations, and of the fable on which the explanations of the Occult Degrees are founded. But the following is a striking proof of their descent from Manes. In the degree of Master every thing denotes mourning and sorrow. The Lodge is hung in black, in the middle is a *Sarcophagus* resting on five steps, covered with a pall. Around it the adepts in profound silence mourn the death of a man whose ashes are supposed to lie in this tomb. This man is at first said to be Adoniram, then Molay, whose death is to be avenged by that of all tyrants. The allegory is rather inauspicious to Kings; but it is of too old a date not to be anterior to the Grand Master of the Templars.

The whole of this ceremonial is to be found in the ancient mysteries of the disciples of Manes. This was the ceremony which they called *Bema*. They also assembled round a *Sarcophagus* resting on five steps, decorated in the like manner, and rendered great honors to him whose ashes it was supposed to contain. But they were all addressed to Manes. It was his death that they celebrated; and they kept this feast precisely at the period when the Christians celebrated the death and resurrection of Christ.[13]

The Christians frequently reproached them with it; and in our days the same reproach is made to the Rosicrucians, of renewing their funeral ceremonies precisely at the same time, that is, on the Thursday in Holy Week.[14]

XI. In the Masonic games *Mac Benac* are the two words which comprehend the secret meaning of this mystery. The literal signification of these words, we are told by the Masons, is *the flesh parts from the bone*. This very explication remains a mystery, which only disappears when we reflect on the execution of Manes. This Heresiarch had promised by his prayers to cure the King of Persia's child, on condition that all the doctors were dismissed. The young Prince died and Manes fled; but, falling again into the hands of the King, he was flayed alive with the points of reeds.[15] Such is the clear explanation of *Mac Benac*, the flesh leaves the bones, *he was flayed alive*.[16]

XII. The very reeds bear testimony of the fact. People are surprized at seeing the Rosicrucians begin their ceremonies by seating themselves sorrowfully and in silence on the ground, then raising themselves up and walking each with a long reed in his hand.[17] All this is easily explained again, when we reflect that it was precisely in this posture that the Manichæans were used to put themselves, affecting to sit or lay themselves down on mats made of reeds, to perpetuate the memory of the manner in which their master was put to death.[18] And it was for this reason that they were called *Matarii*.

Were we to continue our comparative statement we should meet with many other similarities; we should find, for example, that Fraternity so much extolled by the Craft, and which would be deservedly applauded were it not confined solely to their own body. A similar reproach was made to the Manichæans, that they were always ready to succour one of their own sect, but extremely hard on the poor of other descriptions.[19]

The same zeal for the propagation of their mysteries is also observable in both. The modern adepts glory in their Lodges being spread all over the world. Such also was the propagating spirit of Manes and of his adepts. Addas, Herman, and Thomas went by his orders to establish his mysteries, the first in Judea, the second in Egypt, and the third in the East, while he himself preached in Persia and Mesopotamia. Beside, he had twelve Apostles, though some say twenty-two; and in a very short space of time we see his doctrines, like the Free-masons, spreading all over the world.[20]

Attending only to the most striking similarities, we have seen the Occult degrees of Masonry founded on the *Bema* of the Manichæans. It was Manes whom they were to avenge on all Kings, on Kings who had condemned him to be flayed alive, and who, according to his doctrines, had only been instituted by the evil spirit; and the word to be recovered was that doctrine itself, to be established on the ruins of Christianity. The Templars, taught by the adepts dispersed throughout Egypt and Palestine, substituted, at their dissolution, their Grand Master Molay for Manes, as the object of their vengeance; and the spirit of the mysteries and the allegory remained the same. It is always Kings and Christianity that are to be destroyed, Empires and the

Altar to be overturned, in order to re-establish the Equality and Liberty of human nature.

The result of these researches are certainly not flattering to the Craft; it traces the origin of their Lodges and of their doctrines on Equality and Liberty to a slave flayed alive for his impostures. However humiliating such an origin may be, still such must be the result of the researches of him who seeks the source whence all their mysteries are derived. Their Occult secrets are all founded on this man who is to be avenged, and on that word or doctrine which is to be recovered in their third degree. The whole of this third degree is an evident repetition of the *Bema* of the Manichæan degree of *Elect*, the famous Mac Benac is clearly explained by the species of punishment inflicted on Manes, and every thing leads us back to the Palestine Widow's slave.[21] We may defy the Masons to find any ceremony similar to theirs of *Mac Benac* either before or since the *Bema* of the Manichæans, if it be not the *Bema* itself; it is to that therefore that we must refer back; it is there we must rest to find the source of the Masonic mysteries.

The silence observed on this origin by the most learned Masons proves that they were ashamed, but not that they were ignorant of it. It must at least have been difficult for them to have so often in the mysteries of the cabal commented on the *Jehovah* of Manes, subdivided like their own, into the *Good* and *Evil* principle, without knowing the grand author of this system, and who has given his name to the Sect of the twofold God; without recognizing him, otherwise so famous as a profound adept in all the mysteries of the cabal, or of magic and astrology.

It could hardly be possible for the Hero of the Martinists not to have seen that his Apocalypse was nothing but the Heresiarch's code. It cannot be supposed that Condorcet, tracing the origin of the secret associations, and bringing the Templars so near to the *Albigeois*, could have been ignorant of what all history asserts, that the *Albigeois* and all the ramifications of those sects of the South (the *Vaudois* excepted) were really no other than Manichæans; beside, that all those infamous proceedings of the Templars had long since been attributed to the children of Manes; and that all those horrors are easily explained by his doctrines.

When we see the principal adepts of Masonry, such as Lalande, Dupuis, Le Blond, De Launaye, seeking to substitute the errors of the Manichæans and of the Persians, to the mysteries of the Christian religion, it is still more difficult to believe that they had not surmised the real author of their mysteries.[22]

It may be possible that the History of the Templars and of their Grand Master, as more interesting to the adepts, may have obliterated the remembrance of so humiliating an origin.

The object of our researches has not been to humble the Masonic body, but to develop the snares of a Sect justly branded with infamy from the very first days of its existence. Our object is particularly to make men sensible at length how much it interests both religion and the state to investigate the grand object of a secret association spread throughout the universe, an association whose secret is beyond a doubt contained in those two words *Equality* and *Liberty*, confided to the adepts in the very first degrees of Masonry; of an association whose last mysteries are no more than the explanation of these words to the full extent which the Jacobinical Revolution has given to them.

The hatred which a slave had conceived for his bonds makes him invent the words *Equality* and *Liberty*. The detestation of the condition in which he was born makes him believe that the evil spirit alone could have been the Creator of those Empires which contain Masters and Servants, Kings and Subjects, Magistrates and Citizens. He declares Empires to be the work of the Evil spirit, and he binds his disciples by an oath to destroy them. He at the same time inherits the books and all the absurdities of a Pagan Philosopher, a great Astrologer and Magician, and composes his code, a monstrous digest of these absurdities, and of the hatred he had conceived against the distinctions and laws of society. He creates mysteries, distributes his adepts into different classes or degrees and establishes his sect. Though justly punished for his impostures, he leaves them his execution as a new motive to stimulate their hatred against Kings. This Sect spreads itself from the East to the West, and by means of its mysteries perpetuates and propagates itself. It is to be met with in every age. Crushed a first time in Italy, France, and Spain, it spreads anew from the East in the eleventh century. The Knights Templars adopt its mysteries, and the dissolution of that Order lends a pretence to new-model their games. The hatred of Kings and of the God of the Christians is only stimulated by these new motives. The times and manner of the age may vary the forms or modify the opinions, but the essence remains; it is always the pretended light of Equality and Liberty to be diffused; it is the Empire of pretended Tyrants, whether religious or political, of Pontiffs, of Priests, of Kings, of Christ himself, which are to be destroyed, in order to re-establish the people in that two-fold Equality and two-fold Liberty, which proscribes the religion of Christ and the authority of Kings. The degrees and mysteries are multiplied and precautions are redoubled lest they should be betrayed; but their last oath is always hatred to the God who died on the Cross,—hatred to the Monarch seated on the Throne.

Such is the historical sketch of Masonry, and the main point of its secrets. Let the reader compare the proofs we have adduced from the very nature of its degrees, the proofs taken from the dissertations of the most learned adepts of the most zealous Masons on their mysteries; all those, in fine, which we have drawn from their various opinions on the origin of their association; and I do not think he can entertain any doubt as to the grand object of this institution. Let him then reflect on the manner in which we were led back by Condorcet from the Masons of the day to the slave Curbicus, and how we discover in this Heresiach and his adepts the real authors of the code and mysteries of Free-masonry; and I do not apprehend that he can any longer entertain a doubt as to their first and real progenitors.

Still it remains for us to show how these same mysteries promoted the plans of the Sophisters of Impiety united with those of Rebellion, in the execution of their plots for effecting the grand Revolution. But let us not terminate this chapter without repeating our protestations in favor of the immense number of Masons who have never been initiated in the Occult Mysteries of the Sect. Let us admire the wisdom of English Masonry in rejecting all those degrees where an explanation of the mysteries begins to develop their dangerous principles. Let us admire and applaud them for having transformed this conspiring Sect of other states into an association evidently useful to their own. The more strongly we have insisted on the importance to all Empires of investigating the dangerous principles of the Occult Lodges, the better pleased and the more ready we are to do justice to those whom we have seen so generally adopting the principles of a benevolent Equality, and of a Liberty secured by subjection to the laws.

1. Esquisse d'un Tableau, &c. Epoque 7.
2. All this would be amply proved had we published our Memoirs on Ancient Jacobinism. In the mean time our readers may consult what remain of the contemporary writers or those who lived soon after, for the opinions and actions of these sectaries. Such, for example, as Gläber, who witnessed their first appearance at Orleans 1017; Reinier, who was one of their adepts during seventeen years; and Philichdorf, Ebrard, and Hermangard, who lived with them. They may also consult St. Antoninus, Fleuri, Collier, Baronius; but above all let the Councils which condemned these Sects be attended to, and their decrees compared with history; and then will vanish many false prejudices imbibed against the means adopted both by church and state for the irradicating of those sectaries, who, truly Jacobins, aimed at the absolute destruction of all civil society, and of Christianity itself. How is it possible to doubt of the tendency of their disorganizing Equality and Liberty, when we know that the proof necessary and pointed out to the Judges for the conviction of these sectaries, consisted in showing that the accused was one of those who held that *no obedience was due to the civil or spiritual powers, and that no authority was entitled to punish any crimes*. Such is precisely the doctrine of the Council of Taragone, to know whether the famous degrees of the third and fourth Councils of Lateran are applicable to the accused—*Qui dicunt potestatibus ecclesiasticis vel sæcularibus non esse obediendum et pœnam corporalem non esse infligendam in aliquo casu et similia* (Concil. Tarag. anno 1242). How then can it be asserted, that the furies of these sectaries were only in reprisal of the Crusade published against them, when we see that the very first decree issued in this crusade was precisely to rid Europe of their rebellious principles, and of the cruelties which they were already exercising in the states of Thoulouse under the title of *Coteraux*, in Biscay under that of *Basques*, and in many other countries under different names, *Brabantionibus, Aragonensibus, Navariis, Bascolis, Coterellis, et Triaverdinis, qui tantam in Christianos immanitatem exercent, ut nec Ecclesiis nec Monasteriis deferant, non viduis non pupillis, non senibus et pueris nec cuilibet parcant ætati aut sexui, sed more Paganorum omnia perdant et vastent* (Conc. Lateran. 1179). Such nevertheless is the first

motive stated and the first decree issued of this famous crusade. What have Robespierre and the other Jacobins done more to deserve it?

It is inconceivable how much people have been mistaken both with respect to this decree and to that issued on the same subject by the fourth Œcumenical Council of Lateran, anno 1215. They were represented as the church assuming the power of deposing Sovereigns, as usurping all civil and temporal power. And such is the interpretation given to those very decrees which hindered the Jacobins of those days from executing the very plans which our contemporaries have carried into effect against the altar, the throne, and all civil society! Had I but leisure for digesting the materials I have collected, both the church and her councils would be amply avenged of such calumny. I hope hereafter to publish a particular dissertation on that subject, and to be able to show how strangely those decrees have been misconceived, from a want of knowing the history of those times and of the men against whom they were issued.—Let us suppose for an instant Philip D'Orleans, in virtue of the oath of allegiance common in the Feudal System, summoning all his vassals to follow him and unite with his Jacobins in the destruction of the throne, of the laws, of all society and of religion; will any man of sense believe the vasssals to be bound, by their oath, to carry arms under and to follow Philip's standard and thus second his Antisocial Conspiracy? Is it not evident, on the contrary, that no oath can bind subjects to support such a war, that all oaths are null, which can only be fulfilled by the destruction of the throne, the annihilation of the laws, and of the basis of all civil society; that in such a position, it is the cause of the sovereign, of the laws, and of society, that is to be defended in spite of all oaths? Well, I will pledge myself to prove that the famous decrees of the Councils of Lateran against the *Albigeois* were no more than a similar decision, that, so far from encroaching on the authority of Kings, they were issued in their defence, in defence of their persons, of their authority, of the laws, and of civil society; that had it not been for those decrees both sovereignty and the empire of the laws would long since have been at an end.

I should have numerous errors to combat, and one in particular which I shall not forget. I know there are men so much biassed in favour of the Albigeois and the Vaudois, as to represent them as the ancestors of the Anglican Church, in proof of its antiquity. Such were the pretensions of the English Editor of the translation of Mosheim's Ecclesiastical History. (*See his notes on the articles Vaudois and Albigeois*). Though the cause of the Anglican Church is not my own, still I will serve it better than all those feeble writers.—I will avenge it of the shame of such an origin. I will prove, that, so far from descending from the Vaudois, they openly condemned their disorganizing principles both before and after the reign of Henry VIII, and that there never existed the least connection between it and the Albigeois. It is the exclusive privilege of the Jacobins, and Condorcet's secret associations, to descend from and glory in such progenitors.

3. Est valde notandum quod ipse Johannes et Complices sui, non audent revelare prædictos errores credentibus suis, ne ipsi discedant ab eis—Sic tenebant Albanenses, exceptis simplicioribus quibus singula non revelabantur (*Reinier de Cataris Lugduni & Albanenses.*) Such are exactly the secrets of the first and of the Occult Lodges, of the simple dupes and of the consummate adepts.

4. Philichdorf, *contra* Waldenses, Chap. 13.

5. Magorum quoque dogmata Manes novit, et in ipsis volutatur. (*Centuriatores Magdeburgenses ex Augustino.*)
6. V. Baronius in Manetem.
7. Magistratus civiles et politias damnabant ut quæ a Deo malo conditæ et constituæ sunt. (*Centuriatores Magdeburgenses, Tom. II, in Manetem.*)
8. Nec domos, nec agros, nec pecuniam ullam possidendam. (Ibid. Ex Epiphanio & Augustino.)
9. Hieronimus, Prœmium Dialogorum contra Pelagium.
10. Jura, perjura, secretum prodere noli. (*Augustinus de Manichæis.*)
11. Signa, oris, manuum et sinus. (*Centuriatores Magdeburgenses ex Augustino.*)
12. Manichæorum alter alteri obviam factus, dexteras dant sibi ipsis signi causa, velut a tenebris servati. (*Ibid. ex Epiphanio.*)
13. Plerumque Pascha nullum celebrant—sed Pascha suum, id est diem quo Manichæus occisus, quinque gradibus instructo tribunali, et preciosis linteis adornato, ac in promptu posito, et objecto adorantibus, magnis honoribus prosequuntur. (*August. contra Epist. Manich.*)
14. See Mr. Le Franc's Degree of Rosicrucian.
15. Epiph., Baronius, Fleuri, &c.
16. Were it objected, that every thing in this degree appears grounded on the story of Adoniram and Solomon's Temple, I would answer, Yes, as to words; but as to facts nothing relating to the death of Adoniram is to be found in the History of Solomon or of his Temple. All is allegorical, and entirely applicable to Manes. The *Mac Benac* is inapplicable to the Templars. Beside, the whole of this ceremony is far anterior to them. They may have shaped the fable according to their own profession; but they have preserved the leading feature, the Mac Benac, which carries us back immediately to Manes.
17. Mr. Le Franc's Degree of Rosæ Crucis.
18. Centuriatores Magdeburgenses, Baronius, &c.
19. Quin et homini mendico, nisi Manichæus sit, panem et aqua non porrigunt. (*Augustinus de Moribus Manichæorum et contra Faustinum.*)
20. Centuriatores Magdeburgenses ex Epiphanio.
21. Will not this circumstance of the Widow explain a custom with the Masons, who, when they find themselves exposed to any danger, and that they have hopes of being heard by any of the brethren, in order to make themselves known and to obtain succour they hold their hands on their heads and call out, *help from the children of the widow*? If the modern Masons are ignorant of the fact, the ancient adepts were well acquainted with it; and all history asserts, that Manes was adopted by the widow to whom Budda, Scythian's disciple, fled for refuge, and that this Heresiarch inherited all the riches he had left her. *Help from the children of the widow*, therefore, naturally alludes to the children of Manes.
22. See Remarks on the General and Particular History of Religion, by Mr. Le Franc.

CHAP. XIV.

Sixth Degree of the Conspiracy against Kings.

Coalition of the Sophisters and of the Freemasons.

THE generality of Free-masons of the present day do the Scotch the honour of looking upon their Grand Lodge as the stock whence all the others sprang: It is there, they tell us, that the Templars convened for the preservation of their mysteries: it is thence that they suppose Masonry spread through England into France, Germany, and other states. This is not an improbable conjecture with respect to the actual form[1] and present aspect of their mysteries; but, from whatever part they may have spread throughout Europe, it is an undoubted fact, that Lodges existed in France and in most other states in the beginning of this century.

In 1735 they were proscribed by an edict of the States of Holland; two years later they were prohibited in France by Lewis XV; and in 1738, Clement the XII published his famous Bull of excommunication against them, afterwards renewed by Benedict XIV. In 1748, they were proscribed in Switzerland by the Council of Berne.

From the very nature of their mysteries, this association could long resist the storms by which it was assailed. Men trained to the art of hiding themselves had no other precautions to take than to avoid the publicity of large assemblies. It was in the very nature of their tenets that they found the greatest obstacles to their propagation. England, it is true, disgusted with an Equality and Liberty which the civil feuds of its Lollards, Anabaptists and Presbyterians had taught it to appreciate, had rejected from its Masonic games all explanations tending to the overthrow of Governments; but it did not clear itself of all the adepts who still remained attached to the disorganizing principles of the ancient mysteries. It was this species of adept that preserved the greatest zeal for the propagation of its tenets; it was some of these who, wishing to attract Voltaire into their party, had made Thiriot write, that notwithstanding the title of *Equality and Liberty* given to his Letters, he did not go to the point.

Unfortunately for France and for the rest of Europe, such was the species of adepts which took the lead in the propagation of their mysteries—*at first their progress was slow and imperceptible.*—It had cost Voltaire much to adopt their disorganizing principles, and it would necessarily cost many young men much more, who, not having stifled all sentiments of religion, repressed not only that spirit of independence but even that of curiosity and the desire of knowing a secret only to be acquired by an oath which might be perjury in itself.

In France particularly it must have been difficult to inculcate mysteries, whose last secret was apostasy and rebellion, in men as yet unaccustomed to declamations against Sovereigns and the social order. Policy at first, and afterwards the progress of the Sophisters, removed every difficulty. The Freemasons, according to custom, sought to gain an ascendancy over the mind of some man who might protect them against and avert the indignation of the Sovereign; and with the apron they request the Prince Conti to accept the title of Grand Master of the French Lodges. The Prince consented to be initiated, and on that occasion the construction was put upon the mysteries which is artfully given whenever a candidate is received, whose sentiments, rank, or grandeur, is known to militate against the disorganizing principles of Equality and Liberty. Many Princes and some Sovereigns fell into a similar error. The Emperor Francis I would also be initiated; and he protected the brethren, who never revealed any secret to him which could shock his known piety. Frederic II was also a Free-mason. The adepts told him all their secrets against Christ, but guarded against the most distant hint of applying Equality and Liberty to the rights of the throne, which he was so jealous of maintaining.

In fine, the policy of the Craft went so far as to gain protectors even among the Princesses by initiating them in the lesser mysteries. Maria Charlotte, at present Queen of Naples, believed, without doubt, that she was only protecting most faithful subjects; she petitioned in favour of the proscribed brethren, who were even in danger of suffering. A medal struck on the occasion, her health drank with that of the Grand Master at the Masonic feasts, appeared to be an infallible pledge of the gratitude of the Craft: and under her auspices they spread far and near. But when the Conspiracy burst forth at Naples this protected brotherhood were found to be a nest of conspiring Jacobins. The plot had been contrived in their Lodges, and the protecting Queen stood foremost on the list of proscriptions.

Many Lords and Noblemen, true and accepted Masons, had joined in the conspiracy; but the Court soon discovered the *occult* plot, in which it had been decided that all the nobles, though Jacobin Masons, should be massacred immediately after the Royal Family by the equal and clouted-shoed brethren.

In animadverting on these facts, of which the Historians of the Revolution will have to treat hereafter, my design is to draw the attention of my reader to that policy of which so many great personages have been the miserable dupes. The Occult Masons would go in quest of them, and initiate them in all the mysteries against religion.—The initiation of these Noblemen quieted the fears and averted the attention of Government from the Lodges, seeing them frequented by men who were the natural allies of the throne. And this policy of the Occult Lodges proved one of the most successful tools for their success. The names of the most faithful servants of the crown screened the rebellious plots of their occult mysteries; and that of *Conti* easily quieted Lewis XV with respect to the Masons. The Police of Paris made no farther enquiries, and the Lodges were tolerated. The Sophisters and the progress of Impiety furnished them with new and more efficacious means of multiplying their Lodges.

According as Voltaire and Holbach's club succeeded in inundating Europe with their impious writings, the Craft extended its conquests. It was then easy for the Philosophists to make themselves be listened to by men already disposed to the secret mysteries by their Antichristian and Antimonarchical publications, and to inspire them with desire for a new order of things to be learned in their Lodges. Curiosity, stimulted by impiety, daily made new converts to the Sect. Impiety continued, propagated, and spread wide the spirit and fashion of Masonry, and that was the great service rendered to it by the Sophisters of the age.

On their side, the Sophisters of Impiety and Rebellion soon perceived the connection between the mysteries of Masonry and their Philosophism. They were desirous of being acquainted with those mysteries whose profound adepts were their most zealous disciples; and soon all the French Philosophists became Masons. Many years before the Revolution, it was difficult to meet with a Sophister who was not a Free-mason. Voltaire alone had not been initiated. The Craft had too great obligations to him; it was indebted to him for too many of their adepts, not to testify their gratitude to him. Scarcely had this octogenary infidel arrived at Paris when they prepared the most pompous *fête* for his admission to the mysteries. At eighty years of age he was *admitted to the light*. After having taken the oath, the secret which flattered him the most to learn was, that the adepts, in future his brethren, had long since been his most zealous disciples. That their secret consisted in that *Equality and Liberty* which he had himself opposed to the Gospel of his God and to the pretended Tyrants of the Earth. The Lodge resounded with such applause, the adepts rendered him such honours, and he so perfectly felt the cause of them, that, thinking his pride gratified and his vow of hatred accomplished, he blasphemously exclaimed, *This triumph is well worth that of the Nazarene*. The sacred formula of the mysteries was so dear to him, that the ancient adept Franklin having meanly presented him with his children to bless, he only pronounced over them the words *Equality and Liberty*.[2]

If, after all the proofs we have given of the meaning attached to those words of the profound adepts, any one should doubt of their application to Christ and the throne, let him reflect on the interpretation of them given by Voltaire to the Genevese; and particularly what extent he gave them on his admission among the brethren of *Equality and Liberty:* let him be carried back to this initiation, let him behold the crowned adept, those who crown him, and those who surround him, and can any other proof be required of the object of their mysteries than the list of these attendant brethren. There on the same line he would behold Sophisters and Masons, and particularly those who by their writings have prepared the downfall of the Altar and the Throne, who by their votes have decreed it, and by their crimes have consummated so iniquitous an undertaking. There he would meet the impious brethren, such as Voltaire, Condorcet, Lalande, Dupuis, Bonneville, Volney, and all the other blasphemers both modern and ancient; there again he would see the rebellious brethren, a Fauchet, Bailly, Guillotin, La Fayette, Menou, Chapellier, Mirabeau, and Syeyes; there in the same Lodge he would find the adepts of Holbach's club, and those of *Philip l'Egalité*. Whence this concord, what object can unite so many *impious* brethren, so many *rebellious* brethren in the same Lodge, if not the identity of their secret mysteries? and why this concourse of the Sophisters to the Masonic Lodges, if not for the mutual succour they are to afford each other?

It was not sufficient for the heroes of the Encyclopedia to unite under their standards against Christ the infidels of the court and of every class. Many in all classes who had remained faithful to their God were also true to their King. Even in the impious part of the Aristocracy many men were to be found, whom fortune, ambition, or custom attached either to the person or to the existence of the Monarch. There existed a public force, which the duty or interest of its chiefs might oppose to their machinations; and a multitude of Citizens might have risen against the Conspirators.

But however numerous the disciples of impiety may have been, still the multitude sided with the altar and the throne. The Sophisters saw they had not as yet sufficiently triumphed over the public opinion; they felt that it was necessary to acquire strength.

Having long meditated on the arts of rebellion, they soon perceived what advantages might be drawn hereafter from the Masonic Lodges. From the period of their coalition a revolution was made in the French Masonry, the adepts of which soon became the children of the Encyclopedia. The Martinists alone, with some few Cabalistic Lodges, remained true to their slave Curbicus; all others adopt the impiety of Voltaire. The real source of the mysteries was to be traced by the forms preserved; but it was at this period that all those novelties were introduced which make it more difficult to trace them. It was on this coalition that all our Duallist Masons were transformed into Atheists, Deists, or Pantheists. It was then that the degrees of *the Knights of the Sun and of the Druids* were added to the former ones; but they are nothing more than the impious degrees of modern Sophistry.

Be they however children of Manes, or the offspring of the Encyclopedia, it was always the same conspiracy which constituted the grand object of the Occult Lodges. To secure the triumph of Holbach's club, the Sophisters had only to assure themselves of the support of the pikes[3]; and by means of the interior intercourse of the Masonic Lodges they hoped to effectuate it. At the head of this correspondence was a general office called the *Grand Orient*, apparently under the direction of the Grand Master, but really conducted by the most profound adepts. This was the seat of Government, the high tribunal where all the Masonic differences or suits were settled; it was also the supreme council whose orders could not be violated or disobeyed without incurring the penalties of perjury.

It was to this tribunal that the different Lodgees spread throughout the country sent their deputies, who, residing there, were entrusted with the forwarding of orders, and with notifying their execution. Every Lodge had its president called the *Venerable*, whose duty consisted in forwarding the orders of the *Grand Orient*, or in preparing the brethren for the orders they were to receive. All instructions were transmitted in a secret language, in a particular cypher, or by private means. Lest any false brother or Mason, not subject to the inspection of the *Grand Orient*, should intermix with the real adepts without being discovered, there was a watch-word which changed every quarter, and was regularly sent by the *Grand Orient* to every Lodge under its inspection.

Every branch of this government was bound by the oaths of not revealing to the prophane the secrets of Free-masonry. Each lodge sent its contributions quarterly for the maintenance of the central office, and to cover all expences which this office judged necessary to be incurred for the general interest of the craft. Those Lodgees that were not under the inspection of the *Grand Orient*, were under a similar government of a Mother Lodge, which also had its Grand Master and kept the same sort of correspondence.

This part of their constitutions was generally known to all the brethren; but I have often repeated that with respect to the Occult Lodges they were in the dark. The day was to come when the greatest novice in the art was to show as much zeal as the most profound adept. To effectuate this, it was only necessary to fill their ordinary Lodges with hair-brained young fellows, ignorant citizens, and even thick-headed workmen, who had been previously misled by the impious doctrines of the Sophisters, and with all those who were carried away by that torrent of declamation, calumnies, &c. directed against the altar, the throne, and all the higher orders of society.

With such a species of brethren the Occult Mysteries were unnecessary, and without any further instructions the warhoop of Equality and Liberty was more than sufficient to excite their enthusiasm and direct their blows. A chief in each Lodge, or a very few adepts in direct correspondence with the central office of the Conspirators, might easily be informed of the day and hour on which it was necesssary that the minds of these underling adepts should be worked up to revolutionary fury, and to point out the objects and persons on whom they were to vent their rage. Nor was it impossible to organize those bands of *Brigands* and firebrands into Lodges, and thus distribute to each the different parts of levelling butchers and of revolutionary executioners. These Lodges, multiplied throughout the state in the towns and villages, might, under the direction of the central office or committee, turn out at the same instant all over the country, thousands and tens of thousands of adepts all enthusiastically arrayed under the banners of Equality and Liberty, armed with pikes, hatchets, and torches, carrying fire and desolation wherever their course was traced, knowing beforehand what victims were to be sacrificed, what castles and country houses to be burnt, and what heads to be carried before the triumphant levellers of Equality and Liberty; thus preserving the most exact accord in the midst of rebellion, levelling at one blow all public force, all public justice, disorganizing every thing and throwing every thing into confusion. But, in order to establish its new empire and organize its own power, it only had to transform its secret dens of conspiracy into Jacobin clubs, and its grand adepts into municipal officers. Thus at length, it gave birth to a Revolution irresistible, consummated, and irreparable even in the first hours of its existence, and before any one had though of measures to oppose it.

In thus describing what might have been done by means of that tenebrous secrecy of the Masonic government and Lodges, I have only anticipated what really was done by the Sophisters to effectuate the French Revolution. As early as the year 1776 the central Committee of the *Grand Orient* instructed the directing adepts to prepare the Brethren for insurrection, and to visit the lodges throughout France, to conjure them by the Masonic oath, and to announce that the time was at length come to accomplish *it* in the death of tyrants.

The adept who was intrusted with the visitation of the Northern provinces was an officer of infantry called Sinetty. His Revolutionary Apostleship led him to Lille. The regiment of La Sarre was at that time in garrison there. The Conspirators wished particularly to gain proselytes among and make sure of the military brethren; Sinetty was far from succeeding according to his wishes; but the method and plans he adopted are all that can be necessary for our object. To explain this matter to our readers, we will lay before them the relation made by one of the officers of La Sarre, the eye-witness, and one of the many whom Sinetty had chosen to be present at the meeting where he was to disclose the object of his Apostleship.

"We had," said this worthy officer to me, "our Lodge. It was to us, as to most other regiments, a mere plaything. The trials to which the new candidates were subjected afforded us much amusement. The Masonic feasts made us spend our leisure hours agreeably, and refreshed us from our labors. You very well understand that our *Equality and Liberty* was not that of the Jacobins. The greatest part and nearly the whole of the officers gave proofs of this at the Revolution. We indeed little thought of any such Revolution when an officer of infantry called Sinetty, a famous Mason, presented himself at our Lodge. He was received as a brother. At first he did not appear particular. A few days after he invited about twenty of us to meet him at a tea-garden called the Bonne Aventure, a little out of Lille. We thought he wished to return the compliment of the feast we had given him, and expected a common Masonic repast, when on a sudden he holds forth, declaring he had important secrets to communicate from the *Grand Orient*. We listen to him; but judge of our surprize when we heard him in the most emphatic and enthusiastic tone declare, 'That at length the time was come, that the plans so ably conceived and so long meditated by the true Masons were on the eve of being accomplished; that the universe would be freed from its fetters; Tyrants called

Kings would be vanquished; religious superstitions would give way to light; Equality and Liberty would succeed to the slavery under which the world was oppressed; and that man would at length be *reinstated in his rights*.'

"While our orator continued these decalmations we stared at each other, as much as to say, 'What is this madman about?' We hearkened to him for a whole hour, and silently; meaning afterwards to joke among ourselves. What appeared to us the most extravagant was the confident manner in which he asserted, that it would be vain in future for Tyrants or Kings to pretend to oppose their vast plans; that the Revolution was infallible and near; and that the altar and the throne would be overturned.[4]

"He soon perceived that we were not Masons of his stamp, and left us to go and visit other Lodges. After having laughed for some time at what we conceived to be the conceits of a heated brain, we forgot the scene till the Revolution (which convinced us but too forcibly how much we had misconceived the man) recalled it to our minds."

When I had determined on publishing this fact, I knew how necessary it would be to authenticate it by the signature of him to whom we are indebted for the above acocunt; but it may easily be conceived that he did not wish to have been looked upon as having betrayed the secrets of the Lodge. Fortunately there are now in London many who were present at that meeting; for example, Mr. de Bertrix, Mr. Le Chev[r] de Myon, all formerly officers of the regiment of La Sarre. Though I have not the honour of their acquaintance, and that they may be a little surprized at seeing themselves named here, still I am not afraid of being contradicted by them, either as to the mission or the manner in which Sinetty fulfilled it; and especially when I add that it was their attachment to their King which misled them with respect to this designing madman. So far were they from any revolutionary ideas, so well did they know the dispositions of the French officers, and so firmly did they think the authority of the King established, that they believed this Sinetty to be a madman, and all his message from the Master Lodge to be no more than the reveries of a heated brain. Now that the Revolution has dissipated the illusion, I leave the historian and the reader to meditate on so important a fact. The consequences flow of themselves. They manifest all that the Brethren, either Sophisters or Masons, coalesced in their central committee, expected from the chosen adepts which they had sent into the provinces to prepare the insurrection. But it was reserved to Syeyes and Condorcet to establish in the very centre of Free-masonry an Apostleship much more general, whose object was to Jacobinize not the Lodges only but the whole Universe.

That Condorcet, whom we have observed so jealous of fraternizing with the *Albigeois, Patarins,* or *Catares,* in short, with all the Jacobins of the middle age, had, without doubt, studied their means. What history relates of them, to inflame the indignation of the reader, is exactly what he adopted and imitated of their abominable artifices; and he even surpassed them.[5] This zeal so common to the adepts did not appear active and ardent enough for him. He joined with Syeyes to found in Masonry itself a true Apostleship of Jacobinism.

The Lodge established at Paris, Rue Coq-heron, and presided over by the Duke de la Rochefoucault, was more particularly frequented by the profound Masons. After the *Grand Orient*, this was the Lodge wherein the deepest plots were contrived, where Syeyes and Condorcet, with the most zealous of the brethren, held their meetings. This was also the hotbed whence sprung the Propaganda. Of all the writers who have treated of this establishment, none were better acquainted with it than Mr. Girtanner, who lived at Paris in the midst of the Sophisters and Masons. He afterwards lived with the Jacobins, and pryed into every thing with the eye of a correct observer. A learned Foreigner and a Physician were qualities which rendered him less suspicious, and he was much in their confidence. What we are about to lay before our readers concerning the Propaganda is nearly all extracted from his Memoirs on the French Revolution.

"The Club of the Propagandists is widely different from that of the Jacobins, though both frequently unite. That of the Jacobins is the grand mover of the National Assembly; that of the Propaganda aims at nothing less than being the mover of all human nature. This latter was in existence as early as the year 1786. The Chiefs are the Duc de la Rochefoucault, Condorcet, and Syeyes."

For the honour of this unfortunate Duke, we hasten to say, that the Revolution soon reclaimed him from his errors. He had made himself Grand Master of several Lodges, and was the tool of Syeyes and Condorcet, who made use of his riches to forward their plans. When he beheld the disorganization of France succeeding to the first Constitutionalists, his zeal for the Propaganda was greatly abated. He at length abandoned it, and Condorcet and Syeyes remained the sole Chiefs.

"The grand object of the Propagandists' Club," says Girtanner, "is to establish a philosophical order of things, paramount to all the received opinions of human nature. To be admitted into this society it is necessary to be a stickler for the Modern Philosphy, that is to say, Dogmatic Atheism; or else be ambitious, or discontent with the present Government. The first requisite on your initiation is, a promise of the most profound secrecy. The candidate is then informed, that the number of adepts is immense, and that they are spread all over the world. That all are perpetually in quest of false brethren to make away with them, and to revenge themselves on any who should betray their secret. The candidate then promises to keep no secret from the brethren, but always to defend the people against the Government; to oppose all arbitrary orders, and to do all in his power to introduce a general toleration of religions.

"This association is composed of two sorts of members, those who pay and those who do not. The first class subscribe at least three Louis a year, and the rich double the sum. The subscribers are about five thousand; all the rest engage to propagate the principles of the society, and to act according to its views. These latter may be fifty thousand.

"In 1790, the general fund of the order amounted to twenty millions of livres (900,000l.) in specie; and according to statements made, they were to be ten millions more before the end of 1791.

"They have two degrees, that of *candidate* and that of *initiated*. Their whole doctrine rests on the following basis, *want and opinion are the two agents which make all men act. Cause the want, govern opinions,* and you will overturn all the existing systems, however well consolidated they may appear.

"They will also add, it is impossible to deny that the oppression under which men live is most frightfully barbarous. It is incumbent on the lights of philosophy to quicken the minds of men, and to spread the alarm against oppressors. That once done, it will need only to wait the favorable moment when all minds will be disposed to embrace the new systems, which must be preached throughout all Europe at the same time. If any opponents obstruct the way, let them be gained by *conviction* or by *want*. If they persist in their opposition, treat them like Jews, and refuse them every where the rights of Citizens."

A very curious article in their code, and which should not be overlooked (as being probably suggested by the little success they obtained at the outset), is that which instructs the brethren not to try their plan until they are certain of having *created want*. It also says, that it would be better to defer the scheme for fifty years than fail in it through too much precipitation.

"The Propaganda found much difficulty in gaining footing in Holland; and it only succeeded at last by persuading the people there that they must be led away by the general torrent.—At present it draws large sums of money from all those provinces for the general fund."[6]

Such is the account given by Mr. Girtanner as early as the month of February 1791. A letter, dated Paris, September 1, 1792, confirms them all, saying, "You may rest assured, that all that I wrote to you concerning the Propaganda is perfectly exact. At most there are but a few slight errors in the figures, as in the round numbers, which must be taken as approximations. *The Propaganda is at present in full activity.* YOU WILL SOON PERCEIVE ITS EFFECTS."

At the very period when Mr. Girtanner was writing this, it is easy to perceive to what extent they flattered themselves with success. The orator of the club established at Bruxelles under the name of THE FRIENDS OF THE PEOPLE had already exclaimed:

"Every where fetters are forged for the people; but Philosophy and Reason shall have their turn; and the day shall come when the Supreme and Sovereign Lord of the Ottoman Empire shall lie down to rest a Despot, and find himself on waking a simple Citizen."[7]

As a corroborative proof, let the reader recall to his mind what I said concerning that adept who was for a long time an unheeding Mason; was only initiated in the last mysteries when, on his reception to the degree of *Kadosch*, he was judged a proper person to be admitted into the Propaganda; and who had it left to his choice to go to London, Bruxelles, or even to Constantinople; and, provided he would but propagate the principles of the French

Revolution, was certain of repairing from the fund of the brotherhood the loss that his fortune had sustained.

It was thus that many new degrees had been added to Masonry, and even a new society, which the restless enthusiasm of the Sophisters of Impiety had invented to spread the ancient systems of disorganizing Equality and Liberty, and to ensure their triumph. It was to the Propaganda that they were indebted for the immense number of their adepts; or rather, in rendering impiety so common, the spirit of Philosophism had gained so much ground, that it was scarcely necessary to be initiated into the Occult mysteries to be a complete conspirator.

At that time few novices were to be found either in the Grand Lodges of the *Orient* or of the *Contrat Social*. The Revolution was so openly carried on there, that the Court could not be ignorant of it. Among the number, it was impossible that some should not look upon the Revolution as a most dreadful scourge, and in reality several were of this opinion. With certainty I may number among these latter the French nobleman who received the letter mentioned before, from Alfonse Le Roi.

Being questioned, whether he had not observed something among the Masons tending towards the French Revolution, he made the following reply: "I have been the orator in many Lodges, and had got to a pretty high degree. As yet, however, I had observed nothing which in my opinion could threaten the state. I had not attended for a long time, when in 1786 I was met in Paris by one of the brethren, who reproached me for having abandoned the association; he pressed me to return, and particularly to attend a meeting which he told me would be very interesting. I agreed to attend on the day mentioned, and was extremely well received. I heard things which I cannot tell you; but they were of such a nature, that, full of indignation, I went immediately to the Minister. I said to him, *Sir, I am not entitled to question you; I am aware of the importance and of the consequences which may result from my intrusion; but were I to be sent to the Bastille, I must ask you (because I believe the safety of the King and of the State is at stake), whether the Free-masons are watched, and whether you are acquainted with what is contriving in their Lodges?* The Minister turned upon his heel, and answered, *Make yourself easy, Sir, you shall not go to the Bastille, nor will the Free-masons trouble the State.*"

This Minister was not a man who could be suspected of having in any degree tampered in the Revolution; but he most certainly thought it chimerical even to surmise a plan of overthrowing monarchy, and concluded, like the *Comte de Vergennes*, that, while he had the control of an army of two hundred thousand men, a revolution was little to be feared.

Lewis XVI was himself warned of the dangers which threatened his throne, but continued in that security which only ceased to delude him on his return from Varennes, when he said to a person in whom he confided, *Why did I not believe, eleven years since, what I so clearly see to-day! for I had been warned of it so long ago as that.*

If any one was entitled to disbelieve plots formed against his person or his throne, it was certainly the unfortunate Lewis XVI. Seeking only the happiness of his subjects in all sincerity of his heart, never having committed a single act of injustice, perpetually sacrificing his own interest to that of his people, and ambitious of nothing so much as of the love of that same people, how was it possible for him to conceive that the conspirators could succeed in representing him as a tyrant? Lewis XVI had not one of those vices which draw down hatred on the Monarch's head. Publicly proclaimed the justest of Princes, and the most honest man of his empire, he was unfortunately the weakest of King—But if ever Ministers prepared a Revolution, it was certainly those in whom he placed his confidence. He began by entrusting himself to *Mr. de Maurepas*, whose inactive and careless disposition, dreading nothing so much as violent shocks or tempestuous broils, quietly permitted all those to gather which were only to burst forth when he was gone. The Sophister *Turgot* appeared but for a moment, as it were to make an essay of those systems which silently sapped the throne. The sordid œconomy of *Mr. de St. Germain* only served to deprive the Monarch of his bravest supporters. The quack *Necker* showed no talent but that of ruining the public treasury with his loans, and of accusing *Mr. de Colonne*'s profusion of the fact. Under Mr. de Vergennes, false policy fomented external Revolutions, but to infuse the spirit for, and prepare interior ones. Greedy courtiers disgust the Monarcy with their intrigues, alienate the people by their scandals, corrupt them by their impiety, and irritate them by their luxury. The assembly of the *Notables* convene with the apparent intention only of repairing great errors, at the sole expence of the Nobility and Clergy; and nothing guaranteed that great sacrifices would not prove a great source for new dilapidations. New dissentions threatened to break out between the King and the High Courts of Judicature, when Brienne was on the eve of making his appearance to complete the ruin by turning on the Monarch all that contempt and hatred which should justly have been heaped upon himself. Not a single minister attempted to brook the torrent of Rebellion and Impiety; not one reflected on the inefficacy of the laws for a people who hated their chiefs, and had lost all tie of religion. The Sophisters of Holbach's club, those of Masonry, and all the mal-contents of all classes, whether noble or plebeian, had but little to do to create the desire of a Revolution; and that was the period which our conspirators waited for to consummate their plots; that was what the Propagandists called *creating want*. Every thing denoted that the time was come, and they applied themselves to muster up their forces for the completion of the catastrophe.

In the year 1787, about the same time that Mr. de Calonne, anxious to retrieve the finances from the disorder into which Necker had thrown them, was convening the *Notables*, a secret association, supposed of new invention, established itself at the *Hotel de Lussan* in the street *Croix des Petits Champs*, under the name of *Amis des Noirs* (Friends of the Blacks). There was nothing new in this association but the name. All sectaries of Liberty, whether ancient or modern, every class of Sophisters, and all the Revolutionary Masons, had adopted this appellation only the better to conceal the grand object of their conspiracy under the specious pretext of humanity. While occupying all Europe with the question they had proposed, on the slavery of the Negroes in America, they never lost sight of that Revolution which they had so long meditated, and which was to liberate all Europe from the pretended slavery of the laws and of supposed tyrants. Their Lodges might become suspicious by their daily meetings, and they wished not to lose sight for a single hour of the grand object of their plots. The adepts did not agree as to the *method* of the Revolution, or as to the laws to be substituted to those of the Monarchy. All however were unanimous on *Equality and Liberty*, the grand secret of their mysteries. They also agreed, that both Equality and Liberty were at an end, wherever the people were not sovereign, and did not make their own laws, wherever they could not revoke and change them at pleasure, and particularly where the people were subjected to a Monarch or Magistrates who governed in their own right, or who were not the agents and the executors of their will, and subject to be recalled whenever it might please the people. But among the adepts were many Sophisters who shaped out *Equality and Liberty* according to their own interests, their dispositions, their rank and their fortunes. They were in some sort the Aristocratic Jacobins. The adept Counts, Marquisses, Dukes, Knights, and wealthy Citizens, all these were perfectly of opinion that they were to lose nothing of their rank or fortune in this new system of Equality, but that, on the contrary, they were to share among them all the rights, authority, and influence which they were to wrest from their unfortunate Monarch. In a word, they wished for such a King as the first Jacobin Legislators dreamt of, a King whom they could domineer over, and who had no authority over them. Others wished for an Equality of Liberty in the grandees or wealthy, counterpoised by an Equality of Liberty in the plebeians, and concentrating in a common chief the King. This was the Equality of the *Monarchists*, who thought themselves guiltless rebels because they were not sufficiently powerful to direct the course of the rebellion. As for the last class, they wished neither for a constitutional nor any other King. With them every king was a Tyrant, and every tyrant was to be overthrown; all Aristocracy was to be exploded; all titles, rank, or power was to be levelled; and this last class alone was initiated in the profound secrets of the Revolution. They conceived that they could only proceed by degrees; that it was necessary to unite in order to compass the overthrow of the existing order of things; and, that accomplished, to wait the favourable moment for accomplishing their ultimate designs.

It was with this view that Brissot, Condorcet, and Syeyes proposed to form a general union of all the adepts, whatever might be their Revolutionary Systems, under the title of *Friends of the Blacks;* it was even agreed, that every man who had any serious cause of complaint against the court should be invited to join them. This was the reason why they invited the *Marquis de Beaupoil de St. Aulaire*, whom they supposed to be imbued with their principles through desire of revenge. But they were grossly mistaken. The Marquis had great reason to complain of the Ministry; but no one could better distinguish the cause of the Monarch from the injustice of his Ministers.

This, however, proved a fortunate error for history. What I am about to present to the reader concerning this association is made public by permission of Mr. de Beaupoil. He was kind (and I will say patriotic) enough to favor me with an account of what he had been eye-witness to in that secret society; and in vain would the historian seek a better authority.

Consonant with the wishes of its projectors, the association of the *Friends of the Blacks* was composed of all the adepts who had imbibed the principles of modern Philosophism, and they were generally initiated in the mysteries of Free-masonry. In the multitude of brethren were many thousands of dupes, all ardent for, all ready to second the Revolution, and all promoting it with their utmost exertions. Each member subscribed two guineas, and was entitled to attend the deliberations. That the plans might be better digested, a *regulating committee* was formed of the following persons, viz. Condorcet, Mirabeau the elder, Syeyes, Brissot, Carra, the Duc de la Rochefoucault, Clavieres, Pelletier de St. Fargeau, Valadi, La Fayette, and some others.

Had I not even mentioned the French Revolution, this list of its prime movers must naturally make it occur. And what could be the object of such a society, which begins by giving itself a *regulating committee* composed precisely of all those men who, in the course of the Revolution, have shewn themselves its greatest abettors? A Condorcet, who would have smiled at the conflagration of the universe, provided neither Priest nor King could spring from its ashes![8] A Mirabeau, who to the impiety, the ambition, and all the other crimes of a Cataline, had nothing of his own to add but cowardice, and still retained all the daring profligacy of his patron.[9]

When the historian shall depict a Syeyes, let him begin with the visage of a snake; for it is solely to the art of hiding his venom that that abominable character is indebted for his reputation of a profound genius. Like Mirabeau, he had long studied the Revolutionary arts; he left to the latter the more striking features of crime, reserving to himself those luxuries of obscure criminals, who point out to the ruffians the crimes to be committed, and then sculk behind their blood-thirsty cohorts.[10]

With all the desire of operating a Philosophical Revolution, and of conducting it with profound policy, Brissot only dared appear on the second rank: But he had already formed the plan of his Republic, and his Philosophism only shrunk from the horrors of the Revolution, when the axe, with which he had himself assailed the throne, was suspended over his own head.[11]

Claviere, a greedy and frigid stock-jobber, comes from Necker's own country to sell to the Parisians the Revolutionary arts which he had practised there. Moderate in his expressions, even when he insinuated the most treacherous and ferocious means, he seemed to have secretly watched Syeyes to learn the art of forming disciples.[12]

After having kissed the gallows, Carra appears to revenge himself on those laws which had not punished him for his thefts, and he seems to enjoy the liberty to which he is restored only to blaspheme like a demoniac both God and King.[13]

He that is ignorant of the effect of flattery on a weak mind, will be surprized to see the name of Rochefoucault among beings of this species.—Condorcet wanted a tool; as long as he could direct this unfortunate Duke he led him every where, to the Lodges, to the Clubs, to the National Assembly; he even persuaded him that he was leading him through the paths of virtue and honour.[14]

As to La Fayette, on his white horse at the head of the Revolutionary bands, he thought himself the favorite child of Mars; seated near the Sophisters, he believed himself a Philosopher; and the Hero of the Fish-market, he affects to rival Washington. Happy for him if his misfortunes have inspired him with a due sense of shame and sorrow for having been so long a time the puppet of the Sophisters and incendiary firebrands.

Lastly, the Advocate Bergasse was called to this regulating committee. This man had neither the folly of La Fayette nor the wickedness of Condorcet, but he believed in Revolutionary Equality and Liberty as he did in the *Somnambules*, who had persuaded him that he was their Messiah. He even expected to act the part. When, in the first days of that Assembly which was called National, he was entrusted with the care of framing the code of Equality and Liberty, he was quite surprised to find himself coupled with Mounier and several other co-deputies. He meant alone to restore the people to Equality and Liberty, and to triumph over Despotism. It was not the superiority of talents nor his high repute for honesty that acquired him his seat in this committee, but the wild enthusiasm of his ideas and his thirst after a new order of things. Happily for him, what made him quit the new Legislators, made him also abandon the Conspirators. His secession only left Condorcet, Syeyes, Mirabeau, and the other rebels, more at liberty to act.

When the Marquis de Beaupoil was invited to inscribe his name on the list of this association, he candidly believed that its object was the consideration of those questions, so worthy a generous soul, on the means to be proposed to the King of alleviating or perhaps abolishing the slavery of the Negroes. He did not however remain long in his error. The establishment of Equality and Liberty, and the compiling of the Rights of Man, were the leading features of all their deliberations, and consequences of the most alarming nature to Sovereigns were drawn and debated without the least hesitation.

"Notwithstanding my professed aversion for such opinions," says the Marquis, "I had the constancy to attend the meetings of the regulating committe till I was perfectly master of their plans. I remarked that all the members of the association were also members of the Masonic Lodges, and particularly of that society actuated by the same principles called *Philantropes*. I also observed, that there already existed a close correspondence with the other associations of the same sort both in Europe and America, and the general talk was on the certainty of a Revolution which was nigh at hand. Those brethren who did not belong to the committee came to bring their money, and repeat their most ardent wishes for the success of its arduous undertakings. They then mixed in the different Lodges and Clubs, which in fact professed the same principles, and the regulating committe maintained its primacy over these various Clubs, merely by being a selection of the most wicked members from them all."

"Their grand object known, I might have pryed into their most secret mysteries; but I disdained dissimulation; and had I remained longer in this haunt of Conspirators I must have adopted it. Full of indignation, I declaimed vehemently against their plots; I required that my name should be erazed from the list; I blotted it out myself, and left their den forever.

"I ought certainly to have hastened to inform Government of the doctrines and plans of this Association;[15] but to denounce a society which had admitted me to its mysteries, bears a face of perfidy which I should have rejected had the idea occurred. I confined myself therefore to printing a sort of antidote under the title of *Unity of the Monarchical power*. Some time after that, I printed a work called *Of the Republic and of the Monarchy*, with a view to warn the King, and the nation at large, of the consequences pending on the Revolution. This was more than necessary to expose me to all the vengeance of the Conspirators. I was acquainted that the very day after my erazure, the whole sitting was spent in suggesting means of punishing what they called my treachery; many violent opinions were broached; but Mirabeau only voted for calumny and other means of representing me as a dangerous man, and one to whom no credit was due. Carra and Gorsas were entrusted with the commission, and it was from their pens that flowed the most violent declamations against me; and when the proscriptions began, my name was to be found foremost upon the list."

If the candour and loyalty of the Marquis hindered him from staying any longer among these Conspirators, his acount at least demonstrates that he had remained long enough to remove all doubt as to the grand object of their mysteries. I really believe myself entitled to announce to the public, that a day will come when even all the most secret deliberations of this den of Conspirators will be made public.

When the Revolution rendered it unnecessary for the prime agents to wear the mask any longer, the name of *Friends of the Blacks* was thrown aside and the association appeared to be dissolved. *The regulating committee* remained, and only enveloped itself in greater darkness the more surely to direct all the Parisian Clubs, the Sections, the Revolutionary Societies, and even the Jacobins themselves. If Gobet,[16] the too famous intruded Archbishop of Paris, was not a member of this committee, he knew their plans; he must even have been present at their meetings more than once. He would not otherwise have spoken so emphatically of what was contriving there at the time this unhappy apostate requested some secret conferences with me, concerning his reconciliation with the church.—I am at present perfectly persuaded, that it was the fear of the Regulating Committee which hindered him from keeping his word, and in some sort atoning for the horrible scandal he had given. It is true, that he never spoke to me of the committee but in general terms, yet it was always with so much terror that I could easily surmise the atrocity of their plans: "No," said he, "no, you cannot conceive, you could not give credit to the lengths they mean to go, what plans, what means, they have in agitation. You have seen nothing as yet." We were, nevertheless, in April of the third year of the Revolution, and I had witnessed many horrid scenes.

Long before this period I was acquainted with an adept, a great Mason and Deist, but an enemy to carnage and plunder. He wished for a *Philosophical Revolution* conducted with more order and less violence, and was a member of the regulating committee. I shall never forget what he told me one day, when speaking of the committee, in nearly the same terms as Gobet had done. I could have foretold all that has since been done against the Nobility, the Clergy, and the King. "I go there," said he, "but with horror, and to oppose their frightful projects. Hereafter shall be known all that is carried on there, and how those savage minds add to the horrors of the Revolution. It shall be known, but after my death. I am too wise to publish it during my life. I know too well what they are."

I will not attempt to supply from my imagination what might be surmised from such a speech, respecting a committee entirely composed of the most inveterate enemies of the Altar and of the Throne which Masonry or the Sophisters could produce. But I will lay before my readers what I have learned from various adepts concerning that part of the Conspiracy to which this volume has naturally led us.

Of all the means adopted by the regulating committee, that which contributed the most to form the immense multitude of armed men which they wanted, was their correspondence with the Masonic Lodges dispersed at that time all over France in great numbers. In Paris alone there were one hundred and fifty, and as many in proportion, if not more, in the other towns and even in the villages.

Deliberations taken at the *regulating committee* were transmitted to the *central committee of the Grand Orient*; thence they were sent to the *Venerables* or Masters of the different Lodges in the Provinces. The very year in which this regulating committee was established, a great many of the *Venerables* received instructions accompanied by the following letter: "As soon as you shall receive the enclosed packet you will acknowledge the receipt of it. You will subjoin the oath of punctually and faithfully executing all orders which you shall receive in the same form, without making any inquiry whence they come or by whom they shall be sent. If you refuse this oath, or if you are not true to it, you will be looked upon as having violated the oath[17] which you took at your initiation. Remember the *Aqua Tophana* (the most subtle of poisons).— Remember the *poignards* that will start from their sheaths to pierce the heart of the traitor."

Such nearly were the contents of a letter received by a man formerly a most zealous Mason, and of whom I learned that similar orders had been sent to the other Masters of Lodges. For nearly these two years past I have been in possession of a memorial which names several of the *Venerables* who received these instructions and faithfully complied with them. Such was the conduct of La Coste, a Physician of Montignac-le-Comte, in Perigord, originally the founder of the Lodge in that town, a Deputy at the second Assembly, and finally voting the King's death in the third. I can also name the Attorney Gairaux, who did not show less zeal for the Revolution. He was not the Master of the Lodge when these first instructions were sent. The packet was delivered to the Chevalier de la Calprade, at that time intrusted with the hammer at the Lodge at Sarlat; but, surmising to what lengths these first letters might lead him, he very providently resigned his place to Gairaux.[18]

I am thus minute in my accounts, because it is essential that history be informed how so deep a plot was carried on, and how those millions of armed men appeared to second it at the same instant in every part of France.

Lest their numbers should not be sufficiently great, *the regulating committee* resoved on admitting a class of men, which had long since been excluded, to the lesser mysteries of Masonry. It was that of the day labourers, and all the lower classes of mechanics, even vagabonds and ruffians. With these men *Equality and Liberty* needed no farther explanation. It was easy for the adepts to infuse the revolutionary enthusiasm into them by the power of these words alone.

The Masons of a higher rank in Paris did not like to fraternize with such brethren. It was necessary to call some from the Provinces, and in a short time the suburbs of *St. Antoine* and *St. Marceau* were entirely Masonized.

Many years before the formation of this Regulating Committee, the well-informed adepts would write that the number of Free-masons was *incomparably* greater in France than in England; that the hair-dressers and valets, and every sort of profession flocked to the Lodges.[19] It will not be an exaggeration therefore to calculate the number of Free-masons at six hundred thousand; and at that period it could not be supposed that the generality of this immense number were averse to the plans of the Occult Lodges. Impiety and the declamations of the Sophisters supplied the last mysteries. The greatest novices were enthusiastically wedded to the ideas of Equality and Liberty. Let a hundred thousand of the brethren be subtracted as untainted with these principles, it will be the most the historian can do in favour of our youth who remained faithful to the spirit of their forefathers. Thus the *Regulating Club* could rely upon the support of five hundred thousand brethren, at that time spread all over France, all zealous for the Revolution, all ready to rise at the first signal and to impart the shock to all other classes of the people. The Sophisters already boasted that it was not such an easy thing to triumph over three millions of men.

This was the plan adopted by the Committee to organize the Revolutionary bands. The Sophisters had cleared the way by perverting the public opinion. The hiding places and dens of a Sect, the sworn enemies to Christianity and Sovereigns, had opened and expanded themselves. The adepts of Occult Masonry had multiplied; their ancient tenets of Impiety and

Rebellion had identified them in the new Lodges with that of modern Philosophism. Opinion had gained the heart; but plots, cunning, and secret artifice, had mustered up the forces. Had *Necker, Briennes,* the *Deficit* or the *Notables* never been mentioned in France, had Lewis XIV been upon the throne when the *Regulating Committee* and the *Central Club* of Masonry should have completed the organization of their skulking adherents, Lewis XIV himself would not have stopped the Revolution. It would have found chiefs. Public opinion would have named them, and the banners of truth would have been deserted. At the sound of *Equality and Liberty* he would have seen his legions disband, and rally under the standard of revolt. Had Lewis XVI refused to convoke the States General, the Regulating Committee would have convened them; five hundred thousand adepts under arms would have supported the convocation, and the people would have flocked to the elections.

Such was the progress of this twofold Conspiracy at the time of the convocation of the States General. The skulking Sophisters of Masonry and the barefaced Sophisters of Holbach's Club perceived that it would be necessary to choose a chief who might be made the stalking-horse, and give them a sanction by his name. He was to be powerful, that he might forward the crimes which they had planned; he was to be cruel, lest he should flinch at the sight of the numerous victims that were to be sacrificed to their horrid plots.—He needed not the talents, but the vices of a Cromwell. The conspirators soon cast their eyes on *Philip D'Orleans,* the pupil of some evil Genius.

D'Orleans, for his part, was conspiring as well as the combined Sophisters. More wicked than ambitious, he aspired at the Throne; but, like the evil genius, he delighted in ruin and devastation, even though he should not thereby exalt himself; *Philip* had sworn to seat himself on the Throne, or to overturn it though he were to be crushed under the ruins. For a long time had this unparalleled monster been callous to honor or remorse; a brazen front repelled the shafts of contempt or of disdain, nor was he to be affected by the hatred of man or of heaven. A youth spent in debauchery had deadened every honorable sentiment of his heart, and by the blackest deeds he sought to ensure his expectations of fortune. At an age when the love for riches is scarcely known, public report accused him of having enticed the young Prince of Lamballe into debauchery merely to secure to himself the immense fortune of this young Prince, who fell a victim to his cunning, while in quest of pleasure. Nor is there an action of his life which could render at all improbable such atrocious perfidy. Time only more and more developed a heart capable of such designs; he was cowardly and revengeful; ambitious and cringing; prodigal and avaricious. Proud of his name and the rank of Prince, he was the humble servant of the vilest populace; choleric and impetuous before his friends, cool and dissembling before those whom he wished to ruin, callous to all good actions if he saw no direct means of directing them to evil purposes, and never meditating such dark and hideous plots as when he assumed the character of sensibility and benevolence. Little capable (from cowardice) of daring crimes, he was wicked enough to dedicate his riches to the completion of them. His heart, in a word, was the common sewer of every baleful passion, and of every vice. He needed but the opportunity to discover his bias to evil; and such was the chief with which Lucifer presented the Conspirators.

During the contentions which subsisted between the Court and the Parliaments *Philip* had leagued with several of those Magistrates who were more worthy of being seated in the Regulating Club of the Conspirators than in the first Tribunal of the kingdom. He was much more employed as their tool to insult the Royal Majesty in the very sanctuary of the laws, than as a leader against the encroachments of Briennes.[20]

Lewis XVI for the first time showed his resentment, and Philip was exiled to Villers-Coterets. This was the spark that fired D'Orleans heart with vengeance. He already hated Lewis XVI because he was King; he hated Marie Antoinette because she was Queen; he swore their ruin; he swore it in the transports of rage and fury; nor did his agitation cease but to leave him at liberty to meditate the means of vengeance. His first step was to call to his councils the greatest villains France could produce. That Laclos whose fable genius seemed to rise from the Stygian Lakes to guide the venemous and tortuous course of the blackest crimes.

Mirabeau and Syeyes flocked thither, nor was it difficult for them to point out the great helps to be acquired from the Masonic Lodges, of which he had been chosen the honorary chief. The Legions of Hell are bound by the bonds of friendship when evil is their object, and the grand plan was combined during the short period that Philip remained in exile. At that time he was initiated in the Occult Mysteries, but not as men of his rank formerly were; for it is certain that the brethren had considered him as sufficiently wicked to be admitted to their deepest mysteries. It is certain that the King-killing trial of the Vault in the degree of *Kadosch* was a voluptuous one for him.—In pronouncing those words, *Hatred to all Worship, Hatred to all Kings*, he must have seen all his hopes vanish of seating himself on the throne of the unfortunate Lewis XVI, but he breathed vengeance; and, though he were to expend his life and fortune in the pursuit, he would not relent. He renounces the throne under the penalty of perjury, and was overjoyed at having associated with men who had sworn to destroy all thrones, provided they would first strike that of his own relative and King.

This oath discovered to him an ocean of crimes, but he did not shrink at their sight; they only served to stimulate him to the perpetration of them. Brissot declared that he subscribed to them all at that period, but that *the Court was too strong as yet*, and that he only retired to England to gain time, and to let the Revolution ripen. The Marquis de Beaupoil attests this fact, in his memorial, as having heard Brissot himself declare it.

The time was not yet come upon which the Regulting Committees had decided. They waited for the States General; their artifices, their clubs, and a cloud of writers had nearly made the demand general. The Parliament of Paris called for them. France looked up to them as the regenerating power; but I have not as yet enumerated all the plots nor all the Sects which clamorously called for them to entomb the Monarchy and all its laws.

In these divers plots the Sophisters of the Encyclopedia, opposing the rights of Equality and Liberty to the Altar, had thrown themselves headlong into the gulph of hatred to Royalty.—The Tenebrious and Occult Lodges of Masonry, the antique mysteries of the adopted slave, had received the disciples of Voltaire and Diderot into their bosom, but to connect and more secretly invigorate that hatred of Christ and of Kings. The Sophisters of Impiety and of Rebellion had only intermixed their plots with those of the Lodges, or rather dens, ready to cast forth their Legions of adepts and firebrands enthusiastically armed to establishy their Equality and Liberty on the ruins of the Altar and the Throne. The frightful Propaganda appeared with its treasures and its apostles.—The *Central* and the *Regulating Committees* could boast of their *Secret Correspondences*, their council, and their chief—all the forces of Rebellion and of Impiety were organized—still those were not the only scourges that were to desolate France.

Under the name of ILLUMINEES a band of Conspirators had coalesced with the Encyclopedists and Masons, far more dangerous in their tenets, more artful in their plots, and more extensive in their plans of devastation. They more silently prepared the explosions of the Revolutionary volcano, not merely swearing hatred to the Altar of Christ and the Throne of Kings, but swearing at once hatred to every God, to every Law, to every Government, to all society and social compact; and in order to destroy every plea and every foundation of the social compact; they proscribed the terms MINE *and* THINE, acknowledging neither Equality nor Liberty but in the *entire, absolute and universal overthrow of all* PROPERTY *whatever*.

That such a Sect could have existed; that it could have acquired power; that it does exist; and that it is to this Sect that the most terrible scourges of the Revolution are to be traced, are without doubt among those extraordinary phenomena, of the reality of which the most incontrovertible proofs alone can convince the reader. Such will be the object of the third Part of these Memoirs.

After having successively developed the Conspiracy of the *Sophisters of Impiety,* that of the *Sophisters of Rebellion,* and that of the *Sophisters of Anarchy,* it will be easy for us to apply the different disastrous consequences of each of these conspiring sects to the French Revolution, and to prove that the Monster called JACOBIN is no other than the aggregate of the triple conspiracy and of the triple sect.

1. I say with respect to the *actual form of their Lodges,* and not as to the substance of their mysteries; for there had existed Free-masons long since in England who pretended neither to descend from the Knights Templars nor the Grand Lodge in Scotland. This is to be seen in a manuscript written two hundred and fifty years ago and still preserved in the Bodleian Library at Oxford. This manuscript is a copy of certain

questions written about a hundred years before by Henry VI in his own hand. The date then of the original is about three hundred and thirty years back, as Henry VI departed this life in 1471. (*See Mr. Locke's Letter and this Manuscript in W. Preston's Illustrations of Masonry, Book III, Sect. I.*)

There are two important remarks to be made on this manuscript. First, that the adept questioned on the origin of Masonry makes no mention of the Templars; on the contrary he says, that all the important secrets of which it is in possession were brought into Europe by Venetian merchants coming from the East. (*Comed ffyrste ffromme the este ynn Venetia—3d answer.*) Locke suspects that in those times of *monkish* ignorance, the Masons might have mistaken the Venetians for the Phenicians. Mr. Locke could not have chosen a more unfavourable moment for his suspicion, as the Masons and even *the Monks* had by means of the crusades learned to distinguish between the *Phenicians and Venetians*, and particularly between *Tyr* and *Venice*—Nothing was more natural than the answer made by the Mason to Henry VI, 'That the mysteries had been brought from the *East* by the *Venetians*.' All Masons agree that the Templars learned them in the *East*. It is very natural that the *Venetians*, so famous in those days for their commerce in the East, should have taken these mysteries whence the Templars afterwards did, and whose history had not yet been incorporated with that of Freemasonry. But the reader will remark, that every thing leads us back to Manes, to the countries whence, it is well known, the sect and its mysteries spread into Europe.

The second observation to be made on this ancient Manuscript is, that even in England Freemasonry already comprehended all those systems of *Cabal*, of *Astrology*, and of *Divination*, sciences all founded on the twofold principle of Manes. The art of living *without fear or hope* is also to be remarked, the grand object of Manes, as well as of all impious wretches; the art of making perfection and true liberty consist in disbelieving a future state, which may constitute the hopes of the just man and the terror of the wicked. And this is confounded in the general terms of the Manuscript—*The art of wunderwerckynge, and of foresayinge thynges to comme—the skylle of becommynge gude and parfyghte wythouten the holpynges of* FERE *or* HOPE (*8th answer*). Amidst all the panegyrics bestowed on Masonry in this ancient record such are the documents contained in it. Though so much extolled by Masons, the reader will certainly not receive it as a proof of the pretended innocence of their mysteries.

2. See the Life of Voltaire.
3. I hope the reader will remark here, that the swearing in of the multitude is the last step of a conspiracy, and not the first, as some (little versed in these black arts) are perpetually repeating; and that as long as the authors remain undiscovered, it is but of little avail to discover the vulgar and often misled agents. T.
4. Nothing perhaps can show the danger and impolicy of oaths of secrecy more than this passage: For, any rebel, provided he be bound by the same oath, may come and make propositions to you of the most dangerous tendency; and if, through weakness or depravitiy, they are hearkened to, he finds Conspirators ready made; if rejected, they are still kept secret by those who are supposed to be bound to secrecy, forgetting that in this case by the very act they become perjured to their oath of allegiance and to their God. T.

5. Notwithstanding I have already given various proofs of the coincidences between the modern Jacobins and those of the middle ages, I think it proper to lay before my reader an historical fragment very precious, though little known. It is a letter written in 1243, by one Yvon of Narbonne to Gerald Archbishop of Bourdeaux, and preserved by Matthew Paris, a contemporary author. In this letter Yvon says, that, accused of leaning towards the Errors of the *Patarins*, he thought it prudent to seek safety in flight. Arrived at Come, in Italy, he meets with some *Patarins*, and declares himself to be persecuted for professing their doctrines. He is received as a brother, sumptuously treated, and entrusted with information, of which he gives the following account: "For three months," says he, "I was among them, well fed, splendidly and voluptuously feasted; learning each day some new error or rather horror against faith, to all which I pretended to assent. *By dint of good treatment they obliged me to promise, that in future, whenever I was in company with Christians,* I would do my utmost to prove that the faith of Peter never saved any body. *As soon as they had wrested from me this oath,* they began to discover their secrets to me. They told me, among other things, that from several towns in Tuscany and from almost all the towns in Lombardy, they carefully sent some of their most docile disciples to Paris, who were there to apply to all the subtilties of Logic and intricate questions of Divinity, in order to prepare them for maintaining their own errors and combating the Apostolic Faith. That beside this they had a great number of merchants whom they sent to the different fairs with a view of perverting the richer laity, and in a word all those with whom they conversed or associated at table. Thus by the extent of their commerce they on one hand enrich themselves by other men's money, and on the other pervert souls."

This, beyond a doubt, is a secret society, a perfect Propaganda. When we reflect that this society was entirely composed of Manichæans, teaching that all men were free and equal, and were to obey neither *the spiritual nor temporal power,* one an hardly view them in any other light than as Jacobin Masons. Still less can we mistake them when we observe the new adept travelling from Come to Milan, to Cremona, to Venice, and even to Vienna, always received and feasted by the Brethren, only making himself known and getting himself acknowledged by *means of certain signs which were always secretly given to him,* Semper in recessu accepi ab aliis ad alios inter signa. (*Math. Paris. Hist. Ang. ann. 1243*).

It is true, that this is a letter written by a penitent adept, who is sorry for having swerved from the true faith, lamenting the horrors he had been guilty of with the other brethren, and only consoling himself with the happy recolletion of having reclaimed several from their errors, and craving pardon and penance for his past wickedness. But these circumstances all become new proofs of his sincerity, and only depict in stronger colours the connection between the secret associations of the children of Manes, the true Jacobins of the middle age, and the secret associations of the Occult Masons, or of our modern Jacobins.
6. See Girtanner, Vol III, in German, from page 470 to 474.
7. Ibid.——It is worthy the attention of every Englishman, that the work on the Rights of Man, which appeared under the name of Thomas Paine, was published as early as the year 1791; that it was profusely spread all over Great Britain and Ireland (in the latter of which places it may be said to have been the forerunner of the unhappy broils we have since witnessed), and it was sold (as I am credibly informed) as low as for 3d. or 4d. to the Irish Peasantry. We should swell this note to a volume were we

to enumerate the miserable or rather the abominable penny publications that prove the almost *licentious* liberty of the press, and that have been and continue to be sold of late. Even Newspapers have taken up the task. The GAZETTEER at this moment comes to hand (Saturday the 16th September 1797), in the third page and fourth column, &c. of which I read in large letters, "We live in an age pregnant with the seeds of destruction *to one class of men*, and with the means of triumph to another. The energies of men are all actuated, they are embattled against ERROR, and *Superstition, along with its hideous train of Mitres, Diadems, and Sceptres, is* DESTINED TO VANISH, overwhelmed and exploded by the intrepid reasonings of all good, virtuous, independent friends." The writer then talks of *Scourges of Industry* and of friends of man; but, alluding to the French Revolution of the 4th of September, he continues: These "events will be found to be highly conducive to the promotion of the final success of *those schemes which have been conceived and arranged in the retreats sacred to Philosophy,* and to the description we thus allude to. *The* PROJECT *is the* EMANCIPATION *of a world.*"

In the next column we find, that mankind are not only indebted to them (the French Government) for Liberty; but "they owe it to them, that the horrible reign of Priest-craft and MONARCHIC INSTITUTIONS have not been restored in one country and established for centuries in every quarter of the globe. To them we owe the renewed guarantees of *ultimate victory in the struggle* TO PULL DOWN AND DESTROY THRONES. To them ENGLISHMEN CAN ONLY LOOK WITH CONFIDENCE *for a redress of those grievances which have been* GENERATED IN THE LAP OF MONARCHY, and nourished and fostered from the cradle, to a state of manhood by wicked Ministers, and *the sycophant eulogists* OF A WORTHLESS COURT. *From them, Europe is yet destined to receive the* PALM OF LIBERTY, &c. &c. Glorious events! and glorious times, in which men live *only to witness the downfal of some pretender* at (probably misprinted for *as*) *the prelude to* THE OVERTHROW OF SOME THRONE."—Such are the doctrines forced upon that part of the public who support this Paper. They need no comment, but are such as should rouse the attention of every Englishman to oppose them. T.

8. He murdered himself. T.
9. Died in great agonies of pain, 3d April 1791, supposed to have been poisoned by the Jacobins. T.
10. Still exists, 20th September, 1797. T.
11. Was guillotined 31st of October 1793. T.
12. Murdered himself the 1st of December 1793. T.
13. Guillotined the 31st of October 1793. T.
14. When he could lead him no longer he sent assassins to murder the Duke, who was torn to pieces by the mob, September 2, 1792. T.
15. This is a most awful example of the fatal consequences of oaths of secrecy. T.
16. I may now declare it, since this unhappy Gobet has fallen a victim to his vain terrors and mean apostasy. It was he whom I would not name when speaking (in my *History of the French Clergy during the Revolution*) of the Constitutional Bishops that wished to retract. Gobet was at their head. He requested several conferences with me, and we had three, which lasted two hours each. Every thing was prepared. Rome had answered with all the tenderness imaginable to Gobet's promises. His retraction was comprised in six letters, which were already written and directed to the Pope, the King, the Archbishops, the Clergy, the Department, and the Municipality of Paris.

But the unfortunate man wished first to quit France, to be out of the reach of the Jacobins. The report of his departure was whispered about, he was frightened, he remained, and Robespierre ordered him to be guillotined on the 9th of April 1794.
17. This is another example of the fatal consequences of binding oneself by oaths of the tendency of which we are ignorant. It may also serve to explain the question before noticed in page 284 [p. 308, Ed.], as being put at the initiation of the Fellow-craft to the degree of Master: *Brother, are you disposed to execute all the orders of the Grand Master, though you were to receive contrary orders from a King, an Emperor, or any other Sovereign whatever?*—The danger of such oaths will receive a still stronger demonstration in the Third Part of this Work, when we come to treat of the dark and iniquitous Cabals and menacing Conspiracies of the *Illuminees*.   T.
18. I was in possession of another memorial which I am sorry to say has been mislaid. It was the account of a gentleman, who, having refused to continue the correspondence with the Masonic Central Committee, was punished for it by him to whom he delivered it over. At the first dawn of the Revolution he was thrown into prison as an Aristocrate. Orders were sent for his delivery. The master, now become a Municipal Officer, changed the order for that of letting him walk upon a very high terrace. At the same time orders were given to the sentry to throw him off it, and these latter orders were executed. He did not die however of the fall, and I believe he is at present living in Spain.
19. Uber die Alten und Newen Mysterien bey Frederich Maurer, 1782.
20. History of the Conspiracy of the Duke of Orleans.

END OF THE SECOND PART

MEMOIRS,

Illustrating the

HISTORY of JACOBINISM,

Written in FRENCH by

THE ABBÉ BARRUEL,

And translated into ENGLISH by

THE HON. ROBERT CLIFFORD, F.R S. & A.S.

Princes and Nations shall disappear from the face of the Earth... and this REVOLUTION shall be the WORK OF SECRET SOCIETIES.
Weishaupt's Discourse for the Mysteries.

PART III.

THE ANTISOCIAL CONSPIRACY.

Second Edition, revised and corrected.

LONDON:
Printed for the TRANSLATOR,
By T. BURTON, No. 11, Gate-street, Lincoln's-Inn Fields.
Sold by E. BOOKER, No. 56, New Bond-street.

1798.

THE
ANTISOCIAL CONSPIRACY

PRELIMINARY OBSERVATIONS

On the Illuminees[1] and on the different Works whereon these MEMOIRS *are grounded.*

THE third conspiracy, which I am now about to investigate, is that of the *Atheistical Illuminees*, which at my outset[2] I denominated *the conspiracy of the Sophisters of Impiety and Anarchy against every religion natural or revealed; not only against kings, but against every government, against all civil society, even against all property whatsoever.*

The name of Illuminee which this Sect (the most disastrous in its principles, the most extensive in its views, the most atrociously cunning in its means) has chosen, is of ancient standing in the annals of disorganizing Sophistry. It was the name which Manes and his disciples first affected, *gloriantur Manichæi se de cælo illuminatos.*[3] The first Rosicrucians also, who appeared in Germany, called themselves Illuminees. And later, in our time, the *Martinists* (with many other sects) have pretended to Illuminism. As an outline for history I distinguish them by their plots and tenets, and will reduce them into two classes, the *Atheistical* and the *Theosophical* Illuminees. These latter more particularly comprehend the *Martinists,* whom I have already mentioned in my second volume, and the *Swedenbourgians,* whom I shall mention in thier proper place, where also I shall give what information I have been able to collect relating to them. The *Atheistical* Illuminees are the objects of the present volume, and it is their conspiracy that I mean to disclose.

The very numerous letters, books, and manuscripts, which I have received since the publication of my proposals, has rendered it impossible for me to comprise the proposed investigation in one volume. The baleful projects of the Sect and the laws for their execution are so strangely combined, that I thought it necessary to begin by making my reader perfectly acquainted with its code; that is to say, with the regular progression of its degrees, mysteries, and government.

This alone requiring an entire volume, I am reduced to the necessity of giving a *fourth,* in which I shall develope the history of Illuminism, and make an application of the triple conspiracy to the French Revolution. I have more particularly applied myself to the investigation of the legislative part of this conspiring Sect, as no work has yet been published in which the whole of their code is to be found. Detached parts only were to be met with scattered throughout the papers which had been seized by the public authority. These I have collected and digested; thus enabling the reader more easily to judge what has been and what must have been the result of such laws. In such an undertaking, I feel myself bound to lay before the public an account of the documents on which I ground my proofs. The following then is a list of the principal works, with a few observations on each, that the reader may form his own judgment as to their authenticity.

I. The first is a collection entitled "Some of the Original Writings of the Sect of Illuminees, which were discovered on the 11th and 12th of October, 1786, at Landshut, on a search made in the House of the Sieur Zwack, heretofore Counsellor of the Regency; and printed by Order of His Highness the Elector.—Munich, by Ant. Franz, Printer to the Court."[4]

II. The second is a supplement to the *Original Writings*, chiefly containing those which were found on a search made at the castle of Sandersdorf, *a famous haunt of the Illuminees*, by order of His Highness the Elector. Munich, 1787.[5]

These two volues contain irrefragable proofs of the most detestable conspiracy. They disclose the principles, the object, and the means of the Sect; the essential parts of their code, the diligent correspondence of the adepts, particularly that of their chief, and a statement of their progress and future hopes. The editors indeed have carried their attention so far, as to mention by whose hand the principal documents or letters were written. At the beginning of the first volume, and on the frontispiece of the second, is seen the following *remarkable advertisement* by order of the Elector:—"Those who may harbour any doubt as to the authenticity of this collection, have only to apply to the office where the secret archives are kept at Munich, and where orders are left to show the originals."[6]

I entreat that my readers will recollect this advertisement whenever they shall see the *Original Writings* cited.

III. "The *True Illuminee*, or the real and perfect *Ritual of the Illuminee*; of the Illuminee; comprehending the *Preparation*, the *Noviciate*, the *Minerval Degree*, that of the *Minor* and *Major Illuminee*, all without addition or omission."—With respect to the authenticity of this work, we need only quote the testimony of the Baron Knigge, surnamed *Philo*, the most famous of the Illuminees after the Founder of the Sect; and who was actually the chief compiler of its Code, as he tells us himself: "All these degrees (says he), such as I composed them, have been printed this year at *Edesse* (Frankfort on the Mein) under the title of the *True Illuminee*. I am ignorant of the author; but *they appear exactly as they flowed from my pen*; that is to say, as I compiled them."[7] This certainly is an authenticated document *on the Sect*, and recognized by the compiler himself.

IV. I now proceed to a work which was published by this same Philo,—under the title of "*Last Observations, or Last Words of Philo,* and Answers to divers Questions on my connections with the Illuminees." In this work *Philo-Knigge* gives us an account of himself and of his Illuminism, of his agreements with the chiefs of the Sect, and of his labours for it. His vanity, however, makes this narrative fulsome. The reader will observe in his writings one of those pretended Philosophers who treat all religious objects with that contempt which they themselves deserve. This is of no consequence; he attempts to justify his own conduct; his avowals may therefore be received in testimony against the Sect.

V. "The last Works of *Spartacus* and *Philo,*" *Die neusten Arbeiten des Spartacus und Philo.* Except the *Original Writings,* this is the most intelligent and important work that has been published on the Illuminees. It contains the two degrees of the greatest consideration both on account of the mysteries revealed in them by the Sect, and of the laws laid down for the adepts.—Not a shadow of doubt can be maintained as to the authenticity of this work. These degrees and laws are published with a certificate of *Philo* attesting their conformity with the original, and under the seal of the Order. This certificate was scarcely necessary. *Whoever can read* must easily perceive that these degrees and these laws are no other than a compilation, and often (in the most essential parts) but a copy of the discourses, precepts, and principles, contained in the *Original Writings.* The publisher is a man who has passed through all the degrees of Illuminism. More dexterous than *Philo,* he makes himself master of his secret, and of that of the whole Sect. The better to unmask Illuminism, he becomes an Illuminee; and he has so well succeeded, that no member of the Order was better acquainted with it than himself.

VI. The same writer has published *A Critical History of the Degrees of Illuminism,* a valuable work, in which every thing is proved from the very letters of the grand adepts.

VII. The *Directing Illuminee,* or the *Scotch Knight.* This may be said to be the counterpart of the *Last Works of Philo and Spartacus.* It is a description of the most important intermediary degree of Illuminism. The Editor does not indeed publish it under the signet of the Order; but when the reader has compared it with the *Original Writings,* and even with the criticism on it by the chief, who was not much pleased with the compiler, he will soon decide that the grand seal of the Order is not necessary to authenticate it.

VIII. *Remarkable Depositions respecting the Illuminees.* These are three juridical depositions on oath, and signed 1st by Mr. *Cosandy,* Canon and Professor at Munich; 2dly by Mr. *Renner,* Priest and Professor of the same Academy; 3dly by Mr. *Utzschneider,* Counsellor of the Electoral Chamber; 4thly by Mr. *George Grümberg,* a member of the Academy of Sciences, and Professor of Mathematics. As every thing is juridical in these depositions, it would be useless for me to insist on the weight they must carry with them. These were four pupils, who did not wait to be initiated in the grand mysteries of the Sect to form their judgement on, and to quit the Sect. They were cited at a tribunal to declare all they knew, and they answered with moderation and truth. Their depositions will find a place in the historical part of this work.

IX. The *Apologies* published by some of the leaders of the Sect are also to be classed among the incontrovertible evidence which we have acquired. These gentlemen will not be expected to have aggravated their own wickedness.

X. The list would be endless were I to subjoin all the works that have been written against the Sect. But I must distinguish in this place the works of Mr. *Hoffman*, Professor at the University of Vienna. I am but little acquainted with those of Doctor *Zimmerman*, though I have been informed by letter, that he furnished many valuable articles in a journal published at Vienna, and chiefly directed against the Sect. I often find Mr. *Stark*'s name mentioned as a strenuous opponent of the Sect. I have seen no publication with his name to it, except an Apology in Answer to the Calumnies of the Sect, which it continues to repeat, notwithstanding the victorious manner in which he has answered them.

Among the anonymous writings I find an excellent work entitled the *Ultimate fate of the Free-masons (Endliches schicksal des Frey-maurer Ordens).* It is a discourse pronounced at the breaking-up of a Freemason's Lodge. The writer of this discourse gives an excellent statement of the reasons why the Lodges should suspend their labours since Illuminism had intruded itself into Masonry.—I believe he would have pronounced this discourse much sooner, had he known that all Lodges were not so pure as his own.

I have also perused the *Biographical Fragments* of the Sieur *Bode*, a famous Illuminee; these will be very useful in our Historical Volume. As to numberless other works which I have read on the same subject, it will suffice to give the titles of them when quoted. I have said more than enough to show that I am not in the dark with respect to the subject on which I am writing.

I could wish to express my gratitude to those virtuous men who, by their correspondence, and the memorials which they have sent me, have greatly advanced my undertaking. But open expressions of such a gratitude would prove fatal to them. To have contributed to the public utility is a sufficient reward for their virtue; and if my work is not so perfect as it ought to be, it arises not from any want of energy in their endeavours.

I find myself much against my will obliged to answer certain objections which my Translator has made, and which will, doubtless, be repeated by many other readers, grounded on the work of Mr. *Robison*, entitled *Proof of a Conspiracy against all the Religions and Governments of Europe, &c. &c.* That work was published just as this Third Volume was going to the press. Its author had not then met with my two first Volumes; but in a second Edition he is pleased to mention them in his Appendix. I am much flattered by his approbation, heartily congratulate him on the zeal he has himself shown in combating the public enemy, and am happy to see that he has wrought on the best materials. Without knowing it, we have fought for the same cause with the same arms, and pursued the same course; but the public are on the eve of seeing our respective quotations, and will observe a remarkable difference between them. I fear lest we should be put in competition with each other, and the cause of truth suffer in the conflict. I entreat the reader to observe, that these differences arise from the different methods followed by him and myself. Mr. Robison has adopted the easiest, though the most hazardous method. He combines together in one paragraph what his memory may have compiled from many, and sometimes makes use of the expressions of the German author when he thinks it necessary. Beside, he has seen much, and read much, and relates it all together in the paragraphs marked by *inverted Commas*. The warning he has given in his preface will not suffice to remove the objections of some readers. In some passages he has even adopted as truth certain assertions which the correspondence of the Illuminees evidently demonstrate to have been invented by them against their adversaries, and which in my Historical Volume I shall be obliged to treat in an opposite sense. Nor will I pretend to say, that Illuminism drew its origin from Masonry; for it is a fact demonstrated beyond all doubt, that the founder of Illuminism only became a Mason in 1777, and that two years later than that he was wholly unacquainted with the mysteries of Masonry.[8]

I know perfectly well, that this will not make Illuminism less disastrous; nevertheless I am obliged to differ from Mr. Robison when treating on that subject, as well as on some other articles.—So much for objections; here is my reply.

In the first place Mr. Robison and I always agree as to the essential facts and the Conspiracy of the Illuminized Lodges; we also agree on their maxims and degrees; and this must be sufficient to convince the reader.

In the next place, in his general view of the Sect he has observed its detestable and most dangerous principles. Like a traveller he has seen the

Monstrum horrendum, informe, ingens . . .

But he has not described its forms, its manners, and its habits. Nor would it be very prudent to reject his narrative because some few circumstances are not perfectly authenticated, or because here and there some want of order may be observable.

In short, if we except one or two letters, which may be said to be translations, all the other quotations (though in the form of letters) cannot be called so, for they are not to be found in the letters of the Illuminees. They are Extracts from different parts, all brought together under one head; Mr. Robison has given them to the public in his own stile, and sometimes makes the Illuminees speak in clearer terms than is done in the Originals. His addition in the Translation of the famous letter from Spartacus to Marius, page 165-6,[9] has given rise to numberless questions, how the—*even d*— was expressed in the German text. A parenthesis follows (*can this mean death?*). I was obliged to answer that the *even d*—, as well as the parenthesis, were additions; but at the same time that they were not additions contrary to the sense of the letter. I could willingly have attributed these deviations to a difference in the editions of the Original Writings; but a new work must be supposed, as well as new letters, to justify the quotations, and all Germany must have noticed such changes. In the first place, the Court of Bavaria would have protested against such a supposition; as the Original Writings could not have coincided with an edition so dissimilar; next, the Illuminees who have not spoken in such clear language, though clear enough in their letters; in fine, the authors who have combated Illuminism, and whose quotations all exactly agree with the Edition of Munich. The Pages may change in different Editions; but whole Letters and Discourses cannot, especially when the public may, as we have seen above, have access to the Originals.

As for myself, whose name cannot be expected to have such authority as Mr. Robison's, I have taken all the precautions of which I felt myself to stand in need.[10] I never make a quotation but with the Original before me; and when I translate any passage which may stagger the reader, I subjoin the original, that each may explain and verify the text. I follow the same line of conduct when I compare the different testimonies. I never mention a single law in the code without having the original before me, or the practice of it to vouch for my assertion. Hence it will be perceived, that we are not to be put in competition with each other; Mr. Robison taking a general view while I have attempted to descend into particulars: as to the substance we agree. I heartily congratulate him on his zeal in combating the monster; and though we do not agree in certain particularities, we both evince the monstrous nature of the Sect, and the certainty of its horrible Conspiracies.

1. The Translator thinks it proper to inform the Reader, that, considering how much the abuse of terms, such as of *Philosophy, Reason,* &c. &c. has contributed to diffuse the new-fangled doctrines, he has adopted in the present volume (which may be said to be the first methodical work published on the subject of which it treats) the words *Illuminee, Illuminize,* and *Illuminization,* though *Illuminate* and *Illumination* might perhaps be more correct expressions. Every reader will feel, that the illumination of the world, and to illuminate mankind, are objects worthy of the true philosopher. But may the man be ever accurst who shall attempt to *illuminize* his countrymen, or aim at the *illuminization* of the world! T.
2. Vol. I. page xxii [p. 6, Ed.].
3. Gaultier, Verbo Manichæi, Sect. 3.
4. Einige original schriften des Illuminaten Ordens, welche bey dem gewesenen regierungsrath Zwack, durch vorgennommene haus visitation zu Landshut den 11 und 12 Octob. 1786, vorgefunden worden. Auf höchsten befehl seiner churfürstlichen Durchleucht zum druck befördert. München. Gedruckt bey Ant Franz churfl: hof-buchdrucker.
5. Nachrichten von weitern Original schriften, &c. &c.
6. Wer an der aechtheit dieser versammlung einen zweifel trägt, mag sich nur bey den hiesigen geheimen archiv melden, allwo man ihm die urschrifften selbst vorzulegen befehligen ist. München 26 März 1787.

7. Philo's Endliche erklärung, &c. Page 96.
8. Original Writings, Vol. I. Let. 6, to Ajax.—Ibid. Let. 36 to M. C. Porcius—and the first Pages of the Critical History of the Degrees.
9. See Page 4 [p. 401, Ed.], of this Volume.
10. I am also afraid that the difference that exists between the degrees of Rosicrucian, of which Mr. Robison is in possession, and those which I have mentioned, may give rise to argument. I answer, 1st. That I am acquainted with three degrees of Rosicrucians, very different in themselves; 2dly. That the Cathechisms, Questions, and Rituals for the same degree greatly differ in different countries: 3dly. That I have followed the works of *Mr. L'Abbe Le Franc*, which Mr. Robison has quoted: 4thly. That Mr. Robison allows the degree of *Knights of the Sun* as described by me to be similar to that which he is in possession of. Since the publication of my Second Volume, I have received an account of the same degree which coincides with what I had said, and this degree is a sufficient ground for all that Mr. Robison or myself have asserted on the attack carried on by Masonry against Religion and Governments.

CHAP. I.

Spartacus-Weishaupt, Founder of the Illuminees.

THERE sometimes appear men formed with such unhappy dispositions, that we are led to consider them in no other view than as emanations from the evil genius, bereft by the avenging God of the power of doing good. Imbecil in the sphere of wisdom, such men are only efficient in the arts of vice and destruction; they are ingenious in those conceptions, skilful in that cunning, and fruitful in those resources which enable them despotically to reign in the schools of falsehood, depravity, and wickedness. In competition with the Sophisters, these men will surpass them in the arts of exhibiting error in false and delusive colours; of disguising the vicious passions under the mask of virtue; and of clothing impiety in the garb of Philosophy. In the den of conspirators they are pre-eminent by the atrocity of their deeds; they excel in the arts of preparing revolutions, and of combining the downfal of the Altar with that of Empires. If their career be ever impeded, it is only when they approach the paths of virtue and of real science. When Heaven in its wrath permits a being of this species to appear on the earth, it has only to put nations within the sphere of his activity, and it will be awfully avenged.

With such qualities, and under such auspices, was born in Bavaria, about the year 1748, ADAM WEISHAUPT, better known in the annals of the sect by the name of SPARTACUS. To the eternal shame of his Serene protector, this impious man, heretofore Professor of Law at the University of Ingolstadt, but now banished from his country as a traitor to his Prince and to the whole universe, peacefully at the court of Ernest Lewis, Duke of Saxe Gotha, enjoys an asylum, receives a pension from the public treasury, and is dignified with the title of Honorary Counsellor to that Prince.

An odious phenomenon in nature, an Atheist void of remorse, a profound hypocrite, destitute of those superior talents which lead to the vindication of truth, he is possessed of all that energy and ardour in vice which generates conspirators for impiety and anarchy. Shunning, like the ill-boding owl, the genial rays of the sun, he wraps around him the mantle of darkness; and history shall record of him, as of the evil spirit, only the black deeds which he planned or executed. Of mean birth, his youth was passed in obscurity, and but a single trait of his private life has pierced the cloud in which he had enveloped himself—but it is one of hateful depravity and of the most consummate villany.—Incestuous Sophister! it was the widow of his brother whom he seduced.—Atrocious father! it was for the murder of his offspring that he solicited poison and the dagger.—Execrable hypocrite! he implored, he conjured both art and friendship to destroy the innocent victim, the child whose birth must betray the morals of his father. The scandal from which he shrinks is not that of his crime; it is (he says and writes it himself) the scandal which, publishing of the depravity of his heart, would deprive him of that authority by which, under the cloak of virtue, he plunged youth into vice and error.—Monstrous Sophister! he accuses the devils of not having skreened him from this scandal by those abominations which called the vengeance of the God of Nature on the son of Judah.—Then, impudently daring, he perjures himself; he calls every thing that is sacred to witness, that neither he nor his friends ever knew of the existence of those poisons or secret means of skreening him from infamy, much less that they had ever proposed, sought, or employed them. He challenges, and at length forces, the magistrates to prove the accusation; they produce the letters of the perjured Sophister, and therein we behold him entreating a first, a second, and even a third confidant, to seek, or cause to be sought, and to communicate to him, these horrid arts. We see him recalling promises of three years standing with respect to these means. He complains of the little success of his attempts, he accuses the agents of timidity or of ignorance; he entreats and conjures them to renew their attempts, telling them, that it was not yet too late, but that expedition was necessary. Who can paint the depravity of this single trait. How monstrous the being who could have combined such depravity! That the God who humiliates the Sophister should have permitted this single trait to have been brought to light, will suffice to show how far wickedness may be carried by the man who, with virtue on his tongue, and under the shade of that sacred name, was forming and fanaticising the blood-thirsty legions of a Robespierre.

After so shocking an accusation the reader will naturally expect us to produce incontrovertible proofs. We will, therefore, first lay before him the letter of *Weishaupt* to his adept *Hertel*; it is the Third Letter in the Second Volume of the *Original Writings* of the *Illuminees* in Bavaria.

"Now," says Weishaupt to this adept, "let me, under the most profound secrecy, lay open the situation of my heart. It destroys my rest, it render me incapable of every thing. I am almost desperate. My honour is in danger, and I am on the eve of losing *that reputation which gave me so great an authority over our people. My sister-in-law is with child.* I have sent her to Athens (Munich) to *Euriphon*, to solicit a marriage licence from Rome. You see how necessary it is that she should succeed, and that without loss of time; every moment is precious. But should she fail, what shall I do?—How shall I restore the honour of a person who is the victim of a crime that is wholly mine? *We have already made several attempts to destroy the child*; she was determined to undergo all; but *Euriphon* is too timid. Yet I scarcely see any other expedient. Could I depend on *Celse's* secrecy (the professor Bader at Munich), he could be of great service to me; *he had promised me his aid three years ago*. Mention it to him if you think proper. See what can be done. I should be sorry that Cato knew any thing of it, lest he should tell all his friends. If you could extricate me from this unfortunate step, you would restore me to life, to honour, to rest, and to authority (that is over his people). If you cannot, I forewarn you of it, I will hazard a desperate blow, for I neither can nor will lose my honour. I know not what devil".... [Here decency obliges us to be silent; but he continues] "As yet nobody knows any thing of it but *Euriphon*; it is not too late to make an attempt, for she is only in her fourth month, and the worst of it is, that it is a criminal case, and that alone makes the greatest efforts and the most extreme (or boldest) resolution necesssary. Be well and live happier than I do, and do think of some means which can extricate me from this affair. I am yours, &c. SPARTACUS."

Notwithstanding his repugnance to let Cato into the secret, Weishaupt is at length obliged to write to him on the subject, and, after repeating that which through decency we have omitted above, this monster of hypocrisy says, "what vexes me the most in all this, is *that my authority over our people will be greatly diminished*—that I have exposed a weak side, of which they will not fail to advantage themselves whenever I may preach morality, and exhort them to virtue and modesty."[1]

Now let us observe the same Weishaupt barefacedly saying in his apology, "I think and declare before God (and I wish this writing to be looked upon as a most solemn declaration), that in all my life I have never heard of those secret means (of abortion) nor of those poisons; that I have never seen nor had knowledge of any occasion when I or my friends could even have thought of advising, administering, or making any use whatever of them. *And this I say in testimony and affirmation of the truth.*"[2] It is thus that by the most abominable hypocrisy he sustains a barefaced and detestable perjury.

So much for the moral virtue of this man; but our chief object is, to consider him in his character of a Conspirator. Let us then descend into that baleful abyss, and observe him in the schools of impiety, rebellion, and anarchy. Here again he appears to have been ignorant of the gradations of crime, of the space that lies between the slightest deviation from rectitude and the most profound wickedness. Here, scarcely have the magistrates cast their eyes upon him when they find him at the head of a conspiracy which, when compared with those of the clubs of Voltaire and D'Alembert, or with the secret committees of D'Orleans, make these latter appear like the faint imitations of puerility, and show the Sophister and the Brigand as mere novices in the arts of revolution. It is not known, and it would be difficult to discover, whether *Weishaupt* ever had a master, or whether he is himself the great original of those monstrous doctrines on which he founded his school. There exists, however, a tradition which on the authority of some of his adepts we shall lay before the reader.

According to this tradition, a Jutland merchant, who had lived some time in Egypt, began in the year 1771 to overrun Europe, pretending to initiate adepts in the antient mysteries of Memphis. But from more exact information I have learned that he stopped for some time at Malta, where the only mysteries which he taught were the disorganizing tenets of the antient Illuminees, of the *adopted slave*; and these he sedulously infused into the minds of the people. These principles began to expand, and the island was already threatened with revolutionary confusion, when the Knights very wisely obliged our modern Illuminee to seek his safety in flight. The famous Count (or rather mountebank) Cagliostro is said to have been a disciple of his, as well as some other adepts famous for their Illuminism in the county of Avignon and at Lyons. In his peregrinations, it is said, he met with Weishaupt, and initiated him in his mysteries. If impiety and secrecy could entitle a person to such an initiation, never had any man better claims than Weishaupt. More artful and wicked than Cagliostro, he knew how to direct them among his disciples to very different ends.

Whatever may have been the fact with respect to this first master, it is very certain that Weishaupt needed none. In an age when every kind of error had taken root, he did what is naturally to be expected from men who, guided by their unhappy bias, both in religious and political opinions, always select the most abominable. He must have had some notion of the ancient Illuminées, for he adopted their name, and the disorganizing principles of their horrid system. These notions were then strenghtened, without doubt, by his favorite application to the disorganizing mysteries of *Manichæism*, since we may observe him recommending the study of them to his disciples as a preparatory step for, and as having a close connection with, those for which he was preparing them.[3] But perfect Atheist as he was, and scorning every idea of a God, he soon despised the twofold God of Antient Illuminism, and adopted the doctrines of Manes only in as much as they threatened every government, and led to universal anarchy. He was acquainted with the systems of the modern Sophisters; but, notwithstanding all their democracy, he did not think they had given sufficient latitude to their systems of Liberty and Equality. He only adopted their hatred for God, or pure Atheism. One class led to the destruction of all civil and political laws, the other to the overthrow of all religion; he combined them both, and formed a monstrous digest, whose object was the most absolute, the most ardent, the most frantic vow to overthrow, without exception, every religion, every government, and *all property whatsoever*. He pleased himself with the idea of a distant possibility that he might infuse the same wish throughout the world; he even assured himself of success.

With the talents of a vulgar Sophister such a hope would have been the summit of folly; but with a genius like that of Weishaupt, formed for great crimes, it was the confidence of unlimited wickedness. The Bavarian Sophister knew his powers; he believed no crime impossible; he only sought to combine them all to reduce his systems to practice. The mediocrity of his fortune had obliged him to consecrate the latter years of his education to the study of the laws. Whether by dissimulation he concealed the plans fostered in his breast, or whether he had not as yet digested them all, he however found means of getting himself named to the chair of Laws in the University of Ingolstadt, before he had attained his twenty-eighth year. On the 10th of March, 1778, he writes to *Zwack* that he was not yet thirty years of age; and in the same letter he informs him, under secrecy, of his future projects on Illuminism, which he had founded two years before.

He must have known himself possessed of profound dissimulation; he must have been master of strange resources, to ground his plans for the subversion of all laws throughout all empires, on the very function of public interpreter of the law. It was nevertheless at the college of Ingolstadt that Weishaupt, affecting the greatest zeal for his duty, conceived himself to be admirably situated for forming and conducting by invisible means the great revolution which he had planned. He justly estimated the influence which his office of teacher gave him over his scholars, and he had the courage to supply in private the *deficiency* of those lessons which he was obliged to give to them in public.

But it would have been too poor a conquest for Anarchy or Impiety to have gained only those who were under the eye of the founder. Weishaupt beheld mankind subject to religious and political laws from pole to pole, and his jealous zeal weighed the means which the saints had employed to extend the faith of Christ. There still existed the scattered remnants of an Order which the imprudent policy of Kings had obliged the Sovereign Pontiff to sacrifice to the machinations of a Philosophism, the professed enemy of both Kings and Pontiffs. Weishaupt knew how to appreciate the support which the laws had acquired from men who were heretofore spread throughout all Catholic countries, and who, in the towns and villages, publicly taught youth, thundered from the pulpit against vice, directed Christians toward the path of virtue, and went to preach the faith of Christ to idolatrous and barbarous nations. He well knew how much empires were indebted to religious Orders, that in preaching the duty which each man owed to his God, strengthened the ties that bound him to his neighbour and to his Prince. Though he in his heart detested the children of Benedict, Francis, or Ignatius, he admired the institutions of these holy founders, and was particularly charmed with those of Ignatius, whose laws directed so many zealous men dispersed throughout the world toward the same object and under one head: he conceived that the same forms might be adopted, *though to operate in a sense diametrically opposite.*[4] "What these men have done for the Altar and the Throne (said he to himself) why would not I do in opposition to the Altar and the Throne? With legions of adepts subject to my laws, and by the lure of mysteries, why may not I destroy under the cover of darkness, what they edified in broad day? What Christ even did for God and for Cæsar, why shall not I do against God and Cæsar, by means of adepts now become my apostles?"

In attributing such a wicked emulation to Weishaupt, I will not leave the historian to fruitless conjectures. No, these very wishes in plain language are contained in his confidential letters to his disciples; and he even reproaches them with not imitating the submission of the followers of those holy founders.[5] His most celebrated adepts have declared, that they had observed him copying them throughout his code;[6] they must also have remarked, that Weishaupt, in planning his systems according to the forms adopted by those religious founders, had reserved it to himself to add all the artifices which the most infernal policy could suggest. At the actual period when this conspirator formed his plans, he was ignorant of the object of Freemasonry:[7] He only knew that the fraternity held secret meetings: he observed that they were bound by mysterious ties, and recognized each other for brethren by certain signs and words, whatever might be their country or religion. In his mind, therefore, he combined the plan of a society, which was at once to partake as much as convenient of the government of the Jesuits, and of the mysterious silence and secret conduct of Masonry. Its object was, the propagation of the most Antisocial Systems of ancient Illuminism, and of the most Antireligious Systems of modern Philosophism.

Brooding over this disastrous project, Weishaupt cast his eyes on the young pupils whom government had entrusted to his care to form them for magistrates of their country, and defenders of the laws, and he resolved to begin his warfare against both by the perversion of these youths. He beheld in distant succession his first disciples seducing others, those again, subject to his laws, forming further adepts; and thus by degrees he came complacently to view his legions multiplying and spreading from the towns to the country, and resident even in the courts of Princes. He already heard those oaths which, under the secrecy of the Lodges, were to bind the minds and hearts of those new legions who, replete with his disorganizing spirit, were silently to undermine the Altar and the Throne. He calculated the time necesssary, and smiled to think that he would one day have only to give the signal for the general explosion.

Scarcely had this modern Eratostratus attained his eight-and-twentieth year, ere he had laid the foundations of those laws which he meant to give to his disorganizing Sect. Though he had not actually written his code, he had arranged it in his mind, and he made his first essay on two of his pupils, one named *Massenhausen* (whom he surnamed *Ajax*), about twenty years of age, and afterwards a Counsellor at Burkhausen; the other called *Merz* (whom he surnamed *Tiberius*)[8] nearly of the same age, but whose morals and character proved so abominable, that they made even his vile seducer blush. These two disciples soon vying with their master in impiety, he judged them worthy of being admitted to his mysteries, and conferred on them the highest degree that he had as yet invented. He called them *Areopagites*, installed himself their chief, and called this monstrous association THE ORDER OF ILLUMINEES.[9]

It was on the first of May, 1776, that the inauguration was celebrated. Let the reader well observe this epoch. It indicates a feeble beginning; it preceded the French Revolution but by a few years; that however was the time when that abominable Sect first started into existence, which was to combine all the errors, all the conspiracies, and all the crimes of the adepts of Impiety,

Rebellion, or Anarchy, and which, under the name of Jacobin, was to consummate the dreadful Revolution. Such was the origin of that Sect which I had in view when I proclaimed to all nations, and unfortunately with too much truth, "That whatever their government or religion might be, to whatever rank they might belong in civil society, if Jacobinism triumphed all would be overthrown; that should the plans and wishes of the Jacobins be accomplished, their religion with its Pontiffs, their government with its laws, their magistrates *and their property*, all would be swept away in the common mass of ruin! Their riches and their fields, their houses and their cottages, their very wives and children would be torn from them. You have looked upon Jacobinical faction as exhausting itself in France, when it was only making a sportive essay of its strength."[10]

According to the wishes and intentions of this terrible and formidable Sect, nations, astonished, have yet only seen the first part of the plans formed for that general Revolution which is to beat down every Throne—overturn every Altar—*destroy all property*—blot out every law—and conclude by the total dissolution of all society!

The omen is fatal;—but (more fatal still!) I have numberless proofs to demonstrate the truth of this assertion. With respect to the Conspiracies of Illuminism, I shall draw my proofs from their own code and their archives. I will begin with their code; it will lay open the object, the extent, the manner, the means and inconceivable depth of the Conspiracies of the Sect. This First Part will comprehend the plan of their conspiracies, the extract and analysis of the code of laws which they had constructed for attaining their ends. The Second Part will show their progress and their successes from their first origin, till that period when, powerful in Revolutionary Legions, without leaving their secret dens, they unite and confound themselves with the Jacobins, and in unison with them prosecute that war of desolation which menaces with total ruin the Altar of every God—the Throne of every Monarch—The Law of every Society—and the Property of every Citizen. O! that I could in delineating what the Sect has done, what it is doing, and what it still meditates to do—that I could but teach nations and the chiefs of nations what they themselves ought to do, to avert the impending danger; those, I say, who have mistaken these disasters for a sudden explosion, while they are in fact but an essay of the strength of the Sect, and the commencement of their general plan.

1. Original Writings, Vol. I. Let. 61, to Cato.
2. Introduction to his Apology, p. 6.
3. See the degree of *Directing Illuminee*, oder Scottischer Ritter (Scotch Knight) page 72.
4. Mirabeau de la Monarchie Prussienne, vol. V. P. 97.
5. Vid. Original Writings, Vol. I. let 27, to Cato.
6. See the Original Writings, Vol. I *Instructio pro recipientibus*, art. B—Let. 2, to Ajax.—Divers letters to Cato.—Last Observation of Philo.
7. See hereafter the chapter on *Masonry illuminized*, Vol. IV.

8. Weishaupt, in a letter to Zwack, says, "My three first colleagues were *Ajax, you, and Merz.*" (*Let.* 15, Feb. 1778). This clearly states, that *Merz* was the *Tiberius* who was illuminated with *Ajax*; for it is clear that *Zwack* was only initiated ten months after the two adepts *Ajax* and *Tiberius*. *(See Orig. Writ. Vol. I. Sect. IV.)*
9. Orig. Writ. Vol. I. Sect. IV.—Let. 2, to Philip Strozzi.
10. Vol. I, page 23.

CHAP. II.

Code of the Illuminees.—General System, and division of the Code.

BY the code of the sect of Illuminees I mean the principles and systems which it had formed to itself on Religion and Civil Society, or rather against all Religion and Civil Society whatever; I mean the government and the laws which it has adopted to realize its plans, and to guide the adepts in bringing the whole universe into its systems. This was not so much a code springing from an ardent mind, and an enthusiastic zeal for a great revolution, as the offspring of reflection on the means of rendering it infallible; for no sooner had Weishaupt conceived a plan, than he foresaw the obstacles which might thwart its success. Though he decorated the first pupils whom he had seduced with the title of his profound adepts, yet he did not dare unfold to them the vast extent of his plans. Pleased with having laid the foundation, he did not hurry the elevation of that edifice, which might have been exposed to fall for want of the proper precautions; no, he wished it to be as durable as time itself. For five whole years he meditated; and he foresaw that he should still have to pause for many a tedious day on the means of securing the success of his plans. His plodding head silently ruminated and slowly combined that code of laws or rather of cunning, of artifice, of snares and ambushees by which he was to regulate the preparation of candidates, the duties of the initiated, the functions, the rights, the conduct of the chiefs, and even his own. He watched every means of seduction, weighed and compared those means, tried them one after the other; and when he had adopted any of them would still reserve the power of changing them, in case he should happen to fall upon any that would be more disastrous.

Meanwhile his first disciples, now his apostles, gained him many partizans; he seduced many himself, and directed their conduct by letter. His advice was adapted to circumstances, and, artfully husbanding his promises, he kept the minds of his disciples perpetually in suspense as to the last mysteries. To his trusty adepts he promises *systems of morality, of education, and of polity, all entirely new*; and they might easily surmise that this future code would be no other than that of a morality without restraint, of a religion without a God, and of a polity without laws or any dependence whatsoever;[1] though he did not dare entirely to throw away the mask. But his laws appeared imperfect, his snares were not sufficiently concealed; and he was convinced that time and experience alone could perfect the work on which he had so long meditated. Such are the colours, at least, in which we see him representing himself when his adepts, impatient to be initiated in the last mysteries, reproach him with the slowness of the proceedings: "It is from time and experience," says he, "that we are to learn. I daily put to the test what I made last year, and I find that my performances of this year are far superior. Give me then time to reflect on what may forward and on what may delay the execution of our plans; to weigh what may be expected of our people left to themselves or led and conducted by us.—Remember that what is done in haste, speedily falls to ruin. Leave me then to myself, let me act alone; and believe me, *time and I are worth any other two*."[2]

Let not the reader imagine that these meditations of Weishaupt alluded to the objecct of his views; that never varied; the destruction of Religion, the destruction of Society and the civil Laws, the destruction of property,—that was the point at which he always aimed; and this impious man too well knew his crime, not to be alarmed; we see him writing to his confident, "You know the situation in which I stand. I must direct the whole by means of five or six persons. It is absolutely necessary that I should during my life remain unknown to the greater part of the adepts themselves.—I am often overwhelmed with the idea that all my meditations, all my services and toils are perhaps only twisting a rope or planting a gallows for myself; that the indiscretion or imprudence of a single individual may overturn the most beautiful edifice that ever was reared."[3]

At other times wishing to appear above such fears, but still reproaching the adepts with want of caution, he says, "If our affairs already go on so ill, the whole will soon be undone: the fault will be thrown upon me, and, as author of every thing, I shall be the first sacrificed. Yet that is not what frightens me; I know how to take every thing on my own score; but if the imprudence of the Brethren is to cost me my life, let me at least not have to blush before men of reflection, nor to reproach myself with an inconsiderate and rash conduct."[4] Thus does every motive stimulate this famous Conspirator to transfuse into his code every precaution that could at the same time skreen him from condign punishment, and secure the success of his plots. At length, after five years meditation on his side, and numerous consultations with his trusty adepts, particularly with *Philo*, or the Baron *Knigge*, who acts a very exalted part in *Illuminism*, Weishaupt had regulated the mode of his mysteries, and had digested the code of his Sect, that is to say, the principles, the laws, and government adopted by the Illuminees to accomplish the grand object of their Conspiracy. Before we lead our readers through the immense labyrinth of this code, let us give a general idea of the system which stimulated its author to the formation of those laws.

The more we meditate on that part of the code which we shall lay before our readers when we come to treat of the mysteries of Illuminism, the more clearly we observe Weishaupt adopting the principles of *Equality* and of *Liberty*, (propagated by modern Philosophism) in order to present them in a new light, and to lead his disciples to the ultimate consequences of the most absolute Impiety and Anarchy.

The modern Sophisters, some following Voltaire, others Rousseau, had begun by saying, that all men were equal and free; and they had concluded *with respect to Religion*, that nobody, though speaking in the name of a God who reveals himself, had the right of prescribing rules to their faith. The authority of revelation being cast aside, they left no other basis for Religion to rest upon, than the Sophistry of a reason the perpetual prey of our passions. They had annihilated Christianity in the minds of their adepts. *With respect to Governments* they had also asserted, that all men were equal and free, and they had concluded that every citizen had an equal right to form the laws, or to the title of Sovereign; this consequence abandoning all authority to the capricious fluctuations of the multitude, no government could be legitimate but that founded on Chaos, or the volcanic explosions of the democratic and sovereign populace.

Weishaupt, reasoning on the same principles, believed both the Sophisters and the Democratic Populace to be too timid in drawing their inferences, and the following may be said to be the essence of all his mysteries.

"Liberty and Equality are the essential rights that man in his original and primitive perfection received from nature. *Property* struck the first blow at *Equality*; political Society, or Governments, were the first oppressors of *Liberty*; *the supporters of Governments and property are the religious and civil laws*; therefore, to reinstate man in his primitive rights of Equality and Liberty, we must begin by destroying all Religion, all civil society, and finish by the destruction of all property."

Had true Philosophy but gained admittance to these lodges of Illuminism, how clearly would she have demonstrated the absurdity of each and all of these principles, and the extravagance and wickedness of such consequences, both to the master and his adepts! She would have shewn, that the rights and laws of primitive man alone upon earth, or parent of a scanty generation, neither were nor ought to be the rights and laws of man living on an inhabited globe. She would have proved, that Nature, when she ordained that man should increase and multiply on this earth, and that he should cultivate it, clearly announced that his posterity were hereafter to live under the empire of social laws. She would have observed, that without property this earth would have remained uncultivated and uninhabited; that without religious and civil laws the same earth would have only nurtured straggling hordes of vagabonds and savages. Then would our Bavarian Illuminee have concluded, that his Equality and Liberty, far from being the essential rights of man in the state of perfection, would only be the instruments of his degradation, and assimilate him to the beasts of the earth, if they were to be incompatible with Property, Religion, and Society. But true Philosophy was an alien to his school; and Weishaupt, with his detestable genius formed for error, applauds the sophism, makes it the basis of his system, and the ultimate secret of his mysteries.

I am not simply to prove that such is the grand object of the Conspiracy, and of the ultimate revolution which he is preparing with all his adepts. Were that my only task, I should cite the blessings which the hierophant of Illuminism pours out on those hordes that roam without laws or society, and the curses which he vents against those men who, fixing their abodes, name chiefs and constituted states. The very menaces of the teacher unfold the whole of the Conspiracy. *"Yes, princes and nations shall disappear from off the face of the earth; yes, a time shall come when man shall acknowledge no other law but the great book of nature: This revolution shall be the work of the* SECRET SOCIETIES, *and that is one of our grand mysteries.*[5] This single passage of the code is sufficient to demonstrate both the object of the Conspiracy and the extent of the projects of the sect; but though the Conspiracy should be clearly proved, still that would be doing little for the public good. Instead of a terrible and formidable Sect, nations and chiefs of nations might mistake the Illuminees for a band of senseless madmen, plodding without means a chimerical Revolution; therefore little to be feared, and too despicable to deserve notice. Thus would wickedness find a cloak in its excesses; the Sect would prosecute its hellish plots more actively, more confidently, and more successfully, merely because their object was supposed impossible. Society would be dissolved; our laws, our religion, and our property, would be wrested from us, because we believed them proof against any attempt. Nations would tranquilly slumber on the brink of the precipice, and be plunged into destruction while they considered the fatal cause as the delusion of delirium, and smiled on the plots of Illuminism. And its founder foresaw this: for he says to his adepts, *"Let the laughers laugh, let the scoffers scoff; he that compares the past with the present, will see that nature continues its course without the possibility of diverting it. Its progress is imperceptible to the man who is not formed to observe it; but it does not escape the attention of the Philosopher.*[6]

Society then calls upon me to develop more than the existence, or even the extent of the plots of the Sect—I say, it calls on me loudly to proclaim the dangers which threaten us; yes, the evils which threaten all society must be clearly shown. A manner of proceeding and an artful cunning big with crime, which will speedily plunge nations into those disasters which they may believe chimerical, is to be clearly ascertained. I have to unfold the whole of a system, an entire code, in which each institute, each maxim, each regulation, is a new step towards a universal revolution which shall strike society a mortal blow. I am not then about to inform each citizen that his religion, his country, *his property*, that every society, people, or nation, are menaced; unfortunately that would be a task too easily performed. But I am bound to say, "In this horrible plot, such are the dangers which threaten your country, and such the perils that hang over your persons." I must show extensive resources combined with consummate villainy, where *you* imagined that nothing existed but the delirium of modern Philosophism, destitute of means.

Weishaupt, like yourselves, had foreseen numerous obstacles to his conspiracy; and it appears that he had even exaggerated them. That for which his most famous adepts seem to despise their countrymen, should be mentioned here as redounding to their honour. Weishaupt, surrounded by the faithful Bavarians, faithful to their God and to their country (rather speculating on the human heart from his books, than closely observing men in the common intercourse of life), was not aware of how very much Philosophism had forwarded his systems.[7] The generation which had attained the age of manhood appeared too much infected with the antiquated ideas on religion and government. But, unfortunately, facts soon undeceived him; and this error only served, by deferring his hopes, to turn his mind to farther precautions and meditations, which sooner or later were to render his success infallible. He would say to himself, he would say to his trusty brethren, *"According to my views, I cannot employ men as they are; I must form them*; each class of my Order must be a preparatory school for the next; and all this must necessarily be the work of time."[8] But to accelerate the time he cast his eyes on that class of young men, which, just entering the world, easily fall a prey to error, because at that age they are under the influence of their passions. I shall hereafter show what it was that both shortened the time, and abridged their education, in presenting him with whole legions of adepts ready formed to his mysteries. It is first necessary, however, that the reader should be acquainted with the profundity of his system; because, had the French Revolution not taken place, that system would alone have sufficed to render it certain and infallible; for, could the French Revolution be done away at the present moment, and the ancient regimen be restored, this code would furnish Illuminism with all the means of effectuating one that should be still more disastrous. Let us then study it, let us dissipate the cloud in which it is enveloped. Reader, your own interest requires that you should follow our steps; and observe all the snares that have been laid for you; see with what art its disciples are beguiled, with what precaution it chooses, calls, and disposes its adepts. Its proceedings appear indeed to be slow, but they are nevertheless sure. It seems to exhaust all its art to acquire a single proselyte, but the same allurements attract whole legions. Its springs are secret, but the reader must know their power and with what constancy they move toward and direct the common ruin. He has seen the people agitated, animated, and even misled to ferocity; but he must also be informed how those adepts were created who fanaticised the people and rendered them ferocious.

Weishaupt lays down as an invariable and infallible principle, that "the grand art of rendering any revolution whatsoever certain—is to enlighten the people;—and to enlighten them is, insensibly to turn the public opinion to the adoption of those changes which are the given object of the intended revolution.

"When that object cannot be promulged without exposing him that has conceived it to public vengeance, he must know how to propagate his opinion IN SECRET SOCIETIES.

"When the object is an universal Revolution, all the members of these societies, aiming at the same point, and aiding each other, must find means *of governing invisibly, and without any appearance of violent measures, not only the higher and more distinguished class of any particular state, but men of all stations, of all nations, and of every religion*—Insinuate the same spirit every where—*In silence, but with the greatest activity possible, direct the scattered inhabitants of the earth toward the same point.*" This is what he calls the grand problem on the polity of states, on which he grounds *the force of secret societies*, and on which the empire of his Illuminism was to rest.[9]

"This empire once established by means of the union and multitude of the adepts, let force succeed to the invisible power. *Tie the hands of those who resist; subdue and stifle wickedness in the germ;*" that is to say, crush those whom you have not been able to convince.[10] He that teaches such doctrines is not to be looked on as a weak enemy. When Weishaupt reserved them for his mysteries, as well as the revelation of his ultimate object, he knew too well that they were only fitted for men who had long been trained to view them as the lessons of nature and of Philosophy, and should he meet with any who had anticipated them, it would only abridge their novitiate. But he needed nothing less than a whole generation. It was therefore to multiply the number of adepts, to dispose them by insensible degrees to receive his doctrines; by an invisible hand to direct their ideas, their wishes, their actions, and their combined efforts, that the code of laws which he framed for Illuminism constantly tended.

According to these laws, the sect is divided into two grand classes, and each of these again subdivided into lesser degrees proportionate to the progress of the adepts.

The *first class* is that of PREPARATION. It contains *four* degrees, those of *Novice*, of *Minerval*, of *Minor Illuminee* or *Illuminatus Minor*, and of *Major Illuminee* or *Illuminatus Major*.

Some intermediary degrees belong to the *class of* PREPARATION, which may be called of *Intrusion*; such are those which the sect have borrowed from *Freemasonry* as a means of *propagation*. Of these masonic degrees the *code of Illuminees admit the three first without any alteration:* it adapts more particularly to the views of the sect the degree of *Scotch Knight* as an ultimate preparation for its mysteries, and it is stiled the degree of *Directing Illuminee* or *Illuminatus Dirigens*.

The *second class* is that of the MYSTERIES, and this is subdivided into the *lesser* and *greater mysteries*. The *lesser* comprehend the priesthood and administration of the sect, or the degrees of *Priests* and of *Regents* or *Princes*.

In the *greater mysteries* are comprized the two degrees of *Magi* or Philosopher, and of the *Man King*. The *Elect* of the latter compose *the council and the degree of Areopagites*.[11]

In all these classes, and in every degree, there is a part of the utmost consequence, and which is common to all the Brethren. It is that employment known in the code by the appellation of Brother *Insinuator* or *Recruiter*.[12] The whole strength of the Sect depends on this part; it is that which furnishes members to the different degrees; and Weishaupt, well knowing the importance of the task, turned all his genius toward it. Let us therefore begin by directing our attention to the discovery of it.

1. Original Writings, Vol. I. Let. to Marius and Cato.
2. Original Writings, Vol, I. Letters 3, 4, 47, 60 &c to Marius and Cato.
3. Original Writings, Vol. I. Lett. 11 and 25, to Cato.
4. Let. 22, to Cato.
5. See hereafter the Discourse on the Mysteries.
6. See hereafter the Discourse on the Mysteries.
7. See the Last Observations of Philo.
8. Original Writings, Vol. I. Let. to Cato.
9. See the Discourse on the Mysteries.
10. Ibid.
11. See the Original Writings, Chap., II. Part II. page 8. and the last ObservationS of Philo, page 89, &c. &c.
12. This is not a term of my invention; it really is to be found in the code. Insinuator or *Anwerber* (signifying *Recruiter*) are the two words generally made use of to express this character.

CHAP. III.

First Part of the Code of the Illuminees.—Of the Brother Insinuator, or the Recruiter.

By the appellation of *Brother Insinuator*, is to be understood the *Illuminee* whose peculiar office is to make proselytes for the Sect. Some brethren were more particularly instructed for that end; they might, indeed, be called the Apostles or Missionaries of the Order, being those whom the superiors sent to the different towns and provinces, and even into distant countries, to propagate its doctrines and to establish new Lodges. These had received, in addition to the common rules, farther instructions peculiar to the higher degrees. "These (as Weishaupt writes) may sometimes be the most *imbecile*, and at other times the most ingenious of the Brotherhood." From the former he can depend on a blind obedience to the rules he lays down, which are never to be deviated from; and with respect to the latter, provided they be zealous and punctual, should they even transgress any of the laws, it would not be in such a manner as to commit either their own safety or that of the Order; and they would soon make amends for their indiscretion by some new artifice. But, whatever may be the sense of the Illuminee, he is obliged once or twice in his life to act the part of Brother Insinuator, and that with a certain success, by the acquisition of two or three proselytes, under pain of perpetually remaining in the lower degrees. Some Brethren of high rank may have been dispensed from this formality; but as to the generality of them there exists a positive law on that point.[1] To stimulate the zeal of the Brethren, the Insinuator is by the laws of the code established superior over every novice that he has gained to the Order: It is expressed as follows: "Every Illuminee may form to himself a petty empire; *and from his littleness, emerge to greatness and power.*"[2]

Such then is the first duty imposed upon every Illuminee for the propagation of the Sect; and this is the part which first claims our attention, in order that we may be able to form an idea of the immensurable powers of Weishaupt for seduction.

This part may be said to be subdivided into three. The rules laid down are, first, those which are to guide the Brother *Insinuator* in the choice of persons to be admitted or excluded; then follow those which are to teach him how to entice into the order those persons whom he has judged proper for it;

and lastly come those rules and arts by which novices are to be formed, and even involved in Illuminism before they are officially admitted.

In order to judge of the qualifications of the persons whom he may enlist, every Illuminee is to begin by procuring tablets, which he is to keep in the form of a Journal; and this is *his Diary*. Assiduously prying into every thing that surrounds him, he must vigilantly observe all persons with whom he becomes acquainted, or whom he meets in company, without exception of relations, friends, enemies, or entire strangers; he must endeavour to discover their strong and their weak side; their passions and prejudices; their intimacies, and above all, their actions, interests, and fortune; in a word, every thing relating to them: and the remarks of every day he must enter in his Diary.

A twofold advantage is to be reaped from these particulars of information; first, by the Order in general and its superiors; secondly, by the adept himself. Twice every month he will make a general statement of his observations, and he will transmit it to his superiors. By these means the Order will be informed what men, in every town or village, are friendly or inimical to it. The means of gaining over the one or destroying the other will naturally occur. With respect to the *Insinuator*, he will learn how to judge of those who are proper persons to be received or rejected, and he will carefully insert his reasons for the admission or rejection of those persons in his monthly statements.[3]

The Recruiting Brother will carefully guard against giving the most distant hint that he is an Illuminee. This law is peremptory for the Brethren, but more particularly for all the *Insinuators*, whose success may often essentially depend on it. It is to them that the legislator so strongly recommends all that exterior of virtue and of perfection, that care of shunning all public scandals which might deprive them of their ascendancy over the minds of those whom they seek to entice into the Order.[4] The law expressly says, "*Apply yourselves to the acquiring of interior and exterior perfection;*" but lest they should conceive that this perfection even hinted at the mastering of their passions, and at renouncing the pleasures of the world, he adds, "Attend particularly to the art of dissembling and of disguising your actions, the better to observe those of others, and to penetrate into their inmost thoughts. *"Die kunst zu erlernen sich zu verstellen, andere zu beobachten, und aus zu forschen."* It is for that reason that these three great precepts are to be found in the summary of the Code: HOLD THY TONGUE—BE PERFECT—DISGUISE THYSELF—almost following each other in the same page, and serving as an explanation of each other.[5]

Having made himself perfect master of these precepts, and particularly of the last, the *Insinuator* is next to turn his attention to those persons whom he may admit or ought to reject. He is not to admit into the Order either Pagans or Jews; but he is equally to reject *all religious*; and above all to *shun the Ex-Jesuits as he would the plague. Ordens geistliche dürfen nie aufgenommen werden, und die Ex-Jesuiten soll man wie die pest fliehen.*[6]

The cause of such exclusions is obvious. To speak of religion, and admit, without any precaution, Jews, Turks, and Pagans, would be too open a manifestation of what their religion was; and not to reject religious, would be exposing themselves to be betrayed by their own adepts.

Unless they gave evident signs of a sincere amendment, all indiscreet talkers were to be rejected; and also those men whose pride, or headstrong, interested, and inconstant minds denoted that it would be impossible to infuse into them that zeal so necessary for the order; all those again, whose drunken excesses might injure that reputation of virtue which the Order was to acquire; all those, in short, whose meanness and grossness of manners would render them too untractable to give hope for their ever becoming pliant and useful.[7]

"*Leave those brutes, those clownish and thickheaded fellows!*" he exclaims in his Chapter on Exclusions; but, though he excluded these thickheaded fellows, Weishaupt was aware that there existed a good sort of being which some might call stupid, but who are not to be told so, as advantage may be taken of their stupidity. Such were, for example, a Baron *D'Ert*, and many others, who holding a certain rank in the world, though destitute of common sense, have at least their riches to recommend them. "*These are a good sort of beings,*" says our illuminizing legislator; "they are necessary beings. They augment our number and fill our coffers, *augent numerum et ærarium*. Courage then! and make these gentry swallow the bait; but beware of comunicating to them our secrets; *For this species of adept must always be persuaded that the degree they are in is the highest.*[8]

Indeed, there is a sort of half exclusion for princes. The Code ordains that they shall seldom be admitted, and even when they are, shall scarcely ever rise beyond the degree of *Scotch Knight*; or, in other words, they are never to pass the threshold of the mysteries. Hereafter we shall see the Legislator finding an expedient for introducing them beyond that degree, but still without giving them any further insight into the mysteries;[9] and being particularly careful to hide from them certain laws of the Order.[10]

I cannot take upon myself to say, whether a similar expedient had been found as an exception to the general rule which excluded women; but it is certain, that this law was, during a long time at least, only provisional; and many of the brethren sought to revoke it. Freemasonry had its female adepts, and the Illuminees wished to have theirs. The plan is written in *Zwack*'s own hand-writing, and he was the most intimate friend and confidant of Weishaupt, in short, his *incomparable* man. It is couched in the following terms:

"*Plan for an Order of Women.*—This Order shall be subdivided into two classes, each forming a separate society, and having a different secret. The first shall be composed of virtuous women; the second, of the wild, the giddy, and the voluptuous, *auschveifenden*.

"Both classes are to be ignorant that they are under the direction of men. The two superiors are to be persuaded that they are under a mother Lodge of the same sex, which transmits its orders; though in reality these orders are to be transmitted by men.

"The Brethren who are intrusted with this superintendance shall forward their instructions without making themselves known. They shall conduct the first, by promoting the reading of good books, but shall form the latter to the arts of *secretly gratifying their passions, durch begnügung ihrer leidenschaften im verborgenen.*"

A preliminary discourse prefixed to this plan points out the object and future services of these illuminized sisters. "The advantages which the real Order would reap from this female Order would be, first, the money which the sisterhood would pay at their initiation; and, secondly, a heavy tax upon their curiosity, under the supposition of secrets that are to be learned. *And this association might moreover serve to gratify those brethren who had a turn for sensual pleasure.*"[11]

A list and description of eighty-five young ladies of Manheim accompanied this project of Zwack, very properly surnamed the *Cato* of Illuminism; from among whom, in all probability, the founders of these two classes were to be chosen. Circumstances not having favoured our modern Cato's views, we observe several other adepts proposing similar plans. An assessor of the Imperial Chamber at Wetzlaar of the name of *Dittfurt*, known among the Illuminees by that of *Minos*, and who rose to the degree of *Regent*, and to the dignity of Provincial, seemed to dispute the honor of this invention, both with Brother *Hercules* and even with *Cato* himself: We must allow, at least, that nobody was more anxious for the execution of the project than he was. He had already submitted his ideas to the Baron Knigge, and he applies anew to Weishaupt. He even despairs of ever bringing men to the grand object of the order without the support of the female adepts. Indeed, so ardent is his zeal, that he makes an offer of his own wife and his four daughters-in-law to be the first adepts. The eldest was exactly the person for the philosophized sisterhood; she was four-and-twenty years of age, *and with respect to religion her ideas were far above those of her sex;* they were modelled on her father's. He had attained to the degrees of *Regent* and *Prince* of the Illuminees, and she would have been *Regent* and *Princess*. In the higher mysteries, together with Ptolemy's wife, we should have seen the one corresponding with her father, the other with her husband. These illuminized Princesses would be the only two persons of the order who should know that they were all under the direction of men. They would preside over the trials and receptions of *Minervals*, and would initiate those whom they judged worthy into the grand projects of the sisterhood for the reform of governments and the happiness of mankind.[12]

But, notwithstanding all the plans and zeal of the Brethren, it does not appear that the legislator ever consented to the establishment of the Sisterhood. Yet he supplied the want of such an institution by secret instructions which he gave the *Regents* on the means of making the influence of women over men subservient to the order, without initiating them in any of the secrets. He says, that the fair sex having the greatest part of the world at their disposition, "*no study was more worthy of the adept* than the art of flattery in order to gain them; that they were all more or less led by vanity, curiosity, the pleasures or the love of novelty; that it was on that side they were to be attacked, and by that they were to be rendered serviceable to the order."[13] He nevertheless continued to exclude great talkers and women from all the degrees, nor was the sixth article of his instructions for the *Insinuator* rescinded.

Notwithstanding all these exclusions, the legislator leaves a sufficient scope wherein the Insinuator may exercise his zeal. He recommends generally young men of all stations from eighteen to thirty; but more particularly those whose educations were not completed, either because he thought they would more easily imbibe his principles, or would be more grateful and more zealous for doctrines for which they were indebted solely to him.[14]

But this preference is not an exclusion for men of a certan age, provided they are not past service, and are already imbued with the principles of Illuminism.[15] This, however, chiefly regards those persons whose rank in life can give *consequence* and afford *protection* to the order. The Recruiters are particularly instructed to insinuate themselves into the good opinion of such persons, and if possible to entice them into the Order.

There is yet another species of men, who have speech as it were at command; such are attornies, counsellors, and even physicians. "Those are worth having," says Weishaupt; "but *they are sometimes real devils, so difficult are they to be led; they however are worth having when they can be gained over.*"[16]

The *Insinuator* is also to admit artists, mechanics of all professions, painters, engravers, white-smiths and black-smiths; but above all booksellers, those who keep post-horses, and school-masters. Hereafter the reader will see the use for which these men were intended.[17]

To yet another class of men our legislator often calls the attention of the *Insinuator:* "*Seek me out, for example,*" says Weishaupt, "*the dexterous and dashing youths. We must have adepts who are insinuating, intriguing, full of resource, bold and enterprising; they must also be flexible and tractable, obedient, docile, and sociable.* Seek out also those who are distinguished by their *power, nobility, riches, or learning,* nobiles, potentes, divites, doctos, quærite—Spare no pains, spare nothing in the acquisition of such adepts. If heaven refuse its aidance, conjure hell.

"*Flectere si nequeas superos, Acheronta moveto.*"[18]

With respect to religions, he prefers the disciples of Luther and Calvin to the Roman Catholics, and greatly prefers the former to the latter. This distinction should alone suffice to open the eyes of many who wish to persuade themselves that the whole of the revolutionary fury is aimed at the Roman Catholic religion. This motley crew certainly did the Catholics the honour of directing their shafts more pointedly at them, as strenuous opponents of their impiety and of their religious and civil anarchy; but was it to preserve the Protestant religion that Weishaupt gives them such a preference, in hopes of making them subservient to his plots? That he did give such a preference cannot be doubted, when we see him expressly writing to an adept whom he had commissioned to look out for a person proper to be received into the higher mysteries and to found a new colony of Illuminees —*were this man a Protestant I should like him much better.*—*Wäre es ein Protestant, so wäre es mir um so lieber.*[19] Weishaupt's most famous adept constantly manifests the same predilection; he even wishes to retrench certain parts of the mysteries that he may not alarm the Catholics, and seems always to hint at Frederic the IId's saying, *We Protestants go on brisker.*[20] Most certainly this proves beyond a possibility of doubt, that the destruction of all Protestant laws, whether civil or religious, had place in their plans. Nor were the Protestants of Germany the dupes of such a policy, as many of the most determined antagonists of Illuminism were of that religion.

Further, he wishes to entice men into his order who have fixed residences in towns, such as *merchants* and *canons*, who might assiduously propagate his doctrines, and establish them in their neighbourhoods.[21]

The Recruiter must use every art (for an obvious reason) to engage *schoolmasters*, and to insinuate his doctrines into, and gain adepts in the *military academies*, and other places of education; he is even to attempt the seduction of the *superiors of ecclesiastical seminaries.*[22]

"He will spare no trouble to gain the Prince's officers, whether presiding over provinces, or attending him in his councils. He that has succeeded in this has done *more*," says the code, "than if *he had engaged the Prince himself.*[23] In fine, the Provincial, or the chief Insinuator, is *to recruit* every thing that can be tainted with Illuminism, or can be serviceable to its cause."[24]

The following extraordinary instructions are also given by Weishaupt respecting the choice of adepts: "Above all things (he says to his Insinuators) pay attention to the figure, and select the well-made men and handsome young fellows. They are generally of engaging manners and nice feelings. When properly formed, they are the best adapted for negotiations; for first appearances prepossess in their favour. It is true, they have not the depth that men of more gloomy countenances often have. They are *not the persons to be entrusted with a revolt, or the care of stirring up the people*; but it is for that very reason that we must know how to chuse our agents. I am particularly fond of those men whose very soul is painted in their eyes, whose foreheads are high, and whose countenances are open. Above all, examine well the eyes, for they are the very mirrors of the heart and soul. Observe the look, the gait, the voice. Every external appearance leads us to distinguish those who are fit for our school."[25]

"Select *those in particular who have met with misfortunes, not from accidents*, but by some act of injustice; that is to say, in other words, the DISCONTENTED; *for such are the men to be called into the bosom of Illuminism, as into their proper asylum."*[26]

Let not the reader already exclaim, How deep are the views of this illuminizing Sophister? How has he foreseen every point! With what discernment does he lay his snares to entrap those who are to be the future agents of his plots! The reader has as yet seen merely a schedule of those persons who may be admitted or rejected; but that does not sufficiently secure the order with respect to the elections which the Insinuator may have made. Before he undertakes the initiation of any person whom he may have thought proper, he is to make a statement from his diary of every thing that he may have observed with respect to his morals, opinions, conduct, and even of his connections in life. He is to submit this statement to his superiors, who will compare it with the notes they are already in possession of, or may acquire from other adepts, respecting the candidate, or even with a new statement, in case they judge the last to be insufficient. Even when the choice made by the Insinuator is approved of, all is not settled; the superiors have to determine which of the Insinuators is to be entrusted with the care of enticing the approved person into the Order: for all this is foreseen in the code. It is not allowed to all the brethren to exercise promiscuously so important a trust among the prophane, though they may have pointed out the person proper for reception. The young adept is not to measure his strength with the man who has the advantage over him in years and experience, nor is the tradesman to undertake the magistrate. The superior is to name the most proper Insinuator, judging from the circumstances, age, merits, dignities, or talents of the future candidate.[27] At length, when the mission is given, the Insinuator begins to lay his snares.—Such is the second part of this extraordinary functionary, and all his subsequent steps are regulated by the code.

Candidate, in the ordinary acceptation of the word, means a person who has shown a desire or taken some steps into some order, or to acquire some dignity. In Illuminism it means the person on whom the Order has fixed its attention. It often happens, that the candidate is ignorant of the very existence of the sect. It is the Insinuator's business to inspire him with the wish of entering it. To accomplish this grand object, two different methods are inculcated. The first is for the Insinuator who has some candidate in view remarkable for his science or of a certain age. The second, for him who is entrusted with young men from eighteen to thirty, and who are susceptible of a second education. A third method was proposed for workmen, and those clownish fellows whose education had been but little attended to. We may observe Weishaupt consulting with his confidant Zwack on this part of the code; but whether it was never digested, or that he saw the Insinuators could easily supply the defect, no further mention is made of the third method. Let us then examine the essence of the first two.

To exemplify the first method, let us suppose one of those men who have gone through a complete course of modern Philosophism, who, should they not scoff at Christianity, would at least hesitate at every thing which is called religion; for the code forewarns the Insinuator, that his efforts would be vain should he attempt to seduce Philosphers of another stamp, men of sound judgment, and who would never be partizans of doctrines which could not endure the light of broad day. But when he shall have discovered one of the former who has already pretty well imbibed the principles of the sect, he will assume the character of a Philosopher well versed in the mysteries of antiquity. He will have little difficulty in acting such a part, as he will find ample instructions in the code. To follow those instructions faithfully, he must begin "by descanting on the supreme felicity of being versed in sciences which few can approach, of walking in the paths of light while the vulgar are groping in darkness. He must remark, that there exist doctrines solely transmitted by secret traditions, because they are above the comprehension of common minds. In proof of his assertions he will cite the Gymnosophists in the Indies, the Priests of Isis in Egypt, and those of Eleusis and the Pythagorean school in Greece."

He will select certain sentences from Cicero, Seneca, Aristides, and Isocrates; and, lest he should ever be taken unawares, he will learn those by heart which the legislator has carefully inserted in the code. Though it would be very easy to demonstrate from those very authors, that the ancient mysteries laid down no fixed principles on the important points of the *Providence of God*, and of the *origin and order of the universe*, the Insinuator is nevertheless to quote those texts to prove that there exists a secret doctrine on these objects, and above all a doctrine calculated *to render life more agreeable, and pain more supportable; and to enlarge our ideas on the majesty of God*. "Let him add, that all the sages of antiquity were acquainted with these doctrines; let him insist on the uncertainty that man is in with respect *to the nature of the soul, its immortality*, and *its future destiny*. He will then sound his candidate, to know whether he would not rejoice at having some satisfactory answers on objects of such great importance. At the same time he will hint that he has had the happiness of being initiated into these doctrines, and that, should the candidate wish it, he would do his best to procure him the same felicity; but that it was a science gradually imparted, and that certain men possessed the talent of guiding him from a distance, of leading him to the discovery of this new world, and that without being ever in his presence."[28]

When the Insinuator has by such language succeeded in exciting the curiosity of his candidate, he must then ascertain his opinions on some particular articles. He will propose the discussion of certain questions in writing, and of certain principles, as the groundwork on which they are in future to proceed. The code does not determine what these questions are to be, because they vary according to the political and religious dispositions which the Insinuator may have observed in the candidate. Should these dissertations noway agree with the principles of the sect, the Insinuator will abandon his prey. Should the sophisticated candidate, or the man of importance, be found properly disposed, he will be admitted to the very threshold of the mysteries. The Insinuator will simply explain the inferior degrees to him, and mention the divers trials which the order has dispensed with in consideration of his merit.[29]

Notwithstanding the artifice observable in this method, it is still reserved for those who need only to be acquainted with Illuminism to adopt its tenets. But should the Insinuator be entrusted with a young candidate, or with one whose principles noway coincide with those of the sect, and who is yet to be formed; it is then that Weishaupt develops that immense theory of art and cunning by which he is insensibly to ensnare his victims. "Let your first care," he says to the Insinuators, "be to gain the affection, the confidence, and the esteem of those persons whom you are to entice into the Order—let your whole conduct be such, that they shall surmise something more in you than you wish to show—hint that you belong to some secret and powerful society—excite little by little, and not at once, a wish in your candidate to belong to a similar society—Certain arguments and certain books which the Insinuator must have, will greatly contribute to raise such a wish; such are, for example, those which treat of the union and strength of associations." The Legislator then carefully adds a list of those books, and the Order charges itself with the care of furnishing a certain number of them to the adepts. The works of *Meiners*, and particularly of *Bassadows*, are frequently recommended by Weishaupt, as the best fitted to inspire their readers with the love and principles of secret societies. But nothing can equal the art with which he himself has drawn up the reasons, by the help of which the Insinuator is to persuade his young candidate of the pretended necessity for these mysterious associations.

"One represents, for example," says the code, "a child in the cradle; one speaks of its cries, its tears, its weakness—One remarks how this child, abandoned to itself, is entirely helpless; but that by the help of others it acquires strength—One shows how the greatness of Princes is derived from the union of their subjects—One exalts the advantages of the state of society over the state of nature—Then one touches on the art of knowing and directing mankind—How easily, you will say, could one man of parts lead hundreds, even thousands, if he but knew his own advantages. This is evidently proved by the organization of armies, and the amazing power which princes derive from the union of their subjects."

After having descanted on the advantages of society in general, touch upon *the defects of civil society, and say how little relief is to be obtained even from one's best friends,—and how very necessary it would be to support each other in these days. Add, that men would triumph even over heaven were they but united—That it is their disunion which subjects them to the yoke.*—This is to be explained by the fable of the wolf and the two dogs, the latter of whom could only be vanquished by the former after he had parted them; and by many other examples of the same kind which the Insinuator will collect.[30]

As a proof of what great and important things secret societies can effectuate, he will adduce the examples of the Freemasons, of the mysterious societies of antiquity, and even of the Jesuits. He will assert, that all the great events of this world are dependent on hidden causes, which these secret societies powerfully influence; *he will awake in the breast of his pupil the desire of secretly reigning, of preparing in his closet a new constitution for the world, and of governing those who think they govern us.*[31]

"When you shall have got thus far," says the code, "begin to show (as it were unguardely) that you are not entirely ignorant of those secrets; throw out some half sentences which may denote it. Should your candidate take the hint, press him, and return to the charge, until you see him betray symptoms of a desire instantaneously to unite with such a society.

"The Insinuator, however, who has thus far succeeded in inspiring his pupil with such a wish, has not played off every engine with which the code has furnished him. To sound the very bottom of his mind, he will pretend to consult him as if he had been entrusted with certain secrets, he will make objections on the secrecy of these societies; but should they make too much impression he will resolve them himself. At other times, to stimulate the curiosity of his pupil, he will hold a letter in his hand written in cypher, or he will leave it half open on his table, giving his candidate sufficient time to observe the cypher, and then shut it up with all the air of a man who has important correspondences to keep secret. At other times studying the connections and actions of his pupil, he will tell him of certain circumstances which the young man will think he has learned by means of these secret societies, from whom nothing is hidden, though *they* are concealed from all the rest of the world."[32]

These artifices may be greatly abridged, according as the friendship or communicative disposition of the candidate shall have laid him more open; but on the other hand, should they not suffice, the Insinuator is not on that account to abandon his purpose; let him try to accomplish by others what he has failed in himself.—Let him examine his own conduct, and see if he has not neglected some one or more of the rules prescribed in the code; let him redouble his attention and his complaisance. Should it be necesssary to humble himself in order to command, let not the Insinuator forget the formal precept of his legislator, "Learn also to act the valet in order to become master." *Auch zu weilen den knecht gemacht, um dereinst herr zu werden.*[33]

After such a long series of condescensions and discussions the candidate at length must pronounce. If he submit to all these insinuations, he is admitted among the novices of the order; but should he persist in his refusal, let him learn the fate which awaits him from those who have experienced it. "*Unhappy, supremely wretched is the youth whom the Illuminees have sought in vain to entice into their sect. Should he even escape their snares, do not let him flatter himself with being proof against their hatred; and let him take care. The vengeance of* SECRET SOCIETIES *is not a common vengeance; it is the hidden fire of wrath. It is irreconcilable, and scarcely ever does it cease the pursuit of its victims until it has seen them immolated.*"[34] Such at least is the account which history gives us of those who have been guarded enough to withstand the insinuations of the Sect, and particularly of those who, after having gone the first steps with the Insinuator, have refused to proceed any farther with him.

I could cite divers examples; though I once thought that I had met with one of a quite opposite nature, in the person of *Camille de Jourdan*, the same deputy who was to have been involved in the sentence of transportation against Barthelemy and Pichegru after the revolution of the 4th of September, but who luckly escaped from the grasp of the triumvirate. I hear him speaking in the highest terms of one of these Insinuators, who had for a long time endeavoured to entice him into the order. He was much astonished at hearing me speak of these men as consummate in all the artifices of the most villanous hypocrisy. He maintained that his Illuminee was mild, modest, and moderate; full of respect for the Gospel, in a word, one of the most virtuous men he had ever known. In reply, I enumerated all the proceedings of the Insinuator, and the artifices he had played off before he quitted his prey. To all that Mr. Camille answered, "It is true; such was his behaviour; but it was his zeal for the sect which blinded him, and made him have recourse to such expedients in order to work what he called my conversion; yet, with all that, it was impossible for any body to speak of virtue and religion in so impressive a manner as he did without being at least an honest man."—"Well," said I, "I will venture to assert, that the last attempt of your Insinuator was as follows. He proposed to you to give your thoughts in writing on certain questions; you did so; your opinions proved directly opposite to his; he never saw you after, became your implacable enemy, and has never since ceased calumniating you." "All that again," answered Mr. Camille, "is very true; nor was it his fault that I did not lose both friends and fortune. Before that affair he used to praise me; afterwards, however, he represented me as a most dangerous man. You cannot conceive what lies he invented about me, and I was unfortunate enough to observe that they had made impression."— Is it possible to be believed? Mr. Camille could not yet be persuaded but that his Insinuator was a virtuous man; so profound are the arts of hypocrisy which are to be imbibed from Weishaupt's laws! I was acquainted with two bishops, who had as completely mistaken the characters of their Insinuators as Mr. Camille de Jourdan.

But I will cite the example of Mr. Stark. I never could conceive what this Mr. Stark was whom I saw perpetually abused by the Illuminees. Nicolai and Mirabeau spared no pains to render him odious to the Protestants in Germany; they said he had received the Catholic orders of priesthood privately,[35] though every thing seemed to denote that he was a Protestant. I took some pains to inform myself who this Mr. Stark was, and I found him one of the most learned Protestant ministers in Germany; that his zeal for his religion had acquired him the degree of Doctor, and had preferred him to be Grand Almoner and Counsellor to the Landgrave of Hesse Darmstadt; but that in common with several other learned men, such as Hoffman and Zimmerman, he had had the misfortune of being sought after by the Illuminees; that he would not hearken to them; that the Illuminees had expressed a wish to have an Adept near the person of the prince, and that he had been bold enough to answer his Insinuator, "*If you seek support, I am too little and my prince too great to protect you.*"—And every candidate who will make the same resolute stand against the agents of the order must expect to be repaid with similar calumnies. The law of the order is invariable and precise, particularly with respect to those whose talents may be obnoxious to Illuminism. *They must be gained over, or ruined in the public opinion.* Such is the text, *so soll man den schrift steller zu gewinnen suchen, oder verschreyen.*[36] But it is now time to follow the candidate who has shown himself more docile through the various preparatory degrees.

1. Original Writings. The Statutes reformed, Art. 18.
2. Ibid.
3. Original Writings.—The Statutes reformed, Art. 9, 13, and following.—Instructions for the Insinuators, Sect. XI, No. I.—for the Insinuated Nos. 1, 3, 5, &c.—Let. the 4th to Ajax.
4. See Original Writings, Vol. II. Lett. 1, and 9.
5. Original Writings, Vol. I. p. 40. Nos. 4, 6, and 8.
6. The Last Works of Spartacus and Philo.—Instruction for the Stationary Prefects and Superiors, Page 153, Let. the 2d.—And Original Writings, Instructio pro Recipientibus, Nos. 1, and 5.
7. Instructio pro Recipientibus, page 94, and Weishaupt's Letters, passim.
8. Original Writings. See the first Letters to Ajax and Cato.
9. See Degree of Regent, page 154, Letter N.
10. See Instructions for the Provincial, No. 16.
11. Original Writings, Vol. I. Sect. V.
12. Original Writings, Vol. I. Let. of Minos, p. 169.
13. See the New Works of Spartacus and Philo, and Instructions for the degree of Regent, No. 6.
14. Orig. Writ. Instructiones pro Recipientibus, Page 54, No. 4; and Page 55, No. 18.
15. Ibid. Vol. II. Part the 2d, Section and Degree of Regent.
16. Orig. Writ. Vol. I. Let. to Ajax.
17. See Instructions for the Insinuator, No. 4.—Weishaupt's Letters, passim—and the Degree of Regent.
18. Ibid. Let. 3d to Ajax.
19. Orig. Writ. Vol. I. Let. to Tiberius, P. 223.
20. See Vol. I. page 33 [p. 20, Ed.].
21. Instructions for the Provincial and Orig. Writ. Vol. I. Part II, No. 3, page 26.
22. Ibid. Nos. 11 and 13.
23. Ibid. No. 15.
24. Ibid. No. 18.
25. Let. 11th to Marius and Cato.
26. Instruction for the Local Superiors, Letter H.
27. Instructiones pro Recipientibus. Orig. Writ. Vol. I. Nos. 1 and 7, page 54.
28. Original Writings, Vol. II. Part II. Sect. I.
29. Original Writings, Vol. II. Part II. Sect. I.
30. Extract of the Instructions for the Brethren charged to enroll and receive the candidates —Original Writings, Vol. I. Sec. IX. and XII.—Also in the degree of Illuminatus Major; instructions on the same object, Document A.
31. Original Writings, ibid. No 11 and 12.—Illuminatus Major, Document A, and Letters K, L.
32. Original Writings, ibid. No. 17 to 22.
33. Ibid. Let 3d, to Ajax.
34. Important Advice, &c. by Hoffmann. Preface to Vol. II.
35. Mirabeau Monarchie Prussienne, Vol. V. art. Religion.
36. Instructions for the Regent, No. 15.

CHAP. IV.

Second Part of the Code of the Illuminees—First preparatory Degree, of the Novice and of his Teacher.

IN the early stages of Illuminism the duration of the time of trial for the Novice was three years for those who were not eighteen years of age; two years for those between eighteen and twenty-four; and one year for those who were near thirty.[1] Circumstances have since occasionally caused the time to be abridged; but, whatever may be the dispositions of the Novice, though the time may be dispensed with, he must go through the different trials, or have got the start of them before he is admitted into the other degrees. During the interval he has no other superior but the Insinuator to whom he is indebted for his vocation, and during the whole time of the noviciate, the Insinuator is expressly forbidden to inform his pupil of any other member of the Order. This law was made to skreen the order from the dangers which might result from an indiscretion of the Novice, and to render the Insinuator alone responsible in such cases; for, should the Novice unfortunately be an indiscreet talker, the code expressly says, his imprudence would at most betray only one of the brethren.[2] The first lessons of the Insinuator (in future his teacher) treat entirely on the importance and the inviolability of the secrecy which is to be observed in Illuminism. He will begin by telling his Novice, "Silence *and secresy are the very soul of the Order,* and you will carefully observe this silence as well with those whom you may have only reason to suppose are already initiated, as with those whom you may hereafter know really to belong to the Order. You will remember, that it is a constant principle among us, that *ingenuousness is only a virtue with respect to our superiors, but that distrust and reserve are the fundamental principles.* You will never reveal to any person, at present or hereafter, the slightest circumstance relative to your admission into the order, the degree you have received, nor the time when admitted; in a word, you will never speak of any object relating to the order even before Brethren, without the strongest necessity."[3]

Under the restrictions of this severe law, one Illuminee will often be a stranger to another; and the Novice will see in this no more than a measure of safety for the order, which might be ruined by the least indiscretion.[4]

More certainly to assure himself of the discretion of the Novice, the Insinuator will give him no further insight, nor entrust him with any writing relative to the order, until he has obtained the following declaration: "I, the undersigned, promise upon my honour, and without any reservation, never to reveal either by words, signs, or actions, or in any possible manner, to any person whatever, either relations, allies, or most intimate friends, any thing that shall be entrusted to me by my Introducer relative to my entrance into a *secret society*; and this whether my reception shall take place or not. I subject myself the more willingly to this secresy, as my *Introducer assures me that nothing is ever transacted in this society hurtful to religion, morals, or the state.* With respect to all writings which I may be entrusted with, any letters which I may receive concerning the same object, I engage myself to return them, after having made for my sole use the necessary extracts."[5]

These writings or books relative to the order are only lent to the Novice at first in small numbers, and for a short time; and then he must promise to keep them out of the reach of the prophane; but as he is promoted in rank, he may preserve them for a longer time, and is intrusted with a larger quantity; though not without having informed the Order of the precautions he shall have taken, lest in case of his death any of these writings should fall into prophane hands.[6] He will afterwards learn, that the Brotherhood take many other precautions for secresy, not only respecting the statutes, but even with regard to the very existence of the Order. He will see, for example, in its laws, that should any of the brotherhood fall sick, the other brethren are assiduously to visit him, in the first place *to fortify* him, that is to say, to hinder him from making any declarations at the hour of his death; and secondly, to carry away whatever writings relative to the Order the sick man may have had in his possession, as soon as any symptoms of danger appear.[7]

He will at length learn, that to frustrate all attempts to trace even their very existence, the *Order does not exist every where* UNDER THE SAME NAME, but that they are to assume the name of *some other Order*, perhaps even of a literary society, or meet without any name which can attract the attention of the public.

The first writing delivered to the Novice, to accustom him to profound secrecy, is what may be called the Dictionary of Illuminism. He must begin by learning the language of the Sect, that is to say, the art of communicating with the superiors and other adepts without the possibility of being understood by the prophane. By means of this language, the Illuminees are to be able to correspond with each other, without running the risk of its being discovered of what Brother they speak; from what place, in what language, at what period, and to whom, or by whom the letter is written.

To avoid the discovery of persons, the Novice will learn, that no Brother bears the same name in the Order which he does in the world; indeed, had he been initiated in the higher degrees of Masonry, he would have seen the same precaution taken, where the Rosicrucians receive what they call *their Characteristic* or their adoptive name. The Novice will receive the characteristic immediately on his admission, and it will in some measure imply the parts which he is in future to act in the general conspiracy. It will be his task hereafter to study and write the history of his new patron he will by this method recognize in the qualities and actions of his hero the particular services which the order will expect from him.[8] This name will be chosen as conformably as possible to the dispositions observed in him. Has he shown any propensity to repeat the impieties of Philosophism against the Gospel, he will be classed with the Celsi and Porphirii, or with the Tindals and Shaftsburys; should his turn be toward the hatred of Kings, or should his talents be judged useful for the polity of the Order, then his characteristic will be of the Brutus, Cato, or Machiavel tribe. He will not be told what he is to do to deserve his name, but they will contrive that it shall occur to him. Neither will he be told why Weishaupt assumed the name of Spartacus (a name so famous in Rome because he waged the war of the slaves against their masters); but should he ever be admitted to the higher mysteries, he will easily recognize the reason.[9]

The place from whence they write, as well as the persons of whom or to whom they write, is in like manner to be kept secret; a new Geography is therefore taught the Novice. He will thence learn, that *Bavaria*, the country of their founder, is denominated *Achaia; Swabia, Pannonia; Franconia, Austria, and Tyrol* are denoted by *Illyria, Egypt, and Peloponnesus; Munich* is called *Athens; Bamberg, Antioch; Inspruck, Samos; Vienna* in Austria, *Rome; Wurtzburg, Carthage; Frankfort on the Mein* becomes *Thebes;* and *Heidelberg, Utica.* Ingolstadt, the natal soil of the Order, was not sufficiently denoted by *Ephesus;* this privileged town was to be decorated with a more mysterious name, and the profound adepts bestowed on it that of *Eleusis.*

Should the Novice ever be sent on a mission out of his own country, or to distant shores, he will then receive further instructions in the Geography of the Sect.[10]

He must also learn how to date his letters, and be conversant with the Illuminized Hegira or Calendar; for all letters which he will receive in future will be dated according to the Persian era, caled *Jezdegert* and beginning A.D. 630. The year begins with the Illuminees on the first of *Pharavardin*, which answer to the 21st of March. Their first month has no less than forty-one days; the following months, instead of being called May, June, July, August, September, and October, are *Adarpahascht, Chardad, Thirmeh, Merdedmeh, Shaharimeh, Meharmeh:* November and December are *Abenmeh, Adameh*: January and February, *Dimeh,* and *Benmeh:* The month of March only has twenty days, and is called *Asphandar.*[11]

The Novice must next learn how to decypher the letters he may receive; in order to which, he must make himself master of that cypher, which is to serve him until initiated into the higher degrees, when he will be entrusted with the hieroglyphics of the Order.[12]

He will also remember, that he is never to write the name of his Order; so venerable a word cannot be exposed to prophane eyes, and a circle ⊙ with a point in the middle of it will supply this sacred word, and a long square or parallelogram ⊐ will denote the word Lodge.

After these preliminary studies, the young brother receives a part of the code, under the title of *Statutes of the Illuminees*. But these first statutes are nothing more than a snare, and the young Novice, with pleasure no doubt, sees them begin with the following words:

"For the tranquillity and security of all the Brethren, whether Novices or active Members of the Society, and to prevent all ill-grounded suspicions, or disagreeable doubts, the venerable Order declares, that it absolutely has *in view no project, enterprize, or undertaking hurtful to the state, to religion, or to good morals; and that it favours nothing of that nature in any of its members.* Its designs, all its toils, solely tend to inspire men with a zeal for the perfection of their moral characters, to impregnate them with humane and sociable sentiments, to counteract the plans of the wicked, to succour oppressed and suffering virtue, to favour the advancement of men of merit, and to render those sciences universal which are as yet hidden from the generality of men. Such is not the *coloured* pretext, but the real object of the order."[13]

Even should the Novice not have entirely laid aside all suspicions respecting the intentions of the Order, still so positive a declaration he must think would guarantee him as to all obligations which might be imposed upon him. His grand aim is to be, to *form his heart* in such a maner as to gain not only the affection of his friends but even of his enemies. He is positively ordered to endeavour *with all his might to acquire both interior and exterior perfection.* It is true, he is soon after as positively ordered *to study the arts of dissimulation and disguise*; but then the Brother Insinuator is at his elbow to explain to him how that art coincides with true perfection, and thus suppress any suspicions which might arise from a comparison of these two injunctions. Beside, the Novice has many other duties to fulfil, which will deprive him of opportunity for such reflections.

He is next told, that the Brethren must have but one mind, one will, and similar sentiments; that, to effectuate this, the Order has made choice of certain works, to which he must apply with the greatest attention. Should the Novice be one of those men whom an attachment to the Gospel rendered more circumspect as to the snares laid for his belief, the very choice of the books would suffice to show him, that the first object of the Insinuator was to persuade him, that it is not even necessary to be a Christian to acquire the perfection enjoined by the statutes. The *Morality* he is taught is that of *Epictetus, Seneca, Antoninus*, and *Plutarch*, all foreign to Christianity. He will also receive the works of modern Sophisters, such as *Wieland, Meiners*, and *Bassadows*, who by no means make perfection to consist in Christianity. Under the soothing and mellifluous language of a moderate and specious Philosophy, he will be led to lubricity and impiety, traced by the sophisticated pen of Helvetius in his celebrated work *De L'Esprit*.[14] But the Insinuator must previously have sufficiently studied the dispositions of his pupil to know whether such propositions would any longer startle him. Beside, nothing is better calculated to dissipate all such fears, than the constant application that is required to those books which are put into the hands of the Novice, added to the care taken to deprive him of all such as might inspire him with contrary ideas. The Teacher is carefully to attend to all the rules laid down in the code on this subject, and to see that his Novices fulfil the intentions of the Order in this respect. He is frequently to converse with them; he is to mark out their occupations for them; he is even to make them unexpected visits to surprize them, and thus to see in what manner they apply to the code and other writings with which the Order has entrusted them. He is to require an account of what they have read, and extracts from the different works; he will assist them by his explanations; in short, nothing is to be neglected which can secure their progress in the spirit and morals of the Order.[15]

An object of far greater importance next attracts the attention of the Novice; it is that which the code calls *the greatest of all;* it is, *the knowledge of men.* The teacher will represent this to his pupil *as the most interesting of all sciences.*[16] To make himself master of this science, the Novice receives the model of a journal in the form of tablets, and his teacher shows him how they are to be used. Provided with this journal, he is to make his observations on every body he finds himself in company with; he is to trace their characters, and account to himself every thing he has seen or heard. Lest his memory should fail him, he must always be provided with a loose paper or small tablets, on which he may at all hours note his observations, which he is afterwards carefully to digest in his journal. To be certain of the Novice's attention to this point, the Brother Teacher will examine his tablets and his journal from time to time. To render him more expert in the art of drawing the characters of the living, he will exercise the Novices on ancient authors, and on the heroes of antiquity. No study or custom is so frequently recommended as this in all the code of Illuminism. It is to be the grand study of the Novice, and the prime occupation of every degree.[17]

It is by his assiduity in this great art that the Novice will learn how to distinguish those whom he may hereafter judge proper to be admitted into or rejected from the Order; and it is with that view that the Preceptor perpetually presses him *to propose those whom he may think fit for the Order.*[18] By this means a double object is attained; first, the propagation of the Order; and, secondly, a knowledge of its friends or enemies; the dangers it may be threatened with; and the means to be adopted, or the persons to be gained or courted, to avert the impending storm; in fine, of extending its conquests. Whether the Illuminee be a Novice, or in any other degree, he is bound by the laws of the Order to make his report in the prescribed forms at least once a month.[19]

While the Novice is perpetually making researches of this nature, he is not aware that he is as carefully watched by his Insinuator, who on his side notes and writes down every thing that he observes either as to the failings or the progress, the strong or weak side of his pupil, and these he as regularly transmits to the superiors.[20]

The pupil little suspects that the grand object of his Insinutor is *to bind him* in such a maner to Illuminism, *even long before he is acquainted with its secrets,* that it shall be impossible for him to break those bonds which fear and terror shall have imposed upon him, should he ever wish to shrink from the horrid plots and systems which he might thereafter discover.

This profound policy of binding the Novices to Illuminism consists, first, in giving them a magnificent idea of the grandeur of the projects of the Sect, and, secondly, in a vow *of blind obedience* to the superiors in every thing which they judge conducive to the ends of the Order, which vow the Insinuator is to find means of extorting from his pupil.

It is here particularly that Weishaupt appears to wish to assimilate the government of his Sect to that of the religious orders, and especially to that of the Jesuits, by a total sacrifice of their own will and judgment, which he exacts of the adepts; and to the exercising of the Novices in this point, he expressly adverts in his instructions to the Insinuators.[21] But this is precisely the place to remark on the amazing difference between the illuminized and the religious obedience. Of that immense number of religious who follow the institutes of St. Basil, St. Benedict, St. Dominic, or St. Francis, there is not one who is not thoroughly convinced that there exists a voice far more imperious than that of his superior, the voice of his conscience, of the Gospel, and of his God. There is not one of them who, should his superior command any thing contrary to the duties of a Christian, or of an honest man, would not immediately see that such a command was a release from his vow of obedience. This is frequently repeated and clearly expressed in all religious institutes, and no where more explicitly or positively than in those of the Jesuits. They are ordered to obey their superior, but in cases only where such obedience is not sinful, *ubi non cerneretur peccatum.*[22] It is only in cases where such obedience can have no sinful tendency whatever, *ubi definiri non possit aliquod peccati genus intercedere.*[23] And, as if this were not sufficiently expressed, we hear their founder, at the very time when he recommends obedience to his religious, expressly saying, *but remember that your vow is binding only when the commands of man are not contrary to those of God, ubi Deo contraria non præcipit homo.*[24] All those person therefore who, like Mirabeau, surmised certain coincidences, or as he calls them *points of contact*, between the religious institutes and the code of the Illuminees, should have begun by observing, that religious obedience is in its very essence an obligation of doing all the good which may be prescribed without the least taint of harm. It was easy for them on the contrary to demonstrate, that the obedience sought for by Weishaupt's code was a dispositon to obey every order received from the superior in spite of conscience, and unheedful of the most iniquitous guilt, provided it tended to the good of the Order. "Our society (for such are the expressions of the code) exacts from its members the sacrifice of their liberty, not only with respect to all things, *but absolutely with respect to* EVERY MEANS *of attaining its end.* Yet the presumption on the goodness of the *means prescribed is always in favour of the orders given by the superiors.* They are clearer-sighted on this object; they are better acquainted with it; and it is on this very account that they are nominated superiors—It is their business to lead you through the labyrinth of errors and darkness; and in such a case obedience is not only a duty, but an object for grateful acknowledgment."[25]

Such is the obedience of the Illuminees; nor is there a single exception to be found in all their code. We shall see the Novice, before he terminates his trials, obliged to explain himself explicitly with respect to orders which he may receive from his superiors, and which he may think contrary to his conscience. In the first place his teacher is to intangle him, and make himself perfectly master of his most secret thoughts. Under the pretence of knowing himself better, while studying the art of knowing others, the Novice is to draw a faithful picture of himself, to unfold his interests and connections, as well as those of his family.

Here again the Insinuator furnishes him with the tablets in the requisite form, that he may give this new proof of confidence to the Order; but this will neither be the last nor the most important one for which he will be called upon.

On these tablets, the Novice is to write down his name, age, functions, country, and abode; the species of study in which he occupies himself, *the books of which his library is composed*, and the secret writings of which he may be in possession; his revenue, his friends, his enemies, and the reason of his enmities; in fine, his acquaintances and his protectors.

To this table he is to subjoin a second, explaining the same objects with respect to his father, his mother, and all their other children. He is to be very explicit with respect *to the education they received, to their passions and prejudices, to their strong and weak sides*.

We will exemplify this second table by an extract from the Original Writings, by which the reader will perceive that parents are not very much favoured—"The Novice, Francis Antony St. . . . . aged 22, represents his father as *violent, and of soldierlike manners*; his mother as *a little avaricious*; the weak side of both to be flattery and interest; both living after the old fashion, and with an antiquated frankness; in their devotion, headstrong, arrogant; with difficulty abandoning an ill-conceived project, and still more unforgiving to their enemies; that they nevertheless were little hated, because little feared; and hardly in the way of doing any body any harm."

While the Novice is thus occupied in revealing all his secrets, and those of his family, the Insinuator on his side is drawing up a new statement of every thing he has been able to discover during the whole time of his pupil's trial, either with respect to him or to his relations.

On comparing the two statements, should the superior approve of the admission of the Novice to the last proofs, he is then to answer the grand questions. It is by these questions that the Novice is to judge of the extent of the sacrifice he is about to make, and of the awful subjection of his whole will, conscience, and person, to Illuminism, if he wishes to gain admittance.

The Questions are twenty-four in number, and couched in the following terms:

I. Are you still desirous of being received into the Order of the Illuminees?

II. Have you seriously reflected on the importance of the step you take, *in binding yourself by engagements that are unknown to you?*

III. What hopes do you entertain, or, by what reasons are you induced to enter among us?

IV. Would you still persevere in that wish, though you should find that we had no other object or advantage whatever in view but the perfection of mankind?

V. What would be your conduct should the Order be of new invention?

VI. *Should you ever discover in the Order any thing wicked, or unjust to be done, what part would you take;* Wenn unanstandige, ungerechte sachen vorkamen, wie er sich verhalten wurde?

VII. *Can you and will you look upon the welfare of the Order as your own?*

VIII. We cannot conceal from you, that Members, entering into our Order without any other motive than to acquire power, greatness, and consideration, are not those whom we prefer. In many cases one must know how to lose in order to gain. Are you aware of all this?

IX. Can you love all the Members of the Order, even such of your enemies as may be members of it?

X. Should it so happen that you should be obliged to do good to your enemies who are of the Order, to recommend them, for example, or extol them; would you be disposed to do so?

XI. *Do you, moreover, grant the* POWER OF LIFE AND DEATH *to our Order or Society?* On what grounds would you refuse, or recognize in it such a right; Ob er dieser geselschaft, oder order auch das JUS VITÆ ET NECIS, aus was grnden, oder nich zugestehe?

XII. *Are you disposed on all occasions to give the preference to men of our Order, over all other men?*

XIII. How would you wish to revenge yourself of any injustice, either great or small, which you may have received from strangers or from any one of our Brethren?

XIV. What would be your conduct should you ever repent of having joined our Order?

XV. Are you willing to share with us happiness and misfortune?

XVI. Do you renounce the idea of ever making your birth, employment, station, or power, serve to the prejudice or contempt of any one of the Brethren?

XVII. Are you, or have you any idea of becoming a Member of any other society?

XVIII. Is it from levity, or in hopes of soon being acquainted with our constitution, that you so easily make these promises?

XIX. Are you fully determined to observe our laws?

XX. *Do you subject yourself to a* BLIND OBEDIENCE WITHOUT ANY RESTRICTION WHATEVER? *And do you know the strength of such an engagement?* Ober unbedingten gehorsam angelobe, und wisse was das sey?

XXI. Is there no consideration that can deter you from entering into our Order?

XXII. *Will you, in case it is required, assist in the propagation of the Order, support it by your counsels, by your money, and by all other means?*

XXIII. Had you any expectation that you would have to answer any of these questions; and if so, which question was it?

XXIV. What security can you give us that you will keep these promises; and to what punishment will you subject yourself in case you should break any of them?[26]

In order to judge of the nature of the answers written and signed by the Novice, and confirmed by his oath, it will be sufficient to cast our eyes on the account of the reception of two Brethren, as it is contained in the archives of the Sect. To the VIth questrion, *should you ever discover in the Order any thing wicked, or unjust to be done, what part would you take?* The first of these two Novices, aged 22, and named *Francis Anthony St.... answers, swears, and signs,* "I would certainly execute those things, if so commanded by the Order, because it may be very possible that I am not capable of judging of what is just or unjust. Besides, should they be unjust under one aspect, *they would cease to be so as soon as they became a means of attaining happiness, the general end.*"

The Novice Francis Xaverius B.... answers, swears, and signs, in like manner, "I would not refuse to execute those things (wicked and unjust) provided they contributed to the general good."

To the XIth question, *on life and death,* the first Novice answers with the same formalities, "Yes, I acknowledge this right in the Order of Illuminées; and why should I refuse it to the Order, should it ever find itself necessitated to exercise it, as perhaps without such a right it might have to fear *its awful ruin. The state would lose little by it, since the dead man would be replaced by so many others.* Besides, I refer to my answer to question VI.;" that is to say, where he promised to execute whatever was just or unjust, provided it was with the approbation or by order of the Superiors.

The second answers, swears, and signs to the same question, "The same reason which makes me recognize the right of life and death in the governors of nations, leads me to recognize most willingly the same power in my Order, which really contributes to the happiness of mankind as much as governors of nations ought to do."

On the XXth question, on *blind obedience without restriction,* one answers, "Yes, without doubt, *the promise is of the utmost importance; nevertheless I look upon it as the only possible means by which the Order can gain its ends."* The second is less precise: "When I consider our Order as of modern invention and as little extended, I have a sort of repugnance in binding myself by so formidable a promise; because in that case I am justified in doubting whether a want of knowledge or even some domineering passion might not sometimes occasion things to be commanded totally opposite to the proposed object of the general welfare. But when I suppose the order to be more univerally spread, I then believe, that in a society comprehending men of such different stations, from the higher to the lower, those men are best enabled to know the course of the world, and how to distinguish the means of accomplishing the laudable projects of the Order."

This doubt of the Novice as to the antiquity of the Order must have displeased Weishaupt, who spared no pains to make it appear that Illuminism was of ancient date, the better to excite the curiosity and the veneration of the pupils; being content to enjoy the glory of his invention with his profound adepts, to whom only he revealed the secret of the invention of the highest degrees and the last mysteries. But our Novice went on to say, that on the whole he rather believed the Order to be of ancient than of modern invention; and, like his fellow Novice, he "promises to be faithful to all the laws of his Order, to support it with his counsels, his fortune, and all other means; and he finishes by *subjecting himself to forfeit his honour, and even his* LIFE, *should he ever break his promise*.[27]

When the Insinuator has found means of binding the Novice to the Order by such oaths, and especially when the young candidate shall have recognized without hesitation that strange and awful right which subjects the life of every citizen to the satellites of Illuminism, should any be unfortunate enough to displease its Superiors; when the Novice is blinded to such a degree as not to perceive that this pretended right, far from implying a society of sages, only denotes a band of ruffians and a federation of assassins like the emissaries of the Old Man of the Mountain; when, in short, he shall have submitted himself to this terrible power, the oath of the modern *Seyde* is sent to the archives of the Order. His dispositions then prove to be such as the superiors required to confer on him the second degree of the preparatory class; and the Insinuator concludes his mission by the introduction of his pupil.

At the appointed time in the dead of the night, the Novice is led to a gloomy apartment, where two men are waiting for him, and, excepting his Insinuator, these are the first two of the Sect with whom the Novice is made acquainted. The Superior or his Delegate holds a lamp in his hand half covered with a shade; his attitude is severe and imperious; and a naked sword lies near him on the table. The other man, who serves as Secretary, is prepared to draw up the act of initiation. No mortal is introduced but the Novice and his Insinuator, nor can any one else be present. A question is first asked him, whether he still perseveres in the intention of entering the Order. On his answering in the affirmative, he is sent by himself into a room perfectly dark, there to meditate again on his resolution. Recalled from thence, he is questioned again and again on his firm determination blindly to obey all the laws of the Order. The Introducer answers for the dispositions of his pupil, and in return requests the protection of the Order for him.

"Your request is just," replies the Superior to the Novice. "In the name of the most Serene Order from which I hold my powers, and in the name of all its Members, I promise you protection, justice, and help. Moreover, I protest to you once more, *that you will find nothing among us hurtful to Religion, to Morals, or to the State;"*—here the Initiator takes in his hand the naked sword which lay upon the table, and, pointing it at the heart of the Novice, continues, "but should you ever be a traitor or a perjurer, assure yourself that every Brother will be called upon to arm against you. Do not flatter yourself with the possibility of escaping, or of finding a place of security.—Wherever thou mayst be, the rage of the Brethren, shame and remorse shall follow thee, and prey upon thy very entrails."—He lays down the sword.—"But if you persist in the design of being admitted into our Order, take this oath:"

The oath is conceived in the following terms:

"In presence of all powerful God, and of you Plenipotentiaries of the most high and most excellent Order into which I ask admittance, I acknowledge my natural weakness, and all the insufficiency of my strength. I confess that, notwithstanding all the privileges of rank, honours, titles, or riches which I may possess in civil society, I am but a man like other men; that I may lose them all by other mortals, as they have been acquired through them; that I am in absolute want of their approbation and of their esteem; and that I must do my utmost to deserve them both. I never will employ either the power or consequence that I may possess to the prejudice of the general welfare. I will, on the contrary, resist with all my might the enemies of human nature, and *of civil society*." Let the reader observe these last words; let him remember them when reading of the mysteries of Illuminism; he will then be able to conceive how, by means of this oath, *to maintain civil society*, Weishaupt leads the adepts to the oath of eradicating even the last vestige of society. "I promise," continues the adept, "ardently to seize every opportunity of serving humanity, of improving my mind and my will, of employing all my useful accomplishments for the general good, *in as much as the welfare and the statutes of the society shall require it of me.*

"*I vow* (ich gelobe) *an eternal silence, an inviolable obedience and fidelity to all my superiors and to the statutes of the Order*. WITH RESPECT TO WHAT MAY BE THE OBJECT OF THE ORDER *I fully and absolutely renounce my own penetration and my own judgment.*

"I promise to look upon the interests of the Order as my own; and as long as I shall be a Member of it, *I promise to serve it with my life, my honour, and my estates*. Should I ever, through imprudence, passion, or wickedness, act contrary to the laws or to the welfare of the Serene Order, *I then subject myself to whatever punishment it may please to inflict upon me.*

"I also promise to help the Order, to the best of my power, and according to my conscience, with my counsels and my actions, and without the least attention to my personal interest; also, to look upon all friends and enemies of the Order as my own, and to behave to them as the Order shall direct. I am equally disposed to labour with all my might and all my means at the propagation and advancement of the Order.

"*In these promises I renounce every secret reservation, and engage to fulfill them all, according to the true purport of the words, and according to the signification attached to them by the Order when it prescribed the Oath—*

"*So help me God.*" N. N.

The oath being signed by the Novice, and enregistered in the minutes of the Order, the Initiator declares his admission, telling him at the same time that he is not to expect to know all the members, but those only who, being of the same degree, are under the same Superior.—From that moment advanced to the degree of *Minerval*, he is instructed in the signs of his new degree, which are much of the same nature as those of Masonry. He is then enjoined to give an exact *list of all his books*, particularly of those which might be precious or useful to the Order. He also receives the following questions which he is to answer in writing.

I. What should you wish to be the object of our Order?

II. What means, either primary or secondary, do you think most conducive to the attainment of that object?

III. What other things would you wish to find among us?

IV. What men do you either hope to meet, or not to meet, among us?[28]

The answers given to these questions will enable the Superiors to judge how far the young adept has imbibed the principles of the Order. But other helps are preparing for him, that he may be able to demonstrate by his answers both the progress he has made and that which he may be expected to make.

Thus admitted to the degree of *Minerval*, he will find himself in future a Member of the Academy of the Sect. Let us then observe well both the Scholars and their Masters; for they still belong to the class of preparation.

1. The Statutes reformed, No. 7.
2. The Statutes reformed, No. 16.
3. Original Writings, Statutes, No. 20. Statutes reformed, No. 27. True Illuminism, General Statutes, No. 31, 32.
4. Summary of the Statutes, No. 15. B.
5. Original Writings, and the true Illum. Art. *Reverse*.
6. Institutes of the Insinuated, No 8. Orig. Writ. the real Illuminee No. 7.
7. Statutes of the Minerval, No. 12.
8. Original Writings, Vol. I. Instructions for the Insinuated, No. 7, and Vol. II. Let 13.
9. Original Writings, Vol. I. Sec. 4.
10. Original Writings, Sect. 2 and 3.
11. See the real Illuminee first degree.
12. The common cypher of the Illuminees consist in *numbers* corresponding to letters in the following order:

12.	11.	10.	9.	8.	7.	6.	5.	4.	3.	2.	1.
a.	b.	c.	d.	e.	f.	g.	h.	i.	k.	l.	m.
13.	14.	15.	16.	17.	18.	19.	20.	21.	22.	23.	14.
n.	o.	p.	q.	r.	s.	t.	u.	w.	x.	y.	z.

The hieroglyphics [reproduced at the end of this edition, Ed.] are contained in the opposite Plate, and are copied from those published at the end of the degree of Scotch Knight or Directing Illuminee. There is a third cypher, but that has never been published.

13. The True Illuminee, General Statutes—Original Writings, Vol. I. Sect. 8.
14. See the list of these works in the Original Writings in the Statutes reformed, No. 25.
15. See Instructiones pro Insinuantibus et Recipientibus.
16. The true Illuminee. Instructions on the Art of forming Pupils, No. 12.
17. See Ibid. No. 13,—Original Writings, the Statutes reformed, No. 9, 10, 13, 14.—Instructiones pro Insinuantibus, No. 5, pro Recipientibus, No. 16, &c. &c.
18. Instructiones pro Recipientibus, No 13.
19. Instructions for the Insinuated, No. 5. C. and Original Writings, &c.
20. Instructions for the Insinuator, No. 3 and 4.—The real Illuminee, Instructions on the Art of forming the Brethren, No. 1, 2.
21. Mirabeau, Monarchie Prussienne, Vol. V. and Essay on the Illuminées, Chap. III.—Last Observations by Philo, page 61.
22. Constitution of the Jesuits, Part. III. Chap. I. Parag. 2, Vol. I. Edition of Prague.
23. Ibid. Part VI. Chap. I.
24. Epist. Ignatii De Obedientia.
25. Statutes reformed, No. 1, 4, and 25.—The true Illuminee, General Statutes, No. 11, 12.
26. Original Writings. The account of the reception of two Novices, Vol. I. Sect. 17.
27. See the two accounts.
28. True Illuminee, 1st initiation, Page 51 and following. Original Writings, Vol. I. Sect. 15.

CHAP. V.

Third Part of the Code of the Illuminees—Second preparatory Degree—The Academy of Illuminism, or the Brethren of Minerva.

WEISHAUPT, ruminating on what turn he should give to his Code of Illuminism, that its progress might be more subtile and infallible, expresses himself in the following terms, on the preparatory degrees which were to succeed to the novitiate of his pupils. "I am thinking of establishing, in the next degree, a sort of an academy of Literati. My design would include the study of the Ancients, and an application to the art of observing and drawing characters (even those of the living); and treatises and questions, proposed for public compositions, should form the occupations of our pupils.—*I should wish, more especially, to make them spies over each other in particular, and over all in general.* It is from this class that I would select those who have shown the greatest aptness for the Mysteries. My determination, in short, is, that in this degree they shall labour at the discovery and extirpation of prejudices. Every pupil (for example) shall declare, at least once a month, all those which he may have discovered in himself; which may have been his principal one, and how far he has been able to get the better of it."

Ever influenced by a bitter hatred against the Jesuits, he does not blush to say—"I mean that this declaration shall be among us, what confession was among them." Her was, however, unfortunate in his application; for in the Order of the Jesuits, no superior could ever hear the confessions of the Inferiors; and thus their very institutes rendered impossible the horrid abuse, under which Weishaupt affected to cloak the abominable breach of confidence with respect to his pupils, when he says, "by these means I shall discern those who show dispositions *for certain special Doctrines relative to Government or to Religion.*"[1]

The statutes of their Minerval degree are drawn up with a little more circumspection, and simply declare, "that the Order in that degree wishes to be considered only as a learned society or academy, consecrating its toils to form the hearts and minds of its young pupils both by example and precept."[2] These are called the Brethren of *Minerva*, and are under the direction of the *Major or Minor Illuminees*. The academy properly so called is composed of ten, twelve, and sometimes fifteen *Minervals*, under the direction and tuition of a *Major Illumin ee*.

In the kalendar of the Sect, the days on which the academy meets are called *holy*, and its sittings are generally held twice a month; always at the new moon. The place where they meet is called, in their language, *a Church*. It must always be proceded by an anti-chamber, with a strong door armed with bolts, which is to be shut during the time of the meeting; and the whole apartment is to be so disposed, that it shall be impossible for intruders either to see or hear any thing that is going forward.[3]

At the commencement of each sitting, the President is always to read, and, after his fashion, comment on some chosen passages of the BIBLE, or *Seneca*, of *Epictetus, Marcus Aurelius*, or *Confucius*.[4] The care he takes to give to all these works the same weight and authority, will be sufficient to make the pupils view the *Bible* in a similar light with the works of the Pagan Philosophers.

This lecture over, each pupil is questioned "as to the books which he has read since the last meeting; on the observations or discoveries he may have made; and on his labours or services toward the progress of the Order."

Nor are the studies and the books of which the Brethren are to give an account, left to their own choice. To each of these academies there is appropriated a particular library, whenever circumstances will permit, calculated to insure the spirit of the Order; and this collection the Sect takes care to furnish. By three different means it is accomplished. First, by the money which the Brethren contribute; secondly, by the list of his own private Library, which is exacted from each candidate, who is obliged to furnish therefrom such books as may be required of him; the third means is derived from Weishaupt's grand principle, that EVERY THING WHICH IS USEFUL IS AN ACT OF VIRTUE. Now as it would be very useful for the Order to get possession of those rare books and precious manuscripts which Princes, Nobles, and Religious Orders keep shut up among their archives or in their libraries; all Illuminees acting as librarians or archive-keepers are admonished, exhorted, and seriously pressed not to make any scruple of secretly stealing such books or manuscripts, and putting them into the possession of the Sect. This is one of the most explicit lessons that Weishaupt gives to his adepts; at one time telling them not *to make a case of conscience* of giving to the Brethren what they may have belonging *to the library of the Court*; at another, sending a list of what should be stolen from that of the Carmes, he says, "*all these would be of much greater use if they were in our hands.—What do those rascals do with all those books?*"[5]

Yet, notwithstanding the caution with which the founder as yet withholds certain books from the hands of the *Minerval*, it is clear from the very assortment of the libraries of the Order, that he does not hesitate at giving the pupils a certain number directly tending to the grand object, and particularly those which may create a contempt for religion. He wishes much to see *an impartial history of the Church*; and he even proposes hereafter to publish one himself, or at least to contribute many articles toward such a work. He calls the attention of the young adepts to *Sarpi*, to *Le Bret's arsenal of calumnies*, and in short to all that has been written against Religious Orders.[6] He had even put on the list those impious works which appeared under the name of *Freret*. He seemed to have forgotten for a moment his ordinary prudence; but, warned of it by *Knigge*, he corrected his error.[7] Many other books, however, were to be comprehended in the Minerval library, which were to disguise the object of it; and it was one duty of the Presiding Illuminee to select such as would gradually direct his pupils to the grand object of the Sect; always remembering, that the most impious and seditious *were reserved for the higher degrees*. Should the President chance to find *the System of Nature, Natural Polity, Helvetius on Man*, or other such books, in the hands of his pupil, *he was to avoid showing his pleasure or displeasure*, and leave them.[8] In short, it is in the Minerval schools that the teachers are in a particular manner to practise that great art of making the adepts rather as it were *invent* than learn the principles of the Order; because they will then, looking upon them as the offspring of their own genius, more strongly adhere to them.

There is yet another scheme in these schools for attaching the young adepts to the Order.—Every brother is, at his first reception, to declare to what art or science he means principally to apply, unless his station, genius, or particular circumstances, debar him from the literary career; in which latter case, *pecuniary contributions* are to be an equivalent for those services which his talents cannot contribute.[9] If the Brethren adopt literary pursuits, then the Order enters into engagements to furnish them with all possible assistance to forward their undertakings in the art or science on which they shall have determined; unless they should have chosen *Theology* or *Jurisprudence*, two sciences which the Order absolutely excepts from any such agreement.[10]

Their succours for the Minerval have a two-fold tendency. On the one side, they serve to prove that the adept does not *neglect* the science he has determined on, as he is to give an annual account of the discoveries he has made, and of the authors from which he has made selections. On the other hand, the brethren following the same branches of study are desired to help him with all the means in their power. Should he meet with difficulties which he cannot solve, he may apply to his Superior, who will either solve them himself, or send them to other members of the Order, who, better versed in those sciences, and bound to enlighten their Brethren, will send the required solutions.[11]

That his degree of Minveral may have all the appearances of a literary society, the Superiors annually propose some question for a public composition. The answers or dissertations are judged as in academies, and the discourse which obtains the prize is printed at the expence of the Order. The same advantages are held out to all adepts who wish to publish their works, provided they are not foreign to the views of the Founder.[12]—They are sure to coincide with his intentions should they be of the nature of those which he calls *pasquils*, or such as would create mirth among the people at the expense of the priesthood, and of *religious truths; such as parodies on the Lamentations of Jeremiah, or burlesque imitations of the Prophets*; in a word, all such *satires* as dispose the people to the grand object of the Sect. The Minerval can give no better proofs than these of his progress. The Sect has booksellers who put these works into circulation, and the profits are transmitted to the coffers of the Order.

It is, however, to be observed, that should a *Minerval*, or any other of the Brethren, make a discovery in any art or lucrative science, he is obliged, under pain of being looked upon as a false Brother, to impart the secret to the Order, who will look upon itself as proprietor of such secrets should they have been discovered by a Brother after his admission among them.[13]

Lest he should be unobserved *when travelling*, the *Minerval* is never to undertake any journey without previously informing his superiors, who will send him letters of recommendation for different Brethren on the road. He, in return, must carefully report every thing that he shall discover during his travels, which may be to the advantage or disadvantage of the Order.[14]

But we must not forget to mention, that during the academic sittings, the presiding Illuminee is at least once a month to take a review of the principal faults which he may have observed in any of his pupils. He is to interrogate them concerning those which they may have observed themselves; "and it would be unpardonable neglect," says the statutes, "should any pupil pretend that during the space of a whole month he had remarked nothing reprehensible. This would be a proof of the *utmost negligence in the training of his mind to observation; and the Superior must not suffer it to pass without reprehension*. He must also make his observations in such a manner as to excite their serious attention, and effectually to impress them with proper notions, so that each on returning home shall be ready to put in practice his advice for the advantage of the Order.[15] Beside, the Superior is as much as possible to avoid letting a day pass without seeing his pupils, either he visiting them, or they him.[16]

But what can be the object of such vigilance, such unremitting attention to the *Minerval* Academy? A single word from the adept who, under the inspection of Weishaupt, organized its laws, will explain the enigma. It is, to adopt *Knigge's* expressions, by the works required ot the young Academicians that the Order will be able to judge whether they are *of that sort of stuff* (that is to say of that turn of mind, susceptible of all the principles of Impiety and Anarchy) which is necessary for the higher degrees. After all these labours, should the *Minerval adept* still retain any of what they call *religionist inclinations*, he will then receive the three first Masonic degrees, and in them he may moulder during the rest of his life *in the insignificant study of all their hieroglyphics*. He will indeed still continue under the inspection of the Superiors of the Order; but he may rest assured, that he will always remain a *Minerval*, with a brevet of imbecility, on the registers of the Sect.[17] On the contrary, should he have shown a sufficient want of attachment to religion or to his Prince; should he enthusiastically imbibe the principles of Illuminism,—he will certainly be promoted to higher degrees. During his academical course the

Sect has had unerring means of judging him; viz. by the questions he has solved (and which were put by the Order, not so much with a view of exercising his talents as of prying into his opinions), and by the statements delivered in by the *Scrutators*, of the impression made by the different principles which they had disseminated either in the shape of conversation, or by way of refutation, to try the young *Minerval*.

The questions which he has had to investigate during his course sometimes regarded the secret of the Sect; at others, the security of the adepts, and of the Superiors. To envelop the chiefs in impenetrable darkness, and that their asylum may be proof against all attempts, death itself is to be divested of its horrors. The *Minerval* must not finish his Academical course till he has shown how far such fears have lost their influence over him; he shall declare whether he is ready to submit to every torture, rather than give the least information concerning the Order; or even evade the temptation by poison or suicide. A dissertation upon *Cato*, for example, will be given him as a task, and his management of it will show whether he is ready to fall by his own hand for the preservation of the Brethren. The *patet exitus*, or the *exit is free*, that is to say, that every man is free to leave this life at his pleasure, is one of those grand principles which must be advanced; it must be commented on and discussed by the young adept; and should any of those puerile ideas appear, which lead to believe in a God the avenger of suicide, he is not the man to be entrusted with the secret, and he shall be rejected.[18]

Many other questions are proposed in order to convince the Sect of the principles of the young Academician. It must sound his opinions on the means it employs, and on those in which he may hereafter be instrumental. He will be ordered to discuss Weishaupt's famous doctrine, that *the end sanctifies the means*; that is to say, that there are no means, not even theft, poison, homicide, or calumny, but are just and laudable when used for the attainment of objects which the Order may chuse to style just or holy.[19]

After all this, the *Minerval* shall furnish some dissertation from which his opinions on Kings and Priests may be ascertained;[20] but the presiding adept must carefully avoid compromising himself; he must not openly applaud the epigrams, sarcasms, or even blasphemies of his pupils; that must be left to the brethren visitors, who will insinuate and encourage them without ever hinting that they are in perfect unison with the mysteries of the Order. He must not fail, however, to observe which of his pupils are the most zealous for such doctrines, and who complacently repeat these sarcasms or blasphemies; those, in short, who enthusiastically blend them in their Academical compositions. This accomplished, they have run their Academic career, and are next promoted to the degree of *Minor Illuminee*.

1. Orig. Writ. Vol. I.—Let. 4, to Cato.
2. Statutes of the Minveral, No. 16.
3. See the Minerval Ritual.
4. Ibid.

5. Orig. Writ. Vol. I. Let. 4.
6. Ibid.
7. Letter of Philo to Cato.
8. Letter 3, to Cato.
9. Orig. Writ. Vol. I.—Summary of the Institute, No. 9.
10. Statutes of the Minerval, No. 1.
11. Ibid. No. 2.
12. Statutes of the Minerval N°s 6, and 10.
13. Summary of the Institutes, No. 11.—The true Illuminee.
14. Statutes of the Minerval, No. 11.
15. Instructions for the Minerval, No. 4.
16. Ibid. No. 3.
17. Last word from Philo, Page. 90.
18. See hereafter the Chapter on Juridical Depositions, in Vol. IV.
19. Ibid.
20. Ibid.

CHAP. VI.

Fourth Part of the Code of Illuminees.—Third preparatory Degree—The Minor Illuminee.

THE object of the degree of *Minor Illuminee* is not only to dispose the Brethren more and more for the secrets which have not yet been revealed to them; but it has also in view their preparation for presiding over the *Minerval* Academies in which they have already shown their talents, and their zeal for the Sect. The means which are to produce this double effect are worthy of remark, on account of one of those artifices which Weishaupt alone could have invented.

The Minor Illuminees hold sittings similar to those of the *Minerval* Academy. The President must necessarily be one of those adepts who, initiated in the higher mysteries of Illuminism, have attained the degree of *Priest*. He, alone having any knowledge of these higher mysteries, is particularly enjoined to keep his pupils in the persuasion that beyond the degree in which he is there is no farther secret to impart to them. But he is to spare no pains to infuse those opinions into their minds, of which the last mysteries are but the development. The Minor Illuminees are imperceptibly to become as it were the inventors and authors of Weishaupt's principles; that, believing them to be the offspring of their own genius, they may more zealously defend and propagate them. "It is necessary," says the code, "that *the adept look upon himself as the founder of the new Order,*" that hence he may conceive a natural ardor for its success. To effectuate this object, an exordium is appropriated to the initiation in this degree. It is one of those discourses which, replete with *voluntary obscurities*, presents the most monstrous errors to the mind, but expressly mentions none. The veil which is thrown over them is neither coarse enough to hide, nor fine enough clearly to shew them; all that the new adepts can observe at a first hearing is, that *the object of the Order* is worthy of admiration and zeal; that an ardent enthusiasm should inflame the mind of the young adept for the attainment of the grand object of all the labours of Illuminism; that the enjoyment of this happiness depended much more on the *actions than on the words* of the adepts. What then is this object, and what are the obstacles that are to be overcome? Of what species are those actions, those labours of the adept, which are to forward its views? It is in these points that enigma and obscurity veils the intent, and it is here that genius is to invent.

That the errors of the Sect might be considered as originating with the adepts, it goes on to say, *the same discourse shall serve in future as a text for all those which the Brethren shall prepare for the meetings of the Order.* The President will select the obscure passages, which may lead to the development of those opinions which he wishes to instil into his pupils; such will the the *subjects chosen for their themes*, and he will carefully exact *practical conclusions*.[1] But to give the reader a better idea of what these themes or commentaries are to be, we shall quote a part of the original text.

"There certainly exist in the world *public crimes which every wife and honest man would wish to suppress.* When we consider that every man in this delightful world might be happy, but that their happiness is prevented by the misfortunes of some, *and by the crimes and errors of others*; that the wicked have power over the good; that *opposition or partial insurrection is useless*; that hardships generally fall upon men of worth;—then *naturally results the wish of seeing an association formed of men* of vigorous and noble minds, capable of resisting the wicked, of succouring the good, and of procuring for themselves rest, content and safety—of *producing all these effects, by means drawn from the greatest degree of force of which human nature is capable.* Such views actuating a SECRET SOCIETY would not only be innocent, but most worthy of the wise and well-inclined man."[2]

What an ample field already opens itself to the commentating genius of the young adept! The Minor Illuminee will begin by investigating those *general crimes* to which the Sect wishes to put an end. And what are the *crimes*, who are the *wicked persons* that disturb the peace of mankind by means of *power exercised over the good*? What SECRET SOCIETIES are they which are destined to consummate the wishes of the sages, not by *partial insurrections*, but *by the greatest degree of force of which human nature is capable*? In a word, what is that new order of things, which are by such unheard of exertions to be substituted in place of existing institutions?

The greater progress the adept shall make, and the nearer his commentaries shall coincide with the spirit of the Order, so much the more worthy shall he be judged to fulfil the second object of this degree. He is not yet to preside over a *Minerval* Academy, he is too inexperienced in the arts of a Superior; and the Order only entrusts him with two or three of those pupils; but, as a consolation for the smallness of his flock, he reads in his instructions, *that should he have only formed one or two men for the Order during his whole life he will have done a noble act.*

Small as this mission is, still the adept is not left to his own prudence in the execution of it; he receives instructions by which he is to be guided. I forewarned my reader, that in this part of my Memoirs on Jacobinism, my object was, not solely to prove the Conspiracy of the Illuminees, but to render conspicuous the dangers which threatened society, while I was unveiling the means adopted by the Sect. Among these means, the laws laid down by Weishaupt for the Minor Illuminees are to be eminently distinguished; as the authority given, and the manner in which it is to be exercised (at first over two or three adepts only), naturally prepare them for more extensive commands. These laws and these instructions seem to be traced with the venom of the prudent serpent, unfortunately so much more active and ingenious in the arts of vice and seduction than good men are in the cause of virtue. This part of Weishaupt's Code is called—*Instructions for forming useful labourers in Illuminism*, and from it I shall make a large extract. Let the reader meditate on the tendency and probable consequences of such precepts, such laws, and artifices, all designed to form adepts for the most general, most astonishing, and most dreadful Conspiracy that ever existed.

"Assiduously observe (say these instructions) every Brother entrusted to your care; watch him particularly on all occasions where he may be tempted not to be what he ought to be; that is precisely the moment when he must show himself; it is then that the progress he has made is to be discovered. Observe him again at those times when he least suspects it, when neither the desire of being praised, the fear of being blamed, nor the shame of, or reflexion on the punishment, can actuate his conduct. Be exact on such occasions in making your notes and observations. You will gain much both with respect to yourself and to your pupil.

"Be careful lest your own inclinations should bias your judgment. Do not think a man excellent because he has a brilliant quality, nor judge him to be wicked because he has some striking defect: for that is the grand failing of those who are captivated at first sight.

"Above all, guard against believing your man to be a transcendant genius because his discourse is brilliant. We are to judge by facts alone, whether a man is deeply interested.

"Have little confidence in rich or powerful men; their conversion is very slow.

"Your chief object must be to form the heart. He that is not deaf to the cries of the unfortunate; he that is constant though in adversity, and unshaken in his plans; he that feels his soul glow for great enterprizes; and he, particularly, who has formed his mind to observation, is the man of whom we are in quest. Reject those feeble and narrow minds who know not how to quit their usual sphere.

"Read with your pupils those books which are easy to be understood, which abound in the picturesque, and are calculated to elevate the mind. Speak to them often; but let your discourses proceed from the heart, and not from the head. Your auditors easily kindle when they see you full of fire. *Make them thirst after the moment when the grand object is to be accomplished.*

"Above all, stimulate them to the love of the object. Let them view it as grand, important, and congenial to their interests and favourite passions. Paint in strong colours the miseries of the world; tell them what men are, and what they might be; what line of conduct they should adopt; how little they know their own interests; how anxiously our society labours for them; and desire them to judge what they may expect from it, by what we have already done in the first degrees.

"Shun familiarity on all occasions where your weak side may be seen; always speak of Illuminism in a dignified style."

"Inspire esteem and respect for our Superiors; and dwell strongly on the necessity of obedience in a well-organized society."

"Kindle the ardour of your pupil by laying great stress on the utility of our labours; avoid dry and metaphysical discussions. Let what you require of your pupils be within their means. Study the peculiar habits of each; *for men may be turned to any thing by him who knows how to take advantage of their ruling passions.*

"To infuse into them a spirit of observation, begin by slight essays in conversation. Ask some easy questions on the means of discovering the character of a man notwithstanding all his dissimulation. Affect to think the answer a better one than you could have given yourself; that gives confidence, and you will find some other opportunity of delivering your own sentiments. Inform them of what observations you may have made concerning their voice, gait, or physiognomy. Tell them also, that they have the best dispositions, and that they only want practice. Praise some in order to stimulate others."

"Having thus become acquainted with the immense difficulty attending on the art of bringing men to the point whither you wished to lead them, neglect no occasion of disseminating the good principles wherever you can, and of inspiring your pupils with courage and resolution: but never forget, *that he who wishes to convert too many at once will convert nobody.* In the towns where you reside, divide the task with the other Illuminees of the same degree as yourself. Chuse one or two, at most three, Minervals among those over whom you have the greatest influence or authority; but spare neither labour nor pains. *You will have accomplished a great undertaking if, during your whole life, you form but two or three men. Let those whom you have selected be the constant object of all your observations. When one method does not succeed, seek out another; and so on, till you have found a proper one.* Study to find out what your pupil is best fitted for; *in what intermediary principles he may be deficient, and therefore inaccessible to the fundamental ones.* The grand art consists in profiting of the right moment; at one time it is warm, at another cool reasoning which will persuade.—Let your pupil always think that it is to himself, and not to you, that he is indebted for the progress he makes. *If he falls in a passion, never contradict; hearken to him though he be in the wrong. Never controvert the consequences, but always the principle. Wait for a favourable moment when you may explain your sentiments without appearing to contradict his. The best method is to agree with another person, whom you will pretend to attack on those subjects, while the Candidate whom you really wish to convince is only a stander-by and takes no part in the dispute: then support your arguments with all the vigour of which you are capable.*

"Whatever failings you wish to correct in him, speak of them as if they were not his; tell the story as if somebody else had been guilty of them; then take his advice on the subject; and by these means he becomes his own judge.

"All this, it is true, requires time: hurry nothing; it is solidity and *facility of action* that we want in our adepts. Often to read, meditate, hearken to, see the same thing, and then to act, is what gives that facility which soon becomes natural...."

"Do you wish to draw forth his opinion? Propose a dissertation on certain questions relative to your object, as it were merely to exercise his genius. He thus learns how to meditate on the principles while you make a discovery of those which it is your object to eradicate from his mind."

"Instruct, advise; but beware of cold declamations: drop a few words to the purpose when you shall perceive his mind to be in a proper state to receive them."

"Never ask too much at once; let your conduct be provident, paternal, and solicitous.—Never despair; *for one may do what one pleases with men.*

"Make yourself master of the motives of the principles your pupil has acquired from his education. If they be not consonant with our views, weaken them by insensible gradations, and substitute and strengthen others. But great prudence is necessary to operate this."

"Observe what religions, sects, and politics, make men do.—One may enthusiastically wed them to follies; it is therefore in the *manner* of leading them that the whole art of giving the upper hand to virtue and truth consists. *Only employ the same means for a good purpose which impostors employ for evil*, and you will succeed. If the wicked are powerful, it is because the good are too timid and too indolent. *There may be circumstances also, under which it will become necesssary to show displeasure, and even anger, in defence of the rights of man.*"

"Tell your pupils, that they are only to attend to the purity of the views which actuate the Order; and that antiquity, power, or riches, should be perfectly indifferent to them."

"Tell them, that should they find elsewhere a society which would lead them with greater speed or with more certainty to the desired end, the Order would eternally regret the not having been acquainted with it before—That in the mean time we obey the laws of our Superiors, labouring in peace, and persecuting no man.—Follow these rules of conduct, and once more remember, that you will have rendered an essential service to the world, though you should form but two men according to our principles.

"*Carefully profit of those moments when your pupil is discontented with the world, and when every thing goes contrary to his wishes; those moments when the most powerful man feels the want of the support of others, to attain a better order of things.* It is then that you must press the swelling heart, stimulate the sensibility, and demonstrate how *necessary secret societies are, for the attainment of a better order of things.*"

"But be not too easy in your belief with respect to the reality or constancy of such feelings. Indignation *may be the effect of fear, or of the fleeting hopes of some passion which one wishes to gratify.* Such feelings are not naturalized; men are not perfect in so short a time; *prepare for the worst, and then insist.* A heart which easily melts easily changes."

"Never promise too much, that you may be able to perform more than you promise. Rekindle exhausted courage; repress excessive ardour; inspire hope in misfortune, and fear in success."

"Such are the rules which will form you for a good preceptor and a leader of men. By an exact attention to them you will add to the number of the elect. If your own happiness be dear to you, labour (under our direction) at delivering many thousands of men, who wish to be good, from the dire necessity of being wicked.—Believe us, for it is the precept of experience, *bereave vice of its power,* and every thing will go well in this world: for if vice be powerful, it is only because one part of the good is too indolent, while the other is too ardent; or else, that men suffer themselves to be divided, or leave the care of Revolutions to futurity; *the fact is, that in the mean time they had rather bend under the yoke,* than efficaciously resist vice. If they once became sensible that *virtue does not entirely consist in patience, but in action also,* they would start from their sleep.—For your part, unite with the Brethren; place your confidence in our Society; nothing is impossible to it, if we follow its laws. We labour to secure to merit its just rewards; to the weak support, to the wicked the fetters they deserve; and to man his dignity. Such is the new Canaan, the new land of Promise, the land of abundance and blessing; though as yet, alas! we discover it but from a distance."[3]

I was frequently tempted to interrupt the course of this extract by my reflexions; but what reader is there that will not ask himself, What zeal, what strange ardour is this, that can have led Weishaupt to combine and dictate means so powerful to captivate the minds of his pupils? Is there a parent, is there a preceptor, whose love for his child or his pupil ever suggested more efficacious rules? These, however, are only a few of the lessons which the Minor Illuminee is always to have present to his mind to direct him in the training of the young adepts. He is not alone entrusted with the task. All the Brethren of the same degree partake in the care of watching over the lower ones, and each notes on his tablets even the most insignificant circumstances. Their several observations are compared, and of the whole a general statement is formed, according to which each pupil will be judged by his superiors.[4] Meanwhile, it is natural to ask, what can these principles be for which the youth is so carefully trained? What can be the *sublime virtue* that is to be the result of so much care? We shall soon discover them, the principles of shameless villainy. This *sublime virtue* is the combination of every art that can plunge mankind into corruption, and immerse him in all the horrors of universal anarchy. Yes, we shall see the man who says to his disciples, *employ the same means for a good purpose which impostors employ for evil,* proved to be the arch-impostor, training his disciples to every crime, and preparing the most terrible disasters for society with more ardour and more artifice than ever the upright man has been seen to employ zeal and wisdom in the cause of virtue and the support of the laws.

The better to dispose the young adepts, the Minor Illuminee is assisted in his functions and overlooked by the Major Illuminee, that is to say, by the adepts of the highest degree among those of the preparatory class.

1. The true Illuminee, Instructions for the Superiors of this degree.
2. Discourse on this Degree.
3. Extract from the Instruction C. and D. for the Minor Illuminees.
4. Instruction C. Sect. II. A. 2.

CHAP. VII.

Fifth Part of the Code of Illuminees—Fourth preparatory Degree—The Major Illuminee, or the Scotch Novice.

THE degree which follows that of *Minor Illuminee* is sometimes called *Major Illuminee*; at other times, *Scotch Novice*. Under this two-fold denomination a double object is comprized. As Scotch Novice, the adept is turned in upon Masonry; and it is only a snare for imposing upon the credulity of those, who have not given the requisite symptoms for being initiated in the higher mysteries of the Sect. It is an introduction to the degree of *Scotch Knight,* which terminates the career of the dupes. But as a degree of Illuminism, it will encompass the adept with new bonds, more extraordinary and more firm than the former; it is a more immediate preparation for the grand mysteries; in short, it is from this degree that the masters of the Minerval Academies are selected.

Let us begin by laying open the artifice of that strange bond which the adept will never dare to rend asunder, though he should wish to withdraw from Illuminism, or more particularly should he be tempted to reveal what he may have already discovered of the artifices, principles, or grand object of the Sect.

Before the candidate is admitted to the new degree, he is informed that his reception is resolved on, provided he gives satisfactory answers to the following questions:

I. Are you acquainted with any society grounded on a better constitution, or more holy and solid than ours, and which tends with more certainty or expedition to the object of your wishes?

II. Was it to satisfy your curiosity that you entered our society? or, was it to concur with the chosen among men to universal happiness?

III. Are you satisfied with what you have seen of our laws? Will you labour according to our plan, or have you any objection to propose against it?

IV. As there will be no medium for you, declare at once, whether you wish to leave us, or whether you will remain attached to us for ever?

V. Are you a member of any other society?

VI. Does that society impose any thing detrimental to our interests; for example, the discovery of our secrets; or, does it require you to labour for itself exclusively?

VII. Should such things be ever required of you, tell us upon your honour, whether you would be disposed to acquiesce in them?

These questions answered, there still remains another proof of confidence which the Order expects from the candidate. This is nothing less than an exact and candid account *of his whole life*, written without any *reservation or dissimulation* whatever. The necesssary time is given him; and this is the famous bond, or rather snare, into which when Weishaupt has once brought the candidate he exultingly exclaims, "*Now I hold him; I defy him to hurt us; if he should wish to betray us, we have also his secrets.*" It would be in vain for the adept to attempt to dissimulate. He will soon find that the most secret circumstances of his life, those which he would most anxiously wish to hide, are all known by the adepts. The arts which he has hitherto practised to pry into the most secret motions of the hearts of his pupils, into their tempers and passions, their connections, their means, their interests, their actions and opinions, their intrigues and faults, have all been more artfully employed by others in watching himself. Those who compose the lodge into which he is going to be received, are the very persons that have been scrutinizing his past life.

All the discoveries made by his Insinuator, all the statements he has been obliged to give of himself as required by the Code, every thing which the *Brother Scrutators*, either known or unknown, have been able to discover concerning him during his degrees of Minerval or of Minor Illuminee, have been accurately transmitted to the Brethren of the new lodge. Long before his admission, they had accomplished themselves in the scrutinizing arts. ——These wretches then will mimick even the canonization of the saints! The very precautions which Rome takes to discover the least taint in those whom it proposes to the veneration of the faithful, this illuminizing Sect will adopt, in order to satisfy itself that in its adepts no civil nor religious virtue can be traced. Yes, the villains in their dens wished to know each other, and smiled to see their accomplices as wicked as themselves.

I cannot conceive whence Weishaupt could have taken this part of his Code; but let the reader form an idea of a series of at least fifteen hundred questions on the life, the education, the body, the mind, the heart, the health, the passions, the inclinations, the acquaintances, the connections, the opinions, the abode, the habits, and even the favourite colours of the candidate; on his relations, his friends, his enemies, his conduct, his discourse, his gait, his gesture, his language, his prejudices, and his weaknesses. In a word, questions which relate to every thing that can denote the life or character, the political, moral, or religious sentiments, the interior or exterior of the man; every thing he has said, done, or thought, and even what he would say, do, or think under any given circumstances. Let the reader form an idea of twenty, thirty, and sometimes a hundred questions on each of these heads. Such will be the Catechism to which the *Major Illuminee* must be able to answer; such are the rules he is to follow in tracing the lives or characters of the young Brethren, or even of those prophane of whom the Sect wishes to have particular information. Such is the scrutinizing Code which has directed the researches made as to the life of the candidate antecedent to his admission to the degree of *Major Illuminee*. These statutes are called by the Order the *Nosce te ipsum* (know thyself). When one brother pronounces these words, the other answers *Nosce alios* (know others); and this answer denotes much better the object of the Code, which might very properly be styled the *perfect spy*. Let it be judged by the following questions:

"On the *Physiognomy* of the Candidate:—Is he of a florid complexion, or pale? Is he white, black, fair, or brown? Is his eye quick, piercing, dull, languishing, amorous, haughty, ardent, or dejected? In speaking, does he look full in the face and boldly, or does he look sideways? Can he endure being stared full in the face? Is his look crafty, or is it open and free; is it gloomy and pensive, or is it absent, light, insignificant, friendly, or serious? Is his eye hollow, or level with the head, or does it stare? His forehead, is it wrinkled, and how; perpendicularly, or horizontally? &c.

"His *Countenance:*—Is it noble or common, open, easy, or constrained? How does he carry his head; erect or inclined, before, behind, or on one side, firm or shaking, sunk between his shoulders, or turning from one side to the other? &c.

"His *Gait*:—Is it slow, quick, or firm? Are his steps long, short, dragging, lazy, or skipping? &c.

"His *Language:*—Is it regular, disorderly, or interrupted? In speaking, does he agitate his hands, his head, or his body, with vivacity? Does he close upon the person he is speaking to? Does he hold them by the arm, clothes, or button-hole? Is he a great talker, or is he taciturn? If so, why? Is it through prudence, ignorance, respect, or sloth? &c.

"His *Education:*—To whom does he owe it? Has he always been under the eyes of his parents? How has he been brought up, and by whom? Has he any esteem for his masters? To whom does he think himself indebted for his education? Has he travelled, and in what countries?"

Let the reader, by these questions, judge of those which treat of the mind, the heart, or the passions of the Candidate. I will just note the following:

"When he finds himself with different parties, which does he adopt, the strongest or the weakest, the wittiest or the most stupid? Or does he form a third? Is he constant and firm in spite of all obstacles? How is he to be gained, by praise, flattery, or low courtship; or by women, money, or the entreaties of his friends?" &c.—"Whether he loves satire, and on what he exercises that talent; on religion, superstition, hypocrisy, intolerance, government, ministers, monks?" &c.

This however is not all that the scrutators are to note in their statements. They are to elucidate each answer by a fact, and by *such facts as characterize the man at a moment when he least suspects it*.[1] They are to follow their prey to his bolster, *where they will learn whether he is a hard sleeper, whether he dreams, and whether he talks when dreaming; whether he is easily or with difficulty awakened; and should he be suddenly, forcibly, or unexpectedly awakened from his sleep, what impression would it make on him?*

Should any of these questions, or any part of the Candidate's life, not have been sufficiently investigated by the Lodge, divers of the brethren are ordered to direct all their enquiries toward that point. When at length the result of all their researches is found to coincide with the wishes of the Sect, the day for his reception is appointed. Neglecting all the insignificant particularities of the Masonic rites, we shall attend entirely to those circumstances which peculiarly belong to Illuminism.

The adept, introduced into a gloomy apartment, reiterates his oath to keep secret whatever he may see or learn from the Order. He then deposits the history of his life (sealed up) in the hands of his introducer. It is read to the Lodge, and compared with the historical table which the Brethren had already formed respecting the Candidate. This done, the Introducer says to him, "You have given us a welcome and valuable proof of your confidence; but indeed we are not unworthy of it; and we hope that it will even increase in proportion as you become better acquainted with us. Among men whose sole object is to render themselves and others better, no dissimulation should subsist. Far be any reserve from us. We study the human heart—and do not hesitate or blush at revealing to each other our faults or errors.—Here then is the picture which the Lodge had drawn of your person. You must own that some features are not unlike. Read, and then answer, whether you still wish to belong to a society which (such as you are represented here) opens its arms to receive you."

Could indignation operate more powerfully on the mind of the Candidate at the sight of his having been so treacherously watched, than the fear of abjuring a society which henceforth possesses such arms against him, he would not hesitate at asking for his dismission; but he sees the consequences of such a step, and feels that it might cost him very dear. Beside, he is so familiarized with the scrutinizing system, that he can scarcely be offended with it, though operating on himself. He is left for a certain time to his meditations. The desire of acquiring a new degree works upon him and at length turns the scales; he is introduced to the Lodge of the Brethren; and there the veil which hides the secrets of the Sect is partly raised; or, rather, he is himself still more unveiled, that the Sect may discern whether all his views and wishes coincide with theirs.

After a suitable preamble, the Initiator tells him, "that he has still some few questions to answer, relative to objects on which it is absolutely necessary that the opinions of candidates should be known."

The reader is desired to pay particular attention to these questions; as it will enable him, when he shall come to read of the mysteries, more clearly to observe the succession and gradation with which such principles are infused into the mind of the adept, as if he had invented and conceived them all himself.

"I. Do you find that, in the world we live in, virtue is rewarded and vice punished? Do you not on the contrary observe, that the wicked man is exteriorly more comfortable, more considered, and more powerful, than the honest man? In a word, are you content with the world in its present situation?"

"II. In order to change the present order of things, would you not, if you had it in your power, assemble the good and closely unite them, in order to render them more powerful than the wicked?"

"III. If you had your choice, in what country would you wish to have been born rather than your own?"

"IV. In what age would you wish to have lived?"

"V. Always premising the liberty of choice, what science and what state of life would you prefer?"

"VI. With respect to history, who is your favourite author or your master?"

"VII. Do you not think yourself in duty bound to procure all the exterior advantages possible for your tried friends, in order to recompense them for their probity, and to render life more agreeable to them? *Are you ready to do what the Order exacts of each member in this degree, when it ordains that each one shall bind himself to give advice every month to the Superiors, of the employments, support, benefices, or other such like dignities, of which he can dispose, or procure the possession by means of his recommendations; that the Superiors may present worthy subjects of our Order to all such employments?*"

The answers of the candidate are to be returned in writing, and inserted in the registers of the Lodge. It will naturally be expected, that the greatest dissatisfaction with the present order of things is to be expressed, as well as an ardent wish for a revolution which shall change the whole face of the Universe. He will also promise to support, by all the means in his power, the election of none but worthy brethren to offices of emolument and trust, or such as may augment the power or credit of Illuminism, whether about the court or among the people. On his declaring such to be his sentiments, the Initiator addresses him in the following discourse:

"Brother, you are a witness, that it is after having tried the best of men, that *we seek little by little to reward them, and to give them support, that we may insensibly succeed in new modelling the world.* Since you are convinced how imperfectly men have fulfilled their real destiny; *how every thing has degenerated in their civil institutions*; how little the teachers of wisdom and of truth have enhanced the value of virtue, or given a happier disposition to the world; you must be persuaded, that the error lies in the means which the sages have hitherto employed. Those means, therefore, must be changed, in order to reinstate in its rights the empire of truth and wisdom. And this is the grand object of the labours of our Order. Oh, my friend! my brother! my son! when here convened, far from the prophane, we consider to what an extent the world is abandoned to the yoke of the wicked, how persecution and misfortune is the lot of the honest man, and how the better part of human nature is sacrificed to personal interest. *Can we at such a sight be silent, or content ourself with sighing? Shall we not attempt to shake off the yoke?—Yes, my brother, rely upon us.* Seek faithful co-operators, but seek them not in tumults and storms; *they are hidden in darkness. Protected by the shades of night, solitary and silent, or reunited in small numbers, they, docile children, pursue the grand work under the direction of their Superiors.* They call aloud to the children of the world, who pass by in the intoxication of pleasure——how few hearken to them! He alone who has the eye of the bird of Minerva, who has placed his labours under the protection of the star of night, is sure of finding them."

But, lest this discourse should not have given the Candidate a sufficient insight as to the object of the new degree, the Secretary opens the Code of the Lodge, entitled *A general view of the system of the Order.* Here the young Illuminee learns, that the object of the Order *is to diffuse the pure truth, and to make virtue triumph.* Nothing, however, is explicitly said on what is to be understood by *the pure truth.* He is only told, that in order to diffuse it, "he must begin by liberating men from their prejudices, and by enlightening their understandings; then reunite all the common forces for the refinement of all sciences from the dross of useless subtleties, and for the establishment of principles drawn from Nature.—To attain this," continues the Secretary, "we must trace the origin of all sciences; we must reward oppressed talents; we must raise from the dust the men of genius; *we must undertake the education of youth*; and, forming an indissoluble league among the most powerful geniuses, we must boldly, though with prudence, combat *superstition, incredulity, and folly*; and at length form our people to true, just, and uniform principles on all subjects.

"Such is the object of our *Minerval Schools*, and of the *inferior degrees of Masonry*, over which our Order wishes to acquire all the influence possible, in order to direct it towards our object. We also have our superior degrees, where the Brethren, after having passed through all the preparatory degrees, become acquainted with the ultimate result of the labours and of all the proceedings of the Order."

To obtain the completion of that result, "it will be necesssary to divest vice of its power, that the honest man may find his recompense even in this world; but in this grand project, *we are counteracted by the Princes and the Priesthood; the political constitutions of nations oppose our proceedings.* In such a state of things then what remains to be done? To instigate revolutions, overthrow every thing, oppose force to force, and exchange tyranny for tyranny? Far be from us such means. Every violent reform is to be blamed, because it will not ameliorate things *as long as men remain as they are, a prey to their passions; and because wisdom needeth not the arm of violence.*"

"The whole plan of the Order tends to form men, not by declamation, but by the protection and rewards which are due to virtue. *We must insensibly bind the hands of the protectors of disorder, and govern them without appearing to domineer.*"

"In a word, we must establish an universal empire over the whole world, without destroying the *civil ties. Under this new empire, all other governments must be able to pursue their usual process, and to exercise every power, excepting that of hindering the Order from attaining its ends and rendering virtue triumphant over vice.*"

"This victory of virtue over vice was formerly the object of Christ, when he established his pure religion. He taught men, that the path to wisdom consisted in letting themselvees be led for their greater good by the best and wisest men. At that time preaching might suffice; the novelty made truth prevail; but at present, more powerful means are necesssary. Man, a slave to his senses, must see sensible attractions in virtue. *The source of passions is pure; it is necessary that every one should be able to gratify his within the bounds of virtue, and that our Order should furnish him with the means.*"

"It consequently follows, that all our brethren, educated on the same principles, and strictly united to each other, should have but one object in view. *We must encompass the Power of the earth with a legion of indefatigable men, all directing their labours, according to the plan of the Order, towards the happiness of human nature*——but all that is to be done in silence; our brethren are mutually to support each other, to succour the good labouring under oppression, *and to seek to acquire those places which give power, for the good of the cause.*"

"*Had we a certain number of such men in every country,* each might form two others. Let them only be united, and nothing will be impossible to our Order; *it is thus that in silence it has already performed much for the good of humanity.*"

"You behold, Brother, an immense field opening to your activity; become our faithful and worthy co-operator, by seconding us with all your might; and remember, that no service will pass without its just reward."

After this lesson, two chapters directly treating on the functions of the *Major Illuminee* are read to him. With the first he is already acquainted: it is the Code of the *Insinuator* or *Brother Recruiter*. He is also now entrusted with it, as it is part of his duty in future to judge of the pupils of all the Insinuators. The second treats of the duties of the *Scrutator*; this is also delivered into his care, because he must particularly exercise that art while presiding over the Minerval academies: and he must necessarily learn how his new brethren found means of tracing so exact an historical portrait of himself, and of penetrating even more successfully than he could into the interior recesses of his heart; he must also learn to distinguish such pupils as, with dispositions similar to his own, are worthy of being admitted to his new degree. He now has but one more degree to go through, before he is admitted into the class of the mysteries, and this is termed by the Sect *the Scotch Knight*.[2]

---

1. See Weishaupt's Letters.
2. The whole of this chapter is nothing more than an extract from the *degree of Major Illuminee*, and from the instructions contained in the ritual of that code in *The True Illuminee*.

CHAP. VIII.

Sixth Part of the Code of the Illuminees.—Intermediary Class—The Scotch Knight of Illuminism; or Directing Illuminee.

UNDER the appellation of *Intermediary Class* of Illuminism might be comprehended all the Degrees which Weishaupt had borrowed from Freemasonry. In that case we should comprize under this denomination the three degrees of *Apprentice, Fellow-Craft, and Master.* But it has been already said, that these degrees are simply a passport for the Sect into the Masonic Lodges; and that its object may be less conspicuous, it leaves them in their original Masonic state. This, however, is not the case with the higher degrees of Scotch Masonry. The Sect shrewdly surmised that the views of these degrees coincided with their own: beside, it wanted some of these superior degrees, either for the direction of those Masonic Lodges which it composed of its own members, or who were to gain admittance, dominate, and preside over other Lodges which were not devoted to Illuminism.—The great veneration in which the *Scotch Knights* are generally held by Masons, more strongly determined the Baron Knigge to make himself master of this degree, and engraft it on Illuminism. The Sect has constituted this into both an *intermediary* and a *stationary* degree. It is *stationary* for those into whom it despairs of ever infusing the principles required for a futher admission to the mysteries; but it is only *intermediary* for those who have shown dispositions more accordant with the pursuits of the Sect.[1]

Whatever may be his destiny, no Brother is ever admitted into this new degree, until he has previously given proofs of the progress he has made in the arts of *Scrutator*, whose code must have been his chief study since his admission to the degree of Major Illuminee. The secret Chapter of the Knights has had the precaution to propose certain questions to him to ascertain how far he is capable of judging *of the state of the mind by exterior appearances.* He will have had to answer, for example, to the following ones:—"What is the character of a man whose eyes are perpetually in motion, and whose countenance is changeable? What features denote voluptuousness, melancholy, and pusillanimity?"[2]

As a further proof of the progress he has made, he is to transmit to his superiors another dissertation on the life of the hero whose name he bears for his characteristic. The history of his own life, which he had delivered in the antecedent degree, had laid open the whole of his existence, and all his actions through life. This new dissertation will show the Order what he admires or disapproves of in others, and will particularly demonstrate whether he has discovered those qualities in his patron which the Order wished he should imbibe and imitate when it gave him his characteristic.[3] Should any part of his life have escaped the vigilance of the Scrutators, he is still at liberty to give a new proof of his confidence in the Order; and this is described as a meritorious act; but he may reserve it for the cognizance of the Superior of the Order only.[4] He is then to declare under his hand-writing, that he looks upon the Superiors of Illuminism as the *secret* and *unknown* though *legitimate* Superiors of *Freemasonry*; that he adheres and always will adhere to the illuminized system of Masonry, as the best and most useful existing; that he utterly renounces every other association; that he is, in short, so persuaded of the excellence of Illuminism, that he fully adopts its principles, and firmly believes himself bound to labour, under the direction of his superiors, *at the object and according to the intentions of the Order* for the happiness of mankind.[5]

After having received these numerous pledges, the Scotch Knights invite the new Brother to a *secret Chapter*, for such is the name given to the Lodges of this degree. It is hung with green, richly decorated and brilliantly lighted. The Prefect of the Knights, booted and spurred, is seated on a throne erected under a canopy all of the same colour. On his apron a green cross is seen, and on his breast the star of the Order; he wears the riband of St. Andrew in salter from right to left, and holds a mallet in his hand. On his right stands the brother sword-bearer, holding the sword of the Order; on his left the master of the ceremonies with a stick in one hand, and the ritual in the other. The Knights assembled are all booted and spurred, each girt with a sword, and all wear the cross suspended at their necks by a green riband. The Officers of the Order are to be distinguished by a plumage, and a priest of the Order compleats the Lodge. The Prefect then delivers himself as follows to the Candidate:

"You here behold a part of those unknown legions which are united by indissoluble bonds to combat for the cause of humanity. Are you willing to make yourself worthy of watching with them for the sanctuary? Your heart must be pure, and a heavenly ardour for the dignity of nature must fire your breast. The step you are taking is the most important one of your life. Our games are not vainly ceremonial. In creating you a knight we expect of you that you will perform exploits grand, noble, and worthy of the title you receive. Long life to you, if you come to us to be faithful; if honest and good you answer our expectations. Should you prove a false Brother, be both cursed and unhappy, and may the grand Architect of the Universe hurl you into the bottomless pit! Now bend thy knee, and on this sword take the oath of the Order."

At these words the Prefect seats himself, the Knights are standing with their swords drawn, and the Candidate pronounces the following oath:—

"I promise obedience to the excellent Superiors of the Order. In as much as it shall depend upon me, I engage—never to favour the admission of any unworthy member into these holy degrees—to labour at rendering the Ancient Masonry triumphant over the false systems which have crept into it—to succour, like a true Knight, innocence, poverty, or oppressed honesty—*Never to be the flatterer of the great, nor the slave of Princes*;—to combat courageously, though prudently, in the cause of *Virtue, Liberty, and Wisdom*—to resist boldly, both for the advantage of the Order and of the world, *Superstition and Despotism*. I never will prefer my own private interest to that of the Order. I will defend my Brethren against calumny. *I will dedicate my life to the discovery of the true Religion and real doctrines of Freemasonry, and I will impart my discoveries to my Superiors*. I will disclose the secrets of my heart to my Superiors as to my best friends. So long as I shall remain in the Order I shall look upon the being a Member of it as a supreme felicity. I also engage to look upon all my domestic, civil, and social duties as most sacred. So help me God, both for the happiness of my life, and for the peace of my mind."

In return for this oath the Prefect declares to the Candidate that he is going to create him a Knight of St. Andrew, according to the ancient usage of the Scotch—"*Rise*," he says, "and in future beware of ever bending thy knee before him who is only man like thyself."[6]

To these ceremonies the adept Knigge added a certain number of others which were mere derisions of the rites of the Church. Such, for example, was the triple benediction which the Priest pronounced over the new Knight, such the atrocious mockery of the last supper, which terminated the ceremony. But, impious as is the imitation, Weishaupt declares it to be *disgusting* because it is still *religious, theosophical*, and *borrowed from superstition*.[7] But what perfectly coincided with the views of the Bavarian founder were, the instructions given to the new Knight. He is enraptured with that discourse, where one may observe the Illuminizing Orator selecting the most impious, artful, and disorganizing systems of Masonry, to make them at once the mysteries of their Masonic Lodges, and an immediate preparation for those of Illuminism.

Let the reader recal to mind what was said in the Second Volume of these Memoirs[8] concerning the Apocalypse of the Martinists, entitled *Of Errors and of Truth*. He will there have read of a time when man, disengaged from the senses and free from matter, was still more free from the yoke of the laws and from political bondage, to which he was only subjected by his fall. He will there have seen, that the daily efforts of man should tend to the overthrow of Governments, that he may recover his former purity and ancient liberty, and thus retrieve his fall. I might there have demonstrated that absurd *Idealism* reducing our senses to vain fictions, that the prostitution of them might be but a chimerical crime;[9] there, in short, I might have shown, according to the Martinist, that in all ages this system of corruption and disorder has been the doctrine and secret of true Philosophy. This intermediary degree was destined by Weishaupt to serve as a point of union between the Masonic Lodges and Illuminism. It was but natural that the should have selected the most monstruous and most artful system of the Craft. Let not the reader therefore be astonished when he sees the Antitheosophist, the Atheist, the Materialist Weishaupt borrowing in this degree the doctrines of the Martinists on the twofold principle or double spirit. But let it be also remembered, that whenever, in consequence of this artifice, he is obliged to use the words *spirit* or *soul*, he informs the candidate, that such words are employed in the Code only to conform to the *vulgar expression*. This precaution taken, the Initiator may without apprehension repeat the sophisticated lessons on the twofold principle. And indeed one might be tempted to think, that the doctrines he lays down as the grand object of Free Masonry had all been copied from the Martinist system. He begins by deploring a great Revolution which had in former ages deprived man of his primitive dignity. He then represents man as having had the faculty of recovering his ancient splendour; but that by the abuse of his faculties he had again immersed himself still deeper in his defiled and degraded station. The very senses are blunted, and said to lead him into error on the nature of things. Every thing that he beholds in its actual state is *falsehood, show,* and *illusion*; and he lays particular stress on those schools of sages which had, ever since the time of the grand Revolution, preserved the secret principles of the antique doctrines, or of true Masonry. Nor does the montrous Hierophant blush at placing JESUS OF NAZARETH among those sages, and blasphemously numbering the God of the Christians among the Grand Masters of Illuminism. But soon was the doctrine of Christ falsified, and Priests and Philosophers raised on these divine foundations an edifice of *folly, prejudice, and self-interest. Soon also does the tyranny of Priesthood and the Despotism of Princes coalesce in the oppression of suffering humanity.* Free Masonry opposes these disastrous attempts, and endeavors to preserve the true doctrine; but it has overburned it with symbols, and its lodges gradually subside into seminaries of ignorance and error.—The Illuminees alone are in possession of the real secrets of Masonry; many of them are even still to be the objects of their researches; and the new Knight is to devote all his attention to their discovery. He is particularly recommended *to study the doctrines of the ancient Gnostics and Manichæans, which may lead him to many important discoveries on this real Masonry.* He is also told, that the great enemies which he will have to encounter during this investigation will be ambition and other vices which make humanity *groan under the oppression of Princes and of the Priesthood*.[10]

    The obscurity which enwraps these lessons on the new and grand Revolution which is to counteract the ravages of the former, is not the slightest of Weishaupt's artifices. With respect to Princes, this is the last degree to which they are admitted. They are to be persuaded, that the antique Revolution was no other than the coalition of the powers of the earth with the Priesthood, in order to support the empire of religious prejudice and superstition; and that the new Revolution to be effected is the re-union of Princes with Philosophy, to overthrow that empire and ensure the triumph of reason. Should the serene adept be startled at his having sworn *never to flatter the great, nor to be a slave of Princes*, he will be reconciled again by the latter part of the oath, where he *engages to look upon his domestic, civil, and social duties as most sacred*. But let him form what opinion he may as to his initiation, he has nevertheless sworn, that he will protect the Brotherhood from superstition and despotism; *that he will obey the most excellent superiors of the Order*; that he will favour its progress with all his power, and that he believes it alone to be in possession of the secrets of real Masonry.

In the less important class of adepts, should any still hanker after their *Theosophical* ideas, that is to say, should Weishaupt despair of ever infusing into them its Anarchical and Atheistical principles, they are condemned to become *stationary* in this degree; and he imposes on them as a task the explication of all the Hieroglyphics of Masonry, which they may set to the tune of the grand Revolution. Under pretence of discovering a more perfect religion, he persuaded them that Christianity was at this day nothing more than superstition and tyranny. He has infused into them his hatred for the Priesthood and the existing forms of Government. That will suffice to procure him agents of destruction; as to re-edifiction, he has not so much as mentioned it to them.

But should there be found among the number of Knights men who of themselves dive into the meaning of that great Revolution which only deprived man of his primitive dignity by subjecting him to the laws of civil society, should they have comprehended the meaning of this other Revolution, which is to restore every thing by re-establishing man in his primitive independence, such men will be pointed out by the Scrutators. It is at them that the Code particularly aims when it says, *Let the Scotch Knights seriously reflect, that they are presiding over a grand establishment, whose object is the happiness of mankind*. In short, these Knights have to act the parts of Superiors in the Order; they are the Inspectors or the *Directors* of all the preparatory class. They have on that account assemblies peculiar to themselves, called *Secret Chapters*. The first duty of these chapters is to watch over the interests of the Order within their district. "The Scotch Knights," says their first instruction, "are to pay particular attention to the *discovery of any plans which may contribute to fill the coffers of the Order. It were much to be wished that they could devise means of putting the Order into possession of some considerable revenues in their province.—He that shall have rendered so signal a service must never hesitate at believing that these revenues are employed in the most noble purposes.—The whole must labour with all their might to consolidate the edifice little by little within their district, until the finances of the Order shall be found to be competent to its views.*"[11]

The second part of the Code entrusts these Knights with the government of the preparatory class. Each Knight is to correspond with a certain number of Brethren who have the direction of the *Minerval* academies. The Code contains instructions which point out to them upon what objects they are permitted to decide; what Brethren they are to forward or thwart in their promotion; and what reports they are to make to their Superiors. In their correspondence with their Inferiors they make use of the common cypher, but when they write to the chiefs they employ a peculiar character which may truly be called Hieroglyphic.

They are particularly charged with the inspection of the Major Illuminees. "The Scotch Knights," says the Code, "shall be particularly attentive that the Major Illuminees do not neglect to mention in their monthly letters such employments as they may have to dispose of."[12]

I have shown, in the foregoing chapter, how useful and indeed how necessary this precaution proved for recompensing the zeal of the Brethren. The adept Knigge wished to demonstrate that it might be equally useful for princes, when combined with the scrutinizing Code. "Let us suppose," says he, "that a Prince, having an Illuminee for his Minister, wishes to find a proper person to fill any vacant office; by means of the *Scrutators*, the Minister may immediately present the faithful portrait of divers personages, from among whom the Prince will only have to make his election."[13]—But every reader, I hope, will recollect, that in consequence of the oath that has been taken by the Minister to dispose of all places in favour of the Brethren, and that according to the direction of the Knights, he will only present such adepts for those offices as the Order shall have chosen; and thus will Illuminism soon dispose of all benefices, employments, and dignities, and have the entire direction of the whole power of the State.

Meanwhile, until the Sect shall exert this influence over Courts, the Scotch Knights are to acquire an absolute sway in the Masonic Lodges. Their laws on this head deserve particular attention. We shall select the following:

"In every town of any note situated within their district, the Secret Chapters shall establish Lodges for the three ordinary degrees, and shall cause men of sound morals, of good repute, and of easy circumstances, to be received in these Lodges. Such men are much to be sought after, and are to be made Masons, *even though they should not be of any service to Illuminism in its ulterior projects.*"[14]

"If there already exists a Lodge in any given town, the Knights of Illuminism must find means of establishing a more legitimate one; at least, they should spare no pains to gain the ascendancy in those which they find established, *either to reform or to destroy them.*"[15]

"They must strongly exhort the members of our lodges not to frequent (without leave of their Superiors) any of those pretended constituted lodges, *who hold nothing of the English but their diplomas, and some few symbols and ceremonies which they do not understand.* All such Brethren are perfectly ignorant of true Masonry, of its grand object, and its real patrons. Though some of the greatest merit are to be found in such lodges, we nevertheless have strong reasons for not readily allowing them to visit ours."[16]

"Our Scotch Knights must pay great attention to the regularity of the subordinate lodges, *and must above all things attend to the preparation of candidates.* It is here that *in a private intercourse* they will show a man that they have probed him to the quick. *Surprise him by some ensnaring question* in order to observe whether he has any presence of mind. If he be not staunch to his principles, and should expose his weak side, make him feel how great his necessities are, and how necessary it is for him to be guided entirely by us."[17]

"The Deputy Master of the Lodge (who is generally the auditor of the accounts) must also be a member of our Secret Chapter. *He will persuade the lodges that they alone dispose of their funds; but he will take care to employ them according to the views of the Order.* Should it at any time be necesssary to help one of our brethren, the proposition is made to the lodge; though the brother should not even be a Mason, *no matter, some expedient must be found to carry the point.*"

"No part of the capital, however, must in any case be alienated, *that hereafter we may find the necessary funds for the most important undertakings.* The tenth part of the subscriptions of these lodges must be annually carried to the Secret Chapter. The treasurer to whom these funds must be transmitted, shall collect them, and endeavour *by all kinds of expedients to augment them.*"[18]

"But before any part of our own funds are appropriated to the help of any of our Brethren, every effort shall be made to procure the necessary succours from the funds belonging to lodges which do not pertain to our system.—*In general, the money which these lodges spend in a useless manner, should be converted to the advancement of our grand object.*"[19]

"Whenever a learned Mason shall enter our Order, he must be put under the immediate direction of our Scotch Knights."[20]

From what code can Weishaupt, or his compiler Knigge, have selected such laws as these for their Scotch Knights? Many readers will be ready to answer, that they must have learned them from a Mandrin, a Cartouche, or some hero of the gibbet. But it is no such thing:—their own ingenuity was sufficient to invent such doctrines. Weishaupt lays down as a principle, that *the end justifies the means*: he made the application of it when he taught his adepts to rob the libraries of Princes and Religious Orders; his compiler Knigge applies the same principle to the funds of the honest Masons; and we shall soon see what use they made of those funds. It will be in vain for the Illuminee (more zealous for the honour of his founder than for that of the compiler Knigge) to object, that Weishaupt never approved of the degree of *Scotch Knight*. It is true, he never much admired it. But it is not the system of theft (evidently deduced from his own principles) that he reprobates; not a single expression in any of his letters can denote that he did so; for Knigge might have answered, *what do those fools of Masons do with that money?* just as Weishaupt had written *what do those rascals of Monks do with their rare books?* He blamed it not for its principles, but because he thought it *a miserable composition: der elende Scottische ritter grade* are the terms in which he expresses his contempt. When he corrected this degree, the thefts were not the parts which he expunged; they were too serviceable to the order. Weishaupt, however, consented to let this degree (such as it was) serve as a preparation for the mysteries of his *Epoptes*; that is to say, for his *priests* of Illuminism; and when considered in that light it may be truly said, that the *Knights brigands* were but pitiful and miserable indeed. I will, however, give the reader an opportunity of judging for himself.

1. Original Writings, Vol. II. Part I. Sect. 11.
2. See this degree, Sect. 4, No. 2 and 3.
3. See second Instruction for this degree, No. 8.
4. Ibid.
5. Ibid. Reversal Letters.
6. Ibid. Sect. 7.
7. See the Last word of Philo, Page 100.
8. Chap. XI.
9. When treating in the Second Volume of the religious and political tenets of the Martinists, I did not extend my reseraches to their doctrine of *Idealism*, and I frankly confess that I did not sufficiently understand that part of their Apocalypse. Since the publication of that Volume, however, I have met with a Gentleman perfetly capable of comprehending any intelligible system whatever; I mean the Abbé Bertins, residing at present at Oxford. He reproached me in terms similar to those in which some other people had reproached me respecting the Rosicrucians. *What you have written, said he, is ALL true, but you have not told the WHOLE truth.* I had indeed said a great deal of those gentry, and I never will advance any point which I cannot prove. The Abbé Bertins condescended to give me some little insight into the doctrines of this famous St. Martin. It fully confirmed every thing which I had advanced on the tenets of the Martinists, with respect to the nature of the soul, and to the pretended origin of that soul forming *a part of God, of the essence of God, and of the same substance*—But what I had not said was, that according to the same system matter has no real existence, or at least has such a separate existence, and is so entirely null with respect to the soul, that there neither is nor can be any relation whatever between it and the soul; in fine, that *it is*, with respect to us, as if *it were not*. I had surmised these consequences in a converssation which I had had with an estimable young man, the Vicomte de Maimbourg, whom the Martinists had endeavoured to taint with their erroneous doctrines. When they came to treat of the pleasure of the senses, *throw that to the fire*, they say in their treatise of morality; *to the fire: give to the fire all it asks; that is not the spirit*, all that *does not affect the soul; and this fire is matter; it is the senses, the body*. It is not in the same sense that the Martinist tells us, "It is in vain that the enemy pursues me with his illusions. Matter shall not have remembrance of me here below. Does man taste the pleasures of matter? When the senses feel pain or pleasure, is it not easy to perceive that it is not man that feels this pain or pleasure?" (No. 235, *of the Man of Desire, by the Author of a work On Errors and on Truth*). How frightful is this enigmatical language! If all the passions and senses are foreign to man, if he may gratify them with affecting his soul either for the better or for the worse, what monstrous consequences must ensue to morals! And indeed a Danish Martinist was consulted by the Viscount, who, more candid than the recruiting Brethren, answered, "Beware, dear Sir, of ever entering into our mysteries;—I am unfortunately engaged, and should in vain attempt to withdraw myself from them. I could not succeed; but, for your part, take care never to deliver yourself over to those men." The Viscount followed his advice. As to the Abbé Bertins, he was too much for Mr. de St. Martin, who had to argue with a man that perpetually objected—if my soul is part of God, and of the substance of God, my soul must be God. After three months lessons, which the reader will readily suppose the Abbé Bertins only submitted to through curiosity, the *learned* teacher violently exclaimed, "*I see I never shall be able to convince*

a Divine:" and thus Mr. de St. Martin took leave of a scholar far more fitted to teach him real knowledge than to receive his sophisticated lessons.
10. See this degree, Art. 8. Instruction on the Masonic Hieroglyphics.
11. See First Instruction for this degree.
12. Second Instruction, No. 12.
13. Last Observations of Philo, Page 95.
14. Third Instruction for the same degree, No. 1.
15. Third Instruction for the same degree, No. 3.
16. Ibid. No. 5.
17. Ibid. No. 9.
18. Third Instruction for the same degree, No. 12.
19. Ib. 13.
20. Third Instruction for the same degree, No. 16.

CHAP. IX.

Seventh Part of the Code of the Illuminees.—Class of the Mysteries.—Of the lesser Mysteries; the Epopt or Priest of Illuminism.

HOWEVER accurately the Sect may have ascertained the progress of its adepts in the preparatory degrees, still Weishaupt seems to fear that some may be startled when they come to be acquainted with the ultimate views of Illuminism. He wishes therefore to lead them to his darkest plots by gradual shades. Hence the division of lesser and greater mysteries, and the subdivision into degrees. The first degree into which the adepts are initiated in this class is that of *Epopt*; but these new dignitaries are only known by that title to the inferior class; the higher degrees call them *Priests*.[1]

Let not the reader take alarm at the denomination of *lesser mysteries*, as if they were of no consequence; for he will gradually, as he ascends, discover their dark designs and dealings. But before the adept is allowed to proceed, he must collect every thing that his mind, his memory, or all his former lessons can afford, of anti-religious and anti-social principles, to enable him to give written answers to the following questions:

"I. Do you think the present state of nations corresponds with the object for which man was placed upon earth? For example, do governments, civil associations, or religion, attain the ends for which they were designed? Do the sciences to which men apply furnish them with real lights; are they conducive (as they ought to be) to real happiness? Are they not, on the contrary, the offspring of numberless wants, and of the unnatural state in which men live? Are they not the crude inventions of crazy brains, or of geniuses laboriously subtle?"

"II. What civil associations and what sciences do you think tend or do not tend to the grand object? Did there not formerly exist an order of things more simple? What sort of an idea can you form of that ancient state of the world?"

"III. Now that we have passed through all those nullities (*or through all those useless and vain forms of our civil constitutions*), do you think that it would be possible to return back to the original and noble simplicity of our forefathers? Supposing we had returned to it, would not our past misfortunes render that state more durable? Would not all mankind be in a similar state with an individual who, having enjoyed the sweets of innocence during his childhood, and fallen a prey to error and his passions during his youth, at length, instructed by the risks he has run, and by experience, endeavours to return to that innocence and purity which rendered his childhood so happy?"'

"IV. What means were best to be employed for restoring mankind to that happy state? Should it be by public measures, by violent revolutions, or by any means that should ensure success?"

"V. Does not the Christian Religion in all its purity afford some indications, does it not hint at some state or happiness similar to this? Does it not even prepare it?"

"VI. Is this holy and simple religion really what different Sects profess it to be at this present day, or is it more perfect?"

"VII. Can this more perfect Christianity be known or taught? Could the world (such as it now is) support a stronger degree of light? Do you not think that, before the numberless obstacles could be removed, it would be proper to preach to mankind a religion more perfect, a philosophy more elevated, and the art of each one's governing himself according to his greatest advantage?"

"VIII. Would not our moral and political views lead men to oppose this blessing? From our political and moral views then, or from an ill-judged interest, or even from deep-rooted prejudices, these obstacles originate. If men, therefore, oppose the renovation of human happiness, is it not because, slaves to ancient forms, they reject and reprobate every thing which is not to be found in those forms, though it should be the most natural, the grandest, and most noble of all possible things? Does not personal interest, alas! at present predominate over the general interest of mankind?"

"IX. Must we not then silently and gradually remedy those disorders before we can flatter ourselves with the re-establishment of the golden age? Meanwhile, is it not adviseable to *disseminate the truth in Secret Societies*?"

"X. Can we trace any such secret doctrine in the ancient schools of the sages, or in the allegorical lessons given by Jesus Christ, the Saviour and liberator of mankind, to his most intimate disciples? Have you not observed a sort of gradual education in that art which you see has been transmitted to our Order, from the highest antiquity?"[2]

Should the answers of the Candidate to all these questions show that the progress he has made in his gradual education is not what the Order had reason to expect, he will solicit in vain the advancement he hoped for. Should his answers be equivocal, he will receive orders to prepare new ones, or to be more explicit.[3] But if he show the proper dispositions, and the Sect foresee no probability of his being startled at the lessons of the Hierophant on those grand objects which are to be disclosed to him, the Superiors give their assent, and a synod of the illuminized priesthood is held. The day of the initiation is fixed. At the hour agreed upon, the introducing adept waits upon his new proselyte and takes him into a carriage. The windows being closed, the Candidate blind-folded, and the coachman continually winding and varying his course, are precautions more than sufficient to hinder the proselyte from ever being able to trace the spot to which he is conducted. Led by the hand, and still blind-folded, he slowly ascends to the porch of the temple of the mysteries. His guide then divests him of the Masonic insignia, puts a drawn sword into his hand, takes off the bandage from his eyes, and leaves him, strictly forbidding him to proceed a step until he hears the voice which is to call him. He is then left to his reflections.

With respect to the pomp of the mysteries, when the Brethren celebrate them in all their splendour, the walls of the temple are hung in red, and lighted up with an immense number of candles or lamps. A voice is at length heard, saying, "Come, enter, unhappy fugitive! The fathers wait for you; enter and shut the door after you." The proselyte obeyes the voice which calls him. At the bottom of the temple he beholds a throne under a rich canopy with a table before it, on which lie a crown, a sceptre, a sword, some pieces of gold money, and precious jewels, all interlaid with chains. At the foot of this table, on a scarlet cushion, is thrown a white robe, a girdle, and the simple ornaments of the sacerdotal costume. The proselyte, standing at the bottom of the temple and in front of the throne, is addressed by the Hierophant as follows: "Behold and fix thine eyes on the splendour of the throne. If all this childish mummery, these crowns, these scepters, and all these monuments of human degradation, have any charms in your eyes, speak; and it may be in our power to gratify your wishes. Unhappy man! if such are your objects, if you wish to rise to power that you may assist in the oppression of your Brethren, go, and at your peril make the trial. Are you in quest of power, of force, of false honours, and of such superfluities, we will labour for you; we will procure such transient advantages for you, we will place you as near the throne as you can desire, and will leave you to the consequences of your folly; but observe, our sanctuary shall be for ever shut against you.

"On the contrary, do you wish to be initiated into wisdom, would you teach the art of rendering men better, more free and more happy, then be welcome, be thrice welcome. Here you behold the attributes of Royalty, and there, on the cushion, you see the modest vestment of innocence; make thy choice, and let it be the choice which thy heart shall dictate."

If, contrary to all expectations, the Candidate should make choice of the Regalia, he hears a thundering voice exclaim, "Monster, retire! cease to pollute this holy place! Begone, fly, before it is too late." At these words he is led out of the temple by the Brother who introduced him.—But should he chuse the white robe, how different will be the language! "Health and salutation to thy great and noble soul! Such was the choice we expected from you. But stop; it is not permitted to you to invest yourself with that robe, until you have learned to what you are in future destined by us."[4]

The Candidate is then ordered to be seated. The Code of the Mysteries is opened, and the Brethren in silence attend to the oracles of the Hierophant.

Now, reader, you who have been through so long a course of trials, questions, rituals, and insidious degrees; who have been led through all the preparatory labyrinth of illuminized education, if still you be in the dark as to the object of such precautions and artifices, follow me into this den which the Sect dares to call the *holy place*; seat thyself by the adept, and listen to their Oracles.—This is the master-piece of the founder. Hear with patience, though your indignation should be excited by his monstrous fertility in Sophism, in impiety, in blasphemy against your gospel and your God, treachery against your Magistrates, your country, and its laws, against your titles and your rights, against those of your ancestors and your progeny—Let Kings and Subjects, the rich and poor, the merchant and the labourer, let every class of citizens attend; let them hearken, and learn at length what hellish plots are contriving against them in the dark recesses of these diabolical dens. In vain shall the lethargic soul accuse us of credulity or groundless terrors. Those lessons which the Sect view as the master-piece of their code lie before me, such as they flowed from the pen of the Legislator, such as they were published by order of the Sovereign who seized the archives of the Sect, that all nations might learn the dreadful dangers with which they were menaced.[5] I have them again embellished by the compiler of the Sect, corrected and reviewed by the Council of the Areopagites, attested by the compiler as true and conformable to the copy signed and sealed with the signet of the Sect.[6]

Read then, and rock thyself to sleep in the cradle of voluntary ignorance if thou canst, content with having assured thyself that every conspiracy against the *existence of civil society* or of all government whatever, every conspiracy against the *existence of property*, can be but a chimera.

It is to the Candidate, and in presence of the Brethren already initiated to these mysteries, that the Illuminizing President addresses the following discourse:

Discourse of the Hierophant for the Degree of Priest
or Epopt of the Illuminees.[7]

"At length (he says) the time of your reward succeeds to the trials of an assiduous preparation. At present you know yourself, and have learned to know others; you are what you ought to be, such as we wished to see you. It will now be your duty to conduct others.—What you already know, and what you are about to learn, will expose to your view the extreme weakness of human nature. In this advantage alone lies the true source of power which one man exercises over another. The dark clouds dissipate; the sun of light rises; the gates of the sanctuary unfold; a portion of our mysteries is going to be revealed to you. Let the gates of the temple be shut against the prophane; I will only speak to the Illustrious, to the Holy, to the Elect. I speak to those who have ears to hear, who have tongues which they can command, and who have minds sufficiently enlightened to understand.

"Surrounded by the Illustrious, you are about to enter into that class which bears an essential part in the government of our sublime Order. But do you know what it is to govern, can you conceive what this right can be in a secret society? To exercise such an empire, not over the vulgar or the grandees of the people, but over the most accomplished men, over men in all stations, of all nations, of all religions; to reign over them without any exterior constraint, to keep them united by durable bonds, to inspire them all with one spirit; to govern with all possible precision, activity, and silence, men spread over the whole surface of the globe, even to its utmost confines. This is a problem which no political wisdom has ever been able to solve. To reunite the distinctions of Equality, Despotism, and Liberty; to prevent the treasons and persecutions which would be the inevitable consequences; of nothing, to create great things; to stand firm against the swelling torrent of evils and abuse; to make happiness universally shine on human nature; would be a master-piece of morality and polity re-united. The civil constitutions of states offer but little aid to such an undertaking. Fear and violence are their grand engines; with us, each one is voluntarily to lend his assistance.... Were men what they ought to be, we might on their first admission into our society explain the greatness of our plans to them; but the lure of a secret is perhaps the only means of retaining those who might turn their backs upon us as soon as their curiosity had been gratified: The ignorance or imperfect education of many makes it requisite that they should be first formed by our moral lessons. The complaints, the murmurs of others against the trials to which we are obliged to condemn them, sufficiently show you what pains we must bestow, with what patience and what constancy we must be endowed; how intensely the love of the grand object must glow in our hearts, to make us keep true to our posts in the midst of such unthankful labour; and not abandon for ever the hope of regenerating mankind."

"It is to partake with us of these labours that you have been called. To observe others day and night; to form them, to succour them, to watch over them; to stimulate the courage of the pusillanimous, the activity and the zeal of the lukewarm; to instruct the ignorant; to raise up those who have fallen, to fortify those who stagger; to repress the ardour of rashness, to prevent disunion; to veil the faults and weaknesses of others; to guard against the acute inquisitiveness of wit; to prevent imprudence and treason; in short, to maintain the subordination to and esteem of our Superiors, and friendship and union among the Brethren, are the duties, among others still greater, that we impose upon you."

"Have you any idea of secret societies; of the rank they hold, or of the parts they perform in the events of this world? Do you view them as insignificant or transient meteors? O, Brother! God and Nature, when disposing of all things according to the proper times and places, had their admirable ends in view; *and they make use of these secret societies as the only and as the indispensable means of conducting us thither.*"

"Hearken, and may you be filled with admiration! This is the point whither all the moral tends; it is on this that depends the knowledge of the rights of secret societies, of all our doctrine, of all our ideas of good and bad, of just and unjust. You are here situated between the world past and the world to come. Cast your eyes boldly on what has passed, and in an instant ten thousand bolts shall fall, and thousands of gates shall burst open to futurity—You shall behold the inexhaustible riches of God and of Nature, the degradation and the dignity of man. You shall see the world and human nature in its youth, if not in its childhood, even there where you thought to find it in its decrepitude and verging toward its ruin and ignominy."

Should this long exordium, which I have nevertheless abridged, have fatigued the reader, let him rest and reflect for an instant. The enthusiastic strain which predominates in this first part pervades the whole. Weishaupt thought it necessary to his object to afford his proselytes no time for reflection. He begins by inflaming them; he promises great things; though this impious and artful mountebank knows that he is going to fob them off with the greatest follies, the grossest impieties and errors. I have called him an impious and artful mountebank; but that is falling far short of what the proofs attest. Weishaupt knows that he deceives, and wishes to delude his proselytes in the most atrocious manner. When he has misled, he scoffs at them, and with his confidants derides their imbecility. He has, however, his reasons for beguiling them, and knows for what uses he intends them when he has infused into them his erroneous and vicious principles. The greater the consideration they may enjoy in the world, the more heartily he laughs at their delusion. He thus writes to his intimate friends: "You cannot conceive how much my degree of Priest is admired by our people. But what is the most extraordinary is, that several great protestant and reformed divines, who are of our Order, really believe that that part of the discourse which alludes to religion contains the true spirit and real sense of Christianity; *poor mortals! what could I not make you believe?*—Candidly I own to you, that I never thought of becoming the founder of a religion."[8] In this manner does the impostor delude his followers, and then scoffs at them in private. These great divines were probably of that class among the protestants which we should, among us, call apostates, a Syeyes or an Autun, for example; for it is impossible that any man endowed with common sense or candour could avoid seeing that the whole tendency of this long discourse is the total overthrow of all religion and of all government.

A second observation well worthy the notice of our readers is, the extreme *importance* which the Sect gives to *secret societies*, and what mighty expectations it grounds on their mysterious existence. Let nations and chiefs of nations examine themselves, reflect whether they have ever calculated the means and importance of these secret societies so well as those who founded them; and say, whether fear and diffidence on the one side should not keep pace with the expectations and confidence of the other. But let us return to the Lodge wherein Weishaupt initiates his adepts.

Continuing his enthusiastic strain, the Hierophant informs the proselyte, that Nature, having a great plan to develope, begins by the lesser and most imperfect parts; that she then regularly proceeds to the middle terms, to bring things to a state of perfection; which state may serve as a point whence she may again depart, to raise them to a higher order of perfection.

"Nature (says he) makes us begin at infancy, from infancy she raises us to manhood. She at first left us in the savage state, but soon brought us to civilization, perhaps that we might be more sensible, more enraptured and tenacious of what we are, from viewing the contrast of what we were. But to what changes, and those of an order infinitely more important, does our future destiny lead us!"

Were the candidate master of his own reason, he must conclude from these principles, that human nature had acquired perfection when passing from the savage state to that of civil society; that if he is still to acquire perfection it can never be by returning to his primitive state. But sophisters have their tortuosities, and the adepts are involved in a folly and blindness, with which the Almighty God permits them to be stricken, since they prefer error to truth, and impiety to Christianity.

"As has the individual man (continues the Hierophant) so human nature in the aggregate has its childhood, its youth, its manhood, and its old age. At each of these periods mankind learn and are subject to fresh wants—hence arise their political and moral revolutions—It is at the age of manhood that human nature appears in all its dignity. It is then that, taught by long experience, man conceives at length how great a misfortune it is for him to invade the rights of others, to avail himself of some few advantages, purely exterior, to raise himself, to the prejudice of others. It is then that he sees and feels the happiness and dignity of man."

"The first age of mankind is that of savage and uncouth nature. A family is the whole society; hunger and thirst easily quenched, a shelter from the inclemency of the seasons, a woman, and, after fatigue, rest, are then the only wants. *At that period men enjoyed the two most inestimable blessings* EQUALITY and LIBERTY; *they enjoyed them to their utmost extent; they would have forever enjoyed them, had they chosen to follow the track which Nature had traced for them*—or had it not entered the plans of God and Nature first to show man *for what happiness he was destined*; happiness the more precious, as he had begun by tasting it; happiness so early lost, but instantaneously regretted and fruitlessly sought after, until he should have learned how *to make proper use of his strength*, and how to conduct himself in his intercourse with the rest of mankind. In his primitive state he was destitute of the conveniencies of life, but he was not on that account unhappy; not knowing them, he did not feel the want of them. Health was his ordinary state, and physical pain was his only source of uneasiness—*Oh happy mortals! who were not sufficiently enlightened to disturb the repose of your mind*, or to feel those great agents of our miseries *the love of power and of distinctions*, the propensity to sensuality, the thirst after the representative signs of all wealth, those *truly original sins* with all their progeny, envy, avarice, intemperance, sickness, and all the tortures of imagination!"

Thus we see this primitive and savage state, this first essay of Nature, already transformed (in the mouth of the Hierophant) into the happiest state that man ever knew: *Equality and Liberty* are the sovereign principles of happiness in that state. Should the reader be as much blinded as the proselyte, and not see whither all this is tending, let him proceed, and hear how man was deprived of this happiness by the institution of civil societies.

"An infortunate germ soon vivifies in the breast of man, and his primitive peace and felicity disappear."

"As families multiplied, the means of subsistence began to fail; the *nomade* (or roaming) *life ceased, and PROPERTY started into existence*; men chose habitations; agriculture made them intermix. Language became universal; living together, one man began to measure his strength with another, and the weaker were distinguished from the stronger. This undoubtedly created the idea of mutual defence, of one individual governing divers families reunited, and of thus defending their persons and their fields against the invasion of an enemy; *but hence* LIBERTY *was ruined in its foundation, and* EQUALITY *disappeared.*"

"Oppressed with wants unknown until that period, man perceived that his own powers were no longer sufficient. To supply this defect, the weakest imprudently submitted to the strongest or to the wisest; not however to be ill-treated, but that he might be protected, conducted, and enlightened.—All submission, therefore, even of the most unpolished mortal, has an existence only in as much *as he wants* the person to whom he subjects himself, and on the express condition that that person can succour him. *His power ceases when my weakness no longer exists, or when another acquires superiority. Kings are fathers; the paternal power is at an end when the child has acquired his strength. The father would offend his children if he pretended to prolong his rights beyond that term. Every man having attained to years of discretion may govern himself; when a whole nation therefore is arrived at that period, there can exist no further plea for keeping it in wardship.*"

In putting such language into the mouth of the Hierophant, the founder of Illuminism had too well studied the strength and illusion of words; he had been too cautious in the choice and preparation of his adepts ever to fear that any of them would answer, "You who thus give oracles, what do you understand by nations having attained their majority? Without doubt such as, having emerged from ignorance and barbarism, have acquired the lights necesssary for their happiness; and to what can they be indebted for these lights and this happiness, if not to their civil association? It will be then, if ever, that they will find it both reasonable and necessary to remain under the *guardianship* of their laws and of their government, lest they should fall back into the barbarism and ignorance of the roaming clans, or be precipitated into the horrors of anarchy, from revolution to revolution, under the successive tyrany of the brigand, of the executioner of the sophisticated despot, or under that of a sophister Syeyes and his colegislative Marsellois, of a Robespierre and his guillotines, of the Triumvirs and their proscriptions. The populace alone in the *minority* of ignorance, the sophisters alone in the *majority* of wickedness and corruption, shall applaud thy mysteries."

Certain of not meeting with such reflections from the adepts, the Hierophant continues to inculcate his principles by attributing every thing to strength, and destroying all principles of morality or of reason, though he will affect the tone of both; and ends by forming his judgment on man in society, as he would judge tigers and wild beasts in the forests.—These are his new doctrines.

"Never did strength submit to weakness.—Nature has destined the weak to serve, because they have wants; the strong man to govern, because he can be useful. Let the one lose his force, and the other acquire it, they will then change situations, and he that obeyed will command. He that stands in need of another, also depends upon him, and he has renounced to him his rights. Hence few wants is the first step towards liberty. *It is for this reason that the savages are the most enlightened of men, and perhaps they alone are free.*[9] When wants are durable, servitude is also lasting. Safety is a durable want. Had men refrained from all injustice, they would have remained free; it was injustice which made them bend beneath the yoke. To acquire safety, they deposited the whole force in the hands of one man; and thus created a new evil, that of fear. The work of their own hands frightened them; and to live in safety they robbed themselves of that very safety. This is the cause of our governments.—*Where then shall we find a protecting force? In union*; but how rare, alas! is that union, except in our new and secret associations, better guided by wisdom, and leagued in straiter bonds! and hence it is that nature itself inclines us toward these associations."

Subtle as is the artifice in this description of human nature, and in that affectation of beholding on the one side nothing but tyrants and despots, and on the other only oppressed and trembling slaves in the state of society; whatever share Nature may have had in the institution of social order, or in reclaiming mankind from forests and wildernesses to live under laws and a common chief; the Hierophant nevertheless exultingly exclaims, "Such is the faithful and philosophic picture of despotism and of liberty, of our wishes and of our fears. Despotism was engrafted on liberty, and from despotism shall liberty once more spring. The re-union of men in society is at once the cradle and the grave of despotism; it is aso the grave and cradle of liberty. *We were once possessed of liberty, and we lost it but to find it again and never lose it more; to learn by the very privation of it the art of better enjoying it in future."* Reader, observe these words; if they do not evidently point out the object of the Sect, if you do not perceive the wish of bringing mankind back to those times of the *nomade herds* of *savages*, and of men destitute of *property*, laws, or government, read and convince yourself by what follows: "*Nature drew men from the savage state and re-united them in civil societies; from these societies we proceed to further wishes, and to a wiser choice (aus den staaten tretten wir in neue klüger gewählte). New associations present themselves to these wishes, and by their means we return to the state whence we came, not again to run the former course, but better to enjoy our new destiny*——let us explain this mystery."

"*Men then had passed from their peaceable state to the yoke of servitude; Eden, that terrestrial paradise, was lost to them. Subjects of sin and slavery, they were reduced to servitude and obliged to gain their bread by the sweat of their brow.*—In the number of these men some promised to protect, and thus became their chiefs—at first they reigned over herds or clans—these were soon conquered, or united together in order to form a numerous people; hence arose nations and their chiefs—kings of nations. At the formation of states and nations, the world ceased to be a great family, to be a single empire; the great bond of nature was rent asunder."

The impudence of such assertions must astonish the reader; he will ask himself can there possibly exist beings thus belying evidence itself, and pretending to show the universe forming but one and the same family, and the grand bond of nature in those roaming and scattered herds, where the child can scarcely walk when he is separated from his father? How is it possible to represent mankind as divorcing from the great family, at the very period when they unite under the same chiefs and the same laws, for their mutual protection and safety? But, reader, suspend thy indignation. Let us call up in evidence against the Sect those brigands and sophisticted murderers which it decorated with the high-sounding title of *Patriots*, and which it stimulated to bloodshed and methodized murder by the fanaticizing sounds of *people, nation, country*. At the very time that they rend the air with such accents, with names so dear as they pretend, hear the maledictions which their mysteries heap upon every *people*, every *nation*, every *country*.

At that period, when men re-united and formed nations, "they ceased to acknowledge a common name—*Nationalism, or the love for a particular nation*, took place of the general love. With the division of the globe, and of its states, benevolence was restrained within certain limits, beyond which it could no longer trespass.—Then it became a merit to extend the bounds of states at the expence of the neighbouring ones. Then it became lawful to abuse, offend, and despise foreigners, to attain that end—*and this virtue was styled patriotism*; and he was styled *a patriot* who, just toward his countrymen, and unjust to others, was blind to the merits of strangers, and believed the very vices of his own country to be perfections.—In such a case, why not restrain that love within a narrower compass, to citizens living in the same town, or to the members of one family; or why even should not each person have concentrated his affections in himself. *We really beheld Patriotism generating Localism, the confined spirit of families, and at length Egoism. Hence the origin of states and governments, and of civil society, has really proved to be the seeds of discord, and Patriotism has found its punishment in itself....Diminish, reject that love of the country, and mankind will once more learn to know and love each other as men*. Partiality being cast aside, that union of hearts will once more appear and expand itself—on the contrary, extend the bonds of *Patriotism*, and you will teach man that it is impossible to blame the closer contraction of love, to a single family, to a single person, in a word, to the *strictest Egoism*."

But let us abridge these blasphemies. The Hierophant, under pretence of his universal love, may vent his spleen against the distinctions of *Greeks* or *Romans*, of French or English, of Italian or Spanish, of *Pagan* or *Jew*, of *Christians* or *Mahometans*, which denote nations and their religions: he may repeat, if he pleases, that amidst these different denominations that *of man is overlooked*; what will be the result of such declamation?—With our illuminizing doctor, in common with every class of the disorganizing Sophisters, is not this pretended universal love to be a cloak for the most odious hypocrisy? He only pretends to universal philanthropy, that he may dispense with loving his neighbour. He detests the love of one's country, only because he detests the laws of nations; he cannot even brook the love of one's family (he has given us a fine specimen in the person of his sister), and he will substitute that universal love because he is no more attached to them than he is to the Chinese, the Tartar, or the Hottentot, which he neither has seen nor ever will see, and that all human nature may be equally indifferent to him. He extends the bond that it may lose its elasticity and discontinue its action.—He calls himself citizen of the universe, that he may cease to be a citizen in his own country, a friend in society, or a fond father and dutiful child in his own family. His love, he tells us, extends from pole to pole, that he may love nothing that is near him. Such is the philanthropy of our Cosmopolites!

The proselyte stands astonished in stupid admiration at these expressions of universal love.—The Hierophant proceeds to the *Codes of Nations*. Still in extasy at these doctrines, he learns that they are in direct opposition *to the laws of nature*; nor will he even perceive that his new code is in direct opposition to the very first laws of nature, as it eradicates the love of one's own family and that of one's country. Nor will he ask, why the fulfilling of his duty toward his fellow-countrymen should hinder him from treating the barbarian or the savage with proper affection? Then follow new sophisms, to persuade the adept that the original fault of man was, the dereliction of the Equality and Liberty of the savage state by the institution of civil laws.

Here, more than ever, are calumny and hatred blended with enthusiasm by the Hierophant, who, reviewing the different ages of the world since the existence of civil institutions, pictures nations as groaning under oppression, despotism, and slavery, or glutted with the blood of wars and revolutions, which always terminate in tyranny. At one time it is the representation of Kings surrounding themselves with herds or legions called soldiers, in order to gratify their ambition by conquests on strangers, or to reign by terror over their enslaved subjects; at other times, it is the people themselves brandishing their arms, not to attack tyranny in its source, but merely to change their tyrants. If they think of giving themselves representatives, it is these very representatives, *who, forgetting that they only hold their missions and powers from the people, form Aristocracies and Oligarchies*, which all end by flowing into the general reservoir of Monarchy and Despotism. He never loses sight of his sophism of human nature degraded and vilified under the yoke of tyranny. These declamations, enthusiastically pronounced, at length make the proselyte exclaim, in unison with his master, *"Are such then the consequences of the institution of states and of civil society? O folly! oh people! that you did not foresee the fate that awaited you; that you should yourselves have seconded your despots in degrading human nature to servitude, and even to the condition of the brute!"*

Could a true Philosopher have been present, his heart must have burst with generous indignation; he would have abruptly challenged the Hierophant to declare whence he had learned to metamorphose the annals of society into those of brigands and monsters? Is the history of man then reduced to the records of plagues, famines, storms, tempests, or of convulsed elements? Have no serene days shone on man? Shall the sun be represented as a malevolent object, because it is sometimes obscured by fogs or clouds? Are we to fly from our habitations because many have been destroyed by fire? Shall we curse life and health because we are subject to pains and infirmities? Why else this fable painting of the disasters which have in the course of ages befallen civil society? Why are we to be silent on the misfortunes from which it has preserved us, or on the advantages which it has heaped on man, in reclaiming him from the forests?

But the voice of reason cannot penetrate into the den of conspiracy. The oracles of Weishaupt shall there be confidently repeated by the Hierophant. He draws nigher and nigher to the grand object, to the means of making those misfortunes disappear, which originate, as he pretends, in the institution of laws and governments. "Oh nature!" he continues, "how great and incontestible are thy rights? It is from the womb of disaster and mutual destruction that the means of safety spring! Oppression disappears because it meets with abettors, and reason regains its rights because people wish to stifle it. He, at least, who wishes to mislead others, should seek to govern them by the advantages of instruction and science. Kings themselves at length perceive, that there is little glory in reigning over ignorant herds—Legislators begin to acquire wisdom, and they favour *property* and industry:—perverse motives propagate the sciences, and Kings protect them as agents of oppression. Other men profit of them to investigate the origin of their rights. They at length seize on that unknown mean of forwarding a revolution in the human mind, and of thus triumphing for ever over oppression. But the triumph would be of short duration, and man would fall back into his degraded state, had not Providence in those distant ages husbanded the means which it has transmitted down to us, of secretly meditating and at length operating the salvation of human kind.

"*Those means are, the secret schools of Philosophy. Those schools have been in all ages the archives of nature and* OF THE RIGHTS OF MAN. These schools *shall one day retrieve the fall of human nature,* AND PRINCES AND NATIONS SHALL DISAPPEAR FROM THE FACE OF THE EARTH, *and that without any violence.* Human nature shall form one great family, and the earth shall become the habitation of the man of reason.—Morality shall alone produce this great Revolution. *The day shall come when each father shall, like Abraham and the Patriarchs, become the Priest and absolute Sovereign of his family.* REASON SHALL BE THE ONLY BOOK OF LAWS, *the sole Code of man.* THIS IS ONE OF OUR GRAND MYSTERIES. *Attend to the demonstration of it, and learn how it has been transmitted down to us.*"

I have already said, that had my object been only to prove the reality of a Conspiracy formed by Illuminism against the existence of every society, every civil Code, and every nation; these lessons of the Hierophant would render every other proof superfluous. But that the reader may know the full extent of the dangers which threaten us, it is necesssary that he should be shown how those plots of frenzy become really transformed into plots of profound wickedness; that he should be acquainted with the means employed enthusiastically to inflame the minds of whole legions of adepts. Let us then attend to the Hierophant. If patience be necessary to follow him, greater still has it been necessary to enable me to transcribe such doctrines.

"What strange blindness can have induced men to imagine that human nature was always to be governed as it has hitherto been.

"Where shall we find a man acquainted with all the resources of nature? Who dare prescribe limits, and say *thus far shalt thou proceed, and no farther*, to that nature, whose law is unity in the variegated infinite? Whence shall issue the command, that it shall always run the same course, and for ever renew it again—Where is the being who has condemned men, the best, the wisest, and the most enlightened of men, to perpetual slavery? *Why should human nature be bereft of its most perfect attribute, that of governing itself? Why are those persons to be always led who are capable of conducting themselves? Is it then impossible for mankind or at least the greater part, to come to their majority?* If one be enabled to do it why should not another; show to one person what you have taught another; teach him the grand art of mastering his passions and regulating his desires; teach him, that from his earliest youth he stands in need of others; that he must abstain from giving offence if he wishes not to be offended; that he must be beneficent if he wishes to receive favours. Let him be patient, indulgent, wise, and benevolent. Let these virtues be made easy to him by principles, experience, and examples; and you will soon see whether he needs another to conduct him? If it be true, that the greater part of mankind are too weak or too ignorant to conceive these simple truths, and to be convinced by them; Oh then our happiness will be at an end, and let us cease to labour at rendering mankind better, or at seeking to enlighten them."

"Oh prejudice! oh contradiction of the human mind! shall the empire of reason, the capacity of governing ourselves, be but a chimerical dream for the greater number of men, while on the other hand prejudice leads us to believe that such is the inherent right of the children of Kings, of reigning families, and of every man whom wisdom or particular circumstances render independent!"

What horrid artifice is contained in these sentences! The poor proselyte really imagines that he sees the most striking contradictions in the very foundations of our civil societies. He really thinks that we believe them to rest on the hereditary privilege of Kings and of their children, to be born with all the necessary wisdom to conduct themselves, while nature has refused such gifts to other mortals; though Weishaupt, who scoffs in private at the credulity and folly of his adepts, knows as well as we do, that such has never been the idea even of the most ignorant populace. He knews that we believe Kings to be born children like other men, with the same weaknesses, the same passions, and like incapacity; he knows as well as we do, that the gift of conducting ourselves and others is to be acquired by education, and by the helps and lights with which a man may be encompassed; and we know as well as he does, that the child of the most obscure parentage would often make a better king than many Sovereigns; as he might also be an excellent magistrate, or a great general, had he received a proportionate education. But does there hence follow any contradiction in civil society, because, uncertain as to the persons who would be the most proper for governing, but certain of the intrigues and broils which would accompany the election of Kings, it has obviated those inconveniencies by hereditary crowns and empires? And after all, what is the meaning of that sophisticated pretence founded on the poeer of being able to conduct oneself? Question the most prudent and the wisest of men, and he will readily say, though I do not stand in need of laws, magistrates, or Kings, to restrain me from being unjust toward others, or from oppressing and plundering, I yet want their assistance to secure me from being oppressed or plundered. The less I am inclined to injure others, the more I need the protection of the law from all injury. You are pleased to call my submission to the laws slavery; I, on the contrary, look to it as my safety, and as the guarantee of that liberty which enables me to do good and to live happy and at peace in society. I have never heard of laws which forbad me to live like an honest man. It is the wicked man only who recognises liberty but in the impunity of his crimes; I scorn such liberty, and bless the hand that deprives me of it. You call him a tyrant and a despot, I call him my King and my benefactor. The better I know how to conduct myself with respect to others, the more thankful I am to him who hinders others from behaving ill to me.

The reader must pardon me these reflections; I know they are superfluous to those who think; but may not this work fall into the hands of persons as credulous as the unhappy proselyte. In exposing the envenomed weapons of the Sect, let it not be said that I withhold the antidote. Should any be still blind enough not to perceive the tendency of all these sophisms of Illuminism, let them hearken to the Sect ardently declaring their hopes; the Hierophant continues:

"Are we then fallen from our dignity so low as not even to feel our chains, or to hug them, and not cherish the flattering hope of being able to break them, or to recover our liberty, not by rebellion or violence (for the time is not yet come), but by force of reason. Because a thing cannot be accomplished to-morrow, should we despair of ever being able to effect it? *Abandon such short-sighted men to their own reasonings and their own conclusions; they may conclude again and again; but nature will continue to act. Inexorable to all their interested remonstrances, she proceeds, and nothing can impede her majestic course. Some events may take place contrary to our wishes; but they will all rectify of themselves; inequalities will be levelled, and a lasting calm shall succeed the tempest.* The only conclusion to be drawn from all these objections is, that we are too much accustomed to the present state of things, or perhaps self-interest has too great sway over us, *to let us own that it is not impossible to attain universal indepen-*

dence—Let then the laughers laugh and the scoffers scoff. He that observes and compares what Nature has done with what she does at present, will soon see, that in spite of all our intrigues she tends invariably toward her object. Her proceedings are imperceptible to him who reflects but little; they are visible only to the sage whose mind's eye penetrates even to the womb of time.—From the summit of the mount he discovers in the horizon that distant country, the very existence of which is not surmised by the servile multitude of the plain."

The principal means which Weishaupt offers to his adepts for the conquest of this land of promise, this soil of independence, are, to diminish the wants of the people, and to enlighten their minds. Hearken to his lessons, you who, heretofore protected by your laws, peaceably exercised an honourable and lucrative profession, and you who, once rivals of the flourishing commerce of Great Britain on the immensity of the ocean, are now but the sorrowful and dejected coasters of the Texel, imprudent disciples of a disorganizing Sect.—Learn, that it is in the secret hatred sworn against you by the Sect in its mysteries that you are to seek the destruction of Lyons, the pillage of Bourdeaux, the ruin of Nantes and Marseilles, the fate, in short, of so many other towns flourishing in commerce, even the fate of Amsterdam itself; and then let your aching eye glance on your trees of Equality and Liberty. At the very time when you thought that you were seconding the views of the Sect against the Nobles, Priests, and Monarchs, only to reinstate the people in their rights of Equality and Liberty, the Sect was aiming its blows at you as the grand artificers of Despotism. At that very period your profession was already proscribed by the mysteries, as that which of all others most surely tended to retain the people in slavery; the Illuminizing Jacobin was teaching his adepts, that "he who wishes to subject nations to his yoke, need but to create wants which he alone can satisfy.—Erect the *mercantile tribe* (die kaufmanschaft) into an hierarchical body; that is to say, confer on it some rank or some authority in the government, and you will have created the most formidable, the most *despotic* of all powers. You will see it giving laws to the universe, and on it alone will rest the independence of one part of the world and the slavery of the other. For that man dictates the law who has it in his power to create or foresee, to stifle, weaken, or satisfy want. And who are better enabled to do this than merchants?" Thus we see that those men who were such ardent supporters of Jacobinism in our commercial towns, with a view to partake of the government, are precisely those whose profession the profound Jacobin chiefly detests in every form of government. May the elucidation of this mystery inspire the industrious inhabitants of hospitable Britain with new zeal for their laws! The discovery of such a snare is of too great importance to their safety, to allow me to conceal it from them.

In the next place the Hierophant proceeds from the art of diminishing wants in order to operate the independence of nations, to the duty of diffusing what he calls light. "He on the contrary (those are his words) "who wishes to render mankind free, teaches them how to refrain from the acquisition of things which they cannot afford: he enlightens them, he infuses into them boldness and inflexible manners. He that teaches them sobriety, temperance, and œconomy, is more dangerous to the throne than the man who openly preaches regicide.—If you cannot diffuse at the same instant this degree of light among all men, at least begin by enlightening yourself, and by rendering yourself better. *Serve, assist, and mutually support each other; augment our numbers; render yourselves at least independent, and leave to time and posterity the care of doing the rest.* When your numbers shall be augmented to a certain degree, when you shall have acquired strength by your union, *hesitate no longer, but begin to render yourself powerful and formidable to the wicked* (that is to say to all who will resist their plans); the very circumstance of your being sufficiently numerous to talk of force, and that you really do talk of it, that circumstance alone makes the prophane *and wicked* tremble—That they may not be overpowered by numbers, many will become good (like you) of themselves, and will join your party.—*You will soon acquire sufficient force to bind the hands of your opponents, to subjugate them and to stifle wickedness in the embryo.*" That is to say, as it may be understood in future, you will soon be able to stifle every principle of law, of government, of civil or political society, whose very institution in the eyes of an Illuminee is the germ of all the vices and misfortunes of human nature. "The mode of diffusing universal light, is not to proclaim it at once to the whole world, *but to begin with yourself; then turn toward your next neighbour; you two can enlighten a third and fourth; let these in the same manner extend and multiply the number of the children of light, until numbers and force shall throw power into our hands.*"[10]

I observe in the ritual of this degree, that should the Hierophant be fatigued by the length of this discourse, he may take breath, and let one of the adepts continue the instruction of the proselyte.[11] Our readers also may avail themselves of this permission, and they have copious matter for reflection in what they have hitherto read. They may perhaps be inclined to ask, to what degree the people must dinimish their wants not to stand in need of laws? They will perceive that bread itself must be denied them; for as long as fields are cultivated, laws will be necessary to protect the crops and to restrain men from reaping that which they have not sown; and if on the first view the Sophism appears wicked, the reader will soon perceive that it is but folly in the garb of Sophistry.

The better to form their judgments on the lessons of the Hierophant, they will have to compare that Revolution, *which is to be the effect of instruction alone, and which is insensibly to take place without the least shock or rebellion*, with that period when the adepts shall have acquired *numbers, force,* and power, enabling them to *bind the hands of their opponents,* and *to subjugate* all who may still show any affection for their laws, or for that civil order in society which the Sect wishes to suppress.

---

1. Philo to Spartacus.—Instructions for this degree.
2. Instruction for this degree.

3. Ibid. Further instructions on the admission to the degree of Priest.
4. Ibid. Further instructions on the admission to the degree of Priest.
5. Original Writings, Vol. II. Part 2.
6. Last works of Philo and Spartacus, from Page 10 to 70, and certificates of Philo at the beginning of this degree.
7. I have compared the two editions of this discourse. The first gives it just as Weishaupt composed and pronounced it at his first initiations. The second has been corrected by his adept the Baron Knigge, known by the characteristic of Philo. All the difference that I could observe was, a slight refinement of the style in some parts, while prolix passages had been added in others. I remarked, that the Compiler Knigge had literally copied all the impious, seditious, and frantic lessons of the original—I have given the preference to the original. In place of adding, I shall rather retrench, and only mention the most striking passages, making such reflexions as circumstances may require. Weishaupt, according to the idiom of the German language, always addressed the Candidate in the third person plural: in this particular, we have followed Knigge's correction, as more suitable with our language.
8. Orig. Writ. Vol. II. Let 18, from Weishaupt to Zwack.
9. Darum sind wilde, und im höchsten grad aufgeklärte, vieleicht, die einzige freye menschen.
10. See Discourse on the lesser Mysteries of Illuminism.
11. This Discourse actually requires at least two hours to read it. That part from which I have made extracts extends in Vol. II. of the *Original Writings*, from Page 44 to 93, and in the *Last works of Philo and Spartacus*, (which are in much smaller print) from Page 10 to 48. I mean to abridge the remaining part still more; but shall be scrupulously exact in the translation of all remarkable passages.

CHAP. X.

Continuation of the Discourse on the Lesser Mysteries

IN that part of the discourse which remains to be laid before the reader, the Hierophant, insisting on the necessity of enlightening the people to operate the grand revolution, seems to fear that the Candidate has not clearly conceived the real plan of this revolution, which is in future to be the sole object of all his instructions. "Let your instructions and lights be univerally diffused; so shall you render mutual security universal; *and security and instruction will enable us to live without prince or government.* If that were not the case, why should we go in quest of either?"[1]

Here then the Candidate is clearly informed of the grand object towards which he is to direct all his future instructions. To teach the people to live without *princes or governments*, without laws or even civil society, is to be the general tendency of all his lessons. But of what nature must these lessons be to attain the desired object?—*They are to treat of morality, and of morality alone.* "For (continues the Hierophant) if light be the work of morality, light and security will gain strength as morality expands itself. *Nor is true morality any other than the art of teaching men to shake off their wardship, to attain the age of manhood, and thus to need neither princes nor governments."*[2]

When we shall see the Sect enthusiastically pronouncing the word *morality,* let us recollect the definition which it has just given us of it. Without it, we could not have understood the real sense of the terms *honest men, virtue, good* or *wicked men.* We see that, according to this definition, *the honest man* is he who labours at the overthrow of civil society, its laws, and its chiefs: for these are the only crimes or virtues mentioned in the whole Code. Presupposing that the Candidate may object that it would be impossible to bring mankind to adopt such doctrines, the Hierophant anticipates the objection, and exclaims, "He is little acquainted with the powers of reason and the attractions of virtue; he is a very novice in the regions of light, who shall harbour such mean ideas as to his own essence, or the nature of mankind....If either he or I can attain this point, why should not another attain it also? What! when men can be led to despise the horrors of death, when they may be inflamed with the enthusiasm of religious and political follies, shall they be deaf to that very doctrine which can alone lead them to happiness? *No, no; man is not so wicked as an arbitrary morality would make him appear.* He is wicked, because Religion, the State, and bad example, perverts him. It would be of avantage to those who wish to make him better, were there fewer persons whose interest it is to render him wicked in order that they may support their power by his wickedness."

"Let us form a more liberal opinion of human nature. We will labour indefatigably, nor shall difficulties affright us. May our principles become the foundation of all morals! *Let reason at length be the religion of men, and the problem is solved.*"³

This pressing exhortation will enable the reader to solve the problem of *the altars, the worship, and the festivals of Reason,* in the French Revolution; nor will they be any longer at a loss to know from what loathsome den their shameless Goddess rose.

The Candidate also obtains the solution of all that may have appeared to him problematic in the course of his former trials. "Since such is the force of morality and of morality alone (says the Hierophant), since it alone can operate the grand revolution which is to restore liberty to mankind, and abolish the empire of imposture, superstition, and despotism; you must now perceive why on their first entrance into our Order we oblige our pupils to apply closely to the study of morality, to the knowledge of themselves and of others. You must see plainly, that if we permit each Novice to introduce his friend, *it is in order to form a legion that may more justly be called holy and invincible than that of the Thebans*; since the battles of the friend fighting by the side of his friend are those which are to reinstate human nature in its rights, its liberty, and its primitive independence."

"The morality which is to perform this miracle is not a morality of vain subtleties. It is not that morality which, degrading man, renders him careless of the goods of this world, forbids him the enjoyment of the innocent pleasures of life, and inspires him with the hatred of his neighbour. It must not be a morality favouring the interests only of its teachers, which prescribes persecution and intoleration, which militates against reason, which forbids the prudent use of the passions; whose virtues are no other than inaction, idleness, and the heaping of riches on the slothful.—*Above all, it must not be that morality which, adding to the miseries of the miserable, throws them into a state of pusillanimity and despair, by the threats of hell and the fear of devils.*

"It must, on the contrary, be that morality so much disregarded and defaced at the present day by selfishness, and replete with heterogeneous principles. It must be a divine doctrine, such as Jesus taught to his disciples, and of which he gave the real interpretation in his secret conferences."

This sudden transition naturally leads Weishaupt to the developement of a mystery of iniquity for which we have long since seen him preparing his *Major Illuminees,* and particularly the *Scotch Knights* of illuminization. The better to understand this mystery, let us recall to mind how the *Insinuators* or the teachers began by solemnly assuring their different Candidates, Novices, or *Minerval* Academicians, that in all the lodges of Illuminism there never arises a question in the least degree prejudicial to religion or the state. All these promises have been gradually lost sight of, and the proselyte has had time to accustom his ears to declamations against the priesthood and royalty. It has already been insinuated, that the Christianity of our times is very different from that taught by Jesus Christ; the time was not arrived for numbering Christ himself among the impostors; his name, his virtues, might still be venerated by certain adepts. Some there were, perhaps, who would be shocked at bare-faced Atheism; and it is on their account that Weishaupt has thus treated of Christ. In the preceding degree he had contented himself with hinting, that the doctrines of this divine teacher had been perverted; nor had he declared what species of political revolution was (as he pretended) pointed out in the Gospel. But here the execrable sophister apostrophizes the God of the Christians in language similar to that in which we have since seen the too famous Fauchet declaiming in the revolutionary pulpit. It is here that Weishaupt declares Jesus Christ to be the Father of the Jacobins, or rather (to speak the revolutionary language) the great Doctor of the *Sans-culottes*. But, to enable us the better to judge of the cunning and premeditated villainy of this detestable artifice, let us first attend to the correspondence of the adept who, under Weishaupt, is charged with the compiling of the Code. Knigge, like the monstrous prototype of Illuminism, subdivides the adepts into those who scoff at and detest revelation, and those who stand in need of a revealed religion to fix their ideas. It is to explain this that Knigge writes the following letter to Zwack:

"To unite these two classes of men, to make them concur and co-operate toward our object, it was necessary to represent Christianity in such a light as to recall the superstitious to reason, and to teach our more enlightened sages not to reject it on account of its abuse. This should have been the secret of Masonry, and have led us to our object. Meanwhile despotism strengthens daily, though liberty universally keeps pace with it. It was necessary then to unite the extremes. We therefore assert here, that Christ did not establish a new religion, but that his intention was simply to reinstate natural religion in its rights; that by giving a general bond of union to the world, by diffusing the light and wisdom of his morality, and by dissipating prejudices, *his intention was, to teach us the means of governing ourselves, and to re-establish, without the violent means of revolutions, the reign of Equality and Liberty among men*. This was easily done by quoting certain texts from Scripture, and by giving explanations of them, *true or false is of little consequence*, provided each one finds a sense in these doctrines of Christ consonant with his reason. We add, that this religion, so simple in itself, was afterwards defaced; but that, by means of inviolable secrecy, it has been transmitted in purity to us through Freemasonry."

"Spartacus (Weishaupt) had collected many materials for this, and I added my discoveries in the instructions for these two degrees. Our people, therefore, being convinced that we alone are possessed of the real secrets of Christianity, *we have but to add a few words against the Clergy and Princes*. In the last mysteries we have to unfold to our adepts *this pious fraud*, and then by writings demonstrate *the origin of all* religious impositions, and their mutual connexion with each other."[4]

If the reader be not too much disgusted with *this pious fraud*, but can still attend to the declamations of the Hierophant, let us once more enter that den of demons wherein presides the triple genius of impiety, hypocrisy, and anarchy.

The Hierophant is about to say, "that their grand and ever-celebrated master, Jesus of Nazareth, appeared in an age when corruption was universal; in the midst of a people who from time immemorial had been subjected to, and severely felt the yoke of slavery;[5] and who eagerly expected their deliverer announced by the Prophets. Jesus appeared and taught the doctrine of reason; to give greater efficacy to these doctrines, he formed them into a religion, and adopted the received traditions of the Jews. He prudently grafted his new school on their religion and their customs, which he made the vehicle of the essence and secrets of his new doctrines. He did not select sages for his new disciples, but ignorant men chosen from the lowest class of the people, to show that his doctrine was made for all, and suitable to every one's understanding; to show too, that the knowledge of the grand truths of reason was not a privilege peculiar to the great. He does not teach the Jews alone, but all mankind, the means of acquiring their liberty, by the observation of his precepts. He supported his doctrines by an innocent life, and sealed them with his blood."

"His precepts for the salvation of the world are, simply, the love of God and the love of our neighbour; he asks no more. . . . Nobody ever reduced and consolidated the bonds of human society within their real limits as he did—No one was ever more intelligible to his hearers, or more prudently covered the sublime signification of his doctrine. *No one, indeed, ever laid a surer foundation for liberty than our grand master, Jesus of Nazareth*. It is true, that on all occasions (*in ganzen*) he carefully concealed the sublime meaning and natural consequences of his doctrines; *for he had a secret doctrine, as is evident* from more than one passage of the Gospel."

It was during the time that he was writing this hypocritical history of the Messiah, that Weishaupt was turning the credulous proselyte into ridicule; as to the other adepts, he well knew that they anticipated such explanations, or at least would be delighted with them. Hence that impudence with which he falsifies the Scriptures. To prove the existence of this secret school, the doctrines of which are reserved for the initiated alone, he cites these words of Christ: "To you is given to know the mystery of the kingdom of God; but to them that are without, all things are done in parables."[6] But he carefully avoids mentioning the order which Christ gives to his disciples, "That which I tell you in the dark, speak ye in the light; and that which you hear in the ear, preach ye upon the house-tops."[7] Weishaupt then proceeds to these words: "And their princes have power over them—but it is not so among you; but whoever will be greater shall be your minister."[8] This precept, as well as all those on Christian humility, he transforms into principles of disorganizing equality inimical to all constituted authorities.—With equal ease he avoids all those lessons so often repeated both by Christ and his Apostles, on the obligation of rendering to Cæsar what is Cæsar's, of paying tribute, and of recognizing the authority of God himself in that of the law and of the magistrates. If Christ has preached the love of our neighbour, or fraternal love, his words are immediately perverted by *Weishaupt* into a love of *his* Equality. If Christ exhorts his disciples to contemn riches, the impostor pretends it is *to prepare the world for that community of riches* which destroys all property. In fine, the conclusions drawn from these impious and deriding explanations, and from many others of a similar nature, are contained in the following words:

"If therefore *the object* of the secret of Jesus, which has been preserved by the institution of the mysteries, and clearly demonstrated both by the conduct and the discourses of this divine master, *was to reinstate mankind in their original Equality and Liberty*, and to prepare the means; how many things immediately appear clear and natural, which hitherto seemed to be contradictory and unintelligible! *This explains in what sense Christ was the saviour and the liberator of the world. Now the doctrine of original sin, of the fall of man, and of his regeneration, can be understood. The state of pure nature, of fallen or corrupt nature, and the state of grace, will no longer be a problem. Mankind, in quitting their state of original liberty, fell from the state of nature and lost their dignity. In their civil society, under their governments, they no longer live in the state of pure nature, but in that of fallen and corrupt nature. If the moderating of their passions and the diminution of their wants, reinstate them in their primitive dignity, that will really constitute their redemption and their state of grace. It is to this point that morality, and the most perfect of all morality, that of Jesus, leads mankind. When at length this doctrine shall be generalized throughout the world, the reign of the good and of the elect shall be established.*"[9]

This language is surely not enigmatical. The proselyte, once master of the mysteries it contains, needs only to be informed, how the great revolution, which they foretell, became the object of secret societies, and what advantages accrue to these societies from the secresy in which they exist.

The Hierophant then, for the instruction of the proselyte, goes back to the origin of Masonry; he declares it to be the original school and depository of the true doctrine. He takes a view of its hieroglyphics, and shapes them to his system. The *rough stone* of Masonry becomes the symbol of the *primitive state* of man, *savage but free*.—*The stone split or broken is* the state of *fallen nature, of mankind in civil society, no longer united in one family, but divided according to their states, governments, or religions. The polished stone represents mankind reinstated in its primitive dignity, in its independence.* Yet Masonry has not only lost these explanations; but the illuminizing orator goes so far as to say, "*The Freemasons, like Priests and chiefs of nations, have banished reason from the earth. They have inundated the world with tyrants, impostors, spectres, corpses, and men like to wild beasts.*"

Should any reader be surprised at seeing the Hierophant give this account of Masonry, let him reflect on the hatred which Weishaupt had sworn against every school where the name of any deity was preserved. The *Jehovah* or the *Grand Architect* of Masonry, the *two-fold God* of the Rosycrusian magicians, still render the occult lodges a school of some sort of Theosophy. But how reserved soever the Hierophant may be with regard to Atheism, the proselyte must, nevertheless, foresee, that should he be admitted to one degree higher, neither the *Grand Architect* nor the *two-fold God* will meet a better fate than the God of the Christians. And therefore it is that Weishaupt declaims against those *spirits, apparitions*, and all the *superstitions* of Freemasonry; hence the theosophic Masons are involved in the general malediction pronounced against the priesthood and the throne.

It can be easily conceived, that Weishaupt must represent true Masonry, or the pretended real Christianity, as solely extant in Illuminism. But the Hierophant enjoins the proselyte *not to think that this is the only advantage which the Order and the whole universe draw from this mysterious association.*

Here let magistrates, the chiefs of nations, every man who still retains any regard for the support of laws and empires, and of civil society, let them, I say, read and meditate on these other advantages. The lesson is of the utmost importance——Whoever you are, all honest citizens, whether *Masons, Rosycrusians, Mopses, Hewers of Wood, Knights*; all you who thirst after the mysteries of the lodges, cease to accuse me of conjuring up chimerical dangers. I am not the man who speaks: it is he who of all others has been the *best acquainted* with your association, and has known what advantages could be drawn from them by able and patient conspirators.—Read; and tell us which is the most impressive on your mind, the pleasures you may find in your lodges, or the dangers of your country. Read; and if the name of citizen be still dear to you, reflect whether yours should remain inscribed on the registers of a secret society. You were ignorant of the dangers; the most monstrous of conspirators will lay them open to you, and he will call them advantages. He literally says, "Though these mysterious Associations should not attain our object, they prepare the way for us; they give a new interest to the cause; they present it under points of view hitherto unobserved; they stimulate the inventive powers and the expectations of mankind; *they render men more indifferent as to the interests of governments*; they bring men of divers nations and religions within the same bond of union; *they deprive the church and the state of their ablest and most laborious members*; they bring men together who would never otherwise have known or met each other. *By this method alone they undermine the foundation of states, though they had really no such project in view. They throw them together and make them clash one against the other.* They teach mankind the power and force of union; they point out to them the imperfection of their *political constitutions*, and that without exposing them to the suspicions of their enemies, such as magistrates and public governments. They *mask our progress, and procure us the facility of incorporating in our plans and of admitting into our Order, after the proper trials, the most able men, whose patience, long abused, thirsts after the grand ultimatum.* By this means they weaken the enemy; and though they should never triumph over him, *they will at least diminish the numbers and the zeal of his partizans*; they divide his troops *to cover the attack.* In proportion as these new associations or secret societies, formed in different states, shall acquire strength and prudence at the expence of the former ones (that is to say, of civil society), *the latter must weaken, and insensibly fall.*"

"Beside, our Society originates, and must naturally and essentially deduce its origin from those very governments whose vices have rendered our union necessary. We have no object but that better order of things for which we incessantly labour; *all the efforts, therefore, of Princes to stop our progress will be fruitless; the spark may long remain hidden in the ashes, but the day must come in which shall burst forth the general flame.* For nature nauseates always to run the same course. The heavier the yoke of oppression weighs on man, the more sedulously will he labour to throw it off; and the liberty he seeks shall expand itself. *The seed is sown whence shall spring a new world; the roots extend themselves; they have acquired too much strength, they have been too industriously propagated, for the day of harvest to fail us.*—Perhaps it may be necessary to wait thousands and thousands of years; but sooner or later nature shall consummate its grand work, and she shall restore *that dignity* to man *for which he was destined from the beginning.*"

Reader, you have heard them. These conspirators have said more than I should have dared to hint at on the nature and danger of these associations. It would be useless for me to rest longer on that point. I shall end by showing by what artifices the Hierophant endeavours to tranquilize the consciences of those adepts who may have been startled at these predictions. Notwithstanding all that he has said of those times when Illuminism shall find means of *binding hands and subjugating*; notwithstanding all that aversion against governments which he seeks to infuse into the adepts, he concludes in a hypocritical strain peculiar to his wickedness. "We are here at once the observers and the instruments of nature.—We do not wish to precipitate her steps. To enlighten men, to correct their morals, to inspire them with benevolence, such are our means. Secure of success, we abstain from violent commotions. To have foreseen the happiness of posterity, and to have prepared it by irreproachable means, suffices for our felicity. The tranquility of our consciences is not troubled by the reproach of aiming at the ruin or overthrow of states and thrones. Such an accusation could with no more propriety be preferred against us, than it might against the statesmen who had foreseen and foretold the impending and inevitable ruin of the state.—As assiduous observers of Nature, we admire her majestic course; and, burning with the noble pride of our origin, we felicitate ourselves on being the chidlren of men and of God."

"But carefully observe and remember, that we do not impose our opinions; we do not oblige you to adopt our doctrines. Let the truth you can acknowledge be your only guide. Free man, exercise here thy primitive right; seek, doubt, examine; do you know of, or can you find elsewhere, any thing that is better?—Make us acquainted with your views, as we have exposed ours to you. We do not blush at the limits of our understandings; we know that we are but men; we know that such are the dispositions of nature, such the lot of man, that he is not to expect to attain perfection at his outset; he can attain it but by degrees. It is by gaining experience from our errors, by profiting of the lights acquired by our forefathers, that we shall become at once the children of wisdom, and the parents of a still wiser progeny. If, therefore, you think that you have found truth in the whole of our doctrine, adopt the whole. Should you perceive any error to have stolen in with it, remember that truth is not the less estimable on that account. If you have met with nothing that pleases you here, reject the whole without fear; and remember, that in many things, at least, we only need further research, or a new investigation. Do you observe any thing blameable or laudable, see and make choice of what you approve. Should you be more enlightened yourself, then your eye may have discovered truths which are still denied to us. The more art we employ in the instruction of our pupils to lead them to the paths of wisdom, the less you will be inclined to refuse us a portion of your applause."

Thus ends the discourse of the Hierophant.—The proselyte who has heard it without shuddering, may flatter himself with being worthy of this priesthood. But before he is sacrilegiously anointed, he is led back to the porch, where he is invested with a white tunic. He wears a broad silken scarlet belt; the sleeve is tied at the extremity and middle with bandages of the same colour, which make it bulge out.[10] I am particular in the description of this dress, because it was in a similar one that, during the French revolution, a comedian appeared personally attacking Almighty God, saying, "No! thou dost not exist. If thou hast power over the thunder bolts, grasp them; aim them at the man who dares set thee at defiance in the face of thy altars. But no, I blaspheme thee, and I still live. No, thou dost not exist." In the same costume, and to prepare him for the same blasphemies, the Epopt is recalled into the temple of mysteries. He is met by one of the Brethren, who does not permit him to advance till he has told him, "that he is sent to enquire whether he (the proselyte) has perfectly understood the discourse which has been read to him—whether he has any doubts concerning the doctrines which are contained in it—whether his heart is penetrated with the sanctity of the principles of the Order—whether he is sensible of the call, feels the strength of mind, the fervent will, and all the disinterestedness requisite to labour at the grand undertaking—whether he is ready to make a sacrifice of his will, and to suffer himself to be led by the most excellent superiors of the Order."

I will spare the reader the disgusting impiety of the ceremonial which immediately follows.—The rites of the preceding degree were in derision of the Last Supper; these are an atrocious mimicry of the sacerdotal ordination. A curtain is drawn, and an altar appears with a crucifix upon it. On the altar also is a Bible; and the ritual of the Order lies on a reading desk; on the side a censer, and a phial full of oil. The Dean acts the part of a Bishop, and he is surrounded with acolytes. He prays over the proselyte, blesses him, cuts hair from the top of his head, clothes him in the vestments of the priesthood, and pronounces prayers after the fashion of the Sect. On presenting the cap he says, "*Cover thyself with this cap, it is more valuable than the crown of kings.*" The very expressions of the Jacobin with his red cap. The communion consists in honey and milk, which the Dean gives to the proselyte, saying, "This is what Nature gives to man. Reflect how happy he would still have been, if the desire of superfluities had not, by depriving him of a taste for such simple food, multiplied his wants, and poisoned the balm of life."

All the preceding part of this degree sufficiently explains the real meaning of these words. The ceremonies are terminated with delivering to the Epopt that part of the code which relates to his new degree. I shall relate all that is necessary for the reader to be informed of, when, after having treated of the degree of Regent, and of the Grand Mysteries, I shall come to investigate the government of the Order.

1. Und allgemeine aufklärung und sicherheit machen fürsten und staaten entbehrlich. Oder wo zu braucht man sie sodann.
2. Die moral ist also die kunst welche menschen lehrt volljährig zu werden, der vormundschaft los zu werden, in ihr männliches alter zu tretten, und die fürsten zu entbehren.
3. Und endlich macht die vernunft zur religion der menschen, so ist die aufgabe aufgelösst.
4. Orig. Writ. Vol. II. Letter from Philo to Cato, page 104, and following.
5. Here is another example of the manner in which history is falsified—The Jews were enslaved from time immemorial! Does this nation then make its whole history consist in the years of its captivity? Had it forgot its liberty and its triumphs under Joshua, David, Solomon, and its other Kings? Was it just emerged from its captivity when it fell under the dominion of the Romans, a dominion under which it remained at the time of Christ's birth? The adept has heard talk of the captivity of the Jews, of those periods when Almighty God, as a punishment for their crimes, delivered them over to their enemies; and he inconsiderately concludes, that their whole history is but one continued scene of bondage.
6. St. Mark, Ch. iv. V. 11.
7. St. Matthew. Ch. x. V. 27.
8. St. Mark, Ch. x. V. 42, 43.
9. Orig. Writ. Part II. P. 106,7.—The last Works of Spartacus, P. 58.—The author has transcribed the whole of what is printed in Italics in German, lest his translation of this extraordinary passsage should be suspected of being exaggerated. As he perfectly understands the German language, and is a man of undoubted veracity, I have omitted it, but in so doing think it my duty to mention it. TRANS.
10. Last Works of Philo and Spartacus, at the end of the Discourse.

CHAP. XI.

Eighth Part of the Code of Illuminees—The Regent, or the Prince Illuminee.

"WHEN one of our Epopts has sufficiently distinguished himself to bear a part in the political government of our Order; that is to say, when he unites prudence with *the liberty of thinking and of acting*; when he knows how to temper boldness with precaution, resolution with complaisance; subtlety with good nature; loyalty with simplicity; singularity with method; transcendency of wit with gravity and dignity of manners; when he has learned opportunely to speak or to be silent, how to obey or to command; when he shall have gained the esteem and affection of his fellow-citizens, though feared by them at the same time; when his heart shall be entirely devoted to the interests of our Order, and the common welfare of the universe shall be uppermost in his mind;—then, and only then, let the Superior of the province propose him to the National Inspector as worthy of being admitted to the degree of *Regent*."

Such are the qualities required by the Sect for the admission of its adepts to the degree which in the Code is sometimes termed *Regent*, at others the *Prince Illuminee*. Such are the very words to be found in the preamble of the rules of this degree.

"Three things of the utmost consequence (says the Code) are to be observed. In the first place, the greatest reserve is necesssary with respect to this degree. Secondly, those who are admitted into it must be as much as possible *free men and independent of all Princes*: they must indeed have clearly manifested their *hatred for the general constitution* or the actual state of mankind; have shown how ardently they wish for a change in the government of the world; and how much the hints thrown out in the degree of Priest has inflamed their wishes for a better order of things."

If all these requisites are to be found in the Candidate, then let the National Inspector once more examine, in his records, every thing relative to the conduct and character of the new adept, let him inspect the divers questions which have been put to him, and discover where he has shown his strong or his weak side. According to the result of this examination, let the Inspector propose some new questions on those articles on which the Candidate may have shown the greatest reserve. For example, some of the following:[1]

"I. Would you think a society objectionable, which should (till nature shall have ripened its grand revolutions) place itself in a situation, that would deprive Monarchs of the power of doing harm, though they should wish it; a society whose invisible means should prevent all governments from abusing their power? Would it be impossible, through the influence of such a society, to form a new state in each state, *status in statu*;" that is to say, would it be impossible to subject the rulers of every state to this Illuminizing Society, and to convert them into mere tools of the Order even in the government of their own dominions?

"II. Were it to be objected, that such a society would abuse its power, would not the following considerations do away such an objection?—Do not our present rulers daily abuse their power? And are not the people silent, notwithstanding such an abuse? Is this power as secure from abuse in the hands of Princes, as it would be in those of our adepts whom we train up with so much care? If then any government could be harmless, would it not be our's, which would be entirely founded on morality, foresight, wisdom, liberty, and virtue?"

"III. Though this universal government, founded on morality, should prove chimerical, would it not be *worth while to make an essay of it?*"

"IV. Would not the most sceptical man find a sufficient guarantee against any abuse of power on the part of our Order, in the liberty of abandoning it at pleasure; in the happiness of having Superiors of tried merit, who, unknown to each other, could not possibly support each other in their treasonable combinations against the general welfare; Superiors, in short, who would be deterred from doing harm by the fear of the existing chiefs of empires?"

"V. Should there exist any other secret means of guarding against the abuse of that authority entrusted by the order to our Superiors, what might they be?"

"VI. Supposing despotism were to ensure, would it be dangerous in the hands of men who, from the very first step we made in the Order, teach us nothing but science, liberty, and virtue? Would not that despotism lose its sting, in the consideration that those chiefs who may have conceived dangerous plans will have begun by disposing a machine in direct opposition to their views."[2]

To understand the tendency of these questions, let us reflect on the meaning given by the Sect to *liberty* and *general welfare*. Above all, let us not forget the lesson already given to the adepts on morality; the art of teaching men to shake off the yoke of their minority, to set aside Princes and Rulers, and to learn to govern themselves. This lesson once well understood, the most contracted understanding must perceive, in spite of the insidious tenour of these questions, that their sole tendency is to ask, whether "a Sect would be very dangerous who, under pretence of hindering the chiefs of nations, Kings, Ministers, and Magistrates, from hurting the people, should begin by mastering the opinions of all those who surrounded Kings, Ministers, or Magistrates; or should seek by invisible means to captivate all the councils, and the agents of public authority, in order to reinstate mankind in the rights of their pretended majority; and to teach the subject to throw off the authority of his Prince, and learn to govern himself; or, in other words, to destroy every King, Minsiter, Law, Magistrate, and public authority whatever?" The Candidate, too well-trained to the spirit of Illuminism not to see the real tendency of these questions, but also too much perverted by it to be startled at them, knows what answers he is to give to obtain the new degree. Should he still harbour doubts, the ceremonies of his installation would divest him of them. These are not theosophical or insignificant ceremonies;—every step demonstrates the disorganizing genius, and the hatred for all authority, which irritates the spleen of their impious author; and it is therefore that Weishaupt, when writing to Zwack, represents them *as infinitely more important* than those of the preceding degree.[3]

When the admission of the new adept is resolved on, he is informed, "that as in future he is to be entrusted with papers belonging to the Order, of far greater importance than any that he has yet had in his possession, it is necessary that the Order should have further securities. He is therefore to make his will, and insert a particular clause with respect to any private papers which he may leave in case of sudden death. He is to get a formal and juridical receipt of that part of his will from his family, or from the public Magistrate, and he is to take their promises in writing that they will fulfil his intentions."[4]

This precaution taken, and the day for the initiation fixed, the adept is admitted into an antichamber hung with black. Its furniture consists in a skeleton elevated on two steps, at the feet of which are laid a crown and a sword—There he is asked for the written dispositions he has made concerning the papers with which he may be entrusted, and the juridical promise he has received that his intentions shall be fulfilled. His hands are then loaded with chains, as if he were a slave; and he is thus left to his meditations.[5] The Provincial who performs the functions of Initiator is alone in the first saloon, seated on a throne. The Introducer, having left the Candidate to his reflections, enters this room, and in a voice loud enough to be heard by the new adept, the following Dialogue takes place between them.

"*Provincial.* Who brought this slave to us?"

"*Introducer.* He came of his own accord; he knocked at the door."

"*Prov.* What does he want?"

"*Introd.* He is in search of Liberty, and asks to be freed from his chains."

"*Prov.* Why does he not apply to those who have chained him?"

"*Introd.* They refuse to break his bonds; they acquire too great an advantage from his slavery."

"*Prov.* Who then is it that has reduced him to this state of slavery?"

"*Introd.* Society, governments, the sciences, and false religion." *Die geselschaft, der staat, die gelehrsamkeit, die falsche religion.*"

"*Prov.* And he wishes to cast off this yoke to become a seditious man and a rebel?"

"*Introd.* No; he wishes to unite with us, to join in our fights against the constitution of governments, the corruption of morals, and the profanation of religion. He wishes through our means to become powerful, that he may attain the grand ultimatum."

"*Prov.* And who will answer to us, that after having obtained that power he will not also abuse it, that he will not be a tyrant and the author of new misfortunes?"

"*Introd.* His heart and his reason are our guarantees—the Order has enlightened him. He has learned to conquer his passions and to know himself. Our Superiors have tried him."

"*Prov.* That is saying a great deal—Is he also superior to prejudice. Does he prefer the general interest of the universe to that of more limited associations?"

"*Introd.* Such have been his promises."

"*Prov.* How many others have made similar promises who did not keep them? Is he master of himself? Can he resist temptation? Are personal considerations of no avail with respect to him? Ask him, whether the skeleton he has before him is that of a king, a nobleman, or a beggar?"

"*Introd.* He cannot tell; nature has destroyed all that marked the depraved state of inequality; all that he sees is, that this skeleton was man like us; and the character of man is all that he attends to."

"*Prov.* If such be his sentiments, let him be free at his own risk and peril. But he knows us not. Go and ask him why he implores our protection?"[6]

This dialogue ended (and the reader will not be at a loss to perceive the drift of it), the Introducer returns to the Candidate, and says, "Brother, the knowledge you have acquired can no longer leave you in doubt as to the grandeur, the importance, the disinterestedness and lawfulness of our great object. It must therefore be indifferent to you whether you are acquainted with our Superiors or not; nevertheless, I have some information to impart to you on that subject."

This information is nothing more than a summary of a pretended history of Masonry, going back to the deluge; and of what the Sect calls the fall of man, the loss of his dignity, and of the true doctrine. The story then continues to Noah and the few who escaped the deluge in the ark; these, he says, were a few Sages or Freemasons, who have maintained the true principles in their secret schools. It is for that reason, says the Instructor, that Masonry has preserved the denominations of *Noachists* and *Patriarchs*—Then comes a recapitulation of what had been said in the degree of *Epopt* on the pretended views of Christ, on the decline of Masonry, and on the honour reserved to Illuminism to preserve and revive these true and ancient mysteries—"When questioned (says the Instructor) as to whom we are indebted to for the actual constitution of our Order, and the present form of the inferior degrees, the following is the answer we give:

"Our founders, without doubt, had extensive knowledge, since they have transmitted so much to us.—Actuated by a laudable zeal for the general welfare, they formed a code of laws for our Order; but, partly through prudence, and partly to guard against their own passions, they left the direction of the edifice they had raised to other hands, and retired. Their names will for ever remain in oblivion—The chiefs who govern the Order at present are not our founders; but posterity will doubly bless those unknown benefactors who have despised the vain glory of immortalizing their names. Every document which could have thrown light on our origin has been committed to the flames."

"You will now be under the direction of other men; men who, gradually educated by the Order, have at length been placed at the helm. You will soon make one of their number—Tell me only, whether you still harbour any doubt as to the object of the Order."

The Candidate, who has long since been past all possibility of doubt, advances with his Introducer toward another saloon; but, on opening the door, several of the adepts run and oppose their entrance.—A new dialogue takes place in the style of the first—Who goes there? Who are you?—Is it a slave who fled from his masters—No slave shall enter here—He has fled that he might cease to be a slave; he craves an asylum and protection—But should his master follow?—He is safe, the doors are shut.—But should he be a traitor?—He is not one, he has been educated under the eyes of the Illuminees. They have imprinted the divine seal on his forehead.—The door opens, and those who opposed the Candidate's entrance escort him to the third saloon. Here new obstacles occur, and another dialogue takes place between an adept in the inside and the Introducer. In the mean time the Provincial has left his former station, and has seated himself upon a throne in this third room. [It is worthy of remark that these enemies of thrones are themselves always seated on a throne.] The Provincial gives orders that the Candidate may be admitted, and desires to see whether he really bears the print of the seal of liberty. The Brethren accompany the new adept to the foot of the throne,

"*Prov.* Wretch! You are a slave: and yet dare enter an assembly of free men! Do you know the fate that awaits you? You have passed through two doors to enter this; but you shall not go hence unpunished, if you prophane this sanctuary."

"*Introd.* That will not happen; I will be his guarantee. You have taught him to thirst after liberty; and now keep your promise."

"*Prov.* Well, Brother, we have subjected you to various trials. The elevation of your sentiments has made us conceive you to be both proper and worthy of being admitted into our Order. You have thrown yourself with confidence and without reserve into our arms: and it is time to impart to you that liberty which we have painted to you in such bewitching colours. *We have been your guide during all the time that you stood in need of one. You are now strong enough to conduct yourself; be then in future your own guide, be it at your own peril and risk. Be free; that is to say, be a man, and a man who knows how to govern himself; a man who knows his duty, and his imprescriptible rights; a man who serves the universe alone; whose actions are solely directed to the general benefit of the world and of human nataure. Every thing else is injustice—Be free and independent; in future be so of yourself.—Here, take back the engagements you have hitherto contracted with us. To you we return them all."*

As he pronounces these words, the Provinical returns him all the writings which concern him, such as his oaths, his promises, the minutes of his admission to the preceding degrees, the history of his life which he had transmitted to the Superiors, and all the notes taken by the Scrutators concerning him.

This perhaps is one of the most delicate traits of policy of the Sect. The chiefs have had full leisure to pry into the most secret recesses of his heaert, and the Scrutators have no further discoveries to make. The Candidate may take back his oaths and his secrets, but recollections (perhaps copies) still remain, and the Initiator may well continue: "In future you will owe us nothing but that which your heart shall dictate. We do not tyrannize over men, we only enlighten them. Have you found contentment, rest, satisfaction, happiness, among us? You will not then abandon us. Can we have mistaken you, or can you have mistaken us! It would be a misfortune for you; but you are free. Remember only that men free and *independent* do not offend each other; on the contrary, they assist and mutually protect each other. Remember, that to offend another man, is to give him the right of defending himself. Do you wish to make a noble use of the power we give to you? rely on our word: you shall find zeal and protection among us. Could a disinterested zeal for your brethren glow in your heart, then labour at the grand object, labour for unfortunate human nature, and thy last hour shall be blest. We ask nothing else from you, we ask nothing for ourselves. Question your own heart, and let it say whether our conduct to you has not been noble and disinterested. After so many favours, could you be ungrateful, your heart should avenge us, and chastise you. But no; many trials have proved you to be man of constancy and resolution. Be such your character, and in future govern with us oppressed man, and labour at rendering him virtuous and free."

"Oh, Brother! what a fight, what hopes! when one day happiness, affection, and peace shall be the inhabitants of the earth! when misery, error, and oppression, shall disappear with superfluous wants! when, each one at his station labouring only for the general good, every father of a family shall be sovereign in his tranquit cot! when *he that wishes to invade these sacred rights shall not find an asylum on the face of the earth*! when idleness shall be no longer suffered! *when the clod of useless sciences shall be cast aside*, and none shall be taught but those which contribute to make man better, and to reinstate him in his primitive freedom, his future destiny! when we may flatter ourselves with having forwarded that happy period, and complacently view the fruits of our labours! when, in fine, each man viewing his brother in his fellow-creature, shall extend a succouring hand—with us and ours you shall find happiness and peace, should you continue faithful and attached to us. You will also remark, that the sign of this degree consists in extending your arms to a brother with your hands open, to show that they are not sullied by injustice and oppression, and the *gripe* is to seize the brother by the two elbows, as it were to hinder him from falling. The *word* is *redemption.*"

The foregoing passsages so clearly demonstrate the meaning of this word *redemption,* that the reader must be surprised at learning that there still remain further mysteries to be revealed.—The candidate is not yet admitted into the highest class. He is only the Prince Illuminee, and has to gain admission to the two degrees of *Philosopher,* and of the *Man King.* He is invested in his new principality by receiving a buckler, boots, a cloak, and a hat. The words pronounced at the investiture are worthy of the reader's attention.

On presenting the bucker, the Initiator says, "Arm thyself with fidelity, truth, and constancy; *be a true Christian,* and the shafts of calumny and misfortune shall not pierce thee." *Be a Christian! (und sey ein Christ)!* ! What a strange Christian; what a wicked wretch then must be the Initiator who dares carry his dissimulation to such lengths, and prophane that sacred name in mysteries so evidently combined for the eradication of every trace of Christianity! But the adepts smiles, or his stupidity must be beyond expression if he does not see through so miserable a cant.

On presenting the boots: "Be active in the service of the good, and fear no road which may lead to the propagation or discovery of happiness." This will recall to our minds the principle, *whatever may be the means,* fear not to employ them when they lead to what the Sect calls happiness.

On giving the cloak: "*Be a prince over thy people*; that is to say, be sincere and wise, the benefactor of thy brethren, and teach them science." The reader will not be at a loss to understand what science.

The formula of *the hat* is, "Beware of ever exchanging this hat of liberty (*diesen frey heitshut*) for a crown."

Thus decorated, the Prince Illuminee receives the fraternal embrace.—He then hears read the instructions for his new degree; but as they entirely relate (like those of the preceding degree) to the government of the brethren, they will be treated of in the last part of the code. It is now time to proceed to the Grand Mysteries.

1. Instructions for conferring the degree of Regent, Nos. 1, 2, 3. Last works of Philo and Spartacus.
2. Instructions for conferring the degree of Regent, Nos. 1, 2, 3. Last works of Philo and Spartacus.
3. Original Writings, Vol. II. Letter 24, from Weishaupt to Cato.
4. Instructions for conferring this degree, No. 5.
5. Ritual of this degree, No. 1.
6. Ritual of this degree, No. 1.

CHAP. XII.

Ninth Part of the Code of the Illuminees.—Class of the Grand Mysteries; the Mage or the Philosopher, and the Man King.

BY the great importance which the Sect places in the last mysteries of Illuminism, and the many precautions it has taken to conceal them from the public view, I am compelled to begin this chapter with candidly declaring, that every attempt to discover the original text of this part of the Code has been fruitless. Such an avowal, however, should not disconcert the reader. Though the real text may be wanting, we have abundant matter to supply its place. We have Weishaupt's familiar correspondence; we are in possession of the letters of many of the adepts who enthusiastically admired them; and the avowals are still extant of other adepts, who indignantly beheld such abominations. Our judgement will be guided by laws laid down by Weishaupt himself; and the famous apology of this monstrous legislator will teach us how to appreciate them. Such materials are more than sufficient to supply the deficiency of the literal text. It is true, that the crafty cant and affected enthusiasm of the Hierophant will be wanting; but the substance of his declamation, the extent and monstrosity of his ultimate plots will lose nothing of their evidence. Let us begin then by attending to their author, and from him receive our first impressions.

Weishaupt, when writing to *Zwack*, his *incomparable* man, and speaking of the degree of *Epopt*, wherein impiety and rebellion seem to have strained every nerve to disseminate their venomous principles against church and state, says, "One might be tempted to think that this degree was the last and the most sublime: I have, nevertheless, THREE MORE *of infinitely greater importance, which I reserve for our Grand Mysteries*. But these I keep at home, and only show them to the Areopagites, or to a few other brethren the most distinguished for their merit and their services.—Were you here, I would admit you to my degree, for you are worthy of it—But I never suffer it to go out of my hands. *It is of too serious an import*; it is the key of the ancient and modern, the religious and political history of the universe."

"That I may keep our provinces in due subordination, I will take care to have only three copies of this degree in all Germany; that is to say, one in each Inspection." He soon after writes again to the same adept: "I have composed four more degrees above that of *Regent*; and with respect to these four, even the lowest of them, our degree of Priest will be but child's play"—*Wogegen den schlechesten der priester grad kinder spiel seyn soll.*[1]

Before we draw any conclusion toward forming our judgment, let me recall to the mind of the reader those letters wherein Weishaupt declares, that every degree shall be an apprenticeship for the next, *a sort of Noviciate for the higher degrees*. That these degrees were always to be *in crescendo*; in fine, that in the last class of the mysteries a perfect statement of the maxims and polity of Illuminism was to be given. *Und am ende folgt die totale einsicht in die politic und maximen des ordens.*[2] After such letters, the text of these mysteries is scarcely necessary. I know that these degrees were reduced to two for the last class of the mysteries; I know, from the agreement made by the founder and his intimate adepts, that the first was the *Mage*, or *Philospher*; the other, the *Man King*.[3] I will start from these data, and shall not hesitate to say, that this monster of impiety and of wickedness imposes on himself when he speaks of *degrees infinitely more important* for the higher mysteries, or when he pretends that those of *Epopt* and *Regent* are but *puerile* in comparison with those which he reserves for his intimate adepts. His execrable pride may flatter him with surpassing even the devils themselves, in his wicked inventions for sending forth the pestiferous blast; but their combined efforts could not suggest more hideous plots than those in which Weishaupt glories when calling them his *lesser mysteries.*—What! the vow of annihilating every idea of religion, even to the very name of a God; the plan for overthrowing every government, even to the obliteration of every vestige of laws, authority, or civil society; the wish of destroying our arts and sciences, our towns, and even villages, that they may realize their systems of Equality and Liberty; the desire of exterminating the greater part of human nature, to work the triumph of their vagabond clans, over the remaining part of mankind. These vows and wishes, these plots and plans, have already appeared in the lesser mysteries, and his adepts must have been as stupid as he wishes them to be impious and wicked, if they have not seen through the web that veils from their sight the baleful abyss. And, after all, it is not the *object* or the *substance* of their plots which is thus slightly veiled; the *terms* alone are concealed. There only remains to say, that all religion shall be destroyed for the adoption of Atheism; every constitution, whether Monarchical or Republican, shall be overthrown in favour of absolute Independence; property shall be annihilated; science and arts shall be suppressed; towns, houses, and fixed habitations, reduced to ashes, for the re-establishment of the roaming and savage life, which the hypocrite, in his cant, calls *the patriarchal life*. Such are the terms; and the scroll of this hideous pantomime needed only to be unrolled, to tell the names of those who were to appear on the gloomy stage of the last mysteries. The adept had long since inhaled the deleterious air with which Weishaupt had spared no pains to surround him; and could he nauseate this, or turn away from these disastrous machinations, the gates of the mysterious pit were shut against him. At such a sight nature shudders—The reader will cry out, None but monsters could have conceived or abetted such plots. Be it so; I will not contradict him; I only wish to name these monsters.—Behold Weishaupt and his profound adepts! The reader will find the proofs of this exclamation in their own writings.

Weishaupt, who divided his mysteries into two classes, also distributed his last secrets under two heads. First, Religion; which was the object of the *Mages*: The other comprehended what he called his Polity; and he reserved it for the *Man King*. Let us separately investigate each of these degrees, commencing with that principle which he himself lays down, and from which he never deviates, that each degree shall be a preparatory concatenation of principles and doctrines, the ultimate tendency of which was to form the object of the last mysteries. Such a principle is more than sufficient to demonstrate that the secret to be imparted to his *Mages* can be no other than the most absolute Atheism, and the total subversion of every Religion. The adept, however, has already imbibed such horrid principles; and the secret consists in telling him, in plain terms, that it was toward that point the Sect had long since been leading him, and that in future all his thoughts, words, and actions, must tend to second the views of the Sect in their monstrous undertaking; that in the preceding degrees the name of *Religion* had only been preserved the better to destroy the thing; but that in future the very name would only be the expression of chimeras, of superstition, of fanaticism, supported by despotism and ambition, as a tool for enslaving mankind.

This explication is no vain fancy of mine. See Weishaupt confidentially writing to his intimate and incomparable *Cato*-Zwack:

"I firmly believe, that the secret doctrine of Christ had no other object in view than the re-establishment of Jewish Liberty, which is the explanation I give of it. I even believe, that Freemasonry is nothing but a Christianity of this sort; at least, my explanation of their Hieroglyphics perfectly coincides with such an explanation. In this sense, nobody could blush at being a Christian; *for I preserve the name, and substitute reason,—denn ich lasse den namen, und substituiere ihm die vernunft."*—He continues: "It is no trivial matter to have discovered a new Religion and a new Polity in these tenebrous Hieroglypnics;" and he goes on to say, "One might be induced to think that this was my highest degree; I have, nevertheless, three of infinitely more importance, for our grand mysteries."[4] Here then is Weishaupt's decision on the degree of *Epopt* or *Illuminized Priest*.—It is Christianity preserving *the name of Religion*, with the Gospel converted into a Code by means of which Christ taught the Jacobinical *Equality and Liberty*.[5] Here Weishaupt is transcendant in his wickedness and his impiety; it is under the sacred name of Religion that he teaches his disorganizing principles of *Equality and Liberty*. After having led his Epopts to the pinnacle of Impiety, to what farther lengths can he possibly lead his *Mage*?—He may erase the *names* of *Religion* and *God*? And this he will do in his higher mysteries; for who can expect to find them when he says, "You know that the *Unity of God* was one of the secrets revealed in the mysteries of Eleusis; *as for that, there is no fear of any such thing being found in mine."*[6]

After this, can the name of God be expected ever to be found in the mysteries of the *Illuminized Mage* for any other purpose than to be blasphemed? We see this same Weishaupt reserving all the Atheistical productions for this degree; he writes again to his incomparable man: "With our beginners let us act prudently with respect to books on Religion and Polity. *In my plan, I reserve them for the grand mysteries*. At first we must put only books of history or of metaphysics into their hands. Let Morality be our pursuit. *Robinet, Mirabeau* (that is to say, the System of Nature written by Diderot, though attributed to Mirabeau), *the Social System, Natural Polity, the Philosophy of Nature*, and such works, are reserved for my higher degrees.—At present they must not even be mentioned to our adepts, and particularly *Helvetius on Man*."[7] The reader here sees a list of the most Anti-religious and the most Atheistical works,[8] and that they are reserved for these last mysteries. As a preparation for them (*horribile dictu!*) the very idea of a God must be eradicated from the mind of the adept. Can we doubt this, when we see Weishaupt thus write: "Do put Brother *Numenius* in correspondence with me; I must try to cure him of his Theosophical ideas, and properly prepare him for our views.—*Ich will ihn suchen von der Theosophie zu curieren, und zu unseren absichten zu bestimmen*."[9] The Theosopher, or the man still believing in a God, is not fit for these mysteries; Religion then must, of course, be irreconcileable with them. Were the consequences less evident, and should we reject these secret correspondences, or condemn the last oracles of the Hierophant to remain *within the hundred bolts* which keeps them hidden from the adepts; I say, even then, to ascertain what the tenets of the Sect are as to any worship or religion, we should not be necessitated to enter that den of mysteries. Though Weishaupt had not mentioned Religion in his intimate correspondence, the Atheistical Conspiracy of his mysteries would be evident, and why seek private documents when he has given us irrefragable proofs of guilt in that which he publishes as his apology?

Two years after his flight, Weishaupt most daringly asserts, that the Systems of his Illuminism (as published by the civil powers) are but a mere sketch, a plan as yet too ill-digested for the public to form any judgment either on him or his adepts, from the Original Writings or his Confidential Correspondence. He publishes a new Code, and calls it *The corrected System of Illuminism, with its Degrees and Constitutions, by Adam Weishaupt, Counsellor to the Duke of Saxe Gotha*. Here at least we have a right to judge him and his mysteries, both in his apology and his corrected degrees. But the reader will now view him in a new light. He is not only the conspiring infidel, but the insolent Sophister, insulting the Public with all the haughtiness of the most daring Atheist, shrugging his shoulders in disdain at the rest of mankind, and with impertinent pity saying to us all, as he did of the adepts whom he had duped, *poor creatures! what could one not make you believe!*

I deign to cast my eyes on this apology, or the Illuminism corrected. He begins by telling us, that to have supposed him capable of composing so extensive a work in two years *was doing him the honour of supposing him gifted with most extraordinary talents*; and it is in such terms that the Sophister informs the public that he takes them for great fools. Let the contempt with which he treats his readers be retorted upon himself; let neither him nor his accomplices expect to descend to posterity with any other distinction than as the phenomena of vice and infamy. Are we to crouch in token of homage before the men who insolently scoff at their God and at the public weal? I know not whether Weishaupt needed extraordinary talents or not, though I grant him all the art and cunning of the Sophister; but most certainly he must have presumed much on the force of impudence when he flattered himself that the public would inevitably find that his corrected Code contained no principles but such as would elevate the mind and tend to form great men.[10] What I find is, that it is nothing more than a medley of all the arts of his original Code for the education or rather depravation of his Adepts. Did I wish to form a stupid atheist, this would be the work I should chuse to put into his hands. As early as the third degree, in place of a God reigning as freely as he does powerfully over this universe, I find the universe transformed into a vast machine, in which every thing is held together or put in motion by I know not what fatality, decorated sometimes by the appellation of God, at other of nature. Again: did I wish to decorate with the name of providence a destiny *which cannot annihilate a single atom without depriving the stars of their support and involving the whole universe in ruin*, this would be the work I should recommend: I would give it to the narrow-minded adept, who, in a world where every thing is said to be necessary, should still pretend to talk of virtue or vices, or who could comfort himself for all the harm which the wicked could do him, by learning that the wicked like the virtuous man only followed the course which nature had traced for him; and that they would both arrive at the same point as himself: In fine, I would put it into the hands of the imbecile, who would call *the art of making merry the art of being always happy (ars semper gaudendi)*; the art of persuading oneself that one's misfortunes are incurable, or that they are all necessary.[11] But what reader will brook the impudence of that conspiring infidel, who, dedicating his mysteries as an apology to the whole world and all mankind—*der welt und den menschlichen geschlecht*—and pretending to prove that his original mysteries are not a conspiracy against Religion, puts a discourse in the mouth of his new Hierophants, whose very title characterizes the most determined one both against God and Religion; he calls it, *An Instruction for the adepts who are inclined to the fancy of believing in or of adoring a God!* I know it may be also translated, *An instruction for the Brethren inclining toward Theosopohical or Religious enthusiasm.*[12] But if both these translations be not synonymous in the language of the Sophisters, let the reader judge, from the exordium of the discourse, which is the most accurate.

"He who wishes to labour for the happiness of mankind, to add to the content and rest of the human species, to decrease their dissatisfaction (these are literally the words of our Antitheosophical Sophister), must scrutinize and weaken *those principles* which trouble their rest, contentment, and happiness. Of this species are all those systems which are hostile to the ennobling and perfecting of human nature; which unnecessarily multiply evil in the world, or represent it as greater than it really is: all those systems which depreciate the merit and the dignity of man, which diminish his confidence in his own natural powers, and thereby render him lazy, pusillanimous, mean, and cringing: all those also which beget enthusiasm, which bring human reason into discredit, and thus open a free course for imposture: *All the Theosophical and Mystical Systems; all those which have a direct or indirect tendency to such Systems; in short, all the principles derived from Theosophy, which, concealed in our hearts, often finish by leading men back to it, belong to this class."*

In the course of his instructions, the reader is not to expect that Weishaupt will make any exception in favour of the revealed Religion, not even a hint at such an exception is to be seen.—The Religion of Christ is represented as a medley of the reveries of Pythagoras, of Plato, and of Judaism. It is in vain for the Israelites to believe in the Unity of God, in the coming of a Messiah; it is in vain to assert that such was the faith of their forefathers, of Abraham, Isaac, and Jacob, long before they entered Egypt or Babylon; it is in vain to prove, that the adoration of the golden Calf, or of the god Apis, was punished by the Almighty as a prevarication of their Religion: Nothing will serve the Sophister; he will declare in his *corrected Code*, that the Religion of the Jews was but a modification of the reveries of the Egyptians, of Zoroaster, or of the Babylonians. To *correct* his adepts, he teaches them to cast aside the Creation as a chimera unknown to antiquity, and to reduce all Religion to two Systems—The one, that of matter co-eternal with God, a part of God, proceeding from God, cast forth and separated from God, in order to become the world—The other, matter co-eternal with God, without being God, but worked by God, for the formation of the universe. On these foundations he builds a general history of all Religions, and makes all appear equally absurd. The reader might be tempted to think that these lessons had been composed before the hegira or rather proscription of the author of Illuminism. They may have been compiled for one of those discourses which he declares to be of more importance than that of the Hierophant in the degree of Epopt.—He precisely follows the course which Knigge represents as the grand object of the last mysteries. He makes, after his fashion, a general compilation of all the schools of Philosophism and of its Systems; and hence he deduces Christianity and all Religions. The result of the whole is, that all Religions are founded on imposture and chimera, all end in rendering man *cowardly, lazy, cringing,* and *superstitious*; all degrade him, and trouble his repose.[13] And it is thus that this Sophister, under pretence of his justification, daringly acts that part in public which before he had only ventured to act under the cover of his mysteries. He sallies forth from his baleful abyss but to proclaim to the world what heretofore he had only hinted to his adepts in private,—that the time was at length come for the overthrow of every Altar, and the annihilation of every Religion.

Are any further proofs necessary to demonstrate the object of the grand mysteries? The testimony of Knigge cannot be objected to, nor can Knigge pretend or wish to mislead Zwack when confidentially corresponding with him. Both had signed the agreement of the Areopagites respecting the compilation of the degrees of Illuminism.[14] Let us then attend to these two adepts—Philo-Knigge has been exhibiting all that he has done, according to Weishaupt's instructions, in the degree of *Epopt*, to demonstrate that Christ had no other view than the establishment of natural Religion, or, in the language of Illuminism, the rights of Equality and Liberty. Knigge then continues: "After having thus shown to our people that we are the real Christians, we have only a *word to add* against Priests and Princes. I have made use of such precaution in the degrees of Epopt and of Regent, that I should not be afraid of conferring them on Kings or Popes, provided they had undergone the proper previous trials. In our last mysteries we have to acknowledge this *pious fraud*; to prove, upon the testimony of authors, the origin of all the religious impostures, and to expose the whole with their connections and dependencies."[15]

Such, reader, is *that word to add*, which was to be spoken only in the last mysteries of Illuminism! That *word* against Priests and the Ministers of every worship! That *word* on the *pious fraud*, or rather labyrinth of impiety, in which the Sect had involved the Candidate on his first entrance into the Order, only to extricate him when he was judged worthy of their last mysteries! The adept must certainly be of weak intellects, and his credulity must border on stupidity, if he has not in the degree of Epopt, and long before, observed whither they were leading him. But should he really be still in the dark, or could he view with indignation the artifices which had been used with him; if all reflection have not abandoned him; what will not the very term of *pious fraud* discover to him? Will it not recall to his mind, "that on the first invitations of the Sect, to entice him into their Order, they began by telling him, that nothing contrary to Religion would ever enter the projects of the Order? Does he not remember, that this declaration was repeated on his admission into the noviciate, and reiterated when he was received into the minerval academy? Has he forgotten how strongly the sect enforced the study of morality and of virtue in the first degrees, and how carefully it isolated both from religion? When pouring forth its encomium on religion, did not the Sect insinuate, that true Religion widely differed from those mysteries and worship which had degenerated in the hands of the priesthood? Does he remember with what art and affected respect it spoke of Christ and his Gospel in the degrees of *Major Illuminee*, of *Scotch Knight*, and of *Epopt*; how the Gospel was insensibly metamorphosed into illuminized reason, its morality into that of Nature; and from a moral, reasonable, and natural religion, how a religion and a morality of the rights of man, of *Equality and Liberty*, were deduced? Does he reflect how all the different parts of this system and opinions of the Sect were insinuated to him, how naturally they occurred and appeared to have been fostered in his own breast? Could not the Sect say to him, 'tis true, we put you on the way, but you were much more earnest in solving our questions than we in answering yours. When, for example, we asked whether the religions which nations had adopted fulfilled the objects for which they were intended; whether the pure and simple religion of Christ was really that which different Sects professed at this present day, we knew what to believe, but we wished to know how far you had inhaled our principles. We had a multitude of prejudices to conquer in you, before we could succeed in persuading you that the pretended Religion of Christ was but an invention of Priestcraft, imposture, and tyranny. If such be the case with the much-admired and loudly proclaimed Gospel, what are we to think of all other religions? Learn, then, that they are all founded on fiction, all originate in imposition, error, imposture, and chimera. Such is our secret. All the windings we made; the hypotheses we assumed; the promises set forth; the panegyric pronounced on Christ and his secret schools; the fable, of Masonry being for a long time in possession of his true doctrines, and our Order being at present sole depositary of his mysteries, can no longer be subjects of surprise. If, to overturn Christianity and every Religion, we pretended solely to possess true Christianity, the true Religion, remember that the *end sanctifies the means,* that the sage *must make use of all those means for good purposes, which the wicked do for evil.* The means we have employed to rid you, and which we continue in order to rid mankind of all Religion, are but a *pious fraud,* which we always meant to reveal to you when admitted to the degree of *Mage,* or of *Illuminized Philosopher!!!*"

To these reflections *on the word to be added* in the last mysteries (sufficiently demonstrated by the ascension of the degrees, by Weishaupt's apology, by his intimate correspondence, and that of his most perfect adepts) let us subjoin the avowal of a man little calculated indeed for a Member of such an abominable tribe, but who has better than any person known how to tear the mask from their hideous countenances, and expose their wickedness. I am acquainted with his real name; I am aware that it would greatly add to the confidence of the public; but I also know that could Illuminism discover his asylum, it would follow him to drink his blood, though it were to the southern pole. He is then entitled to secrecy; till now it has been observed, nor will I be the first to infringe his right. The Germans have paid him homage, and, ignorant of his name, they have surnamed him *Biederman,* or Man of Honour; at least, it is under that denomination that his works are generally cited. All that I can say in addition to what the public is already in possession of respecting this gentleman is that nothing could have induced him to continue so disgusting a course, but a zeal for the public welfare, and a just opinion, that the only means of preventing the effects of the conspiracy of the Sect was to make their machinations public.—Having passed through all the degrees, he was at length admitted to the last mysteries. He published those of *Epopt or Priest, and of Regent,* under the title of *Last Works of Philo and Spartacus.* He subjoined the instructions belonging to those degrees, with *a Critical History of all the Degrees of Illuminism.* Had I no other guarantee of the veracity of his assertions, than their glaring coincidence with the original writings, which is beyond all doubt with the attentive investigator, I should not hesitate in declaring him to be the man that has given the truest account, and was best acquainted with the Sect. The certificate at the head of the degree of *Epopt and Regent*, for a more perfect knowledge of which the public is indebted to him, I look upon as undoubtedly genuine. I know a person who has seen and read this certificate in the original, in *Philo*-Knigge's own hand-writing, and who has seen the seal of the Order attached to this certificate. I thus particularize because the public is entitled, in discussions of this importance, to know how far I have extended my researches, and how far the grounds I work upon deserve to be credited.—The passage I am about to quote is looked upon as fundamental by all German authors; it is from Biederman, and occurs near the end of his *Critical History*:

"With respect to the two degrees of *Mage* and of *Man King*, there is no reception, that is to say, there are no ceremonies of initiation. Even the Elect are not permitted to transcribe these degrees, they only hear them read; and that is the reason why I do not publish them with this work."

"The first is that of *Mage*, also called Philosopher. It contains the fundamental principles of Spinosism. Here every thing is *material*; God and the world are but one and the same thing; all religions are *inconsistent*, chimerical, and the invention of ambitious men."[16]

"Divers principles," continues the author, "thrown out in the preceding degrees might in some measure point out the object the Sect had in view." Certainly nothing could be better grounded than such a surmise—Nature, so often united with God, represented active like God, following with the same immensity of power, the same wisdom as God, the course which it had traced; a hundred such expressions in the mouth of the Hierophant evidently indicated, that the God of Weishaupt was that of Spinosa or Lucretius, no other than matter and the universe; in fine, the God of Atheism. Let the Sieur D'Alembert assert, that nothing can be more opposite to Atheism than Spinosism;[17] or let Spinosa say, that, so far from being an Atheist, he converts every thing into God; will such an excuse raise pity or indignation in the reader? To deny that there is any other God than the world, is evidently denying the only being that can justly be called God. It is laughing at men, to wish to make them believe, that the person is preserved because they do not dare destroy the name, at the very time that the name of God is only used as an agent for the annihiliation of every idea of a Deity.

I think I have sufficiently demonstrated, that the first object of these grand mysteries of Illuminism, prepared with so much art and cunning, is no other than to plunge the adepts into a monstrous Atheism, to persuade all nations that religion is but an invention of ambitious impostors, and that to deliver nations from this despotism of imposture, and recover the famous rights of man, Equality and Liberty, they must begin by annihilating every religion, every worship, every altar, and cease to believe in a God.

Let us continue the declaration of *Biederman*, and the object of the last part of the mysteries (or the degree of the Man king) will be equally clear.

"The second degree of the grand mysteries," he says, "called the *Man King*, teaches that every inhabitant of the country or town, every father of a family, is sovereign, as men formerly were in the times of the patriarchal life, to which mankind is once more to be carried back; that, in consequence, all authority and all magistracy must be destroyed.—I have read these two degrees, and have passed through all those of the Order."[18]

How well authenticated soever this testimony may be, still one is loth to think that there could have existed men at once so absurd and so wicked as to take such exquisite pains to educate their adepts merely to address them in the end to the following purpose: "All that we have done for you hitherto was only to prepare you to co-operate with us in the annihilation of all Magistracy, all Governments, all Laws, and all Civil Society; of every Republic and even Democracy, as well as of every Aristocracy or Monarchy—It all tended to infuse into you and make you insensibly imbibe that which we plainly tell you at present—All men are equal and free, this is their imprescriptible right; but it is not only under the dominion of Kings that you are deprived of the exercise of these rights. They are annulled wherever man recognises any other law than his own will. We have frequently spoken of Despotism and of Tyranny; but they are not confined to an Aristocracy or a Monarchy: Despotism and Tyranny as essentially reside in the Democratic sovereignty of the people, or in the legislative people, as in the legislative King. What right has that people to subject me and the minority to the decrees of its majority? Are such the rights of nature? Did the sovereign or legislative people exist any more than Kings or Aristocratic Legislators at that period when man enjoyed his natural Equality and Liberty?—Here then are our Mysteries—All that we have said to you of Tyrants and Despots, was only designed insensibly to lead you to what we had to impart concerning the despotism and tyranny of the people themselves. Democratic governments are not more consonant with nature than any others. If you ask, How it will be possible for men assembled in towns to live in future without laws, magistrates, or constituted authorities,—the answer is clear, Desert your towns and villages, and fire your houses. Did men build houses, villages, or towns in the days of the Patriarchs? They were all equal and free; the earth belonged to them all, each had an equal right, and lived where he chose. Their country was the world, and they were not confined to England or Spain, to France or Germany; their country was the whole earth, and not a Monarchy or petty Republic in some corner of it. Be equal and free, and you will be cosmopolites or citizens of the world. Could you but appreciate Equality and Liberty as you ought, you would view with indifference Rome, Vienna, Paris, London, or Constantinople in flames, or any of those towns, boroughs, or villages which you call your country.—Friend and Brother, such is the grand secret which we reserved for our Mysteries!!!"

It is painful indeed to believe, that stupidity, pride, and wickedness, should have thus combined to prepare adepts, who, attending Weishaupt's Mysteries, could mistake them for the Oracles of true wisdom and transcendant Philosophy. How many Jacobins and those pretended patriots of Democracy blush, when they learn the real object of the Sect which directs their actions; when they learn that they have only been the tools of a Sect whose ultimate object is to overturn even their Democratic Constitutions!—But in attributing such language to the Hierophant of the last Mysteries, what more have I said than the Illuminizing Legislator has already declared? What other can be the meaning of his *Patriarchal* or of his *Nomade* or *roaming life*, of those vagabond clans, or of man still in the savage state?[19] What Democracy even could consist with the Patriarchal life or the vagabond clan? Where is the necessity for attending the last Mysteries, to learn from the Sect itself the extent of their conspiracies? We have seen Weishaupt cursing that day as one of the most disastrous for mankind, when, uniting themselves in civil society, they instituted Laws and Governments, and first formed *nations and people*. We have seen him depreciate *nations* and the *national spirit* as the grand source of Egoism; call down vengeance on the *laws* and the *rights* of nations as incompatible with the *laws and rights of nature*. What else can the Sect mean by saying, that *nations shall disappear from the face of the earth*, but the annihilation of all civil or national society? Why those blasphemies against the *love of one's country*, if not to persuade the adepts to acknowlege none?—Have we not heard the Hierophant teaching that true morality consisted *in the art of casting Princes and Governors aside and of governing oneself*; that the *real original sin* in mankind was their uniting under the laws of civil society; that their *redemption* could be accomplished only by the abolition of this civil state? And when his frantic hatred against all government exalts his imagination, does he not enthusiastically exclaim, *Let the laughers laugh, the scoffers scoff; still the day will come, when Princes and Nations shall disappear from the face of the earth; a time when each man shall recognize no other law but that of his reason*? Nor does he hesitate to say, that *this shall be the grand work of* SECRET SOCIETIES. They are to reinstate man in his rights of Equality and Liberty, in an independence of every law but that of his reason. Such he formally declares to be one of the grand mysteries of his Illuminism;[20] and can the reader quietly sit down and think that all these declarations of the author of Illuminism, who must be superior to his Mysteries, have not the absolute ruin of every law, government, and civil society, in view? Has he not seen the Sect anticipating those objections which evidence might have suggested against systems still more wicked than stupid; forewarning the adepts, that independence once more restored among men, it was not to meet the same fate it formerly had, and was never to be lost again;—teaching that mankind, having acquired wisdom by its disasters, will resemble a man corrected of his errors by long experience, and who carefully avoids those faults which were the cause of his past misfortunes? Has not the reader heard him proclaim to his elect, that this independence once recovered, the empire of the laws and all civil society would cease; and will he still continue to disbelieve the existence of the most deliberate and most dangerous Conspiracy that ever was formed agaisnt society!

Should any of my readers be weak enough to be seduced by the imaginary sweets of a patriarchal life, so artfully promised by Weishaupt, let them receive the explanation of that life from these pretended Apostles of Nature.

At my outset I did not only declare, that the destruction of civil society was the object of their views; I did not confine myself to saying, that should Jacobinism triumph every Religion and every Government would be overthrown; but I added, *that to whatever rank in society you may belong, your riches and your fields, your houses and your cottages, even your very wives and children would be torn from you*.[21] I also rejected *fanaticism and enthusiasm* in my own and my reader's name. I have said it, and adopting the simplest construction, do not proofs of the most extensive plots croud upon us from the very lessons of the Sect? Can common sense, nay can the strongest prejudice, refuse to admit such powerful evidence?

Let him who may wish to preserve his field, his house, or the smallest part of his property, under this patriarchal life, go back to the *lesser Mysteries*; there let him hear the Hierophant teaching the adept, that it would have been happy for man, "Had he know how to preserve himself in the primitive state in which nature had placed him!—But soon the unhappy germ developed itself in his heart, and rest and happiness disappeared. As families multiplied, the necessary means of subsistence began to fail. *The Nomade or roaming life ceased; Property began; Men chose fixed habitations; Agriculture brought them together.*" What were in the eyes of the Sect the dreadful consequences of this deviation from the Nomade or Patriarchal life?—Why the Hierophant hastens to tell us, *Liberty was ruined in its foundations, and Equality disappeared.* This *Patriarchal or Nomade* life is then no other than that which preceded *property*, the building of *fixed habitations*, of houses, cottages, or *the cultivation of your fields*. It was this beginning of property therefore, the building of habitations, the cultivation of lands, which struck the first mortal blow at Equality and Liberty. Should any one wish to return to the *Patriarchal* or *Nomade* life with such wretches as these apostles of Equality and Liberty, let him begin by renouncing his property; let him abandon his house and his field; let him, in unison with the Sect, declare, that the first blasphemy which was uttered against *Equality and Liberty* was by the man who first said *my* field, *my* house, *my* property.

It must be voluntary blindness, indeed, in the man who will not see the hatred conceived and the Conspiracies entered into by the Sect against titles or pretensions to, nay against the very existence of property. It will acknowledge none, nor can it in any shape be compatible with their explanations of Equality and Liberty, or with that primitive state of nature which no more entitles you or me to the possession of this gold or silver, or that field, than it does a third person.

Here it is not simply the question of establishing the *Agrarian Laws*, where lands, riches, and other properties are to be equally distributed among all; it is not simply to abolish the distinction of *rich* and *poor*; no, every property is to be destroyed, that of the poor like that of the rich. The first man who was weary of the *Nomade*, roaming, vagabond, and savage life, built a cot and not a palace. The first who furrowed the earth was in quest of bread and not of gold; but he nevertheless, according to the principles of the Sect, was the man who struck the first deadly blow at Equality and Liberty. Poor or rich man then, according to the doctrine of the Sect, the field you have recovered from the waste, and that you have cultivated, belongs to me equally as to you, or else to nobody; I, though idle, and inactive, am entitled to the fruit of your labours; I have a right to share those fruits which you have raised on the land which I left uncultivated. Does not *Equality* disappear, whether it be a poor or rich man who shall pretend to be entitled to or say this field is mind, I have that property? If the poor man has a title to his property, has not the rich man also one? Treasures and palaces are no more property than the cot or cottage. Here an Illuminee spies want, there abundance; Equality and Liberty are every where banished; Despotism or Slavery is universal. Nevertheless, Equality and Liberty in his eyes are the rights of Nature, and he beholds them mortally wounded on the first appearance of property, when man became stationary. Poor or rich, you all imbrued your hands in this foul assassination of Equality and Liberty when you pretended to property; from that instant you are both involved in the curse pronounced in the mysteries; you are both objects of the Conspiracies of the Sect from the first instant that you dared assert your right to your habitations whether cots or palaces, to your properties whether fields or domains. But these cannot be the whole of the secrets; they are only those of the lesser mysteries. Weishaupt has revealed them to his Epopts; he reserves the grander secrets for his *Mage* and *Man-King*; then let any man rich or poor harbour, if he can, a hope of seeing the Sect respect his property. Or rather, let him behold the Sect at present pillaging the rich in favour of the poor. The last mysteries or ultimate conspiracy will take place; and then the poor man will learn, that if Illuminism begins by pillaging the rich, it is only to teach him that he is no better entitled to his property than the rich man was, and that the time is near when he will also be pillaged and fall a victim to the curse which has been pronounced against every proprietor.

The progress of this Sophism is worthy of remark. If we judge by its present growth, what a gigantic form will it assume for posterity! The Genevese Sophister of Equality and Liberty, anticipating the modern *Spartacus*, had already dogmatically asserted, "That the man who, having enclosed a piece of ground, first took upon himself to say *this is mine*, and found beings *simple enough to believe him*, was the true founder of civil society." He then continues:—"What crimes, what wars, what murders, what miseries, what horrors would that man have spared mankind, who, tearing down the fences or filling up the ditches of this new enclosure, had called out to his equals, beware of hearkening to this impostor, you are ruined if ever you forget that *the fruits belong to all, though the land belongs to none.*"[22] How many crimes and spoliations would Rousseau have spared the French Revolution, if, contemning so disastrous a paradox, he had said with more judgement and veracity, "The first man who enclosed a piece of land and took upon himself to say, *this belongs to nobody*, I will cultivate it, and from sterile it shall become fertile; I will follow the course which nature shall point out to me, to raise sustenance for me, my wife and children, and this *land will become my property*. The God of nature, who as yet has given it to nobody, offers and will give it to him who shall first cultivate it in reward for his labour.—The first man who held such language, seconding the views of nature, and meeting with beings *wise* enough to imitate him, was *the true benefactor of mankind*. He taught his children and his equals, that they were not made to dispute the wild fruits of the earth one with another, nor with the savage beasts of the forest; no, he taught them, that there existed social and domestic virtues far preferable to the roaming and often ferocious life of the *Nomades*. His posterity was blessed, his generations were multiplied. If it was not in his power to avert all the evils, he at least destroyed the first of them, that sterility which stinted the very growth of life and drove the scanty population of the earth into the forests like wild beasts, and too often assimilated them to the lion or the tyger, to whom they frequently fell a prey.

Had the Sophister of Geneva held this language, he would not have exposed himself to the ignominy of being the precursor of Weishaupt.—But human imbecility has lavished its praises on this paradox, and have decorated it with the name of Philosophy! The Bavarian Sophister adopts the doctrine of Rousseau, and the delirium of pride has only refined on the phrenzy of wickedness. That which in the mouth of the master had been but a paradox in support of the wildest independence, becomes in the scholar (without divesting itself of its folly) the blackest of conspiracies.

It is now too late to say, that those were the wild chimeras of the Sophisters; at present we are compelled to say, such are the plots contriving against all and each one's property, plots which have been awfully illustrated by the spoliation of the Church, of the Nobility, of the Merchants, and of all rich proprietors—Let them be called chimeras if you are so determined; but remember, that they are the chimeras of Weishaupt, of the genius of conspiring brigands, of a genius the most fertile in sophisms and artifice for the execution of those plans supposed to be chimerical. What Jean Jaques teaches his Sophisters, the modern Spartacus infuses into his Illuminized legions, *The fruits belong to all, the land to none*. He farther states in his dark recesses, When property *began, Equality and Liberty disappeared*; and it is in the name of this Equality and of this Liberty that he conspires, that he invites his conspirators to restore mankind to the Patriarchal or wandering life.

Let not the reader be imposed upon by the term *Patriarchal life*. The illuminizing Hierophant speaks of Abraham and of the Patriarchs, of the father *priest and king*, sole *sovereign* over his family. He is not to expect to see the father surrounded by his children, exercising the sweetest of all dominions, and each child, docile to the dictates of nature, revering the orders and anticipating the will of a beloved father. No; this empire is as imaginary as his priesthood. We have seen in the degree of *Mage*, that the iluminized Patriarch can no more pretend to the acknowledgement of a God than can an Atheist. We must then begin by withdrawing from the Patriarchal life that interesting sight of the father offering up to heaven the prayers of his children, sacrificing in their name, and exercising in the midst of them the functions of the priest of the living God. In the next degree of the mysteries all his dominion over his children is to disappear, as his priesthood has already done. Nor was I afraid to assert in the beginning of this work, *If Jacobinism triumphs—your very children shall be torn from you.* I now repeat it; all this pretended sovereignty of the father is but a conspiracy against the paternal authority. The proofs are extant in the codes of the Sect.

Here again is Weishaupt deprived of the glory of the invention. Rousseau and the Encyclopedists had long since told us, that *the authority of the father ceased with the wants of the son*; this was one of their principles of rebellion. The man who invented his Illuminism only to convert it into the common sewer of every antichristian and antisocial error, could not leave your children in the dark as to these lessons of independence, though under the sanctuary of the paternal roof; nor with respect to the pretended right of governing themselves, and of acknowledging no other law than that of their reason, as soon as they were strong enough to disobey, or no longer needed your assistance. Tell the illuminizing Hierophant, that your children belong to you; it will be useless, for he has already answered, *"The paternal authority ceases with the wants of the children; the father would wrong his children, should he pretend to any authority over them after that period."* This is but a principle laid down in the lesser mysteries. Follow up the consequences, or rather leave it to the revolution to develope such a principle. The reader will soon see to what this authority of the father is reduced. Scarcely can the child lisp the words Equality and Liberty, or that of Reason, when the commands of his parents become the most horrid despotism, oppression, and tyranny.—Nor is the Patriarchal sovereign to expect any more affection than obedience from his subjects or his children. In imparting the doctrines of Equality and Liberty, the Hierophant had taught them to blaspheme the *love of one's family* even still more than *the national love, or the love of one's country*, as being the more direct and immediate principle of the most disastrous *Egoism*. Let the father then enquire by what bonds his children still remain united to him, or how they are subjected to him, when, without fear, they may openly resist his Patriarchal power as soon as their feeble arms have acquired sufficient strength to gather the fruits which were to serve them as food. No, this hellish Sect acknowledges no ties. All those of nature, as well as those of government or religion, were to be dissolved in Weishaupt's last mysteries. The child, like the savage tyger of the forest, was to abandon his parents when strong enough to go alone in quest of his prey. And this is what the Sect calls restoring man to his primitive state of nature, to the Patriarchal life, to those days when filial piety compensated for all the necessary laws of civil society. Yes, it is by the most abandoned depravation of all morals, by the extinction of the purest and justest sentiments of nature, that these conspirators consummate their last mysteries. In the name of Equality and Liberty, they abjure the love and authority of their country; in that name they curse the authority and love of their own family.

As I proceed in revealing these plots, I know not whether the reader does not frequently ask himself, What then can these men want? Have they not fortunes to preserve in our state of society? Have they not children in their families? Can they be conspiring against themselves? or, are they ignorant that their conspiracies will fall back upon themselves?—Those who can propose such questions are little acquainted with the enthusiasm of error when inflated by the spirit of independence and pride, of impiety and jealousy. They have not, like us, heard the cant of the heroes, demi-heroes, and *sans-culottes* of the revolution—They will be equal and free; they will it above all things.—It must cost them many sacrifices, but they are ready to make them—They will lose their fortunes in the pursuit, but you will not preserve yours—He that served will become the equal, nor will he recognize either God or man above him.—Have we not seen the prince of the fallen angels exclaiming in his pride,

—Here at least
We shall be free;—
Here we may reign secure, and in my choice
To reign is worth ambition, tho' in hell:
Better to reign in hell, than *serve* in heaven.

It is not to one of Weishupt's adepts that the ties of nature are to be objects. He must be as heedless of the duty he owes to his parents as of the affection due to his children, or the baleful consequences of the mysteries cannot affect him. Can the reader have forgotten the precept laid down for the *Insinuators* or *Recruiters?*—*The principles; look always to the principles, never to the consequences.* Or, in other words, strenuously support and insist upon these great principles of Equality and Liberty; never be frightened or stopped by ther consequences, however disastrous they may appear. These wretches, blinded by their pride, do not know, then, that one single consequence proved to be false, contrary to nature, or hurtful to mankind, is a sufficient demonstration that both nature and truth hold the principle in detestation as the prime mover of these disasters. These madmen, with all the confidence of an atheistical Condorcet, when once become the adepts of Weishaupt, will exclaim even in the very tribune of the National Assembly, *Perish the universe, but may the principle remain!* They will not see, that this principle of Equality and Liberty, devastating human nature, cannot be an Equality and Liberty congenial to mankind. These unhappy men fall victims, perishing under the axe of these disorganizing principles, and spend their last breath in crying, *Equality and liberty* for ever. No; they are all ignorant of the power of error stimulated by pride, who could think of counteracting the plots of the Sect by the cries of nature, or even by the self-interest of the illuminized adept.—They have not sufficiently comprehended the artifice with which the Hierophant insinuates, vivifies, and inflames the enthusiastic zeal of his adepts.

The reader may rest assured, that villany never slumbers; it watches incessantly the opportunity for the completion of its views. It will persuade the imbecile adept, that all his wants are to disappear on the establishment of the reign of Equality and Liberty; that he will be as free from wants as the savage; that Nature shall provide for them; and this heedless adept thirsts after such an Equality. If the adept ruffian be taught that *the fruits belong to all, though the land to none*, he will easily find means of obtaining his share.

But am I really thinking of reconciling the adepts with their plots? What is it to them whether you see any agreement between them or not? Villany, we all know, is replete with contradictions; but is it the less wicked on that account, or are its crimes less real? In vain would the reader object and say, What can these men want with their monstrous Equality, with their plots against our civil laws, our title to even the very name of property? Must we then, to please them, abandon our habitations; must we renounce all arts and sciences, and end with burning our cities, towns, and villages, to follow them in herds like the savage and Nomade clans?— Are half the inhabitants of the globe to be slaughtered, the better to scatter these roaming herds? What can be the object of those arts and sciences, and particularly of those *Minerval* academies of Illuminism? Can it be for the propagation of science, or the involving mankind again in the disasters of barbarism, that all this parade of science is made? Can these Illuminees resemble the Goths, Huns, or Vandals? And is Europe once more threatened with an inundation of barbarians like those which formerly sallied from the North?—In answering such questions, the reader may expect that I would put certain restrictions on the views of the Sect. Nothing like a restriction or qualification. No; you must renounce all the arts, all the sciences; you must begin by firing your habitations, not only your cities, towns, and villages, in short all your fixed habitations, unless you stop the disorganizing career of the Sect. Yes, wherever its legions shall be at liberty to act and accomplish the grand object of the Sect, there you may expect to see those scenes of plunder, rapine, and devastation, which heretofore traced the awful progress of the Huns, Goths, or Vandals; and this inference is fairly drawn from the very Code of the Sect.

Has not the reader heard the Hierophant insinuating the designs of the Sect upon the arts and sciences? Has he not taught the adept to answer, when asked what misfortunes reduced human nature to slavery, that it *was civil society, the state, governments, and sciences?* Has he not heard him exclaim, When shall the day come when, *the clod of useless sciences banished form the earth,* man shall recognize no other but the savage or nomade state, and which the Sect styles patriarchal, primitive, natural? Has he not declared, that the happiness and glory of the Sect would be at its zenith when, beholding those happy days, it could say, *This is our work? (Wenn die beschleünigung dieser periode, unser werk ist?)*[23] Are we to be duped by the name of *Minerval Academies*, with which the Sect decorates its schools? Can we observe there any other study than that of applying the sciences to the subversion of science, as well as to the total annihilation of all religion or society, when we remark the anxiety with which the Sect puts the following questions to the adept on his coming out of these academies, wishing to know what progress he has made in its principles before he is admitted to the illuminized priesthood:

"Do the *general* and *common* sciences to which men apply infuse real light? Do they lead to true happiness? Are they not rather the offspring of variegated wants, or of the anti-natural state in which men exist? Are they not the invention of crazy brains laboriously subtle?"[24] The reader has heard these questions, he has heard the Sect blaspheme science, and will he still believe that Illuminism recognizes any other sciences but those of the man-savage equal and free, roaming in the forests? Have not the revolutionary devastations, the multitude of monuments fallen beneath the hatchet of the Jacobin brigand, already demonstrated the frantic hatred of the modern Vandals? But the mysteries elucidate this enigma in a clearer manner.

Reader, give vent to your indignation. Ask again, What can this Weishaupt be? What are these adepts of Illuminism? Treat them as barbarians, as Huns, as Ostrogoths; but see him smiling at your contempt, and teaching his adepts to honour themselves by imitating, and glory in the hope of hereafter surpassing, the disastrous devastations of those barbarians.—Do you know in what light the illuminizing legislator views these northern clans sallying from their forests and desolating the most flourishing countries of Europe, firing its towns, beating down its empires, and strewing the earth with ruins? He complacently beholds the precious remains of the patriarchal race, the true offspring of Nature; it is with their hatchets that he means to regenerate mankind, and shape them out to the views of the Sect. I did not note the lessons of the Hierophant on this subject, when lecturing the future Epopt.—Hear the account which Weishaupt gives of these clans, when he pretends to historify human nature, at that epoch marked in the annals of Europe as a scourge, and called the inundation of the barbarians. Here is his description:

At that period when all Europe had fallen prey to corruption, "Nature, which had preserved the true race of men in its original vigour and purity, came to the assistance of mankind. From distant, but poor and sterile countries, she calls those *savage nations* and sends them into the regions of luxury and voluptuousness to infuse new life into the enervated species of the south; and with new laws and morals to restore that vigour to human nature which flourished until an ill-extinguished germ of corruption infected even that portion of mankind which originally arrived in so pure a state," or those barbarians the pretended regenerators of Europe sent by Nature.

Such are the encomiums lavished by the Sect on the Goths and Vandals. You thought it would be offending this illuminized tribe to compare them to barbarians; whereas they glory in the comparison. History has described these northern clans as carrying every where fire and sword, as ravaging countries, firing towns, destroying the monuments of the arts, depopulating empires; their course is to be traced by ruins and wastes, and in their train appear ignorance and the iron age. But in the eyes of the adept this is not the exceptionable part of their conduct; on the contrary, it was by such means that they were to regenerate mankind, and second the grand object of nature. These barbarians leave the regeneration in an imperfect state; in time they adopt our usages and manners; they are civilized; the plains rise once more in fertile crops; society is re-established; science returns; the arts flourish under the protection of the laws; towns are re-peopled; the *savage and primitive* race, confounded among the citizens, is subjected to the same laws, and governments acquire their pristine lustre.

Here, in the eyes of the adept, is the grand crime of these barbarians; the Hierophant, deploring their fall, exclaims, "Oh had there remained any sages among them, happy enough to have preserved themselves from the contagion, how would they sigh after, and ardently wish to return to the former abodes of their ancestors, there again to enjoy their former pleasures on the banks of a rivulet, under the shade of a tree laden with fruit, by the side of the object of their affections! It was then that they conceived the high value of Liberty, and the greatness of the fault they had committed in placing too much power in the hands one one man—It was then that the want of Liberty made them sensible of their fall, and seek means of softening the rigour of Slavery;—but even then their effors were only aimed against the tyrant, and not against tyranny."

It is thus that the insidious and declaiming Sophister, but able Conspirator, leads the adept through the labyrinth of his lesser mysteries, not barely to imitate these barbarians, but to surpass their devouring rage, by constancy, perseverance, and the perpetuation of their devastations. Thus are to be explained all those questions on the danger of reconquering *Equality and Liberty* only to lose them again. Hence those exhortations "to unite and support each other; to increase their numbers; and to begin by becoming powerful and terrible—You have already done it, for the multitude sides with you—The wicked, who fear you, seek protection beneath your banners—Henceforward your strength will be sufficient to bind the remainder of mankind, subjugate them, and stifle vice in its origin."[25]

Such will be the explanation of the revolutionary rage and madness which has levelled beneath its blows such a multitude of majestic and invaluable monuments of the arts and sciences—The cry of indignation rising from every class suspends for a moment the sanguinary crimes of the Jacobin Vandal, and he even pretends to weep.—Wait, and the last mysteries shall be accomplished; wait, and you shall see the awful bodings of the Hierophant fulfilled, and with fire and sword shall he annihilate your laws, your sciences and arts, and erase your towns and habitations.

Here in particular is to be found the origin of that revolutionary ferocity, that thirst of blood, those insatiable proscriptions, those incessant executions, and finally those banishments more artfully cruel than the relentless guillotine. Yes, the time draws near when they shall *bind the hands, subjugate, and crush* in their origin, what the Sect calls the *wicked*, or, in other words, all who are proof against their vile efforts; the time for *subjugating* and *destroying* every citizen zealous in the cause of Religion, or wishing to support the laws, civil society, or property. Like Huns and Vandals, the Sect has begun its career; but it will carefully avoid terminating it like them; the devastations of its followers shall be perpetuated, and they will be Vandals to the last, until Religion, property, and the laws shall be irrecoverably lost. Such atrocious plots are only the consequences of the lesser mysteries; but trust the author of the Sect, the modern Spartacus, for the farther developement of them. Has he not told you, that his last mysteries were but the consequences, a clearer and more absolute exposition of the foregoing secrets of the Order? He informed you, that nations, together with their laws and social institutions, shall vanish, and that they shall disappear before the all-powerful arm of his adepts, or his modern Vandals. What new secret then remains to be discovered, unless it be that no time shall blunt the sword or slack the unrelenting fury of his proselytes; that they shall persevere until the end of time in their Vandalism, lest Religion, society, science, arts, the love of their country, and respect for property, should shoot forth again, and overshadow the venemous growth of his Illuminized Equality and Liberty?

But Spartacus is not to be contented with these last secrets of the Conspiracy; his pride cannot endure that others shoud usurp the glory of the invention. Hitherto we have seen him play upon the credulity of his adepts, inflame their zeal, and acquire their respect by the pretended antiquity of his Order; and successively attribute the honour of instituting his mysteries to the children of the Patriarchs, the Sages, even to the god of Christianity, and to the founders of the Masonic Lodges. But now the time is come when the adept, initiated in the higher mysteries, is supposed to be sufficiently enthusiastic in his admiration of the Order for the chiefs no longer to fear *to disclose the real history of Illuminism.*[26] Here they inform him, that this secret society, which so artfully led him from mystery to mystery, which has with such persevering industry rooted from his heart every principle of Religion, all false ideas of love of the country or affection for his family, all pretensions to property, to the exclusive right to riches, or to the fruits of the earth; this society, which took such pains to demonstrate the tyranny and despotism of all that he calls the laws of empires; this society, which has declared him free, and teaches him that he has no sovereign but himself, no rights to respect in others, but those of perfect Equality, of absolute Liberty, and of the most entire independence; this society is not the offspring of an ignorant and superstitious antiquity, it is that of modern philosophy; in a word, it is of our own invention. The *true father of Illuminism is no other than* SPARTACUS WEISHAUPT.

We must also perceive by many of Weishaupt's letters, that this latter part of the secret, which attributed to him the whole honour of the invention, always remained a mystery to the greater part of his *Mages* and *Men-Kings*. Those alone who, under the title of Areopagites, formed the grand council of the Order, were to be made acquainted with the real chief and founder, except in certain cases where an adept was judged worthy of so distinguished a mark of confidence.[27] Whatever merit the adept might boast, Weishaupt knew no higher recompence than to tell them in the end, "This general overthrow of the Altar, of the Throne, and of all Society, is a conception of my own; to me and to me alone is due the whole glory."

I have revealed the disastrous secrets of Illuminism; I have laid open the gradation and progressive degrees, the long chain of artifice, by which the Sect prepares its adepts for the last mysteries, to behold them stript of their veil without shuddering, and to embrace them with enthusiastic ardour.—We must either commit the Code of the Sect to the flames, and deny the truth of its annals; even refuse the evidence of the familiar correspondence of *Spartacus* Weishaupt the founder, and of *Philo*-Knigge the principal compiler; we must dispute all the agreements of its most arduous co-operators, or else must we wait, as the only possible demonstration, the entire and fatal execution of these disastrous plots, before we positively pronounce, that the sole object of their infernal plans and of their frantic wishes is no other than the total overthrow of every Altar, of every Throne or Magistracy; the annihilation of all authority and of all civil or religious society; the destruction of property whether in the hands of the rich or of the poor; and the very arts and sciences which can only be cultivated in civil society are to be banished from the face of the earth. *Equality and Liberty*, together with the most absolute independence, are to be the substitutes for all rights and all property: Our morals and social intercourse are to make place for the savage, vagabond, roaming life, which the Sect alternately decorates with the name of *Nomade* and of *Patriarchal*. The means to be employed in operating this change will be found in the artifice, deceit, illusion and wickedness which the Sophisters are masters of, until the force of numbers shall have declared for the Sect; but when at length, powerful in numbers, the Sect shall have acquired strength, it shall not only *bind hands, subjugate*, murder, ravage, and renew all the horrors and atrocities of the barbarians of the North, but also surpass those Vandals in the arts of destruction, and without pity or distinction butcher all that part of mankind that shall dare to oppose the progress of the Sect, presume to heave a sigh over the ruins of religion, society, or property, or attempt to raise them from their ashes.—If I have not proved that such are the wishes, the secret machinations of the Sect and of its flagitious principles, let me be informed what is to be understood by proof, or what is to be the operation of evidence on the human mind.—Were it possible that any of my readers still consoled themselves with the idea that the frantic extravagance of these plots surpassed their wickedness, let them remember that I have still something more to say.—I have still to investigate the laws and interior government of the Sect, laws adopted for the destruction of every other law or government, and that it might hereafter prove, that however monstrous the object of the plots of the Sect may be, it was far from being chimerical.

1. Orig. Writ. Vol. II. Let. 15, 16, 24, to Cato-Zwack.
2. Ibid. Vol. I. Let. 4, to Cato.
3. Ibid. Vol. II. Let 1, to Philo, and Second Part of Agreement of the Areopagites.
4. Original Writings, Vol. II. Let. 15, to Cato.

5. See the Discourse on the Degree of Epopt.
6. Original Writings, Vol. I. Let 4, to Cato.
7. Ibid. Let 3, to Cato.
8. See the Helvian Letters on these Works.
9. Ibid. Vol. II. Let. 15, to Cato.
10. So hoffe ich doch sollen alle darin übereinkommen, dass die in diesen graden aufgestellten grund-säze fähig seyen, grosse und erhabene menschen zu bilden—*Introduction to his corrected System*.
11. See in the corrected System the Discourse on the third class.
12. Unterricht für alle mitglieder, welche zu Theosophischen schwärmereyen geneight sind.
13. See the last Discourse of Illuminism corrected.
14. See this agreement in the Original Writings, Vol. II. Part II. signed the 20 *Adarmeth* 1551, or Anno Domini 20 December, 1781.
15. Da nun die leute sehen dass wir die einzigen ächten wahren Christen sind, so därfen wir da gegen ein word mehr gegen pfaffen and fürsten reden; doch habe ich diess so gethan, dass ich päpste und könige nach vorhergegangener prüfung, in diese grade aufnehmen wollte. Indem höheren mysterien sollte man dann A diese *piam fraudem* entdecken, und B aus allen schrifften den ursprung aller religiözen lügen, und deren zusammenhang entwickeln—*Original Writings, Vol. II. Let. I., from Philo to Cato*.
16. Der erste, welcher *Magus* auch *Philosophus* heist, enthält spinosistische grund-sätze, nach welchen alles materiell, Gotz und die welt einerley, alle religion unstatthaft, und eine erfindung hersüchtiger menschen ist.

   I might have quoted the testimony of another adept, who writes as follows to the authors of the Eu-demonia: (Vol. III. No. 2, Art. 4.) "I can also declare that I have been present at the grand mysteries; particularly, that in 1785 I was entrusted with the instructions of the degree of *Mage* or *Philosopher*, and that the short description given in the ENDLICHES SCHICKSAL (or the last object of Freemasonry) is perfectly exact and well grounded." The author of the *Endliches Schicksal* has only, like myself, copied the text from *Biederman*. I have no knowledge of this new adept. I see he has signed his letter, desiring the authors of the Eudemonia not to make use of his name without an absolute necessity. "Besides," he adds, "I am a Roman Catholic; and in the country in which I live might find disagreeable consequences from not having asked to be absolved from my oath, *before I published what I had promised to keep secret*." Sir, I am a Catholic as well as yourself, and should wish to know where you have learned, that the oath you had taken to the Illuminees was superior to that you had taken to the state. How then could you reconcile with your conscience the keeping back from the magistrate or the prince such proofs as you had acquired of a conspiracy against the state? Yes, do penance, and ask absolution for having taken such an oath, and for not having been true to the oath of allegiance which you had sworn to the state, and from which you could not be absolved by *any power on earth*.—What singular ideas are sometimes formed of probity! To persuade oneself that one is bound by an oath to a band of conspirators, while the oath of allegiance is overlooked!—Sir, you had said, that it was necessary to take proper precautions for your security, that *wretches pretending to the power of life and death* might not assassinate you, nothing could be more natural; take your precautions while informing the public magistrate, but do not come and give us as an excuse your fidelity to an oath, which in itself is nothing less than a perjury to the state.

Notwithstanding, however, the reproach justly merited by this adept, his testimony is not to be neglected, since he has sent his name to the editors of the Eudemonia, a journal printed at Franckfort on the Mein, and highly deserving of encouragement for the vigour with which the editors combat the Illuminees. Their writings have frequently corroborated materials that I had received from Austria and Bavaria, which give me great confidence in the researches I have made.

17. Panegyric of Montesquieu.
18. Der zweyte, *Rex* gennant, lehrt dass jeder Bauer, Bürger und hausvater ein *souverain* sey, wie in dem patriarchalischen leben, auf welches die leute wieder zurück-gebracht werden müsten, gewesen sey; und dass folglich alle obrigkeit wegfallen müsse—Diese beyden graden habe auch ich, der ich in dem orden alles durchgegangen bin, selbst gelesen. *Ibid.*
19. Original Writings, Vol. II. Let. 10, to Cato.
20. See the Degree of Epopt.
21. Chap. I.
22. Discourse on the Inequality of Stations, Vol. II.
23. See above, the Prince Illuminee.
24. Befordern die gemeine wissenschaften warhafte aufklärung, wahre menschliche glückseligkeit; oder sind sie viel mehr kinder der noth, der verfielfältigten bedürfnisse, des wiedernatürlichen zustandes erfindungen spitzfindiger eitler köpfe?
25. Nun seyd ihr stark genug den noch übrigen rest die hände zu binden, sie zu unterwerfen, und die bosheit eher in ihrem keime zu ersticken.
26. Original Writings, Vol. II. Letter from Knigge to Zwack.
27. Original Writings, Vol. I. Let. 25, to Cato.

CHAP. XIII.

Tenth and Last Part of the Code of the Illuminees.—Government of the Order—General Idea of that Government, and of the Share which the Inferior Classes of Illuminism bear in it.

IT is not enough for the founder of a Sect of Conspirators to have fixed the precise object of his plots, the trials and degrees through which his adepts are to rise insensibly to the acquisition of his profoundest mysteries. His accomplices must form but one body animated by one spirit; its members must be moved by the same laws, under the inspection and government of the same chiefs, and all must tend toward the same object. Such a genius as Weishaupt's could not be suspected of having overlooked in his Code so important a means of success. From what I have already said, the reader will have observed what connection and subordination subsisted in the gradation of his mysteries; how all the adepts of a given town formed, notwithstanding the inequality of their degrees, but one and the same academy of Conspirators, while each one laboured separately at the overthrow of religion and the laws in the state in which he lived. In this academy the *Candidate* and the *Novice* are under the direction of the *Insinuator*, who introduces them into the *Minerval Lodges;* these Lodges are governed by the *Minor Illuminees*, who in their turn are inspected by the *Major Illuminees*. Next to these preparatory degrees follow the intermediary or Masonic degree, called the *Scotch Knight*; and his power extends on the one side over the *Major Illuminees*, and on the other over the Illuminized Masons; or, in general, over all that part of the Order stiled in the Code the *lower part of the edifice*. After these we meet the *Epopts* and *Regents* or *Princes* of the lesser mysteries, and lastly, in the higher mysteries, the *Mage* and *Man-King*.

The aggregate of all these degrees forms a complete academy of Conspirators, and impendent ruin threatens the country where such a one exists. The Magistrate and the Citizen may expect to see their property and their religion annihilated. The Sect recognizes no country but the universe, or rather acknowledges none; the very term *country* is a blasphemy against the rights of man, against Equality and Liberty. What each member in his particular academy performs by himself, is performed throughout all of them by the Sect in general, and the combined efforts of the whole are regularly directed toward the concerted plan of devastation. The Miners have received their instructions, that each may bore his subterraneous galleries, and lodge the chamber of his mines in such a manner that partial explosions may forward the views of the Sect, without endamaging the grand chamber, which shall involve the whole world in the premeditated explosion of universal destruction. To produce this effect, general laws and mutual communications, common chiefs and directors are requisite. Each Conspirator, wherever his field of action may lie, must be certain that he acts in concert with his Brethren, that he will not be crossed in his plans, but on the contrary meet every where with support and corresponding agents.

Weishaupt was aware, that the farther the sphere of disorganization was to extend the more perfect should be the organization of his power. The more eager he was to call down universal anarchy, and make it take place of all laws, the more did he wish to establish subordination, and concentrate the forces of the Order, the better to direct its motions. To accomplish this, the oath of implicit obedience to Superiors was not enough.—It was not sufficient for the adept to have blindly submitted his life and fortune to the despotic power of unknown chiefs, should they ever suspect him of treachery or rebellion. The Superiors themselves were to be bound by laws and principles common to all, that they might proceed in all points by a regular and uniform impulse.

It cost Weishaupt much meditation before he could perfect his plan of government as he wished. Five years after the establishment of the Sect, he writes *"This machine of ours must be so perfectly simple that a child could direct it;"* and still later he writes, "allow me time to digest my speculations, that I may properly marshal our forces."[1]

So preoccupied was Weishaupt with his speculations on the government of the Sect, that all his letters written to his principal adepts are replete with his maxims and political councils. One must have heard or read them one's self to credit the deep-laid villany of his means and his infernal policy. Here is an example:

In the same letter which I have justed quoted of the 15 Asphandar 1151 he gives two rules to be inserted among the instructions of the Areopagites—The one, to be on the reserve with Candidates *from among the class of the rich, because that sort of men, proud, ignorant, averse to labour, and impatient of subordination,* only seek admission to our mysteries in order to make them an object of ridicule and mockery; the other, not to take the smallest pains to prove, that Illuminism is in the sole possession of the true Masonry, *because the best possible demonstration is to give none.* Let Weishaupt himself explain a third law, which is to make a part of his political collection.

"*That we may be uncontrolled in our discourse, let our pupils remark, that the Superiors enjoy a great latitude in that respect; that we sometimes speak in one way, sometimes in another,* that we often question with great assurance only to sound the opinions of our pupils, and to give them an opportunity of showing it by their answers. This subterfuge repairs many errors. Let us always say, that the end will discover which of our observations conveys our true sentiments.—Thus we may speak sometimes in one way, at others in a quite different one, that we may never be embarrassed, and that our real sentiments may always be impenetrable to our inferiors. Let this be also inserted in the instructions, *etiam hoc inseratur instructioni*. It would still have a better effect, if you gave in charge to our *Major Illuminees* to vary their conversation with their inferiors, for the above reasons, *ex rationibus supra dictis*." These insertions of Latin are from Weishaupt, who frequently makes use of that language in his letters. It is immediately after having given these principles of government to the Areopagites, the chief superiors of his Illuminism, that Weishaupt adds, "I entreat that the maxims which are so often to be found in my letters may not be lost. Collect them for the use of our Areopagites, as they are not always present in my mind. With time they might form an excellent *political* degree. *Philo* has long since been employed about it. Communicate also your private instructions to each other, which may in time grow into an uniform Code. Read them attentively, that they may become familiar to you. Though I know them well and practise them (*und auch darnach handle*) they would take me too much time to digest them systematically. These maxims once engraved in your mind, you will enter better into my plans, and you will proceed more comfortably to my mode of operation."[2]

Let the reader also profit of these instructions. They must bear evidence in my behalf while revealing all the monstrous artifices of the remaining part of the Illuminized Code. From these long meditated combinations, sprang forth that chain of laws which was to direct each Illuminée in all his procedings.

We first remark in this government, as a means of subordination, a general division of command, as well as of locality. Each department has a particular *Lodge* for its adepts; each *Minerval* Lodge has a Superior from among the preparatory class, under the inspection of the intermediary class. In the second place, we find the division into districts which contain several Lodges, all which as well as the Prefect are under the direction of the superior of the district whom the Order calls *Dean*. He is also subjected to the *Provincial*, who has the inspection and command over all the lodges and deanries of the province. Next in rank comes the *National Superior*, who has full powers over all within his nation, Provincials, Deans, Lodges, &c. &c. Then comes the supreme council of the Order, or the *Areopagites*, presided by the real *General* of Illuminism.

The same hierarchy is preserved in their communications. The simple Illuminee corresponds with his immediate superior, the latter with his Dean, and thus gradually ascending to the National Superiors. These latter are in direct correspondence with the Areopagites; and they alone are acquainted with their residence. In this council there is always a member whose particular office is to receive and answer their letters, and to transmit orders, which gradually descend to the person or persons who are the objects of them. The Areopagites alone are entrusted with the name and residence of the General, excepting in cases which I have already noticed, where particular confidence or remarkable services have gained for an adept the signal honour of knowing and approaching the modern Spartacus.

It is easy to perceive, from the very regulations of the first degrees, how voluminous this correspondence must be. Each brother, in the first place, as the *natural Scrutator* of his co-adepts and of the prophane, is bound to transmit at least one letter each month, with a statement of all the observations he has made, whether favourable or detrimental to the Order. He is also to give an account of the progress which himself and his brethren have made; of the orders he has received, and of their execution; and he is each month to inform his higher superiors whether he is pleased with the conduct of his immediate superior. Each brother Insinuator is to report the progress of his Candidates, and the prospect he has of adding to their number. Next, to swell the volume, come all the portraits of the adepts, the extracts of tablets or daily observations made on the friends or enemies of the Order: also the minutes of initiations, the characters and lives of the initiated, the returns made by the Lodges, those by the superiors, and an infinity of other articles which the Illuminee is bound to make known to his chiefs.—All this occurs without noticing the numberless orders and instructions which are perpetually transmitting to the inferiors.

Beside the secret language already explained, and of which the grand object was to render this correspondence unintelligible to the prophane, the Sect had secret means of transmitting their letters, lest they might be intercepted. The Order styles these letters relative to their illuminism *Quibus Licet's* (or to those who have a right). The origin of this appellation is the direction of these letters which consists of the two words *Quibus Licet* or simply the initials Q. L. When, therefore, we find in the Original Writings, that such an adept has been fined in such a month for having neglected his Q. L., it must be understood that he let such a month pass without writing to his superiors.[3]

When the letter contains secrets or complaints which the adept chooses to keep from the knowledge of his immediate superior, he adds to the direction *Soli* or *Primo* (to him alone, to the first); this letter will then be opened by the *Provincial*, the *National Superior*, or will reach the *Areopagites*, or *General*, according to the rank of the person from whom it comes.

Next to these general means of graduated correspondence, come the meetings proper to each degree, and their respective powers. We have already seen, that those of the *Minerval* academy are regularly held twice a month. The *Minor* Illuminees, who are the magistrates of this degree, and the *Major* Illuminee, or the *Scotch Knight*, who presides in them, have no direct share in the government, farther than to inspect the studies and watch over the conduct of the young *Minervals*, and report to the lodges of the *Major* Illuminees. It is in that degree that the authority begins to extend beyond the limits of the assembly. It is to the *Major* Illuminees that all the tablets or instructions relative to the brethren of *Minerva* are sent. Here these statements are digested, and receive additions and notes, before they are forwarded to the assembly of the next superior degree. Here are judged and determined the promotions of the *Novices*, *Minervals*, and *Minor* Illuminees; and also all differences and contests which may arise in the inferior degrees, unless the importance of the debate be such as to require the interference of a higher tribunal. They are the guardians of the first tablets and reversal letters of the brethren.—As to what knowlege a Major Illuminee may have acquired either relative to other secret societies, or to employments or dignities which might be obtained for adepts, he is bound to report it to his lodge, which will note it, and inform the assembly of the *Directing* Illuminees or *Scotch Knights*.[4]

When treating of the intermediary degree of *Scotch Knight*, I gave an account of their particular functions, and especially their *charge of superintending the Masonic Lodges*. The part they act in the general government of the Order chiefly consists in hearing all the *Quibus Licets* of the preparatory classes read in their chapters, even those of the Novices which had already been opened by the officers of the Minerval school: the latter having only the power of deciding provisionally on these letters.

The authority which the *Scotch Knights* exercise over this correspondence seems to give still more propriety to their denomination of intermediary degree. Their *Quibus Licets* are directly sent to the Provincial Lodge, which is composed entirely of adepts initiated in the mysteries of the Order. But the Knights read all letters coming from the preparatory class which have not the distinction of *Primo* or *Soli*. They classify and make extracts from all the *Quibus Licets* of lesser importance coming from the inferior degrees, and send the general extract to the Provincial. To these extracts they subjoin a circumstantial account of every thing that is going forward in the lodges of the preparatory class, to which they transmit all the orders coming from the adepts initiated in the mysteries, even from those of the highest degrees with the very names of which they are unacquainted, and thus constitute a link between the two extremities.[5]

Both the intermediary and preparatory classes, however, form but the lower part of the edifice. The Prefects of the *Chapters* of the *Scotch Knights* are rather tools than superiors; they receive their impulse from the higher mysteries. It is there that the grand polity of the Order is to be sought for in the instructions laid down for the Epopt and the Regent, and these are the instructions which, beginning with those of the Epopt, demand our utmost attention.

1. Letters to Cato, 15th March 1781, and 16th February 1782.
2. Letter to Cato, 15th March, 1781.
3. Vol. II. Let. 2, from Spartacus to Cato.
4. Degree of Major Illuminée, Instruction 4th.
5. See this degree, Instruction the 2d, No. 2.

CHAP. XIV.

Of the Government and Political Instructions for the Epopts.

ENLIGHTEN *nations*; that is to say, efface from the minds of the people what *we* call religious and political prejudices; make yourself master of the public opinion; and, this empire once established, all the constitutions which govern the world will disappear.—Such are the grand means, such the hopes, on which Weishaupt has been observed in his mysteries to have grounded his hopes of success. We have seen even the sciences involved in the vortex of his conspiracies. They were to be swept into the common mass of ruin with religion, laws, Princes, nations, our towns and stationary habitations. —Vandalism and the era of barbarism were to be revived, and science was to be reduced to that of the *nomade* and *savage* clans *equal and free*. This gigantic mass of destruction could be the operation but of a general corruption and perversion of the public opinion, which is itself dependent on science, or at least upon the reputation of wisdom and knowledge which he possesses who pretends to instruct us. To prepare the attack, therefore, it was necessary to make the sciences serve under the banners of the Sect in the cause of their own annihilation, and through their means captivate the public opinion in favour of the Sect. Its errors once triumphant, and every thing dear and sacred to man *vandalized* and overthrown; sciences would of themselves shrink back and vanish from before the man savage and free. Such were the fruits of Weishaupt's meditations, such the spirit which dictated the laws given to his *Epopts*. This degree was to extend the conquests of the Sect over public opinion by science, or, in other words, to dispense its anti-religious and anti-social doctrines under the bewitching name of science. He entirely devoted his degree of *Epopts* to the sciences, and may be said to have forestalled them all, that he might usurp and dictate to the public opinion; or, rather, tainted them all, to make them subservient to his views; well assured that they would not survive the contagion. In his *Minerval* degree, it was the minds of the young adepts that he wished to pervert; but in his degree of *Epopt*, his means and views expand, and, under the same mask, he aims at nothing less than the perversion of the whole universe. He formed it into a secret academy, whose hidden ramifications, widely spreading throughout the globe, were, by means of the disastrous laws he had combined, at one blow to annihilate all society and the empire of science.

The plan may appear inconceivable, and above the reach of the most disorganizing genius; but let the reader remember how clearly it has been proved in the mysteries, that Weishaupt and his followers were firmly resolved to bring back the human race to the days of the Huns and Vandals, and, by means of this Vandalism, to all the ignorance of the *nomade* and *savage clans*; and to reduce the standard of science to that of the Equality and Liberty of *Sans-culotism*. Let the reader now condescend to follow me in the exposition of the lessons which the Sect has appropriated to the instruction of its Epopts, and the organization of their academy.

"The illuminized Priests, or Epopts, are presided over by a Dean chosen by themselves. They are to be known to the inferior degrees only under the appellation of Epopt—their meetings are called *Synods*. All the Epopts within the circle of the same district compose a Synod; but each district shall contain no more than nine Epopts, exclusive of the Dean and Prefect of the Chapter. The higher superiors may attend these Synods."

"Of the nine Epopts, seven preside over the sciences distributed under as many heads in the following order:

"I. *Physics.*—Under this head are comprehended Dioptrics, Catoptrics, Hydraulics and Hydrostatics; Electricity, Magnetism, Attraction, &c."

"II. *Medicine*—comprising Anatomy, Chirurgery, Chymistry,&c."

"III. *Mathematics.*—Algebra; Architecture, civil and military; Navigation, Mechanics, Astronomy, &c."

"IV. *Natural History.*—Agriculture, Gardening, Economics, the Knowledge of Insects and Animals including Man, Mineralogy, Metallurgy, Geology, and the science of the earthly phenomena."

"V. *Politics* —which embraces the study of Man, a branch in which the Major Illuminées furnish the materials; Geography, History, Biography, Antiquity, Diplomatics; the political history of Orders, their design, their progress, and their mutual dissentions." This last article seems to have the divers Orders of Masonry in view. A *nota bene* is added in the original, with a particular injunction *to attend to this article,* which the dissentions of the Illuminees and Freemasons had probably rendered of great importance to the Sect.

"VI. *The Arts.*—Mechanics, Painting, Sculpture, Engraving, Music, Dancing, Eloquence, Poetry, Rhetoric, all the branches of Literature; the Trades."

"VII. *The Occult Sciences.*—The study of the Oriental tongues, and others little known, the secret methods of writing, the art of decyphering; the art of raising the seals of the letters of others, and that of preserving their own from similar practices; *Petcshaften zu erbrechen, und für das erbrechen zu bewahren.* The study of ancient and modern hieroglyphics; and, once more, of secret societies, Masonic systems, &c. &c."

Should the reader feel his indignation roused by the art of raising the seals and violating the secresy of letters, and at seeing an adept named in each district to preside over this strange science, let him not forget that I am but the translator and transcriber of the code of the Sect.[1]

The two remaining Epopts, who in the synod are named to preside over any particular science, are made secretaries to the Dean, and serve him as coadjutors. These functions once distributed, the Epopts are to renounce all other business political or domestic, and every care but that of perfecting themselves in the branch of science which they are to superintend, and of secretly forwarding the brethren of the inferior degrees in the sciences to which they had devoted themselves.

The grand object of this institution is to inspire the pupils with the greatest confidence in the Order, from an idea that it will furnish them with all the means and lights necessary for the prosecution of the study they have adopted. The Insinuators have held out the promise to them, and the Order has engaged to fulfil it. This idea of a scientific society, and of which they have the honour of being members, is to encourage in them a docility and veneration for their chiefs naturally due to men whose precepts appear to be emanations of light and of the most transcendent wisdom. The artifice in some sort answers to the promise.

Every Novice, on being admitted into the *Minerval* schools, was to begin by declaring to what art or science he meant to devote himself, unless indeed his pocket was to be assessed for the tax which his genius could not pay. This declaration is transmitted from the inferior lodges to the Provincial, who forwards it to the Dean; by whom notice of it is given to the Epopt who presides over that particular branch of science; and he inscribes his name on the list of those pupils whose labours fall under his inspection. In future, and by the same conveyance, all the essays, discourses, treatises, &c. which the Sect requires of the young Minerval are transmitted to the same Epopt. The first advantage accruing to the Order from this law is the pointing out to the inspecting Epopt those whom the code calls the *best heads of the Order.*

Should any doubts arise in the minds of the pupils, any difficulties to vanquish, or any questions to propose; they have been taught that the Order is the fountain of science, that they have but to apply to their superiors, and light will instantaneously shine upon them. They are ignorant as to who these superiors may be; but that will not hinder their doubts and questions from reaching the presiding Epopt: and he has divers means of solving them, and of never being taken unawares.

In the first place the Epopt must have prepared himself for certain questions, which he either has or ought to have foreseen. Many of them will have been already solved by his predecessors, by his brother Epopts of other districts or even nations. The Order is exceedingly careful in collecting all these answers, and putting them into such hands as may employ them according to the views of the Sect. Each Epopt is particularly enjoined to study those which relate to his branch; he is even to make an alphabetical entry of them on his tablets, that he may always have them at hand whenever he wishes to turn to them. If, notwithstanding all these precautions, the Epopt should find himself unprepared or unable to solve the difficulty proposed, he will apply to the Dean, who will send the required solution or have recourse to the Provincial. But, lest the Superiors should find their occupations too often interrupted by such applications, it is expressly enjoined to the Epopt not to have recourse to them but in cases of absolute necessity, and not to make the acquisitions of their Superiors an encouragement to their own negligence.—It may so happen, that the Provincial is not able to give the required solution; he will then propose it to all the Epopts of his province. If that does not succeed, application is made to the National Inspector, and from him it is referred to the Areopagites and General. On such occasions all the learned men of the Order are consulted. Before this last appeal, it is ordained in the statutes, that the Epopt may propose the questions to the prophane; but in so doing he is on no account to discover that the *Sect* has recourse to, or stood in need of their information, nor what use it makes of it. This is particularly enjoined to the presiding Epopt in the following terms:—"As often as your own knowledge and that of your pupils shall not suffice, you may ask the advice of learned strangers, *and turn their knowledge to the advantage of our Order, but without letting them perceive it:*" (*ohne dass sie es bemerken.*) This precaution is the more to be insisted on, as one of the grand objects of the Epopts must be, "to attain such perfection in science, that Illuminism shall never be beholden to the prophane; but that the latter, on the contrary, shall perpetually stand in need of the lights of the Order."[2]

That the Epopt may not recur too frequently to the superiors, or to the prophane, an artifice has been invented by which he may profit of all the acquisitions of the pupils of his district, while he makes them believe that the whole flows from the unknown superiors. This artifice consists in proposing such questions as he is not perfectly master of, to the different lodges, and then studying and combining the various answers that he receives. All the Epopts of the province do as much in their several districts. Each one selects those parts which he has judged worthy of notice in the productions of the lodges; these he inspects, and lays them before the provincial and annual assembly. There other Epopts are employed in compiling from these selections, and in preparing the required solutions of the proposed questions, or in commenting on such passages as may elucidate others that may hereafter arise. The same plan is followed in all the provinces, and the reports of the provinces will form a new collection to be digested under the inspection of the National Chief, or even of the Areopagites. This will be a new treasure for the secret library of the Epopts, and furnish them with new means of maintaining in the minds of their pupils the high idea they have conceived of the knowledge of their Superiors.[3] It will also furnish materials for the formation of a systematic Code or complete course of study for the use of the Sect.[4]

Here we cannot but remark how much arts and sciences would be benefited and promoted by the labours of a society which, actuated by quite other views, and despising that affectation of secrecy, should employ the same means and be animated with a similar zeal in the discussion of useful truths. But the united efforts of the Epopts are concentrated in their pursuit of science, only to debase it, by directing all its powers toward the overthrow of Religion and Governments, the triumph of their disorganizing systems, and always under the stale pretext of subjecting mankind to Nature alone.[5]

Should the reader be curious to know to what uses the Epopt turns all the science which he is supposed to acquire daily, let him observe the questions which this presiding Illuminee either solves himself, or proposes for the solution of the adepts. Let his judgement on the questions and on their tendency, be guided by the expressions of the Code:

"The Epopt," says the Code, "must keep a list of a very great number of important questions proper for investigation, and which he may eventually propose to the young adepts.—In the branch of practical Philosophy, for example, he will propose for investigation the question, how far the principle is true, *that all means are allowable, when employed for a laudable end*? How far this maxim is to be limited to keep the proper medium between Jesuitical abuse, and the scrupulosity of prejudice?—Questions of this nature shall be sent to the Dean, who shall transmit them to the *Minerval* schools for the investigation of the young adepts, and their dissertations will swarm with a multitude of ideas, *new, bold, and useful*, which will greatly enrich our *Magazine*."[6]

We despise this infamous aspersion on the Jesuits. Let those pass sentence on them who have learned to judge them by their conduct and by their real doctrines, and not by calumnious assertions, or satires which, in spite of all the powers of genius and irony, have been justly condemned by various tribunals as replete with falsehood and misrepresentation.[7] Let those who have been educated by the Jesuits pronounce on these atrocious imputations of the Illuminees; I do not think myself bound to follow the example of the celebrated Hoffman, Professor at the University of Vienna, one of the most formidable adversaries of the Illuminizing Sect, by inserting a long justification of that persecuted Order.[8] But it is impossible not to observe, that the legislator of Illuminism has not the most distant idea of modifying or limiting this famous principle, *the end sanctifies the means*; his object is evidently to give rise to ideas, *new, bold*, and *useful* to the Sect; or, in other words, to dispose the young adepts hereafter to decide as he has already done, that *nothing is criminal*, not even robbery or theft, provided *it be useful* to the views and forward the grand object of Illuminism. He wishes by means of these questions to acquire an early insight into the minds of the adepts, and to distinguish those who will hereafter be the most worthy of his higher mysteries, by the greater or smaller disposition they show to stifle the cries of conscience and remorse in the perpetration of the crimes necessary for the future success of his plots. This is the sum total of the science to be carefully inculcated by the Epopts in the branch of *practical* Philosophy.

With respect to Religion, it is not even admitted among the sciences to be studied by the Epopts; the Code has, however, furnished them with a means of traducing and blaspheming it.—That the Epopt may never be at a loss for questions of this nature to solve or propose, he will have them noted on a register in alphabetical order. "For example," says the Code, "at the Letter C in the register of secret sciences and hieroglyphics the word Cross is to be found, and under it is the following note—For the antiquity of this hieroglyphic, consult such a work, printed such a year, such a page, or else such a manuscript, signature M."[9] It is not necessary to be endowed with any extraordinary share of perspicacity to see that the whole object of these pretended *secret sciences*, or hieroglyphics, is merely to teach the young pupils to view the Cross in no other light than as an ancient hieroglyphic erected by ignorance and superstition into a symbol of the redemption of mankind. The illuminized explanation of this glorious symbol will, doubtless, long remain buried in the Occult Sciences of the Order. Meanwhile we may defy them to point out in the history of mankind any nation whatever revering the cross as the symbol of salvation anterior to the grand epoch when the Son of Man died on the cross to consummate the triumph of Christianity.

The Epopts have also their historians and annalists, and their duties are laid down in the Code. The following rules may be remarked:——Each province of Illuminism must have its historian, in imitation of the ancient annalists and chronologists. He is to keep a journal, in which, beside facts of public notoriety, he will particularly collect, and even give *the preference to, anecdotes of secret history*.—He will endeavour to redeem from oblivion all men of merit, however deep they may have sunk into obscurity—He will make them known to the Provincial, who will inform the Brethren of their situation—Each Provincial will have a Calendar of his own, in which (instead of saints) for each day of the year shall be inscribed the name of some man as an object of veneration or execration, according as he has merited or demerited of the Sect.

My name may perhaps be inscribed under the black letter; but I anticipate the glory and consolation of seeing it by the side of that of Zimmerman and of Hoffman, who, like myself, are entitled to the sable wreath twined by Illuminism for its most strenuous opponents. But how different is that to which the Code declares that all the Brethren *may aspire*!—Probaby, to be seated beside a Brother *Mirabeau* or a *Marat*.

The same laws ordain, that the Chronologist shall inform the *Minerval* Lodges of all memorable facts.—He will not fail to insert all mean and odious actions, nor to paint them in their proper colours. He will not pass unnoticed *those of men occupying the first dignities, or enjoying the highest consideration*.[10]

Next to the laws of the historian follow those for the Epopt who superintends that branch of science relating to politics, and particularly to the knowledge of mankind. The reader has already seen what stress the Order lays upon this science, and how much they make it depend on the spirit of observation—Let no Brother pretend to the dignity of Epopt, nor to the honour of presiding over any branch of science, until he has answered the three following questions—What is the spirit of observation?—How is this spirit to be acquired, and what constitutes a good observer?—What method is to be followed, in order to make just and exact observations?—When an Epopt has sufficiently distinguished himself by his answers on these heads, to be judged worthy of being chosen the chief of the observers or scrutators, he is entrusted with all those notes which the reader has seen the Sect so carefully collecting on the character, the passions, the talents, and history of the Brethren. When these notes contain the portrait or life of any adept more than commonly interesting, he will make him (without naming him) the object of various questions to be proposed to the *Minerval* Schools. He will ask, for example, What are the ideas which a man, with such and such passions or dispositions, will adopt or reject?—How on such data can such and such inclinations be encouraged or weakened?—What adept could be employed with most advantage in such a business?—What must such a man's ideas be on Religion and Governments?—Can he be looked upon as being superior to all prejudices, and ready to sacrifice his own personal interest to that of Truth?—Should he be deficient in confidence and attachment, what means should be employed to invigorate them, and what sort of man would be the fittest for such an undertaking?—Finally, *what employment in the state, or in the Order, would he fill to the greatest advantage, or in which would he be the most useful?*

The Scrutator in chief digests these answers into a proper statement, which he sends to the Dean. The Provincial receives it from the Dean, and is thus enabled to form his judgement, whether that particular adept *be a moral, disinterested, beneficent man, and free from all prejudice; whether he can be useful to the Order, and in what way he can be best employed.* —From the result of such observations, the scrutinizing Epopt will carefully select rules and general maxims on the knowledge of mankind. He will make a compilation of them, and transmit them to the Superiors.[11]

"By means," says the Code, "of these and such like observations, the Order will be enabled to make discoveries of every kind, to form new systems, and to give on all subjects irrefragable proofs of its labours and its immense fund of science; and the public will give it credit for being in possession of all human knowledge.[12]

Lest any of the prophane should partake of this honour, or that any one of the members should not direct these sciences toward the object of Illuminism, precautions are taken in the Code to assure the exclusive advantage of these labours to the Sect. "Particular parts of these sciences and discoveries may be printed by permission of the Superiors; but the law adds, not only these books shall not be communicated to any of the prophane, but as they will never be printed elsewhere than at the presses of the Sect, they will only be entrusted to the Brethren according to the rank they hold in the Order."[13]

"That our worthy co-operators may not be divested of the glory of their labours, every new principle laid down, machine invented, or discovery made, shall for ever bear the name of its inventor, that his memory may be revered by future ages."[14]

"On the same grounds it is strictly enjoined, that no member shall ever communicate to the prophane any discovery that he may have made in the Order—No book treating of these discoveries shall be printed without the permission of the Superiors; and hence arises the general regulation, that no Brother shall publish any of his productions without leave of the Provincial. He also is to decide whether the work is of a nature to be printed by the secret presses of the Order, and what particular Brethren may be allowed the perusal of it—Should it be necessary to dismiss any of the Brethren from the Order, the local Superior is to receive notice that he may have the necessary time to withdraw from him not only the manuscripts, but even the printed works of the Order."[15]

The Illuminizing Legislator, in justification of all these precautions, alledges, in the first place, the undeniable right vested in the Order to all the labours of its Brethren; then the lure of secrecy, which stimulates curiosity and the thirst of science; finally, the advantage accruing to the sciences themselves, by being preserved among men who only impart them to others so prepared as to render them of the greatest possible utility—Beside, says he, every man has it in his power to make himself an Illuminee if he pleases, and to partake of their science; and who better able to render them useful to mankind, or to preserve them, than we are? After this justification, which the reader may appreciate, he returns to his Epopts, and tells them, that it is incumbent on them to direct and turn all the sciences toward the views of Illuminism. "The wants of every country are to be maturely considered, as well as those of your district; let them be the objects of deliberation in your Synods; and ask instructions of your Superiors." Then the Legislator makes a sudden transition, and expands his views far beyond his Lodges. The reader will scarcely suspect whither they tend. Let him read, and learn the grand object of the Epopts, what conquests they are to make for the Order, and whither they are to extend the systems of Illuminism. "You will," abruptly exclaims the legislator, "incessantly form new plans, and try every means, in your respective provinces, to seize upon the public education, the ecclesiastical government, the chairs of literature, and the pulpit."[16]—This is one of the grand objects of the Sect; and we shall see the Code treating of it again in another part.

To enhance the merits of his plans, and to insinuate his adepts into the ecclesiastical seminaries, and even into the pulpit, under the shadow of his pretended science, "the Epopt must find means of *acquiring* the reputation of a man of transcendent learning; wherever he appears, whether walking or stopping, sitting or standing, let *rays of light* encircle his head, which shall enlighten all who approach him. Let every one think himself happy in hearing the pure truth from his lips. Let him on all occasions, combat prejudice; *but with precaution*, and according to the rules laid down, *with dexterity and with all the respect due to the persons he is addressing.*"[17] Who could believe that these were lessons given to a modern Vandal by his disorganizing legislator, whose heart thirsts after the *happy* period when that *encircling light* of his Epopts shall have *Vandalized* the whole universe, and nations shall have disappeared from off the face of the earth?

But the Epopt has yet to aim at another conquest, that of the empire over the literary world. "In the literary world certain writings generally take the lead for a time, according to the fashion, and inspire feeble minds with admiration. At one time the enthusiastic productions of Religion, at another the sentimental novels of wit, or perhaps philosophical reveries, pastorals, romances on chivalry, epic poems, or odes, will inundate the republic of letters. The Epopt will turn all his skill toward bringing into fashion the principles of our Order, the sole tendency of which is the happiness of mankind." Or, in other words, those baleful principles which, under the pretence of rendering human nature more happy and united in one family, aim at nothing less than destroying every Religion, every title to *property*, every town, every fixed residence, and every nation.

"Our principles must be made fashionable, that the young writers may diffuse them among the people, and serve the Order without intending it."[18]

"In order to raise the public spirit, he must with the greatest ardour preach up *the general interest of humanity, and inculcate the utmost indifference for all associations or secret unions which are only formed among the subjects of one particular nation.*[19] Here the impious legislator blasphemously cites for an example Christ, and his pretended indifference for his family. Because Christ died for the redemption of *all* mankind, because his affection for the most holy of mothers never made him lose sight of that great work, is that a ground on which the illuminizing Epopt shall persuade his simple auditory, that to love all mankind is to dissolve the bonds of nations?

As a farther rule for acquiring this literary empire, "He will take care that the writings of the members of the Order shall be cried up, and that the trumpet of fame shall be sounded in their honour. He will also find means of hindering the reviewers from casting any suspicions on the writers of the Sect."[20]

With respect to the *Literati*, and *writers who*, without belonging to the Order, *show principles coinciding with ours*, should they be what we call GOOD, "*class them among those who are to be enrolled. Let the Dean have a list of those men, and from time to time he will hand it about among the brethren.*"[21]

Let us now take a cursory view of these laws, and of their gradual tendency to infect the whole literary world. In its *Minerval* academies the sect begins by forming its pupils; and the care with which its disorganizing principles are instilled into the young adept has already been displayed. Lest any of these principles should swerve from the grand object, the Epopts oversee all the schools of the same district; these latter have their provincial assemblies, where every thing is prepared, combined, and foreseen. At this assembly the Epopt attends, bringing with him *his notes* and observations on his particular district, and on those means which may there contribute to the advancement or disparagement of the Illuminizing principles and science. The minutes of these assemblies are sent to the National Inspector, who overlooks the whole, and sees that the original spirit is every where preserved; and the Areopagites hold the same line of conduct with respect to all nations that he does within his particular one. Hence then the *Minerval* academies, the Epopts, the Provincials, the National Inspectors, in a word, the disorganizing whole, form but one and the same invisible academy, spreading its subterraneous ramifications, every where infusing the same principles, actuated by the same spirit, and subjected to the same laws: and these laws, this science, are but the machinations and the forebodings of universal impiety and disorganization.

But the union and universality of this conspiring academy is not sufficient for the Sect; it extends its views to the public schools and to the pulpit. The man of letters, the transcendent genius, all are to bend beneath its laws, and fashion is to aid its plots. From the child that spells, to the Doctor enveloped in mazy science, all are to be subjected to Illuminism; and science itself, so instrumental to the progress of the Sect, shall sink beneath the effort of bringing forth that Vandalism which is to annihilate the altar and the throne, all laws, individual property, and national society.

Let the reader compare the mysteries of the Sect with the code of its Epopts, and pronounce if such be not the real tendency of this Empire of Science. Horror impresses the mind, and indignation rises at such a sight.—But the monstrous legislator who has compiled them pretends that they are entitled to the admiration of the young adepts; and it is his Epopts who are to inspire them with this admiration. "You must," says he, "infuse so great a respect for the sublimity and sanctity of our Order, that a promise made by the adepts on the honour of Illuminism shall be more binding than the most sacred oath."[22] At length the Atheist has found an equivalent for the name of God. He seeks bonds to bind his followers, and he has broken those of conscience; he appeals to honour, and perverts it into a bond of villany. "He (says Weishaupt) *who shall dare violate the oath he shall have sworn on the honour of my Society, shall be declared infamous. I care not what his rank may be, his infamy shall be proclaimed throughout the whole Order, and it shall be so without remission or hope of pardon. My intention is, that the Members should be informed of this, that they should deliberately reflect on the sacredness of this oath in my Order, I mean that the consequences of it should be clearly and warmly represented to them.*"[23]

The Epopts charged with this mission are of a degree too much revered in the Order to compromise their dignity. They attend, at pleasure, the meetings of the inferior degrees, but they are never to occupy any office in them, excepting that of Prefect of the *Scotch Knights*. Their presence might overawe and intimidate the young adepts, and thus be detrimental to the observations they are ordered to make; for (so far from constraint), the Epopt is to endeavour to study them in their most unguarded moments. He is therefore never to intermix with them but as their equal. There is a particular law forbidding him to disclose the degree or the class to which he belongs, or even his costume.[24] Thus, hiding his superiority, and seated on the same benches beside the young adepts, he exercises his functions of Scrutator more freely among them in thier mutual intercourse, and he judges better of the talents of each. His lessons, coming apparently from an equal, will sink deeper into their minds; and, without betraying his authority, he will the better observe their progress and their failings.—Should any of these pupils have shown a zeal and fidelity beyond all doubt, he may take them into his confidence; he will point them out to the Dean, who may call them about his person and make them his *Acolites*. The Dean may even throw a great part of the weight of his correspondence on them, and carry them to the Synod of the Epopts, until they shall have shown themselves worthy of being initiated to all the mysteries reserved for this class.[25]

Thus ends that part of the Code which is to be communicated to the Epopts. The following Chapters will delineate the laws and instructions which are to guide their conduct when admitted to the degree of *Regent* or *Prince* of *Illuminism*.

1. Instructions for this degree, Nos. 1, 2, 3, 4, 11.
2. Instructions for ths degree, No. 2, 5, 6, 9.
3. Nos. 5 and 12.
4. No. 15.
5. Das der Order die bisherigen systeme entbehren, und eigene, auf die natur allein gegründete systeme seinen anhänger vorlegen könne.
6. Ibid. No. 7.
7. See Art. Pascal in the Historical Dictionary of Flexier Dureval, last Edition.
8. Vide Hoch wichtige erinnerungen—Von Leopold-alois—Hoffman. Sect. V. Page 279 to 307.
9. Ibid. No. 15.
10. Ibid. No. 18.
11. Ibid. No. 18.
12. Ibid. No. 20.
13. Ibid. No. 17.
14. Ibid. No. 23.
15. Ibid. No. 24.
16. Müssen stets neue plane entworfen und eingeführt werden: Wie man die hände in erziehungswesen, geistliche regierung, lehr, und predigt-stühle in der provinz bekomme. *Ibid. No. 28.*
17. Ibid. No. 2.
18. Damit junge schriftsteller dergleichen unter das volk ausbreiten, und uns, ohne dass sie es wissen, dienen.
19. Ibid. No. 3.
20. Ibid. No. 4.
21. Ibid. No. 5.
22. Ibid. No. 29.
23. Original Writings, Vol. II. Let. 8, to Cato.
24. Ibid. No. 31.
25. Ibid. No. 32.

CHAP. XV.

Instructions for the Regent or Prince Illuminee, on the Government of the Order.

THE prominent feature of all the instructions given by the Illuminizing Legislator to his Epopts is the consecration of their degree to the perversion of the public opinion, and to the attainment of the empire of sciences, that he may direct them all to the support of his disorganizing Equality and Liberty and to universal anarchy. This mission of perversion requires an assiduity to which not many men are equal; but adepts may be found, who, unable to distinguish themselves in such missions, may yet be endowed with a sufficient zeal and with the necessary talents for the superintendance and direction of the Brethren. There are others again whose disastrous successes are to be recompensed by the higher employments in the Order; and it is from these *two classes of Epopts* that the Order *selects its Regents*. It is also for their instruction that the Legislator descends into all the gubernatory minutiæ of his Illuminism.—His instructions are comprised under four different heads. I. General System of Government for the Order.—II. Instructions for the degree of Regent.—III. Instructions for the Prefects or Local Superiors.—IV. Instructions for the Provincial.[1]

I have, it is true, been obliged to anticipate many parts of this Code when unfolding the artifices of the lower degrees; but as a confirmation of what has already been exposed, in order to bring the different objects within one point of view, and to show the dangers of his disastrous combinations, let us attend to the Legislator when treating of the whole collectively. What particularly endeared this degree of Regent to Weishaupt was, that part of his instruction which takes a general view, and which lays open the progressive plan to be observed in the government of the Brethren. The reader perusing the instructions in the same order in which Weishaupt has written them, will more easily conceive the cause of his predilection.

Instruction A. Plan of the General Government of the Order.

"I. The most high and excellent Superiors of the illustrious Order of *true Freemasonry* do not immediately attend to the minutiæ of the edifice.—They must not, however, on that account be considered as contributing less to our happiness, by their counsels, their lessons, their plans, and the many and powerful resources with which they furnish us.

"II. These excellent and most gracious Superiors have established a class of Masons to whom they have entrusted the whole plan of our Order. This class is that of the *Regents*.....

"III. In this plan our Regents hold the first dignities. Until admitted to this degree, no person can hold the office of *Prefect* or of *Local Superior*.

"IV. Every country has its national Superior, who holds an immediate correspondence with our *Fathers*, at the head of whom is a General who holds the helm of the Order.

"V. Under the *National* and his *Assistants* are the *Provincials*, who each govern their Circle or their Province.

"VI. Every Provincial is surrounded by his Counsellors.

"VII. Each Provincial also commands a certain number of Prefects, who may in like manner have their coadjutors in their districts. All these, as well as the *Dean*, belong to the class of Regents.

"VIII. All these offices are for life, excepting in cases of deposition or ejectment.

"IX. The Provincial is to be chosen by the *Regents* of his province and the *National Superiors*, and approved by the *National*.—[I do not understand how the Code distinguishes between the several *National Superiors* and the *National* in chief; unless it be, that it denotes in this place as *Superiors* those who are called a little higher up *Assistants (Gehulfen)* of this chief.]

"X. The whole success of Illuminism depending on the *Regents*, it is but just that their domestic wants should be provided for. They shall therefore be the first supplied from out of the funds of the Order.

"XI. The Regents of each Province form a particular body immediately under the Provincial, whom they are to obey.....

"XII. The offices of Illuminism not being considered in the light of dignities, nor of *places of honour*, but as mere *employments* freely accepted, the Regents must be always ready to labour for the good of the Order, each according to his situation and to his talents. Age is never to be set forth as a title. It may often happen, that the youngest is chosen Provincial, and the eldest only a Local Superior or Counsellor, should the one live in the center, while the other only inhabits the extremity of the Province; or, should the former, on account of his natural activity or his station in life, be more fitted for the place of Superior than the latter, though far more eloquent. In many cases, for example, a Regent is not to think it beneath his dignity to offer himself to discharge any of the lesser offices in the *Minerval churches* (lodges) in whch he may be useful.

"XIII. That the Provincial may not be overburdened with too extensive a correspondence, all the *Quibus Licets,* and all the letters of the Regents, shall pass through the hands of the Prefect, unless the Provincial gives Orders to the contrary.

"XIV. But the Prefect shall not open the letters of the *Regents*. Those he must transmit to the Provincial, who will forward them to their proper destination.

"XV. The Provincial has the power of convoking the whole of his Regents, or merely those whom he may think proper, considering the exigencies of the Province. He who cannot attend according to his summons must give the proper notice at least four weeks prior to the meeting. Beside, he is always to be ready to give in an account of what he has done for the Order until that period, and show willingness to fulfil the intentions of his Provincial and of his high Superiors. The convocation of Regents must take place at least once a year.

"XVI. The following instruction (B) will point out more particularly to the Regents those objects to which they must chiefly attend.

"XVII. It has been already observed, that great attention is to be paid to the gradually procuring of funds for the Order. This may be accomplished by attending to the following rules:

"Each province is to be entrusted with the expenditure of its own monies, and only remit small contributions to the Superiors for the expences of postage. Each Lodge also is to enjoy the *full propriety* of its funds (*eigenthümlich*)—when *for any great enterprize* the assembly of the Regents levy contributions on the funds of the different Lodges, they shall be considered but as loans, and shall be made good to the Lodges with full interest."

Has the Illuminizing Legislator then forgotten, that it was PROPERTY which gave the first *deadly blow to Equality and Liberty*? Certainly not; but more than ONE *great enterprize* will be necessary to prepare the LAST, which is to *annihilate all property* whatsoever; meanwhile the Order is glad to enjoy its own, and to make the inferior Lodges believe that they are not to be pillaged of any thing that belongs to them.

"The Provincial has no fund allotted to him, but he has an exact return of all those of his province."

"The general *receipts* will consist—1°. In the contributions paid on the receptions of Masons *(freymaurer-receptions-gelder)*—2°. In the over-plus of the monthly contributions—3°. In voluntary subscriptions—4°. In fines—5°. In legacies and donations—6°. In our commerce and traffic (*handel und gewerbe*)."

"The *expences* are—1°. The expences of the meetings, postage, decorations, and some few journies—2°. Pensions to the poor brethren who have no other means of subsistence—3°. Sums paid for the *promotion of the grand object of the Order*—4°. Sums paid for the encouraging of talents—5°. The expences of experiments and trials—6°. For widows and children—7°. For foundations."

Thus terminates the first part of the instructions for the Regent. After the reading of this, which takes place on the day of his inauguration, his attention is called to the following:

Instruction B for the whole degree
of Regent

The reader has seen (*ut supra*, art. xvi.) the Regent forewarned to pay a particular attention to this second part of the instructions. Let the reader also profit of the hint. He will see that many of the *arcana* of the Sect still remain to be revealed.

"I. The object of the Order being to render man more happy, virtue more attractive, and vice less powerful, it is necesssary that our brethren, the *teachers and governors of mankind*, should publicly assume an unimpeachable character. A Regent of Illuminism therefore will be the most perfect of men. He will be prudent, provident, ingenious, irreproachable, and of manners so urbane that his company shall be courted with avidity. He is to acquire the reputation of being enlightened, benevolent, honest, disinterested, and full of ardour for great and extraordinary enterprises, all contributing to the general good."

It would be useless to recall to the mind of my reader what is to be understood, in the language of Illuminism, by virtue, vice, or public good. He will therefore on reflection be the less surprised at perusing the following instructions framed for these *virtuous teachers and governors* of mankind.

"II. The Regents are to study the means of ruling and governing without betraying any such intention.[2] Under the mask of humility, but of a real and candid humility, grounded on the persuasion of their own weakness, and on the conviction that their *whole strength rests on our union*, they must exercise an absolute and boundless dominion,[3] and must direct every thing toward the attainment of the views of the Order."

"Let them avoid a pedantic reserve, at once disgusting and ridiculous in the eyes of the sage. Let them give the example of a respectful submission to the Superiors. Should they be possessed of the advantages of birth, it will be an additional reason for showing their obedience to a Superior born in a lower station of life—Let their conduct vary according to the persons with whom they have to deal. Let the Regent be the confidant of one, the father of another, the scholar of a third; very seldom a severe and inexorable Superior, and even on such occasions let him show with how much unwillingness he exercises such severity. He will say, for example, that he sincerely wishes the Order had given so disagreeable a commission to some other person; and that he is weary of acting the part of schoolmaster with a man who should long since have known how to conduct himself.

"III. The grand object of our *sacred legions spread throughout the universe* being the triumph of virtue and of wisdom, every Regent must endeavour to establish *a certain equality* among men.—Let him take the part of those who are too much debased, and humble the proud. Let him never suffer the fool to lord it too much over the man of wit, the wicked over the good, the ignorant over the learned, nor the weak over the strong, though the latter should in reality be in the wrong.[4]

"IV. The means of acquiring an ascendancy over men are incalculable. Who could enumerate them all?... They must vary with the disposition of the times. At one period it is a taste for the marvellous and extraordinary that is to be wrought upon. At another the lure of secret societies is to be held out. *For this reason it is very proper to make your inferiors believe, without telling them the real state of the case, that all other secret societies, particularly that of Freemasonry, are secretly directed by us.* Or else, and it IS REALLY THE FACT IN SOME STATES, THAT POTENT MONARCHS ARE GOVERNED BY OUR ORDER. *When any thing remarkable or important comes to pass, hint that it originated with our Order.—Should any person by his merit acquire a great reputation, let it be generally understood that he is one of us.*"

How smoothly flows this combination of artifice from the pen of the Illuminizing Legislator! But I hope that my reader will not expect to find a method in my translation, where the Legislator has disdained method. It is easy to perceive, that to heap artifice upon artifice is much more his object, than to give a studied connection to principles with which he supposes his adepts to be sufficiently impressed. Or may it not be said, that this disorder is the effect of studied art? But let us proceed and trace the steps of Weishaupt.

"With no other object than to give your orders the appearance of coming from a mysterious hand, you may, for example, put a letter under the plate of an adept when dining at an inn, though it might have been a much less trouble to forward it to him at his own lodgings—You may attend large and commercial towns during the time of fairs in different characters, as *a Merchant, an Officer, an Abbé*. Every where you will personate an extraordinary man having important business on your hands.—But all this must be done with a great deal of art and caution, lest you should have the appearance of an adventurer. It is to be well understood, that these characters are not to be assumed in towns where you are likely to be discovered either by the Police or the standers-by.—At other times, you may write your orders with a chemical preparation of ink, which disappears after a certain time.

"V. A Regent is as much as possible to hide from his inferiors all his weaknesses, even his ill-health, or disgusts; at any rate, he is never to complain.

"VI. Here he repeats the instruction on the art of flattering and gaining over women to their cause, already transcribed, page 43.

"VII. You must also gain over to the Order the COMMON PEOPLE. The great plan for succeeding in this is to *influence the Schools*. You may also attempt it by liberalities, or by great show and splendour; at other times by making yourself popular, and even tolerating, with an *air of patience, prejudices which may hereafter be gradually eradicated*.

"VIII. When you have succeeded any where in making yourself master of the public authority and government, you will pretend not to have the least power, for fear of awakening the attention of those who may oppose us. But, on the contrary, when you find it impossible to succeed, you will assume the character of a person who has every thing at his command. That will make us both feared and sought after, and of course will strengthen our party.

"IX. All the ill success or disgusts which may befall the Order are to be concealed with the utmost caution from the inferiors.

"X. It is the duty of the Regents to supply the wants of the Brethren, *and to procure the best employments for them*, after having given the proper intimation to the Superior.

"XI. The Regents shall be particularly cautious and discreet in their discourse;—but shall carefully avoid any thing denoting the least perplexity of mind—There are even some occasions whereon an extensive genius is to be affected; on others, they may pretend that their friendship has made them say a word too much; by these means the secresy of the inferior is put to the test. They may also spread certain reports among our people, which may prepare them to receive ideas which the Order wishes to infuse into their minds. On all doubtful occasions, the Regent will consult his Superiors by means of a *Quibus Licet*."

"XII. Whatever rank or station a Regent may hold in the Order, he will seldom answer the questions of the inferiors verbally, but generally in writing, that he may have time to reflect or even consult on the answers he should give."

"XIII. The Regents will unceasingly attend to every thing relating to the grand interests of the Order, to the *operations of commerce*, or such things as may in any way contribute to augment the *power* of the Order. They will transmit all plans of that nature to the Provincial. Should it be a case requiring expedition, he will give him advice of it by some other channel than the *Quibus Licets*, which the Provincial has not the power of opening.

"XIV. They will follow the same line of conduct with respect to every thing that tends to influence the Order in general; and find means of putting its united forces in motion at one and the same time.

"XV. When an author sets forth principles true in themselves, *but which do not as yet suit our general plan of education for the world; or principles the publication of which is premature; every effort must be made to gain over the author; but should all our attempts fail, and we should be unable to entice him into the Order, let him be discredited by every possible means.*"

"XVI. *If a Regent should conceive hopes of succeeding in suppressing any religious houses*, and of applying their revenues to our object, for example, *to the establishment of proper* COUNTRY SCHOOLS; he may depend on it, that such a project would be particularly grateful to the Superiors.

"XVII. The Regents will also turn their attention toward a solid plan for establishing a fund to support the widows of the brethren.

"XVIII. *One of our most important objects must be, to hinder the servile veneration of the people for Princes from being carried too far.* All such abject flattery tends only to make those men worse who are already for the most part of very common and weak understandings. You wil show an example of the proper conduct to be held in this respect. Shun all familiarity with them; behave to them politely, *but without constraint, that they may honour and fear you.* Write and speak of them as you would of other men, that they may be made to recollect that they are but men like other people, and that their authority is a thing purely conventional.[5]

"XIX. When there happens to be a man of merit among our adepts but little known by or entirely unknown to the public, no pains are to be spared to acquire celebrity for him. *Let our disguised brethren* every where sound the trumpet of his praises, and force envy and party spirit to be silent.

"XX. The essay of our principles and of our schools is most easily and most successfully made in small states. The inhabitants of capitals and commercial towns are too corrupt, too much a prey to their passions, and think themselves too much enlightened, to submit to our lessons.

"XXI. It is useful to send visitors from time to time, or to give a Regent that is travelling the commission to visit the meetings, to ask for the minutes, and to call on the brethren in order to examine their papers or journals, and receive their complaints.—These Plenipotentiaries, presenting themselves in the name of the high Superiors, may correct many faults, and boldly suppress abuses which the Prefects had not the courage to reform, though ready to enforce the commands of the visitor.

"XXII. If our Order cannot establish itself in any particular place with all the forms and regular progress of our degrees, *some other form may be assumed. Always have the object in view; that is the essential point. No matter what the cloak may be, provided you succeed; a cloak is however always necessary, for in secrecy our strength principally lies.*"

"XXIII. For this reason we should always conceal ourselves under the name of some other association. THE INFEERIOR LODGES OF FREEMASONRY ARE THE MOST CONVENIENT CLOAKS *for our grand object,* (das schickliche kleid für unsere höhere zwecke) because the world is already familiarized with the idea that nothing of importance, or worthy of their attention can spring from Masonry.—The name of a literary society is also a proper mask for our first classes. Under such a mask, should our assemblies be discovered, we may confidently assert, that the reason of our holding secret assemblies was partly to give a greater interest and charm to our pursuits; partly to keep off the crowd, and not to expose ourselves to the bantering and jealousy of others; in short to hide the weakness of an association as yet but in its infancy."

"XXIV. It is of the utmost importance for us to study the constitutions of other secret societies and to *govern* them. The Regent is even bound, after having obtained leave of his superiors, to gain admittance into those societies, but he must not undertake too many engagements. This is an additional reason why our Order should remain secret.

"XXV. The higher degrees must always be hidden from the lower. *A person more willingly receives orders from a stranger than from men in whom he gradually discovers a multitude of defects.* By this precaution one may keep the inferiors in a more proper awe; for they naturally pay greater attention to their behaviour when they think themselves surrounded by persons who are observing them; at first, their virtue may be the effect of constraint, but custom will soon make it habitual."

"XXVI. Never lose sight of the military schools, of the academies, printing presses, libraries, cathedral chapters, or any public establishments that can influence education or government. Let our Regents perpetually attend to the various means, and form plans for making us masters of all these establishments."[6]

"XXVII. In general, and independent of their particular employment, the grand object of our Regents must be an habitual and constant application to every thing which can in any way add to the perfection and to the power of our Order, that it may become for future ages the most perfect model of government that can enter the mind of man;" or, in other words, that it may be hereafter said, such was the famous association which, by perpetually perfecting its laws and governments, at length taught mankind to cast off every law and every government. It would be useless for me to think of adducing farther proofs to demomstrate that such is the real object of the pretended perfection of Illuminism. The mysteries of the Sect have been too clearly laid open for us to harbour the smallest doubt of their intention. But to acquire this perfection and power for the Sect, Weishaupt has modelled still farther laws for his Regents, according to the different offices they hold in the Hierarchy of the Order.[7]

1. Last works of Philo and Spartacus, degree of Regent.
2. Die Regenten sollen die kunst studieren zu herschen, ohne das ansehen davon zu haben.
3. Sollen sie unumschränkt regieren.
4. Er soll nicht leiden dass der dümmere über den klügern—der Schwächere über den stärkern, auch wenn dieser unrecht haben sollte, zu sehr den meister spiele.
5. Eine unserer vornehmsten sorgen muss auch seyn, unter das volke sclavische fürsten verehrung nicht zu hoch steigen zu lassen, &c. &c.
6. Militair-schulen, academien, Buchdruckereyen, Buchläden, Dom-capitel, und alles was ein einfluss auf bildung und regierung hat, muss nie aus den augen gelassen werden; und die Regenten sollen unaufhörlich plane entwerfen, wie man es anfangen könne, über dieselben gewalt zu bekommen.
7. For the whole of the Second Part of this Chapter see the *Instruction B for the Degree of Regent*, of which it is nearly a literal translation.

CHAP. XVI.

Continuation of the Instructions on the Government of the Illuminees—Laws for the Local Superiors.

GREAT as the authority of the *Major Illuminees* over the *Minerval* Academies may appear at first sight, no person of the *preparatory class* is in fact entrusted with any real authority. Even the *Scotch Knight* in his *intermediate* class does not enjoy any. The Order recognizes as real Superiors none but those who have been initiated into the class of the Mysteries. Even in that class the adept must have attained the degree of Regent before he can be named Prefect for the *Scotch Knights*, or Dean of his district. Those are the first two offices which the Order considers as having any real authority over the Brethren.

Though the Code expressly declares, that each Superior shall find in his instructions the respective laws concerning his particular duty, it certainly contains none for the office of Dean. A single Chapter is indeed to be found in the Code on his election and consecration. On the first establishment of a new district he is elected by the Provincial; but on his deposition or death the Epopts assemble and choose a successor by the plurality of votes, the Provincial only having the right of confirming such an election. With regard to what the Code terms his *consecration (Weihung des decani)*, it is generally performed by what is called a Plenipotentiary, and in a sort of barbarous Latin, extremely inelegant. Were not the impiety of it as abominable as the ceremonial is low, it might form an excellent scene for the theatres of Bartholomew fair. The Illuminizing Legislator, a very inferior copyist of Moliere's *Malade Imaginaire*, ridicules St. Paul, Moses, and all religious ceremonies, as Moliere did the quack disciples of Hippocrates. Little wit is required to scoff at religious rites, and yet our Legislator has only succeeded in being disgustingly impious. Such turpitude is not worthy of our notice, for none but Epopts can admire it; this nevertheless is all the information the Code can give us respecting the Dean.[1]

The same cannot be said of the instructions for the *Prefects*. These Local Superiors may have as many as eight Lodges at a time under their command, *partly Minerval*, and *partly Masonic*. The Prefect is the first Regent within his prefecture, and has the direction of all that part of the Order stiled in the Code *the lower part of the edifice*. All the *Quibus Licets* of his district pass through his hands. He opens those of the *Scotch Knights*, and the *Solis* of the Novices and Minervals; but every thing else he transmits to the higher Superiors. When he founds new Lodges, or receives new Brethren, he gives the new *Geographical* names and *Characteristics*, which he selects from the list that he has received from the Provincial. He makes a general report to the Provincial of every thing that has happened within his Prefecture once a month; and every three months transmits the reversal letters, the tablets sent by the Scrutators with notes on their *political and moral* conduct, and an exact return of the state of the funds belonging to each Lodge. He decides on the promotion of the Brethren as far as Scotch Knight, but can confer the latter degree only with the consent of the Provincial.—He has the right once a year of commanding all the adepts under his direction to return whatever writings the Order may have entrusted them with—He returns them to those on whose fidelity he has reason to rely, *but not to those whom he may have any reason to suspect, or who are intended to be dismissed.*[2]

The foundation of the Edifice rests solely on the vigilance, experience, and zeal of the Prefect.—And it was to the direction of their conduct in every part of the Government that Weishaupt dedicated his lessons under the following heads:—I. *Preparations.*—II. *Tuition of the Pupils.*—III. *Spirit or love of the Order*—IV. *Subordination.*—V. *Secrecy.*—Each of these articles contains a cloud of those artifices which the reader has seen interspersed in divers parts of the Code, but which now become the peculiar study of the Prefect. I shall only extract the most striking, or those on which the Legislator particularly insists; such, for example, as the following, to be found in the first pages of the head *Preparation.*

"Our strength chiefly consists in numbers; but much will also depend on the means employed to form the pupil—Young people are pliant and easily take the impression.—The Prefect will therefore spare no pains to gain possession of the *Schools* which lie within his district, and also *of their teachers.* He will find means of placing them under the tuition of members of our Order; for this is the true method of infusing our principles and of training our young men: it is thus that the most ingenious men are prepared to labour for us and are brought into discipline; and thus that the affection conceived by our young pupils for the Order will gain as deep root as do all other early impressions."

Under the same head are to be found instructions for the Prefect equally curious, on the propagation of the Order.

"When a new colony is to be founded, begin by choosing a bold and enterprizing adept entirely devoted to the Order. Send him some time beforehand to live on the spot where you intend making the new establishment."

"Before you proceed to people the extremities, begin by making your ground good at the centre."

"Your next object must be, to gain over such persons as are constant residents, as *Merchants* and *Canons.*"

"Such missions should only be entrusted to *brethren of independent fortune,* and who would occasion no expence to the Order; for though all the brethren are entitled to succour when in real want, yet those of one province are as seldom as possible to be an expence to the neighbouring ones. Nor are the other districts by any means to be made acquainted with the weakness of the Order in yours. Beside, the funds must find a sufficiency to succour those of the *Minerval* school who may stand in need of it, that our promises in their case may be performed."

"You will not seek to extend yourself till you have consolidated your establishment in the capital of your district."

"You will seriously examine and cautiously select from the Brethren those who are the most able to undertake such a mission.—You will next consider whether it will be proper to begin your establishment by a *Minerval Church* or a MASONIC LODGE."

"Pay most particular attention to the man whom you place at the head of the new colony; observe whether he is courageous, zealous, prudent, exact, and punctual; whether fitted for the forming new adepts; whether he enjoys a good reputation or is much considered; whether he is a man of business and capable of a serious and constant application; in short, whether he has all the necessary qualifications for an undertaking of such high importance."

"Consider also the locality. Is the place proposed near to or distant from the capital of your district?—Is it a dangerous or safe situation for such an undertaking?—Is it great or small, more or less populous?—By what means can you best succeed, and which can be easiest employed?—What time would be requisite for the perfecting of such an establishment?—To what persons can you apply on first setting off?—If your first applications be ill made, all future attempts will be fruitless.—What pretence or what name is to be assumed?—How is the new colony to be subordinated or *co-ordinated*? that is to say, what Superiors shall it be under, and with what Lodges shall it correspond?"

"When you shall have acquired sufficient strength in your new colony, and particularly if our Brethren enjoy the first dignities of the state, if they may freely and openly show themselves formidable to their opponents, and make them feel the painful consequences of counteracting the views of the Order; if you have wherewith to satisfy the wants of the Brethren; if, so far from having to fear from the government, the Order directs those who hold the reins—Then be assured that we shall not be wanting in numbers or in the choice of adepts; we shall soon have more than we have occasion for. *I cannot too strongly recommend this method of proceeding.*"

"If it be necessary for us to be masters of the ordinary schools, of how much more importance will it be to gain over the *ecclesiastical seminaries and their superiors! With them, we gain over the chief part of the country; we acquire the support of the greatest enemies to innovation; and the grand point of all is, that through the clergy we become masters of the middle and lower classes of the people.*"

"But remember that great caution is necessary with the Ecclesiastics. These gentlemen are generally either too free or too scrupulous; and those who are too free have seldom any morals." The legislator then proceeds to the exclusion of the religious, and tells the Insinuator to avoid the Jesuits as he would the plague.

While perusing these laws, I suppose the reader makes nearly the same reflections which I am tempted every instant to commit to paper.—Should the following article ever meet the eye of a Prince, it will give him ample room for reflection.

"When the Prefect shall have gradually succeeded in placing the most zealous members of the Order in the councils and offices under the Prince, he will have arrived at the full extent of his commission. He will hve done much more than if he had initiated the Prince himself."[3]

"In general, Princes are not to be admitted into the Order, and even those who are received are seldom to be permitted to rise above the degree of *Scotch Knight.*"

After what has been seen of this degree and those that precede, it is rather extraordinary that Weishaupt should deign to grant admission to Princes; for he did not wait for this degree before he clearly insinuated his plans. Princes, at least, who had not surmised them before their admission to that degree must have been void of penetration indeed. What hopes then could the Legislator entertain of their not perceiving his plots against all legitimate authority? His confidential letters will explain the enigma:—"Brethren," he writes to his Areopagites, "you will take care to have the following corrections made before you show the constitutions of our degrees to the Elector.—In the degree of *Minor Illuminee* in place of the words *imbecile Monks* say *imbecile men*—In the degree of *Major Illuminee* blot out the words *Priests and Princes are in our way.*—With respect to the degree of *Priest* show no part of it *excepting the discourse on sciences,* and read that over carefully lest any *allusion or reference to any other part of the degree should remain.*"[4] These corrections begin to clear the enigma; a more insidious expedient will veil his plots in complete darkness. "I *mean,* says Weishaupt when speaking to the Areopagites of the inferior degrees, *to revise the whole system.*" Then, attributing to the Jesuits his own immorality, he says, "I mean that it should be a complete Jesuitical piece; not a single word shall be found in it that can in any way be cavilled at by religious or political governments. Let us act with caution; do nothing without a reason; things must be prepared and brought on step by step."[5] The adept who has given us the most complete and candid account of the degrees of Illuminism assures us, that he had seen a discourse for the degree of Epopt in which every thing respecting religion and government was omitted.[6]

Here then we find Weishaupt not only correcting but even forming fictitious degrees to dupe the princely adept, and to persuade him that the dark and mysterious recesses of the hireling crew have been laid open to him, while the real adept smiles at his credulity. Such artifice certainly aggravates Weishaupt's criminality. But will that excuse the princely adept? Notwithstanding the veil artfully thrown over the impious and seditious principles of the sect, did he not begin by swearing *obedience and protection* to the Order? His court soon swarms with Illuminees; he thinks he reigns over them, but is no more than their stately captive. And should he fall their victim, will it not be said that he met with his just fate? What strange madness can induce Princes to inscribe their names on the registers of secret societies! Have they not duties to fulfill toward the public? On what right can their oaths of submission and protection be grounded, sworn in the recesses of secret Lodges, to men who hide themselves from public view, when their labours, cares, and protecting power, are to extend over the whole state and to all its citizens? On the throne, or with pretensions to it, do they not degradingly swear obedience and protection to Masters of Lodges! By what right will they promulgate laws emanating from Lodges? When their subjects swore allegiance and fidelity to them, did those subjects expect to be governed by a slave, or be subjected to laws proclaimed indeed by their Prince, but dictated by some *Master Illuminee* or *Rosicrucian*? And ye, magistrates of the people, who are to sit in judgment over the mutual and disputed claims of the citizens in general, what confidence can be placed in you after you have sworn *obedience* and protection to this illuminizing Sect, even in actions just or *unjust*? Such reflections will rise refulgent from the page of history; and would to God that the Revolution had not already indelibly engraved them!

If ever self-love should have directed the actions of men, and supplied the place of nobler motives, the princely dupe will have found ample matter in the laws of Illuminism to stimulate his, when he but casts his eye on the following article contained in the instructions for the Prefects, or local Superiors, under the head *formation of pupils:* "What will numbers avail us, if unity and similarity of sentiment do not prevail?—*No rank, no state of life, can dispense the Brethren from our labours or our trials.* To accustom them to despise all distinctions, and to view the world and human nature in the grand scale, the Prefect shall carefully collect all the anecdotes he can, remarkable either for their generosity or meanness, not regarding to whom they relate, whether Princes or Citizens, rich or poor. He will transmit them to the Masters of the *Minervals*; and these will expose them in a proper manner to their pupils. They will not forget to give the name of the Prince of great personage, though the trait should dishonour him; for," says the Code, "every member must be made sensible, that we distribute impartial justice, and that among us the wicked man upon the throne is called a villain (*ein schurke heist*) just as freely, if not more so, than the criminal who is being led to the gallows."

Under the same head we may observe another article remarkable enough, on the means of rendering the language of the adepts more uniform when speaking before any of the Order, or of facts relating to it.

On these occasions the Prefect will take care secretly to instruct the *lower Superiors* in what stile they are to hold forth, what ideas to propagate, and in what manner they should make their pupils speak. "Hence the pupils will constantly accord themselves in every thing, whether in language or action, with the Superiors, though their motives may be unknown to them. But these means we shall all tend toward the same object; the young adepts will accustom themselves to search and dive into the intentions of the Order; to refrain from acting; or to be silent on all doubtful occasions, till they have received the advice or orders of their Superior as to what they ought to do or say."

Under the head *Love or Spirit of the Order*, the Prefect is instructed, that such *Love or Spirit* is to be infused by descanting on the beauty and importance of the object of the Sect, the integrity of its members, the greatness and certainty of its means, the utility of the instruction imparted, and security promised to all its pupils by the Order.—This *Love* will always be proportionate to the certainty of *being happy while attached to the Order, and of finding real happiness in no other place*. To stimulate it, *he must always feed them with the hopes of new discoveries more and more important*; and, lest their zeal should diminish, "*try to keep our pupils constantly occupied with objects relating to the Order; make it their favourite pursuit.*—See what the Roman Catholic Church does to make its religion familiar to its followers, how it keeps their attention incessantly toward it; model yourself by that.—It would be impossible to foresee all cases and lay down rules for them;—Let it then be the constant study of the Prefects and other Superiors to prepare themselves for unforeseen events—Let them propose and distribute prizes for the best compositions on such cases. Perpetual vigilance will render it impossible for the edifice not sooner or later to succeed, and to take a proper consistency according to the local circumstances. Exhort the Brethren to complacency, beneficence, and generosity toward each other *and toward the Order.*"

The next article treats of *Obedience*. Here the Prefect is informed, "That should he have been diligent and successful in impressing the young pupils with the grandeur of the views of the Sect, they will doubtless obey the Superiors with pleasure. How can they do otherwise than submit themselves to be conducted by Superiors who have so carefully guided them hitherto, who contributed so much to their present happiness, and who promise to perpetuate it in future? May the man who is not to be enticed into obedience by such advantages be rejected from among us; *let him be cast out from the society of the elect!* The spirit of obedience is to be more particularly infused by *example* and instruction—by the conviction, that to obey our Superiors is in fact only fulfilling our own inclination—by the gradual progress of the degrees—by the hopes of discovering more important truths—by fear properly managed—by honours, rewards, and distinctions granted to the docile—by contempt cast on the stubborn—by avoiding familiarity with the inferiors—by the exemplary punishment of the rebellious—by the selection of those whom we know to be devoted to us and ready to execute all our commands—by a particular attention to the *Quibus Licets* whereby we may see how far the Orders of the Superiors have been executed;—and by the punctuality of the intermediary Superiors in sending the *tablets* or reports respecting their inferiors. *The more particular those tablets are, the better they will be; for it is on them that all the operations of the Order are grounded*. It is by their means that the progress and number of the Brethren are to be known; that the strength or weakness of the machine, and the proportion and adhesion of all its parts are to be calculated, and that the promotion of the Brethren, the merits and demerits of the assemblies, of the Lodges, and of their Superiors, are to be judged.

When treating of *Secrecy*, "The Prefect is informed, that *this is the most essential article*; and it is on that account that even in countries where the Sect may have acquired sufficient power to throw off its mask, it is to remain veiled in darkness."

"The Prefect is always to hide with dexterity the real object of his views according to local circumstances. Let him agree with the Provincial on what shape he shall assume to conceal the Order.—As in the religious institutions of the Roman Church, where religion, alas! is but a pretext; exactly so, only *in a nobler manner, must we enwrap our Order in the forms of a mercantile society, or some other exterior of a similar nature.*"

In vain would the reader ask me, whence the Illuminized Code had taken the idea of Religion being only a *pretext* for the religious institutions in the Catholic Church. It has not come to my knowledge, that the most barefaced Sophisters have ever advanced a calumny of this sort. I have seen the religious founders, such as St. Francis, St. Benedict, or St. Basil, and other founders of orders, described by the Sophisters as superstitious enthusiasts. But even among the apostates who must have been acquainted with the Orders they had lived in, we have never heard one pretend that Religion was only a *pretext* either for the institution they abandoned, or for their ancient brethren. Did any of them ever assert, that ambition, avarice, or any pretext beside Religion, had given rise to the foundation of the Order of the Capuchins, Friars, Benedictines, or Carmelites, and of so many other convents destined for men or women? This, however, is not a calumny originating with Weishaupt; it is not to be found in his instructions sent to Knigge, and on which the latter formed the Code of Laws for the Regents and Local Superiors, though he subjoined many of his own ideas. Knigge was totally ignorant of every thing relating to religious Orders. Weishaupt was born a Roman Catholic, and might indeed, in his impiety, have repeated the ideas of many apostate Sophisters, or have left this strange comparison of his Illuminism with the religious institutes, since it was in the Code: but I should be truly surprized were I to find that it was a Calumny of his invention. He knew too well how much he stood in need of darkness to envelope his designs; and he also knew, that in the Roman Catholic Church no religious institute was adopted, until it had been made public and examined by the constituted authorities.

After this absurd calumny follows a recapitulation of every thing we have already exposed to our readers in the first Chapters of this Volume, on the necessity of hiding the proceedings and even the very existence of the Lodges. But I find the following additions in this place.

"Lest the number of the Brethren should expose them to discovery, by their assemblies being too numerous, the Prefect will take care that no more than ten members shall assemble in the same *Minerval* Church."

"Should any place contain a greater number of pupils, the Lodges must be multiplied, or different days of assembly must be assigned, that all may not meet at once; and should there be several *Minerval Churches* in the same town, the Prefect will take care that those of one Lodge shall *know nothing* of the others." For the better direction of the lower part of the edifice, he will observe the following rules—He is to nominate the Magistrates of the *Minervals*; but the chief of these Magistrates can only be named with the consent of the Provincial. He will be responsible for those he names.—He will overlook the MASONIC and *Minerval* Lodges, to see that every thing is regularly and punctually executed. He will not permit any discourses to be delivered there which may give any strong suspicions of what is contriving against Religion, the state, or morals.—He will suffer no Brother to be advanced to the higher degrees before he has acquired the requisite qualities and principles; on this point, says the Code, he cannot carry his precautions, *anxiety*, and *scrupulosity* too far.

"It has already been stated in the rules, that persons not belonging to the Order may be received into the MASONIC Lodges of Illuminism—The Prefect will carefully watch lest any of these strangers should take the lead in the Lodges.—They should as far as possible be honest men, sedate, and quiet; but by some means or other they should be made useful to the Order.—Without leave of the Provincial, the Prefect shall hold no correspondence on matters relating to the Order with any person out of his province—as his peculiar object will be, to watch over and to instruct the Superiors of the *Minerval* and MASONIC Lodges, he will have recourse to the Provincial in all doubtful cases of any importance.

"Let the Prefect make himself perfect master of these rules; let him follow them with precision; let him always attend to the whole of the object; let him take care that each one may attend to his duty, *doing neither more nor less than the law requires;* and he will find in this instruction all that is necessary for the regulation of his conduct."

Such is the promise which terminates the laws for the Prefect of Illuminism. The five articles treated of in these regulations are prefaced by a far more pompous promise: "If, it is said, we have exactly foreseen every thing relating to these *five articles*, nothing will be impossible for us in any country under the Sun."[7]

---

1. Should any adept wish for a specimen of this miserable farce, let him figure to himself an assembly of Epopts in their sacredotal habits. The Delegate opens the piece by Domine aperi os meum: The two Assistants repeat the same—*The Plenipotentiary* Fili mi quid postulas? *The Delegate* Ut Deus et Superiores nostri concedant nobis Decanum hunc quem ad te duco.—*Plenip.* Habetis decretum?—Habemus—Legatur——Communi voto atque consensu superiorum elegimus nobis in Decanum Fratrem N. N. Presbiterum Nostræ Provinciæ, Majoris Ordinis verum atque prudentem hospitalem, moribus ornatum, sapientem, illuminatum et mansuetum, Deo et superioribus nostris per omnia placentemque ad Celsitudinis vestræ dignitatem

adducere, quatenus autore Domino nobis velut idoneus Decanus præ-esse valeat ut prodesse, nosque sub ejus sapienti regimine in securitate ac quiete magnis scientiis aliisque operibus curare possimus—*Plenip.* Disposuisti domui tuæ?—*The Elect Disposui*—Nosti quanta sit Decani cura et qua pœna infligantur infideles et delatores?—Duce me Domine—Ego auctoritate superiorum inductus firmiter sub interminatione anathematis, inhibeo tibi, ne quid de scientiis occultis, vel secreta tibi revelanda abducas, surripias, vel alicui profano communices. Si tu autem aliquid attentare præsumseris, maledictus eris in domo et extra domum, maledictus in civitate et in agro, maledictus vigilando et dormiendo, maledictus manducando et bibendo, maledictus ambulando et sedendo, maledicta erunt caro et ossa, et sanitatem non habebis à planta pedis usque ad verticem. Veniat tunc super te maledictio quam per Moysen in lege filio iniquitatis Dominus promisit. Deleatur nomen tuum in libro viventium, et cum justis non amplius scribatur, fiat pars et hereditas tua cum Cain fratricida, cum Dathan et Abiron, cum Anania et Saphira, cum Simone Mago et Juda proditore. Vide ergo ne quid feceris, quo anathema mereris.—*Here follow the imposition of hands, the exhortations, and the benedictions, all in Latin. The Officiator, extending his hands again on the head of the Elect, terminates the ceremony with the following words:* Sicut ros Hermon qui descendit in montem Sion, sic desecendat super te Dei summae sapientiæ benedictio *(see the last works of Spartacus—Nachricht von Weihung eines Decani).*—What execrable impiety must the Sect have infused into its Epopts to expect that such an impious derision of the Scriptures and of the most sacred rites could give them pleasure? Let not the reader think that I have exaggerated this barbarous cant. The whole ceremony is a buffoonery of the lowest class. Impiety depraves every thing, even the taste for literature.
2. Instructions C for the Regents, and No. I—X.
3. Kann der Präfect die fürstlichen Dicasterien und Räthe nach und nach mit eifrigen ordens mitgliedern besetzen, so hat er alles gethan, was er thun konte. Es ist mehr, als wenn er den fürsten selbst aufgenommen hätte.
4. Orig. Writ. Vol. II. 2d Jan. 1785.
5. Ibid.—Weishaupt's Let. 15th March, 1781.
6. Geschichte der illumin. Grad. Page 66.
7. Ist nun in diessen fünf stücken alles gehörig besorgt, so ist in iedem lande unter der sonne nichts unmöglich—The whole of this Chapter is extracted from the Instructions C for the Prefect, from Page 145 to 166.

CHAP. XVII.

Instructions for the Provincial.

BY far the greater part of the code of laws which has just been laid before the reader as relating to the *Regents* and *Prefects* of the Illuminées, was originally written by Weishaupt for the instruction of his Provincials. This is evident from the first digest of these laws, as they appear in the second part of the second volume of the Original Writings of the Sect, from page 17 to 43. It is even one of those parts which Knigge looked upon as a master-piece of politics.[1] So replete with artifice did he think it, that he deemed it a pity to circumscribe the knowledge of it to the Provincials alone. The reader has seen what use he has made of them, thoroughly persuaded that the Regents in general, and particularly the Local Superiors, could greatly benefit the Order by attending to them. The Areopagites and General consented to these new dispositions; but the following part of this chapter remained appropriated to the Provincials.

"I. The Provincial shall make himself perfect master of the whole constitution of the Order.—The system of it should be as familiar to him as if he had invented it."

"II. As a guide for all his actions, he shall adopt the whole government and the instructions already laid down for the Regents and Local Superiors, not neglecting a single rule."

"III. The Provincial shall be chosen by the Regents of his Province, and be confirmed by the National Superior. . . .[2] The high Superiors (the Areopage and General) have the power of deposing him."

"IV. He shall be a native of, or at least be thoroughly acquainted with the province under his inspection."

"V. He shall be engaged as little as possible in public concerns, or in any other enterprize, that he may devote all his time to the Order."

"VI. *He shall assume the character of a man retired from the world, and who only seeks rest.*"

"VII. He shall fix his residence as nearly as possible in the centre of his province, the better to watch over the different districts."

"VIII. On his being named Provincial, he shall leave his former characteristic, and assume that which the high Superiors shall give him.—The same Superiors will send him the impression of the seal he is to bear, and he will wear it engraved on his ring."

"IX. The archives of the province, which the Regents will have taken care to seal up and carry away on the demise of his predecessor, are to be entrusted to him on his nomination."

"X. The Provincial will monthly transmit the general report of his province to the National Inspector immediately over him. As he himself only receives the reports of the Local Superiors a fortnight after the month is up, he will necessarily be always a month behind-hand, making, for example, the report of May about the end of June, and so on. This report will be subdivided into as many parts as he has Prefects under his inspection. He will carefully note every thing of consequence that has happened in any of the schools or lodges: also the names, ages, country, station in life, and the date of the *reversal* letters, of each new adept; the high Superiors wishing to have no further information concerning the new adepts until they come to the class of Regent, unless on some particular occasion."

"XI. Beside this monthly report, he is to apply to the National Superior in all extraordinary cases which are not left to his decision. He is also to send in his personal tablets every three months; and he will undertake no political enterprize without having first consulted."

"XII. He has nothing to do with the other Provincials. Let things go on well or ill in a neighbouring province, it is no business of his. If he wishes to ask any thing of the other Provincials, let him apply to the National Inspector."

"XIII. If he has any complaint to make against the Inspector, he will direct his letter *Soli* or *Primo*."

"XIV. All the Regents of the province are his counsellors; they are to second and help him in all his enterprizes. If it be convenient to him, he should have two of them near his person to serve him as secretaries."

"XV. He confirms the nominations of all the Superiors of the inferior degrees. He also names the Prefects, but they must be approved by the Director, who can refuse his sanction."

"XVI. He has a right to send the brethren *who are pensioned* by the Order, and to employ them in those parts of the province where he may think them most useful."

"XVII and XVIII. He transmits the characteristics of the brethren and geographical names of the lodges to the Prefects, as he receives them from the high Superiors."

"XIX. He is also to send the names of the excluded brethren, that an exact list may be preserved in all the assemblies."

"XX. When he has any reprimand to make to a Brother, whom it may be dangerous to offend, he will assume an unknown hand, and the signature of *Basyle*. This name, which no member of the Order bears, is peculiarly preserved for that object.

"XXI. He will sometimes write to the Inferior degrees; and on the proposition of the Epopts he will decide what books are to be put into the hands of the young adepts according to the degrees they are in.—He is as much as possible to promote libraries, cabinets of natural philosophy, *Musæums*, collections of manuscripts, &c. in the most convenient parts of his Province; these, it may easily be conceived, are only intended for the adepts.

"XXII. The Provincial opens the letters of the *Minor* and *Major* Illuminees which are directed *Soli*. He also reads the *Quibus Licets* of the Epopts and *Primos* of the Novices; but can neither open the *Primo* of the Minerval, the *Soli* of the Knight, nor the *Quibus Licet* of the Regent."[3] This gradual power of opening the letters of the Brethren according to the degree they belong to, plainly indicates that some mark peculiar to each degree is made use of; but I have not been able to discover that mark. The reader will have observed, that all the letters, even the *Quibus Licets*, are opened by Brethren of a higher degree than that of the adept who writes; and consequently he can never know who it is that answers him, as the rules of this Hierarchy are only made known to the Brethren in proportion as they rise in dignity. The Provincial himself can only form a conjecture as to the persons who open his letters and those of the other Brethren which he is not permitted to open himself.

"XXIII. He shall raise no Brother to the degree of Regent, without having first obtained the consent of the National Inspector.

"XXIV. He is to inform the Dean of the branch of science which each new adept has made choice of on his admission into the Minerval Academy.

"XXV. Lest any of the Archives should be mislaid, he will take care to form but one bundle of all the tablets, reversal letters, and other documents relating to the same adept.

"XXVI. He will apply himself to procure as many co-operators as possible for the Order, in the scientific branches.

"XXVII. He will transmit to the Deans all remarkable treatises or discourses, and every thing relative to the degree of Epopt; for example, the lives historical or characteristic, dissertations, &c.

"XXVIII. If among the Epopts any men be found endowed with great talents, but little fitted for the political government of the Order, the Provincial must devise means of removing them from such functions.

"XXIX. When the Chapters of the Scotch Knights are composed of more than twelve Knights, he will raise the ablest among them to the degree of Epopt.

"XXX. In each Chapter he will have a confidential Epopt, who will be his *secret censor* or spy.

"XXXI. The Provincial will receive his letters patent from the National Superior—When he issues those for the Chapters of the Scotch Knights, he will make use of the following formula: 'We of the Grand Lodge of the *Germanic Orient*, constituted Provincial and Master of the district of N N, make known that by these presents we give to the venerable Brother (here is the characteristic and true name of the new Venerable or Master) full powers to erect a secret Chapter of the *most holy* SCOTCH MASONRY, and to propagate this *Royal Art* conformably to his instructions by the establishment of new Masonic Lodges of the three symbolic degrees—Given at the Directory of the District—

(L. S.)   SECRET PROVINCIAL
                                                                              OF THE DIRECTORY.

without any further signature."

"XXXII. To say every thing in a few words, the Provincial has the special charge of putting his province in a proper situation for attempting every thing for the general good, and for preventing all evil.—*Happy the state where our Order shall have acquired such power!* Nor will it prove a difficult task for the Provincial who shall implicitly follow the instructions of his high Superiors.—Seconded by so many able men *deeply versed in moral sciences*, submissive and secretly labouring like himself, there can be no noble enterprize which he may not undertake, nor evil design which he cannot avert—Therefore let there be no connivance at faults; no *Nepotism*, no private piques; no views but for the general good; no object, no motives but those of the Order. And let the Brethren rely upon us, that we shall never create any Provincials but such as are capable of fulfilling these duties; *but let it be also remembered, that we reserve in our hands all the means necessary for chastising the man who should presume to abuse the power he has received from us.*"[4]

"XXXIII. This power must never be employed but for the good of the Brethren. We should indeed help all whom we can help; but when the circumstances are similar, the members of our society are always to have the preference.—Particularly as to those whose fidelity is proof against all the powers of seduction. In their support let us be prodigal of our toils, our money, *our honour*, our goods, even our blood; and *let the least affront offered to any Illuminee be the general cause of the Order.*"

Thus terminate the instructions for the Provincial. They forewarn us of the existence of a most tremendous power above him whence all the authority of the Order emanates; a power which reserves to itself the means of chastising whoever shall abuse that portion which it has entrusted to any of its adepts; that is to say, who shall not have made it subservient to the grand object and to all the plots of the Sect.—There are, in fact, three offices in the hierarchal Orders of Superiors above the Provincial. First, the *National Directors*, then the *Supreme Council* called the *Areopagites* by the Sect, the authority of which extends over the Iluminees of all nations; and that is presided over by the *General of the Order*. The following Chapter will give every light on these supreme Magistrates of Illuminism which the known Archives of the Sect can reflect.

1. See his last Observations.
2. There is an omission in the copy from which these rules have been printed, which makes part of this article unintelligible.

3. This article is extracted from the instructions for the Prefect; but, being directly addressed to the Provincial, I have placed it here.
4. See the Instruction D for the degree of Regent.

CHAP. XVIII.

Of the National Directors, of the Areopagites, and of the General of Illuminism.

IN the general plan of the Government of the Illuminees it is said, that every Brother shall receive particular instructions according to the rank he holds in the Hierarchy of the Order: Yet I have never been able to discover those intended for the use of the National Directors. This part of the Code is not to be found either in the *two volumes* so often quoted of the *Original Writings*, or in that of *Philo and Spartacus* which has thrown so much light on the mysteries. It does not appear, that any of the German writers who have been the best informed on, and the most strenuous opponents of, Illuminism have ever been able to discover them. For some time I even entertained doubts whether the *Superiors* called *National Directors*, and those styled *Inspectors*, were not of the same degree in the Hierarchy of the Sect.—They were certainly distinct employments in the year 1782; for Weishaupt's letters at that period mention Germany as divided into *three inspections*, each *Inspector* having several Provincials subordinate to him.[1] But, on the other side, the general account which the Order puts into the hands of its Regents, and the last works of Philo printed in 1788, mention no intermediate office between the *Provincials* and the *Nationals*, which latter are sometimes described as *National Superiors*, at others as *National Inspectors*. Their correspondence and subordination is direct from the Supreme Council.[2] It is therefore evident, that in the last digest of the Code the two offices of *National Inspector* and *Director* were united. But in vain would the Sect conceal the instructions which it has appropriated to the functions of these *National* Superiors. The denomination alone testifies the importance which attaches to their office; and if the precise nature of their duties be wanting, it is easy to supply the deficiency, by what has already escaped the vigilance of the Sect in the foregoing parts of the Code.

Let the reader recall to his mind what has been said in the Chapter on the *Epopts*, of the systems which they were to form in order to seize on the empire of the Sciences and direct them all toward the accomplishment of the plots of the Sect. In the same degree we have seen them annually assembling in each province, and compiling from their partial attacks every means that their inventions could furnish, insensibly to enslave the public opinion, and to eradicate from the minds of the people what the Sect is pleased to call religious prejudices. We have seen the class of Regents more particularly occupied in sapping the foundations of the throne, and in destroying that veneration in which nations held the persons and functions of their Sovereigns—Nay, there exists a particular law framed for the Epopts which has not yet been cited, and which must here be introduced. It is to be found *in the Second Volume of the Original Writings, second Section, intitled*—*Articles agreed upon by the Areopagites in Ardameth* 1151 (A.D. December 1781)—There under the article HIGH MYSTERIES, I read, "If among our Epopts *any speculative geniuses* are to be found, they shall be admitted to the degree of *Mage*.—These adepts shall be employed in collecting and digesting all the grand philosophical systems, and will invent or compile for the *people a system of religion* which our Order means as soon as possible to give to the universe."[3]

I do not forget that I am to treat of the *National Directors*; but am somewhat afraid that my readers may adduce this plan for giving a new religion to the whole universe, as invalidating their plot for the destruction of every religion. Let such readers, however, reflect on the religion which Weishaupt has himself laid down for his *Mages*. It is the rankest *Spinosism*, admitting of no God but the world itself; that is to say, absolute Atheism. Let them also remember, that one of the last secrets of the Grand Mysteries, is to reveal to the adepts that all religions are grounded on and are the invention of imposture. Nor is it by any means difficult to account for these two schemes of the Sect, the one for the creation of a new religion, the other for the destruction of all. These plans are to be successive in their operations. Sentiments of Religion are too deeply engraven in the minds of the people for Weishaupt to flatter himself with suddenly eradicating it, or at least without substituting some capricious and sophisticated faith, which in reality would no more constitute a religion than the *Worship of Reason*, of which the French Revolution has given us an impure essay. The religion, therefore, to be invented by the Mages of Illuminism is no more than a preparatory step that should destroy the religion of Christ throughout the universe. This advantage gained, it will remain no very difficult task to open the eyes of the whole world on the inanity and imposture of their own; and thus it will have served as a scaffolding which naturally disappears with the edifice that is to be pulled down. This religion to be invented may be considered as on a parallel with those new governments, those democracies, which are to amuse the people until the period shall come when their Illuminizing Equality and Liberty shall have taught them, that each one is essentially his own sovereign, that this sovereignty is an imprescriptible right inherent in each man, in direct opposition to democracy, and even to all property or social compact.

Such is the general tenour of the systems to be invented and prosecuted by the Sect, for attaining the grand object of these Conspirators. All the adepts which the Sect comprises under the denomination of *speculative geniuses* are perpetually labouring at these systems under the direction of the Provincials. But they are not the persons who complete the plans; they are only to present the first sketch, which each Provincial is obliged to transmit to the *National Directory*, there to undergo a further investigation and receive its final polish.[4] One of the first duties, therefore, of the *National Director* will be to collect all these anti-religious and anti-social systems, to pass judgment on them, and to declare how far they can contribute towards the universal disorganization. But even these could not alone suffice for so great a work; they are surrounded by the Elect of the nation as the Provincial is by the Chosen of the provinces. This council of the Elect, after mature deliberation, declare which are the systems that are worthy of being adopted by the Order; and they will make all the additions and corrections that they may conceive conducive to the success of the general plan. Thus corrected and digested, these systems of impiety and disorganization are deposited in the *archives* of the Director, which now become *national*. It is to these that the Provincials have recourse in all their doubts, and hence flow all those lights which are to expand themselves throughout the nation:—it is hence also that the National Director[5] will take all the new regulations which he may judge necessary for the better combination and concordance of the efforts of the National Brethren.—But the Sect does not confine its views to one nation. It has formed within itself a supreme tribunal, which has subjected all nations to its inquisition. Composed of *twelve Peers* or *Fathers* of the Order,[6] it is presided over by the General; and, under the name of Areopagites, it becomes the common centre of communication from the adepts of all nations, as the *National* is the centre of one particular nation, the *Provincial* of one province, the *Local Superior* of the lodges of his district, the *Minerval Master* of his academy, the *Venerable* of his Masonic Lodge; and, finally, as the *Insinuator* or *Recruiter* is of his novices or candidates. Thus, from the first step to the pinnacle of the Order, every thing is connected and gradually ascends by means of the *Quibus Licets, Solis* and *Primos.*—Every thing that happens in each nation gradually ascends to the *National*, and from these *Directors* all is transmitted to the centre of all nations, to the supreme council of the Areopagites, and the General in chief, the universal Director of the Conspiracy.

The grand point, therefore, to be observed in the code concerning the National Director is, his direct correspondence with the Areopagites. It is evident from the terms expressed in the general plan of the government which the Sect reveals to its Regents. "In every nation there shall be a National Director associated and in direct communication with our Fathers, the first of whom holds the helm of the Order."[7] This accounts for the injunction given to the Provincial, to make frequent and exact returns to the National Director of every thing that may take place in his province; to have recourse to him on all doubtful occasions, or in cases of especial importance; and never to take any step in politics without having first consulted him.[8] This explains why the choice of those adepts which are to be advanced to the political degree of Regent, or to the Prefectships of districts,[9] is left to the option of the National, or even the nomination of the Provincials.[10] This informs us why all the *Quibus Licets* of the Regents are reserved to the Director, that is to say, that all the secrets of their political discoveries may more certainly reach the hands of him who is to leave no secret hidden from the Fathers of the Order.[11]

Such then are the rights of, such the laws for the National Inspector of Illuminism; and so great is the importance which the Sect attaches to this office. To him are forwarded all the secrets of the brethren spread throughout the provinces, the Courts, or towns; to him are sent all the projects, all the reports on the successes gained by, or dangers impending over the Order; on the progress of its plots; on employments, dignities, and power to be acquired for the adepts; on the candidates to be rejected, the enemies to be crushed, the councils and state offices of princes to be seized. To him, in short, are reported all the means which can retard or accelerate the fall of the Altar and of empires, the disorganization of every church and state within his inspection.—It is by means of his direct correspondence, and that of his Co-nationals, that the discoveries of the Scrutators, the political plans of the Brethren, the speculations of the plodding *geniuses* of the Order, the plans proposed and debated in the councils of Princes, and every thing, in short, which can weaken or strengthen the opinion of the people; which is to be foreseen or hindered, to be anticipated or hastened in each town, court, or family, are concentrated, and subjected to the views of the supreme council of the Sect. Hence no sovereign, no minister of state, no father of a family, no man in the bonds of the most intimate friendship, can say, My secret is my own, it has not, it will not, come to the knowledge of the Areopagites. By means of these same National Directors too, we behold all the orders of the Illuminizing Peers gradually descending to the adepts of all nations, of all provinces, academies, and lodges, whether *Minerval* or MASONIC; and immediately re-ascending through these same Nationals an exact statement to the Areopagites in what manner each command has been executed. It is by the Nationals too, that the supreme council is informed of the negligent Brethren who need to be stimulated, of the transgressors and stubborn adepts who deserve punishment, and stand in need of being reminded that they have sworn to submit both their lives and fortunes to the commands of the high Superiors (the unknown Fathers) of the Areopagites. In vain would the Sect strive to conceal the laws which the code lays down for these Inspectors. After what the reader has already seen of the laws of the Order, he must naturally conclude that such are evidently the mysteries comprehended in those words, *There shall be in each empire a National Director associated or in direct correspondence with the Fathers of the Order.*

With respet to the laws and interior economy of the councils, it is easy to be conceived, that the Sect has succeeded in encompassing them with impenetrable darkness. Some few rays of light, however, have been cast on it, and that by the Fathers themselves.

In the first place, we see *Philo*-Knigge, in his Apology, speaking as follows of these supreme magistrates of Illuminism: "Their labours, with regard to the parts purely speculative, were to have in view the knowledge and the tradition of all the important, holy, and sublime discoveries to be made *in the religious* mysteries and in the higher philosophy. Twelve Areopagites only are to compose this tribunal; and one of them is to be the chief. When any one of the members dies, or retires, his successor is chosen from among the Regents."[12] This general idea given by Knigge of the Supreme Council is indeed mysterious;—but he could scarcely be expected to *publish* more, knowing as he did the fate which awaits those who betray the secrets of the Sect. He has, however, at least said enough to give us clearly to understand, that all the religious and philosophical or rather impious and sophisticated speculations of the Epopts, perpetually perverting the sciences and operating the extinction of all religious ideas, are concentrated within the council of the Areopagites; we have seen them combining, digesting, approving, or rejecting *those plans of a new religion* which the *Mages* are directed to invent, and which the Sect *means incontinently to give to the world.*

In his familiar correspondence, Spartacus speaks more openly and with greater latitude to his beloved Cato. Therein it appears, that anti-religious systems do not alone employ the meditations of the Fathers; for, soon after having mentioned the object of those *Quibus Licets* in wich the young adepts were to give an account of the prejudices they might have discovered in themselves, which of them predominated, and how far they had succeeded in destroying them, he proceeds to say, "It is by these means that I discover such of our Order as have the proper dispositions for adopting certain *special* doctrines, and more elevated, on governments and religious opinions."[13] He then continues, "*The maxims and politics of the Order* are completely explained *in the end.* Here, in the *Supreme Council,* they project and examine the plans to be adopted for gradually enabling us to attack the enemy of reason and human nature *personally (auf den leib)*. Here also the mode of introducing such plans into the Order is discussed, and it is decided to which brethren they are to be entrusted, and how far each one can be employed in their execution, in proportion to the insight given to him."[14]

The reader is already too well acquainted with the maxims and policy of Illuminism, not to join with me in saying, Here then is the grand object of this Supreme Council of the Sect! It is in that dark recess that all those artifices are devised for rendering the disorganizing systems of Equality and Liberty familiar to the Illuminizing adepts: There is exactly ascertained the proportion which each class of the Brethren can bear in this universal destruction of religion, empire, society, and property; there again is the day anxiously sought and the means prepared, for hereafter throwing off the mask, and attacking *personally* the defenders of religion, laws, and property, as so many enemies to reason and humanity; there concentrate all the declarations, the reports, the plans of all the brethren dispersed throughout the universe, that the Sect may judge of its own strength, and compare it with that of the friends to the Altar and the Laws. To sum up all, it is there that the artifices and means are determined on, and the merits and powers of the higher adepts are investigated prior to their being entrusted with that part of the grand conspiracy to which their abilities are best adapted. Let the reader remember, that it is not a stranger to the Sect who has thus described the Areopage; it is the grand Legislator of Illuminism himself. Can we any longer stand in need of the regulations for this council? No; we well know what they must be; we know that impiety, and the most consummate arts in seduction and sedition, are to be their leading features; we further know, that its members must resemble Weishaupt himself, before they can be permitted to sit with him in council. What other bond of union do they need, beside the machination of the most hideous plots, the just or unjust means of forwarding the interests of the Sect as much as circumstances will permit, and the ensuring of success by the blackest and most profound artifices that depravity can invent? The fertile genius of the Legislator, however, would not commit the success of the least of his crimes to chance. He attempted to sketch a code of laws for his Areopagites, and for any future *Spartacus* that might succeed him. The code contains but a *sketch* of what he calls *laws ad interim*. It is to be found in the ninth section of the first volume of the Original Writings, and is addressed to the Areopagites. Many other passages of his letters relate to the same object.—I have transcribed the following articles:

"The Areopagites shall form the Supreme Council (literally, the Supreme College).—Their occupations shall relate to affairs of the greatest importance, and they shall pay little or no attention to such as are less essential.—They may *recruit*, it is true (*können sie zwar recroutiren*); that is to say, they may entice Candidates into the Order; but they must leave the care of their instruction to some intelligent adept. From time to time they will visit these Candidates, to inspire them with fresh ardour, to stimulate their zeal—They will be particularly careful in seeing that the progress and method of our Illuminées is every where uniform—They will more particularly watch over Athens (*Munich*, the principal Lodge after that of Ingolstadt, where Weishaupt resided at the time he wrote these instructions). They will make no reports concerning that Lodge to any body but Spartacus. They will send monthly a statement of all the principal events, *a sort of Gazette (Ein art von Zeitung)*, to the Brethren (*Conscii*); that is to say, to those only who are initiated in the last secrets. But (continues Weishaupt) *nota bene*, this Gazette as yet has been no more than our common journal; the *Conscii* must compose one for the use of the Areopagites. These latter will labour at *projects, ameliorations*, and other objects of a similar nature, which are to be made known to the *Conscii* by circular letters. They are the people who are to bear a part of the weight of the general correspondence—They are not allowed to open the letters of complaint (*die litteras gravatoriales*); that is to say, those containing any complaints against them. These are to be transmitted to the general, to Spartacus, as a sure means of informing him that they fulfil their duty. This instruction being only provisional, and relating solely to the Areopage, shall not be circulated; but the council will take a copy and send back the Original to Spartacus.[15]

"The assembling of the council is to be regulated according to the feasts marked in the calendar of the Order. (*Nach dem calendario Illuminatorum an*

Ordens festen)." But this was soon found to be insufficient, and Weishaupt exhorts his Areopagites to meet in their senate every post-day, and at the hour of the delivery of the letters.

Short as this sketch of a Code for the Areopagites may seem, it clearly denotes the essence of their functions, and shows how they are to act as a central point for the whole Sect. A grand question was still undecided when *Spartacus* gave these laws to the council; which was nothing less than, Whether *Spartacus* was to preserve a legislative and sovereign power over the Members of this Council, similar to that authority which they were to exercise over the rest of the Order?—Great Conspirators will seldom brook control even by their fellows. They will be equal among themselves and in their dens of conspiracy. *Spartacus*-Weishaupt was naturally of a despotic disposition. His Areopagites for a long time complained of it.[16] But he contended, that as founder, he had the indefeasible right of giving to the association those laws and regulations which he judged necesssary for its perpetuation. He soon, indeed, repented of the decision he had given against himself in favour of his Senate, "That the *plurality* of votes should dictate the eternal laws of the Sect" (*Lex semper valitura*)[17] Notwithstanding these complaints of the Areopagites, however, he speedily found means of re-instating himself in that authority, the privation of which only thwarted his artful conceptions, by subjecting them to the opinions of persons less consummate in the conspiring arts than their master. He sometimes submits to the justification of his conduct; but that is the very moment in which the reader should observe him artfully reclaiming all the rights and pretending to the exercise of unlimited despotism, though his cant appears to reject the very idea of it. Addressing his opponents in the shape of his pupils, he recalls to their minds the monstrous services he has rendered them in their youth, as so many benefactions of the most tender friendship, and asks them "of what they can in their consciences complain?" "When (says he) did you ever observe harshness or haughtiness in my conduct, with respect to you? When did I ever assume the tone of Master? Is it not rather with an excess of confidence, of goodness, of openess with my friends, that I may be reproached?"—When in this manner Weishaupt has captivated his Areopagites, he comes to the point: "Read then (he says) my letters over and over again. You will therein perceive that the grand object of our Society is not a thing of small consequence for me; that I know how to view it, and treat it also, in the most serious manner; that I have always aimed at the establishment of order, submission, discipline, and activity, as the sole means that can lead you to the grand object. In undertaking a work of such vast importance, was I not obliged by prayers, exhortations, and advice, to maintain and stimulate the ardour of my first, my dearest companions, on whom every thing depended?—If I wish to keep the *supreme direction* in my own hands, hear my reasons, which are most certainly of great weight:

"In the first place, I must necesssarily know with whom I have to deal, and must be ascertained of the fidelity of our people; and, to effectuate this, I am not to receive reports from a sixth hand, or perhaps one still more remote, on the execution of my plans, which have been approved of by the Elect of our Mysteries. . . *In the next place, am I not the Constructor of this grand Edifice?* Is there no respect due to me?.... When my system shall be completed, will it not be necessary for me to inspect the whole, and keep every man at his station? It is a great and radical defect in a society, where a Superior is dependent on the Inferiors, as it has been attempted to render me.

"But, to show you how much I value the friendship of my former friends, above all the authority I may exercise over others, I renounce all my rights, all my authority. Accept my warmest acknowledgements for all your past labours and patience. I flatter myself they have been hurtful to nobody, and that many have acquired from me lights on secret societies which they would not easily have found elsewhere. The purity of my intentions is my consolation and my recompense. From this instant I betake myself to obscurity and repose, where I shall not meet with zealous and envious opponents. There I shall be my own master, and my own subject."[18]

The Illuminizing Despot thus artfully pleaded his cause. The Areopagites were impatient of his authority, but at the same time felt the want of so disorganizing a genius; and that they might not be deprived of its co-operation they reproached the Legislator with the extinction of his zeal.—The fire, however, was only hidden beneath the embers; they once more submit to the yoke of their former chief, who, inflamed with zeal, dictates the conditions on which alone he will deign to place himself once more at their head. Every thing is worthy of being remarked in them. The haughty spirit in which they are conceived, the nature, object, and extent of the power he assumes over the Supreme Council and Elect of the Order, are all worthy of our attentive notice.

"I begin (says he) by telling you before hand, that it may not any more be a subject of surprize, that I will be more severe than ever. I will not overlook a single fault, and shall in that respect be much more strict toward persons whom I know rather than toward those with whom I am not so familiar. My object and views require it. And to whom would you have me address myself, if not to the chiefs of the Order, since they alone are in direct correspondence with me? That things may succeed, it is necessary that we should be actuated but by one opinion, one sentiment, and be acquainted but with one language! And how can this be accomplished, if I cannot freely speak my mind to our people? I will then re-assume my post of General on the following conditions:

"I. That you will execute neither more nor less than what I shall command. I shall expect it in future; at least, should any change be thought necessary, I am to receive previous notice of it.

"II. I expect that every Saturday a proper report shall be sent to me of every thing that has taken place during the week, and that it shall be in the form of *Minutes* signed by all the Elect present.

"III. That I shall be informed of all the Members that have been recruited, or persons that are to be recruited, with an outline of their characters; and let some particulars concerning them be added when they are admitted.

"IV. That the statutes of the class in which you labour be punctually observed, and that no dispenssations be granted without previous investigation. For should each one take upon himself to make such changes as he pleased, where would be the unity of the Order.—What I exact from you, you shall exact from those that are subject to you. If there be no order and subordination in the higher ranks, there will be none in the lower."[19]

It was on the 25th of May 1779, that Weishaupt dictated these laws to his Areopage. A fifth condition seems to have made them merely provisional, and to have entrusted the despotic power in Weishaupt's hand only until the order had acquired a proper consistency; but he took care not again to lose the newly-acquired supremacy; though the Areopagites still regretted the loss of their Aristocracy, and the being reduced to be the mere agents or prime ministers of the *Spartacus* of the Order. But let us attend to that *Spartacus*, who has always represented the most legitimate authority as an outrage on human nature. Let us hear him invoking Machiavel in support of that which he wishes to exercise over the Order. He pleads his own cause with Zwack, who is also jealous of his Master, by showing all the disorder it occasioned, by every body wishing to introduce his own ideas into the Order, and then quotes the following passages from Machiavel: "It must be laid down as a general rule, that it seldom or never happens that any Government is either well-founded at first, or thoroughly reformed afterwards, *except the plan be laid and conducted by* ONE MAN ONLY, who has the sole power of giving all orders and making all laws that are necesary for its establishment. A prudent and virtuous Founder of a State, therefore, whose chief aim is to promote the welfare of many rather than to gratify his own ambition, to make provision for the good of his country, in preference to that of his heirs or successors, ought to endeavour by all means to get the supreme *authority wholly into his hands*: nor will a reasonable man ever condemn him for taking any measures (even the most extraordinary, if they are necessary) for that purpose: The *means* indeed *may seem culpable*, but the end will justify him if it be a good one;—for he only is blameable who uses violence to throw things into confusion and distraction; and not he who does it to establish peace and good Order." After this long quotation which Weishaupt has made from a French transation of Machiavel, *Chap. IX. Discourses upon the first Decad of Livy*, he continues in a sorrowful tone: "but I have not been able to obtain so favourable a decision. The Brethren have viewed that which is but a necessary law in the art of governing, in the light of ambition and a thirst of dominion."[20] In the midst of this contention for power, he felt himself so superior in the art of governing conspiring associations at least, that he did not hesitate at writing to his Areopagites, *As to politics and morality, Gentlemen, you must confess that you are as yet at a great distance behind me.*[21] He at length succeeded in persuading them, that it was necessary that the General of the Order should also, as president of the Areopagites holding the *helm of the Order*, be the absolute director.[22]

Weishaupt, who left nothing relating to the disorganizing arts in an imperfect state, must, no doubt, have composed instructions to guide his successors in the exercise of their supremacy, and to teach them how to make the same use of it which he intended. But the reader will easily conceive, that these never could have escaped the vigilance of the Sect, nor pierced the dark cloud with which it had enveloped itself. It may even be possible that Weishaupt had not sufficient confidence in his Areopagites to entrust them with the entire plan. Throughout the whole hierarchy of Illuminism the lower degree is entirely ignorant of the particular instructions of the superior degrees; and why should not Weishaupt, who wished to perpetuate his disorganizing genius in all the succeeding Generals, have followed the same plan? He undoubtedly dictated laws and rules for their conduct, gave them rights which were to maintain both themselves and their Areopagites in their hierarchical superiority, and second them in the pursuit of their grand object; and these were entitled Instructions for *the General of the Illuminees*. No historian can flatter himself with the discovery of such a code of artifice and cunning; the most unrelenting wickedness and hypocrisy had invented it; and genius alone can pretend to dive into such secrets. The historian can only pretend to collect those articles which are to be found in Weishaupt's familiar correspondence, or in other parts of the code or writings of the Sect. Were we to throw this compilation into the form of instructions, the following might be nearly the result of our research.

I. The General shall be chosen by the twelve Peers of the Areopage, on the plurality of votes.[23]

II. The Areopagites can only elect one of the members of their senate for General; (*ein aus ihrher mitte gewähltes oberhaupt*);[24] that is to say, a man who has sufficiently distinguished himself among the Regents to be admitted among the twelve supreme adepts of Illuminism, and who has afterwards made himself so eminent in their council, that he is judged to be the first Illuminee in the world.

III. The adept is supposed to possess qualities requisite for a General in consequence of those he may have evinced before he was called to the Supreme Council. As he is to preside over the whole Order, he must (more than any body else) be impressed with the principles of the founder, and be divested of all religious, political, or national prejudices. The grand object of the Order must be more particularly inculcated into him, namely, that of teaching the whole universe to set aside all government, laws, and altars; and he must perpetually attend to the grand interests of human nature. His zeal is to be stimulated at the sight of every man who is subjected to any authority. It is to reinstate the inhabitants of the earth in their original Equality and Liberty that he is constituted General of all the Illuminees that are or will be spread over the world during his reign, all labouring at the accomplishment of the grand revolution of the *Man-King*.[25]

IV. The General shall have immediately under him the twelve *Peers* of the Supreme Council, and the various agents and secretaries which he shall judge necesssary to second him in the exercise of his functions.[26]

V. The better to secure himself from the notice of the civil and ecclesiastical powers, he may assume, after the example of the founder, some public office under the very Powers the annihilation of which is to be his sole object. But he will be only known to the Areopagites and to his agents and secretaries in his quality of General.[27] The better to conceal the residence of the General, the town where he has fixed will have three names. The common name known to all; the geographical one peculiar to the Order; and a third known only to the Areopagites and the *Conscii* or Elect.[28]

VI. Our success greatly depending on the moral conduct of the Areopagites, the General will pay particular attention to prevent all public scandals which might hurt the reputation of the Order. He will represent to them in the strongest colours how much bad example will contribute to alienate from the Order the kinds of persons who might otherwise prove its most useful members.[29]

VII. The better to preserve that respect which virtue commands from inferiors, the General will assume the character of austere morals. That he may always have the grand object present to his mind, and be wholly occupied with the duties he has to fulfil; let him never lose sight of that great maxim so frequently inculcated in his letters by the founder, as the leading feature to which he owed all his successes. *Multum sudavit et alsit, abstinuit venere et vino. He neither feared heat nor cold; he abstained from wine and women*, that he might always be master of his secret, always be master of himself, and prepared for all exigencies where the interests of the Order might require it.[30]

VIII. The General shall be the central point for the Areopagites, as the latter are for the whole body of Illuminees. That is to say, each Areopagite holding correspondence with the National Inspectors is to make a report of all the *Quibus Licets* sent, and of all the secrets discovered by the corresponding Inspector; the secrets thus flowing from all parts will ultimately settle under the eye of the General.[31]

IX. The functions of the General, and the success of his dispositions, greatly depending on the information he receives by means of this correspondence, he will distribute it among his Areopagites, assigning to each that of a particular nation whose Inspector is to transmit all his reports to him.[32]

X. The principal heads of this correspondence shall be—Ist, The number of the brethren in general, that the force of the Sect may be ascertained in each nation.—2dly, Those brethren who distinguish themselves the most by their zeal and intelligence—3dly, Those adepts who hold important offices about the Court, in the Church, Armies, or Magistracy: also what kinds of services might be expected from or prescribed to them in the grand revolution which our Order was preparing for human nature.—4thly, The general progress which our maxims and our doctrine were making in the public opinion; how far nations were prepared for the grand revolution; what strength and means of defence still remained in the hands of the civil and ecclesistical powers; what persons were to be placed or displaced; what engines were to be played off, to hasten and secure the success of our revolution; and the means necessary to bind the hands of those who might resist.[33]

XI. If from this correspondence he should judge it necesssary to dismiss any of the brethren from the Order, (and all the rights recognized by the adepts as inherent in the Order, particularly that of *Life and Death* being in the hands of the General) he will have to decide what further punishment is to follow the ejectment: whether the culprit is to be declared infamous throughout all the lodges of the Order, or whether the pain of death is to be pronounced against him.[34]

XII. The General, after having chastised the imprudent, cowardly, and treacherous adepts, will turn his attention toward the discovery of those brethren who may be best fitted for seconding his views in each empire. Without making himself known to them, he will establish a line of communication between them. He will himself prepare the links of this immense chain after the manner laid down by our founder as the grand means of governing, from his mysterious centre, all the diverging ramifications of the Sect to the extremities of the earth; as a means of vivifying invisible armies in an instant, of putting them in motion, of directing their course, and of irretrievably executing the most astonishing revolutions, even before the very Potentates whose thrones are overturned have had time to surmise their danger.

XIII. The use of the chain is obvious and easy. To touch the fist link is all that is required. A single stroke of a pen is the grand spring that imparts motion to the whole. But the success depends on the choice of the time. In his hidden abode the General shall medidate the means, and catch the propitious moment. The signal of universal revolution shall not be given till a time when the combined force and instantaneous efforts of the brethren shall be irresistible.

The illuminizing General who shall have managed this chain with the greatest art, who shall have spread it both far and near, who shall have imparted to it a sufficient power of action to bear away and overturn at a single effort every throne and every altar, all political and religious institutions, and shall strew the earth with the ruins of empires—He will be the creator of the *Man-King, sole king, sole sovereign* of his actions as of his thoughts. To that General is reserved the glory of consummating the grand revolution which has so long been the ultimate object of our mysteries.

Whatever proofs I may have adduced, that must naturally lead my readers to such a conclusion, it may nevertheless be an object of surprise to them to see that Weishaupt had really planned this long chain of subterraneous communications, by which himself and his successors were empowered invisbly to actuate thousand of legions, which instantaneously, on a day prescribed, might burst into existence armed with pikes and torches, and all the horrid implements of universal revolution. Let my readers then cast their eyes on this *series of progression*, which Weishaupt has with his own hand traced in his letters first to *Cato*-Zwack and afterwards to *Celsus*-Bader. The explanations are his own, and let them be particularly attended to.

"For the present, direct nobody to me but *Cortez*, that I may have some leisure to digest my speculations, and determine each one's place; for every thing depends on that. My operations with you shall be directed by the following table:

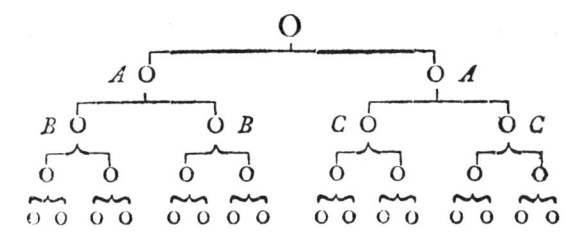

```
                          O
              ┌───────────┴───────────┐
            A O                       O A
         ┌────┴────┐             ┌────┴────┐
       B O         O B         C O         O C
       ┌─┴─┐     ┌─┴─┐        ┌─┴─┐      ┌─┴─┐
       O   O     O   O        O   O      O   O
      ~~   ~~   ~~   ~~      ~~   ~~    ~~   ~~
      OO   OO   OO   OO      OO   OO    OO   OO
```

"Immediately under me I have two adepts, into whom I infuse my whole spirit; each of these corresponds with two others, and so on. By this method, and in the simplest way possible, I can inflame and put in motion thousands of men at once. It is by such means that orders are to be transmitted and political operations carried on."[35]

A few days after he writes to *Celsus*-Bader, and tells him, "I have sent to Cato a table (*schema*) showing how one may *methodically* and without much trouble *arrange a great multitude of men in the finest order possible*. He will probably have shown it to you; if he has not, ask for it. Here is the figure (*then follows the figure*).

"The spirit of the first, of the most ardent, of the most profound adept daily and incessantly comunicates itself to the two A, A; by the one to B, B; by the other to C, C: B B and C C communicate it to the eight following; these to the next sixteen, from thence to the thirty-two and so downwards. I have written a long explanation of it all to Cato. In a word, *every man has his Aide-Major, by whose means he immediately acts on all the others. The whole force first issues from the center and then flows back again to it.* Each one subjects, as it were, to his own person, *two men whom he searches to the bottom, whom he observes,* disposes, inflames, and drills, as it were, like recruits, that they may hereafter exercise and fire with the whole regiment. The same plan may be followed throughout all the degrees."[36]

This is not a document which, like many others, flowed unintentionally from Weishaupt's pen, and which he left his disciples to collect, in order to form the political Code—*Give me leisure to digest my speculations, and to determine each one's place*—*It is by such means that orders are to be transmitted, and political operations carried on.* These words evidently demonstrate, that it is not a provisional law which he is about to pronounce, but a premeditated one, that is to last till that fatal period when whole legions, fired with his spirit, are to be led to that terrible exercise for which he had so long been drilling them;

that time so expressly foretold by Weishaupt and his Hierophants, when they were to *tie hands,* to *subjugate, fire on, and vandalize* the whole universe.

When this fatal law shall be fulfilled, then will the last *Spartacus* sally forth from his baleful den, and triumphantly claim the sanguinary palm of murder and destruction from the Old Man of the Mountain, who would scarcely have been worthy of being his precursor. The earth loaded with the ruins of laws and empires; mortals blaspheming their God; nations lamenting over their conflagrating towns, their palaces, public monuments, and arts, and even their cottages, all overthrown; society weeping over its laws;—such shall be the sight which the last *Spartacus* will contemplate with joy, when he shall exultingly exclaim, "At length, my Brethren, the long-wished for day is come; let us celebrate the name, and dedicate this day as sacred to the memory of Weishaupt, our founder. We have consummated his grand mysteries; no laws shall exist, but those of his Order. Should nations be ever tempted to *return to their wickedness,* (to laws and society) this code, which has once destroyed their bonds, may do it again.

Will not hell vomit forth its legions to applaud this last *Spartacus,* to contemplate in amazement this work of the Illuminizing Code?—Will not Satan exclaim, "Here then are men as I wished them. I drove them from Eden; Weishaupt has driven them to the forests. I taught them to offend their God; he has made them reject their God entirely. I had left the earth to repay them for the sweat of their brow; he has stricken it with sterility; for it will be in vain for them to pretend to till and sow that which they shall not reap. I left them in their inequality of riches; but he has swept all away; he has destroyed the very idea of property; he has transformed mankind into brigands. Their virtues, happiness, and greatness under the protecting laws of society or of their country, was an object of jealousy to me; but he has cursed their laws and their country, and has reduced them to the stupid pride and ignorance of the roaming, savage, and vagabond clans. In tempting them to sin, I could not deprive them of repentance and the hope of pardon; but Weishaupt has taught them to scoff at crime and despise repentance. Villany without remorse, and hopeless misfortune, are all that he has left to the miserable inhabitants of the earth!

Meanwhile, before Satan shall exultingly enjoy this triumphant spetacle, which the Illuminizing Code is preparing, let us examine how far success has hitherto attended on its footsteps?—What share has it borne in that revolution which has already desolated so many countries and menaces so many others.— How it engendered that disastrous monster called *Jacobin,* raging uncontrouled, and almost unopposed, in these days of horror and devastation—In short, what effects this Code of the Illuminees has produced, and what effects it may produce.—This will be the object of the *historical part* of the Sect, and of the IVth and last volume of these Memoirs.

---

1. Original Writings, Vol. II. Let. 15, to Cato.
2. Directions System, No. 5, and Philo's Endliche erklärung, page 81.

3. So werden die selben *Magi*—Diese sammeln und bringen die höhere philosophische systeme in ordnung, und bearbeiten ein *volks-religion*, welche der Orden demnächsten der welt geben will.—In the original, which is in Cato-Zwack's handwriting, the words *volks-religion* are in cypher, thus 20, 14, 2, 3, 18,—17, 8, 2, 4, 6, 4, 14, 13.
4. Instructions for the degree of Epopt, No. 12 and 14.
5. Deswegen kommen jährlich ein mal alle Presbyter einer provinz auf der grossen Synode zusammen, machen ein grosses verzeichniss der in diesem jahr gesammlten beylagen *an die National Direction* wo selbst es in die haupt-katalog eingetragen, und damit ein schatz von kenntnissen formirt wird, woraus jeder befridigt werden kann: denn daraus werden die regel abstrahirt, und was noch fehlt, weitere beobachtungs aufgaben, wie schon erwähnt worden, aufgeschrieben um feste sätze zu bekommen. *Ibid.* No. 15.
6. Philo's Endliche erklärung, Page 119.
7. *Directions System*, No. 4.
8. Ibid. No. 10 and 11.
9. Ibid. No. 15 and 23.
10. Ibid. No. 9.
11. Ibid. No. 22.
12. Last Observations of Philo, Page 115.
13. Aus diesen kann ich ersehen welche geneigt sind gewisse sonderbare staats lehren, weiters hinauf religions meynungen anzunehmen.
14. Und am end folgt die totale einsicht in die *Politic* und maximen des Ordens. In diesen obersten *Conseil*, werden die project entworfen, wie den feinden der vernunft und Menschlichkeit nach und nach *auf den leib* zu gehen seye: Wie die sache unter den Ordens mitgliedern einzuleiten, wen es anzuvertauen? Wie ein jeder *a proportione* seiner einsicht känne dazu gebraucht werden.—*Original Writings, Letter to* Cato-*Zwack, 10th March, 1778.*
15. Extracts from the Instruction to Cato, Marius, and Scipio, Original Writings, Vol. I. Sect. ix.
16. Letters of Philo to Cato and last Observations of Philo.
17. Letter of the 8th November, 1778.
18. Original Writings, Vol. I. Sect. 49.
19. Original Writings, Vol. II. Letters 49 and 50.
20. Original Writings, Vol. II. Let. 2, to Cato.
21. Ibid. Let. 10.
22. General Plan of the Order, No. 5.
23. Last Observations of Philo, Page. 119.
24. Ibid.
25. See the Mysteries.
26. See above.
27. Orig. Writ. Spartacus' Letters, passim, et supra.
28. Orig. Writ. Vol. I. Sect. 3.
29. Ib. Vol. II. Let 9 & 10.
30. Ibid. Vol. I. Let 16, &c
31. Vide supra.
32. Ibid. Vol. II. Let 6, 13, &c.
33. See the different degrees and the views with which the *Quibus Licets* and tablets, &c. &c. are written.

34. Orig. Writ. Vol. II. Let 8, et supra, Oath of the Novice.
35. I here feel it incumbent on me to insert the original text, to show that I do not exaggerate Weishaupt's meaning. The following are the terms in which he writes to Cato:—"An mich selbst aber verveisen sie dermalen noch keinen unmittelbar als den *Cortez*, bis ich schreibe, damit ich indessen speculiren, und die leute geschickt rangieren kann; den davon hängt alles ab. Ich werde in dieser figur mit ihnen operiren." (*Here stands the figure already inserted above: The Letters A B C allude to the explanation given in the Letter to Celsus*). "Ich habe zwey unmittelbar unter mir welchen ich meinen ganzen geist einhauche, und von diesen zweyen hat wieder jeder zwey andere, und so fort. Auf diese art kann ich auf die einfachste art tausend menschen in bewegung und flammen setzen. Auf eben diese art muss man die *ordres* erheilen, und im politischen opieren." *Original Writings, Vol. II. Let 8, to Cato, of the 16th February 1782*. It may be remarked that Weishaupt's style is none of the purest.
36. The original text of this letter is to be found in the Original Letters, Vol. II. Let 13, to *Celsus* without any date. It is as follows: "Ich habe an Cato ein *schema* geschickt, wie man planmässig eine grosse menge menschen in der schönsten ordnung...abrichten kann... Es ist diese forme."

"Der geist des ersten, wärmsten, und einsichtsvollesten communicirt sich unaufhörlich und täglich an *A A—A* an *B B*: und das andere an *C C—B B*, und *C C* communiciren sich auf die nämliche art an die unteren 8. Diese an die weitere 16, und 16 an 32, und so weiter. An Cato hab ich es weitläufiger geschrieben: Kurz! Jeder hat zwey flügel adjutanten, wodurch er mittelbar in all übrige wirkt. Im centro geht alle kraft aus, und vereignigt sich auch wieder darinn. Jeder sucht sich in gewisser subordination zwey männer aus, die er ganz studiert, beobachtet, abrichtet, anfeuert, und so zu sagen, wie recruten abrichtet, damit sie dereinst mit dem ganzen regiment abfeuern und exerciren können. Das kann man durch alle grade so einrichten."

I do not find the long explanation mentioned as sent to Cato by Weishaupt, nor do I remember to have seen it. It would most certainly be curious, and we should see in a clearer light how he was to infuse his spirit into and fire the minds of thousands of men; but still these two letters are proofs more than sufficient for our purpose.

END OF THE THIRD PART

MEMOIRS,

Illustrating the

HISTORY of JACOBINISM,

Written in FRENCH by

THE ABBÉ BARRUEL,

And translated into ENGLISH by

THE HON. ROBERT CLIFFORD, F.R.S. & A.S.

Princes and Nations shall disappear from the face of the Earth... and this REVOLUTION shall be the WORK OF SECRET SOCIETIES.
Weishaupt's Discourse for the Mysteries.

PART IV.

ANTISOCIAL CONSPIRACY; HISTORICAL PART.

Second Edition, revised and corrected.

LONDON:
Printed for the TRANSLATOR,
By T. BURTON, *No. 11, Gate-street, Lincoln's-Inn Fields.*
Sold by E. BOOKER, *No. 56, New Bond-street.*

1798.

THE ANTISOCIAL CONSPIRACY

HISTORICAL PART

PRELIMINARY DISCOURSE

Object and Plan of this Volume.

CONCEIVED but a short time before the French Revolution, by a man whose ambition seemed confined within the narrow compass of the town of Ingolstadt and to the dusty folios of his schools, by what strange means did Illuminism, in less than fifteen years, become that formidable Sect which, under the name of *Jacobin*, rides triumphant over ruined altars, shivered scepters, and scattered crowns; over the wrecks of nations and their constitutions; over the bodies of potentates fallen beneath their poisons or their poignards, while they drag others in their train, craving a servitude termed *peace*, or branding themselves with the infamy of what they call an *alliance*?

Under this name of JACOBIN absorbing all the mysteries, plots, and combinations of every sectary against every religion, government, and society, by what artifice could Illuminism acquire that dominion of terror which forbids any sovereign within the astonished universe to say, Tomorrow I shall continue seated on my throne; which forbids nations and citizens to say, that their laws and religion, their houses and property, will not be torn from them; which forbids the peaceful inhabitant to lie down to rest with any assurance that he will not rise in the morning beneath the shade of that symbol of blood called the *The Tree of Liberty*, and threatened by the axe of the devouring guillotine? How is it possible, that the secret adepts of the modern *Spartacus* should be the invisible and exclusive movers of that long chain of crimes and calamities, that disastrous torrent of ferocity and rapine, which is called the revolution? How do they continue to direct those machinations which are to consummate the dissolution and misery of human society?

In dedicating this Fourth Volume to the investigation of these questions, I do not flatter myself with the hopes of illustrating them with all that precision and of pointing out those particularities which other men might have done who have had it in their power to follow the Sect of Illuminees into their dark abodes without ever losing sight of the adepts or their teachers. The monster has taken its course through wildernesses, and darkness has more than once obscured its progress. Weishaupt had adopted the bird of night for his emblem, because he courted darkness; but the screechings of this ominous bird, rending the air in spite of him, discover his secret retreat. The venomous reptile is often discovered by the stench of its poison; the beaten and blood-stained track leads to the discovery of the cavern inhabited by brigands; and, notwithstanding all the efforts of the wicked, an all-powerful God will sometimes in his mercy permit a ray of light to shine on their tenebrous recesses, which may suffice to develope their pots. Many horrid particulars, no doubt, have been lost under the veil of darkness; but in classing those which have come to my knowledge, I find abundance of proofs to trace the Sect wherever crime has pointed out its fatal influence. In vain does the black cloud hover round the summit of the volcano, the bituminous and sulphureous vapours which it exhales, bear testimony of the interior combustions, till at length the erruption denotes the abyss where so great a convulsion was generated.

Hence without flattering myself with the hopes of seizing every link of that horrid chain of iniquity which must blacken the page of history when treating of the Sect, or of decyphering the assumed names of all its adepts, I shall proceed to lay before my readers what has already come to light. Asserting nothing but what will bear the strictest scrutiny, I shall still find matter sufficient to trace the progress of the Sect from its origin to that congress to which, at the present moment, it calls the vanquished sovereigns, not so much to quell the horrors of the field of battle, as to enjoy that dominion of terror which it despotically sways without, and to prepare within new resources to extend its triumphs; not so much to restore to nations the tottering remnants of their laws and religion, as to invent means of obliterating the very traces of either that may yet remain. I shall here attempt to lead the historian through these mazy windings lest he should lose himself when in pursuit of the Sect. The reader has already seen (in our remarks on the Code) its oaths and threats against every religion, all society, and property. Now, when reading of what the Sect has done, of the plots and machinations it has successfully undertaken and executed, may nations and their rulers acquire new ardour, and be stimulated to oppose their future projects with all the courage and all the means they are masters of. It is to triumph over Jacobinisin, cost what it may, that nations are to study the records of this Sect, and not to sink meanly into despair. I know I am but mortal, and that ere long I shall descend into the grave; and I calmly wait my dissolution; but should that consideration prevent my weeping over the general dissolution which threatens society, after I have awakened my readers to the dangers which threaten them, only to see them sinking once more into that apathy which portends ruin, under pretence that it is too late, that it is useless to resist the fate which the Sect has decreed for all nations? God forbid that I should hold such language! Cannot the good be fired with that zeal which consumes the breast of the miscreant heaving for wickdness. Let the rules of nations *will it*, let nations *will* to save their religion, their laws, their property, as this infernal Sect *wills* the destruction of them all, and success must infallibly crown their endeavours. It is only in hopes of contributing to their success, that I once more consent to sully my pen with the names of *Weishaupt*, of *Iluminee*, and of *Jacobin*, and to wade through their disgusting annals.

The order to be observed in treating of the history of the Sect shall be regulated according to its most remarkable epochs.

The first shall shew Weishaupt laying the foundations of his Iluminism, preparing and initiating his first adepts, founding his first Lodges, trying his first apostles, and preparing every thing for great conquests.

The second shall treat of that fatal intrusion which embodied thousands and thousands of adepts under Weishaupt's banners; and this epoch will be called the *Illuminization of Free-masonry*.

Very few years suffice to extend these tenebrous and mysterious conquests; but the thunderbolts of heaven warn mankind of their danger. The Sect and its conspiracies are discovered in Bavaria, and it speaks of this discovery under the appellation of *its persecutions*; nations and their rulers have been led to believe that it was the death-blow and extinction of the Sect.

Shrinking back, however, into its dark recesses, with unabating ardor, it crawls from den to den until it attains those of Philip of Orleans, who, joining the Sect with all the adepts of his occult Lodges, gives it sovereign sway over the whole of French Masonry. From this monstrous association sprung the JACOBINS, with all the crimes and horrors of the Revolution. This constitutes the fourth epoch of Illuminism; for as the lion, feeling his strength sufficient, sallies from his den, roars loudly, and victims must be sacrificed to him; so the Jacobins, or Illuminized Masons, quit their lurking places, and with horrid yell announce to nations and their rulers that they may tremble, for the day of revolution is come. This is the epoch at which the Sect begins the execution of its plots. He only knows how low the earth is condemned to bend beneath their yoke, who in his vengeance permits the plague and other scourges to devastate empires until he has been avenged of an impious generation. I neither pretend to be a prophet nor descendant of a prophet; but in treating of the numerous crimes already committed by the Sect, it will be but too easy to point out those that it has still to commit, and that it will commit, if princes and their people disregard the lessons of that same God, teaching them the conduct they should hold, in order to avert the impending scourge.

CHAP. I.

First Epoch of Illuminism.

FOR many years past, and particularly since Free-masonry had aquired such repute throughout Europe, a multitude of petty secret societies had been formed in the Protestant universities of Germany, each having its lodge, its master, its mysteries, all modelled on those founded by masons coming from England and Scotland. Hence sprung those various Orders *of Hope, of Harmony, the Constantists, the black Brethren,* and the like. The disputes and quarrels, nay, the disorderly behaviour of these young brethren attracted more than once the attention of the magistrates; some few attempts were made to crush these meetings, but being made without energy they were of course useless. Governments had not sufficiently considered, that the most dangerous abuse of these societies was not so much the quarrels and the boyish battles which ensued, as the taste which they inculcated for societies impervious to the eye of the magistrate, and under the cover of which their secrets were so easily transformed into the mysteries of impiety and the plots of rebellion.[1]

It would, however, be difficult I believe to prove, that any systems or opinions militating against religion or governments had as yet been introduced into these puerile associations. Many were even known to profess principles conducive to good manners and morality. The remedy may be found in the very source whence sprung the evil, that is to say, from the constitution of those universities, which on the one side leaves the choice of the different professors in each branch to their scholars, and on the other does not sufficiently provide for an honest teacher to place him beyond the powers of want or the temptations of avarice and vanity. Hence it followed, that masters, little delicate as to the means of obtaining a nomination, and nearly destitute of talents, had only to show great zeal for one of these little societies, or invent some new mystery more enticing than the rest, and his Lodges immediately filled; the scholars formed parties for him; in a short time his schools were as much flocked to as his Lodges, and contributions in his favour kept pace with his growing reputation. The fear of passing for a seducer of youth was a bar against his making use of these societies for instilling bad principles into his young followers, however much he might have wished it; and on the other side, the authority which he had acquired in the schools gave him a sufficient power in the Lodges to thwart any perverse intentions of the young adepts;

and these opposite reasons proved in general a sufficient guasrd against the introduction of great abuses.²

The time was not yet come, however, when proofs were to be acquired of the use to which the great conspirators were to turn these mysterious nurseries.

When public report spread the news in Germany, of a new order of Illuminees having been founded in the university of Ingolstadt by Weishaupt, many people supposed it to be one of those little college Lodges, which could no longer interest the adepts, when once they had finished their studies. Many even thought that Weishaupt, who was at that time a sworn enemy to the Jesuits, had only founded this Lodge with a view to form a party for himself against those fathers who after the destruction of their order had been continued in their offices of public teachers at the university of Ingolstadt.³ The Illuminees successfully availed themselves of this opinion on an occasion which we shall hereafter see to have been decisive as to their future existence in Germany. Had not the nature of their code and of their mysteries demonstrated views of far other importance both for nations and their governments to have been the grand object of the founder, the Archives of the Sect would show beyond all doubt that from its first institution Weishaupt had conceived the hopes, and determined on means for extending the plots of the Sect to the utmost boundaries of Empires.

It was on the 1st of May, 1776, that Weishaupt laid the first foundations of his Illuminism. The list of adepts seized among their archives shows his name inscribed on that day at the head of the Register; on the same day *Ajax*-Massenhausen and *Tiberius*-Merz were declared Areopagites.⁴ It is true that he selected these two first adepts from among his pupils who were studying the law under him at the university of Ingolstadt; these were generally young men from eighteen to twenty, a most dangerous age, when the passions easily lay open the unguarded mind to the seduction of Sophistry. Weishaupt could not overlook so fair an opportunity for forming apostles, who returning home when they had finished their studies might, under his direction, continue the same career of seduction which he himself carried on at Ingolstadt. Atrociously impious, we see him in the first year of his Illuminism aping the God of Christianity, and ordering *Ajax*-Massenhaussen in the following terms to propagate the doctrines of his new gospel: "Did not Christ send his Apostles to preach his Gospel to the universe? You that are my Peter, why should you remain idle at home, go then and preach."⁵

The modern Cephas had not waited for the orders of his master to give him proofs of his zeal. In the enthusiasm of his first fervor, and during the very month of his installation, he had acted the part of Insinuator to Xaverius Zwack.⁶ We shall soon see him outwitted by his pupil; but so great a conquest covered a multitude of sins of which he was afterwards guilty. By the name of *Cato* we see Zwack pass under the direction of Weishaupt himself, and he soon became his favorite disciple. He may be said to have robbed his Insinuator of the honor of having founded the Lodges of Munich; and it was through the means of this new apostle that the Sect made this rapid progress which Weishaupt boasts of in his letter to *Tiberius*-Merz, 13 May, 1778:

"It is with great pleasure that I can inform you of the happy progress my Order is making: knowing how anxious you are for its welfare, and that you have promised to contribute to its success by all the means in your power, I must inform you, that in a few days I shall be able to found two Lodges at Munich. The first will be composed of *Cato*, of Hertel, to whom I have given the name of *Marius*, and of Massenhausen, whom we call *Ajax*. These three will receive their instructions in a direct line from me. You also shall have a seat in their council when at Munich. I have been obliged to fix *Ajax* there, though he might have been of greaet use to me; for he was the first to whom I opened myself on the subject, and he also recruited *Cato* for me. Had I to begin again, I certainly would not make choice of him; but I have so clipped his wings that he can no longer play off any of his intrigues. I don't leave him in possession of a single half-penny of our funds; they are entrusted to *Marius*. Cato is the main spring at Munich, and the man who conducts every thing. It is for that reason that you must in future correspond with him. It is in this Lodge that all is regulated with regard to the general direction of the Order; but then every thing is to be submitted to me for approbation.

"The second college (or Lodge) shall consist of the above-named brethren, of Berger, under the name of *Cornelius Scipio*, and of a certain Troponero, whom we have surnamed *Coriolanus*, a most excellent man for us, about forty years of age, and who has been for a long time concerned in the Hamburgh trade, he is an able financier, and at this very time reads public lectures on finance at Munich.

"To these will soon be added Baader and Werstenrieder, both professors in the same town. This Lodge is to attend to all local concerns, that is, to all that may be of service or disservice to us at Munich. *Claudius*, one of *Cato's* cousins, and the young Sauer, an apprentice to a merchant, are in the Noviciate. Beieramer, surnamed *Zoroaster*, who was initiated a few days ago, is going to try his luck at Landshut, whither we send him to see how it will be received there. Michel, under the name of *Timon*, and Hohenaicher set off to the attack of Freisinguen.

"You are but little acquainted with the people of Aichstadt. It is enough to say that (counsellor) Lang, surnamed *Tamerlane*, is Director there. His zeal has already gained over to us *Odin, Tasso, Osiris, Lucullus, Sesostris,* and *Moses. This is going on pretty well, I think.* I forgot to say, that we have our printer at Munich. We are now making a new edition, and at our own expense, of *Alphonsus de Vargas* on the *stratagems* and the *sophisms* of the Jesuits.[7] You shall soon receive a copy of it. If you will send your contribution in money to *Cato*, as you promised, I shall be obliged to you. He will send you a receipt for it.

"If, through your zeal and by your means we could obtain a footing in Suabia, it would be a great step gained for us. Let me then beseech you to set to work. In five years you will be astonished to see what a progress we shall have made. Cato is really incomparable. *The greatest difficulties are over.* You will now see us advancing with gigantic strides. Do set to work then. *It would be vain for you to expect a better occasion for acquiring power.* You are endowed with all the necessary talents for such an undertaking; and to neglect building in the Elysian fields when the occasion offers is to be doubly criminal. There are a vast number at Aichstadt; and could not your natal soil rival an Aichstadt. With respect to myself, the services I can render here can be but of little avail. Answer me soon; make an extract of this letter as usual, and then send it back to me, &c."

The grand object of such intimations on the progress of Illuminism was not so much to satisfy the curiosity of the adept, as to stimulate his zeal by the example of *Cato* and *Tamerlane*, those active recruiters for the Sect, the former at Munich, the latter at Aichstadt. Though he owned that *Tiberius* had not been altogether unserviceable to him, nevertheless Weishaupt did not think he had made a sufficient return for the honor conferred on him in being nominated at once second Areopagite and second Apostle of the Order; it was with much concern (to use Weishaupt's expression) that he saw this apostle had neither *son nor nephew* in the Order, that is to say, that he had not founded a Lodge nor recruited a single novice.[8] Wholly absorbed in his pleasures, Weishaupt had hitherto made but fruitless attempts to stimulate his zeal, nor had he succeeded better through Cato's means; but this news had the desired effect. These intimations on the progress of Illuminism finished by requesting *Tiberius* to seek out a proper person to be sent to found new colonies in Suabia. This fired the sluggard apostle with emulation; *Tiberius* undertook the task himself, and in a short time we find him represented in the annals of the Sect as at the head of a new colony at Ravensburg in Suabia, and as fulfilling perfectly the functions of his apostleship.[9]

But this zeal of *Tiberius,* as well as that of *Ajax,* was but of an intermittent nature. The latter had robbed the funds of the Order; and Weishaupt, speaking of himself, complains that *he had done him more mischief both in men and money than three years could recruit again."*[10] As to *Tiberius,* he had so thoroughly imbibed the iniquitous doctrines which he was to infuse into the young adepts, and the scandalous publicity of his character militated so much against that hypocrisy which Weishaupt judged necessary for the propagation of his Illuminism, that we shall see him hereafter expelled from the Order. Notwithstanding the seeming impropriety of such a choice for the two senior apostles, it was to them nevertheless that the Sect was indebted for the two colonies of Munich *Athens,* and of Ravensburgh *Sparta*. As to Aichstadt *Erzerum,* Weishaupt himself was the founder. He profited of the first vacation he had from the schools to make an excursion to that town, and there employed all that time which the generality of professors dedicate to the recruiting of their health after the labours of the past year, in the propagation of his doctrines. An assiduous scrutator, he sought among all ranks of citizens and of all ages those whom he could hope to captivate. The first person on whom he cast his eyes, was one of the principal magistrates, of the name of

Lang. But a few days sufficed for this conquest, and this is the *Tamerlane* whose successes are so much extolled in the above-mentioned letter to *Tiberius*. He next began to exercise his talents as Insinuator with all the artifice and according to the laws laid down in the code, on men who bearing a certain character, and habitually residing among their fellow-citizens, could the more effectually influence the public opinion. He made an attempt to seduce the Chapter of that town, for it was from thence that he writes, "I even think that I shall be able to recruit two others, and what is more two *Canons*. Can I but execute my designs on the Chapter, then we shall have made a great step."[11]

It does not appear that he succeeded with his two Canons; but we see him on the other hand making numerous conquests. He begins by a certain Schleich, with whom he is much delighted, and who on this first admission presented the Order with whatever books Weishaupt chose to select from his library. Then comes a man surnamed *Lucullus*, who, while only in his novitiate, begins by Weishaupt's express command to act the part of Insinuator to the Baron Eckert, who was supposed to be a *great prize*. In short, there was a number of young men whom Weishaupt persuaded to come and finish their educations at his university, that he might be able to complete their initiation. Such was the success he met with during the few months he remained at Aichstadt; and he was so overjoyed with it that he writes to *Ajax*-Massenhausen, "I have most certainly done more during this vacation than all of you have done together."[12] Though obliged to return to his public functions of teacher at the university of Ingolstadt, he left this new Lodge in possession of such a fund of illuminized instruction, that Aichstadt was soon looked up to as the model of Lodges; and the predilection which Weishaupt ever after retained for it is observable. He often proposes it as an example to those adepts who became lukewarm in the service of the Sect. It was also the Lodge which he had the most grossly imposed upon as to the origin of the Sect, and which he most ridicules in his confidential letters to *Cato*-Zwack, when he says, "The greatest of our mysteries must be the novelty of the Order. The fewer persons there are in the secret, the better we shall thrive; at present, you and Merz are the only two that know the secret, nor do I mean to tell it to any one else for a long time to come. *As to our fellows at Aichstadt, there is not one of them that knows it, nor is there one who would not swear on his life and death that the Order is older than Methusalem.*"[13]

On his return to Ingolstadt, Weishaupt applied himself to the means of combining his functions of Doctor of Laws with those of Founder of a Secret Society, whose future purpose was the total subversion of every law. He fulfilled the former part of his duty with such assiduity, and with such an appearance of candor, that he was chosen Superior of the university. This new dignity only added to his hypocrisy. The same year, so far was he from losing sight of his tenebrous plots, that he formed a secret school, wherein he amply counter-balanced the lessons he was obliged to give in public; and by means of this new species of scholars he stored up an abundant means for the propagation of his Illuminism. At once Superior and Professor of the university, he made use of this double title to inspire the parents of his scholars with new confidence. He converted his house into one of those boarding-houses where young men, perpetually under the eyes of their masters, are supposed to be better preserved from the dangers which threaten them at that age. Several letters demonstrate the intention of this monstrous pedagogue to offer his house and table to the young students of the university as a means of attaining his baleful ends. He solicited fathers and mothers to entrust their children to his care; and, over-joyed at having obtained so precious a deposit, he exultingly writes to his adepts, "that the young Baron of Schroeckenberg, and the young Hoheneicher, are to be boarded with him." He then adds, "*And these gentlemen also must swallow the bait that is thrown to them.*" When he had observed the great facility that this secret school gave him of seducing his disciples, he writes, "Next year also I will take boarders at my house, *always with a view to forward the grand object.*"[14] Should it come to pass that he could not persuade the parents to intrust any of his young auditors to his care, especially when he had cast his views on them, he then had houses near him and in his interest, to which he would entice the young pupils, lest he should lose sight of them. It is on a similar occasion that he writes to *Ajax*, "I see no other lodging for you in our neighbourhood but at my mother's. I should be excessively happy if that would do for you; and more particulrly so, as she would make no difficulty in allowing you the key of the house-door. I do not wish to force you to go there if you can find a better; but *the great advantage of this would be, that I should always have a pretence for going to your chamber; and there we could more easily than at my house discourse together without any one's knowing a word of the matter. Our union would be more secret.*"[15]

Let not the reader be surprized at seeing me descend to all these particulars. I am describing the infant state of the Sect, and the founder forming his first disciple. Such means might be despised by some; but this was not the case with our prototype of rebellion; he scarcely appears to venture beyond the porch of his own habitation. Let the wolf alone; in the thickets of the forest she suckles her young; they grow in strength, and we soon behold them carrying the palpitating remnants of flocks to gorge the ravenous maw of her who taught them to devour. Scarcely had Weishaupt dedicated his secret school for the space of two years to his Illuminism, when his adepts, worthy of such disastrous plans, sallied forth to spread the baneful poisons. Let the reader judge of the importance of his means by the successes attending on them; let him reflect on them while Weishaupt shall be his own historian in the following letter:

"In future," says he to his two famous Areopagites *Cato* and *Marius*, "you will assume a different tone with *Timon* and Hoheneicher, as I have let them into the whole secret; I have even disclosed myself to them as founder of our Order; and I have done it for many reasons.

"First, Because *they are to be themselves founders of a new colony at Freysinguen, their native country,* and on that account stand in need of more particular instructions as to the whole tendency of the Order, which were much too long to have been given by letter. I profit of every instant while they remain with me, to prepare them for every thing.

"Secondly, Because they must in the mean time insinuate the Baron D'E...and *some other students*.

"Thirdly, Because H— —" (this H— — is evidently the above-mentioned Hoheneicher, the very person of whom Weishaupt says, when enticing him to board with him, *He shall swallow the bait*) "is too well acquainted with my style of writing and of thinking, not to have soon found out that the whole was of my own invention.

"Fourthly, *Because of all my boarders of last year he was the* ONLY ONE *who had not been made acquainted with the whole business.*

"Fifthly, Because he has offered to contribute to our secret library at Munich, *and will furnish us with several important articles belonging to the chaper of Freysinguen.*

"And, Lastly, Because after three months more instruction, which I have to give them, they will both be enabled to render us the most important services."[16]

From this letter we may evidently infer, first, that of all the youg men who boarded with Weishaupt during the first year of his conspiracy not a single one escaped his dark designs: Secondly, that they were not only initiated in the mysteries, but even in the most profound mysteries, that, for instance, in which he reveals himself to be the founder of Illuminism, which is pointed out in the Code as the last secret, and only to be imparted to the most consummate adepts.[17] Thirdly, that before he had initiated his boarders into all his secrets, he used them as tools for the seduction of other students of the university, whom he had not been able to entice to his table.—Fourthly, that at the very period when Weishaupt restores his pupils to their parents, their seduction is complete; and that when these young men quit the university, as having accomplished the study of the laws of their country, they depart for their natal soil imbued with the principles and initiated in all the means by which they are to overturn those very laws which they are supposed to have been studying, and annihilate all religion, society, and property.—Fifthy, the reader is not to forget the *important articles* which the young Hoheneicher promises to steal from the library of the Chapter of Freysinguen, and with which he is to enrich the secret library of the Sect. Such an action could only be a consequence of Weishaupt's grand principle of morality, that *a useful theft could not be criminal*, or that those same means which the wicked employ for an evil end are justifiable when employed for the attainment of a good end. It is the same principle which begins by plundering the libraries of the clergy, as the first step towards the plundering of their estates; which soon, under the pretence of general utility and necessity for the support of the premeditated revolution, wil invade the property of the Nobles and of the Rich, of the Merchant, the Husbandman, and the Mechanic, pillaging all, and blasting the most distant hope they may have conceived of preserving the smallest remnant of their shattered fortune from the general wreck. When the historian shall come to treat of these great revolutionary spoliations, reverting to the prime source, he will find himself in the midst of a Sect calling itself Illuminees, a school of methodized robbers thieving by principle, whence Weishaupt sends his apostles of depredation, and brigand adepts. Soon we shall behold them boasting of other spoliations. The lessons of the secret cavern shall spread around, and the adept, annihilating all property as well as blaspheming all government and all religion, shall do homage to their master presiding over his secret school.

The two new adepts, formed with so much care to the arts of seduction, at length received their mission, and the town of Freysinguen, under the appellation of *Thebes*, becomes the fourth colony. About the same time the adepts of the two Lodges at Munich showed so much zeal for the propagation of the mysteries, that Weishaupt, after having calculated on their and his own success, did not hesitate at writing to them, "If you do but continue with the same zeal, we shall in a little time be masters of our whole country;"[18] that is to say, of all Bavaria.

Wenn sie so fortfahren, wie seit einiger zeit so gehört in kurzer zeit unser vaterland uns.

The reader must not, however, think that his views were circumscribed to this Electorate; he soon writes to his Areopagites, desiring them to make choice, from among the foreigners who were then at Munich, of persons who might be instructed, initiated, and sent to found new colonies at *Augsbourg, Ratisbon, Saltzbourg, Landshut, and in different parts of Franconia.*[19] At the time he wrote these instructions he had already sent his missionaries to the *Tyrol* and into *Italy*.[20] The part, or rather the multiplicity of parts, which he acted at Ingolstadt to ensure the success of his undertaking are as inconceivable as they were real. He gives us a small sketch of his activity when he writes to Cato, proposing himself as a model: "Do as I do, avoid large companies. But do not think of remaining idle if you wish to acquire any influence in this world. Wait a while; the hour is coming, and it will come soon, when you will have a great deal to do. Remember Sejanus, who so well assumed the character of an idle man, and who transacted so much business without appearing to transact any; *erat autem Sejanus otioso simillimus, nihil agendo multa agens*;[21] never had a conspirator better laid down the precept or given the example than Weishaupt.

Apparently tranquil at Ingolstadt, Weishaupt had a far better cloak for his conspiracies than Sejanus's idleness. A seeming assiduity in his duty, a great show of zeal and erudition in his expounding of the laws, easily misled people to believe that his whole time and talents were engrossed with the study of them; and, if we are to credit his own account, Ingolstadt had never witnessed a professor so well calculated to add new lustre to its university. The public functions of professor of the laws, and the secret arts or seducer in private, had not made him forget that he was also the founder of Illuminism, and that in this latter quality he had to form a code of laws, which were at once to annihilate every other law, all religion, and all property. At the time when he initiated his first adepts, he was far from having perfected that code of iniquity; and perhaps in the strict sense of the word Weishaupt had deviated from the common rules of prudence, in giving way to such ardour for the propagation of the Order, sending his apostles and initiating his disciples before he had completed the code of laws which was to regulate their conduct. But such an impetuosity cannot be considered in this prototype of rebellion as a want of foresight, or as an excess of confidence. He knew that years and experience were necessary to perfect that gradual system of initiations and of trials which his Novices were to undergo; and artfully to prepare those impious and sophisticated discourses to be pronounced by his Hierophants; in a word, to complete that concatenation of artifice which was to regulte the condict of his Regents, Directors, and Areopagites. He could not endure the idea of ssacrificing so many years to mere theoretic projects. He would, in his first essays, make conquests that were to ensure him still greater ones on a future day, which he had already calculated. He knew his own talents too well to entertain the least doubt of success; he foresaw how far he could perfect those systems which he had as yet only conceived, and he wished to have ready at hand a numerous clan of disciples disposed to receive his new gospel, and apostles who should need only to be initited in his last mysteries, when his code, completed, was to be sent to the tenebrous recesses of his different colonies.

Such were his views, and such the confidence he had in the transcendency of his own genius for wickedness, when he wrote at different times to his first adepts, "Do not trouble yourself about future degrees. The day will come when you shall view with astonishment what I have done on that score. In the mean time, *be it your care to enlist men for me, prepare knights for me, instruct them, dispose them, amuse them, and leave the rest to me.*—The whole of your business consists in adding to the numbers. Allow yourselves to be directed, and obey for a year or two longer, *and give me time to lay my foundations, for that is the essential point; and nobody understands that part better than I do.* If these foundations are once laid, you may then do what you please; *and though you were to try I would defy you to overthrow my edifice.*"[22]

This desperate method of proceeding must have given rise to many difficulties; but Weishaupt overcame them all. By provisional regulations and private instructions he supplied the deficiency of this incomplete code, and he was equal to the task. The greatest obstacles he met with came from those very Areopagites from whom he had expected the greatest support. Villains will dissagree even in their villainy; and, impatient of the laws of the state, they become impatient of the laws of their own leaders. Weishaupt wished to take advantage of their views, but had no intention of imparting his to them; he knew his own superiority in the black arts too well, he wished for agents and not counsellors and co-legislators. Jealousies and intestine broils rose to such a height, that any other but Weishaupt would have thought his infant association must have been crushed in its very cradle; but he found means of weathering the storm; now negotiating, then despotically commanding;

suppliant like, he enters into agreements, and ends by dictating conditions; prayers, excuses, all are means with him to command submission; he even showed himself disposed to sacrifice all the fruits of his past labours; he threatened to abandon his rebellious brethren to themselves, and to undertake the direction of a new society more powerful and stronger still, in as much as he would render it more submissive.[23] In the midst of all these broils, he continued and perfected that code which would have required the talents of twenty Machiavels. Storms indeed appeared only to stimulate his ardour and activity; and he says himself, when writing to his dear *Cato*, "I am once more at open war with all our people; *that does no harm, it enlivens the machine*; I can neither praise nor wink at faults committed. Meanwhile our affairs go on very well; and provided they follow my directions the general system will have lost nothing."[24] *Night and day*, in the midst of these broils, as he says, *meditating, writing*, and *combining*, all that could perfect, strengthen, or propagate his Illuminism either in the whole or part, he nevertheless held his professorship with applause, he overlooked his secret school, he formed new adepts, and from his sanctuary watched and overlooked his missionaries in their provinces and new colonies. By means of the *Quibus Licet's* he would descend into the minutest particulars of their conduct, direct them in their undertakings, point out to them what might be done, and reprimand them for what they had not done to promote his views. Voltaire's correspondence under this head is immense; but it is not to be compared to Weishaupt's; not a letter of all those seized by the arm of the law but bears the stamp of the consummate conspirator; not a letter that does not allude to the mysteries or to some new artifice; that does not point out the candidates to be enticed, the adepts to be advanced, animated, repressed, or reprimanded; in short, the enemies who are to be guarded against and the protectors to be courted. His apostles are on the spot in their different missions, while he, from his head-quarters, appears to be better acquainted with those who surrounded them than they are themselves. He goes so far as to inform them of the rank, political or civil station, even of the private characters of those whom they are to recruit; he gives them the means, mentions the persons who are to second them, and what companies they ought to frequent, in order to succeed in their undertakings; in fine, he animates, threatens, and reprimands his adepts, just as if they were still boarding with him, though perhaps at many hundred miles distance. Scarcely have they made any new conquest when he directs them in the same manner and at once governs the main spring and every subservient power throughout the whole Order. His correspondence will show him on the same day writing of the laws necessary for the further establishment of his Order, of treaties to be made, of plans of commerce, and of the most impious commerce, to enrich his Illuminism. At length, with all the hypocrisy of a man who assumes the character of an idler, or at least of one only fulfilling that which his public duty exacts from him, he aims at the supremacy over every conspiring Sect. He gets himself received a Free-mason, he dives into the secrets of the occult lodges of the Rosicrucians, and blends their conspiring arts with his own.[25]

He next forms an alliance, and from the bottom of Bavaria corresponds with those federations which the free-masons of Poland were preparing; and lest any of these revolutionary arts should be lost, he makes large collections, which might be called the grand arsenal for the seduction of nations; and these are to become the foundations of secret libraries for the use of the adepts. He never loses sight of those profits which accrue from the secret presses, which were perpetually disgorging poison into the minds of the people. For the further replenishment of his coffers, he sets all the talents of his adepts to work; some are to contribute pamphlets, prose or verse, or journals, while others are to collect all the impious doctrines and calumnies of antiquity, or to compose libels on subjects which he gives them; and, for his own part he undertakes to burlesque the Prophets and the Lamentations, and to convert the history of the church into a romance replete with calumny.[26] The sacred writings mention a Devil that was named *Legion*, from the innumerable evils he brought upon mankind; were we to consider the fatal activity of Weishaupt in every impious and rebellious art, we should be tempted to believe that he had been possessed by this evil spirit, and that it was to that devil he owed all his success.

As yet the very existence of the Order had not been suspected at Ingolstadt, though there were already in Bavaria alone, five Lodges at Munich; other Lodges and Colonies at Freysinguen, at Landsberg, at Burghausen, and at Straubing. Weishaupt was on the eve of founding others at Ratisbon and Vienna; many had been established in Suabia, Franconia, and Tyrol. His apostles were working at the same time in Holland and at Milan. His Illuminism had not been founded three years, when he writes to *Cato* that he has more than *a thousand adepts*.[27] He was much indebted to his own zeal and activity for such a rapid progress. I cannot flatter the historian with the hopes of an accurate account of the whole Legion; but I can satisfy his curiosity, I think, with respect to those who the most actively seconded Weishaupt, and who after their founder appear the most conspicuous on the records of the Sect.

---

1. The sophisticated masons of France were not strangers to these boyish Lodges. A few years before the destruction of the Jesuits one of these lodges was set on foot in their college of Tulle, styling its members the *Chevaliers de la Pure Verité, (Knights of the Pure Truth.)* The Jesuits soon perceived whither this doctrine of *pure truth* and its secret meetings would lead. Before any other method for putting a stop to this new establishment was proposed, they resolved to try the power of ridicule which was almost infallible in France. Accordingly, one of the masters undertook to compose a most sarcastic song on our young Knights, and copies were secretly distributed to all the young men who did not belong to the Lodge. Scarcely could one of the juvenile Knights make his appearance without hearing some ridiculous line of this song hummed in his ears; and in a short time squares, compasses, Lodge and all, disappeared.
2. See the Memoirs of a Protestant Minister on the Illuminees.
3. See the Memoirs of a Protestant Minister on the Illuminees.

4. Original Writings, Sect. IV.
5. Hat doch Christus auch seine apostel in die welt geschickt, und warum sollte ich meinen Petrus zu hause lassen? *Ite et predicate.*—*Original Writings, Letter to Ajax, 19th Sept. 1776.*
6. In the Third Volume of these Memoirs, page 15 [p. 405, Ed.], in the Note [note 8, Ed.], it is said, "it was clear that *Zwack* was only initiated "*ten* months after the two adepts *Ajax* and *Tiberius*." In place of *ten* we should read *twenty-two* months, as I meant to speak of his installation among the Areopagites, which only took place on the 22d of Feb. 1778. *(Original Writings, Vol. I. Sect. IV.)*; but he had been received into the order on the 29th May, 1776, as may be seen by the tablets of *Ajax*. Beside, these tablets and the list just mentioned do not perfectly coincide. The reason of this difference will be explained when treating of the first adepts.
7. This supposed *Alophonsus de Vargas*, whose calumnies against the Jesuits Weishaupt renews with so much eagerness, is no other than *Gaspar Sciopius*, far better known for the grossness and virulence of his tedious discourses against those who dare to differ with him in opinion, than by his erudition. He was particularly abusive against *Scaliger* and *James I* King of Englnad; the latter had him answered in Spain by a severe bastinado. This was also the man who revenged himself in so virulent a manner on *Casaubon* and *Du Plessis Mornai*, his best friends, but who contradicted him on a point of literature; in short, the man who has been alternately called the *Attila*, the *Cerberus*, and even the *public executioner* of all literature. See *Moreri*'s and *Fuller's Dictionaries*.
8. Let. 3, to Cato.
9. Original Writings, Vol. I. Let. to *Cato*, 25 Aug. and 2 Sept. 1778.
10. Original Writings, Let. 3, to *Cato*.
11. Let. 3, to *Ajax*.
12. To the same, Let. 4.
13. Orig. Writ. Let. 2, to *Philip-Strozzi* or *Cato*-Zwack.
14. Orig. Writ. Vol. I. Let. I. to *Ajax*, Let. 20, to *Cato*.
15. Orig. Writ. Let. 5, to *Ajax*.
16. Original Writings, Vol. I. Let. 12. to *Cato* and *Marius*.
17. See the Code, Vol. 3. Chap. 12, on the Grand Mysteries, Page 288.
18. Orig. Writ. Vol. I. Let. 26, 14th of Nov. 1778.
19. Ibid. Let. 39.
20. Ibid. Let. 36.
21. Let. I. to Cato.
22. Extracts from Let. 8, to *Ajax*, from Letters to *Cato*, and to the Areopagites particularly from Let. 59, Vol. I.
23. Vol. I, Let. 25, 27, 60; Vol. 2, Let. 11, 19, 21, &c. &c.
24. Vol. 2. Let. 19.
25. Let. 6, to *Ajax*, and Let. 36, to *Cato*.
26. Vol. I, Let. 6, to *Ajax*, to *Cato*, 36, &c. To *Philip-Strozzi*, Let. 2, & passim, Vol. 2, Let. 22, et passim.
27. Orig. Writ. Vol. I, see Let. 25, to *Cato*, 13 Abenmeh 1148, that is to say, 13 Nov. 1778.

CHAP. II.

Of the principal Adepts during the first Epoch of Illuminism.

OF this legion of Conspirators, which, as early as the third year of Illuminism, Weishaupt computes at more than *a thousand*,[1] XAVERIUS ZWACK is certainly the most conspicuous among the adepts. He is styled the *incomparable*; and the greater part of the letters printed in the *Original Writings* are written to him, particularly those which comprehend the clearest account of the mysteries; in short, his favour was such, that the founder of the Sect apostrophises him saying, "Now you are in a post where nobody can be above you but myself; you are exalted above all the Brethren; an immense field opens itself for you to exert your power and your influence, should we succeed in propagating our systems."[2] Such a distinction and such favor naturally suppose great merit. Happily, an incontrovertible monument exists which will direct the Historian in his judgment, and render unnecesssary any further research. It is to be found at the end of the first Volume of the Original Writings, under the title of *Tablets relating to Danaus, written by Ajax 31st Dec. 1776*. *Danaus* is the first characteristic name that was given to Zwack when only a candidate. The fact is evident, as in the first column of the Tablets we find the brother *Danaus* described by his own name; *Ajax*, that is, Massenhausen, acts the part of Scrutator.—Should this statement not be very flattering, we may at least conclude that the failings and vices of the adept are not exaggerated, since the Scrutator declares, that it is by the extreme intimacy and friendship in which he lived with the Candidate that he has been enabled to make this conquest, and terminates the tablet by stating the Candidate to be one of those Sages who has all the necessary qualifications to be admitted into the Order.—These tablets are also a lasting monument of the rapid progress Weishaupt had made, even in these early days of Illuminism, in the scrutinizing arts; nor will they prove an unfaithful standard by which the Historian may judge of the merits of those conspirators, whom the founder selects as worthy of his most intimate correspondence. Let us begin by suppressing that disgust which naturally drives the honest heart from dwelling on such despicable engines of rebellion remarkable only for their vices, and proceed from these tablets to depict the features which are in future to stand as the model for all those who are to recruit Candidates for the Sect. Let nations and the people at large learn what a miserable banditti of thieves and libertines pretend to regenerate them, and how basely they are duped by them when stirred up to Revolution.

The Tablets, whence Weishaupt is to learn of the merits and demerits of the future *Cato* of his Order, are divided into seventeen columns, each relating to a different head. The name, the age, the civil dignity, the description of his person, the civil and moral character of the candidate, are all treated of separately. Then follow the studies he is addicted to, the services the Order may expect from him, the progress he has made, the degrees conferred on him, the secret manuscripts or books left to him, the contributions he has paid; his friends, his protectors, his enemies, and the persons with whom he corresponds, are each separately treated of.

Under these columns is to be found a second table also subdivided, and containing observations on the family, and particularly of the father and mother, of the candidate, made by the same Scrutator. Combining these two tables, we find, "that Francis Xaverius Zwack was son of Philip Zwack, commissary of the *Chambre des Comptes*, and was born at Ratisbon; that at the time of his initiation (29 May 1776) he was twenty years of age, and had finished his college education."

"*The description of his person.* He was then about five feet high. *His person emaciated by debauchery*, his constitution bordering on melancholy;[3] his eyes of a dirty grey, *weak and languishing,—his complexion pale and sallow;*—his health weak, and much hurt by frequent disorders;—his nose long, crooked, and hooked.—Hair light brown:—gait precipitate—*his eyes always cast towards the ground;*—under the nose and on each side of the mouth a mole. *The moral character, religion, conscience.* His heart tender, and most extraordinarily philanthropic; but stoic when in a melancholy mood;—otherwise a true friend, circumspect, reserved, *extremely secret,*—often speaking advantageously of himself,—envious of other people's perfections—*voluptuous*, endeavouring to improve himself—little calculated for numerous assemblies—*choleric and violent*, but easily appeased—willingly giving his private opinions, *when one has the precaution to praise him, though contradicting him*—a lover of novelties—*on religion and conscience widely differing from the received ideas; and thinking precisely as he ought, to become a good member of the order.*"

"*His favourite studies, and the services he can render to the order.* Most particularly addicted to philosophy—having some knowledge of the laws—speaking French and Italian very correctly—at present attempting to get himself placed in the foreign department—*a perfect master in the arts of dissimulation; a proper person to be received into the Order,* as applying himself particularly to the study of the human heart."

Friends, correspondence, company.—Here the Insinuator names five or six persons friends to the candidate. Among them we find a certain *Sauer* and a *Berger*, both of whom soon after appear on the registers of the Sect.

These three columns contain the name of *Ajax* as Insinuator—The day when the candidate was insinuated—and when received.

"*Of the means of gaining and leading the Candidate, and whether he is acquainted with any other secret societies*—Here it appears that Zwack was already connected with other secret societies, which made the conquest rather more difficult—*The intimacy of our friendship*, (says the Insinuator) and particularly the care which I took to assume a mysterious tone and appearance, levelled many difficulties—at present he expresses a great ardor and zeal for the Order."

"*Predominant passions—Pride, love of glory, probity, easily provoked*—an extraordinary propensity for mysteries—*a perpetual custom of speaking of himself, and of his own perfections*."

In the eleventh column we are informed, that the candidate had received a *pensum* to fill up, or a discourse to make, and that it was to be finished on the 29th April 1778.

The twelfth mentions the fortune and revenue of the candidate; but the Editor has left the figures in blank.

The two next show, that the day on which Zwack engaged to pay his contribution for 1777 was the 29th of May, but for 1778 was the 1st of April. That on the 19th July 1776, he sent a Dutch Ducat, and some time after two books on Chymistry.

The column in which the Insinuator notes the progress of his candidate shows, that the secret books which had been given him to read were those numbered 1, 2, 4, and 9—the orders which he had received are only numbered, as also *the leave given to recruit other Brethren*. As this column is made use of to note the successive progress of the candidate, the Brother Insinuator at length arrives at that period when Zwack has received all the information necessary to his admission into the Order. He then declares that it is time to impart more essential secrets to him and to promote him to higher degrees.

The sixteenth column enumerates his enemies, and the reason of their enmities. In the last we find the names of his friends and protectors.

I should not have insisted so much on these Tablets, had I not thought it necessary to give one specimen at least of these inquisitorial instruments, on which Illuminism grounds the choice of its adepts and the future success of its conspiracies.[4]

When we reflect on the leading features of these tablets, what idea are we to form of Zwack's character? Inordinate debauchery, extreme fatuity, jealousy, dissimulation, and a sullen melancholy.—Such features are more than sufficient to banish him from all good company. He also thinks on matters relating *to religion and conscience* as the adepts do; or, in other words, is a downright Atheist. With an insatiable thirst after *novelties*, he has all that admiration for secrecy which the revolutionist can desire. He, moreover, professes universal philanthropy for all mankind, that he may the better succeed in his plots against every social law; and this could suffice to obliterate all other failings in Xaverius Zwack, and constitute him the favourite adept.

Meanwhile the lessons of the Insinuator, together with that black melancholy which reigned in his heart, had nearly deprived Illuminism of the important assistance of this beloved adept. To despise death was one of the important lessons that we have seen given the novices; and to die by their own hands rather than disclose the secrets of their teachers, was particularly instilled into them. Weishaupt had conceived this maxim in two words, *Patet*

Exitus (the exit is free), *or destroy himself who will*, particularly if he finds himself unhappy in this life. It is a part of that convenient maxim afterwards decreed by the Jacobins, *That death was only an eternal sleep.* Full of this principle, and weary of his existence, our new candidate had persuaded himself that should he die by his own hand he would die the death of a sage. He composed his work entitled *Thoughts on Suicide.* They are the sentiments of an Atheist worn out with debauchery, and almost mad with impiety.[5] He made his will, and wrote the following letter to Brother *Ajax.*

"Munich, the 30th Oct. 1777.—Friend, I am on my departure. It is the best step I can take. Fare thee well; doubt not of my probity, and let it not be doubted of by others. Confirm the Sages in the judgement they are going to form on my death, and look on those who blame it with pity. Be thou an honest man; think sometimes on me, and do not let me be forgotten by the small number of our friends. Beware of pitying me. ZWACK."

In a postscript he bequeaths a ring as a keepsake to Brother *Ajax*, and begs him to forward a second letter to the whole brotherhood of Illuminism; it is as follows:

"And you also, Brethren, I salute you for the last time; I thank you for your good intentions towards me. I declare to you, that I was worthy of them, I declare it upon my honour; which is my only worth, *and which alone I held sacred.* Let my ashes be honoured by your remembrance; *bless them, while superstition shall curse me.* Enlighten yourselves mutually, labour to render mankind happy, esteem virtue and reward it; punish crime, and behold with pity the failings of human nature. On the brink of his grave, descending into it deliberately, and making choice of death through *conviction,* through *demonstration,* choosing it *for his happiness,* it is thus that he makes his adieu, who ever remains your friend and Brother, ZWACK."[6]

Illuminism must have lost its favourite adept, had he proved as constant in his resolution as he was serious when he took it. No reason is given why he condescended to live; but in like manner as Weishaupt has found a protector in the person of the Duke of Saxe Gotha, so has he been created a Privy Counsellor to the Prince of Salm Kirbourg, and is his ordinary agent at the Imperial Chamber of Wetzlar. At this present moment he is deputy for the House of Salm Kirbourgh at Radstadt, at the General Congress of the Germanic Empire treating of peace with the triumphant Illuminees of the French Republic. He is accompanied by a Sieur Ambmann, a citizen of Darmstadt, and an Illuminee like himself. History, I suppose, will at some future time explain how he contrived to combine the interests of the Sect with those of the Powers which he had sworn to annihilate. But let us return to Zwack at a time when he little expected to be carried by the Brethren to that exalted station where he was to decide on the fate of Sovereigns.

His *Thoughts on Suicide*, however, were not lost on his sister-in-law, for she really sought death, and, throwing herself from the top of a tower, dashed her brains out.[7] But he, who had chosen to live, took umbrage at the great length of his noviciate, and at the many trials *Ajax* made him undergo. He writes directly to Weishaupt, who, taking him under his direction, begins by telling him that *Ajax* had imposed upon him by not forwarding the letter he had written to the brethren; *but since he has imposed upon you*, says the instructor, *trick him in your turn*; and the following was the method adopted on Weishaupt's proposal. Zwack is established Inspector over his own Insinuator;[8] and he then gave the most evident proofs that his character had been well drawn, when it was said that *he was a perfect master of the arts of dissimulation*; for although he now became the confidant and bosom friend of *Spartacus*, and was consequently initiated in all the mysteries of the Sect, he nevertheless continued to act the part of a Novice with his Insinuator. He was not only at that time a member of the College of Areopagites, but also the superior of it, and in a perpetual and direct correspondence with Weishaupt. He acted his part so well, that *Ajax*, still considering him as his scholar, thought to do him a great favour in showing him a few of Weishaupt's letters; but they had already passed through the scholar's hands, as did every writing coming from *Spartacus* to *Ajax*.

This part which Zwack acted, of inspecting him who thought himself his inspector, explains that apparent contradiction between the tablets written by *Ajax* and the list of the first adepts, which is to be seen in the Original Writings.[9] In the former *Ajax* looks upon Xaverius Zwack as a mere candidate till the 29th May, 1778, and in the latter he is styled an Areopagite on the 22d Feb. 1778, under the characteristic of *Cato*; and in a few months after he appears to be the next in command after the *Spartacus* of the Order.[10] Never was an Insinuator better undermined by his novice.

The different names under which this adept appears in the Original Writings has been a matter of some difficulty to many readers; but on paying attention to that predilection, always increasing, which Weishaupt had conceived for this adept, the difficulty vanishes. At first Zwack had received the insignificant name of *Danaus* but no sooner was *Spartacus* made acquainted with his hatred for kings, than he surnames him *Philip Strozzi*, after that famous Florentine Conspirator, who, having murthered Alexander de Medicis, was afterwards taken in open rebellion against his sovereign, and plunged a dagger into his own breast, reciting that verse dictated by all the fury of vengeance:

Exoriare aliquis nostris ex ossibus ultor.

The suicide, though it did not take place, was equally meritorious in Weishaupt's eyes; and hence Zwack is created the *Cato* of Illuminism. It is under that name that he becomes the principal agent and beloved disciple of the founder at Munich, and their mutual sympathy in wickedness has perpetuated their intimacy.

Though he had not all the genius of Weishaupt himself, he was as much prone to the commission of crime. Scarcely had he entered the Order when for his first essay he declares himself a downright Atheist;[11] he at the same time makes known his hatred for kings and his admiration of the people in rebellion against their pretended tyrants.[12] We may observe some of the first adepts astonished at the immensity of the crimes and disasters which Weishaupt was preparing for the universe; and it requires some management to prepare them for such horrid plots. But his *Cato* is always ready for every thing. The incomparable *Cato* was *arrived at the height of his mysteries*, and Weishaupt had but to unroll his code of iniquity, for his scholar could only be surpassed by the criminality of invention.

This sympathy for impiety and wickedness, however, could not suffice for Weishaupt's policy. His views required a senate of Conspirators; but a senate of agents, and not of equals. The better to be obeyed by the Areopagites, he commands them to meet at a distance from him; for he well understood the nature of secret societies, and knew that his order would be better obeyed the more he enveloped himself in mystery and hid himself from public view. If, in spite of his invisibility, jealousy should arise on the part of the Areopagites, he will have an agent at their head, that *Cato*, who holds the exalted station of president from him, and is therefore most interested to support the authority of the founder, his protector. And it is to preserve this president in his interests, that we see Weishaupt using every artifice, and even supplication: "*support me then*," he says; "do dispose things so, and prepare their minds, that my dispositions may be received."[13]

Weishaupt had no reason to regret his choice; for during all those intestine broils which arose between him and his Areopagites on account of his despotism, Zwack always took the part of his benefactor, was the pacificator, and, stimulating their zeal for his plots and conspiracies, brought them back to that respect due to the *Spartacus* of the Order. It is to him also that Illuminism is indebted for the progress it made in Munich. *Cato* was so zealous a Recruiter, that Weishaupt was obliged several times to repress his ardor. He wanted his assistance for the digesting of his code, and for the government of the Order. In short, the result of their correspondence proves, that no Areopagite either entered so completely into his views, or so justly deserved his confidence as *Cato-*Zwack.[14] And it may be said with truth, that no conspirator ever acted the part of a zealous servant of his prince with so much success as this man. In the midst of his plots of Illuminism, Xaverius Zwack found means of getting himself named *Counsellor to the Court and Counsellor to the Regency, with a salary of twenty thousand florins*. Weishaupt, overjoyed at his promotion, compliments him, saying: "Accept my felicitations on the new appointment. I could wish that all my Areopagites were privy counsellors with salaries of twenty thousand florins; but I could also more ardently wish, that their employments required but little time and labor, as they could then apply more closely to the grand object."[15] The very letter in which Weishaupt compliments his president is one of those to his Areopagites in which he enter into the particulars, and boasts of the progress of his conspiracy.

The second of these Areopagites was a priest of the name of HERTEL, surnamed *Marius* by the Illuminees. It is of this person that Weishaupt writes to *Cato*-Zwack, "Our *Marius* is superlatively reserved. On most occasions he advances with the greatest *circumspection; and with respect to religious matters let us flatter his weakness. His stomach is not strong enough as yet to digest the tougher morsels.* On all other subjects you may rely on him. Do not give him too much work until he has acquired the habit of business, and taken a liking to the affair. If he be once broke in properly, he can render the greatest services."[16]

Notwithstanding all his *circumspection*, Hertel soon suffered himself to be carried away into all the dangers of secret societies, and fell a prey to their machinations. Since he had some conscience left, Weishaupt thought that he could not turn it to a better account than by making him treasurer to the Order, that he might by his economy and honesty repair the numerous breaches that had been made in its funds by the thefts of *Ajax*. The illuminized *Marius* acquitted himself of his office much to the satisfaction of the founder. In recompence for his services, the brethren get him nominated to a canonicate at Munich; and he was so much amused with this intrigue, that he wishes to divert *Cato* with a recital of it, but does not dare commit it to paper.[17] At the period when he came to take possession of his canonicate, all those *circumspect* ideas of religion had vanished. He describes himself as going from the altar to the dens of Illuminism, as publicly investing himself with an ecclesiastical benefice, while in secret he extolls the great services he has rendered to the brood conspiring against the church; *but these also are services,* he says, *too important to be committed to paper.*[18] They are services, however, which I am sure no reader can mistake, when he sees him partaking with Zwack and Weishaupt's intimacy. In the correspondence of the latter are a multitude of letters to be found directed in common to Zwack and Hertel; there are also many instructions; both absolute and provisional, directed to the Areopagites; and in these, it is no longer the conscientious but the apostate Hertel, who, after Zwack, is to occupy the next place and act the principal part.[19] It is this unfortunate priest who appears to have been more particularly charged with the care of stealing or buying for the use of the secret libraries all those miserable productions which might form an arsenal of impiety and rebellion for the corruption of all morals.[20] In short, it is he whom *Spartacus* selects from among the brethren as the most proper confidant when premeditating that horrid infanticide mentioned in the beginning of the Third Volume of these Memoirs; and he behaves himself in such a manner as to deserve the thanks of the incestuous parent.[21]

We find a still stronger proof of what horrid monsters were seated in this senate of rebellion in the person of *Celsus*-BAADER. Even before he is admitted into this association, we see him offering the depraved secrets of his art to murder the innocent offspring of incestuous parents; for he is that *Celsus* who had promised Weishaupt two years before to use all the powers of his art to preserve his honor for him at the expence of the most horrid of crimes. Without doubt it is in return for these offers of his services, that Weishaupt is so eager to number him among the adepts, and to grant him those dispensations of which he speaks when writing to Zwack: "If I could but succeed in enrolling the Physician Baader, tell me beforehand what dispensations and privileges we could grant him among the Areopagites; for unless some dispensations were granted to him, we could not employ him so actively as I could wish."[22] This letter was soon followed by a second, in which he expresses in still clearer terms the high value he places on this conquest, and describes the intrigues played off to ensure success. "In order (he writes to his Athenians) to carry my plan into execution in *Athens* (Munich) I stand in need of two men—The one a *Nobleman*, the other a *Physician*. *Cato's* unremitting zeal will soon acquire the means, and he will soon make a conquest of what is wanting to us. The Count S. . . . (*Savioli*, whom *Cato* had just insinuated) shall assume the characteristic of *Brutus*, and he is one of the most important conquests we could have made in *Athens*. The following shall be your method of proceeding with him. Let *Cato* continue to act with him as usual, and particularly attend to his secrecy. After that, let him read our *reformed* statutes to the new candidate, and question him whether he thinks them useful and proper. Should *Brutus* answer in the affirmative, *Cato* will ask the Count whether he is ready to second us in our labours; he will then tell him, that in consideration of the important services he has it in his power to render to the Order, by permitting us to make use of his name, we shall be much less severe with regard to him, in the usual trials, and that he shall be immediately initiated into the higher mysteries. But as a preliminary step he will be required either to deliver Baader over to us, or some other person. That we are very well apprized that he is not to be overloaded with work, and that it is on that account he is dispensed from the usual tasks prescribed by our statutes; that he will comply with them only as far as he pleases; and that we have made a particular choice of him to help us in the *Government of the Order*. Should he deliver Baader over to us, he should also be entitled to the same dispensations, which are to be granted to no other person in *Athens*. You will read the *Degree of Minerval* to the Count with every thing that precedes; if he shows a liking and zeal for the cause, you will also read the *Degree of the Illuminee*; and when you shall have acquired evident proofs of his zeal, and that he shall have made common cause with us by recruiting for us, you may let him into the whole secret.—Hold a similar conduct with Baader."[23]

Whether the Brethren at Munich had already adopted this mode of acting, or whether they had followed some other of a similar nature, is not known; but in a very short time after we find Weishaupt's views on Baader accomplished; for on the 13th of December 1778, only three days after the foregoing letter, we find him inscribed on the list of Areopagites. Ever after we find his named mentioned in the correspondence as one of the most active adepts, and as one of those who had the most deeply imbibed the horrid mysteries.[24]

Another reason, which made Weishaupt more eager for this conquest, was, that Baader read public lectures on medicine at Munich, and therefore had an opportunity of seducing his young pupils, after the example of his master, who had so efficaciously and fatally made use of his influence to seduce the young students of the law at the University of Ingolstadt.

A similar reason had made him ardently wish to initiate BERGER who also read public lectures at Munich, though I do not find on what science.—His characteristic is *Scipio*, and he was inscribed on the list of Areopagites on the 28th July 1778. A Freemason before he became an Illuminee, he was some time before he could overcome his predilection for his former lodges, in so much even that he asked for his dismissal. *Spartacus* was furious at such a preference. Without showing his desire of retaining the discontented Brother, and not having him sufficiently in his power to make use of threats, he commands Zwack to declare to the Candidate in the *name of the Order*, that he was at full liberty to follow his predilection; but the same letter contains all that is to be hinted underhand to the discontented adept, all that was to be thrown on the pre-eminence and advantages of Illuminism over Masonry. The Professor Berger was so perfectly convinced of this *pre-eminence*, that Weishaupt, *to give him the preference over all the other Areopagites*, only required of him *a little more activity*.[25]

The want of activity was not a fault with which Illuminism could ever upbraid its adept *Coriolanus*. He was a merchant of the name of TROPONERO retired from Hamburgh to Munich. At the time of his initiation he did not employ his talents in that line which Weishaupt judged to be useful for the propagation of his hireling doctrines.—Zwack bethought himself of setting up this Troponero for a public lecturer on finance, and made the proposition to *Spartacus*, who immediately answered, "It is a very good plan *both for him and for us, to make Coriolanus read lectures on finance*; only do you spare no pains to get him scholars. *It is a fine occasion for recruiting young men*; nor would it be a bad plan if you became one of his pupils yourself, in order to entice others."[26] It does not appear whether Zwack relished the descending from the bench of the Areopagites to attend the schools of the new lecturer; but certain it is that the Archives of Illuminism bear testimony of the great services rendered by this *Coriolanus*; and Weishaupt frequently extols his merits. He was particularly useful at all the receptions, assuming that air of ceremonious gravity so becoming in the Grand Master of a Lodge, and so well did he impose on the young adepts, that they had not the least suspicion of the Occult Mysteries of the Rosicrucians, much less of those of Illuminism.

About the same time we meet the names of the two first Illuminized Noblemen whom Weishaupt had initiated into his last mysteries—the one *Hanibal*, the Baron BASSUS; the other *Diomedes*, the Marquis of CONSTANZA. Illuminized Barons and Marquisses, certainly, are a sort of phenomena not easily to be conceived. That men who are never called by their names without being reminded of the great stake they have to lose should property and the social order be overthrown, that such men should plunge themselves into the most horrid conspiracy ever framed against both, can only be believed by those who have attended to the amazing cunning of Weishaupt's Code and the artifice with which it is put in execution. In short the Archives of Illuminism, the letters, nay the apologies of these *titled* Illuminees, bear too strong proofs of the fact, and must quash all objections. The Baron Bassus, in his pretended justification, owns that he was the person known under the characteristic of *Hanibal*;[27] and the letters of this Hanibal not only show that he was an Illuminee himself, but also an apostle of Illuminization, giving an account to the Brethren of his successes at Botzen in Tyrol, and boasting of the important conquests he had made in that town, having enlisted and imbued the *President, the Vice-President, the principal Counsellors of the Government*, and *the Grand Master of the Posts*, with the most enthusiastic admiration for Illuminism.[28] A little farther, the letters of this same *Hanibal* bear testimony of his having gone into Italy, and of his having initiated at Milan *his Excellency the Count W . . Imperial Minister*. Then, meditating new conquests, he proceeds to Pavia, in hopes of enlisting several of the Professors of that University, and finishes by requesting that the geography of the Order be enlarged, that he may have a greater scope for his illuminizing talents.[29]

With respect to *Diomedes*, or our illuminized Marquis, his letters also bear testimony of his enthusiastic zeal in the service of Weishaupt. He held this Arch-Conspirator in such great veneration that, *with the exception of some few insignificant weaknesses*, he looked upon Weishaupt as the *most perfect, the most profound*, and *the most extraordinary mortal on earth*. The hours he had the happiness of spending in his company were too short in his opinion, but unhappily long enough to fire him with all that zeal which sends him frantic to Deux Ponts, then to *Nauplis* or Straubingen, and at last to Munich, replete with all that hireling cunning with which the young candidates are to be so completely duped, that they are not *even to surmise that their credulity is to be imposed upon*.—So deeply are the true principles of the Sect rooted in his breast, that to revenge the Order on some Brother who, probably disgusted with the abominable tendency of these mysteries, had made some discovery of them to the Magistrates, he writes to one of the brethren, "Oh the rascal! might not a person, or, to be more correct, *would it be a crime to send such a Devil as this into the other world?*"[30]

Neither do the Original Writings nor my privsate correspondence inform me of the real titles of the Areopagite *Solon*-MICHT. He does not appear to have acted any very conspicuous part in the history of the Order. He is only stated to have worn the ecclesiastical habit at Freysinguen; happy for him if it is to this dress that he is indebted for his apparent nullity in Weishaupt's plots.

Next appears HOHENEICHER under the title of *Alcibiades*, who, though seated in the conspiring senate with the Illuminees, does not blush to hold a seat in the senate of Freysinguen as counsellor.

The Eleventh of the Areopagites is *Mahomet* the Baron SCRÖCKENSTEIN. We shall soon behold him presiding over whole privinces that are subject to Illuminism. A few days after his initiation we meet another Areopagite characterized *Germanicus*. Not having been able to discover his real name, I will not give way to conjecture.[31] At this same period we find a numerous list of persons of consequence initiated in the lower degrees. Such, for example, were the magistrate of Aichstadt, *Tamerlane*-LANG, and the private secretary GEISER. The characteristic of this adept does not appear; Weishaupt's letter on the great acquisition he had made in this adept sufficiently demonstrates the importance he attached to conquests of this nature, and how far he could turn them to the advantage of his Order.

This letter is of the 10th *Chardad*, 1148 (10th June, 1778); and it is worthy of remark, that it is the first letter which we find in the Original Writings dated according to the Persian Æra. It is to his dear *Cato* that Weishaupt writes:—"The acquisition we have made of the private secretary (*secretaire intime*) Geiser is an event of such consequence to us, that our affairs will soon assume quite a different aspect. It obliterates that appearance (much too conspicuous) of novelty. It is for this reason that we ought to mutually congratulate each other and the whole Order. We may now expect to do something great. By enticing men among us of his stamp and of his consequence, we add great weight to our object, and they are useful in keeping our youngsters within bounds. Do not forget to thank and make my most sincere compliments to the private secretary. Men of his importance must have a right to choose their own characteristics, their employment, and the species of labour that they would prefer. You will remember to inform me of it, that I may take the proper steps in consequence."[32]

In this class of Brethren of consequence, we must not forget *Brutus* Count SAVIOLI, *Sylla* the Baron MAGGENHOFF and *Alexander* Count PAPPENHEIM. Meanwhile, till we come to treat of ministers and princes drawn into this vortex of sedition, let us hear Weishaupt develop his views, and observe him marshalling his troops; particularly when he takes measures to ensnare those noblemen whom he wishes to make the prime agents and the propagators of the very conspiracies to which they are to fall the first victims. On the 10th *Pharavardin*, 1149 (31st March, 1779), he writes to his *Athenians* of Munich, "Have you not in all your town of *Athens* any strangers who may be immediately admitted into the Order, advanced as soon as possible to the degree of *Minerval*, and then simply instructed in the mysteries of that degree? Such persons may, without any further initiation, be sent to found the system in other countries and make recruits; for example at Augsbourg, at Ratisbonne, at Saltzbourg, at Landshut, and other towns. To meet with such persons it would be proper for you to go into company, and to frequent assemblies and places of public resort. Since you have done so many others things you may very well do this. At *Erzerum* (Aichstadt) *and throughout all Franconia I could make a rapid progress if I could but initiate two gentlemen of that country whom I am well acquainted with, and who are men of great wit and much esteemed by the nobility there.* This acquisition would soon procure us adepts from among the nobility, men of wit who would recruit for us in their own class throughout Franconia. —When we initiated any one at *Athens* to a new degree, these two gentlemen might be called to assist at the ceremony, and would then become candidates for the higher degree. The rank they hold, and their nobility, would also be of use to curb the petulance of your young *Brutus* and other gentry.—In short,

Tamerlane (or the counsellor Lang), who thinks that there are no other adepts at *Erzerum* but those with whom he is acquainted, would be thunderstruck at finding persons in a higher degree than himself, though he had not the least idea they belonged to the Order, and men also of whom he has the highest opinion. Do reflect and deliberate on this."[33]

In the following letters it appears that *Brutus* no longer needed any curb; for he becomes an apostle of the Sect, and sets off on an expedition from which Weishaupt augurs great success. He is even so zealous, that *Spartacus*, on the eve of dismissing several other adepts, mentions him as an useful member who is to be preserved,[34] and desires that he may as soon as possible be advanced to the degree of *Major Illuminee*.[35] To enable the reader to judge how far he was disposed to serve the Order, it will suffice to record the terms in which he expresses his gratitude for favours received, and the promises he makes in hopes of obtaining new ones. His letter to the *Most Excellent Superiors of Illuminism* is couched in the following terms:

"Most Excellent Superiors!

"Receive my most grateful acknowlegements for the *third degree* with which you have just honoured me. Every part of it is noble, grand, and beautiful; it has perfectly answered the expectations I had formed of it from the *second*. I shall most undoubtedly do every thing that lies in my power to deserve your confidence. In future rely on mine, and believe me to be perfectly devoted to your service.—Nothing in the world shall ever withdraw me from my allegiance to your laws, or make me cease to be guided by you.

"You wrote to me some time since, desiring me to seek for no further advancement at Court, as I could not expect any. I obeyed that order; but as the ministers of the regency have lately paid me some marks of attention, my affairs have assumed a different aspect.—The serious illness of the Emperor having given rise to the idea of a vicarage of the Empire, Brother *Pericles* and myself have been mentioned as counsellors in that court; and I have great hopes of being made a privy counsellor (*conseiller intime*). S. . . . has taken my cause in hand, and I am indebted to the brothers *Celsus* and *Alfred* for it. *If ever I get into power, the most excellent Order will soon see how much I am devoted to it, and how entirely I belong to it*. In the mean time I can but express my sincerest wishes."[36]

Though the advancement which had inspired the Count *Brutus* with so much zeal for the Order left him still at a great distance from the higher mysteries, he nevertheless had a brother who could not flatter himself that he should arrive at even this *third degree*. The insinuator had made a distinction between them. The letter in which he announcs their initiation to *Spartacus* will show the reader what other services the Order had to expect from such kinds of adepts.

Cato writes to *Spartacus*: "Here are my new hopes for the Order. After a long perseverance I have at length engaged the young S—(Savioli). He will deliver his brother over to us, who may set our affairs a going at Augsbourg. They are both rich. The first I recruited as a *Sta bene*, that is to say, one who is never to pass the lower ranks. I also engage him, because on certain occasions he will lend us his house, which is very convenient for our meetings; and more particularly because, being rich, he can help us with his purse."[37]

The same letter mentions a similar *sta bene*: "The Brother *Livius* (RUDORGER) is in future to be looked on as belonging to the same class. He frankly owned to me, that he neither had the time nor inclination to give himself up to our labours. But that he was willing to contribute towards the progress of the Order with his purse, and that he would even furnish us with books for our libraries, and instruments for experiments.—I gave him to understand, that certainly he might remain a member of the Order; but that he could only be classed in future with those who seconded its views with their money."[38] Thus did Weishaupt turn the stupidity and ignorance, the impiety and money of his Marquises, Barons, Knights, and Magistrates, to the advantage and propagation of his disastrous plots.—He had already made converts of this nature in the imperial chamber of Wetzlar; for, as early as the 29th of Aug. 1778, we find that *Minos*, the Assessor DITTFURTH, inscribed on the list of Illuminees, the same person whom we have already seen so zealous for the foundation of an illuminized sisterhood.[39] At first we find him under a *suspension*, as not to be trusted by the Brethren;[40] but very soon his zeal makes him at once the admiration and laughingstock of *Spartacus*. The reader must have already observed the art with which Weishaupt obliges every candidate to give the history of his life, with an exact description of his passions and prejudices. The Assessor *Minos* complied with this regulation in so scrupulous a manner, that Weishaupt could not refrain from writing to the Areopagites in the following terms: "*Minos*, that man who bears so high a character, is at present writing the history of his life. *He is as yet only arrived at his seventeenth year, and he has written ninety-three sheets of paper. He is now forty-five years of age.* This will be something more than a general confession. You see what may be done with men if one *does but know how to gain their confidence, and to convince them of the excellency of the object.*"[41] So completely did the imperial Assessor imbibe this principle and learn to convince others of it, that we shall hereafter see him raised to the dignity of Provincial.

However much Weishaupt may have wished to make proselytes among the great, we nevertheless see him recommending to his insinuators to recruit more particularly among the *professors* and *schoolmasters*, as a sure means of gaining over to his views the youth of all classes. Hence it is that *Hermes Trismegistes*, whose real name was SOCHER, and who was superior of the college at Landsberg, receives the special commission to watch and guard against the Jesuits, as sworn enemies to the education he is to give to his pupils.[42] For the same reason does Weishaupt strain every nerve to fill his university of Ingolstadt with professors and prefects belonging to the Sect. He entreats the adepts at Munich to beset the ministers, and obtain the expulsion of all Jesuits, because these fathers had retrieved the four professors SCHOLLINER, STEINGENBERGER, WURZER, and SCHLEGEL, from Illuminism; and because he had but three professors left in the university to resist Jesuitism.[43] The List of Professors soon swells to an alarming height in all towns where Illuminism makes any progress. On this black list we find *Armenius*-KRENNER; *Cortez*-LEMMER; *Pythagoras*-WESSENREIDER; this latter soon abandoned the Order when his characteristic was given to the Priest and Librarian DREXL; but as professor we find three to replace him, KUNDLER, LOLLING, and above all BAIERAMMER, at first called *Zoroastre*, but afterwards *Confucius*. It is this adept that Weishaupt brings at length to Ingolstadt, that he might have for his collegue in the seduction of youth, a man that he himself had initiated in the black arts of his Illuminism.[44] This serves to account for that zeal with which he sends his adepts into all houses of education, and that solicitude with which he entreats *Cato* and *Marius* to seek out some brethren well drilled to the arts of Insinuators, who might be sent *to the* UNIVERSITIES *of Saltzbourg, of Inspruck, of Fribourg, and of other places*.[45]

To select the following will suffice to show to what extent these missionary professors succeeded, according to the views of the Order; *Saladin*-EKEL; *Thales*-KAPFIMGER; *Timon*-MICHL; *Euclid*-RIEDL; all from eighteen to twenty years of age: SAUER, surnamed *Attila*; and the Emperor *Claudius*, or SIMON ZWACK, cousin to the incomparable *Cato*, were of the same age; an age sought after by Weishaupt, as he could the more easily twine the young adept to vice. This docility was far from being the leading feature of his other adepts; they were not all enthusiastically wedded to his plots at this dawn of Illuminism; nor could he make them the passive instruments of his conspiracy. He describes the proselytes he had made among the aristocracy "*as rich, therefore given to all the vices of their state; as ignorant, proud, cowardly, and lazy in the superlative degree*; *as only seeking their advancement in the mysteries, in order to gratify their curiosity, or even to scoff at the ceremonial of the different degrees*;[46] and he wished to find men who would be struck with awe, and be fired with enthusiasm at the sight of these ceremonies. The style of reproach in which he writes to many other of the adepts clearly depicts a set of men destitute of all morals, and having no other views in the Order than to gratify their passions and their avarice; seeking none but their own interests, and often, through their dissolute and immoral conduct, exposing the *founder of the Order* to be looked upon as a *corrupter of youth*.[47] He was willing to have none but followers that could, like himself, gratify the most infamous passions in private, and who, under the mask of virtue, moderation, and wisdom, imposing on the public, would accredit his Illuminism. With respect to the founder, we have seen him already describing the turpitude of his morals, and the atrocious means to which he had resorted to preserve the mask of his pretended virtue; let us now hear him upbraiding his first adepts with the public depravity of their morals as being prejudicial to his Illuminism: "I have received," says he, "the most fatal intelligence from *Thebes* (Freisinguen). They have given a public scandal to the whole town, by admitting into the Lodge that vile *Propertius, a libertine loaded with debts, and a most detestable being*. In that same town is to be found the Brother D——, who is nothing more than a wicked fellow; our *Socrates*, who could be of the greatest use to us, is always drunk; our *Augustus* has acquired the worst of reputations; the Brother *Alcibiades* is perpetually fighting and pining away at the feet of his landlady; *Tiberius* attempted to lay violent hands on *Diomedes's* sister, and suffered himself to be caught by the husband; *heavens! what men have I there for Areopagites!* What! we sacrifice our health, our fortune, our reputation, to the good of the Order; and these gentry give themselves up entirely to their pleasures and ease, prostitute themselves, give public scandals, and still wish to be acquainted with all our secrets! From this instant I shall look upon *Tiberius* (Merz) as erased from our list. O Areopagites, Areopagites! I would much rather have none at all, than not have men *more active* and *more submissive*."[48]

This is not the only letter in which Weishaupt plainly shows what opinions he had himself of his horde of adepts. The following gives as clearer insight into the cause of the alarm he had taken from their public scandals, and their evil tendency for the general good of the Sect. After having told them, *With regard to politics and morals, you are as yet far behind indeed*, he says, "Judge yourselves what would be the consequence, if a man such as our *Marcus Aurelius* (he was a professor at Gottinguen, and his real name was FEDER) were once to know what a *set of men, destitute of morals, what a set of debauchées, liars, spendthrifts, braggadochios, and fools replete with vanity and pride*, you have among you; if such a man, I say, were to see this, what opinion must he form of us! Would he not be ashamed to belong to a society whose chiefs *promise* such great things, *and execute so ill the most beautiful plans*; and all from obstinacy, and because they will not sacrifice one tittle of their pleasures; now frankly declare, am I not in the right? Do you not think that, in order to preserve a man, such as *Marcus Aurelius*-Feder, whose name alone is worth the best part of Germany, I ought to sacrifice and rescind all your whole province of *Greece* (Bavaria), the innocent as well as the guilty? And should I take such a step, who would be to blame? Is it not better to cut off the gangrened members, than to lose the whole body? Can you be so void of all feeling, as to see a select society of men dissolve, *and abandon the reformation of the world*, and that on account of the vices you have plunged yourselves into, and the scandal you give? That would be still worse than an Herostratus, worse than all the wicked men of all times and of all ages. Those of you, gentlemen, therefore, who do not approve of this plan, who will not sacrifice your ease and miserable passions, those in short who are indifferent to the praises of the best of men, and who will not labour with us *at making all mankind but one and the same family*, those, I not only pray, but conjure, at least not to impede our labours, and not to entail on the Order the infamy and shame of their public scandals. *Such conduct would be worse than that of real assassins, worse than the plague.*"[49]

However well-founded Weishaupt may have been in making use of such reproaches, the rapid progress made by his Illuminism should have convinced him, that his adepts, in the midst of their debaucheriees, never lost sight of the grand object of his mysteries. The reader may judge of their progress by the following note; which, at the same time that it denotes their successes, will show in what manner they reported them to each other. This document may also begin to explain various mysteries of the revolution.

> NOTE, *on the progress of Illuminism, found among the papers of* Cato-Zwack, *written in his own hand, and contained in the first volume of the Original Writings.*

"We have[50] at *Athens* (Munich), 1st a regular Lodge of *Major Illuminees*; 2dly, a lesser meeting of *Illuminees*, very well adapted to our purposes; 3dly, a very large and remarkable *Masonic* Lodge; 4thly, two considerable *Churches*, or Minerval Academies.

"At *Thebes* (Freysinguen) also there is a *Minerval* Lodge, as well as at *Megara* (Landsberg), at Burghausen, at Straubing, at *Ephesus* (Ingolstadt), and in a short time we shall have one at *Corinth* (Ratisbonne).

"We have bought a house (at Munich) for ourselves; and we have taken our precautions so well, that the inhabitants not only do not cry out against us, but speak of us with esteem, when they see us going publicly to that house, or to the Lodge. *Certainly that is a great deal for this town.*

"We have in this house a cabinet of natural history, instruments for experimental philosophy, and a library; and all this is daily augmented by the gifts of the Brethren. The garden is to be turned into a botanical one.

"All the scientific journals are procured for the brethren at the expence of the Order.

"By means of different pamphlets we have awakened the attention of the princes and citizens to certain remarkable abuses; we oppose religious Orders with all our might; and we have good reason to be pleased with the success of our endeavours.

"We have entirely new modelled the Lodge on our plan, and have broke off all communication with Berlin.

"We have not repressed all the enrollments of the R. C. (Rosicrucians), but we have succeeded in casting suspicions on them.

"We are in treaty for a strict and effective alliance with the Lodge of ———, AND WITH THE NATIONAL LODGE OF POLAND."

> *Another* NOTE *written by the same hand, on the political progress of the the Order.*

"Through the intrigues of the Brethren the Jesuits have been dismissed from all the Professorships; we have entirely cleared the university of Ingolstadt of them.[51]

"The Dowager Duchess has modelled her *Institute for the Cadets* entirely on the plan prepared by the Order. *That house is under our inspection; all its Professors belong to our Order; five of its members have been well provided for, and all the pupils will be ours.*

"On the recommendation of the Brethren *Pylades* is made the *ecclesiastical fiscal counsellor*. By procuring this place for him, we have put the church monies at the disposal of the Order: and by means of these monies we have already repaired the mal-administration of our ——— and of ——— and have delivered them from the hands of the usurers.

"With these monies, also we support new Brethren.

"The Brethren who are in orders have all been provided with *livings* and *curacies*, or with preceptor's places.

"Through our means too, the Brothers *Armenius* and *Cortez* have been made *Professors in the University of Ingolstadt*. We have also got purses for all our young candidates in the same university.

"On the recommendation also of our Order, two young men are travelling *at the expense of the Court*. They are at present at Rome.

"The *Germanic schools* are all under the inspection of the Order, and have no other prefects than our Brethren.

"*The Benevolent Society is also under our direction.*

"The Order has obtained an augmentation of pay and salaries for a great number of Brethren who are employed in the *Dicasteres* (that is to say, at the Boards of Administration).

"*We have obtained four ecclesiastical chairs for as any of our Brethren.*

"We shall shortly be *masters of the Bartholomew Institution for the education of young ecclesiastics*. All our measures are ready for that purpose. The business has taken a very favorable turn; *by this means we may stock all Bavaria with priests both clever and proper* (for our object).

"We have similar hopes and views on another house of priests.

"Through incessant application, indefatigable efforts, and the intrigues of *different —— ——*, we have at length suceeded in not only maintaining the Ecclesiastical Council, which the Jesuits wished to destroy, but also in assigning over to this council, to the colleges and universities, all those goods which had still remained under the administration of the Jesuits in Bavaria, such as the institution for the mission, the golden alms, the house of retreat, and the funds for the newly-converted. Our Major Illuminees, to effectute this, *held five meetings; several of them remained there whole nights;* and —— ——."

This latter article is also mutilated by the editor of the Original Writings. The Court of Bavaria did not think proper to publish the names of those *different persons* (ministers and others) who so well seconded Weishaupt and his adepts on this occasion. The Jesuits at least strongly suspected the Count of SENSEIM to be one of the *different* ——— ———, and those of the English college of Liege, in particular, had reason to believe that he was one of those to whom they were indebted for the loss of a pension of ten thousand florins, which had always been paid to them by the Court of Bavaria. How far these suspicions are grounded I do not pretend to say; but certain it is, that this Count Senseim appears on the list of adepts under the characteristic of *King Alfred*. But without our entering into any discussion, the two notes I have just translated clearly evince, that the adepts did not deserve to be so frequently reprimanded for inactivity as Weishaupt seems to have thought.

What a strong light is thrown on the secret history of the Revolution by these two notes, even in their mutilated state! A large portion of the clergy, it is true, have been faithful to their duty; but Europe has been astonished at seeing so many of them plunged into the most horrid scenes of impiety. We here learn from *Cato-Zwack* who those false pastors were. These atrocious hypocrites are selected by the Sect, imbued with all the venom of its principles, and then ushered into the bosom of the church under its baneful protection. It had said to them, assume the appearance of piety and zeal, and pretend to believe in the symbol of the priesthood, and we shall find means of installing you in the livings of the church, and of making you the rectors and pastors of the flock. You shall publicly preach the doctrine of the Gospel, and your exterior shall coincide with the duties of those stations; but in secret you shall second our views, and prepare the way for us. It would be a futile objection to ask how it was possible to find monsters whose depravity could make them consent to act such scenes of hypocrisy even in the Holy of Holies! We have the authority of *Cato-Zwack*, who tells us that they assumed the characters and functions of rectors and curates, of canons, professors, and teachers in the *Catholic* Church. We shall soon see the same game played with respect to the *Protestant* Church; and thus were both churches ministered to by wretches who had sworn their destruction.

A similar mode of proceeding was adopted for the destruction of the state, and that at the first dawn of Illuminism. It is *Cato* again who informs us of the intrigues, views, and successes of the Sect, insinuating its adepts into the *Dicasteres*, the councils, and boards of administration, which are paid by the prince and state; he points them out as having gained access into the councils of the prince and of the state, carrying with them all the treacherous plots of the most disastrous conspiracy against both prince and state.

Many readers have been astonished at seeing whole generations rise imbued with the principles of the most rank jacobinism, and that from schools founded by princes for the instruction of youth; but *Cato* again solves the difficulty, when he speaks of the *Institution* founded by the Dowager Duchess.

In short, it will be incumbent on future historians to tell their readers whence were obtained those treasures spent in the propagation of the principles of the Sect, in the peregrinations of its apostles, and in the support of its pennyless adepts; they will find the talk already completed by the Sect itself, which tells us, *that its novices are supported at the expence of the public foundations*; that its millionaires are paid and sent to foreign parts by the prince, who has been misled to believe that he was sending men in the pursuit of arts and sciences. Moreover, does not the Sect betray itself, when introducing its adepts into the *administration of the ecclesiastical property*, and with that property paying the debts of its Lodges, supporting the apostles of its conspiracies, re-establishing its former clubs, and erecting new ones. Let the historian reflect on the conditions under which such a multitude of adepts have been ushered into livings and other employments, and he will soon perceive the funds of the Sect swelled to an immense bulk by those shares which it preserves for its own use out of all the emoluments which it has procured for its adepts either in church or state.

But in this same note an enigma occurs of a quite different nature. The reader may have observed *Cato*-Zwack at once exulting in having founded a *masonic Lodge* at Munich for the Illuminees, and in the victories gained by the Illuminees over the *Rosicrucian Masons*. What can have given rise to this contradiction, at the same time to imitate the Freee-masons, and to declare war against the most famous adepts of Masonry. These questions naturally lead us to the investigation of the most profound device that Weishaupt ever invented for the propagation of his plots. They relate to his first attempt, to the diversity of the means used, his success, and finally to his triumphant intrusion into the masonic Lodges. In order to solve them, I shall in the following Chapters lay before my reader the most remarkable passages of the Archives of the Sect, or of the letters and avowals of the most celebrated adepts relating to that famous plan, the execution of which belongs to the second epoch of the Sect; and unfortunately it may be too truly called the epoch of the Illuminization of Free Masonry.

1. Original Writing, Let. 25, to *Cato.*
2. Ibid. Vol. I, Let. 27.
3. Der ganze bau seines durch debauche mager gewordenen körper incliniert nun zum melancolischen temperament.
4. Many readers may be curious to know what is contained in the second table, subjoined to that which describes the candidate. It is in ten columns, comprehending the names and rank of Zwack's relations, an account of their children, their fortune, their alliances, friends, and enemies; the company they keep, particularly the education they have received, and their moral character, which is called *their strong or their weak side.* The Editor has thought proper to omit some articles in this table—The two which appear to be the most perfect are on *the strong and weak side* of Zwack's parents, who, according to the Insinuator, have received an *antiquated education not worth much.* The father is described as "jealous of his honor, honest, zealous in the discharge of his duty—apparently harsh to his inferiors, but really loving them to excess—speaking to every body with a tone of authority and in a pedantic style—In his habits and speech impoliticly frank—secret, and sparing even to the want of necessaries when he can serve his Prince, zealously serving him without distinction of persons, to the risk even of losing all his employments—feeling, humane, mysterious, officious, and proud of his experience—carefully attentive to the whole of his affairs."

As to the mother, "*She is a good housekeeper—absorbed in her dear child Xaverius Zwack,* and so forth"—Many other things have been suppressed in this latter table. But there still remains more than sufficient to give all relations of Illuminism an idea of the methods used by the scrutinizing Brethren to pry into their most secret conduct, and to describe their most private interests to the Order.
5. See Orig. Writings, Vol. I. Sect. 20.

6. See Orig. Writings, Vol. I, Sect. 20.
7. Ibid. in the Note.
8. Let. I, to Philip Strozzi.
9. Vol. I, Sect. IV.
10. Letter 27, to Philip Strozzi.
11. See his Disc. on Societies, Orig. Writ. Vol. I. Sect. XXII.
12. See his Thoughts on Suicide.
13. Orig. Writ. Vol. I. particularly Let. 55.
14. See the Original Writings, Letters to *Cato*.
15. Ibid. Vol. III. Letter 2.
16. Ibid. Vol. I. Letter 7 to *Cato*, 27 March 1778.
17. Ibid. Letter from *Marius* to *Cato*, 3d Nov. 1783.
18. Letter from *Marius* to *Cato*, 3d Nov. 1783.
19. Ibid. Vol. I. Sect. IX. See the Instructions for *Cato*, *Marius*, and *Scipio*.
20. Ibid. Vol. I. Letter 46, and Vol. II. Letter 3, &c.
21. Ibid. Vol. II. Let 3 and 4.
22. Ibid. Vol. I. Let 29, of the 30 Dec. 1778.
23. Ibid. Vol. I. Let. 33, 11th Dec. 1778.
24. Vol. II. Let. 13, from *Spartacus* to *Celsus*.
25. Ibid. Vol. I. Let. 46 and 58.
26. Ibid. Let. 3, to *Cato*.
27. Page 6.
28. Original Writings, Vol. I. Sect XLV.
29. Ibid. Vol. II. Sect. IV. Let. 1 and 2.
30. Oder Schurkl! Könnte man nicht, oder um besser zu sagen, wäre es nicht erlaubt, so einen Teufel in die andere welt zu schicken—*Original Writings, Vol. I. Sect. XLIV. Letters 1 and 2.*
31. In order to discover the real name of an adept, it will often suffice to combine their letters, and particularly those in which Weishaupt declares the characteristics to be given to candidates, with what is afterward said of them under their new names. The German journals, and divers other writings in that language, my own private correspondence with, and memorials that I have received from men who, living on the spot, have been enabled to procure more accurate documents with respect to thesse different personages, have furnished me with the means of discovering many others on whom no shadow of doubt can be entertained.
32. Orig. Writ. Vol. I, Let. 13, to *Cato*.
33. Ibid. Vol. I. Let. 39.
34. Orig. Writ. Vol. I, Let. 58.
35. Ibid. Vol. II. Let. 13.
36. Orig. Writ. Vol. II. *Quibus licet* from *Brutus*.
37. Damit er an geld beytraget.
38. Orig. Writ. Vol. I. Sect. xxxii. Letter from *Cato* to *Spartacus*.
39. Vol. III. of these Memoirs, page 41 [p. 418, Ed.].
40. Orig. Writ. Sect. iv. See the List.
41. Orig. Writ. Vol. II. Let. 7 and 10.
42. Vol. I. Let. 28.
43. Vol. I. Let. 36, 30 Jan. 1778.

44. See particularly Let. 24, Vol. I.
45. Ibid. Let. 40.
46. Vol. II. Let. 1.
47. Ibid. Let. 11.
48. Ibid. Vol. II. Let. 9.
49. Original Letters, Vol. 2, Let. 10.
50. This note begins with these words: *The number in Greece consists of*—whether *Cato* did mark the number or not, I know not; but the editor has left it in blank, and the sentence is incomplete. Mr. Robison has inserted the *number* 600; but as he does not give his authority, I shall content myself with translating, and shall continue with Zwack.
51. Durch die verwendung der Br. Br. (Brüdern) wurden die Jesuiten von allen professor stellen entfernt, die Universtät Ingolstadt ganz von ihnen gereinigt.

CHAP. III.

Epoch of the Illuminization of Free-masonry.—
Weishaupt's attempts on the Masonic Lodges.—
Acquisition of Knigge, and his first Services.

LET us for a moment suppose every thing that has been said in these Memoirs relating to the nature, object, origin and secrecy of Masonry, to be no more than a conjectural system; let it still further be supposed, that the cloud which encompasses the origin and history of Masonry is for ever impenetrable; let even the Brethren and their Masters exalt still higher the merits and glory of their ancestry; yet, for the misfortune of our contemporaries, the day is come when all this glory is sullied, when the Orators of their own Lodges with grief exclaim "Brethren and Companions, give free vent to your sorrow; the days of *innocent Equality* are gone by. However holy our mysteries may have been, the Lodges are now prophaned and sullied. Brethren and Companions, let your tears flow; attired in your mourning robes attend, and let us seal up the gates of our temples, for the prophane have found means of penetrating into them. They have converted them into retreats for their impiety, into dens of conspirators. Within the sacred walls they have planned their horrid deeds and the ruin of nations. Let us weep over our *legions* which they have seduced. Lodges that may serve as hiding places for these conspirators must remain for ever shut both to us and to every good citizen."[1] These complaints and awful lamentations are not mine; they proceed from the mouth of the venerable Master of a Lodge; they are contained in the funeral oration pronounced on Masonry in presence of the Brethren assembled for the last time in a Lodge in Germany, and fighting over the sorrowful destiny of their Confraternity. Unfortunately for the honour of the Brotherhood, their sorrow was but too well-grounded; and it is our duty to adduce proofs of it. Whatever may have been its mysteries heretofore, FREE-MASONRY *is now become criminal*. If it be not so in itself, it is become so through Weishaupt's means; it has brought about, or he has brought about through its means, the most disastrous of all revolutions. This awful truth can no longer remain hidden. History must sound its trumpet, and let it adduce its proofs; for never has it yet given so awful a lesson to nations on the fatal effects of secret societies.

From the commencement of his Illuminism Weishaupt had foreseen the great support he could draw from the multitude of Free Masons dispersed throughout Europe, should he ever be fortunate enough to form an alliance with them. "Let me tell you a piece of news," he writes to *Ajax* as early as the year 1777: "Before the next carnival I shall go to Munich, and shall get myself admitted a Free-mason. Do not let this alarm you; *our business will not suffer in the least; but by this step we become acquainted with a tie or new secret, and by that means shall be stronger than the others.*[2] Weishaupt accordingly received the first degrees of Masonry at Munich, in St. Theodore's Lodge. At first he could only observe the bagatelle of an innocent fraternity, yet even then he perceived that *Equality* and *Liberty* were the ground-work of all amusements of the Brotherhood. He surmised further mysteries. In vain they assured him, that all political or religious discussions were banished from the Lodges, and that every true Mason was essentially a staunch friend to his prince and to Christianity. He had said the same thing to *his Novices* and to *his Minervals*; and he knew too well what became of all these protestations in his Illuminism. He easily conceived that a similar fate awaited these declarations in the higher degrees of Masonry. Soon his faithful Zwack furnished him with the means of penetrating into the higher mysteries of Masonry without subjecting himself to all the necessary trials. This latter adept had made acquaintance at Augsbourgh with an Abbé of the name of MAROTTI. At one of their interviews Marotti had *initiated him into the higher degrees, and even into those of the Scotch Lodges. He had explained to him all the mysteries of Masonry, absolutely founded*, as he said, *on religion and the history of the church*. Cato-Zwack shows us, by the eagerness with which he announces his discovery to *Spartacus*-Weishaupt, how much this explication coincided with the plots of his impiety.[3] No sooner has Weishaupt (who on his side was making all possible enquiries) received the news of this interview, though no particulars were mentioned, than he immediately answers, "I doubt much whether you are acquainted with the real object of Masonry; but I have acquired some information on that subject, which I mean to make use of in my plan, and *which I reserve for our higher degrees*.[4] *Cato* soon sent a circumstantial account to his master of the *explanation* that had been communicated to him, and received for answer, "the important discovery you have made at *Nicodemia* (Augsbourg), in your interview with the Abbé Marotti, *gives me extreme pleasure. Profit of this occasion, and get all you can from him.*"[5]

In reading such passages of their most intimate correspondence, one is naturally led to ask what can occasion this extreme joy in the two most monstrous conspirators that have ever appeared on earth, at the mere discovery of the mysteries of the occult Lodges of Masonry, and of those even of the *Scotch* Lodges! Has Weishaupt then been anticipated by the Masons in the explanation he had given of their symbols, and which he has actually inserted in his mysteries?[6] Could there have pre-existed in these occult Lodges of Masonry an impiety and plots strangely preparatory for that infidelity and those plots of *Cato* and *Spartacus*? The consequence is frightful; but is that a reason why nations should be blind and deny the testimony of truth; are we, for the honor of Masonry, to be silent on the hidden snares laid for them, and which will continue to be laid not only for them but for all nations in general.[7]

Well satisfied with the discovery he had made, Weishaupt begins to press the establishment of a Masonic Lodge for his pupils of Munich. He immediately ordered all his Areopagites to get themselves made Masons; he laid his plans for similar initiations at Aichstadt; and in all the other colonies of the Order.[8] Notwithstanding all his efforts, success declared but slowly in his favour. He was in possession of the secrets of the Masons, but they were not initiated in his. The Rosicrucians saw with regret another secret society rising, which drew its members from their Lodges, which already began to bring their meetings into disrepute by bragging that it alone was in possession of the real secrets of Masonry. Notwithstanding the impiety of the secrets of the Rosicrucians, and though their systems all had a similar tendency with respect to the annihilation of Christianity, still the path they had chosen was quite different from that which Weishaupt had adopted. He despised all the nonsense of their Alchymy; above all he detested their Theosophy. He laughed at the double principle, at the *good* and *evil* genii, and at all those demons on which the Rosicrucian founds his Magic, Cabal, and Mysteries of ABRAC;[9] in short, notwithstanding all the benefit Weishaupt expected to reap from these mysteries, symbols, and explanations of Masonry, he treated with the most sovereign contempt every thing that is purely cabalistic folly and reverie in the Rosicrucians. He adopted all their means of impiety and laughed at their fooleries. It was the contention of impiety, fallen on the one side into the most absurd Atheism, and on the other into the most miserable superstition. Hence arose those dissentions and jealousies mentioned by *Cato*-Zwack when tracing the progress of Illuminism; and it was for a long time doubtful which of the two competitors was to be crowned with success. During the conflict we see Weishaupt daily inventing new means of triumph; but he was undecided as to the use he should make of his victory, "In the first place," he writes to Zwack, "I should have wished to send to London for a constitution for our Brethren; and I should still be of that opinion if we could make ourselves masters of the Chapter (the Masonic) of Munich. You would do well to try. I can come to no determination on that subject until I have seen what turn our affairs take. Perhaps I shall only adopt a reform; or it may be better to create a new system of Masonry for ourselves; or, may it not be thought convenient to incorporate Masonry into our Order, and thus to make but one body of them both. Time alone can decide this."[10]

To relieve the Founder from this state of indecision, it was necessary that he should become acquainted with a man who laid less stress on difficulties, and who knew how to cut them short. The demon who wields the fiery sword of revolutions throws a Hanoverian Baron in his way, of the name of KNIGGE. At this name every honest German Mason will start back, as at the man who corrupted *even* the fraternal bagatelles of the *first degrees* of Masonry, and consummated the depravity of their impious Rosicrucians. The honest Brethren, in their indignation, would almost forget Weishaupt to overpower Knigge with the whole weight of their hatred; and to heap on him alone all the opprobrium of the Lodges now become the great seminaries of Illuminism.

The truth obliges us to say, that *Philo*-Knigge was no other than the worthy tool of *Spartacus*-Weishaupt in this grand intrusion. That which was executed by the one had long since been conceived by the other; and, in all probability, had it not been for the profound combinations of the one, the wicked activities of the other would have proved fruitless in its attempts. Unfortunately in the re-union of their baneful talents were to be found all the requisites for the most consummate conspirators; in the one, for the directing of the most disastrous of all Sects; in the other, for the propagation of its mysteries and in the recruiting of its conspiring bands.

Weishaupt, like Satan, profoundly meditated the destruction of mankind, while Knigge may be compared to those Genii winged like the plague, ever hovering and impatient to receive the Orders from the King of Hell to bend their course wherever he will point out evil to be done. Weishaupt proceeds slowly in his combinations, weighs his resources, compares the different essays, and, lest he should mistake, defers and suspends his choice. Knigge, in his levity, has sooner acted than deliberated; he sees where evil can be done; he does it, and is ready to sound a retreat, should his first attempts fail of success. The one foresees the obstacles he may have to encounter, and seeks to evade them; the other proceeds boldly in spite of all, and looks on the time spent in reflection as so much lost from the execution. The former is aware of every fault that can impede his progress; the latter proceeds heedless of the false steps he may have taken.

Encompassed with darkness, how great would have been the happiness of Weishaupt could he but have been gratified with a sight of the world in ruins, and that without being himself seen! The consciousness of his crimes would have been to him that grateful sensation which virtue raises in the honest heart. The power of doing harm is more dear to him, than a celebrity which might have proved fatal to the execution of his plots. Knigge, on the contrary, shows himself every where, meddles with every thing, his utmost ambition was to appear to have been the agent in whatever was done. Both are impious, and both have sworn the overthrow of the laws; but Weishaupt from the very beginning had laid down his principles; he had followed them through all their consequences; his revolution is to be the accomplishment of them all; and he will think his attempt fruitless, should a single law, social or religious, escape the general wreck. With Knigge, both his impiety and his plans of rebellion have had their gradual progression; he successively attended all the public and occult schools of the Infidelity of the age. He can vary his means and adapt himself to the different characters he has to deal with. He also wishes for a revolution, but he will not lose the occasion of one that offers, in hopes of that particular one which he wishes to operate. Where he cannot form an Atheist, he will form a Deist or a Sceptic; as circumstances may require, he will act the part of any species of Sophister, or engage in any degree of rebellion. Weishaupt wishes to involve in universal ruin religion, magistrates, society, and property, that he may install his *nomade* clans, his *Men Kings*, and his *Equality* and *Liberty*. Knigge is content to destroy less, provided he despotically sways over all that has escaped destruction. In the silent shades of his retreat, the one has more accurately studied the nature of man, and has laid his plans for new-modelling human nature according to his views. The other is better acquainted with them from his habit of intrigue, and is easier pleased with the ascendancy he can acquire over them. In short, the former may be said to prepare his poisons with more art, while the latter retails them better; and between them they wield the mighty power of destruction.

When the common enemy of human nature brought these two fiends of rebellion in contact with each other, they had already acquired all those habits and means which must render their union fatal to mankind. The Hanoverian Baron had been cast upon the earth nearly at the same time that the Bavarian monster had been engendered. His whole life appears to have been but one continued preparation for the part he was to act in seconding Weishaupt, and particularly to open the gates of the Lodges from the North to the South and from the East to the West to receive the founder of Illuminism, and deliver over to him all those adepts who, trained by the higher mysteries of Masonry, had long since been prepared to receive those of the modern *Spartacus*.

Knigge informs us, that from his youth he had always had an invincible propensity towards secret societies; and that while a boy he had founded one of those little societies so common in the Protestant Universities, and of which we have before spoken. He had acquired this turn from his father, whom he had observed spending his time in the study of the Masonic Mysteries, and his money in the vain pursuit of the Philosopher's Stone. The father's gold had vanished in the crucible, and the son reaped nothing but the dross. No sooner had he attained the necessary age, than he got himself made a Freemason in one of those Lodges called of the *Strict Observance*. He rose to the degree of *Templar*, that is to say, of those Masons who, still flattering themselves with the hopes of recovering the possessions of that once celebrated Order, distribute in the mean time the different titles formerly borne by those Knights. Knigge became one of these Brother Commanders under the title of Eques a Cygno (*Knight of the Swan*). Contrary to his expectations, he found this to be but an empty title without any emolument. Wishing to make up for this deficiency, and still more actuated with the desire of acquiring that importance in the Lodges at least, which he could not acquire elsewhere, he made himself the disciple of the famous Mountebank SCHROEDER at Marbourg. When in company with this Schroeder, or the Cagliostro of Germany, *What man*, as he says himself, *would not have been fired with zeal for Theosophy, Magic, and Alchymy?* These were the mysteries of the Masons of the *Strict Observance*. *Violent, fantastical,* and *restless,* as he describes himself, he at the age of five-and-twenty was a firm believe in all these mysteries; he even practised all the evocations of spirits, and other follies of ancient and modern Cabal. Soon he began to doubt whether *he really believed or ought to believe* in all this stuff. *He flattered himself* with the hopes that, in the midst of these enchantments and magic spells, *the chaos of his ideas would subside.* To gain knowledge, and put his mind at ease, he would willingly have gained admission into every Masonic

Lodge. He found means of getting admitted into the higher degrees, *procured the rarest and most mysterious manuscripts*, and even studied all their different Sects.[11] Then, as he wished to convert himself into a vast emporium of every error, he applied to the doctrines of the modern Sophisters, and thus plied his unfortunate brain on the one side with all the delirious conceits of Cabalistic Masonry, and on the other with the impious doctrines of the self-created Philosophers. His attempts at fortune were similar to those he had made for the acquisition of science, nor was he more successful.—A courtier without favor, he deserts his Prince to take the direction of a Playhouse; thence he accepts a commission in the service of the Prince of Hesse Cassel; but is soon dismissed, in consequence of the violence and restlessness of his temper. He then turns author, and writes violent declamations against the Roman Catholics; then, in consequence of some hope of preferment (I know not what), he makes a public profession of their faith, but, not succeeding as he hoped, he deserts them, abuses them more scurrilously than ever, takes part again with the Protestants, but writes in favor of Deism.[12] Such had been the restless education for the man who was to prove the most worthy supporter and the most active co-operator that Weishaupt yet had found.

By a strange coincidence, just at the very time that these two Conspirators met, Knigge had been projecting a conquest of Masonry, and had formed such plans for an universal conspiracy, that he scarcely leaves the honor of invention to Weishaupt. The account given by Knigge will best explain the coincidence.

It was in the year of our Lord 1780; and a general assembly of Masons had been convoked at Willemsbaden for the next year, under the protection of the Duke of Brunswick and of the Landgrave of Hesse Cassel. "On the news of this," says *Philo*-Knigge, "I cast an eye on the immense multitude of Brethren: I observed it to be composed of men of all stations in life, of noblemen, of men of great riches, of great power, and also of Brethren possessing great knowledge and activity. I saw these men all actuated by one common sentiment, though I could not very well conceive the object of their union. I saw them all bound by an oath of the most profound secrecy, without being able to form any better idea as to the object of it. I beheld them divided in their opinions, nor could I comprehend on which side the error lay; still less could I surmise what had been the grand obstacle that had impeded the advantages which mankind had reason to expect from Freemasonry.... Nevertheless how great would these advantages have been, if, distinguishing actions from speculations, opinions had been left to each individual, while a regular system of conduct was followed, perpetually tending towards the advantage of humanity in general, *and of the Brethren in particular*! Had they agreed on a system of laws for the mutual and general support of each other; to raise depressed or obscure merit; to second with all the power and influence of Masonry all plans for general utility; *to favor the advancement of the Brethren; to measure out the different employments in the State to the Brethren, according to their capacities, and in proportion as they should have profited of the advantage to be reaped from* SECRET SOCIETIES *in the arts of knowing men and of governing them without constraint.*"[13]

"Meditating and musing on these ideas," continues Knigge, "I had resolved on all my plans of reform, and had sent them to Willemsbaden. I received polite answers; they promised to take my work into consideration at the general meeting that was about to be held. But I soon had reason to believe, that the benevolent and disinterested views of the illustrious chiefs and protectors of Masonry would be but very ill seconded; that partial views and discordant interests would play off every artifice to make the systems of particular Sects predominate; and I foresaw how difficult it would *be to make one cap fit so many heads*. Meanwhile I communicated my plans to different Masons, and repeatedly expressed my fears; when, in July 1780, I made acquaintance with *Diomedes* (the Marquis of Constanza) in a Lodge at Franckfort on the Mein, who had been sent from Bavaria by the Illuminees to establish new Colonies in the Protestant States. I informed him of my views with respect to a general reform of Freemasonry; and that, perfectly convinced of the inutility of the meeting at Willemsbaden I had resolved to work at the establishment of my system seconded by a few Masons my particular friends, and who were spread throughout Germany. After having heard me explain my intentions, "Why," said he, "should you give yourself the trouble to found a new society, when there already exists one which has undertaken all that you wish to do, which can in every way gratify your thirst for knowlege, and open a wide field for your activity and desire of being useful; a society, in short, which is in possession of all the sciences and all the authority necessary for the accomplishment of your object."[14]

The Marquis was correct; for there existed a most striking coincidence between the plots of his master and those proposed by Knigge to raise depressed or obscure merit, and succour suffering virtue; to teach the adepts the art of knowing men; to conduct mankind to happiness, and to govern them without their perceiving it. Like Knigge, Weishaupt also had invented that invisible concatenation which, proceeding from the tenebrous meeting of his lurking senate, was to extend its ramifications over every class of citizens, and, dictating laws from these dark recesses, the Brotherhood was to leave no art untried to cause them to be promulgated by the councils of the Prince.[15] Thus far the two Arch-conspirators follow the same plan; but the truth is, that Weishaupt only seeks power to destroy, and gives laws but to annihilate every law; while *Philo*-Knigge will look upon nations as sufficiently free, provided he can but subject their magistrates and rulers to the decrees of the Masonic Lodges; though the Liberty, therefore, sought by the one be the death of society, that of the other will be its eternal shame. Two such men could not long remain separate; pride may give rise to temporary disagreements; but they will co-operate sufficiently for the misery of mankind.

Knigge could scarcely express the joy of astonishment with which he learned that the plans he had conceived were already executing. He threw himself into the arms of the Illuminizing Apostle, and immediately received the degrees of Candidate, of Novice, and was even admitted into the *Minerval* Academy. Weishaupt soon felt the importance of such an acquisition, though in Revolutionary Impiety he found Knigge even more advanced than he wished. This latter immediately set to work for the Illuminees with as much zeal as if he had been prosecuting his own plan, and took upon himself the mission on which *Diomedes* had been sent. Never had Illuminism beheld so active and insinuating a Recruiter. The list of Novices and Brethren was swollen with amazing rapidity, nor did he, like Weishaupt, merely enlist youths coming from the College, but men who had attained the age of maturity, and whose impiety was already known to him.—He more particularly selected those whom in the Lodges he had observed to have a greater propensity for the Occult Mysteries.

Weishaupt in his first surprize could not help admiring his new Apostle; and thus extolls him to his Areopagites: "*Philo*-Knigge alone does more than all of you put together could even hope to do.... *Philo* is the master from whom you all should take lessons.... Give me only six such men, and I will engage to change the whole face of the universe."[16] The grand point which gave Weishaupt so much pleasure was the *discovery of that generation of men* who were already prepared for his plots, and which in part dispensed with the laborious education he had found necessary for the preparation of youth; and indeed we soon after see him instructing his recruiters to follow Knigge's method of proceeding.[17] Nor was he less pleased to see the Sect daily gaining ground, and that without any violence, in those very Lodges which he wished so much to reduce under his subjection. This rapid success, however, gave rise to difficulties which must have disgusted any other man; but Knigge was exactly the person to remedy them.

Tricked by the Apostolic Marquis, as the latter had been before by Weishaupt, with regard to the antiquity, omniscience, and power of Illuminism, Knigge had only been admitted as yet to the preparatory degrees; nor had he the least suspicion that the remaining degrees had no existence but in the brain or portfolio of the modern *Spartacus*.—He expected grand mysteries; he asked for them, both in his own name and in the name of the Old Masons who were not to be treated like boys from the college in their *Minerval* Academy.—Weishaupt had recourse to all those subterfuges by which he had heretofore succeeded in keeping his pupils in suspense with respect to the higher mysteries; and the more he extolled them by asking for new trials the more pressing Knigge became, who told him that such trials might be *necessary in the Catholic countries, but were by no means so in the Protestant ones*, where the spirit of Philosophy had made a much greater progress.[18] —Weishaupt continued to shift his ground, and Knigge became more pressing in his demands.—The old Masons, famous for decyphering the hieroglyphics, asked for some which might answer to the enthusiasm with which he had inspired them. They threw out hints of abandoning him as an impostor who had deluded them with idle promises, unless he kept his word with them; and Illuminism must have been irreparably undone had so many Brethren abandoned him under that persuasion. These perpetual solicitations at length forced Weishaupt's secret from him: "His letters (says Knigge) at length informed me, that this Order, professedly so ancient, had no other existence than in his own head, and in the *preparatory classes* he had established in the Catholic countries; but that he had a large quantity of excellent materials for the higher degrees. In making this avowal, he begged me to pardon his little finesse; for (said he) I have sought in vain after worthy co-operators; no person has ever entered so deeply into my views as you have; nor has any person seconded me with so much activity. He told me, that I was a man sent from Heaven to second him in his undertaking; that he threw himself upon my honor, and was willing to give me up all his papers; and that in future, not looking upon himself as my superior, he would be content to work under my direction; that the Brethren were expecting me in Bavaria, where all the necessary steps could be agreed upon, and that they were ready to pay my expences there."[19]

Had Weishaupt thought Knigge to be a man less to be depended upon, this would have been the only error we should have seen for this conspiring genius fall into. He must have been the only man on earth who could have looked upon his higher degrees and means of seduction as incomplete. The mysteries and the discourse for the degree of Epopt were finished; all that has been laid before the reader on this degree was already composed;[20] Knigge may have ornamented the impiety and disorganizing principles; but neither Knigge nor all the powers of hell could have added to them. The same may be said of the means of seduction. All the cunning of the *Insinuators* and *directing Illuminees* is to be found either in his first degrees, or in the instruction for the Provincials; his irresolution can only be attributed to the immensity of his powers for seduction, which no other person but himself could conceive. Hence he was led to suppose that what he had done was incomplete, because he thought he could do still better. In a word, had he sent his code as it was, Knigge would have profited of what had been completed, and would never even have surmised that he could have perfected it. Elated to a great degree at the idea of extricating from a difficulty a man whose plots and systems so perfectly coincided with his own, he hastened to his succour. He had soon run over all the papers that Weishaupt entrusted him with; made his appearance at the Council of the Areopagites; and in a few days got the better of all their irresolution with respect to the division of classes and degrees, and of the higher and lower mysteries. The chief point, and which in these circumstances acquired an immediate decision, was to know what rank should be given to the Freemasons in the Order, as a mode of facilitating the general intrusion into the Lodges. Knigge had already proved that they might entirely rely on him as to the number of Masonic brethren to be gained over to Illuminism; his vote carried the point, and the *Intermediary Class* of Masonry was irrevocably determined.

About this time the deputies of the Lodges flocked from all parts to Willemsbaden. It was an object of great importance for Weishaupt and his

Council, that no steps inimical to their views on Masonry should be taken at that assembly.—To obtain an account of all their proceedings, *Philo* had taken care to have *Minos* named a deputy. As to himself, he preferred being in the neighbourhood of the congress, there to watch its motions, and only to act by his agents. He had received full powers from Weishaupt and the Council of Areopagites to take such steps as circumstances might require.

The article which required the greatest expedition was, to complete the higher parts of the code, and to decide on what degrees were to be given to the Masons, who were too far advanced in the mysteries to be subjected to the trials of the Minerval School; and Knigge had speedily executed this first part of his mission. His active pen had soon made choice of its materials from Weishaupt's portfolio. According to his agreement with the Areopagites, he left all the preparatory degrees, such as *Novice, Minerval,* and *Minor Illuminee*, which had already been conferred on several of the adepts, in their primitive state. It had also been agreed, that the *first three degrees* of Masonry (now become the intermediary degrees of Illuminism) should not be touched. He united the *Major* Illuminee to the Scotch degrees. In the degree of *Epopt* and *Regent*, he condensed every seditious and impious principle, as well as every artifice that he could find in Weishaupt's works; and hence arose that astonishing code already investigated in the foregoing volume.

It was not long before Weishaupt again gave way to his irresolution; for he was always inventing some new art of seduction; but while he was deliberating Knigge was acting. The success of the second part of his mission, or his views on the Masons of Willemsbaden, entirely depending on the final determination of the mysteries for the degrees of *Epopt* and *Regent*, Weishaupt was pressed once more, and approving the whole, *he signed and sealed them with the grand seal of the Order.*

Knigge now had only to attend to his mission at Wilhemsbaden. We shall soon follow him to that Congress of Masonry; but we must first explain to our readers of what species of men this grand assembly was composed; and what the great agents were, that had already prepared the success and ensured the triumph of the new mysteries over those of Freemasonry.[21]

---

1. See the discourse of the Orator on the shutting up of a Lodge.
2. Original Writings, Vol. I, Let. 6, to *Ajax*.
3. See *Cato's* Journal, *Diarium des Cato,* Original Writings, Vol. I.
4. Ibid. Let. 31, 2 Dec. 1778.
5. Original Writings, Let. of the 6th Jan. 1779.
6. See Vol. III of these Memoirs, *Degree of Epopt.*
7. Ibid. Let. 32.
8. Let it be always remembered, that we continue to except the Masons who only acknowledge the first three degrees; but EVEN THESE *ought never to forget, that it was precisely their first three degrees which served as* A CLOAK *to the grand intrusion of Illuminism.*

HISTORICAL PART

9. The word *Abrac* is derived from *Abraxas*, which is only a set of Greek letters put together by BASILIDES, a famous Sophister of Alexandria, and an heresiarch of the second century, expressing the number of 365 *Intelligences* or spirits which constituted his God. St. Jerome says, that *Abraxas* was the fictitious God of *Basilides* expressed in Greek numerals Α Β Ρ Α Ξ Α Σ (1 2 100 1 60 1 200). Basilides grounded all his magic on the number of his genii; and hence the term *Science of Abrac* is used for the science of Magic (*Vide Hieronimus adversus Luciferum—Augustinus liber de haeresis—-Tertullian de Basilide*). MANES adopted many of his errors from this Basilides, and particularly his *Eons* and his magic. These *mysteries of Abrac* are mentioned in the Masonic manuscript of Oxford, which bears testimony that some Brethren were as much addicted to these *mysteries of Abrac* three hundred years ago, as many of our modern Rosicrucians.
10. Original Writings, Let. 57, to *Cato*, March 1780.
11. See his Last Observations, P. 24.
12. See his Last Observations, P. 25.
13. See his Last Observations, P. 28.
14. See his Last Observations, P. 32.
15. Original Writings, first Statutes of the Illuminee, and Instructions for the Regent.
16. Original Writings, Vol. I. Let. 56, and Last Observations, P. 49.
17. Original Writings, Vol. II. Let. 7.
18. Last Observations of *Philo*, from P. 35 to 55.
19. Last Observations of *Philo*, from P. 35 to 55.
20. See the original of this discourse in the Original Writings, Vol. II. Part II.
21. For the whole of this chapter, see the Last Observations of *Philo*, from P. 55 to 123; also his first Letter to *Cato*, Original Writings, Vol. II, and his convention with the Areopagites, Ibid.

CHAP. IV.

Congress of the Freemasons at Wilhemsbaden—Of their divers Sects, and particularly of that of the Theosophical Illuminees.

IT was by no means the deputies of an insignificant society that were flocking from all parts of the universe to Wilhemsbaden. At that period, many masons conceived their numbers to amount to *three millions* of brethren; and the *Lodge de la Candeur* at Paris, in its *Circular Letter of the 31st May, 1782,* supposes that France alone contained *one million.* Doctor Stark (one of the most learned writers of the Order) in his work on the ancient and modern mysteries, positively says, that at the lowest computation *the number of masons at that time must have amounted to one million.*[1] Let the historian abide by this estimate, let him be ever so partial, yet at the sight of these deputies sent by a *Secret Society* composed of at least a million of adepts, all flocking to their mysterious congress, what serious reflections must arise, and how important the consideration both to nations and their rulers!

What inconceivable motive is it then that draws forth these agents and deputies from all parts of the globe, from Europe, Asia, Africa, and America, agents of men all bound by the oath of secrecy, both as to the nature of their association and the object of their mysteries? What intentions can actuate, what plans are brought by these deputies of so formidable an association secretly spreading its ramifications around us, throughout town and country, creeping into our habitations, and encompassing empires? What do they meditate, what are they going to combine either for or against nations? If they thus convene for the general good of humanity, and the welfare of nations, whence do they derive their right of deliberating on our religion, morals, or governments? Who has entrusted them with our interests? Who has subjected the world to their decrees and their pretended wisdom? Who has told them that we wish to act, to think, or to be governed according to their decisions and subterraneous machinations; or, in their language, according to their *industrious and secret influence?*

Should their plans be conspiracies, arising in a wish to change the nature of our worship and of our laws, insidious Brethren, perfidious citizens, by what right do you pretend to live among us as children of the same society, or subject to the same magistrates?

But should it neither be for nor against nations, should their only object be to draw more close the bonds of their fraternity, to propagate their benevolence, and their general love of mankind, then will I answer, Amuse the populace with such bubbles, *ad Populum Phaleras*! What! you that live on the banks of the Thames or of the Tagus, in the plains watered by the Tiber or the Vistula, are you to emigrate to the Rhine or to the Elbe, there in the dark abodes of Masonry to coalesce and deliberate with men whom you have never before seen nor will ever meet again? There is great occasion for you to go there to learn how to love and succour those with whom you daily cohabit! The Englishman, the Russian, or the American, is to go and bury himself in a German Lodge to learn how to be charitable at home!—The voice of nature and of the Gospel then is only to be heard within the secret recesses of Masonry? Or are we to be told, that men have braved the dangers of the Ocean and crossed whole empires to assist at a fraternal banquet, there to drink a toast given in a *zig-zag* or a *square*; or perhaps to chant some hymns sacred to innocent Equality; and that for these harmless amusements they should have chosen a den only worthy of the deepest conspirators! Let them find other pretences, or not wonder at being suspected of conspiring. Such language every citizen, every magistratte, every sovereign, was entitled to hold to these deputies flocking to Wilhemsbaden. Happy would it have been for Masonry had such language been held; for it might have saved the Brethren the eternal shame of having become the vile instruments and accomplices of Weishaupt.

Had any religious body, had even the Bishops of the church, held a general meeting, the civil power, without doubt, would have used its right of sending its commissaries to such a meeting, and they would have been instructed to watch, lest, under pretence of debating on ecclesiastical affairs, the rights of the state should be infringed. But all governments permitted the masons peaceably to proceed to the congress of Wilhemsbaden. The brethren even had passports from the civil powers. For more than six months did these deputies deliberate in their immense Lodge, without any sovereign harbouring the least suspicion as to his own safety, or that of his people. They all relied on those princes who were themselves initiated in the mysteries of Masonry; they were in all probability ignorant that *Brethren of that rank are but partially admitted to the secrets of the Sect*; nor were they aware, that great names are only cloaks under which secret societies often conspire against their very protectors. They had not conceived, that the *only means of escaping* the vengeance of such societies was TO TOLERATE NONE, not even those that are known to be innocent; for the conspirator, ever watchful, can have no more favorable opportunity of assuming the garb of innocence, than in these secret recesses, where sooner or later he will find means of involving the undesigning members in his criminal plots.

Sovereigns were equally ignorant of the state in which Masonry was at the time of the too famous meeting at Wilhemsbaden; had they but known it, the utmost severity might have become a duty on them. To judge by the writings of the Sect, it never had been less disposed to a reform, which some it would seem wished to promote, and which Sir Andrew Michael Ramsay, a Scotch Baronet, had attempted to bring about forty years before; nor is it clear that the reform he had attempted was favourable to religion. In order to unite the efforts of the Brethren towards some useful object, he had conceived the plan of an Encyclopedia, which was to have been executed by all the learned Masons of the world.[2] If the posthumous works attributed to Ramsay are really his (such as *The Philosophical Principles of Natural Religion and of Revelation*, printed under his name in 1749, six years after his death) I could not venture to say, that he had not forgotten the greater part of those lessons which he had received from Fenelon, or that the Masonic Encyclopedia would have been a better work than that executed by the Sophisters D'Alembert and Diderot; neither would I vouch that any reform was intended even at that time in the ancient mysteries of the Lodges, other than the introduction of many anti-Christian errors, together with those of the Metempsichosis. But, whatever may have been the reform projected by Ramsay, every thing denoted that that which the Brethren were about to accomplish at Wilhemsbaden would be no other than the consummation of the mysteries or plots of the Rosicrucians. (*See Note at the end of the Chapter.*) In reality, these mysteries as well as those of the Scotch Knights had only been new modelled, the better to meet the wishes of the Sophisters, and of the impostors of the age. In France alone, under the successive protections of the Princes of Clermont, of Conti, and of the Duke of Orleans, all Grand Masters of the Order, the *Clermontois Brethren*, The *African Brethren*, the *Knights of the Eagle*, the *Adept*, the *Sublime Philosopher*, were so many national inventions added to Masonry; and all these degrees were steps towards our Revolution. In Germany we see *Rosa* combining all these French inventions with the ancient Scotch mysteries; the Baron *Hund* and *Shubard* subdividing Masonry into the *Strict Observance* and the *Lax Observance*. Under the name of *Templar Masons*, it daily beheld new degrees invented, more and more threatening to Kings and Pontiffs, who had suppressed the Templars. There also appeared the physician *Zinnendorf*, and with him were introduced the modern *Rosicrucians* from Sweden, and their new mysteries of the *Cabal*, while the impostor *Jaeger* was propagating his at Ratisbon.

There was not one of these new masonic Sects that did not revive some ancient system of impiety or rebellion. But the worst of the whole clan was a sort of *Illuminees* calling themselves *Theosophs*, whom I find continually confounded by some people with those of Weishaupt. They are certainly no better; but they are a different Sect. The necessity under which I lie to distinguish them, lest the historian should be misled, obliges me to trace them to their origin, and to give a short account of their mysteries.

All the *Theosophical Illuminees* of this age in England, France, Sweden, or Germany, have drawn their principles from the *Baron Emmanuel Swedenborg*. This name, to be sure, does not seem to denote the founder of a Sect. Swedenborg became one, perhaps, without dreaming of any such thing, and through one of those extraordinary incidents which Providence in an age of impiety permits to humble the pride of our Sophisters. He was son of the Lutheran Bishop of Skara, and was born at Upsal in 1688. After having passed the greater part of his life in the most incongruous pursuits, as a Poet, a Philosopher, a Metaphysician, a Mineralogist, a Sailor, a Divine, and an Astronomer, he was attacked by one of those violent fevers, which leave the organs of the human frame in a very deranged state.[3] His meditations, or rather reveries, took the form of those speculations to which he had formerly been addicted, on the Infinite, the Creation, the Spirit, Matter, God, and Nature. All on a sudden he thought himself inspired, and sent by God to reveal new truths. The following is the account he gives of his apostleship:

"I was one day dining very late at my hotel in London, and I ate with great appetite, when at the end of my repast I perceived a sort of fog which obstructed my view, and my floor was covered with hideous reptiles. They disappeared, the darkness was dispersed, and I plainly saw, in the midst of a bright light, a man sitting in the corner of my room, who said in a terrible voice, *Do not eat so much*. At these words my sight was bedimmed; but I regained it little by little, and then found that I was alone. The next night, the same man, resplendent with light, stood before me, and said: *I am the Lord, Creator, and Redeemer; I have chosen you to explain to men the interior and spiritual sense of the sacred Scriptures. I will dictate what you shall write.* This time I was not affrighted; and the light, though very vivid, did not affect my sight. The Lord was clothed in purple, and the vision continued for a quarter of an hour. This very night the eyes of my *interior* were opened and enabled to see into heaven, into the world of spirits, into hell, in which places I found many of my acquaintances, some who had long since been dead, others only a short time."[4]

This vision would appear more worthy of a man to whom one might say in a less terrible voice, *Do not eat so much*, but rather, indeed, *Do not drink so much*. Swedenborg declares it to have been in the year 1745. He lived till 1772, perpetually writing new volumes of his revelations, travelling every year from England to Sweden, and daily from earth to heaven or to hell. It requires exceeding great patience to wade through all these works; and when one has studied them, it is difficult to form an idea of their author. In this Theosophical Illuminee some will behold a man in a constant delirium; others will trace the Sophister and Infidel; while others again will take him for an impostor and a hypocrite. Is it the madman, the visionary madman in the regions of Folly, that is sought? Let the reader follow him in his frequent journies to the world of spirits, or let him have the patience to hear him tell what he has seen. On one side he shows us a Paradise perfectly corresponding with the earth, and the angels doing every thing in the other world that men do in this. On the other, he describes heaven and its plains, its forests, its rivers, its towns, and its provinces; he then proceeds to the schools for the infant angels; to the universities for the learned angels; to fairs for the commercial angels, and particularly for the English and Dutch angels. The spirits are male and female; they marry, and Swedenborg was present at a marriage. This marriage is celestial; "but," says he, "we are not to infer that celestial couples are unacquainted with voluptuousness.... The propensity to unite, imprinted by the Creator, exists in the *spiritual bodies,* as it does in the material bodies. The angels of both sexes are always in the most perfect state of beauty, youth, and vigor. They enjoy therefore the utmost voluptuousness of conjugal love, and that to a much greater degree than is possible for mortals."[5]

From this delirium let us proceed to the impostor. The whole life and writings of Swedenborg depose against him. To begin with his writings, it is always God or an angel that speaks. Every thing that he tells us, he has seen in heaven himself, and he is at liberty to go there as often as he pleases. He has spirits at his command; and they reveal to him the most secret transactions. The Princess Ulrica, Queen of Sweden, sends to consult him why her brother the Prince of Prussia had died without answering a certain letter which she had written to him. Swedenborg promises to consult the deceased. The following day he returns, and addresses himself as follows to the Queen: "Your brother appeared to me last night, and ordered me to inform you, that he had not answered your letter because your imprudent politics and your ambition were the causes of the effusion of blood. I command you therefore, in his name to meddle no more in state affairs, and particularly not any more to excite troubles to which you would, sooner or later, fall the victim." The Queen was astonished; Swedenborg told her things that she alone and the deceased could know; and the reputation of the prophet was much increased. For my readers to form their judgement, it will be sufficient for them to know that the letter the Queen had written had been intercepted by two senators, who profited of this occasion to give her the above lesson through the medium of Swedenborg.[6]

Take another trait of the Impostor:—The Countess of Mansfield is afraid of having to pay a sum of money a second time, the receipt being mislaid at her husband's death. She consults Swedenborg, and in the name of the deceased he comes to acquaint her where the receipt was to be found. He could very readily give the information to be sure, for he had found the receipt in a book which had been returned him by the Count.—It was the Queen Ulrica who gave this natural explanation of the fact; yet she is nevertheless quoted by the disciples as an authority to prove the miracle.[7] Certainly we have shown enough of the impostor; but the important person for our consideration is the Illuminizing law-giver, the Sophister of Impiety; and Swedenborg's character partakes much more of this than is generally supposed. His manner would lead us to think that his hypocrisy was not inferior to his impiety.—Never did any man speak more of the love of God and of the love of his neighbour; never did any person more frequently quote the Prophets and the Scriptures; or affect more respect for Christ and more zeal for Christianity; never did any one better assume the character and tone of a sincere, religious, and upright man: Nevertheless, I must say, never did any man show more duplicity and impiety; never did any one conceal the most resolute design of annihilating Christianity and every Religion, under the mask of zeal, more completely than he did. Let all his followers protest against this assertion; to expose the *two systems* of their master will amply suffice to justify the imputation. I say *two systems*, because as Swedenborg always had *two senses*, the one *internal* and *allegorical*, the other *external* or *literal*, to explain and overthrow the Scriptures; so he has also *two systems*, the one apparent, for fools and dupes; the other secret and hidden, and reserved for the adepts; the one tending only in appearance to reform Christianity on the reveries of Deism; the other leading to all the Impiety of Atheism, Spinosism, Fanaticism, and Materialism.

I lament with my readers that such is the nature of our revolutions, that to know and unfold their causes it is necessary to study manifold Sects and wade through disgusting systems. Few people are aware of the multitude of Antichristian, impious, and tenebrous factions that had overrun the earth to prepare the advent of our disasters. I myself for a long time despised these *Theosophical Illuminees*. But I found them at Wilhemsbaden; and the part they acted at first in concurrence with Weishaupt, and afterward in union with him, obliged me to investigate their Sect; and my reader must have a short and precise idea of each of their two systems. The first, which I call *apparent*, is compiled for men who still wish to preserve the words of God, Religion, Spirit, Heaven, and Hell; but who, swerving from Christianity, are abandoned by the Almighty to all the absurdities and follies of *Anthropomorphism*. For such persons Swedenborg has invented *two worlds*, the one *invisible and spiritual*, the other *visible and natural*. Each of these worlds has the *form of a man*; together they compound the universe, which has also the *form of a man*.

The spiritual world comprehends *Heaven; the world of spirits, and Hell*. This Heaven, World of Spirits, and Hell, are formed *to the Image of Man*, that is to say of God himself.

For God is also man; indeed it is only the Lord or God, that can be properly called man—This God man *is uncreated, infinite, present everywhere by his humanity*—Though God and Man at the same time, he is but of one nature, one essence, and particularly *but one in person*. It is true, there is a God the Father, a God the Son, and a God the Holy Ghost; but Jesus Christ alone is the Father, the Son, and the Holy Ghost, according as he manifests himself by the creation, redemption, or sanctification; and *the Trinity of persons in God*, according to Swedenborg, *is an Impiety which has produced many others*.

This doctrine against the Trinity is one of those articles to which the Sophister and his disciples most frequently advert, and particularly insist upon, even in their Catechisms for children.

Though we are to believe the existence of but one nature and of one person in this *God-Man, Father, Son,* and *Holy Ghost*, yet in each man we are to conceive two distinct men; the one *spiritual* and *interior*, the other *exterior* and *natural*. The *Man-spirit* or *interior*, has a *heart, lungs, feet* and *hands*, and all the different parts of the human frame, which belong to the *visible* and *exterior* man.[8]

There are also three distinct things in every man, *the body, the soul, and the spirit*. We are all acquainted with the body, and Swedenborg makes no change in it; but his *spirit* is that *interior man*, who has *a heaert, lungs, and a spiritual body* entirely modelled on the natural body. But the *soul*, that is the man himself, *children receive from their father; the body is the envelope and is of the mother*.

Notwithstanding this body, this spirit, and this soul, *every thing than man thinks or that he wills is infused into him through the influence of Heaven or of Hell*. "He imagines that his thoughts are actually his own, and his volition in himself and from himself, while nevertheless the whole is infused into him. If he believed the real fact, he would not then appropriate evil actions to himself, for he would reject them from himself to Hell, whence they came. Neither would he appropriate to himself good actions, and for that reason would pretend to no merit from then. He would be happy; he would see, according to the Lord, the Good and the Evil;"[9] or, in other worlds, he will find that he is master neither of his thoughts nor actions; that he is deprived of free-agency, and that he can neither merit nor demerit.

This poor being, who so grossly mistakes himself when he believes himself to be thinking or acting of himself, has also fallen into a multitude of other religious errors, because he does not rightly undertand the sacred scriptures. In the Book of Revelation every things is *allegorical*, every thing has two senses, the one *celestial, spiritual, interior*; the other *natural, exterior, literal*. It is from not having understood the spiritual and celestial sense that Christians have believed in the Son of God made Man, and in his death on the Cross for the Redemption of mankind. Swedenborg, one day present in Heaven at a great council, heard and repeats these words of an angel, who was a great divine: "How is it possible that the Christian world can abjure sound reason, and rave to such a degree as to establish the fundamental principles of their belief on paradoxes of such a nature, which evidently militate against the divine essence, the divine love, the divine wisdom, the omnipotence, and the universal presence of God? What he is supposed to have done, a good master would not have done against his servants, nor even a wild beast against its young!"[10] The same angel told him many other things, which overturn all the remaining articles of the Christian belief. One point in particular he asserts, which must give pleasure to the wicked, when he teaches them to scoff at Hell, particularly when he says *that it is contrary to the divine essence to deprive a single man of his mercy; that the whole of those doctrines are contrary to the divine nature, which the Christian world does not seem to be aware of*.[11]

Another part of the doctrine which must be also very acceptable to the wicked, is the state with which Swedenborg flatters them in the other world, and the time he gives them after death to gain Heaven. According to his new Gospel, the instant that man believes to be that of his death, is the moment of his resurrection; and no other resurrection is allowed of. At that very instant *he appears in the spiritual world under the human form*, exactly as if he was in this world; under *this form*, he becomes an angel, and no other angels exist but those who become so at their departure from this world. All these angels inhabit the world of spirits, and are received there by other angels, who instruct them in the *spiritual sense* of the Scriptures. They are allowed till the age of thirty to learn this *sense*, and to repent in the world of spirits. But lest we should revert to the delirious Illuminee, let us hasten to that part of his doctrines which constitutes the grand hopes of his disciples on earth. After having expounded all the mysteries of Christianity according to his spiritual and allegorical sense, that is to say, after having substituted his doctrines to those of the Gospel, Swedenborg informs them, that the day will come when the whole of his doctrine shall be received in this world. This happy day will be that on which the *New Jerusalem* shall be re-established on earth. This New Jerusalem will be the reign of the new church, of Jesus Christ reigning alone over the earth, as he formerly did over our forefathers before the deluge. It will be the golden age of true Christianity; and then the revolution foretold by Swedenborg will be accomplished with his prophesies.

Such is that which I have denominated the *apparent system* of the Baron de Swedenborg. My readers may easily observe, that such tools in the hands of the adepts must suffice to eradicate true Christianity from the minds of their dupes, and to make their New Jerusalem a plea for those revolutions which, in order to recall ancient times, are, in the name of God and of his prophet, to overthrow all the altars and thrones existing under the present Jerusalem, that is to say, under the present churches and governments.

From the midst of this chaos of delirium, and these prophecies of rebellion, let us bring forth that other system, which appears to have been reserved to the profound adepts. It is that of Materialism and of the purest Atheism. This system is occult in Swedenborg's works, but it is wholly contained in them. Here we should no longer have to deal with the prophet in delirium, but with the most artful Sophister, were I not aware that such hypocrisy is not entirely incompatible with a disordered mind. I will explain: it sometimes happens, that the minds of men will rave on certain questions, though perfectly sensible and reasonable on others. There are also madmen who will constantly pursue their object; their principles may be extravagant, but they never lose sight of their consequences. They will even reason on them, and combine them with all the art of the most subtle Sophister. I think it is in this class that Swedenborg is to be ranked; I believe it, because not only his writings, but many circumstances in his life, serve to confirm the conjecture. For example: at Stockholm, after having made a general officer (who came to pay him a visit from Mr. Euler, the Prince of Orange's librarian) wait in his antichamber for a considerable time, he at length came to him and made his excuses, by saying, Indeed, General, just at that moment St. Peter and St. Paul were with me; and you easily apprehend, that when one receives such visitors one is in no hurry to dismiss them.—My readers must as easily conceive the opinion the General formed of the Baron, and the account he gave of him to Euler.

At another time, on a journey from Stockholm to Berlin, one of his companions, awakened by a noise which Swedenborg was making, and thinking he was ill, went into his room. He there found him in bed, fast asleep, very much agitated, and in a great heat, repeating in a loud voice the questions and answers of a conversation which he dreamt he was holding with the Virgin Mary. The next day his fellow-traveller asked the Baron how he had slept the night before; he answered, "I had yesterday asked a favour of the Virgin Mary in the most pressing manner; she paid me a visit this night, and I had a long conversation with her."

The first of these facts will be vouched for by Mr. Euler; and with respect to the second I think it is as well founded.

We will now show how these anecdotes are blended with the history of a Sect that has powerfully contributed towards the Revolution.

Swedenborg, anterior to the derangement of his mind, had formed a system leading to Materialism; and this continued deeply rooted in his mind after his illness. He then added his male and female spirits, and some extravagances of the same nature. With respect to the remainder of his system, he follows up his principles in a consequent manner, and unfortunately the whole tends to Materialism. Sophisters and infidels, no doubt, soon perceived that they could make a tool of this unfortunate man; they set him up as a Prophet, and his reveries were opposed to the truths of Christianity. Let us for a moment attend to his most zealous and artful apostles. It is thus that they speak of his first works, in order to captivate the reader's mind in favour of his subsequent writings: "According to the discoveries made by the Baron de Swedenborg, every human body consists of several orders, of forms distinct among themselves, according to the apparent degree of purity respectively belonging to each; that is to say, in the inferior degree is to be found the basis or receptacle of the second degree, which is more pure and more *interior* than the first. In the same manner, the second serves as the basis or receptacle for the third, which is more elevated, and is the purest and most *interior* of the three. It is in the latter that resides *the human spirits, which is an organized form* ANIMA, *corresponding with the corporal spirit* ANIMUS, *and vivifying it, while it derives its own life directly from the spiritual world.*"[12]

After having seen this famous discovery of the master, and on which the disciples lay so much stress, let us inquire what the true significations of or real expressions appropriate to this *human spirit* or *organized form*, which Swedenborg calls the *soul*; or to this *corporal spirit* denominated *animus*. This *soul* and this *spirit* will be found to be no other than organized matter, one of those *bodies* which is called the *germ*, and which are as much matter, both in the animal or vegetable reign, as the body, the branch, or the fruits they produce. It is easy then to conceive what Swedenborg means by *form* or *soul*, or by that *spirit* which has lungs, feet, and all the different parts of the human body. The soul is *organized matter*, and the spirit is *living matter*. Terms may be changed, but in fact nothing is to be found but matter, and a monster of hypocrisy, who, after the example of the soul, will reduce his God to matter also. To prove this assertion, let the following proposition be noticed—*God is life, because God is love—Love is his essence, wisdom his existence—The heat of the spiritual Sun is love, its light is wisdom.*[13] What a deal of twisting and turning to say, that God is no more than the heat and light of a *Sun* supposed to be *spiritual*; for if God is *love and wisdom*, and that this *love and wisdom* are only the *heat and light* of this Sun, is it not evident that God is nothing more than the heat and light of the Sun. When, therefore, the reader shall, in Swedenborg's works, meet with expressions such as these, *God is life, because God is love, and he alone is life*, he will naturally substitute *God is life because he is heat; he alone is life because life is only supported by heat*; and he will have Swedenborg's real meaning. This might still leave some idea of a spirituality, if this sun, whose light and heat are God, was really spiritual; but for the solution of this question let us again appeal to Swedenborg, and we shall find that the *spiritual sun* is nothing more than *atmospheres, receptacles of fire and of light, the extremity of which produces the natural sun.* This also has its *atmospheres, which have produced by three degrees material substances.—These same atmospheres* of the natural sun, *decreasing in activity and in expansion, ultimately form masses whose parts are brought together by the pression of weighty substances that are fixed and at rest, and which we call matter.*[14] In clearer and more intelligible language, here will be the Deity and its generations according to Swedenborg. In the first place, a Sun, supposed spiritual, forms itself in the higher regions of the most ardent and luminous fire: the heat and light of this fire is God. This God, in this state, as well as this Sun, is nothing more than matter in a state of expansion, agitation, fire, and incandescence. As long as matter remains in these burning regions, Swedenborg does not chuse to call it matter, but the *spiritual sun*. Particles less subtle, or not so much heated, are carried to the extremity of these regions. There they cluster together, and the *natural sun* is formed. They are not matter as yet; but the grosser particles of this second sun unite together at the extremity of its atmospheres; there they clump together, cool, thicken, and form heavy masses, and at length acquire the appellation of matter. These particles are no longer God, or the spiritual sun, because they are no longer in a state of fire. What then is this God of Swedenborg, if it is not fire, or all matter in a state of fire, ceasing only to be God, when it ceases to be burning and luminous? And what abominable hypocrisy is this, where, under the cloak of thus changing the terms, the most downright materialism is preached?

Let my reader form what opinion he pleases as to the man who has broached such impious absurdities; he must never forget that there exist men always ready to adopt the most extravagant errors. Some because they are unable to distinguish a sophism, others because their impiety leads them to rejoice at every new blasphemy. Swedenborg has met with disciples of both these descriptions; and hence arose two distinct Sects, the one public, the other occult. The first comprehends those men so easily imposed upon by hypocrisy, and by their own credulity; they had called themselves Christians and adored Jesus Christ; but when Swedenborg had called his God *heat and light*; or his *spiritual sun* by the name of Jesus Christ, they still continued to think themselves the followers of Christ, though they were only the Sectators of Swedenborg's reveries. He evidently is the declared enemy of the principal mysteries of revelation, particularly of the Trinity, and of the Redemption of mankind by the Son of God dying on a cross for the salvation of sinners; he nevertheless talks a great deal about revelation; he assumes a devout tone, and with his *allegorical* and *spiritual sense* would appear rather to reform than to destroy all; and his followers do not perceive that with his allegorical sense he is only repeating the arguments of the Sophisters against revealed religion, in order to renew all the follies and impieties of the Persians, Magi, and Materialists.[15] They tell these poor people of his miraculous visions, of his prophesies, and of his discoursing with the angels and spirits; they are ignorant of the first principles of criticism, and believe in all these marvelous stories of Swedenborg, just as children do in the history of Raw-head-and-bloody bones told them by an old nurse.

The *new Jerusalem* in particular has gained over many proselytes to Swedenborg. I observe in one of the most famous abridgements of his works, that so early as the year 1788, *the single town of Manchester contained* SEVEN THOUSAND *of these illuminized Jerusalemites, and that there were about* TWENTY THOUSAND *in England*.[16] Many of these beatified beings may be very well intentioned; but with this new Jerusalem they daily expect that great revolution which is to sweep from the earth every prince and every king, that the God of Swedenborg may reign uncontroled over the whole globe.[17] And that revolution, which they saw bursting forth in France, was nothing more in their eyes than the fire that was to purify the earth to prepare the way for their Jerusalem. Should they still remain in the dark as to the menacing tendency of such doctrines for every state, let them learn it from the revolutionary Sophisters. They have publicly declared the hopes they have conceived of those *Sects that are springing up on all sides, particularly in the north of Europe* (Sweden) *and in America*. They even in plain terms express their expectations grounded on the *great number of Swedenborg's sectators and commentators*.[18]

And indeed if we do but cast our eyes on those that are most admired by the Sect, we shall find all the grand principles of the revolutionary Equality and Liberty, and those Jacobinical declamations against the Great, the Noble, and the Rich, and against all governments. We shall find, for example, that their *Religion*, or their new Jerusalem, *cannot be welcomed by the Great, because the Great are born transgressors of its first precept*. Neither can it be approved by the Nobles, because *when mortals aspired at nobility, they became proud and wicked*. Still less can it be admired by those who do not delight in the confusion of ranks, because *the pride of ranks produced inhumanity and even ferocity*; and even long before the revolution we shall see the adepts inculcating that grand principle of anarchy and revolution, that *the law is the expression of the general will*, and thus preparing the people to disregard every law that had been made heretofore, either by their sovereigns, their parliaments, or their senates;

encouraging them to sound the alarm, to overthrow them all, and to substitute the decrees and capricious conceits of the populace in their stead.

But all this revolutionary concatenation as yet only characterizes *the dupes* of the Sect of Illuminizing Jerusalemites. The profound adepts had taken refuge in the dens of the *Rosicrucian masonry*. Those were their natural asylums, the greater part of their tenets perfectly coinciding with those of the ancient Rosicrucians. After the example of their Doctors, Swedenborg tells us, that his doctrines are all of the highest antiquity, and similar to those of the Egyptians, the Magi, and the Greeks; he even asserts them to be anterior to the deluge. His new Jerusalem has also its JEHOVA, its *lost word*, that has been at length revealed to Swedenborg. Should any person be tempted to seek it elsewhere, he must go in quest of it among those clans where Christianity and political laws are not known.[19] Swedenborg tells us that it might be found in the north of China and in Great Tartary, that is to say, among that species of men who have preserved the most of that Equality, Liberty, and Independence, which the *learned* Jacobins pretend to have been anterior to civil society, and which most certainly is incompatible with it. Here then it appears, that Swedenborg's views coincide with those of the occult lodges, aiming at the overthrow of every religious and civil law, and at the downfall of every throne. His God *heat* and *light*, his God fire and spiritual sun, his twofold world and twofold man, are only modifications of the God light and the twofold principles of Manes. The Rosicrucians must then have found in Swedenborg's systems what they so much admired in the Manichæans. Their Magic, Evocations, *Eons*, Cabal, &c. were to be traced in the male and female spirits. In short, what numberless adepts must not this *new Jerusalem*, or revolution, carrying man back to primitive Equality and Liberty, have found in the occult Lodges? It was there indeed that Swedenborg's mysteries become connected with those of the ancient Brethren. These new or compound adepts styled themselves *Illuminees*. Notwithstanding the Atheism and Materialism of their master, they, after his example, perpetually talked of God and of spirits; they even affected to speak much of God, and people were persuaded that they believed in a Deity; hence they received the denomination of *Theosophical Illuminees*. Like the writings of their founder, their history is a mere labyrinth of impiety and imposture. It will suffice for our readers, at this period, to know that their head quarters was at Avignon;[20] that they had a famous lodge at Lyons; that they were spreading chiefly in Sweden, and were making progress in Germany. Their mysteries at that time had mingled with those of the Martinists; or it might be more correct to say, that the Martinists were only a reform of the Swedenborgians; and in France the appellations of Illuminee and Martinist were synonymous. In Germany they began to distinguish themselves under the names of *Philaletes* and *Benevolent Knights*. But whatever may have been their assumed names, they most certainly of all the modern Masons were the nearest of kin to Weishaupt. Systems and means may have differed sufficiently to excite jealousies; but on both sides we find the same determined wish for a revolution as antisocial as it was antireligious.

They were equally ardent in their desire of multiplying their adepts by a general intrusion into the Masonic Lodges. Both Sects had their deputies at Wilhemsbaden, and I will describe their mutual contests and successes in the following Chapter.

Note to CHAP. IV. *vide* Page 118 [p. 630, Ed.]

I think it incumbent on me in this place to mention the observations which I have heard and the strictures that I have received from divers Masons on what has been said of their degrees in the second Volume of these Memoirs. According to some of the Brethren, *I have said a great deal too much*; according to others, *I have not said enough*. The reader will easily conceive, that the former consists of those Brethren in whose favour an exception has been made, as too honest and upright to be admitted to the higher mysteries; and that the latter are men who, after having been admitted into the occult Lodges, blush to think that they could ever have deserved such an admission. Both are entitled to my thanks; I also owe them an answer; more particularly those German observers, who have been kind enough to send me some very important discussions on Masonry, and whose learning can only be equalled by their politeness. They are persons of too accurate understandings not to perceive that their negative testimony must naturally vanish before the positive evidence of those who confess the whole. A very ancient Mason, speaking of a particular Lodge of which he had been a member, told me, "He was perfectly aware, that several Masons, respectable for the purity both of their religious and political principles, and of their general conduct, had often attended a certain Lodge; but that *he also knew what precautions were taken when they were present*; and farther he could assert, that the generality of the Brethren belonging to that Lodge had been the most ardent promoters of the Revolution. Some of them had held high stations in it, and one of them had become minister." These *precautions taken* are more than a sufficient answer to those who have not seen any thing improper, though admitted to the Lodges.

In the second place, my German observers, though they wish to justify the institution and views of Free-masonry, candidly confess, *that Masonry has been corrupted for more than these three hundred years past*; and this is more than sufficient to prove the intrigues to which it has been subservient.

The principal objection made by these gentlemen is, that I have confounded Free-masonry, which has but three degrees, with the new and ancient Rosicrucians, and other degrees of modern creation. My answer is, that if ALL *Masons* are not *Rosicrucians*, ALL *Rosicrucians* are *Masons*; that I have made the proper exceptions for the first three degrees; but that will not hinder these first degrees from being, as they really have been for this long time, a noviciate for the Rosicrucian degrees. I will not dispute upon terms; let any person give me a name by which I may call this body of *Apprentices, Fellow-crafts, Masters, and Rosicrucians*, and I will with pleasure admit it; but till that be done I must speak such a language as my readers can understand. In short, I know that Masonry formerly existed without Rosicrucians; but I should be glad to see it proved, that those occult mysteries now removed to the Rosicrucian degrees did not belong to the first three degrees. I think I could prove that they did; and the inference would be, that Masonry at no time could have been free from those dangerous mysteries or real plots. At present it suffices for my object, to have proved what the Masonry of the present day is; and that it most certainly demonstrated by the very nature and the authentic documents of its higher degrees. To the proofs already adduced I am now enabled to add (if I chose it) memorials, letters, and formal declarations of repenting Masons, certainly not men whose testimony could be questioned. One of these is a worthy magistrate, who, admitted a Free-mason about the

HISTORICAL PART 641

year 1761, had passed a great part of his life in the dark recesses of Masonry. The other is a military man, at present as zealous for his religion as he formerly was for the mysteries of Masonry. The first declares, that what I have said of Masonry is true, but that I have not said *all*. The latter writes me word, that I have rather *softened* than exaggerated the occult degrees. In fact, the former gives me a clearer insight into the three *Rosicrucian* degrees; the first is entirely *Christian*; the second is denominated the *Founders*, or the *Cabal*; the third is that of the *Natural Religion*. The particular object of this third degree was, 1st, to avenge the Templars, 2dly, to seize on the island of Malta, and to make it *the 1st seat of natural religion*. He told me indeed things scarcely to be credited. For example, and these are his words, "That about the end of the year 1773, or in the course of 1774, the Lodge of which he was Master received a letter from the *Grand Orient*, purporting to be a copy of a letter which it had received from the King of Prussia. It was only to be communicated to the *Knights of Palestine, the Knights Kadosh,* and the *Scotch Directory*. This letter was transmitted to us by the *corresponding Lodge*; and though it had already been read in several Lodges, it only contained three signatures. It exhorted us, *in order to fulfil the oath we had taken*, to sign an obligation to march at the first requisition, and to contribute both by our *persons and our moral and physical powers*, to the conquest of the island of Malta, and of all the former possessions situated in the two hemispheres which had formerly belonged to the *ancestors of the Masonic Order. The object of our establishment at Malta was the possibility of converting that island into the seat of natural religion*." I objected to the author of this memorial, that if I wrote this account nobody would believe me. Let people believe, or not, as they please, he answered, I *both saw and received the letter*; my Lodge, however, refused to sign it.—I also say, let it be believed or not, I have the memorial and can attest, that the author is a man much and deservedly esteemed by all who know him.

The second Observer, who is also a repenting Mason, informs me, 1st, That in the hypothesis I had advanced on the origin of Masonry, I had only copied one of the Masonic Traditions, which taught that *Manes* was the real founder of Masonry. 2dly, That, "in the Lodges of the Knights *Kadosh,* after all the oaths, ceremonies, and trials, more or less terrible, wicked and impious, three Manikins are shown to the Candidate, representing *Clement V, Philippe Le Bel,* and the *Grand Master of Malta*, each attired in the attributes of their dignities. The unhappy fanatic is here to swear eternal hatred and death to these three proscribed persons, *entailing that hatred and death on their successors in their default*. He there strikes off the three heads, which, as in the degree of *Elect*, are real when they can be procured, or filled with blood if fictitious. He does this, crying out *vengeance, vengeance! &c.*" It is evident that I had softened the barbarity of this degree, for I had spoken but of one head to be struck off, when in reality there are three. I am not at liberty to name these two Memorialists; but two other witnesses I may name. The first is the Count de Gilliers, who living on intimate terms with great and profound Masons, had so well laughed them out of their secrets, that he gained admission into the Lodges without undergoing any trials; and he makes no difficulty in saying, that he has been an eye-witness to three-fourths of what I have said. The other, the Count D'Orfeuille, gives me leave to say, that though he was for a long time the Master of a Lodge, he can observe but slight differences between the Rosicrucian degrees which he has given and seen taken, and those which I have described.

I am at present in possession of twenty original Masonic degrees; and of four accounts of the *Rosicrucian* degrees, two in manuscript and two printed. The first was sent me from Germany, the second from America, the third was printed in France, and the fourth in England. They differ considerably from each other; but all of them coincide in about fifteen lines, precisely the most impious, those which contain the Masonic explanation of INRI. The account which I followed in my second volume was that published by the *Abbé Le Franc* in his *Voile Levé,* and his *Conjuration découverte*. Several Masons had informed me, that he had accurately delineated the proceedings of the Lodges; but I am now able to say whence he had procured those Masonic degrees whose ceremonies he had so well described; and I learned in the following manner: One of those respectable Ecclesiastics who have found a retreat in the generosity of the English nation from the persecutions of his countrymen, and who to the greatest simplicity of manners joins the knowledge and practice of his duties, Mr. De La Haye, Curate of Fié in the diocese of Mans, hearing that I was writing on Free-masonry, was kind enough, before he had seen my work, to send me some Memoirs that he had written on the same subject. When he came to ask me my opinion on them, I told him, "that, allowing for difference of style, his work had long since been printed, and the Jacobins in return had massacred the Author at the Carmes on the famous second of September." I then showed him the Abbé Le Franc's work, who had added but little to his, and both had fallen into the same error in attributing the origin of Masonry to Socinus. This worthy ecclesiastic answered me, "That he had been perfectly unacquainted with the existence of the Abbé Le Franc's work, but that he could easily account for its coincidence with his. I had, said he, several Free-masons in my parish. In my neighbourhood in particular was that unfortunate Fessier, a famous Brother of the Lodge at Alençon, since become such a terrible Jacobin, and the intruded Bishop of Séez. Several of these Masons renounced their errors; and, as a proof of their total renunciation of the Lodges, they gave me up all their papers and Masonic degrees. I had made a digest of these degrees. Mr. Le Franc, who was at that period in our diocese, pressed me to publish them; but I did not dare do that, for fear of the Masons, and I rather chose to give a copy of the whole to Mr. Le Franc, requesting him to use it as he thought fit. Mr. Le Franc went to Paris; the Revolution took place; and he doubtless thought it would be useful to publish the work I had given him, having first improved it by the polish of his style; and he certainly has done it better than I could. If his work has done any good, I am happy that he published it; but I am very sorry to reflect that it caused his death."—This latter sentiment, and the fear lest I should suspect the Abbé Le Franc of a breach of confidence, seemed solely to occupy this worthy man's mind. I could not help praising M. Le Franc for having had more courage in publishing the work than he had had; and he had besides given it the style of a Man of Letters. The point, however, most interesting for our object is, to find in this anecdote a new proof of the authenticity of the degrees published by the Abbé Le Franc, which I had quoted with so much confidence. The testimony of repenting Masons is far more to be relied on than the assertions of those who continue to be dupes or persist in their errors.—I address this note to those readers who may still entertain any doubt of the authenticity of the degrees as I have published them. I also declare to the adepts, that nothing would give me greater satisfaction than to see an answer founded, not on nonsense and scurrilous abuse, but on good reasoning. I am perfectly aware, that a very excellent work on Masonry might be made. Their Letters and my Answers, with other materials that I have by me, may, perhaps, at some future time, furnish the subject for such a work.

1. Chap. 15.
2. See Der auf gezogene vorhang der Frey Maurery, P. 302.
3. I do not see that any of his adepts have mentioned this illness; but indeed I am not suprised at it. I quote it on the authority of a Physician, who learned it from several other Physicians of London.
4. See the Preface to the Abridgement of Swedenborg's Works.
5. Swedenborg on the celestial Jerusalem—of the spiritual world—of the English—of the Dutch, &c.—Art. Heaven.

HISTORICAL PART 643

6. See Mr. Rollig's letter in the *Monat Schrifft* of Berlin, January, 1788. When the disciples of Swedenborg saw Mr. Rollig's letter appear, they gave a new turn to the story. It was no longer the Queen questioning Swedenborg about the letter; she simply asked, *Whether he had seen her brother?* Swedenborg is said at the end of a week to return to the Queen, and tell her things that she believed herself to be alone conversant with, after the decease of the Prince. This contrivance gives a whole week in place of a day to prepare the trick. I now learn a third; according to Dr. Mainauduc, the letter was scarcely written when Swedenborg, without even seeing it, divines the object and dictates the answer before hand. When this scheme is exploded, it is to be hoped that the brethren will invent another.
7. Preface to the Abridgement of Swedenborg's Works—the Edition of them by Pernetti—Essay on the Illuminees, written by Mirabeau, Note 8.
8. Every thing that is said here of this system is extracted either from the Works of Swedenborg, which I have in my possession, such as his *Doctrine of the New Jerusalem*, his *Spiritual World*, his *Apocalypse Revealed*; or from divers abridgements of his Works in French and English, made by his disciples.
9. Extract from the New Jerusalem and from the Arcana, *Art.* INFLUENCE, No. 277.
10. See Abridgment of Swedenborg, *Art.* REDEMPTION.
11. Ibid.
12. Dialogues on the nature, the object, and evidence of Swedenborg's theological writings, London 1790, Page 24 and 25.—Also the Animal Reign, and the Oeconomy of the Animal Reign, by Swedenborg.
13. See the Abridgement of Swedenborg, *Art.* GOD.
14. Ibid. *Art.* CREATION.
15. Some readers, I know, will be surprised to see me charge with materialism a man who talks so much of the spirit, soul, God, and religion. But I must request them to weigh the proofs adduced before they decide against me. Had I been writing another sort of work I might have prolonged the discussion; but I think I have said sufficient to prove, that Swedenborg never acknowledged any other spirit but matter, or the elementary fire.
16. Ibid. Preface in a note, Page lxviii.
17. See his Apocalypse Revealed.
18. Preface to the *Physical Observations*, an. 1790, by La Metherie.
19. Swedenborg's expressions are, De hoc *verbo* vetusto quod ante verbum Israeliticum in Asia fuerat, referre meretur hoc novum; quod ibi adhuc reservatum sit, apud populos qui in Magna Tartaria habitant. Locutus sum cum spiritibus et angelis qui in mundo spirituali inde erant, qui dixerunt quod possideant verbum, et quod id ab antiquis temporibus possederint—Quærite de eo in China et forte invenietis illud apud Tartaros. *Apocalipsis Revelata, Chap.* I. *No.* II.) Is not this a continuation of that same plan, always holding out nations plunged in the most savage ignorance, and a perpetual prey to anarchy, Equality and Liberty, as the models to which we ought to look up?
20. In a work under the title of *The Red Lodge discovered to Sovereigns*, I read, that "the Rite of the Theosophical Illuminees appears to have taken its origin at Edinburgh, *where the Red Lodge* was formed by a scission from the *Blue Lodge*; that this Red Lodge (of the Theosophical Illuminees) had immediately established a subordinate Lodge at Avignon." (*page* 9 *and* 10).—I should have been very glad to have found proof of this

origin, as at present it rests on the bare assertion of the author. Be that as it may, however, the Illuminees of Avignon are sufficiently well known in France. Ever since the year 1783, that Lodge has been looked upon as the parent stock of all those that have since spread over France with their abominable mysteries.

And here I think it right to say, that this *Red Lodge discovered to Sovereigns* is by no means the work that I mentioned in my second volume under the title of *Depositions made by Kleiner*. The extracts made from this latter work, and which are in my possession, give me reason to think, that it contains details of a very different nature. The author there speaks as an eye-witness; and, among other things, gives the tradition current in his Lodge, with respect to the lessons that Weishaupt is supposed to have received from a certain Kölmer. These depositions would be a valuable document; and it is perhaps on that very account that the Illuminees have destroyed it. At least I am obliged to say, that, notwithstanding the numerous inquiries which I have made, I have not been able to procure it.

CHAP. V.

*Knigge's Intrigues and Successes at the Congress.—
Official Reports of the Superiors of the Order.—
Multitude of Masons illuminized at this Period.*

OF all the general assemblies that had been held by the Masons for these last twenty years, whether at Brunswick, Wisbaden, or in any other town in Germany, none could be compared with that of Wilhemsbaden, either for the number of the deputies or the variety of Sects of which it was composed. One might say, that all the incoherent elements of Masonry had been thrust into one den. Knigge informs us, that he had had the honour of being deputed by his ancient brethren; that he might have taken his seat and been present at the deliberations; but, foreseeing the issue of it, he thought he could more usefully serve the cause of his new Illuminism by directing the part that *Minos*-Dittfurt was to act in the interior of the Meeting, while he himself would hover around and observe the exterior. His first plan of attack was to gain the *Templar Masons of the Strict Observance*, with whose secrets he was well acquainted, and he had frequently attended their Lodges, that he might through their means ensure a majority of votes. Had he succeeded in this plan, Weishaupt's code would have been decreed at this general congress, and would have become at once the standard law for millions of Masons scattered throughout the globe, who would thus have been illuminized and ready to sally forth from their lurking places at the Command of their Antisocial Chief.

When describing this plan of attack, Knigge takes care to inform his readers why he abandoned it:—"I own (says he) that I always retained a certain predilection for my former brethren of the *Strict Observance*; I had already illuminized so great a number, that I was in hopes of uniting their system with ours. My intention most certainly could never be to deliver up to the Congress all our papers, and thus to put ourselves at the mercy of the deputies. I had not received such powers from those who sent me. *And beside, we, who did not seek after that power that gives greatness, rank, or riches; we, who did not seek to reign in splendour and in the eyes of the public; we, in short, whose constitution was to act in silence and with secrecy;* how could we go and make ourselves dependent on an Order so destitute of unity in its systems.

"I made, however, an offer of my services; I made it both in writing and by word of mouth; and all the answer I received was, that I might send or present my papers to the congress, and that they would judge of those parts that were to be approved or rejected."[1]

Stung to the quick at such contempt, Knigge conceived himself absolved from all his oaths, and from every duty toward his ancient brethren. Abandoning all hopes of conquering the whole body, *he resolved to attack them one by one, and then to gain over the whole body Lodge by Lodge.* He agreed with the assessor *Minos* to direct their whole attention in future towards two points; the first, to hinder the assembly from passing any resolutions detrimental to the interests of their Illuminism; the other, to facilitate its intrusion into the Lodges, and that with so much art that no degree, nor any Grand Master, could be an obstacle to the domination of the Bavarian Brethren; and that means should be found sooner or later to unite the code of the Illuminees with that of the Masons.—Such was the object of the mission entrusted by Knigge to his co-adept *Minos,* whom he charged to get the following resolutions passed: "1st. A sort of union of all the Masonic systems in the first three degrees, so that a Mason admitted to these three degrees should be acknowledged as a true brother of every Lodge of whatever class or system it might be.—2dly, That in common Masonry no mention should ever be made of the higher degrees or of the unknown Superiors.—3dly, That all transmitting of money to the Masonic Superiors should be forbidden.—4thly, That a new code should be prepared for the brethren.—5thly, That every Lodge should choose its own Superiors and Directory, that is to say, should declare to which Grand Lodge they chose theirs should be subject."[2]

While *Minos* was thus following his instructions within, Knigge was without acting the part of Insinuator and Scrutator. "I sought to know (says he in the same report to the Areopagites) and I knew what turn things were taking in the assembly. I knew all the different systems that different parties wished to make predominate; I then entered into a correspondence, which I still continue, with the Chiefs of Zinnendorf's party.[3] I also sounded the Chiefs of other parties by various means. Several came of themselves and disclosed themselves to me, entrusting me with all their secrets because they knew that I was solely actuated by a wish for the general good, and not by personal considerations. In short, some of the deputies learned (*I know not now*) that our Illuminism was in existence. They *almost all* came to me to entreat me to admit them;—I thought it proper to exact the *reversal letters* (of our candidates) from them, commanding them to keep absolute silence on the subject; but I took care not to entrust them with the least part of our secrets. I only spoke to them of our mysteries in general terms, during the whole time that the congress continued."[4]

This method of proceeding, and the art with which he insinuated that Masonry, undoubtedly, was in possession of mysteries of the highest importance; but that the profound Masons, who were in possession of such mysteries, were not to be met with at the congress, greatly augmented the curiosity and stimulated the ardour of the deputies for his Illuminism. The care with which he took the *reversal letters,* the character of candidate, the promise he exacted at the same time of all the deputies not to second any proposition detrimental to the new brotherhood, were sufficient to ensure him against any resolutions that might be entered into by the meeting. Beside, the dispositions he observed in these deputies were sufficient to strengthen his hopes. "I owe them the justice to say," he continues in his report, "that I found *the greatest part of them in the best dispositions*; that if their conduct was not effective it was for want of having been nurtured in a better school[5].... It was with pleasure I observed, that if the *excellent intentions* that had brought these men together *from all corners of Masonry*, were not more efficacious, it was because they could not agree on principles. *Most of them* appeared to be ready to follow any system that they judged conducive to give to their Order that utility and activity that was the object of all their wishes."[6]

Whatever may be the partiality of the historian for the Masonic Brotherhood, it will be impossible for him to invalidate this terrible evidence of Knigge against their chosen and privileged members; against those whom the Order judged most worthy of representing it in solemn congress. No man can misconceive the signification of *best dispostions* or of *excellent intentions* in the mouth of *Philo*-Knigge. They evidently demonstrate men who needed only to be made acquainted with the means of working a revolution of impiety and anarchy, to undertake it. This vast Brotherhood of Masons must, at this period at least, have been sorely affected in its higher mysteries. It was prepared for conspirators even of Weishaupt's stamp.

Certain of success, Knigge seems to have left the assembly to its disorderly deliberations; and, notwithstanding the imprudence with which he taxes *Minos*, the latter succeeded in obtaining the decree of the principal particulars agreed between them. It was forbidden that any brethren should call each other Heretics (*Verketzern*). It was decided that the first three degrees alone should be looked upon as essential to Masonry. Commissaries were named to digest certain regulations, the plan of which had been given by the assembly, as well as of a general code. The choice of the higher degrees and of systems was left to the decisions of each Lodge. The rest of the deliberations were as boisterous as might be expected from the variety of Sects. I have before me a manuscript acount of this assembly written by a very learned Mason, and it contains nearly as much lamentation as it does instruction. Among other things I find, that the Duke Ferdinand of Brunswick was proclaimed Grand Master of all Masonry and that few members recognized him as such. Again I see, that it was wished to abrogate the system of the *Templar Masons*, whose abominations and secrets had been exposed by some false brother in a work called *The Stone of Scandal*, but that few Lodges would obey the abrogation. Moreover, an attempt was made to quash all Sects and Schisms; but they neither could be overpowered, and confusion continued to prevail with redoubled force.

Let us however observe, that if any system can be said to have gained a preponderance it was that of the *Philaletes*, a sort of spurious offspring of Swedenborg. The most famous Illuminees of that set, *Wilhermoz, St. Martin*, and *La Chappe de la Henriere*, had made an attempt to connect themselves with the Hero of Crevelt and Minden; it is even asserted, that he was misled by their appellation of *Philaletes* and of *Benevolent Knights*. Strong, however, in his protection, neither they nor their agents spared any pains to carry the day at Wilhemsbaden; they were well supported, and victory must have infallibly declared in their favor had not Knigge already gained over so many of the deputies. Hence the result of this too famous congress was to have been the delivery over of all the Masonic Lodges, and, with them, of all the governments of Europe, to two Sects of Illuminees, the most impious and the most disastrous in their views, and most unrelenting in their zeal for the overthrow of every religion and of every government whatever.

I know not into which of these two Sects the Count de Virieux had been initiated; but either might have suggested the manner in which he described the result of this Masonic Congress. On his return to Paris, being complimented by the Count de Gilliers on the sublime secrets he had been in quest of at Wilhemsbaden, and pressed a little by the sarcastic style with which the Count was wont to jeer the Brotherhood, he at length answered, "I will not tell you the secrets I bring but what I think I may tell you is, that it is all much more serious than you think. *The fact is, that a conspiracy is now contriving, and that with so much art and of so profound a nature, that it will be very difficult for Religion and Nations not to sink under it.*" Happily for Mr. de Virieux, said Mr. de Gilliers when he told me this anecdote, the Count had a great fund of probity and uprightness. What he had learned on his mission so disgusted him with the mysteries, that he abandoned them and became a very religious man. It was to this event that his great zeal against the Jacobins may be attributed.

Unfortunately for all nations, these plots did not inspire the other Masonic Deputies with a similar horror. The Congress being terminated, *Philo-Knigge* hastened to reap the benefit of his intrigues; and his harvest was much more plentiful than he expected. On the breaking up of the assembly, the deputies flocked to him to beg admission to the mysteries. Such candidates needed no long noviciate, or tedious trials in the minerval schools; they were to be conducted quickly to the mysteries; and Knigge admitted them to the degrees of Epopt and Regent, *which they all received* (he tells us) *with enthusiasm*.[7] "All of them *were enraptured* with our degrees of Epopt and of Regent; all were enchanted with these *master-pieces*; for so they styled these degrees. Two only made some slight observations on certain expressions, that may be easily changed according to local circumstances, and particularly in Catholic countries."[8]

Were it not that all honest Masons would sink under grief and astonishment, I should conjure them to weigh for a moment these words, *all were enraptured, all received them with enthusiasm*; all Elect, Rosicrucians, Templars, Brethren of Zinnendorf, Brethren of St. John, Knights of the Sun, Knights Kadosh, Perfect Philosopherrs; all hearken, and receive with enthusiasm those oracles of the Hierophant which cast such light on their antique mysteries, and, expouding the meaning of their *Hiram*, their *Mac Benac*, and their *Polished*

Stone, show that they contain nothing more than primitive Equality and Liberty, as well as that Morality, which entirely consist in the art of annihilating princes, governments, religion and property! When these Deputies shall return to their *Orients*, and spread themselves throughout the Masonic Directories and Provinces, will not these original plots be intruded on your Lodges under the pretence of mysteries? Fly then such dens of sedition; and learn once for all, that those men in whom you place such confidence, are profound conspirators abusing your confidence, just as they will that of princes at a future day. View then this pretended Brotherhood as a hoard of conspirators, who have long waited only for the baleful genius of a Weishaupt to launch out into all the crimes of revolution.

From the period when these Masonic Deputies were illuminized, the Bavarian Sect assumed a menacing aspect; and its progress is so rapid, that the universe will soon be overrun with Conspirators. The center of action may be said to have been at Frankfort, where Knigge resided, and he computes the number of persons he had illuminized, and nearly all of whom were Masons, at five hundred.[9] There is scarcely a town in his neighbourhood, but has its Epopts and Minerval Schools; Franconia, Swabia, the Circles of the Higher and Lower Rhine, Westphalia, &c. swarm with them.

The towns of Vienna and Berlin almost immediately showed that Austria and Prussia were falling a prey to Illuminism. Tyrol had been already infected, and the same apostle had proceeded to carry it into Italy. In the north adepts were making their attacks on the Lodges of Bruxelles and of Holland, while others were preparing *to introduce Weishaupt's mysteries into England*. In Livonia they had gained footing; and treaties were making in Poland, to throw the whole power of the Confederations into the hands of the Illuminees. If the day of France was not yet come, it was because they entertained deeper views on her; but the day was to come, and all Europe shall now know why it had been deferred.

It would be of little avail for me to have produced Weishaupt's code, were I not also to produce demonstrative evidence of its progress and continuation. History will demand that I prove the existence of this Sect, its mysteries, and conspiracies, ranging from the north to the south and from the east to the west, enlisting under its banners that multitude of hands which it needed to work revolutions. To effectuate this, I shall again appeal to their own annals; they are mutilated, it is true; but notwithstanding that, they are menacing, and they are demonstrative.

In the very year after the congress of Wilhemsbaden we find five provinces completely organized according to the Laws of the modern *Spartacus*, under the general direction of *Philo*-Knigge, and in full correspondence with the illuminizing Areopagites.[10] Even during the time of the congress we find in the *Original Writings* not only simple letters on the progress made by a few candidates, but official reports, and statements made by the Provincials of their provinces, relating to the progress of their novices, of their initiated, and of their emissaries. Let us cast our eyes on these documents, for none can be better authenticated. Perhaps I might have done well to have translated the whole of them; but though I abridge them, they will still retain the whole force of evidence.

The first of these reports is from *Mahomet*.[11] This Provincial of a new species was the Baron SCHROECKENSTEIN, the same whom Weishaupt so early as the first year of his Illuminism, enlisted at Aichstadt, and whom he classed among those foolish Aristocrats who were *to swallow the bait*. The Baron so completely swallowed the bait that in six years we find him one of the Chiefs of the Conspiracy. The Province he presided over in the Illuminized Geography was denominated *Pannonia*, comprehending the districts of *Morea* and *Latium*, which comprise the Lodges of *Olympia, Damietta, Tibur, Hispalis, Damascus, Sichem, Nicomedia,* and *Surentum*. I find that his residence is at Aichstadt; and he informs the Areopagites, that he has given the name of *Surentum* to the new colony of Mompelgard, which he looks upon as belonging to the Duchy of Wurtenberg, and therefore should be comprised within the district of *Latium*. I also find that *Nicomedia* is Augsbourg; hence I conclude, that the Lodges under the inspection of this adept were so many conquests made by Illuminism, partly in Bavaria, and partly in Swabia.

The report contains strong proofs of this Provincial's zeal for the propagation of the Order. We may observe him threatening two adepts with their immediate dismission unless they show more activity, and promoting two others because they excelled in the arts of insinuation. As a proof of the care with which he describes his inferiors, and of the precautions he takes according to their characters, let the reader peruse the account he gives of the Brotherhood at *Olympia*, which he has just been inspecting: "I have learned," he writes, "to know the Brother *Zeno*. I did not find him to be a *thinker*, and much less a *scrutator*....He does not like to meddle with things that are above the human understanding; and he contents himself with the degree of Minerval, but *promises to enlist us some good novices....Crantor* has more ardor; I initiated him myself into the Minerval degree. You may easily conceive how much he is displeased with all his science, and how much his wit disconcerts him, when I tell you that he is furious at his father for having had him taught to write.... *Speusippus* was ill; the others though young are full of ardor....The colony is weak as yet.... *Be guarded in yours letters to Zeno. He told me, that he would not lodge in the same house with a man who doubted of the immortality of the Soul*.... All these Brethren hold their regular meetings, but don't dare enlist their novices under the name of Masonry. *They prefer doing it under the pretence of a Literary Society*, and I made no difficulty in permitting them to continue their practice."

In that town of *Latium*, or of the Duchy of Wurtemberg, which *Mahomet* calls *Damietta*, there is an academy and a college; and one of the professors is the adept *Phirro*, whose *honesty* and *activity* could not be sufficiently praised by the Provincial. The following institution may serve as a specimen of this man's honesty: "By means of this Brother, says *Mahomet*, the whole academy of this town is become a real nursery for us (*eine pflanz schule für uns*). Pythagoras-

DREXL is the unknown superior of *this assembly, which is entirely composed of young pupils of noble birth*. He has under him an apparent superior to conduct and form them, *chosen from among the young men*. No *reversal letters* are required of them; they are only flattered with the hopes (should they prove faithful to the lessons instilled into them) of *being hereafter admitted into an Order composed of the best men."*

Lest such lessons should be lost to those who were educated at Court, the adept *Epimenides*-FALK, aulic counsellor and burgo-master of Hanover, has taken care to illuminize the sub preceptor of a young Prince designed by the initials T. H.... After having told all this news to the Areopagites, *Mahomet* at length informs them, that *Machiavel*, one of his emissaries, has sent in a list of the honest men with whom he has made acquaintance in Switzerland; and that things would take a good turn there, provided *Philo*-Knigge would stimulate a little the zeal of the Helvetian apostle.

The next official report is from *Minos*-DITTFURT the Assessor. This man was also a Baron. As a recompense for the pains he had taken at Wilhemsbaden, Knigge had made him the Provincial or Superior of Veteravia, and probably of part of Westphalia. His command comprised two districts, *Dacia* and *Lydia*. Overburdened with business, and more attentive to that of Illuminism than to the affairs of the Empire, he gives but a brief account of the present. He names about a dozen Brethren, among whom are four novices. He distinguishes the Brother *Bentharith* in particular, whom he means to entrust with the establishment of a Minerval school at *Bensabè*.—Meanwhile, till he can report further progress, he proposes his plan for *an illuminized sisterhood*, which he promises to place under the direction of another Baron, who, like himself, is an Assessor at the Imperial Chamber. About the same time (*Merdemeh* 1152, August 1782), Knigge's report states, that *Minos* was in correspondence with Doctor Stark, in hopes of making a conquest of the Landgrave of Hesse Darmstadt by means of his grand Almoner. The Illuminizing Assessor does not report the progress of this negociation; but Knigge appears to have foreseen the success it would have, when he writes to the Areopagites, "I am much pleased to see that Brother *Minos* has entered into a correspondence with Doctor Stark; it will teach him, that to be able to treat with a man of wit one must have some one's self." Though it seems that Knigge did not allow any great share to this Provincial, yet he founded great hopes on his services, especially if *his too great zeal could be repressed*.

The third report is from the adept *Epictectus*-MIEG, Provincial of Albania, the same Brother whom we shall find mentioned by Knigge as founding the Lodge at Manheim surnamed *Surinam*, and at Frankenthal that called *Parmaribo*, within the prefecture of *Paphlagonia*, or of the Palatinate. It would seem, that at that period *Albania* had passed under the inspection of some other Provincial: This *Epictetus*-Mieg was a counsellor and Protestant Minister of Heidelberg, his habitual residence, and had been instructed in the arts of Insinuator by Weishaupt himself.

The reader may judge of this man's merits from the following eulogium that Weishaupt makes on him when writing to *Celsus*: "Do not forget, when at Munich, to do every thing in your power for our *Epictetus*. He is nearly the best of the adepts. He has a little too much ardor, but in all other points he is incomparable. He has already *made a conquest for the Order of nearly the whole Palatinate*. Not a country town but contains one or two adepts at least."[12] This letter being of the same year as the report, it would be useless to particularize. Some, however, of the Brethren mentioned by *Epictetus* deserve our attention: such, for example, as a certain Brother described by the initials B. E. under the direction of *Diodorus*, who in a Catholic University and of the Catholic Religion himself until that period, thought he could not give a better proof of his zeal for Illuminism, than by attempting to defend a Protestant thesis, and that under a pretence that denotes neither a Catholic nor a Protestant, but a man who views Religion only as a political invention.—He gives for reason, that the *College of the Counts of Westphalia must be a Protestant College*.—Next the Brother *Erastus*, of the same degree, who asks advice as to the best means to succeed *in illuminizing the Preceptor of the Prince of Dupont's son*, and by that means to educate the young Prince according to the views of the Order. And lastly the Brother *Pic de la Mirandole*, or Brunner, a Priest at Tiefenback, in the bishopric of Spire. "This man," says the Provincial, "is as yet a novice, but full of zeal for the Order. The tenth of September he defended his Thesis in spite of the Jesuits. In his *Quibus Licet he begs the Order to take precautions lest the fortress of Philisbourgh*, which the Austrians had abandoned, *should fall into the hands of a bigoted officer, who was petitioning for the government of it*; and to have it given to another officer (more worthy of it, I suppose) who aspired to it."—This Illuminized Novice, who already pays so much attention to fortresses, will appear on the stage again with the Brethren of Mentz, conspiring and delivering up that town to the French Jacobins.

The fourth official report is made by the adept *Agis*-Kröber. He does not take the title of Provincial; he only acts for *Alberoni*-Bleubetreu, originally a Jew, and who afterward made himself a Christian to become Aulic Counsellor to the Prince of Neuwied, and a Provincial of the Illuminees. *Agis* was governor to the Count Stolberg's children, and the memoirs I have before me declare him to have been afterward charged with the education of the young Prince of Neuwied, to have gained the good graces of the Princess, sowing discord in that court, and destroying the internal happiness of that family; in short, he was known to all Germany by a name that could not reflect honour on his protectrix.—As news, he informs the Areopagites that the Baron de Witte, at Aix-la-Chapelle, is much more zealous than was expected; that he has undertaken to illuminize his Masonic Lodge there; and that from his letters they may hope to see that of Bruxelles share a similar fate.... The Brother *Agis* enquires whether they think it proper that he should enter into a correspondence with *those fools of the Hermetic Cabal*. Before he initiates them in the secrets of the Order, he wishes to present himself at their Lodges as one acquainted with theirs. He owns, that he is not sufficiently master of all their systems. He asks for some instruction, that he may perfect himself in them, lest he should be discovered by those Masons for whom he has a sovereign contempt, but with whose jargon it is necessary that he should be acquainted, to make a conquest of them for the Order. These instructions are the more necesssary, as a Brother of the district has just applied to him for leave to show some of his letters to the Venerable of the Masonic Lodge at *Iris*, to enable him to make but one draught of the whole Lodge, Venerable and all.

In the same report the Brother *Agis* recommends to the Areopagites the adept *Archelaus*-BARRES, heretofore a major in the French service, at present throwing himself on the protection of the Order to obtain a place in some court of Germany, and the Cross of Merit from that of France, with a brevet of *Major à la suite*: "I had taken it into my head (says he) that the Ambassador Ch...was one of ours; that he had great influence with....(the court or ministers), therefore I did not refuse our protection. If we succeed in this business, *the fame of our power will be greatly extended*. Scarcely a week passes without somebody coming to solicit our protection at the courts of Versailles, of Vienna, or of Berlin. It is enough to make one die of laughing. We take great care, however, not to dismiss those people without hopes; we only say, that we do not like to importune those courts every day."

A marginal note is found opposite to this article in Knigge's own handwriting, saying *Who the devil has put into their heads this fable of our omnipotence?* The man who wrote the question might also have written the answer; for we may observe him long before this period straining every nerve to give the Brethren a high opinion of the power of the Order, and even flattering himself, that through the exertions of his agents he had obtained for the adepts *honourable situations, livings, and dignities, which he distributed in the names of the unknown superiors; who were not even in existence at that time*; and when these superiors do exist, we see him acting precisely as the Brother *Agis* had done, procuring from an adept Count the place of *Chancellor Director*, with a salary of twelve hundred florins, sending the nomination to his candidate *Wundt, ecclesiastical counsellor at Heidelberg*; and to show the candidate the great power of the Brethren, informing him, *that the Order had got him named to this dignity*.[13]

The very article on which Knigge had made this note is followed by another, which will sufficiently demonstrate the credit they had acquired in certain courts, and the use they could turn it to for the propagation of their mysteries. "This week (continues *Agis*) we shall receive a Lutheran minister, who by *slight of hand has collected about nine thousand florins* for the community (the Lodge) of this place. *As soon as peace is made, he is* TO SET OFF FOR LONDON, *with a multitude of letters of recommendation*. The Pr——F——O. B., uncle to the reigning Duke, has promised to second him with all his might.[14] It is our intention also to employ him in that country for the Order. HE MUST SLILY ILLUMINIZE THE ENGLISH.... A large Dutch wig, a sallow and meagre complexion, large eyes widely opened, a fertile imagination, a perfect knowledge of men, acquired by roving about the world for the space of two years under the disguise of a beggar.... Do not you think that with such qualifications this man will do wonders?—During this winter we will drill him, as the Hernuti used to do their apostles."

The adept so well described by *Agis*-Kröber, and on whom he grounds his hopes of the *Illuminization of England*, is not mentioned even by his characteristic; but a manuscript marginal note informs me, that his real name was RÖNTGEN, a Dutch protestant of Petkam, in East Friesland.

The fifth report is mutilated, and is without the name of any Provincial. Such as it is, however, it forcibly evinces the progress of the Set during the last three months of 1782 in the Electorates of Cologn and of Treves, called *Picinum*. At this epoch the Provincial is much elated at the high repute Masonry has acquired in those parts since it has been illuminized. "Here (says he) a Mason was formerly a laughing-stock, whereas now a man who does not belong to a Lodge is pitied. Every body flocks to us; and the prophane thirst after our mysteries.—Every body comes to crave the protection of an Order that is so powerful."

A very unexpected proof of their power is to be found in their Archives; it is the disgrace and exile of the Abbé Beck, whom the Prince Clement of Saxony and Elector of Treves had till then favoured with his confidence. I had not the honour of being acquainted with this venerable ecclesiastic; but I remembered to have seen some of his friends at Paris, who augured ill from his disgrace. I little expected at that time to find his apology in so complete a style in the report made by the Provincial to his superiors: "The famous executioner of the Elector's conscience, the Abbé B. has at length received his dismission, and an order to leave the country. Ever since the Elector has had this *Jesuit*[15] in his service; he has been a declared enemy to Freemasonry, and generally speaking, to every thing that tends to enlighten mankind. Now that this Jesuit is out of the way, *we have the greatest hopes* of making a glorious harvest in Treves and the Electorate." How indignant must his Electoral Highness have been when he discovered in this official report the true origin of all those insinuations to which one of his most faithful servants had fallen a victim; and particularly when he observed the advantages that his real enemies, and enemies of all governments, promised themselves in consequence of an illusion originating, in all probability, entirely with themselves.

We shall here give another proof of the omnipotence that the Order was acquiring in the different courts of Germany. The Provincial, under the head of the Lodge of *Pinna*, that is to say Hachenburg, gives an account of the inauguration of Doctor Vogler, physician to the Count of Kirthenberg, and then continues, "Here the affairs of the Order prosper amazingly well; *the Count is entirely surrounded by Illuminees. His private secretary, his physician, his pastor, his counsellors, are all ours.—The Prince's favorites are our most zealous adepts; and we have taken our precautions for the future. Let the Order establish itself as well elsewhere, and the world is our's.*"

This wish of the illuminizing Provincial would soon have been accomplished, had the adepts been every where as zealous as those whom he mentions of the provinces of *Picinum* and *Dacia*. One adept in particular had made thirteen novices in three months; and it is not unworthy of remark, that eleven were already Free-masons, and two Lutheran ministers, who were *characterized* in the Order by the names of *Averroës* and *Theognis*. The first showed so much zeal, activity, and intelligence, and the principles of the Order appeared to have taken such deep root in his heart, that the superiors hastened his initiation into the higher degrees, that they might admit him to the council, and ease themselves of some part of their labours on him. The other, *Theognis*-FISCHER, became curate of Wölsbrück in Austria, near Lintz, by means of the intrigues of the adept *Rausanias*. In Knigge's report to the Areopagites, I find the following note on this adept:

"*Theognis*, at the time of his promotion to his curacy, received a letter from the bishop of K——, the principles of which appear to be copied from our code. The prelate mentions a secret project of reform, and begs *Theognis* not to show his letter to any body. The Brethren of this colony are firmly persuaded that the Bishop is one of our adepts; and to that circumstance they attribute his having given a benefice to *Theognis*; and in consequence of it they labour with redoubled zeal."

What can have induced the editor of the Original Writings to give only the initial letter of this Bishop's name? Have not the Evangelists named Judas Iscariot at full length? Why not then name the prelate HASLEIN, vice-president of the spiritual council at Munich, afterwards Lord Bishop of KHERSON for the church, and Brother *Philo of Byblos* for Weishaupt? With a little less respect for persons, would mistrust fall on those who deserve it, and who so little respect their own dignity; and the world would know the man who was foremost in the conspiracy against God, though he might wear a mitre.

Before I undertake to present a list to my reader, I will mention the last official reports recorded in the annals of the Sect. They are made by Knigge himself, and are dated *Thirmeh, Merdedmeh, Dimeh*, 1152, that is to say July and August, 1782, and the January following. We there find, that his mission at Wilhemsbaden did not hinder him from overlooking the provincial superiors, whose reports I have just stated. It was to him that their reports were first sent; he transmitted them to the Areopagites, after making such remarks as his zeal for the propagation of the Sect might suggest. What he particularly blames in his inferiors was, a want of method. That want of regularity in their proceedings appeared to him to impede their success, and to render it less certain than he could wish. And he writes to his senate, "I cannot sufficiently repeat it; when we shall have organized the whole body, when every province shall have its Provincial, and every Inspector shall have three Provincials under his inspection; when our National Directory shall be established at *Rome* (that is to say, Vienna); when our Areopagites shall be freed from all the tiresome detail (and by that means certain of remaining known) and shall only have to inspect the whole, to perfect the system, and to direct the propagation of it in other countries; when the Order can give proper help to the directing Brethren, then, and not before, shall we be able to do some thing."

Soon after these lessons, and under the head France, we read, "With respect to that country, I would not advise you to undertake any thing, until I shall have disposed of the multiplicity of business that overpowers me at present. I have even laid aside for the present my projects on Alsace and Lorraine." Meanwhile, till that day comes, Knigge takes a view of the reports returned to him by the Provincials and subjoins to the number of their Novices those whom he had made himself. But the grand object that absorbs all his attention is the means of consummating the intrusion into the Masonic Lodges, which is at once to enlist millions of men under the standard of his Areopage, and to effectuate his Illuminizing revolution.

At the period of this last report, that is, January 1783, this intrusion had made great progress; and it was to that circumstance that Weishaupt was indebted for the multitude of adepts who already had spread his conspiracy throughout Germany. Let the reader cast an eye on the map of Germany, and on the Lodges already Illuminized. It is true, that many towns are at present unintelligible, in consequence of the geographical nomenclature adopted by the Sect; but every one of these names denotes an Illuminized Lodge, a town where the conspirators have gained a hold; and hence we may observe, that scarcely a canton is to be found where this baleful Sect has not penetrated. Let us attend only to those towns that, in spire of all their precautions, have been discovered either by the writings or habitual residence of the great adepts; —what a formidable alliance have they already formed! The first of the Provincials immediately under the direction of Weishaupt has under him alone the Lodges of Munich, of Ratisbon, of Landsberg, of Burghausen, of Straubingen, and of Freysingen.—In the Circles of Franconia and Swabia, the Baron *Mahomet* presides, at least over those at Aichstadt, his habitual residence, at Bamberg, at Nuremberg, at Augsbourg, at Mompelgard, and over those of the Duchy of Wurtemberg.—In the Circles of the Upper Rhine and of the Palatinate of the Lower Rhine the Sect has established itself, at Deux-ponts, Manheim, Frankenthal, Heidelberg, Spire, Worms, Wetzlar, and Franckfort on the Mein.—The Electorates of Mayence, of Treves and Cologne, have, with their capitals, shared a similar fate.—In Westphalia, this distemper rages at Aix-La-Chapelle, at Neuwied and at Hachenburg.—In Higher and Lower Saxony, at Kiel, at Bremen, at Brunswick, at Hanover, at Gottinguen, at Gotha, at Jena.—The great adepts Nicolai and Leuchsering, establish Illuminism at Berlin, and the adept *Brutus* reports that the Minerval Schools are in as full activity at Vienna in Austria, as they were at Lintz. *Hannibal*, or Weishaupt's grand commissioner the Baron Bassus had established it at Inspruck and Botzen, and at many other towns in the Tyrol. From the bottom of his den at Ingolstadt, Weishaupt presides over his conspiring crew; and through their means he commands, as it were, Germany and its confines, and might be called its Emperor of Darkness. He has more towns in his conspiracy than the Chief of the Empire has in his dominions.

At this period a great revolution took place in the code of the Illuminees, which only contributed to augment the strength of the Sect, and which I hope the historian will not overlook, as it will furnish him with an answer to those who may repeat an objection that has often been made to me. "Weishaupt's Illuminism only began in Bavaria about the middle of the year 1776; the Sect chiefly attached itself to youth. It required a long noviciate, and many years for its Minerval schools to form the adepts and prepare them for the degrees where the conspiracy is entered upon. It must have required therefore generation after generation to form that multitude of conspirators whose marshalled cohorts rise triumphant at a time when Illuminism is still in its cradle."

This objection may have appeared forcible; but at the period where we now stand it solves itself. Knigge has answered it when he enumerates that multitude of Masons who have already attained the years of discretion, and did not stand in need of those long trials, and who, in the protestant countries particularly, disdained the Minerval schools *only the more to show their ardour to be admitted to the higher degrees* of the conspiracy.[16] Weishaupt soon understood the reason of this rapid progress; and it was on that account that he dispensed with the severity of the code and the trials of the Minerval school, and that he exhorted his Insinuators to enroll, after Knigge's example, men who could be quickly advanced to the higher mysteries: Such was the new method of recruiting that was adopted at this period. When the Provincials mention the ages of the Novices, we find few that have not attained the age of manhood, generally of twenty-five, thirty, forty, and even fifty years of age, and whose occupations in life denote years of discretion. Thus then does the Sect enlist multitudes of hands that do not wait for age to enable them to prepare for, or even to act when the day of revolution shall be come.

Another consideration that should not escape the historian is, the avowal (frequently repeated by the Adepts in the Original Writings) "that the great progress they made was in consequence of the facility with which they introduced themselves into the Masonic Lodges, and of the preponderance that the mysteries of Illuminism daily acquired in the Lodges." One of the Illuminees, *Lullus*, tells us, that since several Masons and some even of the most zealous Rosicrucians, have been initiated in our mysteries, *one would think that the Order had acquired new life, and a much increased force of expansion or of propagation.*[17] The Areopagite *Hannibal* attributes the success of his mission to the same cause. In the report he makes of his proceedings, he begins by congratulating himself on having found Masonic Lodges already established in the Tyrol. It was in them that he made his great conquests, that he recruited Counsellors of the Regency, Professors of Colleges, Counts, Excellencies, Ministers of the Emperor, Presidents, Vice-Presidents, Masters of the Post Office, Counsellors of the Government, all enthusiasts for the new mysteries of Illuminism. At the sight of such unexpected success, he openly confesses that they are all due to the new method introduced by *Philo*-Knigge. He then informs the Areopagites "that *the experienced Masons are turning themselves on all sides in quest of light*, that scarcely had he given the slightest indication of it, before their hearts were inflamed, and their entreaties to be initiated were most pressing. That it was just the moment for making great conquests at Vienna, *where there must be more than four hundred Masons.*" If at Milan he has not so good a prospect, it is because no *Masonic Lodges* have been established there; but he will find some at Cremona, Pavia, and other parts of Italy; and he ends by requesting that the other towns he means to visit may be comprehended in the new Geography of the Sect.[18]

In short, how does Knigge himself account for that prodigious multitude of adepts recruited in so short a period for Illuminism? "When I entered the Order (he writes to *Cato*-Zwack) you were all in the dark with respect to the *Masons of the Strict Observance.* I told you so, and was positive that among them there were excellent men (for us). *Spartacus* believed me; and the event has proved it. Our best adepts at Neuwied, at Gottingen, at Mayence, at Hanover, at Brunswick, and in the Palatinate, *were all formerly Free-masons of the Strict Observance.*"[19]

Nevertheless, these conquests on Masonry made by Illuminism do not satisfy either *Philo*-Knigge or *Spartacus*-Weishaupt. They will not even let the name of Masonry exist, but as a cloak for their Illuminism. Let us then consider of their new means and further successes in the following Chapter.[20]

1. Last Observations of *Philo*, Page 83.
2. Orig. Writ. Vol. II. Knigge's Report of *Dimeh* 1132, or January 1783.
3. This system of Zinnendorf was an incoherent medley of the Scotch and Swedish degrees, of the Knights Templars, of the *Confidants of St. John*; and at that time was the predominant system in Germany.
4. Original Writings, Vol. II. Knigge's Report of *Dimeh* 1132, or January 1783.
5. Ibid.
6. Last Observations, page 85.
7. Die höheren graden wurden mit enthusiasmus aufgenommen.
8. Jeder mann war zufrieden—Meine Leute waren entzückt über diese meister stücke. *Last Observations, Pages* 125 *and* 132—and *Original Writings, Let.* 1, *of* Philo *to* Cato.
9. Original Writings, Vol. II. Let from *Philo* to *Cato*.
10. Original Writings, Vol. II, let. 3, from *Philo* to Weishaupt.
11. This report is of the month of *Chardad* 1152, that is to say June 1782, consequently anterior to the breaking up of the Masonic Congress. *Mahomet* is nevertheless in direct correspondence with *Philo*-Knigge; for we may observe the latter pointing out to the former novices to be initiated.—*Original Writings, Philo's Report.*
12. Hat schier die ganze pfaltz unter das commando des O's (*ordens*) gebracht. In jedem Landstädtchen sind ein oder zwie—*Original Writings, Vol. II. Let.* 13, *anno* 1782.
13. See Last Observations of Philo, Page 45.—Original Writings, Vol. II. Page 202.
14. In my copy of the Original Writings I find a manuscript note in the margin, by a man who is very conversant on these matters; it states, that these initials stand for the *Prince Ferdinand of Brunswick.* Pr—— F—— V. B—— *hat ihm alle unterstützung versprochen.*

HISTORICAL PART

15. The appellation *Jesuit* is here used by the Illuminees as a term of scurrilous reproach, as it frequently is against any person inimical to their principles, for the Abbé Beck never was a Jesuit.
16. Knigge says, that in the Catholic countries the Philosophical writings, the light of the age, (the impiety of the day) had not made near so much progress as in protestant countries. This was true with respect to Bavaria; would to God that the same thing could have been said of France! Be that as it may, "The Minerval schools, says Knigge, did not take at all in the Protestant countries; and in fact, says he, such institutions could only be of use in Catholic countries buried in darkness, and for indifferent old-fashioned beings. But the greater aversion shown by the Brethren for these assemblies of Novices, the more earnestly they solicited to be admitted to the higher degrees;—*Mit der Minerval classe wollte es in protestantischen länder durchaus nicht fort, und würklich war auch diese anstalt verzüglich nur in ferfinsterten catholischen provinzen, und auf mittelmässige altags menschen anwendbar—Je weniger aber die mietglieder geneigt waren versammlungen der Pflanz-schule anzulegen, um desto eifriger drangen sie in mich, ihnen endlich die höhere grade mitzutheilen."* Philo endliche erklärung, P. 52, 53, *et passim*. The reader will not forget that Knigge speaks particularly of those sophisticated Masons among whom he was making recruits, and who were better prepared for the mysteries than the others because they were more accustomed to the secrets of the Lodge.
17. R. *Lullus's* Journal, Orig. Writ. Vol. II. Sect. VI.
18. Orig. Writ. Vol. I. and II. *Hannibal's* four Letters.
19. Unsere besten leute in Neuwied, Göttinguen, Mainz, Hannover, Braunschweig, Pfaltz, sind ehemalige mitglieder der Stricten Observanz.
20. For the whole of this chapter let the Reader apply to the Original Writings, Vol. II. Part I. and the Reports of the Provincials (*Provincial-Berichte*) from P. 159 to 221.

CHAP. VI.

New Means practised, and new conquests made by Knigge and Weishaupt on Masonry—Disputes between these two Chiefs of Illuminism—Their designs on the German Masons consummated before Knigge's Retreat.

NOTWITHSTANDING the immense number of Masons that had flocked to the standard of Illuminism, Weishaupt and Knigge laboured under some apprehensions with respect to a new congress that had been appointed for the following year at Wilhemsbaden. Knigge particularly dreaded that new Code and new form that was in agitation for the Lodges. He knew that some of the Brethren had been named to make a digest of laws; nor could he forget, that others had received instructions from the Congress to gain admission into, *and get themselves received members of all the secret societies, in order that they might be initiated into their mysteries,* and make their report at the following congress. Lest all the fruits of his last mission at Wilhemsbaden should be blasted in the bud at this new meeting, Knigge sought to make himself acquainted with the dispositions, with regard to his Illuminism, of the commissaries nominated to make the new digest of laws.

The chief of these commissaries was a man of the name of BODE, already famous in the annals of Masonry, and who was soon to become more so in those of Illuminism. The son of a common soldier of Brunswick, he was brought up as a fifer of a regiment, but he soon thought himself destined to act a higher part in the world than to accompany a drum with the shrill sounds of his fife. He had learned to read, and was sufficiently acquainted with the French and English languages to undertake some translations. Those of Tristram Shandy and Yorick's Sentimental Journey gained him more credit than money; he then set up as a bookseller at Hamburg; but soon becoming the widower of a rich heiress he abandoned trade, and was decorated by the Duke of Weimar with the title of Counsellor of Embassy. At length he was declared Privy Counsellor to the Landgrave of Hesse Cassel.

Created a *Commander* among the *Templar Masons* under the title of Knight of the Lillies of the Valley, *Eques a Lilio convallium,* Bode had brought with him all that genius necessary to give importance to the games of their Equality and Liberty, and, above all, that concern which impiety and independence manifest, to discover their mysteries in the symbols of that same Equality and Liberty. The services that he rendered to the Brethren may be appreciatred by that which Knigge believed to be so much to his honor, when he says, that *nearly all the little good that is to be found in the system of the Strict Observance is to be attributed to Bode*; or, in other words, every thing that assimilated their system to that of Weishaupt. After having closely scrutinized his man, Knigge declares him to be advanced in years, but still in quest of truth which he had not yet been able to find, though he had been forty years a Mason; he depicts him as indifferent to all systems, though petulant, fiery, and jealous of dominion; and as loving to be flattered by Princes. To this description I may add from my German Memorials, that his exterior was unpolished and almost deformed, which, however, did not hinder this old Mason from acting the part of a wit and of a man of sentiment with the Ladies. They also describe him as a pedant, with an appearance of frankness that Princes mistook for openness of character; but with which they might not have been so easily duped had they known, that though he sought their favor, he as cordially hated them as he did what he called the *Mummeries of Religion, of Jesuits, and of Priests*. Such sentiments must necessarily have endeared him to the Illuminees. Knigge more particularly courted him on account of the great influence he enjoyed over the German Masonry. These two men scrutinized each other, and Knigge at length declares, that "after many mutual explanations he had admitted him to the degree of Scotch Knight."—Here Bode found all those promises to forward the views of the Order, to reveal all his discoveries on Masonry to his new Superiors, to install the Illuminees in all the principal posts of the Lodges, and to embezzle their funds. *None of these obligations appear to have given him any uneasiness*; but he feared, that in the end those unknown superiors would turn out to be Jesuits and Priests. It was necesssary, therefore, to remove such fears, and to guarantee to him that those superiors detested Priests and Jesuits as much as he did himself. "On this condition (says Knigge) he promised, 1*st*, To labor for us, and, by means of the new System or Code to be formed for Masonry, to throw the empire over the Lodges into our hands. 2*dly*, To put the Directories and provincial inspections, in as much as depended on him, into the hands of the Illuminees. 3*dly*, To prevail on the Brethren of the *Strict Observance* to fraternize with us. 4*thly*, In the forming of the new Masonic Code, never to lose sight of the illuminized plan for the choice of Masters or Venerables of Lodges. 5*thly*, To lay before the Superiors all the knowledge he has acquired concerning the origin of Masonry and of the Rosicrucians; and to cause the *Deductions* promised for the *Strict Observance* to be printed at our presses, and to distribute them to our Brethren according to agreement."[1]

Such promises from Bode were of too much consequence to be rejected by the Illuminees; he was received with open arms, and under the characteristic of *Amelius*, was ushered into the higher degrees. We shall soon see how faithfully he acquitted himself of his promises.

While Knigge was making such important acquisitions from Masonry, Weishaupt was meditating another plan, that was to install him Master of all the Lodges of Poland. The Areopagite *Cato-*Zwack received nearly at the same time both Knigge's official note relative to Bode, and the following letter from

Weishaupt: "I have a mind to undertake the Polonese Confederation, not precisely to Illuminize them, but merely as Free-masonry to establish *the System of Confederate Lodges*; to select the ablest persons; to get the start of the *Strict Observance*, and to destroy it. Write immediately to Warsaw, that you are acquainted with several Lodges at Munich and other towns, that are willing to confederate with them on the following conditions:—1*st*, That they should acknowledge but the first three degrees—2*dly*, That each Lodge should be at liberty to have what Superiors and as many of them as they pleased—3*dly*, That all Lodges should be independent of each other, at least as much so as the Lodges of Germany are of those of Poland—4*thly*, That all their union shall be carried on by the correspondence and visits of the Brethren.—If we can but gain that point, we shall have succeeded in all we want; *leave the rest to me.*

"*Philo* has already received instructions to prepare our Lodges of the Rhine and of Lower Saxony for this plan. Don't lose a day; for both time and danger press. *John is coming*, and the confederation will take place at Vienna before that time. The Lodge ★ ★ appears as if it would accede...Send to Warsaw the manifesto that is to be immediately circulated in the Lodges on the occasion. Without doubt the federation will be numerous. *See how I can seize every occasion and turn every circumstance to use.* As soon as you shall get an answer send it to me; don't lose a minute. The most important business for us is, to establish an *Eclectic* Masonry; if we succeed in that, 'tis all we want. Do not mention our Order in Warsaw; it is always desirable to gain so essential a point. Send all your documents on Poland to *Philo*. A multitude of Lodges would have joined us had they not dreaded to be taken for *blind Lodges*. This arrangement will raise the difficulty. The English Lodge of *Edessa* (Frankfort) has already promised to accede to these conditions. Send your dispatches off immediately for Warsaw, without transmitting them to me, that they may get there sooner; and desire an immediate answer."[2]

Though persons who cannot gain admission to Weishaupt's secret councils may not foresee why he so earnestly interests himself in this plan for the propagation of the conspiracy, we may, however, remark, that Knigge had conceived the full importance of the measure when a week after he writes to Zwack, "*That plan on Poland is a most masterly blow. I have already sent my draft of the circular letter for the Lodges to Spartacus.*" According to Weishaupt's plan, this circular letter was not intended for the Polish Masons alone, but was to be sent to all the Lodges of the Order. It is to be found in the second volume of the Original Writings, and is exactly that medley of artifice for the seduction of Masons which might be expected from its author. Knigge begins with a fulsome eulogy on their institution. He tells them, that their society *was intended by God and nature to reclaim the rights of humanity oppressed, of virtue persecuted, and of science degenerated.* In a story artfully intermixed with truth and falsehood, he endeavours to demonstrate how much the Order had swerved from its grand object for about twenty years past. To restore it therefore to its ancient splendor, he invites all Brethren fired with a true zeal to unite with those Masons who alone have remained in possession of the real mysteries, with a society formed for their preservation about the year 1762, and whose special object was to oppose the tyranny of the Brethren of the *Strict Observance*; in short, to join a society which he declares to be composed of the best heads of the Order, and of men whose science and experience would command the eteem and veneration of all that approached them. At length, giving the plan for his new association, "In the new regimen admitted by these real Masons (says he) we invariably hold to the first degrees. Several Lodges unite together in the choice of one for their *Scotch directory*, or chief place of their district, to which each sends a Deputy. This Directory decides on money matters, overlooks objects of economy and the raising of contributions, and grants powers for the erecting of new Lodges. Above this tribunal we have no Superiors who have a right to raise contributions; they are not entitled to an exact account every three months of the moral and political state of every Lodge. A certain number of *Scotch Directories* join to chuse a *Provincial Directory*, three of the latter elect an Inspector, and three Inspectors choose the National Director.

"This is not the place for expatiating on what we have already done in the silent abodes of secrecy, or on what we mean to do. It will suffice to say, that we have schools to form the young men whom we afterward admit into our Order, and who are destined to labour to procure happier and more tranquil days for the rising generation. The care we bestow on these pupils is in our eyes the most honorable part of our labours. Should the Lodges wish for any further particulars, they shall receive them from the very persons who have thought proper to propose this plan."[3]

The memorials before us are not sufficiently explicit to enable us to decide what effect Zwack's and Knigge's letters produced on the Polish Masons. In Zwack's note, however, on the *progress of the Brethren*, we may observe *that the Areopage was in treaty for a strict alliance with the National Lodge of Poland*. With respect to Germany, we are not left in the dark as to the success of these artifices; but then it is to Bode particularly that such successes are attributed. Through his means it was, that Knigge acquired powerful protectors with the masons of high rank, and particularly with the committee that was to frame the new code. By the help of such protection he so amazingly extended the number of the adepts, that Weishaupt pretended to be alarmed, or was so in reality. The despotic founder viewed with a jealous eye the ascendant that Knigge was daily acquiring, and the great encomiums bestowed on him by the adepts in their *Quibus Licets*. Beside, his profound policy led him to conceive that his power would be too much divided by that of Knigge's, to ensure him sovereign sway over his tenebrous meetings, and to preserve that unity of object and action which his plots required. This multitude of adepts suddenly initiated to the higher mysteries kept him in a state of continual alarm. Among these new disciples some might be found who, not having undergone the necessary trials, might expose both himself and all the conspiracies of his Sect to be discovered. Though Knigge had faithfully copied (as the reader has seen) all the profligate mysteries that Weishaupt had invented in the degree of Epopt, yet this illuminizing chief did not scruple to accuse the Baron of having weakened them; the fact was, that he could not forgive him for having participated in the glory of founding the Order. He even pretended that Knigge was privately laying the foundations of another secret society.[4] These reflections weighed so heavily on the mind of the despotic chief, that all on a sudden Knigge found himself deposed at the very instant when he was most elated with his successes in the service of the Order.

Weishaupt took from him the direction of his provinces, and made him subject to some of his own pupils. The manner in which Knigge received this humbling news cannot be better described than in his own letters to Weishaupt and to Zwack. The latter had attempted to reconcile these two terrible competitors, particularly by affecting to throw the whole blame of their disagreements on *Mahomet* and another brother, "It is neither *Mahomet* nor that other brother (says Knigge to *Cato*), but it is that *Jesuitism* of Weishaupt, that occasions all our broils and disputes. It is that despotism which he exercises over men perhaps less powerful in imagination, art, and cunning than himself, but equal to him at least in good-will, prudence, uprightness and probity; over men who have rendered the most important services, without which his Order would still have been a pitiful medley of boys. Long since have I observed his intention of deceiving me; but I am firmly resolved to make him feel, notwithstanding my excessive patience and obedience, that there are men who are not to be played upon with impunity. I therefore declare, that nothing can ever put me again on the same footing with *Spartacus* on which I was before; *but as long as I live I will do every thing in my power for the good of the Order; and ye* (The Areopagites), *my best of friends*, ye shall always find me ready to obey ye in every thing conducive to the same object."

After this exordium Knigge proceeds to enumerate every thing that he had done for Weishaupt, in the perfecting of the Code, the founding of Lodges, and the recruiting of Brethren. "I had actually recruited *five hundred* (he continues) when he chose to view me in the light of an indifferent being, who was ruining his affairs by my want of reflection. Without giving me any intimation, he began to correspond with my inferiors. I have seen some of his letters to my pupils, in which he treats me as a novice.—At present I am under the direction of *Minos*, and am to send him my *Quibus Licet* every month. Without being an ambitious man, I see no reason why I should put up with such affronts, and allow myself to be led like a scholar by a professor of Ingolstadt. And certainly with respect to him I look upon myself as dispensed from all obedience. With regard to you, ready to obey the slightest intimation of your wishes, I consent to continue to direct the provinces of *Hesse* and *Upper Saxony*, until every thing is properly organized in those countries. I shall then retire, prompt, notwithstanding, to serve you with all my might, either by night or by day."

This letter is dated the 20th of Jan. 1783, and is immediately followed by another to the same adept. The latter shows how painful it was to Knigge to abandon the Brethren; but at length he writes to Zwack, "Were I to give way to an imprudent vengeance? reflect on this at least."

"It was by order of *Spartacus* (auf Spartacus geheiss) that I wrote against the *ci-devant Jesuists* and against the *Rosicrucians*, neither of whom had ever done me any harm. It was by his orders that I spread dissensions among the Masons of the *Strict Observance*, and seduced their ablest brethren. I instilled into them strong ideas of the antiquity, the excellence and power of our Order, of the perfection of our Superiors, of the irreproachable manners of the Brethren, of the importance of our mysteries, and of the sincerity and purity of our intentions. Many of those who at present labour most efficaciously for our Order were under constant apprehensions that we were leading them to Deism. *Little by little, however, I do what I please.* Now were I to inform the Jesuits and the Rosicrucians of their real persecutor; were I simply to let some certain persons into the secret of the insignificant novelty of the Order; were I to inform them that I composed parts of the degrees; were I to tell them how I am treated after the many services I have rendered; were I to make them acquainted with the *Jesuitism* of that man who leads us all by the nose, and sacrifices us to his ambition whenever he pleases; were I to inform the secret-hunters that they will not find that which they are in quest of; were I to let those who love religion into the secret of the founder's religious principles; were I to sound the alarm to Free-masons concerning an association set on foot by the Illuminees; were I myself to establish an Order on a more solid, clear, disinterested plan, whose object should be honesty and liberty; were I to attract the many able men whom I am acquainted with into this new Order; were I to place certain persons in your's who would inform me in future of every thing that was transacting in it; were I to give a hint only in *Greece* (Bavaria) that should at once disclose the founder and his Order; were I to sound the alarm to Princes by means of *Numenius* and the Rosicrucians at *Rome* (Vienna): I shudder at the idea! No, I will not carry vengeance to such lengths; but if I do not obtain satisfaction, I will take such steps as my honor requires. Let me once more enjoy that unlimited confidence that I formerly enjoyed, and then I shall be ready to undertake great things for the Order again. I am perfectly acquainted with our people; I know what attaches each one to the Order, and what engines should be set in motion either to excite their enthusiasm or suddenly to crush it. Once more I repeat it; If I am left at liberty to act I will answer upon my head to put the Order immediately in possession, 1st *of most important secrets*; 2dly, *of a strong preponderance over the Masons of the* Strict Observance, *or, rather, of means absolutely to destroy them;* 3dly. *of a great influence over the Masons of* Zinnendorf's system; 4thly. *I promise to put the Order in possession of great riches and of great power, and that without making any alterations in our constitutions.*"

So far from allowing himself to be soothed by these promises, or affrighted by these menaces, which Zwack was to transmit to Ingoldstadt, Weishaupt appeared to become more inflexible. He knew his agents too well; he was certain that Knigge could never bring himself to betray him; and indeed he must have betrayed himself in denouncing his chief. That adept, without doubt, might have deserted him and carried many of the brethren with him; and Weishaupt would have preferred such extremities rather than have had rebel adepts, particularly competitors, under him. "What care I (he writes) for all that multitude of unmanageable adepts who wish to be guided by no other rule than their fancy?"....At other times he would write, "It is by means of those who will obey me, that *I must perform most astonishing things*. I answer for nothing when I meet with resistance from my adepts; I have foreseen every thing, and I have prepared every thing. Let my whole Order go to rack and ruin; in three years I will answer to restore it, and that to a more powerful state than it is in at present—Obstacles only stimulate my activity. I know how to turn them to my advantage; and when people shall think that I am undone, even then shall I rise stronger than ever. Let that person leave me who thinks he can better himself elsewhere; and time will shew who is mistaken. I know how to find men more docile. I can sacrifice whole provinces, the desertion of a few individuals, therefore, will not alarm me."[5]

Thus firm and constant in his determination to enforce obedience, Weishaupt left Knigge under an interdict; he continued to transmit all orders to him through the medium of his inferiors; he even so far set him at defiance, as to refuse to give him the watchword and the quarterly sign; so that he might almost look upon himself as expelled the Order. If he deigned to write to him, it was in a tone only calculated to add to his humiliation; and Knigge himself actually thought all his intercourse with this overbearing Despot had been broken off when he received a letter still more imperious and injurious than ever. *Philo*'s answer is remarkable and I will lay it before my readers; not that I think it important to describe all the jealousies and intestine broils that may very well be called the rogues quarrel, but because it shows how well in the midst of all their disputes these fellows knew each other, and how they drew together when misfortunes of nations were in question; it shows also how they vied with each other, and placed all their merit in the destruction of the altar and the throne, and in having abused the confidence of Princes; such were the mighty deeds on which they grounded their rights of preeminence in their dark dens of rebellion.

This letter from Knigge to Weishaupt was written at successive periods during his excursion from Frankfort to Cassel, to Brunswick, and Neuterhausen. He begins it, dated at Cassel, 25th Feb. 1783.

"An unforeseen circumstance occasions my writing to you. Read my letter without passion, with impartiality, and as coolly as you are able. I own that, as late even as yesterday, until I had received your Excellency's letter, I little thought we were ever to correspond together again. I am perfectly resolved to wait but for one more answer; and if it is in the same tone that you have lately taken with me, nothing shall hinder me from absolutely breaking off all connection with you. Do not pretend to think that this is an idle threat. I am aware that you can do without me; but I also know, or am at least willing to think, that your conscience will rise in judgement against you, if you continue without reason to reject a man who has been your most active co-operator. What am I to understand when you say that you can begin the whole over again, and that with new agents? To be sure you may try; but were you really to undertake it, you would cease in my eyes to be that man whom I was willing to believe endowed with prudence. The points to which I wish to call your attention require a general view of our respective situations. Let us address each other freely.

"*You* have injured me; you know it; but you will not own it, because you are afraid of losing your consequence were you to say, I have really behaved shamefully ill to that man. You wish to persuade both yourself and others that you are indifferent to my staying with you or not, for that I am not fit for so great an undertaking; though you well know, that we both have our failings; that men must be taken as they are; that no one would proceed far, if he were to change co-operators every six months. To make short of the matter, you would be sorry to see me abandon you, and found another society; but you are unwilling to appear to stand in need of me.

"Now for *Me*: I have not the vanity to pretend, that a man of superior understanding to my own should so debase himself as to ask me pardon. But I could wish you to reflect on the following circumstances: I am certain that I have acted according to my conscience, and on a solid plan. I defy any person to point out to me those indiscretions by which I am supposed to have done the Order irreparable evil. So far from it, I have engaged men of the most transcendent merit in its service. If in many hundred recruits any are to be found who are not exactly what they ought to be, your own conduct will plead my excuse, since you have entrusted *me* with the government of five provinces, a *person* that you at present upbraid as a heedless giddy young fellow. In short, I have acted as I ought to have done. That you should acknowledge this, I do not desire; but I really wish to see you convinced of it. Our union should be grounded on a reciprocal and boundless confidence. If you are unwilling to grant me yours, remember at least that I am not to be led like a machine. I therefore retire, not through an ill-judged delicacy, but because I can be of no use to you, and that I know persons to whom I can be of great use, and who place unbounded confidence in me.

"Now to the point: *I can inform you, that last night I brought my grand plan to a state of maturity*. Mark me therefore: since I have quitted the government of my provinces, *great things have been the objects of my labors, letters, and conferences. For this week past I have had here (at Cassel) several private interviews with the P——C——of H——C——,*" (Prince Charles of Hesse Cassel, brother-in-law to the King of Denmark). "*All this taken together* has enabled me to fulfil the following promises, *provided I am treated as I think I am entitled to be.*"

The promises of Knigge are nearly the same as those already mentioned in his letter to *Cato*-Zwack. He adds, however, some few points that are essential; for example, he does not only promise to discover to the Illuminees *the real object of Masonry and of the Rosicrucians*, but *to make it a part of the higher degrees of Weishaupt's mysteries*. This addition is not an indifferent indication on the occult mysteries of Masonry. Without having been a Rosicrucian, *Philo-Knigge* had long applied to their mysteries before his admission into Illuminism. He had studied them as *Commander* and *Knight Templar*, but had not been able to dive into their last mysteries. It was reserved to Bode, to that man known by all Germany to have been one of their most zealous and learned Masons, to initiate Knigge in these mysteries; and we must hence conclude, that few of the brethren were acquainted with them; but no sooner are they discovered to *Philo*, than he conceives them to be worthy of being blended with those of Weishaupt. These occult mysteries, therefore, of the Rosicrucians can fall little short of the baneful machinations of Illuminism; and all that jealousy that still rages between the Rosicrucians and Illuminees may be said to be only a rivalship for hireling primacy. No longer do I pretend to dispute with Brother Dupe on the existence of these hideous mysteries; on the contrary, I will compliment him on his still having sufficient virtue left to be refused admission; but I will insist on the absolute necessity and duty of abandoning an association that can have nurtured the abominable and impious plots the discovery of which is the cause of so much exultation in these arch-conspirators.

On the same conditions Knigge promises Weishaupt *to discover to the Order certain secrets of Nature, secrets* (says he) *at once astonishing, marvellous, and productive*, and all this without being miracles.[6] He also specifies the means by which the Illuminees are to acquire power and wealth; it is *the liberty and a licence to trade in Denmark, Holstein, and other states, with the necessary funds for the enterprize*. In short, his promises against the Rosicrucians is accompanied with the promise of a powerful party against the Jesuits.[7]

This letter remained in his port-folio until his return from Cassel to Brunswick; he there continues it on the 10th of March: "The D———F———of B———, (Duke Ferdinand of Brunswick) has called me to this town to confer with me on different subjects. I will say more of this on a future occasion, let us revert to the most pressing business. I have already said it, and I repeat it again without any disguise, here are my conditions: If you restore me to your confidence, all will be terminated, and this whole business remains a secret between us. From this instant I not only engage to attach myself stronger than ever to the Order, but I also promise and guarantee to it a power of which it can have no conception.

"Should you refuse to rely on me, from that instant our union is dissolved; I erect another society on much stronger bonds. But no threats. Think of it and weigh it coolly."

Knigge also takes time to reflect; and on the 26th of March he continues from Neuterhausen: "I am here again...Once more, I say, *if you know your own interest the world is ours*; if not, may the consequences of your scandalous proceedings fall upon you. But no; I still rely on your prudence, fate leads us admirably. I have great things before me; I have prodigious ones in view.—It is in your power to partake of them. I have not as yet taken a single step against you. I hope your conduct will give me reason to write to *Athens*, that I had formed a wrong opinion of you."

On the 27th of the same month another postscript in the following terms: "I was just going to send my letter, when I received this Order, which you send me by F... Oh! you ought not to have taken such a step. You wish then to drive me to all extremities? Upon my word you will gain nothing by it. Reflect on the importance, I may venture to say, that I have given to your association. Were I now to discover to certain persons your whole history, and *your principles so dangerous for the world*, and declare that I was obliged to moderate them by every means in my power, who would not shun you? *What is your degree of Epopt in comparison with your means of attaining a good object* (that is to say in comparison to the principle, *all means are good when the end is good?*) What is it, I say, when compared with your scandalous injustice towards Wolter and Levelling? O! what are men? Good God! were you a Jesuit yourself? I tremble to think of it; but should that be the case all Hell should not save you from my claws."

Last postscript of the 31st: "Do not hurry yourself to answer me. *Cato* may transmit certain things to you that may make you change your mind. Take care of yourself *cave ne cadas*. Vengeance is a thing that I shall with great difficulty resist."[8]

All these letters depict Knigge as an adept determined to withdraw himself at length from the despotism of the modern *Spartacus*; not indeed to abandon his plots, but in order to lay the basis of new associations of Conspirators: In the midst of all these broils, it is worthy of remark, that the injured competitor in his letters to Weishaupt and to Zwack intermixes answers and advice on every thing that can tend to propagate the Order. In his postscript of the 26th of March, forgetting on a sudden all his anger against Weishaupt, he informs him, that Brother *Accatius* solicits letters of recommendation and directions to the Brethren of Italy for another adept who is going to second Brother *Hannibal* in his mission to those countries. "This affair (says Knigge) is of the highest importance to the Order; for our man is an excellent Scrutator; and I do assure you that special good news is come relating to the Monks of Italy." Most certainly, discontented Monks of the stamp of Dom Gerles might be found there; but before they could be enrolled an article of the Code which excludes them from the Order was to be dispensed with. As I have already observed, however, Knigge was always less scrupulous than Weishaupt on the article of exceptions. In these same letters he warns the Areopagites to pay particular attention to the affairs of the Order at Vienna; and informs them, that he has important news from that country; and with respect to Poland, though he may be acquainted with no person who could forward the federation, he had *people at least in Livonia*. And in his official reports we find that he had a missionary in that part of Russia, *who from so great a distance perhaps might not send his Quibus Licet exactly and monthly*; but who would labor for the Order perhaps with more success than any of its Apostles.[9]

Such tenderness for the welfare of the Order, and zeal for the propagation of its plots, evidently demonstrates that Knigge, so far from abandoning it, expected to re-assume his former rank. It appears still clearer in the letter he wrote to *Cato* by the very same post, by which he had sent all his menaces to Weishaupt: "I have great views indeed for our Order, and that makes me forget all the injuries I have received from Spartacus. I do not wish him to own that he is in the wrong, but only that he should know that the fault lies with him." The letter ends by constituting *Cato* judge of the contest.[10] Weishaupt needed no more to convince him that this warfare would terminate to his advantage. He did not wish to lose *Philo*, but still less could he bear him as a rival. "If *Philo* (Weishaupt says to Zwack) will return to me, and confess that he is in the wrong, he will find me such as I formerly was in his regard. But for your part do not show the least eagerness to reclaim him. I wish to prove to him that I can do without him; his vanity must not be flattered; he wants to be entreated; and it is exactly for that reason that he should not be entreated.—If he has the good of the cause at heart, he will return of his own accord, and I will receive him with open arms."[11]

The *good of the cause*, as Weishaupt calls it (that is, the propagation and triumph of Illuminism with all its impious plots), was evidently as dear to Knigge as to himself. This mutual bias to crime reconciled them together again, at least, for a space of time sufficient to acquire for Illuminism the greater part of that authority which Knigge had promised to the Areopagites. It is true, that he tells us he had obtained his dismission, and an honorable testimony of his services. It may be a fact that he received his dismission, as he says, on the express conditions, that he would never undertake any thing detrimental to the interests or *plans* of the Illuminees; that he would keep a profound silence with respect to the secrets of the Brethren; that he would never do any thing that could commit the superiors, and not even so much as name them;[12] but certain it is, that the date coincides with the time of the discoveries made at Munich, which must have induced him to take such precautions as he judged necessary to avoid being implicated with the other chiefs of the Illuminees. He declares that he received his *congé* on the first of June 1784, and the first decrees issued by the Elector of Bavaria against Secret Societies bear date of the twenty-second of the same month. Four months after we see *Philo*-Knigge mentioned by Weihaupt as an adept, without the least allusion to his retreat, and this may create some doubt at least as to the date. Whatever may have been the case, fourteen months elapsed from the time of their grand disputes, till that when Knigge declares he broke off all connection with the Illuminees. Hereafter we shall see what is to be understood by this pretended dereliction of his former Brethren. It is however certain, that during those fourteen months, he but too well entitled himself to the gratitude of the Sect by the new services he rendered, and more particularly by his intrigues with Bode, by means of which he consummated Weishaupt's plan of confederation or of intrusion in all the Lodges of Germany.

The grand obstacle to these plans was the jealousy of the Rosicrucians, of the Brethren of *the Strict Observance*, and of the *Philaletes*, calling themselves the Theosophical Illuminees. But the acquisition of Bode; Knigge's frequent visits to their Highnesses the Duke Ferdinand of Brunswick and the Prince Charles of Hesse-Cassel; the manner in which he imposed on these two chiefs of German Masonry; the influence acquired by *Philo* through the means of Bode over the Commissaries who were named at Wilhemsbaden to frame the laws, are circumstances more than sufficient to account for his success in spite of such numerous opponents. When Bode was thoroughly convinced that Illuminism, so far from being an invention of Jesuits and Priests, was no other than a most determined conspiracy against Princes and the Priesthood, which he equally hated; when he beheld the means of it developing themselves in the degree of *Epopt* and of *Regent*, he then had no other view than to perform the promise he had made to Knigge, *to dedicate his life entirely* to the service of the Order, and particularly *to have its interests at heart in the framing of the new Code*. Never was promise more religiously kept, nor attended with greater success. With respect to those Brethren whose antique mysteries perpetually recalled to their minds Equality and Liberty, nothing could be more seducing than Knigge's circular letter on *Eclectic* or *Elective* Masonry. Many Lodges had of their own accord acceded to his federation. Bode introduced its laws into the *new Masonic Ritual*. It was on seeing these laws that the Mason who best foresaw their consequences exclaims, in the bitterness of his heart: "Oh my Brethren! At what point shall I begin, or where shall I end, when I speak to you of that Bode known among the Illuminees by the name of *Amelius*? Judge, my Brethren, of the important, I would say disastrous services he went to render them; he, who has been in habits of intimacy with so many of our Brethren; he who had taken so great a lead in most of our general meetings; he who, under an affectation of good nature and of German uprightness, concealed a heart replete with the most heinous impiety, and a frantic enthusiasm for Naturalism; he again who had taken offence at the Brethren of the *Strict Observance* because they had not satiated his ambition. What an acquisition in all respects was this man for the Illuminees!—His first efforts were directed against us. He acted where Knigge could not gain admittance. *It was through his means that the Illuminees gained their ascendancy in the new system that was to have been established at Wilhemsbaden; that they gained admittance into our Directories; and that they succeeded in fraternizing with the greater part of our Brethren of the Strict Observance.* His Insinuator Knigge had left him no alternative but to bring over Freemasonry to this unfortunate alliance, or to crush the Brotherhood. To the astonishment and grief of every true Mason, it was by the combined efforts of Bode and Knigge, that the greater part of the Lodges throughout Germany were tainted and infected with this baneful Illuminism."[13]

I often meet with similar avowals and lamentations in the different letters and memorials that I have received from German Masons, heretofore zealous for the honour of their Brotherhood, but now lamenting the intrusion of the

Bavarian pest among them. Some few Lodges, however, held out against it. That of Berlin, called *of the Three Globes*, in 1783, published a circular letter, anathematizing all Brethren who should pretend to degrade Free-masonry so as to transform it into a society of men conspiring against their God and their country. Whether this Lodge had not been initiated into the last mysteries of the Rosicrucians and other conspiring degrees, or whether this anathema was but a sham, the circular letter had but little effect. The intrusion continued, and became so general, that the illuminizing Sect in its instructions to the *Directing Illuminees* makes use of the following formidable expressions:—"*Of all the legitimate Lodges in Germany, there is* ONLY ONE *that has not coalesced with our Superiors,* and this Lodge has been obliged to suspend its labours."[14]

This declaration does not imply that the greater number of the Brethren were already illuminized, but only denotes that the Superiors, whether *Masters, Wardens,* or *Treasurers,* of almost every Lodge had entered into the federation with Weishaupt.—But what an awful aspect does this subterraneous power present! A multitude of emissaries and agents dispersed throughout the tenebrous recesses of Masonry. The Superiors once gained over, the Lodges would make but a feeble and short resistance.

The greater part of these successes were to be attributed to *Philo*-Knigge; neither did he hide those pretensions that could indicate the rival.—Weishaupt could not brook the most distant appearance of rivalry; new contests arose between the two chiefs. Knigge at length abandoned, or pretended to abandon, the Order. It does not appear that Weishaupt showed the least regret. His power seemed to be built on foundations that could not be shaken by any storm:—it was no longer confined to a corner of Germany.[15] The Danube and the Rhine could no longer bound it. In the North and the East he had his emissaries, in Holland, Poland, and Livonia.[16] His apostles in the South had already advanced from Milan to Venice.[17] On the West he was beginning his attacks on France by the way of Strasbourg.[18] But just at this period was preparing that storm which in the annals of the Sect shall be called the Third Epoch.

1. Original Writings, Vol. II. *Philo's bericht uber jonien; Dimeh.* January 1783.— If by *Deductions* the account of the contributions to be *deducted* for the *Grand Observance,* and afterward to be delivered over to the Illuminees, be not meant, I do not understand the meaning of them. But Bode reserves to himself the discretionary power of letting other persons participate of them; that is to say, he wishes to serve the Illuminees without appearing to have abandoned his former Brethren. (*See Vol. III of these Memoirs,* P. 154 [p. 465, Ed.]).
2. 11th January, 1783.
3. Extract from the Circular Letter, Original Writings, Vol. II. Part. II. Sect. VI.
4. Original Writings, Vol. II. Let. 20.
5. Original Writings, Vol. II. Let. 8, to *Cato.*
6. Erstaunlich und einträglich, obgleich keine wunder.
7. Eine mächtige parthey gegen jesuiten.

8. Original Writings, Vol. II. Lett. 1, 2, and 3, from *Philo*.
9. Aber er wird würken wie noch keiner gewürkt hat.
10. Worüber sie, bester *Cato!* Richter seyn mögen.
11. Original Writings, Vol. II. Let. 24.
12. Seine obern weder zu nennen noch zu compromittiren.
13. Discourse of a Master on the ultimate fate of Freemasonry.
14. Degree of Directing Illuminee, Sect. 3, No. 5.
15. That the reader may form a clear and precise idea of the manner in which these different Lodges and Illuminees on their several missions corresponded with their chief, I think it right to subjoin the *Geographical and Political Chart* of the Sect, such as it was drawn out by Knigge in the Original Writings. I know this plate only comprehends Germany, and that without the Austrian Provinces, "because (says Knigge) *the Brethren of those Provinces have petitioned to have a separate National Director.*" But every reader can apply a similar one to any other state. To complete it, I have added Weishaupt in direct communication with the Areopagites, and the latter with the National Directors.—A very slight inspection will suffice to show, how instructions, communications, &c. pass to and from the General, down to the Scotch Directories, and from the latter to the lowest individual of Illuminism.
16. Philo's Bericht.
17. See Juridical Depositions made at Munich.
18. Orig. Writ. Vol. II. Let. 23, to *Cato*, 28 Jan. 1783.

CHAP. VII.

Third Epoch of Illuminism.

Discovery of the Sect.

IT was not without reason that Weishaupt had expressed his apprehensions as to the precipitate manner in which Knigge had admitted so many candidates to the mysteries of the Sect: on the other hand, Knigge might with equal reason upbraid Weishaupt with want of prudence in recommending to the adepts such books as those published under the name of Boulanger; and thus disclosing his Atheism previous to the last mysteries.[1] But success had so emboldened Weishaupt, that he kept no farther reserve on the score of religion, even with his Minerval scholars; and so early as the year 1781, the court of Bavaria entertained some suspicious of this new Sect. It had even ordered certain inquiries to be made; but the Illuminees had art enough to baffle these inquests.[2] Lest, however, any inquiries should at any future time take place, Weishaupt bethought himself of making the Elector the tutelary adept of his conspiracies. "I am of opinion (would he write to his Areopagites) that, in order to strengthen ourselves, you should send a deputation to the Elector, to offer him the Protectorate of the Eclectic Lodges. The Brethren *Ulysses, Apollo,* and some others of the most distinguished members, even *Celsus* for instance, might be deputed for this purpose. Should the Prince accept it, we shall be effectually skreened from any future persecution, and nobody will then be afraid of joining you, or of frequenting your Lodges."[3]

The reader may easily judge how such a deputation would have been received by the Elector, when he is informed of the manner in which he had formerly received a similar proposition while residing at Manheim. One of his ministers at that time, under a far more plausible pretence, proposed to him to call to his court the most famous Philosophers of the day, and to grant pensions to these pretended great men, after the example of Lewis XIV, who had been the protector of the learned men of his age. The glory of such an undertaking seemed at first to flatter the Prince; but on consulting men of real learning he soon perceived that such a measure would only end in multiplying a Sect equally inimical to their God and their country; and Charles Theodore would no longer hear of the Protectorship of Philosophism. This anecdote was sent to me by a person who heard it from the very minister that had made the proposition to the Elector.

It is not understood how the court of Munich acquired its first knowledge respecting Illuminism; the information it received was not sufficiently explicit indeed to describe the spirit of the Sect, but it gave a general idea of the danger of secret societies. On the 22d of June 1784, His Electoral Highness published an Edict absolutely forbidding all *secret communities, societies, and confraternities*, other than those by law established. The uncontaminated Masons shut up their Lodges; the illuminized Masons, who had many of their adepts about the court, thought themselves strong enough to bid defiance to the Edicts, and continued their meetings. A work published by Mr. Babo, a Professor at Munich, entitled *The first warning on Free-masonry*, began to disclose more clearly the plans of the new adepts. Soon after the Count Joseph Törring made a more vigorous attack on them. The Illuminees not only wrote apologies in answer to these attacks, but set many other engines to work, the artifice of which cannot be better described than by Weishaupt's own letters to his adepts.

"Listen for a moment to my advice," he writes on the 18th Dec. 1784. "If any inquiry be set on foot; I am of opinion that none of the Chiefs should suffer themselves to be led into the detail and particulars of the Order; and they must positively declare, that no power on earth should force them to make any discoveries excepting to the Elector personally; the two degrees of the higher mysteries should then be submitted to him. At least such shall be the line of conduct which I will hold, if ever I am called upon. You will then see what a happy turn our affairs will take. You have read what Brother D...thought of the first degree. I am certain the Elector will view it in the same light. I shall place all my hopes in the goodness of my cause. Boldly and without the least apprehension, I can declare beforehand, that if I am to fall it shall be in an honourable manner, though it were to cost me my head. Deport yourselves in the same manner, and instil courage into the others. This is an admirable opportunity for showing your magnanimity; do not let it pass by without avail. I have mentioned my plan for the Elector to Brother *Cromwell*, and he augurs fortunately from it:—but he very well knows that such a measure will only be resorted to in the last extremity."

What an extraordinary mode of defense must this appear to those who do not know that these two degrees which he intended to show to the Elector were the corrected ones, such as he had prepared for Princes and certain candidates who would have been disgusted with them in their real state. Sometimes the whole of that part relating to the mysteries, and the discourses of the Hierophants, were retrenched, and nothing but the idle ceremonial preserved. A second letter of Weishaupt's to his Areopagites dated the 2d February 1875, will more clearly explain the whole of this artifice. "My Brethren (he says), the step you are going to take is proper, and such as the circumstances require. The Memorial of our *Menelaus* (WERNER, Counsellor at Munich) is very fine and very judicious. I only wish you to add, that you will show your degrees to nobody but to the Elector; and those that may be submitted to his inspection are — 1st, The *Novice*; 2dly, The *Minerval*; 3dly, The *Minor Illuminee*. [*Nota bene*, that the words *dummster mönch* (stupid monk) are to be changed into *dummster mensch* (stupid men)]. 4thly, The *Major Illuminee*, entire, except these words, which you will efface: *the Priests and bad princes are in our way.* 5thly, The *Directing Illuminee*; but in this degree you will only show the ceremonial of the reception, and my discourse; *not a word of the rest.* 6th, The degree of *Priest* or *Epopt*; here you will only *show our instructions that relate to sciences; and you will carefully read those over, lest any allusion or reference to the rest should subsist.*

"As all the packets for *Ephesus* (Ingolstadt) are opened, I plainly see that I am the person at whom they aim. To-morrow I will write to *Alfred* (the minister Seinsheim); and that letter will inform the court beforehand how I mean to behave on this occasion. Openly declare to the Elector, *that the Order is a produce of his own states, and that I am the author of it.* Then the whole affair will turn upon me; but I am much mistaken if they will proceed to a personal inquest until they have further proofs, which can only be acquired by opening the letters. Show yourselves great, firm, and undaunted. *My conduct will prove to you what I can be.* In the instruction for the degree of *Epopt* take great care of the part that *relates to History*; leave nothing that can lead *to the discovery of the theft committed on the Archives.*"

All this artifice, however, proved useless. The court had acquired sufficient proofs to take such steps against the hero of the Sect as prudence might require. A few days after he had written these instructions to his Areopagites, he was dismissed from his chair of Professor of Laws in the University of Ingolstadt; only, however, as famous *Master of Lodges*, and as disobedient to the Edict suppressing all secret societies. The mysteries of his Lodge had not yet transpired; it was only known, that several members of his Illuminism, disgusted with his doctrines or his plans, had abandoned his Lodges as early as 1783. Among others were to be found COSANDEY, a Priest, and the Abbé RENNER, both of them Professors of the *Litterae humaniores* at Munich. But, great as might be the horror which they had conceived of what they had seen of the Sect without having attained the grand mysteries, it does not appear that they had as yet taken any steps against it; at least they had not given such details as might direct the arm of the law. On the 30th March 1785, however, they received a summons from His Electoral Highness, and from the Bishop of Freysinguen, to appear before the Tribunal of the Ordinary, and there to declare whatever they might have observed in the Sect of Illuminees contrary to religion and good morals. Nobody, even then, had the least idea that the conspiracy was pointedly directed against the government. Messrs. Cosandey and Renner made their depositions, the one on the 3d the other on the 7th of April following. I must give extracts from both, though perfeclty agreeing with each other. That made by Mr. Cosandey is more ample on the principles of the Illuminees, while Mr. Renner descends more particularly into their constitution and the education of their pupils. I shall therefore begin by an extract from the latter; and then revert to that made by Mr. Cosandey.

Juridical Deposition made by the Professor RENNER *on the Illuminees.*

After having stated the orders he had received to appear before the Tribunal, and the subject on which he was to give evidence, Mr. Renner begins by declaring that

"The Order of the Illuminees must be distinguished from that of the Free-masons. But this distinction is a secret to mere Masons, as well as to Illuminees of the Minerval degree. I was myself in the dark respecting it, and, after a long trial, they thought proper to advance me to the degree of *Minor Illuminee*, the first degree in which they take the name of *Illuminee*. I was even constituted Superior over a small number of the Brethren."

Here the deponent, who thought he was to become a Mason on his first entrance into the Sect, learns that he is not yet one; and tells us, that many of the Brethren had complained heavily that they had not been admitted as yet to the *Intermediary Degrees*. He himself is admitted to them, and does not find them satisfactory: but he adds, "The advantage I reaped from them was, that I discovered the benefits which the Order derived from Free-masonry. The Illuminees fear nothing so much as to be known under that name. They assume the cloak of Masonry, only because they believe themselves more secure when masked under the appearance of an association that is looked upon as insignificant.—The Masonic Lodges, according to their expression, only contain the *dross of the people* (der tross von leuten) or the bulk of the army, among whom a few persons may be found, that may look upon themselves as very happy, after long and severe trials, to be secretly admitted into the sanctuary of the Order. All the other Free-masons, Apprentices, Fellow-crafts, and Masters, are to content themselves with idle ceremonies, and remain under the yoke, either because their eyes are not strong enough to bear the light, or because their love for the Order, and their secrecy, two essential requisites in every adept, cannot be sufficiently depended on. When once they are condemned to linger in obscurity, they can never have hopes of rising to the mysteries; and this is expressed by the superiors in the following sentence, *Ex inferno nulla est Redemptio.*

"Meantime, these Masons, without knowing it, are under the direction of the Illuminees, who reap great advantages from their reputation and their riches. These men (say the Superiors) are sufficiently recompensed by being admitted to converse with the adepts of light, and to learn enough from such conversations to appear enlightened to the prophane.

"The Illuminees, who at first only show themselves under the appearance of a literary society, gave themselves the following constitution: Their Order is subdivided into different classes, called *degrees*, because the light expands itself according to these classes.—The first degree is a sort of Noviciate, though every person reported as *insinuated*, and recommended by some member of the Order as worthy of being admitted, must have been prepared and instructed to a certain point by his Insinuator or Recruiter. It is a constant rule in the Order, that every Candidate should undergo a year's trial, that his Insinuator may observe him accurately, according to the regulations of the Order, and in a *Quibus Licet* draw an exact picture of his person, his character, his talents, and his conduct. If the Candidate is judged to be worthy, he is admitted into the class of *Preparation*.—In my time there were two of this nature, called *Churches*. Each was directed by four men, forming what was called the *Magistracy*. They were the *Superior,* the *Censor,* the *Treasurer,* and the *Secretary*; and all these were adepts of higher degrees. We held at least one meeting every month, at which all the members of the same *Church* were to attend, to give their Superiors a sealed letter directed *Quibus Licet, Soli,* or *Primo,* containing an exact statement of the conduct, discourse, &c. of those whom they had *observed* during the month.

"No member is dispensed from these *Quibus Licets,* which ascend from Degree to Degree, and are only opened by those who have a right to read them. The other occupations of the meeting were, after some ceremonies, to read the statutes, a few passages from the ancient Philosophers, and a discourse on various subjects, composed by the different members in rotation. As the Brethren in general do not like religion, the greater liberty the writer uses on that subject, he is the more applauded, and acquires a higher reputation of being enlightened. Sometimes, however, the presence of certain brethren, either feeble as yet, or not to be entirely depended upon, cause the Superiors at such lectures to give signs of apparent satisfaction. It would be a violent breach of their policy to give way to intemperate language, and to express the principles of the Order too openly, as each member might look upon such talk as part of their system.

"To avoid suspicion, and to attain their ends more certainly, they hold weekly meetings, whence all ceremony and constraint is discarded. Here the pupils hold disputations among themselves on all sorts of subjects. It is on these occasions that the superiors, and those who have imbibed the true principles of the Order, sneer at what they call *Religious prejudices*; for in their language every thing that can obstruct their views are *prejudices*. It is then that by means of the most seducing subterfuges they represent their principles in such poignant language, that the most timid, encouraged by their example, and purified from all dross and religious prejudice, become perfectly like the rest. He that can withstand such artifice is a man lost in the eyes of the Order.

"That which made the greatest impression on me, among the Illuminees, was certainly their method of binding down their adepts and subduing their minds. They extoll the greatness and power of the Order; they speak of its dignity with the utmost respect; they stun you with the most magnificent promises, and assure you of the protection of great personages ready to do every thing for the advancement of its members at the recommendation of the Order; till at length each pupil really considers, or appears to consider, the interest of Illuminism as his own, and views all the propositions and orders he receives from his superiors as duties which he has to fulfill. Should a pupil under this idea have the misfortune to declare, in a *Quibus Licet*, a *Primo*, or a *Soli*, some misconduct of his own, or some secret that he has been entrusted with or that he has extorted from any body, the unhappy confident is lost to himself, for he thenceforth belongs wholly to the Sect. When once they have thus tied him down, they assume a very different tone with him. They care very little about him; 'He may abandon us (they say), we stand in no farther need of him.'—I do not think that any one has yet dared or will ever dare to show the least discontent, much less a desire to quit the Order; especially if he reflects on the dictatorial threat, *It shall be in vain for any prince to pretend to save him who shall dare to betray us.*[4]

"They select their pupils with great caution, and only entice into their Order those whom they think can be useful to the attainment of their ends. Statesmen, persons distinguished by rank or fortune, archivists, counsellors, secretaries, clerks, professors, abbés, preceptors, physicians, and apothecaries, are always welcome candidates to the Order.

"The degree of *Major Illuminee* is, if I may make use of such an expression, a school in which the candidate is trained like a true *Bloodhound.*"[5]

Here the deponent relates their method of watching their adepts and of describing both them and the prophane. He also mentions some few of the thousand or fifteen hundred questions that are to be answered on the character, the habits, &c. of any person whom an adept is ordered to scrutinize. He then continues:

"This method of enlightening the pupils always goes on increasing in every degree. A Brother may know those of his class and those of an inferior one; but, unless his Superiors have conferred on him the commission of Director, Visitor, or Spy, all other adepts are, in their language, *invisible* to him. This, without doubt, is the point that constitutes the great strength of the Order. The chiefs, by this method, watch an inferior without being known; they know how far he is devoted to the Order and true to his secrecy; and a point of still greater importance is, that in case of any explosion (of which they have been long apprehensive), and on all occasions, they can support the brethren without any one entertaining the least suspicion of their being connected with the system, since they are unknown even to the Brethren, and of course to the prophane.

"*There are men, and they may be easily discerned, who defend the Order* (of Illuminism) *with great warmth, though they do not declare themselves to belong to it.* Such conduct certainly deserves a little animadversion. Either these defenders belong to the Order, or they do not; if they do not, can they pretend to defend that which they neither know nor have any possibility of knowing. If they belong to the Order, that very circumstance renders them unworthy of belief, though they should adduce as proofs some few works thrown out to baffle any attempt to investigate the plan of the Order, or should protest on their words of honour when they speak so highly in its praise. When a person comes seriously to consider the impossibility of knowing any thing of Illuminism but by being a member of it, and when we compare the many advantages derived from their *invisibility*; if we should be tempted to draw any conclusions on these defenders, we might (and that without reasoning ill) suppose they belonged themselves to the Order, and to that particular species of adept which the Illuminees term *invisible*."[6]

After having thus given as much of the general plan of the Illuminees as he could know without having been admitted to the higher degrees, the Deponent comes to the principles which the Superiors wish to inculcate in their pupils; and in the first place he mentions the following, of which they have made a sort of proverb:

> Tous les Rois et tous les Pretres
> Sont des Fripons et des traitres.[7]

With regard to *Suicide*, the Superiors preach to their brethren *to prepare them for more tempestuous times*. "They have the art of representing suicide as so easy, and so advantageous in certain circumstances, that I should not be surprised (says Mr. Renner) to see some adept carried away by the lure of a certain voluptuousness which they pretend to be peculiar to suicide; and they even pretend to prove their assertions by examples.

"But of all their detestable principles the most dangerous in my judgement is this: *The end justifies the means*. In consequence of this morality, and ACCORDING TO THEIR CONSTANT PRACTICE, the mere suspicion that a man will at any future period be in a position to obstruct the views of the Order will be a sufficient reason to calumniate him, however virtuous he may be. They will cabal to drive one man out of his place; they will poison another; a third they will assassinate; in short, they will do any thing to attain their ends. Suppose the crime of the Illuminee should be discovered, he always has the *Patet-exitus* as a resource. *It is only a ball through the head*, and he escapes the rigour and ignominy of the law."

Mr. Renner next alludees to what the Sect calls its *Moral Government* or *Commission of Morals*, or its *Fiscal*, "This comission is a college formed of the most able and honest men, that is, in their language; of men chiefly belonging to the class of *Invisibles*, and who, enjoying the confidence of the sovereign, would, according to the views of their commission, inform him of the morals and honesty of each of his subjects; but as probity is necessary to fulfill the divers stations of the state, each person should be prepared beforehand for the office he is to occupy. An admirable plan! But should they ever accomplish it, should their rule ever be adopted, what would become of all those men who did not belong to Illuminism? Happily, the plan is discovered in time; otherwise they might have verified what a Superior just returned from visiting a Superior of a higher degree had foretold: *All the Posts once properly filled in succession to each other, should the Order be composed of but six hundred members, no power on earth could resist them.*"

Mr. Renner finishes by declaring, that he is unacquainted with the ultimate object of the Order; that the Superiors were perpetually talking of that object, but never mentioned what it was. He believe it to be of the utmost consequence; but he leaves every one free to conceive, after what he has said, how that object can accord with the civil and religious duties. He affirms on oath the particulars contained in the above declaration, and which he leaves written and signed by his own hand.

Juridical Depositions of Mr. Cosandey,
3d April, 1785.

My reason for placing Mr. Renner's deposition first was, because he is more explicit on the government of Illuminism; while Mr. Cosandey chiefly dwells on the principles of the Sect. After having shown in a few words how Free-masonry serves as a cloak to the Sect, how the candidate is gradually fettered in the bonds of the Superiors, and how dangerous must be a servitude to men who from principle wish to appear idlers though in the most active pursuits; he proceeds with the unfortunate *Minerval* to the degrees of *Minor* and *Major Illuminee*. "It is here (says he) that the pupil is a little further initiated into the systems of the Order. Light, however, is imparted to him but slowly, and with all possible precautions. He is here made acquainted with a greater number of Adepts and Under-Superiors; but the Chiefs always remain *invisible*.

"In order to be advanced to the higher degrees the candidate must, in the language of the Sect, have got rid of all religious prejudices, or at least he must assume the appearance of one who has so done when in the presence of his Superiors; as no *religionist* (such is their expression) can be admitted to the higher degrees.[8]

"The most excellent Superiors are the persons that give the ton in all these degrees. Their orders, their maxims, their opinions, their doctrines, are the soul, the standard, the spirit, the main spring of this institution. The lower class of Superiors and Chiefs, are cunning knaves, and black and systematic villains, or sometimes misled enthusiasts, spurred on and abominably deluded by the others. As a proof, I will relate some of their principles in the form of proverbs, which are never given in writing, but are perpetually inculcated in the adepts by these Superiors.

"I. *When nature lays too heavy a burthen upon us, it is to suicide that we are to apply for relief.* Patet exitus. An Illuminee, they would tell us, should make away with himself rather than betray his Order; and they also represent a secret voluptuousness to be inherent to suicide.

"II. *Nothing through reason, every thing through passion*, is their second maxim. The end, the propagation, and the advantage of their Order, supplies in the minds of the adepts the place of God, country, and conscience. Every thing that obstructs the progress of the Order is the blackest treason."

"III. *The end sanctifies the means*. Thus calumny, poison, assassination, treason, revolt, wickedness, and any thing that can lead to this end, is laudable.

"IV. *No Prince can save the man who dares to betray us.* Things then are carried on in this Order that are adverse to the interests of Princes; things that from their importance might be discovered to Princes; such a discovery (in the language of the Sect) would be the blackest treason; and the traitor is beforehand threatened with vengeance. They must also have means of destroying their accusers with impunity; and such means are easily surmized.

"V. *All Kings and all Priests are rascals and traitors*; and in another place, *All Priests are knaves.* The total annihilation of religion, of the love of the country, and of princes, enters into the plans of the Illuminees, because (say they) religion, as well as love of the country, and of princes, restrains the affections of men to particular states, and diverts them from the more extensive views of Illuminism.

"Among their plans I observed one which they called their *moral Empire* or *Government.* This government, which would throw the whole force of every state into the hands of their *college* or *council* of Illuminism, would *without any appeal to the prince,* name to all promotions, and grant or refuse all the favors of the state. By these means they would be entrusted with the absolute right of definitively pronouncing on the honesty or the capability of each individual. By these means too all the prophane would be discarded from the court and other employments; and, to use their expression, a holy legion would surround the prince, master him, and dictate his edicts according to their own will and pleasure. This Regimen or Moral College, also called the Commission of Morals, or the *Fiscal* (being a sort of exchequer chamber for the government of the people), would invest the Sect with a most formidable despotic power over the four quarters of the globe, and would reduce sovereigns to the despicable state of mere phantoms, or of crowned slaves."

This College or *Moral Regimen*, will occur again in another juridical deposition; and I will then explain how it served to veil the future projects of the Sect for the disorganization and absolute destruction of all society whatever. Mr. Cosandey concludes with saying, that he is ready to affirm on oath the truth of all that is contained in the above declaration.

These depositions, notwithstanding their importance, seemed to make but little impression. Whether the tribunals were beset by, or in great part composed of Illuminees, or not, I cannot know; but they affected to treat these declarations as containing nothing either very serious or menacing; or whether the removal of Weishaupt had made them view the Sect as destroyed, and the conspiracy as counteracted, I do not pretend to say; but certain it is, that at length Heaven by its thunderbolts warns nations and their rulers of the plots contriving against them, of the extent of which plots they were ignorant; neither had they surmized the baneful activity of the conspirators. Dismissed from his public functions at Ingolstadt, Weishaupt had taken refuge at Ratisbon. This town becomes his new *Eleusis*, his center of mysteries; all his plots had followed him thither; and so far was he from looking upon them as baffled, that he pursued them with redoubled ardour. Vengeance had rendered him more terrible from the recesses of his new retreat; and now, entirely liberated from all public duties, he gives up his whole time to the preparation and drilling of emissaries, and to teaching them the means of sapping, when on their different missions, the foundations of the altar and the throne, of civil society, and of all governments whatever.

Among his adepts was one LANZ, an apostate priest. Weishaupt designed him as the person to carry his mysteries and conspiracies into Silesia. His mission was already fixed, and Weishaupt was giving him his last instructions, when a thunderbolt from Heaven struck the apostate dead, and that *by the side of Weishaupt.*[9] The Brethren, in their first fright, had not recourse to their ordinary means for diverting the papers of the deceased adept from the inspection of the magistrates. The perusal of some of his papers furnished new proofs; and, being transmitted to the Court of Bavaria, induced it to take the determination of following up the discoveries made in the depositions of Messrs. Cosandey and Renner.

The enquiries made, chiefly related to those who were known to have had connetions with Weishaupt at Ingolstadt. The adept FISCHER, first judge and Burgo-master of that town, and the Librarian DREXL, were banished. The Baron FRAUENBERG and fifteen other of Weishaupt's pupils were expelled from the university. But neither their punishment nor the circumstance of the adept being struck by lightning, could raise any symptoms of remorse in the mind of their master. The following letter to Fischer may serve as a specimen of the manner in which he wished to support their courage, stimulate their enthusiasm, and infuse all the rage and vengeance of his plots into their minds.

"*I salute you, my dear martyr,*" it is thus he begins his letter. He then reminds his pretended martyr of that passage in Seneca where the just man struggling with adversity is represented as the sight most worthy of Heaven: He then continues: "Am I to congratulate you, or am I to condole with you on your misfortunes? I know you too well to indulge in the latter sentiment—Receive then my most sincere congratulations on seeing you among those to whom posterity will render justice, and whose constancy in the defence of truth it cannot fail to admire—You are triply and quadruply more dear to me, now that you share my fate and that of so many other magnanimous persons. I leave it to your prudence to decide whether you will commence a prosecution against those who have been guilty of such an abominable injustice against you; or whether, submitting to your exile without murmur or complaint, you will wait for better times. You shall not want; I and the Brethren will provide for your expenses. *The public papers also shall represent the whole of this business in its proper light.* Drexl in the mean time will retire to Brunn. *Let laughers laugh, and our enemies rejoice. Their joy ere long shall be converted into tears. Look upon yourself as happy to suffer with the better part of the nation.* If I have the power of giving my benediction to any body, I give you mine with both my hands. *O be thou blessed, most worthy and most constant of my Heroes*.... I am sorry that all this has happened just at the time when I am setting out for the banks of the Rhine. I depart next month and shall not return till a few months hence. *In the mean time I shall not be idle; and it is not without a reason that I go to that country. Acquaint the Brethren of it.* Be always firm and constant. No dishonour can attach to you; continue as you have begun, and your enemies will be obliged to admire you. Adieu, learn to appreciate and feel your own greatness. Your enemies are little indeed in their triumph.—(Ratisbon this 9th April 1785).

"P. S. If you want money I will have proper measures taken at Munich to supply you."

This letter was either intercepted or fell into the Elector's hands by some other means;[10] and he there saw how dangerous a man this must be who could thus infuse his enthusiasm into the minds of his Conspirators. A secret commission was named to receive further depositions. The aulic counsellor UTZSCHNEIDER and Mr. GRÜNBERGER of the Academy of Sciences, who were known to have abandoned the Order of the Illuminees about two years before, were summoned to make their depositions. The Priest Cosandey was called upon once more. The declaration made in common by these three Gentlemen will recall to the minds of the readers many of the particulars already stated in the foregoing declarations, and in the Code of the Illuminees, with respect to the means employed by the Sect, for making themselves masters of the Masonic Lodges; for appropriating to themselves their funds, to provide for the expence of their travellers; and for multiplying the number of their adepts.— The same method for the scrutators is observable, the same oaths, almanacks, and cypher for the first degrees. The deponents had abandoned the Order before they were admitted to the higher degrees. The principles that had been laid down to them are on that account the more remarkable. I shall, therefore, translate that part of their evidence as being of the utmost consequence. Some persons may be of opinion, that to have simply stated the perfect coincidence of this new declaration with those already seen would have sufficed; but they should consider that repetitions of objects of such importance may be insisted on by many readers, because the proofs are strengthened by the number, the character, and concordance of the witnesses.

The Juridical Deposition made in common by the Aulic Counsellor UTZSCHNEIDER, *the Priest* COSANDEY, *and the Academician* GRÜNBERGER, *on the 9th of Sept. 1785.*

"The object of the first degrees of Illuminism is at once to train their young men, and to be informed of every thing that is going forward by a system of *espionage*.[11] The Superiors aim at procuring from their inferiors diplomatic acts, documents, and original writings. With pleasure they see them commit any treasons or treacherous acts, because they not only turn the secrets betrayed to their own advantage, but thereby have it in their power to keep the traitors in a perpetual dread, lest, if they every showed any signs of stubbornness, their malefactions should be made known.—*Oderint dum metuant*, let them hate, provided they fear, is the principle of their government.

"The Illuminees from these first degrees are educated in the following principles:

I. "The Illuminee who wishes to rise to the highest degree must be free from all religion;[12] for a *religionist* (as they call every man who has any religion) will never be admitted to the highest degrees."

II. The *Patet Exitus*, or the doctrine on Suicide, is expressed in the same terms as in the preceding deposition.

III. "*The end sanctifies the means*. The welfare of the Order will be a justification for calumnies, poisonings, assassinations, perjuries, treasons, rebellions; in short, for all that the *prejudices* of men lead them to call crimes.

IV. "One must be more submissive to the Superiors of Illuminism, than to the sovereigns or magistrates who govern the people; and he that gives the preference to sovereigns or governors of the people is useless to us.[13] Honor, life, and fortune, all are to be sacrificed to the Superiors. The governors of nations are despots when they are not directed by us.—They can have no authority over us, who are free men."[14]

The Marquis of Costanza used to say, "that there ought to be but two Princes in Germany—These Princes should be Illuminees, and so surrounded and led by our adepts, that none of the prophane could approach their persons. The greater and lesser offices of the state should be solely entrusted to members of our Order; and the advantage of the Order should be attended to, though in direct opposition to the interests of the Prince.[15] Sovereigns should also pass through the lower degrees of the Order, and they should only be admitted to the higher degrees when they properly apprehend the holy designs of the Order,—which are no other than to deliver the people from the bondage of their Princes, Nobles, and Priests; to establish an equality of stations and of religion; and to render men both free and happy. Should we ever have six hundred Illuminees in Bavaria, nothing could resist us."

I promised to make a few reflections on this article; and to those persons I address them, who would immediately lay hold of it to prove that the Illuminees, so far from wishing to annihilate every government and civil society itself, had no other view than to re-unite Germany under one and the same government.[16] Most undoubtedly such views were held out to the deponents in their lower classes; but let it be remembered, that none of them had been admitted to the higher mysteries. It is in the degree of *Epopt* that the designs of the Order for the total destruction of *Civil Society* are manifested. There the illuminizing Hierophant no longer says, that Germany ought to be under the government of *one* Prince; but he says THAT NATIONS AND PRINCES SHALL DISAPPEAR FROM THE FACE OF THE EARTH; *that every father shall, like Abraham, be at once the priest and sovereign of his family; and* REASON *shall be the sole Code of Man*. The Hierophant there declares, that SECRET SOCIETIES are the agents that are to produce this revolution, and *that it is one of the grand secrets of Illuminism*. There, in short, is clearly to be seen the plan of bringing men back to the pretended *Patriarchal nomade* and *savage* life; and it is even expressly asserted, that the original cause of the fall of man was their *re-union in civil society*. The depositions, therefore, of Messrs. Utzschneider, Cosandey, and Grünberger, are perfectly correct so far as they relate to their degrees; for such was the doctrine taught in the degrees of *Major* and *Minor* Illuminee. Another remark may also be true, that as a preparatory step the Illuminees only seek to destroy all the lesser powers in order to form one or two great states in Germany; but that will not change the fate decreed in the higher mysteries for these greater Princes of the German nation, or for all Princes and nations in general. This single Potentate will then share the same fate as Religion. We have heard them talk of reducing the world to the *unity of Religion*, as well as to the unity or equality of *stations*. But has not the Sect already declared, that in order to be admitted to the last secret one must begin by *getting rid of all religion*? This plan, therefore, for reducing Germany under the dominion of one Prince, is evidently nothing more than a preliminary step, in like manner as their plan of subjecting Princes to the government of their Order. When the proper time comes, all these plans are changed, in the lessons of the adepts, to the total annihilation of every state, prince, and civil government on earth.

The Reader may easily perceive how the Sect, even so early as the degrees in which the three deponents had been admitted, prepares them for the last secrets; especially when he sees immediately following the pretended union of Germany, that maxim which has already appeared in the first deposition:

V. "The love of one's prince and of one's country are incompatible with views of an immense extent, with *the ultimate ends of the Order*, and one must glow with ardour for the attainment of that *end*."[17]

In the Degrees also to which the deponents had been admitted we see the Superiors incesssantly declaiming on that *end*; but they never mention what it really was. They even confess that they are not in the secret; they say that the knowledge of it is reserved to the higher degrees; their own declaration, therefore, proves that it cannot be this unity of Religion or of Government to be established in Germany, as they are not strangers to that plan. Besides, how can it appear, that the love of one's country, or national love, is incompatible with the wish of uniting a great nation under the dominion of one Prince. On the other hand, we see these maxims in perfect accord with the views of Illuminism, when, advancing toward the higher degrees, we hear the Sect pouring for its blasphemies against Princes and Nations, and positively declaring, as one of their mysteries, that Secret societies were only contrived to sweep Nations and Princes from the face of the earth. Such are the plots to be discovered to nations; such have been the tricks employed by the Illuminees to lull nations to sleep on their dangers; and, English Reviewers having hearkened to such insinuations, I am obliged to have recourse to repetitions in the midst of a nation whose ruin is now become one of the chief objects of the Sect.—But let us return to the depositions of our witnesses.

"The Superiors of Illuminism are to be looked upon as the most perfect and the most enlightened of men; no doubts are to be entertained even of their infallibility.[18]

"It is in these moral and political principles that the Illuminees are educated in the lower degrees; and it is according to the manner in which they imbibe them and show their devotion to the Order, or are able to second its views, that they are earlier or later admitted to the higher degrees.

"They use every possible artifice to get the different post-offices in all countries entrusted to the care of their adepts only. They also boast that they are in possession of the secret of opening and reclosing letters without the circumstance being perceived.

"They made us give answers in writing to the following questions: How would it be possible to devise one single system of morals and one common Government for all Europe, and what means should be employed to effectuate it? Would the Christian Religion be a necessary requisite? Should revolt be employed to accomplish it? &c. &c.

"We were also asked, in which Brethren we should place the most confidence if there were any important plan to be undertaken; and whether we were willing to recognize the right of life and death as vested in the Order; and also the right of the sword, *Jus Gladii.*

"In consequence of our acquaintance with this doctrine of the Illuminees, with their conduct, their manners, and their incitements to treason, and being fully convinced of the dangers of the Sect, we the Aulic Counsellor Utzschneider and the Priest Dillis left the Order. The Professor Grünberger, the Priest Cosandey, Renner, and Zaupfer, did the same a week after, though the Illuminees sought to impose upon us shamefully, by assuring us that his Electoral Highness was a member of their Order. We clearly saw that a Prince knowing his own interests, and wholly attending to the paternal care of his subjects, would never countenance a Sect, spreading through almost every province under the cloak of Free-masonry; because it sows division and discord between parents and their children, between Princes and their subjects, and among the most sincere friends; because on all important occasions it would install partiality on the seats of justice and in the councils, as it always prefers the welfare of the Order to that of the state, and the interests of its adepts to those of the prophane. Experience had convinced us, that they would soon succeed in perverting all the Bavarian youth. The leading feature in the generality of their adepts were irreligion, depravity of morals, disobedience to their Prince and to their parents, and the neglect of all useful studies. We saw that the fatal consequence of Illuminism would be, to create a general distrust between the prince and his subjects, the father and his children, the minister and his secretaries, and between the different tribunals and councils. We were not to be deterred by that threat so often repeated, *That no Prince can save him that betrays us.* We abandoned, one after the other, this Sect, which *under different names,* as we have been informed by several of our former Brethren, has already spread itself *in Italy, and particularly at Venice, in Austria,* in Holland, in Saxony, on the Rhine, particularly at Frankfort, and even as far as America.—The Illuminees meddle as much as possible in state affairs, and excite troubles wherever their Order can be benefited by them."

Here followed a list of a great many *invisibles*, of several superiors, and of some of the most active members. A second list contained persons who, though as yet unacquainted with the ultimate views of the Order, were zealous and active Recruiters, but the government thought fit to keep those two lists secret. The deponents then proceed.

"We are not acquainted with the other *Invisibles*, who in all probability are chiefs of a higher degree.

"After we had retired from the Order, the Illuminees calumniated us on all sides in the most infamous manner. Their cabal made us fail in every request we presented; succeeding in rendering us hateful and odious to our superiors, they even carried their calumnies so far as to pretend that one of us had committed murder. After a year's persecution, an Illuminee came to represent to the Aulic Counsellor Utzschneider, that from experience he must have learned that he was every where persecuted by the Order, that unless he could contrive to regain its protection, he would never succeed in any of his demands, and that he could still regain admission."

Here ends the deposition signed by the three deponents. After their signature follows the attestation, that each of the deponents had been called in separately in presence of the Commissary, and their respective declarations read to them; and that each had affirmed the truth of the contents on oath, as witnesses, the 10th of September, 1785. I leave the reader to make his reflections on the strength and nature of these first proofs acquired against Illuminism; and proceed immediately to the circumstances which disclosed the ulterior projects of the Sect.

1. Original Writings, Vol. II. Let 2, from *Philo* to *Cato*.
2. Ibid. Let. 1, from *Epictetus*.
3. Orig. Writ. Let. 1 to *Epictetus*, 7th Feb. 1783.
4. Kein Fürst kann den schützen der uns verräth.
5. Wie die wahren spürhunde abgerichtet werden.
6. Und zwar von iener art der verschwundenen, wie man sie in der ordens sprache nennt.—Were I to request certain English reviewers, and particularly Dr. Griffiths, or his assistants in the *Monthly Review*, to read and weigh this observation of the German deponent, those gentlemen might perhaps wish to retort it on me; but let them recollect, that when men who have associated with robbers are seen to depose against them, or when the writings of conspirators are produced in evidence, a person may easily prove their criminality without being an accomplice. But you, Gentlemen, who were not with them, yet pretend to prove their innocence, will your assertion invalidate the evidence of eye and ear witnesses? If you are of their party, all that can be concluded from your denials is, that you are still very faithful and much devoted to them, since in their defence you resist the demonstration of evidence.
7. All kings and all priests are rascals and traitors.

8. Dann kein *Religionär* (es ist ihr ausdruck) wird in die höhere grad auf genommen.
9. See the Apology of the Illuminees, P. 62.
10. See Original Writings, Vol. II. last Letter and Note.
11. Und zu gliech zur auskundschaftung aller sachen.
12. Der Illuminat, der in die höhern grade kommen will, muss von aller religion frey seyn.
13. Vollte jemand den Regenten mehr anhängen, so taugt er nicht für uns.
14. Sie haben kein Recht über uns, freye Menschen.
15. Alles was beste des Ordens besördert, muss man thun, wenn es gleich dem besten der Regenten zuwider lauft.
16. This is precisely what has been lately attempted to divert the eyes of the public from their monstrous and Antisocial plots; and even in England this plea has been set up, in hopes of invalidating the proofs adduced in these Memoirs. I know not who is the *invisible* writer of such paragraphs; but though even the *Sieur Boettiger* himself, famous among the German Illuminees, were the author of them I should little fear his arguments. Let my readers compare his proofs with mine: I ask no more.
17. Fürsten und vaterlands liebe wiedersprechen den weitaussehenden gesichts puncten des Ordens—Man muss glühen für den zweck.
18. An deren untrüglichkeit man nie zweifeln dürfe.

CHAP. VIII.

Continuation of the Discoveries made in Bavaria as to the Illuminees.—Proceedings of the Court with respect to the Chiefs of the Sect.—A few Remarks on and a List of the principal Adepts.

NOTWITHSTANDING the important discoveries made by the court of Bavaria, proofs were still wanting of the plans and of the ultimate views of Illuminism, which the Sect concealed with so much care, and of which none of the witnesses could give any satisfactory account. The court had neglected to seize Weishaupt's papers at the time; and it was clear that the adepts had taken every precaution to put theirs beyond the power of the most diligent search. The court even appeared to pay little or no attention to the proper steps that should be taken, and only watched the motions of those adepts who still kept up a correspondence with their chiefs. If we are to credit the apology published by the Illuminees, it was for no other reason that DELLING, municipal officer of Munich, and KRENNER, professor at Ingolstadt, were dismissed from their employments. On the same account, they tell us, were the Count Savioli and the Marquis Constanza exiled from Bavaria, and the Baron Maggenhoff condemned to a month's imprisonment in a monastery.

This apologist also pretends, that the Canon Hertel was deprived of his benefice, because he would not give an account of the funds belonging to the Illuminees. But after the different parts that we have seen these adepts perform, it appears that the court was pretty well informed; and it certainly gave a great proof of its clemency when it allowed *Brutus*-Savioli and *Diomedes*-Constanza a pension which they were at liberty to expend wherever they chose, excepting in Bavaria. Light, however, as these punishments were for conspirators of their stamp, the Illuminees filled all Germnay with their reclamations, crying out against a persecution which they represented as the height of despotism, oppression, and injustice. The depositions that had been made were published, and the authors of them were immediately assailed with a torrent of abuse, sophistry, and calumny; nor was the court spared. The whole business appeared to be changed into a literary war, in which the impudence of the apologists had very nigh succeeded in casting doubts on the wisdom and justice of his Electoral Highness;[1] and it was high time to have recourse to such measures as could incontestably prove the guilt of the Sect.

At length, on the 11th of October, 1786, the magistrates, by order of the Elector, made a visit at *Cato*-Zwack's house, at a time when he least expected it. Others went on the same commission to the castle of Sanderdorf, belonging to *Hannibal* Baron Bassus. The result of these visitations was, the discovery of a multitude of letters, discourses, rules, plans, and statues, which may be looked upon as the archives of the conspirators, and have been published under the title of *Original Writings of the Order and of the Sect of the Illuminees*. The conspiracy, of which Weishaupt was the chief, now appeared in such horrid colours, that one could scarcely believe human wickedness to have been able to devise it. But at the head of each of these two volumes is an advertisement, informing all readers, that orders have been given by the Elector to the keeper of his archives to show the originals to whoever might wish to verify them. The only resource now left to the conspirators was to complain of the violation of domestic secrecy. Pretended justifications swarmed again from the adepts; and they had the impudence to assert, that these letters, so far from containing any thing militating against society or religion, only contained views for the happiness and amelioration of mankind. They made every attempt possible to give plausible interpretations to their letters; but they never dared assert that any of these writings had been forged. Their own avowals are to be found in their apologies; and the proofs of their anti-religious and anti-social conspiracy rest upon such incontestable grounds, that their sophisms can never invalidate them.[2]

The court of Bavaria, when it gave so great a publicity to the proofs it had thus acquired, was not actuated solely by a view of justifying its own conduct; but it was desirous also to warn every state of the dangers with which it was threatened. The Elector, therefore, sent a copy of these Original Writings to all the powers of Europe; and the answers of the different ministers proved, that they had all received these documents of a most monstrous conspiracy against every church and state. The historian will naturally ask, how it came to pass that the knowledge of these proofs of a conspiracy, at once so evident and so threatening to every state in the world, should have been so long confined to Germany. And how it happened, that these Original Writings did not become the daily lectures of every family. Should not every father have read it to his children, and explained to them the horrid machinations that were contriving against their God, their country, and their property? Universal indignation must have seized every mind, and crushed these illuminizing monsters in their cradle. Such at least were the fears which the conspirators themselves had conceived on seeing their plans and means discovered. Unable to destroy the proofs, they did every thing in their power to hinder their circulation. On the other hand, few ministers were aware of the immense influence and power of secret societies; and the Bavarian association appeared to them more despicable than dangerous; the very excess of their conspiracy gave it a more chimerical appearance; and the policy of some statesmen might have made them believe that the publication of the archives of these conspirators would only serve to accredit their sophisms, and add to the danger by divulging their principles. Lastly, the language in which they were written was little known in the other parts of Europe; and it was thought best to leave them in a profound oblivion. Such may be the explanation of this species of phenomenon, or of this total ignorance in which the rest of the world were, with respect to the nature and views of the Illuminees, when I announced to the public the use I intended to make of them in these Memoirs.

A mystery still more astonishing, and which could not have been believed, had not the progress of the Illuminees proved it, is that inactivity or somnolency in which all the German courts appeared to be buried in the midst of the dangers that had been so clearly pointed out to them by the court of Bavaria. Unfortunately for the Empire, Frederic II of Prussia died a little before these last proofs were acquired against the Illuminees. No sooner did this Prince hear of the conspiracy, than he immediately traced all those principles of sedition and anarchy which he had already been obliged to divulge as the tenets of the Sophisters; the Illuminees even pretend it to have been at his instigation that the court of Munich prosecuted their chief and the first adepts who were discovered.[3] What would he not have done himself against this Sect, if he had but seen in the Original Writings the progress that it was making in his own states! Ministers, under a Prince so tenacious as he was of the authority necessary to support his Government, and so justly offended as he was against the Sophisters of Rebellion, would not have sneered or replied sarcastically to those letters which the court of Bavaria transmitted as introductory and explanatory, together with the proofs acquired against the Sect. But the archives of Illuminism were not discovered till the 11th and 12th October 1786, and Frederic had died on the 17th August of that year. His successor was a prey to adepts of another species, almost as great knaves as those of Bavaria. The Emperor Joseph had not yet been undeceived with respect to the Lodges that surrounded him. Many other Princes were either seduced, or so fettered by the Illuminees that they could not act. This may serve to account for their apparent indifference; and it also explains the circumstance of several of them having viewed the proceedings of the court of Munich in the light of an absolute persecution of their own Brethren. The Prince Bishop of Ratisbon was the only one who seemed to know his danger, and who published edicts in support of those issued by the Elector.

Nevertheless, the proofs published by the court of Bavaria are those whence the most evident demonstration of the plots of Illuminism have been deduced in these Memoirs. The very scraps of paper found among the archives indicate the most consummate villainy. Among these were, chiefly in *Ajax*-Massenhausen's hand, and in the cypher of the Order, *receipts* for making the *aqua toffana*, the most acute of all poisons; for *procuring abortion in women*; and for *poisoning the air of an apartment*: also a collection of *one hundred and thirty seals of Princes, Noblemen, and Bankers*, with the secret of taking off and imitating all those for which the Order might, according to circumstances, have occasion. The description of a lock, of which the adepts only should have the secret, was likewise contained in these papers; also the model of a coffer wherein to preserve their papers, and which should take fire immediately if any of the prophane attempted to open it. On other detached papers were to be seen the plan for placing some adepts in the suite of an ambassador, who should then carry on some commerce as fraudulent as it was lucrative for the Sect. Also the secret intimation, that all the Superiors of Illuminism should know how *to write with both hands*. A manuscript also was found entirely in Zwack's handwriting, and looked upon as very precious by the Order, because, under the title *Better than Horus*, it contained all the blasphemies of Atheism.[4]

Notwithstanding the little impression the publication of these discoveries had made on the other Princes of Germany, the court of Bavaria continued its prosecutions against the Sect. About twenty of the adepts were cited to appear; some were dismissed from their employments; others condemned to a few years imprisonment; and some, particularly Zwack, saved themselves by flight. The Elector's Tribunal could not by any calumny be accused of being sanguinary, as not one of the adepts was condemned to death. This punishment seemed to be reserved for Weishaupt alone, and a price was set upon his head. The Regency of Ratisbon, which in the first instance had refused to drive him from their territories, no longer dared to support him, at least not openly; and he took refuge under his Highness the Duke of Saxe Gotha. The reason why the Founder of Illuminism, and a number of his proscribed adepts, found protection and still continue in favour at so many courts, may be explained by the numerous disciples who enjoyed places of high importance in the different courts, and some of whom indeed were the Princes themselves. The list of these latter, were it accurately made out, would astonish posterity; more particularly, should the art with which Weishaupt seduced them, by truncating the mysteries, have escaped the notice of the historian; or should the means have remained a secret by which he blinded them and bound them to the Order, by surrounding them with adepts who knew how to seize on the ministry, on the *Decasteres*, or councils, and occupied all the places of consequence by themselves or their creatures.

I will not pretend to say, that these artifices of Illuminism can excuse those Princes for becoming disciples of Weishaupt. But most certainly they were rendered the dupes of his impiety before they became the sport of his conspiracies; and undoubtedly the latter was but the just punishment of the former. However this may be, we find LEWIS ERNEST of SAXE GOTHA at the head of these adepts under the characteristic of *Timoleon*. According to all the letters that I have received from Germany, this Prince is at length conscious of his error. He at present pays much greater attention to the happiness of his subjects than to the mysteries of the Sect. Weishaupt is not even allowed to appear in his presence; but the goodness of his heart will not allow the Prince to withdraw his benefactions even from those who have incurred his displeasure. It is thus, at least, that the pension he allows to the Founder of Illuminism is explained.[5] But on the other hand, Weishaupt is far from being excluded from the presence of Maria Charlotte Meinungen, the wife of His Highness; and thus is explained the asylum which the contriver of such horrid plots still finds at that court, notwithstanding the conversion of the Prince.

I will not pretend to pronounce, whether AUGUSTUS of SAXE GOTHA has imbibed a similar disgust for Illuminism, as has his Brother the reigning Prince. At the time of Weishaupt's arrival, however, he was also an adept under the characteristic of *Prince Walter.*

CHARLES AUGUSTUS DUKE OF SAXE-WEIMAR was also initiated under the title of *Eschylus*; but he renounced the mysteries of the Sect.

The late PRINCE FERDINAND OF BRUNSWICK, at once the martial hero of Minden, and the Masonic leader at Wilhemsbaden, fell a prey to all sorts of Illuminism. Wilhermots had begun by initiating him in the Illuminism of Swedenborg, and of the Martinists. His freqnet conferences with Knigge seduced him into that of Weishaupt, who created him his Brother or his High Priest *Aaron*, and His Highness died during his Priesthood.

As to the late PRINCE OF NEUWIED, I know not what name was given him in recompense for his devotion to the Sect; but at his court it might with truth be said, the Illuminees had acquired such an ascendancy, that if they had gained a similar one in other parts, the world must have been theirs. This unfortunate Prince little thought that his own son would be deprived of all power in his own states, and that he would be reduced humbly to solicit the Comitia of the Empire for leave to assert his own rights, and to drive out from his states those adepts that had been protected by his Father, and his Uncle the Count Stolberg; or at least for leave to dismiss them from the employments they occupied, even from that of education of his children, which they had seized upon in spite of him.[6]

Another species of adept is My Lord the BARON OF DALBERG, Coadjutor to the Sects of Mentz, Worms, and Constanz, and Governor of the town and country of Erfort. We are led to shrink back in astonishment, and examine whether our eyes did not impose upon us, at the sight of a Bishop, intended to occupy the first Ecclesiastical and Electoral See in Germany, ranking among this Illuminized Brotherhood. Morever, persons who had often been in company with His Lordship insisted on my effacing his name from these Memoirs. They asured me, that he held the principles of the modern Philosophers in the utmost detestation and that to them he attributed the French Revolution. I then produced a pamphlet published by His Lordship, with all his titles and his name at the head of it, entitled, *Of the Influence of Sciences and of the Polite Arts on the Public Tranquillity—At Erfort*, 1793. They then saw that the object of this pamphlet was *to stifle in the germs* what His Lordship calls *the noxious prejudices of some short-sighted good people*, by proving to them that neither the Philosophers nor the Sophisters of the age had given rise to the French Revolution, and *that Condorcet himself had but little contributed towards it*. This pamphlet also abounded in those arguments of Illuminized Philosophism which the Sect set forth to dupe nations as to the tendency of their conspiracy; I did not therefore efface the name of His Lordship; I on the contrary subjoined that of *Crescens*, his characteristic among the Illuminees. How it is possible that at such a name he could refrain from shuddering with horror! and what services could the Order expect from him under such a characteristic? The name of *Crescens* has only been transmitted to posterity by his addition to the infamous debauchery of the Cynic Philosophers, and by his calumnies against the Christians, which obliged St. Justin to write his Second Apology for Christianity. A protestant who is eager to see that of His Lordship tells us, that it will most certainly appear in its proper time, and we impatiently await for it![7] We shall there find, I hope, that His Lordship had not been initiated into all the secrets of the Sect. They must at least have concealed from him their designs upon the Sees of Mentz, Worms, and Constanz, to which His Lordship was Coadjutor.—In all probability, these were not the secrets of which his Secretary *Crysippus*-KOLBORN informed him, who, admitted to the degree of Epopt, *was already become a half-naturalist without knowing it*, and from whom Knigge expected the greatest services.[8] But can this characteristic of *Crescens* denote any other view than that of seducing His Lordship into an apostacy similar to that of his Secretary? We can only repeat, that it is with great anxiety we wait for His Lordship's Apology.

But what other apology, than a clear and public profession of faith, and an abjuration of Illuminism, can reinstate the honor of the Prelate HASLEIN, known in the Sect as the Brother *Philo of Byblos*! The Original Writings describe this adept prelate as overloaded with work. It is an unfortunate circumstance for him to have been able to find time to pen letters and plans that could have placed him in such great estimation with the chiefs of these conspirators.[9]

Among the higher class of adepts may be ranked *Alexander*, or the general Count of PAPPENHEIM, Governor of Ingolstadt, and *Alfred* the Count of SEINSHEIM, Minister and Vice-President of the Council at Munich. At getting possession of this latter Minister Weishaupt exults, and on giving him the characteristic of *Alfred* he thus writes to *Cato*: "What great men we daily gain over to our party at *Athens* (Munich), and that without its being perceived! Men much considered, ready formed, and perfect models!" Weishaupt does not wish to see this adept in *leading strings*, and therefore dispenses with his noviciate. He also hopes, with a little care on the part of the recruiters, *to see his Excellency become one of his greatest enthusiasts*; and he soon found that he had judged accurately of his pupil. The adept Minister goes of his own accord to Ingolstadt to be present at the inauguration of an illuminized church, where Weishaupt does the honors in a new discourse prepared for the occasion. Full of admiration at the lessons of the Chief, the illuminized Minister becomes the carrier of this discourse to the Brethren at Munich and all the town of Ingolstadt were surprized at seeing the Minister, with so many other of the Brethren, come to visit Weishaupt.[10] At length the day arrives when the object of this visit ceases to be a mystery, and the adept Minister is condemned to a short exile: but it still remains to be known, whether it is a sincere repentance for his past enthusiasm, or some new intrigue or secret influence of the

Brethren, that has recalled him and reinstated him in his former dignities at the Court of Munich. All that I can gather from my correspondence at Bavaria is, that Illuminism is very far from having lost its influence in that country.

Another adept, dear to the Sect, is the Count KOLLOWRATH, the *Numenius* of Knigge, and whom Weishaupt wished to cure of his theosophical ideas. He was, however, entrusted to the care of *Brutus* Count SAVIOLI, who observing him pass too suddenly to doubts on *the immortality of the soul*, began to suspect that his sudden conversion to the systems of Illuminism was only pretended, in order that he might gain admission to the secrets of the Order. If he ever attained the higher degrees, it was not at least with the enthusiasm of *Alfred*.[11]

Weishaupt also classed *Chabrias*, the Baron WALDENFELS, at Cologne, among the adepts of high rank: he was the Minister of the Elector; but no sooner had he discovered the knavery of the higher mysteries than he abandoned the Order. *Ptolemeus Lagus*, or that same Baron RIEDSEL, who in *Minos*-Dittfurt's plan was to have had the direction of the Illuminized Sisterhood, imitated this example. We cannot hope, however, to tear the mask from all those conspirators whom Weishaupt has encompassed with darkness, and who should rank among the higher class of adepts. The list that was published soon after the Original Writings contains chiefly those whom my reader have already seen in the course of this work. I shall, however, subjoin it here with such observations as time has since enabled me to make. There will appear adepts scattered throughout the Councils, the Magistracy, the Army, and the houses for public Education; and this general view will better enable the reader to judge of the care with which the Conspirators sought to occupy the most important posts of society while they planned its run.

List of the principal Illuminees from the Foundation of the Sect in 1776, till the Discovery of the Original Writings in 1786.

Characteristics	Real Names of the Adepts
Spartacus	WEISHAUPT, Professor of Laws at Ingolstadt, and Founder of the Sect
Agrippa	WILL, Professor at Ingolstadt
Ajax	MASSENHAUSEN, Counsellor at Munich
Alcibiades	HOHENEICHER, Counsellor at Freysinguen
Alexander	Count PAPPENHEIM, General and Governor of Ingolstadt

Alfred	Count SEINSHEIM, Vice-President at Munich, first exiled as an Illuminee, then sent from Deux-Ponts to Ratisbon, and at length returned to, and in place at Munich
Arrian	Count COBENZEL, Treasurer at Aichstadt
Attila	SAUER, Chancellor at Ratisbon
Brutus	Count SAVIOLI, Counsellor at Munich
Cato (also *Danaus & Phil.-Strozzi*)	XAVERIUS ZWACK, Aulic Counsellor, and Counsellor of the Regency. Exiled as an adept
Celsus	BAADER, Physician to the Electress Dowager
Claudius	SIMON-ZWACK
Confucius (at first *Zoroaster*)	BAIERHAMMER, Judge at Diesen
Coriolanus	TROPONERO, Counsellor at Munich
Diomedes	Marquis of COSTANZA, Counsellor at Munich
Epictetus	MIEG, Counsellor at Heidelberg
Epimenides	FALK, Counsellor and Burgomaster at Hanover
Euclid	RIEDL, Counsellor at Munich
Hannibal	Baron BASSUS, a Swiss from the Grisons
Hermes Trismegistus	SOLCHER, Curate at Haching
Livius	RUDORGER, Secretary of the States at Munich
Ludovicus Bavarus	LORI, Dismissed from the Order
Mahomet	Baron SCHROEKENSTEIN
Marius	HERTEL, Canon of, and exiled from Munich
Menelaus	WERNER, Counsellor at Munich

Minos	Baron DITTFURT, Assessor to the Imperial Chamber of Wetzlar
Moenius	DUFRESNE, Commissary at Munich
Masee	Baron MONJELLAY, exiled from Munich, received and placed at Deux-Ponts
Numa	SONNENSELS, Counsellor at Vienna and Censor
Numa Pompilius	Count LODRON, Counsellor at Munich
Pericles	Baron PECKER, Judge at Amberg
Philo	Baron KNIGGE, in the service of Bremen
Philo of Byblos	The Prelate HASLEIN, Vice-President of the Spiritual Council at Munich, and Bishop *in Partibus*
Pythagoras	DREXL, Librarian at Munich
Raimond de Lulle	FRONHOWER, Counsellor at Munich
Simonides	RULING, Counsellor at Hanover
Solon	MICHT, an Ecclesiastic at Freysinguen
Spinosa	MÜNTER, Attorney at Hanover
Sylla	Baron MAGGENHOFF, Captain in the Bavarian service
Tamerlane	LANG, Counsellor at Aichstadt
Thales	KAPFIMGER, Secretary to Count Tattenbach
Tiberius	MERZ, exiled from Bavaria, since Secretary to the Ambassador of the Empire at Copenhagen
Vespasian	Baron HORNSTEIN, of Munich★

★This list is taken from that published in the German Journals.

This List appears to have been chiefly compiled for the Bavarian adepts in the first volume of the Original Writings. The second volume might furnish us with the following additions, besides a multitude of other adepts whose true names have not been discovered. Those whose names are not followed by the page quoted from the Original Writings in this list, have been sent to me in Private Memorials and Letters, or are extracted from Public Journals.

HISTORICAL PART 699

Characteristics	Real Names of the Adepts
Aaron	This adept is only mentioned under the initials P. F. V. B. (*Prince Ferdinand von Brunswig*), both when he sends for Knigge, and when he promises his protection to the adept who is to *Illuminize* ENGLAND, (P. 122 and 184)
Accacius	Doctor KOPPE, Superintendant first at Gotha, afterwards at Hanover (P. 123)
Agathocles	SCHMERBER, Merchant at Frankfort on the Mein (P. 10)
Agis	KROBER, Governor of the Prince of Stolberg's children at Neuwied (P. 181)
Alberoni	BLEUBETREU, formerly a Jew, afterwards a Counsellor of the Chamber at Neuwied (P. 181)
Amelius	BODE, Privy Counsellor at Weimar (P. 213 and 221, &c.)
Archelaus	DE BARRES, formerly a Major in the French service (P. 183)
Aristodemes	COMPE, High Bailiff at Weinburg in the Electorate of Hanover
Bayard	Baron BUSCHE, a Hanoverian in the Dutch service (P. 195)
Belisarius	PETERSON, at Worms
Campanella	Count STOLBERG, the maternal uncle of the Prince of Neuwied; and with him may be comprised the whole court, the favorites, secretaries, and council without exception (P. 69 and 189)
Cornelius Scipio	BERGER, a Lecturer at Munich (P. 220)
Crescens	Baron DALBERG, Coadjutor of Mentz (*from Memorials, Letters, and German Journals*)
Chrysippus	KOLBORN, Secretary to the Baron Dalberg (P. 73 and 100)

Cyril	SCHWEICKART, at Worms
Gotescalc	MOLDENHAUER, Protestant Professor of Divinity at Keil in Holstein, (P. 198)
Hegesias	Baron GREIFENCLAU, of Mentz (P. 196)
Leveller	LEUCHSENRING, an Alsacian, and Preceptor to the Princes of Hesse Darmstadt; driven from Berlin, he took refuge at Paris.
Lucian	NICOLAI, Bookseller and Journalist at Berlin (P. 28)
Manethon	SCHMELZER, Ecclesiastical Counsellor at Mentz (P. 196)
Marcus Aurelius	FEDER[12], Professor at Gottinguen (P. 81)
————	MÜNTER, Professor of Divinity at Copenhagen (P. 123)
Numenius	Count KOLLOVRATH, at Vienna (P. 199)
Peter Cotton	VOGLER, Physician at Neuwied (P. 188)
Pic de la Mirandole	BRUNNER, Priest at Tiefenback in the Bishopric of Spire (P. 174)
Theognis	FISCHER, a Lutheran Minister in Austria (P. 204)
————	RONTGEN, Protestant Minister of Petkam in East Friesland, and *the* ENGLISH APOSTLE of *Illuminism*
Timoleon	ERNEST LEWIS, Duke of Saxe Gotha (*Private Memorials*)
Prince Walter	AUGUSTUS of Saxe Gotha (*Ibid*)

We do not add to this List *Eschylus*, or Charles Augustus of Saxe Weimar, as he has declined the honor of continuing one of Weishaupt's disciples. The late Prince of Neuwied might be subjoined for many reasons, and he would make the fifth Prince well known to have been connected with the Sect; but he is no more; and we have not sufficient proofs to inscribe on the list several others of that class who in Germany are supposed to belong to the Sect.

1. For the whole of this literary war, see the *Apologie der Illuminaten*, and the addition *Nachtracht zu der Apologie*, &c. and the answer of the deponents *Grosse absechten des Orders der Illuminaten*; the addition to these answers *Nachtrach*, &c. No. 1, 2, 3.
2. For these avowals see the Apology of *Cato-Zwack*; the Preface of Weishaupt's *Illuminism corrected*; the Baron Bassus's Defence; and particularly the *Last Observations* by Knigge. *Philo*, in this latter work, very frankly acknowledges all the letters that are attributed to him in the Original Writings, and he frequently quotes Weishaupt's letters as being equally authentic with his own.
3. See Memorial inserted in No. 12 of the *Weltkunde*, the *Tubingen* Gazette.
4. Orig. Writ. Vol. II. Sect. 18, 19, 21.
5. I am also informed, that this pension is not taken from the *public treasury*, (as I said in my third volume, page 2) but from the Duke's private purse. Those indeed who look upon the superfluities of this purse as foreign to the duties that a Prince owes to the public, to decency, or to his own honour and reputation, may make the distinction. I, for one at least, shall never adopt it.
6. This law-suit between the Prince and Illuminism is of a most extraordinary nature indeed. The reader shall hear him state his case himself to the Diet of Ratisbon in the year 1794:—

    "Every one is acquainted with what this Sect has done in France. We have also seen extraordinary instances of its power at Neuwied: it has a Lodge here called the *Three Peacocks*. My Father and my first Wife greatly favoured these adepts, and my present one in particular is the great protectrix of several of them; of that Pastor WINZ for example, who, notwithstanding the great service I rendered him in stifling a prosecution against him for Sociansm, is now one of my greatest enemies. She was also very closely connected with the Aulic Counsellor KRÖBER (the adept *Agis*). One SCHWARTZ, from Brunswick, and a titular major of Weimar, to whom my Father entrusted the education of one of my children, and who to my great grief has still two of them under his care, is also a great favourite of the Princess's; she has placed her whole confidence in him, and sees him very often, although letters from Brunswick depict him in the light of a most detestable intriguer. Several Counsellors and various officers and other inhabitants of Neuwied are, like him, members of the Sect, and are in agreement with the Princess. It is notorious, that they are all bound by oath mutually to support each other. They have also gained over various other persons who do not belong to their Order; and thus an association has been formed for my destruction."

    In fact the Illuminees had succeeded in getting this Prince placed under an interdict in his own states; he accused several of his first judges as being adepts; it cost them little to declare on their oaths that they were not, and some indeed no longer continued attached to the Sect. This incident occasioned him much unpleasant trouble; but at length he was reinstated in his possessions after a very long law-suit, which must have taught the German Princes how well Illuminism can take advantage of its power when once it has succeeded in surrounding them.
7. See the Eudemonia, Vol. IV. No. 5, Letter of Doctor J. H. Jung.
8. Orig. Writ. Vol. II. Let. 1, from *Philo*.
9. Original Writings, Vol. I. Let. from *Diomedes*, and Vol. II. Let. 1. from *Philo*.

10. Original Writings, Vol. II. Let. 7, 9, 18.
11. Original Writings, Vol. II. Let. from *Brutus*.
12. It was on seeing the strong illusion of his degree of Epopt (so strangely impious) on the doctors Feder and Koppe, and some others of the University of Gottinguen, that Weishaupt wrote to *Cato*, "You cannot conceive how much my degree of *Priest* or *Epopt* is admired by our people; but what is the most extraordinary is, that several great Protestant and Reformed Divines, who are of our Order, really believe that that part of the discourse which alludes to religions contains the true spirit and real sense of Christianity. *Poor mortals, what could I not make you believe!*" Original Writings, Vol. II. Let. 18.

CHAP. IX.

New Chiefs and new Means of the Illuminees.—Device of the Jesuits Masonry and Success of that Imposture

AMONG the secret writings that the Sect had in vain sought to conceal from the eyes of justice, was one on which was found, in *Cato*-Zwack's handwriting, this remarkable marginal note: "In order to re-establish our affairs, let some of the ablest of those brethren who have avoided our misfortunes take the places of our founders; let them get rid of the discontented, and in concert with the new elect, labour to restore our society to its primitive vigour."[1] Weishaupt had scarcely left Ingolstdt when he threatened those who dismissed him, that ere long *their joy should be converted into sorrow;*[2] and it was evident, that the Illuminees were far from having abandoned their conspiracy. Notwithstanding, however, the awful and menacing aspect which it presented, the different powers, it would seem, affected to leave the conspirators in possession of means to prosecute their illuminizing plans with greater activity.

If we except Weishaupt, no adept in Bavaria had been condemned to a severer punishment than exile or a short imprisonment. In other parts, from Livonia to Strasbourg, and from Holstein to Venice, not a single inquiry had been made concerning their lodges. Many of those adepts who had been convicted of the deepest guilt had met with protection instead of indignation in the different courts. Notwithstanding that the clearest proofs of his guilt had been adduced, we see Zwack, a very few days after, producing certificates of his probity and fidelity to his prince, which had more the appearance of having been issued by his accomplices than by the Aulic Council;[3] and the Prince of Salm Kyrbourg calls him to his court, in all probability to be served with a similar sort of fidelity!! The conspirators *Brutus*-Savioli and *Diomedes*-Constanza might continue to recruit for the Sect, provided it was not in Bavaria, and that at the expence of the Prince who had discovered their plots. *Tiberius*-Merz, whose infamous morals are recorded in the Original Writings, barefacedly escorted them in the retinue of the embassador of the empire to Copenhagen. *Alfred*-Seinsheim merely bartered the favour of his Prince for that of the Duke de Deux-Ponts, and an intrigue was immediately set on foot to reinstate him at Munich. *Spartacus* himself tranquilly enjoyed his asylum and a pension at a court, though he had conspired to annihilate every Prince. Never had so monstrous a conspiracy been discovered or so publicly denounced; yet never were conspirators so amply supplied with the means of continuing their plots by those even against whom they were conspiring. Thus plainly did every thing denote, that the flight of Weishaupt would be to Illuminism, what the *Hegira* of Mahomet had formerly been to Moslemism, only the prelude to a greater and more splendid success. Experience now taught Weishaupt to combine new means, according to his favorite maxim of *appearing idle in the midst of the greatest activity*. Perhaps also, content with having laid the foundations of his conspiracy, and with having arrived at that day which he had long since foretold, when he could defy the powers of the earth to destroy his fabric; or, perhaps, satisfied at seeing he had now formed men able to preside over his Areopage; he simply gave his advice on important occasions, leaving the common details, the functions of an ordinary chief, to other adepts. However that may be, though it were proved that he had given up the dignity of chief, though the archives of the Sect were more deeply concealed than they are, yet proofs of the plots which they are now prosecuting would not be wanting. Their public actions shall in future depose against them in default of their secret archives. The adepts were known; it was therefore easy to watch their labours and compare their devices. The German writers have had the start of us in that career; history, therefore, will not be destitute of demonstrative proofs.

The grand object of the Illuminees, after the discovery of their secret papers, was to persuade Germany that their Order was extinct; that the adepts had not only renounced all their illuminizing mysteries, but even all intercourse among themselves as members of a secret society. These are not the first Brigands or the first Sectaries on record that have wished to make the world believe the idea of their existence to be chimerical, even at the very time when they were most actively promoting their plots and propagating their principles. But here error has belied itself even in the mouths of its most zealous advocates. On the first appearance of those works that denounced to the British nation at large the conspiracy of the Illuminees, and shewed how they were prosecuting their plots in the occult Lodges of Masonry, the zealous brethren inhabiting the banks of the Thames called on their German allies for succour, in order to destroy those ill impression which the *Life of Zimmerman, Mr. Robison's Proofs,* and these *Memoirs,* were making. The complaints of the English fraternity, and the answer of their auxiliary Brother Boetiger, are inserted in the German Mercury, No. 11, page 267. Nearly the same answer has crossed the seas, in order to inform the English, through the channel of the *Monthly Magazine* of January 1798, page 3, that whoever should turn his researches toward Illuminism would be in pursuit of a chimera, "as *from the beginning of the year* 1790, EVERY CONCERN OF THE ILLUMINATI HAS CEASED, *and no Lodge of Free-masons in Germany* has, since that period, taken the least notice of them. Evident proofs of this assertion are to be found among the papers of Mr. Bode, late Privy Counsellor at Weimar, *who was at the head of the Order* in this part of Germany, and who died in 1794."

The foregoing passage, written by Mr. Boetiger, may be observed to include a very singular avowal, which has already been noticed in Germany to the great confusion of the adepts. Some zealous writers have told them: You now own then, that the mysteries of Illuminism had become those of the Masonic Lodges, and that they had continued to be so till the year 1790; those journalists and other authors, therefore, who incessantly called the attention of sovereigns to the Illuminees, were not mistaken; and Zimmerman, Hoffman, and Dr. Stark, with so many other writers, whose works the Sect wished to suppress, were correct in publicly proclaiming that this disastrous Sect had not been annihilated when its plots were discovered in 1786, and much less so in 1785, as the adept writers of the Brotherhood or their hirelings had attempted to persuade the world.[4] Now the conspirators think that it will suffice for their purpose to make the world believe that the idea of their existence *since the year 1790* is chimerical. This artifice also shall be unmasked, and nations shall be convinced that though this Sect may have changed its form, yet that in so doing it has only invigorated itself, and acquired new means of corruption.

The *Sieur Boetiger*, the Quixotte of the Illuminees, and of the Brother Bode in particular, also makes another avowal, viz. That his hero Bode really became the chief of the Illuminees in his part of Germany.[5] No Brother before him had ever made this avowal, but it perfectly coincides with the information that I had received concerning this infamous Illuminee. It is under the direction of this adept, therefore, whose talents for conspiracy were so much admired by *Philo*-Knigge, that we are now to trace the labours and progress of the Sect.

To avert the public attention by means of fabulous plots, and to conceal their own that they might prosecute their conquests in the masonic Lodges; to ensnare that class called men of letters, and at length taint the whole mass of the people with their principles; were the objects of *Amelius*-BODE, and of the new Areopagites who presided over Illuminism after Weishaupt's flight and the dispersion of the Bavarian adepts. Among the various means devised, *one might appear singularly ridiculous but for the astonishing advantages drawn from it by the Sect:* I mean the fable of the *Jesuits Masonry*. A prodigious number of volumes have been written in Germany, both by those who invented the fable, and by others who thought it incumbent on them to warn the public of this new artifice of Illuminism. I will not wander into useless detail, but will simply lay before my reader the leading points by which he may trace the Sect until it attains the period of its power in our revolutions.

As an act of homage to the despot Weishaupt, *Philo*-Knigge was the first who, in the year 1781, and under the name of ALOYSIUS MAYER, published this ideea of the Jesuits Masonry. He took it up again in the *circular letter* written by order of *Spartacus* to the Masonic Lodges; he again insists on it in his *Additions to the History of Freemasonry*.[6] The adepts OSTERTAG at Ratisbon, NICOLAI and BIESTER at Berlin, and a swarm of other Illuminees, sought to give sanction to this Fable by their writings. As yet, however, it was difficult to form a precise idea of this story of the Jesuits Masonry; or whether it was true or false. Bode at length made a collection of every thing that could be said on the subject, and sent the whole of these materials to the Brother BONNEVILLE at Paris.[7] He soon published his work, entitled *The Jesuits expelled from Free-masonry*; and this production, sent to all the *regular* Lodges, was supposed to be the death-blow to this terrible phantom.

On investigating these different productions, we observe, that their drift was to make the Free-masons believe that all their Lodges were secretly under the direction of the Jesuits; that each Mason, without suspecting it, was but the slave and instrument of that society which had long since been looked upon as extinct, but whose members, though dispersed, still preserved an ascendancy disgraceful to Masonry, and dangerous to nations and their rulers. The result of all this tended to persuade the brethren, that true Masonry was not to be sought for either among the Rosicrucians or the Scotch Knights, and still less among the English Masons, or those of the Strict Observance; but solely among the *Eclectic Lodges* that were under the direction of the Illuminees.[8]

The name of Jesuit is certainly a formidable bug-bear to many people, especially to those who could never pardon their zeal for the Roman Catholic faith; and it cannot be denied, that if constancy in the cause of that religion was hateful, they were well entitled to the hatred of the enemies of the Catholic faith. It is observable, that it was in those very parts of Germany where the Lodges were chiefly composed of Protestant brethren, that this fable made the most astonishing impression, nothing being talked of but Jesuits under the cloak of Masonry, and their great conspiracy. One might have thought that the conspiracy of the Illuminees was entirely forgotten; but that was not their only object. The Masonic Brethren of the ordinary Lodges heard so much of their being the dupes of the Jesuits, that they abandoned the Strict Observance and the Rosicrucians, and flocked to the Eclectic Masons, then under the direction of the Illuminees. The Masonic Revolution was so complete and so fatal to ancient Masonry, that its zealous Masters and Venerables declared this fiction of Jesuits Masonry to be a conspiracy truly worthy of a Danton or a Robespierre.[9] In vain did the more clearsighted Masons point out the snare, to vindicate their reputation and put a stop to the general desertion. Their demonstrations came too late; beside, they were written by Protestants, who were strongly prejudiced against the Jesuits or knew but little about them.[10] But, unfortunately, when Germany really discovered the drift of the fable, the greater part of the Masons had united with the Illuminees for fear of falling a prey to the Jesuits, and many others had entirely abandoned the Lodges, chusing to be neither Illuminees nor Jesuits. Thus was that threat of Weishaupt accomplished, that he would either conquer the Strict Observance and the Rosicrucians, or destroy them.

Were it not that prejudice often deprives men of the use of their reason, one should be astonished to see the Masons fall into such a paltry snare. Supposing that I were to go to the Mother Lodge of Edinburgh, the grand Lodge of York or that of London, and say to their Directories and Grand

Masters, you thought that you presided over the Masonic World; you looked upon yourselves as the guardians of the grand secrets of Masonry, and as the granters of the diplomas, but all this time you were mistaken, and little suspected that you were, and still continue to be nothing more than puppets put in motion by the Jesuits. Could one, I ask, invent any thing more degrading either to the human mind, or to that common sense which must, I suppose, be granted to the heroes of Masonry! Such, however, was the whole fable of the Jesuits Masonry. When speaking of the *English Masons*, the authors and abettors of this fable say, "*It is true, there are some* (of those English Masons) *who suspect that they are led by the nose, but these are few*... It is more common among them than *any where else*, for certain members to renew from time to time the idea of unknown Superiors;" and those unknown Superiors who lead the English *by the nose* are always the Jesuits.[11] Ere long the reproach becomes general; all that multitude of degrees invented in France, in Sweden, and in Germany, becomes an invention of the Jesuits, as well as the English and Scotch degrees;[12] and a sort of epidemical stupidity alone hinders the Brotherhood from feeling their bondage; at least such must be the natural consequence of this fable. How could the German Masons possibly avoid perceiving the absurdity of it?—Their profound adepts and the Elect of all nations flocked to Wilhemsbaden, and in the space of thirty years they held five or six general assemblies; how came it to pass that all these brethren combining their secrets, their government, and their laws, revising, meditating, and correcting, not only their mysteries but their whole code, were purblind enough not to surmise at least that of which they were afterwards so fully persuaded when they returned to their Lodges, viz. "that they were but the vile instruments and slaves of the Jesuits?" There can be no medium; either the Masons must be the offspring of the grossest stupidity and folly (and then what becomes of their great lights and their science of sciences so much extolled), or, the invention of the Jesuits' Masonry must be a most absurd fable (and in that case why do they flock to the Lodges of the Illuminees for fear of meeting a bugbear in their own?)

This fable too appears still more absurd when we reflect that such men as Philippe D'Orleans, Condorcet, Syeyes, or Mirabeau, with so many other Deists, Atheists, and most inveterate enemies and assassins of the Jesuits, and of all those who preached the same doctrines, *were at the head of Masonry!*

It may also be worthy of remark, at what period these Religious are transformed into the Grand Masters and Directors of that multitude of Lodges spread from East to West? It is after they have been abolished; it is when, forbidden to form a community, they are dispersed throughout the different dioceses acting the part of private missionaries under the inspection of their Bishops: this is the period chosen for installing them governors and directors of a vast confraternity of Masons! It is when stripped of every thing, driven from their habitations, having scarcely wherewith to procure the necessaries of life, that they are supposed to command all the funds of the Masonic Lodges! It is when, under the yoke of persecution, they continue to preach the doctrines of the Gospel, that they are accused of a supposed secret impiety and of a profound policy! If they are impious, at least we must allow them to be as aukward in their impiety and as imbecile as those who could suppose them to have possessed some ingenuity; for in the midst of their supposed impiety, of their Deistical and Atheistical, their rebellious and anarchical principles, they have been aukward enough always to have for their greatest enemies not only the Deists and Atheists of Masonry but those of every other class! On the other hand, they are supposed to be the authors of the new mysteries of Masonry, and they are artful enough to introduce them by means of protestant leaders, such as a Baron HUND or a ZINNENDORFF; beside, these mysteries are only multiplied in the divers Lodges in order to create intestine jealousies, hatreds, &c. which all the general meetings of the Sect could not repress! This also must be the work of a body profoundly politic! Did these terrible Jesuits then think to add to their power by thus destroying the Masonic puppets which they had so long governed, in place of uniting those millions of brethren or slaves under one law, who might have formed an impenetrable phalanx against their enemies?

Certainly we must be astonished at the absurdity of this fable of the Jesuits' Masonry; but our astonishment increases on examining the proofs whereon it is grounded.[13]

Let us suppose that Nicolai, Knigge, Bode and the other writers of the Brotherhood, had made a compilation of every thing that was odious in Masonry, and had substituted the word *Jesuit* for that of *Freemason* or *Rosicrucian*, we shall then have a pretty accurate idea of the general course followed by the Illuminizing Masons. It would be exactly as if any historian were to take it into his head, when treating of Weishaupt's Code, to substitute the word Jesuit in lieu of Illuminee, and that without being able to name a single Jesuit against whom the accusation could be preferred, notwithstanding the ardent desire of these barefaced calumniators to mention some one at least of the culprit Jesuits. It is a long series of contradictions. Neither do they agree as to the time, the degrees, or the mysteries of this Masonry of the Jesuits. The sole fact that might deserve to be investigated, had any proof been adduced in confirmation of it, was that of the Jesuits converting Masonry into a conspiracy for the reinstatement of the Stuarts on the English Throne. But of what consequence could their reinstatement on the throne, or a secret of that nature, be to the Swedish, Russian, Polonese, or Dutch Masons; and how could one pretend to persuade the English and Scotch Masons that their Masonry, Code, and Emblems, long anterior to the catastrophe of the Stuarts, were only mysteries invented to reinstate the Stuarts on the throne? Should an historian ever undertake to write the history of the extraordinary reveries of the human mind, let him not forget those set forth by the Illuminees on this occasion; and were it not for the eminent use it was of to them for the propagation of their plots, I should never have thought of troubling my reader with it, or of seriously refuting so incoherent a fable. We must next turn our attention to a coalition more real and far more disastrous, I mean that known under the name of the Germanic Union.

1. Original Writings, Vol. I. last pages.
2. His Letter to Fischer.
3. See his Appendix in the Original Writings, P. 35 and 36.
4. See Eudemonia, Vol. VI. No. 2.
5. The Sieur Boetiger, Director of the Gymnasium at Wiemar, and the auxiliary adept so famous for his Eulogy on Bode, which was only laughed at in Germany, has many other claims to ridicule beside those recorded in his writings. The English may overlook the numerous demands of this kind that he has upon us in about half a dozen Magazine and Reviews in which he co-operates, for his dissertations on the *Roman Ladies*, on their *toilets*, and on their *fans*; on *America* and on *China*; on the *Etruscan Vases*, on the *Acting of a Player*, and in short on many other subjects. But what it most concerns the English people to know, is, that the man, whose authority is set up in favor of the Brotherhood, is as well known in Germany for his talents as a leader of faction as he is for his treatises on toilets and fans. Nor did he on the news of the immortal victory of Admiral Duncan restrain his Jacobin rage in his journals, or blush at saying *that it was doubtful whether* the English had gained this victory by the interference of heaven or hell, *whether it came from above or below* (von oben oder von unten); and that it was opinion of many that it would have been a greater happiness for the *English to have lost the battle than to have gained it*. Such, nevertheless, is the man whom we find placed in competition with, and even set up as an authority against the patriotism of Mr. Robison.

    This very same man moreover writes to inform the English that he is no Illuminee. He may gain credit in England; but in Germany he is asked what business he had with the *Minerval Lodges of Weimar*? In what quality could he pretend to inherit the papers of a chief of Illuminism, which, according to the laws of the Sect, could only be entrusted to brethren? Or for what reason, after having been so intimately connnected with Bode, does he still continue to be the laborious co-operator of the adept WIELAND in the *New German Mercury*?

    This auxiliary adept also writes to the English, that the Duke of Saxe Gotha, *on application* to him for that purpose, *would doubtless permit the inspection of those papers of* Bode's. But no such invitation is made to the Germans; to them he talks of *a Prince* being in possession of all Bode's papers, but does not venture to name the prince. He knew too well that persons on the spot might attempt to gain that admittance to inspect the papers, if Boetiger's word could be a sufficient incitement to those, who think they have acquired a certainty that the prince possessor has powerful reasons, for *not showing* the *two trunks* full of papers that he bought at such an immense rate, and for *not giving* an invitation to the public similar to that which the court of Bavaria ordered to be inserted at the head of the Original Writings.

    I, in my turn, invite the Author of the *Monthly Magazine* to insert these reflections in his publication, as he did Boetiger's letter in opposition to Mr. Robison in that of Jan. 1798. My reason for making this invitation is, because I have been informed that some persons have been duped by that letter, and really thought that the existence of this Sect and of its plots, the most monstrous and most subtle that ever existed, was chimerical.

I can also inform my readers, that all the Secret Writings of Bode are not at Gotha. Many of his letters are at this moment printing; and my correspondents inform me, that they perfectly accord with the statements in my Memoirs.

6. See these works and the Original Writings, Vol. II. Let. 22, from Weishaupt and Let. 1 from *Philo*—Also the Circular Letter, Part II. Sect. VI.
7. Endliche Schicksal, Page 38.
8. See *Philo*'s Circular Letter and his conclusion.
9. Wahrlich ein project eines Dantons oder Robespierre Wardig (*Endliche Schicksal*, Page 32).
10. See on this subject the *Endliche Schicksal*, the work entitled *Der aufgezogene Vorhang der Frey Maurery, &c*—And particularly the last hundred pages of the work *Uber die Alten und Neuen Mysterien*, Chap. XVI. &c.
11. See the *Jesuits expelled Masonry*, Part I. P. 31 and 32.
12. *Philo*'s Circular Letter.
13. Some readers may perhaps tax me with treating this fable, and the proofs adduced by the Illuminees, as absurd and inconceivable, only that I might be dispensed from trouble of refuting demonstrations, perhaps difficult to be answered. Should any such be found among my readers, let them turn to those writings which some of the most famous adepts, such for example as *Mirabeau*, or rather his initiator and recruiter, *Mauvillon*, extol in the highest terms; and which are not (he says) to be looked upon as *a mere system*, but *as a complete digest and exact statement of the principal facts that led in Germany to the discovery of this Masonry of the Jesuits. (See Mirabeau's Prussian Monarchy, Vol. V. Book VIII. Page 77)*. This famous book is entitled *The Jesuits expelled from Masonry, and their Poignard broken by the Masons*. In the very first page we see engraven on a plate this poignard with the compass, the square, the triangles, the eagles, stars, and every thing that he supposes to be the emblem of Scotch Masonry. Should it be asked where this poignard was found, no answer is given; but in the following very *ingenious* manner the writer pretends to demonstrate that the great authors and directors of Scotch Masonry were Jesuits:

1st. Bonneville declares this Masonry to consist of four degrees, the Apprentice, the Fellow-craft, the Master, and the Scotch Master. The pass-word in these degrees are *Boaz* and *Tubal-cain* for the first; *Shiboleth, Chiblin, Notuma* for the others. Boaz seems to have puzzled him; he therefore rejects it, and only takes the four initials, T.S.C.N.

The Jesuits also had four degrees, the Lay Brothers (that is to say those who, as in all religious Orders, were only admitted as servants, such as the cooks, gardeners, &c. These the Jesuits called *Temporal Coadjutors*. Bonneville overlooks Coadjutor, but takes the initial of *Temporal*; and he thus gets T which demonstrates that the Lay Brother Jesuit is the same as the Apprentice Mason, also denoted by T. The second degree among the Jesuits is that of the young students, and these were called *Scolastici* or Scholars; but when they had finished their studies, and taught in their turn, they became *Magistri*, or Masters. The S in *Scolastici* is convenient for Bonneville's demonstration, and it becomes the S of the Shiboleth of the Fellow-craft. The third degree of the Jesuits is that of *Spiritual Coadjutor*, who took the three common religious vows; here the C initial of Coadjutor is the C of Chiblim, and Bonneville had not the slightest doubt but the spiritual Coadjutor of the Jesuits is the *Master* in Freemasonry. At length comes the fourth degree, or the professed Jesuits, that is, those who to the three first vows have added that of going to preach the Gospel in whatever part of the world the Pope chose to send them. These were alled the *professed* Jesuits; but the word *professed* would not serve Bonneville's purpose, he wanted an N; he says therefore, that these *professed* were called *Nostri*, he then gets an N, the evident Notuma of the Scotch Master in Masonry. Thus it is that by comparing the T. S. C. N. of Masonry with the T. S. C. N. that he had discovered among the Jesuits, he proves that the degrees of Scotch Masonry are the same as those of the Jesuits. *See the Jesuits expelled from Masonry, Vol. II. Page* 5 *and* 6.)

Should the reader desire to know how the word *Mason* precisely answers to the *perfect degree* of the Jesuits, or to their *professed*, Bonneville will tell him that the letters A. B. C.&c. stand for numbers 1, 2, 3, &c. Suppose the Jesuits have adopted this easy cypher, and then the four letters M. A. S. O. will give 12 + 1 + 18 + 14 = 45, and then remains N, the very initial letter of the NOSTER *the perfect degree of the Jesuits, to which they could only be admitted at the age of forty-five! (Ibid. Page 9.)* What a pity (exclaims Bonneville) that this *Noster* should be the *professed Jesuit, professus quatuor votorum (Ibid. Page 6)*; and a still greater pity (say I) for his position, that, according to the constitutions of the Jesuits, at the age of twenty-five they might be admitted to take the fourth vow, provided they had finished their course of divinity. (*Constit. Societ. Je. Part I. Chap. II. No. 12, de Admittendis.*) Another misfortune was, that even those Jesuits who had taught in their colleges had generally terminated their course of divinity and taken their last vow by the age of *thirty-three.*

Were I to go on to show, that the G, or the *God* of the Masons becomes the General of the Jesuits, because General begins with a G.—that the *Jubal*, or the musician of the Masons, is a Jesuit, because *Jubal* and *Jesuit* both begin with a J.—that the *Hiram-Abif* also of the mysterries is a Jesuit, because H = 8 and A =1 and the total 9 = J.; in short, were I to proceed to enumerate five or six hundred follies of the same nature, all given as proofs of the Jesuits' Masonry, my reader would be almost tempted to believe that I was traducing Bonneville. I must, therefore, refer him to the author himself; and let that man read and study him who is not disgusted at the reading of the first pages, and at the impudence with which this author wishes to impose upon the public.

CHAP. X.

The Germanic Union—Its principal Actors, and the Conquests it prepared for the Illuminees.

AFTER having described so many plots, unmasked so much artifice, and disclosed such various means of delusion and seduction, all issuing from the dens of impiety, why am I forbidden to lay down my pen, and, abandoning these dark haunts of vice, to assume the pleasing talk of describing the habits of the virtuous man, or of a nation happy, and enjoying the sweets of peace beneath the shadow of its laws, and that under a beloved monarch, revered still more as the father than as the sovereign of his peaceful empire? Alas! the sight of such a nation has vanished from the face of the earth; thrones totter and disappear; states weep over the ruins of their religion and of their laws, or are yet painfully struggling with the devouring monster. Danger stalks on every spot; and if happier days are mentioned, it can only stimulate us to denounce the too long concealed causes of our misfortunes, in hopes of seeing once again those nearly-forgotten days return. Though the mind revolts at the idea, yet for the public good we will pursue that tribe of Weishaupt; and, so far from giving repose to our thoughts, we shall be once more hurried into new plots and machinations invented by the most profound adepts of Illuminism, and horridly famous in Germany under the name of the *German Union*. To understand perfectly the object of this Union, the historian must revert to conspiracies anterior to those of Weishaupt.

We have often seen Voltaire boasting of the progress that Infidelity was making in the north of the German Empire. This progress was not solely to be attributed to his labours, nor had he the least suspicion of the many co-operators that were seconding his views.

In the very heart of Protestantism and of its schools, a Conspiracy had been formed against the Protestant and every branch of revealed religion, inveterate in its means and agents as that formed by Holbach's club. The Parisian Sophisters openly attacked Jesus Christ and all Christianity. The clubs, or rather schools, of the North of Germany, under pretence *of purifying the Protestant Religion*, and of restoring it to the principles of true Christianity, stripped it of all the mysteries of the Gospel, reduced it to that species of Deism which they decorate with the name of *Natural Religion*, and thus hoped to lead their adepts to a negation of all Religion. These new lawgivers did not absolutely proscribe revelation; but revelation was to be subjected to the judgment of their reason.

The Antichristian Conspiracy had originated in France with those men who styled themselves Philosophers, and who professsed to be strangers to all theological erudition. In Germany it took rise in the heart of the Universities, and among their Doctors of Divinity. In France the Sophisters conspiring against all Religion cried up the toleration of the Protestants, in hopes of destroying the Catholic faith; in Germany the Protestant Doctors abused that toleration in order to substitute Philosophism to the tenets of their church.

The first of these German Doctors who, under the mask of Theological disquisitions, engaged in this Antichristian Conspiracy, was SEMLER, professor of Divinity in the University of Halle, in Upper Saxony. The only use he appears to have made of his knowledge would lead us to suppose that he imbibed his principles from Bayle, rather than from the true sources of Theology. Like Bayle, we may observe him here and there scattering a few useful truths, but equally inclining toward paradox and scepticism. Rapid as Voltaire, but destitute of his elegance, he can only be compared to that Antichristian Chief for the multitude of contradictions into which he stumbles at every step. "*It is not uncommon to see him begin a sentence with an opinion that he contradicts before he concludes it.* His predominant system, and the only one that can be gathered from his numerous reveries, is, that the symbols of Christianity and of all other Sects are objects of no consequence; that the Christian Religion contains but few truths of any importance; and that every person may select these truths and decide upon them as he pleases. His scepticism has never permitted him to fix upon any religious opinion for himself, unless it be when he clearly professes, that Protestantism is not founded on better grounds than any of the other Sects; *that it still stands in need of a very great reform*; and that this reform should be effected by his Brethren the Doctors of the Universities."[1]

This new reformer began to propagate his doctrines as early as the year 1754, and continued to circulate them, in German and in Latin, in a thousand different shapes. At one time in an *Historical and Critical Collection*; at another, in *Free Disquisitions on the Canons or Ecclesiastical Laws*; then in an *Institution of the Christian Doctrine*; and, above all, in an *Esssay on the Art and School of a Free Theology*. Soon after a new Doctor appears, attempting to make this desired reform, or to suppress the remaining mysteries that Luther and Calvin had not thought proper to reject. This was WILLIAM ABRAHAM TELLER, at first Professor at Helmstadt in the Dutchy of Brunswick, afterwards Chief of the Consistory and Provost of a Church at Berlin. He made his first essay for destroying the mysteries by publishing a *Catechism*, in which, scoffing at the divinity of Christ, he reduces his religion to Socinianism. Soon after this, his pretended *Dictionary of the Bible* was to teach the Germans "methods to be followed in explaining the Scriptures; by which they were to see no other doctrine in the whole of Christianity than true Naturalism, under the cloak and symbols of Judaism."[2]

About the same time appeared two other Protestant Doctors, who carried their new-fangled Theology *still nearer to the state* of a degraded and Antichristian Philosophism. These were the Doctors DAMM and BAHRDT; the former the Rector of a College at Berlin, the latter a Doctor of Divinity at Halle, but a man of such infamous morals, that even *Philo*-Knigge was ashamed to see his name among Weishaupt's elect, and did not even dare to pronounce it.[3] LOFFLER, the superintendant of the Church of Gotha, ran the same career of impiety, as well as many others whose writings might have been taken for the compositions of the Illuminizing Epopts. The fashion of investigating religion merely to overturn its mysteries became so common in the German provinces, that the Protestant Religion seemed to be doomed to fall by the hands of its own Doctors, when at length a few of those Ministers who were still fired with zeal for their tenets raised their voices to denounce this conspiracy.

The Doctor DESMARÉES, superintendent of the Church of Dessau, in the principality of Anhalt, and the Doctor STARK, famous for his erudition and his conflicts with Illuminism, first called the attention of the public to this rising Sect; the former in his *Letters on the New Pastors of the Protestant Church*, and the latter in his Appendix to the pretended *Crypto-Catholicism and Jesuitism*. Nothing can better probe the wound which the Protestant Church had just received, than the summary view taken of the doctrine of these new pastors, by the superintendant of Dessau in the following terms:

"Our Protestant Divines successively attack all the fundamental articles of Christianity,—They do not let one single article of the general symbol of faith subsist. From the Creation of Heaven and Earth to the Resurrection of the Body, they combat every single article."[4]

While these theological adepts were perverting their science to inundate Germany with their crafty Philosophism, a second confederation was forming at Berlin for the propagation of these works, extolling them as the only productions worthy of the public attention. At the head of this league was one NICOLAI, a Bookseller. Before this man's time we had often seen Booksellers who, actuated by avarice, indiscriminately sold books of the most impious and seditious and others of the most pious tendency; but a phenomenon that had never been seen before, was a Bookseller whose impiety overcame his love of gain, and who would rather sacrifice the profits to be acquired by the sale of religious works, than allow them to be dispersed among the people. Nicolai was a Bookseller of such a stamp as D'Alembert wished to find, and such as he would have been himself had it been his profession. It was exclusively to the propagation of Impiety that he had dedicated his commerce and his literary talents, for he would also be a sophisticated writer. He was not even initiated into the mysteries of Weishaupt, when he had actually formed the plan for overturning the Christian Religion in Germany by one of those means which governments have never yet sufficiently attended to, or been aware of. At the head of his business as a Bookseller, he also undertook to be the compiler of a sort of weekly Enclyclopedia, which he entitled *The Universal German Library*.[5] At once the compiler and salesman of Impiety, he engaged several

Sophisters to co-operate with him. He also leagued with many men of great learning and merit, whose articles being inserted in his Journal were to serve as a cloak for the more impious ones, whence the readers were to imbibe his baneful principles—The most dangerous articles of this sort were those written by himself, by the famous Jew MENDELSOHN, by BIESTER, Librarian to the King, and by GEDIKE, Counsellor to the Consistory of Berlin. It was not long, however, before the tendency of this Journal was discovered. It was observed, that all their praises were lavished on those very men whose doctrines were levelled at the total overthrow of those mysteries of Christianity which had been preserved by Luther and Calvin. The man who so well seconded the views of Weishaupt without knowing it could not long escape the notice of the Scrutators. The Sect had one in particular whose name will hereafter become famous; this was the Brother *Leveller*-Leuchsenring, who had been Preceptor to the Princes at Berlin, and afterward to those of Hesse Darmstadt. A fanatical recruiter, and, though loquacious, very reserved on the mysteries, this Leuchsenring was then travelling as an Insinuator. Hanover and Neuwied already bore testimony of his zeal. He had attempted in vain to insinuate the Chevalier Zimmermann; but Nicolai afforded an easy conquest. It was soon complete; Gedike and Biester, following his example, only combined their conspiracy with Weishaupt's mysteries. The Doctor BAHRDT had fallen as easy a prey to the Assessor *Minos*; but the Doctor viewed what had been done by his new Brethren, to second his views and writings against Christianity, as of little avail—He thought he could surpass all the artifices of Weishaupt, Knigge, and Nicolai; and his evil genius afforded him the means.

The plan that he had conceived was nothing less than to reduce Germany, and by process of time the whole world, to the impossibility of receiving any other lessons, or of reading any other productions than those of the Illuminees.—The means of reducing the literary world to this new species of slavery are all contained in the laws laid down by this strange adept for a coalition famous in Germany under the title of the Germanic Union, *Die Deutsche Union*.[6]

This confederacy was to be governed by twenty-two adepts chosen from among that species of men, who by their functions, their knowledge, or their labours, had acquired a greater facility in directing the public opinion toward all the errors of the Sect. The other brethren, dispersed through the different towns, were to contribute by different means toward the grand object under the direction of the *twenty-two*, each of whom had his department assigned to him, as in Weishaupt's Areopage.

The persons who were chiefly to be sought after were authors, post-masters, and booksellers. Princes and their ministers were absolutely excepted against; and people in favour at court, or in the different public offices, were not to be chosen.

These confederates were divided into *simple associates* and *active Brethren*; and the latter alone were initiated into the secret, means, and object, of the coalition. The instructions imparted to the brethren were drawn up in the same style and method that had long since been adopted by Bahrdt, and other apostates from the protestant universities, to reduce Christianity to their pretended natural religion, by declaring Moses, the Prophets, and even Christ, to have been men distinguished, it is true, by their wisdom, but who had nothing divine either in their doctrines or their works. "To root out superstition, to restore mankind to liberty by enlightening them, to consummate the views of the founder even of Christianity without violent means, such is our object," would they say to the Brethren. "It is for that purpose that we have formed a secret society, to which we invite all those who are actuated by the same views, and are properly sensible of their importance."

As a means of accomplishing these objects, and of propagating their pretended light, these active brethren were to establish in every town certain *literary societies*, or *reading clubs* (lesegeschaften), which were to become the resort of all those who had not the means of procuring the daily publications. These were to attract as many associates as possible to these reading-rooms; watch their opinions, imbue them with the principles of the Order, leave those whose zeal and talents gave but little hopes, among the common brethren; but initiate, after certain preliminary oaths, those who could be of any real service, and who entered fully into the views and plans of the Order.

The society was to have its gazettes and journals, which were to be under the direction of those adepts whose talents were the most conspicuous; and no pains were to be spared to destroy all other periodical prints.

The libraries of these literary societies were to be composed of books all according with the views of the Order. The choice of these books and the care of furnishing them were to be left to the secretaries, and particularly to booksellers who were initiated in the mysteries of the coalition.

The hopes conceived by the man who had planned this association were held out to the elect as an incitement to the founding of new ones. What advantages (would he say) shall we not gain over superstition by thus directing the lectures in our museums? What will we not do for men who, zealous in our cause, and dispersed in all parts, circulate every where, even in the cottages, the productions of our choice? Should we ever be masters of the public opinion, how easy will it be for us to cover with contempt, and bury in oblivion, every fanatical work that may be announced in the other journals, and on the contrary extol those works that are written according to our views. By degrees we shall become masters of the whole trade of bookselling. Then will it be in vain for fanatics to write in defence of superstition and despots, as they will neither find sellers, buyers, nor readers.

Lest booksellers themselves should protest against an institution of this nature, they were to be drawn into it by advantages proposed to them, and by the fear of being ruined should they not accede to the views of the coalition. They were to be assured, that the brethren would employ every possible means to encourage the sale of works that met with the approbation of the union; but would also impede the circulation of, and discredit by their journals all such as were hostile to their views. Neither had they to fear a diminution in their trade; the association could encourage writers to multiply their productions by ensuring their sale; indeed, funds were to be established to indemnify any bookseller who, in place of selling such works as were inimical to the views of the Union, would leave them concealed in his shop, pretend that he had never heard of such works, or flatly refuse to sell them, thus abusing by every possible means the confidence of authors and of the public.

Such was the plan of *the Germanic Union*, or Dr. Bahrdt's master-piece. Never had the desire of tyrannically governing the public opinion invented a more perfidious plan. One might be left to think it the reverie of some evil genius who had sworn to extirpate from the minds of the people all ideas of any social or religious doctrine. There do, however, exist crimes which in the eyes of the honest man are almost chimerical, but which present little difficulty when undertaken by a villain. He that had conceived the plan was with mischievous propriety placed at the head of the association. The dissoluteness and infamy of his morals had not left him wherewith to subsist in any decent way, when on a sudden he purchased, near Halle, a large mansion which he called after his own name *Bahrdts-ruhe*. This was soon converted into the head quarters of the new Union. But it could never have acquired any great consistency had it not been for Nicolai, who had long been labouring according to Bahrdt's views. The immense correspondence that he had by means of his commerce with the other booksellers of Germany; the sort of dominion that he enjoyed over the literary world by means of his *Universal Library*; the court paid to him by different authors whose fortunes depended on the rank he chose to assign them in his *Library*, or in the Berlin Journal, the *Monathschrift*; and more particularly the art with which he contrived to gain over a great number of booksellers, gave him a power that no sovereign could ever pretend to. His illuminized co-operators, Biester, Gedike, and Leuchsenring, became more ardent, daring, and impious, than ever in the journals which they compiled. Bode likewise would have one at Weimar under the title of *the Universal Literary Gazette*. Another of the same nature was set on foot at Saltzbourg, by HUBNER, who was also an Illuminee. The offspring of Weishaupt were all warned of the stress which they were to lay on these publications, and they soon became a most terrible scourge on all writers who would not sacrifice their principles to impiety. The fable of the Jesuits' Masonry was now improved by a new fiction that spread dismay in the mind of every writer who wished to oppose the progress of Illuminism.

Those very Jesuits who have just been seen represented as the most artful infidels, and as secretly presiding over the Masonic lodges, were now become most zealous Catholics, who had secretly mingled among the Protestants, in order to bring these provinces back to the Roman Catholic religion and subject them to the dominion of the Pope. Every man who dared defend any one of those mysteries that can only be known either to Catholic or Protestant through Revelation, every man who preached submission to sovereigns and the laws of the state, was immediately proclaimed a *Jesuit*, or the servile slave of Jesuitism. One might have thought that all the protestant provinces were filled with these Jesuits, secretly conspiring against the protestant religion; and my readers will easily conceive what an impression such a charge must have made to the disadvantage of any writer in those provinces. Neither the office of minister nor of superintendant of a church could screen a person from so terrible an imputation. Even that man was not proof against it, who, out of zeal for Luther and Calvin, had given full vent to all his hatred and prejudices against the Jesuits; I mean Dr. Stark. In his work on *The Ancient and Modern Mysteries* he had declared, "that sovereigns had, by the destruction of the Jesuits, rendered an ever-memorable service to religion, to virtue, and to humanity." Nevertheless, M. Stark, at that time, as he still continues to be, a preacher and doctor of the Lutheran church, and also counsellor of a Consistory at Darmstadt, was obliged to employ many pages of his apology in proving that he was neither a Roman Catholic nor a Jesuit, and particularly that he was not *one of the professed Jesuits, who, having taken the four vows, were obliged at the command of the Pope to go and preach the catholic faith wherever he chose to send them.*[7]

The Chevalier Zimmerman met with a similar fate, merely because he had laid open the plots of the Illuminees, and dared to ridicule the adept *Leveller*-Leuchsenring, who had proposed to initiate him into the Brotherhood that was soon to reform and govern the world.[8] That celebrated man, an ornament to the Royal Society of London, is nevertheless represented by the journalists of the Sect as an *ignorant fellow, wallowing in superstition,* and *an enemy of Light.*[9]

The Professor Hoffman, notwithstanding the high encomiums that had been lavished on him by these very journals, no sooner gave proofs of his zeal for religion and social order, than he was represented in similar colours. Never had the disciples of Weishaupt so well practised that law laid down by their teacher, "Discredit by all means possible every man of talents that you cannot bring over to your party." Nicolai gave the signal in his *Germanic Library,* or in the *Berlin Monatschrift.* The brethren of Jena, of Weimar, of Gotha, of Brunswick, and of Slewick, immediately obeyed the signal, and repeated the same calumnies. "Shortly there were no means of screening oneself from a swarm of periodical writers, who had leagued with the modern *Lucian;* they praised what he had praised; they condemned what he had condemned; the same turn in their phrases, even the same terms are to be observed when they praise or when they blame an author, and particularly the same sarcasms and grossness of abuse."[10] Scarcely could there be found in all Germany above two or three journals that were not in the hands of the united brethren, or persons of the same cast.

Meantime the adept writers, together with Bahrdt, Schultz, Riem, an even *Philo*-Knigge, who, in abandoning the Illuminees had not renounced their plots, with hundreds of other writers of the Sect inundated the public with their libels in verse or prose, under the forms of comedies, romances, songs, and dissertations.—All the tenets of religion Catholic and Protestant were attacked with the most bare-faced impudence. Now the scene began to change; it was no longer to defend the Protestants against the attacks of the Catholics; but the obliteration of every religious tenet became their obvious design. The most pompous eulogiums were pronounced by the journalists of the Sect on all those productions of the brethren that openly disseminated every principle of Impiety and Sedition.[11] But what must appear a still more astonishing contradiction, though perfectly coinciding with the views of the Sect, is, that these very men who wished so despotically to sway the public opinion, and crush every writer that had not imbibed their principles, would pretend to persuade the Sovereigns that their sole object was to obtain that right inherent to them from nature, 'to publish their opinions and systems without danger or constraint.' Bahrdt in particular vindicated this pretended right, in his publication *On the Liberty of the Press*. It contained the sentiments of a rank Atheist, who wished to imbue his reader with all the most abominable principles of Anarchy and Impiety; the author, nevertheless, was extolled by the hebdomadary adepts, and notwithstanding Bahrdt's vindication of the liberty of the press, they united all their efforts to crush every writer that dared to assert an opinion contrary to theirs.

The use which the brotherhood made of this liberty at length aroused the attention of some few sovereigns. Frederic William, King of Prussia, alarmed at the progress which these impious and seditious writings were making, thought it necessary to put a curb on them. He published some new regulations, called the *Edicts for Religion*. This was received by the Illuminees with an audacity which seemed to denote that they had already acquired a strength sufficient to bid defiance to sovereigns, and both the Prince and the Edict became the objects of their sarcasms and most violent declamations. At length appeared a work attributed to Bahrdt, that was the acme of insolence, and, through derision, was also called the *Edict for Religion*. The magistrates ordered to take cognizance of this insult seized on the person and papers of Bahrdt, and all the necesssary proofs of his coalition and of its object were acquired. It might seem that the court of Berlin would have done well to have imitated the example of that of Bavaria by making them public; but the adepts had too powerful agents about the ministry; and numerous arguments were invented for condemning to oblivion these archives of a new species of conspiracy. All that transpired was, that the plan had been really formed, and that a number of authors, booksellers, and persons even who could scarcely have been suspected, had entered into the association. It is not known how far Weishaupt had contributed personally to it; but it appears that he twice attended at the head-quarters of the united brethren; that he spent several days with Bahrdt; and that the most zealous and active of the united brethren were also disciples of Weishaupt. If we are to believe Bahrdt, his secret was betrayed by two associates well worthy of their master. These were two young libertines, nearly beggars, but who had the talents and meanness necessary to become the clerks of his impiety. Notwithstanding the proofs adduced against him, he got off with a slight imprisonment, and spent the remainder of his existence in distress, but without atoning for his vices. He was reduced to keep a coffee-house at Bassendorff near Halle, where he ended his days as miserably as he had lived. The Illuminees have thought fit to abandon his memory to that contempt which his vicious life had entailed upon him; but, though they affected to blush at his name, they nevertheless continued to prosecute his plans.

Indeed, at the time of the discovery of this monstrous conspiracy, it had gained too much ground to be crushed by the fall of its first contriver; and Prussia, and all Germany, soon became infected with those literary societies which were nothing more than a modification of Weishaupt's *Minerval* schools. Nor was there in a short time a town or large village more free from this species of literary societies than from the Illuminized Lodges; and they were all under the direction of the followers of the modern *Spartacus*.

Bahrdt's great object was, to place the associates and other readers under a sort of impossibility of procuring any other writings, or of applying to any other studies, than those of the Sect; and the precaution it had taken to initiate so many booksellers proved a powerful support. The conspiracy might have assumed a new form; but it still continued active, and its effects became more perceptible after its discovery. It was then that the coalition appeared between the booksellers and the journalists of the Sect to suppress all books that counteracted the progress of Sedition and Impiety. It was in vain for virtuous and pious men to attempt to open the eyes of the people; they could scarcely find a bookseller or a printer who would sell or print their works; or if any had consented they would endeavour to disgust the author by delays, and a hundred other pretexts. Did the author undertake to print it at his own expence, the work was then thrown by in some obscure corner of the shop and never exposed to sale, nor would any bookseller attempt to sell it; and the whole work would be sent back to the author under pretence that nobody would buy it. The very existence of such works was not mentioned at the fairs held in Germany for the sale of books. At other times the author was strangely betrayed, the printer giving up his manuscript to the writers of the Sect, and the refutation (if the most scurrilous abuse can deserve that name) was advertised on the back of the book as soon as the first edition made its appearance. Many authors might have brought actions against their printers of a similar nature to that which Doctor Stark was obliged to bring, and demonstrate a similar connivance with the Sect and breach of trust. "At least it is an undeniable fact, that many learned writers made fruitless applications to different booksellers for publications that had been suppressed solely because they gave umbrage to the Illuminees. Their letters were never so much as answered; and the very booksellers who refused to send these books to those who applied for them, affected to defer the sale till the next fairs, as no buyers were to be found." Many others of these works had scarcely been delivered to the booksellers when they were sent back under the most opprobrious pretences; and what may surprise the reader is, that no persons were so certain of receiving such refusals as those who most openly defended their Princes. In the very states of the King of Prussia it was found impossible to get this sovereign's *Apology* and his *Edict for Religion* sold in the common way. Scarcely had the author sent a few copies to the booksellers when they were all returned to him. But did the writers of the Sect wish to publish the most scandalous disputations and the most scurrilous abuse against sovereigns and religion, or against men in office or of high respectability, the booksellers were alert in selling them, the journalists extolled their excellence, and sought numerous readers for the author.[12]

On one hand, the great trade in these productions carried on by the Sect, with the certainty of selling them to the literary clubs; and on the other the great pecuniary contributions made by the rich brethren, formed large funds for the coalition. To these if we add the sums contributed by the brethren whom the Sect had stationed at different courts, in the church and the councils, either out of their own emoluments, or the revenues of church and state, the reader will easily conceive how well these funds sufficed for indemnifying those booksellers who had suffered losses by restraining their commerce to works approved of by the Areopage. A particular fund was established for this purpose. At the appointed time the bookseller had but to produce the list of the works he had suppressed or refused to sell, with the proper proofs, and he received a sum of money sufficient to indemnify him for such losses. The memorials which I have received from Germany, as well as several letters, inform me that this fund still exists in that country; and the French Revolution has only furnished it with many other means of enriching itself.

Among the great advantages reaped by the Sect from this plan which had been so well concerted, we may first observe the impossibility under which authors lay of warning the public against the artifices of Illuminism. In the next place, it drew over to their interest that swarm of writers who, more hungry than honest, are regardless of truth or falsehood, provided they obtain a good price. In short, it emboldened that multitude of Sophisters, more numerous still in Germany than they were in France; Poets, Historians, and Dramatists, nearly all of whom courted the united brotherhood by assuming the tone of impiety and anarchy. The most dangerous device practised by the adepts against society was the great care with which they initiated the different professors of the Protestant universities, the school-masters, and the tutors of princes. It is a painful truth, but we must declare it, and on the authority of those who are best acquainted with the history and progress of Illuminism, that the greater part of the universities of the north of Germany were at that time, and still continue to be, the haunts of Illuminism, whence its baneful poisons are circulated throughout the neighbouring states by the writings and lectures of such men as the Professors FREDERIC CRAMER, EHLERS, and KOPPE.[13]

Let not the reader think that the writers of the Catholic states were exempt from the infection. Vienna was overrun with zealots who sought to diffuse the principles of the Sect. The Chevalier DE BORN, who should have contented himself with the high rank which he held in chymistry, degraded himself in that town by becoming a leader of the adepts; and when the Sect was discovered in Bavaria he was so zealous in the cause, that he sent back his letters of Associate of the Academy of Munich, protesting that he would have no intercourse with men who had been so little able to judge of Weishaupt's merits.

Next on the Vienna list we find the Sieur SONNENFELD, one of those writers who in this age are called wits, though destitute of common sense. He also was one of the propagators of Illuminism under the mask of literary societies. I am informed by persons who attended his clubs, and whom he wished to initiate, that these meetings began and were held as common academies hold theirs: but at the time appointed the sittings broke up, when, only the adepts remaining behind, a secret council was held, in which every thing was concerted and planned according to the laws of the united brethren.

A man whose name would have given great weight to the united brethren, had he hearkened to the praise lavished on him by the Illuminees at that time,[14] is the Professor Hoffman, he who so nobly joined with Zimmerman to tear the mask from these impostors, and has ever since, with his worthy co-adjutor, been the object of their most virulent declamations. In the account given by Mr. Hoffman himself, we find that the Illuminizing recruiters followed him as far as Pest in Hungary. On the 26th of June, 1788, he received from the *twenty-two chiefs* an invitation to become a fellow of the literary society which they had already established in that town. "My answer (says he) was, that I hoped they would give me some further information respecting these societies, and then my duty and my prudence would dictate the answer that I should make...On divers occasions afterward, they gave me distant hints as to the spirit of their system. They also sent me several times a list of the new members; and the signature of the twenty-two authenticated these various documents; but it was this very authentication which made me conceive the horrid plot that was concealed under this association."

The reader will easily conceive, that for a man of his merit and probity, this was more than sufficient to make him reject the offers of such a brotherhood. They had already inscribed his name on their registers, and they were obliged to erase it. As a proof that he had judged rightly of them, he quotes the letter of a virtuous and clearsighted statesman, who, after having *officially* examined the whole plan of the German Union and its mysteries, pronounces them to be *abominations that would make one's hair stand on end!* Such are his expressions!

These abominations, however, were far from making a similar impression on the other apostles of the Germanic Union. Meanwhile Weishaupt, a tranquil spectator of the progress of his Illuminism, seemed to take no part in it. The most active adepts lived round about him at Gotha, at Weimar, at Jena and at Berlin; but one might have thought him quite indifferent as to their success. If we except the visits he received from the brethren, a few journies that he took, and particularly those which he had made to see the founder of the Germanic Union, nothing could depose against him as the founder or chief who continued to direct the plots of the Sect. But let the reader never lose sight of his precepts on the art of appearing perfectly idle in the midst of the greatest activity; let him reflect on those menaces which he issued six months after his flight from Munich: *Let our enemies rejoice. Their joy shall soon be changed into sorrow. Don't think that even in my banishment I shall remain idle.*[15] After this, it is easy to judge of his supposed nullity in the progress of his conspiracy. However secret he may have been in the part he was acting, he could observe but too well the approaching accomplishment of the prediction he had made so early as the second year of his Illuminism, when he wrote to his first adepts, "The great obstacles are overcome; you will now see us proceed with gigantic strides." The Sect had not been in existence twelve years when Germany was overrun with an immense number of adepts and demi-adepts. It was assuming a menacing aspect in Holland, in Hungary, and in Italy. One of the adepts called ZIMMERMAN, who began by being the chief of a Lodge at Manheim, and who soon became as zealous for the propagation of the Sect, as the *famous* ZIMMERMAN had been to counteract their dark designs, would often brag that he had founded more than a hundred of those conspiring clubs known under the name of literary societies, or of Masonic Lodges, during his career through Italy, Hungary, and Switzerland. To give the fatal impulse to the world, it now only remained for the Sect to carry its mysteries into a nation powerful and active indeed, but unfortunately more susceptible of that effervescence which bereaves man of the power of thinking, than of that judgment which foresees disasters; to a nation which, in its ardor and enthusiasm, too easily forgets that true greatness is not that courage which bids defiance to danger (for the vandals and barbarians can boast of such heroes); to a nation, in short, that has ever been prey to illusions, and which, before it would hearken to the councils of wisdom, might in its first fury overturn the altar and shiver the scepter, returning to reason only in time to weep over the ruins, and lament the devastation of which it had been the cause.

This description unfortunately was too applicable to France, which in many respects might claim the primacy among nations, but was too easily led away by illusions. The scrutinizing Areopage had fixed its eyes on her, and now judged it a convenient time for sending its emissaries to the banks of the Seine. This will be the proper commencement of the fourth Epoch of Illuminism. Now let the reader prepare to contemplate states convulsed, citizens butchered, in a word, to ponder over all the crimes and disasters inherent in the very nature of Revolutions.

1. See *News of a Secret Coalition against Religion and Monarchy*. The Appendix, No. 9.
2. Ibid. Appendix, No. 10.
3. Endliche erklarung, P. 132.
4. Protestantische Gottesgelehrten greifen einen grund artikel des Christenthums nach dem andern an; lassen in ganzen Allgemeinen Glaubens-bekentniss vom Schöpfer himmels und der erde, bis zur auferstehung des fleisches nicht unangefochten—(*Uber die neuen wächter der Protestantischen Kirche; erstes heft*, S. 10).

5. I have quoted his *Essay on the Templars*; and I thought myself bound to do so, because I found that his researches perfectly coincided with those which I had made on the accusations preferred against those Knights, and on the proofs that appeared on the face of the most authentic documents relating to their judgment. I was not, however, on that account less concerned to see the Impiety with which these researches are replete. I also observed all that ridiculous display of erudition on the *Baffomet* of the Templars; but I cannot deny that his quotations are perfectly exact.

6. The *Sieur Boettiger* writes from Germany, and his letter is inserted in the *Monthly Magazine for January 1798*, that this plan, and the whole confederation of Doctor Bahrdt, are only known to Mr. Robison through the medium of the *obscure and despicable Journal of Geissen*. This journal of Geissen was never *despicable* in any one's eyes but those of the Illuminees, or of their votaries. They had reasons for crying it down; and those very reasons must enhance its value in the eyes of every honest man. In the next place, how can this Boettiger presume to assert that this Journal was the only source whence Mr. Robison had derived his information? The great number of works quoted by Mr. Robison must evidently belie such an assertion, and I willingly declare that it was difficult to procure more. Had he been in possession of no other than the famous work known in Germany under the title of *Mehr Noten als Text, oder, die Deutsche Union der Zwei und Zwanziger* (More notes than Text; or, the German Union of the Twenty-Two), that work which, according to Boettiger, alone sufficed to open the eyes of the public, is that only known by the Journal of Giessen? With a similar assurance does this champion of Illuminism assert this work to have been written by Bode, as if there could be the least probability that Bode, who had taken so active a part in this conspiracy, would be very forward in laying it open to the public, and exposing the *Baronne de Recke, Countess of Medem*, the daughter of *Wandern* (the *Stroller*), to public ridicule, a woman whose charms he so much admired, and with whose writings he was so well acquainted. If Bode was the writer of this publication, which so well displays the knavery of the German Union, how comes it to pass that Mr. Göschen, a Bookseller of Leipsic, has avowed himself the author of it, and is universally acknowledged as such? My readers must perceive, that by entering into these digressions, I only design to warn the public against the different publications which the Illuminees are daily dispersing to persuade nations that their plots are chimerical, while they are pursuing them with redoubled ardor.

I shall also follow nearly the same documents that Mr. Robison has adopted, as they perfectly coincide with the memorials that I have received from Germany. All that I shall lay before my readers in this chapter may be said to be extracts from the following German writings: *News of a great and invisible confederation against the Christian religion and monarchy.—The System of the Cosmopolitans discovered.—The Vienna Journal by Hoffmann.—Notice given before it is too late*, by the same.—*More Notes than Text, &c.—The Knowlege of the World and of Men, &c.* besides many other private letters and memorials on the Illuminees.

7. See his Apology, Page 52 to 59.
8. Life of Zimmerman, by Tissot.
9. Ibid.
10. The ultimate fate of Masonry, Page 30; and News of an Invisible Association, Appendix, No. 11.
11. Ibid.

12. See Nachrichten von einem grossen aber unsichtbaren Bunde, the Appendix, Nos. 8 and 13, and the Journal of Vienna, by Hoffmann.
13. See Hoffman's admonition, Sect. XVI, XVII, and XVIII.
14. It is really laughable to compare the contempt which the Illuminees affect for Mr. Hoffman at present with the high encomiums which they pronounced on him before he undertook to lay open their imposture, or even with those letters (full of compliments on his wit, style, and talents) which they wrote to him so lately as the year 1790, in hopes of enticing him into their party.
15. Letter to Fisher, 9 Aug. 1785.

CHAP. XI.

Fourth Epoch of Illuminism.

The Deputation from Weishaupt's Illuminees to the Free Masons of Paris.—State of French Masonry at that period.—Labours and Successes of the Deputies.—Coalition of the Conspiring Sophisters, Masons, and Illuminees, generating the Jacobins.

As early as the year 1782, *Philo* and *Spartacus* had formed the plan of converting the French nation to their System of Illuminism; but the vivacity and capricious temper of the people, so difficult to be restrained, made it seem prudent for the two Chiefs at that time not to extend their attempts beyond Strasbourg. The explosion in France might be premature; its too volatile and impetuous people might be unwilling to wait till other nations were properly prepared for the grand object; and Weishaupt, in particular, was not a man to be satisfied with partial or local insurrections, which might only serve to put other Sovereigns on their guard. The Reader has already seen him in secret, preparing his Adepts, and contriving the concatenation of his correspondence, in such a manner, that he had but to give the signal when the favourable moment should come. On the fatal day of revolution, and at the appointed hour, legions of brethren were to spring forth on all sides from their secret recesses, whether Lodges, Academies, or under what other denomination soever, from the North to the South, and from the East to the West. All Europe, in short, was to be revolutionized at the same instant; all nations were to be hurried into a 14th of July; and all kings were, like Lewis the Sixteenth, to awake prisoners in the hands of their own subjects. Altars and thrones were simultaneously to vanish from the earth. According to this plan, as has just been observed, the French were to be the last people initiated in the mysteries, as the Chiefs took it for granted, that with their natural impatience they would never be brought to wait till the explosion could be universally prepared.

Already, however, there existed some adepts in the very heart of the kingdom. Some few had been initiated by Knigge at the time of the meeting at Wilhemsbaden. During that very year, we find on the list of brethren, DIETRICH, that Mayor of Strasbourg who has since in Alsace rivalled Robespierre by his cruelties.[1] Another adept of vast importance to the Sect was the Marquis DE MIRABEAU, who was afterwards to become so famous in the revolutionary annals of his country. What strange infatuation possessed the ministers of the most honest man that ever swayed a sceptre, to entrust this Marquis with the interests of their master at the court of Berlin, well knowing (as they did) the monstrous immorality of his private life, is more than I shall attempt to explain. One might be led to think that it was not deemed sufficient that Lewis XVI had saved him from the scaffold, but his villany was to be recompensed by a secret mission which seemed to denote the utmost confidence of his sovereign. Mirabeau at Berlin conducted the King's affairs just as he had formerly done those of his father and mother, fully ready to sacrifice all parties and to sell himself to the highest bidder. With such a disposition, he could not long avoid the notice of the Prussian Illuminees; and Nicolai, Biester, Gedicke, and Leuchsenring soon became his constant companions. At Brunswick he met with MAUVILLON, the worthy disciple of Knigge, and at that time a Professor in the Caroline College. This was the man who initiated the profligate Marquis in the last mysteries of Illuminism.[2]

Long before his initiation Mirabeau had been acquainted with all the revolutionary powers of the Masonic Lodges; nor did he, when initiated, undervalue those which flowed or might flow from Weishaupt's inventive genius. On his return to France he began to introduce the new mysteries among some of his Masonic brethren. His first associate was the Abbé TALLEYRAND DE PÉRIGORD, who had already begun to act the part of Judas in the first order of the church. But to have only introduced the mysteries was not sufficient for the Marquis; he would have teachers come from Germany, who were better versed than he was in the illuminizing arts. Well acquainted with the reasons that had induced the Chiefs of the Order to defer the conversion of France, he found means to convince them, that the time was now come for the accomplishment of their views; that the whole nation waited for their new revolutionary means, to burst into an open rebellion, for which they had been so long prepared by other conspirators; and that the Illuminees might most certainly turn the scales. A private correspondence then took place between him and Mauvillon;[3] but of this a sufficiency has not transpired to enable the historian to describe the intrigues that took place on the occasion; certain it is, however, that Mirabeau's plan was adopted by the Areopage; and by a plurality of votes it was decided, that France should be immediately illuminized. This was an undertaking of too great importance to be entrusted to a common adept. The man who, since the retreat of *Spartacus*, had been looked upon as the Chief of the Order, offered himself; and *Amelius-Bode*, the worthy successor of both Knigge and Weishaupt, was deputed to the French Lodges, in which the illumination was to commence. Bode received as an associate in this mission *Bayard*, that other pupil of Knigge's, whose real name was WILLIAM BARON DE BUSCHE, a Captain in the Dutch service, heir to a large fortune, a man of talents, and well versed in all that artifice and low cunning which the Insinuators were wont to style prudence and wisdom. This Baron had been formerly employed to propagate the plots of the Sect in those very provinces which had a right to expect from him even the sacrifice of his life in defence of its laws.[4] The zeal with which he had fulfilled his first mission seemed to give him an indisputable title to the honour of attending on the Chief of the Order in his journey to Paris.

Circumstances could not have been more favourable than they were at that time for the deputies, nor more disastrous for France. The Philosophism of the age had operated on the Lodges as fully as could be expected, to prepare the reign of that Equality and Liberty taught by Voltaire and Rousseau, and which only needed the last mysteries of Weishaupt to convert them into the most abominable impiety and most absolute anarchy. A line had been drawn between the degrees of ancient and modern Masonry. The former, with their puerile pastimes, and obscure symbols, were left to the commonalty of the Brethren. The latter, styled *philosophical*, comprehended those which I have described under the titles of *Knights of the Sun*, the higher *Rosicrucians*, and the *Knights Kadosch*. At the head of all these societies (whether ancient or modern) were three Lodges at Paris, particularly remarkable for the authority which they exercised over the rest of the Order, and for the influence that they possessed over the opinions of the Brethren.

The first of these, *The Grand Orient*, was rather *a re-union of all the regular Lodges of the kingdom (represented by their deputies)* than a Lodge. It might be called a sort of Masonic Parliament subdivided into four Committees, which, when united, formed the Grand Council or Lodge, where all the affairs of the Order *were definitely determined*. The Committees were sub-divided into that *of Administration, of Paris, of the Provinces, and of the Degrees*. Of all thesse, the latter was the mainspring and the most impenetrable; for no visitors were admitted to it, as they were to the three others, to the ordinary meetings of which all Masters or *Venerables* of Lodges had free access.

Three great Officers of the Order were attached to this Masonic Parliament; to wit, *The Great Master, the General Administrator*, and *the Great Conservator*. His most Serene Highness *Brother Philip* of Orleans, first Prince of the blood, was Grand Master at the time when the Illuminees arrived in Paris. The two other offices were filled by persons of the first distinction; but their characters are such, that they will ever stand incontestable proofs of what I have already asserted, that even in the very highest degrees of the Order, there were modified mysteries for those who, by their rank, were to serve as a protection for its plots without every surmising their tendency.[5]

Such, however, was not the case with Philip of Orleans. His rank of Grand Master, his impiety, and insatiable thirst for vengeance, sufficiently demonstrated to the Illuminizing Missionaries how well he was qualified and how far prepared to second their designs in the multitude of Lodges that recognized him as Grand Master.—So early as the year 1787 we find that France contained (as may be seen in the statement of its Correspondence) two hundred and eighty-two towns, in which were to be found regular Lodges under the direction of the Grand Master. In Paris alone there existed eighty-one; sixteen at Lyons, seven at Bourdeaux, five at Nantees, six at Marseilles, ten at Montpellier, ten at Toulouse; in short, in almost every town the Lodges were in pretty just ratio to the population. Indeed, it would seem that even

HISTORICAL PART

this vast empire over French Masonry was not sufficient for the Grand Orient, as by the same statement we find the Grand Master issuing out his instructions to the Lodges of Chambery in Savoy, of Locle in Switzerland, of Bruxelles in Brabant, of Cologne, Liege and Spa in Westphalia, of Leopold and Warsaw in Poland, of Moscow in Russia, of Portsmouth in Virginia, of Fort Royal in Grenada, and in short to Lodges in all the French Colonies. Thus did Philip of Orleans and his *Grand Orient* ensure to the Illuminees as powerful an alliance as that formerly made by Knigge with the German lodges under the direction of Weishaupt.[6]

Subject to the Grand Orient we next find at Paris a Lodge called *Les Amis Réunis* (or United Friends), which was more particularly charged with all Foreign Correspondence. The famous Revolutionist SAVALETTE de Lange, was one of its leading members. This adept held under government the office of *Garde du Trésor Royal*; that is to say, he enjoyed that confidence to which none but the most faithful subject could be entitled; yet at that very time was he engaged in the various plots and mysteries of all the different Sects. In order to form an union of them all, he had introduced into his Lodge the different systems of the Sophisters, of the Martinists and of the other Masons; and, the more to impose on the Public, he also introduced all the luxuries and amusements of the Great. Concerts and balls made Brethren of high rank flock to his Lodge, and they came with the most brilliant equipages. Soldiers stood sentry in the avenues, that the multitude of carriages might not occasion disorder; indeed a stranger might have thought that it was under the auspices of the King himself that these balls were given. The Lodge was resplendent, as the more wealthy Masons contributed to the expences of the Orchestra, lights, refreshments, and, in short, of all those diversions which appeared to be the sole object of their union. But while the Brethren were dancing with their female adepts, or were chaunting in the common Lodge-room the sweets of Equality and Liberty, they little suspected that a *Secret Committee* held its sittings over their heads, and were employed in preparing the means for diffusing that Equality and Liberty over all ranks and conditions, from the palace to the cot.

It was actually over the common Lodge-room that the Committee held its sitting, under the title of *The Secret Committee of United Friends*, whose grand adepts were two men equally famous in the mysteries at Lyons and at Paris. These were WILLERMOZ and CHAPPE DE LA HENRIÈRE. During the whole time of the festivity two tylers, with drawn swords, stood, one at the bottom of the staircase, the other near the upper door, to defend the entrance of the new Sanctuary, where were kept the archives of the Secret Correspondence. Even the man to whom all the packets from the Brethren of Germany or Italy were directed, was not permitted to pass beyond the threshold of the door. He was unacquainted with the cypher of the Correspondence; his duty was merely to carry the packets to the door of the Committee,[7] Savalette de Lange came to receive them, and the secret never transpired beyond the walls of the Committee. The Reader may easily conceive the nature of this Correspondence, and of the Councils held in consequence of it, when he is informed, that to gain admittance into this Secret Committee, it was not sufficient to have been initiated in all the degrees of Ancient Masonry, but it was necessary to be *a Master of all the Philosophical Degrees*; that is to say, to have sworn *hatred to Christianity* with the Knights of the Sun, and *hatred to every worship, and to all Kings* with the Knights of Kadosch.

There existed other lurking haunts of rebellion, less known, but still more formidable; such as that in the *Rue de la Sourdiere*, where the Brethren of Avignon, pupils of Swedenborg and St. Martin, came to mingle their mysteries with those of the Rosicrucians and other Masons both ancient and sophisticated. In public, under the disguise of quacks and visionary ghost-raiders, these new adepts spoke of nothing but their powers of evoking spirits, raising and interrogating the dead, and a hundred other phenomena of a similar nature. But in the dark recesses of their Lodges, these new law-givers were fostering plots nearly of the same tendency as those of Weishaupt, but more atrocious in their construction. I have already exposed their disorganizing mysteries in treating of Swedenborg and St. Martin. I scarcely dared to credit the horrid trials and abominable oaths said by several writers to be exacted from the adepts. I could wish to have spoken of them on the authority only of the adepts themselves or of the Code; but those with whom I have as yet been acquainted, had only been initiated in part of the mysteries; yet by what they had learned, it will not be difficult for the reader to form a judgment of the remainder.

It is an incontestable fact to begin with, that Swedenborg's Illuminees, styled in France the Martinists, and also calling themselves the *beneficent Knights*, had their travelling adepts after the manner of the Illuminees of Weishaupt. It is also certain, that these pretended *Philaletes*, or lovers of truth, had formed a code of laws for themselves, had organized societies, and like Weishaupt, had intruded themselves into the Masonic Lodges, there to search after men who might be disposed to receive their mysteries, and adopt their new degrees. Among the latter was one called the *Knights of the Phœnix*. A Knight of this degree giving himself out for a Saxon, and a Baron of the Holy Roman Empire, possessed of the most pompous certificates from several Princes of Germany, came to exercise his Apostleship in France a very few years before the late Revolution.[8] After having spent some time in a *central* town, visited the Lodges, and observed the Brethren, he thought that he had discovered three worthy of being initiated in the higher sciences. The *Venerable* or Master of the Lodge, in whose words we shall relate the story, was one of these worthies. "All things agreed on," said the Venerable, "we three waited on our Illuminee, ardent to be initiated in the new mysteries which he had promised.

"As he could not subject us to the ordinary trials, he dispensed with them as much as lay in his power. In the middle of his apartment he had prepared a chaffing-dish with a brasier full of fire; on his table were various symbols, and among others a Phœnix encompassed by a Serpent with its tail in its mouth, forming a circle. The explanation of the mysteries began by that of the brasier and other symbols. 'This brasier (said he) is here to teach you, that *fire is the principle of all things*; that it is the great agent of nature, and imparts action to bodies. That man receives from that agent life; with the power of thinking and of acting.' Such was the tenor of the first lesson. Our Illuminee then proceeded to explain the other symbols.—'This serpent forming a circle (says he) is the emblem of *the Eternity of the World*, which, like this serpent, has neither *beginning nor end*. The serpent, you may also know, has the property of annually renovating its skin; this will figure to you the revolutions of the universe, and of nature, which appears to weaken and even to perish at certain epochs, but which, in the immensity of ages, only grows old to become young again, and to prepare for new revolutions. This Phœnix is a still more natural exposition of the succession and perpetuation of these phenomena. Mythology has represented this bird as re-vivifying from its own ashes, only to show how the universe is reproduced, and will continue to be so, from itself.'

"Thus far the Illuminizing Baron had taught us, under the common promise of secrecy, when on a sudden he stopped and informed us, that he could not proceed any farther without previously exacting an oath, the formula of which he read to us, to see whether we were disposed to take it. We all shuddered at hearing it. The exact words I do not pretend to state; but it was a promise, in the most execrable terms, to obey the chiefs of his Illuminism. We endeavoured to conceal our indignation, that we might hear to what lengths he would proceed; he then came to the promise *of renouncing and abjuring the most sacred ties, those of citizen, of subject, of one's family, of father, mother, friend, children, husband*. At these words one of the three, unable to endure it any longer, sallied forth from the room, returned with a drawn sword in his hand, and ran at the Illuminizing Baron in a most violent rage. We were happy enough to stop and hold him until he had recovered his senses a little. Then, however, our colleague burst into the most violent passion, abusing the Baron for a rascal, and telling him, that if he were not out of the town in twenty-four hours he would have him taken up and hanged." The reader will readily suppose that the Baron made the best of his way out of the place.

Another affair that may throw some light on this monstrous Sect took place at Vienna. A young man of high birth, and who has signalized himself by his bravery during this war, felt an impulse, like many others of his age, to become a Freemason. His Lodge, though he knew it not, was one of those under the direction of the same species of Illuminees. He had often been made the bearer of letters which he strongly suspected. At length he determined not to deliver them, under pretence that he had not found the persons at home to whom they were directed, but in fact because he did not wish to be made the instrument of treason. Curiosity, however, getting the better of him, he still continued to solicit admission to the higher degrees. At length his initiation was fixed for the next day, when he received a letter demanding an immediate interview, and written in the most pressing style. When he came to the place appointed, he found an adept, the former friend of his father. "I am now taking such a step (said he), that the least indiscretion on your part will most certainly cost me my life; but I thought myself bound to it in consequence of the friendship which your father always shewed me and the regard that I have personally for yourself. I am a lost man if you do not keep my secret; but on the other hand, you are for ever undone if you prsent yourself at the Lodge to receive the degree for which you have been soliciting. I know you too well to think that you would take the oath which will be proposed to you: You cannot dissemble; and still less will you be able to think or act as they would wish to make you. Horror will betray you, and then all will be over with you. You are already on the BLACK LIST *as suspected*. Knowing you as I do, I can assure you that you will soon be on the *Red*, or BLOOD LIST (*blode list*); and then never flatter yourself with a hope to escape the poisons or the assassins of the Sect." This youth's resolution was not to be subdued by fear. Before he would acquiesce, he wished at least to be made acquainted with some of those terrible engagements in which he was to bind himself, and which he should not be able to keep. His friend then explained the oath that would be required, and he found it to be no other than the utter renunciation of all the most sacred ties of Religion, of Society, and of nature; and a vow to recognize no other law than the commands of the Illuminizing Superiors. He shuddered at hearing of such bonds; he found means of deferring his initiation, and abandoned the Lodges entirely before it was too late. Since the Revolution, circumstances have induced this Gentleman to leave the Austrian service and engage in the English; but it was from his own mouth that I learned how much he feared that his friend had been put on the *Red List* for the friendly service he had rendered him. Certain it is that he heard of his death a short time after this interview had taken place.

The reader will naturally wish to return to our Bavarian Illuminees; but that he may better understand what was and what ought to be the effect of their mission, I must first describe the composition of the Lodge in which they were to be received; and for that purpose, I must again insist on those Illuminees so well known in France under the name of *Theosophes*. Let us compare the above-mentioned *black list* and BLOOD LIST with an anecdote that indeed I could never credit until I was at length informed of the circumstances by men who were perfectly well acquainted with them. Every body knew that the large mansion of Ermenonville, belonging to Mr. Gerardin, and situated about thirty miles from Paris, was a principal haunt of Illuminism. It is also well known, that there, at the tomb of Jean Jacques Rousseau, under pretence of regenerating man and restoring him to the age of nature, the most horrible dissoluteness of morals was practised.—The famous impostor *Saint Germain* presided over these mysteries; he was the God of them, and he also had his *blood list*. The Chevalier de LESCURE fell a fatal victim to it. He wished to withdraw from this horrid society; perhaps even to discover its abominations. Poison was mingled with his drink, and he was not a stranger to the cause of his death. Before he expired he positively declared to the MARQUIS DE

MONTROI, a general officer, that he fell victim to this infamous crew of Illuminees.[9]

Having ascertained these facts, I shall no longer hesitate to consider as so many historical truths, first, all the oaths and wishes for the destruction of the Altar and the Throne; secondly, all those doctrines so exactly coinciding with what has been already extracted from the works of the Sect; and, lastly, all those abominable oaths and horrid trials described by a multitude of authors. Nor shall I be guilty of calumny when I declare, that the sole difference between this Sect and Weishaupt's lies in the ceremonial. Atheism is as precisely the ultimate object of their theosophy, as it is of Weishaupt's mysteries. Neither will allow, that the man of nature can be bound by the laws of society; both declare, that sovereigns are nothing more than tyrants; and both agree, that all means of annihilating Priests, Kings, Altars, and Laws, (however atrocious they may be in themselves) become meritorious and noble when directed to that end. But they excel even the modern *Spartacus* in their arts for kindling and inflaming the zeal of their assassins and parricides. That the means of the former are not to be compared with those of the latter, let the reader decide on the following statement.

When one of those unfortunate men who have been led away by the Sect into all the illusions of their visions wishes to be initiated into the art of prodigies, the science of sciences, in short into the last secrets of the adepts, the proposition is made to him to consummate his devotion to the superiors who are entrusted with these sciences. This will be a new contract, and will make him the blind instrument of all the plots into which he will soon be plunged. On the day appointed for his initiation he is led through dark windings to the den of trials. In this cavern the image of death, the mechanism of spectres, potions of blood, sepulchral lamps, subterraneous voices, every thing, in short, that can affright the imagination, and successively hurry him from terror to enthusiasm, is put in action, until at length, worn out by fright, fatigue, hope or enthusiasm, the candiate is so perfectly deprived of his reason, that he cannot help following any impulse that he may receive. Then it is that the voice of the invisible Hierophant bursts forth from this abyss, makes the vaults resound with its menaces, and prescribes the following execrable oath, which the Candidate repeats after him:

"I here break all the ties of the flesh that bind me to father, mother, brothers, sisters, wife, relations, friends, *mistresses*, kings, chiefs, benefactors; in short, to every person to whom I have promised faith, obedience, gratitude, or service."

"I swear to reveal to the new chief whom I acknowledged every thing that I shall have seen, done, read, heard, learned or discovered; and even to seek after and spy into things that might otherwise escape my notice. I swear to revere the *Aqua Tophana*, as a certain, prompt, and necessary means of ridding the earth, by the death of stupefaction of those who revile the truth, or seek to wrest if from my hands."[10]

Scarcely has the candidate pronounced this oath when the same voice informs him, that from that instant he is released *from all other oaths that he had taken either to his country or to the laws*. "Fly (it says) the temptation of ever revealing what you have just heard; for lightning is not more instantaneous than the dagger that shall reach you in whatever part of the world you may be."

Thus did this atrocious Sect form its adepts. Springing from the delirious reveries of a Swedenborg, it travels from England to Avignon, Lyons, and Paris. In this latter town, and as early as the year 1781, a club of this species of Illuminees (to the number of 125 or 130) had formed itself, holding its sittings in the above-mentioned Rue de la Sourdiere. Savalette de Lange, the same man whom we have seen so immersed in the correspondence of the Committee of the *Amis Reunis*, presided over this club. The famous Count St. Germain often held meetings at this same Lodge. CAGLIOSTRO was invited to it by a special deputation for the purpose. Hitherto this man's mysteries had only been those of an impostor; but here he soon learned to be a conspirator. It was from this Lodge that he derived that knowledge of the revolution which he pretended to foretel in a sort of prophetic cant when he made his appearance in London after he had been liberated from the Bastille. It was thence that he received his missions for Rome, where he was to sow the seeds of Revolution. One of the Adepts that had been deputed to him was a Mr. RAYMOND, who had been the master of the Post-office at Besancon. He was an enthusiast, and his imagination was bewildered with Swedenborg's visions. From him the knowledge was derived of this Lodge having had a hundred and thirty resident members at Paris, and more than a *hundred and fifty* travelling members or correspondents in different parts of the Globe; that, after the example of Holbach's club, they had their compilers and printers who were circulating their revolutionary poisons among all classes of the people.[11] In the person of DIETRICH, Secretary to the Lodge, we find every species of Illuminism. CONDORCET also was a member; he who needed only to be made acquainted with Weishaupt's plots to belong to every conspiring Sect; though it is not certain, that Dietrich had not already put him in direct correspondence with the modern *Spartacus*.—Let the reader mark well of what persons this Lodge was composed. We shall have occasion to advert to it again for the illustration of many a sanguinary scene. In the mean time let us take a view of other masonic haunts, that we may discover all these different Sects, the harbingers of such horrors, uniting and combining into one hideous mass of conspirators under the disastrous name of Jacobins.

Beside the lodges that I have already named, there existed two others in Paris, the more remarkable as they shew how the conspirators would as it were class themselves according to the degree of error they had adopted, or the views that had prompted them to engage in the general conspiracy. One of these Lodges was called *the Nine Sisters*. This was the re-union of the Masonic brethren who styled themselves Philosophers. The other was named the *Lodge of Candor,* and was chiefly composed of those Masons who in the world held a high rank and bore titles of nobility, while in the Lodges they traiterously conspired against Nobility, and more particularly against the monarchy and against religion.

The unfortunate *Duke de la Rochefoucault*, at once the dupe and protector of the Sophisters, belonged to the Lodge of the *Nine Sisters*. *Pastoret* was the Master of it, he who in public appeared to sacrifice to rank and riches, and even to court religion; but whose revolutionary career would have caused less surprise had the active part he had taken in the dark recesses of this Lodge been more generally known. The name of *Condorcet* also appears here, as it does in every haunt of rebellion. Together with him we find a long list of all the Sophisters of the day, such as *Brissot, Garat,* the commander *Dolomieu, Lacepede, Bailly, Camille Desmoulins, Cerutti, Fourcroi, Danton, Millin, Lalande, Bonne, Chateau Randon, Chenier, Mercier, Gudin, La Metherie,* and the *Marquis de la Salle,* who, not finding the Lodge of the Social Contract sufficiently philosophized, had come over to Condorcet. There was also *Champfort*, who never could think that the revolution of Equality and Liberty advanced with sufficient rapidity, till at length, fettered in its chains, he could find no other resource in his Philosophism than suicide. Among the apostate clergy that had flocked thither, we find *Noel, Pingré,* and *Mulot*. The two latter, together with *Lalande*, were also members of the Secret Committee of the *Grand Orient*. Dom *Gerles*, in company with *Rabaud de St. Etienne* and *Petion*, came and joined the Lodge of the Nine Sisters in the early time of the revolution. *Fauchet* took his station at the *Bouche de Fer*, with *Goupil de Preseln* and *Bonneville*. As to *Syeyes*, the most zealous of this brotherhood and of the whole revolutionary crew, he had formed a new Lodge at the *Palais Royal*, called the *Club of the Twenty-two,* and composed of the chosen of the Elect.

Such persons as wish to form a precise idea of the revolutionary spirit that predominated in this Lodge, need only to consult those works published by its members, when the court, at the instigation of Necker, imprudently invited all the Sophisters to lay before the public their views on the composition of the States General. A work of this nature, written by La Metherie, being read at the hotel, and in presence of the Duke de la Rochefoucault, a French nobleman, who has since mentioned it to me, ventured to say, that the positions laid down in that work were derogatory to the rights of the sovereign and to religion, ' Well, (said the duke, a mere dupe of his Sophisters,) *either the court will admit of these plans, and then we shall be able to arrange matters as we please; or else, the court will reject them, and in that case we must do without a king.*' Such, indeed, was the opinion generally entertained and declared by the sophisticated Masons, such as Bailly, Gudin, La Metherie, Dupont, &c.[12] They wished to establish a king subjected to all their theory of Equality, Liberty, and Sovereignty of the people; but it was only through them that the people were to dictate the laws; and some of these *soi-disant* sages wished to annihilate royalty entirely. Several of them, such as Brissot and his faction, already showed dispositions to reject all terms with the throne; and reviling it was only the prelude to its utter subversion.

There was another set of brethren, who frequented the *Loge de la Candeur*, but, following other plans, they sought to combine their ambition with the Masonic Equality and Liberty. There did *La Fayette*, the disciple of Syeyes, lisping the *Rights of Man*, and already asserting that *insurrection was a most sacred duty*, dream that he was the rival of the immortal Washington. The Brothers *Lameth*, surnamed the *ungrateful*, flocked thither to punish the court for the favors conferred on them; so did the *Marquis de Montesquiou, Moreton de Chabrillant*, and *Custines*, in hopes of revenge for having been slighted by that same court. Here also were seated many agents of Philip D'Orleans, such as his counsellor *La Clos*, his chancellor *La Touche, Sillery* the vilest of slaves, and *D'Aiguillon* the most hideous of mummers.[13] Thither also had resorted the Marquis de *Lusignan* and the Prince of *Broglio*, whose youth was about to tarnish the glory of a name that deserved a better fate. The Physician *Guilletin* is the only brother that I can find in this Lodge who did not bear a title. He soon felt the effects of its power, when cited before the Parliament to answer for a seditious publication; he beheld thousands of adepts flocking in on all sides and threatening the magistrates, who might now plainly perceive that it was too late to contend against the federated bands of Masonry.

Such was the state of the Lodges, and of the most remarkable Brethren at Paris, when the Deputies of Illuminism arrived from Germany. Most authors make them alight at the Lodge of the *Contrat Social, Rue Coq-heron*. I fear that I have myself prepared my readers for a similar error, when speaking (in Vol. II, Chap. XIII of these Memoirs) of a Lodge established in that same street. I recollect, however, that I particularly mentioned them to be the Sophisters adherent to the Duke de la Rochefoucault; and none of those belonged to the *Contrat Social*. Though I may have mistaken the street in which they assembled, I was not in any error with respect to the persons of the Conspirators. The better to distinguish them, and that I might not confound them with another species of Masons, I made the strictest inquiries. Among other documents, I procured a very numerous list of the Brethren of the *Social Contract*.[14] I therein found men who are well known for their attachment to royalty, and not a single one who had distinguished himself by his zeal for the revolution. I also found, that this error (so scandalizing to the *Social Contract*) originated in a work called *Les Masques Arrachés*, published under the feigned name of *Jacques le Sueur*, which is nothing but a scurrilous libel on persons of the highest respectability. This author transforms men whom I have known to be the most violent enemies to the revolution into the most zealous abettors of it. He also makes the Duke de la Rochefoucault, the Abbé Fauchet, Bailly, and La Fayette, members of the *Social Contract*, though they never belonged to it. He places it under the direction of the Grand Master Philip of Orleans, whereas it never filiated from any Lodge but that of Edinburgh. He paints the venerable Cardinal of Malines in the falsest colours, as will evidently appear to every person who is acquainted with his high reputation for virtue and wisdom. On the whole, I do not think that this supposed *Le Sueur* can be quoted as an authority in any thing, except in what he says on the reception of the *Philalete Illuminees*; and even there he is most abominable in his personalities, and pretends to have been an actor in the scene when he is but the plagiary copyist of Mirabeau.

I have besides acquired a certainty, that Weishaupt's emissaries could not have applied to men more inimical to his systems, whether Masonic or Anarchical, than the members of the *Social Contract*, as by their orders the famous work written by Bonneville, Bode's great friend, was burnt in open Lodge. In short, I have in my possession the *original letter* (or, in Masonic language, the *planche tracée*) written by a man with whom I was acquainted, and on the formal deliberation of the *Social Contract* transmitted to several other lodges, to engage them to join in a federation for the support of Louis XVI against the jacobins. It is true, that the royalist brethren of this Lodge were the complete dupes of this projected federation, for they invited the Lodges to form an union for the maintaining of the King according to the constitution of 1789. Louis XVI, who really wished to keep the oath that had been forced from him, to be true to the constitution, was very pleased with the list of the federated Masons; but Mr. de La Porte, then minister, was of a different opinion. When he saw the *circular letter*, and the number of persons who had subscribed to it, he said, "It is impossible that these persons can be other than constitutionalist, or that they can ever become staunch royalists."—"Let us begin (rejoined the agents of the Social Contract) by maintaining the king in his present state, and we will afterwards find means of re-establishing the true Monarchy." This answer may serve as a vindication for the members of the *Social Contract*; but their good intentions did not make their delusion the less complete. In the first place, they *might* have seen, but they *did not* see, that the greater number of those who had signed the letter were men who wished to continue to enjoy their Equality and Liberty under a King reduced to the condition of a mere Doge to the sovereign and legislative people; and that La Fayette, Bailly, and many other revolutionists, would have signed this letter, without ceasing on that account to be jacobins and rebels. Neither did they reflect, that many of those constitutional brethren would have turned against the *Social Contract*, as soon as they perceived the plan for reinstating the Monarch in his ancient rights; nor that it was far more easy to entice these constitutionalists into the most outrageous democracy of the great club, than to bring them back to the principles of real monarchy. In short, they had overlooked the vast number of adepts of democracy who would infallibly denounce them as traitors to Equality and Liberty, which afterwards proved to be the case. It was to very little purpose that the abettors of this federation terminated their letter with the following words:—"This *table* is only for your chapter. Make discreet use of it. We have *two sacred interests* to manage, that of the French Monarchy and its King, and that of Masonry and its Members." The interest of Masonry carried the day; for, at the very time that the demi-adepts were subscribing the letter, the more profound adepts were from every quarter denouncing the federation to the great club, and the *Social Contract* was itself proscribed.

Certain of this fact, and observing that the brethren of the *Social Contract* positively declare, in the *table tracée* (which I have before me) *that all political and deliberating clubs should be suppressed*; being also assured, by several Masons, that it was from the Committee of the *Amis réunis* that the invitations were sent to go and deliberate with the German deputies, I find myself obliged to differ with those writers who declare the Emissaries of Illuminism to have alighted at the Social Contract, and who attribute to that Lodge the political committees established on their arrival. It may very possibly have happened, that some one of these committees may have taken its station in the same street; but certain it is, that such committee was not composed of members from the *Social Contract*. So likewise is it a mere fable that has been spread, with regard to the inscription supposed to have been written by Philip of Orleans on the door of this Lodge, *Hither each brings his ray of light*. Let it then be remembered, that it was to the Committee of the *Amis réunis* that Mirabeau had directed the illuminizing brethren from Germany.—Savalette and Bonneville had made this committee the central point of revolution and of the mysteries. There met in council, on the days appointed, not only the Parisian adepts, but those of all the provinces who were judged worthy of being admitted to the profound mysteries of the Sect. There were to be seen for the Elect of the Philaletes, the profound Rosicrucians and Knights Kadosch, the Elect of the *Rue Sourdière*, of the *Nine Sisters*, of the *Lodge of Candour*, and of the most secret committees of the *Grand Orient*. This was the landing-place of the travelling brethren from Lyons, Avignon, and Bourdeaux. The emissaries from Germany could not find a central point better adapted to their new mysteries than this committee; and there it was that they unfolded all the importance of their mission. Weishaupt's code was ordered to lie on the table, and commissioners were named to examine it and make their report.

But here the gates of this secret senate are shut against us. I do not pretend to penetrate the dark recess, and describe the deliberations that took place on this occasion. Many brethren have informed me, that they remember the deputation, by they scarcely recollect *Amelius*-Bode and *Bayard*-Busche under any other denomination than that of the *German brethren*. They have seen these deputies received in different Lodgees with all the etiquette due to visitors of high importance; but it was not on such occasions that a coalition was debated on, between the ancient mysteries of Masonry and those of the modern *Spartacus*. All that my memorials say on the subject is, that negotiations took place; that the deputies reported to their Areopage; that the negotiations lasted longer than was expected; and that it was at length decided, that the new mysteries should be introduced into the French Lodges, but under a Masonic form; and that they should all be illuminized, without even knowing the name of the Sect whose mysteries they were adopting. Only such parts of Weishaupt's code were to be selected as the circumstances would require to hasten the revolution. Had not the facts that immediately followed this negotiation transpired to point out its effects, we should still have been in the dark as to its great success; the news of which *Amelius* and *Bayard* carried back to their illuminized brethren in Germany. But happily for history, facts have spoken; and it will be easy to see how far this famous embassy influenced the French Revolution.

At the time of their arrival Paris swarmed with impostors, all raising spirits or conjuring up the dead, in order to pick the pockets of the living; or magnetizing and throwing *into a crisis* certain *knowing dupes*, or knaves who well knew the parts they had to act. Others again would work cures on *healthy dupes*, to swindle away the money of those who were really ill. In a word, *Mesmer* presided there in all his glory. I make this observation, because the illuminizing deputies pretended that they had been attracted from Germany by the fame of *Mesmer's* science, which had spread throughout their country; it also serves to show, that their arrival could not have been later than the year 1787, as in the very next year *Mesmerism* and its *tubs* were entirely abandoned, or confined to a few adepts, the object of public ridicule, who resorted to the hotel of the Duchess of Bourbon. Such a pretext, therefore, at that period would have been as much ridiculed as were *Mesmer's* dupes. The *Notables*, the Parliament, Brienne, and Necker, at that time furnished the Parisians with more important matter for consideration.—Beside, my instructions, as well as many persons the best informed on the subject, even Masons at whose Lodges these German brethren attended as visitors, state their arrival to have taken place about the time of the convocation of the first assembly of the *Notables*, which opened on the 22d February 1787. And, in fact, it is from that very year that we may observe the code of Weishaupt influencing French Masonry.

In that year we see all the mysteries of the *Amis réunis*, and of the other Lodges that had adopted the pretended mysticity of the Martinists, disappear. The very name of *Philalete* seems to have been forgotten. New explanations are given to the Masonic secrets; a new degree is introduced into the Lodges; and the brethren of Paris hasten to transmit it to those in the provinces. The adepts flock to the new mysteries. I have now before me a memorial written by an adept, who about the end of 1787 received the code at his Lodge, though he lived at eighty leagues distance from Paris. According to the agreement made with the Deputies, all the forms of Masonry were preserved in this new degree; *the ribbon was yellow, the badge was a star, and its festivals were kept at the Equinox*; but the ground-work of its mysteries was a discourse entirely copied from that pronounced by the illuminizing Hierophant in the degree of Epopt. *The dawn of a great day begins to break upon us, when the secrets of Masonry, hitherto unknown, shall become the property of all free men.* In short, it contained all the *principles of Equality and Liberty, and of natural religion*, detailed in the degree of Epopt; and even the enthusiasm of style was preserved. The discourses pronounced by the *Knights of the Sun*, or Knights *Kadosch*, on similar occasions, were not to be compared to this. The very Mason who has given me this information, though he had been admitted to all the other degrees, was so disgusted with this, that he refused it; but the greater part of the brethren of his Lodge were so much electrified by it, that *they became the most zealous sticklers for the revolution.* Some have even held conspicuous places in it, *and one actually became minister.* In this new degree, the reader must remark, the very name of Illuminee was not mentioned; it was merely a farther explanation of the origin and secrets of Masonry. The French Masons were now ripe for such an explanation; they were in a state similar to that described by Knigge when speaking of the Brethren who inhabited the protestant parts of Germany; they needed no long trials; they were illuminized with the same facility; the name signified little; they received the degree, and ran wild with the same enthusiasm.

It was difficult, however, as yet, to judge by the dispositions of the different Lodges what turn the revolution would take. The Masons in general wished for a change in the constitution; but the chosen of the Elect alone were initiated in all the disorganizing plans of their Equality and Liberty. Their mysteries, it is true, were unfolded in the higher degrees; but it must be also remembered, that terror had there much more influence than conviction. I was acquainted with Masons who had sworn *hatred to kings* on their reception to the degree of *Kadosch;* nevertheless I have seen them, regardless of that oath, become the staunch friends of Monarchy. That spirit, inherent to the French nation, got the better of the Masonic views; that was the spirit which was to be eradicated from the minds of the brethren; and all the sophistry and delusions of the illuminizing Hierophants were to be practised for that purpose. It was in his degree of *Epopt* that the modern *Spartacus* had condensed all his poisons by which he was to infuse into his adepts that frantic rage against kings, which he had himself imbibed. Such also was the intention and effect of the degree of the *Masonic Epopt.*

But Illuminism was not to be appeased by seeing the adepts of the antient Lodges sacrificing at its shrine. The Hierophant tells his disciples, that *they are to acquire strength by gaining over the multitude.* This is also the period (at the introduction of the new degree, and the return of the deputies to Germany) when the Lodges are multiplied beyond any former precedent, both in Paris and the provinces, and when the system for the reception of Masons is changed. However low Masonry may have stooped in quest of candidates, it had not as yet been seen recruiting in the suburbs among the lowest rabble; all at once we see the suburbs of St. Antoine and St. Marceau filled with Lodges composed of porters and labourers, now decorated with the levelling badges of Masonry. In the country-towns and villages, Lodges are opened for assembling the workmen and peasantry, in hopes of heating their imaginations with the sophisticated ideas of Equality and Liberty and the Rights of Man. At that same period does Philip of Orleans introduce to the Masonic mysteries those French Guards, whom he destined to the subsequent attack of the Bastille and the storming of the palace of his royal master and kinsman. Let the officers of those legions be questioned why they abandoned the Lodges; and they will tell you, it was because they did not choose to be confounded with their common soldiers in this Masonic Equality.

At that same period is Paris over-run with an immense number of clubs and literary societies, on the plan of the Germanic union, and such as it had already established on the banks of the Rhine. They are no longer Lodges, but Clubs, *regulating committes*, and *political committees*. All these clubs deliberate. Their resolutions, as well as those of the committee of the *Amis des Noirs*, are all transmitted to the committee of correspondence of the *Grand Orient*, and thence are forwarded to the Venerables in the provinces. This is no more than that concatenation of revolt, invented by Weishaupt to revolutionize nations from the north to the south, and from the east to the west, at one and the same hour. The chief committee of these *regulating committees* is no other than the French *Areopage*. In place of *Spartacus*-Weishaupt, *Philo*-Knigge, *Marius*-Hertel, &c. we find, wielding the firebrands of revolution in the capital of France, a *Philip of Orleans*, a *Mirabeau*, a *Syeyes*, a *Savalette de Lange*, a *Condorcet*, &c.

Scarcely is the construction of this chain of rebellion made known to them, before they set about forming it throughout the state. Instructions are sent to the very extremities of the kingdom; all the Venerables are ordered *to acknowledge the reception of them, and to subjoin to their answer the oath of faithfully and punctually executing all commands they may receive through the same channel*. Those who might hesitate at such an oath are menaced with all the *poignards* and *aqua tophana* that await traitors to the Sect.[15]

Those Masters of Lodges who through fear or disgust were unwilling to engage in so awful an undertaking, had no other resource left but to abandon the Lodge and the mallet, under whatever pretence their fears could suggest. They were replaced by more zealous brethren,[16] and the orders continued to be transmitted until the meeting of the States-general. The day of general insurrection is fixed for the 14th of July, 1789. At the same hour, and in all parts of France, the cries of Equality and Liberty resound from the Lodges. Paris bristles up in a phalanx of pikes, hatchets, and bayonets; couriers are sent into the provinces, and they return with the news of a similar insurrection; towns, villages, nay the very fields and cots, resound with the cries of Equality and Liberty, and are thus in union with the brethren of the capital. On this fatal day *the Lodges are dissolved*. The grand adepts are now seated in the town-houses in revolutionary committees. As they predominated in the Electoral Assemblies, so are they now predominant in the assembly styling itself National. Their cut-throat bands have been trying their strength, and the barriers of Paris are beaten to the ground; the country-houses of the nobility are in flames; the lantern posts are put in requisition; and heads are carried in savage triumph through the streets of Paris. The Monarch is attacked in his palace, and his faithful guards butchered; prodigies of valour alone could save the life of his royal consort; and the King himself is dragged a prisoner to his capital. Good God! whither am I proceeding?—all Europe is acquainted with the dreadful tale. Let us return then to the hand that organizes this horrid concatenation of villany.

The Lodges had thus been transformed into a vast corresponding society; and, through the means of that correspondence, France had in a single day been overwhelmed by a million of demoniacs, who with horrid yell proclaimed their Equality and Liberty, while they were committing the most abominable outrages. And who were the men that presided over these primitive disasters? History immediately points to a new den of conspirators, holding their meetings at Versailles, under the title of the *Breton Club*. And who are the members of it? Mirabeau, Syeyes, Barnave, Chapellier, the Marquis de la Coste, Glezen, Bouche, Petion; in short, an aggregate of the most profound adepts, both of the capital and of the provinces, who supply the place of the central committee, and by means of the established correspondence fix the time and manner of the insurrection. They are, however, but at the commencement of that long career of crime and iniquity which they are to run; they must concert new means, and gain over hands and numbers to accomplish the views which they were prosecuting. The better to direct this horrid course, they impatiently wait the day when they may sally forth from their dark recesses; and it is to the temple of the living God, to the church of religious men called Jacobins, that Mirabeau convokes the Parisian adepts; it is there that he establishes himself with the very men who composed the Breton Club. The whole conspiring crew flock around him. From that instant this temple is converted into a den of conspirators, and is only known by the name of Club. The name of those antient religious who heretofore made it resound with the praises of the living God, is given to this horde of blasphemers, the re-union of every class of conspirators. Soon does all Europe designate by the name of *Jacobin* the authors and abettors of the French Revolution. The curse once pronounced on this name, it is but just and proper that the appellation of JACOBIN alone should carry with it the idea of a general coalition of the *Sophisters of Impiety* conspiring against their God and Christianity; of the *Sophisters of Rebellion* conspiring against their God and their King; and of the *Sophisters of Impiety and Anarchy* conspiring against their God, their King, and all civil society whatever.

Let us now enter this den of rebellion, which may be looked upon as the prototype of those numerous associations which are soon spread under the same name throughout the provinces. It is thither, it is to that monstrous union of every species of conspiring Sect, that the talk which I undertook at the outset of these Memoirs leads both me and my readers; to follow those different conspiring Sects from their origin to their terrible coalition in this den of conspirators under the name of *Jacobins*. Darkness may have hitherto encompassed the proceedings of those different Sects; and some readers may have been blind to conviction, and disbelieved the evidence I have adduced to prove that the commencement of this fatal union is to be dated from the intrusion of the Sophisters into the Masonic Lodges, and the consummation of it from the coalition of the latter with the deputies of Illuminism. But broad daylight will now betray their actions; behold the Sophisters, the Rebels, the Adepts of every class assembled, all bound by the same oath, whether Rosicrucians, Knights Kadosch, or disciples of Voltaire and Jean Jacques, whether Knights-Templars, Epopts of Illuminism, or disciples of Swedenborg and St. Martin; here, I say, all are holding council and concerting ruin, devastation, and all that measureless chain of revolutionary crimes.

That impious man, who had first sworn to crush God and his Gospel, was no more; but his disciples were still in life and vigour. We have seen them springing up from their academic meetings, retailing their blasphemies in those petty assemblies pretending to the *bel esprit*, under the auspices of the female adepts, such as the Dutchess D'Anville, the Marquise du Deffant, or the Geofrins, Espinaces, Neckers, and Staels. They then framed their conspiracies at the Hotel D'Holbach. To support the illusions of their Sophistry by the strength of Legions, they obtrude themselves on the Masonic Lodges; but now they have abandoned their pettifogging female adepts, their academies; nay, the Hotel D'Holbach and the Lodges themselves are deserted; the great revolutionary gulph has swallowed them up. Behold them muffled up in the red cap; the cloak of Philosphy has been cast aside; behold them all, Condorcet, Brissot, Bailly, Garat, Ceruty, Mercier, Rabaud, Cara, Gorsas, Dupui, Dupont, Lalande, Atheists, Deists, Encyclopedists, Œconomists, in short, self-created Philosophers of every species and every kind. Here they appear foremost in the ranks of *rebellion*, as they formerly did in those of *impiety*. Behold them intermixed with the dregs of the Brigands and of the Lodges, as well as with the leaders of the bands and the heroes of the mysteries; with the banditti of Philip of Orleans, as well as with his worthy advocate *Chabroud*, or his rival *La Fayette*. Behold them in council with the traitors of aristocracy; as well as with the apostates of the clergy; with the Duke of Chartres, the Marquis de Montesquiou, and de la Salle, the Counts Pardieu, de Latouche, Charles and Theodore Lameth, Victor Broglio, Alexander Beauharnois, St. Fargeau, as well as with Syeyes, Perigord D'Autun, Noel, Chabot, Dom Gerles, Fauchet, and all the *intruding* tribe.

It is not by accident that we see these ancient conspirators, whether literary or masonic, coalescing with the conspiring brethren of the Provinces, such as Barrere, Mendouze, Bonnecarrere, and Collot d'Herbois; it is not by chance that the Jacobin clubs both in Paris and the Provinces become the general receptacle for Rosicrucians, Knights Templars, Knights of the Sun, and Knights Kadosch; or of those in particular who, under the name of *Philaletes*, were enthusiastically wedded to the mysteries of Swedenborg, whether at Paris, Lyons, Avignon, Bourdeaux, or Grenoble. The club having once sounded the trump of rebellion, where else should we go to search for those zealous Martinists, Savalette de Lange, Milanois, Willermoz, and men of their stamp? They had improved on the systems of their forerunners the Rosicrucians; they will, now that they have entered the great club, outstrip them with gigantic strides. They had coalesced with the illuminizing *Spartacus*; and in unison with his adepts they are now become the most ardent Jacobins.[17]

But to whatever cause people may choose to ascribe this general reunion of so many conspirators and of their systems, the fact certainly cannot be controverted. It had been first set on foot on the arrival of Bode; it was completed at the Club of the Jacobins. The list is public, and it contains the names of all the profound adepts who had hitherto been dispersed among the Lodges. But let the reader never forget that it is not a mere local union, or an identity of persons; it is an identity of principles, of method, of oaths, and of means; it is the general concert of these conspirators that proves the coalition.

If we turn to the discourses delivered in the club (for the brethren now have their journals and their public archives) we shall find, that Voltaire and Rousseau are their oracles, just as they were of the Sophisters when in their Literary Societies. In that club do they repeat all the blasphemous sophistry against Christianity which they had formerly uttered at the Hotel D'Holbach; the same enthusiastic declamations in favor of *Equality* and *Liberty*, the grand secret of those Sects that had hidden themselves in the occult Lodges. These adepts found themselves perfectly at home within this new den of conspirators; the *costume* and the symbols had changed, it is true; but in substituting the red, or rather the bloody, cap of liberty for the apron and level, they only adopted a more typical emblem of their antique mysteries. The President is now the Venerable; the brethren ask leave to speak, and he grants or refuses it with all the parade of Masonry. When deliberating, the votes are taken just as in the occult Lodges. The laws of the Freemasons for the admission or expulsion of brethren are the same. As in the *Grand Orient*, or at the *Amis réunis*, and in the Lodges in general, no candidate is received unless he be presented by *two sponsors*, who answer for his conduct and obedience; just so is it in the club. Here the obedience sworn is precisely the same as that sworn in the occult mysteries of Masonry. To be received a Jacobin, as to become a Rosicrucian or an Illuminee, the candidate is obliged to swear implicit obedience to the decisions of the brethren; and also to observe and cause to be observed all decrees passed by the National Assembly *in consequence of the decisions of the club*. He then binds himself to denounce to the club any man who shall to his knowledge counteract the decrees proposed by the club; and that he will make no exception in favor of *his most intimate friends, or his father, mother, or of any part of his family.* In short he will, in common with the disciples of Illuminism, swear to execute or cause to be executed all orders emanating from the privy council of the club, *though they should be repugnant to his sentiments and conscience;*[18] for the Jacobin club, like the *Grand Orient*, has its committees and privy counsellors. The brethren have not abandoned their Lodges, as renouncing all their means of hastening, fomenting, and propagating, revolutions. They have established here, just as at the *Grand Orient*, committees for *the reports*, for the *finances*, for the *correspondence*, and lastly, the grand committee of all, the *secret committee*; and nearly all the members of these different committees are the very persons whom we have seen flocking from the Lodges to the great club.[19]

In this club of Jacobins too is to be found, in common with the Occult Lodges of illuminised Masonry, the laws of exclusion and proscription. They have the *black list* and the *red list*, and this is a *list of blood*. The name of a rejected brother is never inscribed on it without effect. Paris has more than once seen such lists posted up; it has also seen those devoted victims perish, or, at best, save themselves by flight.[20]

Thus, in this den of conspirators do we find every thing in perfect unison with the Occult Lodges, to which it only succeeds. Adepts, object, principles, all are the same; whether we turn our eyes toward the adepts of impiety, of rebellion, or of anarchy, they are now but one conspiring Sect, under the disastrous name of Jacobin. We have hitherto denominated some by the name of *Sophisters*, others by that of *Occult Masons*, and lastly, we have described those men styled *Illuminees*. Their very names will now disappear; they will in future all be fully described by the name of *Jacobin*.

It has been an arduous task to collect the proofs of this monstrous association. When we look back to that day when Voltaire swore *to crush* the supposed *wretch* in support of his Equality and Liberty; to that day when Montesquieu dogmatically asserted, that all nations subject to a Monarch, and to laws that they had not made, were slaves; to that day, in short, when Rousseau points out as a public malefactor against mankind the man who had first enclosed a field and was presumptuous enough to declare that it was his property; from those days, I say, until the fatal period when the disciples of Voltaire, Montesquieu, and Rousseau, in the name of that same Equality and Liberty, flock to the club of the Jacobins, there to repeat their sophisms against Christ and his religion, to prosecute their masonic plots against kings, to propagate the blasphemies of the modern *Spartacus* against their God, their king, their country, and all social order; what systems have we not been obliged to investigate, what artifices to unfold, and into what dark and loathsome recesses have we not been obliged to penetrate, in order to trace their progress! At length we have traced them to their general convention of iniquity and rebellion. History will have no further need of my researches to demonstrate all the crimes and disasters of the French revolution that have issued from this haunt of conspirators. The historian needs only turn to the public records, to their own journals, and he will see what crimes of the French Revolution are to be attributed to them. I might, therefore, look upon my task as accomplished.

There is, however, a certain order to be observed in the very growth and progress of these scourges. In this association appears a monstrous wisdom, that directs the course of the crimes that are successively committed and even at appropriate moments. This wisdom has taught them how to make their least criminal accomplices prepare the way for the blackest deeds; it has taught them how to discard or destroy those agents who, from disgust or any other cause, cease to be their instruments and only become obstacles. Thus, in the very club of the Jacobins, in the centre of iniquity, there exists a progression of wickedness. Each Sect has retained its ultimate object, each conspirator his passions and his private views, just as in the Occult Lodges; yet they are all leagued in one common object, in one common measure, to overthrow the existing government, and erect their Equality and Liberty on the new order of things. But opinions will clash as to the choice of this new order. All detest and hate the God of the Gospel; but some will have a God according to their Philosophism, while the Philosophism of others reject all ideas of a God. La Fayette will have a Doge for a king, subject to the laws and will of a sovereign people. Philip of Orleans will have no king, unless it be himself. Brissot will neither submit to Philip as king, nor assent to La Fayette's Doge; he wishes to exercise the magistracy of his own democracy. Mirabeau will be content with any plan, provided he be the prime minister. Dietrich, Condorcet, Babœuf, and the higher adepts of *Spartacus*, will assent to nothing but the *man-king* of Illuminism, *every where his own master*. Crimes then will be graduated by the mysteries. The grand adepts will be seen to make the mere novices act. Private passions will sometimes clog their progress; I shall, therefore, attempt to point out in what order the French Revolution has brought these mysteries into action, and apply its successive progress to the different Sects that had so profoundly meditated and conceived it.

1. Welt und menschen Kentniss, P. 130.
2. See the Discourse of a Master of a Lodge on the ultimate fate of Masonry; Appendix to this Discourse—Important admonition by Hoffman, Vol. II. Sect. vii. &c. &c.
3. It is to this same Mauvillon that the German writers attribute the greater part of those two works published by Mirabeau, under the titles of *The Prussian Monarchy*, and *An Essay on the Illuminees*. Hence the high encomiums passed on Weishaupt in the former (Vol. V. Book vii), and all the cunning artifice that is observable in the latter, which was written with no other view than to mislead the public, by professing to betray the secrets of the Sect, without, in truth, saying a single word that could expose its views; and by leading astray the reader's attention to far different objects. This device made the French believe that they were thoroughly acquainted with Illuminism, though they were so perfectly ignorant on the subject as to have confounded Weishaupt's Illuminees with the Swedenborgians. The artifice also served as a cloak under which Mirabeau introduced Illuminism into France, at the time when he pretended to write against it. The very appellation of *Philalete* which he gave to his adepts was a trick, as it denoted the Theosophical Illuminees, quite another species.
4. Original Writings and Philo's Berichte, 6.
5. See the Alphabetical Statement of the Correspondence of the Lodges of the G. O. of France.
6. Ibid. Art. Foreign States.
7. I was informed by one of the Brethren who for a long time was the carrier of these dispatches, that, after some time, wishing to become a Member of the Committee, he was induced to get himself initiated in these degrees; but that he forbore doing it, because *an engagement for life was required, and also an annual contribution of six hundred Livres (25l.)* He also informed me, that each Brother paid a similar contribution, and that the whole management of these Funds was left to the Brother Savalette, who never gave in any accounts. This was a Fund to be added to the many means of corruption already in the possession of the adepts of the Occult Lodges. Who can say, how far these resources were extended in the hands of a man who had the care of

the *Tresor Royal?* The Conspirators very well knew how to chuse both their men and their places.
8. I could have named this man, as he is mentioned in my manuscript Memoirs as a *Philalete* Illuminee very famous in Prussia. But the person whom the reader will observe so indignant at these mysteries is at present in France; prudence, therefore, on his account, forbids me to mention names.
9. Nothing can equal the profligacy of morals that raged among these inhabitants of Ermenonville. Every woman admitted to the mysteries became common to the Brotherhood. That which *St. Germain* had chosen for himself was called the Virgin; she alone had the privilege of not being delivered over to chance, or to the commands of these true Adamites, unless St. Germain thought proper to confer the title of Virgin on some other woman. This vile impostor, more adroit than Cagliostro, had actually persuaded his adepts that he was in possession of an *Elixir of Immortality*; that he had gone through several changes by means of the metempsychosis; that he had already died three times, but that he would die no more; that since his last change he had lived fifteen hundred years:—And there were dupes who, too wise to credit the eternal truths taught by a God-made-man, firmly believed in this metempsychosis and in the fifteen hundred years of their God St. Germain!! Neither did they know that that period of time was no more than an allusion to the Masonic degrees. According to the Masonic action, an Apprentice is three years old, a Fellowcraft five, and a Master seven. This age goes on in such an increasing ration in certain degrees, that a Scotch Knight is said to be *five hundred years old*. When a Mason therefore comes and says, I am so many years old, it is no more than saying I am of such a degree. (*See Geschickte der unbekanten on the Scotch Degrees*).
10. See the Red Lodge unveiled, Page 11, and the history of the assassination of Gustavus III, King of Sweden, Sect. 4.
11. I have been informed of all these circumstances by a man who was for a long time connected with the Postmaster Raymond, but who resisted all his arts of seduction. This same person, on whom I can perfectly rely, also informed me, that he had seen the minutes of the Lodge, which were regularly printed by *Clouzier* in the *Rue de Sorbonne*; but that they were so overloaded with *signs* and *hieroglyphics*, that it was impossible for any but the adepts to read them.
12. See the account given of their works in Vol. II. of these Memoirs.
13. All Paris was acquainted with his accoutrements and remembers the hideous figure that he cut on the 5th and 6th of October, 1789, in the midst of the Poissards at Versailles.
14. I should have given this list, but that I could not suppose that so many Dukes, Marquisses, and Barons, would like to see their names made public. Besides, I am not writing the history of the dupes, but of the conspiring brethren.—I think it, however, proper to observe, that when the federation of which I am about to speak was undertaken, they (by the advice of the queen) admitted several members of a less aristocratic turn, lest their Lodge should be suspected of aristocracy.
15. See Vol. II. of these Memoirs, Chap. XIII.
16. These letters and menaces were transmitted during the sitting of the States of Britanny, that is to say, about June or July, 1788; at least it was at that time that a member of those States, a Mason and a Knight Kadosch, received his.—The new degree had been received at his Lodge about six months before.

17. See a List of the principal Jacobins in a work entitled "*Of the Causes and Effects of Jacobinism.*"

It is an observation that did not escape the notice of the German writers, and which I repeatedly find in the memorials sent to me, that the greatest visionaries of the Rosicrucian Masons and of the Philaletes are since become the most zealous apostles of Weishaupt's Illuminism and of his Revolution. The Germans particularly mark out one *Hülmer*, a famous Martinist of Prussia, and a *George Föster*, who in his great zeal for the mysteries of Swedenborg would pass fifteen days in fasting and prayer to obtain the vision of a spirit, or to discover the *Philosopher's Stone*. Since that time, however, they have both turned out to be most outrageous Jacobins.—In France many examples of this kind may be adduced: *Prunelle de Lierre*, for instance; a man heretofore of most amiable character, and a very good naturalist. He first became a recluse Martinist, and soon after as outrageous a Jacobin as *Föster*.—As for *Perisse*, the bookseller, he acted the same part at Lyons for the correspondence of the Martinists, as Savalette de Lange did at Paris; but he did not take the same precautions. One might see him going to the Lodge followed by his port-folio, which a servant could scarcely carry. Weishaupt's code gained admittance to this portfolio; the revolution took place; and Perisse, together with his co-adept Milanois, became as outrageous Jacobins as the rest.—What is there that cannot be said of the Martinists of Avignon? Was there ever such atrocious ferocity shown as by the ringleaders of this Lodge? All this tends to confirm the position, that between the adepts of Swedenborg, and the adepts of Weishaupt, there was but a slight shade of separation. The supposed theosophy of the one differed but little from the atheism of the other. Weishaupt goes more directly to the point; but the annihilation of all religion is the real object of both their mysteries. It is even worthy of remark, that the modern *Spartacus* was on the eve of grounding all his mysteries on that very Theosophy where *fire is the principle*, and on the theology of the Persians, as did the Philaletes and Martinists.—(*See Knights of the Phœnix, Original Writings, Vol. I. Let. 46.*)

18. See Memoirs of the club of the Jacobins.
19. See the list of the committees in *The Causes and Effects of the Revolution*—Montjoie, on the *Conspiracy of Orleans*. Book XIII.
20. Ibid., and *Brissot to his Constituents*, when expelled from the Jacobins.

CHAP. XII.

Application of the three Conspiracies to the French Revolution.

WHILE I have been unfolding the object and means of so many insidious plots, my reader has, no doubt, made frequent applications to facts that have taken place under his own eyes. He will have said to himself, what can be this long chain of crime, destruction, and horror, with which the French Revolution has astonished all Europe, but the consequence of the principles, and plans of these conspiring Sects! *In darkness they were conceived, but in broad day are they executed.* Such may be the succinct history of the Revolution, now that these plots have been laid open. It is so evidently demonstrated, that it would be a useless labour to descend to details; we will also pass over in our narrative those bloody scenes which might rather serve to tear open wounds scarcely closed, than convince my reader. I shall, therefore, consider the French Revolution in its preliminary steps, and in its successive attempts against Religion, against Monarchy, and against Society in general. But a cursory view of these attempts will suffice for the most complete demonstration.

Let us revert for a moment to that period when the conspirators of every class were still lurking in their hiding-places. The disciples of Montesquieu and Jean Jaques had so early as 1771 declared that men could only regain their primitive rights of *Equality* and *Liberty*, and the people their imprescriptible right of *legislative sovereignty*, by means of a general assembly of national deputies. At that time also the sophisticated adepts had pronounced, that the grand obstacle to these pretended rights was to be found in the distinctions of the three estates, the Clergy, the Nobility, and the third Estate.[1] To obtain, therefore, the convocation of the States General, and to annihilate the distinction of the three Estates, must necessarily have been and really were the first steps of the Revolution.

The deficit that Necker had left in the public treasury, the depredations and disorders of an age destitute of morals (because these Sophisters had transformed it into an age of impiety) had reduced a Monarch who shone forth unblemished in the midst of corruption, to summon the *Notables* of his kingdom, that they might consult for the happiness of his people, which seemed to be his only care. The tender wish that he has shown is immediately seized on by the conspirators, and serves as a pretext for them to hasten the convocation of that very assembly where all their horrid plots are to be consummated. Whatever might have been the wisdom of the *Notables*, their plans are rejected beforehand. Philip of Orleans and his political committees are likewise eager for the convocation of the States General. Even the tribunes of the nation will rise in judgment against, and discuss the rights of their Sovereign. Foremost among the conspirators, Philip of Orleans is also foremost in action. For the first time does he pretend to be zealous in the public cause; and the first act of his zeal is to enter a protest against the dispositions made by Lewis XVI to provide for the wants of the state.[2] In these intrigues against his Sovereign, he combined with the different magistrates who were then noted for their factious behaviour, such as DESPREMENIL, at that time infatuated with the visions of the Martinists and revolutionary principles; MONSABERT and SABATIER de CABRES, the most ardent enemies of the Court; and FRETEAU, who in the first assembly was to become the worthy associate of the Constitutionalist CAMUS. Philip so completely misleads this first Parliament of the kingdom, that they at length give the example of a lawful and formal demand for the convocation of the States General. Lewis XVI, seeing the general ferment, hesitates; Philip instigates the people; pays brigands; and mobs are assembled in Paris. The King at length thinks proper to grant the convocation of the States General.—That Sect which was headed by Orleans now only wants a Minister who shall direct the convocation according to the views of their conspiracy; and they turn their eyes on that very man who had hollowed out the abyss, that Necker, whose perfidious policy had been the ruin of the national treasury. He was the man of the ambitious courtiers, who led him toward the throne that they themselves might be drawn nearer to it; the man supported by the Princes de Beauveau and de Poix, by the Mareschal Castries, by the Duc D'Ayen, by Messrs. Besenval and Guibert; the man of the conspiring courtiers, such as La Fayette and the Lameths, the man of the Sophisters of Impiety, whose plots had been contrived in his own house and at the hotel D'Holbach; the man, in short, whose bust was to be carried in bloody and revolutionary triumph by the side of that of his worthy co-operator Philip of Orleans.

Lewis XVI might have known this perfidious minister; the whole plan of the conspiracy contrived by Necker and his adepts of Philosophism had been laid before the King; but, alas! he could not be made to believe that such wickedness and hypocrisy was to be found in man. The day came, however, when he sorrowfully exclaimed, *Why did I not believe it? Eleven years ago was every thing foretold that now befalls me.* It was to Necker that he alluded; for during his first ministry, was that man and the plots contrived in his house and at the hotel D'Holbach, formally denounced in a memorial presented to Mr. de Maurepas and to Lewis XVI. But since that time, the Conspirators had sounded all their trumpets to his fame, and celebrated the supposed virtues and talents of the Genevese traitor. Overpowered by such intrigue, the King was misled to think that this man would prove the Saviour of the state, and he entrusted him with the convocation of the States General. He was precisely the man to throw the whole of these states into the hands of the conspirators.[3] He knew that their hopes were in the multitude, and that the distinction of, and voting by estates, would prove an obstacle to their views against the sovereign. He farther saw, that the spirit of sedition predominated in the third estate, that they were becoming the revolutionary organs of the conspirators; and, to ensure the majority of votes to them, he doubled the number of the deputies to be sent by the third estate. Confident in their numbers, they immediately declare themselves, though alone, to constitute the *National Assembly*. In vain did the clergy and the nobility insist on that right (of far more consequence to the state than to themselves) of deliberating separately, and thus counterpoising the deliberations that might have been too hastily entered upon or guided by passion, interest, or the factious pretensions of party men. In vain did the clergy and nobility sacrifice all exclusive privileges or pecuniary advantages in taxation which they enjoyed, in hopes of preserving their rights in deliberation; for the privilege that Necker[4] and the other conspirators aimed at, was that power of counteracting all resolutions detrimental to religion or monarchy. It was in vain that Lewis XVI, with the tenderness rather of a father than of a king, made those sacrifices (which of themselves might be called a revolution, so much did they curtail his royal prerogative) in his Declaration of the 23d of June. But this was not the species of revolution sought by the conspirators. The sophisters had determined, that, to make their Equality and Liberty triumph, it was necessary to deliberate by *persons* and not by *estates*; that the Nobility and Clergy should be confounded among the multitude; and that the majority, when deliberating by estates, should prove a minority, when united with the great numbers of the third estate. Lewis XVI orders, that in virtue of the antient constitution of the kingdom, the antient form of deliberating by estates should be preserved; but his orders are vain; the conspirators protest against them; their president, BAILLY, calls them to a tennis-court, and there they swear to impose a constitution on France congenial to their views. They immediately set their brigands in motion; the venerable Archbishop of Paris is nearly stoned to death; the life of the Monarch is threatened; the fatal union of the three estates at length takes place, which subjects the two first estates to the will of the multitude; for the conspirators were certain of the support of all those apostates and dastards who by their intrigues had been returned among the deputies of the Nobility and Clergy, because Necker had doubled the number of the deputies of the third estate, to ensure the majority of the vortes in favour of the decrees which the party were to propose. He had organized the States general according to the views and wishes of the sophisters; he may, it is true, whimper and weep over the disasters and crimes of the Revolution; but the hand of time shall engrave on his tomb, *that he was the grand agent of them all.*

Having no farther opposition to fear, and certain of passing whatever decrees they chose, these conspirators proceed to declare themselves *a National Assembly*. They arrogate to themselves the right of making and of pronouncing the law. The secrets of the Lodges constitute the basis of the Revolution under the title of *the Rights of Man*. The first article declares *man to be equal and free; that the principle of all sovereignty essentially resides in the people*; and that *law* is nothing more than *the expression of the general will*. Such had been for nearly half a century the doctrines of Argenson, Montesquieu, Rousseau, and Voltaire. These principles of pride and revolt had long since been the groundwork of the mysteries of every class of Sophisters, Occult Mason, or Illuminee; and now they decorate the title-page of the revolutionary code.

This equal, free, sovereign, and legislative people, may will that their religion should be preserved in all its integrity; and that its monarch should be entrusted with the necessary power to crush sedition and rebellion. Veneration for the altar and affection for their prince still glowed in the heart of the French. But the conspirators wanted an armed force, drawn from the body of that same people, docile, and subservient to the views of the Sect, and that would oppose the will of the people whenever it did not coincide with theirs. This force was entirely to overpower the army of the sovereign. Every thing had been foreseen; for the sophisters had long since said, "Oh that we could but once get rid of these foreign military hirelings! An army of natives might be gained to the side of Liberty, at least a part of them; but the foreign troops are kept on foot for this very reason."[5] Their army of natives is immediately formed, and it is again from the dark recesses of Masonry that the signal is given. That same Savalette de Lange who presided over the secret committee of the *Amis réunis*, and over the correspondence, appeared before the Municipality of Paris, and spoke to the following effect. "*Gentlemen, I am a Corporal.* Here are Citizens to whom I have taught the use of arms, that they might defend the country. I did not create myself a major or a general, *we are all equal*, I am simply a Corporal; but I also gave the example; command that every citizen should follow it.—Let the nation take arms, and Liberty will be invincible." Savalette, in pronouncing this discourse, presented seven or eight brigands accoutred as soldiers. The sight of these few men, and the repeated cries of *Let us save the nation!* excited enthusiasm; an immense mob surrounded the town-hall, and Savalette's motion was instantaneously decreed. The very next day the Parisian army is set on foot, and millions are formed into *Native Battalions* throughout the empire.[6] They are the sworn agents of the conspirators; and it is now time that the unfortunate Lewis XVI should feel their power. He had driven from his person the treacherous Necker; but the Sect still wanted his services, and it forces the Monarch to recal him. The King hesitates at sanctioning the Rights of Man, and the force of the people is immediately put in action.

In support of these *rights*, all the conspirators combine; and it is agreed, that immediately on his return, Necker shall starve the people into rebellion; that the brethren shall collect all the harpies of the suburbs to go and demand bread of Lewis XVI, that Bailly and his assessors, seated at the Municipality, shall order the *legions of natives* to follow and support them; that La Fayette at the head of these legions should march to Versailles, that he should surround

Lewis XVI with these bands under pretence of watching for his safety, *and then retire to sleep*. Mirabeau, Petion, and Chapellier, Montesquieu and Duport, Charles Lameth and Laclos, Sillery and D'Aiguillon, will then inform the Assembly that *victims must be thrown to the people*,[7] and they avail themselves of the darkness of the night to inflame the populace and excite the soldiery. Their hearts were already as hideous as the furies; they now assume their *costume*, to lead their harpies on to the commission of crime.[8] D'Orleans will ply his monsters with the beverage of rage and frenzy, and will point out the Queen as the first victim to be immolated. Syeyes, Gregoire, and a multitude of other conspirators, stand spectators of the contest; but, should the monarch fall in the affray, they will tender the crown to Orleans, as they may be certain of parcelling out its prerogative according to their Equality and Liberty. Necker absconds, but his *virtuous spouse*, decorated with her nosegays, and accompanied by her inseparable companion the Mareschale de Beauveau, will appear in the galleries of Versailles, in the midst of the carnage, and virtuously exclaim, *Let the good people act, there is no danger*, and in fact she had none to fear; she had already written to her brother *Germani*, "*Patience; every thing will go well; we can neither speak nor write.*"[9]

The night from the 5th to the 6th of October reveals the secrets which this worthy confidant dared not write. History needs not our labours to paint the horrors of that awful night; they are described in the juridical depositions taken by the magistrates at the Chatelet. Orleans lost courage at the sight of a few faithful Life-guards, the only adherents of the King that La Fayette had permitted to remain near his person; and never was a more heroic phalanx formed than by these brave men round their royal master and his consort. Though their courage was appalled by the orders of their sovereign, they were still prodigal of their own blood; they resisted a forest of pikes,[10] and Orleans could not consummate his premeditated crime. Day-light arrives to expose the horrors of this night; the brigands, his instruments, are seen to blush, and the National Guards at length reflect that they are Frenchmen. They emit no other wish than to see Lewis XVI living in the midst of them at Paris in the palace of his forefathers. The unfortunate monarch knows not what men had profited of the natural effusions of loyalty of his people to make them emit this wish. He thought that he was entrusting himself to the affections of his people, when he was only obeying the dictates of the conspirators. He knows not that it is the last shift of the conspirators, that the crimes of this horrid night might not be entirely fruitless. The great difficulty they had found in making the monarch sanction the *rights of man* make them perceive that they would frequently stand in need of the same brigands to force his acquiescence to those future decrees which were to be grounded on them. All the decrees that were in succession to annihilate religion and monarcy were to be enforced by an insurrection, and the pikes and lantern-posts were to be in perpetual requisition, to constrain the votes, to intimidate the monarch, and discard all reclamation. In future a captive in Paris, Lewis XVI will be perpetually menaced by the brigands issuing from the suburbs or from the quarries, and paid by Necker and Orleans. La Fayette will proclaim, that *insurrection is a most sacred duty*, and insurrection will become the standing order of the day; Mirabeau, Barnave, Chapellier, will point out the object and fix the hours orders will be sent from their antichambers to the Jacobins and the suburbs, and daily at the hour fixed will the King, the Clergy, the Nobility, and all who may oppose the decrees in debate, find themselves surrounded by a mob that will hoot or act exactly according to the instructions given by the conspirators.[11]

Though they reaped no farther benefit from all the horrid deeds of the fifth and sixth of October, yet the conspirators knew but too well how to appreciate their successes. Madame Necker writes again to her brother Germani: "We are content; every thing went on well. The aristocracy would have had the uppermost, and we were obliged to make use of the rabble."[12] Here terminate what may be called the preliminaries of the revolution. Necker had moulded the National Assembly according to the views of the Sect, and had established it in the town that was judged most proper for enabling him to work the premeditated revolution. We next proceed to the plan traced by the Sophisters for *crushing* the pretended *wretch*; and here begins the war waged against the God of Christianity.

To destroy religious orders; to deprive the ministers of the church of their subsistence under pretence of *the wants of the state; silently to sap the edifice*, then to employ *superior force*, and at length to call in the *Hercules* and the *Bellerophons*; such (as it has been shown) were the means combined by the Sophisters to overturn and annihilate the altars of Christianity. To substitute the worship of the *great architect* of the universe to that of Christ; the *light* of the lodges to the doctrines of the gospel; the god of their pretended *reason* to the god of revelation; such were the most moderate of the mysteries of the occult Lodges of Masonry. To invent and substitute new religions in place of Christianity, and to impose them on the people till every religious principle could be eradicated; in the name of Equality and Liberty to render themselves *powerful* and *formidable*; then to *tie the hands, subjugate*, and *smother in the germ*, every thing that could counteract the empire of impiety and atheism; such were the views and plots of the *Epopt, Regent*, and *Magus* of Illuminism. This code and their oaths have been laid open to our readers; and of all these horrid plots what particle has the revolution left incomplete?

Religious vows were immediately suspended and soon abolished; the clergy were pillaged of their property, and all the possessions of the church were converted into a fund for the security of the assignats; the sacred vessels were stolen and prophaned; the churches were not only robbed of their gold and silver, but the very brass and metal of the bells were carried away.[13] All this however is but a first essay of that war which the revolution is to wage against the Church. Still had the Church preserved its faith, its real treasure, pure and untarnished; but it is at that very treasure that Mirabeau will aim his blows. He declared, that if the Catholic religion were not destroyed in France, the revolution could never be consolidated. Immediately after this decision a code is formed for the clergy, of a long suite of decrees, and it is styled the *civil constitution* of the clergy. But it was merely a constitution of schism and apostacy. This was no more than the first religion, invented as the stepping-stone that should lead the people to a nullity of all religion. Grounded on the principles of Revolutionary Equality and Liberty, it constitutes the people sovereigns in the sanctuary, just as those same principles had constituted them sovereigns around the throne; it endows the people with rights that the gospel has reserved to the ministry; it was no more than a repetition of those errors of Camus, of the apostate of Ypres, and of the schism of Utrecht, long since anathematized. Notwithstanding the disguise it had assumed, the clergy of France soon discovered its real tendency, and at the peril of their lives they refused to take the oath of apostacy. The faithful pastors were expelled from their sees and churches, persecuted, calumniated, and reviled in the grossest manner; for the legislating committee had said to the people, *Dare every thing against the clergy; you shall be supported.* Soon is the national worship converted into that of perjury and intrusion, for the true priests of Christ are driven from his altars; at Nismes and Avignon they are slaughtered; and the man who had sworn *to crush* Christ and his altars, who had declared his gospel to be a gospel of slaves, together with him who had begun the revolution by declaring that France must be *discatholized (decatholisée)* are carried in triumph to one of the most magnifcent temples of the Lord, now converted into a den of thieves, into the pantheon of the gods of the revolution, in short into the burial place of a Voltaire, a Jean Jaques Rousseau, or a Mirabeau.[14] Such were the labors of the first revolutionary legislators.

A new set of legislators succeed to the first, and prosecute similar plots against the priesthood. New oaths are decreed, which show in a still clearer light that apostasy is their object. The constancy of the clergy exasperates them. The apostates represent their brethren as refractory to the laws, and decrees of banishment are passed against those who would not swear to their abominations.[15] But these decrees are only a signal given for the brigands to execute that which these conspiring legislators dare not publicly ordain. Their municipalities had taken the precaution to stow into different churches vast numbers of these valiant confessors of their faith, these clergy who were to be banished. The brigands are then let loose, armed with pikes and hatchets, and the *Herculeses* and *Bellerophons* of the bloody September make their appearance; this is also the day on which those *avengers of Abiram* come forward, those men who in the occult lodges had been taught to strike the victims, to tear out the heart, and bear away in triumph the heads of those proscribed persons stiled prophane. When the historian shall proceed to paint the horrors of those bloody days, let him not forget the oaths of the *Knights Kadosch,* and at whom they were aimed. Let him follow into the Lodges those brigands that Philip of Orleans had initiated, and his astonishment will be greatly abated at the sight of so many pontifs and priests immolated on the same day, to the hatred of the adepts and to the manes of their premier chief.[16]

Contrary to the expectations of the conspirators, the people of the provinces refused to imitate the brigands of Paris; and thus did whole hecatombs of victims escape the fate to which they had been devoted. It was in vain that the municipality of Paris invited *all France* to seek its safety in the death of so many priests alledged to be refractory.[17] In vain did Lafitte and the other commissaries of the conspiring legislators range throughout the towns and the country declaring that the true spirit of the decrees meant the death and not the banishment of these priests; the people were not yet ripe for such atrocities. It was executioners that were wanting to the conspirators, and not the good will of the second assembly; but it is also true, that from that instant they no longer had it in their power to consummate that which the first assembly had begun. The former legislators had ruined and driven the clergy from the altar; the latter had made a hecatomb of them; and it was in vociferating curses on those who fled to other nations, that they beheld them baffling their rage, and submitting to exile rather than deny the faith of their divine master.

Hitherto, however, different pretences had concealed the real motives of their persecutions against the pastors of the church. The Roman Catholics, indeed, could no longer exercise their religion in France; but the *constitutional intruders* and the disciples of Luther and Calvin still continued to pronounce the name of Christ in their temples. The third assembly now throws off the mask. The Hierophants of Illuminism had declared in their mysteries, that a day would come when *reason would be the sole code of man*. The adept Hebert appears with this code, and France recognises no other worship but that of *reason*. It is at once the religion of the Sophister, whose *reason* tells him that there is a God, as well as of him whose *reason* tells him that there is no God; it is the religion of the Sophister adoring himself, his own reason, or his supposed wisdom; as it is that of the vain mortal in delirium; nevertheless, this is the only worship tolerated by the Jacobin *equal* and *free*. The wanton devotees of Venus appear; one is immediately set up on the altar and adored as the Goddess of Reason; and the fumes of incense no longer rise but in her worship. The insatiable Guillotine will now devour whatever part of the clergy had hitherto escaped. The time is now come *for stifling in the germ* every thing that can recal to mind the gospel, the God of Christians, his feasts, or those of his saints. They are now proscribed, and are no longer to be seen on the calendars published for the people; thus assimilating them to those that had long since been in use with the Sect. The very order of the weeks, the months, the year, is overturned. The great day of the Lord, the Sunday, is abolished, for it recalled to the minds of the people the existence of a God and of a Creator; but lest the people should still fear the power of an avenging God after death, they will read engraved on the tombs of their forefathers, and on those even into which they are to descend themselves, that *death is only an eternal sleep*; and this was one of the grand mysteries. The few priests who remained, and who still adored an avenging God and a Creator, were either to abjure the very character of the ancient priesthood or perish, stowed up in loathsome dungeons, beneath the fatal axe of the guillotine, or immersed in the waters of the Loire or of the ocean. Such was the reign of the conspirators Hebert and Robespierre.

The tyrants quarrel among themselves and devour each other; and even the revolution may be said to have its revolutions. Impiety for a time assumes a different shape, but does not relent in its persecution against the gospel and the priesthood. One might have been tempted to think that it was returning on its own footsteps, for the people would still adore a God, notwithstanding this new reign of *Reason*; and Robespierre allows them, for a time, *a supreme being*. Next comes REVEILLERE LEPAUX with his *Theophilanthropic* worship. This was the fourth religion invented by the Sect. It is another tyrant of Israel erecting a golden calf, to hinder the people from adoring the true God. It is the *Magi* of Illuminism inventing religion after religion and god after god, in hopes of disgusting the people with every idea of a god. They, indeed, allow this unfortunate people to pronounce his name again; but let us proceed to this *Theophilanthropic* meeting. There every person who still believes in God is treated as a man imbued with vulgar prejudices, as a fool or a madman. There they make no farther mystery of their designs, that if ever they can infuse their philosophic spirit into the people, all this new worship shall be banished as was the former.[18] It is always the worship of cunning and impious rage against the priesthood of the Lord. The Sect appears for a time to have cast aside the instruments of death; but it is only to condemn its victims to a more slow and cruel end. It never ceases to proclaim its oath of Equality and Liberty;[19] those *two blessings of the revolution*, however, can only be acquired for the priesthood by perjury and apostasy. But wo be to those who refuse it; in vain does the citizen offer them an asylum in his house, domiciliary visits will soon discover them. Do they retire into the forests, into caverns, they are hunted down and banished to the wildernesses of Guyana; and pilots more to be feared than the tempest are sent to convey them.

Thus do all the different plots of the Sophisters of Impiety, which had been so long a time contriving in darkness, burst forth into broad day-light, the object of their mysteries is accomplished; that wish, that oath of *crushing Christ* and his religion, with its ministers, is consummated. But the reader has not forgotten, that the Sophisters of Rebellion coalesced with those of Impiety. The adepts had also sworn to crush the monarch and his throne; here again my reader must have got the start of me, and will immediately say, "but the revolution has also consummated their plots against the throne, as it has those against Christs and his altars."

Here again must the historian wade through scenes of blood and horror, and his sight will be blasted by the most atrocious crimes. If he has the strength and patience he may enumerate them; but, at the same time, let him never lose sight of the Sect that has fostered them. Let him follow its progress; agents may vary, conspirators may succeed each other in the legislative-hall, but they will all proceed from one common den wherein the adepts had contrived their plots. The thread of this horrid catastrophe will always be the same, though held in succession by different hands. Equality and Liberty will always be the principle, and the consequences will always strike at the monarch and monarchy, as they have done against Christ and his religion. In this revolution of Equality and Liberty, crimes against the church and crimes against the state are entwined together; to-day the church, to-morrow the sovereign, the day after proprietors are attacked; and this continues in a long concatenation which always takes its rise, as from its centre, in the club of the Jacobins, in the reunion of every species of conspiring adept. Their first conspiring legislators, such as Mirabeau, Syeyes, Barnave, Orleans, La Fayette, Lameth, Chabroud, Gregoire, Petion, Bailly, Rabaud, Chapellier, and all the deputies of the Mountain, habitually pass from the tribune of the Jacobins to that of the manege. There a first constitution was prepared, that was to overwhelm the throne as it had done the altar; that was to weaken Louis XVI and strip him not only of his authority, but also of the affection of his subjects; that was to take from him the command of the army, and deprive him of the support of his nobility; that was, in short, to rob him daily of some part of that authority which constitutes the monarch. Two years were spent in disseminating calumnies, in stirring up the people, or in passing decrees as derogatory to royalty as they were injurious to religion. This legislative rout had formed a code of laws against the church, that was to leave but the name of religion to the French nation; from the same clamorous multitude are issued laws against monarcy, that reduced the unfortunate Lewis XVI to a mere cypher; a captive in his palace, surrounded by brigands, he is forced, as the clergy had been, to sanction those very decrees that despoiled him; the clergy had pleaded the duties of the priesthood in opposition to the decrees; the king sets forth the duties of the monarch; he claims, as they had done, his liberty, and for a moment thinks he has obtained it by his flight to Varennes. But the traitor[20] La Fayette soon dispelled the illusion, and only permitted him to enjoy it for an instant, that he might drag his royal master back to the capital exposed to every outrage, there to keep him a closer prisoner. Lewis, a prisoner, at length sanctions this constitution of Equality and Liberty; he still bears the title of king, when a new band of ruffians or legislative adepts make their appearance to form the second National Assembly.

The second assembly find Lewis a captive in his palace; and they proceed in the wicked career of their predecessors. Each sitting gave birth to new decrees more and more derogatory to the authority of the monarch; daily were the people stirred up to insurrection against the altar and the throne. At length the day drew near when both were to fall beneath their blows. The long list of clergy that were to be immolated had been already formed by the Jacobin municipality, and the Jacobin legislators surround the palace of Lewis with legions of brigands. He is reduced to seek an asylum in the midst of that very assembly that had sent this mob of miscreants against him; they pronounce his suspension, as according to the new forms they would have encroached on the sovereignty of the people in pronouncing the abolition of royalty; but lest he should mistake the nature of his crime, they proclaim the new era and the new oath of *Equality* and *Liberty*, both of which are to date from this day. They then decree the convocation of a new assembly which is to pronounce definitively on the fate of the monarch. All these decrees are passed in his presence; for they had barbarously shut up him and his family in a tribune appropriated to the writers of a Newspaper, lest he should lose a single word of the outrages and calumnies vented against his person, or of the laws pronounced for the annihilation of the throne. But his death had been already resolved; meanwhile he is sent to the towers of the Temple to await his cruel destiny.[21]

I should be little inclined to insist on the atrocious feats that signalized these horrid triumphs of the second assembly, or on the arts employed to prepare them, were it not that the true thread of such a multitude of crimes has not been properly discovered. The whole was contrived by Brissot. The Sect, it is true, furnished him with agents, but he was constantly the chief of the conspiracy of the 10th of August. During a whole year he was employed in preparing it; he had conceived it even before he was named a legislator. Initiated in all the mysteries of Holbach's club, and even contending with Condorcet for the precedence among the Voltairian Sophisters, no sooner was he deputed to the grand assembly, than he thought himself called to fulfil the decree which he had long since pronounced, *That the sceptre of the Bourbons should be shivered, and France be transformed into a republic.*[22] Scarcely was he seated among these new legislators when he cast his eyes around him in quest of adepts who might cooperate in hurling from his throne that unfortunate monarch whose power the preceding assembly had reduced to a mere phantom. He soon perceived that same hatred to royalty raging in the breasts of a Petion, a Buzot, a Vergniaux, a Gaudet, a Gensonné, or a Louvet, and to them he opened his plans.

According to the plan contrived by the conspirators, we shall see that France was in the first place to be inundated with journals, all stimulating the people to complete the grand work of their liberty. By dint of libels and most odious calumnies against Lewis XVI and his queen, they were to eradicate every sentiment of affection from the heart of the subject. They next bethought themselves of stiring up the foreign powers, that Lewis XVI being engaged in war without, might fall an easier prey to intrigue within. We next hear the club resounding with that very sentence which Brissot afterwards writes to the generals of *his* revolution: *Europe must be set on fire at the four corners; in that our safety lies.*[23] By means of their adepts and clubs they were perpetually exciting the people to insurrection, in order to cast the odium on the king and queen. Under pretence of taking measures against these frequent insurrections, and to ward off the danger to which they exposed France, they formed in the National Assembly a secret committee under the title of *extraordinary commission*, and which was the head of the faction since called the *Girondins*, from the department of the Gironde, in Gascony. It was there that Brissot, at the head of the Elect, and presiding in the *commission*, prepared in silence those decrees that were to consummate the plots against monarchy. He wished to give this revolution an appearance of philosophy, solicited by an enlightened people tired of its kings, and willing to recognize no other sovereign than itself. He sent his emissaries into the provinces; but they all returned, declaring that the French nation was unwilling to sacrifice its king. He then founded the legislative assembly, and the opinions of the majority also coincided with the wishes of the people. What he could not accomplish by his sophistry, he now determined to effectuate by means of pikes and his blood-thirsty legions of brigands. He calls those legions from the South known by the name of *Marseillois*; from the West the Jacobins send up the brigands of Brest; *Barbaroux* and *Panis*, *Carra* and *Beaujois*, the intruded vicar of Blois, *Besse* from the Drome, *Gallissot* from Langres, *Fournier* the West Indian, General *Westerman*, *Kieulin* from Strasbourg, *Santerre* the brewer, *Antoine* from Metz, and *Gorsas* the journalist, combined with the *Girondins*. They hold their councils sometimes at Robespierre's, at others at the *Soleil d'Or* (the Golden Sun), a tavern near the Bastille. *Syeyes* and his club of *twenty-two*, or the occult Lodge of the Jacobins, second them with all their might. *Marat, Prudhomme,* and *Millin*, with all the Journalists of the Party, daily invent new calumnies against Lewis and his royal Consort. *Alexandre* and the renegade *Chalet* stir up the suburbs of *St. Antoine* and *St. Marteau*. Philip of Orleans contributes his money and his party, because he is in hopes of being himself exalted to the throne, as soon as Lewis XVI should be driven from it; and even though he were not to succeed in obtaining the throne, he will at least have gratified his vengeance.

Every thing is agreed on; the Legions are arrived; at ten minutes before one in the morning the alarm bells ring the prelude to the terrible 10th of August. The second Assembly has now fulfilled its task; Lewis XVI is declared to be deprived of all right to the Crown. He is torn from the Palace of his forefathers, and immured within the towers of the Temple. It is there that the third Assembly of Legislators is to find him, and are to lead him from thence to the scaffold to fulfil the oaths of the Occult Lodges.

Should the historian hesitate at recognizing this progression of the Sect, to conduct us to the terrible catastrophe of the 10th of August, let him turn to the avowals of the adepts themselves.—The day is come when they envy each other the commission of such crimes; they had installed Brissot the leader of the Jacobins; but Robespierre, Marat, and Danton snatch the sceptre from him; he wishes to wrest it from them again and he publishes an address to all the Jacobins of France to substantiate his rights. His apology as well as that of his co-adept Louvet are in substance no more than the history of the very conspiracy I have just been describing. Should it be necessary, for the conviction of the reader, to turn to any part of it, let him hearken to Brissot when saying the Triumvirs Robespierre, Marat, and Danton, have accused me "of being the author of the war, and had it not been for the war Royalty would have still subsisted! Had it not been for the war, thousands of talents, thousands of virtues would never have burst forth from obscurity! And had it not been for the war, Savoy and so many other states whose fetters are about to fall, would never have acquired their Liberty—They were fearful of a war conducted by a King—Oh! shallow politicians! It was precisely because this perjured King was to conduct the war, because he could only conduct it as a traitor, because this treason alone would infallibly lead him to his ruin; it was for such reasons, that it was necessary to have a war conducted by the King.—*It was the abolition of Royalty that I had in view when I caused war to be declared*—Men who were enlightened understood me, when, on the 30th of December 1791, they heard me answer Robespierre, who was always talking to me of treasons to be feared, *I have but one fear, which is, that we shall not be betrayed; we stand in need of treachery, for our whole safety depends on our being betrayed*—For treasons would soon make that which thwarts the greatness of the French nation disappear, I mean Royalty."

But while this Sophister is declaiming so much on *treasons*, and glorying in that which he had for so long a time premeditated against his unfortunate Sovereign, which he makes his title of preeminence in the eyes of the Jacobins, he takes care not to mention that he would have betrayed the traitors themselves, had Lewis XVI had money sufficient to supply his extravagant demands. On the 9th of August, the eve of the day when all the Conspirators were to be put in action, he sent to ask the King for *twelve millions* (500,000l.) as a price for withdrawing from the Conspiracy *and for rendering it abortive*.[24]—What extraordinary men are these Sophisters, and what ideas do they form of their own virtues! But truth imposes on us the disgusting task of hearkening to this man, while narrating his own crimes. He will boast of the time that he employed in meditating and preparing them, and will represent the callous indifference with which he viewed the canibal scenes of that bloody day as greatness of soul. "They accuse me (he continues) of having presided over the *extraordinary commission; and if the able heads of that commission had not prepared*, and that a long while previous to the 10th of August, those decrees that saved France, such as the *suspension of the King, the convocation of the Convention, the organization of a Republican Ministry*; if these decrees had not been wisely combined, so as to banish every idea of force or terror; had they not borne the stamp of grandeur and of cool deliberation, the Revolution of the 10th of August would have appeared to the eyes of all Europe to have been a *Revolution of canibals*.—But at the sight of wisdom presiding in the midst of these storms, and staying even the arm of carnage, Europe then believed that France was saved. Let who will calumniate the 10th of August, the valour of the federated bands and the deliberate decrees of the National Assembly, which *had been prepared by the Commission*, will for ever immortalize that day."[25]

Let us follow this strange Sophister; for, after showing how he betrayed Lewis XVI, he will now explain the manner in which he betrayed both the Nation and the Assembly; how he and his adherents gradually led the people, and the majority of the Assembly to the commission of crimes, of which neither approved. "My opinion (of the 9th of July) on the deposition of the King has been much cavilled at. The same has happened to Vergniaux—I here call to witness my Colleagues, all those who were acquainted with *the state of our Assembly, with the weakness and minority of the patriots*, the corruption of terror, the aversion in which the enthusiasts held the court party. Doubtless, it needed no small share of courage to risk that eloquent hypothesis on the crimes of the King in the midst of such an assembly as Vergniaux did. And the day after that coalition, which so much weakened the party of the Patriots, was it not a talk that required courage which I undertook, to give a lively description of the crimes of the King, and to propose his being brought to trial. *This was blasphemy in the eyes of the majority, nevertheless I dared to speak it.*"

When describing the *Girondins*, his chief support, he says, "perpetually occupied in repairing their faults, in union with other enlightened patriots, they *were preparing the minds to pronounce the suspension of the King—They were far from conceiving such a step; and this was my reason for risking that famous discourse of the 26th July on the deposition*, a discourse that in the conception of ordinary minds was a dereliction of principle, but in the eyes of the enlightened, *was only a prudent and necessary manœuvre*. I well knew that the Aristocratical party wished nothing so much as to meet the question on the deposition, because they thought themselves certain of success, and because *the minds were not yet ripe in the Departments—the defeat of the Patriots was therefore inevitable. It was necessary then to tack, in order to gain time, to enlighten the public opinion, or to ripen it for insurrection*; for the deposition of the King could be effected but by one of these two means.—Such were my motives for pronouncing my discourse on the 26th of July, which exposed me to so much reproach, and even ranked me among the secret Royalists, while the *Patriote François* (the newspaper that he published) *never ceased to prepare the minds in the Departments for these extraordinary measures.*"

Amidst the multitude of reflexions that must naturally arise on the perusal of these avowals, the words *it was therefore necessary to tack, in order to gain time, to enlighten the public opinion, or to ripen it for insurrection*, present us with a great axiom in the theory of Revolutions. They show us, that those insurrections represented as the grand movements of a people, as the act of the majority of a nation, are merely the efforts of an united faction against the majority of a nation; that had the opinions of the majority of the nation coincided with the views of the Conspirators, they would not have been obliged to seek the aid of brigands, in order to triumph by arms and terror over an unarmed and unsuspecting people. It may be objected, that France had its National Guards; most certainly it had; but Brissot carefully avoided calling on them for succour. He had seen them flocking from all parts of France to the federation on the 14th of July; but these truly *federated bands* had shown the greatest marks of attachment to Lewis and his Royal Consort; and it was not to such men that the Conspirators dared propose the deposition of the King. What plan do the conspirators adopt? They assemble all those brigands called *Marseillois*, (not because they were inhabitants of Marseilles or Provence, but because the greater part of them had been condemned to the gallies at Marseilles), and surname these brigands of all countries *The Federated Bands*. They oblige the inhabitants of the suburbs to fall into the ranks with them; they cause the commander of the National Guard to be murdered, that, being without a chief, it might have no unity of action, and that those who had been seduced might join the brigands. They then represent as a general insurrection of the people, as the will of the nation, that which they have themselves demonstrated to have been no other than an insurrection of their own cut-throat bands against their King and the nation at large. Such has been the whole progress of the Revolution; all has been done by mobs and insurrection, or, as the chiefs style it, by *means of force and terror*, which have enslaved a nation that had resisted every means of seduction.

Similar proofs relating to that atrocious Revolution of the 10th of August are to be found in Louvet's discourse; he also boasts of his cunning in preparing the plots. "*We Jacobins wished for war*, (he says) because peace must have undoubtedly killed the Republic—because, undertaken in time, the misfortunes inevitable at the first outset could be repaired, and would at once *purify the Senate, the Armies, and the Throne*—Every man *worthy of being a Republican* loudly called for war. *They dared aspire to strike a mortal blow at Royalty itself; to exterminate it for ever, in France first,* AND THEN THROUGHOUT THE UNIVERSE." He then alludes to the parts acted by his accomplices. "Those whom you call my friends (he says to Robespierre) were *Roland*, who had denounced Lewis XVI to all France—*Servan*, who was involved in the honourable retreat of the Minister of the Interior, and only returned into office with him, and that to save France—*Petion*, whose conduct, at once vigorous and wise, was *wearing out Royalty*—*Brissot*, he was writing against Monarchy" (Condorcet was also writing in the same cause)—"*Vergniaux, Gensonné, and many others, were preparing before hand the plan for the suspension*—Gaudet was seated in the chair when the cannon began to roar.—*Barbaroux was advancing at the head of the Marseillois for the 10th of August*; and lucky it is for you that he headed them—I (Louvet) was writing the *Sentinelle*; and your eternal vapourings oblige me to say, that my journal contributed much more to the Revolution of the 10th of August, than your *Defenseur de la Constitution* (written by Robespierre)."[26]

Thus have these sanguinary Legislators furnished the Historian with the proofs of their own guilt, and of their crimes against their Sovereign. Let this Republic then appear, this Republic of Equality and Liberty, so long cherished by the Sophisters and nurtured by the adepts in their Occult Lodges! Lewis is no longer seated on the throne! Let not Lewis, nor any Bourbon, nor any living creature aspire to it in future. *Royalty is abolished*, and France is proclaimed a *Republic*. This is the first decree of those Conspirators styling themselves a *Convention*, and succeeding to those who had called themselves the second National Assembly (*September 21, 1792*). The better to establish Equality, every mark of rank, even the comon marks of civility as well as the title of *king*, are proscribed, and *Citizen* is in future the sole appellation allowed (*October 29*). Lest the very sight of a faithful subject should recal the idea of a King, death is pronounced against every Emigrant who shall dare to set foot on the territories of the Republic (*November 10*). The same punishment is pronounced against any man who should *dare to propose the re-establishment of Royalty in France* (*December 4*).

The Sect now proceeds toward the completion of its mysteries. Lewis, who had been seated on the throne, still exists; and it was not in vain that the adept had been taught in the caverns of the *Knights Kadosch* to trample on crowns and stab Kings. To these atrocious games reality must succeed; *Robespierre* advances; but let him and his hangman range for a time on the field; he is no more than a wild beast that the Sect have let loose. He is not the wretch that devours the captive Monarch; it is the Sect. Even in Lewis are two distinct persons in the eyes of the Jacobins. They would perhaps have loved and revered him in private life; but he was King, and they foam with rage at the very idea; his head falls on the scaffold; their relentless vengeance even strikes the statue of the beloved and great Henry IV; every monument that can recal the idea of a King falls beneath their blows. It was not at Lewis, it was at Royalty, that these modern Vandals aimed. They declared Lewis XVI to be tyrant; they continue to proclaim it; but they have their own interpretation; they style him so just as the Sophisters styled *every King a Tyrant*. They knew well, that Lewis XVI had during a reign of nineteen years signed many a pardon, but had never signed a single death-warrant; and that certainly is not the character of a tyrant. They knew well, that the first act of Lewis on coming to the throne was to release his subjects from the tax customary on such an occasion; he abolished the custom of the *Corvées* (or bind days); neither the accused, nor even the guilty, could be put to the torture during his reign; and do such edicts bespeak the tyrant? They also saw him relinquish in favour of his subjects all the feudal rights on his own domain, that he might obtain by example that alleviation for his people, which he could not establish by authority without making an attack upon private property. They knew well, that Lewis XVI was entirely free from those vices which are either odious or burdensome to nations; he was religious, an enemy of ostentation, compassionate and generous to the poor; they had seen him lavishing his privy purse to warm, to cloath, to feed the indigent; seen him even carry in person succour to the friendless cottager; they had seen the poor raising the snow into a pyramid, and shaping it out into a monument of gratitude to Lewis XVI mitigating the rigours of the winter. They knew well, that the gratitude of the poor is not so industrious to shew attachment to a tyrant. In vain will they upbraid him as a despot or a tyrant; for they cannot deny, that never a Prince was seated on a throne more zealous in his application to his duty, or less jealous of his rights than Lewis XVI; confidence and love seem to be his leading features; and if ever he spoke in that peremptory way which denotes the determination of being obeyed, it was when, surrounded by assassins, he so often repeated to his guards, *If it be necessary to shed but one single drop of blood for my safety, I forbid it to be shed*; and such are the orders of a tyrant!!! Should calumny obstinately persist, let it read these last sentiments of Lewis: "I pray all those whom I may have offended through inadvertency (for I do not remember to have offended any person knowingly), or those to whom I may have given bad example, or scandal, to pardon whatever injury they may think I can have done them. "Let the regicide judges read (for it is of them he speaks and says) "I pardon with all my heart those who have constituted themselves my enemies without my giving them cause, and I pray God that he will pardon them." Let them follow him to the scaffold, and there contemplate, if they dare, that serenity of his countenance, in the midst of his executioners, which so well denotes the tranquillity of his soul: and they dare not hear his last words: Drums are beaten, and trumpets sounded, to drown his voice; for they are conscious that he neither lived nor is about to die the death of a tyrant.

These conspiring legislators, however, knew it long before they sat in judgment on their King; for if you ask them, when in the very act of regicide, of what crime Lewis XVI has been guilty? They will answer, Lewis was a King, and our wish is the death of every King. Hearken to the Jacobin *Robert:* when he comes to vote he says, "I condemn the tyrant to death, and in pronouncing this sentence, *I have but one regret,* which is, that my power *does not extend over all the tyrants, to condemn them all to the same fate."*—Hear, again, the Jacobin *Carra: "For the instruction of nations, in all times, and in all places,* and for the consternation of tyrants, I vote for death."—Or the Jacobin *Boileau:* "*Nations accustomed to consider their Kings as sacred objects* will necessarily say, 'the heads of Kings, however, cannot be so sacred, since the axe can strike them, and that they fall beneath the avenging arm of justice.' *It is thus you are launching nations into the career of Liberty*; I vote for death."[27]

Should the real cause of the death of Lewis XVI not sufficiently appear in such language, let the reader revert to that club of the Sophisters where Condorcet was learning that a day would come *when the Sun would shine on none but free men, and when Kings and Priests should have no existence but in history or on the stage.* Turn back to those conspiring dens haunted by the Occult Masons, and doubt for a moment, if you can, of this historical truth, that Lewis perished upon the scaffold *because he was King*; that the daughter of the Cezars perished *because she was Queen*; and never was the more deserving of that exalted station, than when she showed such undaunted courage and greatness of soul in the midst of her murderers. Madame Elizabeth perished, because neither virtue, innocence, nor magnanimity could efface the stain, indelible in the eyes of the Jacobin, of being the daughter and sister of a King. Philip of Orleans crouched into wickedness and infamy, and sacrificed his immense fortune to the Sect; he cowardly and basely votes for the death of his royal relation to please the Sect; he takes the name of *Equality*, abandoning rank and birth, and even denies his father to court the Sect; but no sooner are his crimes unnecessary for the progress of that Sect, than he is dragged away to the scaffold because he is of royal descent. But the conspirators are fearful, that if they struck at that model of virtue and goodness the Dutchess of Orleans, the axe would fall from the hands of the executioners. The numerous sacrifices made by the Dutchess of Bourbon and the Prince of Conti proved to the conspirators that these remnants of blood-royal were little to be feared; nevertheless they are obliged, with every person of royal extraction, to fly the territories of the new Republic. To cement this hatred for Kings, the day on which Lewis XVI was murdered on the scaffold is declared a perpetual festival for *this people equal and free*; and on this day the *oath of hatred to Royalty* is to be solemnly sworn by all the magistrates; and this oath is to be in future a necesssary qualification for the enjoyment of the rights of Citizen in this new Republic; such are the regulations decreed; and death is pronounced, as we have already seen, against whoever dares propose the re-establishment of Monarchy.

Notwithstanding the rivers of blood that flowed in France, to consummate these plots against Royalty, the Sect and its agents behold these horrid scenes with all the brutal exultation of cannibals. The guillotine is declared permanent in Paris, and ambulant in the Provinces in quest of Royalists and Priests. New words are even invented to denote the butcheries that now take place, for our forefathers had not even formed an idea of cruelties to such an extent. Whole catacombs of victims are shot *in mass*, and this was styled *Fusillades*; hecatombs also were drowned, and that species of murder they called *Noyades*.[28] Is it the Sect then that thus hardens and brutalizes the hearts of the Jacobins? Are we to turn back to their lessons to explain both the number and the choice of victims, the cool wickedness of the adepts, the atrocious joy of the executioners? Yes, all you who seek the cause elsewhere, forget the mysteries; I am obliged to call you back to the true parent of this sanguinary tribe; yes, it was the principles of the Sect that made *Barnave*, at the sight of heads carried on pikes, ferociously smile and exclaim, *Was that blood then so pure that one might not even spill one drop of it?* Yes, it was those principles that made *Chapellier, Mirabeau,* and *Gregoire,* when they beheld the brigands surrounding the palace of Versailles in sanguinary rage, thirsting after murder, and particularly after the blood of the Queen, exclaim, *The People must have victims.* It was those principles that even smothered the affection of Brother for Brother, when the adept *Chenier*, seeing his own Brother delivered over to the hands of the public executioner, cooly said, *If my Brother be not in the true sense of the Revolution, let him be sacrificed*; that eradicated the feeling of the child for his parents, when the adept *Philip* brought in triumph to the club of the Jacobins *the heads of his father and mother!!* This insatiable Sect calls out, by the mouth of the bloody *Marat*, for *two hundred and seventy thousand heads*, declaring that before long it will count only by millions. They know well, that their systems and last mysteries of Equality can only be accomplished in its full extent by depopulating the world; and, by the mouth of *Le Bo*, it answers the inhabitants of Montauban, terrified with the want of provisions, " *Fear not; France has a sufficiency for twelve million inhabitants; All the rest* (that is the other twelve millions) *must be put to death, and then there will be no scarcity of bread."*[29]

We wish to cast the odium of such horrors on a *Marat*, a *Robespierre*, or some such wretches; but *Barnave* preceded Robespierre; and the oath of the Sect to denounce *father, mother, friends, brothers,* and *sisters*, and to look upon every person as proscribed who should not adopt the revolutionary principles, did not originate with them. Such was the oath of the Lodges long before the existence of the Jacobins. It was not from Robespierre, but in Holbach's club, that Condorcet learned to exclaim as he did in the legislative assembly, *Let the world perish, rather than sacrifice our principles of Equality!* It would not be the brigands alone, but Syeyes, Garat, the elect of the Sophisters, and the club of the *twenty-two*, that would smile at the horror we had conceived at such deeds. Thus did Syeyes answer Mallet du Pan, when he expressed his detestation of the means employed in the revolution: *You are always talking to us of the means employed; but, Sir, it is the End, it is the Object, the Ultimate View, that you must learn to consider.* And this very principle, that consoles such men as Syeyes for such a multitude of atrocities, is to be discovered in the Code of the Illuminized Lodges, whence it found its way into the Jacobin club.[30]

A day may come when history will be more accurately informed *how* and *in what haunts* this blood-thirsty Sect pointed out its victims, and taught its adepts not to be startled at the number of them. Meantime I have promised to lead my reader back to that which held its sittings in the *Rue Sourdiere*, where *Savalette de Lange* presided; where the Illuminees were received; and where *Dietrich*, who was one of the first that brought the mysteries into France, was seated. The following anecdote may guide the historian in his researches on that subject.

At the time when the brigands were put into requisition, when the castles of the Nobility were being consumed by fire in the provinces, when the heads of the Nobility were being carried in triumph on pikes, the *Abbé Royou*, well known for his zeal against the Sophisters, was obliged to fly from Paris to escape the fury of the *Palais Royal* mob. He had wandered for some time from village to village, when he privately returned to Paris, and called upon me about four o'clock in the morning. On my questioning him how he had passed his time during his flight, "I lived (said he) chiefly with the curates, and was very well received by them, but could not make any long stay with them, lest I should expose them to similar danger with myself. I soon began to suspect the last curate with whom I took refuge when I saw him receive a letter from Paris. He opened and read it with such an air, that my suspicions were greatly increased. Strongly suspecting that I was the object of this letter, I watched the opportunity when he was gone to the church, to enter his room, where I found the epistle couched in the following terms: *Your letter, my dear friend, was read in presence of the whole club. They were surprised to find so much philosophy in a village curate. Be tranquil, my dear curate; we are three hundred; we mark the heads and they fall; only keep your people ready, dispose your parishioners to execute the orders, and they shall be given to you in time.*

(Signed)   DIETRICH, *Secretary.*"

To the many reflexions that must naturally arise on the reading of such a letter, I shall only add, that the club to which these three hundred belonged had transferred the place of its sittings to the suburbs of St. Honoré, and that it assembled there for a long time without being observed by the court; when a scene of drunkenness apprised the king of the fate that awaited him. At the conclusion of one of those banquets *sacred to fraternity*, all the brethren made a puncture in their arm and received their blood in their glasses; they then drank the toast *Death to kings*, and thus concluded the fraternal repast. This anecdote will easily suggest of what species of men the *legion of twelve hundred*, proposed by *Jean de Brie* to the Convention, was to be composed, who were to be dispersed over the whole globe to murder all the kings of the earth.

Thus did the Sect, under the name of *Fraternity*, by the frenzy of its Equality, by the very nature of its principles, and by the horrid rites of its Lodges, so degenerate the hearts of its adepts, as to form (like the old man of the mountain) clubs of three hundred assassins at a time. Thus do the mysteries explain the ferocious joy of a Marat, of a St. Just, of a Le Bon, of a Carrier, of a Collot D'Herbois, and the still more ferocious serenity of the Sophisters of the revolution in the midst of massacres and rivers of blood.

But the vengeance of that God who has permitted so heavy a scourge to befall France, now appears to have taken another turn. In that country the altar of Christ is overturned, and the throne of its king annihilated. Those who had conspired against the altar and the throne now conspire against each other. The intruded clergy, the Deists, and the Atheists, butchered the Catholics. The Intruders, the Deists, and the Atheists now begin to cut each other's throats. The Constitutionalists drove out the Royalists, and are in their turn put to flight by the Republicans. The Democrats of the Republic *one and indivisible*, murder the Democrats of the *federative* Republic; the faction of the *mountain* guillotines the *Girondin* faction, and then split into the faction of Hebert and Marat, of Danton and Chabot, of Cloots and Chaumette, and in fine into the faction of Robespierre, who devours them all, and is in his turn devoured by the factions of Tallien and Freron. Brissot and Gensonné, Gaudet and Fauchet, Rabaud and Barbaroux, with thirty more, are condemned to death by Fouquier Tinville, just as they had condemned their king; Fouquier is himself sent to the scaffold, just as he had sent Brissot and Co. Petion and Buzot perish with hunger in the forests, and are devoured by the wild beasts; Perrin dies in prison; Valazé and Labat stab themselves; Marat falls beneath the arm of Charlotte Corday; Robespierre dies on the scaffold, and Syeyes alone survives, because the cup of vengeance is not yet exhausted on miserable France. *Pentarques* (or the government of five), with a two-fold senate, are now become a new curse on this unhappy country. A Rewbel, Carnot, Barras, Le Tourneur, and a Reveillère Lepaux, assume the command of its armies, drive away its deputies equal and free, fulminate its Sections, and rule it with a rod of iron. Every thing trembles before them; when they grow jealous of each other, they plot destruction, and drive each other into banishment; but new tyrants succeed and unite together; and at this present time the ruling Deities in France are banishment, stupor, fear, and the Pentarques. Terror has imposed silence throughout the Empire, and this vast prison contains twenty millions of slaves, all sculking into obscurity at the very name of a Merlin or a Rewbel, or at the threat of a journey to Cayenne; such is the *Majesty* of that people so frequently declared *Equal, Free,* and *Sovereign*.

The reader, perhaps, may think that in the midst of such massacres, factions, tyrants, and terror, the Sect must have lost the thread of all its plots; but it has never lost sight of them for a moment. The Pentarques are more than ever stimulated by it against the Clergy and the Nobility; while the ultimate mysteries threaten the Pentarques themselves. In vain shall they attempt to preserve a sufficiency of the Social Order to keep them in possession of that authority which they have erected on the ruins of the throne. The Sect has thus far proceeded successfully toward the accomplishment of its mysteries; but it will not stop here; has it not sworn to annihilate *Property* as well as the throne? During the first assembly, did not those conspirators, now *calling themselves Constitutionalists*, annihilate the property of the clergy; and the next assembly that of the nobility, under the pretence of emigration, while those who remained in France were pillaged under pretence of confiscation? Then come the adepts *Bruisssart, Robespierre,* and the two *Juliens*; and they write that the favourable moment is now come to *extirpate the* MERCANTILE ARISTOCRACY, *as well as that of the Nobles*. In their secret correspondence, just as Weishaupt does in his mysteries, they declare, that *merchantism* (negotiantism) *must be crushed. That wherever a large number of rich merchants were to be found, there were sure to be found as many cheats, and Liberty could not establish its empire there.*[31] Accordingly, spoliations and requisitions have robbed the merchants and citizens of their property, just as the Clergy and Nobility had been robbed before them. But even this is not the accomplishment of the *grand end*, of the ultimate views of the Sect, against all property, against all society whatever. Even under the iron reign of the Pentarques, let us attend to the addresses published by the adepts *Drouet, Babœuf*, and *Langelot*.

Extract from the Address to the French People, found in Babœuf's papers.

"People of France,—During fifteen centuries you lived in slavery, therefore unhappy. It is scarcely six years since you began to breathe in *expectation of independence, of happiness, and of Equality*. At all times and in all places men have been lulled with fine words; never, and in no place, did they obtain the thing with the word. From time immemorial has it been hypocritically repeated, that *men are equal*, and from time immemorial the most monstrous inequality has insolently pressed on mankind. *Ever since the existence of Civil Societies*, the finest appendage of man has undoubtedly been recognized, but has never been once realized. *Equality has never been any thing but a noble and sterile fiction of the law*. Now that it is called for with a louder voice, they answer us, Wretches hold your peace! Equality *in deed* is a mere chimera; be contented with a conditional equality. You are all equal before the law, ye rascals! What more do you want?—What more do we want!——*Ye Legislators, ye Governors, ye Rich, ye Proprietors, now hearken in your turn:*

"*We are all equal.*—That principle is incontestable. - - - *Very Well! We mean in future to live and die as we are born. We will have real Equality, or death.* That is what we want, and we will have that real equality, cost what it will. *Wo be to those whom we shall meet between it and us!* Wo to the man who shall dare oppose so positive a determination! *the French revolution is but the forerunner of a revolution greater by far and much more solemn; and which will be the last.*- -

"What do we ask more than the Equality of rights? Why, we will not only have that Equality transcribed in the declaration of the rights of man and the citizen; we will have it in the midst of us, under the roofs of our houses. We consent to every thing for the acquisition of it, even *to clear decks,* that we may possess it alone; *Perish the arts, if requisite,* provided we do but preserve real Equality!

"Legislators and Governors, *Proprietors rich and bowel-less,* in vain do you attempt to paralize our sacred enterprize, by saying, *we are only re-producing the Agrarian law* that has been so often asked for before.

"Calumniators! hold your peace in your turn, and in the silence of confusion hearken to our pretensions, dictated by nature, and grounded on justice.

"*The Agrarian Law, or the equal partition of lands, was the momentary wish* of a few soldiers without principles, of a few clans actuated rather by instinct than by reason. We aim at something far more sublime, far more equitable, GOODS IN COMMON, or THE COMMUNITY OF ESTATES! *No more individual properties in land, for the earth belongs to nobody. We demand and will enjoy the goods of the earth in common. The fruits will belong to all.*

"Disappear now, ye disgusting distinctions of rich and poor, of higher and lower, of master and servant, of GOVERNING and GOVERNED! *for no other distinction shall exist among mankind, than those of* AGE *and* SEX."[32]

The authors of this address were certainly too hasty in their publication; but every reader will see that their language perfectly coincides with the *Manking* of Illuminism. France, it is true, was not yet sufficiently prepared for this last plot; but it is necessary sometimes to detach certain adepts to sound the way, though afterwards the Sect should find it necessary to disavow and sacrifice its offspring. Though Babœuf may have been sacrificed to the mysteries, his accomplices still live; their legions imposed upon the judges and on the Pentarques themselves, and they dared not condemn *Drouet.* It is to be supposed, that after completely pillaging the Clergy and the Nobility, their successfully despoiling many merchants, tradesmen, and citizens, in the same manner as the Sect had pillaged the two first Orders of the State, a single defeat should suffice to check its views? Or can we say, that it will not one day proclaim that *Equality in deed* which shall banish from the earth all those *distinctions of rich and poor, of higher and lower, of master and servant,* and ultimately *of* GOVERNING *and* GOVERNED?

Some persons may flatter themselves that our sciences may protract the day of barbarism, when men are to roam in clans without laws or magistrates; but have we not seen in the mysteries, that our sciences, in the eyes of the Sect, are no other than the prime cause of our misfortunes, of the alledged slavery of society?[33] And if facts did not speak clearly enough, if the monuments of art falling beneath the blows of the Jacobins did not sufficiently denote the veneration it bears to the productions of genius; if any apparent respect should still be shown to the fathers of letters, let not the reader conceive that the adepts have really blushed at the sight of these modern vandals: Fire and sword have only hastened that progress which they so much extol; it was not Babœuf alone that would exclaim, *Perish the arts, if requisite, provided we do but preserve real Equality!* The Jacobin Philosophist, if sincere, will have no difficulty in saying what the legislators have so often proclaimed from the tribune, "What need have we of all your colleges, academies, and libraries? Needs there so much study and so many books for learning the *only true* science? *Let the nations know the rights of man, and they will know enough.*"[34]

I know that a museum and a national institute are held out as objects of magnificence, in which the revolution would appear to infuse new vigour into the arts and sciences; but let the sage in the midst of this vast museum reflect for a moment. Thunderstruck at this immense assemblage of theft, pillage, and robbery erected into trophies, will he not exclaim, Do these men then barefacedly scoff at every idea of property who thus display the fruits of their rapine and extortion? After having pillaged and destroyed every thing within their own country, they set off to despoil the neighbouring States tranquilly reposing on the banks of the Scheldt, the Meuse, or the Tiber. They divide the gold they have stolen among themselves, and they exalt to public view what they have robbed for the State. Within this temple of the arts, therefore, the idea of property is as much blasted as within the Occult Lodges of those adepts who have sworn to annihilate the social compact.

And what is this national Lyceum, where we find the Geometrician *La Place*, the Astronomer *La Lande*, the Poetaster *Chenier*, the Commentator of the Zodiac *Dupuis*, the Historian of the mountains *La Metherie*, all consecrating their studies and their science to prove that God does not exist? Behold the Sect smiling at their labours, for it is aware, that Atheism will soon annihilate arts and sciences, as well as property and society. Little does it concern itself whether the greater part of the literati stop short in the career of the mysteries; for they are forwarding the views of the Sect without knowing it, even where they have made their stand. Its degrees are progressive, and it well knows that the sophisticated and atheistical Jacobin will beget the disorganizing Jacobin. In the Lyceum, or adhering to Babœuf and Drouet, it beholds its offspring, laborious Atheists professing its principles, and, in short, true Jacobins; and though this *name* should for a time be rejected with contempt, it will not forget that the principles, and *not the name*, constitute the disciple. Some are disgusted with the first consequence flowing from these principles, and they stop; while others complacently proceed to the last. The Sect will therefore fix the former in its first degrees; the latter are initiated in its ultimate mysteries; and whether its agents are literati or brutes, it is of no consequence to the Sect. In the French revolution it has always had the art to distribute the different parts as it does its degrees, and to vary them without every losing sight of its ultimate object.

In its attack upon God, we have seen its intruded Clergy, its Deists, and its Atheists. The first overturned the altars of the Catholic religion; the second, of the Lutheran and Calvinist church, and of every religion adoring Christ; and the third blasphemously proclaimed the non-existence of a God.

In the attack on monarchy the Sect has had successively its *Neckerists*, its *Fayetists*, its *Constitutionalists*, its *Girondins*, its *Conventionists*. Herein it is that the reader may observe the Sect varying and gradually distributing its parts to wind up the horrid scene to the bloody catastrophe. Here we see those different actors faithfully fulfilling the parts that had been distributed to them. Syeyes pronounces that the tyrant shall die: this tyrant is Lewis XVI. Necker seizes on him, and delivers him over to the legislative conspirators of the third order; La Fayette and Bailly, with the Constituent Assembly, leave him but the shadow of a sceptre and his royal robes rent asunder. They then deliver him up, after having taught the people to drag him ignominiously from Versailles to the Town-hall of Paris, from Varennes to the Thuilleries. The unfortunate monarch is now surrounded by banditti, armed with pikes. *Brissot* and his *Girondins* proceed in that career begun by *Necker* and *La Fayette*, and find that with a mere breath the throne can be overturned; Lewis is then dragged from the Thuilleries to the Towers of the Temple. Robespierre, Petio, and Marat, are the next that seize on his royal person; and from the Temple they hurry him to the scaffold. In this long concatenation of seditions, rebellions, and treasons, to the very consummation of the regicide, I see various actors; but the guilt of all and each is equal. They are all agents in the conspiracy of Equality and Liberty; all proceed from the same tenebrous recesses; all are Jacobins.

In the conspiracy against property and all society the same gradation and principles are to be observed; and with a similar constancy does the Sect tend toward the grand *ultimatum*. The irreligious Sophisters of every class despoil the Clergy; the Sophisters commoners plunder the Nobility; next come the sophisticated banditti, who lay violent hands on the riches of the merchant or the wealth of the commoner. Meanwhile the conquering Sophisters display the spoils of foreign nations; and the atheistical Sophisters at length break the last tie of society. The former had only admitted one part of the mysteries; the latter are willing to consummate them all. They will that property shall not exist, either in the church, the nobility, the commoner, or in any mortal whatever. In virtue of their Equality, the earth is to be the property of none, the produce the property of all. In virtue of their Liberty, Condorcet refuses to obey a God, Brissot to recognize a king, and Babœuf to submit to a republic, to magistrates, or to any *governing* power. And whence do all these men come? All proceed from the Jacobin club; they are the offspring of

HISTORICAL PART

Holbach's club, of the Masonic Lodges, and of the Illuminizing Mysteries. Their natural parents are Voltaire, Jean Jaques Rousseau, the Knights *Kadosch*, and the Bavarian *Spartacus*.

Thus do we trace the disciples of the Sect perpetually aiming at the accomplishment of its mysteries; whether in their crimes and success against their God or against their king, whether in their essays against republics or the last vestiges of society; every step in the French revolution demonstrates the activity of its adepts, brigands of every degree, pursuing its ultimate views. Indeed it has not yet accomplished all its designs; and may God grant that they may be foiled in the attempt! But let the mind of man calculate, if it be able, the crimes committed by the Sect, and the disasters that have already befallen France; and when it shall have succeeded in this calculation, will it dare venture to explore those entailed on futurity? Let the father of every family contemplate, and inscribe on the threshold of his house, that threat of the adepts contained in the following sentence: *The French Revolution is but the forerunner of a Revolution greater by far, and much more solemn.*

That nations may be awakened to their danger, let us show them that they are all, without exception, menaced with similar misfortunes to those that have befallen France. Such is their fate decreed by the Sect in its Mysteries; for their views are not confined to any particular people, but aim at all nations whatever. To facts, therefore, I will once more appeal; and my reader shall see how perfectly they coincide with the Code of the Sect on the extent and universality of its conspiracies.

1. See Chap. IV and VI, in Vol. II. of these Memoirs.
2. See the *Sceance Royale* for the Land and Stamp-Tax.
3. I was not sufficiently acquainted with this man's character, when I placed him on the same line with Turgot and Malesherbs.—Let this artful and ambitious intriguer be judged by his own words: *A hundred thousand crowns for you if you will make me Controller General*—*I am rich, but cannot boast of birth; money then must supply the defect of ancestry*—*If one is possessed of money, it is not to be spared when it can serve one's ambition*—*You talk to me of the people: they may be useful to me, and I will make a tool of them; they cannot hurt us, and I will play upon them.*—*As to religion, we must have one for the people, but not their Christianity; we will destroy that.*....Let Necker come to enquire on what occasions or to whom he held this monstrous language and I will begin by naming the person who received the hundred thousand crowns for having procured him the post of *Controller General*; I will in the next place tell him, that he held such language to the Lady who had the courage to upbraid him with it to his face, and in the midst of all his glory; to her whom he reproached with shedding tears over her murdered brother, while she taxed him with his murder, because he feared her brother would betray his secret; to that person who refused to enroll herself in that cohort of flatterers that were to open the way for him, by thousands of calumnious accusations, invented by himself and his emissaries, against persons holding stations that he coveted for himself or his adherents, and which his partizans forwarded to the

unfortunate Lewis XVI; to that person through whose medium he wished to persuade the king that *M. de Sartine* had stolen twenty-two millions out of fifty-three entrusted to him, though the minister needed only to be informed of the plot to show the falsity of the imputation;—in fine, to that person whom he courted as necesssary for his intrigues, who discovered him to be a monster, and who laid open all his plots and iniquities to M. de Maurepas and Leewis XVI. Let him learn, that if his secret crimes are to have a place in history, the proofs of all these are not yet lost.

4. In order to second the views of her worthy father in this warfare on the distinction of estates, while he was intriguing at the palace, Madame de Stael was playing the same part in Paris. She established at her house a sort of Office of Inscription. La Fayette and the Lameths would bring the traitors to her table; and the names of those dastards, who would promise to abandon their Order and pass over to the Third Estate, were immediately inscribed on her list.

5. See the letter attributed to Montesquieu.—In Vol. II, page 94, on the testimony of the Abbé Pointe, I quoted a letter attributed to Montesquieu by an English journalist, but could not name the paper. It has since been discovered in the *Courier*, or *Evening Gazette*, of August 4, 1795. It is there said that Montesquieu wrote it, a few years before his death, to a president of one of the Parliaments of France. I could wish to have seen the person named to whom it was written, or in whose possession it is at present, for it is of a complexion to change our ideas very much as to the moderation of that writer. It would immediately class him among the conspiring sophisters; and, to pass such a sentence on this author, the clearest proofs should be required. But it appears, whoever was the author of that letter, he was far advanced in the plots of the Sect, for he very accurately describes the conduct of the Jacobins with respect to the foreign troops in the French service; neither does he appear to be ignorant of the plan for separating Ireland from England.

6. Many authors have fallen into an error with respect to the first formation of the National Guards; and they ground their assertions on a resolution of the Committee of Electors, sent from the town-hall to all the Sections of Paris, ordering the formation of this guard, and signed *Flesselles*, Tassin, De Leutre, Fauchet, the Marquis de la Salle; but it is a certain fact, and within the knowledge of every body, 1st, That this National Guard was formed only two days after the taking of the Bastille; and 2dly, That Mr. Flesseles was murdered on the day of the taking of the Bastille. But a fact little known is, that the minutes of this resolution, as also the minutes of all the transactions that took place at the town-hall during the first year of the revolution, were not compiled till the second year, by a man of the name of *Verrier*, and by orders of La Fayette, who, notwithstanding many observations made on the subject, would not allow any change to be made in what had been inserted by his orders, and would have been particularly grieved to see the real origin of that National Guard made public, in the command of which he so much gloried.

7. See the Sitting of the 5th October, 1789.

8. See the juridical deposition of witnesses, 157, 226, 230, and 373.

9. See her letter of the 5th October, 1789.

10. The 6th of October 1789 was the last day of the French Monarchy.—Should it ever rise again, let a monument be erected in memory of those brave Knights who would have so gloriously contributed to save it, had not their courage been chained down by the commands of their King. May their names be at least preserved by the

historian! I could wish to insert the names of the sixty heroes who so well served the appellation of *Life-guards* on this awful occasion but I have only been able to obtain the following:

OFFICERS	
Duke de Guiche, *Captain*	Vicomte de Sesmaisons
Marquis de Savonnière, *Chef de Brigade*	Comte de Mauleon
Vicomte D'Agoult	Chev. Dampierre
	——St. George

LIFE GUARDS
Messrs. de Berard, *two Brothers*
Chev. de Huilliers
Marquis de Varicourt, *killed*
Chev. Deshutes, *killed*
——de Miomandre
Baron Durepaire
——Demiers
——Moucheron
Chev. de la Tranchade

Chev. de Duret
——de Valory
Comte de Mouthier
——Bernardy
Messrs. Horric, *three Brothers*
Messrs. Malderet, *three Brothers*
Chev. Renaldy
——de Lamotte
——de Montaut
——de Puget

11. Some of the brigands who were in constant pay for the purpose of these insurrections were retiring home between ten and eleven at night, and I heard them take leave of each other in the following terms: "It has gone on pretty well to-day; we shall expect you to-morrow.—What, to-morrow? at what o'clock?—at the opening of the assembly. *Where do we go for orders?* To Mirabeau's, Chapellier's, or Barnave's, as usual." I own that till I was present at this discourse I never could believe that those legislators had daily interviews with these brigands to fix the hour and object of such insurrections.
12. Let. 8th of Oct.
13. Decrees of October 25, Nov. 2, Dec. 19, 1789; and Feb. 13, 1790.
14. See the sittings of Apr. 10, Aug. 24, 1790; and Jan. 4, Apr. 4, May 30, Aug. 27, 1791.
15. Decrees Nov. 29, 1791, and Apr. 6, May 26, Aug. 26, 1792.
16. I am sorry to say it, but it is a fact that cannot be hidden; honest masons will shudder at it, but they must be informed of what monsters have issued from their Lodges. During the whole of the riots, whether at the Town-hall or at the Carmes, the real signs for rallying and fraternizing with the brigands were masonic. During the time of the butchery the murderers offered the masonic grip to the standers-by, and fraternized with or drove them off according as they answered or misapprehended it. I myself saw a man of the lowest rabble who explained to me how they had offered him their hands, and that not knowing how to answer the grip he was driven away with contempt, while others who were not strangers to the science were admitted in the midst of the carnage, with a smile. I am even acquainted with a clergyman, who by means of the signs of Masonry escaped from the brigands at the Town-hall. It is true, that had he not been disguised, his science would have been but of little avail; for no sooner were those same brigands informed that he was an ecclesiastic, than they pursued him. Neither could the science be of any service to the aristocratic brethren; and this preclusion will suffice to demonstrate to the ecclesiastic and

aristocratic members, that they were but the mere dupes of the occult Lodges of the fraternity.
17. The address of the 3d of Sept. 1792.
18. This is the exact statement of an account that I received from a gentleman who procured initiation into the mysteries of the present *Theophilanthropists* of Paris.
19. Decree Jan. 10, 1796.
20. Lest public documents should not be sufficiently explanatory of the conduct of La Fayette on this occasion, and as several persons have wished to persuade the public that he was perfectly ignorant of the intended flight of the king, I here publish a true statement of facts. A German woman, married to a Frenchman of the name of *Rochereuil*, was employed in the queen's service under the title of *Porte chaise d'affaires*. This woman had shown so much indignation, and had wept so bitterly on the 5th and 6th of October, that the queen, affected at seeing such proofs of attachment in this woman, entrusted her with the care of preparing her broth, and lodged her in a room on the ground-floor of her own apartment, which communicated to the apartment that had been occupied by the Duke of Villequier. In the beginning of June the queen, who began to prepare for her intended evasion, lodged this Mrs. Rochereuil in another room. She immediately harboured suspicions of some intended plan, and watched the king and queen. The great confidence they had had in her gave her the opportunity of knowing the whole scheme of the king's flight. On the 10th of June she informed Messrs. La Fayette and Gouvion of what she had observed, and lodged an information at the *Comité des Recherches* of the National Assembly. She had eleven conferenes with them in the space of nine days. In consequence of these denunciations, M. de la Fayette charged thirteen officers on whom he could depend, to patrole every night within the interior of the Thuilleries, but with secret orders to favor the evasion. His orders had been given in a similar manner along the road. Drouet had been instructed in the part he was to act. The remaining part of that fatal journey to Varennes, and the arrestation of the king, may be all easily conceived, excepting that excess of insolence with which La Fayette used his victory, and the outrages he heaped on the unfortunate Lewis, when dragging him back to his prison of the Thuilleries.

Another anecdote that may surprise the reader is, that when the queen had been informed of the treacherous behaviour of this woman, Rochereuil, and had dismissed the traitor from her service, this wretch had the insolence to present a memorial, that a deputy had penned for her, to the queen, requesting that she might be admitted again into her service, and stating that in her opinion she could not have given her majesty a greater proof of her gratitude and fidelity than by depriving her of the possibility of hearkening to the evil councils of the royalists.—The queen gave the memorial to *Mr. Prieur*, the historiographer of France for the foreign department. The denunciation of this woman is carefully preserved in what are styled the National Archives.
21. Sittings of Aug. 10, 11, and 12, 1792.
22. Lewis XVI, was but a child when Sir Horace Walpole, (since Lord Orford,) after a short stay at Paris, wrote the following letter to Mareschal Conway on the views and plans of the Sophisters. It is dated Oct. 28, 1765.

"The Dauphin (Father to Lewis XVI) will probably hold out very few days. His death, that is, the near prospect of it, fills the *Philosophers* with the greatest joy, as it was feared he would endeavour the restoration of the Jesuits. You will think the sentiments of the *Philosophers* old *state*-news—But do you know who *the Philosophers* are, or what the term means here? In the first place, it comprehends almost every body; and in the next means men, who, avowing war against popery, aim, many of them, *at a subversion of all religion, and still many more at the destruction of regal power.* How do you know this? you will say; you, who have been but six weeks in France, three of which you have been confined in your chamber. True; but in the first period I went every where, and heard nothing else; in the latter I have been extremely visited, and have had long and explicit conversations with many who think as I tell you, and with a few of the other side, who are no less persuaded that there are such intentions. In particular, I had two officers here the other night, neither of them young, whom I had difficulty to keep from a serious quarrel, and who, in the heat of the dispute, informed me of much more than I could have learned with great pains." (*Vol. V.*)

23. See Mallet Du Pan's Considerations on the Nature of the Revolution. P. 37.
24. See the Memoirs of Mr. Bertrand, Vol. III. Chap. XXII.
25. Brissot's Letter to the Jacobins, October 24, 1792.
26. See *Louvet's address to Robespierre*. Should the reader wish for any more of these avowals and vapourings of a multitude of adepts on the art with which they prepared the sanguinary scenes of that day, let them read *Robespierre's Letter to his Constituents; Petion's Observations on that Letter; the Annales Patriotiques*, by Carra and Mercier, 30th November 1792; the *Chronique de Paris* by Millin, and his threats on the 5th of August 1792, &c. &c.
27. See the Moniteur, Sittings of January 2, and following, 1793.
28. Another species of cruelty not mentioned is that which the cannibals of Nantes called *Des Marriages Patriotiques*. The reader will scarcely believe me when I tell him, that women were comprehended in these abominable butcheries. Nevertheless, as a refinement of cruelty, when any young royalist was supposed to have an attachment for any young woman, they were tied together hand and foot previous to their being thrown into the Loire, that they might pass in *Charon's Bark together*; or they would tie some venerable old clergyman to a young woman, that he might be provided with a young wife in the next world. Such were their *Patriotic Marriages*; such the cruelties that must surprize the reader, were he not acquainted with the school whence they proceed. At Arras *Le Bon* would guillotine *by streets*; and one night returning home, a little drunk, he thought an execution by torch-light would have a *Patriotic effect*. The Count de Bethune, who had been brought to trial in the morning and *acquitted*, was immediately named as the victim; but Le Bon was informed that he had been tried and acquitted; no matter, we will try him again (says the Commissary); and the poor Count was condemned and executed because he was *soupçonné d'etre suspect*. This, perhaps, is the most extraordinary crime on record, *suspected of being a suspicious character* for Aristocracy; nevertheless, many hundreds perished on the scaffold for this crime. *Trans.*
29. Report of the *Comité du Salut Publique*, August 8, 1795.
30. I leave to Mr. Mallet du Pan himself the task of revealing what he heard in that club, and the horror he conceived on the occasion. He may also inform the reader with what indignation he received the invitation of the *twenty-two* to become a member

of their club. But it was from the mouth of that justly celebrated author that I learned the answer which Syeyes made to his reproaches.
31. See Papers found at Robespierre's, and printed by order of the Convention, Nos. 43, 75, 89, 107, &c.
32. See the Papers seized at Babœuf's.
33. See the Degree of Regent.
34. I do not exactly remember the particular names of the Deputies who would hold forth such language at the tribune. I can affirm, however, that the sophisticated Legislator *Rabaud de St. Etienne* frequently held such language in company, which has more than once given rise to a good deal of debate. Once in particular, he and *Mr. Desilet*, a man of letters, almost quarrelled on the subject; and that was quite at the beginning of the Revolution.

CHAP. XIII.

Universality of the Success of the Sect explained by the Universality of its Plots.

OF all the phœnomena of the French Revolution, perhaps, the most astonishing, and, unfortunately, the most incontestable, is, the rapidity of those conquests that have already revolutionized a considerable part of Europe, and menace the remainder of the universe. Nothing can be more surprizing than to see the facility with which Jacobinism has erected its standards, or planted the tree of Equality and disorganizing Liberty in Savoy, Belgium, Holland, on the Banks of the Rhine, in Switzerland, on the other side of the Alps, in Piedmont, in the Milanois, and even at Rome. When I come to explain these phœnomena, I shall not allow myself to be carried away by system or by prejudice. I will confess, that genius, bravery, and talents, have frequently wrested the palm of victory. I candidly confess, that many of their triumphs are due to men who by their courage and talents were entitled to serve a better cause. I will not dispute their glory with them; let them entwine their laurels with the red cap; let their glory mingle with remorse at the sight of those vile Jacobins, and tyrannic Pentarques, in whose defence they have rivalled their ancestors, who shone in the days of Henry IV or Lewis XIV. Nevertheless, in the career of their conquests many points, and a large share of their successes, are to be attributed to other causes than to their valour. We have seen chiefs destitute of experience or merit baffling the wisdom and talents of heroes consummate in the military art. We have seen the Carmagnole Bands, soldiers of a day, make their triumphant entry into whole provinces, while all the discipline of the combined legions of Austria, Hungary, and Prussia, could not impede their progress. The military science acquired by those veteran bands in camps and under the tuition of the greatest captains appears to have been useless. In spite of the arts of a Cohorn or a Vauban, citadels have fallen at the sight of the new conquerors; and if a battle is sought, one only victory, or even a defeat, will acquire whole provinces to their new dominion, that would have cost long and painful campaigns to a Marlborough or a Turenne. Another prodigy presses on our notice. These Jacobin conquerors are received like brethren by the vanquished nations, and their legions are swoln in the very places where those of any other Power would dwindle into nothing. They impose the harshest of yokes on their new subjects, are guilty of every species of extortion, devastation, and sacrilege, overturning all laws human and divine, yet are nevertheless received with as loud acclamations by the multitude, as if it was their Saviour that approached. These certainly are phenomena that the historian would in vain attempt to illustrate were he only acquainted with the visible armies of the Sect. To unfold these mysteries, let us boldly declare it; the Sect and its plots, its legions of secret emisssaries, have every where preceded the armies and their thunderbolts of war. It had infested states with its principles long before it sent either its *Pichegrus* or *Buonapartes* to attack them. Its means once prepared, traitors were to be found in the fortresses to open the gates; they were to be found in the armies, and in the councils of Princes, to render the plans of attack or defence abortive. Its subterraneous Clubs, Lodges, Corresponding Societies, Journals, and Propagandists, had already disposed the populace and prepared the way. The day will come when nations shall have written the history of this age. Does it not already appear, that each of them will have to dedicate many pages of that history to unfold the treasons of which it has fallen a victim, to enumerate the traitors that it has been obliged to punish, or to describe the means employed to avert the threatening storm. In order to point out the mainspring of all these machinations, I shall turn back to those days when the French Revolution was first rising into existence.

The adepts of revolutionary Equality and Liberty had buried themselves in the Lodges of Masonry. At the commencement of the Revolution a manifesto is issued to *all the Masonic Lodges* and to all the *Directories* (who are to make the proper use of it among *all the brethren of Europe*), by the central Lodge of France, the *Grand Orient* of Paris, the second Areopage of Illuminism. By this manifesto, and in virtue of fraternity, "all the Lodges are summoned *to confederate together*, to unite their efforts to maintain the revolution; to gain over to it, in all parts, friends, partizans, and protectors; to propagate the flame, to vivify the spirit, *to excite zeal and ardor for it, in every state, and by every means in their power*." This is an indisputable fact; it was sent even into England, where the Lodges were the least disposed to second it. It was dispersed throughout the Lodges in Germany, and Joseph II got possession of one signed *Philip of Orleans*.[1]

Never did any government publish an edict so efficacious. Immediately all the adepts in their public prints begin to cry up the revolution and its principles. In Holland *Paulus* publishes his Treatise on Equality; *Paine*, in England, his *Rights of Man; Campe*, in Germay, his French Citizen; and *Philo-Knigge* even outdoes himself in his *Profession of Political Faith*.[2] In Italy *Gorani* appears; in short, every nation has its apostle of Equality, Liberty, and Sovereignty of the People. These incendiary productions, with thousands of others, are distributed among the people, and are even thrown by stealth into the cottages. These were but the general means of the Sect. Men who despise the powers of opinion, or of public error, may smile at such revolutionary means, but great conspirators know too well how to appreciate them. The title of *French Citizen* now becomes their sole title of Nobility, and *Campe*,

Paine, and *Cramer,* with many others who distinguished themselves by their incendiary writings, are thus rewarded for their villany. Obscure writers, but fanatic Illuminees, are called from the bottom of Germany, such as *Nimis, Dorsch, Blau,* to compile in Paris periodical papers, that are to spread the revolutionary enthusiasm beyond the Rhine. They are surrounded by a *Leuchsenring,* a *Rebmann,* a *Hoffman,* with many other adepts, who flocked to contrive the treasons that were to extend their conquests in those countries where the other adepts were preparing the opinions. So well did they know the importance of being masters of the public opinion, that to conquer it by means of their Propagandists, Journalists, and other writers, they spent no less than *thirty millions of Livres* during the first year of their incursions and during 1797 they lavished *twenty-one millions* for the same purpose.[3]

Let us then follow the army, and combine its marches with the progress of the Sect and the motions of its apostles. Let us follow them into Germany, into Belgium, Holland, Spain, in short, whever its arms have triumphed; and we shall then see whether the revolution does not owe the progress of its arms as much to the occult adepts, as to the courage of its victorious bands.

Of all the French Generals no one, perhaps, was more inflated with his successes than Custine; and certainly he had little reason to expect them, as he was destitute of those talents and that intrepidity which denote the great General. Nevertheless, Europe with astonishment behld him in one campaign making himself master of Worms, Spire, and even Mayence. But when Europe shall know how these conquests were prepared, its astonishment will subside, and its indignation will arise against the treacherous offspring of *Spartacus*-Weishaupt.

Condorcet, Bonneville, and Fauchet, had marked out each department of correspondence for their propagandists. Strasbourg was the center, or directory for the union and communication between the German and French adepts. The Chiefs of Illuminized Lodges, STAMM and *Hyerophiles* HERMANN; who, together with the Illuminee DIETRICH, has justly obtained the surname of the *Guillotiner* of Alsace, had distinguished themselves in that province and at Strasbourg. Beyond the French frontiers, the corresponding adepts for Worms and Spire are the Calvinist minister ENDEMAN, the Syndic *Belisarius*-PETERSON, the Canon *Cyril (of Alexandria)* SCHWEICKARD, *Zeno (of Tharses),* KÖBLER, *LuciusApuleius*-JANSON, *Virgilius*-HULLEN, the Canon WINCKLEMANN, and particularly the Professor BÖHMER at Worms. These adepts are in close connection with the club at Mayence, headed by a man on whom the defence of the town was chiefly to depend, the Lieutenant-Colonel of Engineers EICKENMAYER, together with METTERNICH, BENZEL, KOLBORN, VEDEKIND, BLAU, HAUSER, FORSTER, HAUPT, and NIMIS. It is with regret that I sully the pages of history with such names; but proofs are necesssary, and perhaps no one more apposite can be adduced, than to show that the very names of the vilest traitors are known.[4]

Long before this had all these adepts been occupied with the plan of delivering up the left bank of the Rhine and the fortress of Mayence to the jacobins; they had been disposing the minds of the inhabitants of the towns and country towards the revolution by the encomiums which they were continually pronouncing on it. No sooner does Custine take the field, than his Aid-de-Camp, since become his historian, describes him as placing all his confidence in *Stamm*, the famous adept of Strasbourg. Soon after a deputation of the principal Illuminees *invite Custine to advance into the country,* and assure him that by so doing *he will meet the wishes of the majority of the inhabitants.* They added, that *should he be uneasy as to the means of surmounting certain apparent difficulties, they could assure him, that they and their friends had power enough to engage to remove them all; that they were the organs of a numerous society entirely devoted to him and actuated by the greatest zeal for his success.*[5] At the head of this deputation is the adept *Böhmer,* and, together with *Stamm,* he is entrusted with the whole confidence of the General. These adepts, in conjunction with the subordinate deputies, now take the whole direction of the jacobin army; they lead it into Worms, and propose next to carry it against Mayence. Custine is in a tremor at the idea of such an enterprize; the adepts insist, and he at length resolves to let his army proceed against this bulwark of the empire. But at the very sight of its ramparts his fears seize him again; the brethren sooth him, and dictate the summons that he is to send to General *Gimnich.* The answer he receives makes him prepare for his retreat even before he had thought of an attack, when, lo! during the night a letter from the brethren in Mayence to the adept *Böhmer* transforms his fears into hopes of success. This letter stated, that the *friend* who enjoyed all the confidence of the commander *was determined to employ all his influence to persuade him of the impossibility of defending the place;* that the brethren had so *worked upon the inhabitants,* that it would only need to add *a few more threats* in the next summons that was made. Faithful to his instructions, Custine assumes the tone of a conqueror, who has prepared a general assault, and is on the eve of delivering Mayence over to pillage and all the fury of the soldiery in case of resistance. The Illuminized *friend,* or the Lieutenant-Colonel of Engineers *Eickenmayer,* who enjoyed the whole confidence of the Commander, and the Baron *Stein,* the Prussian Envoy, join in their efforts to prove to the Council of War that it was impossible to defend the place (and this against an enemy who had not the means to attack it, and who was actually determined to take flight should he meet with resistance). The other brethren spread the alarm among the inhabitants. The brave AUDUJAR and his eleven hundred Austrians are indignant, but in vain; the capitulation is signed, and Custine, with an army of 18,000 men, destitute of heavy artillery, trembling lest he should not be able to make his retreat with sufficient speed should he but meet with resistance, obtains possession, within the space of three days, and without firing a shot, of those very ramparts that had struck him with so much terror. In such a manner are towns taken in which the Sect predominates.[6]

Let the historian follow Custine and his successors to Francfort, and he will find in the neighbourhood of that town a principality of *Isenbourg;* he will there learn how the Sect can protect its adepts. Every part around this small principality had been ravaged; but this little town was the seat of the Council for the Illuminees, where *Pitsch* presided. It was from this place that all the necessary instructions were sent for the jacobin army, which in return revered the sanctuary of Isenbourg, and even the lure of pillage could not attract the soldiery. But when *Pitsch* and his council disappear, the charm ceases, and the fertile plains of Isenbourg are ravaged.[7]

The armies are overthrown and driven from Mayence; but the union of the brotherhood does not suffer, and the Sect prepares new means of success for the revolutionary army. Some of these conspiring adepts disappear for a time, and then return to Mayence, while others are received at Paris, there, in conjunction with the Pentarques, to devise new means for retaking that town, which now appears to bid defiance to all the Custines of the revolution; and soon after Europe, with astonishment, learns that Mayence with the whole left bank of the Rhine is once more subjected to the revolutionary power. At first it is the Cis-Rhenane Republic, then it becomes a simple department of the Parisian Republic. But the adepts are to be recompensed for having effected by their black arts of Illuminism, that which the Pentarques must have despaired of, notwithstanding the bravery of their troops. The professor *Metternich* had been employed as Directorial Commissary at Fribourg. *Hoffman* is now installed Receiver General on the Rhine, with a salary of fifty thousand livres. *Rebmann*, the panegyrist of Robespierre, is created head of the Cis-Rhenane judicature. We next find acting in concert with the above-mentioned, the Privy Counsellor to the Elector of Cologne *Kempis*, and his co-illuminees the Professor *Gerhard*; the Advocate *Watterfal*, and the Artist *Conrad*; and that my reader may know by what men revolutions may be brought about, I will name the taylor *Brizen*, the cobler *Theissen*, the grocer *Flügel*, the hair-dresser *Broches*, and the alehousekeeper *Rhodius*.[8]

Other plots of the Sect will bring us back to Germany again; but in the mean time Dumourier triumphs over the stationary hero of Verdun, and flies to take possession of Belgium. Let eternal darkness hover round the machinations that gave this General more time to collect his scattered troops that was sufficient for a victorious army to proceed to Paris, and deliver the unfortunate Lewis. Let no reader pretend to associate the reigning Duke of Brunswick with the brotherhood of the modern *Spartacus*. I have positive proof that he detests them; I also know, that Frederic William III has given various proofs, notwithstanding he may have been played upon by another species of Illuminees, that he hated and abhorred the disorganizing jacobins. But his councils are under the direction of other councils. *Bischofswerder* was at Berlin; *Luchesini* held correspondences; the adepts are in the *Dicasteres* (the Offices). Their influence is most formidable, and the Sect has already declared, that it will be *far stronger when once in possession of the offices and councils under the Prince, than if they had initiated the Prince himself.* The day may come that will explain the enigma of this famous retreat made at the time when all Europe was at the height of expectation, and daily awaited the last accounts of its triumphs; meanwhile I shall proceed to unfold mysteries that, hitherto unknown, have led us to view Dumourier as conquering Belgium in the fields of Jemappe. Here at least the laurels are to be divided, for the conspiring Sect has borne a larger share in this conquest than his armies; and it was in London, rather than at Jemappe, that the Austrian Netherlands were conquered.

The Sect had its Lodges in Brabant, and *Vandernoot* had brought over his party to them. He knew that the brethren sought to represent the French revolution in such colours as to make the people eager in its cause; he was also acquainted with those Lodges that had addressed the National Assembly, humbly petitioning for their revolutionary Equality and Liberty. *Vandernoot* was then in London, under the name of *Gobelscroix*. An emissary from the Parisian club, he was prosecuting his plots, together with *Chauvelin, Perigord D'Autun, Noel, Bomet*, and eight other adepts, sent to spread the revolutionary principles in England. *Vandernoot* entrusted himself to persons with whose principles he was not sufficiently acquainted; but they knew him well; he betrayed his secret, and thus the whole mystery is come to light. During the disputes, and even warfare, carried on between the Belgians and Joseph II, the greater part of them certainly had not the most distant idea of subjecting their country to the revolutionary principles of the Jacobins; but the sect had its partizans, and these adepts left no means untried to persuade the people that the sole resource for recovering their liberty was to unite with the French. "I was well acquainted with these plans (said Vandernoot to his confidant); no sooner were we informed of what had passed between the Duke of Brunswick and Dumourier, than we immediately wrote *to Paris and to the army*. The messenger brought us back the plan of the campaign, and a copy of the manifesto that Dumourier was to publish on his entry into the Low Countries. I saw that the plan had been exactly copied from that followed by Custine in his extortions in Germany. I foresaw that such a plan would appal all the efforts of our people, and would only serve to league the inhabitants against the French, whereas if they would but follow my ideas, derived from the knowledge I had of that people, and of their dispositions, I would answer for their seconding the French invasion, and that it would infallibly turn out successful. At the request of Chauvelin and Noel, I drew up the plan to be followed, and wrote the manifesto that was to be published, framing it according to the local knowledge and experience I had acquired; and the whole was immediately sent off to Paris. They were both adopted on the spot. Dumourier did not change a syllable of the manifesto that I had written in *Portman Square*. The people, gained over by our agents, and by this manifesto, threw themselves into our arms, and Flanders was taken."

No reader can expect that I should name the persons to whom Vandernoot had thus opened his plans; of this much, however, I can assure the public, that the whole was laid before the ministry, who for a time suffered Noel, Vandernoot, and their accomplices to remain in London, but keeping a close watch over them until they were sent elsewhere to conspire, and prosecute their vile machinations, against nations that they dared not meet in the open field.

Next to the conquest of Belgium came that of Holland; and with equal astonishment has Europe seen the formidable bulwarks of that republic falling at the approach of the Jacobin armies. Here again we must resort for the cause to the dark recesses of the Sect. The apostles of Illuminism had been labouring in Holland ever since the year 1781.[9] The immense sums of money drawn from those countries were not the only successes of the Sect. The Stadtholder had already learned, to his cost, how much they could envenom faction and sedition; the French revolution then came to raise their expectations and stimulate their labours. The Low Countries had for a second time received their Jacobin conquerors. The English army fell back to the frontiers of its ancient ally to vindicate its liberties from the attempts of the enemy. Its efforts, however, are useless, for Holland no longer wills the liberty of the true patriot, it wills that of the Jacobin. Its wishes shall soon be complied with; the brethren of Paris shall dictate the law in Amsterdam, and shall seize on its riches; the commerce of Holland shall be annihilated; its colonies wrested from it; and soon shall it rank among the powers of Europe, only as the first slave of the Gallic Pentarques. No matter. Let Pichegru approach, for he is the object of their wishes; and the defenders of their true liberty may seek their safety in retreat; for the countries which they wish to defend are replete with plots against them and conspiracies in favour of the revolution. In Amsterdam alone the Sect has no less than forty clubs, and each club has the direction of two hundred revolutionists. The elect of these clubs form two committees, the central and the corresponding committees; and this latter holds correspondence with brethren both within and without the territories of the republic. These are subject to a supreme council, the true Areopagites, whose resolves are transmitted to the dispersed brethren. Persons who watched over the public welfare have acted the parts of associates in hopes of diving into the mysteries; but the scrutators at Amsterdam were as crafty as those of Munich, and these adepts could never penetrate beyond the first mysteries, while other clubs were composed of men well known by the Sect to be the firmest advocates for Jacobin Equality and Liberty.

Deputies from *Leyden* are delegated to the central committee; and the brotherhood at Leyden had made a great progress in proportion, both in numbers and sedition, than it had at Amsterdam. The adepts of *Utrecht* were still more ardent revolutionists than either. The vigilance of government, and the neighbourhood of the armies, had put them to flight; the chiefs, however, assembled together in country-houses, and their deliberations were transmitted to the Areopage at Amsterdam. *Rotterdam* appeared to be neuter; but it held a neutrality that only waited the propitious moment for declaring in favour of Jacobinism. The minister and adept *Mareux* had made the conquest of three fourths of the inhabitants of *Naarden*. The commissary *Aiglam* would have been restless had he known of a single inhabitant of *Haarlem* that was not devoted to the adepts of Amsterdam.[10]

The better to conduct the proceedings of the faction, the French convention had sent a secret agent of the name of *Malabar* to reside at

Amsterdam; he had two acolytes, called *l'Archevêque* and *Aiglam*. At once enjoying the confidence of Pichegru (then advancing with his vidtorious army) and of the rebels in the interior, Malabar never appeared but at the meetings of the Areopagites, where he dictated the resolves. *L'Archevêque* and *Fresine* were employed in carrying on the correspondence with Pichegru. In Amsterdam and Haarlem *Aiglam* was inspector-general of the subterraneous arsenals whither the brethren were to flock for arms on the signal given. Should they stand in need of the protection of the magistracy, the adept *Dedelle* was burgomaster. If funds were wanting, the counting-houses of *Texier, Coudere*, and *Rottereau*, are open to them, beside the treasure of the Jew *Sportas*, a most vehement revolutionist. Among the clubists the adepts *Gulcher* and *Lapeau* distinguish themselves, as do *Latour* and *Perisse* among their armourers. Next in quest of enthusiasts who shall declaim to the populace, we meet the adepts *Termache, Lekain, Müllner, Schneider*, and many others. On their general roll-call they count 40,000 men ready to march out to meet the advancing Jacobins, or to charge in the rear the armies of the allies, and those legions that might still remain faithful to their duty. Nothing new was wanting but a general capable of directing their march; and *Eustace* was sent from Paris.—On a sudden the vigilance of the English minister and of the Duke of York seemed to have counteracted this conspiracy, that had been so well concerted; and the government was informed of the whole plot. *Malabar*, the hero of the mysteries, *La Tour, Fresine*, and about thirty more conspirators, were arrested; even *Eustace* was among the prisoners, and all true citizens thought themselves delivered from the Jacobin scourge. Proclamations were issued, forbidding any meetings of clubs under any pretext whatever; but, in defiance of the magistrates, the clubists publish a counter-proclamation, inviting the brethren to take arms, and rather to die than abandon their clubs. In vain does the English general demand that these persons should be delivered up to him, that he might secure their persons; the Sect even succeeded in getting the American minister to reclaim Eustace, under pretence that he was a subject of the United States. The others are brought to trial, and are condemned to be exiled into those very towns by which the Jacobin army was to enter the republic, and Willemstadt, Breda, Bergenopzoom, Nimeguen, Gorcum, Utrecht, and Amsterdam, fall, just as Mayence had done before them. Most certainly, had Pichegru no other claims to military glory than this conquest, he might, with Dumourier and Custine, write, "*I came, I saw, I conquered;* but it was because, in place of enemies to combat, I found none but adepts to embrace."[11]

Means of another species will explain the triumphs of the Sect in Spain. The brave RICARDO had restored the Castilians to their ancient valour; he had threatened to retaliate on the captive Jacobins, for the cruelties exercised on the French emigrants that fell into their hands. The *Aqua Tophana* immediately liberates the Sect from so fierce an enemy; he dies by poison. The bulwarks of Spain fall like those of Holland at the approach of the legions of *Equality and Liberty*. REDDELEON sells the fortress of *Figueras* for a million of livres. He values his treason too highly, and going to Paris he receives his million in assignats, then only worth 48,000 livres. He complains, and in compensation is sent to the guillotine, for the Sect need not buy traitors at so exorbitant a price. His treachery, however, left Spain at the discretion of the Jacobins. That unhappy country sought to buy peace, and for a time it is suffered to enjoy a truce; but every thing seems to denote, that the brethren have made a sufficient progress to leave the task of establishing the reign of Equality and Liberty to the adepts of the interior, without resorting to arms.

In Portugal the adepts dare not as yet throw off the mask; but at some future day the Court may judge proper to publish the correspondence found among the papers of the Brabanter *Segre*. This propagandist had been thrown into the prisons of Lisbon. The brethren had not forgotten the doctrine of the *patet exitus*; they send a mattress to the prisoner, and a razor is concealed within it. The wretched Segre understands the meaning of the Sect, and the next morning is found weltering in his blood on this very mattress.

It transpired, however, that the conspiracy in which he had engaged aimed at nothing less than the destruction of the royal family, and the total overthrow of the state. It was further asserted, that a correspondence between him and the *Prince of Peace* was found among his papers, and that the Spanish minister, informed of his arrest, immediately claimed it; but the court of Portugal returned for answer, "That since God had in his goodness preserved the state from the greatest misfortune with which it had ever been threatened, her Most Faithful Majesty would only treat of this business with his Catholic Majesty himself." But even should this fact be well authenticated, are we not sufficiently aware of the intrigues of the Sect? Does it not frequently procure secret commissions from ministers, and then , under pretence of transacting the business of that state, prosecute the most villanous plots? It is sufficient for us to have shown the Sect conspiring in Portugal; the public papers describe it as conspiring in like manner at Turin and at Naples.

Here again the secrecy of courts has debarred us from the details. At Naples attestations were taken respecting the guilty, and the proofs were acquired. By the orders of his Majesty, all the documents relating to the conspiracy had been collected and compiled by a magistrate of great merit and known integrity, Mr. REY, the same person whom Lewis XVI had intended for minister of the police of Paris. From these it appeared, that many noblemen had been led to join in a conspiray against the royal family, while the occult adepts of this conspiracy were to make away with these same noblemen, immediately after the destruction of the royal family. The King and the Queen of Naples both chose to show their clemency to the chief conspirators, and rather let them preserve life in confinement, than send them to the scaffold, which must have been the inevitable consequence of a public trial. The policy that has buried in darkness the details of this conspiracy, has not, however, deprived us of this proof of the universality of the conspiracies of the Sect.

In pursuit of its plans, the Sect marches triumphantly to Milan, Venice, and Rome. Its armies entered Italy with Buonaparte, even more destitute of every thing that can ensure victory, than those which had entered Germany under the command of Custine. But numerous legions flocked to their standards; and the banks of the Po, if we except Mantua, are as well prepared for the revolution as were those of the Rhine. This will cease to be a matter of surprise to those who will reflect that Weishaupt had sent his apostles thither, and that Knigge and Zimmerman had long since boasted of the progress of the illuminizing recruiters in those parts. If we turn back to their reports, we shall find that the Masonic Lodges had, like those of Germany, been initiated into the last mysteries; and the triumphs of Buonaparte will be found to be not more astonishing than those of Custine. Were it necessary to explain how the valour of the Archduke Charles, or of the veteran bands of Austria, was rendered fruitless when in presence of the Jacobin troops; whence it arose that the fastnesses of countries could scarcely serve the wisdom of a prince so worthy of being the leader of heroes; it would not be sufficient to say, that the adjutant-general *Fisher* was accused of having received one thousand pounds a month from the Pentarques; or that, to stifle all prosecution, and baffle any attempt tht might be made to induce him to discover the number or quality of his accomplices, he had recourse to that grand means of Illuminism, the *Patet exitus*, and poisoned himself. No; the reader must reflect, that the Sect had long since been educating its adepts for the armies, procuring possession of the *Dicasteres*, and thus preparing for a future day, when they foresaw that treachery and cowardice would serve them in the armies of princes.[12]

Need we explain why the revolutionary legions proceeded to Rome? Certainly but little resistance could be made there. An aged pontiff raising up his hands to heaven, offering up his prayers for the peace and welfare of the faithful, makes every sacrifice, that of his faith excepted, in hopes of mollifying the obdurate hearts of those barbarians. Buonaparte, no stranger to his virtues, feigns a veneration for them. But Pius VI is the chief of that religion of Christ which the Sect has sworn to crush, and Rome is the centre of it.[13] From the very first moment of the revolution the adepts had made no secret of their hatred against Rome and its pontiff. I was present when Cerrutti insolently accosted the Secretary of the Nuncio at Paris, saying with a sneer, "Take good care of your Pope; take good care of this one, and embalm him after his death; for I tell you, and you may be certain of the fact, that you will never have another." This pretender to prophecy little thought that he would be the first of the two to appear before the tribunal of that God who had promised that the gates of hell should never prevail against his church. But the Knights-*Kadosch*, who had sworn the death of kings and of the chief Pontiffs, still survived; as also that multitude of adepts who had long since been smoothing the way for legions of Impiety. Long since had Rome been the object of their conspiracies; adepts of every species flock thither; and, in spite of every authority, the pupils of Cagliostro open their Masonic Lodges in that capital.

The Illuminees of Sweden, Avignon, and Lyons, there unite in the most secret and most monstrous of Lodges, and form the most terrible tribunal for Kings; that, in short, which pointed out the Sovereign that was to fall, named the assassin, prepared the poisons, or sharpened the dagger.[14]

Many of Weishaupt's adepts were also to be found in Rome, who had been initiated by Zimmerman; and the representative of a King seconds their efforts against the altar. The Spanish Monarch is tottering on his throne, at the very time when the public papers describe DOM AZARA, his ambassador at Rome, felicitating the jacobins on their coming to drive the Sovereign Pontiff from his capital. Buonaparte may send his Lieutenants; their triumph will be easy, for shame alone could impede their progress; but they have stifled every feeling, and scoff at the very idea of the rights of nations, as well as at the overwhelming with affliction an aged pastor turned of fourscore. The upright man and compassionate heart might shed tears at such a sight; but the Jacobin, callous to every feeling, will leap with joy, and the Pentarques will compare their ignominious conquest to the storming of ancient Rome by Brennus and his Gauls. Next in the series we shall turn our eyes to a conquest long since announced in the Lodges of the Templars, Rosicrucians and Knights Kadosch, who had all sworn vengeance against Malta; and the fatal day is now come.

Lest indignation might cause their secrets to be discovered, the cross of Malta had for a long time been a badge of exclusion for those bold Knights from the threshold of the Masonic Lodges. New arts will be now employed to render their courage useless. The adepts have made use of the same artifice against Malta which they had employed against the church. So far, said they, from breaking off all connection with these Knights, let our adepts become members of the Order; through their means we shall become masters of that island that would proudly bid defiance to our combined hostile efforts both by sea and land. Letters from the virtuous and honourable part of that community had already prepared us for the catastrophe that has since befallen them; they had complained that false brethren, particularly of the Spanish and Italian tongues, had gained admittance among them. In the persons of *Dolomieu, Bosredon,* and the cowardly *Hompesch,* may the Sect be said to have reigned. Buonaparte appears; and, as if the Sect wished to shew Europe how it can carry the most astonishing works of nature and art by treason alone, it did not even give the conspirators a cloak for their treachery by the semblance of a siege. The adepts of the exterior fraternize with those of the interior, and thus do we learn that the secret arms of the Sect are more terrible than the fire of the embattled legions. Let the hero of Malta set sail for Alexandria: There he will also find adepts that await his arrival: Then will the Sublime Porte learn how to value those rich presents sent by the revolutionary tribe, all stolen from the royal treasury of the crown; it will understand why such immense sums of money were squandered in its capital, to buy the neutrality of the Divan, and thus to enable the Sect to wrest from its dominion its more distant provinces: It will learn, that the Apostles of the Sect were, during its political lethargy, stealing along the coasts of Africa, and penetrating even into Asia.

It was at Constantinople particularly that the Sect was to be careful in the choice of its adepts and propagandists, and to adapt each person's mission to his talents. To spread the doctrines of Equality and Liberty throughout the states that had long since been subjected to the dominion of the Crescent, it was necessary to find men well acquainted with the language, manners, interests, and the various intercourse of those different nations. In the person of the author of the *Tableau de l'Empire Ottoman*, or *Mouradgea d'Hobson*, a Greek by birth, formerly internuncio, and since ambassador from Sweden to the Sublime Porte, the Sect found all the requisites for such an undertaking. At first, he did not appear to be sanguine in their cause; large sums of money, and pensions then at the disposition of the *Committee of Public Safety* (as we are informed by our Memoirs) at length dispel any further shew of reluctance: On his return to Constantinope, Mouradgea places himself at the head of the Jacobin missionaries for the East. He was greatly indebted for the acquirements that had thus prepared him for his new revolutionary career to a Mr. *Ruffin*, who commenced his career as a teacher of languages in Paris; was afterwards an associate with the Baron Tott in Crimea; then attached to the French embassy at Constantinople; afterwards employed in the Admiralty at Versailles; and finally became Professor of the Oriental Tongues at the *College Royal*. For a long time Mr. Ruffin resisted every temptation to betray the Royal cause; for he was indebted to the king for his education, and for his elevation to be Knight of the Order of St. Michael. Similar inducements, however, make him forget his obligations to his king, and he becomes the co-adept of Mouradgea at Constantinople. *Lesseps*, a young man, and one of the few survivors of La Perouse, was also animated by sentiments of gratitude for Lewis XVI; but, seduced by the two apostles, he joins them, and, under the direction of this triumvirate, one part of the subaltern agents disseminate their doctrines among the people of Constantinope, while others spread themselves throughout Asia, travel into Persia, and to the Indies. Others again preach their rights of man in the Levant, while the united forces of the Sect make their descent on the coast of Egypt, and teach the Ottoman Court the fatal effects of having neglected to crush the first dawnings of the Sect.

But a very few years prior to the French revolution, the Turks abominated Masonry, as much as the inhabitants of the East did the Manichæans for many centuries. The Ottoman court would not have suffered any French Religious to have remained at Jerusalem, had it not known that it was their constant rule to refuse to admit any person known to be a *Freemason* to visit the holy places that were under their care. There was even an agreement between the Sublime Porte and the Court of France, by which the Superior of these Religious might and was obliged to dismiss from the Levant any French Consul that should dare to erect a Masonic Lodge; and I have learned from a Religious who was on that mission for seven years, that the Superior had sometimes exercised this authority. But the revolution has annihilated such precautions, as well as many others. The Propagandists have crossed the Mediterranean with their new-fangled doctrines; they have found brethren in the French merchants, who, under pretence of meeting with friends in all countries, had got themselves initiated in the mysteries, and hence they needed not Lodges to be recognized.

The successes of the brotherhood in France inflamed the zeal of the brethren in Africa; and the very manner in which the Directory announced the progress of Buonaparte in Egypt sufficiently denotes the arts that had been employed by the emissaries of the Sect previous to his arrival. Should he not (like Pichegru) fall a victim to the jealousy of the Pentarques, or (more lucky than Brueys) escape the pursuits of a second Nelson, he will on the coasts of India meet with other brethren, who in the Malabar tongue are circulating the *Rights of Man, Equal and Free*, and those of the *Sovereign and Legislative People*. The English General who took Pondicherry seized both the types and the presses employed in disseminating the principles of the Sect and their revolutionary productions.

As the plague flies on the wings of the wind, so do their triumphant legions infect America. Their apostles have infused their principles into the submissive and laborious negroes; and St. Domingo and Guadaloupe have been converted into vast charnel houses for their inhabitants. So numerous were the brethren in North America, that Philadelphia and Boston trembled, lest their *rising constitution should be obliged to make way for that of the great club*; and if for a time the brotherhood has been obliged to shrink back into their hiding places, they are still sufficiently numerous to raise collections and transmit them to the insurgents of Ireland; thus contributing toward that species of revolution which is the object of their ardent wishes in America.[15] God grant that the United States may not learn to their cost, that Republics are equally menaced with Monarchies; and that the immensity of the ocean is but a feeble barrier against the universal conspiracy of the Sect!

The triumphs of the brotherhood at Geneva, at Venice, in Holland, and at Genoa, are demonstrative proofs that it is not at Monarchs alone that the adepts of the Sect aim their blows. Nations must also learn, that, whether Monarchies or Republics, they are all to be comprehended within the revolutionary vortex; and that neither friendship, alliance, nor the most passive obedience, can make the savage conspirators relent.

In vain did the Swiss Cantons in some sort forget the dignity of their ancestors; they were silent under the humiliating treatment of their brethren at Aix, the butchery of their troops at Paris, and the violation of the most sacred treaties even on their own territories. They bore with resignation the insults perpetually offered to them by the Jacobin dictators, who would sometimes deign to mingle assurances of fraternity and promises of peace with their outrages. While the armies of the Sect were ravaging the neighbouring countries, it would lull the credulous Swiss into a fatal security by their cant of fraternity and affection; but in the mean time the adepts were labouring in the mountains. Weishaupt had made many converts in those parts; and a swarm of Illuminees flocked thither from the *University of Gottingen*, all ready to prosecute the views of the Sect. *Fehr*, curate of Nidau, and after him *Bugg*, corresponded with the brotherhood in Germany; and the moment was approaching when he was about to receive the price of his zeal by being elected chief of the revolutionized Canton of Argau.[16] At Lucern *Pfiffer*, at Bern *Weiss*, at Basle *Ochs*, presided over the clubs of Equality and Liberty. By various artifices, the Jacobins had formed a party of ninety-two in the great council of Berne. The Pentarque Rewbel sent as auxiliaries from Paris, *Maingaud, Mangourit*, and *Guyot*; and in Switzerland (as in Holland and at Mayence) secret correspondence and secret societies were preparing the way for the armies of the Sect. Thus was the fate of Switzerland to be similar and an equal share of glory to redound to the victors.[17]

Yet there are monarchies still in existence, notwithstanding all the efforts of the Sect. True; but, if we except Denmark, whose neutrality appears to be of too great service to the Sect, for it to think of destroying that kingdom at present, what other country is there in Europe that has not been exposed to the machinations of the Sect? Gustavus III fell beneath the blows of an Ankarstroem; but this assassin had come from the great Parisian club. Those very persons who wish to isolate this murder tell us, that adepts had declared, that *they knew of the projected murder of Gustavus beforehand, and that all Europe knew of it*. Who are these men that were so well informed throughout Europe, if not those adepts to whom the Sect had made known their determinations against a Prince whose activity could give them little hopes of retrograde movements when he was about to fight the enemies of monarchy? When those same writers cast suspicions on the Duke of *Sudermania*, they ground their attack on his being *Grand Master of the Swedish Lodges*, as Orleans was in France. They further substantiate their charge on the multitude of illuminized Masons that are spread all over Sweden, and on the horror of their mysteries. Is not that telling us, that Ankarstroem was but a mere instrument of the Sect, which, in recompence for his regicide, erected statues to him in the Club of the Jacobins? I will hereafter show that the adepts had previous knowledge of this foul deed, and that it had even been clearly expressed in the public papers. But at present let us turn our eyes toward Russia.

On the death of Lewis XVI the Empress of Russia ordered that all the French within her dominions should take the oath of fidelity to the lawful heir of the Bourbons, and renounce all connection with France until monarchy was restored; but this was a fruitless precaution. The Sect had many adepts in Russia, whom it had taught to scoff at oaths;[18] and they only took the oath of fidelity to the monarchy, that they might the more easily annihilate the Russian diadem. The conspirators were headed by *Genet*, heretofore the agent for the cabinet of Versailles, but now become the agent of the Jacobins. The zeal with which he served his new masters had already filled Petersburg with clubs composed of that species of men who, having no homes in their own country, travel to foreign parts in hopes of gaining a livelihood. Hair-dressers, Cooks, Valets, Bankrupts, Teachers of the French Tongue, and Street-porters from Paris, all were combining together to prepare a pike-revolution. The most artful and most violent of the conspirators daringly held their meetings in the Hotel of *Sir Charles Whitworth*, the English Ambassador at Petersburg. They met there once a month by means of three French servants, who had been recommended to Sir Charles by some of the party as most excellent characters. Public fame, and soon after the Ambassador, informed the Police of this meeting. On making enquiries after the adepts, and on seizing their papers that had been carefully hidden, it was discovered, that their plot had been contrived according to the general plan and views of the Sect. At Rome, the brotherhood had made use of an Ambassador of the King of Spain; in Russia, it is the Secretary of Embassy and *Chargé d'Affaires* from the Court of Sardinia, a *Mr. Bossi*, who is implicated in their foul projects. The adepts were banished, according to the laws of Russia. The diplomatic character of Mr. Bossi saved him for some time from a similar disgrace; but no sooner was the Czar Paul seated on the throne, than he received orders to quit Petersburg in twenty-four hours, and the territories of his Imperial Majesty with all possible speed.[19]

I shall not dwell long on the labours of the Sect in Poland. Among the numbers of its apostles, I might name *Bonneau*, who was sent to Siberia; *Duveyrier*, who wrote the *Proces Verbaux* at Paris for La Fayette, and who was discovered at Copenhagen on a supposed mission for buying corn, while his real object was to visit the brethren of Poland and Russia, to stimulate them; and our Memoirs inform us, that on the road he was to make an attempt on the life of the Count Artois, just as the German adepts have since done on that of Lewis XVIII. Duveyrier was accompanied by one *Lamarre*, and that *Castella* since arrested in company with *Semonville* when proceeding to Constantinople with the plunder of the French crown, in hopes of bribing the ministers of this country. But to give my reader an idea of the multitude of missionaries employed by the Sect in Poland, it will suffice to advert to *Cambon's* report, where he owns that it has already cost France *sixty millions* of livres to support the brethren at Warsaw. This avowal shows how this Sect employs the public revenues, little caring whether the creditors of the interior are paid, and sending its visible legions to live on contributions levied on the exterior, while it largely pays that crowd of invisible adepts and secret emissaries who prepare the way for its triumphs.

This also demonstrates what great stress the leaders of the Sect laid on the projected revolution in Poland; and, indeed, had they succeeded in revolutionizing that country, the Jacobins might have made a strong diversion on the very territories of the most formidable powers that had entered into the coalition. Equality and Liberty would have infused itself throughout Russia with much greater facility. The Prussian and Austrian brethren began to show themselves more openly. Their hopes already seemed to be crowned with success; Koskiusko had excited to revolt Warsaw, Wilna, and Lublin. The bishop of this latter place, with many other gentlemen, had been hanged; in vain had the unfortunate Poniatowski endeavoured to allay the ferocity of the revolution; Poland was advancing rapidly towards it end, and it finished by losing both its king and its independence. My object is not even to hint an opinion on the conduct of the powers who have divided that country among themselves, but to point out the universal conspiracy of the Sect. Germany, which gave birth to the most profound adepts of the Sect, has already severely felt the effects of its treachery, but has not yet met the fate which the Sect is preparing for it.

Joseph II lived long enough to deplore his miserable policy. He was lamenting his philosophism, and that detestable policy that had induced him to trouble the inhabitants of the low countries in the enjoyment of their religion, thus breaking the most solemn treaties and driving to despair subjects who deserved a better fate, when the manifesto of the *Grand Orient* came to teach him, that his policy had been just as erroneous in protecting the Masonic Lodges. If credit is to be given to *Kleiner's Report*, or at least to the extract from it given me by a nobleman of undoubted veracity, it was in consequence of this manifesto that Joseph II gave orders to *Kleiner* to get himself initiated into the illuminized Lodges, and by this means acquired certain knowledge of the Occult Mysteries of the Sect. He then learnt, that the Swedish adepts had precisely the same object in view as the offspring of the modern *Spartacus*; and the Masonic Lodges were the cloaks for both of them. I have learned from a person who was frequently in company with the Emperor, that nothing could equal his vexation, when he saw that he had been so strangely imposed upon by men whom he had favoured, or when he discovered that, *so far from having himself named persons to the different charges of the State, he had only adopted the choices made by the Sect*. He then openly declared, that the Freemasons were nothing more than a set of sharpers and jugglers; he went so far as to attribute all the thefts that had been committed on the treasury of the state to the Occult Masons; he determined to exclude them from every employment civil and military; he was indignant at seeing an *imperium in imperio* rising in the state. He would have followed up his indignation too, had he not learnt that many of his most faithful subjects, and some even for whom he had the greatest regard, such as the Prince *Lichtenstein*, were Masons. The greater part of these, however, renounced Masonry. Joseph had undertaken to destroy the Lodges and repair the errors of philosophism, when a premature death put a period to his reign.

Leopold his successor, wishing to be informed of the nature and progress of the Sect in his territories, applied to Professor Hoffman. No man was better able than he was to give the desired information, for he had been tampered with by the Sect, who, writing to him in the most highflown phrases, endeavoured to seduce him over to the cause of the revolution; but, on the other side, several Masons, *ashamed of having fallen a prey to the seduction of the Illuminees, had discovered most important secrets to him*, and joined with him in baffling the views of the Sect. He had learned from them, "that Mirabeau himself had declared to his confidants, *that he carried on a most extensive correspondence with Germany, but in no part so extensive as at Vienna.* He knew that the revolutionary system was to be extended throughout the universe; that France had only been chosen as the scene of a first explosion. That the propagandists were busied in disseminating their principles throughout every climate; that emissaries were dispersed through the four quarters of the globe, and particularly in the capitals; and that they had their adherents, and were particularly active in strengthening their party at *Vienna* and *in the Austrian dominions.*—In 1791 he had read, as several other persons also did, two letters, the one from Paris, the other from Strasbourg; *describing in cypher the names of seven commissaries of the Propaganda then resident at Vienna, and to whom the new commissaries were to apply, as well for the wages of their labours, as for instructions how to proceed.*—He had also seen several of those manuscript news-papers that were sent weekly from Vienna, replete with the most abominable anecdotes against the court, and with arguments and principles impugning the government.—These papers were to contribute toward the dissemination of Jacobinism throughout the towns and villages of the empire, and even in foreign countries, as they were sent post-free and without even the subscription being asked for. He had even transmitted some of these letters to government.—He had discovered the object of the frequent journeys of the Illuminee *Camp* to Paris, and his correspondence with Mirabeau and Orleans. He had acquired *certain knowledge* of the plans of the German Mirabeau," that is to say, of Mauvillon, who had been Mirabeau's Insinuator, and the same person who had written thus to the Illuminee *Cuhn* (the letter is preserved in the archives at Brunswick): "*The affairs of the revolution go on better and better in France; I hope that in a few years this flame will be lit up every where, and that the conflagration will become universal.* THEN OUR ORDER *may do great things*"[20] Mr. Hoffman also knew that this very Mauvillon "had drawn up a very explicit plan for the revolutionizing of all Germany; that this plan had been transmitted to the greater part of the Masonic Lodges, and to the clubs of the Illuminees; and that it was circulated among the Propagandists and emissaries, who were already employed in exciting to revolt the people on the outposts and frontiers of Germany."[21] While this zealous citizen was thus unfolding to Leopold the intrigues of the Sect, he corresponded with the Great ZIMMERMAN of Bern, who was ever revered by the learned, beloved by all good citizens, and only hated by the illuminizing Jacobins, because he no sooner became acquainted with their mysteries than he warned the Society of their dangerous tendency. This learned man was also employed in composing a memorial for the use of the emperor, on the means of curbing the progress of the revolution;[22] but the Jacobins were aware of the hatred that Leopold had conceived for them. They knew that the chief instigator of the treaty of Pilnitz was a much to be feared as Gustavus; *and they were determined to show that even an Emperor should not oppose their plots with impunity.*[23]

Just at the time when the two sovereigns were making their preparations, the King of Prussia had recalled from Vienna his ambassador, the *Baron Jacobi Kloest*, who, as the Sect supposed, was favourable to their cause. The *Count Haugwits*, who was more decidedly a friend to the measure of the treaty, was sent in his stead. The journalists of Strasbourg announced this news with the following comment: "Hence politicians pretend, that the union between the two courts will be consolidated. They are certainly in the right to make the French believe so; but in despotic countries, in *those countries where the fate of several millions of men hangs on a bit of paste, or on the rupture of a little vein, one can calculate on nothing.* Let us suppose that the court of Prussia is acting honestly in concert with the court of Austria (which is difficult to be believed), or that the court of Austria is acting so with that of Prussia (which is still more incredible), *a single indigestion, or a drop of blood forced from its proper vessels, will be sufficient to dissolve this brilliant union."* This comment in the *Courier of Strasbourg,* No. 53, was dated from Vienna, *the 26th of February* 1792. Leopold died (poisoned) on the *first of March* following, and Gustavus was assassinated in the night between the 15th and 16th of the same month.[24]

The first precaution taken by his young successor was to dismiss all the Italian cooks, that he might not be exposed to the same fate as his father, and fall a victim to what is called the *Naples broth.* More zealous in the cause, Francis II not only opposed the Sect by force of arms, but, in order to attack Illuminism in its dark recesses, he applied to the Diet of Ratisbon in 1794, for a decree to suppress all secret societies, whether Masons, Rosicrucians, or Illuminees, of every sort. They had powerful supporters in this first council of the Empire, and they intrigued against the proposition of the Emperor. They pretended that these bodies of Illuminees were nothing more than little associations of school-boys, that they were very common in Protestant universities.—Through the organs of the Prussian, Hanoverian, and Brunswick ministers it was objected, that the Emperor was at liberty to forbid these different lodges within his own states; but that, with respect to all others, they could not attempt to curtail the Germanic liberty. All that the Emperor could obtain was a decree for the abolition of those associations of school-boys. This decree not only left the great adepts in full possession of their lodges, but was also unattended to in most of the colleges, where Illuminism continued to make the most awful progress.[25]

While the young Emperor was thus endeavouring to counteract the plots of the Sect, it was conspiring in the very heart of the Austrian states to overturn the government. By the death of the *Chevalier de Born* the Sect had lost at Vienna one of its chief adepts; this gentleman was powerfully rich, yet at his death nothing but immense debts appeared, in consequence of the sums he had spent on the Propagandists. Two other adepts, as zealous at the least, and far more enterprizing, had succeeded him. HEBENSTREIT, the *Lieutenant de place* at Vienna, was one; and the other was MEHALOVICH, an ex-capuchin of Croatia, whom Joseph II had imprudently taken from the cloisters and had given him a living in Hungary, in recompence for the dispositions he had shown to second the Emperor in his pretended reforms in the church. A number of other adepts had joined these two conspirators, among whom we may distinguish the Captain *Billek,* mathematical professor at the Academy of Neustadt, the Lieutenant *Riedel,* the professor of philosophy *Brandstäter,* the stupid but rich merchant *Hackel,* and finally *Wolfstein,* one of those adepts whom the sect had contrived to send on a revolutionary mission throughout

Europe at the Emperor's expence, under pretence of acquiring knowlege in the veterinary art, of which he has since been created professor.

The reader may judge of the number and importance of the conspirators by the plan that was agreed upon in 1795. Through their influence at court, they found means of forming a garrison in Vienna of substantial and honest citizens little accustomed to bear arms. They had selected them from this class, and had got an order to compel them into this sort of duty, under pretence of the imminent danger of the State. Always pretending they had the orders of the Emperor, they treated these new-raised corps with unheard-of severity, in hopes of indisposing them against the Court by the time that their revolutionary plots should be ready for execution. The populace was in their hands, and daily became more attached to their cause, in consequence of their being excluded from the new-raised corps, and by making them partake of the large sums distributed among a banditti who were to be put in possession of the arsenal on the day of insurrection. On that day the insurrection was to be general, during which *Hebenstreit*, followed by a banditti, was to secure the person of the Emperor; other detachments of the banditti were to take possession of the arsenal, and post themselves on the ramparts. The person of the Emperor being in their hands, the conspirators were to oblige him to sign *the Code of the Rights of Man*; that is to say, certain edicts ready prepared, by which the rights of all nobility and great proprietors were to be annulled; all were to be declared equal and free; and the sovereignty of the people proclaimed. These edicts were to be sent into the Provinces in the name of the Emperor, just as if he had enjoyed his liberty. Every outward appearance of respect for his person was to be preserved; in short, he was to have been treated just as the gaoler La Fayette had treated the unfortunate Lewis XVI. It is not known, whether the *Aqua Tophana* was to be administered in such a dose as to *kill*, or to *stupify*; it even appears, that the young prince was to be kept as a hostage; but in all cases, he was only to be restored to his freedom after the people had been well accustomed to the new reign of Equality and Liberty, and had acquired possession of the estates of the Nobility in such a manner that all restitution of property, or revival of the ancient constitution, would be rendered impossible. All the preparatory steps had been taken; the Catechisms of the Rights of Man, and the most incendiary performances, had been profusely dispersed in the villages and cottages. Female adepts in the style of the adepts Necker and Stael made their appearance. The Countess of *Marchowich* distinguished herself by the zeal she showed in distributing the new Catechism. The fatal day was drawing near when a most singular circumstance led to the discovery of the whole plot.

While the ex-capuchin Mehalovich was out one day, a domestic playing with one of his fellow-servants, took into his head to put on the capuchin habit which his master had preserved among his clothes, when all on a sudden Mehalovich knocked at the house door. The servant, who did not understand the nature of the habit, could not get it off again, so sent his comrade to open the door, and hid himself under the bed. *Mehalovich* came in with *Hebenstreit* and *Hackel*; they thought themselves secure; the servant overheard their whole conversation; it related entirely to the conspiracy that was to break out in three days. Hebenstreit renewed the conspirator's oath on his sword; Mehalovich took five hundred thousand florins, which were hidden in a harpsichord, and gave them to him for the execution of the plan; and no sooner did they leave the room, than the servant got from under the bed, and discovered the whole plot to the Ministers of the State.

The councils were immediately called in consequence of so important a discovery, and the chief conspirators were arrested on the day preceding the intended explosion. Hebenstreit was hanged at Vienna; Mehalovich, with seven Hungarian gentlemen, his accomplices, were beheaded at Presburg; and many others were condemned to exile, or to perpetual imprisonment.

The King of Prussia had similar conspiracies to guard against at Berlin. The papers of *Leveller*-Leuchsering which had been seized had already warned William III of the conspiracy that was brewing in the Lodges; but in the month of November 1792, a new plot was contriving. The signal agreed upon for the general insurrection was, the setting fire to two houses in different quarters of the town. On the day appointed the two houses were really set on fire. The brethren expected that the trooops in garrison would be immediately sent, as was customary, to extinguish the flames, and keep order. While absent from their posts the rebels were to seize on them and let their banditti loose. Happily the Governor General Möllendorff had been informed of the plot. He commanded the troops to remain at their posts; the conspirators, finding their plans had been discovered, did not dare to show themselves. The incendiaries were arrested, the plot failed, and William III preserved his Crown.

Having acquired certain knowlege of the views of the conspirators, and of their connection with the French Jacobins, this Prince, as every reader would suppose, ought to have shewn more constancy in the cause of Royalty against Jacobinism. Court jealousies, and differing interests, that perpetually keep the cabinets of Vienna and Berlin at variance, may have led him to agree to a pacification with the sworn enemies of every power; but on the other hand it is difficult to account for the great sway which those very men must have had on his decisions, whose disorganizing principles he so much detested. The reader has seen the adepts of the modern *Spartacus* concealing themselves in the Lodges of Masonry; he has observed *Philo*-Knigge promising discoveries that would give the Sect sovereign sway over credulous minds. Unfortunately for Frederic William III he had become a member of one of those Lodges which the Illuminees, under the cloak of Rosicrucians, had converted into one of their theatres of imposture; and the following is an account given me by a learned Protestant Minister, who had had frequent conversations with his Prussian Majesty on the subject of Freemasonry. He informs me, that to divest his Majesty of any respect he might have for the Scripture, these Rosicrucians succeeded in making him believe that the Bible and Gospel of the Christians were deficient; that a far superior doctrine was to be found in the *sacred books of Enoch and of Seth*, supposed to be lost, but which they pretended to have exclusively in their possession. Had it been possible to undeceive the king, the demonstrations adduced by our learned correspondent must have done so, since he invited his Majesty to read those pretended books of *Enoch* and *Seth*, or those apocryphal rhapsodies which these impostors offered to him as so precious, so secret, and so rare, but which had long since been printed in *Fabricius's collection*. His Majesty seemed to be convinced of the imposture of these empirical mystifiers; but curiosity is weak, and the Rosicrucians regain their ascendancy under the pretence of apparitions. So notorious was the credulity of the Prussian Monarch on this score, that in 1792, at the fair of Leipsic, were sold waistcoats called the *Berlin Jesus waistcoats (Berlinische Jesus westen)*, in memory of the brethren having on a sudden announced the apparition of Christ; and the King asking how he was dressed, they answered, *in a scarlet waistcoat, with black facings and golden tresses*. If I am to credit what I have learnt through the same channel, William III deserved to be imposed upon in so humiliating a manner; for the great influence these impostors had acquired over his mind not only proceeded from their magic arts, but from their flattering his passions and propensity for the fair sex. They carried their impudence so far, as to tell him, that Christ *had granted him permission to have twelve wives at once.*

The most famous of his mistresses was a Madame de Reiz, afterwards created Countess of Lichtenau. Had the matters that appeared on her trial been made public, some light might have been thrown on her supposed understanding with the French jacobins, from whom she is said to have received rich presents, and with *Bischosswerder*, who is now occupied, as we are told, in very different projects. We might then have learned how to reconcile that real hatred which William had conceived for the Jacobins, and the personal courage he has shown in combating them, with the peace he made precisely at the time when his armies could most efficaciously have co-operated for their destruction. But his successor has thought proper to commit to the flames the minutes of this trial, saying, that he would not read them, lest *persons, who might still be useful to him*, should be implicated in these intrigues. Some princes might have thought it prudent to read them, that they might learn who were the persons that could still do them much mischief. Without pretending to comment on the destroying of this monument of history, we are happy to say that William IV has inherited from his predecessor all his hatred for the Sect, without any of his weaknesses. The Freemasons of Berlin went so far as to ask to have their Lodges confirmed by letters patent, but the King dismissed them, saying, that in showing such a marked favour to them, he would be wanting in his duty to his other subjects, and that they would find protetion as long as they did not trouble the public peace. The Masons, we may be sure, in return, promised to be most faithful subjects to his Majesty. They made similar promises during the reign of the late king, yet I have seen very honest Masons in London who were much alarmed at the language they heard in the Prussian Lodges, and that but a short time before the death of William III. By their account, the language of the Masons was as frantic to the full as that of the

Paris Jacobins: "When shall we be delivered from the tyrant? When shall we follow the example of our brethren of Paris? Is it not high time for us to show ourselves worthy of Equality and Liberty, and true Masons?" Such expressions, with many others far more offensive to the dignity and person of the king, were not in the mouths of some few brethren only; but whole Lodges were seized with the phrenzy, which raged most violently among the adepts who were connected with the French. Nor is it a trivial circumstance, or to be overlooked, that has taken place in the Lodge at Berlin calling itself *The Royal York*. Public fame has informed the world, that this Lodge has established within itself *a Directory, a Senate of Ancients, and a Senate of Youngers, modelled on the actual Government of France*. How far this revolution in the Lodge is to contribute towards, or denote the impatience with which the members thirst after the universal revolution which the Pentarques are endeavouring to operate, I shall not pretend to ascertain; but thus much I can positively assert, that the auxiliaries of the Paris brotherhood are not confined to the Lodges. They have their brethren, sent from Paris, in the Prussian armies. On the one hand, these soldiers are paid by his Prussian Majesty to maintain his throne; on the other, they are paid by the Pentarques to corrupt the Prussian regiments, and teach them to revolt against the throne. The generosity of the Jacobins is so great, that the wives of these disguised apostles are pensioned in France. Every one knows, that the arch conspirator Syeyes is gone to Berlin in a diplomatic character. Should his mission be ever accomplished, then will the historian have to explain conquests similar to those of Italy. Germany would certainly have long since fallen a prey to Illuminism had the plots formed met with success.

Tired of such partial treasons, that only threw a single town or a province into the hands of the enemy, the senate of the adepts, at that time holding its sittings at Vienna, had, as early as 1793, either digested a plan themselves, or received one, in thirty articles, that was to revolutionize the whole empire at the same instant.—Letters post-paid as far as Ægra were already dispatched for Gotha, Weimar, Dresden, and a hundred other towns, fixing the day of general insurrection for the first of November, inviting brethren and citizens to arm on that great day, though *it were only with knives*; to assemble in the squares of the towns, or in the fields without; to form into centuries and to elect chiefs; *to seize on the public revenue, on the arsenals, on the powder magazines, and on the members of government*. In compliance with the same plan, *a National Assembly was to rear its head in some town of the empire on the same day*, and the brethren in insurrection were to send their deputies to it. These letters were sent during the month of October; and happily for the state, a sufficient quantity of them were seized to counteract the effects of the conspiracy. The Sect consoled itself in the idea that ten years would not elapse, as Mauvillon had declared, before all Germany would be revolutionized. The adepts, indeed, are so very numerous, that it is almost incredible that the revolution has not already taken place; and the only way of accounting for it, is by considering the inert disposition of the people, who cannot be easily thrown into that strong effervescence necessary for an explosion.

The letters from that country complain bitterly of the progress of Illuminism. To give my reader the means of judging how it comes to pass, that princes who are the best acquainted with the views of the Sect continue to tolerate them, I will transcribe the following passage from the memorials which I have received from Germany, and which have been confirmed by several well-informed persons: "One of the Sovereigns of Germany who has the most wit, the Duke of Brunswick, has suffered, under the auspices of *Campe, Mauvillon,* and *Trapp,* three famous Illuminees, both his capital and his states to become the public school of irreligion and Jacobinism. This might lead us to believe, that the prince was himself tainted with those principles, but it would be calumny to suppose it, for he only tolerates *these rascals* that he may not fall a victim to their plots. *Supposing I was to send them away,* said he, *they would only go elsewhere and calumniate me. A league ought to be entered into by the German princes, to suffer them in no part of the empire.*"

Meanwhile, till such a league is agreed upon, there are other governments in that country that permit the last mysteries of Illuminism to be taught publicly. "At Jena in Saxony for example, a professor is permitted to teach publicly, that *governments are contrary to the laws of reason and of humanity*; and consequently that, in twenty, fifty, or a hundred years time, not a government will exist."[26]

To go still farther: few of the German princes will permit writers to combat either the Sect or its doctrines. A society of men of unblemished principles (if we may judge by their publication, the *Eudemonia* (right genius) had consecrated their labours in that journal to the unmasking of the intrigues, cunning, and principles, of the Illuminees. Not a single prince encourages this publication; several have proscribed it in their states, while the most jacobinical publications are allowed a free circulation. The Eudemonia has just been forbidden in the Austrian States, under the specious pretext, that its object and views are good, but that it makes principles known that are not sufficiently refuted. As a proof, however, that they were much better refuted than the Illuminees could wish, we need only observe, that the *Gazette Litteraire of Gotha,* the leading paper of the Sect, announced the prohibition before it was even known at Vienna. The reader will be less surprised at the artfulness of the pretext when he learns, that two of the *censors* who are to pronounce on the literary productions are the well known Illuminees *Sonnenfels* and *Retzer,* who, had it been for a journal of another stamp, would have reclaimed the liberty of the press in its favour.

We must now turn our attention to a new species of Jacobins who are making an amazing progress in Germany. These are the disciples of a Doctor KANT, who, rising from darkness, and from the chaos of his Categories, proceeds to reveal the mysteries of his Cosmopolitism. According to this system,—I. It *is melancholy* to be obliged to seek, *in the hopes of another world,* for the end and destiny of *the human species.*—II. It is not of man conducted by reason, as it is of brutes led by instinct. The former has each for his end the developement of all his faculties; while in the latter, the end is accomplished in each individual brute. Among men, on the contrary, the end is for the species, and not for the individual; for the life of man is too short to attain the perfection and the complete developement of his faculties. In the class of man, *all the individuals pass and perish; the species alone survives, and is alone immortal.*—III. With respect to man again, the end of the species cannot be accomplished; that is to say, his faculties can only be entirely developed *in the most perfect state of society.*—IV. That perfect state of society would be *a general confederacy* of the inhabitants of the earth, so united together, that dissentions, jealousies, ambition, or wars, would never be heard of.—V. Thousands and thousands of years may elapse before this happy period of perpetual peace may come; but, "whatever may be the idea conceived of the free exercise of our will, *it is nevertheless certain, that the apparent result of that volition, the actions of man, are, as well as all the other facts of nature, determined by general laws.*" This nature proceeds with a slow but certain step toward its object. Vices, virtues, sciences, the dissentions of mankind, are in her hands but the sure and infallible means by which she leads the human species from generation to generation to the most perfect state of civilization. Sooner or later the epoch of the general confederation, of universal peace, must come; nevertheless, even at that period, *the human species will have proceeded but half way toward its perfection.*[27]—I know not whether this doctrineer Kant will inform us in what the other half of the way toward perfection consists; but in the meantime his disciples, who are daily increasing, tell us, "that Europe must necessarily dissolve itself into as many republics as there are now monarchies; and then only will the human species show itself in all its strength and grandeur; then people incapable of governing will no longer be seen at the head of nations; *they will then rise to that high state of perfection at present attained by the French nation, where birth is nothing, but genius and talents every thing."*[28] Other adepts, however, perfectly understand what is alluded to by the other half way toward perfection; and these acknowledge man only to be in a state of perfection when he recognizes no other master but himself, no other law but his reason. In short, it is man according to the professor of *Jena*, it is the *Magus* of Weishaupt or of Babœuf.[29]

Notwithstanding the different methods of proceeding, it is easy to see that the system of *Kant*, at present Professor at *Konigsberg*, ultimately leads to the same end as that of *Weishaupt*, heretofore Professor at *Ingolstadt*. The same hatred for revelation is to be found in both, as well as the same spirit of impiety, which cannot brook the idea of a world to come, where all delusion must cease in the presence of the Creator, and where the end of man and of the human species will be procalimed at the tribunal of a remunerating and avenging God. *Kant* and *Weishaupt*, with similar pretensions to superior genius, are equally baffled in their attempts, falling into the most voluntarily absurd propositions, that leave the present generation no other consolation in its afflictions, than the empty Cosmopolites who, in thousands and thousands of years, are, as we are told, to inhabit this earth. In both we may observe that same hypocrisy pretending to great sensibility and virtue, pretending not to know, that every individual who shall be persuaded that he is not born for any fixed or personal end, will soon shape his conduct according to his views or to his pleasures, and will little regard the future Cosmopolites, their universal peace, or the happiness that is to be spread over the earth twenty or thirty ages after his death. The same inept fatalism is taught by them both, wishing to represent nature as acting exactly as it pleases, in spite of our volition, and prevailing over our passions by its *general laws*; and nevertheless represent mankind as slow in seconding the grand object of Nature, just as if we were free to accelerate or to retard its views, by our actions. The only difference that can be perceived between these two prototypes of German Jacobinism, is, that the one at Konigsberg envelopes his views in a pacific cant; while the other, in his mysteries, animates and infuriates his Epopts, teaching that the day is not far distant when the adepts are to resort to force, in order to crush and stifle every thing that should dare to resist them. But notwithstanding the pacific cant of the former, his doctrines also make his hearers thirst after that great day when the children of Equality and Liberty are to reign. His colleagues in the universities do not teach his principles with his coolness; the disciples become violent; the Jacobins smile; and as the system spreads, the offspring of both these teachers unite and form alliances in their tenebrous abodes. Under pretence of this perpetual peace that is to be enjoyed by future generations, they have begun by declaring a war of cannibals against the whole universe; nor is there to be found scarcely one of their offspring, that is not ready to betray his country, his laws, and his fellow-citizens, to erect that Cosmopolitan Empire announced by the Professor Kant, or to enthrone the *Man-king* of the modern *Spartacus*.

Such is the state of the Sect in Germany: It sways the Clubs, the Lodges, the Literary Societies, the *Dicasteres* or Offices of Government, and even Princes. It appears under variegated forms and names; but, however these may differ, it perpetually keeps that unhappy country in a state of crisis. Every throne is undermined by a volcano that menaces explosion whenever a favourable moment shall offer.

Why will not truth permit me to declare, that the conspiring Sect has respected that nation which, content with the wisdom, and living happy under the shield of its laws, must naturally have been adverse to, and constant in repelling the disorganizing plots and baneful mysteries of Illuminism? But have we not seen that Minister of Petkam, RONTGEN, sent to London under the protection of a great Prince? Nor is he the only apostle of Weishaupt that has crossed the seas in hopes of illuminizing England. The very name of *Xaverius Zwack* in these Memoirs recalled to the minds of many persons the stay which that famous adept of Illuminism made during a whole year at Oxford, just after his flight from Bavaria. The exactness of his description, taken from the Original Writings, left not the least shadow of doubt as to the person of the *Cato* of Illuminism. This has made people understand the real motives that induced this adept to make that famous town his habitation, though he pretended to have been attracted thither by the fame of its science. Neither the place nor the times, however, were propitious to his mission, nor to principles that entailed upon him the just contempt of the doctors. Mr. Hornsby, who had entrusted him with some discoveries in astronomy, will now understand how this adept could barefacedly publish them in Germany as the offspring of his own genius. This will also explain why the *Cato* of Illuminism, who was despised at the university, and nearly expelled, never returned, though he only pretended a short absence to the Continent. Other apostles have succeeded him in his mission; and in gratitude for the asylum which this nation has granted us, I must declare, that the missionaries of Weishaupt have not been foiled in all their attempts.

When Mr. Robison published his assertion, that certain Masonic Lodges had been tainted by the illuminizing brotherhood, patriotism naturally exclaimed that it was impossible. Men who have instituted themselves into a sort of tribunal of public opinion called upon this respectable writer to produce his proofs. I know not what the answer of Mr. Robison was; all that I know is, that he might have replied, "When persons who are entitled to question me shall do so, I will answer." To those who may wish to question me, I will say, that there are circumstances which may forbid me to answer; it is sufficient that those who watch for the safety of the nation should be informed of them, that they may take precautions to counteract the Sect; besides, are there not many historical truths, that cannot be proved in a court of justice?

I make these observations with the more assurance, as Government most certainly have the competent proofs in their hands, which their wisdom, nevertheless, has kept secret. I make them because Mr. Robison has spoken with sufficient clearness, in his Appendix and in his Notes, to show that he was but too well informed when he spoke of the intrusion of Illuminism into certain English and Scottish Lodges, without being obliged to particularize the Lodges. But he certainly acted prudently in not exposing himself to the fate of the celebrated Zimmerman, who, as all the world knows, fell, in similar circumstances, a victim to the Illuminee *Philo-Knigge*; not because he had accused him unjustly, but that legal evidence was wanting to prove that *Philo* and Knigge were names applicable to the same person; a fact now so clear both by his own works and those of the adepts. They who have thus attempted to brand Mr. Robison with the name of calumniator, would have done well to reflect on the many means employed by the Sect to influence such a judgement; that it is a standing law of the Sect, *that where an author of merit cannot be gained over, he is to be discredited by every means possible*; and certainly he has a glorious title to the hatred of the Sect. I willingly confess, that it would have given me great pleasure, had it been consonant with prudence, that Mr. Robison had published all his proofs, as I am persuaded that any of those persons who have been so hasty and intemperate in their judgements would have voted him thanks for the service he has rendered to his country, actuated as I suppose them to be with the same zeal for its happiness, but not equally informed as to the dangers with which it is menaced.

Notwithstanding the variance that is to be found between that respectable author and myself in some articles, (particularly on the Catholic religion,[30] and on the Jesuits, whom he might have represented in different colours, had he had, as we have, the whole history of their pretended Masonry before him, a mere fiction of the Illuminees to dupe the Masons and avert the attention of the public from the true conspirators); notwithstanding this variance, I shall never hesitate to acknowledge that he is entitled to the thanks of his fellow countrymen for having denounced a conspiracy that threatens this, as much as it does any other nation; I shall always bear willing testimony to the justice of his cause, to the ardour of his zeal, and to the uprightness of his intentions. Meanwhile, till he may judge it proper to publish his proofs on the Illuminism of certain English Masonic Lodges, I shall mention a few circumstances that have come to my knowledge.

To my certain knowledge, there are two men in England who have been tampered with by the Apostles of Illuminism. One of these, who belongs to the Navy, still preserves that honest indignation which must naturally arise in an upright heart at seeing itself so atrociously duped by an Insinuator who, under pretence of initiating him into the secrets of Masonry, was plunging him head foremost into Illuminism. The other, a man of great merit, who might have known more had he not discovered his real sentiments; but his letters bear testimony of the following particulars:

Of those books which show the multitude of Illuminized Lodges, there is one bearing the title of *Paragrafin*; and it is often put into the hands of certain candidates by the Insinuators. In this production we may see the travelling adept Zimmerman boasting of having illuminized Lodges in England, just as he had done in Italy and Hungary. In some of these Lodges the tenets of Illuminism were well received; but of five that have come to my correspondent's knowledge, two soon abandoned the mysteries of the modern *Spartacus*, the other three are not known to have rejected them.

Another apostle soon succeeded to Zimmerman; this was a Doctor *Ibiken*, an assumed name, perhaps, as it was customary with the travelling adepts to change their names according to circumstances. Whatever may have been the case, this *Ibiken*, an emissary of the Ecclectic Lodges of Illuminism, began by uniting with some Quakers. He was afterwards received into certain Lodges, and introduced some of the preparatory degrees. He even succeeded in completely illuminizing some of the duped brethren. He also boasted of his successes in Ireland and England. He would foretel to his English pupils, that a great revolution was about to be operated in the pitiful and miserable Masonry of their country. Those to whom this language was perfectly unintelligible at the time, have told me, that they have perfectly understood his meaning since they have perused my publication. They have lost sight of the Doctor, which was the natural consequence of his being admonished to depart with his mysteries by those who watch over the public safety.

Another emissary soon after appeared, and coming from America under the name of *Reginhard*, declared himself an Alsacian, and formerly an Almoner in the French navy. He expected to be well received by certain English Lodges in correspondence with those he had just left at Boston, and which, according to his account, had made a surprizing progress since they had fraternized with the brethren that had gone from France to America. This *Reginhard* did not appear so zealous as the other apostles; he even signified his disgust with a mission that so little became his station in life. It was through him more particularly that my correspondent became acquainted with the existence of Illuminism on the banks of the Thames.

This is certainly enough to prove, that the illuminization of England was not neglected by the conspiring brethren. I will say more, that notwithstanding the honourable exception I have made in favour of the English Lodges, I am no longer surprized to hear of Illuminism being well received by certain Lodges. And I here think it necessary to repeat, that when I made the exception, I only meant to speak of what is called the *National Masonry, restricted to the first three degrees*. I should have been more circumspect in my exception, had I known of a pamphlet entitled, FREEMASONRY: *A Word to the Wise*. Here, in vindication of the Grand Lodge of England, I see the most violent complaints preferred against the introduction of a variety of degrees, of which, in a political point of view, it is certainly the duty of a well-ordered government to repress the vice and immorality; the *impiety* of the Rosicrucians is particularly complained of (page 9); and I think that in the course of these Memoirs I have pretty clearly proved, that from the profound Rosicrucian to the mysteries of Weishaupt there is but a short step.

There is also extant another work, printed *fifty* years ago, *On the Origin and Doctrine of Freemasons*. This work would have been of the greatest use to me had it fallen into my hands a little sooner. Let me no longer be accused of having been the first to reveal, that an impious and disorganizing *Equality and Liberty* were the grand secret of the Occult Lodges. The author of this work was as positive in this assertion as myself, and at that time clearly demonstrated it, by following step by step the Scotch degrees of Masonry as they existed in those days. Time may have changed certain forms; but all the numerous degrees styled *philosophical* have not been able to add an iota to the systems at that time followed in the Lodges of the *Scotch Architects*. That species of Masons is as bad as the Illuminees. It can scarcely be conceived with what art they proceed. As they are still extant in Great Britain, it is not too late to point the attention of the ruling powers toward them. Let us proceed at once to their last mysteries.

"When a candidate presents himself to be received a *Scotch Architect*, the tyler asks him, whether he has a vocation for *Liberty, Equality, Obedience, Courage,* and *Constancy.*" When the candidate has answered *yes*, he is introduced within the interior of the Lodge. Here it is no longer the representation of the Temple of Solomon, but of five animals, the *Fox*, the *Monkey*, the *Lion*, the *Pelican*, and the *Dove*. The *Signs*, and the word *Adonai*, being given to the candidate, the orator begins an enigmatical discourse, of which the following is a part: "*Craftiness, Dissimulation, Courage, Love, Sweetness;* Cunning, imitation, fury, piety, tranquillity; mischief, mimickry, cruelty, goodness, and friendship, are all one and the same thing, and are generated in the same thing. They seduce, inspire joy, give rise to sorrow, procure advantage and serene days. They are five in number, and still they are but one. Soon–soon—soon–by him that was, is now, and ever shall be, &c. &c."

"The remainder of the discourse (says my author) is in the same strain. However obscure these things may appear, they are nevertheless clear as day, if attention be paid to the figures that denote the characters of the Freemasons. The *craftiness of the Fox* denotes the art with which the Order hides its object. The *imitation of the Monkey* typifies that suppleness of mind, that address with which the Masons can accommodate themselves to the various talents and tastes of the candidates. The *Lion* denotes the strength and courage of those who compose the society. The *Pelican* is the emblem of the tenderness that reigns among the brethren.—The peaceable demeanor of the *Dove* is representative of *the peace of the golden age*, or of those serene days that Freemasons promise to the universe."

The author from whom we make these extracts lived for a long time with Masons of this species. He was often present at their Lodges and councils; he attended at their deliberations when contriving the means of accomplishing their plans. He then continues to speak of the initiation of a Scotch candidate: "There is no rule which ordains, that the object of the Society should be made known to him in clear terms; but only in terms that would be insufficient to make him wholly understand the morality and polity that are universally received. On the night of his reception they simply tell him, that *Equality* and *Liberty* among the brethren is the sole object of the Society.—But should the *new Architect* show signs of a perfect preparedness for the ultimate mystery of the Society, *he is then let into the secret, or rather informed of the grand objecty of the Society, which is to reduce* ALL MEN *to a reciprocal* EQUALITY, *and to reinstate mankind in its natural* LIBERTY. In short, after a few days meeting, they openly declare, that the expression of *establishing Equality* among men and of reinstating mankind *in their natural libery, indistinctly comprehends all persons of whatever quality or station they may be, without excepting magistrates, great, or small.*"[31]

The ceremonies and catechism of this degree perfectly coincide with these explanations. In short, every thing so clearly demonstrates *Equality and Liberty* to be the ultimate object of their mysteries, that the author attributes the origin, or at least the restoration, of Masonry to Cromwell and his Independents. The author would have simply attributed the restoration to him, had he been acquainted with the manuscript of Oxford. Inferences of the utmost importance may be drawn from this work, both as to the history of Freemasonry and the interests of Governments. It is easily seen at present, that the disorganizing mysteries of the occult Lodges are at least anterior to the reign of the French Sophisters. These may have new-modelled them after their fashion, and multiplied and varied the degrees; but their principles had been received in the Lodges long before Voltaire wrote. The *Knights Kadosch* was already extant in the *Scotch Architect*. When the latter is asked in his catechism, what he is called, he answers *cunning* and *simple*; the *Kadosch* may answer *bold* and *impatient*. The difference lies in the character, and not in the systems. This degree of *Scotch Architect* also explains whence the pre-eminence of the Scotch Lodges arises, and why the Lodges of other countries are so desirous of corresponding with the mother Lodge called the Lodge *Heredom of Kilwinning*, in Scotland. It is there that the famous *Architects* of *Equality* and *Liberty* are supposed to be the guardians of the last mysteries. It was with this Lodge also, that a number of French Lodges at Marseilles, Avignon, Lyons, Rouen, &c. &c. would be affiliated, notwithstanding the influence of the *Grand Orient* of Paris.[32]

In short, the discovery of this degree of *Grand Architect* is of importance to Governments in general, and particularly to that of England; for it shows the dangers to which a state is exposed where, in the midst of those Brethren who dedicate themselves to an innocent Equality, exist a number sufficient to transmit the Grand Mysteries of the Sect.

In spite of all the secrecy observed by this species of adept, who is there that can view their very existence in any other light than as a perpetual conspiracy against the state? How then can we be surprised if the Illuminees found persons in these countries willing to fraternize with them, and to combine their plots with those of the missionaries? However pure the generality of the English Lodges may be, is not this enough to show that the most disastrous plots may suddenly burst from the Lodges; and that the presence of virtuous men may only serve as a cloak to the designs of the wicked?—Do not let me be told, that the Good counteract the evil intentions of the Wicked; for the latter can find means of meeting unknown to the former, though the same Lodge may be an asylum for them both. There are Lodges now extant, that (to use the expression of a brother who frequented them a few months since) would not admit *a single Aristocrat*. My reader must understand such language? There are Lodges the entries to which are perfect labyrinths. The adepts do not go out by the same house as they entered; and, the more completely to baffle the vigilance of the constituted authorities, they have changed their dresses.

But let us for an instant suppose, that the Sect could make no impression on the English Lodges, we know that *Chauvelin* and *Vandernoot*, on quitting London, left their emisssaries behind; public danger is best probed by private facts; and the reader will not be surprised when he sees me descend to the following particulars relative to the emissaries of Jacobinism in England.

Having been honoured with the acquaintance of Mr. Burke, I introduced to him a gentleman who wished to consult him with respect to a letter written to Manuel, who at that time governed the *Commune* of Paris, in conjunction with *Tallien*, the sanguinary butcher of the bloody September. This was in the first year of my emigration. The letter had been written for a French nobleman, who, wishing to return to Paris, thought it might be advantageous to get a letter of recommendation to Manuel from a Jacobin then resident in London. This nobleman's wife suspected some treachery, and opened the letter. The epistle really began with a sort of recommendation, but ended with saying, "this nobleman is, after all, a rank aristocrat, who ought to be got rid of by the pikes or the guillotine, that he may not return any more to London." In the body of the letter an account was given to Manuel of the state of the brethren in London. Among other things it stated, that *five hundred* persons were present at their last meeting; that they were ardent in the cause; that their numbers daily increased, and that every thing denoted the best dispositions for hoisting the revolutionary standard. This letter was immediately laid before the ministry.

Notwithstanding every method was adopted that wisdom could suggest, the partizans of the Sect increased, instead of diminishing; and in a short time there were at least *fifteen hundred* conspirators in London, worthy of being marshalled by *Jourdan Coup-tête*. There were at the same time in London two men who had been educated in all the arts of the police of Paris, and they were ordered to enquire into the state of the foreigners, and to distinguish the real emigrants from the new comers. It was soon discovered, that a banditti of all nations, criminals from the *Bicetre*, from the *gallies*, and who had escaped the gallows; the chosen bands, in short, of Necker, Orleans, and Mirabeau, had been sent into England by their successors of the great club, to effect a similar revolution. It was in consequence of this that the Alien Bill was enacted.

But the Sect is relentless; it roars at the very idea of the obstacles it has met with in England. At London, at Edinburgh, at Dublin, it has its national brethren, its conspiring and *Corresponding Societies*. In London we see the duped brethren of the highest aristocracy proclaiming the *sovereignty of the people* at their revels; while, in the hidden retreat of their secret societies, other brethren are plotting how to put the fortunes of the aristocratic dupes, of the banker, and of the merchant, in requisition for the use of that *sovereign people*; in those same recesses, under pretence of *Reform*, do they wish to erect on the ruins of the British constitution, the reveries of a Paine, a Syeyes, or of the Pentarques; they wish to plant that tree of Equality and Liberty whose nourishment is gore and pillage, whose fruit is murder, misery, and exile. Others are training their deluded followers to assassination, and are forging pikes—Yes, the scourge has been wafted across the ocean with all its plots; the adepts have not forgotten the land of their ancestors, the Puritans, Anabaptists, and Independants. They have discovered their progenitors in those same dens to which Cromwell had confined them, after having, through their means, dethroned and murdered his king, dissolved the parliament, and seduced the nation to his yoke. The brethren of Avignon recognized the Illuminees of Swedenborg as their parent Sect; neither were they unmindful of the embassy sent them by the Lodge of Hampstead. Under the auspices of *De Mainauduc*, they have seen their disciples thirsting after that *celestial Jerusalem*, that *purifying fire* (for these are the expressions I have heard them make use of) that was to kindle into a general conflagration throughout the earth by means of the French revolution—and thus was Jacobin Equality and Liberty to be universally triumphant even in the streets of London.

But what a concatenation of conspiracies will the historian find when he shall turn to the archives of those societies styling themselves of *Constitutional Information* or *Corresponding*. Here, however, Justice and the Senate have interposed; they have torn away the mask, and behold the brethren of *Edinburgh* bound in the same plots and machinations as those of *Dublin*, of *London*, of *Sheffield*, of *Manchester*, of *Stockport*, of *Leicester*, and of many other towns, all uniting in their wishes, invitations, and addresses to the Jacobin Legislators.[33] The Mother Society at once demonstrates all the arts of the *Secret Committees of the Grand Orient* under Philip of Orleans; the deep cunning of the *Bavarian Areopage* under Weishaupt; and the profligate means of seduction of *Holbach's Club* under D'Alembert. All these they combine in hopes of hurrying away a generous nation into the sink of impiety, and thence to rebellion; they combine, in hopes of uniting the councils and the efforts of the dispersed brethren in the cause of revolution. Subscriptions are raised in Great Britain and Ireland, as they were in France, to print Paine's Code of Rebellion, and circulate it from the town to the village, and even in the very cottage.[34] Others of the brethren are distributing at their own expence all the poisons of infidelity, nor do they blush to go and ask subscriptions from house to house for the reprinting of the most profligate and impious productions of Voltaire, Diderot, Boulanger, La Metherie, and of other Deists or Atheists of the age, and this under the specious pretence of *enlightening ignorance*, and how?, by putting all the blasphemies of the Sophister into the hands of the people.

The brethren of Edinburgh, like those of Berlin, were not to be contented with the mere arts of seduction. One might be led to think that the adepts *Watt* and *Downie* had received their instructions from the Prussian Areopage. Notwithstanding the immense distance that divides Edinburgh from Berlin, they adopted precisely the same plan to draw off the attention of the troops by means of the burning of some house, and while the soldiery should be occupied with extinguishing the fire to fall on them, and in the midst of this popular commotion to proclaim the Jacobin Code. In London, have we not seen regicides? At Paris, Lewis XVI, captive in his capital, was dragged to the guillotine. At Ublingen, Lewis XVIII, when a fugitive, was wounded in the head by a ball. In London, was George III in the midst of the acclamations of his subjects, aimed at by the regicide crew; and if Heaven averted the ball, is the Sect less treacherous or less abominable, because it did not succeed in its foul attempt? At length, disdaining obscure crimes, and aiming at the annihilation of the Throne, of the Parliament, and of the whole British Constitution, they attempt to seduce the legions of the empire from their allegiance by means of the most inflammatory hand-bills; they would persuade gallant troops to shake off discipline and butcher their officers, as had been done in France. Emissaries found their way into the fleets; and the sailors were for a time deluded by the sophisms of those seducers, who wished to pervert the bold opponents of the Jacobins on the ocean, into the treacherous abettors of those same Jacobins that dare not face an honest tar. In Ireland, they assume another form; independence in church and state is held out to a deluded people by the emissaries of those who have obliterated every worship and every law in France, in Corsica, in Belgium, in Savoy, in Holland, in Italy, to subject the miserable inhabitants of those once flourishing countries to the tyranny of the Pentarques. In that unfortunate country all the arts of seduction have been played off that Illuminism could invent, and its perjuries have raged to a frightful excess. There did the legions of the Sect, conceiving themselves powerful in their numbers, sally forth from their lurking places. It was no longer a partial treason to be punished; the force of armies were necessary to crush whole legions of rebels who were daily expecting succour from a foreign foe.

But, Praise be to God on high, who in his mercy has counteracted the malice of such plots, of such seditions: Praise be to the all-powerful God, who has preserved this state from the machinations of its enemies!—May the Historian, after having traced the origin, the code, the re-union, the attempts, and the successes of such numerous conspiring Sects, against God and his Son, against thrones and kings, against society and its laws, repose himself, and complacently view the happiness of these Isles, when he comes to treat of the land that has proved an asylum to so many unfortunate victims! May he triumphantly say, "There it was that the surges of insurrection were dashed back upon itself, the attempts of Jacobinism were as vain as the efforts of its fleets."—Happy shall we be, if, by entering into this disquisition on the fury of Jacobinism, we shall have contributed to awaken the attention of nations to the true causes of all their misfortunes and revolutionary disasters! Thrice happy shall we be, if we shall have succeeded in guarding this nation against the dangers with which it is threatened; a nation to which the world looks up for its safety; a nation which, in its beneficence, is become our adoptive country. May it ever behold us offering up our prayers to heaven for the preservation of its king and for its prosperity, with all that affection and zeal that nature inspires for one's native soil!

To presume that we have fulfilled our task in such a manner as not to stand in need of the indulgence of our readers, would be impertinent. We ingenuously confess the inferiority of our talents, and the many imperfections we are conscious must exist in Memoirs of such high importance to the public cause. But with confidence we assert, that we have never swerved from truth. It has been our constant and only guide in pointing out the causes of the revolution, it shall continue to be so in treating of such means and drawing such conclusions as must necessarily follow from the facts demonstrated in the course of these Memoirs.

1. See Hoffman's Avis Important, Vol. I. Sect. XIX.
2. This work alone might suffice to prove, that if *Philo*-Knigge did really abandon the Order of the Illuminees, he continued at least to propagate their principles. Should the reader wish for a more striking proof, he will find it in the historical Eulogium upon him, written by the Jacobin *George Frederic Rebmann*, who also wrote the Eulogy of Robespierre. (*See his Schildvachte, Vol. I. Art.* KNIGGE, *and* FRANCE, *page 89).*
3. With respect to the 30,000,000, see Dumourier's Memoirs; and for the 21,000,0000 that are included in the accounts of this year, the use to which they were put, was betrayed by one of those deputies whom the Pentarques wished to banish to Cayenne.
4. See Hoffman Avis Important, Sect. XV.
5. Custine's Memoirs, Vol. I. Page 46, 47.
6. Ibid. Vol. I. Page 92, and Desodoard's History of the French Revolution, Vol. I. Book II. No. 24.
7. Appendix to the Ultimate Fate of Masonry, page 17 and Memoirs.
8. Memoirs on Mayence.
9. Original Writings, and Philo's Report.
10. Extract of a Secret Memorial, written a few months before the invasion of Holland.
11. Extract of a Secret Memorial.
12. Just as this sheet was going to the press a publication, entilted *Les Nouveaux Interets de l'Europe,* fell into my hands, and the following passage appeared to me so very applicable to our subject, that I have extracted it: "The Emperor has been blamed for signing the preliminaries of Leoben, on the 18th of April 1798. This certainly appears to have been done precipitately; but are those who blame him acquainted with the reasons that induced him to take that step? The Emperor had been informed by *his Brother, the Archduke Charles, of the bad disposition of a great part of the officers of his army of Italy. He knew that both at Verona and Padua they affected to imitate the French in their discourse, manners, and sentiments; it seemed as if they needed but the tri-coloured cockade to make the semblance complete. He was aware that they fled in the most critical moment of an action; so that, in spite of excellent generals, of a well-appointed staff, and of the bravest men, he was always obliged to retire.* He may perhaps have conceived that he was betrayed by these same officers; for it is well known, that Buonaparte, in an unguarded moment, declared, *that the Austrian army cost him more than his own."* TRANS.
13. When the Author published his First Volume, or Antichristian Conspiracy, in the beginning of 1797, and positively declared, "*the total overthrow of Christianity"* to be "the object of the Sect," his assertion was much cavilled at by those who were eager that this nation should not give credit to an author who was about to lay open the tenebrous ramifications of this universal conspiracy; others again were made to believe, that the Sect only aimed at reforming what they chose to style the errors of the Church of Rome. I here call my reader's attention to an event that has just taken place, and he may then judge whether the author was correct when he said, *that the total overthrow of Christianity* was the object of the Sect. In the *Propagateur 6 Brumaire, Year* 7 (or 15th Oct. 1798), we read, "The following is the distribution of the edifices (of worship) for the use of the citizens of Paris, as determined by the central administration of the Seine." Paris is divided into twelve Wards, in leiu of parishes, each having the following churches annexed to them, and which are in future to be called *Temples:* Ist Ward—The church of St. Philip du Roule *consecrated to concord.* II.

The church of St. Roche *to Genius.* III. St. Eustache *to Agriculture.* IV. St. Germain-L'Auxerrois *to Gratitude.* V. St. Laurence *to old age.* VI. St. Nicolas in the Fields *to Hymen.* VII. St. Merry *to Commerce.* VIII. St. Margaret *to* EQUALITY *and* LIBERTY. IX. St. Gervais *to Youth.* X. St. Thomas of Aquin as *to Peace.* XI. St.Sulpice *to Victory.* XII. St. James-du-haut-pas *to Benevolence,* St. Medard *to Labour,* and St. Stephen on the Mount *to filial Piety.*" This needs no comment, when in the hands of a Christian reader. TRANS.

14. Should the historian of the assassination of Gustavus of Sweden not be a sufficient voucher for the existence of this tribunal, (*Sect. IV*) it is, however, an undoubted fact, that the Sect had most powerful advocates at Rome; for the Nuncio at Avignon, having ordered the Illuminee *Pernetti* and his adepts to leave the country in the space of one month, they procured from Rome a counter-order (real or forged) permitting them to stay. This business was followed up at Rome by the arrestation of an adept, which threw the adepts of Avignon into fears that were only removed by the revolution.

15. See Irish Report, No. XIV.—At Quebec, July 7, 1797, a man of the name of *David McLean* was tried and condemned to suffer on the 21st of the same month, being convicted of having come into Canada, under the disguise of a merchant, with a view of raising the people against the Government, and to deliver over the colony to the French. He had taken all the necessary steps; the oath of secrecy, pikes, and other arms, were to be delivered to the people. The brethren at Montreal and Quebec were by the next spring to prepare the way for an army of 10,000 men that was to be brought over in a French fleet, and attack both these towns at the same time. Mr. Adet, the French Minister at Philadelphia, was implicated in it; thus do the Pentarques convert their embassadors into the ringleaders of the conspiring bands wherever they are received; this may be said to be one of the marking features of Jacobinism.

16. Private Notes on Switzerland.

17. See the History of this Revolution by Mallet du Pan.

18. Knigge's apostles in Courl and Livonia had, doubtless, extended their mission; and a Russian gentleman informed me, that one of the great adepts presided over an academy at Moscow where the young Nobility were educated. Every thing seemed to denote an excellent school, when by degrees it was observed, that the illuminized Rights of Man was the ground-work of the secret lessons of this great teacher. They were obliged to dismiss him, as the only means of restoring his pupils to the true principles of religion and society.

19. Extract from a Memorial on Russia.

20. June 1791.

21. Important notice by Hoffman, Vol. I. sect. 19.

22. Hoffman's Letter in the Eudemonia, Vol. VI. No. 2.

23. Important notice by Hoffman.

24. Travels of two Frenchmen in the North, Vol. V. ch. 12.

25. So late as February last (1798) the magistrates of Jena were obliged to punish about a dozen scholars, who, formed into an association calling themselves *Amicists,* were under the direction of the adepts. To prepare these youths for the mysteries of Illuminism, their secret superiors represented the oath appropriated to this association as the most sacred engagement that could be taken, and the least violation of it as

being immediately followed by the most terrible punishments.—They were then questioned, whether they were sufficiently enlightened to believe that they could, *without scruple*, break the oath which they had sworn to the superior of the college, never to engage in any secret society;—whether they believed themselves sufficiently virtuous to accuse themselves alone, and no other person, in case the magistrates should punish them for a breach of that oath;—whether they thought themselves sufficiently courageous to continue in the association, though they should be compelled to abjure it.—The Illuminee who had questioned them, if satisfied with their answers, gave them the Code of the *Amicists*, and therein they learned that they and their associates formed *a state within the state*; that they had *laws of their own* according to which they judged of *affairs that were beyond their sphere*; and this required the most profound secrecy; that should several of them hereafter meet in the same town, they should establish a lodge, and do all that lay in their power to propagate the society; that if they were perchance to change their place of habitation (which should be only done in some extraordinary case), they should then correspond with their own lodge, while the secretary was to hold correspondence with the other lodges, making his return of the name, quality, and country of every new candidate; that they would obey the superiors of the Order, succour their brethren, and procure advancement for them; in short, they *were to be ready to sacrifice their lives and fortunes for the Order*.

Several of these young *Amicists*, which of all the different associations was supposed to be the most innocent, refused to give the list of the brethren, lest they might be inculpated. They, however, declared that the Order comprehended many *men of quality and of high honour, magistrates and persons in office*. (See the Minutes of the Judgment; or the Staats und gelehrte zeitung *of Hamburg*, No. 45, 13 of March.)

Supposing that the reader may wish to know in what state young men came from these Lodges and Colleges, I will here quote an example from the notes I have received from Germany. "At the time I am writing this (July 13th 1794) at the Baths, four leagues from Hanover, there resides here a young man who arrived a few days since from the university of Jena, where he was educated. It is the reigning Count Plattenberg, one of the richest noblemen of Germany, aged 24, of Catholic parents, and a nephew of Prince Kaunitz, the minister. In consequence of the principles imbibed by this young Count at the university of Jena, he dresses in the complete style of a democrat, and affects the uncouthness of their manners.—He would have his servant sit next to him at the *table d'hote*, but it was not permitted. This young *Egalité* goes about, singing the *Ca-ira* and the *Marseillois Hymn*, with other youths whom he gathers together. Don't let this be taken in the light *of an anecdote relating to a thoughtless individual. His folly is the reigning folly of students in all the universities of Germany; and this folly is the produce of those doctrines taught by the professors, while governments pay no attention to them.*"

The same notes (and they are written by a Protestant) represent the *university of Halle* in Saxony, where the greater part of the King of Prussia's subjects go to finish their educations, as in a state similar to that of Jena. In April 1794 the chiefs of the commission of religion of Berlin, *MM. Hermes & Hilmer*, went by order of the King of Prussia, to visit the Lutheran college at Halle, and they disapproved of many things that were going on. The students received them with the cry of *Pereant* (let them perish), and obliged them to seek their safety in flight. Their ministers of religion are exposed to similar insults. Dogs are set at them when preaching, and indecencies take place in the churches that would not be suffered in the streets. "The *Illuminees themselves publish these abominations*, that their pupils the *Amicists* may be induced to act in a similar manner." Such is the education of youth where the Sect predominates.

26. Memoirs on Jacobinism in Germany. Anno 1794.
27. Plan of a General History in a Cosmopolitical View, by Kant. See The *Spectateur du Nord*, April 1798.
28. Memoirs of the State of Jacobinism in Germany.
29. I was not put to the trouble of reading Doctor Kant's works in German. Mr. *Nitsch* has published a sort of analysis of them in English. Those who might tremble at the idea of bewildering themselves in his chaos of Categories may read the account given of them in the British Critic, August 1796; and the reader may easily judge of the absurdity of the argument which the Prussian Doctor heaps up against the very possibility of revelation. A Doctor *Willich* has lately shown himself a rival of Nitsch in proclaiming the glorious feats of this professor of darkness. I have perused the analysis that Dr. Willich has given us, and the praises bellowed *on the project of a perpetual peace*. I could not understand why he would only give the title of the work that relates chiefly to that point, I mean of that very treatise whence Doctor Kant's principles on Cosmopolitism have been extracted. Was the disciple afraid that it would have exposed the doctrines of his master too much, and opened the eyes of the English reader on this *plan of perpetual peace*, and on the drift of his whole system of Cosmopolitism?
30. I do not here pretend to refute the religious prejudices of certain writers against the Catholics: But what has the French Revolution to do with confession, with monastic vows, with indulgencies, or the jurisdiction purely spiritual of the Pope, and articles of such a nature? The proof that these objects were far from contributing to the Revolution is, that the Jacobins spare no pains to destroy them. In a book combating the Jacobins, what can induce a writer to vent his spleen against the tenets of a Catholic? I might say to many writers who have been guilty of this most extraordinary imprudence, Begin at least, gentlemen, by making yourselves acquainted with our tenets, and then see whether we are able to defend them. To others I would say, For God's sake let us expose our belief ourselves, let us say what we do and what we do not believe. The defence you may with the best intentions set up for us, may be more hurtful than beneficial to our cause. Mr. Robison, no doubt, thought that he was speaking in favour of the church of France, when he said, that that church had long since established its independence of the Court of Rome. If by the Court of Rome he means the temporal dominion of the Pope, the French had no great trouble in establishing such an independence, as it never recognized any such dominion; if he means the purely spiritual jurisdiction of the Pope, neither our Catholic bishops, Clergy, nor Laity, ever wished to throw it off. They all continue to believe what they always have believed, that the Pope, as successor of St. Peter, has the jurisdiction as first pastor over the Church of France, as he has over all others. Every one knows, that this jurisdiction of the sovereign Pontiff is held in our faith as an essential point of the hierarchy established by Christ; but every one also knows, that the jurisdiction of the Pope, as well as that of all Bishops, is not of this world; that it does not militate in any way with the duties we owe to our sovereigns; that it can never

absolve us from the fidelity and submission which we owe to the laws of the State. I, therefore, here protest against all those who may choose to interpret the esteem I have declared to entertain for Mr. Robison's work as alluding to those parts of it that are absolutely contrary to my faith. On this occasion also I beg to observe, that in the case of the present Revolution both Protestants and Catholics should unite, and lay aside their prejudices against each other, to combat the impiety of the Jacobins, as their aim is to annihilate the religions of both. Beside, what party has a right to boast, when the Revolution is considered; *Spartacus*-Weishaupt and *Cato*-Zwack were two apostate Catholics—*Philo*-Knigge and *Lucian*-Nicolai two apostate Protestants—Thomas Paine an apostate Anglican. In France, the Catholic citizens of Paris, the Protestant citizens of Nismes; in Ireland, large portions of a Catholic populace organized into a revolutionary army under Protestant chiefs. In Germany, the Illuminees take their origin in a Catholic University, and all the Lutheran Universities are full of Illuminizing Professors. Such considerations as these should certainly put an end to reproach on either side. I must confess, that the Lutherans and Calvinists with whom I correspond in Germany are much more candid; they spare neither side, and are the first to point out those of their own persuasion who are tainted with Illuminism. They behold the Jacobins as enemies to every religion; and when jacobinism is in question, they wisely confess the necessity of uniting all parties to crush the hydra.

31. Of the Origin of the Freemasons, degree of Architect.
32. I have in my possession, the original of the patents empowering a Brother mason to erect Lodges under the direction of that of Rouen. A Provincial holds his residence at this latter place, and is entrusted with the power of judging the lawsuits or dissensions that may arise within the province; but when any thing of great consequence has happened, it is referred to the Lodge of *Heredom* for judgment. Had *Joseph II* seen this, he might well have called it an *imperium in imperio*, or *an empire throughout* ALL *empires*. The reader will remark, that the brethren say, *Heredom* (Harodim), is a Hebrew word signifying *chiefs* or *governors*. It is also to be remembered, that there is another degree of *Grand Architect* entirely different from that which I have just described. The multiplicity of these degrees only serve the better to hide their object.
33. I have annexed a more extensive application of these Memoirs to Ireland and Great Britain at the end of the fourth Volume. [Because of its length, that application is not reprinted here. Editor.] Let me on this occasion beg and beseech every Magistrate and every Clergyman, whose province it is more particularly to instruct and guide the people at large, and for whom this work is more peculiarly adapted, to read once more and with attention the Reports of the English House of Commons made in 1794. After having perused these Memoirs, they will view them in a very different light from what they formerly did. *Trans.*
34. Thousands of that abominable pamphlet were sent out to the British establishments in the East Indies. *Trans.*

CONCLUSION

WHAT a painful and disgusting course have I at length terminated! Wandering through those subterraneous haunts where, in the shades of darkness, conspirators were plotting against all religion and society, I have frequently shuddered with horror, and felt my courage sinking! Fired with indignation at the sight of such iniquity, such a concatenation of crimes still contriving, how often have I said to myself, Leave this abyss of wickedness, fly the abodes of these vile and monstrous conspirators; it may be better even to fall their victim than to sully one's mind with the recollection of such villany, treason, and impiety, or to be the accuser to posterity of the age in which we live.—But have I not contemporaries to be saved? There still exist nations that have not bent beneath the Jacobin yoke; my fellow-countrymen may, perhaps, be induced to shake off that yoke, when they are made acquainted with the unparalleled plots and artifices contrived for their seduction. And ought not posterity to be informed to what an extent this disastrous Sect raged in our days, that it may guard against a renewal of similar horrors? Such thoughts inspired me with courage; they have carried me through this disgusting task; they were my support when overpowered with the odious sight of legions of conspirators conjuring up every hellish art to heap misery on the inhabitants of the earth: moreover the most convincing proofs have never been wanting.

But can it be possible that my endeavours should prove fruitless? if so, alas! let these pages be rent asunder; commit to the flames these Memoirs which bear testimony of such a multitude of hideous plots that threatened society. Kings, Pontiffs, Magistrates, Princes, and Citizens of every class, if it be true, that I have attempted in vain to dissipate the fatal illusion; if it be true, that the pestiferous blast of Jacobinism has deadened your senses, and plunged your souls into lethargy; if it be true, that the torpor of indolence has rendered you callous to your own dangers, as well as those that threaten your children, your country, your religion, and your laws; if you are incapable of the least effort, of the smallest sacrifice for your own safety and for that of the public; if the world be peopled only by dastards, who are ready to submit their necks to the Jacobin yoke, let them be carried into bondage, let them be slaves to Jacobins and to their principles; may their fortunes fall a prey to brigands; may their temples, thrones, governments, palaces, and habitations, fall beneath the blows of the relentless Sect! When you tear these pages, banish from your mind all presage of disasters; pass your days in joy, festivity, and merriment, till the knell of revolution shall sound and startle ye from your lethargy. The Jacobins will take upon themselves the care of hastening the fatal hour. To announce it beforehand to such torpid souls would be to anticipate their sufferings; no, sleep the sleep of death; may your ears be deaf to the sound of those chains that are forging for you; approach not where truth may undeceive you; no, follow in the retinue of some false prophet that may beguile you.

But should there be found men whose manly courage would be fired with zeal for the public cause at the very recital of such monstrous combinations against church and state; for them I write; it is on them that I call when I say, that notwithstanding all the artifices of the various Sects, and the tremendous power which Jacobinism has already acquired, Europe is not yet subjected to them. It is yet possible to crush that Sect which has sworn to crush your God, plunder your country, and annihilate society.—Your country and yourselves may still be saved. But in the war that the Sect is waging against you, as well as in all other wars, the first requisite for working your safety is the perfect conviction of your danger, and an accurate knowledge of the enemy, of his plans, and of his means. It was not unintentionally that I heaped proof upon proof to demonstrate that Jacobinism was a coalition of the *Sophisters of Impiety* swearing to crush the God of the Gospel; of the *Sophisters of Rebellion* swearing to overturn the thrones of kings; and of the Sophisters of Anarchy conspiring not only against the altar and the throne, but swearing to annihilate all laws, property, and society. I was certain that my readers would neglect all means of self-preservation so long as they were not convinced of their danger. Should the proofs that I have adduced still leave them in doubt as to the reality of the plots of the Sect, I shall have lost my labour; I can but weep over their blindness; they will have already fallen into that state of apathy into which the Sect wishes to plunge them. The less credit my readers shall give to the reality of their plots, the more certain will the conspirators be of success. If then I farther insist, let my instances meet with a candid reception; for, reader, it is your safety and that of the public weal that actuates me.

Let us then suppose, for example, that a person comes to warn you, that you are surrounded by men who, under the cloak of friendship, are only waiting for a favourable moment to execute an old plan which they have contrived of robbing you of your money and property, of firing your habitation, nay farther, perhaps, of butchering your wife, your children, your relations; supposing that the intelligence you have received of such a plot were supported by a thousandth part of the proofs that I have adduced of the plots contriving against your country, and against every state without exception, would you waste that time in idle declamations and superfluous doubts on your dangers, which your perfidious friends were husbanding for your ruin? or would you expect to see persons beseeching you to watch for your own preservation?—Well, I now wish to convince ye, whether princes, nobles, rich, poor, burgesses, merchants, citizens in fine of every class, that all these conspiracies of the sophisticated, masonic, or illuminizing, adepts, are conspiracies against your persons, against your property, (whether hereditary or mercantile), against your families, your wives and children. Are you wild enough to believe, that while your country is delivered over to the revolutionary conflagration, an exception will be made in your favour, because you inhabit such or such a place, counting-house, or cot? In the universal pillage of the state, shall your property be more sacred than that of your neighbour, and escape the rapacity of the brigands or the requisition of their pentarques? The characteristic of a revolution made by sectaries is, not that the danger is diminished by its universality, but that terror, indigence, and slavery, rush down like a torrent, swallowing and beating down without distinction every thing that is to be found on its passage.

In the whole progress of the Sect, wherever it has acquired sovereignty, in France, in Holland, in Brabant, in Savoy, in Switzerland, in Italy, search for a single man of property that has preserved it entire; a poor parent that has not had to fear for the requisition of his children, or his own labor; a single family that has not to weep for the loss or ruin of some one of its branches; a single citizen that can lay himself down to rest with the prospect of being able to say, when he awakes, that his property, his liberty, his wife, is any better guaranteed to him, than was that of the unfortunate victims whom he had seen during the day plundered of their property, dragged in chains, or falling under the insatiable guillotine. No, they are not to be found. Cease then, sluggard, to flatter thyself. The danger is imminent, it is terrible, it stares ye all in the face without exception.

Yet sink not under the pressure of terror; that would be cowardice indeed; for, though so positive as to the certainty of your danger, I may boldly say, *Will* it only, and your salvation is certain. I appeal to the Jacobins themselves; for how often have they repeated, that "it is not possible to triumph over a nation that is determined to defend itself." *Will* as they do and you will have little to fear from them. The true Jacobin is not to be discouraged by opposition. The mysteries infuse into the adepts a uniform, constant, and relentless, determination to attain the grand object in spite of every obstacle; that oath, that irrevocable oath of overturning the whole universe and subjecting it to their systems, is the true principle whence originate their resources; this fires the zeal of the adepts, and induces them to make such numerous sacrifices; it inspires its warriors with enthusiasm; it creates rage and fury in the heart of its brigands. It is this principle which constitutes the Sect; in that its force resides; it is the director and mover of its adepts, whether in arms, in the clubs, in the lodges, or deliberating in the senate.—But what inferences may not nations draw from this very principle as to the nature of their plots? Does it not entitle us to say, that the whole of the French revolution is nothing more than the offspring of that oath, of that premeditated determination of overturning the altar, the throne, and society, which the Sect has infused into its adepts? It triumphs because it knows how to *will*; hence it is evident, that to render their efforts abortive we need only resolutely to *will* the salvation of the altar, of the throne, and of society, and they are saved. Let it not be said, that the Jacobins alone can be steady in their cause and predetermined on their object. To know the evils with which the revolution threatens you, and to determine boldly and resolutely to counteract them, does not certainly dispense us from the obligation of applying to the means and of making the necessary efforts and sacrifices to deliver us from the scourge; yet do not let it be thought, that it is idle in me to insist on that boldness, sincerity, and determination. The French revolution is in its nature similar to our passions and vices: it is generally known, that misfortunes are the natural consequences of indulging them; and one would willingly avoid such consequences: but a faint-hearted resistance is made; our passions and our vices soon triumph, and man is hurried away by them.

But should I, on the contrary, have succeeded in inspiring you with the courage necesssary to make you act with resolution; if you need but to know the true means of counteracting the Sect to adopt a firm resistance; then I may boldly say, the Sect is crushed, the disasters of the revolution shall disappear.—But the reader, whose humanity might be alarmed at my saying *the Sect is crushed*, should remember that when I said *the Sect must be crushed or society overthrown*, I took care immediately to add, "Let it, however, be remembered, that to crush a Sect is not to imitate the fury of its apostles, intoxicated with its sanguinary rage and propense to enthusiastic murder.—The Sect is monstrous, but all its disciples are not monsters;—*yes, strike the Jacobins, but spare the Man*; the Sect is a sect of opinion; and its destruction will be doubly complete on the day when it shall be deserted by its disciples, to return to the true principles of reason and social order."[1] It is to reclaim the unfortunate victims of Jacobinism from their errors, and to restore them to society, not to butcher them, that I have been so long examining and tracing all the tortuous windings of the Sect; and I am overjoyed to see that such weapons for self-preservation are the natural result of these memoirs. How different are these arms from those with which the Sect has provided its disciples.

The Jacobins have seduced nations by means of a subterraneous warfare of illusion, error, and darkness. Let the honest men oppose them with wisdom, truth, and light.

The Jacobins are waging against Princes and Governments a war of hatred of the laws and of social order, a war of rage and destruction; let a war of society, humanity, and self-preservation, be waged against them.

The Jacobins are waging a war of impiety and corruption against the altars and religion of every nation; let morality, virtue, and repentance, be opposed to them.

I explain:—when I speak of a subterraneous warfare of illusion, error, and darkness waged by the Sect, I allude to the productions of its sophisters, to the artifices of its emissaries, and to the mysteries of its clubs, lodges, and secret societies. It would be useless to contest the point; for we have incontrovertibly demonstrated, that those have been the preparatory means for its revolutionary triumphs. It is by such means that Jacobinism has insinuated itself under the specious forms of a disorganizing Equality and Liberty, or of a chimerical

Sovereignty of the People, which has ever been the cant of those factious tribunes, who, by flattering their pride, sought to enslave that same people. It is by retailing all the sophisticated doctrines of the Rights of Man to the multitude, by violent declamations against the existing laws, by captious and fallacious descriptions of a supposed happiness which they are preparing for us, by urging nations on to *certain essays at least*; by such means do the emissaries of Jacobinism seduce nations, and imperiously sway that public opinion which will sooner level your ramparts than all the artillery that they can bring against them. From such incontestable facts I conclude, that if it be your intention to guard against the misfortunes which have befallen France, you must begin by disarming the Sect of all its means of illusion. Snatch from the hands of the people all those incendiary productions; but when I say people, I mean from every class of society; for I know none that are proof against illusion; more particularly would I say, from that class which has been supposed to have been most abundant in learning, that class of literary sophisters, such as our Voltaires, D'Alemberts, Rousseaus, Diderots, our academicians, and our doctrineers of the reading societies; for this is the class of all others that has shown us the example of the powerful illusion of sophistry. It was from this class that the revolutionary ministers Necker and Turgot started up; from this class arose those grand revolutionary agents, the Mirabeaux, Syeyes, Laclos, Condorcets; those revolutionary trumps, the Brissots, Champforts, Garats, Merciers, Pastorets, Gudins, La Metheries, Lalandes, Cheniers; those revolutionary butchers, the Carras, Frerons, Marats; I will also say of that class of advocates so verbose and fertile in delirium; for from among them sprung the Targets, Camus, Treillards, Barreres, and all the tyrants of the revolution, the Reveillère-Lepaux, Reubels, Merlins, and Robespierres. What have all these men proved, whether taken from the academies or from the bar?—that if they were the persons whose talents enable them to represent all this sophistry of impiety, of sedition, and rebellion, in the most seducing colours, they were also the persons that were most easily imbued with and drank most deeply of the poison; they were at once the most readily tainted and the most eager to taint others. No; I can make no exception of classes; none are entitled to an exception when I exclaim to Magistrates and Sovereigns, Will you save the people from the disasters of the French Revolution? then snatch from their hands those incendiary productions, those libels of impiety and sedition. Let that man be punished as a traitor, who writes and circulates such writings, conscious of the injury he is doing to society; let him meet with the fate of a madman, if he thinks he can seduce, and stop the consequences of seduction.

But I hear clamours on all sides arising in the literary world, of intolerance, of tyranny, of cramping genius! I foresaw that I should have to treat with men lukewarm in the cause, saying they were determined, nevertheless unwilling; saying they detested the revolution, but timorous when it is to be crushed in the germ. But you at least who profess to enlighten nations by your writings, to point out maxims to Princes for the happiness of their people, you who demonstrate the goodness of your intentions by the purity of your principles, by your zeal in defence of the laws, by the wisdom of your writings, is it from you, I ask, that such cries arise? No, no: shackles thrown on the venomous writer circulating his poisons, will never give concern to the honest writer; against laws prohibiting poignards none will rebel but the assassin. Let us no longer be led away by the stale cries of Liberty of the Press, Liberty of Genius; such cries in the mouths of the Jacobins will be but a shallow cover to their designs;—see what the Sect does itself, lest any writer should open the eyes of the people by the exposition of real truth; wherever the adepts have acquired dominion, ask what is to be understood by liberty of thinking, of speaking, of writing. They destroy not only the author, but seller and even buyer of every book that combats their systems. The printing presses of Crapard, the publications of La Harpe, or the discourse of Camille du Jourdan, are so many conspiracies punished by the Pentarques with exile to Cayenne. It is high time for nations to open their eyes, and dispel the illusion of all this pretended oppression of thought and genius. If magistrates are the dupes of such outcries, the people are the victims, and nations must be preserved from the illusion that they may be saved from the revolution. It is the act of a father and not of a tyrant, that takes from the hands of its children such instruments as may prove fatal to them.

Let the sophister talk of useful discussions. Go to antiquity, and question the Roman senate why it drove from the soil of the republic that swarm of Sophists[2] just arrived from the Grecian shores, so expert in the quibbling arts; and the senate will answer, that they do not enter into discussions to know whether the plague is useful, that they hasten to separate from their fellow countrymen whoever has been tainted with it, and to destroy whatever may propagate it. Guard the people, therefore, against such vile seducers; tremble at the effects of their discourses; but fear still more the poisons of their impious and seditious productions.

Your laws pronounce death against a traitor, though he betrayed his conspiracy but by a single word; and a conspiring sophister may commune and habitually converse with all your subjects by means of his writings! He is in the midst of your families; he instils his principles into your children; his arguments become more and more cogent; he dwells on them; they are presented under all the dazzling colours that a perfidious genius could invent after a long study how to seduce your offspring, lead them astray, or stir them up to revolt against you! The treason spoken by the Jacobin, and for which he has been punished, may have made but a slight impression on his hearers; but this laboured and studied concatenation of sophisms will make a deep impression. Your laws must be inefficient indeed if the revolutionary writer is not stamped as the most baneful of conspirators; and, Magistrate! whoever you are, you must be most unmindful of your duty, if you allow his writings to circulate freely through town and country.

Are you still a stranger to the immense power that such productions have given to the Sect?—The revolution has not been ungrateful, and its gratitude points out its progenitors. Follow the Jacobin to the pantheon; see to whom he has decreed honours, to whom he does homage; ask him how Voltaire or Jean Jaques can have deserved such tribute, such honours. He will tell you, that those men are no more, but that their spirit has survived them in their writings, and more powerfully combat for the cause of Jacobinism than all their armed legions. Here they prepare the minds and hearts of the people for our principles; there they gain over the public opinion to our cause; and when once that has declared for us, we may boldly proceed to certain triumph. Should such honours dazzle any writer for an instant, let him stop and behold the shades of the victims sacrificed to the revolution flitting round the monuments erected to these revolutionary deities; see them ghastly and enraged, passing from the urn that contains the ashes of Voltaire to that of Rousseau; hear them exclaim in bitter reproaches, "Be satiated with the fumes of Jacobin incense! It is not on Jacobins that we call down vengeance from heaven, for you were our real murderers! You are now the object of their adoration; but you were our first executioners, you brought our King to the scaffold, you still continue to be the butchers of our progeny.—O ye Idols of blasphemy and of anarchy! may their blood, may our blood, may all the blood that shall be spilt by the brigands formed at your schools, fall back upon you!"

Ye whom the God of society has endowed with talents which you may turn to the detriment or conservation of society, beware that such curses do not fall upon you, flee from any thing that may breed remorse. Be not dazzled with the jacobinical tribute paid to these sophisters of darkness; they may have succeeded in obscuring the light; it is your duty to rend the cloud asunder, and bear in triumph the fundamental truths. The God who formed man for society did not give him the code of Equality and Liberty, the code of Rebellion and Anarchy. The God who supports society by the wisdom of the laws, never abandoned the making or sanctioning of those laws to the caprice of the multitude. The God who has pointed out the empire and stability of the laws as inherent to that subordination of the citizens to the magistrates, and to their sovereigns, did not create as many magistrates and sovereigns as he did citizens. The God that has bound all classes together by their mutual wants, and who, in consequence of this diversity of wants, has endowed men with a variety of talents for different arts and professions, has not given the same rights to the mechanic or to the shepherd as he has to the prince that is to preside over the state. Restore to these simple and plain truths, all that resplendency which has for a moment been obscured by the sophisters of rebellion; and the dangers of the revolution will soon disappear. Be as earnest in restoring the people to light, as the Jacobins have been in plunging them into darkness. Restore them to their principles pure and untarnished. There is no compounding with error; the Sect cares not by which road illusion may lead you to revolution, provided you do but fall a victim. Some it will attack with its anti-religious sophisms, while it tampers with others by means of its antisocial sophistry. To some it will unfold but a part of the consequences to be drawn, point out but one half of the career that is to be run, or, under pretence of reform, propose some few essays or new means to be tried. But far be driven from us these demi-geniuses or demi-revolutions with their long train of demi-consequences! This is the tribe whence the Sect will select a La Fayette or a Necker, push them forward as long as they can serve the cause, and then abandon such non-entities; or those open rebels styling themselves *Constitutionalists*, or those others called (probably through derision) *Monarchists*. They were the beginners of the revolution, and are at this present day imbecile enough to testify their surprize at other rebels having shivered a sceptre which they had begun by disjointing. Writers of this species, so far from enlightening the people, only contribute to lead them into the path of error; and that was the task of the first revolutionary adepts.

In your writings beware of falling into an error similar to that of a celebrated author, who thinks he is serving the cause of monarchy when describing religion as a fruitless ally. How is it possible that he should not better feel the consequences of that sarcastic sentence borrowed from Bayle and Rousseau, he who, in the midst of the most pressing and most apposite exhortations to princes to unite and combine against Jacobinism, forgets himself so far as to say, "In a similar crisis, the Romans would have flown to arms resolved to conquer or die, *the primitive Christians would have sung hymns to Providence and rushed to martyrdom;* their successors neither die nor fight."[3] Most undoubtedly, it cannot be the intention of the author to revive that contempt which the Sophisters so much affect for Religion; but what a false policy to represent that alledged nullity as inherent to Christianity at a time when the courage of nations should be stirred up against the revolutionary tyrants! Happily it is not true, that the primitive Christians would only have sung hymns to Providence and rushed on to martyrdom. The primitive Christians were not idiots; they did not confound the legitimate powers, which they could only oppose by the courage of martyrs, with the usurped power of a tyrant or of barbarians that came to inundate the empire. They could only conquer or die under the standard of the Cæsars as manfully as the Romans; nay, they surpassed them in courage and resignation, and their apologists were well grounded when they set the Sophisters at defiance to point out a single coward or traitor among the Christian legions. In our days too, did those heroic Christians of the Vendee content themselves with singing hymns, they whose courage was more terrible to the republicans than all the combined forces of Clairfait or Beaulieu? Where have we seen any of our emigrants that have distinguished themselves by their piety, chanting hymns to Providence during the hour of battle. Whence this triple insult to the Christian hero, to his religion, and to the very evidence of reason? Whence this affectation of representing the powerful and active incitements of Christianity as useless to governments? Is not the crown of a soldier dying for laws or for his king, which his God commands him to defend, as valuable as your laurel-wreath? Tell then the Christian soldier, that the coward and the traitor shall not enter into the kingdom of Heaven, and see whether he will not conquer or die. You think that you are serving the cause of society against Jacobinism by representing Christianity as imbecility. Jacobins would reward such sarcastic sentences, because they foresee their consequences. Are our writers then to be always outwitted by theirs; they can combine their efforts against the altar and the throne; and shall we never be able to defend the one without betraying the interests of the other?

What can be the cause of such imprudence, such false lights? Neither do they study sufficiently the Sect nor its artifices. They wish to be blind to its power, and even to its influence. I also am an admirer of the vigor of that same writer, who seeks to stir up the courage of nations; but should he mistake the real causes of our misfortunes, what have we not to fear from writers who are endowed neither with his knowledge nor his energy? Will not the Sect rejoice to hear him say, "it is far more to that continental fatalism than to the Illuminees, that we are to attribute the lethargy of the higher orders of society?" I know not what *continental* or insular *fatalism* can signify. God forbid that Princes should for an instant believe in it, for it would only be immersing them still deeper in their lethargy. No efforts are made against fatality; I know, at least, that the Illuminees would rejoice to see no credit given to their existing influence; for the less they shall be feared in consequence of your writings, fewer will be the precautions taken to guard against them. I am positive, that had you studied one half of the arts employed by the Insinuators to seduce the higher classes, and even courts themselves, you would be the first to find a very different cause than *fatalism* for the continental lethargy.[4]

Far be from me the absurd pretension of alone enjoying the means of giving useful counsels. It is, on the contrary, because I wish that the public should be improved by yours, that I am eager to see you better informed of the real cause of all our misfortunes. I could wish to see a holy league formed of such men of talents as are really actuated with a true zeal against the revolutionary errors. My reader has seen the baneful effects of that coalition of the sophisticated writers of Holbach's Club, of the Sophisters of the Masonic and of the Illuminized Lodges; he has seen the influence of their principles on the public opinion, and of opinion on our misfortunes; why should not virtuous and learned writers then unite in their efforts to bring back the public opinion and the people to the true principles, by laying open all the artifice and cunning that has been employed by the Sect to seduce them.

The Code has been explicit on the means to be employed for the seduction of youth, a time of life most accessible to illusion. Will not virtuous fathers taken upon themselves to discard from their children masters of suspicious characters, and books that disseminate these poisons? Will not governments take as much pains to drive the adepts from the pulpit, from the chairs of science and professorships, as we have seen the Sect taking to make itself master of education and to corrupt youth. Unhappy we, should the reader be affrighted at the detail of such precautions, while the Sects attends to each particularity, and we have seen it as eager for the nomination of a country schoolmaster, as for the success of an adept at court, or the nomination of the general who is to command its legions.

One species of illusion appears to be the favorite engine of Jacobinism, I mean that theory of essays in government, and those demi-reforms. No art has been more powerfully played off on the English nation than this; let the people be put on their guard against this illusion; let them be taught, that France also began by essays and demi-reforms; I need not hint at their consequences. If it be necessary to humble the pride of the Jacobin Sophister, and blight the very idea of that pretended happiness which they attach to their systems, let the people learn that such essays have long since been made; that the brigands who appeared under the different denominations of Lollards, Begards, followers of John Wall, of Maillotin, and of Muncer, all promised the supreme happiness of Equality and Liberty; that it was perfectly useless to talk to us of the *Philosophy* of a revolution that was nothing more than the repetition of the errors of certain Sects, of which the barbarous and devastating tenets could only be equalled by the horror and contempt in which they were held by our ancestors. When, under the pretence of arguing on certain truths the Jacobin seeks to lead you into discussion, guard against his sophistry, by answering, that no argumentation can be held with Weishaupt or Robespierre; the first will retail all the arguments of former brigands, the latter does what they did; for if our modern Jacobins have invented anything of their own, it is a little more artifice and an unparralleled ferocity. They are then the more entitled to our contempt and hatred.

If every where encountered by this two-fold sentiment, the Sect will soon lose that power of illusion which has prepared its triumphs, and you will see it shrinking back into its subterraneous lurking places, the occult Lodges which have so long since offered it an asylum. There it will once more attempt to recruit its legions, and contrive plots for the subversion of the altar, of the throne, and of society. But here what honest citizen can be blind to his duty? Under whatever name, pretence, or form, the magistracy may have thought proper to tolerate these clubs, subterraneous hiding-places, or Lodges of secret societies, what proofs are they waiting for to proscribe them all, now that they have seen legions of conspirators sallying forth from these recesses? You who look upon yourselves as entitled to an honourable exception, why are you seated there still? You are tender of your personal loyalty, of your fidelity to your religion and to your country, how can you make such sentiments agree with your predilection for Lodges that you know to have been the asylum of the most conspiring Sects? Do not pretend that it is us, for it is the Jacobins, the most monstrous chiefs of the Jacobins, their correspondence, their speeches, and all the archives of their history, that have unfolded to you the immense support they have derived from your mysteries and from all your *secret societies*, in the prosecution of their conspiracies against *society in general*, against all laws, and against every altar. In vain shall you attempt to hide it; no part of history can be better authenticated; these conspiracies are proved at any rate to have gained admittance into your Lodges, and to have acquired strength and numbers from them. Your particular Lodge may not be one of those with whose honor the Sect has tampered; we are willing to believe it; but what proofs can you adduce? the Sect knows too well how to clothe perjury in the garb of innocence.—We are willing to believe it, and that will be another motive why we should conjure you in the name of your country to abandon those Lodges. Your presence is only a cloak for conspirators. The more unblemished may be your character of honor, the more will the conspiring adepts boast of your name, and of the fraternity and intimacy in which you live with them.—We address our complaints to you yourselves, but own that we have sufficient grounds to address them to the prince or to the senate; may we not with truth denounce you as demi-citizens, since by your oath the interests of the brotherhood are more dear to you than those of your fellow-subjects? Are we not entitled to ask, whether you are not a secret enemy to every citizen who has the interests of religion and his country at heart, since you are a member of a secret society, under the cloak of which a multitude of brethren are conspiring against our religion and our laws, and that it is impossible to distinguish the innocent from the guilty. What right would you have to complain if the senate and your prince were to exclude you from the magistracy, or from every office that requires the whole attention of an impartial citizen, and on whom no suspicion can alight, as it appears that your affection is at least divided between society in general and your secret societies, as that affection, according to your own laws, must be greater for the members of your secret societies than for us; since, in short, it has been demonstrated, that a large portion of the members of secret societies are mere conspirators? In vain will you object that you have never witnessed any thing reprehensible in the Lodges. Were you only initiated in the mysteries of the Grand Lodge of London, know, that notwithstanding all the exceptions we have made in its favor, suspicions are even cast upon that Lodge, and a reviewer thinks himself founded in denying the validity of such exceptions.[5] If you are so careless of your reputation as to remain insensible to such suspicions, allow me at least to address myself to you in the name of all mankind, whose interests you tell us are so dear to you.

No longer than a century ago the remaining part of Europe was nearly a stranger to your Lodges and their mysteries. You made it the baneful present; the new-erected Lodges have filled with Jacobins, and from them the most disastrous scourge that has ever befallen the universe has rushed forth to produce these terrible effects; you imparted to them the mysteries of your Equality and of your Liberty; to combine and prepare them, you introduced them into your tenebrous asylums; to prepare their pupils, you taught them your trials and your oaths; and that they might propagate their conspiracies from pole to pole, you lent them your language, your symbols, your signs, your cypher, your directories, your hierarchy, and all the regulations for your invisble correspondence. The offspring may have improved on the mysteries of their progenitors; but has not their conduct been such as to make you abjure all connection with them; have not your Lodges been so prophaned as to make you hasten to abandon them; is not the disastrous scourge that has burst from them a sufficient ground for eternally closing their gates? O you, whose fleets, under the protection of heaven, ride triumphant over the main, dispelling the fleets of the Sect! O grant the universe a victory, perhaps of still greater importance. At the sight of your admirals the Sect disappears; drive then from its recesses that bantling of yours; show that if the abuse of your mysterious associations may in possibility be fatal to the universe, you are willing at least to deprive the vile conspirators of every plea that can tarnish your glory. Show, that if sports, innocent in your hands, could grow into a scourge in the hands of others, you are not backward in making a sacrifice of such utility to nations. Your example would be powerful; and it is incumbent on you to pronounce the anathema on secret societies; to close the gates of the Lodges, to close them all without exception, nevermore to be opened, wahtever may be the nature of their mysteries. None can exist into which the Sect will not attempt to penetrate; none can exist where the magistrate and honest citizen can sit down certain that the Sect has not intruded with its plots and means of seduction. The more zealous you may be for the preservation of our laws, the less will you be enabled to secure us against the plots of the Sect; for though it shall ever commune with you it will not lay its views open to you until it has seduced you. Masons of England, what a fatal gift you have made to the world! May the historian who shall write the annals of this age, when speaking of the scourge that has rushed forth from the Lodges, conclude by saying, if England made the baneful present to the universe, it was also the first to sacrifice its own Lodges for the safety of nations.

Why should not every honest Mason on the Continent address himself in terms similar to those in which we address the English brotherhood? Their presence would no longer be a cloak to the Mysteries of the conspiring Jacobins. Left to themselves, they could no longer plead the innocence of their Mysteries. If the Magistrates treated them with all the severity of the law, he would not have to fear the protests of honest citizens. Then would every thing denote that the time was come to strike all secret societies with the anathema of the laws; then would all the productions of the Sect be suppressed, or thrown away with indignation by every class of citizen. True principles only would be taught, and these would discard from the minds of the people all those disorganizing errors. The Sect once dislodged from its lurking places, truth and light would dispel that warfare of illusion, error, and darkness, which, waged by the Sophisters of Jacobinism, prepares the way for the triumphant entry of its destroying brigands.

But that long-expected day, that day of devastation and plunder foretold in the Mysteries, has dawned. In darkness have the adepts multiplied, and the legions of the Sect have sallied forth. They now wage the war of pikes and destruction, they wave the firebrands of revolution, but have not abandoned the warfare of illusion. Sovereigns and Ministers of Empires! It behoves you to stem the torrent of these men of blood by the marshalled bands of heroes whom you command. I do not pretend to step over the threshold of the chamber where our warriors sit in council to deliberate on the means of vanquishing the Sect in the field of battle. But, to ensure the success of your valorous efforts, may we intrude on your wisdom, to represent that force should not attract your entire attention? The Jacobin is no common enemy. He wages a war of Sect, of proselytism against you; and Sects are not to be vanquished by the same arms as warriors waging a glorious war, or brigands rushing forth from their ungrateful shores in quest of pillage and booty. The seat of conflict lies in opinions. The Jacobin has all the enthusiasm of the Sectary, and has also the force of arms; that you may overpower his arms, you should know the object of his delirium.

I began by declaring, and think I have established the position, that in this warfare of pikes and firebrands the Sect sends forth its legions to shiver the scepter, not to fight the power; it has not promised to its adepts the crowns of Princes, Kings, and Emperors, but has required and bound those adepts by an oath to destroy them all. In the Sovereign, it is not the person that they hate; but it is the chief, the Minister of the Social Order. The war it wages against a nation is of a similar complexion; it is that war of opinion, which hates, not the Englishman, but the laws of the English, which abominates not the German, the Spaniard, or the Italian, but the God, the Altars, the Thrones, the Senates of the German, the Spaniard, or the Italian, in short, of every people. Do not suffer yourself to be misled; the Pentarques will certainly attempt to warp these plans and plots of the Sect, and make them subservient to their own ambition; but have not the mysteries taught us, that the elevation of an Orleans, a Barras, or a Rewbel to the throne, never entered the mind of the adepts when they murdered their lawful Sovereign? It may support its tyrannic Pentarques in the destruction of kings and governments, but it will crush these tyrants in their turn, when they shall have completed the destruction of society. It is not a new Empire that they are seeking to establish; it is at the annihilation of every Empire, of all order, rank, distinction, property, and social tie, that they aim. Such is the Ultimate View of its mysteries of Equality and Liberty. Such is that reign of anarchy and absolute independence, proclaimed in the subterraneous lurking-places, under the appellations of patriarchal reign, of the reign of Reason and of Nature.

Sovereigns, Ministers, You who watch for the safety of the subject! Is it clear to you why we so much insist on this general and predominating hatred as the sole principle and object of this terrible war? Because it immediately points out that it behoves you to combat this relentless foe by an ardour and zeal for the universal maintenance of social order; because now it is more than ever incumbent on you to cast aside all ideas of personal interest, that might counteract the general efforts; because, were it possible that the interests of the Sect could for a moment coincide with yours, it would be only a duty that you would fulfil in suspending those mutual resentments or national jealousies that have but too long nurtured enmities and bloodshed; because much woe will befal you, if you be imprudent enough to think but for an instant that you can either make the principles or the legions of the Sect the instruments of your vengeance, or of your personal views; for the power you put in motion shall soon fall back upon you.

I am not one of those who thought that they could trace such a kind of policy in the first motions of the French revolution, pretending that foreign powers had abetted the Jacobins with a view, if not to crush, at least to weaken the ancient and powerful fabric of the French monarchy. I have probed the strength of the Sect when it rushed from its dens. But let it not be overlooked by history; let the terrible example of that man who was held out as one of the greatest politicians of the age, be ever present to the eyes of sovereigns. The Sect began to demonstrate the first elements of its Code of Equality, Liberty, and Sovereignty of the People; baneful policy ordered La Fayette, D'Estaing, and Rochambeau, to proceed to the succour of a colony asserting its sovereignty against its mother country. I do not pretend to discuss the rights of London or of Philadelphia; but let the minister, the politician Vergennes rise from his grave, he who in America would make, and in Holland abet, revolutions of the people equal and free; let him look to the throne, or seek the sovereign whose interests he thought to serve when using the Sect as an engine of state!! Let the minister of Joseph II, I mean, Mercy D'Argenteau, come forth; let him behold to what an end the services of the sovereign populace would lead which he was about to assemble in Brabant, or the services of *those pretended friends to the public safety*, in other words, of the *emissaries* of the Sect, already omnipotent in Paris, or of those Jacobins that he would receive and support, that he might oppress through the means of anarchy.[6] No, the Sect that has sworn to shiver every sceptre will not avenge any quarrels of yours, or prove a support in danger. Banish then every idea of alliance or union with its principles and means! it can never lose sight of its Ultimate End; and if it should affect to make a common cause with you in the annihilation of the throne that gives you umbrage, it will only be that it may find you standing alone and destitute of allies when it shall turn back upon you.

To renounce such temporary and disastrous services can be no great sacrifice. When the common enemy of society rears its head, is it not the duty of the chiefs of society to forget all private quarrels, and unite in combating so formidable a foe? Every step gained against it, will be a step gained for yourself, for your people, and for that portion of society over which you preside. Still farther from your mind be all those ideas of cold œconomy, calculating the sacrifices or efforts you will have to make, or the indemnities you may claim! When the house that joins your palace is in flames, do you think yourself safe because you have not contributed to the conflagration? Or do you enquire what reward is offered for extinguishing the flames? More wildly avaricious, would you think of pillaging that house while the flames were communicating to your own? Save the universe, and you save your own empire. Every throne beat down by the Jacobin, reduces an obstacle that he has to encounter in the attack of yours. Will the arsenals he shall pillage, will the requisitions of men, and legions raised, in the newly-conquered states, ensure the indemnities you ask; or do you expect, by complacency, flattery, and meanness, to have an exception made in your favour? Can you hope to see the Pentarques always preserving their neutrality in your regard, because for the moment they are pleased not to demand any farther sacrifices from you? Or, when you desert the common cause, will you ground your security on treaties of peace, or even on treaties of alliance offensive and defensive? O virtue! what desertion of the common cause! O shame! O cowardice! No, the very idea of such treaties could never have entered your mind, had you been acquainted with the Sect that proposes them. You have signed them; but you do not enjoy peace, not even a neutrality. You are its slave. You are only the mouth-piece of its imperious dictates, until the Sect shall choose to strip you of even the semblance of authority.—You will tell us, perhaps, that you have been neuter in the contest; that is to say, you have not dared to attack the Jacobin that only waits to drag you into slavery till he shall have crushed those with whom you should have leagued, and who could have defended you or avenged your death.—You have lived in peace with the common enemy of society! You have sworn to abandon society to be butchered, thrones to be annihilated, and sceptres to be shivered; and this without showing the least resistance.—Have you made treaties of alliance? then you have sworn to support the destroying hords, and to contribute towards the destruction and devastation of society.

You are sensible as we are of the shame, of the ignominy, of such a neutrality, peace, or alliance.—But a superior force commands....Then say that you are vanquished, that you are a slave to the Sect, and we shall then ask, if on no occasion a valiant death be preferable to slavery? Is that throne saved, around which you still hover, by permission of the Sect, merely as the mouth-piece of its commands? Are your people saved, who are obliged to sully their hands with the crimes inherent to Jacobins? Is that slave free, who, chained to the bench of the gallies, can only handle his oars in the service of a pirate? If you still preserve any glimmerings of Liberty, if your strength be not entirely exhausted, rise, Oh! rise once more, and fight the battles of society!—Could you still be led astray by that flirting semblance of authority which the Sect has allowed you, hearken to Jean de Brie, proposing in the name of the Sect, in the midst of its legislastors, to raise a legion of *twelve hundred assassins*, and to send them, not to kill *one* king, but to *murder every king*! Did not those legislators announce to you in terms sufficiently clear the fate which they intended for you and your people, when they declared that they would *fraternize* with every nation that wished to shake off its laws or rise against its magistrates and sovereign?[7] Would you wish to persuade yourself that there exists a single king who is not comprehended within the revolutionary proscription, go and assist at the annual celebration of the festival held by the Sect in honour of the murderers of their king; go and hearken to their constituted authorities, and to the ambassadors whom they send to the neutral or allied Powers, all solemnly swearing the oath of hatred to royalty. You have seen the adepts teaching in the universities, that but a few more years will elapse before the last mysteries of the Sect shall be accomplished; then neither king nor magistrate shall exist, nor a single nation, country, or society governed by laws. And with such a prospect before you, do you still hesitate at throwing aside petty jealousies and personal interests? Shall pretensions, mistrusts, and enmities, between king and king, or nation and nation, disunite you, when society calls upon you for the defence not only of your own crown, but of every crown, not only of your own nation but of every nation wherever laws are recognized?

It is not yet too late. Nations are still more powerful than the Sect; let then every nation unite; let their kings, their senates, their people, join in the common cause; let every man living in the state of society consider the warfare waged by the Sect against society and property as aimed at his own person. Shall the heart of the Jacobin alone be inflamed by the fire of enthusiasm? Shall the desolation of your country, the destruction of your altars, of your laws, of your fortunes, the devastation of your towns and mansions, the tearing away of your children, not rouse you from your lethargy? Shall not such sights inspire you with courage, are they not inducements for sacrifices as powerful at least as the enthusiasm of delirium in the Jacobin? Shall it still continue to be said, that the Brigands alone know the power and strength of union? Every where they are one; they have but one object in view; they all serve but one and the same cause; they are brethren wherever they meet, merely because they universally aim at the destruction of the social order. May chiefs of nations then unite in one common tie of affection; for it is the common interest of all and each of them to preserve that social order. Such would be my definition of a war of zeal for society, a war entirely directed against the Sect, and the only means of depriving it of those resources which it may have but too plentifully drawn from politicans hacknied in wars of vengeance, jealousy, and ambition, but little accustomed to the idea of such sacrifices as wars for the general interest of society may require.

When I thus wish to stir up all nations to make but one power, but one nation in the common cause; when I thus wish to see them all actuated by the same zeal and ardor for combating the Sect; the reader may be tempted to ask me, what is become of the war of humanity, of self-preservation, that I wished to see opposed to that warfare of fury, destruction, and of sanguinary rage against society? Doubtless, it must afflict me thus to sound the general alarm, which calls your embattled legions into the field of Mars; but when we behold those of the Sect nurtured on blood and carnage; when thousands and hundreds of thousands of citizens, whose sluggard tranquillity and aversion to resistance could not save them from falling victims; when women, aged parents, and even children, have been butchered so recently in the mountains of Switzerland, just as they had been before in the fields of La Vendée and in divers parts of France; when in every country into which the Sect can penetrate, the inhabitants must either bend the knee to adore the idol, or perish beneath the pikes; who will be the true friend to humanity? Will that man set himself down for a friend to humanity, and as having preserved society, who would let the armies of the Sect successively proceed from Brabant into Holland, from Savoy into Switzerland, from Piedmont into the

Milanois, and from thence to Rome, every where overturning social order, because the Sect every where met but with a feeble and partial resistance? Which then shall be the true friend to humanity, the man who permits the scourge to extend and ravage all Europe, or he who excites you to crush the germ of such horrors? Will the preserver of your life be the man who, fearing to probe your wound, shall let mortification engender in your flesh; or he who, employing the caustic or the blade, shall consume or amputate the decayed part to preserve the body? Had the counsellors of such a cruel humanity foreseen that a Sect whose empire is terror, whose means are those of brigands and assassins, was not to be overpowered by their perfidious complaisance, what horrors and what rivers of blood would have been spared; what numberless citizens has that reign of terror chained to the standards of the Sect, citizens even who abhorred it! And what numbers would have joined your standard, in defiance of the reign of terror, had they seen you waging a war against the Sect, and not a war of ambition. I never assisted at the councils of princes, and am willing to believe that my fellow-countrymen have formed an erroneous judgement, and that the reports of partitioning and of ambitious views may even have originated with the Sect, since it acquires such empire through its means; that error has recruited the ranks of the Sect with soldiers whose courage and lives would have been at your disposal, had you found means of convincing them that you had fled to arms solely to vindicate the cause of monarchy, of their religion, and of their laws; had they not been led to think, that between two enemies they were obliged to repulse that which was coming, not to defend them, but to profit of their dissentions, and deliver up their country to pillage, or make them share the fate of Venice or Poland! Deprive the Jacobins of this vain pretext; let every people that groans under the bondage of the Sect learn from your candid declarations, supported by your deeds, that you only come as their saviour and liberator, that your legions have no other object in view than the restoring of them to the blessings of social order.

But whither am I wandering, and what was I about to promise? Shall the fate of my country, the destiny of empires, solely depend on the strength of armies? There is a war far more terrible than that of brigands, which the Sect wages against us. The amazing progress of impiety, the corruption of morals, and general apostacy of an age styling itself the age of Philosophy; these are the real arms of the Sect, the grand source of all our misfortunes. Ye who may be affrighted at these truths because they may affect you more particularly, turn back to the causes of our misfortunes, and you will trace them all to this apostacy.

Infuriate as a demoniac of blasphemy, a disastrous Sophister exclaimed, I will not serve, my Reason shall be free. The God of Revelation may persecute me, but I will persecute him, I will raise a school against him, I will surround myself with conspiring adepts, I will say to them *Crush the Wretch*—Crush J—C—. This school was established on the earth; kings and great men applauded the doctrines of this demoniac; they relished them because they flattered and unbridled their passions. This was the first step towards the revolution. Do not come and plague me with idle representations; turn to the archives of the impious man whom thou hast idolized; there are my proofs. Princes, Nobles, Lords, or Knights, such was the crime, I will not say of each of you in particular, but so predominant among you, that I may in some sort call it the crime of your corps. The ministers of God whom you abandoned admonished you of the scourges with which apostates are threatened, and told you that your example would be fatal to your people as well as to yourselves. Do you remember how their menaces were received? Attend for a moment to the acts of that school which you set up in opposition to us. Heaven, in its wrath, has permitted the offspring of the sophisters to multiply like unto the locusts. They thought themselves the Gods of Reason; they also raised their voices, declaring that they would not serve; but, turning their eyes toward you, they added, oppression and tyranny has placed men like unto us upon thrones; chance of birth has made men Nobles and Grandees who are not so good as ourselves. They said it; and that Liberty which you asserted against your God, when stimulated by your passions, they now assert against you at the instigation of their pride. They conspire against the throne and the nobility that surrounds it. Abandoned to your blindness, you courteously received this cloud of sophisters, just as you had received their progenitor. The priests of the living God came once more and admonished you, that this school of impiety would not only operate the ruin of the church, but sweep away into the common mass of ruin Kings, Princes, Laws, and Magistrates. Reason called as loudly on you as your priests; but you had turned away from Revelation, and you refused to hearken to the voice of reason.

The God whom you daily irritated by your apostasy permitted this cloud of Sophisters to descend into the abyss of the Lodges, and there, under pretence of Masonic pursuits, the occult adepts combined their conspiracies against the altar, the throne, and all distinctions, with those of the pretended sages whose dupes you had been.—The adepts now multiplied as fast as the Sophisters. Under the auspices of another pretended Sage, who could improve on every species of impiety and blasphemy, a new Sect is fostered under the name of Illuminees. These, like the hero of your apostasy, swore to crush Christ, as his offspring swore to crush you yourselves; and, in common with all brigands, swore to annihilate the empire of the laws.—Such has been the fruit of that Philosophism which you would so obstinately portray as true wisdom. At length to dissipate the illusion, and to call you back to the faith of his Gospel, far more than to avenge himself, what has your God done? He has silenced his prophets and the doctors of his law; he has said to them, "Discontinue those lessons with which you combat the delirium of these impious men. They raise their Reason up against me; it is my Son whom they have sworn to crush. They wish to reign alone over that people. They have taken upon themselves the important task of leading them to true happiness; I will let them act; I abandon that people to the wisdom of their new teachers.

You, my priests and pontiffs, fly from amidst them, carry away with you the Gospel of my Son. Let their sages beat down his altars; let them raise trophies in his temples to their heroes who had sworn to crush him; and let that people proceed under the sole direction of the light of their Reason. Begone, retire; together with my Son I abandon both the people and their grandees to their sages; let those sages be their leaders, since they turn their backs upon me and my Son."

Frenchmen, the God of your forefathers has thus spoken. Oh, how deeply and easily can he confound *the prudence of prudent men and the wisdom of sages!* Go; proceed through that vast empire which he has abandoned to your pretended Philosophy. His priests have abandoned it; his altars are beaten down; his gospel is no longer to be found. Now calculate the crimes and disasters!! Go and wander among those ruins, behold those mazes and shapeless heaps of rubbish. Ask of the people, what is become of those millions of citizens that formerly thronged in their towns and fields; inquire what inundation of Vandals has devastated their land. What has been the fate of that town, that proudly towered in magnificent palaces, or those other towns, the modern rivals of ancient Tyre? By what means have those riches dwindled into nothing, that were annually brought from the shores of the east or the Isles of the west. Those notes of mirth, those rural songs, why have they given place to groans and complaints? Why is that brow, formerly the seat of content, now knitted and downcast with terror; and why those sighs, that even the fear of being heard cannot suppress! All you inhabitants of France, who were formerly so happy under the laws of your forefathers, but at present victims to all the horrors of the revolution, have you not among ye its Philosophers, the wisdom of its Deists, of its Atheists, and of its Philanthropists? And you in particular, the disciples, and for a long time the zealous protectors of all these revolutionary sages, how comes it to pass that you are now dispersed on the face of all Europe, poor and deserted? Is not that Philosophy which you so much idolized now triumphant in the very centre of its empire?

Ah, how bitter would be such language in the mouth of a God but too well revenged! Unhappy victims of your confidence in these false sages! You now conceive how terrible it is to be abandoned to the empire of impiety! Confess at last, that your credulity, your confidence in these heroes of Sophistry has been disastrous indeed! They promised you a revolution of wisdom, of light, of virtue; and they have cursed you with a revolution of delirium, of extravagance, and wickedness. They promised you a revolution of happiness, Equality, Liberty, of the golden age; and they have brought down upon you the most frightful revolution that a God, justly irritated by the pride and wickedness of men, has ever poured down upon the earth. Such is the end of all that impiety which it has pleased you to style Philosophy.

Never let any person pretend to dispute the prime cause of all our misfortunes. Voltaire and Rousseau are the heroes of your revolution, as they were of your Philosophism. It is now time to dissipate the illusion, if you wish to see the scourge cease, and preserve yourself from a similar danger in future.

You must work a revolution that will be the death-blow to that philosophism of impiety, if you wish to appease the God who has only permitted this scourge to befal man to avenge his Son. It is not by persisting in the outrage, by leaving your hearts a prey to the prime cause of all our misfortunes, that you will find the termination of them. The great crime of the Jacobin is his impiety; his great strength rests in yours. The powers of hell will second him when he combats against Christ; and will heaven, think ye, declare for you, so long as your morals and your faith shall declare you an enemy to the Son of God? By your impiety you become the brother of the Jacobin. You are a Jacobin of the revolution against the altar; and it is not by persisting in this hatred against the altar, that you will appease the God who avenges the altar by the revolution annihilating our thrones and our laws.

Such is the last and most important lesson that we are to derive from those scourges that have befallen us in the same gradation as the sophisters of impiety, the sophisters of rebellion, the sophisters of anarchy conspired.—O that I may have succeeded, when terminating these Memoirs, in engraving it deeply on the minds of my readers!—May it more particularly contribute to pave the way for the restoration of religion, of the laws, and of happiness in my country!—May the resesarches that I have made to discover the causes of the revolution, be serviceable to nations that may still preserve themselves, or rid themselves of such disasters!—Then will that God who has supported me in my pursuit, have blessed my labours with an ample recompence.

1. See Vol. I. P. 17.
2. The word *sophister* has been made use of throughout this work, to distinguish the modern rebels from the Greek Philosophers of the school of Sophists. Johnson, in his dictionary, defines SOPHISTER as a *disputant fallaciously subtle; an artful but insidious logician*; such is the species of men that have been described in this work, who, conscious of their own fallacy, but acting the part of Satan to pervert mankind, should never be confounded with those men of antiquity whose systems of disputation may have been fallacious, but whose intentions were upright, and who did not combat every sacred or social principle in hopes of subverting society. *Trans.*
3. *Mercure Britannique*, Vol. I. No. IV. P. 292.
4. It is evident, however, that the author of the *British Mercury* never wished to favour the *Illuminees*. He is as indignant as we are at the successes of the *inept Philosophists of modern republicanism*, of that revolutionary warfare waging against property and the laws, of those young Jacobins just coming from the University of Gottinguen. He is indignant at the audacity of the *revolutionary letters* and of the *northern league*, that is to say, of a *company of Theologians, Professors, and Philosophers of Holstein*, who ask to form a central assembly, having under it subordinate committees to form and direct *public education, without being under any control of government, laws or religion* (P. 292). He would have spoken just as we have done of the *Illuminees*, had he known these *philosophical* absurdities and their successes to be the work of the Sect; that the youths come from Gottinguen were just arriving from a haunt of Illuminism; that the northern league is nothing more than a branch of the *German Union* invented by the

Illuminee Barhdt; that the plan of education originated with the *Illuminee Campe*, heretofore pastor and preacher to the garrison of Potzdam, called to Brunswick, protected by the first minister, and decorated with the appellation of *French Citizen*, in recompense for what he has more particularly written on the independency of education.—(*See the Universal Revision of every thing relating to Schools, Vol. VI.*) I shall therefore repeat, Study the Sect, study its code, its history; study its means for seducing the Great; and, so far from despising the influence of the Sect, you will find the cause of that disastrous lethargy which has seized on men whose duty it is to be most active, far better explained than by your *Fatalism*.

5. See the Monthly Review, Appendix to Vol. XXXV. Page. 504.
6. See Letters of the Affairs of the Austrian Netherlands, Let. II. P. 31.
7. Decree of the 9th November, 1792.

END OF THE FOURTH AND LAST PART

OBSERVATIONS *on some Articles published in the* MONTHLY REVIEW, *relative to the* "MEMOIRS ON JACOBINISM."

THERE are Reviewers of whose approbation I shall ever be proud, because I know the propagation of good principles to be the object of their labors. There are others, however, whose applause would always be hateful to me, because, under the mask of science, they disseminate the principles of Impiety and Rebellion. To which of these classes the *Monthly Review* may belong, I shall not pretend to determine, as I am not in the habit of reading it; but should be sorry to ground my judgement on the account which Dr. Griffiths, or his associates, have given of the *Memoirs of Jacobinism*. In the Appendix to his twenty-fifth Volume, he has loaded me with imputations which I should leave to the good sense of my Reader, were I engaged in a mere literary dispute; but I have denounced the most formidable conspiracy that ever was contrived against Religion and Society. I owe it, therefore, to my cause, and to myself, to prove which of us is most open to the charge of *unfairness,* of *dexterity, or of treacherous ingenuity*. Fortunately the task is not difficult.

Dr. Griffiths is pleased to pass a favourable sentence on my first Volume, treating of the *Conspiracy of the Sophisters against the Altar;* but he says, that the Conspiracy "of the Sophisters of Rebellion against the Throne is so imperfectly supported in the second Volume, that he must still ascribe the extinction of Royalty in France much more to the course of local events in Paris, than to the previous concert and deliberate wish of the leaders of the Revolution." Certainly the Jacobins would not be sorry to see such an opinion become prevalent; for they also claim the right of saying to Kings, if we attack your thrones you may thank yourselves; it was your perfidy and despotism, much more than the efforts of a Brissot or a Syeyes, that dethroned Lewis XVI; it was more owing to you than to Petion or Robespierre that he was led to the scaffold; and, above all, it was the tyranny of Lewis XVI that engraved in our hearts that wish to exterminate every King on earth—Dr. Griffiths also finds it more convenient peremptorily to pronounce on the validity of the proofs which I adduce, than to submit any of them to his readers, lest they should draw a very different conclusion. Not a word does he mention of the Letters, of the Systems, of Holbach's Club, of the Central Committee, of the Emissaries of the Grand Orient, of the Declamations and formal avowals of the adepts Le Roi, Condorcet, Gudin, and his fellow-reviewers of the Mercure. All this must lead us to believe, that Dr. Griffiths is difficult of conviction when he pleases to be so; and that he can withhold proofs when he is not in a humour to refute them. So many persons will take the word of their teachers for granted, that it is unnecessary for him to condescend to give his reasons. We shall see whether he will deign to notice Sir Horace Walpole, who so long since denounced the Conspiracy of the Sophisters of Rebellion. If Dr. Griffiths be determined to be blind, I cannot pretend to make him see.

2dly, Dr. Griffiths also declares, that my position "is wholly erroneous," when I say, *that Equality and Liberty form the essential and perpetual Creed of the Freemasons.* Here I was tempted to recognize a brother dupe; but he had his reasons for appearing to be better informed than I was. He then speaks of a communication opened between the Grand Lodges of London and Berlin in 1776; and Berlin, he says, was at that *æra the very focus of convergence for every ray of modern Philosophy;* and then he asks, *were those embassies mere child's play, or were there Timoleans concealed in the Latomies* (Lodges)? I candidly confess, that had I known of these communications with the very center of Sophistry, so far should I have been from retracting my proofs of the Conspiracy of the Freemasons, that I should have given them a stronger turn. I can also assure him, that I would not have generalized to such an extent my exception in favor of the Masonry of the Grand Lodge of London, had I been informed that it could possibly have contained members so inimical to Kings as that *Timoleon* who assassinated his brother *Timophane*, for that same cause of hatred to Royalty in which the Elder *Brutus* became the executioner of his Children, and the Younger Brutus the murderer of Caesar his benefactor. Let English Masons defend themselves against the imputations of Dr. Griffiths; but every reader will perceive that the method he has adopted to prove that *my position was erroneous* is rather extraordinary; for, according to his assertions, if I am culpable, it is of having generalized my exception too much in favor of those to whom I thought no guilt could attach.

When we proceed to the third Volume treating of the Illuminees, and I speak of their Conspiracy against all society, property, and sciences, then is he far more difficult of persuasion. It is here that I am guilty of *treacherous ingenuity, of partiality*, and of *unfairness*. Let the reader judge to which of us such imputations are the most applicable.

The Reviewer deduces his grand proofs against me from the manner in which I have translated two of Weishaupt's texts. I must own, that one of them gave me a considerable deal of trouble, not on account of the language, for the words are clear enough; but on account of the arrant nonsense, and, to me, irreconcilable contradiction of this text in the place where it stands. To have translated Weishaupt literally, we must have him say, *"few wants; this is the first step towards Liberty. It is for this reason that Savages and the Learnea (or men enlightened in the supreme degree) are perhaps the only free men, the only independent men."* I here saw a great error in stating our men of learning as those who have the *fewest wants*, or as the freest, or as the most independent of Society. To enable them to attend solely to their studies, they stand in need of a sufficient fortune to relieve them from attention to temporal concerns. They stand in need of the labour of others to cloath, lodge, and nourish them. They are above all others dependent on society for that state of peace and tranquillity so necessary to the progress of science. They must, therefore, be monsters of ingratitude if they do not recognize that public authority, without which sciences must vanish. Put the most learned member of the Royal Society into a desert or a forest, and in another put a country clown, and see which of the two will fare best, or stand most in need of the help of others.

But this is not all; Weishaupt positively asserts, that slavery is the offspring of the sciences; and can it follow from such a position, that the most scientific are the freest and most independent of men? As from a variety of other passages I knew that according to the modern *Spartacus* no men were really enlightened, unless it were the savages, or those who wished to carry us back to the savage state; I translated it thus: "*Hence few wants is the first step towards Liberty. It is for this reason that the savages are the most enlightened of men, and perhaps they alone are free*" (page 177 [p. 477 in this edition, Ed.]); but I took the precaution to add the German text ("Darum sind wilde, und in höchsten grad aufgeklärte, vielleicht die einzige freye menschen"), that each reader might give the sense he chose to the original. Dr. Griffiths has done more; he has quoted that other text, in which Weishaupt literally declares slavery to be the offspring of the sciences; he nevertheless makes Weishaupt say, *that savages and the fully enlightened are perhaps the only free men.* This certainly approaches nearer to a literal translation, and the sentence taken in the abstract may be more correct; my translation, however, is conformable to the sense of the discourse; but I have no objection to substitute that given by Dr. Griffiths, provided a N. B. be added, to warn the reader of the nonsense of it, and the gross contradiction it contains.

4thly, Dr. Griffiths, or the writer he employs, next proceeds to page 171 of the French. "The text of Weishaupt expressly says: *out of our present imperfect forms of civil union we shall pass into new and better chosen*: but the Abbé, in order to attribute to him the perverse project of perpetuating anarchy, unfairly renders the passage as if we were to pass back into the savage state." Then, as if he had it in his power to quote numberless examples of my unfair translations, he adds, "On the topic of *Property*, similar freedoms have been used, with a not less *treacherous ingenuity.*"

Upon my word Dr. Griffiths here fathers with great facility his own failing upon others. Sir, notwithstanding the base and calumnious accusations which you chose to vent against me, I wrote to you as a Reviewer upright in his intentions, yet liable to mistake, but who, after such violent imputations, would condescend at least to insert in a future number of his Review the explanation which I had sent him. You denied me this means of defence; I then told you, that I should not leave the public in that error into which your Review might lead them; as in the present circumstances the consequences might be too dangerous. I requested a meeting in order to lay before you *the Original Writings*, and therein to point out evident proofs that your imputations were unjust. You refused these means of rectifying your mistake. What, then, entitles you to better treatment than you have given to a man who was most certainly actuated by no other sentiment than that of the public good, and whom you choose to calumniate in defiance of conviction?

It pleases Dr. Griffiths also to represent my letter (in which I informed him, that I would not leave the public in an error) as a risible threat of denouncing him as an Illuminee (June 1798). He adds, that I am "*at full liberty to accuse or compliment him, by such a description.*" You may, Sir, take what I am going to say as a *reproach* or as a *compliment*; but, without pretending to say whether you are initiated in the secrets of Illuminism or not, this much I can assert, that no Illuminee could have shown less candour than has the author of the article to which I am about to reply.

So far was I from attributing any other intention to Weishaupt, than that which he really had, when he wrote these words, Aus den staaten tretten wir in neue klüger gewählte, which I have translated, *de ces sociétés nous passons a des voeux, a un choix plus sage* (from these societies we proceed to further wishes and to a wiser choice); and as this sentence, taken abstractedly, has no signification either in German or French, I, in a note, called the attention of the reader to the sentence that immediately followed, as explaining the nature of the *wiser choice*. (Fr. Vol. III. 171). The English translator has omitted this note, which in reality was only added through an excess of precaution. But had he inserted it what would it have proved? Nothing but an especial care on my side not to attribute to Weishaupt any meaning that did not entirely coincide with the text. Am I to blame, if what precedes and what follows that sentence evidently demonstrate that this Sophister was endeavouring to lead us back to the savage state? I should spare the Reviewer too much, or should rather hold him out as an *Ignoramus*, were I to say that he could have been mistaken as to the meaning of that sentence. Here it is, with what precedes and follows it: "Nature drew men from the savage state, and re-united them in civil societies; *from these societies we proceed to further wishes, and to a wiser choice.*[1] New associations present themselves to these wishes; and by their means we return to the state *whence we came*, not again to run the former course, but the better to enjoy our destiny." Since the reviewer did not condescend to favour me with the interview I requested, that I might show him the German text, I here print it, that he may get it translated by whom and where he pleases; and I defy him to show that I have either altered or *warped* the sense of that passage: "Die natur hat das menschen geschlecht aus den wildheit gerissen, und in staaten vereinight; *aus den staaten tretten wir in neue Klügergewählte.* Zu unseren wünschen nahen sich neue verbindungen, und durch diese langen wir wider dort an, wo wir aufgegangen sind; aber nicht um dereinst den alten zirkul wieder zurück zu machen, sondern um unsere weitere bestimmung näher zu erfahren." Now I boldly ask, whether natural stupidity can be carried so far, or whether any man can be so totally destitute of every idea of logic, as not plainly to see, that the state from which Weishaupt says that Nature has drawn us, and to which it is leading us back by means of his (secret) associations, is not the savage state. Beside, he adds, *Let us explain this mystery*; and how does he do this? why, by dedicating more than forty pages to prove, that the object of Nature in *Secret Societies* is to eradicate even the very name of *People, Prince, Nation,* or *Country*; and this he positively tells us is *one of his grand mysteries*. This monstrous Sophister also says, that *Original Sin,* the *Fall of Man,* was no other than their reunion into civil society; and that *Redemption* is our reinstatement in that state which was anterior to society. It is even thus that he pretends to explain the gospel; it is thus that he explains the *rough stones, the stone split or broken,* and *the polished stone of Masonry*.—And after this Dr. Griffiths and his co-operators will come and accuse us of *unfairness, dexterity,* and *treacherous ingenuity,* because we unfold the absurdity of his favorite Illuminism! Let our readers assign those epithets to whom in their opinion they belong.

5thly. What can the reviewer mean by that great zeal which he shows for the characters of Weishaupt and Knigge, those two prototypes of Illuminism? In order to justify them, he comes and talks to us of the *Theism* and of the opinions which they affected in their public writings, and acts the brother dupe, grounding his opinion on Weishaupt's giving the writings of the *Socinian Bassedow* to his novices. What does all this prove to a man who is speaking of the secret opinions of Knigge and Weishaupt, and who has demonstrated the whole doctrine of their conspiring mysteries; to a man who proves to you, by the very letters of Weishaupt and Knigge, that after the perusal of the writings of the Socinian Bassedow, these two atheists recommend and give to their adepts the writings of the atheist Boulanger, of the atheist Robinet, of the atheist Helvetius, of the atheist Diderot; and that Knigge even complains, that such a super-abundance of Atheism would betray the tendency of the Sect too soon? (*Original Writings, Vol., I. Let. 3, from Spartacus to Cato.—Vol., II. Let. 2, from Philo to Cato.*)—To what purpose, let me ask, is all the stuff which this reviewer has copied from the German Illuminees about the Jesuits; all those panic terrors which he affects about the return of Catholicism in a protestant country; as if protestants and persons of every religion were not bound in one interest to counteract the plans of Illuminism? If Dr. Griffiths wishes to mislead the English nation, as some of the adepts did for a time in Germany, let him learn that the trick is stale; that it will be in vain for him to copy Mirabeau or Bonneville, and, like them, cry up the alledged proofs of Jesuits Masonry discovered by the Illuminee *Lucian-*NICOLAI. We are on the spot, and can verify these grand proofs. We beg Dr. Griffiths to favor us with a sight of that famous *Pelican* discovered at Oxford; and that he will not forget to tell us how it comes to pass, that this Pelican *is replaced by a Sparrow-hawk,* whose feathers grow again, and *how a Sparrow-hawk, who thus refledges itself,* evidently demonstrates that *Jesuits have long since been hidden in the English Lodges*; and that if great care be not taken, they are on the eve of sallying forth to make a most terrible havock. He will also tell us, how this demonstration becomes evident, when we observe, that Sir Christopher Wren (the architect who built St. Paul's) was professor in one college at Oxford, and that the *Pelican* and *Sparrow-hawk* were found in another college. But I am sorry to consider, that, when Dr. Griffiths shall have ably developed all the grand proofs given by Nicolai, the English reader will be much tempted to rank the inventor and his panegyrist in the same class.[2]

Let not Dr. Griffiths think that while we shrug our shoulders at this miserable fable of Catholicism and Jesuitism latent in Freemasonry, we cannot produce substantial proofs that this fable was only invented to avert the attention of the inhabitants of protestant countries from the progress making by the Illuminees. We can show those leaders of Illuminism *Brunner*, the apostate catholic curate of Tiefenbach; the apostate *Nimis*, the *Chabot* of Germany; the adepts *Dorsch, Blau*, and *Wreden*, the famous Illuminees of Spire, Mentz, and Bonne, meditating and combining among themselves the means of propagating this fable in Germany, just as Dr. Griffiths had done in England. We can produce the letters of the adept *Brunner* to *Nimis*, discovered among the papers of *Blau* and sent by the officers who had seized them to the *Bishop of Spire*. Dr. Griffiths knows many things concerning Masonry and Illuminism; but he may probably be unacquainted with this letter; it would not be right that he should continue so, as he will by the information be better able to judge of the part that he is acting, and of the services that he is rendering to Illuminism.

This dispatch is dated July 9, 1792, that is, just about the time when the coalition of the crowned heads seemed to menace Jacobinism with immediate destruction. The adepts are much occupied with inventing a plan for remodelling Illuminism, that it might acquire new vigor. In this plan a cloak is sought, which, hiding the grand machine, leaves its instruments at liberty to act without being seen, and to attain the object of the Sect without being suspected of meddling with Illuminism.

The cloak that was thus to favour the views of the brethren, was an *Academy of Sciences* formed of two classes of men, the one of men remarkable for their zeal in the cause of religion, the other of profound Illuminees. Honorary members were to be elected as protectors; *and if* (says the author of the plan) DALBERT *once gets to his government* (that is, if the Suffragan becomes Elector of Mentz) *he of all other princes would be the most proper for our object. We may perhaps unfold the whole of our plan to him, and make Mentz the central point of our academy.—To do away every idea of the hidden mysteries of this academy, it would be right that each member should wear on his breast a medal bearing the inscription* RELIGIONI ET SCIENTIIS (to religion and sciences).—*The better to conceal our secret object, we must be careful to engage all the learned Jesuits, such as* SATTLER, SAILER, MUTSCHELLE, *and other learned religious, that are perfectly orthodox, such as* GERBERT, *and* SCHWARTZUEBER.—*It would even be right if it could be brought about, that the establishment of this academy should be announced to the public by a Jesuit, and not by one of us.*

Pray, Dr. Griffiths, has this plan come to your knowledge? Now listen to what the adept author of the plan says, "But if people cry out against *hidden Jesuitism* and against the *progress of Catholicism*, it will be so much the better. That would the better do away all suspicion of a secret association; *one might* (and this is worthy of Dr. Griffith's observation) *one's self help to spread this false alarm.*" I here add the text, for the benefit of a translation from Dr. Griffiths, which if he gives, I hope he will also add the text, that the public may pronounce on *the treacherous ingenuity*: "Wurde über heimlichen Jesuitism, oder über grösere ausbreitung des Katholicism geschrien, desto besser; dadurch würde aller verdacht einer geheimen verbindung nur um so mehr beseitiget. Man konte sogar diesen blinden lärm selbst schlagen belfen." When, Sir, you shall have duly meditated on this plan of the adepts, I should like to know what you could have done more to favor their views than you did in giving an account of Mr. Robison's work, of my work, and of the miserable production calling itself *A first Letter of a Free-mason to the Abbé Barruel*. You will, doubtless, remark, that the date of this plan is June 1792; so you cannot refer your readers to the *Illuminee* BOETIGER to make them believe, that since the year 1790 there has been no farther question of Illuminism in Germany.

I flatter myself that you now coincide in opinion with me, and that you think it might have been better—1st, To have either spoken of the above works with more candour and politeness, or not to have mentioned them at all.—2dly, To have accepted the invitation that I sent you, that I might lay the original texts before you.—3dly, To have published the letter that I requested you would insert in your Review.—And 4thly, Not to have pretended that I had threatened to denounce you as an Illuminee. For really, Sir, I never felt the slightest inducement to pronounce whether the Illuminees had ever initiated yourself or your co-operators in their last Mysteries. You begin with granting that the conspiracy of the Sophisters against the altar really exists; and when you come to the Illuminees you tell us, "*that however extravagant may be the opinions of some* LEADING MEN *among the Illuminees, the average will of the party, the collected pursuit of the confederated Lodges, appears rather to have had* SOCINIANISM *and* REPUBLICANISM *than atheism and anarchy for its objects.*" —(June 1798, p. 240.)—This is avowing at least that there exists in these Lodges a conspiracy against the God of the Gospel, and against the thrones of all sovereigns. This is also abandoning the chiefs or founders of the confederacy of the Illuminees. When you go so far yourself, Sir, as to grant all this, am I not entitled to ask what could induce you to accuse me of so much *treacherous ingenuity*, when you confess yourself that I might be in the right; for you must have seen that I distinguished the degrees; I have shown by the very code of the Illuminees how in their first schools they only infused hatred for kings, and that species of Socinianism which borders closely on rank Deism. This, I think, was sufficiently proving a conspiracy whose trendency well deserved the attention of the public.—When I accuse the Sect of aiming at the wildest anarchy, I show that this mystery was reserved to the profound adepts and chiefs, though their secret at present frequently escapes them before a public audience. Generally, Sir, they make the same avowals as you do. They are pleased to hear it said that Voltaire, and those men whom they denominate *great philosophers*, conspired against Christianity; and that other self-created philosophers of the Lodges conspired against kings. This might contribute to make nations believe that it is not so very criminal a thing to engage in such conspiracies. But it is a more difficult thing to invent a plausible pretext for conspiring against all property and civil society; and for that reason more care is taken to conceal the ultimate views of their plots. Meanwhile, however, they cry down every author that dares to unmask these hideous conspirators. Was it under an illusion, or wittingly, that you followed so nearly the same method in reviewing the works of Mr. Robison and myself? Do not expect a decision from me. My object is, that the public should not be misled to believe that I have exaggerated the mysteries of the Illuminees. I leave to that same public to judge whether any of the Reviewers are dupes or accomplices.

N. B. In support of the account given by the *Monthly Review*, I am threatened with an answer from SPARTACUS-WEISHAUPT. My rejoinder is ready for this personage also. Let him meet me at the archives of Munich, where his letters are preserved. But as that might expose him to the peril of the gallows, I consent that he should act by attorney. Let him prove then that these letters are spurious; and that the Court and Magistrates of Bavaria imposed upon the world, when they published those letters, and invited persons of every country to come and verify the originals; for all other apology on his side must be useless, and any answer on mine superfluous. A complete answer to all his publications, as well as to his first apology, is already published in the code and history of his Illuminism; and all that I can possibly say with reference to his writings may be reduced to three words, *read and verify*.

---

1. The note in question would answer to the word *choice*, Vol. III. page 179 [p. 477 in this edition, Ed.] and is literally as follows: "To a wiser choice; this is the literal translation of the text, *aus den staaten tretten wir in neue klüger gewählte*. The sentence that follows clearly enough expresses what this choice is." I placed the German text between a parenthesis immediately after the word *choice*; and as the sentence alluded to immediately followed, I looked upon the remainder of the note as perfectly useless, and omitted it; for who could have dreamt that any person could have cavilled at so clear a sentence? I only transcribe the note in this place, that every reader may judge of Dr. Griffith's candour. *Trans*.
2. See Monthly Review, August, 1798, pages 460 and 461—See also the miserable discoveries of Nicolai appreciated in a German work called the *Veil torn from Masonry*, page 318, &c.

In the original this chart of hieroglyphics faces the passage marked with note 12 on p. 429 of this edition.